AFTER THE ICE

AFTER THE ICE

A Global Human History, 20,000–5000 BC

Steven Mithen

Harvard University Press
Cambridge, Massachusetts

First Harvard University Press paperback edition, 2006

First published by Weidenfeld & Nicolson Ltd, London

Library of Congress Cataloging-in-Publication Data

Mithen, Steven J.
After the ice : a global human history, 20,000–5000 BC / Steven Mithen.
p. cm.
Originally published: London : Weidenfeld & Nicolson, 2003.
Includes bibliographical references and index.
ISBN 0-674-01570-3 (cloth : alk. paper)
ISBN 0-674-01999-7 (pbk.)
1. Prehistoric peoples. 2. Hunting and gathering societies. 3. Primitive societies.
4. Human beings—Migrations. 5. Antiquities, Prehistoric.
6. Civilization, Ancient. I. Title.

GN740.M58 2004
930—dc22   2004042216

For my parents
Pat and Bill Mithen

CONTENTS

Preface   xi

THE BEGINNING
1   **The Birth of History**   3
    Global warming, archaeological evidence and human history
2   **The World at 20,000 BC**   8
    Human evolution, the causes of climate change and radiocarbon dating

WESTERN ASIA
3   **Fires and Flowers**   20
    Hunter-gatherers and the forest steppe, 20,000–12,300 BC
4   **Village Life in the Oak Woodland**   29
    Early Natufian hunter-gatherer communities, 12,300–10,800 BC
5   **On the Banks of the Euphrates**   40
    Abu Hureyra and the rise of hunter-gatherer sedentism, 12,300–10,800 BC
6   **One Thousand Years of Drought**   46
    Economy and society during the Younger Dryas, 10,800–9600 BC
7   **The Founding of Jericho**   56
    Neolithic architecture, burial and technology of the Jordan valley,
    9600–8500 BC
8   **Pictograms and Pillars**   62
    Neolithic ideology, symbolism and trade, 9600–8500 BC
9   **In the Valley of Ravens**   72
    Architecture, textiles and animal domestication, 8500–7500 BC
10 **The Town of Ghosts**   80
    Ritual, religion and economic collapse, 7500–6300 BC
11 **Heaven and Hell at Çatalhöyük**   88
    Florescence of the Neolithic in Turkey, 9000–7000 BC
12 **Three Days on Cyprus**   97
    Extinctions, colonisation and cultural stasis, 20,000–6000 BC

EUROPE
13 **Pioneers in Northern Lands**   110
    The recolonisation of northwest Europe, 20,000–12,700 BC
14 **With Reindeer Hunters**   122
    Economy, technology and society, 12,700–9600 BC

15 **At Star Carr** 134
*Adaptations to early Holocene woodlands in northern Europe,
9600–8500 BC*

16 **Last of the Cave Painters** 143
Economic, social and cultural change in southern Europe, 9600–8500 BC

17 **Coastal Catastrophe** 150
Sea-level change and its consequences, 10,500–6400 BC

18 **Two Villages in Southeast Europe** 158
Sedentary hunter-gatherers and immigrant farmers, 6500–6200 BC

19 **Islands of the Dead** 168
Mesolithic burial and society in northern Europe, 6200–5000 BC

20 **At the Frontier** 178
*The spread of farming in Central Europe and its impact on Mesolithic
society, 6000–4400 BC*

21 **A Mesolithic Legacy** 187
*The Neolithic in southern Europe, 6000–4000 BC; debates in historical
linguistics and genetics*

22 **A Scottish Envoi** 196
*Colonisation, Mesolithic lifestyles and the transition to the Neolithic in
western Scotland, 20,000–4300 BC*

THE AMERICAS
23 **Searching for the First Americans** 210
The discovery of ice-age settlement, AD 1927–1994

24 **American Past in the Present** 221
*Dental, linguistic, genetic and skeletal evidence for the peopling of the
Americas*

25 **On the Banks of Chinchihuapi** 229
Excavation and interpretation of Monte Verde, AD 1977–1997, 12,500 BC

26 **Explorers in a Restless Landscape** 236
*North American fauna, landscape evolution and human colonisation,
20,000–11,500 BC*

27 **Clovis Hunters on Trial** 246
Extinction of the mega-fauna and Clovis lifestyles, 11,500–10,000 BC

28 **Virginity Reconsidered** 258
Hunter-gatherers of Tierra del Fuego and in the Amazon, 11,500–6000 BC

29 **Herders and the 'Christ-Child'** 266
*Animal and plant domestication in the Andes, and coastal foragers,
10,500–5000 BC*

30   A Double-Take in the Oaxaca Valley   274
The domestication of maize, squash and beans in Mexico, 10,500–5000 BC
31   To Koster   286
Hunter-gatherer lifestyles in North America, 7000–5000 BC
32   Salmon Fishing and the Gift of History   296
Complex hunter-gatherers of the northwest coast, 6000–5000 BC

GREATER AUSTRALIA AND EAST ASIA
33   A Lost World Revealed   304
Tasmanian hunter-gatherers, 20,000–6000 BC
34   Body Sculpture at Kow Swamp   312
Burial and society in Southeast Australia, 14,000–6000 BC, and mega-faunal extinctions
35   Across the Arid Zone   319
Hunter-gatherer adaptations to the Central Australian Desert, 30,000 BC–AD 1966
36   Fighting Men and a Serpent's Birth   327
Art, society and ideology in northern Australia, 13,000–6000 BC
37   Pigs and Gardens in the Highlands   337
The development of tropical horticulture in highland New Guinea, 20,000–5000 BC
38   Lonesome in Sundaland   348
Hunter-gatherers in the Southeast Asian tropical rainforests, 20,000–5000 BC
39   Down the Yangtze   359
The origin of rice farming, 11,500–6500 BC
40   With the Jomon   370
Complex hunter-gatherers in Japan and the earliest pottery, 14,500–6000 BC
41   Summer in the Arctic   381
The mammoth steppe and colonisation of the High Arctic, 19,000–6500 BC

SOUTH ASIA
42   A Passage through India   396
Indian rock art and villages on the Ganges Plain, 20,000–8500 BC
43   A Long Walk across the Hindu Kush   407
Early farming in South and Central Asia; the domestication of cotton, 7500–5000 BC
44   Vultures of the Zagros   420
The roots of Mesopotamian civilisation, 11,000–9000 BC

45 Approaching Civilisation in Mesopotamia 430
The development of towns and trade, 8500–6000 BC

AFRICA
46 Baked Fish by the Nile 443
Hunter-gatherers of North Africa and the Nile valley, 20,000–11,000 BC
47 On Lukenya Hill 453
The development of East African landscapes and faunas after 20,000 BC
48 Frogs' Legs and Ostrich Eggs 462
Hunter-gatherers of the Kalahari Desert, 12,500 BC
49 A South African Tour 469
Changing environments, diet and social life, 12,500–7000 BC
50 Thunderbolts in the Tropics 483
*Hunter-gatherers in Central and West Africa; environmental change in East
Africa, 7000–5000 BC*
51 Sheep and Cattle in the Sahara 490
The development of pastoralism in North Africa, 9500–5000 BC
52 Farmers in the Nile Valley and Beyond 499
The arrival of cereal agriculture in North Africa, 5500–4000 BC

Epilogue: 'The Blessings of Civilisation' 504
Past, present and future impacts of global warming on human history

Notes 513
Bibliography 575
Picture Acknowledgements 611
Index 613

PREFACE

This book is a history of the world between 20,000 and 5000 BC. It is written for those who like to think about the past and wish to know more about the origins of farming, towns and civilisation. It is also written for those who think about the future. The period under discussion was one of global warming during which new types of plants and animals arose – domestic species which underpinned the agricultural revolution. These new genetic variants of wild species have an intriguing resonance with the genetically modified organisms being manufactured today, while global warming has also begun anew. Those concerned with how GMOs and climate change will impact upon our world may wish to know how new types of species and global warming have already impacted upon our past.

The past is worthy of study for its own sake, irrespective of any lessons it may have for the present day. This book asks the simple questions about human history: what happened, when, where and why? It provides answers by interweaving a historical narrative with causal argument. When doing so, it also caters for those readers who will ask 'How do we know that?' – often a very appropriate question when the archaeological evidence appears so scant. And *After the Ice* asks another type of question about the past: What was it like to live in prehistoric times? What was the day-to-day experience of those who lived through global warming, an agricultural revolution and the origin of civilisation?

I have tried to write a book that makes the evidence from prehistory accessible to a wide readership while maintaining the highest levels of academic scholarship. The popularising of archaeology on TV and in many recent books often adopts a condescending attitude to its viewers and readers, providing superficial and inaccurate accounts of our past. Conversely, many of prehistory's most remarkable events remain hidden from all but a few academics and specialist readers in scholarly works of impenetrable and jargon-laden prose. I have endeavoured to make archaeological knowledge more readily available while also catering for those who wish to assess my claims critically and undertake further study of their own. To that end I have included a comprehensive bibliography and extensive endnotes that specify primary sources, discuss technical issues and provide alternative opinions. These are, however, optional extras: my main aim has been to produce a 'good read' about an astonishing period of human history.

This has not been an easy book to write. Having begun work on it several years ago, writing progressed in fits and starts owing to the demands of academic and family life. New themes kept emerging: the history of archaeological thought, the (im)possibility of understanding other cultures, travel as a metaphor for reading and excavation. That I have been able to complete *After the Ice* has only been due to the generous support of family, friends, and colleagues.

As it draws on research and teaching conducted over the last decade I must initially thank my colleagues in the Department of Archaeology, University of Reading, for providing a stimulating and supportive environment for the whole of that time. Of these colleagues I am particularly grateful to Martin Bell, Richard Bradley, Bob Chapman, Petra Dark, Roberta Gilchrist, Sturt Manning and Wendy Matthews who answered specific questions or provided pertinent advice. I am also grateful to Margaret Matthews for her advice and help in preparing the colour illustrations, and to Teresa Hocking for her meticulous care in checking my text. The inter-library loan department of the University Library deserves special thanks for attending so efficiently to my copious requests.

I have benefited enormously from the kindness of archaeologists from around the world who provided advice, unpublished papers, tours of their excavations and visits to archaeological sites. In addition to those mentioned above and below, I would particularly like to thank: Søren Andersen, Ofer Bar-Yosef, Bishnupriya Basak, Anna Belfer-Cohen, Peter Rowley-Conwy, Richard Cosgrove, Bill Finlayson, Dorian Fuller, Andy Garrard, Avi Gopher, Nigel Goring-Morris, David Harris, Gordon Hillman, Ian Kuijt, Lars Larsson, Paul Martin, Roger Matthews, Edgar Peltenburg, Peter Rowley-Conwy, Klaus Schmidt, Alan Simmons, C. Vance Haynes, and Trevor Watkins.

Others kindly answered specific questions about their sites and provided colour illustrations – many of which I was finally unable to use. And so I would also like to thank: Douglas Anderson, Françoise Audouze, Graeme Barker, Gerhard Bosinski, James Brown, the Çatalhöyük Project, Jacques Cinq-Mars, Angela Close, Creswell Crags Heritage Trust, John Curtis, Rick Davis, Tom Dillehay, Martin Emele, Phil Geib, Ted Goebel, Jack Golson, Harald Hauptmann, Ian Hodder, Keiji Imamura, Sibel Kusimba, Bradley Lepper, Curtis Marean, Paul Mellars, David Meltzer, Andrew Moore, J. N. Pal, John Parkington, Vladimir Pitul'ko, John Rick, Lawrence Robbins, Gary Rollefson, Michael Rosenberg, Daniel Sandweiss, Mike Smith, Lawrence Straus, Paul Taçon, Kathy Tubb, François Valla, Lyn Wadly and João Zilhão.

I thank my brother Richard Mithen for advice regarding agricultural practices, plant genetics and crop developments. I am immensely grateful to those who read and commented upon one or more of my chapters: Angela Close, Sue Colledge, Tom Dillehay, Kent Flannery, Alan James, Joyce Marcus, Naoko Matsumato, David Meltzer, James O'Connell, Anne Pirie, and Lyn Wadley. Two of these – Anne and Sue – need special thanks for reading more than their fair share and advising about the contents and style of the book in general. I would also like to thank Toby Mundy who commissioned this book when at Weidenfeld & Nicolson and to Tom Wharton who provided detailed editorial advice on the whole text to its immense benefit.

Four further archaeologists need special mention: Robert Braidwood, Jacques Cauvin, Rhys Jones and Richard MacNeish. All were outstanding archaeologists and died while I was in the latter stages of writing. Their excavations and ideas are documented in *After the Ice* and I wish to acknowledge their seminal contribution to our understanding of the past.

The completion of this book before the end of 2002 was made possible by the British Academy whose award of a Research Readership in October 2001 provided the necessary relief from my normal academic duties. Before this, the vast majority of writing, however, was done in stolen time. It was stolen from my students when I should have been attending to their essays and preparing lectures, from my colleagues when I should have been more punctual for departmental meetings, from my field team in Wadi Faynan when I should have been digging. But most of all, it was stolen from my family.

It is to them that I offer my apologies and greatest thanks. I especially thank Heather (now aged eight) for the afternoon that she came home fresh from a literacy hour at school and reminded me to 'use verbs and nouns, as well as adjectives' in my book. Also to Nicholas (twelve) for his suggested title of 'Trudging Through Mud' – which must sum up his unfortunate experience of archaeology. And to Hannah (fifteen) for being the first to recognise that 'Dad's book is really a family project'. Indeed it was, a project that could not have been completed without their support. It is to Sue, my wife, that I owe my greatest debt simply for being at the centre of my world. And it is with immense love and gratitude that I dedicate this book to my parents, Pat and Bill.

AFTER THE ICE

THE BEGINNING

1
The Birth of History

Global warming, archaeological evidence and human history

Human history began in 50,000 BC. Or thereabouts. Perhaps 100,000 BC, but certainly not before. Human evolution has a far longer pedigree – at least three billion years have passed since the origin of life, and six million since our lineage split from that of the chimpanzee. History, the cumulative development of events and knowledge, is a recent and remarkably brief affair. Little of significance happened until 20,000 BC – people simply continued living as hunter-gatherers, just as their ancestors had been doing for millions of years. They lived in small communities and never remained within one settlement for very long. A few cave walls were painted and some rather fine hunting weapons were made; but there were no events that influenced the course of future history, that which created the modern world.

Then came an astonishing 15,000 years that saw the origin of farming, towns and civilisation.[1] By 5000 BC the foundations of the modern world had been laid and nothing that came after – classical Greece, the Industrial Revolution, the atomic age, the Internet – has ever matched the significance of those events. If 50,000 BC marked the birth of history, 20,000–5000 BC was its coming of age.[2]

For history to begin, people required the modern mind – one quite different to that of any human ancestor or other species alive today. It is a mind with seemingly unlimited powers of imagination, curiosity and invention. The story of its origin is one that I have already told – or at least tried to tell – in my 1996 book, *The Prehistory of the Mind*.[3] Whether the theory I proposed – of how multiple specialised intelligences merged to create a 'cognitively fluid' mind – is entirely right, wrong or somewhere in between is not an issue for the history that I will now recount. All the reader must accept is that by 50,000 years ago, a peculiarly creative mind had evolved. This book addresses a simple question: what happened next?

The peak of the last ice age occurred at around 20,000 BC and is known as the last glacial maximum, or LGM.[4] Before this date, people were thin on the ground and struggling with a deteriorating climate. Subtle changes in the planet's orbit around the sun had caused massive ice sheets to expand across much of North America, northern Europe and Asia.[5] The planet was inundated by drought; sea level had fallen to expose vast and often barren coastal plains. Human communities survived the harshest conditions by retreating to refugia where firewood and foodstuffs could still be found.

Soon after 20,000 BC global warming began. Initially this was rather slow and uneven – many small ups and downs of temperature and rainfall. By 15,000 BC the great ice sheets had begun to melt; by 12,000 BC the climate had started to fluctuate, with dramatic surges of warmth and rain followed by sudden returns to cold and drought. Soon after 10,000 BC there was an astonishing spurt of global warming that brought the ice age to its close and ushered in the Holocene world, that in which we live today. It was during these 10,000 years of global warming and its immediate aftermath that the course of human history changed.

By 5000 BC many people throughout the world lived by farming. New types of animals and plants – domesticated species – had appeared; the farmers inhabited permanent villages and towns, and supported specialist craftsmen, priests and chiefs. Indeed, they were little different to us today: the Rubicon of history had been crossed – from a lifestyle of hunting and gathering to that of farming. Those who remained as hunter-gatherers were also now living in a manner quite different to that of their ancestors at the LGM. The remit of this history is to explore how and why such developments occurred – whether they led to farming or new types of hunting and gathering. It is a global history, the story of all people living upon planet earth between 20,000 and 5000 BC.

This was not the first time that the planet had undergone global warming. Our ancestors and relatives – the *Homo erectus, H. heidelbergensis* and *H. neanderthalensis* of human evolution – had lived through equivalent periods of climate change as the planet see-sawed from ice age and back every 100,000 years.[6] They had responded by doing much the same as they had always done: their populations expanded and contracted, they adapted to changed environments and adjusted the tools they made. Rather than creating history, they simply engaged in an endless round of adaptation and readaptation to their changing world.

Neither was it the last. In the early twentieth century AD, global warming began anew and continues apace today. Once again new types of plants and animals are being created, this time through intentional genetic engineering. Like these novel organisms, our modern-day global warming is a product of human activity alone – the burning of fossil fuels and mass deforestation.[7] These have increased the extent of greenhouse gases in the atmosphere and may raise global temperatures far beyond that which nature alone can do.[8] The future impacts of renewed global warming and genetically modified organisms on our environment and society are quite unknown. One day a history of our future times will be written to replace the multitude of speculations and forecasts with which we struggle today. But before that we must have a history of the past.

The people who lived between 20,000 and 5000 BC have left no letters or diaries that describe their lives and the events they both made and witnessed. The towns, trade and craftsmen had to be in place before the invention of writing could occur. So rather than drawing on written records, this history examines the rubbish that people left behind – people whose names and identities will never be known. It relies on their stone tools, pottery vessels, fireplaces, food debris, deserted dwellings and many other objects of archaeological study, such as monuments, burials and rock art. It draws on evidence about past environmental change, such as pollen grains and beetle wings trapped in ancient sediments. Occasionally it gains some help from the modern world because the genes we carry and the languages we speak can tell us about the past.

The risk in having to rely upon such evidence is that the resulting history may become little more than a catalogue of artefacts, a compendium of archaeological sites or a succession of spurious 'cultures'.[9] A more accessible and appealing history is one that provides a narrative about people's lives; one that addresses the experience of living in the past and recognises human action as a cause of social and economic change.[10] To achieve such a history, this book sends someone from the modern day into prehistoric times: someone to see the stone tools being made, fires burning in the hearths and the dwellings occupied; someone to visit the landscapes of the ice-age world and to watch them change.

I have chosen a young man by the name of John Lubbock for this task. He will visit each of the continents in turn, starting in western Asia and working his way round the world: Europe, the Americas, Australia, East Asia, South Asia and Africa. He will travel in the same manner as an archaeologist digs – seeing the most intimate details of people's lives but being unable to ask any questions and with his presence quite unknown. I will provide a commentary to explain how the archaeological sites were discovered, excavated and studied; the ways in which they contribute to our understanding of how farming, towns and civilisation arose.

Who is John Lubbock? He resides in my imagination as a young man with an interest in the past and fear for the future – not his own but that of planet earth. He shares his name with a Victorian polymath who, in 1865, published his own book about the past and called it *Prehistoric Times*.

Victorian John Lubbock (1834–1913) was a neighbour, friend and follower of Charles Darwin.[11] He was a banker who instigated key financial reforms, a Liberal Member of Parliament who produced the first legislation for the protection of ancient monuments and bank (public) holidays, a botanist and entomologist with many scientific publications to his name. *Prehistoric Times* became a standard textbook and best-seller, with the seventh and final edition appearing in 1913. It was a pioneering work, one of the first to reject the biblical chronology that claimed the world to be a mere six thousand years old; it introduced the terms Palaeolithic and Neolithic, the Old and New Stone Ages, which are now recognised as the key periods of the prehistoric past.

But Victorian John Lubbock's insights were matched by an appalling ignorance. He knew little about the date and duration of the Stone Age; his evidence for ancient lifestyles and environments was scant; he had never heard of Lascaux, prehistoric Jericho and innumerable other sites that are known today as milestones of the human past. When planning this book I considered sending Victorian John Lubbock to such sites in gratitude for writing *Prehistoric Times*. But his time has gone; even with experience of Lascaux and Jericho I thought it unlikely that he would have abandoned the standard Victorian attitude that all hunter-gatherers were savages with child-like minds.

A more appropriate beneficiary of prehistoric travel is one who is yet to make his mark upon the world. And so I will send a modern-day John Lubbock into prehistoric times, carrying a copy of his namesake's book. By reading it in remote corners of the world he will appreciate both the achievements of Victorian John Lubbock and the remarkable progress that archaeologists have made since *Prehistoric Times* first appeared less than 150 years ago.

I make use of John Lubbock to ensure that this history is about people's lives rather than just the objects that archaeologists find. My own eyes cannot escape the present. I am unable to see beyond the discarded stone tools and food debris, the ruins of empty houses and the fireplaces that are cold to the touch. Although excavations provide doors to other cultures, such doors can only be forced ajar and never passed through. I can, however, use my imagination to squeeze John Lubbock through the gaps so that he can see what is denied to my own eyes, and become what the travel writer Paul Theroux has described as a 'stranger in a strange land'.

Theroux was writing about his own desire to experience 'otherness to its limit'; how becoming a stranger allowed him to discover who he was and what he stood for.[12] This is what archaeology can do for all of us today. As globalisation leads to a bland cultural homogeneity throughout the world, imaginative travel to prehistoric times is perhaps the only way we can now acquire that extreme sense of otherness by which we recognise ourselves. And it is the only means that I have found to translate the archaeological evidence I know into the type of human history I wish to write.

When I peer at the deserted dwellings uncovered by my own excavations I often share the thoughts of another great travel writer, Wilfred Thesiger. In 1951 he had lived with the Marsh Arabs of southern Iraq. When returning the following year he arrived at dawn and looked across the vast reed beds silhouetted against the sunrise. Thesiger recalled his first visit – the canoes on the waterways, the crying of geese, reed houses built upon water, the dripping buffalo, boys singing in the dark, the croaking of frogs. 'Once again I experienced', he later wrote, 'the longing to share this life, and to be more than a mere spectator.'[13]

The techniques of archaeology have enabled us all to become spectators of prehistoric life – albeit through a fuzzy lens. Like Thesiger, I long to go further: to experience prehistoric life itself and use such experience to write human history. Thesiger could depart in his canoe; all I have is my imagination, informed by a meticulous and exhaustive study of archaeological evidence. And so, within the pages of this book, John Lubbock fulfils my wish to become more than a mere spectator. Through him, I become like Theroux and Thesiger, a stranger travelling through strange lands – in my case, those of prehistoric times.

2
The World at 20,000 BC

Human evolution, the causes of climate change and radiocarbon dating

The world at 20,000 BC is inhospitable, a cold, dry and windy planet with frequent storms and a dust-laden atmosphere. The lower sea level has joined some land masses together and created extensive coastal plains. Tasmania, Australia and New Guinea are one; so are Borneo, Java and Thailand which form mountain chains within the largest extent of rainforest on planet earth. The Sahara, Gobi and other sandy deserts are greatly expanded in extent. Britain is no more than a peninsula of Europe, its north buried below the ice, its south a polar desert. Much of North America is smothered by a giant dome of ice.

Human communities have been forced to abandon many regions they had inhabited before the last glacial maximum, or LGM; others are amenable for settlement but remain unoccupied because any routes for colonisation have been blocked by dry desert and walls of ice. People survive wherever they can, struggling with freezing temperatures and persistent drought. Consider, for instance, those living at a location in modern-day Ukraine that will become known to archaeologists as Pushkari.

At this period of time five dwellings form a rough circle on the tundra. They face south, away from the biting icy wind and close to the meander of a semi-frozen river.[1] The dwellings are igloo-like but built from mammoth bone and hide rather than blocks of ice. Each has an imposing entrance formed by two tusks, up-ended to form an arch. The walls use massive leg bones as vertical supports, between which jawbones have been stacked chin-down to create a thick barrier to the cold and wind. Further tusks are used on the roof to weigh down hides and sods of turf that are supported on a framework of bones and branches. Smoke seeps gently from the roof of one dwelling; the cries of a baby pierce the thick hide of another.

Beyond the village a sledge loaded with massive bones is being hauled from the river. The faces of those working are misted in clouds of hot breath, behind which thick beards and long hair leave little flesh exposed. They are wrapped in fur-lined clothes. No simple draping of hides but artfully stitched clothing. It is the middle of winter and this village is no more than 250 kilometres south of the glaciers. Temperatures can fall to minus 30°C and there are nine months of it to endure. The river supplies building materials: bones from animals that have died in the north and had their carcasses washed downstream.

Life is tough: hauling the bones, building and repairing dwellings, cutting and breaking tusks into sections so that the village craftsmen can make utensils, weapons and jewellery. Daylight is precious – just a few hours of it each day, and then long hours in the darkness, telling stories around their fires. A small fire is already burning between the huts, its flame provided by a single knotted log. This provides a focus for half a dozen men and women who sit close together, knees drawn up and arms folded, minimising their exposure to the wind while stitching new clothes.

Near the fire an animal is being butchered and the air stinks of flesh and blood. It was a reindeer found wandering in isolation from its herd – a welcome surprise for a party who had gone to collect stone from a nearby outcrop. They killed it and can now eat meat without depleting that stored within their freezer – a hole in the ground. None of the carcass will be wasted. The meat will be shared between the five families who are living at Pushkari this winter. Knife handles and harpoons will be made from the antlers, clothing and bags from the hide, the ligaments and sinews will provide thread and cord. The heart, lungs, liver and other organs will be eaten as delicacies, the teeth drilled to make decorative pendants, the bone saved for fuel.

One of the dwellings has its interior lit by the small flame of an animal-fat lamp. It is warm, stuffy and dingy inside. The floor is soft, carpeted with hides and furs that surround a central ash-filled hearth. Mammoth skulls and leg bones provide furniture; an assortment of leather bags, bone and wooden bowls, antler and stone tools are scattered by the walls and hung from the rafters – a scene of Stone Age domestic clutter. The flickering light exposes a man's face. He looks old, but skin and bone must age rapidly in the ice-age world. This man wears his hair in plaits, has pendants of ivory and pierced teeth around his neck. His fingers work quickly with a needle and sinew thread.

Outside the dwelling, a man and some women and children sit together while striking nodules of stone that rest upon their knees. Flakes of stone are detached, the largest carefully laid to one side; others are left where they fall or casually tossed into the scatter of surrounding flakes. There is chatter and occasional laughter; some cursing as a thumb rather than a stone is struck.

The interior of another dwelling lacks any signs of domestic life. Its floor is covered in thick furs; a particularly large mammoth skull dominates the room, painted with red stripes. Adjacent to it are drumsticks and flutes made from bird bone. Two ivory figurines, each no more than a few centimetres long, rest upon a stone slab. Otherwise the dwelling is quite empty. This is where special gatherings take place; when visitors arrive, almost the entire village meets inside so that their news can be heard and gifts exchanged. It gets pretty hot and smelly; noisy too when they all begin to sing.

But for now the only sound is that of daily life at the LGM: the crack of stone against stone, the gentle chatter of human voices, the huffing and puffing from hard labour. These are carried across the tundra by the icy, relentless wind, one that will gather strength with the howling of wolves as darkness descends. When it does so, the people of Pushkari are clustered around a fire. Roasted meat has been shared, stories have been told. The temperature falls by another fraction to cross an unspoken threshold and causes the people to disperse to their dwellings for the comfort of furs.

Those living at Pushkari are *Homo sapiens* – modern humans, anatomically and mentally the same as you and me. By 20,000 BC all other human species had already become extinct so this is the only type that John Lubbock will encounter on his travels. A brief explanation of when and why this happened is thus a useful prelude to the history that is about to begin.

The fossil record for human evolution begins seven million years ago with a specimen discovered in AD 2002 in Chad, in north central Africa, one of the most important discoveries of all time and designated as *Sahelanthropus tchadensis*.[3] After 4.5 million years ago, several species of ape-like creatures that walked on two legs and used stone tools are known from the fossil record in Africa. Soon after 2 million years ago the first human-like species appeared, one that archaeologists call *Homo ergaster*. This was the first of our ancestors that spread out of Africa. It did so with extraordinary speed, reaching Southeast Asia perhaps as long as 1.6 million years ago.[4]

Homo ergaster had at least two evolutionary descendants, *H. erectus* in eastern Asia and *H. heidelbergensis* in Africa. The latter dispersed into Europe and gave rise to the Neanderthals – *H. neanderthalensis* – at about 250,000 years ago. The Neanderthals were an evolutionary dead-end, as was *H. erectus* in Asia. Nevertheless, both of these were extremely successful species that lived through great swings of climate.

It was during one especially harsh glacial period at *c.* 130,000 years ago that *H. sapiens* evolved in Africa – the earliest specimen being found at Omo Kibish in Ethiopia. This new species behaved in quite a different way to those that had preceded them: the archaeological record begins to show traces of art, ritual and a new range of technology, reflecting a more creative mind. *H. sapiens* rapidly replaced all existing human species, pushing the Neanderthals and *H. erectus* into extinction.

Soon after 30,000 BC *H. sapiens* was the only type of human left on the planet; it was found throughout Africa, Europe and across much of Asia. A remarkable thirst for travel took some of its members to the southernmost reaches of Australasia, which would become the future island of Tasmania. By then, however, the climate was heading to the depths of the last ice age:

temperatures were plummeting; droughts were persisting; glaciers, ice sheets and deserts were expanding; sea level was falling. Plants, animals and people either had to adjust where and how they lived, or become extinct.

How many people were alive on planet earth at the LGM? Taking into account the large areas of uninhabitable regions, the harsh climatic conditions that induced early mortality, and the fact that modern genetics has suggested that only 10,000 modern humans were alive 130,000 years ago, we can guess at a figure of around one million. But this really is a guess; trying to estimate past population sizes is one of the most difficult tasks that archaeologists face.

While the Pushkari hunters build their dwellings and chip their stone, a mammoth herd forages on the other side of the world in North America, in a vicinity that will become known as Hot Springs, South Dakota. It is a winter's afternoon and the sunlight is fading while the great beasts rhythmically sweep the snow away with their tusks to find the grass below. They head towards longer grasses and small shrubs that surround the steaming waters of a nearby pond.[5] At 20,000 BC the Americas remain quite devoid of human settlement, even though its landscapes are rich with game, so these animals have no fear of human hunters.

The forthcoming global warming will not only condition the human history that John Lubbock will experience but that of all other species, some of which – such as the mammoths – will have become extinct before his travels are complete. Unlike the global warming we face today, that which came after 20,000 BC was entirely natural. It was just the most recent switch from a 'warm and wet' to a 'cold and dry' period in the earth's history – from a 'glacial' to an 'interglacial' state. The ultimate cause of such climatic change lies in regular alterations in the earth's orbit around the sun.[6]

The Serbian scientist Milutin Milankovitch first appreciated the significance of such orbital change in the 1920s. By building on his theories, scientists have established that every 95,800 years the earth's orbit changes from being roughly circular to elliptical. As this happens, the Northern Hemisphere develops greater seasonality, while the converse happens in the south. This sparks off the growth of northern ice sheets. When a circular orbit returns, the north–south contrasts in seasonality are reduced, global warming occurs and the ice sheets melt.

Alterations in the earth's tilt during its orbit also have climatic implications. Every 41,000 years, the inclination of the earth changes from 21.39 to 24.36 degrees and back. As this angle increases, the seasons become more intense: hotter summers, colder winters. The earth also has a regular wobble on its axis of rotation, which has its own cycle of 21,700 years. This influences the point on its orbit around the sun at which the earth is tilted with its Northern Hemisphere directed towards the sun. If this happens when the earth is relatively close to the sun, the winters will be short and warm; conversely, if the earth is relatively distant from the sun when tilted in this fashion, winters will be longer and colder.

While these changes in the shape, the tilt and the wobble of the earth's orbit will alter the earth's climate, scientists think that they are insufficient in themselves to account for the immense magnitude and speed of past climate change. Processes happening on the planet itself must have substantially amplified the slight changes they induced. Several of these are known: changes in ocean and atmospheric currents, the build-up of greenhouse gases (principally carbon dioxide) and the growth of the ice sheets themselves (which reflect increasing amounts of solar radiation as they increase in size). The combined impact of orbital change and amplifying mechanisms has been the see-sawing of climate from glacial to interglacial and back every 100,000 years, often with an extraordinarily rapid switch from one state to another.[7] One of the most dramatic of these switches came about in 9600 BC, following on from 10,000 years of ups and downs of rainfall and temperature since the climatic extreme of the LGM.

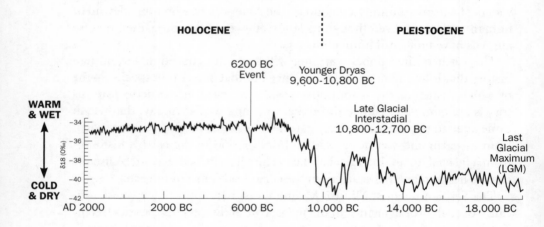

The jagged line in the above figure measures global temperature change between 20,000 BC and the present day. It is based on changes in the chemical composition of ice through a core taken from Greenland, this being a 'proxy' – an indirect measure – for global temperature.[8] More specifically, ratios between two isotopes of oxygen, ^{16}O and ^{18}O, are recorded as relative deviations from a laboratory standard ($\delta18$ O‰). When this value is high, the planet was relatively warm and wet, when low, it was cold and dry. As can be seen in the figure above, the line measuring this value gradually and irregularly increases from a low point at 20,000 BC until 12,700 BC is reached; at that date it shoots upward, marking the start of a period of relative warmth and wetness known as the late-glacial interstadial. There are several small peaks within this period, the first being known as the Bølling, and the second the Allerød, but it is only in Europe that these can be distinguished. The key feature to note is simply the general period of warmth between 12,700 and 10,800 BC.

The big dip that follows is called the Younger Dryas. This plays a major role in human history in the Northern Hemisphere but once again may not be noticeable in the south. Its very cold and dry conditions come to a sudden end at 9600 BC when there is a second dramatic increase in temperature; that marks the true end of the last ice age. In fact, it marks the transition between two major periods in earth's history, the Pleistocene and the Holocene. After that steep rise, the line continues to fluctuate while gradually climbing to a peak at 7000 BC and having a noticeable dip at 6200 BC. Otherwise the earth's Holocene climate has been remarkably stable – although such stability may now have come to an end as a new period of human-made global warming has recently begun.

The construction of mammoth-bone dwellings, stitching of clothes, making of stone tools and acquisition of food are not the only human activities under way on planet earth at the LGM. Artists are at work in the caves of Southwest Europe. A cluster of animal-fat lamps burn on the floor of the cave that will become known as Pech Merle in France. Another lamp is held aloft by a young boy to provide illumination for the quick movements of an artist's hand. The artist is an old but sprightly man with long grey hair, naked but with painted flesh. He is part of a community who live by reindeer hunting on the tundra of southern France. Amidst the lamps are his paints. Lumps of red ochre have been crushed to powder and then mixed in a wooden bowl with water from puddles on the cave floor. Another bowl contains a black pigment; sticks of charcoal are scattered between them along with pieces of leather and fur, frayed sticks and hairbrushes. There is a sweet smell in the air: herbs are smouldering upon a fire. Every few moments the artist kneels and inhales deeply to refresh the vision within his mind.[9]

On the wall two horses have been painted in profile, back to back with hindquarters overlapping. The artist is creating large spots within the outlines; he takes mouthfuls of paint and spits it through a leather stencil to make circles on the wall. His breath is the key ingredient to make the horses come alive. Then he returns to his herbs, changes the pigment and now places his hand against the wall to spit and leave its silhouette.

The artist works hour after hour, pausing only to change his pigment or his stencil, to switch a brush or sponge, to replenish the fat within his lamps and intoxicate his mind. He talks and sings to the horses, he drops to all fours and then rears like a stallion. More spots and hand stencils are made. The horses' heads and necks are painted black. As he comes to an end, the artist is physically exhausted and mentally drained.[10]

Archaeologists have only learned the date at which the mammoth-bone dwellings were built at Pushkari and the paintings were made in Pech Merle by the use of their most precious scientific tool: radiocarbon dating. Without this technique, writing a human history of prehistoric times would be quite impossible, as archaeologists would be unable to place the sites they excavate – the living settlements that John Lubbock will visit – in the correct chronological order. And so, as a final prelude to the history that follows, it is appropriate to provide a brief summary of this most remarkable technique of archaeological science.

The underlying principle is quite straightforward. The atmosphere contains three isotopes of carbon: ^{12}C, ^{13}C and ^{14}C. These are carbon atoms with different numbers of neutrons (six, seven and eight respectively). Living things take the carbon isotopes into their bodies at the same ratio as they exist within the atmosphere. With death, the ^{14}C within the body begins to decay while the other carbon isotopes remain quite stable. The date at which death occurred can be established by measuring the ratio of ^{12}C to ^{14}C and by knowing the rate at which ^{14}C decays.[11]

In order to be dated, an object must contain carbon, which means that it must have once been alive. Stone tools, the most ubiquitous find from prehistory, cannot be directly dated themselves, nor can walls or pottery vessels. Instead, archaeologists have to rely on finding items in close association with datable material such as animal bones or plant remains, ideally charcoal. Also, there must be sufficient ^{14}C remaining in the sample. Unfortunately this is not the case for any sample earlier than 40,000 BC, which provides the chronological limit for radiocarbon dating.

There are two further complications. The first is that a radiocarbon date is never an exact value but simply an estimate defined by a mean and a standard deviation, as in, for instance, 7500±100 BP. 'BP' is the term used by archaeologists to refer to 'Before Present' (with the present having been once agreed upon as 1950). In this example, the 7500 provides the mean and the 100 the standard deviation for a distribution of dates within which the true date lies. This tells us that there is a 68 per cent chance (i.e. two chances out of three) that the true date lies within one standard deviation of the mean, in this case between 7400 and 7600, and a 95 per cent chance that it will lie within two standard deviations, i.e. between 7300 and 7700 BP. The smallest deviation possible is, of course, preferred. But as this is unlikely ever to fall below fifty years, the dates for past events will always remain approximate.

The second complication is that radiocarbon years are not the same length as calendar years, and indeed they are not the same length as each other. An artefact with a radiocarbon date of 7500 BP is not 100 calendar years older than an artefact with a date of 7400 BP. This is because the concentration of ^{14}C in the atmosphere has decreased through time and that makes years appear longer. Fortunately this problem can be resolved by 'calibrating' the radiocarbon date through dendrochronology, otherwise known as tree-ring dating.

With tree-rings, one can count individual calendar years back into the past. By linking up timbers of different ages, a continuous sequence of trees for the last 11,000 years has been established.[12] Wood from any one of those rings can be dated by radiocarbon methods and hence the deviation between the real calendar date and the radiocarbon date derived. So when a radiocarbon date is acquired from an archaeological site, that deviation can be taken into account and a date in calendar years established. When dates are calibrated they are also frequently converted from BP (before 1950) to BC (before Christ, i.e. '0'; sometimes this is expressed as BCE, 'Before the Common Era'). So, after calibration, a radiocarbon date of 7500±100 BP indicates that the true date has a 68 per cent chance of lying between 6434 and 6329 BC. Tree rings are not available before 11,000 years ago but archaeologists have found other means to calibrate their dates. This has shown that the gap between 'radiocarbon years' and 'calendar years' gradually widens (although in an irregular fashion) as one goes back in time. By 13,000 years ago there is more than a 2,000-year difference between a date given by the radiocarbon method and its true age in calendar years. All the dates that follow in this book are in calendar years BC; my endnotes provide the radiocarbon dates themselves along with their precise calibrated values at one standard deviation.[13]

While the people of Pushkari stitch their clothes and the artist paints within Pech Merle, others are stalking wallabies on the grasslands of Tasmania, ambushing antelopes on East African savannahs, fishing in the Mediterranean and the Nile. This history will visit these and other hunter-gatherers, and then examine how global warming changed the lives of their descendants. It begins, however, in the Fertile Crescent – an arc of rolling hills, rivers valleys and lake basins that is today covered by Jordan, Israel, Palestine, Syria, southeast Turkey and Iraq. This is where the first farmers, towns and civilisations will arise.

A hunter-gatherer campsite is flourishing on the western shore of Lake Tiberias, otherwise known as the Sea of Galilee. When excavated by archaeologists, the campsite will be called Ohalo and recognised as one of the best-preserved settlements from the LGM.[14] Being located far from the ice sheets and tundra landscapes, oak woodland is not far away. Its dwellings are made from brushwood, its people wear garments of hide and vegetable fibres. A new hut is under construction: cut saplings have been forced into the ground and are being woven together to make a dome. Piles of leafy branches and animal skins have been prepared to use as material for the roof. Such building work involves far less effort than that required at Pushkari; indeed, life at Ohalo seems far more attractive in every way.

There are many people scattered along the lakeshore: some sitting in groups chatting, children playing games, old men sleeping in the afternoon sun. A woman approaches the huts from the water's edge bearing a basket of freshly caught fish, while others hang nets across coracles to dry. She beckons her children to follow her into their dwelling where the fish will be threaded on to twine and hung to dry.

Two women emerge from the woodland draped with freshly killed fox and hare. Several men follow with a trussed-up gazelle supported on a pole. More women and then children appear with bags and baskets carried in every way imaginable – on their heads, hauled along the ground, slung across shoulders, tied around the waist. The carcasses are placed close to a hearth and the bags and baskets emptied on to hides. Piles of fruits, seeds, leaves, roots, bark and stems have tumbled forth. There will be a feast tonight. A young man stands amidst this busy village scene, quite unnoticed by those at work and play. This is John Lubbock and Ohala at 20,000 BC is where his travels through human history begin.

WESTERN ASIA

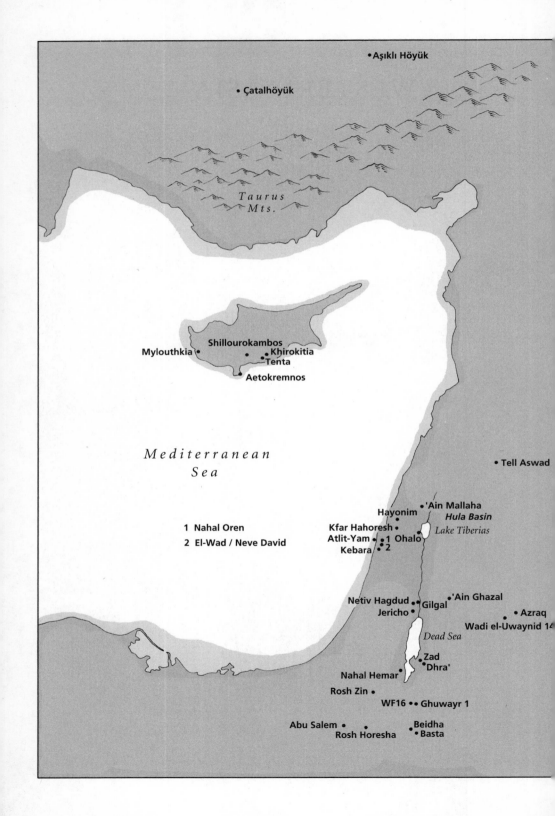

- Aşıklı Höyük
- Çatalhöyük

*Taurus
Mts.*

Shillourokambos
Mylouthkia
Khirokitia
Tenta
Aetokremnos

*Mediterranean
Sea*

- Tell Aswad

1 Nahal Oren
2 El-Wad / Neve David

Hayonim
'Ain Mallaha
Hula Basin
Kfar Hahoresh
Lake Tiberias
Atlit-Yam
1 Ohalo
Kebara
2

Netiv Hagdud
Jericho
Gilgal
'Ain Ghazal
Azraq
Wadi el-Uwaynid 14

Dead Sea

Zad
Dhra'
Nahal Hemar
Rosh Zin
WF16 Ghuwayr 1
Abu Salem
Rosh Horesha
Beidha
Basta

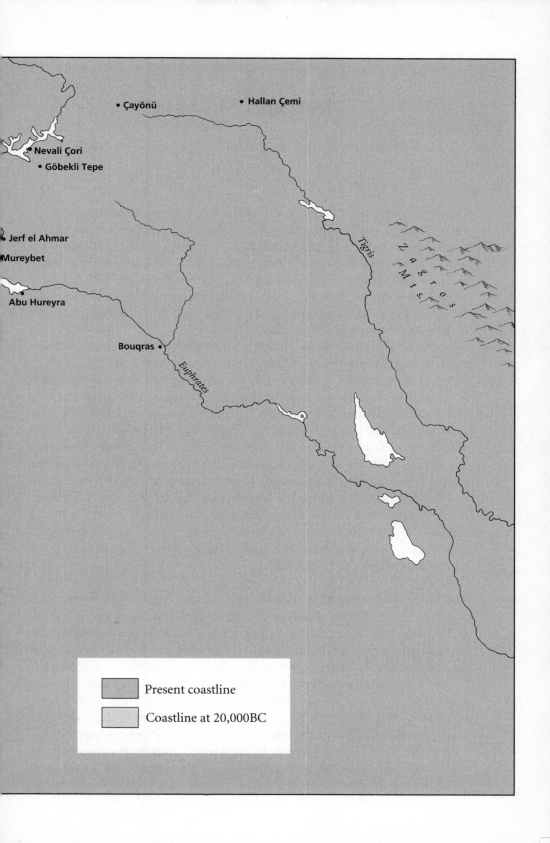

Çayönü

Hallan Çemi

Nevali Çori

Göbekli Tepe

Jerf el Ahmar

Mureybet

Abu Hureyra

Bouqras

Tigris

Euphrates

Zagros Mts.

Present coastline

Coastline at 20,000BC

3

Fires and Flowers

Hunter-gatherers and the forest steppe, 20,000–12,300 BC

Unable to sleep, John Lubbock sits by the lakeshore watching bats at work and enjoying a night-time breeze. Across the water, grazing deer are silhouetted in moonlight at the woodland edge. The Ohalo huts are behind him, a few metres from the shore and now quite empty as the people sleep below the stars and around a smouldering fire. The hut floors are left unclean – some scattered with flint flakes, others with the debris from a recent meal. Strings of fish and bouquets of herbs are hanging from rafters inside, wicker baskets and wooden bowls are stacked by the walls.

Someone sighs and turns, a child cries out and receives comfort. Trees rustle as a stiff breeze blows between the Ohalo huts; the fire gives a crack and a glowing ember is wafted into the air. It spirals upwards and then floats back down, not to the fire but on to the dry grass that covers the roof of a brushwood hut.

Wood smoke. Lubbock inhales it deeply, assuming that it comes as a wisp from the fading fire. But the smoke lingers and then grows; it becomes a pungent, visible cloud. Coughing and turning, he sees the hut ablaze. The people have woken and are pulling it apart, stamping out the flames and rushing for water. But the gentle breeze easily defeats such frantic efforts – it lifts a score of burning stems, leaves and twigs and scatters them all around. A second and then a third hut are now alight. The people retreat. Shielding their faces and holding their children tightly, they gather by the lake to watch their campsite burn.

The fire at Ohalo may have taken no more than a few minutes to reduce a cluster of huts to circles of charred stumps. Whether it began in this fashion or by some other means is quite unknown – perhaps it was a deliberate firing of huts infested with fleas and lice. But what may have been tragic for the Ohalo people was a blessing for twentieth-century archaeologists. Within a few years, water from rising lake-levels had gently flooded the site, protecting it from decay. Ohalo became lost from sight and human memory until a drought in 1989 brought a 9-metre drop in the water level and exposed rings of charcoal where the brushwood dwellings had been.

Dani Nadel of Haifa University began a meticulous excavation of a truly remarkable site; both he and archaeologists throughout the world were astonished at the diversity of plants and animals that had been used by the

Ohalo people at the LGM.[1] After the immense excitement of that first season of excavation there was a ten-year wait until water levels were once again sufficiently low for Nadel to continue. By great good fortune I was there when he began to do so in 1999. His was the most idyllic excavation I have ever seen – hot sun, glistening blue water, shaded trenches revealing the debris of ancient lives.

In the morning the Ohalo people rake through hot ashes and the still smouldering remnants of their settlement. They pick out a few treasured items – a bone-handled knife inset with flint blades, a woven mat that had escaped the flames, a burnt bow that could be repaired. With these they depart, heading westwards into the oak woodland to find another place to camp.

Had they been farmers rather than hunter-gatherers, the fire would have destroyed more than brushwood huts: most likely timber-built dwellings, animal pens, fences, and stored grain; their flocks may have fled or even died in the flames. Rather than abandoning the site to nature, farmers would have had to remain and rebuild because of their investment in the surrounding land: woodland clearance, fence construction and the planting of crops. But the Ohalo people can simply disappear into the woodland, heading westwards towards the Mediterranean coastal plain.[2] Lubbock decides that the woodlands can wait and departs to encircle the lake and walk into the grasslands and among the trees on the gentle hills that lie to the east.

The forest steppe – a landscape of grasses, shrubs and flowers growing lushly below thinly scattered trees – was critical to the course of human history. This is because the immense diversity of plant foods it offered to hunter-gatherers included the wild relatives of the first domesticated crops: wheat, barley, peas, lentils and flax. Comparable plant communities hardly exist today and are certainly no longer found within the Golan Heights, today's name for the hills to the east of Lake Tiberias.

Reconstruction of the vegetation cover of prehistoric landscapes is a requirement for understanding the past. It is often achieved by the analysis of pollen grains: the male reproductive cells, or gametes, of seed plants whose purpose is to reach the female part of the flower where fertilisation takes place. Fortunately, many do not make it and fall unused to the ground. If recovered by scientists, perhaps many thousands of years after the flowers have died, they can fulfil a different role – that of telling us what plants had once flourished in the evolving landscapes of the ice age world.[3]

Pollen grains from different species of plants are quite distinct. They are tiny specks to the naked eye but appear unique when seen below a binocular microscope. The pollen grains of pine, for example, have two wing sacs, while that of oak looks granular with three slits around each edge. When magnified with an electron microscope they present an exotic range of 3D surreal spiky spheres and other wonderful forms.

Pollen grains rain down from the flowers of grasses, shrubs and trees and often become embedded in the mud of a pond or lake. They become buried as further mud, with its own pollen, accumulates. More mud, more pollen, perhaps coming from a quite different set of plants that had begun to grow nearby. And so on, perhaps for many thousands of years until the lake has completely silted up.

A 'core' can be extracted from those sediments, a thin column of the mud or peat, every inch of which takes us back through time. Palynologists – those who specialise in the study of pollen grains – slice up these cores like salami. They remove the pollen grains from each separate slice and discover which plants had been growing in the vicinity when that particular layer of mud had been at the surface. By comparing the pollen from successive slices, they reconstruct how the vegetation changed through time. And by gaining radiocarbon dates from fragments of stem, leaf or seeds trapped within the core, they can work out the history of vegetation change.[4]

When Lubbock travels through Europe there will be many 'pollen cores' for us to examine. These show how its tundras turned to woodland and back again. But western Asia has very few cores, and hardly any of these are very deep or have well-preserved pollen. One core, however, is of immense value, having been extracted from the sediments of the Hula basin 20 kilometres north of Lake Galilee.[5] At 16.5 metres in length, it reaches back to the sediments laid down at the LGM when the Ohalo people were camping by the lake; it can tell us what pollen had been floating in the air.

The pollen evidence makes clear that as the hunters moved eastwards away from the Mediterranean coastal lands, the woodland disappeared, leaving a mere scattering of trees within grasses, shrubs and herbs – a woodland steppe. As soon as the Jordan valley had been crossed trees would have become less abundant, although surviving on the slopes leading to the plateau; and as one moved further east, the grasses and shrubs themselves diminished until there was desert – just as there is today. But within that desert there were oases, notably at Azraq where inland lakes attracted not only many birds and animals, but also hunters and gatherers. And it is to Azraq that Lubbock is now heading after a rest amid an expanse of vibrant red poppies on the steppe.[6]

Pollen evidence by itself is unable to provide an accurate picture of the ice-age steppe. Different species of grasses – including the wild cereals – cannot be easily distinguished by their pollen grains, while any insect-pollinated plants would be under-represented owing to the limited amount of pollen they produce. So archaeologists have examined the few remaining areas of steppe in western Asia, especially those that escape the heavy grazing of sheep and goat, such as nature reserves and military training grounds.

These provide insights into ancient plant communities that cannot be garnered from the archaeological evidence alone.[7]

Gordon Hillman, from the Institute of Archaeology in London, is one of the foremost 'archaeo-botanists' in the world. For more than thirty years he has been studying modern steppe communities, and has influenced a whole generation of students to do likewise. He has shown how the prehistoric steppe would have been composed of knee-high perennial shrubs with small fleshy leaves, known to botanists as wormwoods and chenopods (or members of the goosefoot family), and a rich mixture of grasses. Some of the grasses would have grown in small wiry tussocks, while the taller 'feather' grasses produced – in Hillman's words – a sea of silvery plumes billowing in the wind. Each spring the steppe would have exploded with colour and erupted with scent – the blossoming of thistles, knapweeds, wild fennel and a myriad of other plants.

Archaeo-botanists have studied not only the surviving steppe communities, but also how people from traditional societies, such as Native Americans and Australian Aborigines, have exploited these plants for food. They have shown that the steppe would have been brimming with both staples and delicacies for those with the botanical know-how of what to eat. Plants such as cranesbill, storksbill and wild parsnip could have provided thick, bulbous roots; the chenopods would have yielded abundant quantities of seeds; and wild grasses would have provided grain.

An understanding of the nutritional value of such plants is vital to reconstructing prehistoric life on the steppe. Unfortunately, there is very limited evidence as to which specific plants were gathered. Unlike stone artefacts, plant remains decay almost instantly once discarded unless this is inhibited by extreme aridity, waterlogging or intense charring – as was the case at Ohalo. But even within that site's burnt remains there were no traces of fleshy vegetables and leaves, both of which are most likely to have been collected.

With the hindsight of history we know that wild cereals were the most important plants growing within the forest steppe. The key difference between the wild and domestic varieties lies within the ears of grain. In the wild forms these are very brittle, so that when ripe they spontaneously shatter and the grain is scattered on the ground. Domesticated forms do not do this; their ears remain intact and the grain needs to be removed by threshing. So without human management the domesticated forms cannot survive, as they are unable to reseed themselves.

It is the same with peas, lentils, bitter vetch and chickpeas – the other early domesticates. As Daniel Zohary, a specialist on the genetics of wild and domesticated cereals from the Hebrew University in Jerusalem, once explained, the domesticated forms of cereals and pulses 'wait for the harvester'.[8] He has revealed that the change from one to the other depends on the mutation of a single gene. Another consequence is a change in the pattern of germination. Different individuals within a stand of wild plants will germinate and ripen at slightly different times – this ensures that some of them at least will mature and provide seed for the next year in conditions of unpredictable rainfall. Domesticated varieties, however, all germinate and ripen at the same time; they not only wait for the harvester, but also make his – or probably her – life very much easier.

The origin of agriculture is intimately tied up with the emergence of these domesticated varieties of cereals and legumes, as well as flax which was used to produce the first linen. As we will see, this could only have happened with human intervention in the life cycle of plants – people have been in the business of genetically modifying foods for a very long time indeed.

But not the Ohalo people and their contemporaries. They would have harvested wild cereals by beating the plants with sticks so that the grain fell into baskets held below. This is the method used by many recent peoples, such as the North American Indians, when collecting seed from wild grass. To be effective, one must time the collection just right – if the cereals have not ripened, few of the grains will fall into the baskets; conversely, if the cereals are past their peak, much of the grain would have already fallen to the ground. Some would have entered into cracks, been kept warm and watered by the rain to provide new shoots in the spring; other grain – probably the vast majority – would have been eagerly eaten by birds and rodents.

Plants were important to the Ohalo people; so, too, were the animals that lived in the woodland and steppe. Their favoured prey throughout the region was the gazelle, present as several different species, each adapted to a different habitat: the mountain gazelle in the Mediterranean zone, the dorcas gazelle in craggy regions, the Persian (or goitred) gazelle on the eastern steppe. Fallow deer browsed in the mountainous regions of Lebanon, wild ass grazed on the steppe and wild goat picked its way across the crags of the upland areas. Aurochs (wild cattle), hartebeest and wild boar would have been found within the woodlands, along with many smaller mammals, birds and reptiles.

The animal bones excavated from Ohalo tell us that several of these species were hunted. Fish were caught in the Sea of Galilee, and perhaps in the Mediterranean. That coastline could have supplied many varieties, together with crabs, seaweed and shellfish. But whether these were collected we can but speculate: long before archaeologists could get to work the coastline was flooded and any coastal settlements washed away by rising sea level, caused by the melt waters of the great northern ice sheets.

Azraq, the place T. E. Lawrence called the queen of oases,[9] comes into view as John Lubbock climbs the last ridge of lava pebbles. He has travelled 100 kilometres from the Sea of Galilee, much of it across barren desert with freezing night-time temperatures. Now he looks across lake waters that glimmer in the first rays of the morning sun. Gazelle are delicately picking their way through the surrounding marsh; what had been a single purple blur beyond is turning into foliage, a rich selection of greens, yellows and browns as the trees gain their form; the new day is welcomed by sweetly singing birds and tiny wafts of smoke from fires in the many campsites that surround the lake.

These are of hunters who have gathered at Azraq for the winter months, having spent the summer dispersed throughout the steppe and desert. Now they meet again to exchange their news, to renew friendships and perhaps to celebrate a marriage. They also bring items to trade: shells from the shores of the Red Sea and the Mediterranean, carved wooden bowls and furs.

Lubbock spends the day exploring the marshes, watching the wading birds and swimming in the lake. When resting, he flicks through his leather-bound and rather tatty copy of *Prehistoric Times*, impressed by the elegant drawings of artefacts and burial tombs. Its full title is very telling: *Prehistoric Times as Illustrated by Ancient Remains and the Manners and Customs of Modern Savages*. Much of the book is devoted to the latter, with descriptions of tribal peoples such as the Australian Aborigines and the Esquimaux (Inuit) as living representatives of the Stone Age past. Lubbock picks a chapter to read at random, and finds that even though its Victorian author had thought prehistoric people possessed childlike minds, he had appreciated their tool-making skills, especially in working flint.

In the late afternoon Lubbock arrives at a small campsite just below a basalt outcrop and beside a pool of fresh water that arises from a spring. It has a simple shelter: gazelle hides tied together with sinew and supported by a ridge-pole and stakes wedged upright with stones. Nothing of this shelter will be left for archaeologists to find, in contrast to the activities outside where a man and two women are generating a huge amount of flint flakes as they make stone tools. They sit cross-legged wearing necklaces made from tube-like shells known to us as dentalium. A child sits near them playing with stone nodules and unknowingly learning the arts of tool making. A much younger child sleeps in the shade of the shelter, where an old woman slowly grinds seeds upon a basalt mortar. A hare hangs from the ridge-pole.

Another member of the group is undertaking a task crucial to human survival throughout the prehistoric world: making fire. A young woman squats upon the ground, holding a piece of softwood below her toes. She has a thin stick of a harder wood in her hands that she rotates very rapidly in a small nick in the softwood, having added a few grains of sand to increase the friction. Within a few moments a little pile of dust accumulates; and then it glows. She adds some wisps of dry grass and soon has a light for a nearby hearth. Lubbock will see this technique used repeatedly throughout the world; it is one that he himself will perfect. He will also see another: creating sparks from chipping brittle stones together. But for now, his interest lies in watching the manufacture of stone tools to see whether his Victorian namesake was correct about the amount of skill required.

The nodules of stone – or cores – being worked come from the limestone outcrops close to Azraq that are peppered with blocks of flint. Using hammer-stones of basalt, the cores are shaped by detaching thick flakes of the limestone crust. Once these have been prepared long, thin slivers of flint are carefully removed from around the edges of the cores. These slivers, or blades, vary from five to ten centimetres in length; many are thrown away with the other waste but a few are put aside.

Those working the stone chat as they work, sometimes cursing when a fine blade accidentally snaps, sometimes commenting upon a fossil shell that appears when a nodule breaks in half. Lubbock takes a nodule and hammer stone and tries to make a blade; but all he achieves is a couple of thick flakes and a bloody finger. He recalls a passage in *Prehistoric Times* about flint tools: 'Easy as it may seem to make such flakes as these, a little practice will convince any one who attempts to do so, that a certain knack is required; and that it is also necessary to be careful in the selection of flint.'[10]

The flint knappers shape their selected blades with immense skill, using pointed stones to chip off minuscule flakes and turning the blades into an assortment of tiny tools – some with thin points, others with curved backs or chisel-like ends.[11] More accurately they are tool-parts: these microliths – as archaeologists call them – are inserted into reeds used as arrow hafts and into bone handles to make knives. The broken points and blunted blades will already have been removed and discarded on to the pile of waste. Any new microliths that do not fit are also thrown away – the craftsmen prefer to spend a few moments making another rather than risk damaging the far more precious haft.

The Ohalo people had made similar microliths; indeed, such artefacts have been made throughout western Asia ever since the LGM and will continue to be produced for many thousands of years. Collections of microliths – coming in a variety of shapes and sizes – and the waste from their manufacture dominate the archaeological record of this period in western Asia and are used to define the 'Kebaran culture'.[12]

The particular scatter of microliths and stone flakes that Lubbock watched being created was eventually excavated by Andy Garrard, now at the University of London. In the 1980s, as director of the British Institute in Amman, Jordan, Garrard undertook a major programme of excavations in the Azraq basin, documenting the presence of both hunter-gatherers and prehistoric farmers. In Wadi el-Uwaynid, 10 kilometres from Azraq Lake, he found two dense scatters of flint flakes and microliths, along with a basalt grinding stone, a few dentalium beads, gazelle, tortoise and hare bones.[13]

Garrard's work exposed a great number of such sites, and demonstrated that some had been used repeatedly for many thousands of years, resulting in huge scatters of artefacts.[14] The attraction of Azraq would have been the herds of gazelle which came to drink and graze on the lakeside vegetation; they most likely did so in great numbers and at predictable times of year and day. The hunter-gatherers would have known those times and arrived in large numbers to capture the vulnerable prey, probably returning to the campsite they had used the year before. Worn-out tools, and the waste from making new ones, were discarded on to the vast piles already present – contributing to what would one day be Andy Garrard's excavation challenge.

Almost 20,000 years before Garrard begins his work Lubbock watches two men arrive at the camping site in Wadi el-Uwaynid. They have been hunting with little success. As dusk descends, the hare is roasted on a spit and eaten with a thick porridge served in upturned tortoise shells.[15] Visitors arrive from nearby camps, requiring more food to be prepared and more wood for the fire. Soon at least twenty people are gathered and their talk merges imperceptibly into quiet song. Lubbock climbs on to the nearby basalt crag and looks down upon the flimsy shelter, the fire and the seated crowd. Stars appear and the moon rises. It is a scene repeated not only throughout the Azraq basin but also across western Asia – a world of hunter-gatherers only known to archaeologists by the scatters of stone artefacts they left behind.

Over the next four and a half thousand years, both the plants and the people in this region will become much thicker on the ground. What had been barren desert to the west of Azraq will be covered by grasses, shrubs and flowers by 14,500 BC. Trees will spread on to what had been the open steppe.

As western Asia became warmer and wetter, its plants and animals became more abundant. Direct evidence for such environmental change comes from the Hula core which, from around 15,000 BC, shows a marked increase in thick woodland with oak, pistachio, almond and pear. This period of increasing warmth and wetness culminates at 12,500 BC – the late-glacial interstadial.

These changes in vegetation lead to a vast increase in the availability of plant foods on the steppe.[16] Plants with edible roots that had been rare are now abundant – wild turnips, crocuses and grape hyacinths. The wild grasses are flourishing, enjoying not only the more clement conditions but also an increase in seasonality – cooler, wetter winters and hotter, drier summers. We must envisage vast stands of wild wheat, barley and rye appearing across the steppe, surrounded by a scatter of trees. In effect, there was a massive increase in the availability of wild plant foods for the hunter-gatherers throughout the whole of the Fertile Crescent.

Human population increased in this warmer and wetter world; with improved nutrition women could bear more children, and more of these survived infancy to reproduce themselves eventually. They dispersed into the new woodlands and steppe; they began to hunt in the uplands that had previously been too cold and dry.

Although populations were greater, human lifestyles were little changed from those of the people who had camped at Ohalo and Azraq at the LGM. Nevertheless, archaeologists find a new uniformity in human culture. After 14,500 BC people from the Euphrates River to the Sinai Desert, and from the Mediterranean to Saudi Arabia, had adopted similarly shaped microliths and methods of manufacture. With increased numbers, more extensive travel and frequent gatherings of people, the old diverse traditions of tool manufacture had been eclipsed. People throughout this region chose to use rectangular- and trapeze-shaped microliths. These became favoured over all others for the next 2,000 years.

The largest sites continue to be found within the Azraq basin and in the woodlands of the Mediterranean hills. New settlements appear, such as that of Neve David, established at the foot of the western slopes of Mount Carmel in Israel.[18] Excavations by Daniel Kaufman from Haifa University revealed the remains of a small stone-built circular hut and wall, together with many stone tools, a basalt grinding stone and mortar, limestone bowls, beads made from seashells, and a human burial. The skeleton had been laid on its right side with the knees tightly bent up under the body. A flat grinding stone had been placed between the legs, a broken mortar over the skull, and a broken bowl behind the neck and shoulder. The placement of plant-grinding tools in the grave suggests the importance of this activity and food source to the people of Neve David. Kaufman thinks the fact that the mortar was broken is significant: as such it was 'dead', just as the person in the grave was dead.

From Wadi el-Uwaynid, Lubbock has travelled through 150 kilometres and more than six millennia to arrive back in the thick woodlands of the Mediterranean region. The date is 12,300 BC and he stands on the west bank of the Hula Lake on an autumn afternoon, looking westwards towards the hills covered with oak, almond and pistachio. Nestled into the east-facing slope there is a settlement with the reds, russets and browns of hide and brush dwellings merging almost seamlessly with the surrounding woodland. It is much larger than any other settlement he has seen, one that truly deserves to be called a village.

4
Village Life in the Oak Woodland

Early Natufian hunter-gatherer communities,
12,300—10,800 BC

Through gaps in the leafy trees John Lubbock sees five or six dwellings aligned along the woodland slope. They are cut into the earth itself, having subterranean floors and low drystone walls that support roofs of brushwood and hide. With such well-built and neatly ordered dwellings the village looks quite different to what now seem haphazardly planned and hastily built settlements at Ohalo and Azraq. People have evidently planned to live within this village all year round. It is 'Ain Mallaha, a village of the new lifestyle that has emerged within the oak woodlands that grow across the Mediterranean hills.[1] More than a new lifestyle – a completely new culture, that which archaeologists call the Natufian.[2] Ofer Bar-Yosef, Professor of Archaeology at Harvard and doyen of west Asian archaeology, believes this culture to be the 'point of no turning back' on the road to farming.[3]

As he stands on the threshold of the village, Lubbock watches its people at work. They are tall and healthy, dressed smartly in clothes made from hide, some wearing pendants of shell and bone beads. Just as at Ohalo, their main work is turning wild plants into food, plants that have been gathered in the woodland and on the forest steppe. But their undertaking is now quite different, far larger in scale and far harder work. The stone mortars they use are of boulder proportions. There are many hands at work – grinding, pounding, shelling and cutting. Baskets of acorns and almonds are waiting to be opened and then ground into flour and paste.

Lubbock strolls between the workers, peering over their shoulders, stealing a little almond pulp to taste. Rich crushed-vegetable and wood-smoke aromas meld with the rhythmic pounding of mortars, the gentle chatter of adults and laughter of children. But not all the adults are at work; some sit idly in the afternoon sun, at least two women are heavily pregnant. Another leans against the wall of a dwelling with a dog asleep in her lap. Lubbock passes by, stepping between pits lined with plaster in which nuts are stored for future use, and enters her dwelling. Its remnants will eventually be excavated by the French archaeologist Jean Perrot in 1954 and become known unglamorously as no. 131.[4]

Dwelling 131 is a little larger than the others, perhaps 9 metres across, allowing five or six people to sit or sleep in comfort. Parts of the interior are dark and musty; elsewhere broken beams of afternoon sun enter through the brushwood roof, a roof supported by internal posts wedged upright and stabilised by rocks. The stone walls are draped with hides and rush mats cover the floor.

Just inside the entrance there is a spread of ash where a fire had burned the previous night to keep the biting insects at bay. Another hearth now glows in the centre of the floor; a man squats alongside and plucks a brace of partridges. He cuts the birds into joints and places them to cook on hot stone slabs. Behind him a third fire is burning, providing a focus for a few young people who are repairing bows and arrows. Flat stones with deep parallel grooves are used to straighten thin branches to be used as the shafts; razor-sharp flakes of flint are attached using resin to form points and barbs.

Stone pestles and mortars, wicker baskets and wooden bowls, are stacked around the walls. Hanging from the rafter is a group of tools quite unlike any that Lubbock has seen before – sickles. Their bone handles are either decorated with geometric patterns or have been carved into the form of a young gazelle.[5] The blades are made from five or six flint flakes, set tightly into a groove using resin. As they dangle, spin and catch the sunlight the blades glisten, having been polished by the many thousands of plant stems they have cut.

Jean Perrot found the remnants of this domestic scene when he excavated dwelling 131 at 'Ain Mallaha – holes and clusters of stones where the roof supports had been, bird bones scattered around stone slabs within an ancient hearth, flint cores and flakes, grooved stones, basalt mortars, and flint blades. Many of the blades hold 'sickle-gloss', indicating that they had been used to cut a great number of plant stems, most likely of wild wheat and barley. Of course Perrot did not find the rush mats, the hides, wicker baskets and wooden bowls – we can only guess at the presence of these to provide some comfort, and to make the best use of the many materials available in the woodland.

A short distance from dwelling 131 Lubbock finds another that has been abandoned – its roof and walls have long since collapsed, its stone foundations robbed for use elsewhere. In the absence of the living, this deserted and dilapidated dwelling has become a cemetery. The graves are unmarked but contain richly decorated bodies. Jean Perrot found eleven men, women and children, all from separate graves and probably members of one family. Four of them had worn necklaces and bracelets made from the toe bones of gazelle and seashells, notably the long, thin and naturally hollow dentalium shells, as already seen at Azraq. One woman had worn an elaborate bonnet on her head, made from row upon row of such shells.[6]

Within a few years, dwelling 131 will also be abandoned and will house the dead of another 'Ain Mallaha family. Twelve individuals will be buried there, five of whom will be decorated in a similar fashion. One of the dead will be an elderly woman; she will lie with a puppy, curled up as if asleep. Her hand will rest on its little body – much as it had done throughout the dog's short life.[7]

There is a large stone mortar carved into a protruding piece of bedrock close to the centre of the village, on which Lubbock sits to appreciate the scene. When I sat upon that same stone in 1999, 'Ain Mallaha had just undergone renewed excavations by another French archaeologist, François Valla. It was deserted and silent other than the song of a woodland bird. But Lubbock sees large nodules of basalt being turned into pestles and mortars, the surface of one being decorated with an intricate geometric design.[8] He listens to the chipping of stone, the chatter of voices and bark of dogs. He watches people making beads – cutting dentalium shells into segments and threading them on to twine. The wooden bowl from which the shells are taken also contains a bivalve that had originated in the waters of the Nile. Perhaps it had been traded from person to person, from settlement to settlement until it travelled at least 500 kilometres north; or perhaps it was the memento of a long journey made by one of the 'Ain Mallaha villagers.[9]

As was the case at Ohalo and Azraq, people are chipping stone nodules. At 'Ain Mallaha a new design of microlith is being made: thin rectangular blades of flint are carefully chipped into crescents – or lunates as archaeologists call them. Some are used in sickles, others as barbs on arrows. Why this particular design of microlith gained such popularity remains unclear – probably for no reason other than that people are such compulsive followers of fashion.

Lubbock leaves the village for the woodland as the light begins to fade. The pounding slows, the rhythm is lost, and then it stops, as does the chipping of stone. The 'Ain Mallaha people return to their dwellings or congregate around fires. Gentle chatter turns to quiet song. Mice and rats come out to feed on the nuts and seeds that have been dropped; dogs come to chase them away.

With the last of the light, Lubbock reads some more of *Prehistoric Times*. Although disappointed to find nothing about western Asia, two passages seem pertinent to 'Ain Mallaha. In one, his Victorian namesake has drawn together tiny scraps of evidence to suggest that dogs had been the first domesticated species.[10] But in another he seems to have been completely wrong:

the true savage is neither free nor noble; he is a slave to his own wants, his own passions; imperfectly protected from the weather, he suffers from cold by night and the heat of the sun by day; ignorant of agriculture, living by the chase, and improvident in success, hunger always stares him in the face, and often drives him to the dreadful alternative of cannibalism or death.[11]

Modern John Lubbock wishes that he could show his namesake the substantial houses, the clothing and food now being eaten within the village – all made by people quite ignorant of agriculture but seeming to be both noble and free. He drifts to sleep as the Natufian singing merges imperceptibly with the hooting of owls and scratching of beetles.

'Ain Mallaha was just one of several Natufian villages established at around 12,500 BC in the woodlands of the Mediterranean hills. Another was 20 kilometres to the southwest at Hayonim Cave.[12] Ofer Bar-Yosef and his colleagues began excavating this cave in 1964, and continued for eleven seasons of fieldwork. Six circular structures were found within the cave, each about 2 metres in diameter, some with drystone walls still standing up to 70 centimetres high and paved floors. One had been used as a workshop rather than a dwelling, first as a limekiln and then for working bone. Close to the cave wall a cache of rib bones from wild cattle were found, some partially turned into sickles. Beads made from fox teeth and the leg bones of partridges were also recovered – material never used in this fashion by people at 'Ain Mallaha. Conversely their favoured bones for jewellery, the toe bones of gazelle, were extremely rare at Hayonim.

This difference in jewellery suggests that the Natufian people from each village were concerned with asserting their own identity. Marriage between people from 'Ain Mallaha and Hayonim seems to have been rare, as the two populations were biologically distinct.[13] As evident from their skeletal remains, those from Hayonim were significantly shorter and a large proportion of them had 'agenesis' of the third molar – which means that it simply never grew – a condition that was very uncommon at 'Ain Mallaha. This inherited condition would have been equally present at both villages had there been regular marriages between their peoples. Yet it seems unlikely that either village contained sufficient inhabitants to have been a viable reproductive community in itself. The people at Hayonim may have been linked with those at another Natufian village, known today as Kebara. These two villages share decorated bone objects with almost identical, and complex, geometric designs.[14]

Each village had its own cemetery, often containing richly decorated bodies. Some of the most spectacular burials were found in the cemetery at El-Wad, a site at Mount Carmel in Israel. Almost one hundred Natufian people were buried there, mainly as individuals, although some graves contained several bodies.

El-Wad was one of the first Natufian sites ever found, excavated by Dorothy Garrod of Cambridge University during the 1930s. She was a remarkable figure – the first woman professor at Cambridge University and the leader of several major expeditions to the Near East. She discovered the Natufian culture when excavating in Shukbah Cave in the western flank of the Judaean hills[15] and came to believe that the Natufian people were farmers – an idea now known to be incorrect. Within the El-Wad cemetery Garrod found some particularly ornate decorations on several of the bodies. One adult male alone had worn an elaborate head-dress, a necklace and a band or garter around one leg, all made with dentalium shells.

Whether such jewellery was worn in life as well as in death remains unclear. The most elaborate jewellery adorned young adults, both men and women – although rather more men than women were buried. It may have denoted social identity, perhaps indicating wealth and power. Much of the jewellery was made from dentalium shells, which could have been gathered from the Mediterranean coast by the Natufian people themselves. But Donald Henry, an archaeologist from the University of Tulsa, USA, who has undertaken extensive studies in southern Jordan, suggests another possibility. He thinks that the shells may have been acquired from hunter-gatherers living in the open steppe of today's Negev desert in return for cereals, nuts and meat.

For the Natufians, it may well have been control of this trading relationship that provided individuals with wealth and power – and the key to maintaining these may have been to ensure that limited shells were in circulation within their village. The most effective way of doing that was the regular removal of large quantities by burying them with the dead. Those graves were like our gold-filled bank vaults today, designed to ensure that the small amount remaining in circulation – whether of gold or seashells – maintains its value so that it confers status or prestige on the few that have some to own.

The first rays of sunlight through leafy branches dapple the ground; Lubbock wakes to hear footsteps and voices approaching from the woods. Four men and a couple of boys are returning to 'Ain Mallaha after a hunting trip at dawn. They carry three gazelle carcasses, already gutted and partially butchered but dripping a trail of blood through the trees.

In the village the carcasses are hung within a dwelling, away from the sun and the flies. When roasted, the meat will be assiduously shared between family and friends. The hunters are welcomed back and tell the tale of the kill – how the men had waited in ambush while the boys chased startled animals into a flurry of arrows. There is talk about the various tracks and trails of animals they had seen, and the women learn about any plant foods that appeared ready for collection. Two young women take a wicker basket and leave for a spread of mushrooms that had been seen, hoping to reach them before the deer. Lubbock decides to follow.

All of the Natufian villages shared the same economic base as that of 'Ain Mallaha. Indeed, all the villages are found in very similar settings – at a juncture between thick woodland and forest steppe, localities likely to have had permanent water supplies, suitable for hunting gazelle and providing edible plants from the two contrasting habitats. Gazelle bones are abundant in excavations at Natufian sites. Other animals were also taken, such as deer and small game – foxes, lizards, fish and game birds. The gazelle bones reveal more than just the Natufian diet: they show that people probably lived in the villages all year round.

We learn this from the gazelle teeth. Like those of all mammals, gazelle teeth are largely composed of cementum that grows slowly in discrete layers throughout the animal's lifetime. During the spring and summer, when growth is most rapid, these bands are opaque. During the winter, when growth is restricted, they are black. So by taking a slice through a tooth and inspecting the last cementum band laid down, one can identify whether the animal had been killed in the summer or winter.

Daniel Lieberman, an archaeo-zoologist from Rutgers University, New Jersey, USA, has used this technique to study gazelle teeth from Natufian sites throughout western Asia.[16] At all those he examined, some animals had been killed in the spring/summer and some in the autumn/winter; he took this to mean permanent occupation – or 'sedentism' as it is referred to by archaeologists. His findings on gazelle teeth from earlier sites showed that occupation had occurred either during the winter or the summer, reflecting the mobile lifestyle of these hunter-gatherers.

Further lines of evidence support the idea of Natufian sedentism – although some archaeologists strongly believe that the Early Natufian people remained as mobile hunter-gatherers.[17] It seems unlikely that so much effort would have been expended on the construction of stone houses if they were to be used for only a few weeks or months each year. The many rat, mouse and sparrow bones within the village rubbish are also telling; domestic strains appeared for the first time during the Natufian, and may have evolved to take advantage of the new niche created by permanent human settlement.[18]

This may also have been the case with the dog. The burial of a puppy at 'Ain Mallaha is the most persuasive sign that wild wolves had evolved into domesticated dogs by the time of the Natufian. Another dog burial comes from Hayonim where three humans and two dogs were carefully arranged together in one grave.[19] These animals were not simply tame wolves but truly domesticated dogs – they were much smaller than their wolf ancestors. All animal species become reduced in size when the domesticated variants arise, as we will see later with sheep, goats and cows.

The first villages would have been attractive to wolves, coming to scavenge on the permanent supplies of waste and for the ready supplies of mice and rats. As such, they would have done a service to the Natufian people by keeping the vermin under control; some animals may have been tamed and used for hunting or as companions for the old and sick. Others may have been used as guard dogs to warn of approaching strangers. When isolated from the wild populations, these tame animals may have rapidly become genetically distinct as the Natufian people controlled their breeding to ensure the proliferation of some characteristics rather than others. The consequence was a new species entering the world: the domesticated dog.

Not all the Natufian people lived in villages all year round – perhaps none of them did so. Several settlements on the east side of the Jordan valley, such as Tabqa and Beidha, appear to have been used only for brief periods. These have neither dwellings nor burials and seem most likely to be temporary hunting camps, perhaps little different from those that Lubbock saw at Azraq. The people at Beidha had hunted goat, ibex and gazelle, and had dentalium shells from the Red Sea.[20] Whether they spent part of the year in a proper village or lived an entirely transient lifestyle like that of the much earlier Kebaran people, remains unclear.

A dog decides to follow the two young women. It bounds past Lubbock, looking very wolf-like, and soon disappears into the undergrowth. His attempt to follow is soon abandoned as the women walk quickly using a maze of tiny but well-trodden paths that wind between groves of oak and almond trees, past clusters of lupins and thickets of hawthorn. Lubbock loses their trail and finds himself in more open woodland close to marshes that border the lake of the Hula basin. The paths continue and patches of cultivated plants are found in the under-storey of the oak trees. These include tangled peas and wild wheat with heavy drooping ears of grain. Lubbock sits by one such stand to rest, hearing the dog barking from afar.

Tame dogs, whether treated as pets or kept as working animals, are rather like children. They need to be cared for and can become the subject of intense relationships: dogs were as much 'man's best friend' in the Natufian as they are today. This caring attitude to animals may have spilled over on to the plants gathered by the Natufian people. We should not think of them collecting cereal grains, picking fruit and gathering nuts in bland economic terms – with no concern other than to maximise their immediate yields for the minimum of effort. No hunter-gatherer groups recorded by anthropologists have been like that, and there is no reason to think that they were so in prehistory

The Bushmen of South Africa, the Aborigines of Australia and the Indians of Amazonia have all displayed immense and intimate knowledge about the plants around them, even those that have no economic value. Parts of roots and clusters of seed-heads are often left in the ground to ensure that there will be plants to gather at the same location in the following year. Fire has frequently been used to burn off old stems and encourage the growth of new shoots.

Christine Hastorf, an archaeologist from Berkeley, California, stresses the significance of 'plant nurturing' in understanding the earliest stages of plant domestication.[21] She reminds us that with very few exceptions plants have been gathered and cultivated by women who have often applied the same attitudes and care for the plants in their gardens as they do to the children within their houses. The Natufian women may have been like those of the Barasana people of northwest Colombia who maintain 'kitchen gardens' close to their dwellings. Most of their garden plants are wild species but are nevertheless nurtured for use as food, medicines, contraceptives and drugs. The Barasana frequently exchange cuttings with their friends and relatives so that each plant added to the garden comes with a story that serves to maintain social links. Moreover many plants have symbolic meanings associated with the origin myths of the Barasana people. In the words of Hastorf, 'To walk through a [Barasana] woman's garden is to view her daily life, her ancestral lineage and a history of her family's social relations.'[22]

Any gardener today will understand this: in my own suburban garden, for instance, my wife has plants that have been given as gifts, plants that mark where our deceased pets have been buried, plants that we have uprooted and taken with us from garden to garden as we have moved during the last twenty years. Every year my wife meticulously collects marigold seeds to resow the next. Many years ago her grandmother had given her seeds from marigolds that she had herself collected and resown each year throughout her long life.

We have no knowledge of how the Natufian people thought about the plants around them. But in light of the permanence of their settlements, the many mouths needing to be fed, and the abundance of grinding stones, pestles and mortars, wild plants appear to have been managed in a way that we would recognise as cultivation. I suspect that the stands of wild cereals, the groves of nut trees, the patches of lupins, wild peas, and lentils were treated as a wild garden, and that these were manipulated and managed, used in social relations and infused with symbolic meanings, just like the plants in the kitchen gardens of the Barasana. Dorothy Garrod may have been wrong to think of the Natufian people as farmers; but they were most certainly rather special gardeners.

In this regard some artefacts from Natufian sites take on added significance because they may actually depict the gardens themselves. At Hayonim a rectangular slab of limestone, about 10 by 20 centimetres, was incised with lines that divide the surface into distinct areas. Ofer Bar-Yosef and Anna Belfer-Cohen, a specialist on Natufian art from the Hebrew University in Jerusalem, propose that this pattern 'can be viewed as designating definite territories or "fields" of some kind,'[23] perhaps separated by tiny paths. This slab is not unique; others have similar designs and while they may not be spatially accurate maps of fields or gardens, they may represent these in some abstract form – just like the map of the London underground.

John Lubbock spends the morning reading *Prehistoric Times* and bird-watching in the Natufian world of the Hula basin. After the sun had climbed to burn off the few wispy morning clouds a pair of vultures circled in the clear blue sky; a flight of geese arrived on the lake and then song-birds landed on the wild wheat to feed upon the grain. Just as Lubbock decides to return to 'Ain Mallaha, a party of women arrive and stand right beside him to inspect the wheat. They curse a little as it has ripened more quickly than expected and they know that much will now be lost. Within minutes the women are at work, cutting the stalks with the flint-bladed sickles that Lubbock had seen dangling within dwelling 131. They cut the stalks at their base to acquire straw as well as grain; just as they had feared, the ears shatter when touched, scattering many of the spikelets – the seed with its long spike attached – to the floor. Working quickly, they gather up the bundles of stalks and ears and tie them into sheaths.

Back at the village, the ears are beaten into wooden bowls to release the remaining spikelets; red-hot stones are added and swilled around. Lubbock gathers that this parches the spikelets and turns them quite brittle. Next they are emptied into wooden mortars and crushed to release the grain; the mortars are emptied on to bark trays that are agitated to separate and discard the chaff.[24] The grain goes back into the mortars and is now finely ground into flour; after being mixed with water and made into dough, it is cooked as flat bread-pancakes upon the hot stones, no more than a few hours after growing within the wild gardens of 'Ain Mallaha.

We know that the Natufian people were cutting the wild cereals with sickles. In the light of their decorated handles, this might have been an activity infused with symbolic meaning, just as picking marigolds is for my wife. Cutting with sickles would have been much more efficient than beating the grain into baskets because it reduced the amount falling uncollected to the ground.[25] Another impact of this new harvesting method remained unknown to the Natufian people: cutting with sickles laid the foundations for the transition from the wild to the domesticated forms.

Recall that the principal difference is the brittleness of the ear – the wild strains spontaneously fall apart when ripe, scattering their seed on the ground while the domestic strains remain intact, 'waiting for the harvester'. Within the stands of wild cereals there would always have been a few plants that were relatively non-brittle – rare genetic mutants, estimated by Gordon Hillman as numbering one or two for every 2–4 million brittle individuals.

Those beating the stalks and catching the grain in baskets held below would not have collected it from such genetic mutants. Only when cut by sickles would the grain from these have been collected along with that from the normal brittle plants. Imagine a situation in which a small party of Natufians arrived to begin cutting a stand of wild cereals. If the wheat or barley was already ripe, then much of the grain from the brittle plants would already have been scattered. But the rare non-brittle plants would still be intact. So when the stalks were cut, the grain from those plants would have been relatively more abundant within the harvest than it had been in the woodlands or on the steppe.

Now imagine what would have happened if the Natufian people began to reseed the wild stands of cereals by scattering grain saved from a previous harvest, or perhaps sowing it into holes made with a stick or even into tilled ground. That seed grain would have had a relatively high frequency of the non-brittle variants. When the new stand was cut with sickles, the non-brittle variants would have been favoured once again and hence gained an even higher presence within the harvested grain. If this process had been repeated many times, the non-brittle plants would gradually come to dominate. Eventually they would be the only type of plant present – the domestic variant that 'waits for the harvester' would have arisen. But if abandoned, the domestic strain would gradually disappear; being unable to seed itself new genetic mutants – those with brittle ears just like the original wild plants – would be the only ones able to reproduce and would rapidly come to dominate the stand once again.

Gordon Hillman and Stuart Davies, a biologist from the University of Wales, have used their knowledge of plant genetics and ancient gathering techniques – much of it acquired by experimentation – to estimate how long the change from wild to domestic strains would take.[26] By using computer simulation they showed that in ideal circumstances as little as twenty cycles of harvesting and resowing in new patches could have transformed a wild, brittle type of wheat into the domesticated non-brittle variant. Under more realistic conditions, 200 to 250 years is the most likely period of transition.

The archaeological evidence makes it clear that this transition did *not* happen during the Natufian. There are microscopic differences between the shape of the grain from domestic cereals and wild varieties, and although cereal grains are rare in the Natufian archaeological record all of those known are clearly from wild cereals. Not for another millennium at least do we encounter the first domesticated grains – from the settlements of Abu Hureyra and Tell Aswad in Syria, and Jericho in Palestine. So the Natufian people appear to have cut the wild cereal stands with their sickles for as much as 3,000 years without the evolutionary leap from brittle to non-brittle plants.

There seems to be a very simple explanation for this, identified in some remarkable research by Romana Unger-Hamilton during the 1980s while she worked at the Institute of Archaeology in London.[27] Under the guidance of Gordon Hillman she spent many months replicating the Natufian style of harvesting wild cereals. Using identical sickles made with bone handles and flint blades, she cut stands of wild wheat and barley on the slopes of Mount Carmel, around the Sea of Galilee and in southern Turkey in a series of controlled experiments. The blades were then microscopically examined for signs of 'sickle-gloss' – the texture, location and intensity of gloss will vary with different types of cereals and at different stages of ripeness.

Unger-Hamilton found that the sickle-gloss on the true Natufian blades was most similar to that on the blades she used to harvest cereals that were not yet ripe. In that state, the brittle plants would have shed only a little of their grain, so that it would be collected from the non-brittle variants in virtually the same minute proportion as from those plants within the stand. So even if the Natufian people were sowing seed to generate new stands of wild cereals, non-brittle variants were unable to become dominant. Harvesting the unripe ears was perfectly sensible as it avoided the loss of most of the grain from the brittle plants, which would have already been shed to the ground.

Another factor probably prevented the emergence of domesticated cereals among the Natufians: their sedentary lifestyle. Patricia Anderson, of the Jalès Research Institute in Paris, undertook a similar programme of research to that of Romana Unger-Hamilton and confirmed many of her results.[28] She also found that when wild stands are cut with sickles, even when still in a 'green' stage, the grain that falls to the ground is quite sufficient to provide for the next year's crop. So the Natufians would have only needed to sow if they were beginning a brand-new plot of cereals – otherwise they could have relied upon 'growback' at the existing stands. Even if the grain collected by the Natufian people did have a higher proportion of the non-brittle variants, unless they were creating new plots of cereals in new places these variants would never have had the opportunity to become the dominant form. And as the Natufian people were sedentary, new plots were never made. The Natufians remained as cultivators of wild cereals within the wild gardens of the Mediterranean woodland.

These arguments about the Natufian people, their wild gardens and their plant-gathering activities have one obvious weakness: very few botanical remains have been recovered from their settlements. This is partly due to poor preservation and partly because many excavations predated modern recovery techniques. For direct evidence of the nature of plant-gathering at 12,000 BC John Lubbock has to leave the Mediterranean woodland and the Natufian culture. He has to travel 500 kilometres to the northeast to another hunter-gatherer village, one found on the flood plain of the Euphrates: the astonishing site of Abu Hureyra.

5

On the Banks of the Euphrates

Abu Hureyra and the rise of hunter-gatherer sedentism,
12,300–10,800 BC

The grass and flowers of the steppe are wet with dew as John Lubbock approaches the village of Abu Hureyra. It is dawn on a midsummer's day in 11,500 BC. His journey from 'Ain Mallaha took him from the dense oak forests of the Mediterranean hills, through open woodland and finally into the treeless steppe, into what is northwest Syria today. He passed several villages close to rivers or lakes, all unknown to the modern world. Now he pauses for the view – in the distance there is a plain, beyond which a line of trees borders a wide-flowing river, the Euphrates. Beyond that there are no more than shadowy horizons in the misty light of the breaking day.

Another few minutes of walking brings the village into view; but it requires a double take. It blends into its sandstone terrace just as 'Ain Mallaha blended with its surrounding woods, seeming to have been grown by the sun and moulded by the wind rather than constructed by human hands. With every step the low and flat reed-covered roofs clustered by the rim of the flood plain become a little clearer. Even so, the boundary between nature and culture remains deeply obscure.[1]

The people of Abu Hureyra are sleeping. Dogs are sniffing each other and the ground, some scratching and some chewing at bones. The roofs are at waist-height, supported on the small wooden frames of dwellings cut into the soft stone.[2] Lubbock steps down into one and finds a small, cramped, circular room little more than 3 metres across. A man and a woman sleep on hides and a mattress of dry grass; a young girl does likewise upon a bundle of hides.

The floor is littered with artefacts and rubbish – not pestles and mortars as at 'Ain Mallaha but flat and concave grinding stones. Chipped stone artefacts are scattered across the floor, along with wicker baskets and stone bowls, and even a pile of animal bones crawling with flies. One small bowl contains tiny crescent-shaped microliths made of flint, much like those at 'Ain Mallaha. One side of the dwelling contains a pile of dirt – the wall has crumbled and soil fallen in from outside. There is a nauseating smell of rotting meat and stale air.

Much of village life occurs beyond these walls – they do not enclose houses as we think of them today. In the outside spaces there are cooking places, piles of sticks, bundles of reeds, sheets of bark, and clusters of grinding stones. Evidently many people work together in preparing the plants gathered from the wild gardens on the steppe and the marshy woodland by the river's edge. Lubbock stoops and lets the multicoloured husks, stems, twigs and leaves that surround the stones filter through his fingers. These are the waste, left precisely where they fell from the grinding stones or were stripped from the gathered bundles of plants and flowers. Near by there are baskets and stone bowls brimming with nuts and seeds of assorted shapes and colours.

Elsewhere in the village Lubbock comes across a further cluster of grinding stones; but these are surrounded by lumps of red stone and powder instead of seed husks and plant stems. The grinding stones are stained red from making pigment that is used for decorating human bodies. Close by, three gazelles have been gutted but have yet to be butchered; their carcasses are left hanging beyond the reach of dogs. The Abu Hureyra people are as dependent upon hunting gazelle as on gathering plants. But such animals are only principally hunted for little more than a few weeks each summer when vast herds pass by close to their village.[3]

Daily life at Abu Hureyra begins. The gazelle do not appear and the hunters leave to search the river valley for wild pigs and wild ass. Few animals now live in the vicinity of the village so the hunters will be disappointed. The women and children work in the wild gardens, weeding, killing bugs and collecting whatever has ripened in the sun.

Within days the herds arrive and the annual slaughter of gazelle begins. Visitors are welcomed to the village. They bring shiny black obsidian from southern Turkey as gifts and receive dentalium shells in return, shells that had once been collected on Mediterranean shores and were brought by previous visitors to Abu Hureyra.

For more than a thousand years the hunter-gatherers at Abu Hureyra will continue to hunt the gazelle. The animals are so numerous that their slaughter has no impact on the size of the herds. The women and children will continue to tend their wild gardens and reap a rich harvest. The accumulation of dirt, sand, lost artefacts and other debris within the dwellings will become either unbearable or simply make access impossible. And then the Abu Hureyra people will build new dwellings, this time totally above the ground. But eventually hard times will arrive. The drought of the Younger Dryas will disrupt the gazelle and decimate the productivity of the steppe. The village will be abandoned, the people returning to a life on the move.

At 9000 BC they will return, not as hunter-gatherers but as farmers. They will build mud-brick houses and grow wheat and barley on the alluvial plain. The gazelle herds will have resumed their migrations and be hunted for another thousand years until the Abu Hureyran people suddenly switch to herding sheep and goats. The houses will be repeatedly rebuilt so that a

mound – or tell – is formed, half a kilometre across, 8 metres deep and containing more than one million cubic metres of deposits. The remnants of
the first subterranean dwellings at Abu Hureyra will be deeply buried and
lost from human memory.

In 1972 the archaeologist Andrew Moore excavated part of the tell. As it
was a salvage operation before dam construction, his work was limited to
two seasons. Today the tell lies drowned beneath the waters of Lake Assad.
In the small area that he could excavate, Moore found several dwellings and
rubbish tips of the earliest inhabitants of Abu Hureyra. There was no sign
of a cemetery or indeed of any burials. This left him in a quandary. What
had they done with their dead, and were there the same differences in
wealth as had been evident at 'Ain Mallaha?

Nevertheless, within those two seasons of work a wealth of information
was acquired about the village. It was one of the first excavations to employ
methods to ensure that even the tiniest and most fragile plant remains were
recovered. These included 'flotation' in which charred seeds are literally
made to float away from the sediment that encased them, and then scooped
off and prepared for study. Gordon Hillman found that no less than 157 different species had been brought to the village, and suspected that at least
another hundred species had been collected but left no archaeological trace.[4]

He was able to pinpoint at least two seasons of collection: from spring to
early summer and the autumn. But he thinks the people remained in their
village all year round; where else would they have gone in the winter when
conditions in the steppe and surrounding mountains would have been
bleak? In the high summer the most critical resource was probably water
from the valley. By staying at Abu Hureyra they could have enjoyed plant
foods that reached their prime in the summer, such as the tubers from
club-rush and nut-grass – although neither was found in the archaeological
remains.

Peter Rowley-Conwy and Tony Legge, two of the most prominent
archaeo-zoologists in the United Kingdom, have studied the annual gazelle
slaughter.[5] From two tons of bone fragments, they showed that only adults,
the newborn and yearlings had been killed. This pinpointed the slaughter as
taking place during the early summer: only at that time of year would this
specific range of ages have been present.

This remarkable work by Moore, Hillman, Rowley-Conwy, Legge and
many other archaeologists shows that the hunter-gatherers of Abu Hureyra
enjoyed the most attractive environmental conditions that had existed for
many thousands of years, since long before the LGM. At no other times had
animals and plants been so abundant, so diverse and so predictable in their
availability – just as they were for the Natufian inhabitants of the
Mediterranean woodlands. This provided them with the opportunity to
give up the mobile lifestyle that had served human society since its first
appearance 3.5 million years ago on the African savannah. But why do it?

Why create the social tensions that inevitably arise when one has perma-nent next-door neighbours within a village? Why expose oneself to human waste and garbage and the health risks that accompany a more sedentary lifestyle? Why risk the depletion of the animals and plants near one's own village?

We can be almost certain that people were not forced into this lifestyle by over-population. Natufian sites are no more abundant than those of the previous times; if there had been a time of population pressure it was at 14,500 BC when there is a dramatic increase in the number of Kebaran sites and the standardisation of microlith forms. There is no evidence for a pop-ulation increase two millennia later when the first Natufian villages appear. Moreover, from the evidence of their bones, the Natufian people were reasonably healthy – quite unlike a people being forced into an undesirable lifestyle by shortage of food.[6]

Anna Belfer-Cohen of the Hebrew University in Jerusalem has studied the skeletal evidence and found very few signs of trauma, such as healed fractures, nutritional deficiencies or infectious diseases. People under stress tend to develop thin lines in their tooth enamel – called hypoplasias. These indicate periods of food shortage, often immediately after weaning. The lines are less frequent in Natufian teeth than in those of farming people. But both Natufian teeth and those of early farmers are heavily worn down. This confirms the importance of plants in their diet: when seeds and nuts were ground down in the stone mortars, grit would have become incorpo-rated in the resulting flour or paste. And when the food was eaten, this grit abraded the teeth, often leaving them with hardly any enamel at all.

The Natufian people appear to have been quite peaceable as well as healthy. There are no signs of conflict between groups, such as embedded arrow points in human bones – unlike the situation that Lubbock will find on his European, Australian and African travels. The Natufian hunter-gatherer groups were good neighbours; there was plenty of land, gardens and animals for all.

It is possible that the Natufian and Abu Hureyran people were prepared to suffer the downside of village life – the social tensions, the human waste, depletion of resources – to enjoy the benefits. François Valla, the excavator of 'Ain Mallaha, believes that the Natufian villages simply emerged from the seasonal gatherings of the Kebaran people.[7] He recalls the work of the social anthropologist Marcel Mauss who lived with hunter-gatherers in the Arctic at the turn of the century. Mauss recognised that periodic gatherings were characterised by intense communal life, by feasts and religious cere-monies, by intellectual discussion, and by lots of sex. In comparison, the rest of the year, when people lived in small far-flung groups, was rather dull.

Valla suggests that the aggregation of mobile hunters and gatherers prior to the Natufian may have been similar, and the Natufian people simply had the opportunity to stretch out those periods of aggregation, until they effectively continued for the whole year. Indeed, all the key elements of the Natufian villages were already present at Neve David: stone dwellings, grinding stones, dentalium beads, human burials and gazelle bones. As the climate became warmer and wetter, plants and animals more diverse and abundant, people stayed longer and returned earlier to their winter aggregation sites until some people remained all year round.

The sedentary hunter-gatherers at 'Ain Mallaha, Abu Hureyra and indeed throughout western Asia between 12,500 and 11,000 BC were enjoying the good life. The wealth of the archaeological evidence and the excellence of the research allows us to capture in our minds some vivid images of that life. We can readily imagine the acorns being carried in baskets to 'Ain Mallaha, and then being pounded to a paste, the Abu Hureyran hunters catching their first sight of the approaching gazelle, and the dressing of a dead man with a dentalium shell head-dress, necklace and leg band at El-Wad ready for burial.

But the image to remember is of a few families enjoying a day within the forest steppe – away from the barking dogs, the smelly rubbish heaps, the grumpy stay-behinds of their village. They are neither searching for game nor collecting plants. It is a day of rest and I see them sitting surrounded by a myriad of summer flowers. Children are making garlands while young lovers sneak off to the long grass. Some talk, others sleep. All enjoy the sun. They have full stomachs and no worries.

John Lubbock sits with them, after a few days spent living and working at Abu Hureyra. He reads his book, discovering what his namesake had known about climate change – very little. Victorian John Lubbock appreciated that immense alterations of climate had occurred because he had visited caves packed with reindeer bones in sunny southern France, found oak trees within peat bogs and seen valleys cut by ancient rivers. But in 1865 there had been no awareness of the complexity of climate change, the idea of multiple glaciations only gaining favour in the early twentieth century, and key events such as the Younger Dryas remaining unknown until recent times. Nevertheless modern John Lubbock was impressed with his namesake's book, especially when he read that the suggested causes of climatic change included variation in solar radiation, alteration in the earth's axis and changes in ocean currents – all of which have since been proved and remain at the forefront of scientific study.[8]

For a while Lubbock forgets his place in history; the butterflies, the flowers, the sun and the breeze are quite timeless. But the date is 11,000 BC and a dramatic change in the climate is about to happen; the families sitting on the steppe unknowingly teeter on the edge of an environmental calamity: the Younger Dryas is about to arrive.

For generation after generation since the LGM, life for the people of western Asia had been getting better and better. Ups and downs had occurred: years of relatively cold and dry weather when plant foods and game had been more difficult to find, years when these had been particularly abundant. But the trend was towards a warmer and wetter climate, a greater diversity of plants, increased yields of seeds, fruits, nuts and tubers, larger and more predictable animal herds, and a richer cultural and intellectual life. This had culminated in the village life that Lubbock has seen at 'Ain Mallaha and on the banks of the Euphrates. The families from Abu Hureyra enjoying the summer sunshine on the steppe were certainly the lucky ones and they probably knew it. But they could not have known quite how lucky they were. For within a few generations the tide of climate change had turned and life was never quite so good again.

6

One Thousand Years of Drought

Economy and society during the Younger Dryas
10,800–9600 BC

Once again John Lubbock stands on the west bank of Lake Hula and looks across to the village of 'Ain Mallaha. Fifty generations, 1,500 years, have passed since he watched vibrant activity within the village amidst the oak, almond and pistachio. Times have changed. The woodland is sparse. The trees and undergrowth lack the luscious growth that had seemed to cosset the people of 'Ain Mallaha with a promise of abundant food. Within the village, roofs and walls have collapsed and some dwellings are no more than piles of rubble. There are new circular structures, but these are small ramshackle affairs.

Fifty kilometres to the southwest, the village of Hayonim has been abandoned altogether. After two hundred years of occupation, people left the cave to live on the terrace, using their previous dwellings for the burial of their dead. But even those new houses are now deserted. Brambles and weeds, snakes and lizards, lichens and moss are the only residents as nature begins to reclaim its stone, welcoming the limestone walls, the basalt mortars, and the flint blades back within the earth. Abu Hureyra is the same – the people gone, empty dwellings left to crumble, artefacts abandoned and forgotten.

The date is 10,800 BC. Sedentary village life exists only in the stories, passed from generation to generation, of people who live in transient campsites scattered throughout the struggling woodland and the now desert-like steppe. The cultural achievement of the Natufian remains as no more than a faint echo in the artefacts, the dress and the social customs of these people – people whom archaeologists refer to as the Late Natufians. Many of them periodically meet together at 'Ain Mallaha, El-Wad or Hayonim, bringing the bones of their dead to rebury alongside their ancestors at what have become sacred sites existing in that nether world between history and myth.

The experiment of sedentary village life lasted for close on two thousand years but ultimately failed, forcing people to return to a more ancient peripatetic lifestyle. Before so doing, Natufian culture had spread far beyond the Mediterranean woodlands claimed by Ofer Bar-Yosef to have been its 'homeland'. The signature of this culture – the crescent-shaped microliths

– became widespread throughout western Asia, with Late Natufian settlements appearing all the way from the southern deserts of the Arabian peninsula to the banks of the Euphrates.

The spread of Natufian culture suggests that the sedentary villages were partly victims of their own success. Their inhabitants are likely to have grown in number unremittingly. Mobile hunter-gatherers have a natural constraint on their numbers as they have to carry not only their possessions but also their youngest as they move from site to site. Childbirth must be spaced at three- to four-yearly intervals as it is not possible to carry more than one child at a time. The Natufian residents of 'Ain Mallaha, Hayonim and other villages were able to reproduce more freely.

It seems likely that the spread of Natufian culture arose partly from groups of people leaving their villages to establish new settlements. This may have been the only way that ambitious young men and women could gain power for themselves. But another reason for dispersal also presents itself: there was no longer enough food to go round. Late Natufians heading into the Negev desert to establish villages such as Rosh Horesha and Rosh Zin,[1] or those close to the Mediterranean coast as at Nahal Oren,[2] or at settlements such as Mureybet on the banks of the Euphrates,[3] may have been some of the original economic migrants.

The village people had begun to over-exploit the wild animals and plants on which they relied. The gazelle bones from their rubbish heaps provide a telling story about attempts to manage the herds that ultimately backfired and led to a shortage of food. Carol Cope, from the Hebrew University in Jerusalem, has made meticulous studies of the gazelle bones from Hayonim and 'Ain Mallaha.[4] The mountain gazelles hunted from these villages behaved quite differently to those hunted at Abu Hureyra. They remained in the vicinity of the Natufian settlements all year round, never forming the massive herds that were ambushed near the Euphrates.

Cope found that the Natufian people preferred to kill the male animals. This was evident because the foot bones (the *astragali*) she studied were easily divided into two groups on the basis of size, with the larger bones outnumbering the smaller by four to one. Big feet imply big bodies, and for gazelle those bodies would have been male.

When the Kebaran people had used Hayonim Cave, five thousand years before the Natufian became established, they killed male and female gazelles in equal proportion.[5] By preferentially selecting the males, the Natufians were probably attempting to conserve the gazelle populations. Although both sexes were born in equal proportions, only a few male animals were actually needed to maintain the herds. Carol Cope thinks that the Natufian people decided that the males were expendable while recognising the need to ensure that as many females as possible gave birth to young.

If this was their aim, it went horribly wrong. The Natufians made the mistake of not just hunting the males, but selecting the biggest that they could find to kill. So the female gazelles were left to breed with the smaller males – unlikely to have been their natural choice. As small fathers give rise to small offspring, and as the Natufians killed the largest offspring, the gazelles reduced in size with each generation. Hence the gazelle bones found in the rubbish dumps of Hayonim Cave were from animals much larger than those from the rubbish dumps on the terrace – the two being five hundred years apart.

Smaller gazelles meant that there was less meat available to feed an ever-growing population. This shortage was compounded by over-exploitation of the 'wild gardens': too many stalks of the wild cereals had been cut and excessive quantities of acorns and almonds had been collected for natural replenishment to occur.

The health of the Natufian people began to suffer, especially that of the children. This is evident from their teeth.[6] Those from the Late Natufian people buried at Hayonim have a much higher frequency of hypoplasias than their Early Natufian predecessors. They also had fewer teeth remaining when they died, and those teeth that survived had caries – two further signs of poor health.

Food shortages can also lead to poor physical growth – as is evident among famine victims today. This might explain why many of the Later Natufian people, such as those buried at Nahal Oren, were shorter than those who had first lived at 'Ain Mallaha. Just as in the modern world, the men were affected more than the women, and so the Late Natufian sexes were more similar in body size than had once been the case.[7]

Food shortages within the Natufian villages, leading to emigration and eventual abandonment, cannot be blamed solely on the Natufian people themselves, on their failure to control their own numbers. The problems of population growth are likely to have been eclipsed by something over which people had no control at all: climatic change.

The Younger Dryas, one thousand years of cold and drought, was triggered by the massive influx of glacial melt waters into the North Atlantic when the North American ice sheets collapsed. Its impact on the landscapes of western Asia is readily seen in the pollen grains from the Hula core.[8] The sediments laid down within that lake after 10,800 BC show a dramatic reduction in the quantity of tree pollen, indicating that much of the woodland had died through lack of rain and warmth. Indeed, within five hundred years conditions little different to those of the LGM had returned: a devastating collapse of food supplies just as population levels had reached an all-time high.

With the double-whammy of population pressure and climatic deterioration, we should not be surprised at the collapse of Early Natufian village life. But people could not simply return to how their Kebaran forebears had lived. Not only were population numbers substantially greater but the Late

Natufian people had a legacy of sedentary life: new technology, new social relationships, new attitudes to plants and animals, new concepts about land and dwellings, perhaps even those about ownership and property.

There could be no turning back from such ideas, even though people had returned to the ancient lifestyle of transient campsites and weary feet.

Before we follow the story of the Late Natufian people of the Jordan valley and return to Lubbock's travels, we must make a brief visit 1,000 kilometres to the east. This takes us beyond the now deserted village of Abu Hureyra, beyond the Euphrates and into the foothills of the Taurus and Zagros mountains. Here, rather than villages being abandoned during the Younger Dryas, they were created for the very first time.

The Zagros region has ill-defined boundaries and is topographically diverse; it includes the upper part of the Mesopotamian plain, rolling hills, deep valleys, crags and mountain peaks. The changes in exposure and altitude created dramatic differences in the extent of rainfall and temperature, producing many localised pockets of lush vegetation even when the general conditions were cold and dry.

Throughout the whole region temperatures fell and rainfall diminished, knocking out many of the trees that had recently spread from the Mediterranean coast. But the sheltered lowland valleys provided a refuge for copses of oak, pistachio and tamarisk, as well as for game animals forced down from the now bitterly cold higher slopes.

The hunter-gatherers had to follow the plants and animals and settle within those valleys at much higher densities than when they roamed widely across the hills. Within these valleys they built some of the most elaborate architecture yet seen in the history of the world. Hallan Çemi Tepesi, found on the banks of a small river in the foothills of the Taurus Mountains, is the most intriguing of these new villages.[9] In 1991 the archaeological site was threatened by dam construction. A joint American and Turkish team undertook excavations, they found traces of structures with stone foundations and wattle-and-daub walls. Precisely when these had been built remains unclear; the few radiocarbon dates span more than two thousand years but the major period of occupation seems to have been around 10,000 BC. The people at Hallan Çemi Tepesi had gathered a wide variety of plant foods including almonds, pistachios, plums and pulses. They hunted wild goats, deer and wild boar.

Some of the structures were domestic dwellings containing hearths, grinding stones and utilitarian artefacts. But others had figurines, decorated stone bowls and obsidian that had originated 100 kilometres to the north. Domestic tasks had been excluded from these structures, reserving them for social or ritual activity.

Decorated stone bowls were made from fine sandstone; some had flat bases while others were rounded, with pierced sides for suspension across a fire. Many were decorated with incised hashes, zigzags and meanders. Some had animal images – a line of three dogs parades along the surface of one vessel. A number of the pestles had been highly polished; one had its handle carved into a stylised goat's head. Many beads were found, coming in a variety of shapes and sizes and made from coloured stones. So-called figurines were made from the same white stone used for making bowls.

Hallan Çemi Tepesi appears far too substantial for a seasonal hunter-gatherer camp; considerable labour had been invested in the buildings, and the larger stone vessels had evidently been made as fittings. The highly developed material culture and obsidian trade suggest a society as complex as that which had flourished at 'Ain Mallaha – and perhaps one even more immersed in a world of symbols and ritual. John Lubbock will only discover the consequence of these developments much later in his travels – when he arrives in Mesopotamia in 11,000 BC after having journeyed almost entirely around the world.

Archaeologists are still struggling to understand the new lifestyle that the Late Natufian people of the Jordan and Euphrates valleys adopted during the Younger Dryas. A telling source of evidence is their burial practice, and how this had changed from those of their village-based ancestors.[10] Perhaps the most striking development is that people were no longer interred wearing elaborate head-dresses, necklaces, bracelets and pendants made from animal bones and seashells. The fact that about a quarter of the Early Natufians had been buried in this fashion suggested that some had been much more wealthy and powerful than others.

Wealth and power had evidently been dependent on sedentary village life. This provided an élite with the opportunity to control the trade that brought seashells and other items to the villages. A return to mobile lifestyles swept away their power base and society became egalitarian once again, much as it had been in the Kebaran period. The absence of seashells adorning the dead was not because such shells were no longer available – they are found in abundance in Late Natufian settlements. Rather than being placed with the dead they were simply discarded with the domestic rubbish, along with bone beads and pendants. The shells had lost their value because there was no longer any control over their distribution – mobile hunter-gatherers were able to collect seashells for themselves and trade with whom they wished.

Another sign of a return to a more egalitarian society was a switch from burying people predominantly in groups – probably as members of a single family or lineage – to individual interments. Evidently family membership no longer held the same significance – people were valued on the basis of their accomplishments and personality, rather than their blood ties. But it is a third change in burial practices that is the most telling about changing society during the Natufian. A large proportion of the Late Natufian burials are of jumbled collections of bones, or of a skeleton with parts missing – frequently the skull.

These are known to archaeologists as secondary burials. They show that funeral rites were far more than the single event of placing a body into a grave and leaving it there. Instead there were at least two, perhaps several, stages to the burial ritual – most likely culminating when many groups gathered together for the final passing of the dead.

It is an autumn day in 10,000 BC. Dusk falls across Lake Hula, seemingly announced by a flight of geese. John Lubbock settles down close to his small fire, happy to watch the darkness descend and for sleep to arrive. But within minutes he is disturbed by human voices coming from a travel-weary party who pass by on their way to 'Ain Mallaha. Some are old and walk with sticks; some are young and carried by weary parents. Loud barks come from the dilapidated village, answered with little more than muted yelps by the dogs that travel with these people. To the dogs, 'Ain Mallaha will be just another of many settlements visited in the course of a year. But to the people it is a place with no equal – it is their ancestral home and this is their first visit for many years.

Their journey has taken them to several of their temporary camps – sites abandoned when the local game and plants had become too depleted to sustain their presence. They visited places where people had died and been buried. At each grave, bones were exhumed and placed in baskets to be taken to 'Ain Mallaha. From some, they took near-complete skeletons held together by dried skin and tendons; from others, just the skull. Whenever they rested on their journey, the old recalled the visits that their fathers and grandfathers had made to 'Ain Mallaha, bringing the bones of their own dead for reburial. The young listened eagerly. They knew the stories by heart: how their ancestors had dwelt at 'Ain Mallaha all year round; how there had been an abundance of food; how they had adorned their bodies with elaborate jewellery and clothes; how the wolf had become the dog.

Lubbock joins the party and enters the village of 'Ain Mallaha where respectful and formulaic greetings are made with the handful of people who live in the ramshackle dwellings and guard the site. The baskets and the few belongings they carry are laid to rest. A fire is lit and a little food shared before sleep claims them all.

During the next few days three more groups arrive at 'Ain Mallaha, each bringing baskets with the bones of their dead. Almost one hundred people have now gathered together, ready to relive the ancestral past. Two further days pass by while the woods are scoured for game and plant foods for the feasts. Stories are retold, and then retold again.

Lubbock helps with the clearance of debris from one of the collapsed dwellings: boulders, brambles, rotting timbers and the earth. The ancient cemeteries of 'Ain Mallaha are reopened. Amid singing and chanting, the bones of the new-dead are removed from their baskets and placed within the ground. By doing so, the past and present are joined as one. The act of reburial, the days of celebration that follow, the community life, story-telling and feasting recreate for the living the days of the ancestral past. The challenge of the present – the struggle for survival during the severity of the drought-ridden Younger Dryas – is momentarily forgotten.

The people remain at 'Ain Mallaha for as long their food supplies allow – ten days, perhaps two weeks at most. They talk endlessly about where they have been, who they have seen, and what the future might hold. They exchange gifts: stones, shells and, most intriguing of all, leather pouches of cereal grain, peas and lentils.

Finally the groups depart and go their separate ways, each having gained some new members and lost others. They are all grateful for the return to their transient lifestyle within the arid landscapes of the Mediterranean hills, the Jordan valley and beyond. It is, after all, the only lifestyle they have known and it is the one that they love. Lubbock has grown to love it too, especially when in the company of these people who have a tale to tell about every valley and every hill, every pool of water and every grove of trees. He joins a party that sets off walking towards the southeast, heading for the Jordan valley. Bags of seed dangle from their waists and swing like pendulums, seemingly conscious of time itself, knowing that there is little left for those who hunt and gather for their food.

There is no direct archaeological evidence that the Late Natufian people carried bags of cereal grain, lentils and peas. But if they had done so, and then scattered the seed when arriving at their autumn camps and gathered the summer harvest before moving on to live elsewhere, it would explain how domesticated wheat and barley evolved.

Patricia Anderson's experimental work has shown that the reseeding of existing stands – as the Early Natufians may have done – would have made little difference to the proportion of the non-brittle variants due to the amount of grain already in the soil.[11] What was needed for domestication to occur was that brand-new plots of cereals, peas and lentils were regularly sown and harvested, and this is just what many Late Natufian people are likely to have done. But what could have caused them to do so?

We know that times were hard in the increasingly arid landscapes of the Younger Dryas, but quite how hard remains unclear. The droughts certainly caused many ponds and rivers to disappear completely, and the larger lakes to shrink in size. The people who lived in the south, in today's deserts of the Negev and Sinai, were most likely hit the hardest. They returned to a completely transient hunter-gatherer way of life, one much like that of the Kebaran people. Survival required improved hunting weapons: game had become scarce and consequently success had become essential when a kill was possible. And so we see the invention of the Harif point – a rhombic-shaped arrow-head.[12]

Further north, the impact of the Younger Dryas may have been less severe. Yet survival still required more than just a return to the ancient mobile hunter-gatherer lifestyle, especially as there were many more people now needing food than had been the case during the Kebaran period, before the Early Natufian experiment with permanent dwellings. One response was to hunt a much wider range of animals than before; and hence we find on Late Natufian settlements the bones of many small-game species as well as the ever-present gazelle.[13]

Another response was to continue, and perhaps expand, the cultivation of plants. Wild cereals were particularly hard hit by the Younger Dryas owing to a decrease in the concentration of carbon dioxide (CO_2) in the atmosphere.[14] This diminution, carefully documented from air bubbles trapped in the Antarctic ice, inhibited their photosynthesis and markedly reduced their yields. Consequently, whatever cultivation practices had begun during the Early Natufian – weeding, transplanting, watering, pest control – may have now become essential to secure sufficient food. And these may have created the first domesticated strains.

This appears to be what occurred at Abu Hureyra just before its abandonment. When Gordon Hillman studied the cereal grains from the site he found a few grains of rye from plants that had undergone the transition into domestic forms. When dated, they were shown to lie between 11,000 and 10,500 BC – the oldest domesticated cereal grain from anywhere in the world. Along with these grains, Hillman found seeds from the weeds that typically grow in cultivated soil. And so it appears that, as the availability of wild plant foods declined due to the onset of the Younger Dryas, the Abu Hureyra people invested an ever greater amount of time and effort in caring for the wild rye, and by doing so unintentionally transformed it into a domestic crop.[15] But even this could not support the village – it was abandoned as people were forced to return to a mobile lifestyle, perhaps carrying pouches of cereal grain. The domesticated rye of Abu Hureyra reverted to its wild state.

With their increased interest in plant cultivation, the Late Natufians drifted away from the depleted woodlands where their forebears once flourished. They were drawn to the alluvial soils of the valleys, not only those of the River Jordan, but also those found by the great rivers of the Mesopotamian plain, and in the vicinity of lakes and rivers throughout the Near East. Large expanses of these rich, fertile soils became available as the rivers and lakes shrank in size during the Younger Dryas. Wild, but cultivated, cereals grew well in such soil, especially when close to the meagre springs, ponds and streams that survived in the arid conditions.

The few rye grains from Abu Hureya are the only existing evidence that such cultivation in the Late Natufian created a domesticated type of cereal –

one that 'waited for the harvester'. It is possible that wheat, barley, pulses and flax were similarly transformed by the planting and harvesting techniques employed during the arid Younger Dryas. The plain fact is that at present we simply do not know exactly when or where the very first domestic strains appeared, or whether these evolved just once for each species, or whether they evolved independently or as a package. A pioneering study in 1997 compared the genetics of wild wheat from surviving stands in the Fertile Crescent with those of modern domesticated wheat and claimed that the hills of southeast Turkey, known as the Karacadağ, is the likely location of domestication – approximately 200 kilometres north of Abu Hureyra[16] – although this needs further verification. We shall shortly see that a remarkable archaeological site is found in the vicinity of those hills.

It may have taken another thousand years or more for domestic wheat, barley and pulses to appear – possibly this did not happen until new villages and even towns had been established. But my guess is that somewhere in the Fertile Crescent, at some time during the Younger Dryas, one or more bands of mobile hunter-gatherer-cultivators had begun to carry new types of seed around. They may have noticed how much better their yields had become but they were surely quite unaware that those seeds were cultural dynamite. And their short fuse began to burn when the Younger Dryas came to its dramatic end.

At 9600 BC global temperatures rose by 7°C in less than a decade. It was a phenomenal helter-skelter change in climate. There is a sudden upsurge in the quantity of tree pollen in the sediments of the Hula core, although woodland never returned to the density and lushness that had been enjoyed by the Early Natufian people of 12,500 BC.

The impact upon the Late Natufian people was felt within a generation. Localities that had been able to sustain no more than a seasonal campsite, offered the possibility of a permanent home. Once again wild plant foods were abundant, closely followed by burgeoning animal populations. Streams and rivers flowed with renewed vigour; lakes reclaimed the soils they had for so long abandoned. Wild cereals benefited from increased CO_2 in the atmosphere.

The tricks of cultivation, those that had provided no more than meagre supplements to the diet of wild foods during the drought-ridden Younger Dryas, now produced abundant quantities of grain, peas and lentils. So the opportunity arose for the Early Natufian experiment in village life to be undertaken once again – an experiment perhaps remembered by the stories passed from generation to generation, an almost mythical way of life that could again become a reality. The opportunity was grasped – and this time there really was no turning back.

For the Early Natufians the key to village life had been the gazelle, the produce from the oak, almond and pistachio, and the wealth of plant foods gathered from the woodland undergrowth and the forest steppe. When salvation from the Younger Dryas arrived at 9600 BC a quite different environment was the key: it was on the alluvial valley soils that the new phase of human history began. Archaeologists call it the Neolithic – the New Stone Age.

7

The Founding of Jericho

Neolithic architecture, burial and technology of the Jordan valley, 9600–8500 BC

John Lubbock stands in the evening shadow of the Palestinian hills, looking towards a cluster of small round houses in the valley below. They have flat thatched roofs and are intermixed with brushwood shelters. The latter are not dissimilar to those he had seen at Ohalo at 20,000 BC, but the houses are completely new. Willows, poplars and fig trees surround the village, evidently fed by a local spring and growing luxuriantly in the new warm, wet world of the Holocene. Beyond, there are marshes that reach to the edge of Lake Lissan – known today as the Dead Sea.

Many trees have been felled to provide building material and to create small fields for barley and wheat. Whether such crops are biologically domestic or wild seems quite unimportant, as the new world of farming has certainly arrived. The date is 9600 BC and John Lubbock looks upon Jericho, a village that marks a turning point in the history of western Asia, perhaps the history of the world.

My own first view of Tell es-Sultan, ancient Jericho, was just as striking but rather less picturesque. I too stood within the shadow of the Palestinian hills, about half a kilometre to the west of what had become a great mound constituted by several millennia-worth of collapsed buildings and human debris, eroded by the sun, wind and rain. Far to the east there were bands of brilliant yellows and dazzling whites of the Jordan valley still burning in the sun; immediately below me the drab grey, breeze-block buildings of the Palestinian town that now surrounds the ancient site. But there, in the centre of my view, was Tell es-Sultan, renowned as the 'oldest town in the world'. It looked like an ancient quarry, even a bomb-site.

That, of course, was the fault of my profession – the archaeologists who began to dig the mound in 1867. A few years later Captain Charles Warren had come to search for the walls destroyed by the trumpets of Joshua and his Israelites, believing that Tell es-Sultan was biblical Jericho. A team of German scholars followed him between 1908 and 1911, and then John Garstang of Liverpool University in the 1930s. But it was Kathleen Kenyon's great excavations between 1952 and 1958 that revealed ancient Jericho to the world.[1]

Kenyon had written how 'the oasis of Jericho stands rather as one imagines the Garden of Eden'.[2] The green trees and arable farmland that surrounded the Jericho I looked upon sprawled for many kilometres beyond the neat oasis that Kenyon had seen. Modern irrigation now carries the water of 'Ain es-Sultan – the spring which gave rise to the village – to fields far away in the valley. So I used my imagination to cut down those distant trees and planted many more palms around the mound. I demolished the buildings of concrete and breeze-block, and planted cornfields in their stead. I then pitched the cluster of white tents that Kenyon had used at the foot of the mound. Once erected, I could see a stream of workmen leaving the mound at the end of the day's work, the archaeologists and students settling down for tea before beginning to sort the finds.

This was the day that they gained the first hint of the most ancient buildings within the mound. The Bronze Age town, and that of the Later Neolithic rectangular buildings were already well known. But on that day, one which I knew to be some time in 1956, 'it became clear', Kenyon would later write, 'that we were penetrating down into a different phase... the floors were of mud and not plaster... the walls were curved and the plan of the houses seemed to be round.'[3]

We know that parties of Natufian people had camped by the spring as a scatter of their crescent-shaped tools have been found. They most likely planted cereals, peas and lentils and gained one meagre harvest before departing to live elsewhere in the valley or in the hills.

Around 9600 BC the summer droughts came to an end. Renewed rainfall fed the streams that gushed between the Palestinian hills; the River Jordan began to swell. Thick layers of rich fertile soil were deposited across the Jordan valley by new annual floods, and these were watered by the spring that flowed with a new-found vigour. The cultivated crops flourished, most likely replacing the untended wild plants as the main provider of food. The Late Natufians extended the duration of their stay, until history repeated itself and sedentary village life was reborn far from those Mediterranean woodlands favoured by the Early Natufians. And so Jericho was founded, and with it people became farmers.

People have continued to live at Jericho right up to the present day. The first village was buried below houses, storerooms and shrines built by successive generations, those who used pottery, bronze, and then entered into the annals of Old Testament history. And thus a giant mound was created by the spring of 'Ain es-Sultan, 250 metres in length and more than 10 metres in height. It consisted of collapsed mud-brick walls and layer upon layer of house floors and rubbish pits; but as well as human debris, the mound contained the lost belongings and concealed burials from 10,000 years of human history.

Kathleen Kenyon (1906–78) arrived at Jericho wanting to apply what to her were very modern techniques of excavation. Like Dorothy Garrod, who

had discovered the Natufian, Kenyon was one of the great British archaeologists of the twentieth century. Both women succeeded in what was still
essentially a man's world, Kenyon studying at Oxford during the 1920s, and
then directing excavations in England and Africa. She acted as director of
the Institute of Archaeology at University College, London, during the war
and eventually became principal of St Hugh's College, Oxford. She received
many honours, culminating in being made a Dame of the British Empire in
1973.[4]

Her aim in 1952 was both to further explore the final phases of the
ancient town, that which might relate to the biblical story, and to discover
the earliest remains, which she thought more important and deserving of
'thorough exploration'. She was quite right. This became evident to the
world in 1957 when she published a popular account of her work, *Digging
Up Jericho*. The academics, however, had to wait until the early 1980s before
the suitably massive volumes describing the architecture, the pottery and
the key sequence of layers within the tell, appeared.[5] Sadly, Kenyon had
died a few years before their publication.

John Lubbock is now within the village, helping to construct a mud-brick
house. A great deal of building work is under way as the brushwood shelters
are gradually replaced by more permanent constructions. With the reliable
winter rains, productive harvests and abundant wild game within the
valley, the Jericho people have no need to leave. Whenever they choose to
spend several weeks or even months away, visiting friends and family or on
extensive hunting and trading expeditions, they know that they will return
to Jericho. And so they are quite prepared to invest time and energy in constructing mud-brick houses and clearing fields. Once a few houses had been
built, Jericho attracted new residents who were prepared to leave their own
hunter-gatherer groups to join the novel lifestyle of cultivating crops.

Lubbock has spent his morning digging clay from the valley floor and
hauling it on a wooden sledge to the village; there it is mixed with straw and
cut into oblong bricks which are left to dry in the sun. They will be bonded
together with a mud mortar to make the walls of round dwellings, each
about 5 metres in diameter and with sunken floors. The upper walls will be
constructed from sticks and branches, the roof from reeds smeared with
clay.

That evening, after Lubbock has washed in the spring, he walks around
the village and counts no less than fifty dwellings – some arranged around
courtyards for use by extended families, others standing alone or in isolated
clusters. There are hearths both inside and out and a heavy pall of wood
smoke hangs within the alleys. People sit in the courtyards, some at work
weaving mats and baskets, others exchanging news and devising plans for
the following day. At 9600 BC there are likely to be over five hundred people
living at Jericho – perhaps the very first time in human history that a

completely viable population was living in the same place at the same time.

Within a few hundred years Jericho had grown even larger, to more than seventy dwellings, perhaps with a population of one thousand. A great deal more of the surrounding woodland had been cleared and large areas were under cultivation. Many of the original dwellings had already collapsed or been deliberately knocked down so that others could be built on their ruins. But the most striking difference to the village was that its western side, that which faced the Palestine hills, had been enclosed by a massive stone wall and a large circular tower had been constructed inside.

Kenyon discovered these constructions during her excavations in 1956. The wall, 3.6 metres high and 1.8 metres wide at the base, seems unlikely to have encircled the whole settlement as no trace of it could be found on its eastern side. Inside this wall she found the remnants of the tower, 8 metres in height, 9 metres in diameter at its base, and estimated to weigh 1,000 tons. An internal staircase with twenty-two stone steps led to its summit. Such architecture was completely unprecedented in human history, and is the most remarkable of Kenyon's discoveries – at least a hundred men working for a hundred days would have been necessary to build the wall and tower. As she herself proposed, 'in conception and construction this tower would not disgrace one of the more grandiose medieval castles'.[6] Both the wall and tower remain quite unique for this period.

Kenyon assumed that these had been constructed to defend the town from attack, a seemingly irresistible conclusion, given Jericho's biblical associations. It wasn't until 1986 that Ofer Bar-Yosef asked some obvious questions: who were the enemies of Jericho? Why was the wall not rebuilt after it had become buried by house debris and refuse after no more than two hundred years? Why are there no other fortified sites of the same date in western Asia?

Bar-Yosef concluded that the walls had been for defence but not against an invading army – the enemy was flood water and mud-flows.[7] Jericho was in perpetual danger as increased rainfall and vegetation clearance de-stabilised sediments on the Palestinian hills that could then be carried to the edge of the village by the nearby wadis. By the time the village rubbish had buried the walls, the level of human settlement had literally been raised up by the accumulation of collapsed houses and human debris. This had removed the threats of flood water and mud-flow. A wall was simply no longer required.

Ofer Bar-Yosef dismissed the idea that the tower had been for fortification. He was impressed by its fine preservation, and suggested that this may have been helped by the presence of a mud-brick platform on top of the stone construction. Kenyon herself had found traces of buildings attached to its northern side that she thought might have been used for storing grain.

In this light, Bar-Yosef suggested that the tower had been publicly owned or was at the service of the community, perhaps as a centre for annual ceremonies. It seems unlikely that a definitive answer will ever be found – although further excavations in the vicinity of the tower would certainly help. What is clear is that with the construction of the wall and tower, people were creating architecture and communal activity on quite a new scale. A new phase of human history had begun.

By the late 1950s, comparable village settlements in Europe – although much younger in age – had already been described as Neolithic. During the 1920s Gordon Childe, the leading archaeologist of the pre-war period, had coined the phrase 'Neolithic Revolution' to refer to the sudden appearance of settlements that he believed reflected a complete sea change in the way of life. This not only involved farming but architecture, pottery, and stone axes that had been ground smooth. Childe thought that these formed a 'Neolithic package', one that was always acquired as a single, indivisible whole.[8]

Kenyon discovered that he was wrong. Although their houses, burials and general lifestyle fitted neatly into the Neolithic mould, the first villagers at Jericho lacked one of the crucial elements of the Neolithic package: pottery. Any bowls, vessels, plates or cups that survived were made from stone; many more are likely to have been made from wood or vegetable fibres. And so Kenyon coined a new term for early Jericho culture: the Pre-Pottery Neolithic (PPN). In fact, she designated the first village at Jericho as belonging to 'Pre-Pottery Neolithic A' – a period now known to have lasted for no more than a thousand years after the start of the Holocene.

Those who had lived in the 'PPNA' village of Jericho had literally lived with their dead. Kenyon found no fewer than 276 burials even though she excavated only ten per cent of the settlement. These were all associated with buildings in one manner or another; they were below floors, under house-hold structures, between walls and within the tower. The key Late Natufian burial traditions continued: people tended to be buried alone rather than within groups; very few artefacts, if any, were placed with the dead.

After the burials, and most probably when all flesh had decayed, pits were frequently dug to remove the skulls, many of which were then reburied elsewhere within the village. One collection of five infant skulls had been placed within a pit below what Kenyon believed was an altar. But the majority of the children and infants, who made up forty per cent of the burials, were left undisturbed – it was principally the skulls of adults that were removed for display and eventual reburial.

Why was there such an interest in skulls? It was an interest that would become highly elaborate as the village of Jericho became a town, leading to the covering of skulls in plaster masks with cowrie-shell eyes. Kenyon thought there had been a cult of the ancestors and drew comparison with the people from the Sepik River of New Guinea who in recent times have used the skulls of venerated ancestors within their rituals. But we will never know precisely why the Jericho people – and indeed people throughout western Asia and beyond – exhumed and reburied human skulls, perhaps after a period of display.[9]

As with their burial practices, the tools used by the villagers of Jericho are very similar to those of the Late Natufian, although there are also some major technological innovations. The most dramatic was the use of mud brick for building – labour-intensive work demonstrating a commitment to village life. Yet many of the stone artefacts remained largely unchanged. Microliths were still made, as were a wide range of blades, scrapers and sickles. Stone axes and adzes are, not surprisingly, found in much larger numbers than before. These were used to clear the vegetation for their fields. Such clearance may have contributed towards soil erosion, adding to the need for a defensive wall. One item, though, deserves special attention: a new type of arrow-head, known by archaeologists as the 'el-Khiam' point. These are triangular in shape with two side-notches used for hafting, and were named after the small site of el-Khiam where they had been first discovered.[10]

Just as geometric microliths and lunate microliths had come and gone in fashion, so too did el-Khiam points. They reached the height of their popularity at about 9000 BC when they appear almost simultaneously throughout the western and central regions of the Fertile Crescent. As such, it is not clear where this new design originated, or why it became so widely adopted across this vast region. Many are aerodynamically designed, and may well have led to a substantial improvement in hunting efficiency. But new research employing microscopic study has shown that a great number of these points had been used as awls and bits for bow-drills rather than as the tips of projectiles, as had been traditionally assumed.[11]

Gazelles continued to be the main target for hunters. But with the spread of woodland a wider range of animals had become available as prey – and hence the bones of fallow deer and wild boar joined those of the gazelle and ibex within the rubbish heaps of Jericho. Foxes and birds, especially birds of prey, also became prominent. These are unlikely to have been hunted for food: fox fur, talons, elegant wing and tail feathers may all have been crucial items of body adornment. They may have been part of the trade networks that were rapidly developing within the Jordan valley and beyond. For Jericho was not alone in this new Neolithic world.

8

Pictograms and Pillars

Neolithic ideology, symbolism and trade, 9600–8500 BC

Jericho was the first of the early Neolithic 'PPNA' villages to be discovered and remains the most renowned. But its long-held pre-eminent position, as constituting the origin of the Neolithic and a farming way of life, has become severely challenged in recent years by new discoveries in the Jordan valley and in the northern reaches of the Fertile Crescent. These have also provided new and quite astonishing insights into Neolithic religion.

During the 1980s several PPNA villages were discovered and excavated in the West Bank region of the Jordan valley, most notably Netiv Hagdud and Gilgal.[1] These were no more than 20 kilometres from Jericho and much smaller in size, easily imagined as hamlets in the environs of that thriving village. As these settlements had not developed into tells by the accumulation and then collapse of later prehistoric mud-brick buildings, the excavators were able to expose larger areas of the earliest Neolithic dwellings than was possible at Jericho. Their excavations added clarity and more detail to the types of architecture, burial and economic practices that Kenyon had discovered. And so this West Bank region, rather than Jericho itself, became characterised as the origin and centre of the Neolithic world.

In the late 1990s early Neolithic PPNA sites also began to be discovered and excavated on the eastern side of the valley, to the south of the Dead Sea in modern-day Jordan. These showed that the Early Neolithic flourished over a more extensive area than had once been supposed. Zad, currently being excavated by Phillip Edwards of La Trobe University, Melbourne, Australia, has some particularly impressive architecture, the walls of horse-shoe-shaped structures having been built from stone.[2] No more than two kilometres from Zad the site of Dhra' is under excavation by Bill Finlayson, director of the Council for British Research in the Levant, and Ian Kuijt of Notre-Dame University, Indiana, USA.[3] They have found a particularly impressive circular mud-walled structure with internal pillars that may have supported a wooden floor.

Seventy-five kilometres due south is my own ongoing excavation undertaken jointly with Bill Finlayson at the site of WF16 – the sixteenth site found in a survey of Wadi Faynan in southern Jordan.[4] When we discovered this site in 1996, a prominent archaeologist suggested to me that little of significance would be found as WF16 is located too far from Jericho. But our excavations have revealed some of the best-preserved floors and rubbish pits of the PPNA, a mix of architectural styles and a rich assortment of burials, artefacts and art objects: the earliest Neolithic had evidently flourished in the southern reaches and on the eastern side of the Jordan valley.[5]

All of these excavations, from Netiv Hagdud to WF16, have confirmed the character of the PPNA culture that Kenyon first identified at Jericho: small circular dwellings, burials placed below floors, rituals associated with skulls, reliance on wild game and the cultivation of either wild or possibly domestic cereals together with a diverse range of other plants. There is no question that Jericho remains the largest PPNA settlement known – nothing comparable to its tower and wall have been found elsewhere. But it is clear that we can no longer identify that site with the origin of the Neolithic itself. This has become even more evident in light of excavations in the northern reaches of the Fertile Crescent. These suggest that the Jordan valley as a whole may have been quite peripheral to the social, economic and ideological developments that created the Neolithic world.[6]

Five hundred kilometres northeast of Jericho is the site of Mureybet – or rather was, because it has now been flooded by the creation of Lake Assad by the Tabaka Dam, the same fate that befell Abu Hureyra.[7] The two sites were found less than 50 kilometres apart on opposite sides of the Euphrates. It seems likely that those who abandoned Abu Hureyra simply crossed the river and began a new village at Mureybet. That resettlement occurred during the Late Natufian and the new village developed to form a tell like that at Jericho, constituted by collapsed houses and human debris from several millennia of occupation.

Excavations in 1971 by Jacques Cauvin identified Early Neolithic levels contemporary with the first village at Jericho. But Mureybet's architecture had been more complex, with interlinked dwellings consisting of several rooms. Cauvin reconstructs them as semi-subterranean, with central internal posts holding roof timbers that radiated to rest upon the surrounding walls. The dwellings had raised areas, probably used for sleeping, grinding stones set into the floor and storage areas for grain.

While the range of stone artefacts from Mureybet are similar to those from the Jordan valley sites, Cauvin found a much greater use of baked clay than has been discovered elsewhere. Some of this had been used to make small bowls. These cannot be technically described as pottery because they lack a tempering material such as crushed bone, shell or stone to prevent the clay bursting in the kiln. But the bowls had been hardened by fire and this was perhaps the first step to pottery production in western Asia.

Clay had also been used to mould female figurines, others of which were carved from stone. Although these were schematic in character, with diminutive arms and lacking facial detail, they were more realistic than the almost completely abstract human forms found at Netiv Hagdud. On the basis of these figurines, Cauvin proposed that a cult of the 'mother goddess' had existed not only at Mureybet but throughout the Neolithic world. This deity had – according to Cauvin – been joined by another: the bull. Although no bull figurines or depictions were found at Mureybet, Cauvin had excavated skulls and horns of wild cattle buried below floors and within its walls.[8]

As all plant and animal remains from the site were from wild species, Cauvin argued that the new Neolithic worship of such deities preceded and, by some undeclared means, caused the development of farming. Few archaeologists today subscribe to the notion of a 'Neolithic mother goddess' but the view that ideological change came before economic change has found support from two further Neolithic sites, Jerf el Ahmar and Göbekli Tepe.

Jerf el Ahmar is found 120 kilometres north of Mureybet and is another site that now lies below an artificially created lake.[9] Danielle Stordeur of Lyons University, France, excavated the site between 1995 and 1999 as a rescue operation immediately before the flooding occurred. Its earliest phases are again contemporary with the first village at Jericho. Distinct architectural similarities between the structures of Jerf el Ahmar and those at Mureybet and in the Jordan valley are evident. But once again the architecture is notably complex and two structures are particularly striking.

One was located in the centre of the village and appears to have been used for the communal storage of cereal grain from wild, but cultivated, crops. It was divided into six small rooms around a central area with two benches and was extraordinarily well preserved, having walls standing more than a metre high. This building might suggest a highly co-operative and sharing community. Alternatively, one might take a bleaker view and wonder whether the centralised storage of grain had allowed one individual or family to gain power by controlling its distribution to the community. The final use of this building appears to have been for a ritual act: below the debris from the collapsed roof an almost complete human skeleton was found splayed out upon the floor. Only the skull was missing – the body had been decapitated.

That ritual and ideology played prominent roles in the lives of the inhabitants of Jerf el Ahmar is evident from another building. This was small and round, and had been deliberately burned down. On its floor, Stordeur discovered four large skulls of wild cattle which had once hung upon its walls, providing further evidence that these animals had been of religious significance. This room at Jerf el Ahmar recalls one at the Younger Dryas settlement of Hallan Çemi Tepesi – 300 kilometres to the northwest in the Zagros hills – where a wild ox skull had also been hung upon the wall.[10]

The architecture of Jerf el Ahmar is just one aspect of the site's significance. It also provides several intriguing ritual deposits, such as three human skulls that had been placed on a fire burning within a pit and then sealed with a layer of pebbles. The art works from Jerf el Ahmar are also outstanding, including stone vases intricately carved with geometric decoration and stone figurines of birds of prey. But perhaps the most significant find was four stone plaquettes, each about 6 centimetres long and engraved with signs that look like pictograms: snakes, birds of prey, four-legged animals, insects and abstract symbols.

If these had not been found at an Early Neolithic site six millennia before the invention of writing one would have no hesitation in describing such signs as a symbolic code – Neolithic hieroglyphics. Danielle Stordeur suggested that they appeared to 'evoke some kind of record' and 'carry a message'.[11] Quite what that message was will remain unknown until we learn to decipher this Neolithic code. For that we will need many more pictogram examples, but since Jerf el Ahmar is now below a lake these will have to be found elsewhere.

The closest examples to the Jerf el Ahmar pictograms that I have seen were engraved on stone pillars at a site lying a further 100 kilometres to the north. This has no risk of being flooded as it is found on the summit of a limestone hill in southeast Turkey. It is known today as Göbekli Tepe. Excavations since 1994 have astonished the archaeological world, and given further encouragement to those who wish to make Jericho and the Jordan valley peripheral to Neolithic origins.[12]

Göbekli Tepe had been first located in the 1960s when a survey conducted in its region by Istanbul and Chicago Universities recorded 'a complex of round-topped knolls of red earth' upon the summit of an otherwise barren limestone hill. A dense scatter of flint artefacts and a large number of limestone slabs were recorded. The slabs were assumed to be the remains of a cemetery, probably of Byzantine date, which accorded with the few shards of medieval pottery found by the survey. But no further comment was made about the very high density of flint artefacts. In the 1960s the idea of an Early Neolithic site perched upon a hilltop was simply inconceivable.

The site was ignored or forgotten for thirty years, until Klaus Schmidt of the German Archaeological Institute of Istanbul climbed the hill in 1994. He immediately recognised the flint artefacts as Neolithic and suspected that the limestone slabs were the remnants of contemporary architecture. Excavations have continued every year since then, to reveal a truly spectacular and unique Neolithic site. When Klaus showed me around on an October afternoon at the end of his 2002 excavation season I felt completely overwhelmed by what he had discovered and the grandeur of its setting.

Very soon after 9600 BC, at the same time as the first circular dwellings of Jericho were being built, people had come to Göbekli and carved massive 'T-shaped' pillars out of the limestone bedrock. Many were 8 feet high and seven tons in weight. These were erected within circular structures that had been sunk into the hill to create what looked liked cellars in the earth. Two stone pillars were placed in the centre of each building and up to eight evenly positioned around its edge, between which benches had been constructed. The faces of many of the pillars had been carved to display wild animals – snakes, foxes, wild boar, wild cattle, gazelle and cranes – together with enigmatic symbols like the pictograms of Jerf el Ahmar. The face of one pillar had been carved to depict a human arm and the pillars themselves resembled massive human torsos.[13]

Four adjacent buildings of this type had been exposed when I made my visit and they simply took my breath away. Schmidt suspects there are several more still deeply buried below the surface of the hill. When the site had been abandoned, the Early Neolithic people deliberately buried their ritual buildings and pillars beneath several tons of soil.

The time and effort involved in quarrying, carving, transporting and erecting such pillars by people equipped with no more than flint tools is staggering to consider. And even the 7-ton pillars had not entirely satisfied their needs. When Klaus showed me the quarries located up to 100 metres from the buildings he pointed to an unfinished 'T-shaped' pillar still partly connected to the bedrock – if removed, it would have been no less than 20 feet long and 50 tons in weight. Not surprisingly, our feet crunched over a thick carpet of flint flakes from the tools used to carve the stone. These were made from many thousands of flint nodules that had been carried up the hill from a source several kilometres away.

All of this work had been done by people who relied entirely on wild game and plants for food. Although the excavations have produced a great number of animal bones and plant remains, not a single one of these is from a domesticated species. The people at Göbekli had hunted gazelle, wild cattle and wild pig; we know that they had gathered almonds, pistachios and wild cereals and I suspect that the 'wild gardens' around Göbekli would have easily provided at least as many plant foods as identified at Abu Hureyra 200 kilometres to the south. But while the remnants from such foods were discarded at the mound, there are no traces of any domestic dwellings – no houses, fireplaces or pits.

Schmidt concludes that Göbekli had been a ritual centre, one that he describes as a mountain sanctuary, and consequently unique among all the known Neolithic sites of western Asia. It was, he believes, a meeting place for many different groups who lived in a 100-kilometre radius of the hill, or perhaps even further afield. They had gathered at Göbekli once or twice a year for purposes of an entirely religious nature. Such gatherings are very likely to have involved people from Jerf el Ahmar. As well as similarities in the choice of abstract signs and the range of animals depicted, the two sites share architectural features, especially in the use of circular buildings with benches.

Quite what the animal and symbolic images mean, and what kind of ritual activities took place at Göbekli, we are unlikely to discover. The images may have been clan totems or depictions of Neolithic gods – but there had been no 'mother goddess' at Göbekli. All of the animals are male, and there is a limestone carving from the site of a human figure with an erect penis. Indeed, rather than notions of wholesome fertility and reproduction, the emerging religious themes from both Jerf el Ahmar and Göbekli are about fear and danger of the wild. Nevertheless, Cauvin's idea that ideological change preceded the economic developments that created farming communities has gained further support. Unfortunately he died after a long illness in 2001 and never got to see the pillars of Göbekli Tepe.

That the ideology behind the images and pillars may have played a role in the development of farming came home to me when Klaus pointed at some hills lying no less than 30 kilometres across the flat plain below Göbekli. He casually noted that these were the Karacadağ.

In 1997 the wild wheat still growing on the Karacadağ was identified as being the closest known genetic relative of modern domestic wheat.[14] The need to acquire sufficient food for those who had worked and gathered for ceremonies at Göbekli – perhaps several hundred – may have led to the intensive cultivation of wild cereals that created the first domestic strains. In this regard the domestication of wheat may have had little to do with people struggling against the harsh conditions of the Younger Dryas. It may have been no more than an accidental by-product of the ideology that drove hunter-gatherers to carve and erect massive pillars of stone on a hilltop in southern Turkey.

When standing on that hilltop late on an October afternoon in AD 2002 I truly felt that it had been at Göbekli and not Jericho that the history of the world had turned. As I watched the Kurdish workmen returning to their village and the archaeologists to their camp, I imagined others making a similar departure – the Neolithic people leaving Göbekli once their ceremonies were over. Knowing the heavy yields that the Göbekli Tepe wheat provides, some may have carried bags of grain to sow in their own wild gardens. As they did so, they were spreading not just new seed but also a new way of life to the hunter-gatherer-cultivator villages of Jerf el Ahmar, Mureybet and perhaps even to Jericho itself.

The seed-grain is likely to have featured in the Neolithic trade network that had extended from Turkey to the southern reaches of the Jordan valley. We know such trade occurred because obsidian, a very fine, jet-black and shiny volcanic glass originating from a single source in the hills of southern Turkey, is found on all the Early Neolithic sites. For those who relied upon relatively dull flint in the Jordan valley, obsidian must have been a highly valued material. Many modern hunter-gatherers, such as the Australian Aborigines, have invested shiny stones with supernatural powers and the same must surely have been true of obsidian in the Neolithic period: its thin flakes are effectively transparent; thick flakes can be used as mirrors; it has the sharpest edge of any stone, and can be knapped into intricate forms. It is a truly magical material.

Obsidian was most likely traded from settlement to settlement, along with a host of other goods that are now invisible: furs, feathers, grain, meat and nuts. As the amount of obsidian found at Jericho was disproportionate to the village's size it must have been a key centre for the trading network. It was perhaps within this network of exchange that new seed-grain was gradually spread around western Asia – seed-grain for the plants that, in Daniel Zohary's phrase, 'waited for the harvester' and finally transformed the Neolithic cultivators into fully-fledged farmers. That transition created the earliest settlements of the next phase of the Neolithic, that which Kenyon called the Pre-Pottery Neolithic B. To understand how dramatically these contrasted with the first Neolithic villages of Jericho and its like, we must travel from the northern to the southern end of the Fertile Crescent and visit my own excavation site in Wadi Faynan.

Wadi Faynan is an arid but spectacularly beautiful landscape. One finds it by driving past the southern end of the Dead Sea on the road towards Aqaba, and then heading west through the village of Qurayqira – a sprawl of breeze-block houses built for the local Bedouin, many of whom prefer to remain within their tents. After Qurayqira the road ceases, and one heads on a dirt track (if one finds it) along the base of the dry wadi, to the edge of the steep escarpment that climbs to the Jordanian plateau. It is best to arrive by night, capturing porcupines and jerboas in one's headlights, debating whether it is this track or that, celebrating arrival at the excavation camp with a cold beer in the moonlight.

At Wadi Faynan we sleep under the stars and leave behind the stresses of university and family life to regain the child-like thrill of archaeology – getting our hands dirty, digging things up, exposing the past. By working with Bill Finlayson I am attempting to reconstruct the prehistoric settlement in this wadi from very earliest times to the first farming communities. Many sites have been found, some containing artefacts made by Neanderthals and possibly even earlier human types. But the most important site we have discovered is the Early Neolithic PPNA village to which we have given the unromantic name of WF16.

We found traces of this village on our first ever visit to the wadi, a time when just the two of us had gone to make a reconnaissance. After several exhausting days walking in the unrelenting heat, when we were both feeling dispirited about the lack of finds, I decided to finish the day by examining two small knolls just above the wadi bottom. To my immense excitement the ground was littered with stone artefacts: pieces of chipped flint and grinding stones. Along with these were the faint traces of small circular structures: rings of stones emerging from below sediments that had washed down from the surrounding hills and crags to bury what I hoped might be a village.

Several years later, we know that WF16 was indeed a small Early

Neolithic settlement, contemporary with the earliest phase of Jericho 250 kilometres to the north. It had perhaps ten or twelve circular dwellings, each a mere four metres in diameter and built a few metres apart so that one could wander easily between them. The people of WF16 had hunted wild goats, trapped falcons and dug out foxes from their lairs. They had collected figs, legumes and wild barley. Some of their dead had been buried within their dwellings, sometimes individually and left undisturbed, sometimes as jumbles of bones. They acquired shells from the Mediterranean and the Red Sea, carved geometric designs on to bone and stone artefacts, and made green beads from copper ore in the surrounding crags. Obsidian originating in Turkey had also been acquired – although we have so far found just one single obsidian flake amidst many thousands of those made from flint.

Our excavations are far from complete. We have yet to ascertain whether people had lived at WF16 all year round or whether it had been a seasonal camp. We remain unsure about how many dwellings there were, and whether those present were built together or in a piecemeal fashion between 10,000 and 8500 BC – the period of occupation. Had their inhabitants been hunter-gatherers, cultivators of wild cereals or farmers with domesticated crops?

My own interpretation of the site is changing in the light of new discoveries elsewhere. I once thought the foxes had been trapped simply to provide warm pelts; but having now seen the engravings on the pillars of Göbekli Tepe I wonder whether there had been ideological rather than utilitarian motives behind their capture. I have similar concerns about the many bones we have found from birds of prey – perhaps, in view of the carvings from Jerf el Ahmar, captured for reasons other than merely to provide decorative feathers. Just as at Göbekli, male imagery seems important. We have found a carved stone phallus, while some of the supposed utilitarian pestles are so phallic in appearance as to suggest that the grinding of plant foods may have been invested with some kind of sexual symbolism.

It is 9000 BC and John Lubbock has travelled south from Jericho to stand on what will become the knoll of WF16. He is surrounded by the grandeur of the wadi. It is coloured a vibrant green rather than the parched yellows and browns of today. Where I have looked upon barren desert, Lubbock can see trees of oak and pistachio; fig, willow and poplar trees grow by a river that runs along what is an entirely dry and treeless wadi today. He listens to human chatter, the grating of stone against stone, and the barking of dogs. The scent of freshly cut juniper pervades the air. Neolithic people sit outside their dwellings making and using those very artefacts that we will one day find. They wear shell necklaces and feathers from the falcons whose bones we will excavate. El-Khiam points are being hafted onto reeds and bow-drills; pestles and mortars are in action; walls are being constructed with juniper stakes.

Visitors arrive bringing obsidian to exchange for greenstone beads and parcels of goat hair. Lubbock watches the feasts that take place when hunting has been good and the grinding of tiny dry seeds when it has been bad. He watches the burial of an old man within a dwelling, his head placed upon a stone pillow. When the earthen floor has been beaten flat the skull remains exposed, enabling people to work and sleep around it, comforted by his continuing presence in their lives.

At 8500 BC, WF16 becomes silent and Lubbock finds himself alone. The Neolithic villagers have disappeared and their dwellings have been abandoned to nature and whoever might find and excavate the site. Lubbock hears voices coming from up the wadi, where it winds around a corner and the crags turn into cliffs, and where today it becomes known as Wadi Ghuwayr. Lubbock follows the riverbank, brushing past lush reeds, startled geese and ducks. He walks for no more than 500 metres on the bank of the fast-flowing river and finds people at work. Some are from WF16 but others have come from afar, perhaps from elsewhere in the Jordan valley or from a much greater distance away. Together they are building not only a new village but also a brand-new *type* of village.

They work upon the slope above the riverbank ten or twenty metres from the water's edge. Rectangular houses are being built; houses with solid stone walls and plaster floors. Terraces have been made and the positions of walls for houses 10 metres long and 5 metres wide have been marked out in the earth. Some houses are already half built; their walls are chest-high and constructed with water-worn cobbles. Small stones and mortar are packed between parallel rows of cobbles to make a solid wall 50 centimetres thick – a far cry from the drystone walls of WF16. In some houses timber posts have been set just inside the walls, ready to support the weight of roof beams.

Close to the building site a fire burns to make the lime for plaster floors. Many hundreds of limestone nodules have been collected from the upper reaches of Wadi Ghuwayr and are being burned within a pit. When sufficiently high temperatures are reached the stones will disintegrate into powdered lime. Elsewhere some of this is already being mixed with water and then poured thickly over a foundation of stones upon the floor of a near-completed house. The plaster smothers all corners, cracks, and a central shallow pit that will become the fireplace. Once dry and hard, it will be painted red and then polished. More plaster will cover the walls, both inside and out. This will be kept a brilliant white.

I know this new village well, but neither as a building site nor as a living place. I know it as ruins exposed by excavation. Mohammed Najjar of the Jordan Ministry of Antiquities and Alan Simmons of the University of Nevada[15] have found and excavated the site. They come to Wadi Ghuwayr each year to gradually reveal its architecture, one remarkably different to that of WF16 and yet built within a single generation of its demise.

Such villages with rectangular two-storey houses made their appearance throughout the Fertile Crescent soon after 9000 BC. They most likely originated at Jerf el Ahmar and Mureybet where structures that are transitional from round to rectangular have been found. The new architecture spread rapidly: a sign of the social and economic transformations that occurred now farming with domesticated crops had truly begun, and population numbers had soared. These new buildings typify the phase of the Neolithic that Kathleen Kenyon designated as the Pre-Pottery Neolithic B (PPNB). It is another new Neolithic world that John Lubbock must now explore.

9

In the Valley of Ravens

Architecture, textiles and animal domestication, 8500–7500 BC

Leaving the crags overlooking Wadi Ghuwayr, John Lubbock walks south until dusk begins to fall on a spring day in 8000 BC. That takes him into the spectacular sandstone landscape that runs as a shelf below the Jordanian plateau. He walks through thick woodland following the paths of wild goat. Having criss-crossed western Asia from the Mediterranean to the Euphrates and back again, he is knowledgeable about the trees and easily recognises the oak, pistachio, and hawthorn even though they have yet to reach full leaf. While walking he sees not only wild goats upon the crags, but glimpses a jackal beginning its night's work and a hare finishing for the day. He recognises the tracks of wild boar and the remnants of a leopard kill. With such animals around he sleeps uneasily in the shelter of a sandstone cliff which changes colour as the sun sets across the Jordan valley.

The next day Lubbock continues through the woods, occasionally balancing on the edge of rocky precipices to peer westwards across a vast and treeless gulf to the future Negev desert. After he has travelled about 30 kilometres from Wadi Ghuwayr, he arrives at the entrance of a wide, open valley, one with a thick coverage of trees and defined by high sandstone cliffs. Appropriately he sees a couple of black birds squawking loudly, for this is Wadi Gharab – the valley of ravens. It contains the first town[1] that Lubbock has the opportunity to visit; it is indeed one of the very first towns in the world: Beidha.[2]

The goat track becomes a well-trodden path through woods in which many trees have been felled. This soon gives way to small fields with newly sprouted cereals, peas and little green shoots of an unfamiliar crop – flax. And then he sees, hears and smells the town – a mass of rectangular stone buildings, human voices, dogs barking, goats braying, and wood smoke. Here there is no blurring between the domains of nature and human culture, as there was at 'Ain Mallaha and Abu Hureyra. The town of Beidha is a dramatic statement of human detachment from the natural world, epitomised by the sharp angles and ordered layout of buildings, the goats within their pens, the land cleared for farming.

The opportunity to visit Beidha has been provided by the third member of a trio of remarkable women archaeologists. We have already acknowledged the contribution of Dorothy Garrod and Kathleen Kenyon. Now we must appreciate the work of Diana Kirkbride. After having studied

Egyptology at University College, London, in the 1930s, and worked at Jericho with Kenyon, she spent seven months in 1956 excavating at Petra for the Jordanian Department of Antiquities. During that time she discovered the Neolithic town of Beidha.[3]

The spectacular 2,000-year-old rock-cut temples and tombs of Petra could not hold Kirkbride's interest and on her free days she went looking for nearby 'flint sites'. With help from Bedouin guides several were found, some of which were extremely ancient. She also found a small tell that became the site of Beidha, located about one hour's walk through the sandstone hills to the north of Petra.

Kirkbride began excavating there in 1958, and completed the last of her eight field seasons in 1983, by which time she had uncovered sixty-five buildings. This was, and remains, by far the most extensive excavation of a settlement of the Pre-Pottery Neolithic, providing a unique insight into the layout of an early town. Her work revealed how Beidha had grown from a small village of interconnected circular dwellings to the town of two-storey rectangular buildings at which Lubbock has now arrived.

To enter the town he steps across a low wall that surrounds the buildings. This is a barrier to the sandy soil that threatens to cover the courtyards, now that it has been untethered by the felling of trees. A path takes Lubbock between buildings into a walled courtyard about eight metres in diameter. This is the centre of the town. Opposite him, there are four stone-built chambers that have floors scattered with grain – the remnants of a harvest; to his left/right is the façade of a particularly large building. Lubbock steps through its doorway into a room that is gleaming white – the floor, walls and even the ceiling are thickly plastered. The only colour is a thick red stripe around the base of the walls. In the centre stands a metre-high, uncut stone pillar. Behind it, there is an entrance into a second and larger room. This is just as sparse and dazzling, with the same white plaster and red stripe which also encircles a hearth in the middle of the floor and a stone basin close to the entrance. In the farthest corner there is a stone-lined pit. And that is all. No furniture to suggest a house, no chipped stone or bone fragments to suggest a workshop, no carved effigies to suggest a place of ritual or worship, and – most frustrating of all – no people to watch either at work or play.

Although excavated by Kirkbride, the most substantial attempt to interpret the architecture of Beidha has been made by Brian Byrd of the University of California.[4] He was particularly impressed by the size of the building that Lubbock has entered, estimating that the plaster alone had required more than 2,000 kilograms of quicklime and 9,000 kilograms of wood for the kilns. So, even if individual families had built their own houses within the town, this building had required communal effort, and the key question – not just in the case of Beidha but of all the new towns with such buildings – was whether the work had been done willingly or under the coercion of town leaders. It is indeed difficult to imagine a community the size of Beidha, one with perhaps five hundred people, existing without leadership. Perhaps this came from respected elders who played a prominent role in making the decisions that would affect the community as a whole. Or perhaps there were individuals who wielded power by force.

Brian Byrd thought it likely that this building had been used for making such decisions, a place in which separate households could gather together. It seemed significant that in the courtyard directly opposite its entrance was the storage facility for grain. The encircling wall had been a recent addition – previously people had walked freely across the courtyard. The new courtyard wall, along with other architectural developments, was evidently being used to control people's movements through the town and to influence what they could see. This was, one assumes, to the advantage of those who were in authority: the stores of grain – and knowledge about how much grain they contained – were sources of power to those who controlled its distribution.

Leaving the large building, Lubbock walks between houses until he reaches another courtyard – smaller than the last, unpaved and providing access into two adjacent houses. Each has three or four steps into an upper storey, and a similar number into a basement below. Lubbock chooses a house from which he hears voices, climbs the stairs and enters a room in which eight or nine people sit on rush mats around a central hearth. There are adults and children, men and women; some are sharing bread and meat, others are inhaling from smouldering leaves. The whole room is filled with smoke that can pass only slowly through the reeds that form the roof. Lubbock's eyes stream with tears.[6]

The people are squeezed together; it seems likely that one family is entertaining another. Their clothes are striking – testament to another small revolution that has happened during the last millennium, one that has gone by practically unnoticed by archaeologists. All the previous people in this history have worn clothes made from hides or furs, or very occasionally from knotted fibres. The people of Beidha are dressed elegantly in fabrics made from spun yarn; they are wearing the earliest form of linen, dyed green and turned into tunics and skirts.

Such clothing, made while the arts of spinning and weaving were in their infancy, was unlikely to last even a few generations before rotting or falling part, let alone for the many millennia since people had sat eating at Beidha. Yet some did survive, not in the town ruins but within the tiny cave of Nahal Hemar, located midway between Beidha and Jericho, on the northern boundary of the Negev desert far from any known human settlement. Bedouin had plundered this cave during the 1960s when searching for a further collection of Dead Sea Scrolls. In 1983 it was rediscovered by the

Israeli archaeologist David Alon who excavated the surviving deposits with Ofer Bar-Yosef.[7] They found many pieces of fabrics, cords and baskets. All were contemporary with the first towns of western Asia.

The fabrics had survived because the sediments were bone dry – without moisture, destructive bacteria could not complete their work.[8] They had been made from reeds, rushes and grass, using a variety of spinning, knotting, stitching and hand-weaving techniques. Baskets had been made from plaited plant-fibre cords, coiled into the shape of a vessel and waterproofed by coating with asphalt from natural deposits around the margins of the Dead Sea. Bone spatulas from the cave were most likely basket-making tools.

Some fabrics had been made from linen yarn that came from the strong stem fibres of flax plants. These had been spun and then combined either by knotting or by hand-weaving, using a method known as 'weft twining', which may have been undertaken across a wooden board. This is the simplest type of weaving, and one used until recently by tribal societies throughout the world. Several bone shuttles were found which would have taken the weft, or horizontal yarn, between the warp, or vertical yarn.

Unfortunately the fragments of fabric from Nahal Hemar are too small to reconstruct the items of Neolithic clothing – with one exception, a conical head-dress. A woven band had been made to fit around a forehead and decorated with a single greenstone; the cap had then risen to form a diamond-patterned cone finishing in a topknot and tassels. As it is a unique find, we have no idea whether this was everyday wear for Neolithic people or an item of ceremonial clothing worn only by special persons on special occasions. The latter is perhaps more likely in view of the isolated location of the cave and the other objects it contained.

As with the wheat and barley, flax had also grown as a wild species within the forest steppe of western Asia, and then been cultivated with the cereals and legumes. Fragments of flax have been found at Jericho, Tell Aswad and Abu Hureyra, but it has not been possible to tell whether they come from wild or domesticated plants. My guess is that flax was also grown at Beidha; none has been found, but plant preservation and recovery at this site was particularly poor.

Although the clothing and baskets left in Nahal Hemar may have been used on ceremonial occasions, they remind us of what must have been a pervasive aspect of everyday life during the Neolithic. The cutting of reeds and growing of flax, the spinning, weaving, twisting, sewing and knotting of fibres are likely to have taken up a large part of many people's lives. They would have seen and handled fabrics on a daily basis, feeling their coarse grain against their flesh. The smell of asphalt, wickerwork and linen cloth would have always been with them. And yet practically all that archaeologists know of their clothing are the few fragments discovered in Nahal Hemar Cave.[9]

Lubbock is still inside the house at Beidha, inspecting waterproofed baskets on the floor and a pile of knitting. Hot stones from the hearth are periodically dropped within the baskets to heat the liquid inside – mint tea. A thick pile of furs, hides and fabrics at the far end of the room suggests a sleeping area. A young child lies upon them with a pale and sickly complexion. Just as Lubbock has so frequently seen elsewhere, infant mortality at Beidha is high – something that Diana Kirkbride discovered when she unearthed the many tiny skeletons that lay buried beneath the floors.

Lubbock discovers that work principally takes place in the basement. It has an earthen floor and thick walls that contain six small chambers, three on each side of a short corridor.[10] Stone slabs on the floors provide solid work surfaces – some are covered with stone flakes, others with discarded fragments of cut bone and horn. Some chambers have been used for grinding stone into beads, others for working hide. The two chambers closest to the entrance have large grinding stones used for making flour from wheat and barley.

So here is another radical change, not only from the Natufian settlements but also from the first farming villages of Jericho and Netiv Hagdud. Many activities have moved indoors and rooms within single buildings now have defined functions: some are devoted to eating, sleeping and entertaining, others to craft activities and storage. There seems to be not only a new order in architecture and town layout, but also in people's lives.

The transition from small circular dwellings typical of PPNA settlements such as Jericho, Netiv Hagdud and WF16 to the relatively large, rectangular and often two-storey buildings of Beidha and other PPNB settlements documents a major social transformation.[11] Kent Flannery from the University of Michigan has argued that this reflects a shift from a group-oriented society – in which any food surpluses are pooled and available to all – to one in which families are the key social unit. Rather than being spread out between several small circular huts, such families consolidated their presence with multiple rooms within a single building. They owned and stored some, or perhaps all, of any food surpluses they generated, often constructing special storerooms as part of their houses.[12]

Lubbock's walk through the alleys and courtyards of Beidha provides him with other new experiences. In the hunter-gatherer settlements he had visited there had been few surprises – he could almost always see from one side of the village to another, most of the work occurred in the open air, and everyone seemed to know everyone else's business. Here, as in the other Neolithic towns, turning almost any corner can lead to a surprise – unexpected clusters of people, an outdoor hearth, a tethered goat. People simply cannot know what is happening elsewhere in the town – even just a few metres away – because so much occurs behind thick walls. The number of inhabitants has become too great for people to know one another's business and relations. There is, Lubbock senses, an atmosphere of distrust and anxiety, one brought on by the impact of town life on a mentality that had evolved for living in smaller communities.[13]

Along with sheep, goats were the first animals to be domesticated after the dog, and completed the shift from hunting and gathering to a farming lifestyle. Precisely where, when, and why such domestication occurred is still much debated by archaeologists.[14]

The goat is very rare in the collections of bones from Natufian and Early Neolithic villages, these being dominated by gazelle – the preferred prey ever since the LGM. So the abundance of goats found at Beidha – 80 per cent of all animals bones – suggests herding rather than hunting.

The Beidha goats were also small in size compared to known wild goats. A reduction in body-size occurs with all animals once they become domesticated – pigs are smaller than wild boar, cows smaller than wild cattle. This most likely arises from poor maternal nutrition and the selective killing of the largest adult males for meat. Such a pattern of slaughter is evident at Beidha where most of the bones come from animals of about two years of age, suggesting that they had been kept alive until they reached full size but killed before they ate too much forage. The fact that very few of the bones from Beidha came from young animals is a sure sign that the goats were not being kept for milk; in that practice, the newborn are killed so that the mother's milk can be taken for human use.

The early domestication of goats and sheep is not surprising, as their wild behaviour readily lends itself to human control. Both animals are highly territorial; they are reluctant to stray from their herd and live within strongly hierarchical groups. Hence both goats and sheep are ready to follow the largest ram or ewe, and this makes them susceptible to becoming imprinted with the idea of a human as leader. Stone-built dwellings provided substitutes for the caves in which wild goat and sheep naturally take shelter.

Exactly where and when herding began remains unclear. On the basis of size and abundance, sheep and goats may have been first domesticated in the central (i.e. Syria, southeast Turkey) or eastern (i.e. Iraq, Iran) part of the Fertile Crescent by 8000 BC, possibly much earlier. We know that the occupants of Abu Hureyra by the Euphrates were herding sheep and goats at 7500 BC. By this date, a new set of mud-brick houses had been built, burying the hunter-gatherer village that Lubbock had visited. The new town's people had initially continued the Late Natufian practice of slaughtering the gazelle during their annual migration. By 7500 BC, however, they had switched to killing sheep and goats, animals which had been kept in managed herds.[15] But we must look further east for the earliest domesticated goat, to Early Neolithic villages that are found today in central Iran.

Of these, the village known as Ganj Dareh provides the most compelling evidence.[16] It is a small mound at the southern end of the Kermanshah valley, about 40 metres in diameter and 8 metres high. Most of it consists of collapsed mud-brick buildings that were first constructed at some date between 10,000 and 8000 BC.[17] The people who lived at Ganj Dareh had killed large numbers of goats, providing a collection of almost 5,000 bones for study. Brian Hesse of the University of Alabama and Melinda Zeder of the Smithsonian Institution undertook this work, finding a tell-tale sign of domestication in the presence of large numbers of slaughtered young males.[18]

Either the herds themselves, or simply the idea of herding, may have swept westwards and then to the south, just as the practice of arable farming spread to the east. As such, goat herding would have reached the Jordan valley by around 8000 BC. But it is also possible that goats may have been domesticated quite independently elsewhere, even in the vicinity of Beidha. At present, archaeologists simply do not know.

Quite how the idea of goat/sheep domestication came about and was put into practice is also a matter of debate. Frank Hole of Yale University thinks that hunters became aware of an increasing scarcity of wild animals and took deliberate steps towards their management. This may have involved the provision of winter forage, the construction of fences to control herd movements, and caring for orphan animals.[19]

Many historically documented hunter-gatherers, such as Australian aborigines, kept tame animals as pets and we must assume that this was the case with the Natufian and PPNA people. When their descendants began living in permanent settlements some of these 'pets' are likely to have become sexually mature and to have reproduced within the bounds of the settlement. These animals, isolated from the wild, would have provided the basis for the domestic herds. Selective breeding intentionally developed particular traits – placid temperaments, rapid growth, high milk yield and thick wool. Caring for tame animals in hunter-gatherer groups is often assumed to have been undertaken by women and children, so it may have been these, rather than male hunters, who played the most critical role in animal domestication.

Once sheep and goats had been domesticated, cattle and pigs followed within a few hundred years. But domesticated horses and donkeys did not arrive until several thousand years after the Neolithic towns had flourished. These most probably arose as pack animals for the movement of ore and fuel to smelting centres once metalworking had begun in the Bronze Age.

It is time for Lubbock to leave Beidha. Although new buildings are still being constructed, the town will be abandoned within a few generations. Beidha had not been situated in the most advantageous of locations: the southern reaches of the Jordan valley received barely enough rainfall to support farming, and the nearest permanent spring was more than 5 kilometres and a climb of 400 metres away. Under these conditions the soils of

Wadi Gharab are simply too poor to sustain intensive and repeated cultivation, and too unstable without the trees. Each year goats are being taken further and further from the village to find forage, while crop yields diminish and will soon collapse.[20] And so at around 7500 BC the last inhabitants of Beidha will leave, following a steady haemorrhaging as life had become too hard.

Many people will go to a thriving new town a mere 12 kilometres to the south, known today as Basta.[21] This was only discovered by archaeologists in 1986 and has since provided some of the most impressive surviving Neolithic architecture, with 2-metre-high stone-built walls, complete with windows and doors. Basta grew to more than 12 hectares in extent, one of the largest Neolithic towns. It must have found itself a particularly fertile niche, allowing it to far surpass Beidha in size. But even this town did not survive beyond 6000 BC.

Lubbock's journey is not to Basta but to the north – a return to Jericho and then to the town of 'Ain Ghazal. His time at Beidha has provided only a partial view of the new town-dwellers of the Neolithic age – one largely concerned with their domestic lives – so he must visit these settlements to learn more about their sacred world.

10

The Town of Ghosts

Ritual, religion and economic collapse, 7500–6300 BC

From Beidha John Lubbock heads directly west, following a stream through a wooded valley to the lowlands and eventually the River Jordan. There is lush woodland, reeds and papyrus on either side of the river, but otherwise the landscape is dry and barren. Beyond the Jordan the land climbs and soon becomes today's Negev desert. It is sunrise. Across the river a lazy wisp of smoke rises from a fire.

It burns for a party of men from Jericho who are heading south with baskets of surplus grain. A dozen of them have carried the heavy load, heading for a rendezvous with hunter-gatherers who live within the Negev. The grain will be exchanged for seashells and meat from wild game.[1]

The deserts of the Negev and Sinai were recolonised soon after the Younger Dryas had come to an end. Some new desert settlements were made at exactly the same location as those of the Late Natufian, such as Abu Salem in the central Negev.[2] The new occupants may have remained in the desert all year round, living as hunter-gatherers; alternatively they may have simply been summer visitors, spending winters in the Neolithic towns such as Beidha. In either case they may have supplied the townspeople with meat.

As domesticated animals became the principal source of meat, wild game is likely to have become a prestigious foodstuff for people within the towns. The dwellers of Beidha and other settlements made a variety of very elegant arrow and spear points, suggesting that the killing of wild game had now acquired a special status.[3] At 'Ain Ghazal – a town on the outskirts of modern-day Amman – the remains of no less than forty-five wild species were present, including three species of gazelle, wild cattle, pig and small carnivores.[4] It seems unlikely that such a range could have been hunted in the immediate vicinity of the town and hence some of these bones must have arrived in joints of meat acquired from desert-based hunter-gatherers.

Shells from the Red Sea were also arriving in the towns by some means. The interest in acquiring seashells, whether by exchange or by expeditions to the coast, reaches right back to the LGM, and had previously attained a peak in the Early Natufian. But a change in the most desirable types had occurred: interest in the tube-like dentalium shells seems to have been replaced by a desire for cowries.[5]

As the traders head south, Lubbock travels north to visit Jericho for a second time. He follows the base of the Judaean Hills along the western shore of the Dead Sea. Wadis, some containing small streams that will soon dry out under the hot summer sun, dissect the hills. He passes flocks of goats being taken to pasture by young boys and small groups collecting asphalt and salt.

Lubbock arrives in 7000 BC. The settlement has changed since the time when he watched the first wheat being sown: the clusters of small, circular dwellings have been replaced by sprawling rectangular buildings amidst not just arable fields and flocks of goats, but row upon row of mud bricks drying in the sun. Jericho has turned from a village of hunter-gatherer-cultivators to a town of farmers, craftsmen and traders.[6]

Lubbock wanders through the courtyards and between the houses, engulfed by the clamour of Neolithic life. Much work is taking place out-doors – food preparation, stone-working, the manufacture of baskets, fabrics and leather goods. He is reminded of Beidha; there are similar packs of scavenging dogs, and the same flux between the stench of hanging meat, the earthiness of wood smoke and the fragrance of smouldering herbs as he walks around the town. He stops to watch a woman at work with her quern; it is so large that she sits on one end and repetitively bends her back as she stretches with her hand-stone to the other – the work of countless generations to come.

The houses are built from sun-dried mud brick rather than stone. They are single storey and seem rather simpler in design than those at Beidha, there being no sign of the corridor buildings.[7] Lubbock chooses one at random to enter. Wooden doors lead him through three successive rectangular rooms, each with a burnished red plaster floor and rush mats. No one is at home and there is little in the way of furniture. A pile of mats and hides suggests a sleeping area, baskets and stone bowls appear to be valued possessions.

In the third room three clay figurines, each female and about 5 centimetres high, stand against a wall. One is particularly striking – it is dressed in what seems to be a flowing robe and has been sculpted with arms bent, so that one hand is placed below each breast. Next to them is what looks like a human head. Lubbock lifts it gently – it is literally a human head, or at least a skull on which the face has been delicately modelled with plaster.

As he moves around the town, Lubbock finds more plastered heads in other houses along with plain skulls that have been positioned in corners of rooms or within wall niches. After much searching, he finds a man seated within his house working on a face. It is being modelled on to the skull of his father, the man who had built the house and whose hands had laid the plaster floor below which his bones now rest. After the body had remained entirely buried for several years, the grave was reopened, the skull removed and the floor patched with new plaster.[8] Now the son honours his father.

The man at work squats beside bowls of white plaster, red paint and an assortment of shells. The nasal cavities and eye orbits have already been packed and left to dry; the base of the skull has been levelled so it can stand unaided. Now the final coating of a fine white plaster is being applied which will soon be painted red. Cowrie shells will be inset for the eyes and then the skull displayed within the house. As he moulds, pinches and smoothes the plaster, the man's wife collects lentils in the fields, struggling with the weight of their baby boy strapped to her back. One day that son will loving-ly exhume and model his own father's head to ensure that he too continues to live within the house, even after his bones have been buried under the floor.

The plastered skulls of Jericho were perhaps the most dramatic of Kathleen Kenyon's discoveries. She found seven of them within a single pit, along with various isolated skulls below house floors. Most were rather squat in character as whole faces had been modelled over skulls that lacked their lower jaws. But one skull had been complete and the plaster sculpture appears as an elegant portrait of a revered ancestor. Whether the skulls had been displayed, belonged to the 'founders' of the house and aspired to be portraits, are matters for speculation. All we know is that at some time they were buried in pits, perhaps as a final act of remembrance or as the last step in reaching the afterlife.

Since Kenyon's excavations at Jericho, plastered skulls have been found at numerous Neolithic sites, each settlement making them in a subtly different manner but conforming to the same basic design.[9]

A different type of decorated skull was found in Nahal Hemar – the cave from which the fragments of fabric were recovered. Here remnants of six skulls were found, all of which had strips of asphalt arranged in a net design across the cranium, perhaps once used to attach hair, but with no plaster on the facial bones.

These skulls were joined in the cave by a remarkable array of other ritu-alistic objects, in addition to the pieces of fabric.[10] This included the frag-ments of two stone masks that had been painted in alternating red and green stripes and are likely to have had hair and beards attached. Four carv-ings of human faces were found, each made from a segment of a long bone and decorated with plaster, red ochre and asphalt to mark eyes, hair and beard. These had been applied on several occasions, suggesting that the fig-urines had been intentionally 'aged'. Fragments of plaster were found on wads of grass that, in light of discoveries I will shortly describe, are likely to have been modelled plaster figures. There were a great many beads within the cave, several hundred made from Mediterranean and Red Sea seashells and others from stone, plaster and wood.

David Alon and Ofer Bar-Yosef, the excavators of Nahal Hemar, have struggled to explain why such a precious collection of objects had been placed within a tiny cave located many kilometres from any known settlement. The cave may have been revered because of its location on the boundary between two social territories, and indeed two distinct types of landscape – the Negev and Judaean deserts – and hence used as a store for ritualistic objects. Little more can be said at present. All we can do is to visit the cave, describe its objects and admit to our woeful ignorance about the sacred world of the Neolithic.

From Jericho, a journey of 100 kilometres to the northwest would take Lubbock into the Nazareth hills and to the funerary centre of Kfar HaHoresh. This is looked after by resident guardians and is where the small towns and villages of that region bring their dead for burial – or more frequently reburial after bones have been exhumed. A host of ritual practices occurs at Kfar HaHoresh: facial modelling in plaster, the slaughter and burial of wild animals, the laying of plaster surfaces surrounded by low walls into which bones are sometimes positioned to mimic a recent death, and communal feasting. Indeed, as Nigel Goring-Morris of the Hebrew University in Jerusalem continues his excavations which began in 1991, an ever greater range of exotic practices is coming to light.[11]

From Kfar HaHoresh, a further walk of 30 kilometres would take Lubbock to the Mediterranean coast below Mount Carmel. Providing that took him about five hundred years, he could then visit the coastal community of Atlit-Yam. Although its people grew cereals, and kept cattle, goats and pigs, this was primarily a fishermen's village. Boats departed daily to net the triggerfish that resided on the sandy and rocky seabed.[12] But the sea will eventually bring about the town's demise as rising sea levels flood the Mediterranean coastline, leaving Atlit-Yam entirely submerged.

Lubbock's time in the Neolithic age of western Asia is rapidly running out. He must therefore forgo visits to Kfar HaHoresh and Atlit-Yam and travel 50 kilometres to the eastern side of the Jordan valley where he will find the largest of the Neolithic towns, that known today as 'Ain Ghazal. And so for two days he travels through the thick woodland of the Jordan valley, climbing its steep eastern escarpment into grasslands dotted with scattered trees.[13]

The first sign that a town is near by is when the goat tracks he follows broaden into well-trodden paths between small fields, some planted with lentils and peas, others with wheat or barley. Women and children are at work, harvesting the lentils and departing in twos and threes to carry heavy loads to the town. Many baskets wait to be taken and so Lubbock heaves one upon his shoulders and follows a woman with her two tired children. He follows them into the valley known today as Wadi Zarqa; stepping-stones cross the river where many goats have been tethered. A track then leads directly to the heart of the town.

As he walks, Lubbock notices that every available patch of soil has been planted. The reason soon becomes evident – the town is three or maybe four times the size of Jericho. The nearby valley sides of Wadi Zarqa, however, are quite barren – the soils exhausted by repeated cropping, and then washed away by winter rains after the remaining vegetation had been cleared for firewood. Some of the slopes have been terraced for the construction of new houses, while families live in temporary tents and brushwood shelters. 'Ain Ghazal is 'enjoying' a population explosion, partly from its own inhabitants, and partly from the influx of people whose own villages have already been abandoned due to erosion and exhaustion of the surrounding land.

The date is 6500 BC and the town is a maze of buildings – some brand new, some being repaired, others dilapidated or abandoned. They are built from undressed stone, timbers, reeds, mud mortar and plaster.[14] People are returning to their homes as dusk descends; some are embarking on meals, others preparing to sleep. Lubbock leaves the basket outside the house of the woman he has followed, who will thank her children for carrying it, much to their surprise. For the next hour he explores the town, peering through windows and over people's shoulders. Much is the same as at Beidha and Jericho, with plastered heads and small clay figurines prominently displayed. In one house he sees a delightful model of a fox – indeed, models of animals seem particularly important to the people who live here, especially those of cattle, although whether wild or domestic remains unclear.[15]

In another house a group sits around a flaming hearth as obsidian blades, pieces of coral and brightly coloured stones are passed from hand to hand. These come from a man with distinctive clothes and hairstyle – a trader recently arrived from the north. Peering around the door Lubbock sees small spheres, discs and pyramids of clay being counted and placed in leather pouches.[16] Such items are quite new to him, but tiredness overcomes curiosity and he finds an abandoned house in which to sleep.

The next morning Lubbock awakes to find the town silent and deserted: no cooking in the courtyards, no women setting off for the fields, no men erecting timbers and laying plaster floors. As he wanders through the alleys between the houses, a low murmuring turns into a quiet babbling of voices. On turning a corner Lubbock finds a gathering of several hundred people. Young children sit upon parents' shoulders, older children have climbed upon walls and window-ledges. Everyone is clamouring for a view. Just as Lubbock arrives, the wooden doors of a building swing open and a procession emerges. Silence and stillness descend.

Six men lead the way, dressed in masks, robes and head-dresses much like those discovered at Nahal Hemar. They carry a wooden platform supporting a group of statues, made by plaster-coated bundles of reeds that had been tied to form torsos, arms and legs.[17] There are perhaps twelve plaster statues, some about one metre high, others much smaller. They have flattish bodies, elongated necks, large round faces, wide-open eyes with deep black centres. The noses are moulded as stubs; the lips hardly exist at all. The plaster is pure white; some statues are draped with fine pieces of textile. One has her hands positioned below her breasts, thrusting them towards the viewer whom she entraps with her steely gaze.

The crowd clamours to see the statues, knowing that it will be their last chance as they are going for burial. But the people also know that within a few years another set of statues will be brought through those wooden doors, and eventually another set, and then another: new life will always follow death, just as spring growth always follows the harvest.

Lubbock joins the procession to an abandoned house and squeezes inside to watch the burial ceremony and listen to the prayers and chanting. Each statue is held aloft and then carefully placed into a pit dug in the floor. More prayers, and the pit is closed. The 'priests' return to the building from whence they came, the doors slammed shut. The crowd disperses; some people appear to be in shock, some mournful, others confused.

The town of 'Ain Ghazal was discovered in the late 1970s when the construction of a new road exposed walls and human bones. The plaster statues were found in 1983 during the third season of excavation directed by Gary Rollefson, then of the University of San Diego. He and his colleagues also found several plaster skulls, many human burials, evidence for traded items such as obsidian from Turkey and coral from the Red Sea, together with numerous small clay 'tokens' which may have been accounting devices, perhaps representing the allocation of fields to particular families. A vast quantity of animal bones was excavated, too, the majority coming from goats that had evidently been kept in large herds.

Rollefson was able to document the boom and eventual bust of this farming town. So, even without the plaster statues, 'Ain Ghazal would have provided further insights into the economic, social and religious life of the early Neolithic farmers. But it is the statues that distinguish 'Ain Ghazal from all other Neolithic towns. Although pieces of plaster with impressions of reeds were found at Nahal Hemar and Jericho, it has only been at 'Ain Ghazal that plaster statues have been found intact.

Two caches were discovered. The first consisted of twelve statues and thirteen busts, all of which had been placed in a single pit, with the larger figures aligned on an east–west axis. Two years later a second, smaller cache was found dating from about two hundred years later in the history of 'Ain Ghazal. Its statues were very similar in design, although a little larger and more standardised. Included in this second cache were three spectacular busts of a two-headed figure.

Denise Schmandt-Besserat from the University of Texas has looked towards the religious practices of the much later Babylonian civilisations for clues as to what the statues represented, believing that the origins of those Babylonian beliefs lie within the first farming communities of western Asia.[18] One possibility is that the plaster statues were depictions of ghosts. The early

Babylonian scripts record how ghosts were sometimes banished from houses by burying effigies at a distance from occupied buildings. Schmandt-Besserat is sure that the people of 'Ain Ghazal would have feared these statues, and that their uncanny appearance – big staring eyes, disproportionate heads, and in one case six toes – might suggest ghosts.

So perhaps 'Ain Ghazal had been a town full of ghosts which had to be repeatedly banished from the houses and courtyards, from the goat pens and fields, by encasing them within the ground. But Schmandt-Besserat is more persuaded by another possibility – that these statues represent a pantheon, the gods and goddesses of the Neolithic.

In Babylonian literature the great god Marduk has two heads, much like some of the plaster statues and similar to two-headed figures in the art of the later prehistoric and historic communities in western Asia. The plaster statue exposing her breasts recalls a Babylonian goddess who adopts a similar pose. So the possibility arises that the roots of Babylonian religion lie in the Neolithic culture of the Jordan valley around 6500 BC.

But why would the statues have been buried? The fact that two caches have been found within the tiny excavated portion of the town suggests that many statues were once made. Perhaps this was for no other reason than wear and tear – the plaster constructions would have soon cracked and crumbled, so burial was a way of enabling new statues to be made. Or perhaps, as in later religions, the gods had to 'die' and then be reborn each year to ensure a fertile spring.

The plaster statues indicate a shift to a more public and perhaps cen-tralised form of religious activity than was present earlier in the Neolithic. This is also suggested by the appearance of buildings that were most likely 'temples'. Such buildings have been associated with Jericho and Beidha but the most convincing examples come from 'Ain Ghazal. Towards the end of this settlement's existence, three new types of building appear, diversifying what had been a remarkable degree of architectural homogeneity of rectangular, domestic dwellings.

Gary Rollefson describes the appearance of buildings with apsidal ends that became scattered within 'neighbourhoods' of the domestic dwellings; small circular buildings were also constructed. These were repeatedly refloored and so interpreted by Rollefson as shrines associated with several families or a lineage. Two 'special' buildings are also known from the final phases of 'Ain Ghazal. The most impressive was located high on a slope in full view of the whole settlement. It is unique in lacking a plaster floor and in the nature of its surviving furniture and fittings. A square, red-painted hearth was positioned in the centre of the room, surrounded by seven flat limestone slabs; there were several standing blocks of limestone and an anthropomorphic stone pillar. Rollefson suggests that the building may have functioned as a temple for the whole community.[19]

The town of 'Ain Ghazal made remarkable growth, reaching thirty acres in extent, spilling over to the east side of Wadi Zarqa, housing 2,000 people and more. By 6300 BC, however, it is in an advanced state of terminal decline. There are many abandoned houses and the alleys between them are littered with Neolithic rubbish. There is little more than a faint echo of the once ebullient town in the few occupied houses and the men and women who are still working in the courtyards. Any recently constructed houses are small and shabby compared to those of the original town.[20]

The river within Wadi Zarqa still flows but the valley sides are bare – not just around the village but as far as one can see. Soil exhaustion and erosion had devastated the farming economy of 'Ain Ghazal. Not a single tree remains within walking distance of the town. Its people had travelled further and further every year to plant their crops and to find fodder for their goats. Yields declined, fuel became scarce and the river polluted with human waste. Infant mortality, always high, reached catastrophic proportions, so that population levels collapsed, compounded by the steady departure of people back to a life within scattered hamlets.[21] Such is the story of all PPNB towns of the Jordan valley – complete economic collapse.

Lubbock now stands above the Zarqa valley and stares at the shocking scene of environmental degradation caused by farming.[22] Both he and modern-day archaeologists wonder whether farming could possibly have been the only cause; the ice cores show that between 6400 and 6000 BC there was a period of particularly low temperatures and unreliable rainfall, if not drought. But it seems quite impossible to untangle the relative impacts of human farming and a changing climate on the now barren landscape around 'Ain Ghazal.

In the distance a flock of goats is being herded into the hills. Lubbock watches as they pick their way over the crags and disappear from sight. That flock will return to 'Ain Ghazal, but not for many months as a new economy has arisen. Town life is no longer sustainable in the Jordan valley and has been replaced with nomadic pastoralism, the way of life that continues to the present day. Within a few years 'Ain Ghazal will be no more than a seasonal gathering place for nomadic goat herders who will erect flimsy shelters in the ruins of the town while their animals feed upon the thistles that have grown over the deserted buildings and burial places of the gods.[23]

11

Heaven and Hell at Çatalhöyük

Florescence of the Neolithic in Turkey, 9000–7000 BC

John Lubbock is approaching the end of his journey through the Neolithic revolution of western Asia, that which turned the Ohalo hunter-gatherers into the farmers, craftsmen, traders and priests of 'Ain Ghazal. From that town he has travelled northwest for 500 kilometres in the company of pastoralists and traders, crossing the Syrian desert by moving from oasis to oasis. This has taken him to the Euphrates, where at the confluence with the River Khabur he visits the town of Bouqras, established on a promontory overlooking the flood plain.[1] In its buildings, he finds wall-paintings – pictures of large water birds, storks or cranes – the first sight of an ever-increasing quantity of art work that he is to encounter during the final stages of his West Asia journey.

But Bouqras, like 'Ain Ghazal, has passed its heyday; many of its mud-brick houses have fallen into disrepair. The flood plain had once provided ample land for hunting game, grazing and cultivation. Now hard times have arrived and the population has dwindled from a thousand to little more than a couple of hundred at most. A few specialist craftsmen remain at work, producing fine stone bowls carved from marble and alabaster.

Lubbock leaves and heads northeast, following the Euphrates through the eastern Taurus Mountains and into the rolling foothills of the Anatolian plateau. There it changes direction, making a westwards arc through barren hills of limestone interspersed with wooded plains. Here, no more than three kilometres south of the Euphrates, he finds the village of Nevali Çori[2] straddling the banks of a small tributary stream. There are about twenty-five abandoned buildings – all single storey, rectangular in shape, and built from limestone blocks bonded with mud mortar – but no people. The village is deserted except for scurrying mice and rats.

Several houses had been aligned in a terrace with narrow passages between. Some are particularly large, almost 20 metres in length, and divided into adjoining rooms. Most have thick plaster floors; where these are decayed, stone drainage channels and human burials are exposed.

The floors are scattered with rubbish – animal bones, broken querns, flint tools and worn baskets. Abandonment of the village had evidently been a gradual affair, with a slow decline in standards of hygiene and order. Within the rubbish Lubbock finds clay and stone figurines that had fallen from wooden shelves. One stylised human face looks familiar; it seems to recall the masks worn by the 'priests' of 'Ain Ghazal, which were in turn similar to the masks from Nahal Hemar.

The area outside the houses is also a mess. Several large roasting pits have begun to fill with silt; others still show their cobbled linings. Animal pens have collapsed, while clusters of grinding stones still sit amidst husks and chaff. Whoever had lived at Nevali Çori had evidently been farmers like those at Beidha, Jericho and 'Ain Ghazal; but they had possessed quite different religious beliefs, as Lubbock appreciates when he enters what archaeologists will call the 'cult building'.

It is at the northwest end of the terrace, a square building with its back wall set into the natural slope. The reed-covered roof has almost entirely collapsed and the walls are crumbling. Lubbock has to squeeze his way past fallen timbers to descend the few steps into its interior. As he does so, a host of snakes shoot below the rubble upon the floor.

A stone bench runs around the walls, partitioned into sections by ten stone pillars. There are further slab-like stone pillars in the middle of the room. These have T-shaped capitals and appear like human shoulders; when Lubbock looks closely he sees a pair of human arms carved in low relief upon each face. From the steps he looks towards a niche in the opposite wall. It contains a human head upon which a snake has come to rest – both head and snake carved in stone. The surrounding walls had once been thickly plastered and covered in exotic murals painted in red and black. But most of the plaster has collapsed to the floor, leaving the paintings as the pieces of a broken and jumbled jigsaw.

Lubbock finds more sculptures, some free-standing, some built into the walls and pillars. There is a large bird, perhaps a vulture or eagle; a woman's head is caught in the talons of another great bird; a third bird of prey tops a column carved into two female heads. And so it goes on – more birds, faces that seem part animal and part human, another snake.

Excavations at Nevali Çori were directed by Harald Hauptmann of the University of Heidelberg between 1983 and 1991, prior to the site being flooded by the new lake behind the Atatürk Dam. The settlement had developed at the same time as the PPNB towns of the Jordan valley, between 8500 and 8000 BC. Its inhabitants had been farmers with domesticated wheat and herds of sheep and goat, although hunting and gathering had also been pursued. When first discovered, Nevali Çori's sculptures and carvings were quite unprecedented in the Neolithic, although they now have a clear origin in those at Göbekli Tepe, the hilltop Early Neolithic ritual centre located no more than 30 kilometres away. Indeed, it was only because Klaus Schmidt had excavated at Nevali Çori that he was immediately able to recognise the limestone slabs upon that hilltop as having come from carved Neolithic pillars.

The design of Nevali Çori's cult building, with its standing pillars and benches, is strikingly similar to the PPNA buildings at Göbekli Tepe with the exception of its rectangular rather than circular form. By 8500 BC, however, rectangular buildings were also all that could be seen upon that limestone hill. The circular structures with their massive carved pillars had been deliberately buried by tons of soil and the area where they had been demarcated by a stone wall. New rectangular buildings had been constructed beyond this wall, leaving an empty space where the previous and now buried buildings had stood. Within these new buildings pillars carved with wild animals were once again erected, identical in form to those buried beneath the earth but lacking their monumental size. As Schmidt has yet to find traces of domestic activity associated with these new buildings he suspects that Göbekli had continued as a dedicated ritual centre until it became abandoned, probably around 7500 BC.

The cult building at Nevali Çori, however, had been part of a settlement that was dominated by domestic dwellings, in the same manner that special buildings were found at the hunter-gatherer village of Hallan Çemi Tepsi – the 10,000 BC settlement located 200 kilometres east of Nevali Çori. Cult buildings were also found at a settlement located midway between the two, known today as Çayönü. This provides further evidence for the florescence of Neolithic culture in southeast Turkey.[3]

Çayönü has a much longer excavation history than Nevali Çori and Hallan Çemi Tepsi – it began in 1962 and continued until 1991.[4] The site is found at the most northern extent of the Mesopotamian lowlands, located in the Ergani plain that is cut by both the Euphrates and the Tigris. It lies in the shadow of the Taurus Mountains in what is quite an arid landscape – although a seasonal river still flows by the site. When occupied, there had been marshes and swamps near by where beavers and otters had been trapped. It is a stunning site to visit, a place of immense tranquillity and with a powerful sense of its prehistoric past – a huge relief after having had to pass through several of the military barriers that block the roads of eastern Turkey today.

Occupation had begun at Çayönü by at least 9500 BC, making it contemporary with the first occupations at Jericho and the construction of the ritual centre at Göbekli Tepe. Its first people had also built circular dwellings, cultivated wheat and remained reliant on wild animals, especially pigs, cattle and deer. By 8000 BC, however, they were engaged in a very different form of architecture. Large rectangular stone buildings were made using a 'grille plan' as a foundation – that is, a series of parallel low stone walls on which a wooden and plaster floor had been laid. This was probably a protection from damp ground and periodic flooding. At least forty of these 'grille plan' buildings were constructed, the largest divided into multiple rooms and workshops. Asli Özdoğan of Istanbul University, the most recent excavator, believes that at least six architectural phases are apparent in the slightly new styles and forms of building that were adopted.

The major expansion of the village reflected the adoption of a fully-fledged mixed farming economy – probably one of the first settlements to do so. A central 'plaza' was constructed, presumably for public meetings and ceremonies, along with cult building where multiple burials took place and human skulls were cached – no fewer than seventy were found within a single room. Although no monumental art objects have been found at Çayönü to compare with those from Nevali Çori and Göbekli Tepe, more than four hundred clay figurines, mainly of humans and animals, were excavated from amongst the domestic rubbish. But in spite of this use of clay, and a wide range of craft activities including the carving of stone bowls, no traces of pottery vessels have been found within the village. Nevertheless, the people of Çayönü were certainly pushing forward the boundaries of technology – they took copper ore from deposits 20 kilometres away and beat these into beads, hooks and metal sheets.

Lubbock heads west from Nevali Çori and undertakes a vast journey, crossing the Taurus Mountains and entering the plateau of central Anatolia. He passes several small villages and some larger towns. For parts of the journey he travels with pastoralists and for others with those visiting relatives in distant villages or heading for the 'shiny black hills'.

These hills are made out of obsidian and found in the region that we describe today as Cappadocia. Even at 7500 BC people had already been visiting them for several thousand years to collect the volcanic glass that was then traded and exchanged throughout western Asia.[5] The obsidian that Lubbock had seen at Abu Hureyra, Jericho and 'Ain Ghazal had come from Cappadocia – most likely having passed through many different hands and households on its way.

It is not surprising, therefore, that large heaps of wasted flakes and cores surround many of the obsidian workings, from which only the very best pieces have been taken away. Workshops, from which one can acquire enormous cores of obsidian in exchange for shells, furs, and copper ore, are plentiful. But the obsidian covers far too great an area for all access to be controlled. And so Lubbock passes many small parties either grubbing large nodules from the ground or simply breaking large flakes from outcrops of this highly prized shiny black stone.

His companions are heading to the town that we know today as Aşıklı Höyük, located at the western extent of Cappodocia, a sprawling farming settlement of mud-brick buildings.[6] But Lubbock takes a different route, crossing the Anatolian plateau to its southernmost plain, heading towards the Neolithic town of Çatalhöyük.

Throughout his journey from Nevali Çori the vegetation has continuously changed from steppe to woodland and back again, sensitive to the many variations in topography and water – steep-sided valley, rolling hills and flat plain dissected by many rivers. Some of the woods are now composed of massive oaks, through which Lubbock catches fleeting glimpses of deer and wild cattle. Huge birds of prey seem to be endlessly circling in the sky.

It is 7000 BC and Çatalhöyük is at its peak.[7] As Lubbock approaches, he enters a heavily cultivated landscape. Signs of tree-felling are common – wood is evidently becoming a precious resource as the freshest cuts are on the smallest trees. Small fields appear in which women and children are completing their day's work while young boys steer flocks of sheep and goats back to the night-time safety of the town. This has now become visible, appearing as a solid mass within the half-light of dusk.

Çatalhöyük is quite unlike any place that Lubbock has seen. It appears to have a continuous perimeter wall, one that has no entrance and no desire to welcome uninvited guests. Looking more closely, Lubbock realises that it is not a single wall at all, but the outcome of many abutting walls from individual buildings that cling tightly together as if in fear of what lies beyond. A dirty, rubbish-strewn river stagnates along one side, leading to stinking swamps and marshes behind the town. On the other is a muddy pond around which goats are settled for the night.

Lubbock watches the fieldworkers returning home; they climb wooden ladders on to the roofs, dispersing and disappearing down a maze of rooftop pathways, steps and ladders that lead from tier to tier and house to house. Between the paths are flat mud roofs, some evidently used as workshops for tool-making and basket-weaving. A few have collapsed, leaving gaping holes that expose the rooms below. Sometimes the paths edge around courtyards entirely enclosed by mud-brick walls; from these come the stench of human waste.

Each house has a trapdoor entrance on its southern side and small windows in whatever wall is exposed above the adjacent roof. Some doors are open, releasing smoke and the light of flickering oil-lamps into the cold night air; sometimes a bolder, stronger glow emanates from a well-fuelled hearth.

Choosing an open doorway, Lubbock descends a wooden ladder into the kitchen area of a small rectangular room.[8] Before him there is a raised hearth – a platform with a kerb to prevent any spillage of ash. It gives a deep glow and a low heat from its animal-dung fuel. Near by an oven has been built into the wall, exposing neat mud bricks, and beside that a clay bin with a hole at the base from which lentils are spilling. There are scattered utensils, a basket with root vegetables and a young goat tethered to the wall. As such it is a familiar domestic scene, one that could have been found at Jericho or 'Ain Ghazal. But then Lubbock turns and sees a monstrous scene of bulls bursting from the wall.

There are three of them at about waist-height – white heads striped with black and red, from which sprout enormous pointed horns that seem to threaten all of human life within the room. Beside Lubbock, a woman and a man sit upon a raised platform adjacent to the bulls, their heads downcast, eating bread in silence. Between them a child has left her bread untouched upon its wooden plate.

Around the bulls the walls are painted with bold geometric designs – sharp, oppressive images above handprints in red and black similar to those painted in the French cave of Pech Merle at the LGM. But while those ice-age hunter-gatherer hands were welcoming, outstretched in greeting to visitors within the cave, these farming hands of Çatalhöyük seem to be more of a warning or a plea for help – its people are trapped within a bestiary from which they cannot escape.

And so begins a night-time tour of Çatalhöyük, a nightmare vision of the world that farming has brought to these particular members of humankind. First Lubbock crawls through a small doorway to escape the room, but this leads nowhere, merely into a storeroom where baskets and hides are stacked. And so he returns to the roof and tries another house, and then another and another. In each he finds the same – the hearth, the oven, the grain bin, the platform all positioned identically, in rooms that are near-identical in size and shape. Many rooms have clay figurines placed within wall niches, or simply upon the floor; some are evidently of women, others of men, but many seem quite sexless. The most startling is of a woman who sits upon a throne that had been placed beside a grain bin. At each side of her stands a leopard; she rests one hand upon each head while their tails wrap around her body.[9]

The bulls vary from room to room but are always shocking, especially when encountered in the hard-edged beams of moonlight that now enter through the tiny windows, or by flames that bring the beasts alive.[10] There are bulls' heads with long twisted horns, bulls' heads with faces covered in exotic designs, and bulls' heads stacked one above the other from floor to ceiling. Some rooms have free-standing stone pillars with horns, or long lines of horns set into benches daring anyone to sit within their grasp.

The geometric designs are joined by pictures of great black vultures viciously attacking headless people, and by scenes of enormous deer and cattle surrounded by tiny frenzied people. The real people are asleep upon their platforms. They lie in contorted positions, sometimes jerking awake and staring at Lubbock as he passes, as if able to see yet another intruder in their lives.

Lubbock goes up and down the ladders, from room to room and horror to horror, until he falls exhausted and lies prostrate before another sculptured wall. He heaves himself up on his knees and faces a pair of modelled women's breasts that emerge from the mud-brick and plaster. Both nipples are split apart and peering from within are the skulls of vultures, foxes and weasels: motherhood itself violently defiled. Lubbock can take no more and crawls across the floor into the pitch-blackness of a storeroom. And there he hides, in the hope that daylight will bring release from this Neolithic hell.

It was on a cold November day in 1958 when James Mellaart, a scholar at the British Institute of Archaeology at Ankara, arrived at the mound of Çatalhöyük. He had been searching for archaeological sites on the Konya plain of the Anatolian plateau since 1951, and had in fact seen the mound from a distance in his second year of work. When he eventually examined it, he found the mound covered in grass and weeds, its surface scoured by southwesterly winds. These had revealed the unmistakable traces of mud-brick walls, and exposed artefacts such as obsidian arrow-heads and fragments of pottery. Mellaart immediately knew that he had made an important discovery. To his trained eye, the artefacts were unmistakably Neolithic in date, a period of settlement then unknown in the region. And the mound was vast, 450 metres in length and covering 32 acres. But he had no idea how important it would prove to be. Çatalhöyük turned out to be quite simply the most remarkable Neolithic settlement ever discovered – although that status must now be shared with, or perhaps even surrendered to, Göbekli Tepe.

Mellaart excavated the settlement between 1961 and 1966, exposing no more than a tiny fraction of the southwest corner. His discoveries of painted walls, bulls' heads, human burials and figurines soon became renowned throughout the world. Along with these there was an impressive series of artefacts, including mirrors made from obsidian and daggers with exquisitely carved bone handles.

But what exactly had he found? There was a series of rooms: the larger and more elaborate believed to be shrines, the smaller domestic dwellings. And yet in spite of the sculptures and paintings, signs of craft specialists and architectural complexity, there was no evidence for a priestly caste, political leaders, or public buildings.

Mellaart joined the Institute of Archaeology, London, where his lectures about Çatalhöyük in the 1970s were enthralling, especially to one undergraduate by the name of Ian Hodder. By 1993, Hodder had become a professor of archaeology in Cambridge, and was believed by many to be the most innovative archaeologist of his generation.[11] He had pioneered the study of prehistoric symbolism, and hence it came as little surprise that he was drawn to Çatalhöyük – the ultimate challenge for those who wished to enter the symbolic worlds of people from the past.

Hodder had begun planning his own work at Çatalhöyük in 1991, wishing not only to undertake new excavations but to ensure that the site was properly conserved, restored and managed as part of Turkey's heritage. The result has been one of the largest archaeological projects in the world today, one that applies the latest advances in archaeological science, methods and theories. Some of the most informative results have come from microscopic studies of the floor deposits and wall plaster, undertaken by Wendy Matthews – a colleague of mine at Reading University.[12] These have shown that some walls had as many as forty layers of paint and plaster, suggesting that they may have been retouched annually, or perhaps every time a new burial was placed below the wall.

Hodder doubts if there ever had been public buildings, priests or political leaders at the settlement. He also questions Mellaart's distinction between shrines and domestic houses – the microscopic study of the floor deposits in the so-called shrines has shown that routine activities such as toolmaking took place within those rooms, just as in the others. Hodder believes that ritualistic and domestic activities were so intimately entwined that it is unlikely that the people themselves could make any distinction between the two.[13]

The economic basis of Çatalhöyük has also come into question. Mellaart had little doubt that such a settlement must have been reliant upon an efficient farming economy, based upon cereals and cattle. Yet his evidence was slight. Some charred cereal grains had been found, but grinding equipment is rare within the houses and courtyards in comparison to its abundance in the villages of the Jordan valley. Wild plants and animals, such as tubers and deer, may have been of far greater significance than Mellaart had believed. Initial studies of the newly excavated material suggest an economy no different to any other settlement of its age, based on domestic sheep and goats, cereals and legumes.[14]

Hodder's new work has, however, confirmed many of Mellaart's original views. Mellaart had stressed the order within the settlement, the manner in which each room conformed to the same spatial arrangements, and the remarkable uniformity in artefact design throughout the history of settlement. Hodder has found further evidence for such order. When houses needed rebuilding they were constructed to the same design at the same place, maintaining the same areas for each activity that took place within them. He suggests that different types of people – old and young, male and female, specialist toolmakers and those without skills – were very restricted as to where they could sit and work within each room. To me it seems as if every aspect of their lives had become ritualised, any independence of thought and behaviour crushed out of them by an oppressive ideology manifest in the bulls, breasts, skulls and vultures.

This sounds like living in a Neolithic hell, which is ironic because when I visited the mound on an autumn afternoon in AD 2002, the site looked more like an archaeological heaven. It was deserted except for the custodian and looked splendid in the middle of the Konya plain. Hodder's recently excavated trenches were protected by covers and I could see the wonderfully preserved wall plaster, fireplaces and a whole range of architectural features: wall slots where the ladders had been, entrances into storerooms, grain bins and platforms below which the burials had been made. Just as impressive was the on-site laboratory, workrooms and facilities for the archaeologists, the displays for the visiting public, and the reconstructed dwelling for them to see. I recalled reading an interview that Ian Hodder had given in which he was asked to describe his dream project. Not surprisingly he answered that he had already found it and intended to pursue the excavation of Çatalhöyük for many years to come.[15]

It is dawn at Çatalhöyük in 7000 BC. Weary after his tormented night, Lubbock has climbed on to the roof again and found a vantage point across the plain. The sun is yet to rise and the air is fresh. A goat herder has already left the town to find grazing for her flock; another woman weeds in the fields that surround the town. Lubbock looks east, towards Nevali Çori and Göbekli Tepe whose art works had seemed to forewarn of Çatalhöyük. But so too, he thinks, had the painted birds of Bouqras, the cattle figurines and the plaster figures of 'Ain Ghazal.

Turning to look southeast, to the modern lands of Israel and Jordan where his journey had begun, Lubbock recalls that birds of prey had been revered and heads detached from human bodies at the earliest farming villages: Jericho, Netiv Hagdud and WF16. And so the paintings and sculptures of Çatalhöyük are perhaps not so horrific after all – simply an expression of the mythology that had grown alongside the fields of wheat as farming was invented and developed in western Asia.

He then looks even further back in time, to his arrival at Ohalo before its fire, to his travels across the steppe and desert, to cutting wheat in the wild gardens of 'Ain Mallaha. What would those Kebaran and Natufian hunter-gatherers have thought of Çatalhöyük? Most likely they would have been confused and terrified as they had seemed to trust the natural world, indeed to be part of it themselves. The people of Çatalhöyük, on the other hand, seemed to fear and despise the wild.

With another turn Lubbock looks westwards, towards Europe. A journey through that continent will be the next stage of his travels through global history. This will begin back in the depths of the ice age in the far northwest where people are hunting reindeer and clothed in furs. But first he must visit what still remains a halfway house between European and West Asian culture – the Mediterranean island of Cyprus.

12

Three Days on Cyprus

Extinctions, colonisation and cultural stasis, 20,000–6000 BC

Alan Simmons was perched precariously on a cliff ledge above a brilliant blue Mediterranean sea. I listened intently as he described his 1986 excavation of Aetokremnos[1] Cave at Akrotiri – now little more than a platform in the cliffside, its roof having collapsed many thousands of years ago. I was crouched upon its floor; Alan faced me a couple of metres away with his back to the sea and a strong breeze ruffling his mass of silky grey hair. Way above him birds of prey circled on the thermals – perhaps they knew that Aetokremnos means cliff of vultures.[2]

Alan described how there had been two main layers upon the floor, the upper one with stone tools, a mass of shells and bird bones; the lower stuffed with hippopotamus bones – but not from animals like those in Africa today. These were pig-sized pygmy hippos, and more than five hundred of them had been excavated from the remnants of the tiny cave.

The hippos had been hunted, Alan explained, at around 10,000 BC by the first people to arrive on Cyprus;[3] Aetokremnos was where the carcasses had been brought, roasted and then pulled apart for their meat, fat and bone. He was excited, waving his arms, speculating how the hippos had been chased from their feeding grounds and then forced off the cliff edge to their death. One step backwards, I thought, and he would be joining them on the surf-covered rocks below.

Between 20,000 and 10,000 BC there had been no human inhabitants on Cyprus. Neither had there been any wild goats, wild pig or deer. Being surrounded by deep seas, Cyprus, like other Mediterranean islands, had been isolated from other land masses for many millions of years and so it had hardly any fauna at all.[4]

There was certainly plenty of forage and grazing as the island was covered in a mixture of thick woodland and steppe, their proportions and composition changing as the climate went through its ups and downs towards the Holocene world. By 10,000 BC much of the island was covered with oak woodland; pines were growing in the uplands along with magnificent cedar trees with their great spreading boughs and powerful scent.

Other than mice and their little furry night-time predator, the genet, the only animals that flourished upon the island were pygmy hippos and elephants. Their full-sized cousins had once lived in the coastal marshes of western Asia that had been flooded by the rising sea. At some very ancient date, full-sized elephants and hippos had swum to the Cypriot shore. In the absence of a predator threat, evolution turned their descendants into dwarfs – great bulks being quite unnecessary if the only worry is to procure sufficient food and sex to ensure the survival of genes.[5]

Both elephants and hippos gradually assumed the size of large pigs, the latter far more numerous and seeming to behave like pigs themselves. They were good swimmers but seemed happier scurrying through the under-growth, feeding on leaves and shoots. The hippos had drunk from fresh-water springs on the cliff-tops. In cold weather they had sheltered in coastal caves, being adept at climbing up and down steep slopes. The caves may also have been used for giving birth, nursing the young, and as a place to die in once their hippo life was done.

At 10,000 BC John Lubbock sits unseen upon a scrap of sandy beach with five other travellers – three men and two women. They have just pulled their canoe on to the beach below the Aetokremnos Cave, relieved to arrive on dry land after an exhausting 60-kilometre sea-crossing from the coast of western Asia. Evidently hungry, they quickly begin gathering shellfish from the rocks and shallow pools, knowing exactly where to look. A couple of well-aimed beach pebbles bring down a pair of ducks which had sat bobbing on the water, quite unconcerned by the threat presented by these strange arrivals.

The canoeists had spotted the cave as they skirted the southern coast of Cyprus. Now inside, they find it cramped and stoop to avoid grazing their heads. Using rocks as picks and shovels, they begin to dig out the sandy floor to make a fireplace; as they do so, bones begin to appear which are either discarded or adopted as a better tool. Lubbock crouches in the rear, knees tucked tightly beneath his chest, his head sporting a purple bruise from a knock against the cave roof.

Within their shallow pit, Lubbock's companions light a fire using wood collected from the shore and snapped from desiccated shrubs.[6] While the ducks are roughly plucked, the canoeists take a second look at the bones unearthed within the cave. Lubbock watches them pass a skull around, examining its teeth and then shrugging their shoulders as to what animal it might be. Although experienced hunters, they had never seen such bones before. A few were gathered up, brushed free of sand and placed within the flames in the hope that they would burn, to make the firewood last.

My own arrival on Cyprus had been the day before Alan took me to Aetokremnos Cave. I had no more than three days to spend on the island while attending a conference about its early prehistory. While Alan Simmons was conducting a site tour, another twenty conference delegates were crouching on the cliffside where Aetokremnos Cave had once been located.

The cave was the most controversial site discussed by the conference in September 2001. It had been the subject of almost continual debate since Alan's excavations and his provocative claims that a great number of charred bones from the cave provided conclusive evidence that its occupants had killed and eaten the hippos. How else could the remains of so many pygmy hippos have arrived within a small cave halfway up a steep cliff?[7]

There were some uncontested facts about the site: humans had made a fire in the cave at about 10,000 BC, leaving a scatter of stone tools and beads made from seashells. No one questioned that those people had also been responsible for the thousands of mollusc shells, and the bones from a variety of ducks and birds.[8] Some of the hippo bones had unquestionably been burned, but how they originally came to be within the cave was keenly disputed.

Alan's critics pointed to the rarity of stone artefacts found with the hippo bones themselves, suggesting that the few within the lower layer could easily have slipped down crevasses or been moved by the rodents that had burrowed within the cave. They also pointed to the complete lack of stone-tool cut marks on any of the 218,000 excavated hippopotamus bones. Only cut marks could provide the incontestable evidence that the hippos had been hunted and butchered; without them, the bones might simply be a natural deposit as found in many caves around the Cypriot coast, perhaps accumulating many tens of thousands of years before the arrival of people.

When preparing his report, Alan had invited Sandi Olsen from the Carnegie Museum of Natural History, Pittsburgh, USA – an expert on identifying human butchery – to examine the bones. Unfortunately for Alan, she also became his harshest critic.[9] Olsen suggested that the people in Aetokremnos Cave had simply dug into its deposits to make more room for themselves; this had disturbed the hippo bones, some of which had been burned by their fires and mixed with the debris they left behind. The occupants might even have tried to use the bones for fuel. Olsen thought the hippo bones were likely to be several thousand years older than the human occupation. But any radiocarbon dates on the hippo bones themselves were unreliable, she explained, due to chemical alterations by the fire.[10]

I weighed up both sides of the argument. Alan was a persuasive advocate for the existence of hippo hunters, but without cut marks and reliable radiocarbon dates on the bones I was left unconvinced. The constant changes of climate and ecology between 20,000 and 10,000 BC would have upset the reproductive patterns of pygmy hippos; the spread of thick woodland at 12,500 BC – the late glacial interstadial – may have had a devastating effect. And so I suspect that by 10,000 BC, when the first canoe had reached the Cyprus shore, there had been no pygmy hippos and elephants drinking at the cliff-top springs – merely birds of prey circling lazily on the thermals.

By that date the hippos had already slipped over the edge – not of the cliff, but of existence itself.[11]

Whether they were hippo hunters or not, the stone artefacts from Aetokremnos and the radiocarbon dating of charcoal from their fires of approximately 10,000 BC provide the earliest known evidence for a human presence on Cyprus. Why had they come to the island? The date placed the occupation within the Younger Dryas that had transformed life in western Asia. Whether people had settled at 'Ain Mallaha or Hayonim Cave in Israel, or at Abu Hureyra on the Euphrates, they had returned to a transient lifestyle as the yields from their wild gardens collapsed. Their arrival on Cyprus might have been one further consequence of the economic stress they faced. The island's existence would surely have been known, being either visible itself from mountain peaks or suspected because of distant cloud formations, tell-tale currents or flotsam on the shore.

What the hunters found there must have been a disappointment – no game to hunt, few wild cereals to harvest. As Aetokremnos is currently the only known site of its age on the island, it appears that the first visitors left without delay. Almost two millennia had to pass before people returned to Cyprus; when they did so they came better prepared, bringing not only seed-grain in their boats but wild goats and pigs with which to stock the island.

On the second day of my visit, I stood looking down a Neolithic well with Paul Croft, ex-Cambridge graduate and now a resident archaeologist on Cyprus. He was describing its discovery and excavation. Less than 100 metres away holidaymakers were sunning themselves on the sands of a sheltered bay or drinking cocktails below the fake-straw umbrellas of a beach bar.

Since 1989 Paul had worked with a team from the University of Edinburgh undertaking a 'watching brief' in the fast-developing coastal resort of Mylouthkia in the southwest of the island. An archaeological watching brief is exactly that – watching what quarrying or building work exposes, and being able to call a halt if anything of potential archaeological importance is revealed.[12]

Mylouthkia was already known to be rich in remnants of the Cypriot Bronze Age, beginning around 2500 BC, but the discovery of such ancient wells was a complete surprise. The only other Neolithic examples outside of Cyprus came from the submerged village of Atlit-Yam off the Israeli coast, but these new discoveries were considerably older. In fact, they might be the oldest-known wells in the world.

Paul explained how the wells – there were six of them scattered around and inside a new hotel complex – had been discovered as circles of dark soil on the ground, or as long columns of soil which had been sliced lengthways as their stone surround was quarried away. At first the wells were assumed to be Bronze Age in date and no more than shallow pits. But excavation revealed them to have gone down at least 10 metres into the soft rock. The debris that had filled their shafts contained many tell-tale artefacts of the Neolithic, the complete absence of pottery being particularly significant. Charred grains of domestic wheat and barley were also found. Radiocarbon dates confirmed their early Neolithic age, and by doing so extended the antiquity of farming in Cyprus by two thousand years at least.

Rather than being abandoned when no longer needed, or when the underground rivers had dried up, the wells were deliberately filled in. One well turned out to contain a great number of fragmented stone vessels, together with the hammer-stones and flint flakes used in their manufacture. These had most likely come from a rubbish dump near the well. Another had ritualistic depositions. It contained twenty-three complete goat carcasses, a carefully positioned human skull and an elegant mace-head made from polished pink stone.

Paul described how the shafts had been cut with antler picks and that hand- and foot-holds still survived in their walls for climbing up and down. I felt a strong desire to do just that. But before I had a chance to ask permission, Paul had led the party of conference delegates away. He wished to show us a newly discovered and still unexcavated well in the backyard of a hotel apartment.

It is 8000 BC and Lubbock is peering into the same well. There is a protective wicket fence around the opening that has to be clambered over. Near by three or four adults and a few adolescents are carving stone vessels below a rickety shelter. They use hammer-stones to break and then laboriously peck the stone into rough-outs, and then grind and carve these into bowls and plates. To do so, a continual supply of water has to be poured over their stone. This, Lubbock guesses, is why they sit so close to the well.

There are no buildings around the well, not a single hut let alone a Neolithic village to be seen in the scrubby woodland that reaches to the shore of a sheltered bay, a couple of hundred metres away. Lubbock sits down in the workshop and notices that one of the men has a knife with a glassy black blade stuffed in his belt. As the man is concentrating so hard on his work, Lubbock carefully slips it out and finds, as he had guessed, that it is as sharp as a razor – it is exactly the same stone that he had seen in vast quantities in Cappodocia when travelling to Çatalhöyük. So either these Cypriot craftsmen had once come from southern Turkey or were connected with that region by trade.

Their work comes to a sudden halt when a boat appears within the bay.[13] It is quite different to the log canoe that arrived at Aetokremnos a millennium and a half earlier; this vessel is built with planks and has a mast and sail.[14] Within minutes the boat has been anchored and a dozen or so people are splashing on to the beach, greeted by the craftsmen who run to meet them.

Lubbock also goes to the boat and is soon helping unload – sacks of wheat and barley, a few goats and a young fallow deer, each with their legs firmly tied and looking very poorly. The people – a couple of families – aren't looking much better; the children in particular appear to be quite sick.

As the new arrivals drink thirstily from the well Lubbock reflects on the date, 8000 BC, and what he should expect to find elsewhere upon the island. When in western Asia at this date he had been visiting Beidha – a town with rectangular two-storey buildings, a public meeting-house, granaries and courtyards. Such villages and small towns were found throughout the Fertile Crescent. Lubbock recalled the man plastering his father's skull at Jericho and watching the burial of statues at 'Ain Ghazal. Did Cyprus have similar Neolithic villages or even towns? As the farmers on the island must have come from western Asia, presumably they did. So Lubbock leaves the well, craftsmen and new arrivals at Mylouthkia, heading inland to search for village life.

There are at least two Neolithic settlements on Cyprus contemporary with the wells at Mylouthkia. One, the site of Shillourokambos, is another recent discovery.[15] Delightfully situated amidst olive groves a few kilometres from the southern coast of the island, excavations have been undertaken since 1992 by the French archaeologist Jean Guilaine. We had been to visit this site before seeing the wells of Mylouthkia.

Guilaine, as French as they come with his espadrilles, shrugs and charm, provided a tour of his ongoing excavations. He too had discovered wells, together with the remnants of an enclosure that had possibly been used for penning animals, perhaps those still wild in their habits and form. Guilaine had found cattle bones at his site – another animal that must have been brought in boats from western Asia.

Shillourokambos had a long history of occupation, but architectural preservation was poor; in fact it was almost non-existent, as any useful stone had long been taken away for building elsewhere. As far as Guilaine could detect from post holes and pits, its dwellings had been circular in design. As such they matched the buildings at Tenta, the other Neolithic settlement of a similar date. But they also matched the houses in all Later Neolithic settlements on the island, right up to 5000 BC and beyond.

This long tradition of circular dwellings on Cyprus has been recognised ever since the 1930s when excavations began at the largest-known Cypriot Neolithic site, Khirokitia. The settlement covers the entire side of a hill a few kilometres from Tenta. It was as large as the small Pre-Pottery Neolithic B towns in western Asia – although by the time Khirokitia had reached its peak such towns had long been abandoned. And yet Khirokitia was built from small, circular, single-storey dwellings. These are most comparable to those from the very first villages of western Asia, such as Netiv Hagdud in the Jordan valley and Jerf el Ahmar in the Euphrates valley, both dating to about 9500 BC.

Tenta was the same, providing evidence of an architectural style that had evidently survived for many millennia on Cyprus after it had been replaced elsewhere. Ian Todd, working on behalf of the Cypriot Department of Antiquities, excavated this village during the 1970s. He revealed a cluster of small circular dwellings around the summit of a knoll, some built from stone and others with mud brick. At the summit itself there was a much larger circular structure with three concentric walls surrounded by small cells.[16]

The structure is almost identical in size, shape and design to one found more than 500 kilometres to the east and which may have been constructed one thousand years earlier. This was at the settlement of Jerf el Ahmar, excavated by Danielle Stordeur in the 1990s and now flooded by Lake Assad. With its concentric walls and radial cells, Stordeur suggested that the Jerf el Ahmar structure could have been a central granary for the village, built by communal effort.

The striking similarity between the structures at Tenta and Jerf el Ahmar was noticed by Eddie Peltenburg, an archaeologist from Edinburgh University who directs excavations in both Cyprus and Syria. In a presentation at the conference, Peltenburg pointed to several other connections between Neolithic architecture on Cyprus and that of the earliest Neolithic villages in Iraq, Syria and Turkey, those which date to the Pre-Pottery Neolithic A.[17] Both, for instance, used thick pillars inside their dwellings; these had been found at Qermez Dere and Nemrik in Iraq (as we will see in a later chapter) and at Nevali Çori and Göbekli Tepe in Turkey. Additionally, at least one of the pillars at Tenta had been painted with a dancing anthropomorphic figure that recalled the carvings at the latter two sites. As the dwellings in Cyprus had thick walls, Peltenburg disregarded the idea that the pillars were required as roof supports. He thought they lacked any utilitarian function and were charged with symbolic meaning.

On the basis of such architectural similarities and those found in the technical details of stone tools, Peltenburg proposed that the first farmers on Cyprus had originated from western Syria: not from the settlements of Jerf el Ahmar or Nevali Çori themselves, as these are far inland, but from contemporary settlements near the coast which had the same architectural and cultural traditions. No such settlements are currently known. Any that might have been on the coast itself will now be far under the sea. Peltenburg speculated that others must still exist in the present-day coastal strip of Syria, undiscovered simply because no one has taken the trouble to look for them. That is precisely what he now intends to do.

Peltenburg made a persuasive case that the first farmers of Cyprus had sailed from the Syrian coast. Whereas the very first Cypriot arrivals had been pushed by the economic stress caused by the Younger Dryas, these new arrivals were driven by the opportunity for colonisation that a farming economy provides. They brought with them not only seed-grain, pigs, cattle, sheep and goats, but the architectural and cultural traditions that were also found further east at Jerf el Ahmar, and Göbekli Tepe.

Once these colonists had arrived on Cyprus soon after 9000 BC they maintained their cultural traditions throughout the Neolithic, even though new architectural styles – the rectangular two-storey buildings – developed across the mainland of western Asia. By 6000 BC, when small circular mud-walled houses were still being built at Tenta and Khirokitia, the Euphrates valley was home to substantial towns; even larger and with more impressive architecture than Lubbock had seen at 'Ain Ghazal and Bouqras.

On the third day of my Cyprus visit I went to visit Tenta and Khirokitia. Both were fascinating and disappointing in equal measure. The archaeology itself was outstanding. The mud-brick dwellings at Tenta had walls surviving to waist-height and clustered tightly around the multi-walled stone-built circular structure at the summit of the hill. It looked just like the pictures I had seen of the structure at Jerf el Ahmar. Many of the dwellings had remnants of thick square pillars, leaving hardly any living space for the occupants.

A wooden walkway had been constructed so one had to view the site from above. This was below an enormous conical tent that cut out the sun, the breeze and the view.[18] Such measures served to protect the fragile mud-brick buildings of Tenta. But however fine the buildings looked, as I was unable to walk between or within these dwellings, to touch the stone or crouch down beside the walls, I felt quite unable to imagine the people who had lived inside.

The archaeology of Khirokitia was more impressive and even less evocative of the Neolithic past.[19] As a 'World Heritage' site it was carefully managed with walkways and information boards, guidebooks and reconstructed dwellings. Excavations in the 1930s and 1970s revealed a mass of circular stone-built houses, so tightly squashed together across a hillside that from a distance the site looked more like a scree slope than the ruins of a prehistoric village. On a closer look, the walls of many circular dwellings survived to knee-height; a few had internal pillars, hearths and grinding stones.

I didn't linger. I simply walked the demarcated route up and down the hill to the sounds and smells of motorway traffic that roared near by, then went to drink a beer in the local bar. It advertised a 'Neolithic salad' but this turned out to be like any other salad on the island. Cyprus, it seemed, was determined to keep its prehistoric past firmly in the present: my visit to Aetokremnos Cave had been disturbed by the roar of military aircraft from the nearby air base of Akrotiri, while the Neolithic wells at Mylouthkia were surrounded by tourist development. The terraces of olive groves around Shillourokambos had been pretty but such intensive cultivation left no sense of the prehistoric terrain. Both Tenta and Khirokitia had been admirably conserved and displayed, but in the process they had lost their prehistoric soul.

I should have been with Lubbock, back on the hillside at Khirokitia in 6000 BC. Then the village was crammed with people, who had to squeeze past each other to reach their own dwellings or visit one another after having worked in the fields all day. Clusters of flat-roofed dwellings were arranged around small courtyards, cluttered with the debris of domestic life: stone bowls, grinding stones, flint-bladed sickles. The clusters, housing an extended family, abutted each other so tightly that people were irritable with those who tried to pass through or had discarded their rubbish too near. Fortunately Lubbock was able to sit in a corner quite unseen, sharing it with a couple of farting goats. There was a cacophony of Neolithic noise dominated by barking dogs and crying children. The whole village stank of human and animal waste; it was covered in a thick pall of acrid smoke as each courtyard had its own fire and cooked its own food.

Life at Khirokitia seemed deeply unpleasant to Lubbock – not in a menacing way, as at Çatalhöyük, but in a messy, claustrophobic way. The types of dwellings and courtyards they used had been originally constructed for communities of fifty people at most. Lubbock reckoned there to be ten times that number squatting around their fireplaces upon the hill. Whereas those who lived in western Asia had adopted new types of architecture as their populations grew, the people of Khirokitia had simply kept adding more of the same, resulting in their sprawling, dysfunctional settlement.

The new architecture in western Asia had gone hand in hand with new rules and regulations for living together. These were imposed by the priests such as Lubbock had seen in 'Ain Ghazal, or agreed upon in public meeting-houses such as that of Beidha. But no such authority or decision-making for the common good had arisen at Khirokitia. Each extended family effectively cared for itself alone – producing and storing its own food, burying its own dead, even having its own religious beliefs.

Lubbock had searched in vain for public buildings where communal planning, worship or ritual might have taken place. Neither could he find any sign of authority-figures that might have provided rules and resolved disputes. While such independent family groups had been viable when fresh water, land and firewood were in good supply, these were now seriously depleted. The result was unremitting tension and conflict in the over-populated town.

My plane was leaving from Larnaka airport the next morning. I had one last chance to engage with the Cypriot past. And so I hurried away from the

Khirokitia bar and drove into the Troodos mountains where the ancient forest of pine and oak that had once covered the island has been allowed to grow again.

I arrived at dusk. My destination was Cedar Valley in the heart of the forest, the last natural habitat of the indigenous cedar trees that must once have flourished across the island. Tarmacked roads had long since turned to rough forest tracks which repeatedly grated against my quite unsuitable hired car. The light was fading as the sun sunk below the tree-covered slopes. I was thinking about giving up when, turning one of the endless sharp bends, a mouflon appeared on the track and then ambled into the trees. I stopped, and we stared at each other for an instant; with its great curved horns, powerful forequarters and deep brown hide, this was as close to a Neolithic goat as can be found. Suddenly it turned and fled, leaving me with nothing but the sound of stones kicked down the rocky slope as it disappeared from sight.

Feeling encouraged, I passed a forester and asked the way to Cedar Valley. 'Another twenty kilometres,' he said – at least an hour's drive on the ever-deteriorating track. 'Come back tomorrow,' he continued, 'it will be pitch black when you arrive.'

That wasn't an option. But he was right, for when I finally stepped from my car and turned off the lights there was almost nothing to be seen. I hesitantly walked into the trees, their thick trunks emerging one by one as my eyes adjusted. I looked up, hoping to see the flat, umbrella-like branches of the cedar; but there was neither shape nor form, the branches from pines, planes, cedars and oaks all silhouetted into one dark surround pierced irregularly by the moonlit sky.

I shuffled from trunk to trunk feeling their bark and trying to recall whether the cedar was rough or smooth. Without my eyes, my ears took over: the cicadas reverberated, tiny drips of water splashed loudly, scuffles in the undergrowth – beetles or mice – sounded like mouflon, deer or even wild boar. Quite suddenly I felt closer to the prehistoric world than I had done at Aetokremnos or Mylouthkia, at Tenta or Khirokitia. I had become entirely engulfed in an astonishing scent of cedar and pine, of rotting leaves and decaying bark, of moonlight, spider's webs and forest streams. It was perhaps the one sensation I could share with those who had first arrived to explore and live upon the island.

EUROPE

North
Sea

Staosnaig

Oronsay
middens

Aoradh

1
2 BRG3
3

1 Coulererach
2 Gleann Mor
3 Bolsay Farm

13-24 Castle Street,
Inverness

Star Car

Creswell Crags

Meiendorf

Esbeck

Stellm

Elb

Gough's
Cave

Bois Laiterie

Chaleux

Rhine

Gönnersdorf

Atlantic
Ocean

Téviec

Höedic

Cuiry-les-
Chaudardes

Verberie,
Etiolles

Pincevent

Loire

Seine

Ofnet

Danube

Altamira

La Riera

Pech Merle

Garonne

Rhône

Alps

Mondeval de Sora,

Arene Candide

Sêbrn Ab

Gruta do
Caldeirão

Molta do
Sebastião

Tagus

Pyrenees

Mas d'Azil

Balma Marginada

Roc del Migdia

Mediterranean
Sea

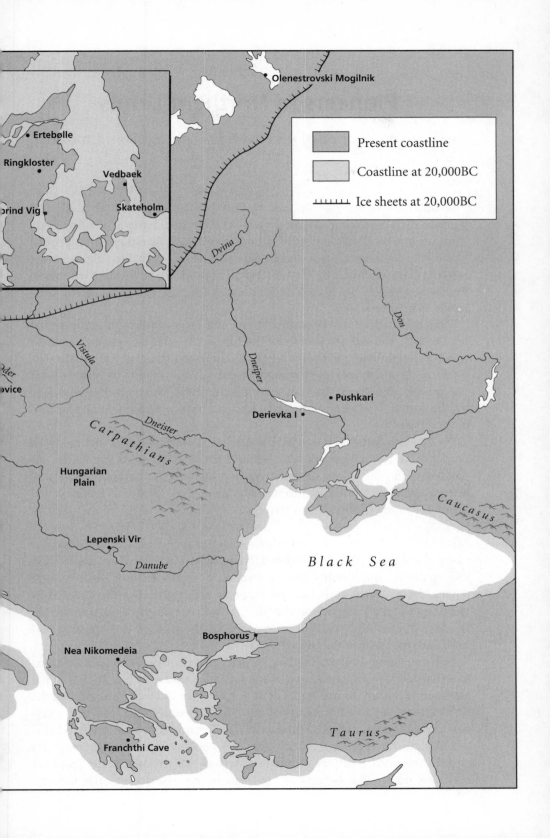

Olenestrovski Mogilnik

Ertebølle

Ringkloster

Vedbaek

rind Vig

Skateholm

	Present coastline
	Coastline at 20,000BC
⊥⊥⊥⊥⊥	Ice sheets at 20,000BC

Dvina

Don

Vistula

Oder

ovice

Dneiper

Pushkari

Dneister

Derievka I

Carpathians

Hungarian
Plain

Caucasus

Lepenski Vir

Danube

Black Sea

Bosphorus

Nea Nikomedeia

Taurus

Franchthi Cave

13

Pioneers in Northern Lands

The recolonisation of northwest Europe, 20,000–12,700 BC

The butchery of human bodies. A flint blade slices through flesh and tendons, first removing the lower jaw and then the tongue of a young man. Another has been scalped. A third body lies naked, face down in a pool of blood, the back split open and gouged by stone tools. Moonlight shines into the cave, illuminating the fur-clad and bloodstained hunters who wield the tools. Crouched within a dark recess, John Lubbock is as fearful to be inside as he is to leave.

This is Gough's Cave in southern England on an autumn night in 12,700 BC. Outside, the limestone cliffs of the future Cheddar Gorge and beyond a windswept landscape with birch trees sparkling in the frosty night air. The men are ice-age hunters – pioneers in the northern lands of Europe after the great ice-age freeze had come to its end. Lubbock creeps by unnoticed by the hunters, whose weathered faces are hidden behind long hair and matted beards.

As he steps into the gorge he shivers in the freezing night air; the grass crunches, a cloud appears with every breath. It is quite silent, the air scented with pine. Now he must resume his travels, for another slice of history awaits, a period of momentous change as Europe is transformed into a continent of forests and farmers.

After my own last visit to Gough's Cave in the spring of AD 2000 I had left along a concrete path below hot electric lights which led to a gift shop selling plastic mammoths and dinosaurs. Outside, further visitors were paying their money and clanking through a turnstile into the cave. They were eager to see stalactites and underground rivers; some hoped to see the resident horseshoe bats. Few were aware of the human carnage that had once occurred within the cave.

For me, Gough's Cave had been a place of historical as well as archaeological interest – it was one of the first localities where archaeologists of the nineteenth century found traces of an ice-age past. By today's standards the first excavations were quite appalling, and probably destroyed more evidence than they recovered. Those early digs left no more than small morsels of sediment for today's archaeologists, who now complement their spades and shovels with a battery of scientific techniques. In 1986 Roger Jacobi, a specialist on ice-age occupation in Britain, excavated one such morsel.[1]

Within a small deposit near to the entrance of the cave he found discarded tools, butchered animal remains, and 120 pieces of human bone.

Jill Cook from the British Museum examined the bones and found them heavily incised. Under a high-powered microscope these grooves proved to contain tell-tale parallel scratches – conclusive evidence that they had been made by stone tools. The position and direction of each cut indicated which muscles had been severed and precisely how the bodies of four adults and one adolescent had been systematically taken apart.[2]

Cannibalism seems the most likely explanation. Some of the cut-marked bones were burnt, suggesting that human flesh had been roasted and eaten. They had been discarded in the debris of occupation, among animal bones and broken tools. We can do no more than guess whether the victims had been deliberately killed or had died from natural causes. The animal bones from Gough's Cave tell us that another activity had also occurred: the removal of sinews from horse bones, probably to be used as cords and threads for sewing shoes and clothing. And so we find a picture of mundane domesticity side by side with human carnage.[3]

Gough's Cave is just one of many archaeological sites in Europe which provides evidence for the recolonisation of northern landscapes as the ice age drew to its close. Those landscapes had become polar deserts when the ice age reached its peak at the LGM, abandoned by people and all but the very hardiest animals and plants. It is with the recolonisation of such lands that this history of Europe must begin, a history of 15,000 years that lasts until a second wave of migrants arrive – the first farmers. But those farmers remain far away in time as we begin at the LGM, when agriculture remained quite unknown throughout the world and northern Europe was a land of glaciers, polar desert and tundra.

The story of how this was returned to the domain of human experience begins in the south, where people survived the ice-age extremes. They had settled in the valleys of southern France and Spain to live by hunting reindeer, horse and bison. Their winters were harsh, with temperatures falling to minus 20°C. Although some remarkable art was created, such as the paintings within Pech Merle, the people were often desperate for food and had to crack open even the smallest bones of reindeer to remove the morsels of marrow inside.[4]

Victorian John Lubbock had visited several caves in southern France and written about them within *Prehistoric Times*. He had travelled with his two friends and colleagues, the great French archaeologist Edouard Lartet and the English banker Henry Christy, who supported Lartet's work.[5] In 1865 many still questioned human antiquity and refused to believe that Europeans had lived as 'savages'. Victorian Lubbock recognised that the reindeer bones found by Lartet provided crucial evidence. Not only were they mixed with stone artefacts, but many still bore cut-marks from flint knives.

Victorian Lubbock had enthused about the beauty of the French landscape, especially the Vézère valley where several caves were found. The residents of the ice-age tundra must also have found generous compensation for winter hardships in the beauty of their world with its herds of bison, horse and deer, with its roving mammoth and woolly rhino, with glimpses of bears and lions, flights of geese and swans. François Bordes, another pivotal figure in French archaeology, one who built upon Lartet's pioneering work during the 1950s and 1960s, had been quite right to describe that tundra as an ice-age Serengeti. After the demands of winter came the annual spectacle of spring.

The first signs of the annual thaw would have been watched for keenly and were celebrated within their art. On one day around 15,000 BC an unknown person carved a host of images on to the surface of a bone – a spawning salmon, a pair of seals, eels emerging from hibernation, flower buds: an invocation of spring that was later lost or discarded at the site of Montgaudier in France.[6]

Although none of the ice-age cave paintings had been discovered by 1865, Victorian John Lubbock was able to describe some ice-age carvings in the pages of *Prehistoric Times*. Ice-age art was a challenge to those who believed that prehistoric men were savages with child-like minds. Victorian Lubbock was more generous than most; he wrote how it is 'natural to feel some surprise at finding these works of art' and went on to state, grudgingly, that 'we must give them full credit for their love of art, such as it was'.[7] Yet statements immediately followed that the cave men were nevertheless quite ignorant of agriculture, domestic animals and metallurgy. The paradox with which he wrestled, the savage with exquisite artistic skill, would reach breaking point within a matter of years: in 1879 a little girl ran shouting to her father about bulls – it was the discovery of paintings in Altamira Cave.

The world of ice-age artists began to change soon after 18,000 BC. Global temperatures began to rise and the northern ice sheets began to melt. By 14,000 BC the glaciers had disappeared from northern Germany and were retreating across Scandinavia and Britain. The artists and hunters in the south felt and saw the effects of global warming at first hand, unaware that the changes they observed – a lusher growth of the grass, earlier nesting times for birds, reduced snowfall – were the harbingers of a new era of climatic, and indeed human, history.

We look back at those ice-age people with knowledge of what their future held – 10,000 years of dramatic climate change. Although the trend was towards warmer conditions it was a roller-coaster ride with huge ups and downs in temperature. But of course those jigs and jags, peaks and troughs of changing temperature that we see recorded in the ice cores taken from Greenland and the Antarctic tell us little about how landscapes evolved and even less about the nature of human experience. For these we need to turn to evidence from Europe itself, especially from the sediments trapped within its caves and deposited within its ancient lakes.

We have seen the value of pollen grains when following the history of changing landscapes of western Asia as recorded by evidence from the Hula basin core. In Europe the tiny pollen grains record the history of plant migration and the development of woodlands across what had once been the barren tundra close to the glaciers themselves. It is a history created by the seeds and spores of plants carried northwards upon the wind, in the feathers and fur, on the feet and in the faeces, of birds and animals. Some of these plants – those most tolerant of conditions that remained cold and dry – found that they could survive, and even flourish, where not long before they would have lain frozen and useless upon the ground.

As these plant pioneers became established they encouraged further birds and animals to venture north. They also helped new soil to develop, soil that was eagerly used by a new set of plants, able to colonise because of increasing warmth and rain. These new arrivals competed fiercely for the sunlight and nutrients, gradually pushing the original settlers northwards, to further lands just released from grip of the ice-age freeze.

By 15,000 BC herbs and shrubs had taken hold of the rolling hills of central Europe, notably artemisia (a spiky knee-high shrub), dwarf willow and mugwort. An acceleration in their northward spread marks the onset of the first major warm phase in the history of global warming, the Bølling. This is the dramatic peak seen in the ice-core record at 12,500 BC and marks the date when those Early Natufian hunter-gatherers in the warmer, lusher world of western Asia were settling down to a sedentary lifestyle. In Europe the Bølling resulted in a scattering of birch trees across the northern tundra and the development of pine and birch woodland further south and within sheltered valleys.

The pollen grains show that there followed a hiatus, and in some areas a reversal, in the spread of woodland. By 11,500 BC, however, full woodland of birch, poplar and pine had penetrated northern Germany, Britain and southern Scandinavia. In some regions, this is identified with a second particularly warm phase called the Allerød, the final peak of climate change before the Younger Dryas began at 10,800 BC.

The pollen grains record that 1,000-year relapse to Arctic conditions by a renewed dominance of grasses, shrubs and only the most resilient of trees – the northern landscapes had once again become open tundra, with copses of birch and pine struggling for survival against the odds. The grasslands would have been dotted with the delicate white flowers of mountain avens, known to botanists as *Dryas octopetala* – from which the name Younger Dryas is derived. And then quite suddenly, at 9600 BC, tree pollen appears once again; it soon becomes abundant as northern Europe is clothed by thick woodland when dramatic global warming brings the ice age to its close.

*

Pollen grains can tell us a great deal: how landscapes changed, what plants and trees the people had seen and burned on their fires as they ventured north. But to truly appreciate how cold these ice-age hunters and gatherers may have felt, archaeologists must turn to another type of pioneer: beetles.

Beetles largely stopped evolving more than one million years ago. Consequently we can be confident that the species identified from the particularities of legs, wings and antennae in ancient deposits are precisely the same as those which live today. This is important because many species are highly sensitive to air temperature and live in very specific types of climate. Consider, for instance, the beetle known as *Boreaphilus henningianus*. Today it is restricted to northern Norway and Finland as it can only survive in extreme cold. But its remains are found in ice-age deposits throughout Britain, indicating temperatures as cold as those of the Arctic today.

The beetle remains from Britain are the best studied of anywhere in the world.[8] More than 350 species are known, from which accurate estimates of past temperatures have been gleaned. The beetles tell us, for instance, that at the LGM winter temperatures in southern Britain routinely reached minus 16°C, and rose to 10°C in the summer. When the warm phase of the Bølling arrived at 12,500 BC, the beetles in Britain were much the same as they are today, indicating that winter and summer temperatures were also similar, 0–1°C and 17°C respectively. But then cold species rose to prominence, indicating a substantial drop of winter temperatures to minus 5°C at 12,000 and minus 17°C at 10,500 BC, the last fitting neatly with the period of the Younger Dryas as seen within the ice cores from Antarctica and Greenland.

Beetles may be precious but they hardly enable us to envision the prehistoric landscapes of ice-age Europe. For that, animal bones are much more useful – for, as soon as mammoths, reindeer and wild boar are invoked those landscapes become alive. Animal bones are principally found within cave deposits, like the hippo bones from Aetokremnos Cave, Cyprus. Some are from the animals that lived and died within the caves, such as hyenas and bears. Others are the prey of carnivores – food taken to feed their young or to be eaten in safety – while the bones of many small mammals arrived via the pellets deposited by roosting owls. Once humans were present they used caves for shelter and discarded within them the bones of animals they killed or had scavenged from frozen carcasses.

Animal bones – whatever their origin – tell us a great deal about the changing environments of Europe. As with beetles, mammals are known to favour different types of habitats – reindeer enjoy cold tundra, red deer prefer more temperate woodland. And so, by arranging the collections of bones in an ordered sequence through time we can reconstruct the changing animal communities, and hence environments, of Europe.

Very few caves, however, have long sequences of deposits. For this reason, collections of bones from different caves must be placed together if we are to reconstruct several thousand years of climate change. Jean-Marie Cordy of the University of Liège conducted one such study.[9] He examined the animal bones recovered during more than a hundred years of excavation from caves in the limestone region of the Meuse basin in Belgium.

Cordy constructed a jigsaw sequence of deposits from 15,000 to 9000 BC, finding that in those dated before 14,500 BC the bones of reindeer and musk ox were dominant – animals of the tundra. From 14,500 BC onwards, they were joined by the remains of grassland and woodland species, such as horse, red deer and wild boar. These came to dominate the collections of bones from 12,500 BC, which coincides with the Bølling phase – a time when reindeer had been forced to travel north to find their favoured lichen and moss-covered tundra.

In the next set of bone collections from the Belgium caves, reindeer once again become abundant, reflecting a drop in temperature and the re-emergence of tundra. Such see-sawing between warm- and cold-loving animals continued as the global climate moved through the Allerød, Younger Dryas, and finally the global warming that brought the ice age to a close 9600 years ago.

Using the bones of large mammals to map the changing environments of Europe is sometimes problematic. They are often found in small numbers and some species, such as red deer, are known to be very adaptable – at home on both open grassland and thick woodland. Moreover, some of these bones may have travelled considerable distances before becoming discarded within a cave: both carnivores and humans can have large hunting territories and bring home animals that are quite different to those in the immediate vicinity of their den or campsite. Consequently, the bones of the small mammals found within cave sediments provide a better index of climate change – for these are generally more numerous, the species more sensitive to environmental conditions, and few travel very far within their short lives.

One of the most useful is the Arctic lemming – the peaks and troughs in the quantity of its bones are almost as good as a temperature gauge itself. Take the cave of Chaleux in the Meuse valley, Belgium, as an example.[10] Before 13,000 BC practically all the small mammal bones in the deposits are those from Arctic lemmings and this denotes a very cold tundra landscape. These are replaced by other rodent species – the northern birch mouse, the bank vole, and even the common hamster – that require much warmer and wetter conditions, and usually inhabit woodland. Their abundance in the sediments at Chaleux marks the start of the Bølling. During the next thousand years the lemmings and the warm-loving rodents keep exchanging places as the most abundant species – a direct reflection of the climatic fluctuations just prior to the environmental crash of the Younger Dryas, marked by the disappearance of all woodland rodents.

*

Pollen grains, beetles' legs, animal bones – it is from the study of these that the environments of the northern lands are reconstructed. Scientists working within sterile laboratories, writing technical reports on specific aspects of the past, do this work. The challenge we face when writing history, however, is not just to combine these sources of evidence so that we can imagine actual communities of plants, animals and insects, but also to gain an understanding of the experience of those who first entered and then became part of those communities. The lists of plants and animals are a poor substitute for the smell of pine needles and the taste of venison roasted under the stars; a report on insect remains cannot evoke the buzz and sting of a horsefly; estimates of winter temperatures fail to convey the numbing pain of fur-clad frozen feet that have walked through snow and waded across icy rivers. Fortunately such sensations are within our grasp: to be a good prehistorian one should not just read the technical reports that emanate from archaeological science, but actually go walking and immerse oneself in the natural world, edging a little closer to the hunter-gatherer experience.

This is precisely what John Lubbock has been doing since leaving Gough's Cave. He headed north, crossing 150 kilometres of rolling hills and plain; the trees became sparse and the wind persistent as he approached the great ice sheet itself. Few people were seen as he crossed the tundra – a party of reindeer hunters in the distance disappearing into the mist, a few families heading south, perhaps to Gough's Cave itself.

When Lubbock rests, or is forced to shelter, he reads *Prehistoric Times* to discover what his 1865 namesake had known about using animal bones and plant remains to reconstruct past environments. Victorian Lubbock evidently knew that certain animals were indicators of past climatic conditions, commenting how reindeer bones provided a clear indicator of a cold climate and even picking out the lemming as a particularly telling species when found in cave or river deposits.[11] There was no mention of pollen grains,[12] but he described how peat bogs in Denmark often have layers of pine near the base, followed by oak and birch, and then beech – trees that he assumed had grown around the edge and fallen in. 'For one species of tree thus to displace another,' he had written, 'and in its turn to be supplemented by a third, would evidently require a great lapse of time, but one which, as yet, we have no means of measuring.'[13]

Elsewhere, Victorian John Lubbock had been just as cautious about estimates of past temperature. Commenting on the proposal from a Mr Prestwich[14] that temperatures had once been up to 29 degrees below that of the present, he had written: 'we are hardly yet in a condition to estimate with any degree of probability the actual amount of change which has taken place.'[15] As with radiocarbon dating, so useful for establishing the lapse of time between one vegetation type and another, palaeoentomology – the study of beetles and other insects from ancient deposits – had yet to be developed.

When not reading, modern John Lubbock watches for people, and is in turn watched by animals of the tundra. As he crunches across the frozen ground, a snowy owl seated upon a tussock pivots its head to fix him in its stare. As it does so, an arctic hare rises and does likewise. Within a moment the tension breaks – the owl silently departs its perch to sweep low across the grass, the hare drops again and disappears from sight. Lubbock walks on.

When no more than a day's walk from the glaciers themselves, he arrives at another limestone gorge, known today as Creswell Crags. It is daybreak on a winter's day in 12,700 BC and he stands upon the edge of its southern cliff looking down among pine and birch that have found shelter in the gorge. Its sides are peppered with fissures and caves. Wisps of smoke wind their way between the trees; tracing back to their source, Lubbock spots a fireplace that smoulders at the entrance to a cave.

A shout draws his gaze away to a man and a boy entering the gorge. Clad in furs, they each have a pair of snow-white hares slung across their shoulders; a spring in their step suggests they are pleased with their kill. Lubbock watches as they climb across the scree-slope towards the cave and dump their catch by the fire. Women and children appear excitedly from within the cave; they admire the hares, stroking their fur and pinching their thighs to feel the meat.

By the time that Lubbock has descended the shallow cliff, crossed the gorge and joined them by the fire, a stone blade has removed the front feet and slit the belly of the biggest hare. Its skin is peeled back, and the front legs eased out, before being drawn over the animal's head. A few minutes later the carcass is on a spit across the fire, its pelt hanging with the other hares inside the cave.

Once roasted, the hare is cut into joints to be shared between all present – except, of course, John Lubbock. Nevertheless he manages to eat some scraps that provide a deeply satisfying breakfast. When all the bones have been chewed quite clean they are gathered and buried in a shallow pit just within the entrance of the cave; if left exposed, they would attract scavenging hyenas and foxes.

Lubbock remains with these people for the next few days, anticipating a chance to hunt big game – some of the reindeer, horse and even mammoths he had seen while travelling north. But no such hunting occurs, as hare is the only game they take. And so, instead of learning how to slay mighty beasts, he acquires some less macho but far more important survival skills: how to extract sinews from a hare to use as sewing thread, how to turn its leg bones into awls and needles, how to make socks, mittens and coat lining from the fur.

One evening he follows a man and a youth to a thicket of stunted willow where the hares are known to feed. The man inspects which leaves have been chewed and which grass stems broken by the resting hares. A branch is torn off, stripped and inserted into the ground. A loop of sinew is then attached just where the man suspects the next feeding bout will occur.[16] At dawn the party returns to find a gleaming white hare caught within the noose, lying exhausted from its struggle but still alive. The man lifts it gently, strokes its fur and whispers kind words in its ear. And then he breaks its neck.

Lubbock leaves what will become known as Robin Hood Cave in Creswell Crags. He heads east; a journey across tundra-covered lowlands awaits. It will take him through the gently rolling hills and valleys of a land that no longer exists – Doggerland, now drowned by the waters of the North Sea.[17] Beyond that, he will arrive in northern Germany and there his wish to see ice-age hunters at work with larger game will be fulfilled.

Creswell Crags is found today amidst a decaying industrial conurbation, a landscape that could hardly be more different from the beauty of ice-age tundra. The gorge is no more than 100 metres long and 20 metres wide; its caves have marvellous names: Robin Hood Cave, Mother Grundy's Parlour, Pin Hole Cave. Once they were full of sediments containing the remains of animals that had lived and died on the tundra. Wolves, hyenas, foxes and bears had used the caves for denning, dragging home the remnants of their prey: reindeer, horse, red deer, lemmings and a vast array of birds. Smaller mammals, bats and owls had also lived and died within these crags, making them a treasure trove for those who wish to reconstruct animal communities of the ancient world.

As at Gough's Cave, the first excavations at Creswell occurred in the late nineteenth century, by the Rev. J. Magens Mello, and then continued periodically until the present day. In 1977 John Campbell synthesised all the data that had accumulated and attributed the presence of animal bones to human activity, principally to those people who came to the crags during the last few thousand years of the ice age. He thought that those pioneers of the north had not only hunted reindeer and horse, but had also slain mammoth and rhino.[18] Recent, meticulous studies, however, have identified which bones carry the tell-tale cut marks of stone tools and which the gnawing of carnivore teeth. This work has downsized human activity to the more modest pursuit of trapping arctic hares.[19]

All of the cut-marked bones dated to a narrow window of time at around 12,700 BC – with radiocarbon dates so similar to those from Gough's Cave that we could be dealing with the very same party of pioneers.[20]

Cut-marked bones can tell us far more than merely what people had once eaten and which animals had once lived in ice-age Europe: they can tell us precisely when people began to spread north from their refuges in the south. The tools themselves are little help – being made of stone they lack the crucial carbon from which an exact date can be acquired. Consequently, archaeologists are reliant upon establishing the age of the animal bones found lying with the artefacts, and then assuming that each is contemporary with the other. Unfortunately this is often not the case.

As happened at Creswell Crags, animal bones can become embedded in cave sediments from a variety of sources and then further muddled together. Stone tools can become intermingled with such bones. So when a radiocarbon date is acquired on, say, the leg bone of a reindeer found next to a spear point, that date would not necessarily tell us when the spear point was discarded or lost within the cave. It might simply tell us when a hyena had used the cave for its den many centuries or even millennia either before or after the human presence.[21]

Victorian John Lubbock, writing in the 1860s, was quite aware of this problem. Indeed, in *Prehistoric Times* he used cut-marks to counter arguments from a certain Monsieur Desnoyers that the bones of extinct animals had lain in caves for thousands of years before the appearance of man, their remains simply becoming mixed together. The association between stone artefacts and the bones of mammoth, cave bear and woolly rhino was crucial to those who argued for an age of human antiquity greater than the few thousand years spanned by the Bible. Victorian John Lubbock did exactly what any modern archaeologist would do: he looked for cut-marks on the bones and provided examples for cave lion, woolly rhinoceros and reindeer.[22] In fact, he anticipated almost all the techniques used by archaeozoologists today. He discussed the impact of gnawing and scavenging by dogs on the bone collections which archaeologists have to study,[23] used different degrees of skeleton fragmentation to assess relative dates of burial,[24] and assessed the seasons in which hunting had taken place by the animals present and a knowledge of their modern counterparts' behaviour.[25]

Today, when the age of human antiquity is no longer in doubt, cut-marked bones remain just as crucial for archaeological study. They provide ideal specimens for radiocarbon dating, as the cut-marked bones are by definition contemporary with a human presence. The possibility of dating what are often small fragments has only arisen by the advent of a new technique of radiocarbon dating known as 'accelerator mass spectrometry' or AMS. This can date samples no more than 1/1000th of the size required by the older, 'conventional' technique, as it is now called.[26]

In 1997 Rupert Housley and his colleagues published the results of more than a hundred new AMS radiocarbon dates obtained from forty-five sites distributed across northern Europe, from eastern Germany to the British Isles.[27] Housley is one of the leading experts on radiocarbon dating and had carefully selected specimens that provided unequivocal evidence for human presence.[28] For the first time, archaeologists had the chance to develop a precise understanding of when and how people expanded northwards from their ice-age refuge in Southwest Europe.

The northern limits of that refuge were the valleys which act as tributaries to the Loire. It was only after 15,000 BC that settlement pushed further north, initially into the upper Rhine and then by 14,500 BC into the middle Rhine, Belgium and southern Germany. This was after grasses and shrubs had travelled north, these closely followed by herds of reindeer and horses eager to expand their range. We can tell that the ice-age pioneers moved at an average rate of one kilometre per annum and, in another four hundred years, had made settlements in northern France, northern Germany and Denmark. At around 12,700 BC the first people returned to Britain after an absence of almost 10,000 years. Not surprisingly, this final big push north-wards coincides with the warm period of the Bølling. At that time Britain was just the most northwesterly corner of Europe – several thousand more years had to pass before it became an island.

The recolonisation of any one specific region was a two-stage process. First came the pioneers. In this phase the archaeological sites are small, usually no more than a scatter of stone tools. Such sites were most likely the overnight camps of hunting parties exploring lands that had lacked any human settlement during the great glacial freeze. The pioneers are likely to have travelled north in the summer, returning to southern base camps to report on what they had seen. Knowledge about topography, the distribution of animals and plants, the sources of raw materials, had to be gradually acquired by these pioneers so that mental maps of the new territory could be constructed. This must have been challenging. Because both the weather and the climate remained so variable, bodies of knowledge built up in one generation of explorers may have been of little value to the next.

The phase of pioneering lasted for about five hundred years, or twenty generations. Only after this had occurred did a shift in human settlement take place – initiating what Housley and his colleagues call the residential phase. At this stage, families and other groups relocated their base camps to live permanently in the north, exploiting the herds of reindeer and horses that had become established on the tundras.

Why did people go exploring in northern lands and then take up residence there? The spores and seeds of plants were carried by the wind; the insects and animals that followed in their wake were unable to resist the ecological imperative to breed and exploit new niches as soon as such opportunities arose. Were the ice-age hunters just as helplessly driven as the beetles, the rodents and the deer? When the thaw arrived, did human populations simply swell just as the rivers had done until they were forced to find new sources of food?

There can be little doubt that human populations did indeed expand. The brilliance of ice-age cave paintings hide the sore truth that life at LGM had been appallingly hard. Winter would have been fatal for many of the babies, children and the infirm as frozen ground and blizzards destroyed food supply and human health. Quite what happened to the bodies we do not know as there are no cemeteries, and individual burials are few and far between.

With even a slight increase in average temperatures, populations would have grown, perhaps rapidly: babies surviving into infancy instead of dying of cold and hunger; women giving birth to a third or fourth child; the elderly surviving the winter while telling tales to the new generation of ice-age hunters.

But factors other than an increase in numbers may have driven people into northern lands. Ambitious young men and women may have left to search for new resources, those that provided prestige and items for exchange rather than food and drink. Hence, as the ice sheets retreated, entrepreneurs may have followed in their wake, searching for mammoth ivory, luxurious pelts, seashells and exotic stone. Social tensions may have been the incentive for others to travel north. As new lands became available, an opportunity arose for young men and women to establish communities of their own rather than remaining under the authority of elders and traditions no longer to their liking.

I doubt if any or all of these explanations are quite sufficient to explain the great northward trek after the ice had gone. There is another driving force that must be invoked, one that we will find behind human dispersal throughout the world as Lubbock's travels take him across the Americas, Australia, Asia and Africa. It is the curiosity of the human spirit: the drive to explore new lands for the sake of exploration itself.

14

With Reindeer Hunters

Economy, technology and society, 12,700–9600 BC

Silence – other than the rhythmic deep breathing of anxious hunters and the thunderous beating of his adrenalin-fuelled heart. Some hunters are crouching behind boulders; others hide among tussocks of grass from the approaching herd. John Lubbock lies flat on the ground, ready to observe the annual reindeer slaughter in the Ahrensburg valley of Schleswig-Holstein.

Through the grass stalks he sees a path winding between two small lakes within the valley bottom. Reindeer use this route every autumn when making their annual northward migration towards new grazing. An icy wind blows the hunters' scent away as the ground begins to vibrate with the pounding of a multitude of hoofs. The ambush is set.

The leading group of deer pass by the boulders and funnel along the narrow path. A signal is made and spears are thrown, striking the animals from behind. More spears come from across the valley – the deer are trapped. Terrorised, they flee into the water and swim for their lives. Within a few minutes eight or nine animals lie upon the ground; some quiver before a final blow to the head. A few carcasses are floating within the lake; they are left to sink, as those on land will provide more than enough food, hides and antlers. The spears are carefully collected – not so much for their points as for their wooden hafts that are precious within the largely treeless landscape of northern Europe.

Alfred Rust excavated the site of Meiendorf in the Ahrensburg valley in the 1930s.[1] In the muddy sediments of the valley bottom he found thousands of reindeer bones, and a great number of stone points that had once been attached to spears. They had been lethal hunting weapons, most likely propelled with the aid of an atlatl – a stick that hooked around the end of the spear – to provide extra power.

These date from 12,600 BC, which was almost at the end of the period Edouard Lartet christened 'l'âge du renne'. Lartet, the French archaeologist so admired by Victorian John Lubbock, had been impressed by the vast quantities of reindeer bones in the caves of southern France. We now know that these had been accumulating since 30,000 BC at least.[2] But Lartet lacked any notion of their age and conceived of L'âge du renne as following L'âge du grand ours des cavernes (cave bear) and L'âge de l'éléphant et du rhinocéros, but preceding L'âge de l'aurochs (wild cattle).

To divide what Victorian John Lubbock had called the Palaeolithic into four phases of this type was a ground-breaking idea in 1865 and yet subject to some criticism in *Prehistoric Times* because of the chronological overlaps of the named species.[3] Of the four phases, L'âge du renne persisted in archaeological thought far longer than the others because many ice-age communities were indeed dependent upon reindeer for their livelihood.

After the ice had retreated, reindeer rapidly began to use the Ahrensburg valley as a major route-way on their annual migrations across treeless tundra to winter pastures in southern Sweden. The tundra landscape was far milder than those we know today: summer temperatures reached 13°C, and fell to a mere minus 5°C in winter. When the pioneers first arrived in this region they must have watched in awe as herds of reindeer passed along the narrow valley – it was a hunting opportunity second to none.

Some of the sites that Rust found, such as Meiendorf, dated to the Bølling, while others were 2,000 years younger, falling within the period of the Younger Dryas. By then subarctic temperatures had returned to northern Germany, although the tundra was now supporting scattered woodlands of pine and birch. The most famous Younger Dryas site discovered by Rust is that of Stellmoor, located on the eastern edge of the valley. Here more than 18,000 reindeer bones and antlers were recovered, together with a vast number of flint tools, and more than a hundred arrow shafts of pinewood, preserved within the waterlogged sediments.

The site had evidently been one of mass slaughter, most likely turning the lake red with blood. The German archaeologist Bodil Bratlund has reconstructed the scene by a meticulous study of the reindeer bones from Rust's collections, concentrating on those within which flint arrow points were still embedded. He identified which parts of the body had been struck and the direction from which the arrows had come.

Hunters had fired their first arrows horizontally into the deer, aiming for the heart to make a direct kill. The deer fled into the lake, terrorised and swimming for their lives – just as their ancestors had done when the spear-throwers of Meiendorf had struck. Other shots followed, from behind and above – flint arrow points have been found embedded in shoulder bones and in the back of the neck – but many arrows clearly missed their mark and sank into the mud. After the carcasses were hauled to the shore and butchered, there is likely to have been feasting among the groups that had gathered for the annual slaughter.

The Stellmoor hunters killed the deer on a far larger scale than those at Meiendorf. Their technology was more effective: spears had been replaced by bows and arrows tipped with the distinctive triangular and tanged points. In fact, archaeologists now call them 'Ahrensburgian' points, and find them across northern Europe during the Younger Dryas. They were most likely a creative response to the severity of the climate and constituted a leap forward in technology.

So far, the campsites where the hunters of Meiendorf and Stellmoor made their atlatls, pine arrows, and planned their ambush have not been found. About 1,000 kilometres to the southwest, however, in the Paris basin – that area bounded by the mountains of the Ardennes in the northeast and the Vosges in the east, the Morvan in the southwest and the Massif Central in the south – the opposite is true.

More than fifty sites have been discovered, mostly consisting of no more than scatters of flint artefacts – any organic materials such as animal bones and wooden arrow shafts having decayed long ago. Three are particularly well-preserved, Pincevent, Verberie and Etiolles, each of which was occupied during the Bølling and its immediate aftermath.[4] They had been located so close to rivers, tributaries of the Seine, that they became covered with fine silts each time a flood occurred – probably every spring. Consequently the stone artefacts, animal bones and fireplaces were sealed and so preserved just as they had been abandoned. They have been meticulously excavated and fastidiously studied, notably by the French archaeologists Françoise Audouze and Nicole Pigeot, and provide vivid snapshots into the lives of pioneers and settlers in Northwest Europe.

John Lubbock steps into one of those snapshots after having left Meiendorf and reaching what will become the archaeological site of Verberie in the Oise valley in the Paris basin. Today this site is located amidst a rich agricultural landscape but Lubbock's visit required a journey across tundra and through scattered pine and birch trees in valley bottoms, trees that provided welcome relief from the biting wind. It is an autumn afternoon and the light is already beginning to fade. He stands on the edge of the campsite and sees people clustered around a fire. They do not live at Verberie; they merely use it for one or two days each year to butcher reindeer ambushed and killed when attempting to ford the nearby river.

Three carcasses have already been brought here and dumped a few metres apart from each other. The hunters have joined their friends around the fire – a short rest before the work begins. Lubbock also sits, taking up a good viewing position so as not to miss this new and vital lesson in ice-age life: how to turn a reindeer carcass into venison steak.

Three or four of them – men and women – begin to cut swiftly and expertly with their stone tools, frequently stopping work to find a better stone knife or a new chopper from a pile of flint flakes prepared while the hunting was under way. Lubbock focuses on the nearest group, eager to learn this hunter's craft.[5] First the animal's head is removed and then the whole body is skinned. Cuts are made around each hoof and along the inside of each leg. The hide is then virtually peeled away – albeit with a lot of tugging and cutting of sinews. It is laid out flat upon the ground. The belly is sliced open from the sternum to the crotch; a mass of innards spills upon the ground and is shoved to one side.

The carcass is taken apart: legs, pelvis, and slabs of ribs, together with the liver and kidneys, are removed and stacked upon the skin. The heart, lungs and bronchial tubes are removed as a single unit, and then separated – the heart added to the pile of meat, the rest put with the guts. As a penultimate act, the cheek of the severed head is sliced open to expose the base of the tongue. This is cut and removed with a sharp tug. Finally the antlers are removed and they crown the pile of meat and organs.

Each party works around their carcass, circling it to make the next cut through the hide or to detach a limb. A couple of larger joints are carried a few metres away to a pair of women who remove fillets of meat. As the reindeer butchers work, they casually toss over their shoulders the bones that have insufficient meat or marrow, littering the floor with short sections of vertebrae, bones from the lower legs and feet, fragments of the rib-cage.

When the work is finished, there is another break during which the fillets, together with some kidneys and liver, are roasted on the fire and eaten. Sledges are then loaded with the reindeer meat, dirt is kicked across the ashes, and the hunters depart, heaving on ropes of twisted hide as dusk descends. Lubbock remains seated. Within a few minutes wolves come to scavenge upon the waste. They have a feast, chewing bones, licking blood and eagerly devouring the innards.

They too move on and leave the butchery site much as archaeologists will one day find it. There is a patch of ash where the fire had once burned; a concentration of flint flakes and broken nodules where tools had been prepared; a light scatter of chewed bone fragments and discarded tools. Three empty circular patches mark where the carcasses had once been dumped and around which the agile butchers had worked. The remaining morsels of meat, skin, tendons and marrow on the discarded bones soon disappear, consumed by birds, beetles and maggots. In the spring the river will burst its banks and deposit fine sediment across the site, leaving all but the smallest chips of flint and fragments of bone undisturbed.

Lubbock visits another settlement, one that will become Pincevent. It lies 125 kilometres due south, but he takes a winding route along the valleys of the Oise and the Seine to its confluence with the Yonne. On arrival, he sees a group of tents made from wooden frames draped with reindeer hide around which people are tending fires and cleaning skins. These are tightly staked and being scraped to remove fat and sinews. Lifting a flap, he looks inside a tent: a small fire is burning next to a baby lying in a canoe-shaped cradle made from animal skins. Another child, a boy aged four or five, plays on the floor dressed in no more than a pair of leggings.

Outside, several of the older men and women are in a cluster discussing whether it is time to leave Pincevent and return to their winter campsites in the south. It is now late autumn and the reindeer have all but gone – mere stragglers are left from the vast herds that have long since passed on their northward journey.

Five families, each of which has its own fireplace built within a hollow in the ground, are using Pincevent. Some men arrive pulling a sledge loaded with joints of reindeer meat and stacked with antlers – much like that which Lubbock had watched leaving Verberie. Everybody crowds round; joints are split apart and the meat is shared. An evening feast takes place – the last before the campsite is abandoned for another year.

When the great French archaeologist André Leroi-Gourhan excavated Pincevent in the 1960s, many fragmented reindeer bones were found clustered around the hollow fireplaces where the meat had been roasted and eaten.[6] Two decades later, the American archaeologist James Enloe found that fragments from different fireplaces could be fitted together, showing how one single joint had been shared.[7] Whole carcasses had been divided in this fashion – the left forelimb of one animal was found beside one hearth, the right forelimb of the same animal at another. Food sharing was at the centre of social life for those who camped at Pincevent – as indeed it has been with all hunter-gatherers throughout human history.

Heading 40 kilometres back north along the Seine valley, Lubbock arrives at a settlement that will become known Etiolles.[8] Here, a quite different activity is under way: tool manufacture. The predictable migrations of reindeer herds had been just one of the attractions of the valleys of northern France to the ice-age hunters. Another was the availability of the massive, fine-quality flint nodules that were exposed within the chalk and limestone outcrops of the valley sides. Flint was the most valuable raw material throughout the Stone Age because it could be worked into flakes and razor-sharp elongated blades by striking the nodules with hammer-stones. From the blades a great variety of tools could be made by delicate chipping: points for spears, scrapers for cleaning hide, chisels ('burins') for engraving bone and ivory, awls for piercing hide. The pioneers who spread into the northern lands would have been on the lookout for sources of flint – the ice-age hardware store. Those found in the valleys of northern France are likely to have been the best they had ever come across.

Lubbock watches large nodules of flint arriving at the site in deerskin bags after having been dug from chalky sediments just a few hundred metres away. Some of these are really large, weighing 50 kilograms and more than 80 centimetres in length, making those Lubbock had seen being worked at Azraq in western Asia seem quite diminutive in size. Many of these massive nodules are also flawless inside, containing none of the hidden fossils, crystals or internal cracks caused by frost that bedevil poorer-quality stone.

The work appears casual, intermingled with chatter and snacking, and yet it is deadly serious: each strike of the nodule is carefully planned. Such fine nodules provide experienced craftsmen with an opportunity to show off their skills, while the abundance of flint allows novices to work with fresh stone rather than with that discarded by the experts. The nodules – or cores as archaeologists name them – are clasped between their knees and struck with hammers made from stone and antler. Thin flakes are systematically detached; most are left where they fall to the ground, but a few are selected and placed to one side. These will either be turned into tools by delicate chipping of the edge to create a specific shape or angle, or more likely used just as they are – nothing could be sharper. Having acquired a nodule and hammer-stone himself, having bruised his thumb and failed to detach a single flake, Lubbock appreciates once again the knowledge and skill that is being effortlessly displayed. At least this time he manages to avoid a bleeding finger and so some progress appears to have been made since his days at Azraq.

The shape and size of each detached flake depends precisely on what type of hammer is used, where the nodule is struck, the speed and the angle of the blow. Tiny flakes are often removed by chipping or grinding the edge before the nodule is struck so that the force of a blow is not deflected. The knappers aim to produce long, thin 'blades' of flint.[9]

The production of blades might appear a rather bland, mechanistic exercise – and that is indeed how archaeologists often describe the work. But from watching the action itself, Lubbock's impression is quite different. The cores are caressed by fingers that enjoy the texture of the stone; the crack from each blow and the tinkle of flakes falling upon flakes upon the ground are listened to intently; the core is constantly turned, inspected, explored, as if it were a new landscape in which to hunt. To call such work 'flint knapping' or 'tool production' seems derisive.

Of course knapping does not always go to plan. Some nodules that seem perfect from the outside have hidden internal flaws and are discarded as soon as they are tapped – they provide a dull thud rather than the resounding 'ping' that comes from the perfect stone. More problematic are the mishits and wrong decisions about which flakes to remove in order to shape the core. As Lubbock watches the knappers at work he hears the odd curse uttered as a core breaks in two, or when a flake is only partly detached, leaving a 'step' on the nodule. Sometimes the core is discarded, simply dropped into the pile of flakes that have accumulated on the floor.

Twenty-five piles of such waste were excavated at Etiolles. Just as James Enloe had rejoined broken animal bones at Pincevent, the French archaeologist Nicole Pigeot rejoined the flakes and nodules from each cluster. She reconstructed the second-to-second decisions and actions made by the individual ice-age flint knappers who worked at Etiolles close to 12,500 BC. Pigeot found that those knappers who had sat nearest the fire had been the most skilful, for their reconstructed nodules had shown the least errors. Progressively less skilful knappers had worked at increasing distances from the fireplace, with the most distant ones making tentative and clumsy attempts to remove blades.[10]

Elsewhere in Europe – such as in the valleys of the Meuse and Lesse rivers of southern Belgium – flint was a far more precious commodity and could not have been wasted on the inexperienced. These valleys were probably first visited by hunters from the Paris basin, making exploratory trips across the Ardennes around 16,000 BC.[11] They found numerous caves that were used as campsites; their fires had burned the wood from small thickets of alder, hazel and walnut. Just as in France and Germany, reindeer were sometimes killed by ambush in natural 'traps' – when the animals were fording rivers or passing through a narrow gorge. At other times the hunters were more opportunistic, stalking and killing a wide range of animals such as wild horses, ibex, chamois and red deer.

The Meuse and Lesse valleys must have been productive landscapes because soon after 13,000 BC the hunter-gatherers began to remain there all year round. We know this from the microscopic examination of seasonal growth-lines within the teeth of the animals they killed. Just as Lieberman had done when studying the gazelle from the Early Natufian site of Hayonim, archaeologists have identified whether the last bout of tooth growth on slaughtered reindeer in ice-age Belgium was made in summer or winter.

As both were found in equal proportions it became evident that the hunters within southern Belgium killed animals throughout the year. They moved between the valleys and may have also hunted on the intervening tundra-covered plateaux. But they had no flint immediately to hand; it had to be collected from sources 35 kilometres to the north or 65 kilometres to the west – a few days' walk at least.

One of the ice-age campsites is now called Bois Laiterie.[12] This is a small north-facing cave situated above a steep gorge and by all accounts draughty, cold and dark. It had been used as a summer camp by the ice-age hunters, probably occupied for no more than a few days while hunting and fishing for salmon and pike in its vicinity. Partially butchered carcasses had been taken there; a bird-bone flute had been played and then either lost or discarded; bone needles suggest that clothing had been sewn. Foxes took up residence when the hunters departed, perhaps initially attracted by the rubbish left behind.

Other cave sites, such as Chaleux located close to the confluence of the Meuse and Lesse, are much larger, south facing, and contain substantial fireplaces lined with stone slabs. These seem to have been the major base camps from which small parties had set out on different tasks – hunting, collecting flint, gathering firewood and going fishing.

While no site was occupied all year round, the valleys of the Meuse and Lesse provided an annual territory for groups of hunter-gatherers who no longer travelled back south to the homelands of past generations. Quite how many people lived within those valleys is almost impossible to say, but a figure of five hundred people is usually taken to be the minimum to ensure that a population remains viable. This figure, derived from mathematical models of dispersed hunter-gatherer groups who periodically meet up to exchange members, corresponds with historically documented hunter-gatherers of North America and Canada.[13] Such gatherings may have happened only once or twice a year; for the most part the hunter-gatherers of the Meuse and Lesse valleys are likely to have lived in groups of between twenty-five and fifty individuals, divided into four or five families.

Although all of Europe other than the far north was habitable at 12,500 BC, much of it is likely to have remained quite empty of people. Ice-age conditions would still have inhibited the rate of population growth and caused severe difficulties during the winter seasons. Additionally, people's dependence on reindeer for food may also have caused problems, for, as we know from modern times, reindeer populations can go through periods of boom and bust.[14] The latter would have left many ice-age hunters desperate for food and cancelled out any population growth that had been made. In such conditions it was essential that groups of people remained in contact with each other – not only those within the same region, but those who may have lived hundreds, even thousands, of kilometres away. The key to survival was information – information about food supplies, environmental conditions, possible marriage partners, and new inventions, such as the bows and arrows used at Stellmoor.

We can guess that people must have travelled many miles to visit their friends and relations, bringing news and gossip, discussing their future plans, what animals and plants they had seen, when the migratory birds had flown, and what had been heard from other groups. Archaeologists have found traces of those journeys in the trail of items that were carried and sometimes lost across large expanses of Europe. A prime example of these are the fossilised seashells brought to, and subsequently found within, the caves of southern Belgium – objects of no utilitarian value but which could have been used to adorn clothes or worn as beads. These shells have been traced to two geological strata, one close to Paris and the other within the Loire valley, distances of 150 and 350 kilometres.

Similar journeys were being made by the hunter-gatherers in western central Europe between the Elbe and the Rhine in the north, and the Alps and the Danube in the south. Flint, quartz, amber and jet, as well as fossil shells, have been found at sites more than 100 kilometres from their sources.

This region of modern-day Germany provides one of the best insights into the communities which had taken up permanent residence in lands that had been polar desert during the glacial maximum.[15] The majority of ice-age sites found within its rolling hills and river valleys date once again to the Bølling period, a time when its landscapes were still quite open, and on which horse and reindeer were the available prey. In the middle Rhine area, several groups of hunters appear to have combined their efforts every autumn and winter to hunt the large numbers of horses that clustered together within the valleys; during the summer they dispersed to hunt reindeer in the adjacent uplands.

The most striking evidence for communal hunts during autumn and winter are the sites of Gönnersdorf and Andernach, found directly opposite each other on either side of the middle Rhine, both dating to between c. 13,000 and 11,000 BC. It is at the former that Lubbock now arrives – having practised his reindeer-hunting, butchery and flint-knapping skills while travelling across Europe from Etiolles.[16]

He finds the settlement located upon a terrace above the valley floor. Winter has set in; the sky is dark and snow is upon the ground. Here he finds neither a damp, dark cave like Bois Laiterie, nor a site of flimsy shelters as at Pincevent. Instead there are several substantial circular dwellings, 6 or 8 metres in diameter, built with solid wooden posts and covered with sods of turf and thick hide. An icy wind blows across the tundra and smoke ekes its way from every roof. From a distant dwelling there is the faint sound of song; from one near by, human chatter.

Lubbock bends low, pushes aside the hides across the door and enters. Ten or twelve people sit on thick furs laid upon a pavement of slate. It is warm inside and the occupants, both men and women, are bare-chested; the smoke-filled air is intoxicating as aromatic herbs smoulder upon the fire. The people surround a central fireplace, over which slabs of horsemeat are roasting, supported on a mammoth-bone grill.

A group of shells is being passed from hand to hand around the circle. They are small, creamy-white hollow tubes, just a few centimetres long. Some have a smooth surface while others are heavily ribbed. The villagers have not seen such shells before; they are dentaliums that originated from the Mediterranean shore and have been brought by a winter visitor to the settlement. Lubbock, of course, has seen such shells around the necks of people at 'Ain Mallaha – a village that is thriving in the oak woodlands of the Fertile Crescent at this very moment.

Night descends, the meat is eaten and candles are lit. One of the men appears older than the others and wears a necklace of pierced fox teeth around his neck. Throughout the evening he has been lowering his face close to the smouldering herbs and inhaling deeply. He now takes a flat slab of slate and draws upon the surface, cutting into it with a flint point. As he does so the other people gently chant. Within a few minutes he has finished, and the engraved slate is passed around the circle. He has drawn a horse; it has been carefully depicted and proportioned quite correctly. The slate is placed to one side. The old man – a shaman – starts again: a deep intake of the intoxicating smoke, a few minutes of intense concentration amid more chanting, another slate to pass around the circle. That too has the figure of a horse. And so this continues for many hours – eventually the old man will collapse upon the floor.[17]

Since 1954, the excavations conducted by Gerhard Bosinski at Gönnersdorf have produced the largest and finest collection of art objects from central Europe. More than 150 slabs have been found with engravings of animals and women. Horses were most frequently depicted, often with a naturalism quite similar to that found in the cave paintings of the Dordogne. The interest in the horse may not be surprising as it was the inhabitants' key food supply; but such economic arguments cannot explain why the mammoth was also frequently depicted with a similar level of naturalism.[18] These drawings demonstrate considerable anatomical knowledge in the detailed depiction of eyes, trunks and tails, even though mammoths would have been very rare or even completely absent from the middle Rhine at this time. Birds, seals, woolly rhinos and lions were also depicted.

Lubbock remains at Gönnersdorf for a few days. On each of these, male hunting parties go searching for horses within the valley. As they do so Lubbock comes to appreciate another key fact of ice-age society, one that has been sorely neglected by archaeologists throughout the last century. It is the pivotal role of women. With such an emphasis on hunting and butchery – tasks assumed to be undertaken by the men and which create the majority of archaeological remains – the critical work of women has been overlooked. At Gönnersdorf, Lubbock sees how they gather firewood, construct and maintain the dwellings, tend the hearths, prepare clothing, make stone, wood and antler tools, cook the food and look after the young, the old and the infirm. At night it is the women who sing and dance around the communal fires. It is they who bear and nurse the newborn. And the women also go hunting.

One evening Lubbock searched the pages of *Prehistoric Times* to discover what his Victorian namesake had written about the role of women in 'savage society'. Very little; they were hardly mentioned at all. On one page he had noted that 'the chastity of women is not, as a general rule, much regarded among savages', although he went on to argue that 'we must not too severely condemn them on this account';[19] elsewhere he casually remarked on how cannibals prefer the flesh of women to that of men,[20] and that women will be preferably eaten to dogs during times of shortage.[21] So the only women's role that Victorian Lubbock appreciated was that of satisfying the hunger, gastronomic and otherwise, of their men.

Modern John Lubbock had found this to be quite wrong; their key role in all aspects of ice-age society may have been the reason why women were the principal subjects depicted by the Gönnersdorf artists. Although never displaying the naturalism of the animals, such images range from near-complete depictions in which heads, bodies, arms and breasts are drawn, to a virtual abstraction in which a single line traces that of the back and the buttocks. Sometimes women were depicted singly, at others in groups of three or four, and in some cases in lines of ten or more with their bodies appearing to sway in a way that is suggestive of dance. In one image a line of women appear to be walking together; one carries an infant on her back, her breasts clearly swollen with milk. The same stylised female form is widely found on sites throughout western central Europe, sometimes engraved on slabs and sometimes carved from antler, but never in such profusion as at Gönnersdorf.[22]

Archaeologists – typically male archaeologists – have traditionally interpreted any female image from the ice age as a fertility symbol, describing many as 'Venus figurines'. But there is nothing overtly sexual about the Gönnersdorf images; indeed, they seem more likely to celebrate the role of women as mothers, carers, providers and workers within ice-age society, rather than only as the bearers of children, let alone as objects of sexual desire.

Throughout the winter people remain at Gönnersdorf; new arrivals swell their numbers to more than one hundred. Much time is spent telling stories and discussing plans for the spring – where each group will go to hunt, which – if any – will remain at the village. The same is happening at winter campsites throughout central and northern Europe. But it will not last. Lubbock sits in the warmth of a dwelling, as he had once done on the steppe close to Abu Hureyra. Just as on that occasion, his companions are quite unaware that the Younger Dryas is about to arrive. This will bring the curtain down for a millennium at least on any singing and dancing in the valley of the Rhine.

At around 10,800 BC the climate of Europe did indeed take a sharp dive back to the most severe of ice-age conditions. This decimated the horse herds that had wintered in the valleys of central Europe and which had sustained large groups of hunter-gatherers. Rather than simply being temporarily deserted for the summer season, Gönnersdorf was abandoned for good.

Throughout Europe the vegetation and animal communities were transformed: areas of woodland returned to barren tundra. Just like the Early Natufian people of western Asia, the ice-age hunters of northern Europe had to adjust to the new conditions and their populations were pushed to the brink of extinction. They lacked any wild cereals to cultivate but exploited the resumption of annual reindeer migrations through the Ahrensburgian valley – this time by using bows and arrows.[23]

With the hindsight of history we know that better times would once again arrive. At 9600 BC, dramatic global warming killed off the bitterly cold winters and provided the thickest covering of woodland that Europe has known for more than 100,000 years. And it is into those woods that we must now travel, skipping over the Younger Dryas. We will leave Lubbock to make a journey into southern Europe and return to the northwest, to that which is today the British Isles.

15

At Star Carr

Adaptations to early Holocene woodlands in northern Europe,
9600–8500 BC

To visit Star Carr in Yorkshire is to visit one of the key archaeological sites in Europe. It has been rightly compared in significance to the painted cave of Lascaux and the tomb of Tutankhamun. Yet when one arrives, there are neither tourist coaches fouling the air nor guides eager for cash. No heritage centres, no gift shops; no signposts, monuments or plaques; just a near perfect corner of the English countryside.

My last visit was on a tranquil summer's afternoon in 1998. I had found the way down an unmarked country lane and through a farmyard, pausing to watch the aerobatics of swallows and house martins. A footpath took me through pasture grazed by cows, and along a hedgerow where my only companions were butterflies and goldfinches flitting between the purple thistles. When this path met the Hertford River, a gentle-flowing stream upon which swans and cygnets were idling, I knew from words exchanged with the farmer that I had arrived.

The site lay to my left, but there was no archaeology to be seen, no tumbled walls or grassy humps to denote a bygone age. Before me there was a field of pasture like any other; behind, a flower-strewn riverbank where bees were working the brambles, buttercups and dog-rose. Looking both east and west, the flat pasture of the Vale of Pickering stretched as far as I could see, interrupted by occasional ditches and small plantations. To the north the land began to climb towards the Yorkshire moors, and to the south the rolling hills of the Wolds. The air was scented with meadowsweet; I was first tempted to swim, and then to snooze.

How could this unmarked corner of Yorkshire be sensibly compared with Lascaux and Tutankhamun? It was surely an absurd comparison. Yet it was made by no less a figure than the late Sir Grahame Clark, Disney Professor of Archaeology at Cambridge University, Master of Peterhouse, Fellow of the British Academy.[1] He was certainly not a rash man; but neither was he modest and Star Carr was his prize excavation.

Just as Tutankhamun's tomb and the paintings of Lascaux are symbolic of lost and ancient worlds, so too is the site of Star Carr – the lost world of forest-dwelling hunter-gatherers of Europe who lived within the period which archaeologists call the Mesolithic. That was the new world of European culture. It was one forged by the descendants of the Stellmoor reindeer hunters and Gönnersdorf dancers after the Younger Dryas had ended as suddenly as it had begun and the ice sheets of Europe had finally melted away.

There are many hundreds, probably thousands, of Mesolithic sites in Europe – an archaeological record quite different to those ephemeral traces of ice-age people who had come before. Some have exotic burials; others striking art. But Star Carr has neither. So why is that site so special?

The answer is simple. Star Carr is where the Mesolithic effectively began. It began here in a literal sense – it is one of the earliest-known Mesolithic settlements in the whole of Europe. It began here for me personally – Star Carr was the first Mesolithic site I ever heard about and was central to my decision to become an archaeologist. And it began here in a historical sense: before Grahame Clark made his excavations of 1949–51 the Mesolithic period was all but ignored in comparison to the Paleolithic, which came before, and the Neolithic, which followed.[2] It was the first site in Europe, of any period, to be radiocarbon dated.

In 1865 Victorian John Lubbock had no inkling of this critical phase of European prehistory. He had written in *Prehistoric Times*: 'from the careful study of the remains which have come down to us, it would appear that Pre-historic Archaeology may be divided into four great epochs.'[3] He went on to describe the Palaeolithic period – 'when man shared possession of Europe with the Mammoth, the Cave bear, the Woolly-haired rhinoceros and other extinct animals';[4] the Neolithic period – 'a period characterized by beautiful weapons and instruments made of flint and other kinds of stone';[5] the Bronze Age and the Iron Age.[6] No mention of the Mesolithic; it simply did not exist in 1865.

Later in the volume, Victorian Lubbock had described how the Danish archaeologist Professor Worsaae wanted to divide the Palaeolithic age into two phases. The first involved stone implements associated with extinct animals, and the second concerned finds from the Danish coast, notably large shell mounds that also contained fishbones, animal bones and artefacts, called Køkkenmøddinger (kitchen middens, or waste dumps). Another Danish archaeologist, Professor Steenstrup, believed the middens belonged in Lubbock's Neolithic, the New Stone Age. Having weighed up the scanty evidence either way, Victorian John Lubbock sided with Steenstrup: although he thought the Kjökkenmöddings represented a definite period of Danish history, this probably came within the Neolithic itself.[7]

We now know that Worsaae had been correct and Steenstrup entirely wrong; the Mesolithic is quite distinct from both the Palaeolithic and the Neolithic periods of European prehistory. It is the period of Holocene hunter-gatherers in Europe, those living in thick forests before the arrival of the first farmers. Grahame Clark pioneered Mesolithic studies in Britain during the 1930s by compiling a catalogue and classification of the stone tools of the period.[8] But it was only with the excavation of Star Carr that his interests turned to the Mesolithic lifestyle and environment. By doing so he was merely catching up with Danish archaeology, which had been tackling such issues ever since the Kjökkenmöddings were first excavated in the 1850s – even though Worsaae and Steenstrup disagreed about their age.[9]

On that peaceful summer afternoon I imagined the activity of the young Cambridge lecturer and his team arriving at Star Carr, setting up camp, and beginning the task of excavation. Clark had chosen Star Carr after stone tools were discovered in a drainage ditch. It turned out to be a shrewd choice. Within the waterlogged peat of that Yorkshire field he found the remains of a hunter-gatherer campsite with an unprecedented degree of preservation, not just of animal bones but of antler and wooden tools. No other Mesolithic site in Britain, found either before or since, has remotely approached its level of preservation.

The Mesolithic inhabitants would have sat precisely where I sat on that delightful afternoon. But the hills they saw to the north and south lacked the Yorkshire field walls and stone-built farmhouses; they looked towards slopes covered with birch woodland and a thick undergrowth of fern. And before them lay not pasture but an extensive lake, the edge marked today by that shallow slope on which I had dozed.

Their campsite had been a base for hunting within the birch woods and along the lakeshore. Red deer was their favoured quarry, but wild boar, roe deer, elk and aurochs (wild oxen) were also taken. They had gathered plants, caught ducks, grebes and divers, and most likely fished from canoes. They came to Star Carr each summer, and one of their key tasks was to burn the dense stands of reeds that fringed the lake. At the campsite toolkits had been made and repaired – new stone points and barbs were fitted to arrows, animal skins were cleaned and then sewn for clothing, antler harpoons were manufactured.

The antlers had been gathered in the autumn and winter, cached at the site ready for this visit. Carving the harpoons was both a skilful and a laborious craft. The antler was worked with stone tools fashioned like chisels. Long parallel grooves were made the length of the antler, and then a flat segment eased out; this was cut, shaped and ground smooth. Some chose to make antler points with many fine barbs, others carved just a few, crudely shaped; perhaps these were designs for catching different types of game or perhaps they were experiments because no one knew which design was the most effective for hunting.

So while sitting within that Yorkshire field I had to imagine the Mesolithic scene: flames crackling through the dry reeds, eyes watering from the smoke, excited children chasing the flushed-out wildfowl, hares and voles. The reeds had burned well, the flames catching overhanging branches so that catkins blossomed in vivid orange, were carried on the breeze and then momentarily floated on the lake before sinking. The reeds were burned to provide a view across the lake and improve access to their canoes. It also encouraged the growth of new shoots so that grazing deer could be relied upon when they returned once again to hunt along the shoreline. Elsewhere in the prehistoric world at this date of 9000 BC, others were also encouraging new shoots – those of wheat and barley in the fields of Jericho.

That night the people may have danced and sung, full of venison and intoxicated with herbal drugs. I could imagine some dressed in hides and antler masks, moving their bodies sensuously, deer-like, to the music of chants, drums and flutes made from reed. The dancers would suddenly halt, sniff the air, dart in panic; then they would die with the hunters' arrow, be thanked and celebrated for giving up their life.

I imagined the people departing the next day after sleeping below the stars – some walking towards the hills, others travelling by canoe, heading eastwards towards the coast. The deer masks were discarded with the butchered animal bones, the rubbish from making the harpoons and stone tools. And there they would remain, quickly forgotten – buried beneath the dead reeds that turned into peat, until their discovery changed our understanding of the European past.

Clark's excavations produced much of the evidence upon which my imagination had worked.[10] He found the deer masks – but they may have been used as hunting disguise rather than as dancing costumes. He also found many different shapes and sizes of barbed antler points and the remains of food plants, although none are known to have had intoxicating properties. There was a wooden paddle, but no canoe.

He finished his excavations in 1951. That, however, was just the beginning of a constant re-analysis and re-evaluation of the Star Carr evidence that has continued to the present day.[11] Clark had thought the settlement was a winter base camp owing to the large amount of antlers – something only present on hunted animals during the latter part of the year. But when in 1985 the archaeo-zoologists, Peter Rowley-Conwy and Tony Legge, re-analysed the animal bones they found nothing to suggest a winter occupation.[12] In contrast there were many indicators of early summer, of which deer teeth were the most telling. By examining which teeth had erupted, and comparing these with known patterns of tooth development in modern deer, Legge and Rowley-Conwy were confident that most animals had been killed between May and June.

The reed-burning was not identified until the mid-1990s. This was by Petra Dark, an archaeologist who specialises in environmental reconstruction and is a colleague of mine at Reading University.[13] She took new samples of the peat from the edge and centre of the former lake and made a remarkably detailed microscopic study of the pollen grains, charcoal particles and plant fragments in a succession of razor-thin slices. The first of these came from a time before people had arrived in the Vale of Pickering and showed that the vegetation had been quite typical of ice-age landscapes – herbs, grasses, scattered dwarf willow, pine and birch.

After 9600 BC the pollen grains within the slivers of peat had changed to include those of poplar and juniper, and then to be dominated by birch. Soon after 9000 BC charcoal particles appear within the peat, blown from the first campfires made close to the lake. A sudden increase in the quantity of charcoal, together with fragments of burnt reed and catkins, reflect the onset of intense activity; an annual clearance of the lakeside vegetation by fire continued for eighty years. People then ignored the lake for one or two generations, to return at about 8750 BC and continue the same activities as before for at least another century. By that time willow and aspen were encroaching upon the lake, turning much of it into 'carr' – dense stands of trees in pools of water. By 8500 BC hazel had taken a hold on the landscape, and after one last burning episode, the people gave up on Star Carr and went to hunt and gather elsewhere. The lake had virtually disappeared.

Trees such as hazel, birch, willow, pine and aspen had re-emerged from their ice-age hide-outs soon after the end of the Younger Dryas, rapidly expanding into extensive swathes of woodland and resuming their northward march.[14]

Once established, the new woodlands had little peace. For coming hard on the heels of those hardy, pioneering species, were the trees that favoured warmer and wetter conditions, their needs provided by ongoing global warming. These included oak and elm, lime and alder which survived within the valleys of southern Europe and whose northward dispersal had been cut short by the Younger Dryas.

As these species travelled from their southern ice-age shelters, they left behind a trail of pollen grains as a record of their journey. Oak trees, for instance, were already found throughout Portugal, Spain, Italy and Greece when the Younger Dryas came to its sudden end. By 8000 BC they had edged up the west coast of France and had reached the far southwest of Britain; by 6000 BC they were across the whole of mainland Europe and the southernmost parts of Scandinavia. By 4000 BC they had reached the northern tip of Scotland and the western coast of Norway. By that time, however, oak trees further south were being felled by farmers who were clearing land to grow crops. Lime made a different journey, beginning in the southeast, having survived the great freeze in northern Italy and the Balkans. It edged its way into eastern and central Europe, and only reached the southeast of England at around 6000 BC. Hazel, elm and alder made similar treks across the continent. The resulting woodland was a rich mix of species, not just of trees but of a vast range of under-storey shrubs and plants, fungi, mosses, and lichens. It engulfed the whole of Europe.

Animals either had to adapt or migrate to survive. Some didn't make it. Mammoths, woolly rhino and giant deer went extinct, perhaps nudged into the abyss by stone-tipped spears. Others, such as reindeer and elk, survived by moving to the far north or to high mountains where thick woodland was unable to prevail. The great beneficiaries of global warming were the red deer, roe-deer and wild boar that soon became the favoured prey for the Mesolithic hunters. Whereas the red deer had lived in large herds on the tundras and in the parkland of southern Europe, the roe-deer and wild boar had survived the LGM and Younger Dryas within the sheltered valleys, amidst the stunted oak and elm.

As the landscape and animal communities evolved, so too did people's lives. For the hunters, changes in animal behaviour were as important as changes in the species themselves. Those who had camped at Etiolles and hunted at Meiendorf were reliant on migratory herds of reindeer. They had waited and watched for the animals to travel well-worn paths, and then slaughtered great numbers at ambushes in narrow valleys or at river cross-ings. But in the new woodlands the deer lived in small and scattered herds, in family groups and sometimes just in ones and twos. So bloody slaughter by brute force had to be replaced by stealth – stalking lone animals, shoot-ing arrows through thick undergrowth, more tracking as the prey fled while trailing blood.[15]

Not surprisingly, such changes in the environment and hunting practices were accompanied by the development of new technology. Chunky spear points and arrow-heads were replaced by microliths: small chipped blades of stone, usually flint, that rapidly became the most important element of stone-tool technology throughout Europe.

In this regard the people of Europe reached the same decision as had been made by the Kebaran people of western Asia at least 10,000 years earlier – that making small blades and chipping these into a series of dis-tinctive shapes was the most effective use of their stone resources. What the resulting weapons lost in terms of brute power and penetrating capacity was amply compensated for by their diversity and flexibility.

Microliths were employed not only as the tips and barbs for arrows, but also as the points for drills and awls for piercing leather, bark and wood. In addition, they made effective knife blades, could be used in leisters for spearing fish and embedded in wooden plaques for vegetable graters. They provided a plug-in pull-out technology – a Stone Age equivalent of the latest DIY or food-processing gadget today with its seemingly endless parts and uses. Nothing could have been better suited to the needs of the Mesolithic people: so many different opportunities arose for its use in any one season, day or even hunting trip – sights of unexpected game, chance encounters with early-ripening nuts, shelter for an overnight camp, a chance to fish.[16]

Microliths are usually found scattered within the domestic rubbish of settlements. Very occasionally they have been recovered still hafted on an arrow shaft, attached with pine resin. And in equally rare cases they have been found still embedded within the animals they killed. At the Danish sites of Vig and Prejlerup, both approximately contemporary with Star Carr, almost complete skeletons of aurochs have been excavated.[17] These had been attacked but escaped capture. The Vig specimen had two stone arrow tips embedded in its ribs, and two further lesions on its bones. One of these had healed – the bone had begun to grow around the wound, showing that this was not the first time the bull had been hit and escaped. The second lesion, which had not healed, was evidently one of the fatal shots that killed the animal. The Prejlerup bull was similar; although arrow tips were only found in its rear end, one must assume that it had also been struck in soft tissue and bled to death. Both finds create images of hunters creeping through undergrowth, striking at the bulls and then stalking the wounded animals – in both cases without success.

Microliths may have been involved in some impressive action, but in themselves they are some of the least striking and complex of prehistoric tools. To find the cutting edge of Mesolithic technology we must look not towards stone, but to those tools made from wood and plant fibres. For the first time in European history these are reasonably abundant in the archaeological record; they seem to testify to a technological revolution.

The presence of these new tools may reflect no more than the wider opportunities available to craftsmen and women in the lush woodland of the Mesolithic, or may even be due to the fact that these people frequently camped next to lakes, leaving their rubbish in the muddy shallows. As invading vegetation turned those lakes into peat bogs, there it remained, quite waterlogged and hence resistant to decay. But while both opportunity and preservation are no doubt important, I suspect there is another critical factor: a new channelling of creative energies into the arts of whittling, binding, twisting, carving and knotting, just as these had once been channelled into painting and sculpture.

The delight of such tools is that they appear to seep from nature itself; they tell of an intimacy with the natural world that is lost today and are the handiwork of people who loved their craft. Archaeologists have found, for instance, the remnants of wicker cages used to catch eels. Some were made from branches of cherry wood and alder, woven together with pine roots – a work of art, natural science and practical need twisted and knotted into one.[18] Willow bark was braided and tied to make fishing nets, used with pine-bark floats and stone sinkers.[19] Such nets were thrown from canoes hollowed from trunks of lime and paddled with heart-shaped blades carved from ash.[20] Hazel rods were used to make fences to divert fish into traps and birch bark was folded and sewn into bags for carrying flint blades.[21]

Not all the tool-making had been successful. There were many fine craftsmen throughout the Mesolithic who could make bows, but this art had to be learned. In one case an elm tree had been felled and the trunk roughly shaped into a bow. The wood was left to season, and then the shaping completed. But perhaps from inexperience, perhaps from knots in the wood, the bow had split during use and was then broken in half, presumably snapped across a knee in frustration.[22]

I fear that the impression so far might be that the Mesolithic diet was all beefsteak and venison, eels and grilled fish. Not true. Remember that we are dealing with people living in vibrant woodlands, surrounded by trees and plants suitable not just for hiding behind when stalking game or for cutting, carving, twisting and knotting when making tools. The woodlands of the Mesolithic provided a feast for the taking: nuts, seeds, fruits, leaves, tubers, shoots. And take they certainly did, sometimes in enormous quantities[23] – as is evident from Franchthi Cave, a site as far from Star Carr as Europe will allow.

While deer were being stalked and reeds burned in the far northwest, the Mesolithic people 4,000 kilometres away in southern Greece were collecting wild lentils, oats and barley; picking pears, gathering pistachios, almonds and walnuts. Excavated between 1967 and 1979 by Thomas W. Jacobsen of Indiana University[24], Franchthi Cave was found to contain a vast number of seeds in the levels belonging to the Mesolithic people, especially those who had lived between 9500 and 9000 BC. In fact he found more than 28,000 seeds coming from twenty-seven different species of plants. The Mesolithic people at Franchthi collected a similar array of plant foods to those who had lived a few thousand years earlier at 'Ain Mallaha and Hayonim in western Asia. Perhaps the Greek coastal lands also supported wild gardens nurtured with care by hunter-gatherers.

Back in northern Europe the key plant foods were hazelnuts and water chestnuts, often exploited in vast quantities. In 1994 I myself found one of the greatest concentrations of waste discarded in a Mesolithic rubbish pit at the settlement of Staosnaig on the tiny island of Colonsay, 40 kilometres off the west coast of Scotland – the remnants of more than 100,000 hazelnuts collected and roasted on the island.[25]

As I left Star Carr, I thought once again about Grahame Clark laying out his trenches, Peter Rowley-Conwy and Tony Legge measuring teeth in their laboratory, and the endless hours that Petra Dark had spent peering down her microscope. A curlew shrieked as I walked across the pasture, just as they had shrieked in the Mesolithic. When approaching the farm I noticed willow, aspen and birch growing in the wet ditches, interspersed with reeds. I stepped among them for a moment and crouched down low. A rich, peaty aroma engulfed me, water oozed from the ground; I touched the reeds and those deer-masked hunters once again danced and sang their way around my imagination.

16

Last of the Cave Painters

Economic, social and cultural change in southern Europe,
9600–8500 BC

The date is 9500 BC. Somewhere in southern Europe the last of the ice-age cave artists is at work. He or she is mixing pigments and painting upon a wall, perhaps a horse or a bison, perhaps a line of dots or merely touching up a painting made long ago. And that will be it: more than 20,000 years of cave painting – perhaps the greatest art tradition humankind has ever known – will have come to an end.[1]

John Lubbock left Gönnersdorf at 11,000 BC and travelled south along the Rhine and then across the hills of eastern France to the limestone valleys of the Dordogne. For a thousand years he watched the landscapes freeze as the Younger Dryas arrived – the retreat of woodland and return of reindeer to the valleys of central and southern Europe. But such conditions were not to last: as Lubbock crossed the Massif Central, global warming returned with a vengeance. And so, instead of joining fur-clad hunters waiting in ambush, Lubbock now trod quietly with those stalking wild boar, helped to gather baskets of acorns and berries, stood upon rocks to spear salmon as they swam upstream to spawn.[2]

Pech Merle – the cave in which spotted horses were painted at the LGM – was no longer used for art, indeed it was no longer used at all. While sitting by its entrance Lubbock watched some children scratch their way through brambles, squeeze between boulders and drop to the floor with muddy, bleeding knees. They had come prepared with a brushwood torch. A flint was struck, the twigs flared and for a few moments the cave walls came alive with bison, horse and mammoth. The children fled in terror, leaving the torch to burn out upon the floor – 10,000 years would have to pass before Pech Merle's spotted horses were illuminated once again.[3]

Lubbock continued to travel south and entered the foothills of the Pyrenees. Here he visited what had been one of the great ice-age meeting-places: a vast tunnel running through a limestone cliff that we know today as Mas d'Azil.[4] A river flowed through the tunnel and people were camped on its left bank. On the right there were entrances to caverns whose walls were decorated with paintings and engravings. When the ice age was at its height, people had largely camped on the right bank where they either lost or discarded some of the finest ice-age carvings ever made: depictions of a braying horse, sprightly ibex, and waterfowl with their young. Groups had gathered at Mas d'Azil during the winter months, often coming from afar and bringing seashells, marine fish, and fine stone as gifts and items to exchange. They decorated their bodies with paint, pendants and necklaces; they may even have been tattooed.[5] It was at Mas d'Azil that initiation ceremonies, marriages and rituals had taken place. Archaeologists describe it as an ice-age 'super-site'.[6]

But when Lubbock arrived in 9000 BC, the heyday of Mas d'Azil had passed. A few family groups were seated on the riverbank near to the vast upstream entrance of the tunnel, quite uninterested in the painted walls near by. Lubbock peered over their shoulders, hoping to see fine animal carvings being made; but they were doing no more than gutting fish that had been caught with very plain and small flat antler harpoons.[7] All except for one man, who was indeed making some art. But this involved no more than the daubing of pebbles. Some got a single blob of paint, others two or three, occasionally a few more. Some blobs were red, some black, some were round and some were striped.

The River Arize still flows through the tunnel at Mas d'Azil and is now joined by the D119 that leads from Pamiers to Saint-Girons, its construction having destroyed some of the archaeology on the right bank. Like Star Carr, Mas d'Azil is a site to which any would-be archaeologist must come as a pilgrim, owing not only to its remarkable ice-age art works but also to its crucial role in the history of archaeology. My own visit was more than two decades ago when I was just embarking on my undergraduate studies, and I have far stronger memories of lying in the glorious French sunshine outside the tunnel, with a bottle of wine and my girlfriend, than whatever I had seen inside the cave. Moreover, at that time I wasn't aware of Mas d'Azil's historical significance: it was here that in 1887 the great French archaeologist Edouard Piette found material that linked the Old and New Stone Ages – the Palaeolithic and Neolithic.

Both his and later excavations revealed a remarkable array of Palaeolithic art objects and occupation debris: stone tools, harpoons, animal bones from reindeer, horse, bison and red deer. The majority of these dated to the final few millennia of the ice age. But lying above this material were layers containing painted pebbles, short flat harpoons and new types of stone artefacts that Piette designated the 'Azilian culture', which is now recognised as the Mesolithic across much of southern Europe.

In 1887 the authenticity of the painted pebbles was questioned by the academic establishment. At that date the only known examples of early prehistoric art were the paintings in Altamira Cave, discovered in 1879. Most French archaeologists were still virulently opposed to the idea that such paintings could have been made by ice-age hunter-gatherers – savages. Piette, however, had never been in any doubt. By the end of the century he had been vindicated: further discoveries made the acceptance of both the Altamira paintings and Mas d'Azil pebbles unavoidable.

From the excavations of Piette and later ones at Mas d'Azil, more than 1,500 painted pebbles were found, while at least another five hundred are known from other sites in France, Spain and Italy. Although these may lack the beauty of the ice-age art they are every bit as mysterious, perhaps more so. Like all Mesolithic art, that of the Azilian is subtle and complex, one that has kept its secrets closely guarded. A study by the French archaeologist Claude Couraud showed that rather than having been randomly applied, the blobs of paint most likely constituted a symbolic code: specific shapes and sizes of pebbles had been chosen; particular combinations and numbers of different motifs had been preferred.[8] Couraud identified 16 different signs but of the possible 246 binary combinations, only 41 were ever used. Numbers of dots between 1 and 4 accounted for 85 per cent of the pebbles, and pairs of dots for 44 per cent. For higher numbers, there appears to have been a preference for numbers between 21 and 29. He suggests that these numbers might refer to lunar phases, but neither Couraud nor any other archaeologists have been able to read the messages on the painted pebbles of Mas d'Azil.

From Mas d'Azil Lubbock headed west, across the rolling, wooded landscapes that bordered the Pyrenees, across rivers that gushed with melt waters from the mountain glaciers that could no longer hold their ice. In northern Spain he visited people camping along wide estuaries that dissected the coastal plain.

As elsewhere in Mesolithic Europe, and indeed the world, these hunter-gatherers had been attracted to estuaries by the abundance and diversity of wild foods to be found there. Its ultimate source lies in detritus – rotting organic matter that arrives within the freshwater rivers on the one hand, and from the sea on the other. This provides food for a host of tiny creatures such as shrimps and snails, which in turn provide rich pickings for crabs and bigger fish and birds, along with mammals such as otters and seals. Migratory birds favour estuaries, their arrival often coinciding with the feeding bonanza of a spawning season. So it is not surprising that hunter-gatherers have been drawn to estuaries – to hunt and fish, gather shellfish and crabs, net birds and collect their eggs.

Despite this bounty, those in northern Spain at 9000 BC regularly went to hunt red deer and wild boar in the foothills of the mountains some ten kilometres from the shore.[9] Sometimes they continued into the crags, cliffs and peaks to search for mountain goats. Lubbock also made a foray inland, not to hunt but to visit the great painted cave of Altamira.

After scrambling through the tangled branches that hid its entrance, he broke through great spider's webs to enter the chamber of the bulls painted by ice-age artists at 15,000 BC. Although quite dim inside, Lubbock could now see the great panorama of bulls – the Sistine chapel of prehistory, as it would later be described. But its heyday had also passed; now only bats and owls came and went, the cave itself home to no more than spiders, beetles and mice.[10] Lubbock wondered whether those living in the surrounding woodlands even knew that the cave was there. With that thought he continued his journey westwards for another 25 kilometres until reaching another cave, one much smaller but evidently still in use: there was debris all over the floor and a stinking rubbish dump of mollusc shells. He settled himself in the shadows, waiting for the occupants to return.

This cave is known today as La Riera, and although lacking spectacular art works its excavation has provided us with the greatest insight into how human lifestyles in southern Europe changed when the ice age drew to a close. Perhaps more than any other individual site, La Riera helps us understand why the tradition of painting caves and carving animals in ivory and bone came to a sudden end.

La Riera was discovered in AD 1916 by Ricardo Duque de Estrada y Martínez de Morentín, the Conde de la Vega del Sella.[11] Already established as a pioneer of Spanish archaeology, he was working on a hunch – that somewhere in a thicket of trees between the towns of Santander and Oviedo he would discover the entrance to a cave.

A crevice was found which became a near-vertical and narrow passage. He squeezed through and entered the rear of a small dark chamber, finding himself right behind a huge mound of limpet and periwinkle shells that had blocked the proper entrance to the cave – a Mesolithic rubbish dump.

Following his discovery, the Conde excavated La Riera and found that the mound of shells capped many layers of occupation that stretched back to the depths of the ice age and beyond. After he had finished, the cave suffered the fate of so many archaeological sites – looted by treasure-hunters and dug out by farmers wanting the shell-rich sediment to fertilise their land. La Riera even became a hideout for soldiers during the Spanish Civil War. Archaeological interest returned in 1968 when a group of paintings was found on one wall, and in 1969 when Geoffrey Clark from the University of Arizona dug a small trench to examine what had survived. In spite of its history, he found that intact deposits remained within the cave.

Between 1976 and 1982 Clark teamed up with Lawrence Straus from the University of New Mexico and conducted a very fine and important excavation.[12] They found no fewer than thirty layers of human rubbish, one on top of another, covering a period of more than 20,000 years. At its base were the stone artefacts and animal bones discarded by some of the first modern humans to live in Spain 30,000 years ago. On top of their rubbish was that of the ice-age hunters of the LGM, which in turn was buried by the debris of those who lived through global warming until, at 5500 BC, the cave entrance became entirely blocked by the quantity of human waste.

La Riera had only ever been a temporary camping place, used for short visits, ranging from a few days to a few weeks. In some years it had been used in the spring, in others during the summer, autumn or winter. Straus and Clark's meticulous work, together with that of an army of specialists who studied their finds, recreated how human lives adapted to dramatic environmental change and revealed another incentive for a new way of life: an ever-enlarging population.[13]

At 20,000 BC, those who used La Riera inhabited a largely treeless landscape. They hunted ibex and red deer with stone-tipped spears and slaughtered herds after trapping them in thick snow or behind brushwood fences positioned to block off narrow valleys.[14] By 15,000 BC, the La Riera occupants had begun to visit the seashore where they collected limpets, periwinkles and urchins, and speared sea bream from rocky promontories. On their return to La Riera they would have walked through pine and birch woodland, visited hazel thickets to collect nuts, and may have glimpsed new woodland occupants such as wild boar. Over the next 7,000 years the rising sea level brought the shoreline closer and closer to La Riera Cave – today it is no more than two kilometres away. Its occupants made ever greater use of its products and a great mound of limpet shells began to accumulate inside. While the mound grew, the limpets themselves became smaller as the intensity of gathering outstripped their rate of growth.

Those who used La Riera were still hunting red deer, but were now stalking them as individuals and using arrows tipped with microliths rather than large stone points. Wild boar and roe-deer were also hunted, wildfowl and other birds were trapped. Although plant remains were scarce within the cave, the appearance of chunky stone picks suggests that roots were dug up, while pitted stones indicate that many nuts were cracked.

After the last dump of shells, fish and animal bones had been made inside the cave, La Riera was abandoned. Its entrance became hidden behind trees and brambles, lost from human memory. Beneath the shell midden there was layer upon layer of human rubbish waiting to be excavated. Geoff Clark and Lawrence Straus dismiss the idea that the changes in diet that this rubbish revealed can be entirely explained by the rising sea level and spread of woodland. The gradual increase in the diversity of foodstuffs, and the intensity with which animals were hunted, and plant foods and shellfish were gathered, suggests that there was an ever-increasing number of mouths to feed.

The animal bones excavated from La Riera, and indeed at sites throughout southern Europe, indicate a gradual evolution rather than a revolution in the lives of people who inhabited southern Europe. Red deer had always been the prime target for hunters, whether the animals were living in large herds upon LGM tundra or in scattered groups within Holocene woodland. The tundra of southern Europe had never been quite as treeless and windswept as those of the north; when temperatures rose and rainfall increased, the woodland had simply to creep out from the shelter of the valleys where trees had survived even the harshest of ice-age winters. Wild boar and roe-deer came with them, providing competition for the red deer and new opportunities for the now woodland-living hunter-gatherers.[15]

Although those using La Riera after 10,000 BC followed the millennia-old tradition of hunting deer, their social and religious lives had changed beyond all recognition. The people who used La Riera at the LGM and 15,000 BC had also travelled to the great painted caves to sing, dance and worship their ice-age deities.[16] But those who hunted wild boar and filled the cave with a mound of shells, had no such obligations to fulfil.

The tradition of painting and carving animals, especially horse and bison, together with abstract signs and human figures, had lasted for more than 20,000 years. It had extended from the Urals to southern Spain, and produced masterpieces by the score: the painted bison of Altamira, the lions of Chauvet, the horses of Lascaux, the carved ibex from Mas d'Azil.[17] For more than 800 generations, artists had inherited the same concerns and the same techniques. It was by far the longest-lived art tradition known to humankind, and yet it virtually disappeared overnight with global warming.

Had the closed woodlands also closed people's minds to artistic expression? Was the Mesolithic a time when ancient knowledge was forgotten – 'the dark age' of the Stone Age? Well, no, not at all. The cave art tradition ended simply because there was no longer a need to make such art. The paintings and carvings had never been mere decoration; nor had they been the inevitable expression of an inherent human creative urge. They had been much more than this – a tool for survival, one as essential as tools of stone, clothes of fur, and the fires that crackled within the caves.[18]

The ice age had been an information age – the carvings and paintings the equivalent of our CD-ROMs today.[19] Ambush and bloody slaughter had been easy: as long as the right people were in the right place at the right time, ample supplies of food could be acquired. Rules were then required to ensure distribution without conflict. An abundance of food in one region had meant scarcity elsewhere – groups had to be willing to join together and then to split apart; to do so they needed to know which group was where, and to have friends and relations that could be relied upon in times of need. Because herds of animals are prone to unpredictable extinctions the hunters required alternative hunting plans, always ready to put into practice.

To solve such problems, information was crucial – knowledge about the location and movements of animals, about who was living and hunting where, about future plans, about what to do in times of crisis. The art, the mythology and the religious ritual served to maintain the constant acquisition and flow of information.

When groups joined together once or twice a year for ceremony, painting and ritual, such as at Pech Merle, Mas d'Azil and Altamira, they also exchanged vital information about animal movements. Such groups would have spent the previous year living apart, some in the uplands, some on the coastal plains; some had made long treks to visit distant relations, others had watched for the arrival of migratory birds. There was a lot to tell and even more to find out. The religious beliefs of the hunter-gatherers provided sets of rules for the sharing of food when necessary. Cave paintings had not only depicted the tracks of animals, but had shown them in the act of defecating, and with their antlers and fatty parts exaggerated.[20] Such pictures were the stimulus for accounts of what had been seen, for teaching the children; they contained the signs that a hunter must look for when searching for prey and selecting a victim in the months to come. The mythological stories contained survival strategies for those inevitable but unpredictable years of hardship.[21]

So, for as long as the annual ceremonies and rituals were performed, and people had opportunities to gossip, to swap ideas and observations, to recount tales of hunters' exploits, to reaffirm social bonds, to learn yet more about the animals around them, information flowed and society flourished – as far as it could under the constraints of an ice-age climate.

Life in thick woodland after 9600 BC did not exact the same demands. Animals were now largely hunted on a one-to-one basis; with no mass kills there were no surpluses to manage. Narrow valleys and river crossings no longer had the same significance; there was no longer a need to have people in precisely the right place at the right time. Neither was there the need to know what was happening many miles away, either in the natural or in the social world. Hunting could effectively take place anywhere, any time, by anyone. And if animals could not be found, there were plenty of plant foods to gather and limpets to collect. Just like the red deer, people began to live in smaller, more scattered groups, becoming increasingly self-sufficient.

Periodic gatherings still took place but these were to solve problems of maintaining social ties, to allow people to marry, to exchange raw materials and food, to learn and teach new techniques of basketry and weaving. There was no longer the need for these group activities to be conducted under the gaze of painted beasts.

The ending of the cave-art tradition should not be attributed to cultural disintegration, social collapse, or the arrival of a dark age when minds were closed to the arts. The cessation of cave painting is a remarkable testament to the ability of people to rewrite the rules of their society when the need arises. It is one that we must recall as global warming threatens our planet today.

17

Coastal Catastrophe

Sea-level change and its consequences, 10,500–6400 BC

Forty millimetres. Perhaps 33 millimetres, or even no more than 23 millimetres. About the thickness of a small pebble on the beach or the depth of a shallow rock pool. Had the people of the Mesolithic been told that these were the best guesses for the average yearly increase in sea level during the century following 7500 BC, I doubt if they would have shown much concern.[1] After all, such statistics are practically identical to the estimated rise in our own global sea level during the next hundred years and none of our governments seem too bothered.

These figures are estimates made in the last few years by scientists who struggle with the imprecision of radiocarbon dates and the sheer complexity of sea-level change in northern Europe. Although they sound small, the implications of such figures for Mesolithic times were extraordinary: coastal catastrophe. Its ultimate cause was the final melting of the great ice sheets, especially those of North America. Millions upon millions of gallons of water poured into the oceans and touched the lives of many thousands of people – sometimes quite literally.[2]

At 7500 BC the coast of northern Europe ran directly from eastern England to Denmark. It was deeply incised with estuaries that led into narrow-sided valleys that in turn wound their way between gently rolling hills. Doggerland – the region now submerged below the North Sea – had a coastline of lagoons, marshes, mud-flats and beaches. It was probably the richest hunting, fowling and fishing grounds in the whole of Europe.[3] Grahame Clark, the excavator of Star Carr, believed that Doggerland had been the heartland of the Mesolithic culture.[4]

The first awareness of this lost Mesolithic world came in 1931. The *Colinda*, a trawler, was fishing at night about twenty-five miles east of the Norfolk coast near the Ower bank. Its skipper, Pilgrim E. Lockwood, hauled up a lump of peat and broke it open with a spade. He struck something hard – not a piece of rusty metal but an elegant barbed antler point.[5]

In the same year Dr Harry Godwin, a botanist from Cambridge University and a colleague of Clark, was about to begin applying the new science of pollen analysis to peat deposits in Britain. Godwin took further samples of the North Sea peat from close to where the *Colinda* had sunk its nets. He found that woodland had once grown there, of a type almost identical to that which grew in east Yorkshire, in Denmark and in the Baltic States, immediately after the ice age came to an end. In effect, Godwin established that these were part of a continuous land mass, one in which people had hunted deer and collected plant foods in mixed oak woodland; one in which they occasionally lost their barbed antler points.

For almost sixty years the harpoon found by the *Colinda* stood as a symbol of a Mesolithic world drowned by rising sea level. But archaeologists got a shock in 1989 when a minute sample of antler was removed from it for radiocarbon dating. To their surprise it proved not to be contemporary with almost identical harpoons from Star Carr, but two thousand years older.[6] Reindeer hunters had lost the harpoon when Doggerland was Arctic tundra – that which Lubbock himself had crossed when travelling from Creswell Crags to the Ahrensburg valley.

The Mesolithic coastal dwellers of Doggerland began to see their landscape change – sometimes within a single day, sometimes within their lifetime, sometimes only when they recalled what parents and grandparents had told them about lagoons and marshes now permanently drowned by the sea. An early sign of change was when the ground became boggy, when pools of water and then lakes appeared in hollows as the water table rose. Trees began to drown while the sea remained quite distant. Oak and lime were often the first to go, alder normally the last, surviving until sea water was splashing upon its roots and spraying upon its leaves.[7]

High tides became higher and then refused to retreat. Sandy beaches were washed away. Coastal grasslands and woodland became salt marsh – land washed daily by the sea which saturated the soil with salt. Only specialised plants could survive, such as the edible samphire and cordgrass that provided a home for an assortment of fleas, bugs and midges. Herons, avocets and spoonbills soon came to feed where, not long before, woodland birds had flourished.

The North Sea invaded Doggerland. Marine waters worked their way into the valleys and around the hills; new peninsulas appeared, became offshore islands and then disappeared for ever. So, too, in the Mediterranean where the sea edged its way closer and closer to Franchthi Cave,[8] where so many plant foods had been collected by hunter-gatherers in Greece. By 7500 BC the seashore was little more than an afternoon stroll away for the occupants of Franchthi; their forebears had required a whole day's hike to reach the coast. Layers of buried food waste within the cave show how the Franchthi people first began to gather limpets and periwinkles and then became sea-going fishermen. They started to visit islands, such as Melos 120 kilometres away where they found obsidian and brought it back to their cave. This new lifestyle favoured exploration and colonisation: Corsica, Sardinia and the Balearic islands were settled for the very first time.[9]

The experience of those who dwelt along the coastlines of Europe varied with time and place. For some, the environmental changes were so gradual as to go unnoticed: minute year-by-year shifts in diet, technology and knowledge – a subtle, unconscious moulding of lifestyle. Others would have stared in amazement as they watched the sea race inland after a shingle ridge or dunes had been breached. Still others – such as the inhabitants of what would one day become the town of Inverness in eastern Scotland – faced catastrophe.

In the 1980s the Scottish archaeologist Jonathan Wordsworth excavated part of the medieval town after the modern houses at nos. 13–24 Castle Street had been demolished.[10] Below were the foundations of thirteenth-century medieval buildings and outhouses that had been built overlooking the estuary of the River Ness. Underneath a layer of stony white marine sand, sandwiched between those worked by the medieval masons, he found a scatter of almost 5,000 flint artefacts, bone fragments and traces of a fireplace – the remains of a Mesolithic hunting

On some day close to 7000 BC a small group of Mesolithic people had nestled themselves into a natural hollow within the dunes overlooking the estuary and most likely with a view out to sea. Perhaps they were waiting for dusk before setting out to hunt seal; perhaps they had spent the day collecting tern's eggs and samphire and were ready for sleep, except for one or two who chipped at beach pebbles, replenishing the store of microliths and scrapers that they carried inside their otter-skin bags. A scene probably repeated a thousand times throughout the coastlands of northern Europe – another normal Mesolithic day in a normal Mesolithic hunter-gatherer's life.

It was not to last. A few hours earlier a massive sub-marine landslide had occurred almost 1,000 kilometres to the north, within the Arctic Ocean midway between the coast of Norway and Iceland. This was the Storrega slide and it created a tsunami, an immense tidal wave.[11] Those who were at the site of the future 13–24 Castle Street, Inverness, are likely to have been startled by the sudden shrieking of gulls; they heard a distant grumbling that turned into a roar. One assumes they first stared in disbelief, and then panic, as 8-metre-high waves approached the estuary mouth. I guess they ran for their lives.

Whether they made it to safety, we cannot know. If they did, and then returned after the water had subsided, they would have found a vast expanse of white, stony sand burying not just their picnic spot but everything as far north and south as they could see. More than 17,000 cubic kilometres of sediment was dumped across the east coast of Scotland and remains buried below farmland, dunes and town houses as a record of a Mesolithic catastrophe.

The impact of this tsunami across the low-lying coast of Doggerland must have been devastating. Many kilometres of coastline are likely to have been destroyed within a few hours, perhaps minutes, and many lives lost:

those hauling up nets from canoes, those collecting seaweed and limpets, children playing on the beach, the babies sleeping within bark-wood cots. Communities of crabs, fish, birds and mammals were wiped out; coastal settlements obliterated – the huts, canoes and eel-traps, the baskets of nuts and racks of drying fish, all crushed and swept away.

Another catastrophe happened on the other side of Europe, 3500 kilometres away. The victims were those who lived upon the lowlands around the freshwater lake that was the Black Sea.[12] These provided flat, fertile soils, covered with oak woodland in which people had hunted and gathered for many thousands of years. By the date of this event, however, a new people had arrived: Neolithic farmers. They had travelled from communities in Turkey, settling upon rich alluvial soils; felling trees to make way for fields of wheat and barley and to provide wood for their houses, fences and pens for their cattle and goats. The story of their journey and their reception by the native Mesolithic people is one for the following chapter. Here our concern is with their tragic end.

The Black Sea had become a freshwater lake during the ice age. The level of the Mediterranean had fallen to below the base of the Bosphorus channel, its link to the Black Sea through which seawater had once flowed. The channel became blocked with silt. Then, when global warming began to melt the ice, the Mediterranean Sea began to rise again. As it did so, the level of the Black Sea was doing the precise opposite – it was falling, due to evaporation and reduced run-off from rivers. As the sea level rose above the base of the channel, the plug of silt held firm. It held, and it held, as a gigantic wall of marine water built up on its western face. And then it began to seep. Then it burst.

So, one fateful day about 6400 BC, a cascade of salty water crashed with the force of two hundred Niagara Falls into the placid waters of the lake – and continued to do so for many months. The roar would have been heard 100 kilometres away – echoing in the ears of those hunting within the hills of Turkey and those who fished around Mediterranean shores. Fifty cubic kilometres of water thundered into the lake each day until the Black Sea and the Mediterranean were one again. Within a matter of months, a staggering 100,000 square kilometres of lakeside woodland, marshland and arable fields had been submerged – an area equivalent to the whole of Austria.

Victorian John Lubbock had not known a great deal about the history of sea-level change. *Prehistoric Times* contains no more than a few comments about how, on the Danish coast, there is 'good reason for supposing that the land has encroached upon the sea', whereas elsewhere the absence of the Køkkenmøddinger (shell mounds) 'is no doubt occasioned by the waves having to a certain extent eaten away the shore'.[13]

For his general understanding of sea-level change Victorian John Lubbock had been dependent upon the views of Sir Charles Lyell, the geologist whose seminal *Principles of Geology* had been published between 1830 and 1833[14] and *Geological Evidences of the Antiquity of Man* in 1863. He quoted Lyell at length from the latter volume about a period when the land was thought to have been at least 500 feet above its present level, followed by one of submergence with 'only the tops of the mountains being left above water' and then by a further period of elevated land when the bed of the glacial sea 'with its marine shells and erratic blocks, was laid dry'. Lyell had suggested that the 'grand oscillation' of submergence and re-emergence had most likely taken 224,000 years.

Victorian John Lubbock didn't add much himself – *Prehistoric Times* came just too early for a more informed view. Had he been writing at the end of the nineteenth century, he may well have quoted Joseph Prestwich, whose estimates of past temperatures he had already commented upon. In 1893 Prestwich published evidence for a major flooding event throughout Europe at the end of the glacial and immediately preceding the Neolithic.[15] Eduard Suess, Professor of Geology at Vienna University, might also have been cited since, in 1885, he had introduced the idea of a worldwide uniform and simultaneous rise in sea level.

It wasn't until the 1930s, however, that the changes in sea level at the end of the ice age began to be well documented.[16] Today they are known to have been extraordinarily complex in some parts of the world, occurring much more rapidly than the maximum figure of 6 feet per century that Charles Lyell was prepared to consider. Victorian John Lubbock would, I suspect, have been astonished had he known about the sequence of sea-level change in the far north of Europe between 10,500 and 8000 BC.

The people who lived to the north of Doggerland, in those regions we now call Scotland, Norway and Sweden, also lost the coastline that their parents, grandparents and earlier generations had so much enjoyed. But instead of becoming the sea floor, their coastal lands became permanently dry; they had quite literally gone up in the world.[17]

The glaciers had weighed heavily upon the land and forced it downwards – causing the land to the immediate south to bulge upwards, just like the unoccupied end of a sofa. And consequently, when the ice got up and left, the land evened out; the bulge fell and the dent rose. Much of Doggerland had been within the bulge, and hence the impact of a rising sea level was exacerbated: just as the bulge was dying away, millions of gallons of melt-water was entering the oceans.

Further north, where the glaciers had once sat heavily, a race was on. Which would rise the quickest, the sea or the land? If the former, then people saw their coastlines flooded; if the latter, the beaches were raised – and 'raised beaches' is precisely the term used to explain expanses of sand and pebbles found around the coastlines of northern Europe today at levels never reached by the sea.

In the far north the land was an easy victor. At the former centre of the ice sheet, somewhere north of Stockholm on the eastern coast of Sweden, the land has risen more than 800 metres since the ice age – and still it hasn't finished. Every year a few more millimetres is added – although that may soon change with renewed global warming and sea-level rise during the century to come.

Further south, along the coastlines of southern Sweden, the Baltic States, Poland and Germany, the sea and the land had a neck-and-neck race, periodically swapping the lead. This caused repeated havoc to all the communities – plant, animal and human, land and water – that managed to establish themselves just before the lead changed again. We know this in part from the work of Svante Björck from the Danish Institute of Geology, who has studied the shells found buried at the bottom of the Baltic Sea, together with the sediments, raised beaches and drowned forests of that region's coastline. The story that they have revealed is a remarkable one of dramatic geographical change, of which only the barest highlights can now be retold.

At the height of the Younger Dryas, 10,500 BC, the Baltic Sea was not a sea at all but a lake, the Baltic ice lake. Its waters were close to freezing; its shores bare rock or arctic tundra. Had anyone visited them, they would have found reindeer and lemming, but would be unlikely to have remained for long. A glacier in the north and solid land in the south blocked any potential exit routes to the North Sea for the Baltic waters. The glacier formed a dam across the low-lying lands of today's central Sweden, while the route taken in the present by the interchanging waters of the North and Baltic Seas, that through the 'Storebaelt' – the island-dotted seascape between Sweden and Denmark – was high and dry, a continuous land mass. Those countries were no more than the eastern end of Doggerland.

By 9600 BC the Baltic ice lake was held by a wall of ice to a depth of 25 metres. This was the precise opposite of what happened in the Black Sea 3,000 years later, when waters strained to get into, rather than out of, a dammed lake. But here, as there, the dam burst, in this case as global warming melted the ice and weakened the wall. The Baltic ice lake drained across central Sweden into the North Sea, leaving boulders, gravels, sand and silt in its path. Within a few years at most, perhaps no more than months, the 25-metre drop in water level produced a vast new expanse of shoreline around the modern-day coasts of northern Germany, Poland and the Baltic States. It was a shoreline composed of muddy clays and silts that had so recently formed the bottom of the lake.

As marine waters began to flow eastwards, the lake became an inland sea. It has been named after a marine mollusc, *Yoldia,* whose shells are found deeply buried within its sediments, indicating that salty waters now lapped the shores of the future Baltic States. It is likely that people came to live on the shores of the Yoldia Sea as soon as its soils had been stabilised by the roots of birch and pine. Rich lagoons and marshes developed around the mouths of the new river estuaries. Mesolithic people crept in and felt at home.

And yet no sooner had they established their communities than the world began to change again. Those living on the southern shores were flooded out by the rising sea level; those on the northern shores saw the sea recede as the land rebounded. It receded by about 10 metres each century – a rate quite noticeable within a human lifetime. At some point midway between those who were flooded out in the south and elevated in the north, there must have been an area of stability, the fulcrum for this see-saw between land and sea.

This continued for twenty-five generations, each of which made subtle alterations to their lifestyle in order to adapt to the ever-changing world. And then, at about 9300 BC, the flooding in the south became more severe. Settlements drowned before people could relocate, and we must imagine them wading to rescue prized possessions. By now, the water was moving inland at an average rate of 3 metres in every generation – a rate that implies periodic catastrophe to people's lives. In the north, where over the decades people had watched the sea recede, it now started to encroach upon the land. They too had to learn how to cope with waterlogged land and flooding.

The cause of the new influx of waters was the rebounding land; that of middle Sweden had now risen so much that it blocked the flow between the Yoldia and the North Seas. Once again the Baltic had a lake, water with no route to escape. As its volume rose with the influx from the many inflowing rivers, its salt was diluted and soon the water became fresh. Another mollusc, *Ancylus fluviatli*, has been honoured by lending its name to this lake – the Ancylus Lake – its shells found within Baltic sediments above the level of *Yoldia*. Once again all living things had to adapt, migrate or die – including human communities, which now went fowling among the reeds rather than fishing for cod from kayaks.

They had about three hundred years – perhaps ten generations – to make the change before there was yet another turnaround. As from *c.* 9000 BC they began to watch the wetlands and lagoons dry out, the shore recede from the lakeside fishing platforms. New expanses of silt and sand were exposed, and new opportunities arose for pioneering plants and insects.

The Ancylus Lake had found an outflow into the North Sea. It certainly needed one, as its level had become 10 metres higher than that of the sea. This outlet was not so much found as forced, in the form of the River Dana, which cut its way through the low-lying land of the Storebaelt, in some places creating a veritable canyon through soft sediments up to 70 metres deep. Riverside woodland, peats and human settlements were washed away or buried by sands and gravels carried by a torrent of water. For two hundred years the outflow continued apace until the Ancylus Lake became level with the sea. And then meanders began, as smaller rivers and streams wound themselves through the woods and around headlands of the Storebaelt.

The final event in this remarkable history was the flooding of the Storebaelt. This began at 7200 BC and was caused by the final stages of the rise in sea level that brought it to its present level, creating the familiar geography of Scandinavia and the Baltic. The inland sea that was created this time is named after the mollusc *Littorina*, whose shells are not only found in sediments above that of *Ancylus fluviatli*, but also continue to adorn the coasts of the Baltic Sea today. Another round of readaptation followed as waterlogging and flooding returned – but the new floods were of such a gradual nature as to be hardly noticeable. Human lifestyles were slowly remoulded once again to those of people who live by the sea.

18

Two Villages in Southeast Europe

Sedentary hunter-gatherers and immigrant farmers,
6500–6200 BC

Fishing trips, barbecues, and pine forests after rain – jumbled memories recalled by the lingering smell of wood smoke. John Lubbock wakes upon a hard plaster floor at the narrow end of a tent-like dwelling. Sitting up and looking out, he sees a broad river with steeply wooded slopes below limestone cliffs. The sun has just risen. There are footsteps and voices.

The brushwood walls of the dwelling pitch towards a long ridge-pole from which wicker baskets and bone harpoons are hanging. Blocks of limestone surround a pit in the floor containing the still warm ashes of pine logs where parcels of fish had been baked the night before. Wooden bowls holding water and herbs sit upon paving slabs by the entrance. Lubbock turns and meets the silent gaze of a rounded river boulder, sculptured with bulging eyes, swollen lips and a scaly body. It is of the owner of the house.

Stepping outside, Lubbock finds that his is just one of twenty such huts arranged upon a terrace above the river. A hunter-gatherer village – the first of his European travels. It initially reminds him of 'Ain Mallaha and Abu Hureyra in western Asia at 12,500 BC. But a second glance shows it to be quite different – canoes are moored and nets are hanging out to dry. This is a fishermen's village, one that is flourishing just as the town of 'Ain Ghazal in western Asia is suffering economic collapse.

Some people work while others idly stand or sit in small groups, enjoying the early sunshine. They chat about the weather, about fishing plans, about their children. Behind the village small trails climb steeply though scrubby hazel trees into woodland of oak, elm and lime, leading towards the pine trees and high cliffs. An eagle soars within a pale blue sky, while cormorants fly low across the water. It is daybreak at Lepenski Vir, 6400 BC.[1]

Sitting by the river, Lubbock recalls the journey from La Riera in northern Spain – a momentous walk across southern Europe. Several of the campsites he shared with Mesolithic occupants have become known as archaeological sites. Many others will never be found – perhaps destroyed by later settlements or buried below deep alluvium of the Rhône delta and Po basin. Still others wait to be discovered.

Lubbock had climbed into the Pyrenees and found rounded grassy summits giving way to splintered stone, the skyline becoming ever taller and more fractured with every day of eastern progress. In the central Pyrenees he had camped with ibex hunters at 1,000 metres, in the base of a great natural amphitheatre known today as Balma Margineda.² Having caught ibex with the men, Lubbock joined the women fishing for trout and picking blackberries. Another 200 kilometres of hiking brought him to Roc del Migdia, a cave at the base of a cliff within thick oak woodland, in what is today Catalonia.³ After having helped fill its occupants' baskets with acorns, hazelnuts and sloes, he sat with them to watch vultures circling lazily on the thermals.⁴

Lubbock's journey across southern France involved walks along sandy beaches, hitchhikes on canoes through the marshes of the Rhône delta, detours inland when the sea washed against the base of cliffs of creamy-white limestone or fiery red porphyry. There was an immense variety of trees and plants but none of those that strike the visitor today – the lemons and oranges, olives, the palms and mimosas. Such trees are all late arrivals to the Riviera. Lubbock was pleased by their absence as it gave space for swathes of wild lilac and honeysuckle that grew within the limestone ravines, in which he listened to thunderous torrents and springs bursting from the earth.⁵

After crossing the marshy lowlands of northern Italy, the haunts of people setting fish-traps and catching waterfowl, Lubbock once again climbed into mountains, the pine-clad peaks of the Italian Dolomites. He did so following the tracks of hunters, who in turn were following red deer to summer pastures. At 2,000 metres he joined their camp below the overhang of a massive boulder – erratically placed by a long-gone glacier. That site is now known as Mondeval de Sora. When excavated in 1986, the burial of a man was found – a hunter laid to rest with an assortment of stone tools and jewellery carved from boar tusks and deer teeth.⁶ From the Dolomites Lubbock headed southeast into the rolling hills and deep valleys of Croatia. There he shared small caves with hunting parties who watched the valley bottoms for game and chipped new stone points for their hunting weapons.⁷

Leaving the mountains and hills, Lubbock travelled to the southern margins of the Hungarian plain and then relieved his tired legs by adopting a new means of transport: a dugout canoe. He found one drifting; it had presumably escaped a mooring downstream. For 800 kilometres he travelled along the rivers of southeast Europe, taking short sojourns into surrounding woodlands with hunters after wild boar and helping passing fishermen to haul in their nets.

At some point on this waterway journey Lubbock's canoe entered the Danube. The river lazily unwound between tree-covered hills, sometimes looping away for a kilometre or two and then meandering back through willows and aspens. Eventually it passed between steep cliffs and Lubbock entered the first of the great canyon-like gorges known today as the Iron Gates. It was now that clusters of dwellings appeared, sprawling along the terraces above the river. These looked quite different to the brushwood huts that Lubbock had seen elsewhere in Mesolithic Europe and so, late one evening, he moored and climbed the bank. It was a cloudy, moonless night and the dwellings appeared as curious shadows, unnatural in their man-made geometry. As he stumbled over fireplaces still warm with ash, and startled rats and mice, Lubbock realised that the entire village was asleep.

The sleeping occupants of Lepenski Vir are hunter-gatherers who have 'settled down' to a sedentary lifestyle. Woodland had survived in the Danube valley throughout the LGM, principally juniper and willow, but also small stands of oak, elm and lime that would help seed the rest of Europe. Ice-age hunters made periodic visits to the valley to stalk ibex and fish for salmon, but they never stayed for very long. As the climate became warmer and the rains more frequent, the broad leaves flourished. The trees climbed the mountain slopes and produced thick woodland containing an abundance of game and edible plants. Red deer and wild boar, otters and beavers, ducks and geese became additions to the ice-age diet. And so people came to the Iron Gates more often and were less inclined to leave. They arrived at their supposedly winter campsites in early autumn and remained until the late spring. Such settlements began to merge with what had once been short-term summer fishing camps. By 6500 BC people found no need to leave the river at all; what had been temporary campsites became the first permanent villages on the banks of the Danube.

John Lubbock wanders around Lepenski Vir, in and out of the dwellings. Although varying in size, they share the same design and furnishings. Carved stone boulders with faces that seem to be part fish and part human, sit looking rather melancholy within each hut. Frequently they are placed beside stone structures that look like altars, supported by pebbles incised with geometric designs. Within the largest hut, located centrally in the village, a few bone amulets and a flute rest upon a slab.[8] This hut is next to an open space, one where the ground seems beaten smooth from dancing feet. Although ritual, religion and performance are always integral parts of hunter-gatherer lives, they have a more pervasive presence than at any other European settlement that Lubbock has visited. Wherever he looks there are stacks of stone-tipped arrows, antler harpoons, net floats and weights, wicker baskets, stone pestles and mortars.

This range of equipment testifies to the varied and abundant foods available to the people of Lepenski Vir – not just meat and fish but nuts, fungi, berries and seeds. Yet despite such gastronomic diversity, several of the children playing in the river shallows appear undernourished. Rickets is prevalent in the village and some children carry horizontal ridges on their teeth – lines where the enamel has failed to grow owing to ill-health. The reality is that the architectural and artistic creativity at Lepenski Vir goes hand in hand with periodic shortages of food.[9]

Three women are halfway through the construction of a dwelling. They have formed a compact, trapeze-shaped platform from a mixture of baked crushed limestone, sand and gravel around stone blocks positioned to form the central hearth. As Lubbock watches, they pause to unwrap a hide bundle, revealing the decayed body of a young infant. Its bones dangle from each other, loosely joined by ligaments and fragments of dried yellow skin.

The body is buried and sealed within the floor. An adult's jawbone is withdrawn from another wrapping and placed between two stones of the hearth.[10] After no more than a tiny pause the practicalities of building work resume: posts are secured within holes to support the ridge-pole that will soon be lifted into place. To Lubbock, the women seem to have switched from the secular to the religious and then back again; but for them such divisions have no meaning. They just get on with life, a life in which every act, every artefact and every aspect of the natural world is just as sacred as it is profane.

Life at Lepenski Vir revolved around the river. It provided food, it was the Mesolithic highway, its flow symbolised the passage from birth to death. At least, that is the belief of Ivana Radovanović, an archaeologist from Belgrade who has undertaken the task of trying to read the symbolic code that was woven as much into day-to-day life as into the ceremonial burials and seasonal celebrations of Lepenski Vir.[11]

Radovanović was a student of Dragoslav Srejović, the Yugoslavian archaeologist who discovered and then excavated Lepenski Vir between 1966 and 1971.[12] He found the site while surveying the banks of the Danube prior to the construction of a dam in 1970 – one that would drown the banks and all that was hidden upon them. It is just one of several sites on both riverbanks that share similar art and architecture – others include Hajdučka, Vodenica, Padina and Vlasac. Some may have been seasonal encampments rather than permanent villages; Lepenski Vir may even have been a ceremonial centre.[13]

Srejović excavated many burials at Lepenski Vir. Those of children were usually placed within the dwellings, either buried under the floor or within the stone hearths and structures Srejović thought were altars. Adults, normally men, were buried between the dwellings. The skulls and jawbones of wild ox, deer or other humans were sometimes placed with the dead, together with tools and necklaces made from snail-shell beads.

Most of the adult burials had their heads pointing downstream so that the river could carry their spirit away – or so Radovanović believes. She thinks the river had also symbolised rebirth, as each spring beluga – the giant sturgeons still revered today as producers of the very best caviar – came upstream to spawn. Their arrival must have been striking, a procession of river monsters growing up to 9 metres long: the spirits of the dead reborn, according to Radovanović, made real by the stone sculptures that blended fish and human into one being.

Lubbock leaves Lepenski Vir on a summer's afternoon, to the sound of nets being hauled from water, of posts being hammered into the ground and human voices chatting. He heads south through the lush woodland of the Balkan hills, walking upon a matted carpet of leaves, cones and acorns, oak-apples, beechmast and the split caskets of chestnuts. He encounters does grazing in sunny glades; catching his scent, they turn in a flurry of white rumps for the underbrush. A stag with candelabra antlers stares severely before following at a stately trot upon his neat and shiny hoofs.

Lubbock is now adept at reading the signs of game, quite unlike when he had begun his European travels across the tundra towards Creswell Crags, illiterate in the language of footprints and turds. He tests himself at tracking deer and calculating where the wild boar will come to feed. He knows where to find nests for collecting eggs, which fungi to take and which to leave. Indeed, he feels quite confident of being able to live by hunting and gathering within these woods and wonders why no one else has chosen to do so: there is a complete absence of people or signs of their presence. At no other time in his European travels can he recall having gone for so long without encountering a single campsite or occupied cave.[14]

This paucity of Mesolithic sites in Southeast Europe, all the way from the Danube to the Mediterranean Sea, has been of considerable worry to archaeologists. Was there a genuine absence of settlements? Have Mesolithic sites been destroyed, or do some remain to be discovered? In Greece, for instance, there are barely a dozen Mesolithic but many hundreds of Neolithic sites, thousands from later periods and a great many from much earlier periods of human evolution. Catherine Perlès, the leading scholar of early prehistoric Greece, recently evaluated all possible reasons for the rarity of Mesolithic sites and concluded that this must genuinely reflect a very small population, one that was almost entirely based on the coast.[15]

After a trek of some 400 kilometres from Lepenski Vir, Lubbock reaches the Macedonian plain of northern Greece. He arrives in the year of 6300 BC, and sits on the branch of a sturdy oak to watch the comings and goings of quite a different kind of village. A cluster of dwellings lie within a clearing upon a small knoll; the ground to one side is marshy, to the other it is divided by criss-crossing paths and fences which define small gardens whose plants have just begun to sprout. The dwellings, ten or twelve in number, are rectangular with thatched roofs and overhanging eaves.

One is under construction: bundles of reeds are being tied between uprights of cut saplings. Although these houses are far larger and of more substance than the dwellings of Lepenski Vir, it is the simple wooden pens attached to their outside walls that attract Lubbock's interest – or rather, what the pens contain. Jumping down, he approaches the village along a pathway that runs from the woods to a gap in a low mud wall that surrounds it. He stoops to examine the plants sprouting in the gardens. Some – wheat or barley – have pointed leaves just beginning to unfurl around the stem; others – peas or lentils – have wispy stems with pale rounded leaves. Women and children are also stooping, weeding around the shoots. Lubbock pulls a few handfuls of grass – not as a gesture of help but so that he can feed the sheep, which look more like goats, that stand idly within the wooden pens.

Lubbock is about to enter one of the first farming villages of Europe, that which archaeologists will call Nea Nikomedeia.[16] Several generations of farmers have already lived and died at this village. Its founders may have come from other farming settlements in Greece, or those of Turkey or Cyprus – perhaps all the way from western Asia itself.

It was from western Asia that the very first farmers to arrive in Europe had once embarked, after loading their small boats with baskets of seed-corn and suitably shackled sheep and goats.[17] Some had crossed the Aegean to the eastern lowlands of Greece; others went to Crete and southern Italy.[18] They cleared woodlands, set their sheep and goats to browse, built their houses and began a new chapter in European prehistory.[19]

The first farmers arrived in Greece at around 7500 BC and found a largely uninhabited landscape.[20] Only in the vicinity of Franchthi Cave in the southern Argolid was there a substantial Mesolithic presence. This is the cave where Thomas Jacobsen found evidence for a diet rich in plant and coastal foods, especially after the seashore had all but reached the entrance of the cave. In the upper layers of Franchthi Cave, those contemporary with the first farming settlements, Jacobsen found a few seeds of domesticated wheat, barley and lentils, but these were vastly outnumbered by the remains of wild plants. Sheep, goat and pig bones had, however, become prevalent, suggesting that the Mesolithic people had begun poaching from the farmers' settlements or were rustling to create flocks and herds of their own. But this made little impact upon their way of life: stone tools, burial practices, hunting and gathering activities continued at Franchthi Cave with hardly any change.[21]

The farmers and hunter-gatherers lived side by side for a whole millennium at least. They had little to do with each other; the flood plains, which provided fertile soils for the farmers, were of little interest to the hunter-gatherers who relied upon the woodlands and the seashore.[22]

Yet this co-habitation of southern Greece could not survive. Around 7000 BC many new farming settlements appeared – one of which was Nea Nikomedeia. Whether these were built by a burgeoning local population or by a new wave of immigrants remains unclear. The latter is perhaps more likely as fine pottery appears – something not found in Greece before this date.

The final deposits at Franchthi Cave contain pottery and stone tools more similar to those found in the farming settlements than those in the lower levels of the cave. Dwellings were constructed outside the entrance and plots created for cultivating crops. The farming culture had finally overwhelmed the Mesolithic hunter-gatherers of Franchthi.

They might have abandoned the cave to the new farmers, gradually dwindling in number and becoming extinct. Perhaps they chose to become farmers themselves. Or the two populations may have become so closely linked by marriage and interbreeding that even they could no longer tell which was which. In this confusion of what happened to the Mesolithic people of Franchthi Cave we find the future history of the European continent as a whole.

The interior of the house that Lubbock has entered at Nea Nikomedeia is dark and quiet, the air stale and smoky – quite different from the light, fresh dwelling at Lepenski Vir. While walking through the village he had paused to help members of a family plaster clay over the reed bundles and oak saplings forming the walls of their new home. Now he discovers how effective such walls can be, creating a space that is isolated from the outside world.

Pottery vessels and wicker baskets are stacked against the walls, rush mats and hides lie upon the floor. A raised plaster platform, about ten or twenty centimetres off the ground, has a shallow basin with a smouldering fire. The smoke seeps through the thatch, killing off pests and waterproofing the reeds. A woman sits by the fire, twisting fibres to make a ball of twine. She pauses to prod the ashes and then to scratch. The bone buckle that fastens her belt looks familiar – Lubbock remembers seeing one similar in design at Çatalhöyük.[23]

Finding pottery is another 'first' for his European journey – all previous vessels had been made from wood, stone or wickerwork. The pots he sees at Nea Nikomedeia come in a variety of shapes and sizes, ranging from open bowls to large storage jars with narrow mouths. Some are plain; others are painted white with geometric designs in red. A few have finger impressions or even human faces in the clay: the noses are shaped by pinching and the eyes are small ovals. Many are large and elaborate; Lubbock guesses they are used for entertaining.

There is one larger building, more than 10 metres square, located in a central position. It is gloomy inside, with no evidence of domestic life and quite empty of people. Clay figurines sit upon wooden tables. Most are of women – moulded to have thin cylindrical heads, pointed noses and slit eyes. Arms are folded, with each hand grasping a breast made from a tiny knob of clay. Their diminutive size is compensated for by enormous, near-spherical thighs. Alongside these figurines are a few crude models of sheep and goats, and, in stark contrast, three polished effigies of frogs, beautifully carved from green and blue serpentine.

Lubbock leaves the village, returning to his lofty seat in the woods, choosing to watch village life from a distance. Within a few days he begins to understand how the village works. Each household is self-sufficient; families tend their own gardens, manage their own livestock, and make their own pottery and tools. At the same time, this household independence is balanced by a culture of hospitality, the outside fireplaces being used for communal meals.

Time begins to move more quickly: the oak comes into full leaf as the crops ripen; the leaves turn brown and fall as the harvest occurs. During the winter Lubbock sits through rain while the marsh becomes a lake and then spills its water across the gardens, depositing a layer of fine silt to fertilise next year's crops. When the oak buds appear, the people of Nea Nikomedeia return to their gardens with spades and hoes, turning the soil before they plant again.

Lubbock watches as visitors arrive bringing stone, shells and elaborate pottery to trade. He sees the dead of the village being buried in shallow unmarked graves or within the debris of abandoned dwellings. It seems a pragmatic affair – getting rid of a body with as limited ceremony as possible, with no graveside ritual or offerings buried with the dead. But people regularly enter and leave the central building which contains the clay figurines and seems to be a shrine. Sometimes many arrive together and Lubbock hears muffled singing and chanting from inside. He suspects that new figurines are taken in, and others are removed or smashed – but from his distant view he gains little insight into the religious life of Nea Nikomedeia.[24]

Acorns drop, seedlings sprout only to have their life snubbed out by the nibbling teeth of deer; any saplings that survive are soon cut and taken to the village. As time passes, Lubbock watches a complete harvest fail owing to a dry winter with late frosts, and the people reluctantly slaughter sheep and goats to survive. The friendships between households, maintained by the constant hospitality, help in times of need: when one household is short of food they can rely on gaining a share of another's.[25]

The overriding impression from his woodland seat is that life at Nea Nikomedeia is hard: tilling fields, weeding, watering, grinding seed, digging clay, clearing woodland. Labour appears to be in short supply as even young children are pressed into weeding and spreading muck. Lubbock recalls the hunter-gatherers of Lepenski Vir, those of La Riera, Gönnersdorf and Creswell Crags, none of whom seemed to work for more than a few hours on any one day. For them, the key to a full stomach had been knowledge, not labour: where the game would be, when the fruit would ripen, how to hunt wild boar and catch shoals of fish.

As the years pass by, Lubbock watches the construction of new houses and the number of gardens increase. Villages throughout the Macedonian plain are similarly increasing in size and soon population limits are reached. The available soils around Nea Nikomedeia cannot support more people and so a group of families leave to find new land. With a herd of goats and a straggle of piglets they head northwards, aiming to create a new settlement on the first suitable flood plain they locate.

The farmers 'leap-frogged' their way from one fertile plain to the next, through the Balkans and on to the Hungarian plain where new farming cultures would develop.[26] Farming settlements were made no more than 50 kilometres from Lepenski Vir, their presence leading to an initial florescence and then to the collapse of its Mesolithic culture. Some of the Lepenski Vir people, most likely the old, elaborated their artistic traditions as a means to resist the new farmers and their way of life. New stone sculptures were made, even larger and more striking than those that Lubbock had seen. They were positioned close to the doorsteps of their dwellings rather than hidden away inside.

But for others, most likely the young, farming settlements provided new ideas and opportunities for trade.[27] Lepenski Vir's fate was inevitable: an increasing number of pottery vessels appeared amidst the hunting weapons and fishing nets; its people became seduced by the farming way of life. There were some good reasons for this: sheep, cattle and wheat could fill the dietary gaps created by the periodic shortages of wild food that had left children undernourished. But very soon the culinary tables had turned – the wild foods became the supplements to a diet of cereals and peas.

Lubbock also leaves Nea Nikomedeia. He travels to the shores of the Black Sea, recently flooded after the Bosphorus had burst. There are vast acres of drowned forests, swathes of silt, fields of great boulders and uprooted trunks.[28] Lubbock continues northwards into the valleys of the Dniester and Dnieper, still untouched by the new farming way of life. There he finds hunter-gatherer villages amid thick woodland and the first cemeteries of his European journey – a sign of what is to come.[29] Buried beneath the river sediments of these valleys are the remnants of mammoth-bone dwellings that had been occupied at the LGM when the landscape was barren tundra.

As Lubbock travels further north, the landscape begins to change. Broad-leafed woodlands with lush understoreys of shrubs give way to dark coniferous forests quite barren below the trees. Elk replace red deer and bear replace the wild boar. Permanent hunter-gatherer villages give way to the more familiar transient campsites of people whose sense of place is a whole forest, a mountain range, a string of lakes or even all three combined, rather than any one culturally demarcated patch of ground. Lubbock continues on foot and by boat through endless marshy lowlands as the seasons turn and turn again until, 2000 kilometres due north of Lepenski Vir, he arrives at a lakeshore from which canoes are embarking to a little island. He steals a ride.

Nea Nikomedeia was entirely abandoned at around 5000 BC – perhaps due to the exhaustion of surrounding soil or endemic disease caused by overwhelming quantities of human waste. Once deserted, the final buildings collapsed; their timbers decayed, the clay plaster was washed or blown away, or simply became compacted on the ground. The pits filled up with silt; blown sand buried fireplaces, post holes and rubbish dumps.

As nature reclaimed its own, Nea Nikomedeia became a small tell; once covered by scrubland and scoured by the sun, wind and rain, it looked little different from the many natural small mounds on the Macedonian plain. By the twentieth century the mound of Nea Nikomedeia was surrounded by orchards and fields growing cotton and sugar beet. In 1953, as a bulldozer began to flatten the land for road construction, fragments of pottery came tumbling from a cutting in the mound, causing the Greek Archaeological Service to halt the work. In 1961 they embarked upon a joint excavation with Cambridge University, led by Robert Rodden. He was assisted by Grahame Clark, whose heart, one suspects, had always remained with the Mesolithic hunters of Star Carr while he excavated in the heat of the Mediterranean sun.

19

Islands of the Dead

Mesolithic burial and society in northern Europe,
6200–5000 BC

The canoe glides across still waters, shattering mirror images of spruce, larch and a steel-blue sky. Water sprayed from the paddles is icy cold; the sun is at its zenith. The woodlands are left behind as the canoe approaches the island. There the body, which the canoe is carrying and Lubbock is squeezed behind, will be buried. It is of a man, clothed as when alive in furs, an elk-tooth necklace, a bear-tusk pendant, a slate knife attached to his belt. This is the last of his many journeys upon the waterways and through the woodlands of northern Europe. He must now join his ancestors, those who inhabit the island of the dead.

Lubbock is heading towards Oleneostrovski Mogilnik – Deer Island cemetery – in the middle of what is today Lake Onega in northwest Russia. The date is 6200 BC.[1] The canoe is paddled by the dead man's sons and is one of many approaching the island. The burial provides an excuse for people to gather after a hard winter in the northern forest, and they come from all directions. They need to catch up on gossip, exchange flints and furs, swap stories and discuss future plans: who will be going where for the summer, for how long and with whom. They must also ensure that the deceased passes safely into the world of spirits and ancestors.

In 1939 Vladislav Iosifovich Ravdonikas, head of the State Institute for the History and Material Culture of Stalinist Russia,[2] received the results of excavations undertaken on Oleneostrovski Mogilnik by his assistant and protégé, I. I. Gurina. She had begun work in June 1936, finding the island covered by spruce and larch. Between the trees were large pits where local people had recently quarried sand and gravel, once deposited by the great glaciers of the north. They had known it as 'the island of the dead' owing to the human bones that their quarrying exposed. Many graves had been dug up out of curiosity and in the search for treasure. But hopes for gold and silver were rapidly dashed. Gurina found archaeological treasures of a quite different kind. Associated with the human burials was jewellery made from animal teeth and bones, carved figurines of elk and snake, slate knives, bone points and flint implements.[3]

During three seasons of fieldwork she excavated 170 burials. Some contained well-preserved skeletons; others mere fragments of human bone.

Some had large quantities of ornaments and tools while others had few or none. Men, women and children had been buried on the island. Eighteen graves had contained two individuals and a few had three. Gurina estimated that the cemetery contained 500 burials in total. She would have excavated more if her fieldwork had not been terminated by state security in 1938 as plans for the Soviet invasion of Finland were being finalised – Lake Onega was *en route*.

The results of Gurina's work caused a dilemma for Ravdonikas. The size and wealth of the Oleneostrovski Mogilnik cemetery implied that its people had been farmers – at least, it did so if one followed the Marxist theory of social evolution and material culture. As he worked in Stalin's Russia and archaeological observations were made to confirm the pattern of social evolution as laid out by Frederick Engels, Ravdonikas had to just that. Primitive communism had supposedly gone through two stages: the Early Clan phase of fully nomadic hunter-gatherers and the Late Clan phase of sedentary farmers and animal herders when people first lived in large communities and acquired material possessions. Where did Oleneostrovski Mogilnik fit in? Its social complexity suggested the Late Clan phase that Ravdonikas dated to 2000 BC. But where, therefore, were the obligatory pottery and the domestic animals?

His solution – and the one still favoured by so many archaeologists today when lost for an explanation – was 'ritual'. The Oleneostrovski Mogilnik people must have had ritual prohibitions about placing pottery and the bones of domestic animals into the graves of their dead. So the problem was solved, and Engels' view of history remained intact.

Ravdonikas was quite wrong. The people in Lubbock's canoe have never heard of pottery and had no conception of a domestic animal. They lived at least 4,000 years earlier than Ravdonikas had proposed, using the island as a cemetery between 6700 and 6000 BC.

The canoes arrive and are pulled ashore. The island is very small, a mere 2.5 kilometres long and less than one kilometre wide, and covered in spruce and larch. The body is placed upon a stretcher and without a word the people proceed along a path between the trees. Lubbock follows, arriving at a clearing where about fifty people have already gathered. This is the cemetery. Low mounds of sandy soil indicate previous burials; some appear fresh while others are overgrown by shoots and seedlings. A new grave has been dug; like the others, it is quite shallow and orientated east–west. The burial rites begin and Lubbock stands within the group of onlookers, watching the shaman at work.

The body is secured within the grave, its head at the eastern end and the deceased man's possessions positioned by his side: a slate knife, bone points, flint implements.[4] The people now disperse to fireplaces at the margins of the cemetery to engage in small talk. Lubbock remains by the graveside, wondering about the dead man's life. In a little over 8,000 years, long after his clothes and flesh have decayed to nothing, Gurina excavated his body. She meticulously drew each bone and artefact; she too wondered who that man had been.

Almost fifty years after Ravdonikas had interpreted Gurina's results, a second attempt was made. This time it was by a pair of archaeologists quite unswayed by the canons of Marxist theory: John O'Shea from the University of Michigan, a specialist in the analysis of cemeteries, and Marek Zvelebil, from the University of Sheffield, the leading expert on the Mesolithic hunter-gatherers of northern Europe.[5]

They took Gurina's information and used sophisticated statistical methods to place the graves into a series of overlapping groups. These groups, they argued, reflected social distinctions within the past society of the Oleneostrovski Mogilnik people. They claimed that the society had been divided into two lineages, one marked by the use of elk effigies and the other by those of snakes.[6] These effigies were only found in certain graves, possibly those who were the hereditary leaders of the lineage.

As some implements were exclusively buried with the men – bone points, harpoons, slate knives and daggers – O'Shea and Zvelebil proposed that a strong sexual division of labour had existed. The women had no specific tools for themselves and were more frequently buried with beads made from beaver teeth. The archaeologists decided that pendants of elk, beaver and bear teeth were indicators of wealth because, when these were plentiful in a grave, so too were artefacts such as knives and points. Those buried with bear tusks were the wealthiest – predominantly young adult males. This suggested that acquiring wealth was dependent upon physical health and, most likely, hunting prowess – the loss of one's vigour with age meant the loss of prestige and power. For women, the pathway to wealth appeared to be either by marriage or from blood ties to males.

Four burials were quite different to the others. Many grave-goods had been placed in the graves and the bodies had been interred in an almost vertical position so that the dead appeared to be still standing on the ground. O'Shea and Zvelebil thought that these were shamans, as Gurina herself had proposed. Finally, eleven graves of older men contained bone points alone – possibly a special group of hunters who were prohibited from accumulating their own possessions and wealth.

O'Shea and Zvelebil concluded that those who buried their dead at Oleneostrovski Mogilnik had more complex social lives than the vast majority of hunter-gatherers both past and present. As such, they had most likely lived all year round in as yet undiscovered villages, away from the island of the dead that appears to have been the provenance of ancestors alone. O'Shea and Zvelebil suggested that the Oleneostrovski Mogilnik people had gained their wealth by acting as 'middlemen' in the trading networks for flint and slate that covered northern Russia and eastern Finland.

Whereas it had taken nearly half a century for Ravdonikas's interpretation of Oleneostrovski Mogilnik to be substantially challenged, that of O'Shea and Zvelebil had less than a decade of grace. In 1995 their conclusions were questioned by Ken Jacobs from the University of Montreal and the cemetery of Oleneostrovski Mogilnik was reinterpreted once again.[7]

Jacobs considered that the similarities between the graves were more significant than the differences. He argued that the island had acted as the 'ritual centre' for many small groups of hunter-gatherers who lived, widely dispersed, along the shorelines and adjacent woodlands of Lake Onega. He thought that this had been a society of equals, attributing differences between the graves in the numbers of beads, pendants and artefacts to variable preservation rather than wealth and status. To Jacobs, Oleneostrovski Mogilnik resembled the sacred places of the Saami people who lived in the region until the nineteenth century. They too had buried their dead on islands within lakes. They did so to prevent spirits returning to settlements, in the belief that they would attempt to take relatives and possessions to the afterworld. By being restricted to an island, the spirits would also leave favoured hunting and fishing grounds undisturbed. Perhaps those who buried their dead at Oleneostrovski Mogilnik had thought likewise – perhaps they were the direct ancestors of the Saami.

As darkness falls, Lubbock watches dancing shadows in the moonlight; he listens to singing but cannot understand the words. And so he would have been in sympathy with the archaeologists of today, with Vladislav Iosifovich Ravdonikas, with John O'Shea, Marek Zvelebil and Ken Jacobs. They, too, are chasing the shadows of past lives and lack translators for the language they attempt to read – that of bear tusks, elk teeth and bone points. As the moon climbs and shooting stars arrive, Lubbock borrows a canoe and paddles into the night.

From the western shore of Lake Onega he travels to the Baltic coast. At times the canoe must be dragged from river to river; there are many woodland floods to negotiate, all created by the dams of beavers – animals that seem far more intent on redesigning nature than does any human being within the northern forest.[8] Lubbock catches glimpses of elk, he lives on fish and berries, and sleeps under the stars – when not woken by screech owls and howling wolves. Were it not for permanently sodden feet, an aching body and unremitting insect attacks, his nomadic lifestyle would be idyllic.

After paddling across the vast Lake Ladoga he enters the Gulf of Finland by the estuary of the River Neva, arriving where St Petersburg will one day flourish. A journey southwards begins.[9] He crosses large river-mouths, weaving between a multitude of tiny islands, and sometimes heads for open water. Porpoises often trail behind and occasionally lead the way; seals are ever vigilant while gulls swoop low over the strange canoeist in their midst. Lubbock passes many coastal encampments, some with wigwam-like tents, others with timber huts. People are sitting beside their canoes and smouldering fires; they mend fishing nets and harpoons, prepare food, tell stories to each other.[10] Lubbock travels for more than 1,500 kilometres south on the Baltic Sea. The date becomes 5000 BC and winter approaches. On the shore great flocks of starlings have appeared, the leaves have turned and the nights are growing long. And so a sprawling settlement around the mouth of a lagoon at the tip of southern Sweden looks most inviting, spirals of smoke suggesting a warm fire and roasted meat.

This settlement is known today as Skateholm, one of the largest Mesolithic sites in the whole of northern Europe. Today's quiet farmland of Skateholm provides no hint of its lively prehistoric past. The sea level has fallen by a few metres since that time, leaving what were once small islands in the lagoon as low knolls in otherwise flat fields. If the soil is scraped or blown away, sand from the prehistoric beach appears. Ploughs drag the debris of Mesolithic life to the surface.

It was indeed during ploughing in the late 1970s that the first traces of Mesolithic Skateholm were found in the form of stone tools.[11] Lars Larsson, Professor of Archaeology at Lund University, investigated. His trial trenches of 1980 recovered not only abundant artefacts, but many animal bones, including those from tiny fish, which indicated excellent preservation. There was more. Just where this Mesolithic debris was becoming sparse, suggesting the edge of the living area, a trial trench exposed a dark patch of sediment amidst the clean yellow sand of the underlying beach. When the top few centimetres were scraped away, a human skull appeared; it was a grave, the first of sixty-four that Lars Larsson would excavate at Skateholm.

Within a few years, he had exposed more than 3,000 square metres of this prehistoric settlement, discovered not one but three cemeteries, and recovered a remarkable collection of tools and animal bones.

At 5000 BC the lagoon entrance is half a kilometre across and interrupted by two small islands, one of which barely clears the water. That had been the cemetery before becoming flooded; now the larger island has been adopted and will be the burial ground that Larsson excavates in its entirety: fifty-three graves. Behind the lagoon thick reeds border the shore, brown and beaten by the winter weather, threaded by winding rivers. Beyond, there is thick woodland, not of pine as in the north but of deciduous trees – Lubbock is back in the world of oak, elm, lime, alder and willow.[12] From his viewpoint, bobbing on the sea a kilometre offshore, he sees people gathered around fires and small brushwood huts. Canoes are moored within the reeds and nets hung out to dry.

The Skateholm people have been attracted to the lagoon by its immense diversity of plants and animals. During the winter months they stalk wild boar and deer within the adjacent woodland, set fish-traps for pike and perch, and net the great shoals of sticklebacks that flourish in the rivers, which they mash for oil. Nets are also used for catching sea birds along rocky promontories: guillemot, razorbill and eider duck. When the sea is calm, they go fishing for herring or harpooning for dolphin and porpoise. Some evenings are spent stalking seals that gather upon the shore.

All such activities were evident from the collection of animal bones that Lars Larsson recovered: the bones of eighty-seven different species. With such an immense range, he thought that people had lived at Skateholm all year round. But then Peter Rowley-Conwy got hold of the bones and analysed them with his intimate knowledge of animal anatomy, reproduction and behaviour.[13]

Rowley-Conwy found that the bones of wild boar told a different story about life at Skateholm to that envisaged by Lars Larsson – or rather their piglets did. Wild boar is an ideal animal for an archaeo-zoologist because of the rapidity of its growth from tiny newborn piglet to large full-grown adult. Consequently, an animal's size is an accurate indicator of its age, not in years but in months since birth. Mesolithic piglets were most likely born in the spring, just like piglets today. By estimating their age when killed, one can establish in what month hunting had occurred. Of course, one cannot measure the actual piglet because only individual bones survive; but some of these – such as the phalanges or foot bones – give a very accurate estimate of the complete piglet. So Rowley-Conwy measured the bones at Skateholm and found that all the wild boar had been killed during the winter months.

The same season was suggested by the study of deer jaws and seal bones. Of the birds, almost all were winter visitors; there were just two bones from possible summer migrants to the Swedish coast: the Dalmatian pelican and the shoveller. Just as telling was the absence of species that would have been caught if people had been at Skateholm during the summer months. Cod, mackerel and garfish, for instance, would surely have been caught in large quantities when they came inshore to breed; but they were represented by only fifteen out of 2425 identified fishbones. This suggests that people were only fishing in the winter, a time when such fish were far away in the Baltic Sea.

From his canoe, Lubbock can see several clusters of huts along the Skateholm shore; some have wigwam-like tents covered with hide, others are dome-shaped brushwood dwellings or rather shaky timber-framed huts. Looking closer, he finds that the people within each cluster are also dressed quite differently – some with long shawls, others with furs. Faces might be painted or plain, necks and waists strung with beads or left quite bare. There seems little contact between each cluster, simply a grudging acknowledgement that they too have a right to camp by the lagoon.[14]

Just as Lubbock raises his paddle to approach the shore, a dog barks. A second joins in, along with a pack on the western headland of the lagoon. Big dogs, rather like German shepherd dogs today. Fierce dogs. Lubbock decides to remain watching from a distance.

The Skateholm cemeteries excavated by Larsson suggest families who were only loosely bound together into a single community, owing to the immense variety of burial practices. This contrasts greatly with the uniformity found at Oleneostrovski Mogilnik. When Larsson had completed his excavations he found that the human graves had been randomly positioned in their cemeteries, with no consistent pattern.[15] People were buried lying on their back, on their front, crouching, sitting, partly reclining, with some limbs bent and others outstretched.

Most graves were of single individuals, about an equal number of males and females, although a few multiple burials were found. Some people had been cremated while others had wooden structures burned over their graves as part of the burial ritual. Some had their bones rearranged or partly removed at a later date.

The range of artefacts and animal bones found within the graves matched the diversity in burial practices – almost every imaginable combination of tools, pendants and antlers. The bones, teeth, tusks and antlers of the large terrestrial game – those coming from red deer, roe-deer and wild boar – were the favoured burial items. But one female body had a container of fish placed by her lower leg; another had the skull of an otter. The impression is of separate families choosing how to bury their dead, only loosely constrained by community-wide convention and ritual practice.

There were few clear patterns between the type of burial and type of person, in terms of age and sex.[16] As at Oleneostrovski Mogilnik, the wealthiest individuals appeared to be those in the prime of life. So power and prestige were again largely a matter of personal achievement rather than inheritance. There were limited differences between men and women, the former more frequently buried with the flint blades and axes, while elk- and auroch- (wild cattle) teeth pendants seem to have been for females alone. There are no examples of individuals with inordinate amounts of wealth or who may have been shamans or chiefs.[17]

The presence of domesticated dogs at Skateholm was one of Lars Larsson's most important discoveries. Some bones were scattered within the household rubbish but proof of domestication came when dog burials were found. In the earliest cemetery, dogs had been sacrificed when their owners had died, joining them in both the grave and the afterworld. But in the second cemetery – that which is in use during Lubbock's visit – the dogs had their own graves and were accorded the same burial treatment as humans. One had an antler placed along its back, three flint blades next to its hip and a decorated antler hammer, and was strewn with red ochre.[18]

Stones are thrown, the dogs yelp and disappear from sight. Once again

Lubbock lifts his paddle and now approaches a little closer to the shore. But as he gains a clearer view of those seated and standing by the fires, he again halts his canoe. One of the men hobbles on a crutch; two others have heavily scarred faces; one may well be blind. Lubbock decides to forsake a visit to this particular settlement, a place of evident social tension and violence. He turns his canoe and heads east towards the Danish coast.

Lars Larsson found disturbing evidence that the Skateholm people had fought aggressively either amongst themselves or with others. Indeed, the accumulation of evidence from cemeteries and isolated burials has shown that violence was endemic within the Mesolithic communities throughout northern Europe.[19]

At Skateholm four individuals were found with depressed skull fractures – at some time they had been hit on the head with a blunt instrument that left a permanent dent. Such blows may have simply rendered the victims unconscious, but they could well have been fatal. Flint arrowheads had hit two others from Skateholm and still lay amid their bones when excavated by Larsson: one had been hit in the stomach, the other in the chest.

These might have been innocent hunting accidents – but that would hardly explain the fractured skulls. Some of the violence may have been ritualistic in nature. At Skateholm, a young adult female had been killed by a blow to the temple and then laid beside an older male within a single grave – perhaps a sacrifice to join her partner, perhaps the ultimate punishment for some unknown crime. But the most likely explanation for the violence is that these Mesolithic communities were fighting to defend their land.

Skateholm must have been highly desirable for hunter-gatherers, with abundant supplies of food in the woodland, the marshes, the rivers, the lagoon, and the sea. When the people dispersed in the summer they would not have wished to relinquish the lagoon to unexpected strangers, or to those who lived in adjacent but less productive regions.

The majority of the head injuries had come from blows to the front and left side – the outcome of face-to-face combat with a right-handed opponent. Males were more involved in fighting than the females, having three times as many head-wounds and four times those from arrows. One can easily imagine groups returning to the lagoon as summer ended, finding uninvited occupants already present and fighting for their land.

When seeking to explain the violence at Skateholm and elsewhere in Mesolithic Europe it is useful to consider the Yanomamö people who lived in the Amazonian forest. Living in villages and having a substantial reliance on wild foods, the Yanomamö have been studied in detail by the anthropologist Napolean Chagnon.[20] Like those of the Mesolithic, violence is endemic within their society, both within and between villages. It ranges from ritualistic duels involving chest-pounding contests, to club fights, raids between villages and outright warfare. Men are responsible for most of the violence, and much of it is about women and sex.

Duels often start when one man catches another in flagrante with his wife. In Chagnon's words, 'the enraged husband challenges his opponent to strike him on the head with a club. He holds his own club vertically, leans against it, and exposes his head for the opponent to strike. After he has sustained a blow on the head, he can then deliver one on the culprit's skull. But as soon as the blood starts to flow, almost everybody rips a pole out of the house frame and joins in the fighting, supporting one or other of the contestants.'[21] The tops of most men's heads are covered with deep, ugly scars of which they are immensely proud. In fact, some men display their scars by shaving and rubbing in red pigments to ensure these are clearly defined.

Many raids between villages were in order to abduct women, even if it was claimed that their purpose was to end sorcery being undertaken by members of one village against another. Chagnon describes extremely violent conflicts, especially those that involve *nomohori* – treachery – in which people visit another village on false pretences and then brutally kill the welcoming residents and flee with their women. A captured woman is typically raped by all members of the raiding party, and then by any other man in the village who so chooses. One of the men then takes her as a wife.

Yanomamö warfare provides an appealing analogy to what might have occurred in the Mesolithic of northern Europe. It is, however, always dangerous in archaeology to take descriptions of living people and impose them on to the past, especially when the two societies come from such different environments – the South American tropics and coastlands of Mesolithic Scandinavia could hardly be more different. And there can be no question that the Yanomamö lived in much larger communities and in more permanent settlements than those of the Mesolithic. Nevertheless, ritualistic club fights and raiding parties are attractive explanations of those fractured skulls and pierced bodies in Mesolithic cemeteries. And men fighting over women is no doubt one of the oldest and most pervasive features of human society.

A raiding party might explain the most dramatic sign of violence from Mesolithic Europe: the skull 'nests' from the cave of Ofnet in Germany.[22] Two shallow pits were found containing carefully arranged human skulls, all apparently cut from newly dead bodies at some date around 6400 BC. One pit had twenty-seven, the other six, and a large majority had come from women and children. Several displayed head-wounds, especially those of the males, one of which had been assaulted with six or seven massive axe-blows. Almost all had been elaborately decorated with ornamental mollusc shells, the pierced teeth of red deer and red ochre. The mollusc shells are remarkable in that they include species coming from far away – eastern central Europe, the Swabian alb, and even the Mediterranean.

These skull 'nests' suggest a raid upon a Mesolithic settlement similar to those undertaken by the Yanomamö. Whether the heads were cut from already dead bodies or the 'prisoners' were executed remains a point of gruesome speculation, especially as so many women and children were involved. Similarly, one can speculate that the careful burial had been undertaken either by the survivors, as an act of mourning and remembrance, or by the victors to appease their spirits. Whatever the case, Mesolithic Europe evidently had its moments of brutal violence and bloody slaughter.

The common explanation among archaeologists for the growth of violence in the Mesolithic societies of northern Europe after 5500 BC concerns population pressure on diminishing resources.[23] Ever since 9600 BC the woodlands, lagoons, rivers, estuaries and seashores of northern Europe had provided abundant wild resources. The populations of the first settlers after the ice age and those of the Early Holocene would have expanded rapidly – they were in a Mesolithic Garden of Eden. But by 7000 BC those living in the lands of modern-day Sweden and Denmark were losing substantial areas of land to the rising sea. People were increasingly crammed into smaller and smaller territories, leading to intense competition for the best hunting, plant-gathering and – especially – fishing locations.

The economic and social problems caused by environmental change had been exacerbated, however, by a new force that had entered these people's lives. It was one that had already overwhelmed the occupants of Franchthi Cave and Lepenski Vir and which had originated far away in western Asia. By 5500 BC, farmers had arrived in central Europe and made contact with the indigenous people, either in person or via traded goods. The farmers' desire for land, for women, for furs and wild game fitted neatly with the Mesolithic people's need for new items of prestige such as polished axes in order to pursue their own internal social competition.[24] They began to trade across a frontier – farmers to the south in what is now Poland and Germany, hunter-gatherers to the north in Denmark and Sweden. But whereas the farming settlements flourished by such contact, it caused further social disruption and economic stress for the Mesolithic people. And it would eventually lead to complete cultural collapse.

20

At the Frontier

*The spread of farming in Central Europe and its impact on
Mesolithic society, 6000–4400 BC*

By 6000 BC the Mesolithic people of northern Europe were listening to fireside stories from visitors about a new people in the east, people who lived in
great wooden houses and controlled the game. Soon they found their own
Mesolithic neighbours using polished stone axes, moulding cooking vessels
from clay and herding cattle for themselves. When farming villages arrived
within their own hunting lands, Mesolithic eyes peered from behind trees
at the timber long houses, the tethered cattle and the sprouting crops with
mixed emotions – fear, awe, dismay, disgust.

The older generation must have struggled to understand what they saw.
Although they had felled trees and built dwellings themselves, the new
farmsteads were quite beyond their comprehension.[1] The farmers appeared
intent on controlling, dominating and transforming nature. Mesolithic
culture had been no more than an extension of the natural world. Its
chipped stone axes were merely an elaboration of nature's work, her use of
rivers and frosts to break stone nodules apart and make sharp edges.
Wicker baskets and woven mats were merely extravagant forms of spiders'
webs and birds' nests made by human hands.

The pottery of the farmers – a product of mixing clay and sand,
firing, decorating and painting – had no precedent within the natural
world. When the farmers ground and polished their axes smooth, they
appeared intent on denying the natural angularity of stone. Building a
Mesolithic dwelling required no more than promoting and combining the
existing suppleness of hazel, the stringiness of willow and the sheets of
birch bark that grew ready-made; a timber-framed long house, on the
other hand, required nature to be torn apart and the world constructed
anew.

The older men and women are likely to have retreated from the forests of
central Europe, relinquishing their hunting grounds and insisting that ever
more time be spent celebrating the natural world. But they sang and danced
against the tide of history: the younger generation had quite different ideas.
Many were born into a world where farmers, pottery, cattle and wheat were
as natural as wild boar and the annual harvests of nuts and berries. And so
they made contact with the new arrivals. They worked for the farmers as
labourers, trackers and hunters. They engaged in trade, learned to make

pottery, to plough the land. Their daughters married the farmers and soon their sons became farmers themselves.

Those who continued with their Mesolithic culture in the northern forests had to adjust their traditional hunting-and-gathering patterns. Furs, game, honey and other forest products had to be procured for trade; the wild resources were fought over and further depleted. And as increasing numbers of women joined the farmers, perceiving agriculture as providing greater economic security for themselves and their children, there were fewer to maintain the Mesolithic populations. Both land and women became sources of tension that often boiled over into the violence so vividly documented within the Mesolithic graves.

By 5500 BC a new type of farming culture had emerged from the fringes of the Hungarian plain: the Linearbandkeramik, which archaeologists thankfully abbreviate to the LBK.[2] It spread with astonishing speed both east and west, into the Ukraine and into central Europe. While Lubbock was canoeing towards Skateholm, the LBK farmers were crossing and clearing the deciduous woodlands of Poland, Germany, the Low Countries and eastern France.

This was a quite different type of Neolithic to that which had appeared in Greece and spread northwards through the Balkans to reach the Hungarian plain. As their LBK name implies, these farmers decorated their pottery with bands of narrow lines; they constructed timber long houses and relied on cattle rather than sheep and goats. Nevertheless, archaeologists have traditionally assumed that the LBK farmers were direct descendants of the original immigrants from western Asia and represented a new phase of their migration across Europe.

Their identity has now been challenged. Marek Zvelebil argues that the local Mesolithic people who lived on the peripheries of the Hungarian plain adopted farming practices for themselves – watching and learning from the new immigrants, bartering for domestic stock and grain.[3] There is likely to have been some mixing of the populations, perhaps through marriage, perhaps through the theft of women Yanomamö-style. But the Mesolithic people did far more than simply copy the immigrants. They adapted the farming lifestyle to suit the soils, climate and woodlands of central Europe – they themselves created the LBK. And when their own new farming populations began to expand they spread both east and west, maintaining a remarkable consistency in all aspects of their new culture – the architecture of their houses, the layout of their villages, their social organisation and economy. And so, according to Zvelebil, the LBK Neolithic farmers of Europe were the direct descendants of indigenous Mesolithic hunter-gatherers rather than of the immigrants who had originally arrived in Greece.

Whatever their ancestry, the new farmers travelled westwards at a remarkable rate, covering 25 kilometres a generation. Just like the original immigrant farmers of Southeast Europe, they filled up each new region of fertile soils with farmsteads and villages and then leap-frogged across less favourable soils to establish a new frontier. Such speed reflects more than the success of their lifestyle – it implies an ideology of colonisation, an attraction to 'frontier life', similar, some have suggested, to that of the Trekboers of South Africa and the pioneers of the American West.

A 'frontier' mentality may also explain the cultural uniformity of the LBK farmers. A house from the village of Cuiry-les-Chaudardes in the Paris basin will appear near-identical to one from Miskovice in the Czech Republic, constructed almost 1,000 kilometres away and several hundred years before. Those at the frontier stuck to a settlement 'ideal' remembered from their homeland, even if that 'homeland' had begun to change – just as the farming colonists on Cyprus had done by persevering with their small circular dwellings while rectangular architecture became ubiquitous in western Asia.

The new farmers of central Europe cleared small patches of woodland and built long houses, usually about 12 metres in length, sometimes three or four times this size. Wheat and barley were grown within small plots, sometimes with peas and lentils. Their cattle browsed within the lush woodlands as their pigs rooted in the leaf litter below the trees. As had been the case at Nea Nikomedeia, the household was the key social unit; it made its own decisions and sought to maintain its independence, while remaining ultimately reliant upon others in times of need.

The long houses were substantial, constructed with three columns of interior timbers, flanked by rows of posts that supported the wattle-and-daub walls. The daubing clay was often dug from immediately outside the walls themselves, creating convenient ditches for dumping domestic refuse. Inside, the long houses were frequently divided into three sections, possibly used for storage, for cooking and eating, and for sleeping. It has to be 'possibly' because all generations of later farmers, including those of modern times, have been attracted to exactly the same fertile soils as those favoured by the LBK. The long-house floors have been destroyed by modern ploughs, leaving archaeologists with no more than the rings of blackened earth which mark where timber posts had once supported roofs and walls.

Some long houses had stood alone within the woodlands; elsewhere twenty or thirty were neatly aligned, each with their door-ends facing east. Within such villages the houses were in various states of repair. When the last member of a household died, their long house was abandoned even if structurally sound. It was simply left to collapse within the village, ending up as a long low mound – a 'dead' house to match the 'dead' family.[4]

The people themselves were buried in cemeteries adjacent to their village. Bone preservation is generally so poor that rarely anything more than faint traces of durable tooth enamel survives within each grave. When bones are found, they suggest that all members of the community were buried together – men and women, the old and the young. Axes, adzes, arrow-heads and shell ornaments were often placed with the men, grinding stones and awls with the women. There are no traces of very wealthy or powerful individuals, little evidence for religious belief and ritual practices.[5]

John Lubbock has yet to encounter any of these farmers himself as he explores the slowly disintegrating Mesolithic world of Denmark. But his journey will soon bring him face to face with the new arrivals.

From the bay at Skateholm, he has crossed to the Danish coast and then travelled northwards and has now reached a narrow inlet that will eventually become boggy land behind the town of Vedbaek, about 20 kilometres north of Copenhagen. At 4800 BC the inlet is much like the Skateholm lagoon – a prized locality for hunting, fishing and fowling, one that people are prepared to fight and die for, one where they will reside long after death. Many small settlements are scattered around its shore; Lubbock chooses one to visit and finds it recently deserted – fireplaces are still smouldering and a tethered dog has just been fed.

Its people are gathered in a cemetery on a low knoll behind their cluster of brushwood huts. Squeezing between them, Lubbock watches a tiny baby boy being lowered into a grave next to his young mother.[6] She looks no more than eighteen years of age; it had most probably been the first as well as the last child she carried. Lying on her back, she looks resplendent – her dress has ringlets of snail-shell beads and a host of pretty pendants. A robe, similarly decorated, has been folded to make a pillow across which her blond hair is splayed. Her checks burn brightly, having been dusted with red ochre; her pelvis has also been made red – perhaps a reminder of the blood that flowed.

The little blue body is laid beside her, not on the ground but in the ultimate soft embrace of a swan's encircling wing. A large flint blade is placed on the body, just as it would have been had the baby boy grown up and died as a man. Lubbock watches as powdered red pigment is blown from a wooden bowl to float down upon the child's dead body.

When excavated in 1975, this burial was simply designated as 'Grave 8' of the Bøgebakken cemetery, located while a car park was being built. Sixteen other graves were excavated; almost all the bodies had been identically positioned – on their backs with feet close together and hands by their sides. The graves were in neat parallel rows, quite unlike the random scattering of bodies in assorted positions at Skateholm.

The swan's wing within Grave 8 may have been much more than a comfortable resting place for the nearly-child. Among the nineteenth-century Saami people of northern Europe, swans and wildfowl were the messengers of the gods.[7] Such birds could, after all, walk on the land, swim on the water and fly in the air – adept at moving between different worlds. Perhaps the

Mesolithic people had similarly revered their swans and let one fly that poor child away to their afterworld where he could have the life denied to him on earth.

From Vedbaek Lubbock travels south, keeping close to the shore and passing dense reed-beds that flourish below the alders which fringe wood-land in summer leaf. A deep mulchy aroma of rotting debris wafts from the shallows, yet all around there is the vibrant buzz of life – fish jumping, frogs plopping, dragonflies, ducks and a seemingly continuous trail of villages and fishing camps along the shore.

Although the people Lubbock meets revere the red deer and wild boar of the woodlands, such animals are infrequently hunted and contribute little to the diet when compared to the constant supply of sea and freshwater foods: fish, shellfish, birds, eels, crabs and the occasional seal or porpoise. Fortunately for archaeologists, this Mesolithic diet will leave a chemical trace within their bones.[8] Had it not been for this, and the scientific tech-niques to analyse the chemistry of bone, archaeologists could easily have thought that the Mesolithic people depended more on hunting than fishing in view of their preference for ornaments made from deer teeth and pig's tusk.[9]

The heavy marine diet might account for the people that Lubbock meets who seem unwell: bloated stomachs, pale faces, diarrhoea and sickness. Copious quantities of fish can lead to an infestation of parasites, which in turn impairs the functioning of kidneys and intestines. An archaeological trace is only left when such infestation becomes severe – skull bones can thicken, as has been found on some Mesolithic specimens from Denmark.[10]

At the settlement of Tybrind Vig, on the west coast of Zealand, Lubbock squeezes into the rear of a canoe as it departs for the shallow waters of a muddy-bottomed bay for night-time fishing.[11] When darkness arrives, a fire is lit upon a bed of sand in the canoe itself and soon a tangle of eels are darting around the boat, drawn to the light. The fishermen stand upright to spear the eels with leister prongs. Lubbock sits tight, watching the moths around the flames and admiring the fine canoe made from a single log of lime – and more particularly the heart-shaped paddles.[12] Each has been carved from ash and then decorated with an intricate geometric design, cut into its surface and filled with dark brown pigment.

Lubbock had seen similar paddles being used while walking on the shore; his Mesolithic companions knew immediately, from their design, where the canoe had come from and where it was likely to be going. Lubbock soon realised that the Mesolithic people were just as intent on monitoring the whereabouts of each other as of fish shoals and animals.

From the islands, Lubbock crosses over to Jutland and the open woodland of its sandy soils. Jutland's northern end is deeply indented with fjords and he finds people creating enormous mounds of mollusc shells, fishbones and other domestic refuse. He had already read about such sites in *Prehistoric Times*.[13] In the 1860s his Victorian namesake made two visits to the shell mounds, or Køkkenmøddinger as the nineteenth-century Danish archaeologists called them. During the course of one visit, Victorian John Lubbock dug his own small section through a mound and collected flint tools.

Modern Lubbock has arrived at what we call today the Ertebølle midden: a continuous mass of shells about 20 metres wide, several metres thick and stretching for more than 100 metres along the shore.[14] One end is boggy and close to the spring which had first drawn people to the site. The vast banks of oysters, mussels, cockles and periwinkles found just offshore had also been attractive – a product of the salty, nutrient-rich and sheltered waters. He sits upon the pile of discarded shells and bones close to where clusters of people are at work. The rubbish-mound stench is almost overpowering, but only Lubbock seems to notice. Some people are working stone; others cluster around fires or gut fish. Lubbock's attention is drawn, however, to an activity he has never seen a hunter-gatherer perform: a woman is moulding a lump of clay into a pottery vessel.

All those who worked on the midden in 4400 BC left traces for Søren Andersen of Aarhus University to find when he excavated Ertebølle in 1983: scatters of flint flakes, animal bones clustered around charcoal-filled pits, thick piles of fishbones. Andersen wasn't the first to excavate the site. Almost a hundred years before, the National Museum had investigated the great shell mound and used its name for the last of the Mesolithic peoples of Denmark: the Ertebølle culture. Modern John Lubbock had read about the Museum's work in *Prehistoric Times*. A committee composed of a biologist (Professor Steenstrup), a geologist (Professor Forchhammer) and an archaeologist (Professor Worsaae) had been formed to examine the Køkkenmøddinger – interdisciplinary research has always been recognised as necessary to investigate the past. As Victorian John Lubbock had written: 'Much was naturally expected of such a triumvirate, and the most sanguine hopes have been fulfilled.'

Søren Andersen, working with his own interdisciplinary team, excavated both within and around the midden as he searched for dwellings and burials. Victorian John Lubbock had assumed that the shells accumulated around 'tents and huts', the mounds being 'sites of ancient villages'. But Andersen found no such dwellings; modern John Lubbock could have told him why. Only flimsy shelters were erected around the midden and, as it expanded, the scant traces of their presence – the holes for supporting posts – were buried by new layers of shell. But modern John Lubbock had seen no signs of a cemetery and remained as ignorant as Søren Andersen as to what happened to the dead.

Like all hunter-gatherers, the Ertebølle people knew just where, when and how to exploit differing animals and plants as the seasons changed. In winter they went to the northern tip of Jutland to catch the whooper swans that arrived as migrants on the Danish coast – leaving a scatter of butchered swan bones and artefacts now known as the site of Aggersund.[15] Some would go to Vaengo Sø, a small island on the east coast and close to the shore of a shallow bay. That was perfect for stranding whales. During the autumn months the small island of Dyrholm was regularly visited. There they caught eels that flourished in the shallows and skinned them with bone-bladed knives.[16]

Such seasonal movements along the coast were identified by a detailed analysis of animal bones by Peter Rowley-Conwy during the 1980s, using the latest techniques of 'archaeo-zoology', and pointed to the likelihood that some people lived permanently at Ertebølle midden. He was, however, merely building on the insights of Victorian John Lubbock, who had already decided that it was 'highly probable that the "mound builders" resided on the Danish coast all year round' on the basis of the traces of swan bones, antlers and the bones of young mammals discovered in the middens. The first indicated winter occupation, as swans were cold-season migrants; the second suggested autumn, when deer shed their antlers; and the third springtime, when the young are born. Victorian John Lubbock was an archaeo-zoologist before the term was known.

He was also attentive to botanical remains, remarking that the absence of grain suggested that 'the men of the Køkkenmøddinger' lacked any knowledge of agriculture. Neither did the shells escape his enquiring mind; Victorian John Lubbock had noted that those in the middens were much larger than can be found on the Danish coast today, and that the oysters had completely disappeared. He put this down to changing concentrations of salt in the water – anticipating by a century Peter Rowley-Conwy's argument that decreasing salinity had caused the abandonment of the shell mounds and the switch to a farming economy.[17]

The Mesolithic pottery made at Ertebølle was quite different to that which Lubbock had seen at Nea Nikomedeia; it was plain, with thick, uneven walls and fashioned by inexperienced hands. Such pottery had not been unexpected since, in *Prehistoric Times*, Victorian John Lubbock describes finding 'small pieces of a very coarse pottery' during his visit of 1863. Modern John Lubbock saw the complete vessels: bowls with pointed bottoms and flat dishes. They were mainly used for cooking, a great advantage over those made from wood and wickerwork.

The sight of hunter-gatherers making pottery is just one of several signs of change that Lubbock encounters as his journey through Mesolithic Denmark continues. Another is young men with ground stone axes ostentatiously tucked into their belts[18] – tall, handsome figures, quite different to the 'race of small men, with overhanging brows' that Victorian John Lubbock had imagined living in Mesolithic Denmark.

The source of these axes begins to become evident at the last of the settlements that Lubbock visits in Mesolithic Denmark: Ringkloster.[19] Surprisingly, this is inland, located beside a lake-edge in northeast Jutland – Victorian John Lubbock had thought it 'evident that a nation which subsisted principally on marine molluscs would never form any large inland settlements'. On this he had been wrong. But only just, as after 150 years of research, Ringkloster is still the only inland settlement of Mesolithic Denmark currently known. Modern John Lubbock finds the settlement amidst a staggeringly beautiful landscape, one with steeply forested hills, wide valleys, bogs and lakes. Many of the woodland trees – oak, elm, lime and hazel – are covered in thick ivy, while dense alder carr flourishes by the lakeside.

Lubbock arrives at Ringkloster at dusk in the middle of winter, finding a cluster of snow-covered brushwood huts. The woodland has been opened up by the felling of lime and elm – the favoured wood for canoes and bows. People are busy around their huts, all finely dressed and decorated with beads. Both men and women are having their hair plaited and their faces painted. Within the huts he sees the now familiar implements of Mesolithic life: bows and arrows, stone axes and wicker baskets. In one, however, there is something new: bundles of thick furs, tied with twine and ready to be carried away. Lubbock watches as baskets of rubbish are taken and dumped into the lake and dogs are tethered to posts. At the centre of the settlement a huge boar is being spit-roasted; the ground around it has been swept of snow and laid with bark mats. Visitors are evidently expected. Lubbock climbs a tree to watch from a distance.

Within an hour Ringkloster is the scene of a great feast; visitors have arrived from the coast and brought many items to trade – baskets of oysters, salted dolphin steaks, beads made from golden amber. These are exchanged for the luxurious winter furs that Ringkloster is renowned to provide. For two months its people have been trapping pine marten, wild cats, badgers and otters. They have accumulated a great store of pelts in readiness for the traders who will arrive throughout the winter and into the spring.

The roasted boar is eaten and liquid refreshment served in strikingly decorated ceramic vessels – a contrast to the plain and drab Mesolithic pottery that Lubbock had seen elsewhere. Some have a chequerboard pattern, others meandering lines of dots made by stabbing the wet clay with a point. Some vessels have parallel lines and appear to be of higher quality – smooth, even surfaces, with thin walls and an elegant form.

The feast continues long into the night and is followed by story-telling, singing and dance. The following morning the traders leave loaded with furs and with Lubbock in tow. Those at Ringkloster continue their trapping and hunting, and will do so long after the first farmers are present in Denmark itself. Søren Andersen excavated the settlement during the 1970s;

Peter Rowley-Conwy analysed the animal bones and found evidence for hunting wild boar and intensive trapping of furry animals. He once described Ringkloster as 'the finest site of all'.[20]

Lubbock remains with the pine-marten furs as they are traded from group to group down the east coast of Jutland, across Zealand and Aerø and finally into northern Germany. As he travels south, the Mesolithic people seem increasingly concerned with identity and territorial boundary: each group can be identified by their distinctive clothes and hairstyles, and by the manner in which they make their tools. Some have made their harpoons straight and others curved; some have made their stone axes with parallel sides while others produce axes with a flared cutting edge.[21] Lubbock recalls the time when the Mesolithic had begun, the time of Star Carr – when a virtual identity in human culture had existed across the whole of northern Europe. The old Mesolithic order had become fractured and would soon be gone.

The bundles of furs gradually diminish in number and increase in value. Finally, no more than a small basket of pine-marten pelts are left. Lubbock watches as these are carried into a forest clearing somewhere in northern Germany at 4400 BC. A hunter, accompanied by his two sons and young daughter, lays them on the ground. A man steps from the trees opposite and lays a polished stone axe next to the furs. Unable to communicate with words, the two men – one Mesolithic and one LBK Neolithic – use subtle nods, narrowed eyes and raised eyebrows to ensure that their views are known. Once the exchange is made, each backs away before raising a hand in farewell. As the hunter-gatherer departs with his daughter and sons, he hears the farmer call. Turning, the farmer points to the girl. The hunter-gatherer pauses and then agrees – next time they meet she can become his wife. The hunter-gatherer takes her still tiny hand for the homeward trek and imagines the axes and cereal grain that the union will bring.[22]

Lubbock is at the frontier – that between the LBK farmers and the remaining indigenous hunter-gatherers of the forests. The clearing is a known meeting-place, but as yet quite unmarked by human structures. Within a few generations, the farmers will build houses and surround them by a ditch. Archaeologists will eventually know their settlement as Esbeck. Some will argue that the ditch was made for defence against the remaining hunter-gatherers who had turned hostile after their Mesolithic culture had almost entirely disappeared.[23]

21

A Mesolithic Legacy

The Neolithic in southern Europe, 6000–4000 BC; debates in historical linguistics and genetics

The final canoe trip of John Lubbock's European travels takes him past islands that sit like giant stepping-stones between the Low Countries and southern England. These, and a larger island off the Yorkshire coast, are all that remain of Doggerland – the lowlands that Lubbock had walked across after leaving Creswell Crags in 12,700 BC. Britain is an island again – for the first time in 100,000 years.[1]

Lubbock has no time to return to Gough's Cave, to walk through the thick oak woodland that now grows where he had trapped arctic hares in the tundra and watched snowy owls. His European journey is nearly at an end. On a black night in the year of 4500 BC, he approaches a settlement now known to archaeologists as Téviec and located on the coast of northern France.[2] His destination is marked by firelight and song. A feast and burial are under way, with perhaps a hundred people focused intently on swaying figures silhouetted by the flames.

The dancing and singing comes to a sudden halt and the elements take over: the crackle of flames, the distant crash of Atlantic breakers, and the howling wind. Lubbock looks at the corpse lying by the fire: a man with bushy beard and thick black hair, his body clothed, decorated with beads and sprinkled with red ochre.

A costumed figure – half man, half antlered deer – leaps across the flames while beating a drum. He addresses the dead man and orders stone slabs to be levered from the ground. Two women step forward and lift them to expose another body within a stone-lined grave. Lubbock leans forward and sees its bones sharply defined beneath a taut yellow skin. The shaman kneels beside the grave and shifts the desiccated corpse to the side – it falls apart, its bones becoming jumbled with yet older bones already stacked inside.[3] The new body is laid to rest. One by one the deceased man's belongings are placed by his side and a collection of fine flint blades are laid upon his chest. After a further dusting with red ochre, the slabs are replaced. A small fire is then lit upon the tomb, into which the jawbones of a deer and wild boar are solemnly placed. When the flames die down, the singing, dancing and feasting resume.[4] John Lubbock joins in – the last dance of his European travels.

The Mesolithic settlement-cemetery of Téviec was discovered and excavated by the French archaeologists M. and S.-J. Péquart in the late 1920s and 1930s, along with a nearby cemetery known as Hoëdic. These sites had once been located on low knolls in an extensive coastal plain, but the rising sea level has left them on small islands off the coast of Brittany.

Study of the burials, skeletons and domestic debris showed that the Mesolithic inhabitants of the Atlantic seaboard shared many features with those of the Scandinavian lands. They had a diverse diet – large mammals, waterfowl, shellfish, fruits and nuts – and fought to protect their territory and women. They too used clothing to announce their identity: the cloak-pins used by those buried at Téviec were made from the bones of wild boar, while the pins of Hoëdic people were made from the bones of deer. Few of us today could tell such cloak-pins apart, but the differences would have been glaring to Mesolithic eyes.

The items that the Téviec people valued and placed within their graves were much as Lubbock had seen elsewhere: flint blades, deer teeth, boar tusks and bone daggers. The wealthiest were once again the younger adults, gaining their wealth by physical strength and mental agility, and then losing it as old age slowed them down. As at Oleneostrovski Mogilnik, the men were buried with more utilitarian items than the women, and the sexes had their own distinctive jewellery: cowries for the men and periwinkle beads for the women.

Multiple burials are one of the most striking features of the Téviec and Hoëdic cemeteries. We must assume – just as the Péquarts and later archaeologists have assumed – that those placed within each stone-lined tomb were members of a single family; blood ties seem to have been particularly important to these people. But not all burials were of this type. Many were of lone individuals and some were covered by tent-like structures made from antlers.

We should not be surprised by the abundant evidence for ritual and feasting at Téviec and Hoëdic: their inhabitants must have felt insecure and needed to appease their gods. Not only did they face the impact of the LBK farmers who were living no more than 50 kilometres to the east, they also faced similar disruption coming from the south.

While the LBK was spreading through central Europe, Neolithic sites were appearing around the Mediterranean coast. Some archaeologists believe that these arose from the arrival of immigrants, the direct descendants of farmers in western Asia whose recent ancestors had made settlements in Greece and southern Italy, such as Nea Nikomedeia. Other archaeologists reject this idea; they believe that the indigenous Mesolithic people of the central and western Mediterranean adopted Neolithic culture themselves after having made contact with farmers in the east.

What is agreed upon is that the Mediterranean Neolithic between 6000 and 4500 BC looks quite different to that of central Europe. In that region there is a clear separation between sites that have the complete Neolithic 'package', on the one hand – those of the LBK with timber-framed houses, cattle, sheep, crops, pottery and polished stone axes – and Mesolithic sites, with microliths, deer and wild boar bones, on the other. In the Mediterranean, however, Neolithic and Mesolithic elements are mixed together at single sites, appearing to have been used by the same people at the same time. These are predominantly cave sites and, to archaeologists such as James Lewthwaite of the University of Bradford, and Peter Rowley-Conwy, they suggest that the indigenous hunter-gatherers choose selectively from the Neolithic package, having no wish to become fully-fledged farmers themselves.

Lewthwaite has argued that the Mesolithic inhabitants of Corsica and Sardinia adopted sheep and goats to compensate for their lack of game – red deer never having colonised those islands. Having done so, they eschewed cereals and timber-framed houses in order to continue their traditional hunter-gatherer lifestyle, one now made more secure by the small flocks they tended.[5]

Other hunter-gatherers picked out pottery from the Neolithic package as something both useful for cooking food and effective for social display. They pressed shells into the soft clay to make vessels of a distinctive design, quite unlike any others made in Europe.[6] Some chose to adopt cereal cultivation to plug seasonal gaps in the availability of wild foods: seed was sown, people dispersed to hunt or gather and returned months later to harvest the wheat or barley just as if it were another wild plant. As a result of this piecemeal and partial adoption of the Neolithic package, people who were neither strictly Mesolithic hunter-gatherers nor Neolithic farmers occupied the Mediterranean.

Those who used the cave of Arene Candide in the landscape of steep cliffs and narrow valleys of northwestern Italy typified the hybrid type of lifestyles that arose. Excavations in the decade following 1946 revealed a long sequence of layers of occupation, beginning with the debris from hunter-gatherers and finishing with that from fully-fledged farmers. Between the two extremes was the debris from people who lived by hunting pigs Mesolithic-style and herding sheep Neolithic-style.[7]

This was Peter Rowley-Conwy's conclusion after studying the animal bones. He could tell that the pigs had been wild and hunted by the large size of their bones. Equally, he could tell that the sheep were kept for milking because so many young lambs had been killed. By that means, the milk from the adult females was available for human use. Just like those on Corsica, the Mesolithic people of Arene Candide had merged elements of Neolithic culture with their traditional Mesolithic lifestyle.

In the 1980s, this type of indigenous piecemeal adoption of Neolithic culture was widely believed to have been responsible for the gradual spread of farming across the central and western Mediterranean, and then along the Atlantic façade of Portugal and France and through the major valleys of the Rhône and Garonne. But João Zilhão of Lisbon University has since challenged this belief.[8] He thinks we should return to the ideas popularised by Gordon Childe in the 1930s about immigrant farmers bringing the complete Neolithic package to Mediterranean shores.

According to Zilhão, the evidence from the cave sites, which supposedly show pottery and sheep side by side with hunted animals and Mesolithic tools, has been misinterpreted. These associations, he argues, are caused by burrowing animals that made a complete mess of any stratigraphy that might have survived. He suggests that bones of wild ibex have at times been mistaken for domesticated sheep, and that radiocarbon dates are either plain wrong, having been contaminated, or misinterpreted; also that they have been used to date fragments of pottery with which they have no real association.

Zilhão stresses that the final rise of sea level flooded the coast where the first farmsteads of Neolithic colonists would have been established. The cave sites that have survived were probably no more than occasional camp-sites used by those farmers either on hunting trips, or when taking their flocks to pastures.

To support his case, Zilhão cites evidence from Gruta do Caldeirão. The finds from this Portuguese cave suggest that one or more boatloads of Neolithic colonists arrived at about 5700 BC and established a farming settlement, while the indigenous Mesolithic people continued hunting and gathering quite undisturbed. By 6200 BC, large thriving communities of hunter-gatherers had arisen within the Tagus and Sado river estuaries of central Portugal. They created shell middens equivalent in size to that at Ertebølle in Denmark.[9] Surveys elsewhere in Portugal have failed to find any other traces of a Mesolithic presence after 6200 BC – the entire population, it seems, had come to live within these estuaries.

The Portuguese middens were used as burial grounds as well as rubbish dumps – much like those in Britanny. The graves are predominantly found below the midden layers and appear to have been arranged in discrete clusters, perhaps in family groups. Some graves were lined with large stone slabs, recalling the tombs at Téviec and Hoëdic. Such similarities should not be surprising. Although we lack any direct evidence from the Atlantic seaboard, its Mesolithic communities must have possessed large canoes and used them to travel long distances around the coast, establishing contacts from southern Portugal to northern France.

Between 1979 and 1988 Zilhão excavated Gruta do Caldeirão, located in a region to the north of the shell middens and one with no known Mesolithic sites.[10] Neolithic debris, including pottery and stone tools, was found directly above that of ice-age hunters, along with many bones from domesticated sheep and wild boar. Shepherds who liked to engage in some occasional hunting had evidently used the cave.

Gruta do Caldeirão was also used as a mortuary. At about 5200 BC, the bodies of three men, a woman and a child had been laid on the cave floor, their heads against the wall, for scavenging animals and the elements to decompose, scatter and bury. Two or three hundred years later, at least another fourteen individuals were left within the cave.

According to Zilhão, these bodies were of farmers whose forebears had arrived by boat on the Portuguese coast. Their farmstead, he speculates, was in the valley, its archaeological traces now deeply buried below river sediments. For several hundred years they continued farming while the Mesolithic people continued hunting and gathering within the river estuaries further south, just as they did further north in Spain. Zilhão implies that similar communities of immigrant farmers, forming enclaves quite separate from the indigenous Mesolithic people, were spread throughout the coastal regions of southern Europe. While those using Gruta do Caldeirão flourished, by 5000 BC the Mesolithic middens in the Sado and Tagus estuaries had been abandoned. What happened to their former inhabitants is unknown; they may have died out or simply gave up on the hunting and gathering lifestyle to become farmers themselves.[11]

The dispute between those who favour colonisation by immigrant farmers such as Zilhão, and those such as Lewthwaite and Rowley-Conwy who believe that the indigenous Mesolithic people adopted Neolithic culture, might be resolved by a completely new type of evidence that has recently become available for studying the past: the genetics of those alive today. This new field of study is known as historical genetics and its influence on our study of the past is bound to become ever more widespread and profound. As we will also turn to historical genetics when considering the peopling of the Americas, a brief introduction to this field will be useful before considering its impact on the European question.

The possibility of tracking population history through human genes arises from the fact that although we are all members of a single species, *Homo sapiens*, and have a high degree of genetic similarity, we vary in specific details. The similarity is present because all people in the world today originated from the same small population that lived in Africa no more than 130,000 years ago. The severe environmental conditions of the last but one glacial maximum had caused that population to fall to no more than 10,000 individuals. This reduced the amount of genetic variation present, being known as a population bottleneck. When global warming occurred at 125,000 years ago, that population expanded. Its people dispersed from Africa and the first *Homo sapiens* entered Europe, Asia and eventually the Americas. Any existing populations, such as those of *H. neanderthalensis* in Europe, were entirely replaced without making any contribution to the modern gene pool.

As a result of this evolutionary history, people who are today found at the opposite ends of the earth are very similar in their genetic constitution. But not identical. Random mutations are constantly occurring, most of which have neither positive nor negative effects on our behaviour and physiology. The likelihood that exactly the same mutation could happen independently in two different people is extremely remote. So if two people have the same mutation, it is likely that they shared a recent ancestor within whom this mutation had occurred. And, of course, if those two people are now living in different parts of the world, this enables geneticists to trace the pattern of human dispersal.

There is more. The rate of genetic mutation can be considered to be constant – although whether this is actually the case remains to be established. By measuring the extent of genetic variability between two human populations, and by having an estimate for the rate at which mutations occur, one can calculate the amount of time that has elapsed since the two populations became isolated from each other.

These stark facts have provided the basis for a completely new method of studying the human past – one that has no need for history books or even archaeological excavations. One simply needs to document, and then interpret, the genetic variability found in living humans throughout the world, and then the patterns and dates of past dispersals, migrations, and colonisations can be established. At least that is the theory when stripped of numerous complicating factors. But, as in all areas of science, putting theory into practice is often far harder than anticipated.[12]

Luca Cavalli-Sforza has championed historical genetics. His 1994 book *The History and Geography of Human Genes*, co-written with two collaborators, is one of the key academic landmarks in the development of our approaches to human history.[13] Within that book, Cavalli-Sforza argued that the modern-day genetic map of Europe shows a gradient of gene frequencies from the southeast to the northwest.[14] This could only, he claimed, be a legacy of Neolithic immigrants who spread from Greece, through eastern, central and southern Europe until they reached the far northwest. This became known as the 'wave of advance' model, one that gave the indigenous Mesolithic people no role at all in the development of the European Neolithic. According to this view, the LBK people had to be descended from West Asian immigrants and not from the local Mesolithic people, as Zvelebil has more recently proposed; Zilhão's interpretation of the Mediterranean region has to be preferred over that of Lewthwaite and Rowley-Conwy.

The 'wave of advance' model gained further support in 1987 from another source of non-archaeological evidence: language. Colin Renfew – Grahame Clark's successor as Disney Professor of Archaeology at Cambridge – tackled one of the key problems in historical linguistics: the origin of the Indo-European family of languages. This family includes almost all of the languages spoken in Europe today and linguists have long argued when and where the original language from which they evolved was spoken.[15]

Renfrew provided a compelling answer: proto-Indo-European, as that original language is known, was spoken by the Neolithic people of Anatolia – modern-day Turkey – and/or western Asia in 7500 BC. It spread across the whole of Europe, and some parts of central and southern Asia, as Neolithic migrant farmers colonised these lands. According to Renfrew, the modern-day non-Indo-European languages, such as Basque and Finnish, reflect the regions where Mesolithic populations survived and contributed to the Neolithic, and ultimately modern-day, cultural and linguistic diversity. But these were few and far between: Renfrew's arguments fitted neatly with Cavalli-Sforza's genetic data indicating a 'wave of advance' of immigrant Neolithic farmers across Europe.[16]

Renfrew's claims came in for immediate attack from both linguists and archaeologists[17] – the key problem being that languages can spread quite independently of people. In 1996 the genetic evidence was also questioned. A challenge to Cavalli-Sforza's claims came from Bryan Sykes and his colleagues at Oxford University. They had studied a different type of DNA to the nuclear DNA relied upon by Cavalli-Sforza – mitochondrial DNA – and reached a very different conclusion.[18]

Most of our DNA is found in the nucleus of each cell and is inherited in equal proportions from our mother and father by a process known as 'recombination'. This involves an unpredictable mixing of genes from both parents, and when repeated in generation after generation the possibility of tracing evolutionary history becomes extremely difficult. Mitochondrial DNA (mtDNA) is found within the cell body rather than the nucleus and is inherited from one's mother alone. I acquired my entire mtDNA from my mother, and none of this has been passed on to my children. Without the complexities of recombination, the genetic relatedness between people is much easier to establish and generally thought to be more accurate.

Mitochondrial DNA also has a much higher mutation rate than nuclear DNA, and a much higher frequency of those mutations is quite neutral, neither benefiting nor detracting from the health of the individual. The value of this is simply that there is the potential for gaining a far more detailed picture of human history than from nuclear DNA simply because, as time goes by, more evidence is being laid down by the random mutations that occur. By this means, lineage groups can be identified – groups of people who all descended from the same female, in effect from the same molecule of mtDNA.

When Sykes and his colleagues examined the mtDNA from 821 individuals distributed across Europe, they found that there were six clear lineage groups; this immediately indicated that Europeans are more genetically diverse than the 'wave of advance' model would suggest. By making the best guess-estimate for the rate at which mtDNA mutations occur, Sykes and his colleagues calculated the date at which each European lineage group had arisen. Just one of these was sufficiently recent to relate to the immigration of farmers from western Asia, and this did indeed have some clear genetic markers that pointed to a West Asian origin. Moreover, its geographical distribution in Europe matched the two archaeologically recognised routes of colonisation: central Europe and the Mediterranean coast. But this group only constituted 15 per cent of the total number of lineages within the six groups. All other lineages dated to between 23,000 and 50,000 years ago, indicating that 85 per cent of the existing mtDNA lineages were already present in the Mesolithic, having originated during the preceding ice age.[19] The wave of advance had been nothing but a tiny ripple.

This was a startling conclusion and led to a lively academic debate between Cavalli-Sforza and Sykes, both questioning the validity of each other's methods.[20] A key problem for the mtDNA evidence is that it only tracks the female line. If West Asian immigrants chose to take indigenous Mesolithic women for their wives – as is quite likely – the mtDNA record will soon have failed to register the presence of the immigrants at all.[21] Nevertheless, Sykes's conclusion strengthened the hand of archaeologists such as Zvelebil, Rowley-Conwy and Lewthwaite. If Zilhão really has identified an enclave of immigrant farmers in Portugal at 5700 BC, then they made little contribution to the overall development of the Neolithic in Iberia. For that we must thank the Mesolithic people, whose forebears had occupied the middens in the Sado and Tagus estuaries.

Sykes and Cavalli-Sforza remain in dispute today, but their most recent results have converged and some archaeologists – such as Colin Renfrew – now find their conclusions quite compatible. While Cavalli-Sforza has reduced the contribution of immigrant farmers to the modern European gene pool to 28 per cent, Sykes has increased his estimate of this to a little over 20 per cent. These figures seem too close for any controversy to be sustained and we must conclude that the indigenous Mesolithic people played a role at least as great as that of immigrant farmers in the development of the European Neolithic.[22]

The genes of Mesolithic hunter-gatherers may be dominant among modern Europeans today, but their way of life failed to survive much beyond 4000 BC. Only in the far north of Europe did hunting and gathering have a longer life, continuing until at least 1000 BC, after which pastoralism took over.[23] For the temperate regions, those who feasted, danced and buried their dead in stone-lined tombs at Téviec and Hoëdic were some of the last Mesolithic people in Europe.

The Mesolithic communities of Sweden and Denmark, those who had lived at sites such as Skateholm, Vedbaek, Tybrind Vig and Ertebølle, eventually collapsed under the new ethic of competition introduced by contact with the LBK. The slow and steady seepage of young women as wives and young men as labourers left their communities depleted. Those who remained no longer continued their kinship with the red deer and wild boar; they too wished for material wealth, social power and control of the natural world. They wished to become farmers themselves, and did so at around 3900 BC.

As farmers, they were quite unlike those of the LBK. They herded cattle, used ephemeral Mesolithic-like dwellings and occupied the same shell middens as their Mesolithic forebears. As if to compensate for the absence of domestic architecture, they built huge burial monuments that we call long barrows – choosing to erect houses for the dead rather than for the living. Their inspiration came from the LBK long houses. The long barrows were an attempt by the new farmers to align themselves with the farmers who had originally come from the east, and to deny their own Mesolithic past.[24]

Much the same happened along the Atlantic seaboard when the hunter-gatherers of Téviec and Hoëdic became engulfed by the new farming way of life.[25] Yet another type of Neolithic arose, one in which people constructed tombs from boulders and great slabs of stone. Rather than alluding to the ancestral farmers of the east, these megalithic tombs recalled the Mesolithic past – the stone-slabbed graves within the Portuguese shell middens and the family tombs of Téviec.[26] In the far northwest of Europe, especially Britain, both long barrows and megalithic tombs were integral parts of the new Neolithic culture. By 4000 BC, Europe was almost entirely inhabited by farmers of one sort or another. A new chapter in its history had begun, one that would remove any remaining vestiges of the Mesolithic world. At least, that is what we thought until an unexpected Mesolithic legacy was found within our genes.

22

A Scottish Envoi

Colonisation, Mesolithic lifestyles and the transition to the
Neolithic in western Scotland, 20,000–4300 BC

My account of European history, from the paintings of Pech Merle to the origin of megalithic tombs, has neglected many regions of the continent, ranging from the far south of Italy to northern Norway, and from the Swiss Alps to the Spanish Meseta. Although these regions lacked the cultural drama that occurred elsewhere, they are nevertheless part of the European story and their archaeology provides further insights into how people responded to global warming and the spread of farming.

Unfortunately, all but one must remain neglected, as this history must soon cross the Atlantic to address the beginnings of American history. The one exception is a region where I have myself spent many years searching for the Mesolithic past: Scotland. Not the whole of Scotland, but two off-shore islands at the southernmost end of the Hebridean island chain off the west coast. These are Islay and Colonsay which, together with the adjacent islands of Jura and Oronsay, form a small archipelago known as the southern Hebrides. Although lying on the geographical periphery of Europe and lacking any sites as spectacular as Lepenski Vir or Skateholm, these islands have their own history that contributes to our understanding of Europe as a whole. So, in this envoi for Europe, I will briefly recount their history from the ice age to the Neolithic, via the story of my own excavations on these islands.

The four southern Hebridean islands share many characteristics that are typical of western Scotland, and yet are quite different from each other. They are largely treeless, with rugged coastlines indented with sandy bays. Their populations peaked in the nineteenth century and have slowly declined ever since; sheep farming predominates but is quite uneconomical to pursue. Islay, covering more than 600 square kilometres, is the largest and most diverse, with extensive heather moorlands and sand dunes, a substantial main town, several villages and the highest density of whisky distilleries in Scotland. Colonsay is far smaller, no more than 13 kilometres long and 5 kilometres wide, while Oronsay – connected to Colonsay at low tide – is a tiny speck of land, less than 5 square kilometres in extent. Jura is another large island and much more rugged than Islay, its landscape dominated by three conical peaks known as the Paps.

At 20,000 BC these islands were almost entirely covered by the ice sheet that extended as far south as the English midlands. There was just one ice-free zone – a hill, known today as Beinn Tart a'Mhill, and its surrounding lowlands that now form 'the Rinns', the westernmost peninsula of Islay. The fact that this escaped the ice is crucial for the later history of human occupation. It left flint-rich sediments intact that would eventually supply raw materials to the first inhabitants of Islay and influence where they chose to live.

For five thousand years the slopes of Beinn Tart a'Mhill rose above surrounding landscapes and seascapes of snow and ice. Fifty kilometres to the east the Paps of Jura pierced the ice and looked like smouldering volcanoes when surrounded by cloud. A sea channel cut the Rinns off from the rest of Islay, turning it into a tiny offshore island.

By 15,000 BC the ice had begun to melt; the glacier front retreated eastwards until, by 12,000 BC, the southern Hebrides were completely free of ice. The lowlands of the Rinns were now smothered by great swathes of sand and gravel. To the east there were bare hillocks of rock and sediment – moraines – that marked where the glaciers had once reached, this having been bulldozed into position by the ice. Further east there was a broken jigsaw of bogs, bare rock, sands, silts and gravels before more sea was reached, the stretch of water which still separates Islay from the Scottish mainland.

Within another thousand years a blanket of soil had formed, supporting a mix of grasses and small shrubs – arctic-like tundra. Relieved of its ice mass, the land had elevated in height, making the sea level fall. The channel that had once flowed between the Rinns and the glacier front became shallow and often dry at low tide.

By this date – 11,000 BC – much of England had been recolonised by people following in the footsteps of the pioneers who had butchered their dead at Gough's Cave and caught arctic hares at Creswell Crags. Scotland, however, remained entirely free of settlement until 8500 BC.[1] But exploratory visits had been made from the south; an ice-age hunting party had come to Islay and lost at least one Ahrensburgian arrow-head – a flint point designed in just the same fashion as those used to hunt reindeer at Stellmoor in 10,800 BC.

One of my students found this point on an August afternoon in 1993 as we collected flint artefacts from a ploughed field near the village of Bridgend on Islay.[2] It was placed in a bag along with a number of undistinguished pieces likely to be Neolithic or Bronze Age in date. I didn't find it until a few days later, after it had been washed and left out to dry in our field laboratory. My colleagues, Bill Finlayson and Nyree Finlay, both from the University of Edinburgh and experts on stone tools, agreed that it might be an Ahrensburgian point. But none of us could be sure. If true, it meant that people had been in Scotland two thousand years before any known settlement.

The Bridgend point wasn't the first possible Ahrensburgian arrow-head found in Scotland; five others of a similar design had previously been discovered – two in the Orkney Islands, two in Jura and one in Tiree, another Hebridean island.[3] But these were either broken, of questionable design, or could not be pinpointed to an exact location, having been found long before modern recording methods were adopted. The new specimen was complete, looked identical to an Ahrensburgian point, and we knew exactly where it had been found. And so we immediately went back to the field and made a more intensive collection of its flint, hoping to find the first ice-age settlement in Scotland. But the only artefacts we found were evidently Neolithic or Bronze Age in date.

The field at Bridgend was just one of many that my survey team searched for prehistoric settlements as part of the project I directed on Islay and Colonsay between 1987 and 1995.[4] Although we recorded sites of Neolithic and later periods, my interest lay in finding those of a Mesolithic and – ideally – an ice-age date. The former were relatively easy to discover. We found more than twenty scatters of distinctively Mesolithic artefacts – tools and the debris from their manufacture.

When on Islay I often left my students working in the fields or washing flints and met up with Alistair Dawson from the University of Coventry, a specialist on reconstructing sea-level change in Scotland. Both he and Kevin Edwards, now of the University of Aberdeen, who was studying pollen grains from Islay peat,[5] were attempting to discover what the island had looked like to its former Mesolithic inhabitants.

Alistair is a Scot who seems more at home in the hills or on wild Atlantic beaches than in the laboratory or conference room. He had his own team on the island and extracted long columns of sediment from Gruinart – the lowest-lying part of the island through which the sea channel that once isolated the Rinns had flowed. As his columns went further down, he found that the sediment changed from the modern-day peat to silt and clay laid down by sea water; below this was more peat, a return to dry land, before the sediments became marine deposits once again. In his university laboratory, Alistair extracted diatoms – fossilised plankton – from the sediments; the succession of different types told him about the subtle changes from dry land, to brackish water, marine water and then back again, in the same manner that pollen grains inform about vegetation history. Alistair also removed tiny twigs and other plant material. These were radiocarbon dated to establish exactly when the flooding events had occurred.[6]

By examining the sediments, diatoms and radiocarbon dates, Alistair reconstructed how the sea level around the Hebrides had fallen immediately after the ice sheets disappeared at c. 13,000 BC, to reach a level similar to that of today by 8500 BC. He discovered that within another two millennia the sea level had risen again, flooding the Gruinart channel to isolate the Rinns from the rest of Islay. But western Scotland had not finished rebounding after having been relieved of the great weight of ice and eventually overtook the rising sea. And so, at about two thousand years ago, the channel once again became dry land and has remained so until the present day.

Alistair could also 'read' the modern landscape in order to understand its ice-age past. There were, for instance, the heather-covered hillocks of rock and gravel that marked the furthest westward extent of the glacier. Near by there was a longitudinal mound of sand and gravel that he described as an esker. It marked where there had once been a tunnel of water flowing below the ice itself, which had become choked full with gravel; when the ice melted, what had once been a tunnel was left as its mirror image, a longitudinal, rounded mound. We walked along the beaches and examined ridges of pebbles several metres above the current high-tide mark that showed how the sea level had once been higher than it is today.

When in the uplands of the Rinns, Alistair showed me a thick orange clay that lay below the heather and would have been washed away if the ice sheet had covered the whole of Islay. This clay had been created many thousands of years before the LGM when the whole island lay below a floating ice sheet during an earlier glaciation. Its interest for me lay in the large nodules of flint it contained, carried by a very ancient glacier from deposits of chalk now below the Irish Sea. For many thousands of years the orange sediment had been eroding into the sea; its angular flint nodules were returned to the beaches of the Rinns as perfectly smooth rounded pebbles.[7]

Nowhere else in Scotland could so many and such large and fine-quality flint pebbles be found. As flint was a key raw material for prehistoric hunter-gatherers, I was sure that if ice-age pioneers had come to Scotland they would soon have discovered the Rinns and remained hunting in their vicinity. But alas, almost a decade of survey and excavation on Islay produced no more evidence of ice-age hunters than the single flint point from Bridgend.

The first people to settle in Scotland arrived in 8500 BC, travelling from the north of England and leaving us their earliest-known site at Cramond, near Edinburgh. No sites are known in the southern Hebrides until 7000 BC. When people finally did arrive they were attracted to the Rinns with its rich deposits of flint pebbles. One of their settlements had been located no more than a hundred metres from a flint-rich beach; it had been a Mesolithic workshop where pebbles were first broken apart.

This site became known as Coulererach, having been discovered by Sue Campbell who farms a small croft of the same name on the western coast of Islay. Over a period of several years Sue had collected flint blades, flakes and fractured pebbles from her drainage ditches and handed them to the island museum in a shoebox. When seeing them in 1993, I immediately knew that she had discovered a Mesolithic site. We dug many small 'test-pits' across her pasture to locate the site and then excavated a long trench, having to dig through two metres of peat before reaching the Mesolithic ground surface. It was scattered with tools and tool-making debris, their edges as fresh as the day they had been made.[8]

Nyree Finlay – now of Glasgow University – examined the collection and found some very skilfully worked pebbles along with others that had been simply bashed about. Some pebbles were so small and had so many crystalline inclusions that no experienced flint knapper would have chosen to work them. Nyree suggested that Coulererach had been where children learned to make stone tools, often using the pebbles rejected by the expert flint knappers or finding their own on the beach. It was the Scottish equivalent of Etiolles in France.

Unlike the excavators at Etiolles, however, we were unable to expose large areas of the Mesolithic ground surface in Sue Campbell's pasture as excavation led to permanent water-logging. So although we found fragments of charcoal we never discovered the Mesolithic fireplaces or learned whether huts had been built at Coulererach. All we acquired was a collection of stone artefacts and we had to guess whether activities other than tool-making had once occurred. I suspect they had, as Coulererach is located close to Loch Gorm which is the largest inland lake on Islay. I frequently saw otters and deer around its margins and suspect that the people who camped at Coulererach in 6500 BC had hunted such animals.

At that time the Islay landscape was quite different to the bleak heather-covered peat bogs of today. The pollen grains sealed within and below the Coulererach peat told us that willow and alder had grown in Mesolithic times, together with birch and oak on the higher and drier ground. The peat also contained tiny fragments of charcoal. Some may have been blown from cooking hearths but its quantity suggested the deliberate burning of trees and reeds around the lake – just as had occurred at Star Carr in 9500 BC.[9]

Coulererach was just one of several Mesolithic sites on Islay that we examined. They all produced vast numbers of flint artefacts but unfortunately no bones (animal or human) as these had been destroyed by the acidic soils of the island. Animal bones would have helped us to discover which sites had been used in which season as Peter Rowley-Conwy has done at Skateholm, Ringkloster and many other Mesolithic sites in Europe. Nevertheless, the stone tools and surroundings of each site suggested what activities had taken place there.

In contrast to those from Coulererach, the artefacts we excavated at Gleann Mor, a site located in the uplands and several kilometres from a pebble beach, consisted of many tiny flint cores that had been thrown away at the end of their useful life.[10] This appears to have been a hunting camp used on just one or two occasions when people had been searching for deer within the Rinns. Some of the tools had been made from tiny flakes, most likely the last of a supply that had been carried around the island. From Gleann Mor the hunter-gatherers must have returned to a site like Coulererach to replenish their toolbags.

We found a site on the eastern edge of Gruinart estuary that we called Aoradh after a nearby farm. This was practically adjacent to a bird-watching hide and we guessed that the Mesolithic people had been doing the same as the modern visitors.[11] Gruinart estuary is famed today for its over-wintering flocks of geese that spend each summer in the Arctic – a migratory pattern that probably reaches back to the start of the Holocene. Just like those of the Mesolithic, the modern-day bird-watchers at Gruinart see far more than geese. Seals frequently congregate on the sandbanks within the estuary and otters play in the shallows; wading birds probe in the mud; kestrels and peregrine falcons swoop down to take rodents in the dunes, while red deer can often be seen among the scattered trees. With no signs of the modern world in sight, one can sit at Gruinart and feel close to what Mesolithic eyes had seen.

The quantity of artefacts at Aoradh also suggested that this site had been used on no more than a few occasions; there are probably many similar scatters of artefacts along the banks of the estuary. But another site we excavated, Bolsay, had evidently been a greatly favoured spot, one repeatedly used over several thousand years. Today this site is located in open pasture and close to a boggy marsh known as Loch a'Bhogaidh; in the Mesolithic it had been in woodland, adjacent to a spring, and Loch a'Bhogaidh had been a freshwater lake. The excavation at Bolsay was the largest I undertook, recovering more than 250,000 flint artefacts, which were but a small fraction of those buried in the ground.

At first we thought that Bolsay had been a Mesolithic base camp, but when the tools were analysed we found them dominated by microliths, many of which had been used as arrow-heads.[12] There were few signs of domestic activity, such as tools for cleaning skins and post holes for dwellings. The microliths had apparently accumulated from a multitude of short visits by hunters who had sat by the spring while repairing hunting equipment, enjoying one of the most favoured places on the island.[13]

Excavations at Coulererach, Gleann Mor, Aoradh and Bolsay provided insights into how different locations on Islay had been used for different activities during the Mesolithic. But people had not restricted themselves to one island alone. During the 1960s and 1970s several scatters of microliths had been found on Jura by a dedicated amateur archaeologist called John Mercer.[14] It was on the much smaller island of Colonsay, however, that we gained a quite unexpected insight into Mesolithic life.

Searching for Mesolithic sites on Colonsay is rather like looking for needles in a haystack as it involves looking for microliths in peat bogs and sand dunes. When we began work there were hardly any ploughed fields to examine as almost all farming had already turned from arable to pasture – a transformation that has occurred throughout the Scottish highlands and islands since the 1960s. We spent many weeks digging test-pits through turf, peat and blown sand to reach the Mesolithic ground surface at locations where we guessed a settlement might be found. A few sparse scatters of flint artefacts were recovered, but none contained microliths and all were most likely Neolithic or Bronze Age in date. It began to look as if Colonsay had been completely deserted during Mesolithic times.[15] That would not have been surprising. Owing to its distance from the mainland many mammals had never colonised the island; without red deer, roe-deer and fur-bearers such as fox to hunt, Mesolithic people would have had little incentive to paddle their canoes the twenty kilometres from Islay or Jura to Colonsay.

Our first impressions were quite wrong however. There had been one very good reason to visit the island – as our excavations at Staosnaig, a small bay on the east coast of Colonsay, would show.

I first saw this narrow bay with its sandy beach from the ferry that makes the three-hour sea-crossing from the Scottish mainland. It arrives north of Staosnaig where the tiny settlement of Scalasaig, with its single shop and luxurious hotel, have grown up around the pier. Within a couple of days I had left my student team digging test-pits in the hotel garden to visit Staosnaig where there was one of the few ploughed fields on the island. 'Ploughed field' is perhaps an exaggeration as the soil was thin and sandy; it had been little more than scratched for planting grass seed. The sand came from the Mesolithic beach that now lay directly below the soil and several metres higher than that of the present day. From the ferry, Staosnaig had looked the ideal place for Mesolithic canoes to arrive and I pictured a thriving campsite upon its shore. So I spent a couple of hours searching the plough, confident that I would find flint artefacts. But there were none.[16]

That was in 1988. I spent three weeks on the island with my students inspecting other scanty patches of ploughed land and digging test-pits at likely settlement locations. On our last day I returned to Staosnaig and searched the field again – this time finding a single flint nodule that had evidently been struck by a hammer-stone.

That find led to three more visits to Staosnaig, in the summers of 1989, 1991 and 1992, during which we excavated test-trenches throughout the field in an endeavour to find the settlement that I believed must be there. The first two visits yielded no more than ephemeral traces of washed-out fireplaces and flimsy windbreaks. But perseverance ultimately brought rewards.

In 1994 we opened a large trench that exposed a 4-metre-wide, circular pit packed full of charred hazelnut shells and stone artefacts. It was a remarkable find – nothing like it had ever been found in Scotland. Surrounding this deposit were a series of smaller and deeper pits, every one of them just missed by all of our previous trenches – appalling bad luck. The new excavation took the whole summer, an idyllic time as Colonsay experienced a heat wave and we swam during lunch breaks and by moonlight after barbecues on the beach.

It took another five years to analyse the material we recovered, requiring a variety of specialists to examine the sediments, plant remains and stone artefacts. The large pit had contained not only burnt fragments of hazelnut shell but also the remnants of apple cores and other plants, especially the lesser celandine. This is a member of the buttercup family, the roots and stems of which have been eaten by many traditional peoples, some of whom believed the plant had medicinal properties – one of its other names is pilewort.[17] The large pit itself seemed likely to have once been a hut floor, although there was a frustrating lack of post holes; but it had been primarily used as a rubbish dump. The small pits that surrounded it had once been ovens for the roasting of hazelnuts – the nuts had been sealed below ground and a fire lit above. Both their shells and the nuts that became accidentally burnt were discarded in the dump, along with other plant waste and tool-making debris.[18]

We estimated that the shells of more than 100,000 nuts had been discarded on to the rubbish dump, probably from several annual visits around 6700 BC. Although scatters of charred hazelnut shells are known from sites throughout Mesolithic Europe, they had never been found in such large quantities as at Staosnaig. Hazelnut harvesting and roasting had been undertaken on an almost industrial scale,[19] the hazel woodland having been decimated for its nuts and firewood. Pollen evidence from a loch close to Staosnaig indicates an almost complete collapse of the woodland just after the intense hazelnut harvests had taken place.[20] So these hunter-gatherers were certainly not living 'in balance' with nature. The destruction of woodland on Colonsay which they began was completed by the arrival of its first farmers.

No hazel trees grow on Colonsay today, but its past is recalled in its name. 'Coll' is the Gaelic word for hazel, so the Mesolithic people must have thought of Colonsay as 'hazelnut island'.

The peripatetic lifestyle of Mesolithic hunter-gatherers in the southern Hebrides, moving between settlements on Islay, Jura and Colonsay, continued for more than a thousand years. Our understanding of how it came to an end is intimately tied up with sites on the fourth island – Oronsay. Although minuscule in size, Oronsay contains no fewer than five Mesolithic shell middens. None are known on the other islands. Although originally explored at the end of the nineteenth century, Paul Mellars of Cambridge University undertook the most extensive excavations during the 1970s.[21] He found that the middens had accumulated between 5300 BC and 4300 BC, just before the arrival of the first farmers.

Mesolithic people had come to Oronsay and gathered a variety of shellfish to use as food and fishing bait; they had caught saithe – a type of cod – from their canoes and trapped a great variety of sea birds; seals were hunted and would have been easy prey if the island had been a breeding ground in the Mesolithic, as it is today. Periwinkle shells had been turned into necklaces and, in light of the bone awls that Mellars found – tools suitable for piercing leather – clothing was manufactured. Jumbled among the animal bones, shells, fireplaces and broken artefacts of the middens were fragments of human skeletons, confirming that people had also died on Oronsay. Whether these were the remnants of ceremonially buried bodies or merely another type of discarded rubbish remains unclear.

Some of the smallest finds were the most important, such as the 'otoliths', or ear bones, from saithe. The size of each otolith was a direct reflection of the size of the fish it came from; that in turn indicated the time of year it had been caught. From this evidence, Mellars revealed that different middens on the island had been occupied at different times and at all seasons of the year. He also suggested that people had lived on the island all year round – sedentary hunter-gatherers.[22]

Mellars published the results of his excavations in 1987. At that time I was a graduate student in Cambridge and highly sceptical of his claims. I was sure that Mesolithic Oronsay would have had little to offer hunter-gatherers in comparison to the wealth of resources on the larger Hebridean islands, and that no more than very short and periodic visits would have been made there. One or two visits each year over the course of a millennium could easily have created the shell middens, these being much smaller than those found in Denmark, such as at Ertebølle. And so when I began working on Islay and Colonsay I was confident that I would find settlements contemporary with the Oronsay middens and prove Mellars wrong.

However, as the radiocarbon dates accumulated from my excavations, not one of them fell in the 1,000-year period of the Oronsay middens. Neither did any of the dated Mesolithic sites on Jura. By 1995 I had more than thirty dates, half of which came before 5300 BC and half after 4300 BC. The gap between was completely empty and this was precisely when the middens had accumulated. I soon had to admit that Mellars had probably been right all along.[23] It seems that after having spent almost two thousand years on Islay, Colonsay and Jura, these productive islands were abandoned for the impoverished, windswept speck of Oronsay. Even if visits had been made to the larger islands, these had been so brief and insubstantial that they left no archaeological trace. In 1998, further confirmation of permanent occupation on Oronsay was published by Mellars: the chemical composition of the human bones indicated an entirely marine diet, one of fish, seals, crabs, sea birds and shellfish.[24]

For hunter-gatherers to swap Islay for Oronsay defies ecological sense. Why would they have done this? When searching for a solution I found myself grasping at the archaeologists' last resort: Oronsay must have been preferred for some ideological reason that remains quite unknown to us.

Although we have no rock paintings or carvings, the Mesolithic inhabitants of Scotland are likely to have had a mythology as complex as any other human society. When climbing the Paps of Jura and Beinn Tart a'Mhill, visiting Loch Gorm and the estuary of Gruinart, sitting in the relict oak woodland on Colonsay and walking on its beaches, I always thought that these were as much the haunts of Mesolithic spirits, ghosts and gods as of its people. The landscape was, I am sure, steeped in origin myths and creation stories; these may have been the inspiration for what seems to be an irrational decision about where to live and what to eat.

After 4300 BC people were again living on the larger islands. The hunting camp of Bolsay was in use once more, with microliths being made and discarded. But the new occupants of Bolsay were also discarding broken pottery vessels and ground stone axes. And as if to replace the shell middens of Oronsay, new types of mounds had appeared on Islay: megalithic tombs.

By 4500 BC, immigrant farmers had arrived in the east of Scotland. They built stone houses that foreshadowed the famous village of Skara Brae on Orkney and timber buildings elsewhere that looked like continental LBK long houses.[25] They herded cattle and sheep, grew fields of wheat and barley. Any Mesolithic hunter-gatherers disappeared without trace.

In the west of Scotland the new farming and old hunter-gatherer lifestyles seem to have blended together, just as they had done in the Mediterranean. While distinctive Neolithic burial tombs were made on Islay, Mesolithic sites such as Bolsay continued to be used in much the same way as before.[26] Only scant traces have been found of any crop cultivation so this must have been on a very small scale; there are no Neolithic houses or villages to compare with those from the east. Scatters of Neolithic chipped stone are sparse, rarely having more than a few hundred pieces – a dramatic contrast to the many thousands of artefacts found at almost any Mesolithic site.

The Neolithic people in the southern Hebrides and elsewhere in western Scotland were nomadic sheep and cattle herders who continued to hunt wild game and collect plant foods. But as if to distinguish themselves from Mesolithic hunter-gatherers, they refused to eat marine foods. At least, that is the indication from the chemistry of the few Neolithic bones that have been recovered from burial tombs.[27] The resources of shellfish, marine mammals and fish that had sustained people on Oronsay were simply ignored. As with the decision of Mesolithic hunter-gatherers to live on Oronsay, this seems to defy economic sense.

What had happened to those Mesolithic people of Oronsay? Had their populations simply withered away? Or had they mixed with new Hebridean arrivals by exchanging goods, providing labour, and by marriage? Both are possibilities, but I suspect a third. My guess is that the people on Oronsay became the Neolithic farmers themselves; they acquired new ideas, new tools and new animals from people in the east and returned to the larger islands. Just like their ancestors had done, they sat by the spring at Bolsay and chipped stone into microliths; but this time there were cattle browsing near by.

THE AMERICAS

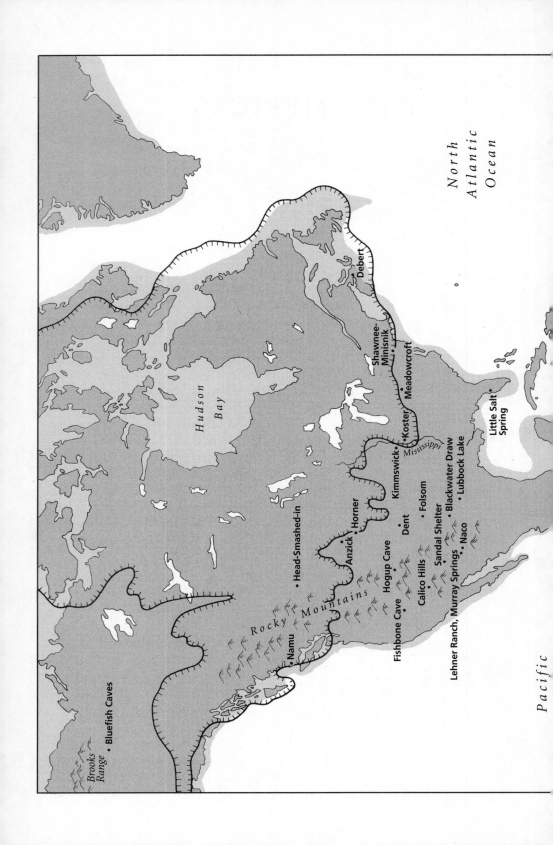

Brooks
Range • Bluefish Caves

Hudson
Bay

North
Atlantic
Ocean

Debert

Shawnee-
Minisnik

Koster• Meadowcroft

Mississippi

Little Salt
Spring

• Head-Smashed-in

Kimmswick•

Anzick• Horner

Hogup Cave • Dent

Fishbone Cave

Calico Hills • Folsom

Sandal Shelter

Blackwater Draw

• Namu

Rocky Mountains

Murray Springs • Naco

Lehner Ranch,

Lubbock Lake

Pacific

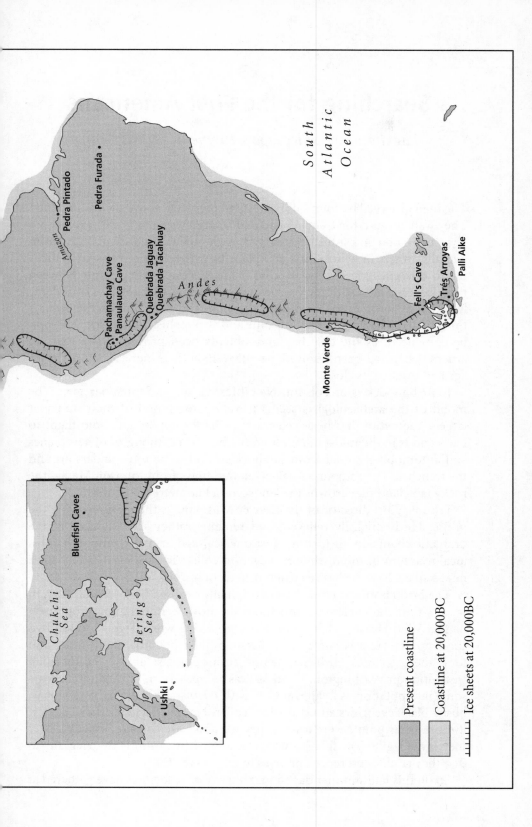

South Atlantic Ocean

Amazon

Pedra Pintado
Pedra Furada

Pachamachay Cave
Panaulauca Cave
Quebrada Jaguay
Quebrada Tacahuay

Andes

Monte Verde

Fell's Cave
Trés Arroyas
Palli Aike

Chukchi Sea

Bluefish Caves

Bering Sea

Ushki I

Present coastline

Coastline at 20,000BC

Ice sheets at 20,000BC

23

Searching for the First Americans

The discovery of ice-age settlement, AD 1927–1994

The men observed by John Lubbock stand pensively above the bison bones. They walk around the trench, bend and scrape away a little soil, exchange a few words, nod and smile knowingly at each other. Some are in blue denim overalls, others in white shirts and black bow-ties. Their eyes keep returning to the centrepiece: a spear point made of stone, sitting firmly between two ribs. One man appears to have made up his mind; he strides confidently across to another, shakes him by the hand and slaps him on the back. A third man draws deeply upon his pipe and strokes his chin; he too will soon be convinced, as the case has undoubtedly been proven. Forty years of ardent debate has been resolved: people were in the Americas before the ice age had reached its close.

John Lubbock is at Folsom, New Mexico, on 30 September 1927. The mood of the archaeologists seems to reflect the mood of the country at large – the nation has been celebrating Charles Lindbergh's solo flight to Paris and is in the midst of an economic boom. Yet thoughts of aeroplanes and automobiles are far from Lubbock's mind as he too wanders around the trenches. They adjoin a small creek that flows from Johnson Mesa – the rocky tableland that crowns the landscape a kilometre to the west.

Jesse Figgins, director of the Denver Museum,[1] is the man receiving the praise. He is mightily relieved, and remains rather shell-shocked at the dramatic change in his fortune. Just one year ago he had no more than his local museum in mind when he began to collect ice-age bison bones for a new display. Now he has rewritten American history.

The bison bones at Folsom were originally exposed by torrential rains in 1908 within the ancient sediments of the now seemingly inappropriately named Wild Horse Valley. Soon after beginning work, Figgins found two spear points. He was immediately aware of their potential importance and took them to Aleš Hrdlička, senior anthropologist at the Smithsonian Institution in Washington. Hrdlička was a Czech-born immigrant, as fearsome in reputation as in appearance, with swept-back hair, furrowed brow, bushy black eyebrows and stiff white collar. He gave Figgins crucial advice: if more spear points were found, they were to be left *in situ*, exactly where they lay. Figgins was then to notify academic institutions by telegram so that they could send representatives to inspect the finds.

So on this late summer day in 1927 a party of academics have gathered at

Folsom – with Lubbock as a privileged onlooker. It includes the pipe-smoking A. V. Kidder, one of the most respected archaeologists of his time, Frank Roberts, a graduate student with a distinguished future, and Barnum Brown, a palaeontologist from the American Natural History Museum. Lubbock watches as Brown clutches a stone point to his starched white shirt and declares that 'the answer to the antiquity of man in the New World is in my hand'.[2]

Barnum Brown was wrong; but his rashness can be forgiven. That sentiment has most likely been felt, if not expressed, by a great many American archaeologists during the last 150 years. Although the Folsom discoveries proved that people were in the Americas before the end of the ice age, the date of their arrival remains unknown – 12,000, 20,000, 30,000, 50,000 BC, or even earlier? Nobody can yet provide a definitive account of how and when the first people arrived in the Americas. I have little doubt, however, that this occurred after the great freeze of 20,000 BC; it was one of the key consequences of global warming for human history.

In place of that definitive account, John Lubbock must visit some of the most intriguing archaeological sites of the ice-age world, from northern Alaska to southern Chile. As he travels between these sites there is a remarkable story to tell, that of the history of prehistory in the Americas – the passions, ingenuity, hard work and sometimes sheer luck of those attempting to establish exactly when the first Stone Age footsteps were made on the last of the habitable continents to be colonised. Robson Bonnichsen, Director of the Centre for the Study of the First Americans, Oregon, described those footsteps as 'the ultimate pioneering event … a brave new people in a brave new world'.[3] From empty continent to global superpower – the ultimate American Dream.

David Meltzer of Southern Methodist University, Texas, one of the fore-most scholars of American prehistory and a historian of archaeological thought, has shown that debates about the First Americans go back to the very beginning of modern America itself. The first contact between European explorers and the Native Americans took place at the end of the fifteenth century. The new arrivals asked the obvious questions: Who were these indigenous people? Where had they come from?

The stock answer for more than three hundred years was that they were one of the Ten Lost Tribes of Israel. In 1590 Fray Joseph de Acosta speculated that this wandering tribe had made an overland migration and arrived in the north of the continent, at a meeting-place between the Old and New Worlds. Meltzer has meticulously documented how such speculations developed up until the discoveries at Folsom.[4] Some of the nineteenth-century scholars – such as Charles Abbott, a physician and keen amateur archaeologist from Trenton, New Jersey – had been adamant that a Stone Age race of people using primitive tools had once inhabited the Americas.

Others were ardently against such views, notably William Henry Holmes of the Bureau of American Ethnology. He was a member of the archaeological establishment and was partly motivated by the audacity of an amateur like Abbott making claims about the human past.

One spur to this debate was the demonstration of human antiquity in Europe, through the discovery of human artefacts in association with the bones of extinct animals. *Prehistoric Times* had explained the significance of such finds, establishing that people had lived in Europe during the ice age – even though nobody knew quite how long ago that had been. Victorian John Lubbock had also devoted a chapter to 'North American Archaeology', being keenly interested in the age of its monuments, burials and artefacts.[5] He was sceptical of two claims for the association of human artefacts with extinct animals in North America, concluding that there was no need to believe that people had been in that continent for more than three thousand years. But he was careful not to reject the possibility of more ancient settlement; he simply noted that the required evidence did not currently exist.

The measured tone of *Prehistoric Times* was typical of an English gentleman writing at a distance – Victorian John Lubbock never crossed the Atlantic. Those Americans at the forefront of the debate, such as Abbott and Holmes, used somewhat harsher language and held dogmatic views. This led David Meltzer to name the few decades before the Folsom discovery as the 'Great Palaeolithic War' – the level of acrimony, accusations of incompetence, and plain insults between the protagonists, makes our current debates about human origins seem the most genial of affairs.

It is not surprising, therefore, that Jesse Figgins felt anxious when several of those protagonists gathered to inspect his excavations on 30 September 1927. His discovery of spear points amid bison bones was quite unexpected, even by those who were ardent supporters of ice-age Americans. They had been anticipating the discovery of crude chopping tools and human remains with 'primitive' features, similar to those possessed by the Neanderthals of Europe. But the skilfully-made stone spearheads found at the Folsom site bore witness to sophisticated hunting.

The spear points were about 6 centimetres long, made by flaking from both faces (a technique known as bifacial working), and had a long groove – a flute – reaching from the base almost to the tip. They became known as Folsom points and the term Palaeo-indian was introduced. Today we know that Folsom points had been made and used between 11,000 and 9000 BC.[6] Within a decade of the Folsom excavation many similar sites were discovered. Now that people knew what to look for, they only needed to explore old river channels and lake sediments for the bones of extinct animals and then search among them for human artefacts.

In 1933 a site was found close to Dent in Colorado.[7] Mammoths rather than bison had been the prey, and the spear points were larger than those at

Folsom. The points soon came to characterise a new culture: 'Clovis'. This name came from a small town in New Mexico near the site of Blackwater Draw where further points and mammoth remains were also found during the 1930s.[8] The Clovis points were larger, had a flute that reached only to the middle of the point and bases ground by a coarse stone to facilitate hafting. The association with mammoths – believed to have gone extinct before the bison from Folsom – suggested that they predated any previous discovery. The excavations at Blackwater Draw confirmed this by providing deposits in which Folsom points and bison bones lay directly above those containing Clovis points and mammoth bones.[9]

During the 1950s several Clovis sites were excavated in the San Pedro river valley of southern Arizona. In 1953 no fewer than eight Clovis points were found intermingled with the near-complete skeleton of a single mammoth at Naco.[10] There were no other archaeological remains and this was soon christened as 'the one that got away' – a mammoth that had been attacked, wounded but then escaped to die unrecovered. Two years later, twelve spear points were found with the remains of eight mammoths at Lehner Ranch, just a few kilometres from Naco.[11]

By the 1970s, numerous radiocarbon dates for Clovis sites were available, indicating that none were older than 11,500 BC.[12] With no traces of any earlier settlement, the Clovis culture appeared to be that of the first Americans. They were the pioneers who originated in Northeast Asia and made that heroic journey first proposed by Fray Joseph de Acosta: across the now flooded land mass of Beringia, that which had joined Siberia and Alaska when the sea level had reached its ice-age low, and then southwards as soon as the ice sheets covering the whole of Canada had begun to melt. There had been two of these: the Laurentide to the east and the Cordilleran to the west. When they began to melt, an 'ice-free corridor' was created between them, through which the Clovis hunters had supposedly passed into the landscapes of North America.

The discovery of sites such as Naco and Lehner Ranch soon led the Clovis people to be characterised as much more than mere pioneers. They had evidently tackled mammoths with no more than stone-tipped spears, and were believed by many to have pushed them into extinction – an idea that became known as the 'overkill hypothesis'. The most ardent supporter of both 'Clovis First' and 'overkill' was – and still is – Paul Martin of Arizona State University. He argues that Clovis hunters arrived at the southern end of the ice-free corridor by 11,500 BC. From there they spread through the woodlands, across the plains and into the forests of both North and South America within a few hundred years, pushing not just mammoths but many other types of giant animal species into extinction.[13]

It is easy to make the postmodernist claim that Paul Martin was simply writing the ideal of the American hero into the Clovis past, but this would be quite unfair. In the 1970s, the 'Clovis First' scenario was the most reasonable interpretation of the existing evidence. It had, however, already been challenged by archaeologists claiming to have discovered pre-Clovis sites on the American continent. Louis Leakey, the revered scholar of human origins in Africa, claimed to have discovered 'primitive' human artefacts at Calico Hills in the Californian Mojave Desert. He was wrong – they were nothing but broken river cobbles.[14] But by the late 1970s far more substantial claims for pre-Clovis settlement had arisen.

It is AD 1978 and John Lubbock finds himself in the Yukon valley, just inside the Arctic Circle. His destination is the far northwest, the land which had remained free of ice throughout the LGM, that of eastern Beringia which today we call Alaska. If people were hunting mammoths at Lehner Ranch in southern Arizona at 11,500 BC, then surely this must be where their ancestors will be found – those who first crossed the now flooded land bridge from Asia.

It is midsummer, the sky remaining light throughout day and night. The high peaks of the Brooks range to the north, the Alaska range to the south and the MacKenzies to the east, protect this landscape, providing it with a modicum of summer warmth. Alaska is vast – almost five times the area of the British Isles but with a population less than one twentieth of London's.

Lubbock has travelled between rolling hills and low mountains, through river basins and endless miles of cottongrass scrub. He has seen many flocks of geese overhead, wolf and bear. But the only creatures on his mind are the demonic mosquitoes and horseflies. These must be tolerated so that he can visit Bluefish Caves in the northwest of the Yukon where, in this year of 1978, another claim to have broken the Clovis Barrier is about to be made.[15]

Lubbock finds the caves after travelling along the Bluefish River to a point about 50 kilometres southwest of Old Crow village. The sides of the spruce-clad valley slope up towards a jagged limestone ridge. He scrambles between the trees and finds the excavation under way. There are two small caves in the base of the crags; the mouth of one is surrounded by buckets, spades and trowels.

This is the work of Jacques Cinq-Mars and his associates of the Archaeological Survey of Canada. Cinq-Mars had first seen the caves when making a helicopter reconnaissance of the Bluefish River in 1975. Today he is digging in one of the caves, thickly clothed as a joint protection against the cold wind and mosquito plague. Outside, there is a growing pile of excavated sediment consisting of loess – wind-blown silt – and rocks that had once collapsed from the roof of the little cave.

Tables, chairs, boxes, sieves, notebooks and the other paraphernalia of excavation are set out in the shelter of the trees. Someone sits and writes labels for large excavated bones, the codes carefully copied into notebooks. The bones are secured inside crates in preparation for the long journey to the laboratory. There are several boxes of heavily fragmented bone, labelled to indicate the layer and area of the cave in which they were found. The bones come from an immense variety of animals: mammoth, bison, horse, sheep, caribou, bear and cougar, together with many small animals, birds and fish. Several specimens are covered in tooth- and gnaw-marks – the debris left by wolves and bears that had used the cave for shelter during ice-age times.

There are also stone artefacts, small flakes and the remnants of the nodules from which they had been detached. Similar types of tools have already been found elsewhere in Alaska and designated as the Denali culture, shown to be no older than 11,000 BC.

A third type of find is being inspected, sorted and labelled: animal bones which are believed by Cinq-Mars to have been shaved and whittled by human hands. When radiocarbon dates are acquired, these 'worked bones' – found immediately next to the stone tools – will be dated to earlier than 20,000 BC.

At the time of Lubbock's visit, these dates are unknown to Cinq-Mars. But he works with the conviction that his discoveries reveal a pre-Clovis settlement in the Americas. Lubbock squeezes inside the cave and experiences the cramped, dark and stuffy working conditions. Rather than being horizontal and neatly stacked, the layers of sediment dip and rise, start and stop in an erratic fashion – almost impossible to decipher. His thoughts are with the wolves that have made their dens within the cave and disturbed the layers, and with the rodents who burrowed through the soft sediments. Tiny stone flakes could easily have moved with them and mingled with bones brought by wolves to the cave several thousands of years before people had come to chip at their nodules of stone.

Ever since the 'worked bones' were found, archaeologists have debated whether the smooth edges were really made by human hands. They might have arisen from constant licking by animals close to starvation, or even by wind or by water before the bone had been scavenged from a rotting carcass and brought in desperation to the cave. If so, the scavenger could have been either man, woman or beast. Almost thirty years after conducting his excavations, Cinq-Mars remains convinced that the smooth-edged bones are true human artefacts and demonstrate that people were present in Alaska before the LGM. I have not seen the bones, but from their descriptions I remain a sceptic – nature seems the most likely workman.

Bluefish Caves is the only site in the whole of Alaska which can make any claim to pre-11,500 BC settlement, and this is sufficiently weak to allow confident dismissal. If such sites are absent in Alaska – or eastern Beringia as we should call it – the likelihood that they exist further south seems limited. Their absence in Alaska cannot be explained by a lack of fieldwork, as might have been expected in such a challenging landscape. Intensive archaeological survey has found more than twenty sites – past camping places – of ice-age date. Several of these are deeply buried in loess with undisturbed scatters of artefacts, fireplaces and butchered animal bones. But not one of these dates to earlier than 11,500 BC.[16]

In fact, the situation for the pre-Clovis advocates is far worse than the absence of evidence from Alaska; there are no known sites in the whole of Siberia – which formed the western portion of Beringia – with an age greater than 15,000 BC. Hunter-gatherer communities were certainly established in Siberia by this date, and it is reasonable to imagine that they eventually spread into Alaska across what to them was a quite invisible and unknown inter-continental barrier. People arriving at that date, however, could not have travelled southwards owing to the massive ice sheets that isolated Alaska from the rich tundra and thick woodlands of North America. The ice-free corridor is unlikely to have been passable until 12,700 BC; if a gap between the ice sheets had existed prior to this, it would have been too inhospitable for travel, lacking in any resources for firewood and food.[17]

But if that is the case, how can there be stone artefacts dated to 16,000 BC at Meadowcroft Rockshelter in Pennsylvania? This is the next contentious site we must consider, one that lay to the south of the Laurentide ice sheet.

In 1973 James Adovasio, from the University of Pittsburgh in Pennsylvania, began excavating a small cave in Cross Creek Valley, a tributary of the Ohio River.[18] Adovasio was to spend the next thirty years studying and debating the significance of Meadowcroft Rockshelter, for the peopling of the Americas – and he is still going strong. His excavations exposed 5 metres of neatly layered sediments from which many radiocarbon dates were acquired. The lowermost layers date to around 30,000 BC and lack any sign of a human presence. Above these is a layer dating to about 21,000 BC, within which a knot of plaited fibres, possibly a fragment of a basket, was found. The next layers have been dated to 16,000 BC and contained what are unquestionably stone tools made by human hands.

Many animal and bird bones were found in the cave; some would have been from roosting owls, denning carnivores and burrowing rodents; others are undoubtedly the remnants of human prey. At face value, Meadowcroft seems to demonstrate human settlement in the Americas by 16,000 BC – at least 5000 years before the date of the first Clovis points. But before we can relinquish the 'Clovis First' theory, a couple of problems must be resolved.

The geology around Meadowcroft is riddled with coal deposits. If coal dust had blown into the cave or seeped into the sediments through groundwater, then the charcoal samples used for dating may have become contaminated. They could easily appear to be several thousands of years older than is really the case. Adovasio rejects such claims by explaining that none of the carbon-rich deposits in the vicinity are water soluble, and that the amount of contamination required to alter a date of, say, 10,000 BC to 16,000 BC would be so great that no dating laboratory could possibly make such an error.

The animal bones also raise a question. At 16,000 BC the cave would have been no more than 80 kilometres from the edge of the Laurentide ice sheet, and hence, one assumes, surrounded by barren tundra. But the Meadowcroft animal bones are from deer, chipmunk and squirrel; the type of animals that live in thickly wooded landscapes. If the radiocarbon dates are correct, shouldn't these come from animals such as mammoth, arctic hare and lemming?

Adovasio accepts that the bones supposedly dating from 16,000 BC come from woodland-living animals, and that oak, hickory and walnut had grown around the cave when it was first occupied. But this, he argues, was because of its particularly sheltered location – Cross Creek Valley today has up to fifty more frost-free days a year than the surrounding area. So even at the height of the ice age, trees and woodland animals could have survived in the vicinity of the shelter, providing hunting-and-gathering opportunities for the First Americans.

By 1993 Adovasio was able to declare that Meadowcroft had become 'the most intensively studied, most extensively written about, and most thoroughly dated of all the putative pre-Clovis sites known in the Americas'.[19] Testing and re-testing of his charcoal samples, and microscopic study of the sediments, has produced no traces of contamination of the charcoal samples from the earliest levels.[20]

But serious doubts remain. If people were at Meadowcroft at 16,000 BC, how did they get there?

An answer to this question had in fact been proposed in the 1970s by Knut Fladmark: the First Americans, coming from Siberia, had bypassed the North American ice sheets by travelling around the coast.[21] This idea has become popular with two archaeologists from the University of Alberta, Ruth Gruhn and Alan Bryan. Rather than arriving via the ice-free corridor, they claim that the First Americans had simply walked or sailed around the west coast, or even crossed the Bering Sea in boats from Kamchatka to California.[22] Consequently, the key sites indicating how people reached Meadowcroft at 16,000 BC have been submerged by the rise of sea level as the ice age came to its end.

As the extent of glaciation is likely to have made any coastal or sea routes impossible between 30,000 and 16,000 years ago, Bryan and Gruhn argue that colonisation most likely happened around 50,000 years ago. To support their claim, they point to the greater diversity of Native American languages found on the northwest coast than elsewhere, which they believe reflects the longevity of human settlement in this region. When one of the first classifications of American languages was made in 1891, no less than twenty-two of the identified fifty-eight language families were found in California.[23]

But if the First Americans had arrived by a coastal route 50,000 years ago, and even if their early coastal settlements have been flooded by rising sea level, why is the earliest sign of their presence at a mere 16,000 BC at Meadowcroft Rockshelter? Could the First Americans have spent more than 30,000 years without travelling inland from the coast? Even to Bryan and Gruhn this seems unlikely. Hence they have a second argument for the absence – or, if one is a Meadowcroft fan, the extreme rarity – of pre-Clovis sites: the First Americans were living in small, highly mobile groups, scattered across the continent at low densities. The archaeological sites they left were highly ephemeral – so Bryan and Gruhn claim – and even if such sites did survive the rigours of time, the chance of their discovery and accurate dating is minimal. The sudden appearance of archaeological sites across the continent at around 11,500 BC reflects, according to Bryan and Gruhn, the passing of a population-level threshold after which a sufficient number of sufficiently large settlements were created to have left a recognisable archaeological record.[24]

Such arguments can appear compelling. But without further early settlements to support the claims from Meadowcroft, and ideally to extend the time of the First Americans to before 20,000 BC, they are not persuasive. And yet, just as Adovasio was completing his major work at Meadowcroft, a new claim was made for precisely that – a site that dated the First Americans to at least 40,000 years ago. This site is called Pedra Furada and is found further from the northern ice sheets not only than Meadowcroft but also the Clovis sites of southern Arizona.

It is 1984 and John Lubbock has travelled to a remote region of northeast Brazil, the state of Piauí with its distinctive caatinga – dry and thorny – woodland and sandstone cliffs. These have many small caves with wall-paintings of the local animals: deer, armadillos and capybaras. Some paintings are hunting scenes with little stick figures; others depict sex and violence. Lubbock finds it a deeply unpleasant land – poverty ridden, dry, hot, and brimming with biting insects and creeping dangers.

The archaeologist that Lubbock is about to visit is Niède Guidon of the École des Hautes Études en Sciences Sociales in Paris. She has worked in northeast Brazil for more than twenty years, principally making a survey of the rock shelters and documenting the art. In a bid to find out when the paintings were made, she began excavating in one of the largest and most brilliantly decorated sites, that known as Pedra Furada.[25] That was in 1978 and now, six years later, her excavations have reached quite momentous proportions. And, as Guidon claims to have evidence that people lived at Pedra Furada more that 40,000 years ago, her interest has shifted from the paintings – which date to around 10,000 BC – to human antiquity.

Lubbock first sees the site from a distance, or rather he sees the sandstone cliff rising above the thorn trees and cacti scrubland. When he arrives, the rockshelter is of a daunting size; he leans back and feels dizzy below the massive towering, tilted wall of stone, rising more than 100 metres to the escarpment above. This shelters an area about 70 metres wide and 18 metres deep, within which the archaeologists are working. There is Guidon herself – a tough lady who survived an attack of two hundred stings by Brazil's infamously aggressive 'killer bees' – inspecting a drawing of the site; she is as energetic and as committed to the excavations as on the day when she first arrived.[26]

Her work has evidently been on a scale to match the shelter itself; more than 5 metres of deposits have been removed from the shelter floor, much of which has been dumped within the trees beyond the excavation. Columns of the floor deposits, bulwarked by cobble walls, have been left as a reference both for the archaeologists themselves and for any visitors wishing to inspect the site. Drawings and photographs are being made to ensure that there is an accurate record of the sequence of layers from which the artefacts have come.

Lubbock has a splendid view of their work from a catwalk positioned just above the original height of the floor level and adjacent to the rock face with its many red-and-white paintings. Massive boulders that had once collapsed from the overhang mark the extent of the sheltered area. At both sides there are heaps of pebbles and small boulders that have evidently eroded from the top of the cliff. Stains on the walls show that water has flowed from above; at times this must have been persistent as there are plunge pools scoured out of the bedrock below.

Although a claim for 40,000-year-old settlement had been made by the early 1990s, detailed reports on the site specifying exactly where the stone artefacts had been found, their relationship to the dated pieces of charcoal, and drawings of supposed fireplaces, had not appeared. Aware of her critics, Guidon invited them to visit the site and inspect the artefacts themselves. Unlike the visit made by distinguished academics to Folsom in 1927, the excavations at Pedra Furada had already been completed by the time three acknowledged experts – David Meltzer, James Adovasio and Tom Dillehay – arrived in December 1993. And Lubbock missed their visit – he departed from Pedra Furada in 1985, heading to Dillehay's own purported pre-Clovis settlement of Monte Verde in southern Chile.

Had Lubbock remained, he would have watched Meltzer, Adovasio and Dillehay make close inspections of the columns, examine the thick layers of charcoal and frown when they found the columns packed full of naturally broken cobbles rather than true artefacts; he would have seen them collect discarded stones from the dirt heaps among the trees and look even more concerned when they found that these were little different to those claimed by Guidon as stone artefacts. Lubbock would also have seen them inspect the water stains on the cave walls, wondering how flowing water might have influenced the layout of rocks and distribution of artefacts within the shelter.

Meltzer and his colleagues came to Pedra Furada with open minds, and left unconvinced. They thought that the stone artefacts could easily be quartzite cobbles that had become broken by the forces of nature rather than the hammer-stones of the First Americans.[27] Meltzer found the source of the cobbles at the top of the cliff, 100 metres above the cave; from here, they had clearly been falling over the edge, to smash on the ground below.

The three archaeologists could find no evidence for contamination of the charcoal samples, as might be the case at Meadowcroft. They readily accepted that many pieces of charcoal really were more than 40,000 years old, but did that charcoal have anything to do with human activity? Arid scrubland, which has surrounded Pedra Furada for at least 50,000 years, is susceptible to natural forest fires created by lightning. If such fires had broken out close to the cave, the resulting wood charcoal could easily have been blown or washed into the sediments. Indeed, the thick and diffuse layers of charcoal in the cave looked to Meltzer quite unlike the thin, concentrated lenses of charcoal seen in authenticated fireplaces at other sites, and indeed at Pedra Furada itself from 10,000 years ago.[28]

In their 1994 report, David Meltzer and his colleagues concluded that they were 'sceptical of the claims for a Pleistocene human presence at Pedra Furada'.[29] That was a measured and generous conclusion, offered with many constructive suggestions to Guidon and her team as to how she could support her assertions – such as by demonstrating how artefacts can be distinguished from naturally broken cobbles. Unfortunately Guidon reacted aggressively to the report, claiming that their 'commentaries are worthless' being based on 'partial and incorrect knowledge'.[30] Having written about the 'Great Palaeolithic War' of the nineteenth century, David Meltzer had become a rather unwilling protagonist in its modern counterpart.

24

American Past in the Present

Dental, linguistic, genetic and skeletal evidence for the peopling of the Americas

While Lubbock is travelling to Monte Verde in southern Chile we must trace other developments in the search for the First Americans. At the end of the 1970s a fundamental shift began in the study of the American past: no longer was it possible to rely on archaeological evidence alone. Linguists and geneticists who were studying living Native Americans also became prehistorians and started asking when the First Americans arrived, and where they came from. And so too did dentists.

The notion of a 'dental prehistory' may sound bizarre but its study is very informative. People's teeth vary in shape and size; incisors come with a particular set of ridges and grooves; the number of roots to each molar can vary, as do the number of cusps. These traits are heavily determined by our genes and evolve very slowly – so two people with similar dental patterns are likely to be closely related.

Christy G. Turner II, an anthropologist from Arizona State University, became a dental prehistorian more than twenty years ago by collecting information about the teeth of Native Americans, and comparing them to the teeth of people throughout the Old World.[1] By 1994 he had measured more than 15,000 sets of teeth. On each set he measured twenty-nine different features such as the length of roots and the shape of crowns. Most of the teeth had belonged to Native Americans prior to European contact and had come from prehistoric burials. That was important, as any new genes arriving into the American gene pool from interbreeding with Europeans, or at a later date with Africans, might have influenced the dental patterns he studied.

The question Turner asked was simple: in which part of the Old World do we find people with dental patterns most similar to those of Native Americans? Although he relied on complex statistical methods, the answer itself was straightforward: northern Asia, and more particularly north China, Mongolia and eastern Siberia. These people share such a distinctive dental pattern with Native Americans that Turner called them all 'sinodonts', contrasting them with people from elsewhere in Asia, Africa and Europe, all of whom he named 'sundadonts'. As such, he was confident that northern Asia was the original homeland of Native Americans.

Differences were also present within the dentistry of the North American sinodonts themselves. Turner identified three distinct groups which, he suggested, related to three different migration events, beginning around 12,000 BC – an idea that really took root when evidence was added from Native American languages.

For more than two hundred years linguists have been trying to reconstruct the history of contacts between human communities and their patterns of migration. They look to the similarities and differences between languages, seeking to group these together into families and then to trace patterns of descent – in much the same way as biologists seek to classify animal species into families and search for evolutionary relationships. Such work should ideally be combined with archaeological study – as we saw Colin Renfrew attempting to do by relating the spread of the Indo-European languages to that of Neolithic farmers across Europe.

The potential for a linguistic prehistory of the New World is considerable, owing to its great number of languages. More than a thousand have been recorded since the time of European contact and six hundred of these are still spoken today. Attempts to classify them into families and to trace their origins began more than three hundred years ago. In 1794 Thomas Jefferson wrote: 'I endeavour to collect all the vocabularies I can, of American Indians, as those of Asia, persuaded, that if they ever had a common parentage, it will appear in their languages.'[2]

Since the 1960s, these attempts have revolved around arguments put forward by the Stanford University linguist Joseph Greenberg. In the late 1950s Greenberg was shifting his attention away from the classification of African languages, on which he had built his reputation, to those of the Native Americans. By the mid-1980s he had concluded that these could be grouped into three families: Eskimo-Aleut, consisting of ten languages and restricted to the Arctic region of North America; Na-Dene, with thirty-eight languages found principally in the far northwest of America, including Native American groups such as the Tlingit and the Haida; and, controversially, Amerind which included all the remaining languages of North, Central and South America.[3]

Greenberg reached this classification by searching for similarities in the sounds and meanings of the basic vocabularies of each language he studied, such as in the words which name parts of the body. He argued that each of the language families derived from a separate migration of peoples into the Americas. The first was of a people who spoke 'proto-Amerind' – the suffix 'proto-' being the conventional way to refer to a language that no longer exists but which was the source from which existing languages have diverged. Greenberg claimed that this first migration event occurred at around 11,500 BC and is represented archaeologically by the Clovis culture. The origins of the people remained unclear; proto-Amerind was said to have similarities with languages found very widely dispersed across Europe and Asia (referred to by linguists as the 'Eurasiatic complex') and hence arose in a time before existing language families had become established.

The next arrival, occurring at about 10,000 BC, was of a people speaking proto-Na-Dene and represented archaeologically by new types of stone tools, referred to by archaeologists as the Denali culture: that which Cinq-Mars excavated at Bluefish Caves in 1978. Greenberg believed that its source had been in Indo-China. Then, about five hundred years later, the final migration happened. These people spoke proto-Eskimo-Aleut, and were believed to have originated in northern Asia.

The idea of this three-event colonisation was published in the late 1980s. It was greeted with acclaim by some academics and despair by others. The most significant article was in the journal *Current Anthropology* in 1986,[4] in which Greenberg collaborated with Turner and a colleague of his, Stephen Zegura, who had been studying patterns in the distribution of specific genes within Native Americans.

Greenberg and his collaborators made a powerful argument. They proposed that those Native Americans within each language family also shared specific patterns in their genes and dental anatomy. In other words, three independent lines of evidence converged to substantiate the claim for three discrete migrations to the Americas, with the first relating to the appearance of the Clovis culture. Finding such a convergence of evidence from diverse sources is the aspiration of all those wanting to establish the truth about American colonisation. But many thought that it was just too good to be true.

Ives Goddard of the Smithsonian Institution and Lyle Campbell of Louisiana University are two vehement critics.[5] They argue that the supposed anatomical-genetic-linguistic correlations do not exist – a close inspection of the data shows a mismatch in distributions, a fact which is actually acknowledged by Greenberg and his collaborators.[6]

The two critics were principally concerned, however, with a far more fundamental problem: Greenberg's classification of Native American languages was simply wrong. The methods employed did little more than make superficial comparisons of similar words and pieces of grammar; no attention had been paid to the study of whole languages, and how languages change over time – a field of study known as historical linguistics. Languages spread, change and become extinct quite independently of genes or the shape of teeth; it is nonsense to search for correlations between these without taking into account the vast amount of intermarriage, slavery, internal migrations and warfare that is known to have occurred during Native American history, let alone prior to European contact.

Writing in 1994, Goddard and Campbell were unaware of any individual specialist working on Native American historical linguistics who thought that the Amerind family had any validity. Its incoherence was neatly demonstrated when they showed that by following Greenberg's methods,

Finnish had to be included as a member. All Greenberg had done, in their opinion, was to collate linguistic coincidences and then misinterpret these as prehistoric derivations.

This dispute is not the only one within the linguistic study of Native American origins. In 1990 Johanna Nichols, a linguist from the University of California at Berkeley, claimed that the large number of languages in the New World – the 'linguistic fact' as she called it – makes it 'absolutely unambiguous' that the New World has been inhabited for tens of millennia, at least since 35,000 years ago – a date that would have made Niède Guidon, who was digging at Pedra Furada in 1990, very happy indeed.[7]

Nichols assumed that the number of languages within any region gradually increases through time at a fairly constant rate. She favoured the term 'stock' to refer to the original language from which a number of existing language families arose. In Eurasia, for instance, Indo-European is the stock from which language families such as Germanic, Celtic and Balto-Slavic arose. These could then function as stocks for new language families. Stocks, she claimed, give rise to an average of 1.6 daughter stocks/families every 5–8,000 years. Nichols argued that the 140 primary languages she recognises within Amerind would have required about 50,000 years to have arisen from the original language spoken by the first people in the Americas. She moderates this figure to a mere 35,000 years ago to allow for more than one colonisation event, and hence more than one original stock.

When Daniel Nettle – a linguist from Oxford – looked at exactly the same data as Nichols, he reached a quite different conclusion. To his mind, the large number of Native American languages must be a sign of relatively recent colonisation, one unlikely to have happened before 11,500 BC.[8] Nettle argued that the rate for the emergence of new languages claimed by Nichols was quite unfounded; he also questioned the whole premise that languages proliferate in this fashion at all. A new language ultimately arises, he argued, only as a result of some particular event, frequently the movement of a group of people into a new area, especially one that requires them to adapt their lifestyles to a new set of resources.

According to Nettle, the colonisation of a new continent would rapidly lead to a proliferation of languages as communities spread out and split up into new 'niches' – areas with their own particular range of resources. Within each 'niche' the settlers would begin a distinctive way of life as hunters, fishermen, farmers or herders, developing their own vocabularies, and, ultimately, languages. All the available niches would eventually become full of people and consequently there would be a slow-down and, finally, an end to the appearance of new languages. And then, Nettle argued, the number of languages would begin to fall; some groups would grow in power and subdue others, while the development of trade would require the sharing of words and a degree of linguistic convergence.

As populations further expanded and people became tightly packed, there would be an ever greater reduction in the number of languages present. This process is readily apparent in the world today where the existing number of languages, about 6,500, is expected to halve in the next hundred years, as a consequence of globalisation. And so Nettle concluded that the high linguistic diversity of the New World indicated a recent colonisation, a view compatible with a Clovis First scenario.[9] This was precisely the opposite conclusion to that reached by Nichols.

How could Johanna Nichols and Daniel Nettle have arrived at such different views? One reason is that they approach the study of language from quite different perspectives. Unlike Johanna Nichols, Daniel Nettle is an anthropologist by training; he is primarily concerned with the way people use language to build and maintain social relationships, and how economic and ecological factors affect the distribution and number of languages within a specific continent. Linguists such as Nichols, however, have only a marginal interest in such issues and see languages as evolving entities with a dynamic quite independent from their social, economic and environmental context.

With all these contradictory arguments on American colonisation, the linguists seem to be in the same boat as the archaeologists – unable to agree with each other on even the most basic facts. Those of us without linguistic expertise are left in a quandary about who to believe. My own inclination is towards the anthropological approach of Nettle and the rather depressing conclusion of Goddard and Campbell: that the extent of reliable knowledge about the linguistic history of the American Indians is so incomplete that it is compatible with a wide range of scenarios for the peopling of the Americas. So much for the linguists. Are the geneticists doing any better?

We have already seen how the genetics of living people can be used by archaeologists when considering whether the spread of farming across Europe arose from the migration of farmers with a West Asian ancestry or from the indigenous adoption of Neolithic culture. The same technique of searching for specific patterns of genetic mutation, especially in mitochondrial DNA, has been used to determine when people may have first arrived in the Americas and where they came from.

Three sources of mtDNA have been studied: that from living Native Americans; that from living people in North and East Asia to enable comparisons with the American data; and that from the skeletal remains of prehistoric Native Americans.[10] The specific types of analyses undertaken, and the specific conclusions reached, have varied widely. But a major finding has been that the mtDNA sequences of Native Americans fall into four major clusters, referred to as groups A, B, C and D.[11]

Native Americans from the Na-Dene and Eskimo-Aleut language families mainly produce mtDNA sequences that belong to the A-group, while – perhaps not surprisingly – the massive Amerind language family has representatives from all four groups. Such genetic diversity – implying contributions from several migrant populations – supports those linguists who doubt the reality of the Amerind family. But just like the archaeologists and the linguists, the geneticists cannot come up with a single answer as to when and how colonisation occurred.

In 1993 one team of geneticists, led by Satoshi Horai of the National Institute of Genetics in Japan, suggested that each of the four groups is a product of a separate migration into the Americas between 21,000 and 14,000 years ago.[12] One year later a team lead by Antonio Torroni of Emory University, Atlanta, USA, analysed the data in a slightly different manner and concluded that Amerinds had migrated into the Americas in two waves: the first carrying groups A, C and D arriving between 29–22,000 years ago, and the second carrying group B alone at a much later date.[13] In 1997 Sandro Bonatto and Francisco Salzano of the Federal University of Rio Grande do Sul, Brazil, concluded that all four groups had a single origin from one migration earlier than 25,000 years ago.[14]

Why should the geneticists find it so difficult to reach a consensus? One reason is that they face several of same problems as the linguists.[15] Just as there is limited understanding of the rate at which the languages diverge from each other, so there is limited agreement about the rate of genetic mutation. Geneticists effectively use their best guesses as to the frequency of mutations, and those guesses may be quite wrong. Moreover, different genes may mutate at different rates, and some mutations might mask others that had previously arisen.[16]

Another reason is that even with our limited knowledge of American history and prehistory, it is clear that there has been an intense mixing of the genes of people who may have originated from separate migrations into the Americas at different times. After such jumbling, it may be quite impossible to identify the number and timing of such migrations from the genes of modern-day Native Americans.

The attempt to reconstruct American prehistory from present-day teeth, languages and genes also comes up sharply against another potential problem, one posed by the scanty skeletal remains of the First and Early Americans. As of AD 2000 there are no more than thirty-seven individuals represented by the entire collection of skeletal remains dating to before 9000 BC. Many of these individuals are known only from a few fragments of bone.[17]

When this collection was studied by D. Gentry Steele and Joseph Powell, anthropologists from Texas A&M University, USA, they made a startling discovery: the earliest Native Americans looked quite different to the Native Americans recorded from later prehistory or historic times.[18] The more recent people are described as having a mongoloid appearance – relatively broad and flat faces and high cheek-bones, clearly indicating descent from northern Asia. But the skeletal sample from pre-9000 BC suggests people with short and narrow faces and quite different dental patterns to those described by Christy Turner for Native Americans. In fact, rather than looking like recent American and North Asian people, those early Americans were far more similar in appearance to the earliest Australians dating to 60,000 years ago, and modern Africans.

In 1996, a precious new skull and the partial remains of a skeleton were discovered in the Columbia River region, Washington State.[19] After conducting a forensic examination, the local archaeologist, James Chatters, concluded from their caucasoid features – those which distinguish people from Europe, North Africa and the Near East, such as a narrow, high-bridged nose – that the bones were of a recent European settler. But when dated, the man was shown to have died at about 7,400 BC – a date that fitted with the style of a stone projectile point embedded in his thigh bone.

Kennewick Man soon became a cause célèbre. No fewer than five Native American tribes claimed him as a direct ancestor. The Umatilla tribe took the lead and, under the NAGPRA (Native American Graves Protection and Repatriation Act) of 1990, demanded immediate reburial in a secret location. Many scientists were horrified. They argued that that would be an abuse of legislation, and that no links to any tribe could be demonstrated: reburial would constitute the loss of priceless evidence about the colonisation of the Americas. The bones were sealed within a vault and protracted court cases conducted to decide their fate, before permission was granted to test the DNA within them; something that has outraged the Umatilla Indians.

When Chatters learned of the date of 7400 BC, he revised his opinion, stating that Kennewick Man was merely caucasoid-*like*. A detailed statistical analysis showed that the shape of the skull was most similar to Polynesian people, particularly those from Easter Island in the Pacific and the Ainu of Japan. The latter are indeed caucasoid-looking and may well have descended from the earliest *Homo sapiens*, to spread into eastern Asia soon after 100,000 years ago. Some of them had travelled to Australia by 60,000 years ago and others may well have been the very first to arrive in the New World.

In the light of their difference in physical appearance, the First Americans, as known from the pre-9000 BC skeletal record, might have been quite unrelated to the Native Americans known in the later prehistoric and historic records, and indeed to those living today. All of those more recent Native Americans evidently originated from migrations – perhaps better described as dispersals – of North Asian peoples after distinctive mongoloid features had evolved. Those already present in the Americas may simply have been subsumed into these new populations, with their own dental, genetic and linguistic traits being swamped by those of the new arrivals. Alternatively, the First Americans might have become extinct, making no linguistic or genetic contribution to future populations. A third – and more unlikely – alternative is that the First Americans were deliberately wiped out by the new immigrants – remember the projectile point in the thigh of Kennewick Man. Whichever scenario is correct, the dental, linguistic and genetic prehistories may never be able to reach back to the First Americans. For that, we will have to rely on the archaeological record. So now we must turn to the last and perhaps the most critical archaeological site in the Americas: Monte Verde.

25

On the Banks of the Chinchihuapi

Excavation and interpretation of Monte Verde,
AD 1977–1997, 12,500 BC

John Lubbock walks along the peaty riverbank of the Chinchihuapi Creek, a shallow meandering offshoot of the Maullín River in southern Chile. It has been his guide through woodlands, marshes, and green cattle-grazed pastures. High snow-capped peaks of the Andes tower above treetops to the east; lower wooded slopes of the Pacific coastal range climb in the west. The Pacific Ocean itself is no more than 30 kilometres away.

Lubbock's destination is Monte Verde where Tom Dillehay, of the University of Kentucky, completed his final excavation season in 1985 – a site that had left him 'overwhelmed and slightly confused' when he began work some eight years earlier.[1] Peat, the compacted remains of marsh and bog plants, had rapidly accumulated over abandoned huts, work areas, cooking places and rubbish dumps, inhibiting the normal processes of decay and creating unprecedented levels of preservation. And so Dillehay not only had stone artefacts and animal bones to excavate, but plant remains, hut timbers, wooden artefacts, pieces of hide, and even chunks of animal flesh.

Dillehay assembled an impressive team of collaborators: geologists, botanists, entomologists and palaeontologists, not to mention his archaeologist colleagues. They had both to analyse the archaeological finds and to reconstruct the landscape in which the inhabitants of Monte Verde had lived. His team had one more important task: to establish the age of the settlement.

As Lubbock follows the creek, the water deepens and flows more swiftly. The air temperature falls and it feels more humid; his footsteps no longer bounce upon springy peat but sink a little into soft sand. There are voices. As Lubbock rounds a bend in the river, he expects to see the excavation in full swing, as he had done at Bluefish Caves and Pedra Furada. But Lubbock has arrived at Monte Verde rather earlier than planned – it is 12,500 BC and the settlement, with its original inhabitants, is thriving.

The people have jet-black hair and olive skins; their bodies are lean and draped in poncho-like cloaks of animal hide.[2] Several are working at the end of a long oval-shaped tent which has been divided into several units, perhaps family houses. This is positioned a few metres from the riverbank and those working appear to be adding another unit on the end, having already laid logs as foundations for the walls and floor. Labouring quickly and efficiently, they sharpen the ends of poles with stone flakes and push them into the sandy soil. Near by a cluster of women sit preparing twine from vegetable fibres for securing hide drapes over the tent frame.

While men and women work, children splash in the creek and an old man tends a large fireplace outside another line of dwellings. He rearranges the cobbles being heated by embers, while two younger men prepare the food. They wrap small potato-like vegetables in large green leaves, stacking them upon a bark platter in preparation for steaming; nuts are crushed in a wooden mortar and emptied into a wickerwork bowl containing sweet-smelling leaves.

A call comes from the woodland that lies beyond the marsh at the back of the village. People peer through the hide drapes of their huts and work is forgotten as a party of smiling figures with heavy bags steps out from amongst the trees, crossing the brushwood pathway into the village. Greetings are shouted, and the whole community – at least thirty men, women and children – rush to meet them.

The new arrivals sit beside the fireplace, the half-prepared food pushed to one side. Everyone gathers around, eager to see what has been brought back from the coast. Lubbock finds himself squeezed among them, rubbing shoulders with the people of Monte Verde – not the first, but the earliest-known Americans.

The bags are opened. One by one the contents are removed, each item being held aloft and presented with a story about its collection. People are attentive. Almost every story ends with peals of laughter as the item is passed around the group and then laid carefully upon the ground: a bladder-skin full of salt, gleefully tasted as it circulates; a gourd shell full of black, sticky bitumen that will be used to haft stone flakes to wooden shafts; a collection of spherical beach pebbles which will be much preferred as hammer-stones to the angular rocks found in the creek.

Once everything has been laid out, the travellers continue talking, answering many questions about what they have seen and who they have met. They had been away for ten days, visiting another settlement and returning via the coast to collect such delicacies as seaweed, shells, cockles and sea urchins along with anything else that they thought useful.

The crowd gradually disperses, only to return as dusk falls to sit and sing around a fire and under a starry sky. Herbs are set to smoulder and the air becomes replete with pungent aromas. One man takes the musical lead while the others are silent; the song switches to the young women, and then back again to the man as others begin to clap. There is dancing, which leaves a patchwork of footprints around the hearth. Food is shared from large leaf plates – the wild potatoes, roasted meat, a mix of leaves, stems, grated roots and the crushed nut salad. When the meal is complete, the singing and dancing resume and continue long into the American night. It is 12,500 BC and as Lubbock drifts off to sleep he recalls where else he has been at this date in human history: trapping arctic hares at Creswell Crags; ambushing reindeer in the Ahrensburg valley; watching the people of 'Ain Mallaha grinding almonds and baking bread.

Meandering rivers are always shifting their course, depositing the sediments they carry to create new sandbanks and channels. The Chinchihuapi Creek had a spate of such activity in 1976, cutting through one of its own previous channels that had long been buried beneath a peat bog. The old banks of the creek became exposed and were cut further back by local woodsmen to make a track for their timber-hauling ox-carts.

Members of the local Gerardo Barria family found bones protruding from the bank, which they gave to a student studying agriculture in the belief that these were from cows. He showed them to Carlos Troncoso, an anthropologist at the University of Valdivia, and his colleague Professor Mauricio van de Maele, Director of the Museum. They examined the site and found further bones, together with stone artefacts. At that stage Tom Dillehay, who was teaching at the university, became interested, intrigued by possible cut-marks on the bones and the peculiarly high frequency of ribs. He surveyed the site in 1976 and soon began the excavation that would take both him and the whole of American prehistory to the far side of the Clovis Barrier.

Even if 'Clovis First' had remained intact, the degree of preservation at Monte Verde would still have ensured its renown as one of the most remarkable archaeological sites in the New World. Dillehay required two massive volumes to publish and interpret the evidence from his excavations, the last appearing in 1997 – more than twenty years after work had begun.[3] With such evidence he could make an elaborate reconstruction of the lifestyle at Monte Verde, arguing that people lived all year round at the settlement, and either traded with coastal dwellers or simply made regular visits to collect food and raw materials from estuaries, rock-pools and beaches. Nevertheless, it is the date of Monte Verde that elevates the site above all others in the Americas.

Dillehay was able to identify two distinct collections of artefacts. The largest, that which included the majority of tools, the remnants of huts and most of the food debris, was referred to as MV-II and dated by radiocarbon methods to about 12,500 BC.[4] The second collection, MV-I, was more ephemeral and came from ancient river sediments. Dillehay found charcoal scatters which may be the remnants of fireplaces next to possible stone and wood artefacts, and these were dated to at least 33,000 BC.[5] He himself remains cautious about MV-I, recognising the need to excavate a larger area before any conclusion can be held with confidence. But by 1985 he was in no doubt about the validity of the 12,500 BC date of the MV-II occupation. The

Clovis Barrier, which had resolutely remained intact for more than fifty years, had been washed away by the waters of Chinchihuapi Creek.

By the time Lubbock wakes the next morning, work on the new hut has already begun again; hides are now being tied on to wooden frames and brushwood placed across the roof. Other people are making and repairing tools with the newly acquired bitumen. The flakes being hafted are hardly worked at all – they could easily have been mistaken for naturally fractured stones. Indeed Lubbock sees that sharp stones collected from the creek bed are used as found – stones that are little different to those at Calico Hills and Pedra Furada.

Most of the activity is taking place about thirty metres away from the huts at what appears to be the settlement's workshop. Lubbock wanders between several clusters of men and women each engaged in a different task, many of whom are chewing as they work. Three men sit cross-legged making bolas stones for hunting. Using the hard beach pebbles, they peck and grind each nodule of softer stone into an almost perfect sphere, before making a groove for a string. Another group chops wood with large stone axes, implements made by flaking from both sides of a nodule – much the same technique as that required to make Clovis points.

There is just one structure in this area of the settlement, one quite different to the others at Monte Verde. It is dome-shaped – bent saplings covered with hides. Lubbock peers inside. Its floor has a raised triangular platform made from compacted sand and gravel, with two curved extensions that protrude on either side of the entrance. Nobody is inside but the floor is littered with an assortment of wooden bowls, pestles and mortars, grinding slabs and wooden spatulas. Hanging from the roof are bundles of leaves, grasses and flowers.

Nearby, animal skins are being worked. Some are tautly pegged to the ground so that their fat and sinews can be scraped away; others are being stretched and pummelled to make them soft and supple for clothing. The bone implements being used have hardly been modified at all, reminding Lubbock of the supposed tools from Bluefish Caves. A less than meticulous archaeologist could easily fail to notice the slightly smoothed ends and tiny notches in their sides.

Scattered among these tool-makers and hide-workers are a number of old fireplaces. One is brought to life again – pebbles are placed within its ashes and covered with dry wood and leaves. When lit, there is a sudden but short-lived blaze. While the fire settles, dry leaves taken from inside the structure are crumbled into a wooden bowl of water and, after about thirty minutes, hot stones from glowing embers added to make the tea. Work stops and the tea is shared, the bowl being passed from mouth to mouth. Before drinking, wodges of chewed plants are spat on to the ground.

Lubbock helps himself to tea. As he sits drinking, a canoe arrives and the two young men occupying it call for help to unload. They have a collection of ribs, and a massive thigh bone from a mastodon – a large elephant-like creature that lived throughout the Americas prior to the end of the ice age. The Monte Verde people had found the carcass some days earlier in a treasure trove that had already provided hair, tusks and hide. The thick footpads have been turned into excellent baskets; selected internal organs have been emptied, cleaned and stitched to provide waterproof bags.[6]

Lubbock recalls a passage from *Prehistoric Times*. Victorian John Lubbock had summarised a published account from 1857 about the remains of a mastodon in Missouri. It had apparently 'been stoned to death by the Indians, and then partially consumed by fire'. The account had been written by a Dr Koch who thought that the Indians had found the huge creature helplessly mired in mud and then hurled rocks at it collected from a nearby riverbank. He also claimed to have found several arrow-heads, a stone spearhead and stone axes among the ashes, bones and rocks. Victorian John Lubbock quoted Dr Koch at length, but seemed sceptical, commenting that such observations had yet to be proved correct.[7]

After the controversies surrounding Bluefish Caves, Meadowcroft and Pedra Furada, it will come as no surprise that not all archaeologists were as convinced as Dillehay that he had broken the Clovis Barrier. Thomas Lynch, an archaeologist now at the Brazos County Museum in Bryan, Texas, suggested that the artefacts must have eroded into the deposits from a much more recent human occupation – although none are known in the area. The University of Massachusetts archaeologist Dena Dincauze thought Dillehay had misinterpreted his radiocarbon dates.

In 1997 a group of acknowledged experts visited Monte Verde to examine Dillehay's claim – following in the tradition of those who had visited Folsom in 1927 and Pedra Furada in 1993. The Monte Verde group included the main protagonists in the debate about the peopling of the Americas for the previous thirty years. There was David Meltzer with his intimate knowledge of the history of archaeological studies; Vance Haynes, a champion of the 'Clovis First' scenario since the 1960s; James Adovasio who had fought his own case at Meadowcroft Rockshelter; and Dena Dincauze who had questioned Dillehay's interpretations.[8]

Their visit was an extremely thorough affair. It began with a study of Dillehay's final publication about Monte Verde, which was about to go to press, and continued with an inspection of the Monte Verde artefacts housed at the Universities of Kentucky and Valdivia. The group then received presentations about the past and present environments at Monte Verde, and finally made a detailed examination of the site itself. At the end of that day the party sat down to discuss their findings, and to decide whether Tom Dillehay had achieved that which had eluded Louis Leakey, Jacques Cinq-Mars, James Adovasio and Niède Guidon: an unequivocal demonstration of pre-Clovis settlement in the Americas.

Unanimity was achieved. None of the party was left in any doubt that Dillehay had indeed broken the Clovis Barrier. There was no question that many of the artefacts, notably the flaked stone tools, the 'bolas' stones and the knotted fibres had been made by humans; similarly, it could not be doubted that these artefacts were found just where they had been discarded, securely sealed by the peat that had grown across the site. The dates were verified as being uncontaminated – unequivocally demonstrating that human occupation had occurred at about 12,500 BC. It could even have been substantially earlier. For although the MV-I remains were sparse and received less attention, some of the party at least were impressed with the evidence for a 33,000-year-old occupation at Monte Verde.

But verification of that particularly early phase of occupation must wait until Dillehay has excavated a larger area. For the needs of this history – and those of American archaeology for at least the next decade – acceptance of occupation at 12,500 BC is momentous enough. It means that the Clovis First scenario is dead and buried.

Until 1927, nobody dreamed that the oldest site in the Americas would produce spear points and bison bones. Folsom delivered a brand-new vision of the First Americans: nomadic big-game hunters of the plains. Monte Verde was equally unexpected and replaced that vision with another: forest-dwelling, plant-gathering people in settled communities.

There is a further dramatic difference between these sites: whereas Folsom is in New Mexico and seems reasonably positioned as a marker of the first people to have arrived in North America, Monte Verde is no less than 12,000 kilometres from the southern end of the ice-free corridor. How much easier it would have been for unravelling the story of American prehistory if Monte Verde had been in Alaska, or even North America. For where are all the other settlements that people made on their southward journey from the north? Perhaps in Bluefish Caves, perhaps in Meadowcroft Rockshelter, perhaps at Pedra Furada. How many settlements should there be? That depends on how long people took to get to Monte Verde and whether they travelled overland or by sea.

David Meltzer thinks that whatever route they took, several thousands of years would have been required. Although in historic times fur trappers had indeed sped across the continent within a couple of centuries, he contends that this could hardly have been true of 'small colonising bands (with children, of course) travelling through changing, diverse and unfamiliar environments across major ecological boundaries, occasionally confronting formidable physical, ecological, and topographic barriers such as ice sheets and the swollen lakes and rivers draining them, all the while maintaining vital kinship links and population sizes'.[9]

The idea that the First Americans were bold explorers, travelling those 15,000 kilometres from Beringia to Monte Verde in less than 2,000 years is, to Meltzer, most unlikely. If he is correct, then people must have entered the Americas before the great LGM freeze of 20,000 BC. But, in that case, the complete absence of validated settlements in the Americas prior to Monte Verde is even more remarkable – much too remarkable for me to believe.

To my mind, the First Americans, those who must have travelled from Alaska to southern Chile within less than a hundred generations, were the most extraordinary group of explorers ever to have lived on this planet. I suspect that the mystery of the peopling of the Americas can only be resolved by invoking those peculiar human qualities of curiosity and thirst for adventure that in recent times have taken men to the poles, to the deep oceans, and to the moon. Did the same notions drive generation after generation of the First Americans to travel ever further southwards from their original homelands, perhaps after having left that land by boat to arrive on the coastal plain of the northwest? Did they then move inland to traverse melt-water lakes, mountain ranges and swollen rivers, to learn how to live in woodlands, on grasslands and in rainforests, eventually arriving on time at Monte Verde? If so, then Robson Bonnichsen was certainly correct when, in 1994, he described the First Americans as 'a brave new people in a brave new world'.

If that journey did indeed occur, a journey through the landscapes of North America in turmoil as global warming took hold, it would have been one of the most momentous events in human history. It is one that we must now visit in order to reconstruct the next chapter of American history after the ice – the extinction of the mega-fauna.

26

Explorers in a Restless Landscape

*North American fauna, landscape evolution and human,
colonisation, 20,000–11,500 BC*

Imagine standing in unfamiliar woodland on a summer's evening as the light is beginning to fade in 12,000 BC. You are in a clearing, surrounded by trees of juniper and ash, hornbeam and mahogany. A river crashes its way through rapids, providing a backdrop to the buzzing of insects and the occasional shriek of an unseen bird. Beyond the trees, massive cliffs tower over the river and woodland, casting long, protective shadows.

Now imagine a new sound, perhaps a new smell. A creature rapidly approaches, snorting its way pig-like through the undergrowth, avoiding the cacti while it searches for edible roots and stems. It stops a few feet away and rears up on to its hindquarters to explore an unfamiliar odour in the air. It stares at you, eye-level, six feet off the ground. Brown and hairy, thickset, a small head with beady eyes and flared nostrils. The front limbs hang motionless; three hook-like claws extend from each shovel-like paw. It grunts, returns to all fours and passes on its way, heading towards its cave within the cliff. There it will empty its bowels and sleep.

Now place yourself upon a small knoll, amidst a stand of cypress trees. The air is sticky with the smell of tar. Beyond you there are ponds; not sparkling with fresh blue water, but oozing, black, oily ponds in which putrid bubbles of gas swell and burst. A camel lies on its side within this mire of pitch. Trapped. Literally stuck to the ground. It cranes it head and makes one last bellow before giving up, exhausted by its struggle. But the tar does not claim its life. A wildcat, the size of a lion with serrated canine teeth 20 centimetres long, pounces. It makes an enormous gape, before it stabs the camel and rips apart its flesh.

A short distance away wings flap furiously, as a vulture also struggles to free itself from the tar. As the wings splash, they themselves become black and heavy. The quest for freedom is quite futile.

Today, of course, it would be something of a surprise to come across a smilodon dispatching a camel (appropriately named Yesterday's Camel by scientists) at the Rancho La Brea tar-pits in downtown Los Angeles, or a shasta ground sloth on its way to the Rampart Cave in the Grand Canyon. To have seen sights such as these, you would have had to have been one of the First Americans.[1]

The present-day American fauna is seriously impoverished compared to that seen by the first human inhabitants. Not only does it lack the shasta ground sloth and smilodon, but also the glyptodon, a type of giant armadillo, and the eremotherium, a giant ground sloth, 6 metres in length and 3 tons in weight. Castoroides, a beaver the size of a black bear, and the teratorns, flesh-eating birds that outstripped condors in size, are nowhere to be seen. Neither are the mammoths and their distant cousins the mastodons, elephant-like creatures with straight tusks and flat skulls.

Not all of the now extinct animals would have been strange to modern eyes. The American dire wolf and cheetah looked similar to their modern counterparts. So too did the five species of horse that became extinct – an animal that had to be reintroduced to its ancestral home by European settlers.

The bewildering variety of animals in North America encountered by the First Americans was a consequence of millions of years of biological and geographical evolution long before the arrival of the LGM. Up until 50 million years ago North America was connected to Europe by a land bridge through Greenland. The two continents shared many of the same animals, such as hyracotherium, or 'dawn horse', a forest-dwelling animal about 30 centimetres high, which would evolve in North America into the horse. Yet as the two continents drifted apart, the land bridge was lost, and the animals in Europe and North America began to evolve in quite different directions. By 40 million years ago, a new land bridge had arisen – one that provided a route from Asia and was taken by many species. The most striking was the mastodon, an animal that both the First Americans and the Clovis people would eventually encounter, whether in the swamps surrounding Monte Verde or in the spruce woodlands of North America.

Between 60 and two million years ago South and North America were quite separate from each other. In the southern continent a remarkable array of animals had evolved – including the giant sloths, the glyptodon and other forms of giant armadillos. When the Panamanian land bridge was formed two million years ago, some of these animals spread to North America, while others such as the horse, deer, sabre-toothed cats and bears spread from the north into the south. Not surprisingly, palaeontologists describe this as the 'Great Interchange'. At around 1.5 million years ago the first of two mammoth species arrived across the Asian–American land bridge, the Columbian mammoth (*Mammuthus columbi*). Its cousin the woolly mammoth (*M. primigenius*) spread into North America around 100,000 years ago and remained in northern regions. The two species effectively shared the continent between them.

The consequence of these periods of isolated evolution and interchange of species is that when the First Americans arrived – some time prior to 12,500 BC – they encountered some beasts that were familiar, and some that they and their ancestors had never seen before. There would have been nothing like the giant ground sloths and giant armadillos in their Asian homelands, although many generations of their forebears would have known, and perhaps hunted, the mammoth.

We know about the extinct animals from more than a million bones excavated from the Rancho La Brea tar-pits.[2] Since at least 33,000 years ago oil has been seeping to the surface where downtown LA is located today. When exposed, it reacted with the atmosphere to become sticky and viscous, eventually turning to asphalt and solidifying. Animals became trapped within these tar-pits, providing today's geologists with a unique record of ice-age fauna – a 'gigantic fossil time capsule' is the way David Meltzer has described it. Excavations occurred throughout the twentieth century and produced a remarkable array of skeletal remains, many in almost perfect condition. Once scientists had worked out how to remove the petroleum from the bones, these became available for radiocarbon dating and showed a gradual accumulation between 33,000 and 10,000 BC.

Another source of evidence for the extinct fauna is the dung they left behind in Rampart and other caves in Arizona.[3] The cave interiors have remained so dry since the end of the ice age that bacteria have been unable to do their destructive work. Consequently the dung balls of ground sloths up to 10 centimetres in diameter and still packed with the twigs on which they fed, have survived – in some cases feeling and smelling as fresh as the day they were produced. David Meltzer once opened a drawer containing sloth dung in the prestigious Smithsonian Institution in Washington and it smelled like a barn. Strands of hair and even bits of hide are occasionally found within them.

Rampart Cave in the Grand Canyon was a treasure trove of such deposits – until destroyed by a fire that burned from July 1976 until March 1977.[4] Before that Paul Martin had had to dig through layers of rat midden and bat faeces to find the dung balls. This cave is at the top of an 8-metre vertical cliff-face and is not easily accessible: the sloths must have had a crevice to climb up and, once inside, were carefully hidden from the prowling wolves and sabre-toothed cats.

The bones of extinct animals have also been found eroding from the banks of ancient rivers and – very occasionally – on archaeological sites of the Clovis period. When all sources of evidence are placed together, it is apparent that after evolution had taken many millions of years to produce a wonderful panoply of animals in the Americas, they became wasted almost overnight as a tragic finale to the Pleistocene in America.[5]

No fewer than 70 per cent of all large mammals of North America – thirty-six species – became extinct: animals described as its 'mega-fauna'.[6] This continent was not unique in its devastation. During the same period of time forty-six large animals became extinct in South America (80 per cent of its mega-fauna). Of the sixteen species that were living in Australia at 60,000 years ago – including giant wombats, giant kangaroos and a marsupial lion – only one has survived into the modern day, the 6-foot-tall red kangaroo. Extinctions also occurred in Europe, which lost seven species including the woolly rhinoceros and the giant elk. Only Africa escaped largely unscathed, losing just two out of forty-four species of 'mega-fauna'.[7] Thankfully, we have been left one place on earth where we can watch extraordinary beasts – those we call hippopotamus, rhinoceros and giraffe.

What happened to all the other ice-age mega-fauna? Their extinction story is a key part of our history, and those extinctions which occurred in the Americas are closely tied to another story – that of the Clovis people. Once fêted as the First Americans, it has long been thought that it was their mighty stone-tipped spears that pushed these beasts into extinction – indeed, the stories of human colonisation and mega-faunal extinction may be so closely interwoven as to be inseparable. But within that weave there is a third story that must be told: the evolution of the North American landscape following its release from the deep freeze of the LGM.[8]

When people first set foot in the Americas the continent was, like most of the world, in the throes of change.

The great thaw had gathered pace by 14,500 BC, pushed along by the shrinkage of the ice sheets themselves. Initially they simply became thinner – at the height of the great freeze the ice sheets are likely to have reached a thickness of 3 kilometres. They began to move, changing their size and shape in a quite erratic manner, contracting in some regions while expanding in others. Their edges can be imagined as active amoeba, unsteadily pulsating, undulating and wobbling.[9] Between 14,000 and 10,000 BC there were at least four advances, as far south as Iowa and South Dakota, with ice sometimes oozing its way across frozen ground, at other times sliding over land which had defrosted.

When the ice sheets lost contact with the sea, icebergs no longer shelved into and cooled the waters, resulting in warmer air being blown inland; this further accelerated the ice-sheet demise. And then the Younger Dryas interrupted global warming soon after 11,000 BC. Although far less severe than in Europe and western Asia, this disrupted the animal and plant communities which for the previous 7,000 years had been adapting to a warmer world.[10] The ecological confusion was made worse by the sudden return of rapid global warming at 9600 BC. And then the Americas, along with the rest of the world, settled down as the Holocene began: a time of relative climatic stability, now threatened by the new man-made bout of global warming that has just begun.

When the ice sheets finally lost the battle against global warming a mighty legacy was left on the landscape of North America; in fact havoc was wreaked on coastlines and coastal communities throughout the world as billions of litres of melt-water poured into the oceans. Those who lived in the far north of the Americas would have seen their homeland of Beringia diminish in size year by year as the coast flooded and salty water seeped across the steppe. I imagine the people standing upon hilltops, old men telling young children how the forests of birch that now stretch before them are quite new to their land. They explain how, during their own childhood, herds of mammoths and musk oxen had grazed on grasslands where the caribou now browse. Settlements were abandoned as communities headed for the coast where they hunted the newly abundant seals and walrus. As they did so, clear icy-blue skies became shrouded in fog and drizzle.

The First Americans who travelled south from Beringia, most likely by boat or foot along the coastal plain, explored the Rocky Mountains as they became free from the Cordilleran ice.[11] I can see them climbing to view the plains to the west and the mass of peaks and the labyrinths of sharp valleys to the east. They crossed rivers that flowed through canyons and visited the glaciers that remained within high valleys. They were not alone: alpine plants and trees also climbed into the Rockies, followed by mountain sheep and an assortment of small mammals. Beyond the mountains, the First Americans found the great basins of the Columbia and Fraser rivers. Once liberated from the ice, these basins soon became covered in coniferous forest and their rivers replenished with fish. And so, picture the First Americans standing knee-deep in the ice-cold water, spearing the salmon as they came to spawn and deciding that this was a good place to settle. When they headed further south, into what we now call California, they found landscapes struggling with a lack of water, trees becoming sparse and stunted. And new plants, such as the cactus and yucca. It was perhaps here that they first encountered the giant shasta ground sloth as it searched for edible roots and tubers.

Settlements would have been located where people found the most abundant plants to gather and animals to hunt; each settlement may then have acted as a base for further exploratory journeys. The fact that none have been found suggest that they were scattered thinly and occupied by relatively small numbers of people, perhaps a hundred at most. Such communities must have remained in touch with each other to ensure that populations were biologically viable: widespread social relations were required to avoid inbreeding and cope with the failure of a group of hunters to return or the fatalities from a hard winter.[12] When food, water and firewood were plentiful, population growth may have been high, readily producing parties of men and women prepared to establish new settlements in recently explored lands. Those lands may not have been the ones immediately next door. Just like the first farmers of Europe, the First Americans may have leap-frogged their way across unproductive regions to find the river basins, prairies, estuaries and woodlands in which food was abundant and the living was easy – at least, as easy as it can ever be for people in an unfamiliar world.[13]

We must envisage parties leaving established settlements and heading

Excavations at Ohalo (occupied *c.* 20,000 BC), Sea of Galilee, in September 1999.

Tell Abu Hureyra, Syria, in 1972, and the excavated remains of its hunter-gatherer dwellings dating to *c.* 11,500 BC.

Tell es-Sultan (initial Neolithic occupation at *c.* 9600 BC), surrounded by the modern town of Jericho, in September 1999.

Wadi Faynan, Jordan, in September 2000. The Land Rover is positioned over the Early Neolithic site of WF16 (occupied *c.* 9500–8500 BC).

Excavation of hunter-gatherer-cultivator dwellings at WF16, in September 2000.

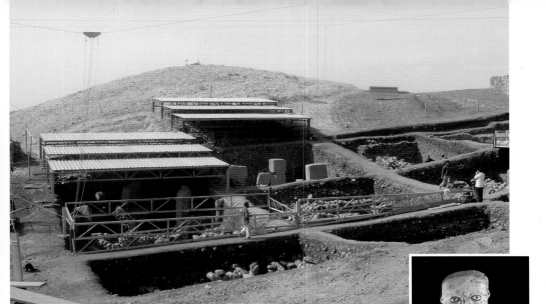

Excavations at Göbekli Tepe (occupied *c.* 9500 BC), southern Turkey, in October 2002.

Right: Plaster figure, *c.* 7000 BC, from ʿAin Ghazal, Jordan.

The site of Ghuwayr I (occupied *c.* 8500 BC), Wadi Faynan, Jordan, in April 2001.

Dr Alan Simmons at the remains of Aetokremnos Cave, Cyprus, in September 2001, and a sample of the excavated pygmy hippopotamus bones, possibly dating to *c.* 10,000 BC.

Excavations at Verberie (occupied *c.* 12,500 BC), River Oise, France, showing a typical hearth.

La Riera Cave, Asturias, Spain: entrance and layers of occupation debris dating from *c.* 20,000 to 7000 BC.

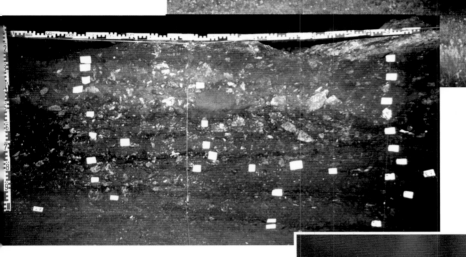

Right: Carved human/fish stone figure, *c.* 6400 BC, from Lepenski Vir, Danube River, Serbia.

Left: Vedbaek, Denmark: *c.* 4800 BC burial of young woman with new-born baby beside her on a swan's wing (grave 8).

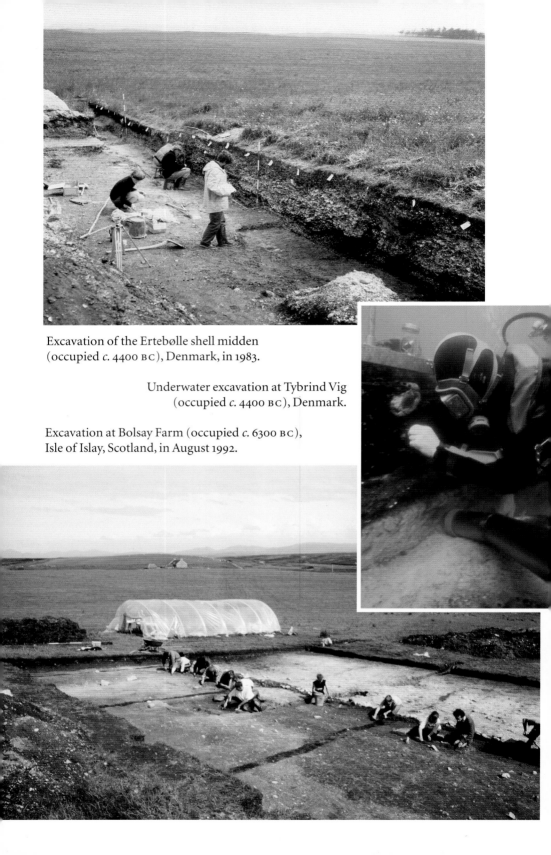

Excavation of the Ertebølle shell midden
(occupied *c.* 4400 BC), Denmark, in 1983.

Underwater excavation at Tybrind Vig
(occupied *c.* 4400 BC), Denmark.

Excavation at Bolsay Farm (occupied *c.* 6300 BC),
Isle of Islay, Scotland, in August 1992.

Excavations at Bluefish Caves (occupied *c.* 11,500 BC, and possibly prior to 15,000 BC), Alaska, USA, in July 1983.

Meadowcroft Rockshelter, Pennsylvania, USA. Excavated from 1973 onwards and possibly occupied prior to 15,000 BC.

Location of Monte Verde (occupied *c.* 12,500 BC), Chile, adjacent to Chinchihuapi Creek, and excavations (below) in 1983, showing preserved wooden timbers from hunter-gatherer dwellings.

south, relentlessly exploring a world that became more exotic with every kilometre they travelled. At some point on their journeys they would have encountered the tar-pits of Rancho La Brea and most likely stopped to watch the futile struggles for life and the bloody scenes of death. Some intrepid groups most likely headed east from the Rockies and trekked close to the edge of the Laurentide ice sheet, through a world dominated by wind and water. Think of a group of men, tightly huddled together with their fur-clad backs turned to the dust storm that had suddenly arrived, and which will just as suddenly cease to blow. At other times such explorers faced winds up to 150 kilometres an hour, similar to those blowing off the Antarctic glaciers today.

The generations that followed had an easier time as the winds eventually relented and the dust settled, to create fertile seedbeds for the hardy shrubs and trees that had edged their way north. And so we can imagine the grand-children and great-grandchildren of the storm-trapped pioneers making camp among trees of poplar, willow and juniper. Other arrivals included insects, always quick to respond to the warmer weather, and birds which soon followed. When our imaginary travellers break camp to continue upon their journey, they will have made their own contribution to the changing world by having carried further seeds and insects upon their leather-strapped feet and leaving them behind to flourish within the new soils.

As the First Americans travelled within Beringia, across the Rockies, along the edge of the ice sheets and then further south, they had to build maps of the New World – mental maps to be wrapped up in stories and songs. For the very first time the Rockies, the Sierra Nevada and the Appalachian Mountains would have acquired names, most probably a whole host of them – one for each peak, valley and cave. And so, too, would the lakes, rivers, waterfalls and estuaries, the forests, woodlands and plains.

But such was the environmental turmoil brought about by global warming that each new generation of travellers would have found a land-scape quite different to that learned from stories around the fire. Where they had expected to find ice, new travellers may have found tundra; con-versely, previous tundra may have become buried beneath an advancing glacier. Where they expected to find stands of poplar and willow, they may have found woodlands of spruce and pine, the trees that crowded out those pioneer species. They may have witnessed unexpected types of insects and birds, and begun to encounter new animals such as mastodons as they came to browse within the fresh spruce woodlands. And sometimes they saw scenes of devastation: I can imagine a party standing aghast at the sight of trees crushed, broken and buried by a new southward surge of ice – trees that had been woodland in which their parents had hunted for deer and gathered plants for food.

But their most daunting vision would surely have been the massive lakes that developed along the edge of the ice sheets.[14] These were vast expanses of water, quite unlike any in North America – indeed the whole world – today. They were formed by the melt-waters, dammed by cliffs of ice on their northern edge and gently rising ground to the south. The first had appeared by 15,000 BC – Lake Missoula at the southern edge of the Cordilleran ice sheet, the size of Lake Ontario today – but their apogee came with Lake Agassiz in the west, which had appeared by 12,000 BC and lasted for 4,000 years. When at its most expansive, it covered 350,000 square kilometres. That is four times the area of Lake Superior today, which is itself equivalent to a medium-sized European country, such as Ireland or Hungary, and currently the largest freshwater lake in the world.

The drainage routes of these lakes were changeable – the most dramatic example being Lake Agassiz which, up until 11,000 BC, had drained to the south, into the Gulf of Mexico. Soon after that date an ice dam at its eastern edge was breached and rather than taking the southern route, billions of litres of water began to flow east, into the St Lawrence River and then the North Atlantic. There it may have had a catastrophic effect on the circulation of ocean waters, which may in turn have influenced the climate, perhaps causing the Younger Dryas itself.[15]

While some North American lakes disappeared completely, creating devastating floods almost as soon as they had appeared, others, like Lake Missoula, could not decide what to do. Part of this lake's western boundary was formed by an ice dam that became increasingly insecure as the lake basin filled with melt-water. When the dam floated, the lake quite suddenly drained, sending many millions of litres of water through its neighbouring lake, and then into the Columbia River valley, violently submerging any woodland that stood within its way. In a mere two weeks the lake bed was dry, and the land beyond had been not only scoured of its trees and plants, but also of much of its soil, leaving exposed bedrock. A new ice advance re-created the ice dam, and Lake Missoula began to refill, only to eventually breach the dam once again. This happened no less than forty times during 1,500 years of the lake's existence, each time destroying the fragile aquatic ecosystem that had just become re-established after the previous catastrophic drainage of the lake.

Such destructive floods were not unique to Lake Missoula – they were a constant feature of life in the vicinity of the receding glaciers. And so we must imagine the First Americans finding huge expanses of mud from which lake waters had recently drained, where the first plants – sagebush and ragweed – were finding a home. As they continued to explore and learn about their world, they would have found lakeshores with no lakes, river deltas with no rivers. Even more dramatically, those who ventured all the way to the eastern seaboard of North America would have witnessed the rapid advance of the Atlantic. As melt-water poured into the sea, the coastline rushed inland, sometimes travelling at a rate of 300 metres a year. To the north of Cape Cod, offshore islands became submerged, while further south an extensive coastal plain of mixed tundra and spruce woodland became flooded and then drowned. Today trawlers haul up mammoth teeth and mastodon bones within their nets as momentary reminders of the lost ice-age world.

When the ice that blocked the St Lawrence valley disappeared in about 12,000 BC, the sea flooded into the interior of the continent. For two thousand years Ottawa, Montreal and Quebec were submerged by the Champlain Sea. I can see the First Americans watching for whales, porpoises and seals, perhaps planning to hunt them from their kayaks. This sea was unsettled, sometimes it was warmed and diluted by drainage from freshwater lakes, at others it was cooled by melt-waters from the ice, and at others still it was salinised by new influxes from the Atlantic. Today, little survives of this lake – unless one has sharp enough eyes to find the sea-water shells and fossilised strands of seaweed buried in sediments now high and dry in the Ottawa River valley. The sea disappeared simply because the land eventually rebounded upwards, relieved of the weight of the ice.

Life at the edge of the ice sheets was not one that could be enjoyed for very long; the woodlands and the plains to the south were the place to live, but these, too, were ever changing. We must picture a party of the First Americans standing bewildered in a new type of woodland – one in which the trees were leaning at all angles or had collapsed into hollows, perhaps to float upon ponds of water. Those First Americans would have been in what ecologists today appropriately call 'drunken woodland', that in which the forest floor was turning to water.

Such woodland had developed on soil which lay upon stagnant layers of ice. Across large areas of Saskatchewan, North Dakota and Minnesota, wind-borne dust, water-borne silt and gravel, deposits of soil and rock shifted by re-advancing ice sheets, had buried and insulated layers of ice. Soil developed, was colonised by pioneering insects and seeds, and within less than a human generation woodland emerged. But as temperatures kept rising the buried ice began to melt, initially where the soil cover was thin so that pools and ponds seeped their way to the surface. The melt-water within these ponds was joined by rainwater warming them sufficiently for life to take hold.

The First Americans were not the only ones to discover these ponds: they would have watched ducks and geese arrive, their muddy feet delivering plant seeds and snails' eggs. The ponds began to flow into rivers which eventually joined the tributaries of the Missouri. Sticklebacks, minnows and other fish could then find their way to new woodland lakes; the fish brought their own host of fellow travellers in the form of parasites. Ecology was blossoming and in the midst of it stood the First Americans.

As they headed further south they would have left coniferous forests behind for open woodland, a botanical mosaic of trees and plants rarely found together today. It was a landscape that provided ideal grazing and browsing for many of the large mammals, such as the mastodons and the Columbian mammoth. This was larger and less hairy than the woolly mammoths of the north, often standing four metres at the shoulder and requiring 225 kilograms of food each day. The First Americans may have found a small group of Columbian mammoths sheltering within a cave on the Colorado Plateau in southern Utah. There they left thick layers of dung, spherical turds up to 20 centimetres across, which shows us that they fed on grasses, sedge, birch and spruce. The quantity is not surprising – we know that a modern elephant has to evacuate 90 to 125 kilograms of the stuff every day. Today we call that cave Bechan Cave; this is the Navajo name – it means 'the cave of the big turds'.[16]

By 13,000 BC, the midwest was a sodden landscape, a broken jigsaw of pools, bogs and patches of spruce woodland. But as global warming intensified, new drainage patterns developed and the midwest began to dry out. Periodic droughts arrived at 11,500 BC, which were exacerbated by the onset of the Younger Dryas a few hundred years later. Trees could no longer survive in the arid conditions and were replaced by an array of grasses and herbs such as sage, ragweed and many flowering plants. The grazing mammals – mammoths, camels, horse, bison and many others – exploited the new prairies, eagerly turning them into a North American Serengeti. The First Americans would have watched those herds with the same awe that we feel when we watch the wildebeest, antelope and zebra on the African plains.

As their relentless southward progress continued, some of the First Americans headed into Central America and beyond, into environments that were fast becoming tropical. This was a new, exotic world in which their ability to learn about new landscapes and new resources must have been pushed to its extreme. The rainforests had remained largely intact throughout the great freeze of 20,000 BC; when entering them, the First Americans must have watched the feeding habits of the deer and monkeys in an effort to identify which leaves and berries were edible and which should be avoided. Here they would have encountered yet more fabulous beasts, including the great glyptodon – the giant armadillo-like creature that foraged along the riverbanks.

First Americans must have suffered many losses in their journeys from Beringia to South America: explorers drowned in sudden floods and mudslides, killed by carnivores, and the victims of new diseases.[17] Some communities are likely to have become isolated. If biologically viable they may have evolved their own distinctive language, culture and even genetic markers. Perhaps such 'lost' people became surprise encounters for new generations of Early American explorers, originating from new dispersals from northern Asia. Some isolated communities may have been too small to survive. For them the future was bleak – one of declining numbers and eventual extinction.

By 11,500 BC the First Americans were dispersed throughout the Americas, from Tierra del Fuego in the south to Beringia in the north. This population had most probably resulted from many migrations and already acquired a multitude of languages, genetic mutations and cultural traditions. Human numbers grew, and were perhaps boosted by new waves of immigrants – or at least bolstered by what David Meltzer describes as migratory dribbles.[18]

In an unknown place and for an unknown reason the Clovis point was invented. This most likely occurred in the forests of eastern North America where the spear points have been found in most abundance. With the new Clovis toolkit and their greater numbers, people suddenly became visible to archaeologists.

Quite why people started to make large stone points from the best stone they could find, is unclear.[19] It is easy to think that they were for hunting – some were certainly used in that fashion. But Clovis points may equally have been knives for cutting plant material or may have been manufactured principally for social display. The remarkable speed with which they spread across the whole continent, presumably as an idea rather than as objects, testifies to the close links between communities that had been essential for survival as the ice age came to its end. Indeed, the numbers, design and distribution of such points suggests to me that they were used as much for building social bonds between groups as for acquiring food from the landscape.

Each group appears to have moulded the idea to their own specific design, and hence there are many subtle variations in point size, shape and style. Archaeologists have given each type a different name: Gainey points in Ontario,[20] Suwanee points in Florida,[21] Goshen points in Montana[22] and so on throughout the continent.[23] Whatever the reason for the spread of this technology, once present we need no longer talk about the elusive First Americans, but can refer to the Clovis people.

Now the exotic North American fauna faced a new type of potential predator, one that came armed with stone-tipped spears, that hunted in large groups, that laid ambushes and set traps. The mammoths, mastodons and other giant herbivores were certainly used to predators that attempted to take their young: wolves, lions and sabre-toothed cats. They had been living and co-evolving with such carnivores for millions of years and had their means of defence: large herd size, massive bodies, lethal tusks, group formations to protect the vulnerable, patterns of movement to enable them to keep out of the carnivores' way. Would these have been any good when a new type of predator arrived? One whose spears were even more deadly than smilodon's teeth, whose group hunting tactics were more sophisticated than that of the wolf, and who had one 'weapon' that the ground sloths, mastodons and even smilodon had never encountered before: a large brain with which to outwit its prey.

27

Clovis Hunters on Trial

Extinction of the mega-fauna and Clovis lifestyles,
11,500–10,000 BC

When the claim that the Clovis hunters had hunted the great beasts of North America into extinction was first mooted by Paul Martin in the 1960s, there was relatively limited understanding of the precise dates at which these extinctions had occurred. Yet, as the evidence has accumulated, the Clovis culture and some mega-faunal extinctions do indeed seem to coincide.

By 1985 David Meltzer and Jim Mead, a geologist from Northern Arizona University, were able to assemble no less than 363 radiocarbon dates on extinct animals, coming from 163 fossil localities, especially the Rancho La Brea tar pits and the bone-dry caves of the southwest.[1] With the radiocarbon dates assembled, Meltzer and Mead weeded out any that they thought might be suspect, such as those possibly contaminated by old carbon in the ground, leaving them with a sample of 307 dates. A few years later Donald Grayson from the University of Washington, another expert on radiocarbon dating, thought it necessary to remove more dates as unreliable, cutting the final sample to a mere 125 radiocarbon determinations.[2]

Such rigour meant that the extinction date for twenty-nine of the thirty-six extinct species could not be ascertained any more precisely than having happened at some time in the last 50,000 years. Grayson cautioned against assuming that these animals went extinct during the final 1,500 years of the ice age when they shared the North American landscapes with the First Americans and Clovis hunters. Nevertheless, this left the 'ice-age seven': mammoth, mastodon, camel, horse, tapir, shasta ground sloth and smilodon. The last living representatives of these North American species were reliably dated to have been living between 11,000 and 10,000 BC[3] – precisely when the Clovis people were at large.

Paul Martin's claim that the Clovis people were responsible for their extinction presents a compelling argument when considered with the evidence from sites in the San Pedro River valley.[4] When faced with the remains of thirteen mammoths, spear points, butchery tools and fireplaces at Lehner Ranch, one can readily imagine the drama: Clovis hunters ambushing a small herd as they came to drink, the resulting blood bath in the creek; fires lit as butchery begins, the smell of roasting meat; vultures circling above and giant teratorns perched upon nearby rocks waiting to feast upon wasted meat and innards. This is precisely the type of scene reconstructed from a study of the mammoth bones by Jeffrey Saunders of Illinois University.[5]

Perhaps such scenes were repeated throughout the continent; not just with mammoths but also with the sloths, the camel, the glyptodon and the giant beaver. Clovis hunters were just too powerful and cunning for their prey; they were guilty of overkill and pushed the ice-age seven into extinction.

A neat scenario, but is it correct? We should give the Clovis hunters a proper trial. Paul Martin himself was aware of a severe weakness in the prosecution's case. While we have some (possible) kill sites for mammoths, similar sites for the thirty or so other extinct animals are absent – with very rare or highly ambiguous exceptions. Martin has a cunning explanation: the apocalyptic slaughters happened so rapidly, and to animals that were so sensitive to predation, that very few kill sites were ever made. Borrowing military terminology, he described it as a 'blitzkrieg'.

Moreover, Martin argued, the chances of archaeologists finding *any* site from the last ice age are so remote that we should be surprised by the number of Clovis/mammoth sites that have been located, rather than bemoan the absence of sloth, camel and glyptodon kill sites. Such animals may have been killed and butchered in grasslands or in the hills, where erosion rather than sedimentation occurs. Here, any cut-marked bones and fireplaces would have long since been broken up and scattered out of sight – part of the dust and the dirt that is blown and washed around the continent today.

Back in the 1970s the idea of Clovis hunters entering a virgin landscape, sweeping southwards and conducting a blitzkrieg of the naïve animals, couldn't be proved or refuted, but it did fit the archaeological evidence. Today, this isn't the case, largely because of Monte Verde – a settlement that tells us people could have been in North America thousands of years before Clovis technology was invented, and more significantly before the mass extinction. If the First Americans had not hunted large game, then those animals could not have been the easy prey that Paul Martin suggests. Conversely, if they had been big-game hunters, then there could not have been a blitzkrieg and we should have sloth, camel and glyptodon kill sites. Martin loses the argument either way round.

It is not just the circumstantial evidence of Monte Verde that comes to the defence of the Clovis people. In fact, they have a great number of alibis throughout the continent – the Clovis archaeological sites themselves. Although those in the southwest have yielded a substantial number of mammoth bones, those elsewhere suggest a lifestyle devoted to hunting small game, catching turtles and collecting plant foods.[6] When at Shawnee-Minisnik in Pennsylvania, the Clovis people had gathered hawthorn berries and blackberries; when at Debert site in Nova Scotia they hunted caribou;

while at Lubbock Lake in Texas it had been rabbits, geese and wild turkeys. Elsewhere, such as at the Old Humboldt site in Nevada, the Clovis people had dined on trout, birds' eggs and clams.[7] Big game was hunted on some occasions. Whether or not the mammoth at Murray Springs in the San Pedro valley had been hunted, a herd of bison had certainly been ambushed and slaughtered in a marsh. But even at the sites where mammoth bones are prominent, such as Lehner Ranch, it is the small game present which may be more representative of the normal Clovis diet.

The Clovis people appear to have been opportunists, gathering whatever plants and killing whatever animals were available, rather than specialising in big-game hunting. It could, therefore, have been no more than a unique opportunity that led them to spear a giant land tortoise at Little Salt Spring in Florida or to kill a mastodon at Kimmswick in Missouri.[8] If they had been particularly searching for big game, then we would expect to have found Clovis points at Big Bone Lick in Kentucky and Saltville in Virginia – natural salt outcrops and magnets for large mammals throughout the ice age that could have provided easy big-game hunting. Although both sites have been searched for two hundred years and provided vast numbers of animal bones, not one single Clovis point has ever been found.[9]

Consequently, the probable mammoth kill sites appear to be the exception rather than the rule for Clovis settlement – and even these may be less indicative of hunting than they first appear. The key problem is that there are several 'natural' accumulations of mammoth bones in North America that look very similar to those on Clovis sites, except for the absence of human debris. These are from natural disasters, for example, when herds crashed through ice when crossing a frozen lake, or became mired in un-anticipated mud. The animals would have died together, quite unaided by any human hand.

This interpretation has found favour with Gary Haynes, an anthropologist at the University of Nevada who studied the natural die-off sites of African elephants during periods of drought in the 1980s. When he examined the accumulation and decomposition of carcasses around dried-up water-holes he found a striking resemblance to the mammoth remains at sites such as Murray Springs and Lehner Ranch.[10]

Haynes suggests that the Clovis people had been the spectators at natural die-offs of drought-ridden mammoths, occasionally making a *coup-de-grâce* killing to send an animal on its way. The carcasses were left largely untouched because there was so little meat on them: it was not worth even cracking the bones for marrow as these animals had starved to death. The mammoths may indeed have been living through a period of drought, either immediately before or during the Younger Dryas – but here again, the evidence is inconclusive, with the severity and even the existence of droughts at this time in much dispute.[11]

Coup-de-grâce killings, or even the passive observation of starving mammoths, present a quite different view of the past to that of Paul Martin and Jeffrey Saunders. Indeed, the Clovis points themselves could have had quite a different role to that first suggested; these valuable stone points might have been laid near, or even on, the dead animals as a mark of respect or as part of a religious observance.

Such speculation is a reminder that there must have been far more to Clovis lifestyles than simply trying to find the next meal. Unfortunately, evidence both of religious beliefs and of the organisation of their societies is very limited. Whatever they did with their dead they certainly did not regularly bury them, at least not in places where they survived or where archaeologists have been able to look.[12] There are just two exceptions: Fishbone Cave in Nevada provided the remnants of a skeleton wrapped in a cedar-bark shroud[13] and the fragmentary remains of two young adults were found at the Anzick site, Montana.[14]

The Anzick site was discovered in 1968 at a small collapsed rockshelter. In the dry dirt a cluster of more than one hundred stone tools was found, including many fine spear points. These had not been haphazardly discarded, but intentionally placed within a cache of tools which had been dusted with red ochre.[15] Similar caches of stone artefacts have been found elsewhere in the continent.[16] If these were simply stores of artefacts to be recovered when a hunting party returned to a region, then the red ochre, the particularly fine workmanship of the stone points and the association with a burial at Anzick remain unexplained.

The striking colours of many Clovis points also suggest that they may have been more than mere utilitarian objects. Points were made from chert coming in alternating red and brown bands, multicoloured chalcedonies, red jasper, volcanic glass and petrified wood. Why choose such an exotic range of coloured raw materials? The Australian Aborigines did likewise because of their religious beliefs. A deep red chert was often used because it had been formed from the blood of ancestral beings; quartz was treasured because the way it shimmered was related to the quality of 'rainbowness', believed by Aborigines to be the essence of life.[17]

Clovis people may have had similar reasons for choosing coloured stone. But if they did so, they failed to leave behind any rock paintings as evidence for their religious beliefs. All we can do is surmise that they had lived in a social and symbolic world in which stone points may have been as meaningful as the carvings of figurines were to ice-age hunter-gatherers in Europe or quartz points to the recent Aborigines of Australia.

Although there is definitely blood on their spears, the archaeological evidence leaves us in considerable doubt about whether the Clovis people played the sole, or indeed any, role in the mass extinction. But if they are innocent – or at least temporarily released on bail – who, or what, else can be taken in for questioning?

There are two alternatives, the first of which can be dealt with quite rapidly as an intriguing but purely hypothetical idea: a lethal plague.

Ross MacPhee, a palaeontologist at the American Museum of Natural History, and Preston Marx, Professor of Tropical Medicine at Tulane University, have suggested that at 11,000 BC in North America a virus jumped from the new human colonists to the large game.[18] This hypothetical 'hyper-disease' would have been more lethal than anything known in recorded history. As yet there is not a shred of evidence, but they suggest that a plague could explain several of the awkward facts about the mass extinction, notably its speed and bias to large animals who, they claim, would be more susceptible because of their slow breeding rates. Theoretically, evidence could be found: fragments of the DNA of the viral infections may survive to be extracted from the bones of the extinct animals. Well, perhaps. It seems a long shot, and recovering DNA from ancient bone has proved immensely more difficult than scientists had thought just a few years ago.[19]

The second alternative to overkill is climate change and for this we have a trio of principal prosecutors: Russell Graham, a palaeontologist from Denver Museum, Ernest Lundelius, Professor of Geological Science from the University of Texas, and Dale Guthrie, Professor of Palaeontology from the University of Alaska. They believe that climate change, and its consequence for animal habitats, was the perpetrator of the mass extinction. According to this formidable trio, the climate did not kill its victims directly by making it too hot, cold, wet or dry for them. Rather it destroyed their habitats.[20] We know that this is the major cause of animal extinction in the modern world and we should be immediately sympathetic to their case. Graham and Lundelius's claim is that severe habitat loss at the end of the ice age was a consequence of changing weather patterns – the summers became relatively warmer and the winters colder. Animal and plant communities which had evolved for many thousands of years in conditions of limited seasonal differences collapsed as some members became unable to tolerate the winters, and others the summers.

It is one of the most astonishing features of ice-age animal communities that species which now live many thousands of miles apart, in radically different environments, then regularly rubbed haunches with each other. The First Americans, touring their new world, would have seen what today are far northern tundra species, such as caribou, musk ox and lemmings, living side by side with what to us are quite southern species (that live in woodland or on the prairies) such as elk and bison. Such animal mosaics could exist in the ice age because the contrast between the seasons was not nearly as marked as it is now.

When the winters became colder, some animals were driven to the south; conversely, warmer summers pushed others to the north. No more could the twain meet in neutral ground, as that place simply no longer existed. Those animals that found new niches were the lucky ones; many that were unable to adapt became extinct.

Dale Guthrie has explained why some animals survived and others didn't by reconstructing the impact of climate change on the distribution of plant communities. In the world today we see these as distinct bands: in the far north there is the band of tundra; south of that coniferous forest; south again deciduous woodland; and then grasslands. The ice-age world of the First Americans was not like this at all; rather than arranged in latitudinal bands, plant communities were found in 'plaids' or mosaics – bits of today's tundra, coniferous forest, deciduous trees and grasslands mixed up together. It was the warmer summers and colder winters that pulled these bands apart.

In the process, the animals that had depended upon this mixture of plant types suffered – and they were predominantly those of very large body-size: the mammoths, mastodons, giant sloths. These animals suffered owing to a shortening of the growing season, restricting the time available to feed their enormous bulk. They also suffered from the marked reduction in plant diversity – they relied on eating a vast assortment of plants to gain sufficient energy and nutrients. As seasons became more marked and plant diversity reduced, specialised feeders rose to ascendancy. In the far north, it was the caribou that could rely on no more than lichen; in the woodlands it was the deer, a highly skilled browser; in the south it was the bison which fed on the few types of short-stemmed grasses that replaced the mix of many long-stemmed varieties and herbs which had been favoured by the generalist grazers. These new plants also came with chemical defences which the bison could tolerate but which were toxic to many others. In effect, everything was stacked against the mammoths, mastodons, and sloths. Guthrie's argument is that extinction was inevitable.

The competition between species reminds us that all animals are parts of communities, and once one element is disturbed there might be a cascade of consequences throughout the food web. So the loss of the carnivores, such as the American lion, cheetah and smilodon, may simply have been due to the loss of their preferred prey. And this may also account for the extinction of giant birds, most of which had been eagles, vultures and condors. These were all flesh-eating birds, as were the teratorns. They may have relied on the vulnerable young camels, horses and even mammoths, either as predators or as scavengers.[21]

The ecologist E. C. Pielou expresses caution in accepting these environmental and ecological explanations for the mass extinctions.[22] Why, she asks, would the small modern beaver have been the victor in the competition against the massive castoroides? Why could not the America lion and smilodon have fed upon the many grazing animals that not only survived but whose numbers flourished, such as the bison, moose and deer? And why could the rotting carcasses of their victims not have fed the teratorns and the vultures? We don't normally think of such birds as fussy eaters.[23]

A strong argument, and with it comes an even stronger one – the simple fact that far from being a unique event, this period of global warming was just the most recent in the roller-coaster of climate change along which our planet has been propelled for at least the last million years. Periods of dramatic global warming have occurred roughly every 100,000 years, only for the planet then to revert back to ice-age conditions. On each of those occasions, the resulting changes in seasonality and plant distributions are unlikely to have been significantly different to those which occurred during our period of interest, the millennia following the most recent glacial maximum of 20,000 BC.

Yet the mega-fauna survived all of these previous climatic turnarounds, habitat loss, and ecological havoc. No doubt their numbers suffered, but they coped, finding refuges, perhaps in the far north, where conditions remained sufficiently similar to those of the preceding ice age. And then, once the climate reverted, they dispersed from those refuges to become a major element of the global fauna once again. Why, then, could the mastodon have not simply shifted their range northwards at the end of the last ice age, to where spruce and pine forests survived, and waited there to see out those ghastly warm and humid days of the post-glacial? Could not yesterday's camel, the giant sloths, castoroides and even horses have found somewhere to survive within the vast and astonishingly diverse continent of North America? Even if nothing ideal was available or accessible, could these animals not have learned to adapt to new habitats, and would not natural selection have provided a helping hand by making subtle changes in their physiology and behaviour? This is precisely what these species must have done many times during the previous millions of years. So why didn't the same tactic work at the end of the most recent ice age?

We have one sensational discovery about an attempt at survival – evidence that shocked scientists when it came to light in 1993. Up until March of that year it was thought that every single mammoth in the world had died by 10,000 BC – or at least very soon after. But then came the announcement from Russian scientists that they had found mammoth bones from animals that had survived long after this date on Wrangel Island – a remote and desolate dot of land in the Arctic Ocean, 200 kilometres north of Siberia.[24] Those mammoths had survived not just for a few hundred more years, but, staggeringly, for another 6,000, to the time of the Egyptian pyramids.

Twelve thousand years ago Wrangel Island was part of Beringia and the mammoths that roamed across its hills were just like those elsewhere, about 10 to 12 feet high at the shoulder. When the sea level rose, those mammoths were isolated – but they paid a price for their survival. For, over the course of about 500 generations, they shrunk in size, becoming dwarves; the last

survivors were no more than 6 feet high. This is not a unique event –
several other cases of mini-mammoths and mini-elephants have been
found from much earlier times in human history, such as on Cyprus, Malta
and islands off the coast of California. Some of those mammoths had been
no bigger than goats.

Becoming a dwarf is a good survival strategy when living on a small,
isolated island. When the quantity of food is restricted, there is a reproductive premium to be gained from reducing body-size – one can become
fully-grown and sexually mature more quickly and, consequently, pass on
one's genes into the next generation faster. And if one of the original
reasons for having a great hulk was to deter predators, this becomes unnecessary when there are no wolves, lions or sabre-tooth cats around. So we
should not be surprised that the mammoths of Wrangel Island were mere
dwarfs compared to those which had been killed by Clovis people at Lehner
Ranch.

Although their discovery was sensational, it has done little to resolve the
mystery of the mass extinction from elsewhere in the world by 10,000 BC.
The mammoths on Wrangel Island most likely survived because it maintained a rich diversity of grasses, herbs and shrubs, owing to its particular
climate and geology. So the island had indeed been a refuge for mammoths
as boggy tundra and woodland spread elsewhere. It was one from which the
mammoths could have expanded their number and resumed full body-size
again – but only if the next ice age, the fall in sea level and the return of
an extensive mammoth steppe had occurred before the Wrangel mini-
mammoths had also fallen into the pit of extinction.

Did they fall or were they pushed? Probably the latter, as the first date for
human occupation on Wrangel Island is coincident with the last date for
the mammoths. We know little about that occupation. We simply have a
few traces of stone artefacts that must have come from people pushed to the
very limits of their own survival in such an inhospitable land. But what
could have been easier prey than mini-mammoths, animals totally naïve
about predators and with nowhere to go?

The Wrangel Island discoveries seem to put the Clovis hunters back into
the dock. These show that mammoths could have found refugia at the end
of the last ice age, but that once humans enter the equation, extinction can
rapidly follow. So perhaps it was just those few animals that the Clovis
people killed each year, represented at sites such as Naco, Murray Springs
and Lehner Ranch, that pushed mammoths over the edge into the abyss of
extinction – animals whose populations had become fragmented and
numbers depleted, animals who were weak and in poor health as they
sought refuge in conditions of ecological chaos.

We must now make one final return to the Northern American continent to investigate what now seems to be the only possible solution to the
extinction. For although neither Clovis hunters nor climate change appear

to have had sufficient impact when working alone, they amounted to a death sentence for mammoths, sloths, mastodons and fellow victims when their forces were combined.

In conducting this final trial of the Clovis hunters and climate change conspirators, I will draw on my own research from the early 1990s. Much as I would love to excavate a Clovis kill site, this work was done with a computer, far from the rigours of fieldwork. Just as economists use computers to predict the future, such as the impact of an increase of interest rates on the level of inflation, so too can archaeologists build models to 'predict' the past. The objective of my research was to explore the impact of slightly increased rates of predation in conjunction with similarly increased frequencies of droughts on the level of the mammoth population in North America.[25]

One of the skills I acquired as a student was that of building mathematical models for animal populations and then using a computer to simulate prehistoric hunting methods.[26] I had worked with an ecologist to write a computer program to simulate the population dynamics of elephant populations in Africa. We had then experimented with the simulated populations in the computer by 'hitting' them with years of drought and with poachers to examine the likelihood that elephants would survive as a living species into the next century.

Mammoths and the Clovis problem were always in the back of my mind. Because of their similarities in body size, the population dynamics of modern-day African elephants and pleistocene North American mammoths will also have been similar. So I developed some alternative versions of the computer simulations geared to Clovis hunting of mammoths. Then, as with the elephant models, I used these simulations to do some experiments: different levels of mammoth hunting, different strategies – such as killing whole herds or just animals of a particular age or sex – different degrees of environmental stress.[27]

The findings were quite startling. It was of course possible to push mammoths into extinction by environmental change alone. Making the intensity of droughts ever more severe and their appearance more frequent, would eventually kill off any mammoth population. Infant mortality would become so high, and the onset of sexual maturity so late, that populations would decline rather than grow. Equally, even without any climate change the mammoth populations were very susceptible to human predation. Even if hunters were randomly taking animals from a herd at a rate of no more than 4 to 5 per cent each year, the populations would enter serious decline and suffer eventual extinction.

The reason for this is simply their slow rate of reproduction. Remove a few of the reproductively active females from a herd and the consequences can be immense. I then combined a small amount of hunting with a slight drought, neither of which would have been sufficient alone to kill off the population. The mixture, however, was potent. Within my computer I could watch mammoth populations of many thousands of animals crashing to extinction within a few decades. A graduate student of mine, Melissa Reed, built more sophisticated models which yielded the same result.

Nothing like a blitzkrieg was required to achieve this – the low degree of opportunistic hunting that is compatible with the archaeological record appears to be quite sufficient. To pursue the military analogy, guerilla warfare had devastating consequences. Moreover, the environmental stress and the hunting do not need to be concurrent. The population consequences of killing a few mammoths, especially the young females, may not be felt until a decade later; if that is when environmental stress also occurs, its effect on the population may be devastating.

The same explanation might suffice for the extinction of the ground sloth, the mastodon, the American horse, camel and tapir. However, it should be remembered that there is a complete absence of archaeological evidence for any of these animals and that the evidence for drought during the Younger Dryas remains contentious. Moreover, we must also attempt to discover why some large mammals avoided extinction, notably the bison which need to consume huge amounts of water to survive.[28]

In the spring of 1997 Melissa and I travelled to Lehner Ranch, Murray Springs and Naco with Paul Martin and Vance Haynes, the geoarchaeologist who excavated the site during the late 1960s.

We had given a seminar about our research at Arizona State University, describing the results of my work and Melissa's new simulations. This involved giving a demonstration on a monitor while we talked, so that Vance, Paul and others could watch our version of prehistory replayed: people colonising Alaska, ice sheets retreating, people passing through the ice-free corridor and dispersing across North America, the emergence of the Clovis culture and the onset of drought conditions in the south, and then mammoth populations collapsing into extinction

We approached the seminar with some trepidation. Vance and Paul had spent more than thirty years involved with the issue of mammoth extinction; they had been working on it before Melissa was born; they had dug and visited the sites, published books and papers, attended the major conferences arguing the odds for or against overkill while I was still at school. So, as we gave our presentation, I kept a watchful eye on them, worried as they whispered to each other, wondered what they thought, and feared we might have made some fundamental error that they alone could detect.

There was no cause for anxiety, as both Vance and Paul proved themselves to be constructive in their criticisms and generous with their praise. And they offered to take us to those classic sites – Murray Springs, Lehner

Ranch and Naco, the site of 'the one that got away'. Before that, Paul provided another treat – a visit to his hilltop laboratory overlooking Tucson and the Arizona desert. In a splendid glass-topped cabinet, in which lesser people would have kept coins, medals or pinned butterflies, he had his treasured collection of prehistoric dung balls.

Vance seemed to want to relive the excavations at Murray Springs. To get there we had to leave the vehicle and walk for a short distance across the scrubby desert. At the site he explained the stratigraphy, pointing to the layers in the exposed sections that might indicate prolonged drought at the end of the ice age, and then the transition to the Holocene. He showed us precisely where Elouise had been discovered – his name for the she-mammoth that he had found intact. She had shown no sign of being killed and was thought to have died a natural death. He supposed that Clovis people had scavenged upon her carcass. We saw where her footprints had been found; perhaps they were her final steps, or those of another animal, curious and maybe caring about the dying beast. Paul drew from his jacket a replica of an enigmatic artefact found at the site: a 10-inch-long piece of mammoth bone that had been carved and perforated with a hole, believed to have been a shaft-straighter. He asked Vance to place it precisely where it had been found, as if this were some ritualistic act. A few metres from the site of Elouise, we were shown the bison kill site; here the remains of a herd of bison which seem to have been driven into a swamp before being slaughtered were found.

The last North American mammoth died at some time around 10,000 BC. Whether it had a violent, bloody death perpetrated by Clovis hunters, or quietly passed away unseen other than by encircling vultures, is unknown. At a similar date, life also departed from the very last ground sloth and mastodon, from the last of the glyptodon, yesterday's camel and American horse. The world became a far poorer and less interesting place without them. The bison dominated the prairies and caribou were the masters of the boggy tundra that replaced the mammoth steppe, once home to such a magnificent array of ice-age mammals.

North America took on its modern appearance. The southwest turned into desert; great plains stretched through the centre of the continent. Deciduous woodland was established in the east and coniferous forest in the north. The ice sheets practically disappeared and the great lakes were rapidly draining to leave those which we know today. The climate settled down, with no more of the violent oscillations of the last few thousand years.

Something else had happened too: the last Clovis point was manufactured, used and discarded. With the passing of the ice-age bestiary and the emergence of a more stable environment, the Clovis way of life had disappeared. As it did so, human culture underwent the exact converse of nature;

it diversified, to make the North American continent a much richer and more interesting place. All its inhabitants continued to live as hunter-gatherers but never again would there be the unity to the North American people that was found during Clovis times.

28

Virginity Reconsidered

Hunter-gatherers of Tierra del Fuego and in the Amazon,
11,500–6000 BC

It is 11,000 BC. The cool water of Chinchihuapi Creek laps across John Lubbock's toes as he sits quietly upon its bank pondering the journey ahead, one that will take him through American history until he reaches 5000 BC. The surface shimmers with light beams that have penetrated the canopy from the newly risen sun. Other than for a kingfisher perching upon an overhanging branch, Lubbock sits alone. Monte Verde has been abandoned, but elsewhere in South America people are living in almost every ecological nook and cranny, and by virtually every type of hunting and gathering imaginable: some survive as big-game hunters, some as fishermen, others as plant gatherers. Their cultures are also varied: some continue to use the crudest of stone tools, others have adopted elegant stone points chipped into a variety of shapes. Indeed, South America at this date is far more culturally diverse than its northern neighbour, a continent where the Clovis point and its minor variants are all-pervasive.

From Monte Verde Lubbock follows the Chinchihuapi into the valley of the River Maullín, and then climbs into and across the Andes. As he does so the temperate forest gives way to beech woodland and then to scattered, stunted pines. Finally he walks across a carpet of grass and flowers, through a mountain pass between glaciers and alongside a crystal-blue lake. Peaks of snow-capped granite tower above, turning from grey to pink in the brilliant sun. The glaciers extend far down the western mountainsides as long tongues of ice that stretch into the valleys and beyond.

Lubbock heads south and begins to encounter abandoned campsites and scatters of charred animal bones. The grasslands on which they lie cover an extensive plateau that is cut by deep ravines. It tilts gently towards the Atlantic Ocean, its coastline located much further to the east than it is today as the sea level remains at its ice-age low. During the next 10,000 years these grasslands will become quite arid, making them so barren that Charles Darwin will consider them cursed by sterility when he too travels through Patagonia in the early nineteenth century.

Lubbock reaches a region of shallow flat-bottomed valleys, canyons and low hills close to the Atlantic coast. The ravine he enters provides shelter from the exhausting wind that has been a constant companion since leaving the Andes. Others are also finding shelter – a group of hunters returning to their cave in the cliff-like wall of the valley side. There are four of them, dressed in furs and hides, carrying segments of a horse. Lubbock follows them inside.

The air is smoky and dense from a fire burning dung. As his eyes adjust, Lubbock sees six others – women, children and an old man – sitting in the cave; to the rear, more bodies shuffle in the darkness. Pieces of precious wood are placed to refuel the fire and steaks of horse meat are set to roast. Lubbock sits close to the fire, as grateful as the hunters for its warmth, and listens to the telling of the hunt. He learns that they trapped the horse in a ravine, ambushed and killed it from above with stone-tipped spears. It was butchered and the best joints carried home. During their return journey, the men had encountered a recently deceased giant sloth. Had they not killed the horse they would have scavenged upon its carcass. Instead they left it for the vultures that they knew would soon arrive.

During the next few days Lubbock learns that this hunter-gatherer group uses several different caves, frequently shifting their few belongings and dependants from one shelter to another. One that is particularly favoured is about 30 kilometres to the west, located in an old volcanic crater. As well as horse and sloth, they hunt guanaco – a llama-like creature that lives in small herds on the grassland. They are effective hunters, making use of spear points as lethal as those used by Clovis hunters far to the north but of a quite different design. Their points lack the Clovis flute, the central shallow groove, but have an elegant long stem.

On one occasion Lubbock travels with a party of hunters to the far south, to what we today call Tierra del Fuego. When sitting in one cramped shelter, that known as Tros Arroyos,[1] near deafened by a howling wind and surrounded by the blackest of black nights, Lubbock knew that he had reached the very end of the earth. Across the glowing embers his companions talk quietly, deciding whether the next day should be spent searching for horse or setting traps for fox. Lubbock opens *Prehistoric Times* and finds sufficient firelight to read what his namesake thought about the nineteenth-century inhabitants of this barren land.

Victorian John Lubbock had no personal experience of the Fuegians and so he drew on the account provided by his great friend and mentor, Charles Darwin, who had arrived in Tierra del Fuego in 1834 during his voyage on the *Beagle*.[2] The people that Darwin met had been living entirely by hunting and gathering, making his account, and those of other Victorian travellers, of great value to modern-day archaeologists when attempting to interpret the prehistoric remains in caves such as Tros Arroyos. Indeed, the nineteenth-century Fuegians were most likely the direct descendants of the very first inhabitants of Tierra del Fuego, those who had used Tros Arroyos and other caves in 11,000 BC. But Victorian accounts need to be read with great caution in order to separate useful observation from racial prejudice.

'While going on shore,' Darwin had explained, 'we pulled alongside a canoe with six Fuegians. They were the most abject and miserable creatures I anywhere beheld ... These poor wretches were stunted in their growth, their hideous faces bedaubed with white paint, their skins filthy and greasy, their hair entangled, their voices discordant, their gestures violent and without dignity. Viewing such men, one can hardly make oneself believe they are fellow-creatures and inhabitants of the same world.' Darwin had continued to describe how they 'slept on the wet ground coiled up like animals', and avoided famine by cannibalism and parricide (the murder of a near relative). Robert Fitzroy, captain of the *Beagle*, thought the women should be called she-Fuegians and that 'they may be fit for ... uncouth men, but to civilized people their appearance is disgusting'.[13]

Victorian John Lubbock had also extracted from Darwin's account descriptions of expertly crafted technology and sophisticated hunting-and-gathering methods – quite the opposite of what one would have expected from poor wretches and uncouth men. The Fuegians had wigwam-like shelters, 'straight and well polished arrows' and 'hooks very nearly the same shape as ours' as part of a wide range of stone-tipped spears, fishing tackle and bows and arrows. They had remarkably well trained hunting dogs, were excellent swimmers, and were evidently adept at ambushing guanaco. 'In reading almost any account of savages,' Victorian Lubbock had concluded, 'it is impossible not to admire the skill with which they use their rude weapons and implements.'[4] He was evidently struggling to reconcile the prevailing Victorian attitudes to savages, epoused by no less a figure than Charles Darwin himself, with his own admiration for the skills required to make and use hunter-gatherer tools.

Modern John Lubbock's journey from Monte Verde to the caves of southern Patagonia had taken him from one of the most recent excavations in South America to two of the earliest. The first cave he entered was Fell's Cave; that in the volcanic crater had been Palli Aike. Both were investigated in 1934 during the pioneering archaeological survey of southern Patagonia undertaken by Junius Bird from the American Museum of Natural History.[5] His excavations uncovered the remains of fireplaces, the distinctive stone tools which soon became known as 'fishtail' points[6] and bones from horse, sloth and guanaco.[7]

Bird knew that these deposits were of great antiquity. He had recognised the bones of extinct animals, and found that the remains in Fell's Cave had been sealed under roof collapse, on which later people had camped. Bird had little idea about the age of the fishtail points, or the means to find out, as radiocarbon dating had still to be invented. It was not until 1969 that this technique revealed that Fell's Cave had been occupied as early as 11,000 BC.[8] That was, of course, long before the discovery of Monte Verde but it remains one of the earliest-dated occupations in the whole of the Americas.[9]

It is now 10,800 BC. Lubbock is in the Amazon, having travelled more than 5,000 kilometres northwards from Tierra del Fuego.[10] He paddles a canoe on a river that will one day be known as the Tapajós, although its course will change many times before it receives that name. In Europe and western Asia the Younger Dryas has just arrived; hunters at Stellmoor in the Ahrensburg valley are checking their bows, while the dwellings of 'Ain Mallaha have been deserted. But here in the Amazon the Younger Dryas will go by quite unnoticed. Lubbock passes caiman basking on sandbanks in the river; a dolphin follows his canoe.

The Amazon today is the greatest museum on earth, with contents worth far more than the combined treasures of the British Museum, the Louvre, and the New York Metropolitan. Its plant communities passed through the whole ice age almost unchanged. And although we are doing our utmost to destroy it today, much of this museum survives as a twenty-first-century prehistoric world.

It was once thought that the Amazon had been decimated by the ice age. Arid conditions were supposed to have broken up the continuous forest into a patchwork of woodlands, savannah and grassland. But when samples of pollen were collected from ice-age sediments, these showed that the forest had remained virtually intact.[11] Practically the same range of plants and trees in broadly the same proportions had continued growing in the basin throughout the collapse of global temperatures that culminated in the LGM and then through the rise of temperatures to the present day. Some developments did occur; at 20,000 BC the Amazon lowlands had been home to several tree species that require a cool climate and are today restricted to the eastern slopes of the Andes. But their exclusion as temperatures rose was a matter of detail – the rainforest has hardly changed at all.

Lubbock entered the Amazon basin after a journey through the grasslands and thorny woodlands of eastern South America, passing close to Pedra Furada where Niède Guidon will one day excavate. He met many communities of hunter-gatherers but passed quickly by, anxious to reach the rainforest. The woodland had gradually become thicker, the temperatures rose and soon he had taken to travelling by water rather than land. Tropical animals and plants appeared as one small tributary led into another and transported Lubbock to the heart of the rainforest.

Lubbock's river joins another, one much larger and flowing more swiftly with dark brown rather than crystal-clear water – the Amazon itself. A troop of monkeys in the tree canopy is alarmed and starts to howl, herons are startled and take flight. Soon after entering the new current Lubbock sees a canoe moored on the far bank, and then two figures standing by the shallows listening to the commotion. They turn and disappear into the trees. Lubbock crosses the river, ties his boat to theirs and follows the trail. It leads through a strip of marshy woodland and then into the thick forest, soon becoming a well-worn path.

Below the trees it is cooler and quite dark as the dense canopy provides few spy-holes for the sun. The ground is soft underfoot from thick layers of rotting leaf litter; the air is thick with the pungency of organic decay. Lubbock passes an immense variety of forest trees, many with massive vertical trunks wrapped in huge serpent-like creepers. Some have buttresses so vast they appear as wooden walls within the forest.

He catches occasional glimpses of the two men and notices that one carries a large fish strung across his back, its tail sometimes dragging along the ground. They walk swiftly, never pausing to rest. After almost 10 kilometres a peak of brilliant red rock emerges triumphantly above the trees, and soon Lubbock faces a warren of caves in a sandstone knoll. The fish-bearers disappear inside, calling out that they have returned. Lubbock hears greetings; a joke is evidently made as hearty laughter follows.

As he approaches the cave entrance Lubbock sees paintings on its sandstone wall: concentric circles in red and yellow, hand-prints and an upside-down schematic figure with rays emanating sun-like from its head. They remind him of those at Pedra Furada.

Lubbock has arrived at Monte Alegre – or Happy Mountain in Portuguese – and is about to join the occupants of Pedra Pintada cave. This is one of the most important archaeological sites of the Amazon basin – indeed within the whole of South America. It was found in 1991 during a survey in the lower Amazon basin, conducted by Anna Roosevelt from the Field Museum of Chicago. When her team excavated the site, they found evidence for human habitation at 10,800 BC,[12] proving – to the surprise of many anthropologists – that people were able to live as hunter-gatherers in the Amazon rainforest. Anthropologists had previously believed that without slash-and-burn agriculture people were unable to acquire sufficient food from the forest and consequently that the Amazon had remained unoccupied until at least 5000 BC. But, as Lubbock is about to discover, those who occupy Pedra Pintada live by hunting and gathering alone.

In the cave's airy interior there are at least ten people standing in a circle admiring the catch. They wear few clothes and are reminiscent of today's Amazonian Indians – stout, with copper skins, straight black hair and elegantly painted faces. The floor is covered with mats made from enormous leaves; there are baskets and bags stacked along a wall; spears, fishing rods and harpoons are propped in a corner. Wooden bowls at the rear of the cave contain lumps of red pigment that have been crushed and mixed with water. Along another wall there are bundles of soft grass, tied with plant fibres into cushions. In the middle, a small smouldering fireplace next to which the fish lies magnificently on the ground.

A woman crouches and with a stone knife removes the fish's head. This is offered to a young man, the fish bearer, who takes it with a grin. He sucks at each eye-socket in turn while blood and juices trickle down his chest. With that preliminary over, the fish is taken outside and gutted.[13]

Lubbock spends the next few days with the people of Pedra Pintada, helping to gather freshwater mussels and collecting a bewildering assortment of fruits, nuts, roots and leaves. Some, such as brazil nuts and cashews, are familiar to him, while others are quite new. He sees a new tool-making technique: flakes of stone are shaped into spear points not by striking with hammer-stones but by pressing pointed pieces of bone against the stone with such force that tiny chips become detached. This is known by archaeologists as 'pressure flaking' and was used throughout the prehistoric world to make particularly elaborate artefacts, such as the triangular points found at this site and the Clovis points of North America.

As Lubbock has already seen a great deal of hunting and plant-gathering in his South American travels, the sophistication of his unknowing host's foraging comes as no surprise. Neither does their skill and ingenuity in using an immense range of plant material for making clothing and equipment. But the extent of freshwater fishing is quite new to Lubbock and at this the people excel. Large fish are speared from boats and smaller ones caught in nets. Recent Amazonian people have used poison to catch fish and it is easy to believe that those who inhabited Pedra Pintada in 10,800 BC did likewise.

Lubbock learns about this when he accompanies a party of men, women and children – about a dozen in all – into the forest. They go to one specific tree about a kilometre from their cave. It is a mighty size, the girth far larger than any Lubbock has seen before. Several metres from its base the forest floor has evidently been disturbed many times before. He watches as the party space out and begin to dig little pits to expose a network of roots. Next, they use stone saws and knives to cut sections, each about the size of Lubbock's forearm, and pile them into baskets. Once these are full, the party departs, with the young women carrying the load upon their heads.

A tiny trail is followed to a small clearing by the edge of a shallow creek where the baskets are emptied on the ground. Both men and women disappear momentarily into the forest; Lubbock remains with the children, throwing sticks into the shallow, murky water. The men return with stout wooden sticks and proceed to smash the roots to a pulp, keeping their mouths firmly closed as bits of fibre and white sap are sprayed into the air.

Meanwhile the women have returned with large flat waxy leaves. Within a few minutes, these have been tied into loose baskets. Root pulp is scooped inside and the men carry these away, taking care to avoid any contact with the oozing, fibrous mush. Lubbock remains with the women and children, passing them branches and leaves to help build a dam across the creek. The men have reached about 500 metres upstream where they wade knee-deep in the water and swish the baskets around to create a milky-white cloud.

Back at the dam the women are now resting while eating some berries.

They are soon joined by the men, who prefer to chew upon wads of leaves. The children peer excitedly into the water and then shriek as they see the first fish arrive. They are literally swimming for their lives, trying to escape the poison that is drifting downstream. Once they reach the dam they have nowhere to go. Some turn and swim back to an immediate death while others flounder on to the sticks and leaves, where they suffocate. Within minutes the surface of the creek is shimmering with the bodies of dead fish. These are collected by the women who thread each fish through its gills on to twine with bone needles. Soon the whole party is returning to Pedra Pintada draped with their silvery catch. Gutting, washing and baking will remove the poison. But Lubbock is no longer with them: he has departed westwards for the distant Andes.

Roosevelt's excavation found the remains of many animals and plants still exploited by Amazonian people today, including the fruits of the tarumā tree which is used for fishing bait. The animal bones were poorly preserved but allowed an immense variety of species to be identified, including snakes, amphibians, birds, tortoises and – in greatest abundance – fish, ranging in types from those just a few centimetres to over 1.5 metres in length.

Amidst the plant remains, animal bones and fireplaces Roosevelt found more than 30,000 stone flakes from tool-making – but no more than twenty-four finished tools – and hundreds of lumps of red pigment. She took immense care to ensure that this was the same pigment that had been used to make the wall-paintings in the cave, examining it microscopically and analysing its chemistry. It did indeed prove identical to that used in many of the paintings, providing one of the most thoroughly documented cases for Pleistocene rock art in the Americas.

Pedra Pintada was abandoned soon after 10,000 BC. As at Monte Verde, quite where the people went we do not know. For more than 2,000 years the cave was empty, while its floor became covered with blown sand. And then new occupants arrived, coming to use the cave on a far more casual basis and having no interest in painting the walls. They left a similar array of plant, animal and fish remains, together with something else, something quite new in the whole of South America – pottery. By 6000 BC those living in the Amazon had invented the use of ceramic bowls, sometimes decorating them with simple geometric designs.[14] As that new technology emerged, so an old one faded as the fine triangular stone points were abandoned and stone stools became no more than simple flakes and unshaped grinding stones. It would take another 1,500 years before pottery was adopted in northern Central America, and another 4,000 years until it was found in the central Andes, even though its people were already domesticating plants and animals.

Fragments of similar pottery are found within shell middens that appear along the riverbanks after 6000 BC, showing how some of the Amazonian people had begun to specialise in river fauna, both the molluscs and the many varieties of fish. As time passed, riverside villages developed, and eventually the cultivation of manioc and maize began.[15] These were the type of people first encountered by Victorian travellers, such as Darwin's intellectual bedfellow Alfred Russel Wallace, long after the hunter-gatherers of Pedra Pintada cave – and presumably elsewhere in the Amazon basin – had faded from human memory.

The triangular stone spear points that were found were assumed to have come from prehistoric horticulturists, living in much the same way as recent Amazonian Indians. And yet both their shape and technique of manufacture were quite similar to points found elsewhere in South America and already known to have a terminal ice-age date.[16] And so Roosevelt's excavations in Pedra Pintada were very special indeed – not only extending the known duration of occupation in the Amazonian rainforest, but adding a further way of life for people who lived as the ice age came to its close.

But perhaps the most intriguing consequence of her work is that it questions the 'virginity' of the forests. Such was the term used by Alfred Russel Wallace in his 1889 account of his Amazonian travels. Like all other nineteenth-century travellers Wallace assumed that the whole forest was quite unaltered by human hands. But now that Roosevelt has revealed an extra 5,000 years of human occupation, this must be questioned. The possibility arises that the distinct clusters of food-producing plants that are found, such as the brazil and cashew nut trees, are as much a consequence of human activity as of nature.[17] The exhibits of the great museum of the Amazon may have been slowly and subtly rearranged by generations of prehistoric foragers.

29
Herders and the 'Christ-Child'

Animal and plant domestication in the Andes, and coastal foragers, 10,500–5000 BC

With aching limbs, John Lubbock shelters from a bitter wind as another spell of dizziness overcomes him.[1] Beyond the rocks there is a grassy plain and then a lake which blends imperceptibly with the distant sky. He is in the puna grasslands of the Peruvian Andes, having left the tropics long ago to climb steep valleys while the forest dwindled to woodland, and then to scattered and stunted trees. The air has become thin, his mind and body aches with fatigue and nausea.

The puna is a 4,000-metre-high landscape of rolling hills and rocky escarpments, one riddled with small streams and pock-marked by lakes.[2] The lake before him is the largest he has seen; it will become known as Lake Junin, located 800 kilometres northeast of its much larger and more famous neighbour, Lake Titicaca.

Lubbock needs to visit the puna as this will eventually become home to the Incas. Their great cities, roads, and temples will appear several thousand years after his travels have come to an end. But a foundation of their civilisation now grazes before him on the plain. Not one, but a whole herd of creatures about the size of a deer, with long necks and pointy ears. They are vicuños, the wild ancestor to the alpaca that will become an essential source of meat and wool.

On his journey to the puna, and indeed throughout his South American travels outside of the tropics, Lubbock has encountered a similar but rather larger type of camelid, as these animals are known, the guanaco, which also lives in herds but prefers lower elevations and is less tied to streams and lakes. It will give rise to the other key domesticate, one which has a broad back and will be the principal means of transporting goods across the high Andes – the llama.

All the animals Lubbock has seen are wild and will remain so for several thousand more years. The date is 10,500 BC and they are hunted by people who have already been living in the puna grasslands for many generations. A group of hunters arrive by Lubbock's side, their footsteps and voices having been silenced by the wind. There are eight of them, dressed in thick hides and armed with stone-tipped spears. Within a few minutes four have left, departing in the opposite direction to the lake. The others sit and check their weapons; they need to ensure that the points are secure and sharp.

One takes a bone awl from his bag and forces it so hard against his spear point that a small flake is removed from near the tip; this perfects its symmetry to enhance its penetrating power.

After an hour's rest the men set off for the vicuña herd; Lubbock's dizziness has passed and so he follows as they clamber over the crag and head towards the lake. They walk slowly and in silence, soon beginning to crouch among the knee-length grass. Before long they are flat on their stomachs, wriggling inch by inch through the wet grass towards a grazing beast. The target is the leader of the herd, the male who rarely moves far from his harem and ensures that they keep within territorial bounds.

Momentarily disturbed, the vicuña raises its head, sniffs the air and looks quizzically around, but with nothing to be seen or heard he soon returns to the grass. Lubbock moves with the hunters once again and eventually draws so close that he can hear the tearing and grinding of tough grass stems by the vicuños' teeth.

A subtle nod is given and the hunters stand and launch their spears in unison. The weapons miss, but all is not lost, for, as Lubbock watches, the hunters take up the chase, scattering the harem and sending the male running straight into a second set of spears. These come from the other hunters who had taken cover in the lakeside reeds on the far side of the harem.

That evening Lubbock sits with the hunters and their families in the mouth of a large cave that is to be found among limestone crags on the southern side of the lake. Small walls have been built in the cave mouth to keep out the wind that persists throughout thier summertime occupation. There is a spectacular northward view across the water to distant peaks, once snow-capped but now fading silhouettes as the day draws to a close.

When John Rick of Stanford University excavated Pachamachay Cave in 1974 and 1975 he found the remains of many vicuña carcasses and the spears used to hunt them.[3] Those from 10,500 BC were deeply buried below the debris left by many later generations of occupants as the cave continued in use for 9,000 years. But whereas the first occupants had been hunters of vicuña and guanaco, the last had been herders of alpaca and llama – an economic switch that probably occurred as a gradual drift from hunting to herding rather than a sudden break in lifestyles. While it is impossible to know exactly when this switch occurred, as the bones from these four animals are nearly identical,[4] the best guess is that it was around 5000 BC. By that date the camelids begin to account for the vast majority of the animals killed, not just in Pachamachay Cave but in all the excavated caves of the Peruvian puna. Before then, the hunters had been killing a greater diversity of game, including deer and birds.

Perhaps more telling is that around 5000 BC the proportion of new-born and young animals increases from about a quarter to a half of the total.[5]

Bruce Smith of the Smithsonian Institution, and a leading expert on the origins of food production in the Americas, suspects that this reflects the increase in infant mortality that arises when animals are kept in crowded corrals and infectious diseases become rampant. Such high levels of disease-induced mortality among young animals are a pervasive feature of llama herds today.[6]

John Rick's studies concluded that the hunters of the puna grasslands took up permanent residence within the largest of the caves soon after 10,500 BC. There were probably several groups, each using a territory centring on a lake basin and containing a cave as the principal residence. The density and range of artefacts within Pachamachay, together with the evidence for walls and constant cleaning, suggest that the cave had been used in a manner quite unlike the temporary, short-term occupations of hunter-gatherers who are always on the move. And hence, just as with the Natufian people in western Asia, sedentism may have been a crucial step towards agriculture. But in this case it was the prelude to animal herding rather than plant cultivation.

One can readily imagine settled hunters developing an intimate knowledge of the herds within the catchment of their cave, most likely identifying many of the individual animals, especially those males who gained control of harems. The other males lived in troops and may soon have become the principal prey as such animals were expendable – their loss caused no threat to the survival and reproduction of the population as a whole. Selective hunting may then have been supplemented by providing forage during harsh winters and so controlling the movements of herds. Injured or orphaned animals may have been cared for, which would ultimately have provided the basis for a domesticated herd. Once present, such herds may have played a significant role in bringing another species in from the wild, not an animal but a plant: quinua.

Quinua is one of two plants that dominated the early prehistoric food-producing economies of the high-altitude basin and valleys of the Andes, the other being the potato.[7] A member of the chenopod group of plants, known more familiarly to many as goosefoot, quinua became a key crop of the Incas and is still grown by subsistence farmers today who value its high protein content. When mature, its multicoloured seed-heads stand waist-high, and can be harvested to make biscuits, bread and porridge. The two key differences between the wild and domestic chenopod variants are the same as those between the wild and domestic wheat of western Asia: both domestic variants 'wait for the harvester' and neither can delay germination, which results in the simultaneous ripening of all plants within a crop.

The earliest quinua has come from another cave in the Junin basin, no more than 30 kilometres from Pachamachay and also excavated by John Rick. This is Panaulauca Cave which contains a similar range of artefacts and animal bones, and was most likely a base camp used by another group of hunter-gatherers who had settled in the puna. The chenopod seeds from Panaulauca of 5000 BC had thin 'testas', or seed coats, comparable to those of domestic quinua and indicative of the reduced ability to delay germination. So, by this date, stands of quinua may have been growing in the vicinity of the cave, perhaps close to corrals where llama or alpaca were being kept – or perhaps actually within old corrals themselves.

Camelids enjoy eating the wild varieties of quinua, but cannot digest the seed. These pass through the animal's gut undamaged and are deposited with a quantity of natural fertiliser, often far from where the plants had originally grown. Bruce Smith suggests that if the early herders had begun to corral their herds at night, then stands of chenopods would have flourished within their organic soils. By simply relocating the corrals, and using the fences to protect the thriving new stands from grazing, a substantial food source could have easily arisen close to their settlement. It would then have been a small step for cultivation – weeding, watering, transporting – to have begun the subtle, unintentional genetic alterations to those plants, turning the wild chenopods into domesticated quinua.

Another plant was domesticated in the Andes, probably in the basin of Lake Titicaca. But unlike quinua, this plant played a major role in global history after it was taken from South America to Europe in the sixteenth century. It was the potato. There are several variants of wild and cultivated potatoes in South America today and the Lake Titicaca basin is the centre of genetic variability – a sign that this is where the first domesticated variants arose.

No archaeological traces of early cultivation have yet been found within the basin and surrounding river valleys. But this most likely reflects the limited search for open settlements. Almost all excavation has taken place in the highland caves which are unlikely to provide a complete picture of prehistoric life in central Peru. Bruce Smith believes that once such open settlements are discovered, the domestication of the potato will be found to have arisen as part of a joint package with the llama, alpaca and quinua.

One more species may also have been involved: the guinea pig. Bones from these animals were found by John Rick in Pachamachay Cave and they are known to have been a much-hunted species throughout the Andes before becoming a domesticated source of meat. Exactly when that occurred also remains unknown. Like the mice and rats of western Asia, the wild variants may have been attracted to the first sedentary settlements due to the reliable food supplies either from human waste or from crops. Guinea pigs were susceptible to domestication because of their high reproductive rate and the ease of being raised in confined areas – which also makes them ideal pets for children today.

The day begins slowly at Pachamachay Cave. John Lubbock wakes at dawn and finds that most others remain asleep. They use the rear of the cave, which is made comfortable and warm by soft bedding and hides. A young woman sits in the entrance nursing her baby; a few children fiddle with sticks close by. A man wakes and invigorates the fire that has smouldered all night. As the others stir, spiny spheres are taken from a wicker basket and tossed into the ashes. These are fruits from prickly pear cacti that grow as rounded mounds throughout the puna zone. After a few minutes they are dragged or flicked out of the ashes. The now spineless but juicy fruits are passed around, wiped clean and eaten whole.

All the plant foods eaten by the residents of Pachamachay Cave are from wild species. Their excavated remnants were analysed by Deborah Pearsall of the University of Missouri who found a great variety of species, even though the opportunity for preservation was limited to what had been accidentally charred in the fire.[8] While some remnants, such as those from prickly pears and chenopods, had most likely come from fruits and seeds collected for food, others may have had a medicinal role. There were, for instance, ninety seeds of a plant from the Euphorbia family. Such plants are widely used in Andean folk medicine today: the white sap from some is used as a laxative, the mashed tubers of others help relieve stomach pains, and provide an ointment for skin eruptions.

Lubbock takes a small portion of dried vicuña meat and a couple of prickly pears and leaves the Junin basin, embarking on a challenging journey across the mountains to Lake Titicaca. From there he descends through a labyrinth of valleys to the coastal lands of modern-day Peru. At 10,000 BC he arrives in a landscape of barren, dusty foothills cut by narrow tree-lined valleys which make ribbon-like oases. It is warmer than in the mountains but surprisingly cool for the tropics, especially when the coastal hills are so frequently covered by a thick grey-fog.

Fishy smells greet Lubbock on his arrival at a small cluster of circular dwellings on the north bank of what will become known as Quebrada Jaguay, or the Jaguay Canyon. Canoes are also arriving, returning from a fishing trip in the estuary mouth about 8 kilometres away. Heavy nets are being hauled ashore in the half light of dusk. Lubbock joins in, emptying the fish into baskets and picking out those trapped between the vegetable-fibre cords.

The semi-subterranean huts are built from brushwood, clay daub and thick wooden posts. Smoke ekes its way through the roofs and soon tempts Lubbock to sit by the fire inside. Between the huts there is the typical debris of hunter-gatherer life: scatters of tool-making waste, piles of roots waiting to be turned into fibres, and of rushes to be made into baskets. Along the riverbank are the remnants of fireplaces and roasting pits.

Lubbock finds these coastal dwellers in the midst of change. People have been living in the same vicinity for almost 1,000 years and throughout that time have been fishing and collecting clams. This settlement was once a campsite used by people who travelled each year from the coast into the mountains. On their highland visits they hunted the guanaco and collected obsidian – that volcanic glass valued throughout the Stone Age world – returning with as much as they could carry.

But such mountain sojourns are no longer made and so there is no obsidian for Lubbock to see. The people now spend all year in the coastal lands, although they occupy three or four different settlements each year. They come to Quebrada Jaguay with a specific purpose in mind: to catch the shoals of drum fish that flourish in the estuary mouth and to collect the abundant clams. While doing so they will also restore the huts and collect gourds from the valley floor. Once the shoals depart, the people leave for the next site in their annual round, perhaps to trap cormorants or to fish for anchovy.[9]

The site of Quebrada Jaguay was discovered in 1970 but excavations only began in 1996 by Daniel Sandweiss from the University of Maine.[10] Because it lacked any distinctively-shaped stone tools – such as the fishtail points Lubbock saw in Tierra del Fuego or the triangular points from the Amazon – Sandweiss had no idea how old the fishbones, clam shells, burnt stones and post holes were before radiocarbon dating. When it was shown that people had lived on the edge of Quebrada Jaguay since 11,000 BC, the site was immediately acclaimed as a major discovery. It demonstrated how the very earliest people in Peru were proficient in the use of marine resources, implying boats and a fishing technology. It also provided further evidence for the diversity in Early American lifestyles.

For the next few weeks Lubbock remains with these coastal people – helping to knot fibres, joining the fishing trips and accompanying them when they visit neighbours and keep watch upon the ever-changing sea and sky. During his travels he notices that much of the landscape is covered by a thick mantle of sediment – sometimes a fine silt, at others a coarse gravel. In the mouth of one valley, this reaches waist height around tree-trunks; in others, the trees have evidently been toppled and crushed. On one occasion he finds a vertical exposure that looks like the side of an extraordinarily deep archaeological excavation. River water had undercut the steep valley side and a mass of sediment had slumped into the river to leave a vertical wall. Within that, he sees the crushed walls, timbers and fireplaces of a hut.

More than 10,000 years later David Keefer of the US Geological Survey made a similar discovery when he inspected a cutting through sediments made for new roads in Quebrada Tacahuay, a valley about fifty kilometres south of Lubbock's fishing village.[11] Sandwiched between thick layers of coarse gravels, he found traces of hearths and rubbish heaps which were dated to 10,800 BC:[12] the remnants of a settlement that had been suddenly inundated by a massive flow of debris caused by violent rains.

After Keefer and his colleagues had acquired more dates, they realised that the coastline of southern Peru had suffered four major debris flows between 10,800 and 8000 BC. There could have been only one cause of such repeated devastation to the landscape. Keefer had found the earliest yet known work of the 'Christ child' – better known by its Spanish name, El Niño – which continues to lay waste to the modern world.[13]

El Niño is caused by a change in the pattern of sea-surface temperatures and atmospheric pressure across the tropical Pacific Ocean. This happens when a large mass of warm water forms off the coast of Central and South America at regular intervals of between two and ten years in length, disrupting the currents and preventing the nutrients from lower, colder levels reaching the surface. As a result, fish populations abandon the region for cooler, nutrient-rich waters. This can have a devastating effect on the fishing industry – something which most likely supported no more than a few hundred people in 10,000 BC but which now sustains millions of lives.

Even more dramatic is the havoc that changing air pressure wreaks on regional weather patterns around the world. The Pacific coasts of the Americas become inundated with El Niño storms, leading to extensive flooding, while Southeast Asia is afflicted with drought. Computer models predict that the frequency and strength of El Niño events are likely to increase with global warming. This appears to have been proved by David Keefer's discovery that such events only occurred every 700 to 800 years at the close of the ice age but have intensified to a mere ten-year cycle during the last 150 years. That development was most likely due to natural global warming alone, which peaked at 7000 BC. And so we are left to wonder about the impact – environmental and economic – of the next hundred years of artificial global warming on El Niño.

While we can only guess at the events and suffering at Quebrada Tacahuay in 10,800 BC, a vivid illustration of El Niño's power is provided by the catastrophe that struck the coast of Peru in 1997–8.[14] A pool of warm water 400 metres deep and the size of Canada had developed in the Pacific. The resulting storms began pounding the Pacific coast in December 1997 and their impact soon reached apocalyptic proportions. Within six months, rain-swollen rivers and mud-slides had destroyed three hundred bridges, swept away entire villages, and made half a million people homeless. The fishing industry was devastated, ports were destroyed, and ideal conditions created for the spread of disease. The sea flooded 15 kilometres inland. The deluge that struck the desert city of Trujillo eroded the city's oldest cemetery and sent ancient coffins and cadavers floating through the streets. When faced with this terrifying spectacle, the city leaders dedicated one stormy Sunday in March 1998 as a day for beleaguered citizens to beg God for relief. Perhaps that is just what people had done in 10,800 BC when their settlement was destroyed. What else can people do when faced with the might of El Niño – the 'Christ Child'?

A pair of cormorants momentarily appear in the moonlight as they fly low across the water, their wing-tips almost touching the sea. They disappear into darkness as clouds engulf the moon and waves suck at the sand as they retreat across the beach. Lubbock sits shivering on a headland in the dead of night, transfixed by the Pacific Ocean.

It is time to leave South America. As Lubbock steps into the darkness, his thoughts return to drinking hot tea at Monte Verde. And then to horsemeat in Tierra del Fuego, fishing in the Amazon, stalking vicuña in the Andes and collecting clams in Quebrada Jaguay. He wonders whether the Monte Verde people really were the First Americans, about the meanings of rock paintings, and why people had become herders rather than hunters. South America after the ice has been a continent of remarkable people and unanswered questions. But now he must travel to Mexico and then North America to discover what happened after the time of mammoths and Clovis.

30

A Double-Take in the Oaxaca Valley

The domestication of maize, squash and beans in Mexico,
10,500–5000 BC

I must confess to a feeling of boyish excitement on a September afternoon in AD 2000 when I sat cross-legged against one cave wall and then leapt up to squat beside another. The desire to perform such antics had overwhelmed me as soon as I had penetrated the last thicket of thorns and manoeuvred around the final prickly pear to arrive at Guilá Naquitz, a small cave in central Mexico.

It was hardly a cave at all – little more than a ledge below an overhang within a cliff face, one located in the valley of Oaxaca. Near by there were proper caves, ones with gaping entrances and tunnels deep into the rock. Further away in the valley there were spectacular archaeological sites, most notably the ancient city of Monte Alban where the Zapotec civilisation had built their capital city 2,500 years ago.

Although Monte Alban's architecture had been impressive, my visit to its hilltop had been of marginal interest. I had come to Oaxaca to visit Guilá Naquitz – the site where the earliest domesticated plants in the New World have been found.[1] And even if its speleological credentials were limited, crouching below the overhang was worth all the sweat, cactus spines and thorn scratches that I had acquired during the long walk in the midday sun.

One moment I imagined myself as one of the hunter-gatherers who had camped in Guilá Naquitz at 8000 BC, and in the next I was the Michigan-based archaeologist Kent Flannery at the moment of his (re)discovery of the cave on 26 January 1966 – thirty-four years and 243 days before my own visit. He would later describe how he had found stone artefacts and plant remains on the surface, the latter surviving due to the extreme aridity of the soil. For me, the cave was bare – except for a pile of goat droppings left by its most recent occupants. Flannery had taken just six weeks to make his excavation in the spring of 1966. He then required another fifteen years to analyse the finds and publish the results.

My fascination with Guilá Naquitz was due to the contrast it provided between ordinary lives and extraordinary events in the history of the world. Between 8500 and 6000 BC the cave had been occupied on several occasions by no more than four or five people, probably members of a single family. They had used the shelter as a place to make and repair stone tools, to cook rabbits and small turtles, to shell, grind, peel and roast an immense variety of plant foods gathered in the vicinity of the cave. They had slept at Guilá Naquitz, using oak leaves and grass as bedding. I imagine much of their time had been spent gossiping, joking, perhaps even singing and dancing. Each visit had been made in the autumn and may have lasted for anything between a few days and a few months. For them, Guilá Naquitz was just one of many camping places in the Oaxaca valley; it had no special significance and those who went there were simply getting on with day-to-day life during the Early Holocene in Central America.

Flannery discovered that while they did so, they were also making history. When they first came to the cave, all of their plant foods had been from wild species. By the time of their last visit, however, some were from domesticated varieties – plants dependent upon humans for their survival. Unbeknown to the Guilá Naquitz people, the new plants they created would eventually support the great Meso-American civilisations – the Olmec, Zapotec and Aztec.

These thoughts had been in my mind when I left my hired four-wheel-drive as far as I dared venture up the dry river-bed of the Gheo-ala, a small tributary of the Oaxaca valley, on my way to Guilá Naquitz. I then followed an overgrown track and at times embarked through the scrubby woodland, not entirely sure of the way and looking out for the distinctive cliff face I had seen illustrated in Flannery's book. Many of the trees and shrubs, let alone the cacti, were quite unfamiliar to me. Some were laden with extraordinary epiphytes – those plants which attach themselves to another for support and extend wandering tentacles through the air. Butterflies and bees abounded.

My inability to identify the plants caused considerable frustration. I loved the exotic yellow and white flowers, the occasional pungent aromas, the small berries beginning to form and seed pods beginning to swell. But I hardly knew what I was looking at. I was annoyed at not having done my homework because the vegetation in this part of the Oaxaca valley is thought to be close to that which had surrounded Guilá Naquitz in 8000 BC. So those ancient foragers would have seen just the same flowers and seed pods, smelled the same aromas and spiked themselves on the same type of thorns. But they, of course, knew exactly what the plants were – which provided the best food and which the best fibres, which had medicinal properties and which were stimulants.

When I arrived at the cave, a pendulous bell-shaped wasps' nest was hanging from the ceiling. It was surrounded by the scabs of previous nests that overlapped and buried each other, just as the layers of debris from successive human occupations had done on the floor. Once my antics were over I scrambled back through the thorn trees and down the boulder-strewn slope below the cliff to find the overgrown track. It was only then that I realised that this was the very track that Kent Flannery and his team had made as they repeatedly drove their vehicles far closer to Guilá Naquitz than I had dared.

I paused to watch a line of ants marching and thought I heard an engine straining its way through ruts and potholes. And then I imagined Flannery and company bumping and bouncing past me in their Ford Pickup after the end of a day's work more than thirty years ago. I strolled on and imagined a second vehicle, one less congruous to the setting: a Mercedes-Benz negotiating its way along the dry river-bed that now stretched out before me. That was Kent Flannery on his first visit to Oaxaca, having been lent a car by a business executive relative – one presumably quite innocent of the ways of archaeologists. Apparently the Mercedes had been more effective than many four-wheel-drives in getting Flannery around the valley, along donkey paths and negotiating canyons. I walked back through the cactus and thorn trees to find my own vehicle, tired but exhilarated to have sat within the cave of Guilá Naquitz.

It is 8000 BC and John Lubbock sits in that cave reading *Prehistoric Times*. Around him is the clutter and debris of a hunter-gatherer camp; its occupants are away gathering plants. The floor has woven mats; piles of grass have been arranged for bedding; a fireplace contains warm ashes. Bowls, baskets and bags sit upon the mats and hang from pegs wedged into the wall. Lubbock has returned to the chapter about North American archaeology to check on his namesake's knowledge of American agriculture and whether he had views on how farming had begun. Victorian John Lubbock knew that it had been founded on maize and commented that 'it resulted from, and in return rendered possible, the gradual development of American semi-civilisation'.[2] Modern John Lubbock pondered these words, which suggested that domesticated crops had arisen in a society far more complex than that he had found at Guilá Naquitz.

Today we know that initial crop domestication happened in central Mexico because the wild ancestors of the three key domesticated plants – maize, beans and squash – are found in this region.[3] Those of maize and beans have been pinpointed quite precisely by locating which of the possible wild populations have the specific genetic markers of the domesticated varieties.

Maize evolved from a wild grass called teosinte which continues to grow in remote areas of Mexico today. Rather than having a single stalk, with its grain packaged in a few easily harvested cobs, teosinte has numerous branching stalks, each with several small grain spikes. That which grows on the slopes of the Balsas River valley in central Mexico is particularly similar – in biochemical terms – to modern maize. So it may have been within that valley that the intense cultivation of teosinte by prehistoric plant gatherers began, with the repeated selection of those plants with the largest gains for both food and seed for new plants.

Wild beans, on the other hand, grow throughout the whole of Central America. A cluster around the modern city of Guadalajara has been identified as the ancestor of the common domesticated bean (*Phaseolus vulgaris*) which comes in many different forms including red, pinto and kidney. All have one key difference from their wild ancestor: just like the barley, wheat and lentils that we examined in western Asia, the domesticated beans 'wait for the harvester'. And if the harvester does not come, the beans cannot spread their seed. As with those West Asian plants, the transition to the domestic bean came about as people repeatedly chose – either intentionally or by accident – those pods which had less tendency to split apart.

The wild ancestor of the third key domesticate, the squash, has not yet been located. There are certainly many wild varieties of squash still growing throughout Mexico, all of which have small, green fruits. It seems likely that one of these will soon be identified as the specific progenitor of the domestic varieties that come with larger orange fruits and which were cultivated by those who had used the Guilá Naquitz rockshelter.

The study of when and why these domesticated plants arose began in the late 1940s when Richard MacNeish, who at that time was a graduate student from the University of Chicago, came to work in Mexico, drawn to the region by its native plants. This was the start of a long and distinguished career, one that was ended by a road accident in January 2001 – while he was still on fieldwork at the age of eighty-two.[4]

MacNeish began work in the northeast, excavating caves with bone-dry sediments in the Tamaulipas mountains. By the early 1960s he had shifted his work further south into the Tehuacán valley of central Mexico. Here he excavated Coxcatlán Cave which provided abundant remains of maize, beans and squash, along with a host of wild plants.

The corn cobs were no more than two centimetres long but undoubtedly from domesticated plants. They were initially thought to date between 6000 and 4500 BC on the basis of radiocarbon dates from pieces of charcoal found near by. But when the cobs themselves were directly dated, they were shown to be considerably younger, dating to no more than 3500 BC. The same happened with the remains of domesticated beans from MacNeish's excavations: they were initially believed to be 4,000 years older than was eventually shown to be the case.

This leaves the cobs found at Guilá Naquitz, which date to 4200 BC,[5] as the oldest currently known. If this is the date at which domestication occurred, then it indicates a very long delay between the end of the ice age and the emergence of domestic maize in Mexico – an altogether different situation to that of domestic cereals in western Asia. But these radiocarbon dates may be providing a quite erroneous picture about when the first domesticated strains arose. That is the message from a recent study of the genetics of modern maize, which indicates that domestication had occurred by 7000 BC.[6]

Flannery also recovered the earliest-known samples of domesticated squash from Guilá Naquitz. Although these samples were no more than fragments of rind, stalk and seeds, they were quite sufficient to differentiate between the wild and domestic varieties. The key difference is simply size: the domestic squash are significantly larger. When the Guilá Naquitz sample was first studied, however, just one seed was thought to have come from a fruit sufficiently large to be labelled domestic. That seed was dated to 8000 BC.

When the sample was restudied by Bruce Smith of the Smithsonian Institution in the 1995, he found a great deal more evidence to support the idea that the Guilá Naquitz people were cultivating squash by that date.[7] Although the squash fragments from the earliest levels were unequivocally from wild plants (except for that single seed), those coming from levels dated to between 7500 and 6000 BC were evidently from domesticated plants. The seeds and stem fragments were significantly larger than those from wild plants; the rinds were thick and bright orange, rather than thin and green as in a wild fruit.

Smith concluded that the Guilá Naquitz people were cultivating squash plants by 8000 BC – weeding around wild plants, selecting seed from the largest squash fruits to replant for next year's crop. And, if so, it seems likely that the Guilá Naquitz people, those in the Tehuacán and Balsas valleys, and those who gathered on the foothills around Guadalajara, were cultivating beans and teosinte/maize. The question then arises of why people had begun to do so. Why were they unwittingly laying the foundations for the future Meso-American civilisations?

There are at present two major, but radically different theories for the origin of domesticated plants in central Mexico. One has been devised by Flannery himself on the basis of his excavations at Guilá Naquitz, the other by Brian Hayden of Simon Fraser University, drawing on extensive knowledge of historically documented hunter-gatherers. These theories hinge not on the contents of the caves but on whether there had been permanent hunter-gatherer villages on the floor of the Oaxaca and other river valleys.[8]

Athough Flannery has the advantage of first-hand field experience of the Oaxaca valley, we need to consider both theories before choosing the one that is most likely to be correct. To enable us to do so, John Lubbock needs to have a double-take on the Oaxaca valley at 8000 BC: he needs to spend ten years living in the world that Kent Flannery has imagined for the Guilá Naquitz people, followed by the same ten years in the one imagined by Brian Hayden.

During his first decade in the Oaxaca valley, Lubbock participates in all the plant-gathering, hunting, singing and story-telling activities of the Guilá Naquitz people. As he does so, he watches children grow up and learn the skills of hunting and gathering for a living. These included the techniques for making hunting weapons, baskets for plant gathering and containers for carrying water. Footwear and clothing had to be manufactured from vegetable fibres, bark, skins and feathers. They also had to learn about medicinal plants, how to care for the very young, the infirm and the old. Hardly any of this was done by instruction. The children simply participated in activities with the adults; they watched, they listened; they tried things out, made mistakes, and gradually became as skilled and as knowledgeable as their parents and grandparents.

Towards the end of that decade, one of the girls left the group to join the families who live in the Tehuacán valley. Soon after that, with the consensus of other members, one of the boys becomes the unspoken leader of the group. He is now allowed to speak first and last when decisions are required that affect the group as a whole, such as when to move camp and where to go. Everybody listens carefully to his views, but they also voice their own. Special attention is paid to the opinions of the older men and women. Decisions gradually emerge from group discussions – the leader's role is essentially that of chairperson, acting to summarise options and expressing the emergent viewpoint.[9]

Summer months are spent on the valley floor at an encampment known to archaeologists today as the site of Gheo-Shih. Squash are cultivated on the alluvial soils, and hackberry and mesquite are harvested. Large black iguanas are hunted and then roasted among hot coals. In some years, the group at Gheo-Shih is joined by another, especially when food is plentiful. Visitors frequently arrive and remain for a few days while news and gossip are exchanged; arrangements are made for communal celebrations when marriages will take place. The couple will then depart as members of a new group, soon to bear children.

Each autumn is spent at Guilá Naquitz. Lubbock soon appreciates its attraction. There is an abundance of plant foods near by – at least, there is if one knows how to distinguish underground tubers from tiny wisps of grass; which berries to eat and which to avoid; where the wild melons, runner beans and onions can be found; and how some plants become edible only after having been baked for many hours in an earth oven. There are animals to hunt, notably the white-tailed deer, collared peccary and rabbits, and birds to shoot – quails, doves and pigeons.

Permanent drinking water is the key resource; it comes from the river that flows below the cliff-face and from a scattering of springs. These are often no more than small ponds, but they make the cave and its environs far more attractive than other places. Turtles are often found within the ponds or on the muddy riverbanks and taken to be roasted whole within their shells. Lubbock soon finds that the region is covered by a network of tiny paths leading between springs, clusters of nut trees, clumps of cacti and patches of squash. It is, in effect, another wild garden – one quite similar to that around 'Ain Mallaha but stocked with an entirely different range of plants.

With the end of autumn, the dry season arrives. By the end of the year the river is often no more than a trickle and the summer springs are only recognisable by patches of damp ground. And so Lubbock travels with the Guilá Naquitz people into the more humid uplands for the winter. Many belongings are left in the cave – it is so dry there is no fear that they will become damp and rot. Indeed, if gathering during the autumn has been particularly fruitful, supplies of seeds, acorns, tubers and especially squash – which they know store particularly well – are left to provide food for when the group return.

Every autumn the people return to Guilá Naquitz, relieved to be back at the centre of their world. They have a life on the move within which the values of sharing, co-operation and consensus are paramount. Although hunting is rarely successful, and sometimes the tubers are small and the seed pods almost empty, people rarely go hungry.

The longer Lubbock lives with the Guilá Naquitz people, the more he appreciates that some years are relatively wet, with abundant food, and others quite dry. The timing of either a wet or a dry year is quite unpredictable and the Guilá Naquitz people have become used to responding to whatever conditions arrive.

When the spring and summer rainfall are plentiful, Lubbock finds that they are prepared to travel further from the cave to experiment with a wider range of plant foods and in an attempt to hunt more exotic species. They are able to do so because there is a guaranteed supply of their traditional foods if these enterprises fail. Such forays are essential to maintaining their knowledge of the landscapes around them, even when they return empty handed. In this respect the people of Guilá Naquitz are much like the Monte Verde people, and indeed like all the other hunter-gatherers Lubbock has visited on his travels – they have an unquenchable thirst for natural history that they attempt to satisfy at every opportunity.

It is during an especially wet year that Lubbock first witnesses another activity. The people are familiar with several patches of squash plants in the vicinity of Guilá Naquitz, knowing that this year these will produce large and abundant fruit. They visit them early in the season to check their flowers and the developing fruits. When doing so they simply pull up any other plants immediately around the squash, and then pinch off and throw away all but the very best of the flowers and fruits. They can afford such waste as there will be plenty of other plant foods that autumn, even if no more than one or two squashes develop on each plant. Any plants with blighted leaves are simply dug up and thrown away.

On one occasion Lubbock arrives at a particularly dense and tangled patch of squash. The women he has followed use their digging sticks to uproot two or three of the strongest-looking plants and place them in a basket. They then proceed to thin out the other plants, and help the pollination of remaining flowers. On the way back to Guilá Naquitz they pause and, in no more than a moment, have replanted the squash, watering them from a large hollow gourd they carry. This takes place in what appears to Lubbock as a nondescript part of the landscape, one that he would have had difficulty finding again. Anyone coming upon these newly planted squash would have had no reason to think that they were anything but entirely wild.

The Guilá Naquitz people never speak about their cultivating activity. They do it as a routine part of their hunting, gathering and travelling. It is not until a particularly dry year that Lubbock appreciates the dividend it provides.

In this year the landscape lacks the vibrancy that Lubbock has come to expect. The yellow and white flowers are scarce, the greens of the cacti are dull, and when their red fruits arrive they are drab and shrivelled in size. Game is especially scarce. But in their parched landscape the people can rely on the squash. As the plants are free of disease and any weak strains have been weeded out, there are always fruits packed with substantial seeds to be collected. Even though the quantity of food they provide is limited, it is quite sufficient to support a short visit to the cave.

During Lubbock's decade with the Guilá Naquitz people he doesn't notice any change in the fruit themselves. But if he had remained not for ten but for a hundred, or even a thousand years, he would have seen the fruit increase in size and change in colour from green to orange. Edible flesh would have developed, growing from the thin layers to which the seeds were once attached. Such plants would have become dependent upon the devoted care of the Guilá Naquitz people. The domesticated strains simply emerged from attempts by these hunter-gatherers to guard against food shortages when the rainfall was scarce.

John Lubbock has spent those ten years living as part of Kent Flannery's reconstruction of the Guilá Naquitz people and watching them act out Flannery's explanation for the domestication of squash – one that could readily be extended to maize and beans. This was a world of mobile, egalitarian plant gatherers who cultivated squash to offset potential food shortages in years when the rain was limited. In that world, Guilá Naquitz was one of their key localities; they returned every autumn to use the cave as a base for hunting and gathering. For Kent Flannery, the origins of domesticated plants lay in the hunter-gatherers' attempts to combat the irregular rainfall and supply of wild foods. But Kent Flannery might be wrong. And so Lubbock must relive that decade in quite a different world – that imagined by Brian Hayden who has very different views about the origin of domesticated plants.

At the start of this second 'take' on life in the Oaxaca valley at 8000 BC Lubbock is sitting on the floor of Guilá Naquitz with three women, one of whom carries an infant strapped to her back. It is late afternoon and this plant-gathering party is resting before the walk back to their settlement in the bottom of the Oaxaca valley. They have been collecting an assortment of seeds, nuts and leaves and each has a bulging sack to carry, one of which contains many small green spherical fruits – wild squash. In the fading light the party sets out, down the steep slope to the river below the cave and then through the scrubby woodland to the valley itself. The women have no difficulty in finding the way even though they have no wild gardens to walk through and no paths to follow – visits to the cave are too infrequent for these to have arisen.

Three hours later Lubbock emerges with them out of the darkness and into the firelit village. There are ten or perhaps a dozen huts forming a rough circle around a central fireplace which radiates with glowing embers. The huts are circular, with brushwood roofs hanging over wattle and daub walls on timber frames. Many people are sitting around the fire; several rise to greet the women, helping to unload their sacks and offering water.

Lubbock's relief is probably greater than the women's as he drops his sack to the ground and watches it taken away for storage. He sits with the women as they tell the other villagers about what they have seen and brought back, answering questions about the state of the cave, of the springs and animal tracks. Lubbock looks around at the timber buildings and courtyards. There had been no such villages in the Guilá Naquitz world established by Kent Flannery's extensive fieldwork – just small campsites such as Gheo-Shih, little different to those within the caves. But Lubbock is living within Hayden's imagination and wonders if this village is the semi-civilisation envisaged by his Victorian namesake, from which he thinks agriculture arose. Lubbock stretches out upon the ground and falls asleep.

He wakes long after preparations have begun for a feast. The seeds and nuts that he helped to carry have already been shelled and are now being ground within wooden mortars into a paste. Several small earth ovens are baking tubers and a large pit has been prepared for roasting a peccary. Lubbock can see many other baskets of food, including one stacked high with large orange squashes, quite different to those collected in the vicinity of Guilá Naquitz. Logs, reed mats and cushions made from bundles of grass are being placed around the fire.

Lubbock wanders around the village and sees that within the largest hut an elaborate robe is being prepared. The basic garment, one woven from twisted vegetable fibres, has been removed from a bark box and is now being adorned with an assortment of brightly coloured feathers, flowers and shells. Immediately behind this hut there is a well-tended garden of squash plants. The largest fruits have already been picked but there are many others beginning to ripen. A brushwood fence encloses the garden, suggesting that it is private property.

The feast begins late in the afternoon. It is for the benefit of a visiting group from the Tehuacán valley who are now seated on one side of the fire. Their leader is also dressed in a colourful robe and is raised above his followers upon a wooden seat. The Oaxaca people sit on the other side of their robed leader, each person positioned according to status. Lubbock also sits near the fire, a prime seat to watch the competition of words, songs and food that is about to begin.

For the next five hours this is precisely what happens: one side will tell a story which is then replied to by the other. At first the stories are short and related quite matter-of-factly; but as the evening progresses they become longer, and are told with more passion, involving sudden bursts of song, dance and dramatic reconstructions of the ancestral deeds being described. Periodically food is brought from the ovens and roasting pits by Oaxacan women and distributed among the guests. Some stories involve the giving of gifts from one leader to the other – precious stones, shells and exotic feathers.

When the Oaxacan leader reaches a climax in his story, a platter of orange squash is brought to the fire and placed to roast in the ashes. Lubbock watches the visitors gasp at the number, size and colour of the fruit.[10] Once roasted, they are split and the seeds distributed throughout the crowd, with the Tehuacán leader being given a whole bowlful to eat. He has never before seen such impressive fruits and such a quantity of seed; he eats them and then admits defeat by telling a final story that exalts the Oaxaca valley and its people.

The feast continues until the moon rises. The Tehuacán people depart to their own temporary camping site; the Oaxacan people retire to their huts, some accompanied by one or more visitors, perhaps to enjoy sex as extravagant as the food they have eaten. On the following day the Tehuacán people depart for their own valley, their obligations fulfilled and their leader's status maintained. When he arrives at his village he will display the gifts received, objects that cannot be found in his own valley. And he will instruct his followers to tend the maize plots in the surrounding hills with ever greater care, to ensure that he has a stack of the largest corn cobs ever seen – perhaps as large as his outstretched thumb – when he entertains the Oaxaca people the following year. Cultivating such plants is serious business – not for the calories they supply but for the status they bestow.

The competitive feasting continues year after year, sometimes with just two groups, sometimes with three, four or five. Lubbock sees a variety of exotic foods brought to these occasions. In addition to squash and maize cobs, there are chilli peppers, avocados and beans – all much smaller than those he knows in the modern world but on the way to becoming fully domesticated varieties. These are eaten as delicacies and used by leaders to impress not only their visitors but also their own people. If they fail to do so, they will be replaced – all the young men have their own gardens behind their huts in which they work at cultivating plants. Unknowingly, they are putting in place the foundations for the Zapotec civilisation that will one day level a hilltop and build its city at Monte Albán with its spectacular view across the Oaxaca valley.

The world imagined by Hayden for the Guilá Naquitz people and the reasons he proposed for plant domestication, were radically different from those of Flannery. Guilá Naquitz was now quite peripheral to the lives of the Oaxacan people. It was only occasionally used as a shelter on hunting and plant-gathering trips away from a permanent village in the valley bottom. In Hayden's imagined world, 'big men' – individuals who wielded authority and power – had the pick of the females as wives and displayed their power through communal feasting and by the acquisition of exotic shells, feathers and stones. In this world, the origins of domesticated crops lay in the hunter-gatherers' attempts to impress their neighbours with ever more exotic foods.

To decide which of these two theories about squash and maize domestication is most likely to be correct we must evaluate Hayden's claim that permanent hunter-gatherer villages had existed on the valley floors, where he believed the competitive feasting had occurred. Although no traces of any such sites have been found, Hayden argues that this is because their archaeological remains have been buried by several millennia-worth of river sediments.

Kent Flannery is an ardent critic of Hayden's views. He argues that while alluvium might exist in places, it is far older than 8000 BC. Consequently, if such villages had existed their archaeological traces would remain upon the surface today. Extensive and detailed surveys of the valley floors have been undertaken and many archaeological sites have been found; but none of these even roughly resembles the type of villages that Hayden envisages being used for competitive feasting in 8000 BC. Gheo-Shih, which was most likely a small summer encampment located just a few kilometres from Guilá Naquitz, was excavated in 1967 and provided a large number of artefacts but no sign of any structures. The activities that had occurred there appear to have been little different to those within the caves.[11] Any substantial hut timbers found eroding into drainage ditches have been dated to 1500 BC at the earliest. This is when the first villages in the valleys appear to arise.

When I drove back to the town of Oaxaca after my own visit to Guilá Naquitz I paid attention to the fields on either side of the road, weighing up the respective claims of Hayden and Flannery. Even though dusk had arrived I could see that these were intensively farmed, growing a range of what seemed to me to be exotic crops – chilli peppers, avocados, beans, maize – together with more familiar carrots and lettuce. I guess squash was also grown. The likelihood that villages had existed at 8000 BC seemed remote and I found myself entirely persuaded by Flannery's scenario for the origin of domesticated plants.

Competitive feasting was certainly important among many historically known Native American communities – but this had only occurred when there was an immense surplus of food. The Indians of the northwest coast had fabulous quantities of salmon from the Pacific and used feasting – or potlatches – to impress and humble rival chiefs. It seems quite inappropriate to impose this lifestyle on to those living in the Oaxaca valley at 8000 BC. Not only do their social lives seem to have been more based around sharing than competition, but it seems unlikely that a rival would have been impressed, let alone humbled, by no more than a handful of squash seeds, however large they might have been.[12]

Before arriving at Oaxaca town I stopped at a roadside bar and tried some of the mezcal – the local tequila. It was unpleasant to taste but looked splendid in a bottle stuffed with herbs and fruits. I bought one to take home – such an exotic drink would be bound to impress when we next had a dinner party.

31

To Koster

Hunter-gatherer lifestyles in North America, 7000–5000 BC

John Lubbock's journey from Mexico takes him through the San Pedro River valley in Arizona, passing the localities of Lehner Ranch and Murray Springs where mammoth bones and Clovis points lie buried in the ground. He encounters people using Folsom points to hunt bison and deer; points like those Jesse Figgins will excavate at Folsom itself. Others use new styles of stone points, all of which lack the characteristic flute of earlier times. Everyone has a much greater reliance on plant foods than in Clovis times, as one day will become evident to archaeologists by the number of grinding stones they excavate at Early Holocene camping sites.[1]

The change in diet reflects the growth of woodland that resulted from warmer temperatures and increased rainfall. Along the river valleys stands of willow, cottonwood and ash have become quite dense, while Lubbock treks through oak and juniper woodlands where the Clovis people had hunted upon open plains. The undergrowth is rich in shrubs and grasses; for those with sufficient knowledge, food, medicine and materials are there for the taking.

Archaeologists refer to the Early Holocene Americans as Archaic hunter-gatherers. This term distinguishes them from Palaeo-Indians, those of the Late Pleistocene, such as the Clovis people, and is a term broadly equivalent to that of the Mesolithic in Europe. And just like those Mesolithic people, Archaic hunter-gatherers were diverse in their lifestyles. Some adopted a sedentary life very rapidly, and eventually became farmers, developing societies which included chiefs, priests and slaves. Others remained as hunter-gatherers throughout the Holocene – right up to the fateful year of AD 1492 when the first Europeans arrived and the decimation of Native American society began.

By 7500 BC Lubbock has passed through Arizona and entered the rugged canyons at the southern edge of the Colorado plateau. He rests in a cave in today's Chevelon Canyon, which archaeologists now know as Sandal Shelter.[2] It was once a crevasse at the juncture of sandstone below and limestone above, but was eroded and widened into a cave when the river flowed several metres above its current height. Behind him on the cave floor are the remnants of a fireplace, a scatter of burnt bones, chips of stone and wooden digging sticks. There is also a pair of sandals beside the cave wall. These are made from tightly woven yucca leaves with open toes and straps to tie around the ankle. Lubbock slips one on and it fits rather well; but he resists the temptation of new footwear in case the owner should return.

A curiously large number of intact Archaic-period sandals have been found by archaeologists in the caves of the Colorado plateau, preserved by the bone-dry conditions and because they were made of tough materials. Other organic remains include fragments of clothing, bags and baskets. We must also thank the pack-rats that still flourish in the caves today. The large nests of twigs and leaves built by these hairy rodents have done an immeasurable service for archaeology. When building their nests they made use of human debris that would otherwise have decayed. In Sandal Shelter they dragged no fewer than nineteen abandoned, forgotten or simply mysteriously lost sandals into their nests.

In 1997 Philip Geib of Northern Arizona University had gone to investigate, after finding a forgotten shelf of sandals in his local museum which had once been collected from a pack-rat midden in the cave. He secured radiocarbon dates which covered a period of almost 1,500 years, the earliest dating to 7500 BC. The sandals were so well preserved that Geib could reconstruct exactly how they had been made, and compare them with sandals from caves further north. He documented how Archaic footwear varied between regions and changed over time – a very welcome alternative to the studies of stone tools which so dominate archaeological research. As a result, we probably know more about the footwear of the Archaic people of the Colorado plateau than any other aspect of their lives.

Dawn breaks and as no one has returned for the sandals Lubbock leaves the cave and follows the Chevelon Canyon to its confluence with Little Canyon, which then takes him 200 kilometres northwest into the Grand Canyon itself. Here he finds hunter-gatherers as much in awe of the huge cliffs, the colours, moving shadows and rapids as any modern-day visitor. Lubbock travels on and begins his crossing of the Great Basin – a misnomer, as it is really an area of many small basins between the Rockies to the east and Sierra Nevada to the west. Today it includes most of Nevada and suffers from extreme aridity.

At the LGM it had many clear blue lakes, notably the vast Lake Bonneville. These were a consequence of the quite different rainfall patterns that arose from the impact of the North American ice sheets on atmospheric circulation.[3] But even at 7500 BC these lakes have all but disappeared and Lubbock crosses a landscape of small ponds, shallow lakes, marshes, streams and springs.[4] Some basins and valleys are completely dry, their soils being slowly colonised by salt-tolerant plants. Elsewhere, there is a sagebrush-dominated scrub already beginning to take on a desert-like appearance. Piñon nut and juniper trees grow on lower slopes of the hills, while pine and spruce woodland flourish at higher elevations.

The hunter-gatherers of the Great Basin are living in small, scattered groups. They hunt a variety of game: deer, antelope, rabbits, squirrels, gophers and the occasional bison. They fish and collect a wide variety of plant foods. As they never remain in one place for more than a few weeks, often no more than a few days, their shelters are flimsy, while any discarded animal bones or plant material soon decomposes in the acidic soils.[5] And hence, the traces left for future archaeologists are minimal: small scatters of broken spear points and discarded grinding stones.

This meagre archaeological fare is supplemented, however, by the finds from still more dry caves. Almost as good as these are their evocative names: Last Supper Cave and Dirty Shame Rockshelter where sixty pieces of cordage have been found; Fishbone Cave and Danger Cave, which provided a cedar-bark mat and willow basketry; Spirit Cave where the only Archaic burial for the region has been found – one with a rabbit-skin robe and a plant-fibre mat for a shroud.

One of the archaeologically richest caves is known as Hogup, located on the northwest edge of Utah's Great Salt Lake.[6] Here the excavated material included grinding stones and remnants from a variety of baskets, bags and willow-bark trays. But perhaps the most significant finds were coprolites – human faeces that had been deposited in the cave.

Eleven coprolites were excavated, along with another six from nearby Danger Cave. When these were pulled apart they were found to contain a diverse assortment of plant remains, notably from prickly pear, bulrush and goosefoot. Pieces of crushed bone, insects and animal hair were also present, the latter possibly arising from the use of teeth as a vice when cleaning hides, while minute fragments of charcoal and gravel most likely derived from methods of food preparation, the gravel having been used to help grind the plants.

Lubbock descends through the eastern foothills of the Rocky Mountains into the High Plains – an immense swathe of rolling hills and grasslands that bisects the continent all the way from Canada to Mexico. It is now 7000 BC and he has arrived in Bighorn basin, northern Wyoming, at what will become the Horner site.[7] A cloud of dust has just settled, to expose a dozen men and women crouched around four freshly killed bison on the floor of a narrow gully. Within the last few moments they have changed from being brutal killers to lovers of nature and are solemnly paying homage to the animals that have given their lives for these people of the plains.

The bravest hunters had positioned themselves behind boulders at the cul-de-sac end of the gully; others had remained on the sides of the inclines looking towards the gully floor; all gripped their spears tightly and had blood pounding through their veins. At first they heard a rumbling and then they gained a taste of dust; there was the roar of galloping hoofs and the panting of mighty lungs. Four rampaging bison charged towards them, running from men and women who were shouting loudly and banging sticks. The hunters waited for the perfect moment – one that made their own potential death just a few seconds away – before they threw their spears. One, two and three bison collapsed to the ground as they struck. Another was wounded; it writhed in pain and bellowed in anger with lethal thrashing hooves. And then, with an almighty roar, the fourth bison died as its heart and lungs were pierced by the final spears to be thrown.

Butchery begins. As stone knives and choppers are withdrawn from leather bags, Lubbock recalls watching reindeer being butchered at Verberie in the Paris basin 5,500 years and one continent ago. The bison hunters face a more urgent task, for they lack the surrounding deep-freeze and flies are already congregating upon the wounds. These beasts are far larger than the bison Lubbock has seen in wildlife parks and Wild West movies before his travels began; they are some of the last members of *Bison antiquus*, a species soon to be extinct. Once gone, the plains will be grazed by the smaller and unimaginatively named *Bison bison*.

The work is undertaken swiftly. Everybody is eager to complete it before the flies lay their eggs and the meat begins to sour. Large stone flakes are used to cut the skin of each animal's belly from tail to throat. The innards are removed – vast entrails spilling across the ground – and left for inevitable future scavengers, while favoured organs are carefully put aside. The butchers constantly clean the grease and blood from the edge of their stone tools by wiping them on the thick bison hide. Some work with bison bones themselves: lower legs, skinned and cracked apart, make skinning and defleshing knives as effective as any stone tool.

The meat is removed in long thin strips and immediately hung from the tree at the gully end. Within a few minutes a hard film will form over their surface and although flies arrive in hordes, they are unable to penetrate this crust to lay their eggs. Soon the tree can take no more weight and so racks are built from branches and boulders. Butchery continues for several hours as windpipes and tongues are removed, pelvises smashed apart, hides partially cleaned and folded. Lubbock lends assistance whenever he can – helping to roll over the beasts after one side has been finished, carrying the meat to the drying racks, throwing stones at the thieving magpies and ravens.

As evening arrives, fires are lit to deter scavengers and to roast some meat. The people are to spend the night in the gully before returning to their settlement at daybreak with their heavy load. As darkness descends and the work is finished, they sit around the fire and relive the hunt. The livers are eaten raw – a favoured delicacy – evenly divided between all present, with Lubbock stealing a tiny scrap. One man leaves the fire to rummage among a pile of wasted innards and returns with a gall-bladder which he squeezes over his sliced liver before chewing it with gusto.

In the morning the hunters head north, returning to their summer-time settlement where the old and young eagerly anticipate bison steak. Lubbock travels south, following the plains into Colorado. Here, he joins another group of hunters, and remains with them as they hunt mountain sheep in the hills and deer within the thickets of woodland. Prairie voles and gophers are sometimes trapped, or dug from their burrows, and plant foods are collected – a rather dismal selection compared to that he helped gather at 'Abu Hureyra, Monte Verde and in the Amazon. But whether stalking deer or grinding seeds, the minds of his unknowing hosts are never far from the bison and the planning of a hunt.

Spears are their prized possessions. The stone points are the finest Lubbock has ever seen, some up to 15 centimetres long and masterfully worked into a perfect symmetry with lethally sharp edges. The spear shafts are treasured – suitable wood is not abundant and the success of a hunt depends as much on the spear flying true as on the point itself. The binding of sinew and resin is also critical. This has to be sufficiently robust for the point to be secure, but also slim and streamlined so that it does not interfere with the penetration of the spear. The knack is to strike the animal between the ribs, let the edges of the point cut a hole through the hide, and then gain sufficient penetration by the shaft so that the lungs or heart are pierced by the point. Within a fraction of a second, the hunters have to aim and throw with both accuracy and power.

Lubbock remains on the plains until the end of the autumn of 6500 BC. During those years, life for the bison hunters becomes harder, and will continue to do so for another two millennia. Every year there is less rain; periodic droughts appear, and then become regular and persistent.

This climatic period is known in America as the Middle Holocene altithermal[8] and its droughts were severe, hitting the whole of the southwest. Water tables plummeted while dust storms became frequent, causing erosion and the establishment of dunes. The marshes of the Great Basin finally dried up, while the gradual drift to desert was accelerated and reached its finale. Although grasslands survived across much of the High Plains, plant diversity collapsed, to leave only the most hardy of species. With poorer grazing, bison gave birth to smaller and weaker calves, fewer of which survived to adulthood.

The bison hunters of 6500 BC have to dig wells to reach the much-fallen water table. Having helped with this, Lubbock takes his turn at the grinding stones as plant foods have become essential to survival. The men talk about searching for bison, but no longer know where to find them and often decide that it is simply not worth the effort. As rivers and springs dry out, settlements become tied to the few remaining water sources. The quality of stone points deteriorates as people are forced to rely on poor-quality local stone.

The droughts will eventually come to an end and bison hunting will return; indeed, it will continue into historic times. But the soils of the plains will always be too dry and the frosts too frequent for the Native Americans to settle down and cultivate the maize, squash and beans that were spreading around the continent by 2000 BC.[9] They will, however, develop new hunting methods: herds of bison will be stampeded off cliffs; when no natural falls are available, fences and corrals will be built as animal-traps; bows and arrows will replace spears. They will burn vast tracts of grassland to encourage new shoots and attract the bison. None of these will threaten the survival of the herds; that apocalypse will only come after horses return to the continent with the Europeans. Then, both Native Americans and Whites will use the horse to rain a hail of bullets upon the bison herds and slaughter them in thousands.

The sun has risen to begin a warm autumn day in 6000 BC and the dry and dusty plains seem a world away. From his seat upon a limestone crag, Lubbock looks west towards a wide, fast-flowing silvery river bordered by marshes and meadows. Beyond that, thick deciduous woodland, soft and golden, thrives now that the rains have returned. Below the crags, a steep slope falls into a grassy tree-scattered hollow. At the bottom, a village – five rectangular huts with thatched roofs whose reds and russets match the leaves and grass of this autumn morn. Smoke rises gently from the first fire of the day; a dog barks, a child cries.

The river is the Illinois and the village Koster, named after Theodore Koster, the farmer on whose land its remnants were found in 1968.[10] Had that been the year of Lubbock's visit, he would have been 80 kilometres northeast of St Louis, and 400 kilometres southwest of Chicago, looking down upon a cornfield undistinguished from the thousands of others that dotted the plains.

The excavation began in 1969 and became one of the largest undertaken on American soil. It revealed that people had first camped in the hollow at 8000 BC.[11] The successive layers of soil and human debris traced how people continued to dwell within the hollow for many thousands of years. With the help of soil washed from the valley sides, they created 10 square metres of deposits as thirteen distinct settlements were built, one upon another. By 5000 BC a permanent village had been established, from which the people hunted game, collected plants and fished without fear of hunger – a Garden of Eden in the American midwest.

The day at that village's predecessor of 6000 BC begins with people pushing back hide drapes and emerging from their dwellings. They sit and talk, brew tea and eat porridge made from mashed seeds and warmed with hot stones from the fire. Some are dressed in neatly tailored tunics and skirts, others eschew clothes, exposing their lithe bodies to the morning sun. An old, arthritic man is sat upon a doorstep by his wife and will remain there for much of the day, doing odd jobs brought to him, telling stories for children and throwing sticks for his dogs.

People gradually disperse to their daily tasks. A party of women and children leave for a grove of nut trees, knowing that they will make a rich harvest, the hickory nuts being the most abundant of their autumn foods. Young men leave with spears to hunt deer; others head towards the river. Work begins in the village – there are wicker baskets to repair and medicine to prepare for a sickly child.

Lubbock watches, now sitting by the fire and happy to rest after his recent travels. A woman comes and sits beside him. She takes a nodule of stone and places it among the hot embers. While it heats, she stirs a little pot of resin and cuts notches in a wooden haft. The nodule is retrieved. While still hot, she holds it in a leather wrap and strikes to remove five or six fine flakes from the now brittle stone. These are set into the notches and stuck firm with the resin. She leaves, her knife complete. A couple of discarded flakes remain by the fire, to be meticulously excavated, washed and labelled many thousands of years later.

The sun begins to set behind the western hills. The nut gatherers return with heavy baskets, the hunters empty-handed and those from the river with bundles of reeds. Rush mats and soft hides are set out round the fire, and a communal supper is followed by stories. When the moon rises and night descends, Lubbock remains seated while others return to their dwellings for sleep.

Night-time brings moths to the glowing embers and bats overhead. It also brings the stars and the cold. Lubbock hears rats scurrying through the grass.

Another day begins as the fire is lit by an early riser and once again Lubbock watches daily life unfold at Koster, one of many hamlets scattered through the valleys of the midwest.[12] Most people remain at home; it is a day for shelling and pounding nuts, for making rush mats and attending to roof repairs. And then another night and another day – one with torrential rain. Through a succession of sunrises and sunsets, Lubbock remains seated at the fireside, watching the kindling as it crackles into flame, basking in the heat of a roaring fire and shivering as cold ashes waft upon a night-time breeze. Day by day he watches village life and the archaeology it is making: tools lost in the grass, rubbish dumped in middens, pits dug to divert the rain. Then the frosts begin. At night he huddles below the hides and woven mats that had been left by the fire.

After one freezing night Lubbock watches as the old man is carried from his bed and laid out on the frosty grass below an ice-blue sky. All day people come and pay their respects beside his body, remembering how he had taught them to hunt and fish; recalling his stories of the 'old days', when people had always been on the move. That night he is buried behind the huts. There is a feast; singing, dancing and prayers from a shaman. In the shadows an old woman weeps.

Winter arrives and still Lubbock remains seated by the fireplace. Now he watches as each family packs their belongings and leaves the village. Some depart together, some go alone – where to, neither he nor future archaeologists can say. But no winters are spent at Koster in 6000 BC except by Lubbock as he waits for their return.

They come back in the spring; repair and clean their huts and begin another year. Some sit next to Lubbock, spending many hours knotting fibres into new fishing nets. On other days he watches the same people return from the river, their nets replete with fish. In the summer, Lubbock listens to their plans for hunting white-tailed deer; throughout autumn, the village reverberates with the pounding of nuts into flour, not just those of hickory but also walnuts and acorns, hazelnuts and pecans. And then, once again, the people leave, while Lubbock remains to face another winter of frost and snow. So it continued year after year until one spring no one returned and the village was left to nature. So ended what the archaeologists will come to call Koster phase 8.[13]

As the years pass, Lubbock watches the dwellings tumble and their timbers rot. Sprouts appear from the middens and become sunflowers and elders, saplings of oak and hickory. Rainwater cascades down the valley sides, bringing silt to bury the grass which had long since hidden those lost tools, drainage pits, and the low mounds which marked the dead. He watches as nature reclaims that which had once been its own: its stone that had been transformed into knives and points; its wood, reeds and bark used for houses; the bones, hides and guts of its animals all turned to human design rather than rotting in the earth.

Year by year the rains increase and the river bursts its banks earlier and with ever-increasing force. The annual floods can no longer drain away so lakes are created on what had been marshes and meadows. Now Lubbock witnesses flocks of geese, ducks and swans discovering the new lakes and adopting them as a summer home. Their waters are soon brimming with fish and edged by mussels.

And then, one spring morning, there is a voice whose peculiar tones wake him with a start. After one thousand years, people are returning to Koster. Lubbock decides to stand up and watch them arrive. He digs his feet free of the knee-deep soil that had accumulated around him as he had been patiently awaiting this moment. Yet all he sees is a couple of men approaching from the river. They walk right past, wondering aloud whether anyone had ever lived within this sheltered hollow, so well served by woodlands, rivers and lakes.

The following week several families arrive. Some erect tents and brushwood shelters while others begin to fell trees, clear scrub and construct their houses. Within days the skeleton of a new village has appeared, that which, to the archaeologists of the 1970s, will be Koster phases 6 and 7.[14]

It is a different phase, but little different in nature as the people continue to live by hunting and gathering. During the summer that follows, a terrace is made in the slope and a trench dug for the posts, as further houses are built. Lubbock helps by holding the timbers steady as they are packed with stones, and with the weaving of saplings for the walls. He spends days with the women at the riverside, holding baskets below the dry heads of marsh elder and sunflowers as they are shaken for their seed. On other days he finds himself at dawn knee-deep in the new backwater lakes, ready to help throw weighted nets over mallards and widgeon. He goes to the woods and stalks deer, stays in the village and sweeps out the houses. At night Lubbock paints his face and joins the Koster people as they sing and dance around the new fire that burns amidst the huts.

The settlement is now larger than before, at least a dozen huts and about a hundred people. A much wider range of foods are eaten, racoon and turkeys joining the deer, many types of fish and mussels which are gently steamed in clay-lined pits. The village is made far busier by the many visitors who arrive by canoe – the river now being a highway as much as a place to fish. They bring items for trade: copper from the Great Lakes, marine shells from the Gulf of Mexico, fine-quality flint from what will be Ohio. Much of this material ends up as bracelets and pendants and seems to be worn by the few, not the many.

So change is under way and cracks appear in the old egalitarianism. Lubbock is reminded of his travels in Mesolithic Denmark at a similar date; how farmers' axes and cereal grain had helped destroy an ancient hunter-gatherer way of life. At Koster he observes another sign of social change: the dead are no longer all buried together. Those with any physical ailments have shallow graves in the dingy area behind the huts and close to the rubbish heaps; those who die with a fine physique are laid in cemeteries upon the headlands overlooking the rivers and lakes and where the sun strikes as soon as it has risen.[15]

The village is thriving, and will continue to do so until finally deserted. Before that date, at around 1000 BC, it will become a village of farmers using a brand-new set of domesticated plants: the descendants of the marsh elder, sunflowers and goosefoot that Lubbock had helped gather. Later still, those in the Illinois valley will finally adopt the cultivars that had originated long, long ago in central Mexico: squash, corn and beans – although the squash may have been independently domesticated in eastern America itself. The tightly woven baskets will be replaced by clay vessels, spear points will be spurned for arrowheads, and great burial mounds will be built for chiefs who claim their power by right of birth. But it will not be until the Europeans have arrived on the continent that the forests will be cleared and the Midwest begins its transformation into today's great corn belt of America.[16]

Such developments are far beyond the scope of this history. Lubbock's last day at Koster is spent in 5000 BC. In the morning he hunts deer and gathers fungi; at midday he climbs on to the limestone crag where he had sat on first arriving in Koster and takes his last look at the village. Later that day he follows a pair of traders to their canoe. They load newly acquired hides and furs and then set off, paddling northwards towards their home on the shore of what will become Lake Michigan.

32

Salmon Fishing and the Gift of History

Complex hunter-gatherers of the northwest coast,
6000–5000 BC

John Lubbock's stowaway canoe ride along the Illinois River begins the end of his travels through American history. After several days he reaches the traders' settlement at the far south of what is now Lake Michigan. It appears to be a place of manufacturing and exchange with people coming from all directions, and where the population will soon be expanding too fast for the hunter-gatherer ethics of equality and sharing to be maintained.

Sitting by the lake on a summer afternoon Lubbock faces a tranquil scene: cloudless skies and still water, children paddling and the smell of wood smoke from huts spread along the shore. It was not always like this, nor will it remain so.

At the LGM this location was covered by thick ice, the southern margin of the Laurentide ice sheet. In the millennia that followed it had been drowned by the vast melt-water lakes, subject to torrential rivers, turned into tundra, battered by violent winds, colonised by pine and spruce, before it was discovered by the First Americans. But perhaps all of that was nothing compared to the future that awaits this spot. It will become Chicago; the canoes and the brushwood huts are the harbingers of steam trains and skyscrapers.[1]

Lubbock, however, must make a return to the west coast, back to the Pacific Ocean beside whose southernmost reaches he had once sat when in Peru. And so he embarks on another enormous trek. It begins by foot until he reaches the Mississippi, and then he continues northwards by canoe between many riverside villages towards the vast Canadian wilderness that will continue, little changed, into the modern day. In this land of lakes, rivers and thick forests, Lubbock finds people living in small mobile groups, little different to the long-gone Clovis people. They hunt caribou and moose, they trap beavers and muskrats and they leave few traces for archaeologists to find.

Lubbock heads due west, eventually leaving the woodlands and crossing the northernmost extent of the Great Plains. Bison are still being hunted and he passes close to what will become a celebrated cliff-jump site of mass slaughter known, appropriately, as 'Head-Smashed-In'. After the plains Lubbock crosses the Rockies, and then the Columbia mountains. The Fraser River is traversed, followed by a plateau with high ridges and meadows where he watches the hunting of mountain goat and sheep. Lubbock descends through a valley with steep gorges and canyons, their tabletops covered in pine forest. The river alternates between slow mean-ders and turbulent rapids. During rainy winter days he follows a well-worn path between thick ferns and below tall evergreens to where the river enters the sea. The waters are shallow and sheltered by a chain of islands. This is the Pacific. Lubbock sits exhausted after the 3,500 kilometres of his journey from Koster.

The land beyond the Fraser River is known to archaeologists as Cascadia. It includes modern-day Washington State and British Columbia, and stretch-es from southern Alaska to northern California. Its Pacific coastline is ragged with deep fjords, convoluted sea passages and many offshore islands. It is pierced by a series of great rivers – the Columbia, Klamath, Skeena, Stikine and the Fraser itself – and a multitude of smaller streams. Cascadia is an appropriate end-place for Lubbock's American journey as this is where the most elaborate hunter-gatherer societies of America, and most probably in the whole history of the world, will develop.[2]

When Europeans first encountered the Native Americans of the north-west coast in the late eighteenth century, they found people quite unlike any they had met before. This was not because of their timber-framed houses and settlements with more than a thousand inhabitants. Neither was it because they found aristocracies, freemen and slaves, and great chiefs who commissioned artists to carve and paint their house-fronts and totem poles in the manner of Renaissance patrons. Nor was it because the people had notions of land ownership and indulged in theatrical feasts, during which immense amounts of food and materials were given away as means to demonstrate wealth and status.

Such houses, towns, art works and customs would have been of no sur-prise had the people been cultivating corn and herding cattle. But the people of the northwest coast were hunter-gatherers. More accurately, they were fishermen: their elaborate cultures were based on the harvesting of salmon. The sea levels of the North Pacific stabilised at around 6,000 years ago, after millennia of rising and falling as the impact of glacier melt-waters was counteracted by the rebound of land once freed of its icy burden.[3] Vast shoals of salmon began to swim with unerring regularity up the great rivers of the northwest coast to reproduce and die. Every year the fishermen were ready; with hooks and lines, with rakes, nets, weirs, clubs, harpoons and traps they harvested the fish just as a farmer would harvest the corn.

Such harvests were only of value if the product could be stored. Fish were filleted and placed on racks to be dried by the sun and the wind; others were suspended from ceilings and preserved in the smoke of household fires. Cascadia had an abundance of resources so salmon was not the only food; many other types of fish were also caught. The people hunted seals and otters, deer, elk and bear; they collected berries, acorns and hazelnuts. Indeed, it might have been the immense diversity of foods they had available, rather than the super-abundance of salmon, that was the key to their success.

With such unlimited wild foods the Native Americans of Cascadia lived in permanent villages, relying on their stored supplies during the lean periods of the year. They could afford to support specialist craftsmen and engage in trade. Their populations grew, uninhibited by the usual constraints on hunter-gatherer numbers: the need to keep on the move and periodic shortages of food. It is hardly surprising that, amidst such wealth, leaders emerged and waged war upon their neighbours.

Such 'complex hunters', as they are referred to by archaeologists, first appeared at around 500 BC. But when Lubbock arrives on the northwest coast at 5000 BC the groundwork for their emergence is already being laid. After having rested, he explores the headland at the mouth of the river that had led him through the canyons and forests. He notices a scatter of oyster shells and some animal bones partially buried by sand and grass. Amongst these are a few broken cobbles and flakes of stone; he finds that some have been chipped into small points. Near by there are the remnants of what were once brushwood huts: a few posts in the ground, some woven branches, pieces of hide still tied to frames but hanging in a dishevelled state. Lubbock takes a couple of the thicker posts, some of the woven branches, collects new brushwood and builds himself a shelter.

The sound of voices interrupts his work. Turning, he finds about a dozen people, a couple of families, inspecting the collapsing huts just as he had done a few hours before. They pull off the fragments of hide and tatters of wall, secure the wobbling posts with rocks and begin to rebuild. A few leave for the shore and return within the hour carrying shellfish. Once eaten, the shells are dumped on to those partially buried below the grass – right next to the small shelter that Lubbock hurries to complete as storm clouds are building in the evening sky.

Throughout the next day more families arrive, all greeting each other after a summer spent scattered along the coast and in the woods. Soon there is a village of brushwood huts housing at least a hundred people. The rubbish dump accumulates and Lubbock finds himself surrounded not only by oyster and mussel shells, but the remnants of butchered deer and porpoise. Unwanted fish stew is poured on to the heap; people use it as their toilet. Sometimes a fire is lit to kill off the maggots and deter scavengers; Lubbock's hut becomes engulfed in smoke as well as the stench of rotting food and human waste.

The people are busy preparing for the salmon run. On some days Lubbock leaves them and explores the woodland. He searches for deer and muskrat among the pine, hemlock and spruce. He finds small red cedars, trees colonising the woodlands whose massive descendants will be prized for their timber when people begin building houses, canoes and totem poles. On other days Lubbock sits among the fishermen as they fashion harpoons and spears, prepare slate knives and use branches to build drying racks. Every evening there are stories, many about the spirits of the woodlands and the sea.

The salmon arrive, initially in ones or twos and then in great shoals of fish compelled to swim upstream. The fishermen are ready – men and women, young and old, all armed with spears and harpoons, standing ankle- or knee-deep in the water. Within a few days the salmon run has ended; hundreds have been killed, but thousands have passed by unharmed. The racks are heavy with fillets drying in the autumn sun.

Some families take their share and depart, but most remain. Soon the herring will become abundant in the estuary and while waiting there are plenty of salmon to eat. On most days it rains; the old and young suffer from constantly damp clothing and bedding; an elderly man will die and be buried in a shallow grave behind the dump. Visitors will arrive and exchange obsidian for dried fish. In the spring the families will go their separate ways, planning to return next autumn when the salmon will once again swim for their lives. In the meantime their shelters will collapse and the rubbish become lightly buried by blown sand.

When the rain is torrential, Lubbock shelters within his rickety dwelling and reads *Prehistoric Times*. Towards its end, his namesake writes about North American Indians as a further example of modern savages.[4] Victorian Lubbock drew his information largely from a publication of 1853 by a Mr Schoolcraft, entitled *History, Conditions and Prospects of the Indian Tribes*. The tone was quite different to the constantly abusive passages about the Fuegians; most of it was a relatively dispassionate description of the clothing, equipment, hunting, fishing and farming practices of various groups throughout the continent.

The rubbish dump around Lubbock's hut became the archaeological site of Namu, named after the river at whose mouth it is located on the coast of British Columbia. When Roy Carlson of Simon Fraser University excavated the midden in 1977–8 he found that it had begun to accumulate at 9500 BC,[5] and continued to do so for 8,000 years. Initially the rubbish had been dumped during brief visits to the river mouth, the remnants of a wide assortment of fish, birds, molluscs and animals. Broken tools and tool-making waste had also been left at the midden, including microliths.

Soon after 6000 BC a change occurs in the composition of the midden as salmon bones suddenly overwhelm all the others. This indicates the start of the salmon runs. The discarded tools also change: no more microliths but increasing numbers of slate points. Fragments of obsidian appear, suggesting that trade and exchange had begun, but other than a few post holes there is no sign of houses. These had probably been too flimsy to leave much trace, indicating that although the salmon run at Namu had been productive, it was not of a sufficient size to allow occupation all year.

Namu is just one of several shell middens along the northwest coast that were accumulating in the Early Holocene. It shows how the people were beginning to specialise in salmon while continuing to exploit an immense diversity of other resources. During the next few thousand years, the salmon runs became bigger, while new technology was invented to harvest them in ever greater numbers. The demand for food grew from a burgeoning population. Some people took their opportunity and claimed ownership of the best fishing spots; others disagreed and began to fight.

Sitting on the headland, Lubbock looks out across what will become the Fitzhugh Sound to a string of offshore islands. Their white beaches glisten in the evening sun; the still water is broken by a lone canoe that crosses from the mainland to an island shore. A few thousand years ago a canoe was quite unnecessary. People could have walked to those islands as they were hills within a wide coastal plain. The first human footstep on American soil may have occurred on that plain, a foot that may have stepped from a boat that had crossed the icy waters of the North Pacific from an Asian shore.

That was the start of American history. It was a time when no human had ever climbed the Rockies, canoed on the Amazon or ventured to Tierra del Fuego. But now, at 5000 BC, people are living from the far north to the far south of the continent, most by hunting and gathering, some by farming. They have given it a history, but taken its nature in return. Their Clovis ancestors may have helped to edge the mammoths and ground sloths into extinction; their Archaic ancestors created new varieties of squash and maize. But the people of Namu – neither big-game hunters nor farmers – have done much more; they have appropriated the whole of nature for themselves. For them, the bear and the raven are no longer mere animals; the mountain peaks and rivers are far more than products of geology and rainfall; the seasons no longer come and go because the earth orbits the sun, and night no longer follows day because the planet spins around.

A few metres away, a fire burns while voices sing. The people of Namu are thanking the spirits who created the mountains and rivers and who visit their world as the bear. They recall how the raven had first come to their land and found it cold and empty of people but with a plentiful supply of game.[6] They sing so that the sun will rise and the spring will come.[7] Lubbock stands, turns and walks to the fire. He sits and helps to sing the new dawn into being.

GREATER AUSTRALIA AND EAST ASIA

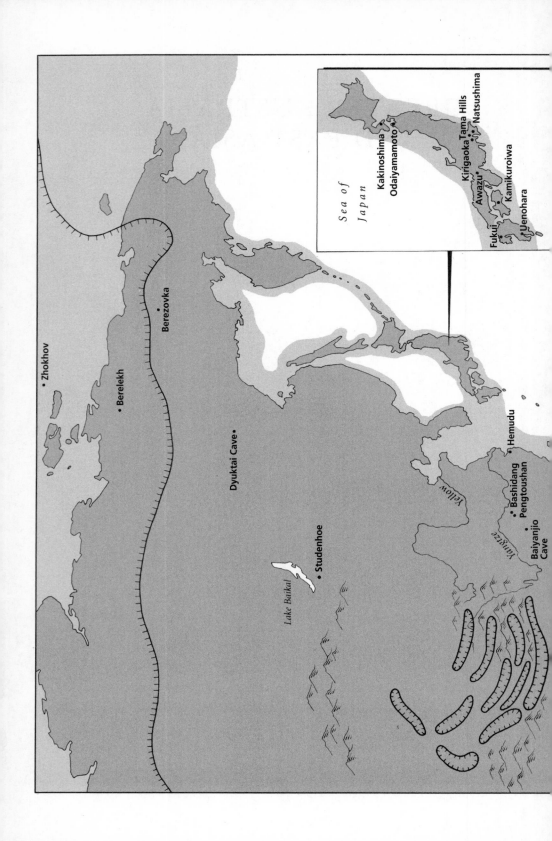

Sea of
Japan

Kakinoshima
Odaiyamamoto

Kirigaoka Tama Hills
Awazu Natsushima
Fukui Kamikuroiwa
Uenohara

Zhokhov

Berelekh

Berezovka

Dyuktai Cave

Studenhoe

Lake Baikal

Hemudu

Bashidang
Pengtoushan

Baiyanjio
Cave

Yellow

Yangtze

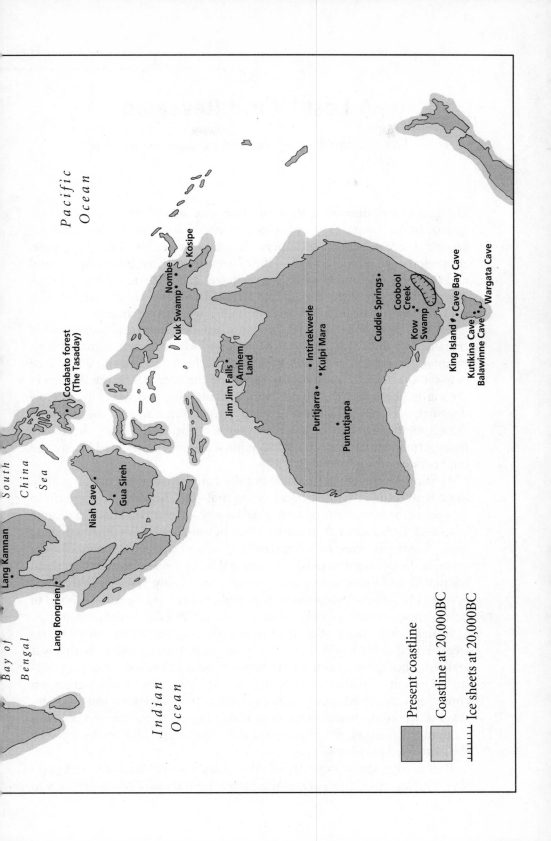

Pacific
Ocean

Cotabato forest
(The Tasaday)

Nombe
Kuk Swamp
Kosipe

Jim Jim Falls
Arnhem
Land

Intirtekwerle
Kulpi Mara

Puritjarra

Cuddie Springs

Coobool
Creek

Puntutjarpa

Kow
Swamp

King Island
Cave Bay Cave

Kutikina Cave
Balawinne Cave
Wargata Cave

South
China
Sea

Lang Kamnan

Niah Cave

Gua Sireh

Lang Rongrien

Bay of
Bengal

Indian
Ocean

Present coastline

Coastline at 20,000BC

Ice sheets at 20,000BC

33

A Lost World Revealed

Tasmanian hunter-gatherers, 20,000–6000 BC

Daylight enters through a shaft to illuminate shiny brown faces and set quartz crystals sparkling as pebbles are split apart. Wallaby fur, wrapped around human bodies, shimmers as muscular hands work the stone. Beyond, there is a brighter light – the cave entrance. That brings an icy wind and so the people sit and work in a sheltered, half-lit corner. John Lubbock steps forward out of the dark, damp recess of the cave. He is shivering with cold but ready to begin his journey through Australian prehistory.[1]

At the LGM, Australia was a continent of hunter-gatherers, and it remained so until 1788, the year of the first European settlement. At least 250,000 Aborigines were living in this southern land mass, distributed between the tropical forests of the north and the edge of Antarctic waters in the south. Lifestyles were varied. In the arid interior, Aborigines lived at low densities, with few possessions, and covered vast distances in the course of their foraging activities; in the river valleys of the fertile south, there were near-permanent villages with wooden huts, their walls plastered in clay and built on stone foundations.

Predictably, the earliest accounts of the native Australians are often little more than dismissive racist tracts. Anthropologists, however, soon began to appreciate the complexity of Aboriginal society. At least two hundred distinct languages were recorded; extensive trade networks were documented along which foodstuffs, axes, grinding slabs and ochre travelled; the mythological world of the Dreamtime, in which Ancestral Beings created the landscape and continued to intervene in human affairs, was partly revealed. What had appeared to be simple depictions of animals, people and signs were found to have complex meanings, often relating to the activities of Ancestral Beings.

Initial assumptions of a hand-to-mouth, catch-as-catch-can existence were revised as the sophistication of Aboriginal hunting and gathering was realised. Aborigines were found to have a profound knowledge of plant distribution and animal behaviour; they were able to adapt to ever-changing conditions, often adopting radically different lifestyles in wet and dry seasons according to the range of available resources. Although they were all hunter-gatherers, many managed their landscapes and food supply by the controlled burning of vegetation.

Recognising the complexity of Aboriginal society was the first of two shifts in European views about the native Australians. The second was to appreciate that these people were not a timeless relict of an original human society, a people without history. Their societies were as much a product of history as those of the European colonists. The start of their history – the date at which Australia was first colonised – has gradually shifted back in time, from an initial guess of 10,000 BC, to 35,000 BC during the 1980s, to almost 60,000 years ago today.[2]

John Lubbock has travelled to Australia to explore part of that history: the developments in Aboriginal society between 20,000 and 5000 BC, between the time of the LGM and the peak in the warm, wet conditions that arrived with the Holocene. Whereas it was the spurt of global warming at 9600 BC which had the greatest impact on people in Europe and western Asia, it was only towards the end of this period that the most fundamental changes occurred in Aboriginal societies. Moreover, while people in all other continents had adopted agriculture by 5000 BC, from either indigenous invention or the spread of ideas and people, all Australian Aborigines remained as hunter-gatherers – although with lifestyles quite different to those of their Pleistocene forebears.

The date of Lubbock's arrival is 18,000 BC; the continent remains as 'Greater Australia' – a continuous land mass from Tasmania in the south to New Guinea in the north. As he travels through the continent and through time, the sea level, which is more than 100 metres lower than today, will rise, temperatures and rainfall will increase, seasonal contrasts in weather will become marked.

Lubbock's encounters with prehistoric Aborigines will depend on the interpretation of a sparse archaeological record. Compared with other continents, there are relatively few Pleistocene archaeological sites and many of these consist of nothing more than a few flakes of stone. Consequently, it is hard to resist the urge to draw on the historical accounts of Aborigines when attempting to translate such mute artefacts into human lives. In that lies the risk of simply writing the Aboriginal present into the distant past and failing to recognise how Aboriginal society has changed through time. It is a risk that cannot be wholly avoided as Lubbock sits on the cave floor and peers over shoulders to watch ice-age hands at work.

He has entered what is known today as Kutikina Cave; owing to its size and location, it is a favoured place for the Tasmanian Aborigines of 18,000 BC. Even so, they will remain for just a few weeks, preferring to keep on the move as they deplete the animals and plants around each of their transient camps.

Those within Kutikina Cave are expecting the return of a hunting party. Lubbock watches as a fire is built in another of its sheltered corners, one where any smoke will disperse through a second and much smaller entrance. With their new set of stone knives and choppers complete, the group shifts to sit around this fire. Lubbock joins them, glimpsing a view across the open valley beyond.

Two remarkable achievements allow him to sit with these ice-age hunters, no more than 1,000 kilometres from the sea ice of the Antarctic Ocean. The first was that of the ice-age Australians themselves. Having arrived in the far north of Australia at around 60,000 years ago, after an island-hopping journey from Southeast Asia involving sea-crossings of at least 100 kilometres, generation after generation kept spreading south and eventually moulded a new lifestyle around wallaby hunting in Tasmania as the southernmost inhabitants of the ice-age world. The second achievement was that of the Australian archaeologists who discovered and began to reconstruct that Tasmanian ice-age world no more than two decades ago.

Today the valleys of southwest Tasmania are uninhabited. Covered by dense and almost impenetrable temperate rainforest, with treacherous swift-flowing rivers, they are one of the last great wildernesses of planet earth. And so when Rhys Jones of the Australian National University observed stone artefacts embedded in the banks of the Denison River on 11 January 1981, and described them as 'a very interesting discovery', he could justifiably be accused of understatement.[3] Those specific artefacts turned out to be no more than a few hundred years old; but their discovery was highly significant.

A few weeks later Rhys Jones and his colleague, Don Ranson, visited Kutikina Cave with Kevin Kiernan, a geomorphologist from the University of Tasmania.[4] Having travelled along rivers for ten hours, sometimes hauling their boats over rapids and wading waist-deep in icy water, they fought through dense vegetation and squeezed behind the trees that now hide the cave entrance.

When a gas lamp was lit, Rhys Jones found himself within a huge cavern with gleaming white walls reflecting the light of the hissing lamp:

> the floor was crumbly orange clay that rose in banks 70cm high on three sides... Protruding from the slightly eroded face and strewn along its base were hundreds of stone tools and burnt fragments of animal bones. Dense layers of charcoal, alternating with burnt red clay, documented a series of ancient hearths. Beyond one of the banks was a trench cut away by water, a 2m section through which clearly showed wallaby skull fragments, jaws and limb bones piled one on top of the other... That night we cooked our food in the shelter of the cave and laid our sleeping bags on hard limestone in a dry alcove at the back of the main chamber. Later we would learn that we were the first people to sleep here in more than 13,000 years.[5]

Jones and his colleagues excavated less than one cubic metre of deposit and recovered a staggering 250,000 animal bones and some 40,000 stone artefacts. These were later dated to around 15,500 BC, and charcoal from a rubble layer below to 20,000 BC. So it was revealed that today's uninhabited forests of southern Tasmania had once been home to ice-age hunters.[6]

The discovery in Kutikina Cave began two decades of research in the rainforests of Tasmania. Led by Jim Allen and Richard Cosgrove of La Trobe University, many seasons were spent in arduous field conditions while archaeological sites were excavated to produce an astonishing record of ice-age life.[7] The date of the first Tasmanians was pushed back to 35,000 years ago, and their tool repertoire expanded from stone artefacts to include fine spear points made from wallaby bone and knives made from naturally occurring glass. Fragments of ochre in Kutikina Cave had hinted at art and this was discovered in January 1986: a panel of sixteen hand stencils, coming from at least five individuals, was seen by torchlight in the deep recesses of Ballawinne Cave in the Maxwell River valley. Iron oxide had been ground, mixed with water and then sprayed across hands placed flat against the wall.

The following year, more hand stencils were discovered in Wargata Cave, 85 kilometres to the southeast. Both adults and children, using human blood as one of their pigments, had made the signs.[8] By the start of the 1990s, Rhys Jones felt able to compare the ice-age archaeology of southwest Tasmania with that of southwest France – Ballawinne and Wargata being the Lascaux and Altamira of the Southern Hemisphere.[9]

This is a generous comparison, to say the least. Although Tasmania has ice-age archaeological sites in which stone artefacts, animal bones, and rock art are found, any similarities with reindeer hunters of northern latitudes are quite tenuous.[10] In any case, the archaeology of each region should be examined on its own terms – the days when ice-age Europe provided the 'gold standard' by which the archaeology of other regions is measured should have ended long ago.

Of greater interest is the detailed work conducted by Allen, Cosgrove and their colleagues on the artefacts and bones excavated from the Tasmanian caves. Their study of wallaby hunting is of particular interest.[11] It required a reconstruction of the ice-age landscape from pollen evidence, a study of modern wallaby ecology and the analysis of many thousands of excavated bones. The ice-age hunters appear to have lived within the valleys during the winter, spring and early summer. They utilised a selected area of grassland until the wallabies became too scarce to justify further hunting; they would then move to another area, perhaps using a new cave as their base. Although other animals were sometimes taken, the wallabies were specially targeted, probably by being driven towards hunters clasping spears and waiting in ambush.

Owing to the rarity of bones from feet and paws within the caves, Cosgrove and Allen learned that the wallabies were partly butchered at the kill sites – only the meatiest parts of the carcasses had been returned. By examining the manner in which limb bones had been broken, they knew that wallaby marrow as well as meat had been eaten. On some occasions, the menu had included wallaby brain. In the late summer the hunters left the valleys for the uplands where plant foods featured more prominently in their diet.

Back in 18,000 BC John Lubbock watches hunters return to Kutikina Cave with a joint of wallaby meat. The group now comprises about thirty people: men and women, old and young. They wear wallaby-fur cloaks and spend much of each year together, one of several groups living in the valleys of southern Tasmania.

After skinning and filleting, roasted meat is prepared with chopped bulbs and then shared between all present. The shin bones of the larger wallabies are set aside to be worked into spear points. Most other bones are cracked open for marrow; even the toe bones are split apart for the morsel inside. The rubbish is dumped in a corner of the cave, along with blunted and grease-covered tools. People disperse to different parts of the cave – some to sleep, taking ashes from the fire to spread upon the floor to keep their children warm, and some to work the bone into elegant points.

Lubbock sits near the fire by the cave entrance. With sufficient light to read, he opens *Prehistoric Times* to find out what his Victorian namesake had known and thought about the Tasmanian Aborigines in 1865. There was a short passage in which two 'authorities' were quoted. According to Captain Cook, who had visited 'Van Dieman's Land', as Tasmania was originally known, during his third voyage between 1776 and 1779, the Aborigines 'had no houses, no clothes, no canoes, no instruments to catch large fish, no nets, no hooks; they lived on mussels, cockles, and periwinkles, and their only weapon was a straight pole sharpened at one end.'[12] Worse was to come. Victorian John Lubbock quoted the Reverend T. Dove who had written in the T*asmanian Journal of Natural Science* that the Tasmanians were 'distinguished by the absence of all moral views and impressions. Every idea bearing on our origin and destination as rational beings seems to have been erased from their breasts.'[13]

Lubbock looks at the Tasmanians of Kutikina Cave sleeping below their thick fur cloaks, having shared their wallaby meat, cared for their children and finished making new tools. Plenty of morality, but not a cockle or periwinkle in sight.

The group plan to remain in Kutikina Cave for the next few days; they have seen several groups of wallabies grazing in the grasslands of the valley bottoms and browsing in the scrub of the ridges between. The next day Lubbock accompanies three men on a 25-kilometre trek along the Franklin River valley, and then one of its tributaries, to what is called today the Darwin Crater.

The route follows well-trodden paths through knee-high grass and thickets of stunted trees in sheltered valley corners. The higher slopes are covered in shrubs while small glaciers can be seen in the uplands. Although Lubbock's companions do not hunt, they nevertheless inspect every animal track and many of the leaves to see where the wallabies have been feeding. They can also tell where the animals have slept and the size of the herd.

Darwin Crater is indeed a crater – a hollow, one kilometre wide and two hundred metres deep, created by a meteorite strike 700,000 years ago. Lubbock's companions climb to the rim and spend an hour collecting nodules of glass – siliceous bedrock that has been melted by the impact. The glass is precious and will be used to make razor-sharp points and knives.[14] It will be traded with people who live further south so that one day archaeologists will find glass points more than 100 kilometres from its source.

Lubbock leaves his companions and journeys into the windswept lowlands of northern Tasmania, a landscape interrupted by sporadic hills and ridges. In 15,000 BC he shelters within a cave upon a rocky outcrop, disturbing a pair of roosting owls as he arrives. There is a scatter of gnawed bones showing that a carnivore, perhaps a Tasmanian devil, had recently used the cave. It may have come to scavenge on the debris left behind by human occupants as ash and burnt stones are also spread across the floor.

From the cave's entrance, Lubbock looks across a vast grassy plain. To the north, east and west the sea has already begun to edge across the plain; it will eventually surround the rocky outcrop and turn it into the Hunter Island of today. Lubbock's land-locked shelter will become a sea cave, battered by the violent waters and winds of Bass Strait that will divide Tasmania from the mainland, and one Aboriginal culture from another.

Cave Bay Cave, as it is known today, is now six kilometres off the northern coast of Tasmania. Its heyday for human occupation had been in the two millennia before the LGM, when visiting hunters lit fires and left their debris behind.[15] They hunted wallabies, wombats and bandicoots in the surrounding grasslands. When the LGM arrived, the landscapes around the cave became too impoverished of animal and plant foods to sustain human occupants. Constant freezing and thawing of water in crevices of the cave destabilised its roof, creating rockfalls that buried all the pre-LGM human debris.

When the extreme ice-age conditions began to relent, the cave was used on just one occasion before it became surrounded by sea. This was at 15,000 BC when a single fireplace was made, created by hunters exploring what had become an unfamiliar land. Such hunters went further north and buried one of their dead in a cave within hills that would eventually become King Island, now 100 kilometres south of the Australian coast.

Archaeologists discovered the burial and examined the skeletal remains after the Tasmanian Aboriginal Centre granted permission to do so. The deceased had been a man aged between twenty-five and thirty-five years, whose bones were bundled together and covered with jagged rocks to make a small mound within the cave. Small lumps of ochre were found among the bones. These may have once been items of body decoration similar to that worn by the Tasmanians when first encountered by Europeans.[16]

The physique of this man was telling: he had short, robust bones giving him a stocky disposition similar to that of modern people who live within cold landscapes, such as the Inuit of the far north. This physique serves to conserve body heat by minimising surface area. The first people to arrive in Tasmania 35,000 years ago must have looked quite different – tall and slender, as is appropriate for those who live in tropical environments. The change in stature was no doubt a consequence of living in the glacial conditions of this southern land.

From Cave Bay Cave Lubbock heads northwest across the north Tasmanian plain until he encounters the sea heading in the opposite direction. Much of the plain has already been flooded but it will take another three thousand years at least to detach Tasmania from the Australian mainland. Lubbock follows the coastline to the east and then northwards, crossing the 100-kilometre-wide isthmus that leads to the hills that will soon become the southern coast of Australia.

The rising sea level transformed the lives of many coastal dwellers in ice-age Australia. But for those in the southwest valleys of Tasmania it was the increasing rainfall and temperature that threatened their way of life and ultimately led to their demise. Each generation of hunters who sat within Kutikina Cave found the valley less attractive than the last. The invasion of the trees and rising of the rivers made getting around and watching for game more difficult. Year by year new saplings of beech and pine appeared, while existing saplings made remarkable growth. Between the trees a thick undergrowth of ferns took hold. Wallaby herds split into small, scattered groups that clung on to patches of surviving grassland; their numbers collapsed as the rainforest took hold. A new, tree-dwelling fauna began to thrive: some familiar-sounding animals such as the long-tailed mouse and ring-tailed possum, together with more exotic creatures like the pandemelon and spotted-tailed quoll.[17]

Soon after 15,500 BC, Kutikina Cave was entirely abandoned; it was the lowest-lying of the caves and the first to drop out of the wallaby hunters' seasonal round.[18] Within a few more generations the rainforest had spread to higher ground and all the caves in the southwest had been abandoned and were soon forgotten. A few caves in the southeast of Tasmania escaped the stranglehold of rainforest and continued to be used for a few thousand more years.[19]

There are hardly any archaeological sites in Tasmania between 10,000 and 6000 BC. Where had the people gone? Perhaps population numbers had declined through falling birth rate or by migration northwards across the remnants of the isthmus into Australia. Or perhaps there had been no population decline and archaeologists have yet more discoveries to make. Archaeological sites dating after 6000 BC are relatively abundant and tell us about a completely new style of Tasmanian life: the descendants of forest dwellers and wallaby hunters had become inhabitants of the coast and gatherers of shellfish.

When European settlers arrive, when the anthropologists and archaeologists begin their work, it will be assumed that such coastal occupation was all that had ever occurred upon the island. That was what Captain Cook believed, his views of the Tasmanians reported so faithfully in *Prehistoric Times*. Only when Rhys Jones and his colleagues penetrated the rainforest to find the wallaby bones, stone tools and fireplaces on the floor of Kutikina Cave would a start be made on revealing a lost ice-age world. Only then would we begin to understand the depth of human history in this southern corner of the world.

34

Body Sculpture at Kow Swamp

Burial and society in Southeast Australia, 14,000–6000 BC,
and mega-faunal extinctions

The band of kangaroo teeth around the dead man's head catches the moon-light as his body is lowered into its sandy grave. He is laid on his left side with knees drawn up under his chin. The singing halts for his moment of release from human care; he now joins the ancestors whose bones also lie within the dunes but whose spirits reside within the night. Silence. And then a shriek reignites the music as painted bodies leap from darkness into firelight and dance to a frenzy as the moon climbs high in the night sky. Sand is spread across the corpse and the dead man has gone for ever.

It is 14,000 BC. John Lubbock's journey from Tasmania has taken him across grassy plains to the Murray River in southeast Australia. Trees, animals and birds became abundant and travel more pleasant. He arrives at a cluster of timber-framed huts with reed and hide coverings in a locality known today as Kow Swamp. Preparations are under way for a burial.

Lubbock spends several hours wandering in and out of the dwellings; he watches paint being mixed and applied to bodies, and the corpse being pre-pared for its grave. Groups of old men sit talking quietly; women are preparing food and keep their children inside. A fire has been built upon an adjacent ridge of sand, close to where the burial pit had already been dug. As darkness descends and the first stars appear, people gather upon the dune. Lubbock sits among them and soon finds the rhythm of their gentle singing, which seems to raise the moon into the night-time sky. The fire is lit, the body buried and the dancing begins.

Not far from him a women presses her thumb against the forehead of the baby cradled in her arms. She begins just above the brow and runs her thumb to the crown of the head, then releases it. And she repeats the action again and again, slipping into a rhythm with the dance. She will do the same the next morning, in pace with the pounding of tubers. There is always some rhythm to follow; if all is quiet she will sing to make her own as her thumb lovingly works against the fragile skin and bone.

At least fifty people are gathered around the fire, their minds consumed by the flames, song and dance that celebrate the passing of the dead. Lubbock stands to look at them, following the light as it flickers from face to face; some have headbands like the deceased, some are painted; there are the faces of the old and young, men and women. Some look shocked, others scared; some sing and clap while others stand in silence, mesmerised by the spectacle.

There is a familiarity about the occasion acquired from Lubbock's travels through prehistory elsewhere in the world. The songs and dances always differ, as do the burial rites and costumes; but the intense emotion, the sense of belonging, the idea of past and present merging into one is always the same. And yet there is something new, something quite different about this particular group of people beneath the moon and stars of the Australian night.

The flames throw light on to the face of an old man; his skin is dry and taut. He has a huge jaw, quite disproportionate to his shrivelled body. The face is large – wide and projecting; the eye-sockets are pronounced, angular at their base and with the bone curving steeply away behind; brow ridges are prominent. Above these, his forehead seems abnormally long, sloping away from his brow.

The flames flicker, returning him to darkness as a young boy is thrown into view; he too has a large and rugged face, his forehead slopes and his jaw seems thickly set. He sings loudly, with lips curled back to reveal teeth that match the jaw in size. And so Lubbock looks from face to face, finding the same features in all, less pronounced in the women and the young, but quite definitely there. Unthinkingly he runs his fingers around his own slender jaw; his tongue explores his teeth. Then he feels his brow, quite flat, his forehead, quite upright; both entirely different to those of the people who are singing and dancing at Kow Swamp in Southeast Australia at 14,000 BC.

In August 1967 Alan Thorne, now retired from the Australian National University, came across fragments of a skeleton and skull lying unregistered and forgotten in a box at the back of a cupboard in the Museum of Victoria.[1] Such bones would have been quite unremarkable to the un-trained eye, but he was intrigued: they reminded him of a skull found in 1925 near the town of Cohuna that had seemed abnormally large for a native Australian. The only label referred to the local police office; Thorne followed this lead, which eventually took him to the find spot that was no less than ten kilometres from Cohuna itself.

By 1972 Thorne had excavated more than forty individuals from a lunette-shaped sand dune at Kow Swamp. Most had been buried in shallow graves between 9500 and 8000 BC in one of the largest hunter-gatherer cemeteries in the world.[2] Some had been buried with artefacts – lumps of ochre, shells, stone artefacts and animal teeth. One had a band of kangaroo teeth around his head. Some burials had been made at an earlier date, most likely reaching back to 14,000 BC.

A study of the remains was made in conjunction with those from 126 individuals collected in 1950 from another cemetery, known as Coobool Creek. Murray Black, an amateur archaeologist, had dug these up on the opposite side of the river but failed to keep any records.[3] Even the specific location of the cemetery remains unclear; but the burials from Coobool Creek are believed to cover the same time-period as Kow Swamp and the two samples can be reasonably placed together. When the most ancient skulls were reconstructed, Thorne found they had large, rugged facial bones, thick craniums, low-set rectangular eye-sockets and strongly sloping foreheads. Their bodies matched their heads in size. He described them as 'robust'.[4]

When faced with these skulls, Thorne made a radical claim: although he did not dispute that the Murray River people were *Homo sapiens*, he proposed that they were descendants of the *H. erectus* populations that had been living in Southeast Asia more than one million years ago. The fossilised skulls of those premodern humans, such as the specimen known as Sangiran 17 from Java, were also 'robust' and Thorne compiled a long list of shared features. In effect, he was challenging the widely accepted view that all *Homo sapiens* had a single origin in Africa at around 130,000 years ago. *Homo erectus* was supposed to have gone quite extinct without contributing to the modern gene pool; but Thorne claimed them as the forebears of the Australian Aborigines.[5]

Thorne is most unlikely to be correct. His claimed similarities between the *H. erectus* specimens from Java and those from Kow Swamp are spurious – or at least the similarities are of no greater significance than between any other *H. sapiens* and *H. erectus* samples.[6] And so the only feasible scenario for the origin of the Australians lies with one or more colonising populations of *H. sapiens*, the first of which arrived around 60,000 years ago.

Why, therefore, are the Murray River skulls so robust and quite unlike those from elsewhere in the continent? The answer seems to lie in the particular nature of the final Pleistocene environments and communities in the Murray River region, amongst whom Lubbock has recently arrived.

As soon as the Kow Swamp skulls were published in the premier science journal *Nature*, the issue of artificial cranial deformation was raised: could the particular shape of the skulls have been a product of culture rather than biology? Peter Brown from the Australian National University compared the Kow Swamp and Coobool skulls with those of the Arawe people of southern New Britain, an island in Melanesia whose inhabitants were known to have practised skull deformation.[7]

Immediately after birth, an Arawe baby's head was tightly bound with a bark cloth for three weeks. Its impact was immediate – even after one day, the skull had begun to take on an elongated form. As the baby's head grew, the bandage was replaced, until the mother felt that the head had been sufficiently moulded. Brown found strong similarities between the Arawe and

Murray River skulls, enough to argue that the people from Kow Swamp and Coobool had also deformed their babies' skulls. But their deformations were more subtle than those of the Arawe, lacking a narrowing of width as well as an elongation of length. Rather than using a tight binding, those who lived by the Murray River appear to have simply used their thumbs and palms to apply constant pressure to the foreheads of their newborn.

Such body sculpture accounts for the sloping forehead but not for the robust features of the Kow Swamp skulls, especially the large jaws and teeth. These can only be explained by genetic inheritance. As contemporary populations elsewhere in Australia lacked such features, the Kow Swamp communities appear to have been genetically isolated, with considerable inbreeding amongst their people. Why should that have been so?

Colin Pardoe of the South Australian Museum explains it by the development of strict territorial behaviour to protect access to the abundant resources of the Murray River region, which were far in excess of those elsewhere.[8] By 14,000 BC, the Murray River was beginning to approach its modern form – one that Pardoe describes as being 'stocked with unimaginable wealth in fish, fowl and invertebrates'. Trees were colonising the well-watered land immediately adjacent to the river and were housing small mammals such as possums and lizards. A wealth of plant foods, such as grass seeds and tubers, were available. Away from the river itself, a large range of mammals lived in the surrounding scrubland: kangaroos, wallabies and bandicoots.

In the early twentieth century, the British social anthropologist Alfred Radcliffe-Brown described the Murray River as 'the most densely populated part of Australia before the days of White Settlement'.[9] He found Aboriginal tribes who claimed exclusive ownership of stretches of river and the surrounding land; people who were prepared to defend their boundaries by force. As such, they were much like the people that Lubbock had observed at Skateholm when travelling in Europe in 5000 BC.

Moreover, the Murray River tribes that Radcliffe-Brown encountered, such as the Yaralde, organised their social lives quite differently to those in the arid deserts of Australia. Rather than having a system in which everyone was related to everyone else in both adjoining and quite distant groups by a complex system of social ties, those in the Murray River region had far fewer outside links. They were more concerned with rules and customs which *excluded* people from their social group, rather than those which would *include* as many people as possible, as found among the desert-living Aborigines.

Colin Pardoe believes that the origin of the Murray River societies described by Radcliffe-Brown is found several millennia before the Holocene began, with the people of Kow Swamp and Coobool Creek. These were, he believes, the first to live at high densities in a resource-rich environment; the first to establish boundaries and develop a social system on the principle of exclusion rather than inclusion. This, he suggests, explains the 'robust' skeletons and skulls: with greater degrees of inbreeding, gene flow became restricted and regional differences in physique appeared. It also explains why cemeteries were made: to invest the land with the bones and spirits of one's ancestors and hence claim ownership. And it explains the body sculpture: this was a means to accentuate existing physical differences from other groups. Having an elongated skull was a mark of belonging to Kow Swamp or Coobool Creek, and with such belonging came rights to hunt and fish.

The people of Kow Swamp and Coobool Creek of 14,000 BC appear to have been the first Australians to live in this manner. During the next few thousand years their lifestyle spread throughout the whole Murray River valley. New methods were adopted to demonstrate group membership, such as tooth avulsion – knocking out particular teeth during a rite of passage from adolescence to adulthood. Both men and women suffered injury as territories were defended. By 6000 BC many cemeteries had been established along the course of the river. It is not unreasonable to surmise that they contained the direct ancestors of the Aborigines that Radcliffe-Brown and other early anthropologists encountered; indeed, the ancestors of today's Native Australians. So it is appropriate that the skeletal remains of Kow Swamp and Coobool Creek have been returned from the museums and laboratories of Western scientists to the current Aboriginal communities.[10]

Back in 14,000 BC the persistent tickle of flies crawling across Lubbock's face forces him to wake. He scrambles up from his sleeping place upon the dune and finds that the sun has risen. The women and children of Kow Swamp have left to gather plants and shellfish, while the men have gone hunting. On the river a canoe is about to depart, heading for a lagoon where its two occupants plan to fish, and so Lubbock seats himself behind them and is paddled downstream.

The canoe moves swiftly, sometimes providing views across open country, sometimes travelling between tree-lined banks and through corridors of reeds. The two men paddling have long and steeply sloping foreheads, like those Lubbock had seen the night before, and he recalls a passage from *Prehistoric Times* about cranial deformation among North American Indian tribes. Various methods had been described: fastening babies to cradle boards, placing bags of sand upon foreheads, binding with tight bandages. Modern John Lubbock recalls, and agrees with, his namesake's last words on the subject: 'It is very remarkable that this unnatural process does not appear to have any prejudicial effect on the mind of the sufferers.'[11]

Lubbock's attention is suddenly drawn to the riverside woodland where he glimpses the movement of what might be a large animal – a very large animal. His eye registers the curve of a shoulder, and then a rump, but it was largely hidden behind the trees. The canoe has passed on and so he turns and strains his neck to get a second look; but it is too late. Perhaps it had been a kangaroo or perhaps there had been no animal at all.

As in America, Australia had an abundance of large animals – mega-fauna – during the Pleistocene, all but one of which became extinct before the Holocene began.[12] Of almost fifty different species, only the red kanga-roo survived, a beast that weighs up to 90 kilograms and stands two metres tall.[13] There had once been kangaroos two, three or even four times as large, as well as giant wombats and a range of other exotic creatures. *Megalania* had been the largest carnivore on the continent: a lizard seven metres in length with sharp teeth and claws; *Genyornis*, a flightless emu-like bird weighing 100 kilograms and with a beak 30 centimetres long; *Diprotodon*, a mammal the shape of a wombat and the size of a rhinoceros; *Thylacoleo*, the marsupial lion.

As with the American mega-fauna, there has been a debate as to whether these animals became extinct owing to the climatic changes associated with the ice age or hunting pressure caused by the arrival of modern humans in the continent.[14] And, as in the American debate, strong evidence on either side is lacking. There is just one site where human artefacts have been found with the bones of extinct animals: Cuddie Springs in New South Wales. Excavations at this water-hole revealed stone artefacts associated with the bones of *Diprotodon* and *Genyornis* dating to about 30,000 years ago. When microscopically examined, blood and hair residues from those animals were found on the artefacts. But as hunting implements were absent, the excavators believe that Aborigines had simply come to scavenge on animals that had recently died of thirst or become trapped in mud at the water-hole.[15]

The key difference between the Australian and American extinctions is timing. Whereas the mammoths survived until the very end of the Pleistocene, all of the Australian mega-fauna, except for the red kangaroo, appear to have gone extinct by 20,000 BC, and perhaps long before. This makes a climatic explanation more persuasive: by 20,000 BC people had already been on the Australian continent for more than 30,000 years and the extinctions may coincide with the development of the extremely arid conditions of the LGM.

The mega-fauna that went extinct are likely to have been particularly susceptible to the loss of water-holes and most probably died of hunger and thirst. But the precise timing of many extinctions remains unclear. The newly available evidence from Tasmania suggests that the mega-fauna of that region had already died out by 35,000 BC. This was before the arrival of people, leaving climate change as the only explanation

Many Australian archaeologists believe that the extinctions throughout Australia occurred at an even earlier date – between 50,000 and 40,000 BC. As such, they point to the coincidence with the arrival of people in the continent.[16] Conversely, Colin Pardoe believes that some of the mega-fauna survived long after 20,000 years ago in the vicinity of the Murray River.[17] And so Lubbock may well have caught a glimpse of *Diprotodon* or some other beast. Or not – the canoe moved too swiftly to tell.

At the lagoon, the men who paddled the canoe begin to unravel a net made from twisted plant fibres. But with another 5,000 kilometres and 9,000 years of Australian prehistory to cover, Lubbock has no time for fishing. He sets off on foot through the thicket of trees around the lagoon and on to the open plain, heading northwest, towards Australia's arid centre.

35

Across the Arid Zone

Hunter-gatherer adaptations to the Central Australian Desert, 30,000 BC–AD 1966

Dusk in the Central Australian Desert:

The western sky is suffused with a rich after-glow, against which the mulga branches stand out sharp and thin. All shrubs and tufts of grass are deep purple in colour as seen against the golden light. Towards the east the scene is changed completely. The white-blue salt bushes, with pale grey patches of low herbage and still lighter tufts of grass stand out in strong contrast to the warm, rich browns of the gibber[1] fields stretching away to the horizon where the sky is a cold, steel blue melting above into salmon pink and this into a deep ultramarine speckled with brilliant stars. Gradually the light fades and the outline of the horizon becomes indistinct. Save for the weird plaintive call of a passing curlew everything is absolutely silent. One after another the stars rise in the east and mount higher and higher in the sky, and then with a feeling of perfect freedom and a delicate sense of absolute fresh air, as the night wind rises and blows over you, gently rustling the leaves of some old gnarled gum tree, you fall asleep.[2]

So wrote Baldwin Spencer and Frank Gillen in their 1912 book, *Across Australia*. Spencer was Professor of Biology at Melbourne University and Gillen had the grandiose title of 'Special Magistrate and Sub-Protector of Aborigines for South Australia'. As well as describing the desert, they wrote one of the first accounts of the Arrente Aborigines of central Australia – whom they referred to as the Arunta tribe – focusing on their religious customs and beliefs.[3]

Whether travelling in the present day, in AD 1912 or 14,000 BC, everything in central Australia is on a vast scale – boundless scrub-covered plains, great valleys four or five hundred kilometres in length, impressive gorges and wide river channels that are either absolutely dry or flooded with water. For urban dwellers such as myself, Spencer and Gillen's descriptions make the desert sound heavenly. Until, that is, one reads about the plagues of mosquitoes and flies. A mouthful of these often accompanied any food they ate; on some occasions they woke in the morning with 'bung eye' – the attempt by a female fly to lay her eggs in the soft and mucous membrane of the eyelid. As soon as the sun had risen, they recalled, the low buzz of mosquitoes began and then grew in intensity, becoming worse and worse until a climax was reached which remained until dusk.

By suffering such conditions, Spencer and Gillen provided some of the earliest accounts of the Central Desert Aborigines, publishing a succession of classics including *The Native Tribes of Central Australia* in 1899, *The Northern Tribes of Central Australia* in 1904 and *The Arunta* in 1927. Spencer had written the texts while Gillen had undertaken most of the fieldwork, sending extensive letters and notes to his colleague and receiving demands for further information and clarification by return. Their books made extensive use of black-and-white plates and contributed to the development of anthropological thought, influencing Durkheim, Freud and Lévi-Strauss.

Across Australia combined accounts from several expeditions into 'a simple narrative of some of the most interesting things we have seen'. That had been a great deal, not only of the Australian landscapes but of the indigenous people. Both Spencer and Gillen had become fully initiated members of the Arunta tribe and were allowed to attend many ceremonies previously unwitnessed by Western eyes.

And yet a lifetime of studying the Aborigines failed to dispel their Victorian notions about tribal people. The introduction to *Across Australia* provided a warning to any unwary reader who might be fooled by their own descriptions of complex ceremony and ritual:

> It must be remembered [the authors wrote] that though the native cermonies reveal, to a certain extent, what has been described as 'elaborate ritual' they are eminently crude and savage. They are performed by naked, howling savages, who have no permanent abodes, no clothing, no knowledge of any implements, save those fashioned out of wood, bone, or stone, no idea whatever of the cultivation of crops, or of the laying-in of a supply of food to tide over hard times, and no words for any numbers beyond three or four.[4]

The irony is that it is precisely these qualities of high mobility, limited possessions and intense ceremony that so impress anthropologists today. By surviving within the Central Australian Desert, the Aborigines documented by Spencer and Gillen had attained one of the greatest achievements of humankind. And yet those alive in the late nineteenth and early twentieth centuries may have had it relatively easy in comparison to their forebears, those who had occupied the desert at – or very soon after – the LGM.

Central Australia has been hot and arid for more than a million years. Today the arid zone of Australia covers five million square kilometres, 70 per cent of the continent.[5] Defined as the region where evaporation equals or exceeds rainfall, summer temperatures pass 35°C, while average annual rainfall is less than 500 millimetres and fails to reach 125 millimetres in the driest parts. Almost 80 per cent of the region consists of 'open desert' – stony or sandy surfaces, bare rock and clay pans which lack defined drainage patterns; surface water may be abundant immediately after rain but rapidly disappears. Scattered between the vast expanses of open desert are the uplands: the Musgrave, James and MacDonnell ranges of the centre, the Pilbara district to the west and the Kimberley ranges in the northwest. Within these uplands, run-off is concentrated into streams that provide the most reliable water sources of the arid zone and support a relative abundance of plant and animal life. Along the margins of most uplands are riverine flood plains. Surface water can be found on these throughout most of the year, providing a surprising source of food for such an arid land: fish, shellfish, waterfowl and aquatic plants.

When people first entered the arid zone close to 30,000 BC, temperatures were little different to those of today but it was much wetter, resulting in widespread lakes and permanent water courses. As global temperatures fell to the LGM, an already meagre rainfall was halved; wind speeds increased, lakes dried up and extensive dunes were formed. The arid zone expanded to cover 80 per cent of the continent, leaving no more than the northern tip and eastern margins with a temperate climate.

When the climate turned after 20,000 BC, conditions began to improve; rainfall increased, leading to reliable water sources once again; plant cover also increased which, together with a decline in the winds, led to stabilisation of the dunes. Conditions for human settlement improved continuously up until 7000 BC. After that, the climate became rather cooler and drier, resulting in today's desert, so evocatively described by Baldwin Spencer and Frank Gillen.

To examine its history of occupation, John Lubbock has arrived in the Central Desert at 13,500 BC. On his journey from Kow Swamp he has crossed a vast extent of scrubland killed off by drought, encountered desiccated carcasses and passed many extinct lakes. These were brilliant white sheets of salt, quite sterile of life but which told of a time when there had been freshwater expanses surrounded by woodland harbouring a myriad of animals and birds. Lubbock crossed clay pans; some had flimsy surfaces, broken into little curled flakes glistening in the sun, others had thick hexagonal pavements of cracked clay, covered by the tracks of emu and kangaroo and surrounded by withered shrubs and the dead shells of snails and mussels.

When the rain came, the normally dry creeks were soon transformed into torrents and the clay pans became pools of water brimming with snails, crabs, mussels and crayfish. Thousands of frogs would emerge from below ground where the sand had been cool with an inkling of moisture.

The frogs would spawn, eggs hatch, tadpoles develop and turn into bright green and orange frogs in time to disappear into the ground when the drought returned. They fed upon caterpillars that appeared as if from nowhere on the revitalised plants and the mass of seedlings that erupted from the ground. Wildfowl arrived – coots, spoonbills, pelicans – as did hawks and eagles, all feeding with a feverish anxiety.

Now Lubbock, sits within a large sandstone rockshelter practically in the centre of the continent. It is in a south-facing escarpment on the southern side of the James mountain range. Lubbock looks across the seemingly endless arid scrubland in which he both enjoyed the dusk and was plagued by flies; it is now baking under the midday sun. By climbing on to the escarpment he has looked north and seen tinted rows of mountains, all shimmering in the heat haze, threatening and yet inviting for the traveller, whether in prehistoric or modern times. Beside him on the cave floor is debris from others who recently sought shelter there: a scatter of ash, burnt fragments of animal bone, a few flakes of quartz.

At the time of Lubbock's visit, the cave walls are quite bare. In the future, though, they will be covered with hand stencils and the rockshelter will gain the name Kulpi Mara, meaning 'cave of hands'. This is how Peter Thorley of Northern Territory University found it when he excavated the cave in 1995–6, discovering the remnants of successive hearths sandwiched in sediment that had weathered from the roof and walls, supplemented by a little blown sand. Radiocarbon dates indicated that people had lit fires within Kulpi Mara at some date prior to 30,000 BC, at around 27,000 BC and between 13,700 and 11,500 BC.[6]

About 200 kilometres to the northwest of Kulpi Mara lies Puritjarra, another and larger sandstone rockshelter, which provides comparable dates for occupation. Located in the Cleland Hills, its name means 'shade area' – an appropriate title as it provides protection both from the midday sun and from the prevailing wind. Its massive entrance is 45 metres long by 20 metres high; paintings and stencils cover the walls. The absence of wind was a blessing for the Aborigines who occupied Puritjarra until the 1930s, but a curse for Mike Smith from the University of New England, the archaeologist who excavated there between 1986 and 1988. With no blown dust, there was such a low rate of sedimentation that artefacts made thousands of years apart could have been separated by no more than a few millimetres of sediment.[7]

Smith believes that the shelter was first occupied about 30,000 years ago, although his oldest radiocarbon date – from a layer containing fragments of charcoal and red ochre, stone tools and waste flakes – is around 25,000 BC. Above this, there were very few artefacts embedded in the cave's deposits before a date of 15,000 BC was reached. The upper horizons covered the last 7,000 years and contained cooking hearths, flaked stone and grinding implements.[8]

Had Puritjarra and Kulpi Mara been used continuously between 25,000 and 15,000 BC, throughout the time of the LGM when the climatic conditions had been most severe?[9] Mike Smith thinks so, proposing that the Cleland Hills had maintained permanent water-holes, creating a refuge for people expelled by drought from the surrounding desert. But whether the few dates from Puritjarra and Kulpi Mara had derived from sporadic, exploratory visits or record a constant human presence in Australia's arid centre, remains unclear. Whatever the answer, Aborigines were evidently using the rockshelters when conditions were far more arid than those that Spencer and Gillen had witnessed a century ago – or even than today. How did they manage to do so?

We know how the recent Aborigines have survived in the Australian deserts thanks to anthropologists who have meticulously studied their adaptations, undertaking quite different types of research to that adopted by Spencer and Gillen. During the late 1960s Richard Gould, who later became Professor of Anthropology at the University of Hawaii, lived with Aborigines in a region to the west of Puritjarra Cave – a region that can claim the most unreliable water supplies and impoverished plant and animal communities of anywhere in the world.[10]

The Aborigines usually lived in groups of around twenty. The men spent several hours each day hunting but rarely killed anything larger than lizards and mice, while the women collected seeds and tubers from more than thirty different plants, of which seven provided the bulk of the food. They too caught small game, along with insects and grubs – in fact, almost fifty different varieties of meat and fleshy food were collected.[11]

The key to survival was opportunism – being prepared to move to wherever rain had been seen to fall, and where a water catchment was known. To do so they needed very few possessions and 'permanent abodes' would have been no use at all. Rainfall could be seen from 80 kilometres away and vast distances were regularly covered; in just three months during 1966, Gould's group moved to nine different campsites spread across 2,600 square kilometres. This lifestyle required a detailed and extensive geographical knowledge that was embedded in the Dreamtime stories. As the younger members of the group learned the mythology and were initiated into sacred knowledge, they had to memorise the names and locations of many landmarks, notably water-holes. Such initiations took place on the rare occasions when hunting was good; up to 150 people would gather and remain together until local game became depleted. And so the story-telling, ceremonies, and dancing – that performed by Spencer and Gillen's 'naked, howling savages' – were absolutely essential to human survival.

Another key ingredient of the desert adaptation was the sharing ethic. All food brought into the camp was meticulously shared between all members of the group, even when it was no more than a small lizard. Beyond this, kin ties between groups served to ensure that one group would be welcomed into another's territory if they were suffering from drought and a shortage of food. These links were established through a 'cross-cousin' marriage system in which a man was expected to marry a woman who was his mother's mother's brother's daughter's daughter. As these relations were understandably not easy to find, men often sought partners among groups living hundreds of kilometres away. And as a man could take several wives, he often became related to different families living throughout thousands of square kilometres of desert. Consequently, there was always the possibility of finding kin, and hence access to water and foraging opportunities, in times of need.

Gould describes fire as the most useful tool of the desert Aborigines. Much of their landscape was covered by spinifex – a spiky shrub that didn't provide any edible material. This was burnt off, resulting in the growth and succession of several productive food plants until spinifex was once again established. Gould watched the Aborigines burn extensive tracts of land, but they never voiced any intention about encouraging the growth of new plants. Fire was also used to flush out small game, and sometimes to smoke lizards and mammals out of their burrows.

Grinding stones were equally essential; without these, many of the seeds collected would have been inedible. Such stones were acquired from quarries or trade and left at campsites in anticipation of a future return. With one exception, all other tools were remarkably simple: stone flakes, often used as found upon the ground and then discarded, digging sticks for plants, wooden spears. The exception was the spear-thrower – a stick up to one metre in length that was used for many tasks other than propelling spears. These were usually flattened to serve as a mixing tray for pigments and tobacco; they were used to start fires and often had a stone flake hafted to one end for woodworking. Surfaces were frequently incised with geometric designs that functioned as maps to sacred landmarks.

The Aborigines of the twentieth century survived in the incredibly difficult environment of the Australian desert with this combination of tools, rules and profound geographical knowledge. But is this how the Aborigines who made the stone flakes and fireplaces in Kulpi Mara and Puritjarra Caves had also lived? We must be extremely cautious about imposing modern patterns of behaviour on to the past – especially when dealing with such archaeologically invisible matters as cross-cousin marriage.[12]

Richard Gould excavated two rockshelters in the desert: Puntutjarpa and Intirtekwerle. Both had long sequences of deposits that stretched back to 10,000 BC. And both had stone artefacts little different to those used by the Aborigines with whom Gould had lived during the 1960s. In his 1980 book, *Living Archaeology*, which described his experiences and excavations, Gould proposed that the culture of seed grinding, marriage networks and Dreamtime mythology stretched back not only to that date but to the very first occupation of the arid zone at 30,000 BC. This was a bold claim as, in the 1960s, the oldest known grinding stones dated to a mere 3500 BC.[13] It wasn't until 1997 that Gould was vindicated by the discovery of grinding-stone fragments at Cuddie Springs – the site in New South Wales where people had once either hunted or scavenged upon the carcasses of now extinct mammals. Excavations by Richard Fullagar and Judith Field of Sydney University have recovered thirty-three grinding-stone fragments from a 150-centimetre-deep trench with layers dating from earlier than 30,000 BC up to the present day. Many of the fragments came from the same layers in which butchered mega-fauna bones were found. Microscopic remains of plant tissues and a distinctive polish on the grinding stone fragments confirmed that they had been used for processing seeds.[14]

The evidence from Cuddie Springs suggests that the Aborigines living in the Australian deserts during and immediately after the LGM had a seed-grinding economy, similar to that observed in the 1960s by Richard Gould. But the fragments of ochre that have been recovered from Kulpi Mara and Puritjarra Caves are hardly sufficient to enable archaeologists to determine whether the desert Aborigines also had similar Dreamtime mythologies and marriage rules – as crucial to recent survival as the grinding of seeds.

For three days John Lubbock remained in Kulpi Mara Cave, hoping for the return of whoever had recently built the fire. He wished to meet them, to travel with them, to discover how they lived. Nobody came. Lubbock gathered his own food: wild figs and roots, a lizard dug from its burrow. While waiting, he opened *Prehistoric Times* to read about his namesake's knowledge and views of the Aborigines. In the few pages devoted to the Australians, the author had drawn upon the accounts from various nineteenth-century travellers[15] – but not those of Spencer and Gillen whose initial publication did not appear until thirty years after the first edition of *Prehistoric Times* (1865).

For Victorian John Lubbock, the Aborigines were – unsurprisingly – 'miserable savages'. But just as modern John Lubbock had found when reading about the people of Tierra del Fuego and the North American Indians, such statements conflicted with Victorian Lubbock's evident appreciation of the many tools which the Aborigines had skilfully made and used. *Prehistoric Times* explained how they were 'well practised' in the use of spear-throwers, boomerangs and turtle spears with moveable barbed blades, describing such implements in some detail. It also seemed difficult to understand how the Tasmanians could be described as being entirely lacking in moral views (as quoted from the Reverend Dove) and yet the Australians as being capable of recognising selfish and unreasonable behaviour. Once again, Victorian Lubbock seemed to be wrestling with how to reconcile the blatantly racist views of those whose journals he relied upon and the evident value he himself attached to the technology and lifestyles of those he called 'modern savages'.

After an early-morning vigil looking for that key sign of human life, a spiral of smoke, Lubbock climbs down from the crags and leaves Kulpi Mara Cave. His direction is due north, across what will become the MacDonnell ranges and through the future Alice Springs. Lubbock has another 1,200 kilometres of desert to cross before he reaches Arnhem Land, a land that will be transformed by global warming.

36

Fighting Men and a Serpent's Birth

Art, society and ideology in northern Australia, 13,000–6000 BC

Two men face each other, ready for combat. They wear ornate clothes with elaborate head-dresses. Their hands grip boomerangs. Lethal weapons. Neither man will think twice about killing the other.

John Lubbock has seen many similar scenes during his last few days of travel. The majority have been one-to-one boomerang and spear contests, happening close to water-holes. The combatants had all been men wearing tunics and trousers of animal hide decorated with feathers and shells; their faces painted red and their statures extended by menacing constructions of plumes, furs, bones and bark. Some men had transformed themselves into beasts by wearing animal masks and yet remained on two legs as they advanced to attack those who dared to stand in their way.

At Deaf Adder Gorge, Lubbock had seen one man running towards another, about to throw his boomerang. His opponent, dressed as a wild animal, stood his ground, ready with a handful of spears. Amongst the rocky crags above Twin Falls two men had stood face to face, each quite intent on bringing the other to a bloody death. One held a spear aloft, poised to strike, while the other gripped a boomerang, ready to assault and break his opponent's arm. Elsewhere Lubbock saw the outcome of these battles: bodies falling to the ground or lying dead, pierced with spears.

Now, though, Lubbock has reached the crags and eucalyptus trees above Jim Jim Falls. It is midday; the sun is scorching and the air bone-dry. A pair of birds, perhaps vultures, are circling in the clear blue sky. Despite the heat, another fight is about to break out – two men dressed, armed and engaged in a battle of minds before the first boomerang is thrown. Lubbock sees it in mid-flight, hurtling off the artist's brush as the rock painting is finished with a deft flick of red paint. There the boomerang will remain, pinned to the wall for many millennia to come. Lubbock turns to the artist; he is an old Aboriginal man with a gnarled face and grey stubble; a peaceful man, one who has never lifted a spear or boomerang in anger throughout his long life but who dwells upon scenes of violence and death.[1]

Lubbock is in today's Arnhem Land, at the 'top end' of the Northern Territories in Australia. It is a landscape of sandstone escarpments, savannah woodland and deep gorges. An arid landscape, one in which rivers struggle to survive and periodically fail. The date is uncertain – it is hard to say exactly when he could be visiting the rock paintings of fighting men and sitting with an artist who quietly mixes his ochre pigment.

The present-day Aborigines of Arnhem Land attribute these paintings, referred to by archaeologists as 'Dynamic Figures', to the work of the Mimi people.[2] These are believed by the Aborigines to have been their forerunners in Arnhem Land, and to have taught them how to paint. The Mimi people decorated high rockshelter ceilings by flying and survive today as spirits, sometimes nestled within the cracks of a rock-face.

'Dynamic' is an appropriate description. Each figure is no more than a few centimetres high; many have legs outstretched as if running with utmost speed, this emphasised by the small dashes close to their feet suggesting movement. Similar marks seem to emanate from their mouths, perhaps depicting heavy breathing or war cries. But not all Dynamic Figures are involved in fighting; some are shown hunting emus; some are depicted simply standing, sitting or tumbling through the air; some hold leafed branches and others are engaged in sex.[3] The simple fact that such paintings were created beyond the time of Aboriginal oral history, and hence have been placed into the mythic world of the Mimi people, suggests great antiquity. Christopher Chippindale and Paul Taçon, archaeologists from Cambridge University and the Australian Museum in Sydney, have attempted to identify exactly how old.

To begin with, the Dynamic Figures are not the first art style in Arnhem Land; below the painted figures one finds faint engraved lines of an older art: depictions of giant kangaroos, wallabies, snakes, crocodiles and fish. We also know such engravings cannot be more than 60,000 years old, as that marks the arrival of people in the Australian continent. But beyond this, things get difficult.

The use of boomerangs as weapons is significant, as all the historically known Aborigines of Arnhem Land have used them as musical instruments alone – clapping boards. The depicted animals are also chronologically suggestive as some are now extinct, such as the thylacine – or Tasmanian tiger – whose striped flanks can be seen in several paintings. This animal had disappeared from Arnhem Land by 5000 BC. A few paintings appear to depict extinct animals of a much earlier time, such as a giant wombat known as *Palorchestes* that became extinct before the Pleistocene had ended. In addition, the absence of certain animals is also helpful; there are few depictions of fish, and when present they are relatively small freshwater varieties. In the later art styles of Arnhem Land, fish become very prominent and this is thought to reflect the rising sea level, development of swamps and changing diet of the Aboriginal people after the ice age had reached its end.

Chippindale and Taçon have taken these few strands of evidence, woven them together and concluded that the Dynamic Figures depict people in the arid landscapes of Arnhem Land before the final spurt of global warming at 9600 BC.

Another hint as to the age of the paintings comes from fragments of red ochre in rockshelter deposits which also contain the stone artefacts left by Pleistocene Australians.[4] The Dynamic Figures were created with the same type of pigment, although this has since turned to a rich mulberry colour and seems to have become embedded within the rock itself. At about 12,000 BC there is a marked increase in the quantity of red ochre in the rockshelter deposits, suggesting the start of intense artistic activity; Paul Taçon believes that this is when the Dynamic Figures were first created.[5]

It seems most likely, therefore, that Lubbock is in Arnhem Land at some date between 20,000 and 9600 BC – I will follow Taçon and place Lubbock close to the end of this period, say at 10,000 BC. But while we know that he has been visiting the painted rocks, and watching the artists at work, has he also seen the fighting in real life? Do the paintings depict the reality of life during the final stage of the ice age in Arnhem Land? They might be a true historical record of public contests by men fighting for access to precious resources, perhaps over the few water-holes that were jealously owned and guarded in the arid landscapes. The fights may have been either bloody and to the death or largely ritualised in nature. Alternatively, they may have been no more than fantasy: depictions of mythical beings, engaged in imaginary battles while wearing costumes quite unlike any seen in the real world. Indeed, the Aboriginal artists of Arnhem Land may have been a peaceful people, who dressed in plain clothing and ensured that all food and water was evenly shared.

Chippindale and Taçon favour the 'art as historical record' interpretation.[6] And hence, on his travels through Arnhem Land, Lubbock has seen not only the fighting men painted in red, but the fighting men themselves.

Lubbock now sits in the shade of a eucalyptus on the banks of a shallow stream. Its course has been his pathway from a deep gorge within the escarpment, past rockshelters where people were chipping at quartz and on to a tree-scattered plain. The stream continues as far as he can see, meandering away for at least another 500 kilometres before it meets the ocean. He intends to follow it to the estuary and then the coastline, until he reaches the snow-covered mountains that lie 1,000 kilometres to the north in today's Papua New Guinea.

But for now it is too hot and Lubbock is tired. And so he rests by a tree and checks a passage in *Prehistoric Times* that he recalls had mentioned Aboriginal art. 'In a cave on the north-eastern coast', his namesake had written in AD 1865, 'Mr Cunningham observed certain "tolerable figures of sharks, porpoises, turtles, lizards, trepang, starfish, clubs, canoes, water-gourds, and some quadrupeds which were probably intended to represent kangaroos and dogs". It is, however, doubtful whether these are the work of the present natives.'⁷ Modern John Lubbock thinks how the paintings he saw on the escarpment had lacked any figures such as these.

He closes the book and begins to doze by the shallow waters of what will one day become the East Alligator River of Arnhem Land. Dreamy memories arrive of his travels elsewhere at this date in human history: watching the reburial of the long-time dead at 'Ain Mallaha by the Late Natufian people who had been forced on the move by the droughts of the Younger Dryas; arriving in southwest France to find that the painted caves are deserted and forgotten; fishing with the people of Quebrada Jaguay of Peru.

He sleeps deeply, not just for the rest of the day but for the rest of the ice age and beyond. New types of dreams: droplets of water from icicles that suddenly balloon in size; melt-water lakes that burst their banks; rivers in spate carrying huge boulders and trees; cliffs of ice collapsing into the sea. That one wakes him with a crash.

Instead of the clear blue sky and eucalyptus shade that sent Lubbock to sleep, he wakes in a gloomy, cavernous world, seated upon a muddy island and surrounded by swamp.⁸ Four thousand years have passed since he began to doze, and it is now 6000 BC. Gnarled and knotted trunks on either side send out contorted and threatening mud-stained boughs. Above, a thick canopy of leaves. The air is stifling, permeated with a hot miasmatic vapour. There is an intense silence, broken only by the quiet gasping of shellfish that lie in the mud or cling to the roots and trunks of the mangroves.

As Lubbock slept, the tide had come in; not the daily tides that lapped the shores of Pleistocene Greater Australia but the tide of post-glacial sea-level rise.⁹ As glaciers collapsed, ice sheets melted, and lakes drained, the southern oceans swelled. Sea levels rose relentlessly, at times flooding 45 metres a year of the plain across which Lubbock had planned to travel. By 6500 BC, the low land between northern Australia and New Guinea was entirely submerged under the Arafura Sea. As the waters inundated Arnhem Land, small interior streams were transformed into wide estuaries; levees developed leading to freshwater wetlands; the mangroves took over.

Lubbock traverses the edge of the swamp, clambering over massive roots and disturbing the turtles that had been resting on sandbanks. For a while the swamps seem endless and threatening, especially the crocodiles that lurk in the shallows. Relief arrives as the canopy is pierced by tiny patches of blue; they grow in number and size. The air freshens, the gloom recedes. Quite suddenly the mangroves end and he steps into sunlight and on to dry, solid ground.

Others have emerged just a few moments before. A few metres away a group of Aborigines have seated themselves on the ground and lit a fire. Lubbock joins them and finds that they have been collecting shellfish from the mangroves. A few will be eaten while they rest before returning to their camping site in the narrow fringe of woodland between the end of the mangroves and the start of the escarpment. When they rise and leave, Lubbock follows.

The next few weeks are spent with these people – fishing, hunting turtles, gathering yams, collecting more shellfish. They have a rich assortment of foods to choose between; middens are accumulating by the riversides, soon to be buried by the mangrove mud as the swamps expand.[10] Lubbock makes a two-day trip with them to the seashore to collect shellfish and salt. On the way a thunderstorm strikes; howling winds and rain cause the party to shelter within a cave and then to find unexpected novelties on the shore. There are great masses of seaweed within which jellyfish and urchins lurk, while the little bodies of seahorses and pipefish are scattered across the sand.

Although such foraging within the mangrove swamps and on the seashore is a new way of Aboriginal life, their stone tools remain little changed from those of their ice-age forebears, principally simple flakes of quartz. Some new types have appeared, such as bone points, and they have an array of artefacts made from organic materials such as woven baskets and wooden spears. But only the stone flakes will survive in the debris left behind for archaeologists to find.[11]

Lubbock returns to the escarpment, the plateau and crags where he had once encountered the Dynamic fighting men. The violence continues, but now takes the form of pitched battles rather than one-to-one contests. In one such battle, two groups are facing each other – perhaps fifty to sixty people in all – armed with barbed spears and hafted axes. Except for a head-dressed man that leads each group, the men are simply clad, if clothed at all. A volley of spears has been launched and one of the leaders receives a fatal strike to his abdomen.[12]

He continues to fall but is destined never to reach the ground, just as the spears are to remain in flight; this battle is another painting found on the rock-faces of Arnhem Land. Chippindale and Taçon think that this and other battle scenes were painted at about 6000 BC. The new paintings are much simpler than the pairs of Dynamic men; many are no more than stick-figures with circles for their heads.

The new artists have done more than bringing whole groups into battle; they have also changed the animals and adopted new artistic styles. Fish, snakes and turtles – animals of the wetlands – are now common in the art; a few are painted in an X-ray fashion which shows their internal organs. Another new feature is the Yam figures – people and animals painted with tuberous-like bodies.

This range of imagery replaces the Dynamic Figures and reflects the animal and plant foods being collected in the wetter and warmer environments of the Holocene. The switch from individual skirmishes to battle scenes suggests that society has also changed. When archaeologists look at these paintings of warriors, spears and death from 6000 BC, they find a remarkable resonance with the twentieth-century warfare practices of Aboriginal groups.

Such warfare was recorded by Lloyd Warner, an anthropologist who lived among the Murngin Aborigines of northeast Arnhem Land in the 1920s.[12] The Murngin had lived by hunting and gathering in a not dissimilar landscape to that reconstructed for 6000 BC. Violence and warfare were endemic in their society; Lloyd Warner estimated that this caused about two hundred deaths of young men each year. He described several types, ranging from *nirimaoi yolno*, one-to-one fights between men seldom resulting in any casualties, to *milwerangel*, a pitched battle between members of several clans arranged to take place at a specified time and place, usually ending in a violent brawl with several fatalities.

A great deal of this fighting originated from disputes over women. *Nirimaoi yolno* usually arose when a man from one camp accused one in another of having been – or at least trying to become – his wife's lover. The two men rarely ever got further than hurling insults at each other, happy at being 'restrained' by their friends so they could feign much bravado without risking getting hurt.[14] In another form of combat – *narrup* – a man will be physically attacked while sleeping. The whole clan of the attacker will be held responsible and the incident may easily escalate into *maringo*, an expedition to revenge the killing of a relative or even *milwerangel*.

Lloyd Warner argued that warfare and killing within the Murngin was a consequence of their marriage system. This was polygyny, which allowed men to have several wives; most middle-aged Murngin men had at least three. As the number of Murngin men and women were approximately equal, and as women married just before puberty, there were simply too few women for the young men to marry. And so, in Lloyd Warner's words, there was a 'seasonal slaying' of young men who had passed into adolescence and were ready to find their first wife.[15] This culling of the young and eligible was presumably in the interests of the older members of society who were happy to encourage the younger men to fight.

There is no direct evidence that the 6000 BC battle-scene paintings of Arnhem Land depicted real life; even if they did so, there is nothing to prove that the battles corresponded to those described for the Murngin or were undertaken for the same reasons. Chippindale and Taçon are confident, however, that this change from paintings of fighting men to battle scenes is indeed a historical record and is ultimately explained by the changing environments of Arnhem Land brought about by global warming.

Exactly how the environmental, social and artistic changes may be related remains unclear. One scenario is that the appearance of wetlands created a new diversity and abundance of plant and animal foods. With better nutrition, the population grew. But the sources of food were not evenly dispersed across the landscape. Instead, the particularly profitable stretches of river, groves of trees, water-holes and animal haunts were highly localised. And so groups became concerned with establishing and defending territories that encompassed these locales. They did so partly through ceremony and partly through warfare. It may have been at this time that the historically known territorial patterns and linguistic divides of Aboriginal groups in Arnhem Land began to emerge: those between-groups known as the Jawoyn, Gundjeibmi, Kunwinjku and the Murngin.[16] Moreover, the modern-day Dreamtime ideology might also find its origins in this time of adjustment to the Holocene world, as Lubbock will discover with his next encounter on the Arnhem Land plateau.

Lubbock has already seen a variety of new paintings on the escarpment in addition to the battle scenes. These included depictions of lizards, turtles and gourds, reminiscent of those described in *Prehistoric Times*. But now he is face to face with something quite new: a strange creature with an elongated body, a head like that of a kangaroo, or perhaps a crocodile, and a pointed tail similar to a snake. It has strange appendages hanging from its body: perhaps other animals or a combination of these, yams and waterlilies. The creature winds it way over the rock surface, having been brightly painted in red and destined to survive for many millennia. Eventually it will be described by archaeologists and recognised as the earliest-known depiction of the mythical Rainbow Serpent from the Aboriginal Dreamtime.

The Rainbow Serpent is one of the key Ancestral Beings, known to Aborigines throughout the continent. It is believed to have played a fundamental role in creating the Australian landscape and is described by Paul Taçon as being among the world's most powerful mythological creatures. As with other Ancestral Beings, its form was not fixed; it could change between that of a snake, a kangaroo and a crocodile and was often depicted as a combination of all three. During the founding days, this serpent wound its way through the country, creating all the water-holes and creeks, stocking them with creatures and placing people in the landscape, each clan in a designated area. Rainbows in the sky were thought to be the soul of the serpent; when these disappeared the Being had returned to the permanent water-holes where it liked to dwell.[17]

Taçon and his colleagues believe that the idea of the Rainbow Serpent was inspired by the pipefish washed up on the newly formed shores by the turbulent seas of the Early Holocene. As these were being found, the Aborigines were also watching snakes slithering away from drowning landscapes and rainbows overhead that followed lightning and thunder. Waterholes were now remaining permanently full and previously dry creek beds had become swift-flowing rivers. And so the Rainbow Serpent and its stories were adopted to make sense of this changing world, of the new landscapes and the astonishing nature of human experience in the first few millennia of the Holocene.

Josephine Flood, a distinguished Australian archaeologist, believes that many other Aboriginal myths also relate to the environmental events at the end of the ice age. The mythological accounts of a great flood are often so detailed and specific that she cannot doubt that they are recalling actual events that occurred thousands of years earlier. Many myths tell how hills were severed from the mainland and turned into islands: Mornington Island in today's Gulf of Carpentaria was created by Garnguur, the seagull woman who pulled her raft backwards and forwards across what had been a peninsula to form a channel for the sea. Elcho Island, now off the north coast of Arnhem Land, was the result of an Ancestral Being tripping and accidentally pushing his stick into the sand, causing the sea to rush in.[18]

In southern Australia there is a widespread myth about the creation of Kangaroo Island, known as Nar-oong-owie by the Aborigines. This tells about Ngurunderi, a great Ancestral figure who became angry when his wives ran away from him. Having found them wading across the shallow channel that divided Nar-oong-owie from the mainland, Ngurunderi 'was determined to punish his wives and angrily ordered the water to rise up and drown them. With a terrific rush the waters roared and the women were carried back towards the mainland. Although they tried frantically to swim against the tidal wave they were powerless to do so and were drowned. Their bodies turned to stone and are seen as rocks off the coast of Cape Jervis, called The Pages or the Two Sisters.'[19]

Other events occurring at the end of the ice age might also be remembered in the Dreamtime myths. One such story begins as follows:

Long ago, many people were camped at the confluence of the Lachlan and Murrumbidgee Rivers. The day was very hot and a haze rose from the windless plain so that the horizon danced, and mirages distorted the landscape. Everyone lay motionless, resting in the heat. Suddenly, a tribe of giant kangaroos were seen away in the distance and the headman leapt to his feet with a galvanising cry. The camp became a scene of wild excitement and fear. Children were quickly seized and everyone dispersed into the bush. In those days, however, the men had no weapons and were defenceless against the enemy. The kangaroos relentlessly advanced on them through the bush and without mercy crushed their victims with their powerful arms. When the animals were finished, few of the tribe survived.[20]

The story continues with the headman devising weapons and camouflage, and using fire to drive the kangaroos away. Josephine Flood wonders whether such stories about giant kangaroos enshrine memories of extinct animals that might have once been feared and hunted. A further story tells how fertile inland lakes dried up and became barren salt-pans – another widespread event occurring at the end of the ice age.[21]

If Josephine Flood is correct, the Aborigines have passed down stories from generation to generation about sea-level change, mega-fauna and the desiccation of inland lakes for ten, perhaps even twenty, thousand years. Such stories may have begun as factual accounts and gradually became embedded within the Dreamtime mythology. Or perhaps – as the pipefish suggests – the environmental transformations that occurred as the ice age came to an end gave birth not only to Rainbow Serpents but to the Dreamtime itself.

By 6000 BC, Greater Australia is no more; one seventh of its land, about 2.5 million square kilometres, has been drowned by the sea. Tasmania, once a southern peninsula, is now an island whose Aborigines have lost all contact with those on the mainland, divided from them by the ferocious waters of the Bass Strait. The people of New Guinea will, however, remain in contact with those of Australia across the more benign and island-spotted Torres Strait.

To approach New Guinea, John Lubbock travels eastwards and then northwards along the edge of the Gulf of Carpentaria and on to the Cape York peninsula. This journey takes him along a coastline of mangrove swamps, freshwater lagoons, estuaries and shallow waters.[22] He departs as the dry season begins in May, a time when the rivers and lagoons are drying up and the people he meets are living in small, nomadic groups. When the drought takes hold, they congregate around the few sources of permanent water. Lubbock finds that they collect many plant foods, notably the seeds and tubers of waterlilies, and hunt wallabies by flushing them out from the edges of the woodland that spreads inland. As the year passes, the climate becomes increasingly hot and stifling. Trees lose all their leaves and under-growth is burned by the Aborigines. Finally the weather breaks with lightning and thunderstorms, which occur every day for several weeks.

By now it is October. The ground and bare branches erupt with new shoots; dry river-beds fill with water and soon burst their banks to flood much of the low-lying ground. The Aborigines Lubbock meets have already established substantial campsites on high ground. They had waited for the first rains and then collected great sheets of bark from the eucalyptus trees, which had become free once the sap began to run. From these sheets of bark, draped over branches, they built conical huts. They also used the bark for building canoes, essential for travel now that so much of the landscape is flooded. Like the Aborigines, Lubbock's diet changes as crabs, shellfish and birds' eggs become available. Hunting continues but the groups under-taking wallaby drives are replaced by individuals who attempt to stalk and kill kangaroos. They know that if they fail – which is usually the case – there will be plenty of plant foods and small game available at the camp, whereas success will bring much praise and status.

By the following March plant foods have become abundant. On his way

Lubbock helps to gather yams, tubers and a multitude of seeds into bark trays, and then to construct weirs and traps for fish as the flood waters begin to recede. As the wet season comes to its end, the camps break up and people disperse by canoes along the waterways, knowing that within weeks the rains will have ended for another year. By then Lubbock has reached the tip of Cape York and is ready to cross the Torres Strait.

Right: The Puna landscape of the Peruvian Andes.

Pachamachay Cave (occupied *c.* 10,500 BC), Peru.

Below: Excavations in Panaulauca Cave, Peru, of deposits dating to *c.* 10,500 BC.

Excavations at Guilá Naquitz Rockshelter (occupied *c.* 8000 BC), Mexico, in April 1966.

Sandal Shelter, Arizona, USA, and woven sandal made from Yucca leaves dating to *c.* 7000 BC.

Excavations at the Koster site (occupied *c.* 8000–5000 BC), Illinois, USA, in 1970.

Inside Kutikina Cave (occupied *c.* 18,000–13,000 BC), Tasmania.

Left: Excavations at Puritijarra Rockshelter (occupied *c.* 13,000 BC) in the Central Australian Desert in 1998.

Rock painting located in Kakadu National Park, Australia. The battle scene probably dates to *c.* 6000 BC

Kuk Swamp in New Guinea. Excavations showing 'island beds' in the grey clay, *c.* 8000 BC, and superimposed ditches.

Below: View from the entrance of Niah Ca
Sarawak, excavated 1954–67 and 2000–3.

Excavations at Uenohara (occupied *c.* 9200 BC), Kyushu, Japan, in 1990, with the distant volcano of Sakura-jima.

Excavation on Zhokhov Island (occupied *c.* 6400 BC), Siberian Arctic, in June 1990, of a hunter-gatherer dwelling made from driftwood.

Excavations at Jeitun, Turkmenistan, in 1994: an Early Neolithic settlement occupied *c.* 6000 BC.

Below: Excavations at Umm Dabaghiyah, Iraq, in 1973: a farming and specialised Onager hunting site, occupied *c.* 7500 BC.

Mud-walled dwellings at Yarim Tepe, Iraq, excavated in the early 1970s and occupied *c.* 6300 BC.

Excavations in Wadi Kubbaniya (occupied c. 20,000 BC), Nile valley, in 1980.

Site of GvJm19 below an overhang of rock on Lukenya Hill, Kenya. Excavated in 1993 and occupied c. 20,000 BC.

Location of Drotsky's Cave (occupied c. 12,500 BC), Kalahari Desert, Botswana.

Rose Cottage Cave (occupied *c.* 10,000 BC), South Africa: view of entrance and 1992 excavation.

37

Pigs and Gardens in the Highlands

The development of tropical horticulture in highland New Guinea, 20,000–5000 BC

Three Aborigines sit in front of John Lubbock, expertly paddling their canoe into currents and away from reefs. He leans back, relaxing; his hand trails through the water while sea birds are gliding in the brilliant blue sky above.

Lubbock is crossing the newly formed strait that separates the northern-most tip of Australia and the southern coast of Papua New Guinea. At the LGM, this 300-kilometre-wide stretch of water had been grasslands, provid-ing hunting grounds for ice-age Aborigines. By 6000 BC, the date of Lubbock's stowaway canoe journey, rising sea levels had flooded the Arafura plain and breached the last remaining isthmus of land. Only the hills escaped, surviving as more than one hundred islands scattered across the Torres Strait. Some have hills of their own, some possess rocky coastlines ringed with mangrove swamps and others are mere islets of sand.[1]

The first islands Lubbock reached are known today as Muralug, Moa and Badu. He found them inhabited by people with lifestyles similar to that he had experienced in Cape York. But as Lubbock travelled further north, the islands became smaller and lacked any sign of human life. Some remained uninhabited until the present day; others were colonised by people from New Guinea, although it is difficult to say when as archaeological research has been so limited.[2] They were certainly occupied by AD 1898, the year that the Cambridge anthropologist A. C. Haddon arrived in the Torres Strait to make a survey of its people. His monumental six-volume work became an invaluable record of traditional Aboriginal lifestyles.

Haddon's studies built on the first scientific observations of the Torres Strait made in 1770 by Joseph Banks who travelled as the naturalist on Captain Cook's ship, the *Endeavour*.[3] Anthropologists, geographers and, most recently, the archaeologist David Harris from University College, London, went on to develop Haddon's work. Since 1974 Harris has been reconstructing the lifestyles of the Torres Strait islanders both at the time of Captain Cook's voyage, and of Lubbock's visit – 6000 BC – so soon after the islands had been formed.[4]

Harris discovered that while the people encountered by Banks and Haddon on the larger southern islands were hunter-gatherers, those further north were farmers, or more accurately swidden horticulturalists. Each year they burned woodland and planted yams, sweet potatoes and taro – tropical root crops that are still dietary staples for much of Southeast Asia today. Groves of banana, mango and coconut trees were also cared for in their gardens. Wild plant foods were gathered, especially from the mangrove swamps that fringed the islands, while dugongs were hunted for their meat and fat.[5]

The intensity of horticulture encountered by Harris was minimal compared with that observed by the first Europeans to visit New Guinea. Both in its lowlands and highlands vast areas of forests had been cleared and turned to garden plots for root crops. In complete contrast to the transient hunter-gatherer campsites of northern Australia, the first European explorers found densely populated villages ruled by powerful chiefs whose wealth was measured by the number of pigs they owned and who regularly waged war against each other. Hence the narrow Torres Strait divided two quite different worlds: Australian hunter-gatherers to the south and New Guinea farmers to the north.

Why hadn't the Australian Aborigines adopted agriculture? Captain James Cook asked this question when he landed on Possession Island off Cape York in 1770 and reflected that 'the Natives know nothing of cultivation' and 'when one considers the proximity of this country with New Guinea … which produces cocoa-nuts and many other fruits proper for the support of man it seems strange that they should not long ago have been transplanted here'.[6] To Cook, and many later anthropologists, the Aborigines appeared quite backward to have remained as hunter-gatherers when they could have adopted a lifestyle 'proper for the support of man'.

From studies of the Aborigines, it became apparent that their devotion to hunting and gathering could not be explained by a lack of farming knowledge, as they were quite aware of how to cultivate plants. When those in Cape York gathered wild yams, for instance, they often ensured that parts of the tubers were left behind, or were even replanted to ensure a supply in the following year.[7] Moreover, substantial trading contacts between the Aborigines and the Torres Strait islanders had brought the hunter-gatherers into direct contact with the farmers. So why had farming not spread from New Guinea to Australia, just as it had spread from Western Asia to Europe?

An answer was provided by Peter White from Sydney University in 1971: the Australian hunter-gatherers were 'simply too well off to bother about agriculture'.[8] By that date, views about farming had changed dramatically from those held by James Cook, and indeed by academics right up until the late 1960s. The view that farming was an inevitable step on the path to civilisation, one that would be grasped at every opportunity, had been overthrown. Western academics who lived with hunter-gatherers in Australia and Africa decided that they had been among what the anthropologist Marshall Sahlins declared to be the 'original affluent society'.[9]

Such hunter-gatherers were found to work for no more than a few hours each day, to be free from the physical ailments caused by back-breaking tillage and harvesting, and unencumbered by the social tensions and violence found in densely populated farming communities. And so the question that Peter White and his colleagues were asking by 1970 was not why had certain hunter-gatherers 'failed' to adopt farming, but what had forced others to do so when it had such disastrous consequences for their quality of life.

Lubbock gains his first sight of New Guinea from afar – green lowlands below pale clouds that had resolved themselves into ghostly-looking mountains. His unknowing companions remain on one of the islands and he paddles on alone towards the mangrove-edged coastline. A wide river mouth takes Lubbock into New Guinea itself. For some distance the river remains broad, winding in fine sweeps below mangrove-covered banks, until, after an hour of paddling, it splits into two. One branch runs with chocolate-brown water, indicating it to be a forest stream rising in the lowlands, while the other is milky-white, revealing that its waters had once flowed across limestone and hence have a mountain source. To find human settlement, Lubbock must follow the latter. While substantial settlements most likely existed in the New Guinea lowlands at 6000 BC, archaeologists have yet to find them.[10] So begins Lubbock's exploration of the highlands.

The first European exploration did not in fact occur until the 1930s. Earlier expeditions to New Guinea, such as that of the British Ornithologists' Union led by A. F. R. Wollaston in 1910, had assumed that 'novelties' other than exotic birds might be found above 1,000 metres. But they had no idea what such novelties might be; nor did they know that fertile inter-montane valleys existed, believing that there was a single mountain chain across the middle of the island.[11]

The first European contact with the New Guinea highlanders who lived within those valleys was by German Lutheran missionaries in 1919. They kept their discovery secret for fear of attracting rivals in the business of winning human souls: the Baptists, Anglicans, Wesleyans and, their most feared opposition, the French Roman Catholics. It was the 1930s quest for gold by Australian prospectors that brought the New Guinea highlanders to public knowledge. In 1935 Jack Hides penetrated into one of the inter-montane valleys with his fellow prospector Jim O'Malley. Hides later wrote that 'on every slope were cultivated squares, while little columns of smoke rising in the still air revealed to us the homes of the people of this land. I had never seen anything more beautiful. Beyond all stood the heights of some mighty mountain chain that sparkled in places with the colours of the setting sun.'[12]

Lubbock's journey also leads to the highlands, but long before such intensive cultivation has begun. As his river journey continues, small trees from which he picks fresh fruit replace the mangroves. When the river runs straight he snatches glimpses of the distant mountains; but such infrequent views are soon lost altogether as the river narrows yet further and begins to meander between huge trees which shut out all but a narrow strip of sky.

Travel becomes monotonous; the riverside vegetation turns to rank undergrowth and rotting trunks protrude from steep muddy banks.[13] On good days the air is musty; on most days it is rife with the smell of organic decay. It rains frequently, and the leeches are relentless for Lubbock's blood. Compensation for such trials arrives in the occasional sightings of exotic birds, especially the grandiloquent plumes of a bird of paradise. As the river begins to climb, exotic birds are rivalled by other natural wonders: iguanas sunning themselves on logs; bee eaters and swallows swooping amongst swarms of bright yellow flies; tree ferns and flowering creepers.

Lubbock is, however, more interested in the first indication that another type of forest dweller is near by. Some of the fallen trees have evidently been cut with stone axes; others have been burned. He passes an abandoned dugout canoe sinking into river mud. And there are paths – small trails where the bush has been cleared or simply beaten back. Some cross the river, others run parallel for short stretches before veering off into the forest. Some must belong to animals but human feet have marked many others.[14]

Lubbock moors the canoe, leaves the river and begins to follow one such path towards what we now call the Wahgi valley. The air remains hot, humid and musty; the light is gloomy and takes on a greenish hue. Only on rare occasions is the canopy incomplete, splashing sunlight on to the forest floor. New odours arise – some like honeysuckle, others like rotting fruit. And new sounds, perhaps of the same birds and animals he has heard before, but now limited and muffled by the confusion of trees. Perhaps human voices. The path continues, through forest, along riverbanks, and on to ridges from which he can see the huge expanse of forest climbing over hills to disappear under heavy cloud.

Below those clouds the forest climbs to 4,000 metres above sea level. At 6000 BC, it has only recently attained such heights; during the LGM, lower temperatures and reduced rainfall had kept the trees below 2,500 metres. Instead of highland forest there had been open grasslands with scattered shrubs and tree ferns. Glaciers had formed on the peaks and extended into the higher montane valleys.[15]

The grasslands might have been good hunting territory. Two sites are known from close to the tree-line, but neither gives much away as to what people had been doing in the highlands. Kosipe yielded a scatter of artefacts including axeheads at 2,000 metres above sea level, some left there as long ago as 27,000 BC. Dense stands of fruit and nut trees still grow close by, suggesting that Kosipe might have been occupied by people on seasonal expeditions to collect their produce.[16] A little lower, at 1,720 metres, the rockshelter of Nombe can be found, which had been sporadically occupied between 27,000 and 12,500 BC. Along with stone artefacts, the bones of several ground- and tree-living animals were found within the cave. The human occupants of Nombe seem to have had a time-share arrangement with the thylacine, the native wild dog otherwise known as the Tasmanian tiger. The bones of various forest-browsing animals were also found, but whether they, and the other animals, had been the prey of its human or thylacine occupants remains unclear.[17]

With the advent of marked global warming at 9600 BC, the trees spread above 3,000 metres, following in the wake of shrubs that had already invaded the higher altitudes. Unlike the global trend, the climate appears to have become less rather than more seasonal.[18] Within a further two millennia the forests were much like those Lubbock viewed on his journey to the Wahgi valley, and much like those one can see today.

The upper reaches of that valley lie about 20 kilometres west of Mount Hagen in the centre of Papua New Guinea. Missionaries first arrived in 1933 and found a series of small empires ruled by dictatorial big-men. Their wealth and power were measured by the number of pigs, women and shell valuables they owned, these being acquired through the complex trading system between tribes known to anthropologists as the *Moka* exchange. The women and low-status men worked in gardens, cultivating crops of yams, sweet potatoes and taro. Warfare between villages was endemic, a means by which the big-men extended and consolidated their power.

The missionaries, closely followed by gold prospectors and government officials, were treated as people from the spirit world. They provided a seemingly unlimited supply of the highly desired steel axes and marine shells. In so doing they undermined the traditional ceremonial exchange system on which the big-men had relied for securing their wealth. Warfare was also suppressed and European administrators began to usurp the authority of traditional leaders. As a consequence, when the anthropologist Andrew Strathern went to live with the Kawelka tribe in the Upper Wahgi Valley in the early 1960s to make a classic study of big-man society, the traditional lifestyle had already been substantially altered by Western contact.[19]

At around that time, members of the Kawelka tribe returned to the part of the Wahgi valley known as Kuk Swamp. They had abandoned this land in 1900 after the loss of a tribal fight, and all signs of previous cultivation had long been hidden by a thick carpet of grass.[20]

Kuk Swamp lies at 1,500 metres above sea level and appears today as an extensive area of grassland with an almost complete absence of trees. North and east of the swamp is a high, narrow ridge known as Ep, covered with much shorter grass and the only trees of the region. These are not, however, part of the original forest of the Wahgi valley; they are a secondary growth that occurred after the area had been entirely cleared for farming. Marshes are found to the south, and low hills separated by drained ground to the west.

The Kawelka tribe began their recolonisation of Kuk Swamp by developing gardens on the surrounding drylands; within three years, confirmation of their territorial rights by neighbouring tribes, and an increase in their number, led them to reclaim the swamp itself by digging substantial drainage ditches. But the government claimed much of Kuk Swamp in 1969 for its own developments, including an agricultural research station, and inhibited the Kawelka expansion. It was excavations at that research station during the 1970s, by Jack Golson of the Australian National University, that exposed a much more ancient history of farming in the New Guinea highlands.

John Lubbock arrives in a clearing above Kuk Swamp in 5500 BC, the path bringing him on to hills to the west of the wetland area itself. The landscape is quite different to the open grassland that will be found by the missionaries and anthropologists of the twentieth century. The forest which had been growing and evolving at this altitude for many thousands, probably millions, of years remains largely intact, having survived throughout the LGM. But on the drylands around the swamp there are clearings where the forest has already gone; within some of these, shrubs and grasses have taken hold to create a tangle of undergrowth. The trees in Lubbock's clearing have only recently been removed – charred stumps suggest the use of both axes and fire. As a result, sunlight floods on to the few trees and plants that remain.

Just as Lubbock crouches to examine one such plant his attention is drawn to something altogether more striking – a pig. A fat, brown, hairy pig with white tusks, sleeping in a hollow of its own making. Lubbock approaches with caution. It stirs and he halts. Grunting, it rises and Lubbock is first astonished by its size and then fearful. The pig steps forward, sniffs and grunts again; it attempts another step but is halted by a tether – a rope of twisted bark fibres that ties it to a stake. The pig tugs but without much vigour and then turns, dismissively, to resume its wallow.

The edge of the clearing looks out across the wetlands where people are at work, the first people Lubbock has seen since canoeing across the Torres Strait.

An area of about half a kilometre square has already been cleared of forest and is now covered with a mosaic of different plants. The men and women, ten or twelve in all, are digging with wooden spades. They are dark-skinned and naked except for short skirts made from leaves and grass. A long, low mound of grey clay marks the trail of their work, a straight ditch that cuts across the wetland from the marshes at its southern end to a river flowing at its northern margin.

Lubbock descends the slope and walks between the plants, finding that many grow on circular islands between a network of channels, which are themselves full with leafy plants. Banana palms have been planted on the islands, along with several other types of green-leafed plants familiar to Lubbock from his journey through the forests. Among these is another tree-like plant that he has also seen in the forest but never quite as large and healthy-looking. These have thick stems, or trunks on the larger specimens, from which leaves have grown and then dropped in a spiral pattern, leaving a corkscrew appearance. Roots are growing from the stem itself and appear to be propping the plants up; indeed, in some of the larger specimens the base of the stem itself has entirely decayed.

The plants in the ditches, growing in much wetter conditions, are dominated by a type that has large, heart-shaped leaves, pale green in colour; many have still to unfold from the end of lengthy stalks. Lubbock snaps a fresh shoot and rolls it between his fingers, squashing out its sap; it smells acrid and his nostrils and skin begin to sting.

An irrigation ditch is being dug; a much larger ditch than those defining the raised beds, it runs quite straight for several hundred metres and is evidently meant to carry a continuous flow of water. Digging is hard work as the ditch is already waist-deep, the clay heavy to remove, and the humidity stifling. The term 'spade' is a kind description for the tools being used, as these are little more than flattened sticks. Lubbock is soon using one just to lever up the clay which he then removes with his bare hands.[21]

While most people dig, others are carrying some of the clay on to the islands to raise them even higher from the surrounding channels. Still others are weeding around the plants, removing diseased leaves, killing some of the bugs they find and leaving others. One woman is walking through the bushy plants in the channels and picking fresh young leaves. She does so with considerable care so as not to damage the plants, and seems quite unaffected by the irritation that Lubbock had felt when touching similar leaves.

After some hours a decision is made that the day's work is done. Lubbock tags behind the other workers as they make their way to the stream where mud is washed from bodies and thirst is quenched. And then they all follow a small path into the trees until another clearing is reached. This one has at least twenty huts, each made with branches bent into domes and covered with banana leaves. There are fences surrounding a patch of cultivated plants and a pen in which a pig is kept. A fire, one of several in the village, is smouldering and children run to greet the returning party. The baskets of leaves collected from Kuk Swamp are passed to an old woman who sits by the fire and the party disperses to rest.

That night, the fire is in flame again and at least thirty people gather to eat the leaves picked from the field and prepared by the old women. They have been crushed, covered with juices from fruits and then wrapped in banana leaves to be cooked on hot stones.

*

Golson's excavations at Kuk Swamp uncovered traces of ancient drainage ditches, hollows and holes from stakes along the bottoms and sides of the modern drainage ditches of the Kuk agricultural research station. Subsequent work exposed more of these and showed that the oldest dated to about 8200 BC, with another set having been made about 3,000 years later.[22] That second set of ditches, those in which Lubbock worked, had consisted of long irrigation channels, up to two metres deep, and a network of much shallower channels creating a maze of small islands. Still later in time, about 2000 BC, the ditches became more numerous, were laid out more systematically and covered a larger area.[23]

Golson believes that these ditches provide evidence for the earliest agricultural activity in the highlands – the first stages in the development of the big-man societies that would be encountered in the twentieth century. Quite what type of farming – if any – was attempted in 5500 BC, however, remains unclear owing to the absence of plant remains, artefacts and traces of settlement. But the soils are very telling.

At the base of the deepest of the modern ditches there is a thick peat, one created by many millennia of rotting plants in the basin. Some of the hollows and stake holes had been cut into this and then filled with grey clay that covered the whole area. This clay had seemed to form quickly, 10 centimetres being deposited every millennium between 8200 and 5500 BC. Golson believes the clay to be the remnants of soil from the dryland area surrounding the swamp that had eroded into the basin after the first clearances had destabilised the soils.[24] The hollows both below and on top of the clay might, he suggests, have been the wallows of pigs, as they look just like those created when animals are tethered to a stake.

Other than native bananas, microscopic traces of which were left in the soil, the plants grown at Kuk Swamp can only be guessed at.[25] The sweet potato, currently the most important crop in New Guinea, was certainly not present as this only arrived on the island three centuries ago.[26] Taro is the most likely candidate – the plant growing within the drainage channels that had stung Lubbock's hands. No remains of taro plants were found in Golson's excavations, but this may be explained by poor preservation.[27] Taro was once thought to have been an introduced plant, having first been cultivated in Indonesia. But it now seems more likely to have been a native of New Guinea and independently domesticated on the island.[28] It is one of the most widespread tropical crops today, and was a key plant grown by the New Guinea highlanders when they were first encountered in the 1930s. Both its leaves and underground stem, or corm, can be used as vegetables. Although it can tolerate high altitudes, taro needs plenty of water to thrive, and so it is perhaps the best candidate for the cultivated plants at Kuk Swamp.

Three other likely candidates are yams, sago and pandanus – those tree-like plants with the corkscrew stems.[29] All three were used in their wild forms by hunter-gatherers in northern Australia and as cultivated plants by the New

Guinea highlanders. Groves of pandanus, otherwise known as screw pines, were jealously guarded and maintained in recent times as they provided substantial quantities of fruit. A wide range of other green-leafed plants, including sugar cane, might easily have been cultivated at Kuk Swamp – plants which had once been gathered from the forests and marshes and were now being irrigated, weeded and perhaps transplanted from elsewhere.[30]

Just as it was for the woodland around 'Ain Mallaha at 12,500 BC and the scrubland around Guilá Naquitz at 8000 BC, the term 'wild garden' is the most appropriate description for Kuk Swamp at 5500 BC. The use of the word 'agriculture' for Golson's discoveries is probably a misnomer for the place and time; the wild gardens of Kuk Swamp constituted a form of intensified plant gathering with no radical break from a hunting-and-gathering past. Indeed, intervention in the forest may stretch back to the time of the very first human arrival in New Guinea.[31]

None the less, there is still the question of what motivated people to undertake wetland cultivation rather than simple gathering. It could have been that a burgeoning population was unable to secure sufficient food from the dryland forest alone.[32] The wetlands are likely to have provided much higher yields – but only after the substantial initial investment in labour to drain the land. And yet, just as we found when considering the origins of squash cultivation in the Oaxaca valley in Mexico, there is no evidence to suggest population pressure; in fact, we have no evidence at all about New Guinea population levels prior to the 1930s.

When Kent Flannery faced this dilemma he suggested that the Guilá Naquitz people from Oaxaca may have been attempting to make the availability of plant foods more reliable. This provides the most effective explanation for the investment made in clearing trees and digging ditches at Kuk Swamp, and presumably elsewhere in the highlands and lowlands of New Guinea at this date.[33] The result is likely to have been scattered localities throughout the island, where high yields of plant foods could be guaranteed at specific times of the year. Such localities would enable normally dispersed groups to meet up and spend time together. Hence the motivation for swamp drainage might have been as much for social as nutritional reasons – just as it may have been for the cultivation of wild wheat in the vicinity of Göbekli Tepe in Southeast Asia at 9500 BC.

The switch from being New Guinea hunter-gatherers who also cultivated plants, to horticulturalists who also collected wild foods, may be attributable to the pigs Lubbock saw wallowing at Kuk Swamp. This animal had to be introduced into New Guinea from Indonesia, where it had either been domesticated or had spread already domesticated from an original source in China.[34] Although pigs are good swimmers, the shortest crossing to New Guinea at the lowest sea level would have been almost 100 kilometres and so they would have had to be transported by boat.

Some archaeologists are confident that such pigs were present in New

Guinea by 6000 BC in the light of pig bones found within rockshelter deposits, which are believed to be at least this old. Indeed, in one case a 10,000-year-old date has been proposed. But of the few radiocarbon dates available, the earliest presence for the pig is a mere five hundred years ago.[35]

Once present on the island, whether by 6000 BC or in much more recent times, pigs would have become a nuisance, if not a serious pest, to those cultivating plants. Whether feral or domestic, they too would have enjoyed many of the native food plants of the forest – and wild gardens. All, that is, except the taro because of its toxins; but pigs when rooting in the drains might have grubbed even those plants up.[36] And so the cultivators would have needed to impose a barrier between the domains of nature and human culture by fencing in their gardens. Such physical barriers may have also created a mental barrier between hunter-gatherers and horticulturalists, with people fencing themselves into one domain or the other.

For the next few days Lubbock remains at Kuk Swamp, helping to complete the drainage ditches and weeding around the taro, bananas and pandanus. He then decides it is time to leave: with the passing of 5500 BC his journey through Australian prehistory is at its end. Not long afterwards the villagers themselves disperse into the hills to resume their hunting and gathering of wild foods. They will return to Kuk Swamp when the bananas are ripe and the corms of the taro are ready to dig. For now they are relieved to depart – living in one place is not in their nature, and will not be for another few thousand years.

On a cloudless day Lubbock climbs the slopes of Mount Hagen, passing beyond the tree-line into an alpine meadow. From a rocky crag he looks east and sees the Pacific Ocean. There are large islands near by, those that will become known as the Bismarck Archipelago, while scattered on the horizon are the future Solomon Islands.

There are people on those islands, and most likely in boats travelling between them. The sea-crossing to the Solomons was first made as long ago as 30,000 BC, although longer voyages into the Pacific would not be attempted for several more millennia. Travel between the islands must have been easier when the sea levels fell during the LGM. During that time a small tree-climbing marsupial known as the phalanger had become another new occupant. Whether the phalanger had been taken intentionally to stock the islands with wild game, or whether the animals had 'stowed away', is unclear. But archaeologists have found their bones in the rockshelters of New Ireland along with the stone artefacts of the tropical ice-age hunters.[37]

Lubbock climbs higher until another crag provides a view southwards: more islands, the Torres Strait, and then northern Australia. It has taken him 12,000 years to travel the 6,000 kilometres from Kutikina Cave in Tasmania to where he is now. Memories of wallaby hunts and a moonlit burial, of deserts and mangrove swamps, of fighting men, Rainbow

Serpents and canoeing along leech-ridden streams are as clear in his mind as the sky is a brilliant blue. He wishes he could have had the time to climb the mountains of eastern Australia, cross the Western Desert, spend longer with the artists of Arnhem Land, and discover whether Diprotodon had really been browsing in the woodlands of the Murray River. After another hour of walking, Lubbock approaches the summit and gains a view to the north and east. In those directions lie not only Indonesia, China and Japan, but also the start of another journey through human history.

38

Lonesome in Sundaland

Hunter-gatherers in the Southeast Asian tropical rainforests,
20,000–5000 BC

In July 1971 Manuel Elizalde, a member of Ferdinand Marcos's government with responsibility for national minorities, made an incredible announcement. The 'Tasaday', a group of cave-dwelling, stone-tool-using hunter-gatherers, had been discovered living in complete isolation from the modern world in the Cotabato forest of the southern Philippines. A report in the *National Geographic* magazine, entitled 'First Glimpse of a Stone Age Tribe', soon followed, illustrating their lifestyle with glossy photographs of bare-breasted women in orchid-leaf skirts.[1]

For eighteen months the Tasaday became media celebrities. Convoys of journalists, photographers, politicians and scientists made well-publicised visits to their caves, all under Elizalde's strict supervision. Newspapers carried their story, books were written about them and films were made. As the gentle peace-loving Tasaday, living in complete harmony with both nature and each other, were the antithesis of life elsewhere in Southeast Asia, such adulation was not surprising. Just a stone's throw away across the South China Sea, America was bombing the Vietnamese.[2]

One voice questioned the Tasaday's authenticity: that of Filipino anthropologist Zeus Salazar. His challenges were immediately suppressed and he was prevented from visiting the Tasaday people. In 1972, access to them was banned completely when President Marcos created a special forest reserve for their protection. Lengthy prison sentences were promised for anyone who dared to enter.

That many archaeologists were as enthralled as the journalists by the discovery of living Stone Age people in the forests of Southeast Asia can, perhaps, be excused. The archaeology of this region – the Malaysian Peninsula and Indonesian islands – between 20,000 BC and 5000 BC almost entirely consists of chipped stone artefacts. As they are some of the least impressive tools made by modern humans, archaeologists politely refer to these as 'unstandardised forms'. Given the uninformative nature of such tools, the Tasaday seemed to offer an unmissable chance to see not only how they had been used but the whole panoply of Stone Age life itself.[3]

Archaeologists have found the stone tools within caves, often deeply buried below multiple layers of bat guano, roof collapse and ancient soil.

The great majority are no more than pebbles from which a few flakes have been removed with little evident intention to impose a form. Some have one or more edges ground smooth; others have been chipped to create a 'waist' around which fibres had tied them to a haft. On the Malaysian peninsula most were made from complete pebbles, whereas on the Indonesian islands a higher proportion of flakes were used. All such tools are often grouped together and called the Hoabinhian culture.[4]

One of the largest collections has come from Niah Cave, now located in Sarawak. It is within this cave that John Lubbock's journey through the prehistory of eastern Asia begins; it will take him from the equatorial tropics to deep inside the Arctic Circle.

Lubbock awakes in a cathedral-like cave and sits at its mouth watching a rainforest dawn.[5] The gorge below and the trees beyond are half-obscured by a heavy morning mist. Swifts are darting in and out, the cave ceiling covered with their nests. Bats disappear down passages in the sloping recess of the cave. It had been a restless night, the unpleasantness of constantly creeping insects matched by the stench of guano from the floor. But in the freshness of dawn, before the appalling heat and humidity begins, the cloudy layers of moisture rising through the trees infuse John Lubbock with energy for the day. The whooping and ringing hoots of a female gibbon suggest that she must be feeling it too.

The date is 18,000 BC, and the cave mouth is light, cool and perfectly dry. It would, Lubbock thinks, provide an attractive shelter for hunter-gatherers – it is certainly better than many he has crouched inside during the course of his travels around the world.

As the sun completes an extraordinarily rapid rise, Lubbock searches for traces of human activity inside the cave. The floor itself is only exposed in the entrance area, where insects and the breeze have taken the guano away. The only bones he finds are those from birds that had once roosted within. Many fragments of rock lie either on, or are partly embedded in, the guano mat but Lubbock cannot decide whether they had been flaked by human hands or fractured by nature. Equally unclear is whether these had been 'made' a few days, years, centuries or even millennia ago.

Tom Harrisson, the curator of Sarawak Museum, undertook the first excavations in Niah Cave, working in its west mouth between 1954 and 1967.[6] His experience is best described by the name he gave his trench – Hell.

Working in conditions of stifling heat, almost one-hundred-per-cent humidity and direct afternoon sunlight, 'Hell' trench produced a human skull likely to be 40,000 years old, one of the first modern humans to have lived in Southeast Asia. Harrisson also recovered vast numbers of stone artefacts and several human burials in the upper deposits of the cave. The material in Niah probably covered the entire duration of human settlement in Southeast Asia, including the 15,000-year period of interest to this history.[7]

But we can't be sure. Tom Harrisson had many remarkable qualities – including, it is rumoured, a palang[8] – but the skill needed to excavate cave sediments was not among them. Although the cave floor was heavily undulating he sliced off its deposits in horizontal layers, most likely mixing up artefacts of a quite different age. The bones he radiocarbon-dated most likely came from animals that had simply lived and died within the cave, rather than having been butchered by human hands. In Harrisson's defence, he was working long before archaeologists had begun to understand the true complexity of how cave deposits and bone collections are formed. Fortunately a new team of archaeologists has recently started work in the cave, applying the very latest techniques of excavation. Led by Graeme Barker of Leicester University, a four-year excavation project was initiated in AD 2000 to unravel Niah's complex history of deposition and record of human activity.

Four years of fieldwork will require at least the same amount of time spent on laboratory study to analyse the finds. So it will be several years before we discover what Niah Cave can reveal about human history as the Pleistocene reached its end. Although Barker has previously worked in the challenging conditions of the Libyan and Jordanian deserts, he describes those at Niah as being by far the hardest he has ever faced. Fortunately he finds that Sarawak provides rich compensation for his toils:

> The cave is an hour's walk and climb through the rainforest ... All the specialist equipment has to be carried to the cave from our riverside camp every day, and then carried back with bags of sediment. Add the cobras in the cave, the crocodiles in the river, and the poisonous ferns and millipedes in between, set alongside the overpowering beauty of the rainforest and the hospitality of its people, and you have an unforgettable and exhilarating experience.[9]

There are two striking features of Hoabinhian artefacts, the first of which is their simplicity. This most likely reflects their minimal role in the day-to-day life of foragers in Southeast Asia as the ice age came to its close. With a wide range of robust plant material available, notably bamboo, there was little need for stone.[10]

The second feature is their consistency through time – a remarkable contrast with technology elsewhere in the post-LGM world. This is because the forests of the region – and presumably the people who lived within them – also remained largely unchanged as the rest of the world went through its roller-coaster ride to global warming.[11] More accurately, the forests of the surviving land masses underwent minimal change – the rising sea drowned those that had covered the extensive low-lying plains.

At the time of Lubbock's visit, Borneo, Sarawak, Java, Sumatra and the Malay Peninsula formed one continuous expanse of rainforest and mangrove swamp, much of which now lies below the South China Sea. Known to archaeologists as Sundaland, this ancient land mass also spread 30 kilometres west beyond the present-day Andaman Sea coastline of the peninsula. The result was more than two million square kilometres of forest – twice the area that exists today and the greatest expanse of forest in the ice-age world.

The flip side of this was a coastline no more than half the length of today's. As is evident from this history, hunter-gatherers are frequently drawn to coastal habitats owing to the abundance and diversity of resources they provide. The poverty of the archaeological record in Southeast Asia might be largely explained by this simple fact: the stone artefacts found within the caves may result from rare inland sorties by people who lived in coastal settlements. Had they survived, archaeologists might also have dwellings, middens and burials to excavate. Such shell-midden sites certainly exist from the relatively recent past, after modern sea levels had been reached at around 6000 BC. Or at least they did so until quarried for their shells – used for making cement – which left no more than huge water-filled holes in the ground.[12]

The forest surrounding Niah Cave is subtly different to that seen by Lubbock in New Guinea: he is now on the western side of 'Wallace's Line' – the boundary between flora and fauna that has an Australian descent to its east, and an Asian descent to its west. But although Lubbock has crossed this boundary, much of his forest experience is entirely familiar. The humidity is extreme and the leeches are just as eager to suck his blood. The forest abounds with gigantic trees with buttressed or furrowed trunks. Some trees appear to begin in mid-air, having an umbrella of aerial roots, while others have their own forest of stems. Palms, creepers, ferns and epiphytes fill the spaces between. Flowers are scarce. Many of the orchids have disappointing inconspicuous blooms; but these make the occasional extravagant displays all the more startling.

The forest is crowded: whenever Lubbock stops, butterflies come to feed upon his sweat; hornbills alternately flap and glide across the rivers with their trailing plumes; orang-utans spy him from the tree-tops; marauding ants attack him from the floor. And yet Lubbock feels alone amidst this abundance of animal life, as there are neither people among the trees nor any signs to indicate their presence.

Having travelled southwest from Niah Cave, Lubbock now sits within another cave, known to archaeologists as Gua Sireh. This is a much smaller one than Niah and even further from the sea, which is now 500 kilometres away. The sky grows black and a silence descends. Huge globules of rain begin to fall; they splash at the cave entrance as thunder rumbles across the trees. A flash of lightning momentarily illuminates every single leaf, tendril and flower of the forest for miles around. Gloomy darkness returns and the rain falls with extraordinary force. Lubbock retreats inside the cave and once again searches for the debris of human life. But he finds neither artefacts nor hearths, neither butchered bones nor piles of vegetable waste. The only possible sign of a recent human presence is a small cluster of broken mollusc shells looking like ones he had seen in the forest streams. Could these have got into the cave by nature alone – perhaps by a bird or a massive flood? Lubbock thinks not. But just like the flaked stone in Niah Cave, there is little to indicate quite how long the shells have been lying on the floor.

Lubbock's journey continues, now heading northwest, across a low-lying forest-covered swamp from which a few isolated hills arise. After travelling 200 kilometres from Gua Sireh he arrives on what will become the Malay Peninsula. The terrain is mountainous, cliffs of granite taking him into deep inland valleys before steep ridges of limestone climb in the west. Naked white precipices sparkle in the sun in stark contrast to the verdant cover that clothes the land elsewhere. After climbing through hanging fronds of ferns and above ravines with foaming white water, Lubbock emerges from the cool, dark forest to be greeted by rhododendrons and spectacular views. In every direction the interminable forest, partitioned by glistening winding ribbons of river water, covers the hills and valleys.

In 17,000 BC Lubbock arrives at another potential site of human habitation: a platform below a massive limestone overhang, known today as Lang Rongrien. To reach it he climbs a steep talus slope and then edges along a narrow ledge. Having hoped to find a flat earthen floor with people gathered around a fire and the usual domestic clutter, he finds it starkly empty, a crude spread of angular boulders and loose rubble.

Looking up, he sees that the roof of the overhang is quite smooth and clean – with no discolouration from centuries of weather, lichens, roosting bats and nesting birds. It appears to have recently collapsed, burying any traces of human habitation that may have existed upon its earthen floor. There is just one such sign among the rubble: a small patch of charcoal and five stones that might have been flaked by human hands. Lubbock guesses that recent visitors had lit a fire, perhaps to cook, have a smoke or just to sit quietly by the flames. And then they must have left to find a more comfortable shelter for the night. Lubbock does the same, returning along the ledge and disappearing once again into the dark and humid forest.

Both Gua Sireh and Lang Rongrien were excavated during the 1980s. The first, located in the southwest of Sarawak, had already been partly excavated – but little understood – by Tom Harrisson during the 1950s. Ipoi Datan, now deputy director of Sarawak Museum, re-excavated the main chamber in 1988, finding successive layers of ash and soil containing many stone artefacts, pottery shards, mollusc shells and a few poorly preserved animal bones.[13] The majority of this debris had accumulated after 4000 BC, deriving from rice farmers who had spread into Southeast Asia from the north. But one of the shells was dated to around 20,000 BC, coming from a freshwater mollusc that still lives in the fast-flowing clear-water streams near the cave. Ipoi Datan thought that it could only have entered the cave by human means. If the shell did indeed arrive in the cave by a human hand, and if the date is accurate, this still only reflects the briefest of visits to the cave – a single overnight camp at most.

Douglas Anderson of Brown University, Rhode Island, USA, excavated Lang Rongrien in 1987 and found traces of human occupation dating back to 40,000 BC.[14] A substantial roof collapse had occurred between 25,000 and 7500 BC – the dates established for layers immediately above and below the rubble. The charcoal within the rubble gave a date of around 42,000 BC, leading Anderson to think it had come from deposits within a fissure or cleft in the limestone that entirely disappeared when the roof collapsed.[15] It was this charcoal that Lubbock had seen and so he had been completely wrong – there had been no other visitors to Lang Rongrien at 17,000 BC.

The absence of occupation in Lang Rongrien at the LGM, or even within several millennia on either side, repeats a pattern found throughout the region. Only in Gua Sireh is there a trace of a human presence at this date: the single freshwater mollusc shell dated to around 20,000 BC. It is not surprising, therefore, that Lubbock is finding the forest lonely as he leaves Lang Rongrien – there may simply be no one else around. One can only guess that the people of Southeast Asia were all living on the coast.

After 17,000 BC, stone artefacts are found within many caves, showing that people were now regularly travelling inland even if they still preferred the shore. The successive floor layers in Lang Rongrien reveal much about the increasing ease and frequency of travel between the coast and inland areas. When the cave was approximately 100 kilometres from the coast, between 30,000 and 25,000 BC, there were no marine shells among the stone artefacts on its floor. These first appear in the successive floor layers after 10,000 BC, and then become increasingly numerous as sea level rises and the coast approaches the cave, finishing no more than 18 kilometres away.

It is unlikely that people stayed for more than a few days on any one visit to Lang Rongrien. But the lack of plant remains and animal bones makes it impossible to identify the season and duration of such visits. About 75 kilometres to the north of Lang Rongrien, Lang Kamnan offers some better evidence. This cave was used periodically between about 30,000 BC and 5,000 BC – although, as elsewhere, the presence of people at the LGM seems doubtful.[16] Rasmi Shoocongdej from Silpakorn University, Bangkok, has excavated the cave and interpreted the animal and plant remains that were found there, together with stone tools and marine shells. The animal bones came from many different species including squirrels, porcupines, turtles and deer; the snails and plant remains suggested that occupation had been within the wet season. This is when today's hunter-gatherer/horticulturalists in the forests of Southeast Asia collect a wide range of plant foods such as vegetable roots and bamboo shoots; they hunt the same types of animals that Shoocongdej found within Lang Kamnan.

The remains in Lang Kamnan suggest that people may have been living in the rainforests of Southeast Asia ever since 17,000 BC, in a similar manner to people of recent times, although without the cultivation of rice and other domesticated plants and animals. Some anthropologists, however, have questioned the ability of people to live there by hunting and gathering alone – just as hunter-gatherer occupation of the Amazon had been doubted until the discoveries in Pedra Pintada.[17]

Robert Bailey, an anthropologist from the University of California, has argued that edible resources in rainforests are so poor, variable and dispersed that viable hunter-gatherer populations cannot survive. Although rainforests are the most productive ecosystems on the planet, their vast stores of energy are trapped within inedible woody tissue – the massive tree-trunks and boughs which are essential in the competition to acquire sufficient light. Very little energy goes into producing edible flowers, fruits and seeds; those that do exist are often inaccessibly located in the canopy. The key dietary constraint, Bailey argued, is carbohydrate: to acquire sufficient amounts, 'hunter-gatherers' either have to engage in horticulture themselves or trade with farming communities.

The Hoabinhian culture shows this view to be quite wrong. Farming, in the form of rice cultivation, did not spread into Southeast Asia until 2500 BC, having originated in China[18] – as Lubbock will discover on the next stage of his travels. Moreover, the viability of rainforest hunting and gathering is quite evident from the existing communities – many of whom are thought to be the direct descendants of those who made the Hoabinhian tools.

One such community is the Batek of the Malaysian Peninsula, with whom anthropologists Kirk and Karen Endicott from Dartmouth College, New Hampshire, USA, spent nine months between 1975 and 1976.[19] They hunted monkeys and birds with blowpipes; they caught turtles, tortoises, frogs, fish, prawns and crabs; they dug wild tubers from the forest floor and collected an immense array of ferns, shoots, berries, fruits and seeds. Even though the Batek sometimes cleared the forest for growing rice, corn and manioc, and regularly traded with farmers for flour, sugar and salt, the Endicotts had no doubt that they could have survived on the wild foods alone, with the wild tubers providing a source of carbohydrates.

The Penan of Borneo are also effectively self-sufficient rainforest hunter-gatherers. Peter Brosius of the University of Georgia lived with the Penan on the Apau plateau between 1984 and 1987.[20] This is a mountainous and forested landscape, several days' walk from the long houses of rice farmers located in the valleys. Although the Penan engaged in trade, they did not rely on the farmers for food. Like the Batek, they gathered a wide array of plants and hunted many animals, with a preference for the bearded pig. Their main source of carbohydrate came from the sago palm, a tree that stores starch within its trunk. These palms grow in clumps, many of which were probably individually owned, and cropped with sufficient care to avoid any long-term depletion. Like so many other hunter-gatherers encountered in this history, the Penan managed the wild plants around them.

Brosius describes the Penan as 'stewards' of the forest. He explains how the network of forest streams provides them with a reservoir of ecological knowledge and memories. Many rivers are named after a particular type of tree or fruit which occurs either near the river-mouth or grows abundantly along its course. Others are named after a natural feature, such as a type of stone, or some event, such as the killing of a rhino, the loss of a favourite dog or an especially abundant fruiting season. A large number of rivers are named for individuals, perhaps signalling the birth and death of a person or their fondness for hunting along its banks. As the Penan do not mention the names of the dead, they often use the name of their river instead.

Both the Batek and Penan provide insights into how the Hoabinhian people may have lived between 17,000 and 5,000 BC. But this leaves us with an even greater dilemma about the effective absence of people from the forests during the LGM. Although Robert Bailey and like-minded anthropologists were wrong to claim that hunter-gatherers could not survive without agricultural products within the rainforest, they were quite correct to stress the relative difficulty in doing so. The open, deciduous forests that were more prevalent during the LGM would have provided a far more productive landscape for hunters and gatherers than the forests of today. Mammals, which then lived in herds and on the ground rather than as scattered individuals within the trees,[21] would have been more abundant and easier to hunt. So why does archaeological evidence only appear after the distribution, density and humidity of the rainforest had reached their peak?

According to Peter Bellwood of the Australian National University and author of encyclopaedic works about the prehistory of Southeast Asia, this may simply be a consequence of the combined pressures of population growth and rising sea level forcing people into the forests after having been quite content at the coast.[22] But without the ancient coastline it seems unlikely that we will ever know.

It is 16,000 BC and passage through the forest has eased. At first Lubbock thinks that the trail he follows is simply another pig track that runs between the trees. But he finds no need to duck below branches and twist between creepers and saplings – the ends of such potential barriers have been cleanly cut, proof at last of a human presence.

It takes several more days of walking through torrential rain and along a network of forest paths that link one river valley to the next before any people are actually found. They are at a campsite in the forest – three shelters made from palm leaves supported on stakes pushed into the ground. A few small trees have been cleared for the camp, which centres around a single smouldering fire – no more than a bundle of sticks and a handful of dry leaves. Standing at its edge Lubbock counts a dozen people – a few squatting around the fire, others sitting by the shelters. They are short in stature, with curly black hair and dark-brown skin. The children are naked. The adults wear no more than small aprons of leaves; some have faces painted red and noses pierced by porcupine quills.

It takes less than five minutes to explore the whole campsite – there is hardly anything else to see. Close to the fire a few wooden blocks have evidently been used as chopping boards. Hanging from the shelters are woven bags and scattered on the floor a few flaked stones. A number of polished wooden sticks and axes with flaked stone heads are propped against a tree. Knives with bamboo blades tucked into belts complete the equipment of this family group.

Having passed the night at their camp, Lubbock rises early as his unknowing hosts gather their belongings together. The group departs in single file along another tiny track, with Lubbock bringing up the rear. A backward glance at the flimsy palm-leaf shelters, and ephemeral scatter of debris on the ground, tells him that archaeologists are unlikely ever to find this site.

The day is spent hunting and gathering in the forest. After an hour or so the women and children go one way, and the men another. Lubbock dithers, follows the men and then turns back to catch up the women. They have stopped at what appears to be a quite undistinguished patch of forest, to dig tubers. Sticks go easily into the soft and stoneless ground; from each hole a woman pulls a swollen knobbly root, pushes it into a bag and then looks for another. By watching closely Lubbock discovers the sign to be no more than a spindly stem, seeming much like any of the other stems growing from the forest floor.

For the rest of the day the group travels from tuber patch to berry bush and bamboo thicket. The women and children eat as they work, particularly enjoying the fresh young bamboo sprouts, and find sufficient also to fill their bags. Although they seem to be following a familiar route, the women are always looking for something new: mushrooms, ferns, frogs and lizards. Camp is made at a riverbank. As palm-leaf shelters are quickly erected, the men arrive with a far-fetched tale about a monkey that got away.

The next day is spent fishing with the men, or rather they fish while Lubbock sits wedged among rocks in the shallows as the current washes away some of the terrible heat from his body. Once again, the camp is abandoned at dawn and the men set off in a different direction to the women. First they cut saplings with stone flakes and fashion barbed points; then they make their way to a deep pool where they dive to spear the fish. These are easily caught and much of the day is spent sitting idly by the pool, smoking and eating the bland and bony fish.

After several days of hunting and gathering Lubbock begins to appreciate that the group is living in a world quite different to his own. Lubbock's is simply one of the humid, dark forest that at times he loves and at times he hates – especially when attacked by leeches, ticks and biting ants. His companions also live in the forest, but to them it is a world replete with spirits, ghosts and gods.

This became apparent from tiny, subtle actions that at first went quite unnoticed.[23] Some foods, for instance, were never cooked on the same fire; the tracks of deer and tapir were ignored, as were – what seemed to Lubbock – quite easy opportunities to make a kill. He guessed there were religious prohibitions against killing such animals or eating certain foods together. On one occasion he watched a young man being admonished by an elder for some food he had cooked; at night the offender cut himself, mixed his blood with water and then threw the mixture to the sky – apparently as a means of assuaging an angry deity. Lubbock becomes aware that singing and speeches by members of the group are often directed to the forest rather than to each other. Sometimes the singing takes place on specially built platforms of tree bark, set on logs close to fruit trees from which the people hope to gather produce later in the year.

As the date moves on to 15,000 BC, Lubbock has to leave. The daily routine of hunting and gathering in the forest will continue undisturbed for many millennia to come and it is time for Lubbock to head into temperate latitudes, those which global warming has already begun to change. And so, when at a juncture of paths, he goes one way while the Hoabinhian foragers go another.

The Tasaday people, mentioned at the beginning of this chapter, were a hoax.[24] When the Marcos regime was overthrown in 1986, their caves attracted a new influx of observers, this time without the strict supervision of Manuel Elizalde. Any claims to authenticity as a long-time isolated group with a Stone Age technology soon unravelled – Zeus Salazar's original suspicions had been correct. The Tasaday language was found to be a dialect of that used throughout the southern Philippines; their caves lacked the debris that would have arisen from generations of occupation; their knowledge of wild foodstuffs appeared quite insufficient for real hunter-gatherers; they were never seen to handle stone tools and, when asked to make some, used quite unsuitable materials with limited skill. The orchid-leaf clothes had simply been worn for the cameras. As one of the Tasaday admitted: 'whenever Elizalde and his companions were coming, he sent a message to tell us to take off our clothes and go to the caves. We had to wait there until all the pictures had been taken. When Elizalde left, we put our clothes back on and came back to our own houses.'[25]

The Tasaday themselves were innocent local horticulturalists who were induced and bribed by Elizalde to act out his Stone Age fantasy. The affair was just one more example of how Philippine minorities were victims of the Marcos regime. It provides this history with another illustration of how the Stone Age past is politically potent, ready to be exploited by politicians for their own ends. Remember the mental contortions of Vladislav Iosifovich Ravdonikas to fit Oleneostrovski Migilnik into his Marxist scheme of human history, and the claims of Native Americans that the bones of Kennewick Man belonged to them? And, of course, the writings of Victorian John Lubbock which espoused the mental superiority of Europeans, conveniently justifying the imperialism of his day.

There are no isolated Stone Age tribes in the world today. The Penan and Batek may be direct descendants of the Hoabinhian people and we may draw upon observations of their lifestyle to propose scenarios for Stone Age gathering, fishing and religion – as I have done above.[26] But we must, as always, be cautious of such accounts. Archaeologists must not be tempted by the present; they must keep returning to the analysis of artefacts and the pursuit of excavation. There are not short cuts to the prehistoric past.

39

Down the Yangtze

The origin of rice farming, 11,500–6500 BC

Lubbock is taking another canoe journey, this time down the Yangzte River. His long trek from the rainforests of Southeast Asia has taken him through the plateaus, broad basins and steep valleys of the Wuling mountains of southern China, from where he followed the valleys that cut through the Yunnan plateau. Much of that journey had been through thick deciduous woodland, the haunts of deer and pig, tapir and pandas. When the trees gave way to grassland he saw larger animals: rhino, and on one occasion stegodons – elephant-like creatures with straight tusks, similar in appearance to the mastodons of North America.[1]

Many groups of hunter-gatherers were encountered. They stalked animals in the woodlands, gathered an assortment of nuts, berries and roots, collected shellfish from rivers and lakes. In 14,000 BC Lubbock spent time with a few families at Baiyanjiao Cave, found today in the Guizhou province of south China. When sitting by their hearth he watched flakes being struck from stone nodules with little apparent concern for the shape and size of detached pieces.

Baiyanjiao was just one of several sites used by those hunter-gatherers during their seasonal round as they moved between hills and valleys, woodlands and plains. At least we must suppose it was. Archaeological sites dated to the end of the Pleistocene are extremely rare in southern China – we know hardly anything about human lifestyles in this region of the ice-age world. Baiyanjiao was excavated in 1979 and provided a precious collection of artefacts made from limestone, chert, sandstone and quartz.[2] The excavated animal bones were equally valuable, representing many species including stegodon, tapir, deer and pig. Those from bear, tiger and hyena were also present. And so until a study of cut-marks and gnawing patterns has been made, we cannot be sure how many of the bones derived from human activity and how many were the debris from carnivore dens.

As Lubbock travelled north from Baiyanjiao, the woodlands became open and the trees changed from broad-leafed species to fir and spruce. Temperatures fell and cold winds began to whip across barren hills. The hunter-gatherers also changed; they had fewer options for finding food and many were now reliant on annual slaughters of migrating horse and deer, much as Lubbock had seen in ice-age Europe. Sewn clothing of animal hides and furs became essential, as did access to caves for shelter during cold winter months.

When Lubbock reached the Sichuan basin he found the vast expanse of the Yangtze River. At its shore was a party of hunters, packing their belongings into a large canoe before heading east, back to the lowlands after having spent the autumn months hunting goats. Lubbock climbed on board, settled down between bundles of goat hides and found a spare paddle to use.

The Sichuan basin marks the limits of navigation for boats on the Yangtze River today. Chang Jiang – the 'Long River' as it is more properly known – rises in the 5,000-metre-high snows and glaciers of the Tibetan plateau and makes a 6,300-kilometre journey to the South China Sea. Very few archaeological sites dating to between 20,000 and 5000 BC are known along its course, although we must imagine that the river had been as important to prehistoric hunter-gatherers as it is to the Chinese people today. Unfortunately we are never likely to know for sure as the Three Gorges Dam is currently under construction. By 2009 this will house the largest hydroelectric generator in the world, requiring the creation of a lake 600 kilometres in length behind the dam. A great number of known archaeological sites will be flooded, and the possibility of new discoveries entirely lost. But the loss of sites potentially equivalent to those of Abu Hureyra, Jerf el Ahmar and Nevali Çori – those flooded by dams across the Euphrates – is the least of the problems facing the Chinese people. More than 150 villages and towns will be inundated by the lake, displacing up to two million people from their homes.[3]

The date is 13,000 BC. Lubbock's fingers and toes are frozen; his stiff joints and tired muscles can hardly work the paddle as the canoe battles against icy winds on the Yangtze River. Fortunately, his companions are hardy individuals and familiar with this route as winter approaches. The canoe turns around a rocky headland and enters a dark and narrow channel between perpendicular limestone cliffs. Fantastic towers of curiously splintered and weathered rock have squeezed the river from many kilometres to no more than 50 metres wide.

This is the Ichang Gorge, one of the great spectacles of the Yangtze River as it leaves the rugged country of the Wushu mountains and approaches the flat wetlands of the Hupei basin.[4] Time moves quickly within this tunnel-like passage. With each drag of his paddle Lubbock sees a decade and then a century pass by. Within minutes he has reached 12,000 BC, and the world beyond the bare walls of rock is transformed. Temperatures have risen, rainfall increased, and thick woodland has spread across what had been barren hills and mountain slopes beyond the gorge.[5]

The late-glacial interstadial has arrived; in western Asia the Natufian culture is flourishing, while people are building dwellings and drinking tea at Monte Verde in southern Chile. Here in China, oak, elms and willows are replacing the scattered pine and spruce, while a thick undergrowth of ferns is developing between the trees. The river rises with melt-water pouring from the mountain glaciers. Streams begin to tumble down the cliffs; rock crevices are suddenly full of maidenhair fern and wildflowers blossom in profusion on narrow ledges. Lubbock's companions also change, their thick furs replaced with tunics of light hide. Whereas once their faces had been hidden below frost-covered hoods and beards, they are now gleaming in sunlight. Parcels of goat fat have been replaced by bamboo baskets containing acorns and berries.

Time moves on to 10,500 BC. The sun disappears behind a cloud and a chilling wind once again blows along the gorge as a cold spell arrives.[6] With another few paddle-strokes the water level falls, leaving the riverbanks stranded high above its course. White clouds of snow swirl around the peaks as the waterfalls freeze and flowers wilt before Lubbock's eyes. Beyond the cliffs, fir and spruce make a comeback as the oak trees and ferns wither in the face of drought and cold. In the canoe, fur clothes and goat fat return.

Soon after 10,000 BC, the dramatic spurt of global warming that begins the Holocene occurs; fir trees and spruce along the Yangtze valley are once again replaced by broad-leafed and evergreen woodland, the herbs overcome by ferns. Lubbock leaves the gorge at 9,500 BC, with his companions once again dressed for life in a warmer world. The baskets have returned and are joined by something quite new – pottery vessels. The river carries Lubbock into a landscape with thickly wooded, rolling hills and lush riverside reeds. It begins to meander, fork and spill across the flatlands of the Hupei basin. In the distance he sees a plume of smoke rising from the middle of the tree-covered plain. This is the village of Pengtoushan, whose inhabitants plant and harvest a wild grass – one known today as *Oryza rufipogen*.[7]

These are important people for Lubbock to meet: through their efforts, along with those of other prehistoric inhabitants of the Yangtze valley, that grass will become transformed. Having once fed a few thousand people living in scattered river- and lake-side hamlets, it now sustains at least two billion people throughout the world as the most important foodstuff on planet earth. *Oryza rufipogen* became *Oryza sativa*, the wild became the domestic.[8] John Lubbock is about to watch the first cultivation of rice, a turning point in the history of the world.

Rice is the most important cereal plant in the world today; China the largest producer and consumer. When the People's Republic was created in 1949, 170 million tons of rice were harvested each year. During the following half-century this output increased at least fourfold, partly due to the system of collective ownership and partly through selective breeding of new strains, double cropping, the use of machinery, fertilisers and pesticides. China is a global power because of its rice and the story of its domestication begins with the people who first cultivated the wild plants that grew in the swamps of the Yangtze valley.[9]

Wild rice comes in at least twenty different variants, all of which can be conveniently called *Oryza rufipogen*.[10] Some flourish as perennials in permanently wet swamps; others grow as annuals, usually where swamps or ditches become dry for part of the year. The domesticated varieties differ from these in much the same way as wheat and quinua differ from their wild ancestors. Not only do the grain-heads 'wait for the harvester' rather than shatter spontaneously, but the plants also germinate within a few days of each other so that the whole crop ripens together. Wild rice, like wild wheat, germinates in a piecemeal fashion, often over many weeks or months. This ensures that at least some of the seedlings will find benign conditions for growth – something that the domesticated varieties can be assured of, due to the farmer's work. A further contrast is simply size – rice grains from domesticated plants are significantly larger than those of the wild.[11]

When the Chinese archaeologist Anping Pei of the Hunan Institute of Archaeology excavated Pengtoushan in 1988, he found what were then the earliest known traces of domesticated rice dating to at least 7500 BC. Before his discovery, most archaeologists believed that rice cultivation had originated either in India or, more probably, mainland Southeast Asia where substantial stands of wild rice can be found today. And so, with the same logic that took archaeologists to the Fertile Crescent to search for the origin of modern wheat and barley, they looked for the origin of rice cultivation at sites far to the south of the Yangtze River.

Initially they appeared to have found success. Grains of rice believed to date to at least 6000 BC were found in Banyan Valley Cave in the uplands of Thailand and from the settlement of Khok Phanom Di on the coast of the Gulf of Siam. But when radiocarbon-dated, these samples were found to be much younger – no more than 1000 BC at Khok Phanom Di and a few hundred years old in Banyan Cave.[12]

In 1984 small stands of wild rice were discovered in the Yangtze River valley.[13] It was soon realised that its rarity in this region is explained by the practices of intensive farming that have destroyed natural habitats. After the excavation of Pengtoushan, the middle stretches of the Yangtze River were confirmed as the likely place of origin of cultivated rice. And so a search began for sites older than Pengtoushan, where the transition from wild to domestic rice could itself be found – a search for the Chinese equivalent of Netiv Hagdud or Guilá Naquitz.

Richard MacNeish – whose work in Central Mexico we have already encountered – and Yan Wenming of Beijing University worked together exploring caves in the limestone hills just to the south of the Yangtze River in today's Jiangxi province.[14] Unlike MacNeish's experiences in the dry caves of central Mexico, they found that plants had almost entirely decayed in the Chinese sites. Fortunately some crucial microscopic evidence had survived within the cave sediments: phytoliths.

Phytoliths are minute deposits of silica that form within plant cells. The silica, originating from groundwater, can sometimes completely fill a cell and then maintain its shape after the plant itself has decayed. Because they are inorganic, phytoliths often survive in the soil long after all other traces of plants have disappeared. Moreover, different species of plants – and indeed different parts of a single plant – produce different shapes of phytoliths. And hence they can be used to identify plants which had once grown in the soil, or had perhaps been placed there as either stored food or discarded waste.

Just as some plants produce more pollen grains than others, some produce more phytoliths. Grasses are big producers and, while the pollen grains from different species are near identical, their phytoliths are quite distinct. Deborah Pearsall from the University of Missouri pioneered the study of those from rice, finding that the most distinctive are produced in the cells of the 'glume', the husk of the grain, as these have large conical hairs or peaks.[15] The presence of such phytoliths in an otherwise empty soil is a definite sign that rice plants had once grown there.

The crux of Pearsall's work, however, is that glume phytoliths can be used to identify whether the long-gone rice plants had been wild or domestic – whether they had grown in a swamp or been cultivated in a paddyfield. The phytoliths from domesticated plants are simply bigger than those from wild varieties, matching the increase in grain size.[16] With this discovery, the cave sediments excavated by Richard MacNeish and Yan Wenming may hold the key to identifying when and where rice cultivation began.

Diaotonghuan Cave is located in the side of a small limestone hill within a region of swamps known as the Dayuan basin, just to the south of the Yangtze River[17] – no more than 50 kilometres from the recently discovered stands of wild rice. MacNeish and Wenming excavated a 5-metre deep trench in the centre of the cave and revealed at least sixteen occupation layers, neatly layered one on top of another. The eight uppermost layers covered the period from 12,000 to 2000 BC; the age of the lower layers was not determined. Each excavated layer contained animal bones and stone tools; fragments of pottery were present in those dating back to 10,000 BC.

While plant remains were entirely absent, the phytoliths from each occupation layer showed that several types of rice had once been gathered. Rice phytoliths were very rare in the lower layers of the cave; the few present might have arrived within dry leaves blown by the wind, on the hoofs or in the faeces of animals while using the cave for shelter. At about 12,000 BC, however, there is a dramatic increase in the number of rice phytoliths, which must reflect rice being gathered and eaten by human occupants of the cave. The phytoliths are small, indicating that they had come from wild plants, most likely gathered from the edge of nearby swamps. The date marks the particularly warm and wet conditions of the late glacial intersta-dial, a time when stands of wild rice may have begun to flourish in the Yangtze basin. After 12,000 BC rice phytoliths remain abundant in the cave, except within layers dating to between 10,800 and 9600 BC – a period coin-ciding with the Younger Dryas. During that period of cold and drought, wild rice, a subtropical water-dependent plant, had evidently, and not surprisingly, become very scarce.

After the return of warm and wet conditions, rice was once again used as a major source of food. Successive layers within Diaotonghuan Cave show a gradual increase in the proportion of large phytoliths, reflecting the appear-ance of the first domesticated plants. By 7500 BC there was an equal use of wild and domesticated rice plants; a thousand years later, all traces of wild rice had completely disappeared.

It takes Lubbock almost 3,000 years to travel the 250 kilometres from the mouth of the Ichang Gorge to Pengtoushan, arriving at 6800 BC. That time was spent paddling slowly along the Yangtze as it meandered through the lowlands of the Hupei basin. His companions had remained at 9,600 BC; having gone to collect walnuts from a grove of trees, they failed to secure their canoe. With Lubbock on board, this was taken by the current downstream and further into the Holocene world.

Each year the river rose a little higher and then fell a little lower as the rainy and dry seasons became more marked. The rains began in late March and reached their peak in August. The waters would rise by ten metres or more, turning much of the lowlands into a seemingly endless expanse of muddy water spotted with little islands that had previously been low hills.[18] When the waters fell they left moist blankets of silt upon the land – foundations for the fertile agricultural soil that supports millions of people today.

In 6800 BC this watery landscape teems with life: shoals of fish, flocks of waterfowl, kingfishers and egrets; deer and tapir in the waterside thickets, horse and rhino on the drier ground. And people. They live in their boats as much as on land and are spoilt by unlimited opportunities for fishing and fowling, hunting and gathering. By following a canoe along an offshoot of the Yangtze, and then through a network of small streams, Lubbock finds the way to Pengtoushan; he does so just as the moonsoons arrive, to turn the network of streams into a single muddy lake.

As he steps on to dry land for the first time in more than six thousand years, Lubbock still has a short walk to reach the village. He follows a well-trodden path that passes through dense ferns and finds Pengtoushan nestled in the side of a knoll, surrounded by trees of fir and pine. As he approaches, no more than two dwellings can be seen above the ferns:

substantial rectangular houses built with timber posts, wattle-and-daub walls, and thatched roofs. After another few steps he sees a further five or six reed-covered roofs belonging to smaller dwellings whose floors must have been sunk into the ground.[19]

Lubbock enters the village as the sun sinks below the trees and a heron flies towards its roost. There are few people to be seen: an old woman sleeping upon a doorstep when she should be minding the children; two men whittling branches with stone blades; a young women kneading clay. The air is thick with pine-scented wood smoke from fireplaces that smoulder between the huts.

The potter sits cross-legged on a bamboo mat. She wears no more than a small leather apron around her slim waist, a string of shells around her neck and a bone point that dangles between her breasts. Her hair is jet black and cut short; she has the high cheek-bones, flat nose and narrow eyes of the Chinese people today; her skin glows in the rays of the evening sun. She squeezes, rolls and kneads her clay upon a wooden board; she sings gently, occasionally giving a huff and a puff as she puts the little weight she has into working the clay.[20]

Lubbock sits by her, careful not to interrupt the last of the sun that she so clearly enjoys. Next to her is a pile of dry crumbly clay, evidently dug from the river-bank some time ago. She gradually adds it to the moist lump being moulded, together with water poured from a wooden bowl. Every few moments she leans forward to reach a basket and takes a handful of its contents to mix with her clay. Lubbock manages to tilt the basket to look inside – chopped pieces of plant stem, husks and grains of rice.

As she kneads her clay, people return to the village from their day in the woods and on the water. A mother who arrives with fish strung around her neck finds her young children playing among the ferns. Hunters arrive with a brace of ducks but without the deer they had gone to kill. Smouldering fires are brought to life; those carving wood finish their work and sit with others by the flames.

The potter has now prepared rolls of clay and begins to coil, pinching and then smoothing across the joins. The clay becomes a thick-walled bowl about 20 centimetres high, with a wide mouth and narrow base. Using her bone point, she incises a wavy pattern in the soft clay; then she stands with hands on hips to admire her work. She takes the new pot to her hut and places it with several others ready to be fired the next day – high-necked jars, shallow dishes, plates and bowls, all marked with the same wavy lines.

Lubbock moves to sit closer to the crackling and jumping flames of a nearby fire; others are also drawn to the light and warmth now that it is dusk. Much about Pengtoushan seems familiar to him – its sounds and smells, the arrangement of huts and communal fires, the way that hides and furs are draped around shoulders as the coolness of evening descends. When he looks around, the semi-subterranean dwellings bring to mind another village where people had also lived at the brink of farming: Abu Hureyra on the banks of the Euphrates at 11,500 BC. But something is missing here. For a moment Lubbock's mind flounders, and then it becomes obvious: there are no grinding stones, no querns, no stone pestles and mortars. There had been so many of these in the villages of the Fertile Crescent, both before and after the cultivation of wheat had begun. And yet there are none at Pengtoushan.

The potter has washed and returns wearing a shawl to sit, unwittingly, by Lubbock's side and among her family who have now gathered to eat. When the flames begin to die, the ducks are roasted upon a spit; once completely gone, the fish, wrapped in leaves and flavoured with herbs, are placed within the embers. Finally a ceramic bowl is wedged upon the hot rocks and glowing wooden stumps. As the ducks and fish are shared and the tales are told, the water begins to simmer. Soon Lubbock, the potter and her family will be eating boiled rice at Pengtoushan, as will every later generation who lives within the Yangtze valley.

That Anping Pei was able to identify rice cultivation at Pengtoushan was solely due to the presence of burnt rice husks, stems and grain within the many pottery fragments that he recovered from the site.[21] The quantity of plant debris trapped within the fired clay suggests that it had not arrived by accident. It had been used as a temper – an addition to prevent pots cracking when fired. While it is quite common for traditional potters to add sand or crushed shell to their clay, the use of plant material is most unusual and probably quite ineffective – later potters in the Yangtze valley had soon adopted sand. And so, at Pengtoushan, Lubbock might have seen some of the trials and errors that had to be endured when people first learned about the art and science of ceramic technology. Another trial is apparent from Diaotonghuan Cave where the first fragments of pottery had been tempered with coarsely crushed stone.

Several shapes of vessel had been made at Pengtoushan. Most were black on the outside because the rice temper had burnt during firing. Many were decorated, either stabbed and incised by sharp points or impressed with twisted cords. Coiling wasn't the only technique employed; some pots had been made by simply pinching the clay or pasting slabs together. This slab technique had first been used at Diaotonghuan at around 10,000 BC to produce the oldest known pottery in China.[22]

The near simultaneous invention of pottery and the first cultivation of rice is unlikely to have been coincidental – the vessels were most likely used to steam and boil the grain.[23] Direct evidence comes from a slightly later village known as Hemudu, located at the Yangtze delta, where cooked rice was found within a pot. Hence the desire to gather and then cultivate rice appears to have been linked to the manufacture of pottery, while the vessels so produced provided new opportunities for storing and cooking rice, thereby encouraging more cultivation. It is likely that the pottery was as essential for the development of rice agriculture as were the grinding stones of the Fertile Crescent for that of wheat and barley. And there could be no better symbol of this intimate relationship than those fragments of rice-peppered pottery excavated by Pei at Pengtoushan.

It is September in 6800 BC and the flood waters are beginning to recede. Lubbock has spent the summer at Pengtoushan, learning how to make and then fire pots, either in an open fire or within a pit dug in the ground. Now there is a new task to be undertaken, one that is eagerly awaited as each day the people watch the riverside mud expand as the waters fall. All the villagers help with this event: the scattering of seed. They take baskets of rice from their store and broadcast it over the newly exposed silt, without preparation of the soil and with neither irrigation ditches nor banks of mud to retain the retreating water. Lubbock joins in – standing ankle deep in mud and making great arcs with his arm to scatter the seed, helping to begin a Chinese farming revolution.[24]

Within a few weeks the boggy ground has become green with seedlings – a mottled green with patches of brown as some seeds take longer to germinate than others, or fail to do so at all. The plants grow slowly through the winter; many of those on the highest land – which had been the first to drain – wither and die. But those on the lower and permanently waterlogged soil have become lush plants by the spring, just as the rains return.

In May, tall weeds are removed from the crop; in June the rice blossoms, and by early August Lubbock is knee-deep in water harvesting the plants as the flood waters creep towards the village. As each plant is pulled from the ground some grain falls and is lost in the mire. Nobody cares as there will be plenty left for threshing. It is exhausting work – not just the bending and pulling, but the weight of the baskets that must be carried uphill and emptied on to an ever-growing mound of rice plants within the village.

Once dry, the plants are threshed by striking the ears of grain; the stalks are kept to use as thatch and matting, and to mix with clay when pots are being made. Having helped thresh the grain, Lubbock next gives a hand with the hulling – removing the tough outer husks by rubbing them with wooden slabs. And then it is winnowed to leave the grain – some will be eaten immediately, some stored for winter food, some put aside to use as seed when the flood waters recede once again.

Whether or not the people of Pengtoushan had sown and harvested their rice in this fashion is conjecture. Broadcasting seed on to land naturally and gently watered by annual floods is the simplest method of rice cultivation, known to have been used by many traditional people of Southeast Asia.[25] There is no evidence from Pei's excavation to suggest the use of irrigation ditches or mudbanks; he found neither spades for digging, hoes for preparing the soil nor knives for cutting the ears of grain. But all such tools might have once been used at Pengtoushan – they could have been washed away, decayed without trace, or become too deeply buried for Pei to discover.[26]

The flood-water 'farming' method described above could easily have provided the required conditions for the domestic strains of rice to evolve. Just like the transformation of wild wheat in western Asia, there had to be some selection by people of those rare mutant rice plants that had non-brittle ears – those which 'wait for the harvester'. Such genetic mutants would not have survived for long in the wild, being unable to seed themselves. But they were the ideal plants for early farmers who didn't want to see ripe grain sinking into the mud as soon as they began their harvest.

The simple fact that much of the grain from the brittle-eared rice would have been lost in this manner meant that any baskets of harvested plants contained a relatively high proportion of the rare non-brittle variants. The key to ensuring that this amount was further increased was not only to use some of the grain as seed, but to plant where there would have been no growth of wild plants.

Only if planted in a wild-rice-free zone could the new crop reflect the relatively high proportion of seed from the non-brittle-eared rice that had been sown; this proportion would have been further enhanced when harvested. Eventually, after many cycles of planting and harvesting, perhaps as many as the two hundred harvests that Gordon Hillman had estimated for the domestication of wheat,[27] the crop would have become dominated by non-brittle, simultaneously ripening and large-grained rice – *Oryza sativa*. If left alone it would have soon disappeared, being unable to seed itself and survive; but by that time, of course, it was being cultivated by farmers.

The Pengtoushan people of 6800 BC may have already become such farmers. Some of the rice grains preserved within their pottery were certainly large enough to have come from fully domestic plants. Unfortunately a detailed study of the grains has not been possible as they become severely damaged when removed from their protective pottery casing. But any doubts that domestic rice had appeared by 6800 BC were removed in 1997 when Pei excavated another settlement located no more than twenty kilometres to the north.

This is the site of Bashidang, which thrived between 7000 and 5000 BC. Here, Pei found the traces of many dwellings, including some built on piles. He excavated about a hundred burials and recovered a remarkable collection of artefacts from waterlogged soil, including part of a wooden plough, a wooden shovel, reed mats, bamboo baskets and cane ropes.[28] Within a nearby riverbed he discovered an abundant quantity of plant remains including 15,000 grains of rice. Studies of these have left no doubts that the Bashidang people were farmers using a fully domestic strain of rice.[29]

Back on the Yangtze River time is moving slowly again. It takes a mere hundred years for Lubbock to complete the 1,000-kilometre journey to the delta, reaching the coastal plain at 6700 BC. He finds a vast patchwork of marshes and lakes, scattered woodland and salt marsh, all criss-crossed by rivers and streams. Sea level still has a few metres to rise before stabilising at its present height; the final inundation will further enlarge the estuaries, create new bays and yet more islands to fringe the coast.

The watery landscape of 6700 BC is a hunter-gatherers' paradise; some are stalking deer, others are fishing or collecting shellfish. But the largest settlements that Lubbock can find are no more than clusters of reed-built dwellings upon islands of dry ground, none of which approach Pengtoushan or Bashidang in size. Their inhabitants are doing no more than harvesting wild, uncultivated rice. The idea of sowing seed on the flood plain and then tending the seedlings has not yet arrived from upstream. When it does so, the results will be dramatic as the coastal wetlands provide the perfect setting for rice farming to take root and flourish.

Had Lubbock followed rather then pre-empted the arrival of farming, not reaching the delta until 5000 BC, he would have found a quite different type of village. He could then have visited Hemudu on the southern shore of Hang-Chou Bay, the remnants of which were excavated during the 1970s.[30] There he could have sat within houses more than 20 metres long, built with wooden planks using mortise-and-tenon joinery and raised on piles at least a metre above the shallow waters below. He could have helped prepare paddy-fields for planting using spades made from the shoulder blades of water buffalo fixed to wooden handles, or even tended the domesticated buffalo themselves.[31] Or perhaps thrown scraps to the pigs. The quantity of rice excavated from Hemudu suggests that Lubbock might have spent the early summer transplanting young shoots from nursery beds to the main paddy-fields – one of the most laborious jobs for twentieth-century Chinese peasants.[32] Alternatively he might have joined parties going fishing and fowling, hunting and gathering in the marshes and woodlands of the Yangtze delta, or perhaps developed his pottery skills to help produce the ornate vessels that were excavated from Hemudu.

But Hemudu is nothing more than a simple hunter-gatherer campsite as Lubbock sits at the mouth of the Yangtze River watching egrets at sunrise on some unmarked day in 6700 BC. It is low tide and glistening mud-flats stretch far to the east. They are cut by meandering silver ribbons of flowing water and it is into one of these that he pushes the same canoe that has brought him from the Sichuan basin. Now it must carry him across 2,000 kilometres of the Yellow Sea so his travels can continue in the lands that today we call Japan.[23]

40
With the Jomon

Complex hunter-gatherers in Japan and the earliest pottery,
14,500–6000 BC

Everybody stops, looks up and stares in silence. For a brief moment John Lubbock's feeling of 'otherness' from his new, unknowing hosts is lost. Rumbling, smoking volcanoes have that effect – emotional responses swell up to override cultural differences. But within an instant it has passed. The people of Uenohara are once again watching and listening to the distant volcano through their own cultural filter – their mythology and ideological beliefs about which Lubbock knows nothing. As voices and the sounds of work begin again, he resumes his status as observer rather than participant in life on Kyushu island, in Japan, 9200 BC. Lubbock has arrived at Uenohara 2,500 years before he left the Yangtze at 6700 BC.[1]

Uenohara is a village on the southern coast of Kyushu, at the head of what is now known as Kagoshima Bay.[2] Its occupants are hunter-gatherers – the ideas and seed-grain for rice cultivation that will spread eastwards along the Yangtze valley from Pengtoushan will not arrive in Japan until 5000 BC at the earliest.[3] To reach the village, Lubbock had trekked through the island's thickly wooded hills after his own arrival on its western shore. A maze of tiny paths took him between oaks and chestnuts; the air was pungent with autumn, the boughs heavy with their seasonal load.[4] He soon discovered unseen companions in the woods by recognising deer tracks in the mud, pig hair on brambles and axe-marks on tree stumps. The paths led him to a clearing with a scatter of thirteen conical huts. It was mid-afternoon; adults were busy tending fires and manufacturing tools, while the village's children chased each other round the dwellings.

A party of the Uenohara people had also just emerged from the woods carrying bundles of reeds and sacks that bulged with the produce of the forest. Lubbock guessed that the reeds were for a new hut whose skeleton of wooden poles had already been tied into a wigwam shape around a circular depression.[5] Several men were felling trees with stone axes to enlarge the clearing. Their work exposed a view across the sea, revealing a distant mountain with its summit surrounded by cloud – or so Lubbock had thought until it rumbled and a new plume of ash-laden smoke issued forth.

The people of Uenohara looked fit, healthy and happy. They wore few clothes. The children and some adults went bare. Most had nothing more than an apron of hide around their waist; a few wore tunics. All except the very old had vibrant yellow-brown skins with jet-black hair either tied into plaits or swept back below headbands. Some wore necklaces made from deer teeth and boars' tusks; a few men had swirls of red paint upon their chests.

Just as at Pengtoushan, Lubbock was drawn to sit next to a potter – this time an elderly lady with wrinkled skin and no teeth. She was completing a vessel far more elegant than any Lubbock had seen during his travels around the world – near spherical in shape with a narrow neck and curved lip, it was about the size of a football. Her bony fingers rolled a thin wooden rod wrapped with cord across the surface of her pot to make an intricate geometric pattern. She then moved her dowel and rolled again, gradually covering the entire surface with her design.

Just as she was about to make the final impressions the volcano erupted and she lost her rhythm, momentarily freezing, with her cord-wrapped dowel hovering a few millimetres above the clay. Her hesitation was brief because she had seen and heard this volcano before – many times. It had never been quiet throughout her long life living in its shadow.

Uenohara is just one of a great number archaeological sites known throughout Japan which are placed into the Jomon culture, many of which appear to have been occupied all year round. The name derives from the Japanese word for the technique that had been used to decorate pottery – *jomon* means 'cord-marks'.[6]

Edward S. Morse, an American biologist and antiquarian, found the first signs of this culture in 1877 – twelve years too late for Victorian John Lubbock's *Prehistoric Times*. He excavated a shell midden at Omori close to modern-day Tokyo City and trained Japanese students in the techniques of archaeology.[7] They were soon excavating further sites and beginning to find the pottery, dwellings and artefacts that became designated as the Jomon culture. Many different designs of pottery were found, leading to numerous cultural subdivisions that have been continually revised throughout the last century as new discoveries were made and radiocarbon dates acquired. Today six cultural phases are recognised, running from the Incipient Jomon which begins with the first pottery, to the Final Jomon which ends at 500 BC. After this date, rice farming appears on a substantial scale in Japan, probably brought by immigrants from China and Korea.[8]

Uenohara falls into the Initial Jomon, during which the first sedentary villages appear. The shift from the traditional mobile hunter-gatherer lifestyles occurred at around 9500 BC and appears to have been a response to the warmer temperatures and increased rainfall of the Holocene – just as was the case with the foundation of Jericho. But the Jomon people differed from those of the Jordan valley by remaining entirely reliant on wild foods, having abundant woodland and coastal resources to exploit.[9] They also made extensive use of pottery.

Jomon pottery is, in fact, the earliest pottery in the world. It provides just one example of the cultural precociousness of Japanese hunter-gatherers as the last ice age came to its close. Fukui Rockshelter in western Kyushu provided some of the earliest-known fragments when excavated in 1960–2.[10] This small cave, found at the base of a sandstone outcrop, is well lit and provides an excellent view across a nearby river. Ice-age hunter-gatherers favoured the cave, resulting in more than five metres of artefact-rich deposits that had begun accumulating before the LGM. The first pottery shards appear in levels dating to 13,000 BC.

Their discovery caused widespread disbelief. In 1962 two distinguished Professors, Suago Yamanouchi and Hiroyuki Sato, published an infamous article entitled 'The Age of Jomon Pottery', concluding that either the dates or the excavation method employed at Fukui must be in error as its pottery could not be any older than 3000 BC.[11] They found it inconceivable that pottery had arisen in Japan at least six thousand years earlier than in western Asia and Europe. Their attitude seems astonishing today when archaeologists are often far too quick to claim that their own region was the source of some cultural innovation. As more radiocarbon dates and pottery finds accumulated, and as confidence in the new dating method increased, Yamanouchi and Sato had to recant: Japan did indeed have the earliest pottery in the world.[12]

Cultural precociousness was not only manifest in pottery. Ice-age hunter-gatherers in Japan were grinding the edges of their stone axes to make better tools several thousand years before this technique was adopted in the West.[13] The Jomon people also invented the use of lacquer, made with sap from the urushi, a type of sumac tree. It needs collecting, heating and filtering before being painstakingly applied to the surface of an object. Recent excavations at Kakinoshima in Hokkaido have found the oldest known lacquered object from anywhere in the world: a red-lacquered comb placed within a burial at 7000 BC.[14]

Why should the Jomon people have been so inventive? Why were they making pottery so much earlier than anywhere else in the world? Only the pottery from China comes remotely close to it in date and there it is explained by the requirements of rice cultivation. Melvin Aitkins from the University of Oregon, an authority on the Jomon period, believes that Japanese pottery was invented to cook and store the produce of the thick broad-leaved woodland that had already covered Kyushu by 13,000 BC. The relationship is evident, he argues, from the simultaneous spread of broad-leaved woodland and pottery into the northern islands of Japan, both appearing on the northernmost island of Hokkaido at around 7000 BC.[15]

There are, however, two problems with this idea. First, there is no necessity for hunter-gatherers to have pottery when living in wooded environments – the inhabitants of 'Ain Mallaha in western Asia at 12,500 BC and Star Carr in northern Europe at 9,500 BC flourished with an entire reliance on vessels made from wickerwork, bark, skins, wood and stone. Pottery no doubt made life easier for those who did the cooking in the woodlands of Kyushu and we know from food residues that pottery vessels had indeed been used to make vegetable, meat and fish stews. But people could have easily survived without such vessels.

A second problem for Aitkins' theory arose in 1999 when a new sample of pottery was found at the site of Odaiyamamoto in northern Honshu. Radiocarbon dates on the residues stuck to the interior of the pot dated to 14,500 BC, pushing back the origin of pottery by at least another thousand years.[16] At this date Honshu would have had no more than a sparse covering of pine and birch. And so the theory that Japanese pottery was invented to store and cook acorns and other produce of broad-leaved woodlands cannot be correct.

Brian Hayden of Simon Fraser University has proposed an alternative explanation. It provides another example of his belief in social competition as the driving force of culture change that we first encountered when considering his theory for the origin of squash cultivation in Mexico.

Hayden suggests that ceramic vessels have a number of important qualities that makes them prestigious objects to own and ideal containers for serving food to guests. At the outset, the potter's art would have been difficult to master; clay had to be carefully selected, tempers prepared, construction and firing techniques explored, practised and refined. Neighbours and more distant visitors would have been struck with the amount of labour and skill required to produce a pottery vessel. The display of novel forms with fancy decoration would have impressed them even more. Most striking of all might have been the dramatic smashing of vessels during feasts as an ostentatious display of wealth.[17]

Theatrical smashing of pots may have occurred in the later Jomon period as immense 'pottery middens' have been found.[18] And as they come in astonishingly elaborate forms, there can be no doubt that many later Jomon vessels were primarily for display. Constructed on a basic flowerpot design, they have spectacular rims modelled as licking flames or serpents winding about the vessel with protruding sculptured heads. Sometimes the decoration is so top-heavy that the pots can hardly stand alone.[19] Lacquered objects must have been very striking, as indeed they still are today. But we must be cautious about applying such interpretations to the earliest, and frankly rather drab, specimens of pottery from Fukui Cave and elsewhere. We currently know too little about the very earliest pottery makers of Japan to decide whether they had been more concerned with impressing their visitors or devising a means to cook vegetable stew. We do know, however, that by 9500 BC many were living sedentary lives in permanent settlements such as Uenohara. Although pottery had already been invented, the sedentary lifestyle must have been crucial in enabling ceramic technology to flourish.

As Lubbock wanders between dwellings, pausing to spy over shoulders and taste titbits of food, the feeling of permanence soon reminds him of his visits to other hunter-gatherer settlements, especially 'Ain Mallaha in western Asia and Koster in North America. A substantial number of trees have been cleared and the dwellings seem built to last. The grinding stones and pottery vessels are certainly not designed for carrying from one camp-site to another. The contents of cooking pots and rubbish heaps show that the Uenohara people have an immense range of food supplies at hand; they evidently take from the woodlands, the freshwater streams, the seashore and the ocean itself. Just like the people at 'Ain Mallaha and Koster, they have used the abundant natural harvests to eschew the mobile lifestyle of traditional hunter-gatherers and enjoy a settled village life.

But just like every other village, Uenohara has a unique atmosphere and a host of cultural particularities. Lubbock watches more potters at work, some using seashells instead of knotted cord to decorate their vessels. Joints of pork are being smoked above ingenious cooking pits that have two open-ings connected by a short tunnel. The joints are hung from branches over one, a fire burns in the other and smoke wafts through the tunnel and over the meat. The stone arrow-heads being made have deeply serrated sides and are quite unlike any that Lubbock has seen elsewhere. Body ornaments are also different: the painted designs are striking and many people wear thick bangles of fired clay as earrings, incised with swirls and spirals.[20]

Although elaborate, such body decorations do not seem to denote status. Uenohara appears to have neither designated leaders nor differences in wealth. All dwellings are similar in size and construction; each of the fires are cooking the same type of food; there seems to be no restriction as to who can sit where and talk to whom.

As the day at Uenohara draws to a close, Lubbock examines the sacks carried by those coming from the woodland when he arrived. These had been dumped next to a series of ready-made clay-lined pits, with their con-tents spilling across the ground. Acorns. Two women are at work, placing layers of crushed rock and then chopped reeds in the bottom of each pit. Acorns are tipped in and packed down into a firm layer. Further layers of reeds and crushed rock are added until the fill is almost level with the ground. Finally the women smother each pit with clay to make a watertight seal. In this manner, the nuts will be safely stored from rodents and the wet for the lean times which come every winter; when eaten, they will have lost their bitter taste.[21]

As work finishes and the sun sets, Lubbock is attracted to a fire and sits within a group that has gathered close to the part-constructed hut. A stack of reeds still waits to be attached to the wooden poles – there seems no hurry to complete the work. Oil oozes and sizzles from parcels of folded leaves containing fish that sit upon hot stones. Some adults and children have already lain down on plant fibre mats to sleep; others talk in hushed voices or sing gently to the young. As Lubbock joins them, the evening sky gives an astonishing display of ever-changing reds and oranges, and then becomes swamped by deep purple and mauves. There is a faintly sulphurous flavour to the air as flecks of volcanic ash fall and fluoresce in the unfolding darkness like a gentle flurry of pyrotechnic snow.

When Koichi Shinto of the Archaeological Centre of Kagoshima excavated Uenohara between 1986 and 1997 he found its archaeological remains sandwiched between layers of volcanic ash. Sakura-jima, the volcano that was billowing when Lubbock arrived, erupted in 9100 BC and buried the settlement below its pumice and ash.[22] It is not known whether Uenohara's people had already left, fled in terror or were buried alive because the acidic ash destroyed all organic material at the site, including human and animal bones. Nevertheless, a great number of ancient hut floors, cooking pits and fireplaces were uncovered. Along with these, Koichi Shinto found an array of artefacts that included ceramic earrings, pots, clay figurines and serrated arrow points. Many had been buried several decades, perhaps centuries, after the 9100 BC eruption had occurred. Without dwellings to accompany them, it seems that Uenohara had become a location of ritualistic deposition.

Sakura-jima was not, however, the volcano that sealed the last of the material remains of Uenohara and the ultimate fate of its people. That came on a day around 5000 BC with the eruption of Kikai volcano, located 100 kilometres off the southern coast of Kyushu.[23] This was one of the biggest eruptions of the Holocene world. Pyroclastic flows travelled across the sea to Kyushu, devastating its southern and central forests and anything they contained; ash from Kikai was even deposited far to the north on Hokkaido island. Uenohara – which might have already been deserted – was buried below one metre of ash. Much of southern Kyushu remained uninhabited for several centuries and people never returned to rebuild the village.[24]

Today, Uenohara has been put on public display and is visited by thousands of people every year who see where the Jomon hunter-gatherers had once built their homes and smoked their pork. In this most recent phase of its life, Uenohara has become quite unlike those other hunter-gatherer settlements of prehistory with which it had once been so easily compared. The excavated remnants of Star Carr, 'Ain Mallaha and many others lie neglected, quite unknown and inaccessible to the public who are denied a knowledge of their hunter-gatherer past.

It is 9100 BC. Having dozed until daylight, Lubbock leaves Uenohara to begin a northward journey through the islands of Japan. First he travels by foot along deer tracks and well-trodden plant-gathering routes to the northern coast of Kyushu. There he arrives at cliffs that tower above the

Bungo Channel, 50 kilometres of island-dotted sea beyond which lies Shikoku, the next of Japan's islands. Its distant coast is lost in a salty haze thrown up by crashing waves below.

He has no choice but to follow the cliff-top, descending into bays and climbing again on to headlands until the far northern point of Kyushu is reached. Jomon campsites are nestled in sheltered coves, some with canoes dragged on to their shore. Borrowing one, Lubbock crosses the narrow strait to the southwesterly tip of Honshu island. From there he follows its convoluted southern coastline, always in the shadow of high inland mountains with stone-grey and purple peaks. Winters come and cover the summits and forest-covered slopes with snow; the summers are hot and humid, their arrival announced by torrential winds and rains blown from the Pacific. Soon 9100 BC becomes 8000 and then 7000 BC.

When the coastline swings to the south Lubbock heads inland; steep, tree-covered valleys lead to passes between mountain peaks. From these he looks eastwards, across the emerald Pacific towards North America. When 6500 BC arrives, Lubbock knows that hunters upon the Great Plains are struggling with the impact of drought as they search for dwindling bison herds.

On another inland sortie from the coast Lubbock arrives at the marshy margins of an enormous inland lake – known today as Lake Biwa. The woodlands are particularly rich, and the lake provides shellfish and many edible aquatic plants. Not surprisingly, there are several Jomon campsites; their inhabitants discard the debris from their plant gathering into the boggy ground – nutshells, unpalatable skins, seeds and stalks. There it will remain preserved in waterlogged sediment, until excavated as the site of Awazu and providing one of the few collections of Jomon plant remains.[25]

After having covered about 850 kilometres as the crow flies from the southwesterly tip of Honshu, and at least four or five times that distance around the intricacies of the coasts and valleys, Lubbock finds himself resting in the gentle Tama Hills above today's Tokyo Bay. He has recently passed close to Mount Fuji, whose perfectly symmetrical and snow-covered peak dominated a landscape of lakes and waterfalls, flowering cherry and wild azaleas. But the view before him now is more prosaic: a troop of wild pigs snorting and snuffling their way through the undergrowth on the opposite side of a shallow valley.

A single large boar with curly and lethal-looking tusks dominates the group; with him are three females and a host of stripy piglets. One of the sows suddenly disappears amid piercing squeals; the others flee, the little ones desperately trying to keep up with the adults that charge into the trees, leaving broken boughs and trampled shrubs behind. The squealing continues from precisely where the pigs had been, a panic-stricken, painful squeal intermixed with desperate grunts that echo through the valley. And yet there is no pig to be seen.

It takes several minutes for the cries to cease, becoming replaced by heavy breathing and sounds of struggle. Slowly, cautiously, Lubbock approaches and learns that the sow had fallen through the brushwood cover of a pit, having been tempted by a bait of nuts. The pig is stuck: her legs dangle helplessly in a ditch, her sides wedged and made firm by her own hopeless efforts to escape.

For the next few hours Lubbock waits by the pit-trap while the pig periodically squeals and frantically thrusts her head around. By the time a party of Jomon hunters step from the woods to check their trap, she is exhausted and quiet. When they use a flint knife to cut a swollen artery there is no more than a whimpering acceptance of death.

The hunters drink a little of her blood from a small pottery bowl and wait for the rest to drain. Work then begins to remove the carcass. They climb on to her back and undertake butchery with stone axes and knives, levering out the partitioned carcass with wooden stakes. Then they return to the woods carrying haunches across their shoulders and the pig's head upon a stake. A scatter of blunted, greasy stone tools and a single bloodstained pottery vessel are left behind.

When Keiji Imamura, now at the University of Tokyo, undertook excavations prior to a housing development in the Kirigaoka area of Yokohama City in 1970, he failed to discover Jomon pit-dwellings in any of the seven localities examined. But he found many oval-shaped pits, most about 1.5 metres long and more than one metre deep. Too small to be houses and with very few artefacts around, Imamura thought he might have found pit-traps for wild boar.[26]

To pursue his idea, Imamura shunned the usual archaeological tools of trowels and dental picks in favour of bulldozers. He stripped a vast area of topsoil from Kirigaoka, removing it from hill slopes, ridges, terraces and the bottoms of small valleys. The whole area proved to be peppered with the oval pits, many close to what Imamura thought might once have been animal trails. The pits came in a range of different designs. One type had once had poles erected in its base. These may have been stakes to kill the animal or perhaps just supports to keep trotters dangling above the ground. Another type was like the one that Lubbock had seen – an elongated oval with narrowing walls to tightly wedge the pig once it had fallen in.

A few of the pits at Kirigaoka contained fragments of pottery. These had presumably been washed in by the rain from broken vessels left around the trap, along with soil and other debris. The style and decoration of the pots suggested that some pits dated to the Initial Jomon, contemporary with the settlement at Uenohara, while others were Early Jomon in date. Further pits were very recent, having been used for boar hunting in historic times, as recorded in Japanese folklore.

During the Japanese economic boom of the 1970s and 1980s, thousands of excavations took place every year in advance of building, and many similar sites were discovered throughout the country. The majority of pit-traps dated to the Early Jomon period and were sometimes found in substantial numbers. One of the most spectacular discoveries was made in the Tama Hills region of Tokyo's southern suburbs, where 30 square kilometres of land was examined prior to a housing development. An astonishing 10,000 pits were uncovered. Those of the Later Jomon period were arranged in lines, suggesting that pigs or deer had been chased towards them, perhaps with the use of fences to channel the animals to their death. But the Earlier Jomon people appear to have been more casual about their hunting – they simply left some bait and let fate play its role as pigs rooted and deer nibbled through the innocent-looking woodland.

From the Tama Hills Lubbock walks to the coast of Tokyo Bay, now always watching for suspicious clusters of nuts. On arrival, the shoreline appears deserted, even though there are many signs of human presence around the bay: old fireplaces, collapsed brushwood huts, canoes dragged on to the sands. As Lubbock sits wondering where to go, a wispy spiral of smoke rises above the trees on a small island within the bay. The water looks warm and shallow and so he begins to wade to its shore. In fact it is cold and deep, requiring Lubbock to undertake an unpleasant and tiring swim.

He finds a few families living on the island; their simple brushwood dwellings built near a diffuse heap of shells, including those of oysters, clams and cockles. Animal bones, some still carrying scraps of skin and sinew, broken tools and pots have also been thrown on to the stinking heap. A fire burns by the midden's edge; women are grinding nuts into a paste and children are playing on the rubbish. They throw old bones around and decimate discarded pots into tiny fragments. Dogs lie close to the women and chew bones. The men sit looking out to sea, wondering whether the incoming tide will reach as high, and perhaps even surpass, that of the night before.[27]

Lubbock has reached what will become the archaeological site of Natsushima. Needing some warmth after his swim he sits by the fire, the stench of the midden reminding him of days spent at Ertebølle and Namu. But although familiar with midden sites, he has previously given little time to learning the arts of coastal gathering. So Lubbock resolves to remain at Natsushima for a few weeks at least – watching and practising this further aspect of Jomon life.

Lessons begin at low tide early the next morning when he accompanies the women to gather shellfish. Many of the small children also come, carried on shoulders or running to play in the water near by. Molluscs on the rocks are easy to find but difficult to remove; Lubbock has to learn how to strike them sharply with a pointed stone but too often scuffs his knuckles on the rock.

The women also search for clams below the sand, looking for small depressions where the shells have burrowed and then testing their potential by dragging their fingers or a digging stick through the sand. If sufficient shells are felt, some women sit and begin to fill their baskets; if not, the search continues – heads and shoulders bent for a better view of the ground. When a particularly dense patch of shells is found, all the women gather together in a circle to pull enormous clams from the sand.

The shellfish culinary lesson follows back at the camp. A patch of clean sand close to the hearth is found and the shells are stacked carefully against each other with their lips in the sand. Small sticks and dead grass are placed upon the shells; once lit, the breeze quickly spreads the flames over the bed of shells. Within minutes sizzling and popping noises begin, as the shells open and juices begin to escape. When cooked, the fire is cleared away and the gaping shells arranged on fresh green leaves to cool.[28]

Although marine fish and coastal foods dominate the diet at Natsushima, Lubbock also joins the hunting parties that regularly leave for the inland hills and forests. They inspect pit-traps and set snares to capture hare – a skill Lubbock had already learned long ago at Creswell Crags. Fresh deer tracks are followed but with little success; dogs flush out game birds; nets are thrown over unwary ducks.

Within a few weeks Lubbock has learned a great deal about how his unknowing hosts acquire their food but discovered little about their social life and religious beliefs. The only death to occur has been that of a dog, its body unceremoniously buried in the midden. So what happened to the human dead remained unclear. There was the familiar story-telling and singing around night-time fires, but no memorable rituals, costume or dance.

Sosuke Sugihara and his colleagues excavated the Natsushima shell midden in 1955.[29] The site played a key role in establishing the antiquity and character of the Jomon culture by providing the very first radiocarbon dates relating to Japanese prehistory. Its lowest layers contained tiny fragments of pottery and charcoal that were dated to 9000 BC; just like at Fukui Cave, excavated a few years later, this combination of pottery and radiocarbon-dated charcoal caused some initial disbelief.

The excavation found traces of many coastal activities: fish hooks, needles, net weights, axe-heads, grinding stones and the bones from an immense array of shellfish, animals, birds and fish. As at the Ertebølle midden in Denmark, no traces of dwellings were found, possibly because they had been erected just outside the excavated area, or because they were too ephemeral to leave a trace. One must guess at the presence of sea-going canoes from the tuna, sea bass and dolphin bones found within the midden. But Jomon canoes have been found elsewhere, notably at Kamo, another shell midden on the Pacific coast.[30]

Lubbock's failure to garner information about the burial customs and ritual activities of those who lived at Natsushima at 6500 BC was a consequence of the short duration of his visit – a summer season alone. He failed to learn whether the families would remain by their midden all year round or whether they would move to another settlement, perhaps joining other families in a woodland winter village. That may have been the time for ceremony and ritual, for dressing-up and dance, a time when marriages were forged and rites of passage passed through. But Lubbock had to leave Natsushima with such questions unanswered – just as they remain unanswered for archaeologists today.[31]

The Jomon culture continued to flourish long after Lubbock's travels came to an end. Its apogee came soon after 3000 BC when Jomon pottery effectively became ornate sculpture, and elaborately carved stone rods and female figurines were produced. In light of a dramatic increase in the number of archaeological sites, the human population had evidently soared in number. The woodlands were intensively harvested, the Jomon becoming wild gardeners, cultivators and managers of their forest.[32] Shell middens grew from the small spreads of rubbish, such as at Natsushima, into great horseshoe-shaped mounds containing many millions of shells and bones. Migratory salmon provided predictable supplies of food, possibly making the same contribution to cultural complexity as they did across the Pacific on the northwest coast of America.[33]

When full-scale rice farming arrived in Japan at around 500 BC, the hunting-gathering-cultivating Jomon lifestyle was replaced by a rural agricultural economy that made use of iron tools and continued into modern times. Incoming people originating in China and Korea brought this new economy to Japan.[34] It is from these people that almost all modern-day Japanese people are descended. Because rice was unable to grow in the colder environments of northern Honshu and Hokkaido the Jomon culture survived a little longer in the north of Japan. Today, the Ainu people who maintain a hunting-and-gathering lifestyle inhabit these regions.[35] Many believe that the Ainu are not only the cultural inheritors of the Jomon way of life, but the biological descendants of the Jomon people themselves.

41

Summer in the Arctic

The mammoth steppe and colonisation of the High Arctic,
19,000–6500 BC

Having once shared a Tasmanian cave with the southernmost people of the ice-age world, Lubbock is now heading for the opposite end of planet earth. His destination is Zhokhov, a peninsula in the Arctic Ocean that will mark the end of his northward journey through eastern Asia – there will simply be nowhere else to go.

Today Zhokhov is a tiny island, detached from the Siberian mainland by a rise in sea-level and no more than 11 kilometres from north to south and 9 kilometres east to west. Its spine of low hills is bordered by entirely flat lowland pock-marked with waterlogged hollows. An impoverished tundra of bogs, mosses, lichens and grass covers the bedrock, except where the basalt has been scraped clean by Arctic storms. Constantly assaulted by a violent northerly wind, it suffers the intense cold and darkness of a long Arctic winter. Few would dispute that Zhokhov island is one of the most inhospitable places on earth; it was little different in 6400 BC. Yet it was home for a Stone Age community – the first people known to live in the High Arctic.

To reach Zhokhov, Lubbock must undertake a journey of some 3,500 kilometres from Natsushima; this begins with a canoe trip from the northern tip of Japan. On his arrival in the Russian Far East, he treks through a thickly forested landscape of oak, elm and birch that provides a perfect habitat for bear, fox and wild boar. As he travels north, this broad-leafed woodland changes to a dark coniferous forest, one of spruce, larch and fir in which Lubbock feels alone, even though there are signs that suggest otherwise.[1] He passes recent fireplaces on riverbanks where stone artefacts have been made, birds plucked and salmon skinned. Plumes of smoke spiral above distant trees; strange unnatural noises seem to announce a human presence. But such echoes are rare additions to the sounds of the Siberian forest – those of trees creaking in the wind and the rustles of wary animals, moose or maybe lynx. And up above there are the cries, the honks and the beating wings of geese; they too are heading north for an Arctic summer.

Halfway through his northward journey a cave provides shelter and a place to wait for others to arrive. It is within a small limestone cliff and close to the confluence of two rivers, the larger of which will one day become called the Aldan and flow through the Sakha Republic of the

Russian Federation. Lubbock scrambles through a thicket upon its steep bank to reach the entrance; the cave is quite small inside – no more than 12 metres to its rear and just high enough to stand upright. The view is daunting: waves of forest-covered hills that rhythmically rise and fall before fading gently into sky.

The cave is warm and dry; if there are people in the vicinity they will be sure to come and use it. And so Lubbock waits, just as he had done elsewhere in the world – at Kulpi Mara in the Central Australian Desert at 13,000 BC and Sandal Shelter, Arizona, at 7500 BC. Once again he waits in vain.

Lubbock's lonesome waiting place is Dyuktai Cave but his arrival is poorly timed to meet any occupants.[2] Having been used at 17,000 BC and 12,000 BC, it then suffered a long period of abandonment until being reoccupied in historic times. So by 6400 BC – the date of Lubbock's arrival – the stone tools and food debris of Dyuktai's ice-age occupants were sealed within the floor deposits: a mix of wind-blown silt, limestone collapse and sand left behind by the river when in flood. The tools remained buried within these sediments until the late 1960s when excavated by the Russian archaeologist Yuri Mochanov.

Mochanov undertook his excavations as part of the Prilensk Archaeological Expedition established in 1964 by the Academy of Sciences of the USSR.[3] The Aldan River valley was chosen in the hope of finding the settlements of people who had migrated to the northeast of Siberia and whose descendants colonised the Americas. This was, of course, long before Monte Verde had been discovered and when the Clovis people were still revered as the first Americans.

The cave contained several metres of floor deposits from which large numbers of stone artefacts and animal bones were recovered. The former came from many different species – both large animals, including reindeer, horse and bison, and smaller ones such as lemmings, hare and fox. These suggested a quite different landscape to the forested hills through which Lubbock had travelled, one of tundra and steppe in which, Mochanov concluded, people had hunted not only bison and reindeer but the woolly mammoth whose bones were also found within the cave.[4]

The stone tools turned out to be quite different from anything previously found in Northeast Asia. Some were stone knives and projectile points made by repeatedly removing chips from the alternate faces of a large stone flake. This was the same 'bifacial' method that the Clovis people of North America used to make their projectile points at least a millennium after the final prehistoric occupation of Dyuktai Cave.[5] Other tools were made from small, thin blades of flint removed from 'wedge-shaped' cores, while antlers and bones had been worked to make a variety of other implements including awls and hammers.

As the Prilensk Archaeological Expedition discovered further sites, similar collections of tools were excavated, which were often associated with the same range of mammals. And so a new culture was defined, named after the cave where such tools were first found: the Dyuktai culture. This was soon recognised as having existed throughout Siberia – or western Beringia as we should call it – during the final millennia of the Pleistocene.

The origins of the Dyuktai culture are now known to stretch back to just a millennium or so after the severest conditions of the LGM. Between 1986 and 1990 Mikhail Konstantinov from the Russian Chita Pedagogical Institute excavated a remarkable open settlement on the ancient banks of the Chikoi River, close to Lake Baikal in eastern Russia, approximately 2,000 kilometres southwest of Dyuktai Cave. Known as Studenhoe, this site revealed that hunter-gatherers had regularly camped upon the river's flood plain, their discarded debris being flooded and then buried in fine sediments immediately after each occupation.[6] The consequence was a tremendous sequence of deposits in which individual hearths and huts were separated by fine layers of silt. One of the dwellings was marked by a ring of seventy boulders with the remnants of five hearths situated in a line. The hearths were rock-lined oval features, containing charcoal, while the hut floors provided thousands of stone artefacts typical of the Dyuktai culture.

In 1996, an American team collaborated with the Russians to secure charcoal samples from the hearths for radiocarbon dating. The results showed that the first riverside campsites had occurred by 19,000 BC, by which date the Dyuktai-type tools had already been adopted. It became evident that Studenhoe and the Dyuktai-type technology provided the basis for the colonisation of the far northeast. Although the Studenhoe people and their descendants must have endured freezing temperatures, violent winds and a constant search for firewood and shelter, they appear to have been driven to colonise the frozen north. By 15,000 BC they were living at Berelekh, a settlement 1,000 kilometres north of Dyuktai Cave and 500 kilometres inside the Arctic Circle. And as we know from sites such as Blue Fish Caves in Alaska, people with a Dyuktai-type technology had crossed the Bering land bridge by 11,000 BC, becoming some of the earliest Americans. By 6400 BC, they had colonised the High Arctic, establishing the settlement of Zhokhov.

Before leaving Dyuktai to resume his northward journey, Lubbock reads a passage from *Prehistoric Times* about the 'Esquimaux'.[7] Writing in 1865, his namesake had known that people were living on the shores of the Arctic Ocean from Siberia to Greenland. Victorian John Lubbock had drawn on the journals of many Arctic expeditions, especially those from Captain Parry's voyages of 1821–3, and was more complimentary about the Esquimaux than any of his other modern savages. His descriptions of their dwellings, tools, clothes, boats, hunting, fishing and burial practices were littered with remarks about ingenuity and skill.

When Victorian John Lubbock found his sources being critical or dismissive, he was quick to defend the Esquimaux. So when various 'disgusting accounts' of meals were cited, along with the Esquimaux habit of eating raw meat, Victorian Lubbock had commented that several of the European Arctic expeditions had also eaten raw meat, this being conducive to good health in high latitudes. Similarly, when describing how the Esquimaux are 'excessively dirty', he stressed how they suffer from a scarcity of fresh water and how the extreme cold, 'by preventing putrefaction, removes one of our principal inducements to cleanliness'. In the same way, after having cited evidence that the Esquimaux are 'great thieves', Victorian Lubbock emphasised that allowances must be made for the temptations offered by ships' stores to people familiar with an extreme shortage of food. He went on to describe the Esquimaux as 'strictly honest amongst themselves, kind, generous and trustworthy'. Some of the women were even 'beautiful and clever'.

Leaving Dyuktai Cave in 6400 BC, Lubbock continues to travel northwards, crossing hills and fording rivers. It is often dark below the trees; the forest floor is springy with a thick mat of pine needles. With every step the rarity of animals becomes more striking. Moose are occasionally seen in small meadows between the trees or browsing in thickets of willow. A bear is sighted, gorging upon berries. But otherwise the spruce woodland seems quite empty, no more than a few birds within the trees and wildfowl around the bogs. Only the insects seem plentiful – biting, drilling and piercing Lubbock's skin at every opportunity.

While following the course of a valley he notices something white, smooth and curved protruding from a gully. After scraping away some dirt it is revealed as a mammoth tusk, exposed after a collapse of sediment to the valley floor. With a stout branch as a pick and a flat pebble as a shovel Lubbock begins to dig. More of the tusk appears and with it part of a skull. Soon an expanse of hairy mammoth hide is exposed. After hours of digging Lubbock gives up on his own allotted task – it would take far more than sticks and stones to expose the mighty beast.

The frozen animals of Siberia are the most evocative reminders of the northern ice-age world. The earliest recorded discovery is a mammoth from Berezovka, located in the far northeast of Siberia. In 1900 an ivory dealer had bought tusks from a tribesman who lived on the Kolyma River and heard how they had been cut from an animal with its hide intact. After months of reports and telegrams, an expedition set out from the Imperial Academy of Sciences in Petrograd to investigate the find. Led by Otto F. Herz, the expedition left in May 1901 and took the whole summer to reach the mammoth. By the time they arrived, the frosts and snows of autumn had cemented the mammoth once again within the refrozen ground. And so a log and canvas structure had to be constructed over the carcass, stoves lit and the ground thawed out before digging could begin.[8]

Although much of the head was missing and other parts had decomposed, preservation of the Berezovka mammoth was remarkable. Large areas of skin had survived with some internal organs, its tongue, tail and penis. The mammoth's last meal remained between its teeth – buttercups and other flowers. Many of its bones were broken and there were large clots of blood. Death seemed to have been almost instantaneous, perhaps from falling into a gully.

During the next fifty years there were several other startling finds, not only of frozen mammoths but of horses, bison, and woolly rhino, all coming from before the ice age had reached its end. Several contained undigested grasses, sedges and flowers within their stomachs – critical evidence for scientists in their quest to reconstruct how the ancient landscape had looked before the forests arrived.

Dale Guthrie, a zoologist from the University of Alaska and one of the most distinguished of such scientists, coined the term 'mammoth steppe' for the ice-age landscapes of northern Asia.[9] Trees had been entirely absent from a landscape of grasses, herbs and shrubs that supported herds of large game. Just like the steppe which Gordon Hillman, the archaeo-botanist from University College, London, has sought to reconstruct for western Asia, this northern steppe hardly exists today but had been a vital component of the ice-age world.

An insight into the animal inhabitants of the mammoth steppe was gained by excavations of a vast natural accumulation of bones at Berelekh, which became known as a 'mammoth cemetery'.[10] Having been first reported in the scientific literature in 1957, a research expedition was launched in 1970 by the Academy of Sciences of the USSR. N. K. Vereshchagin used a water cannon to wash away the enclosing sediments, exposing the remains of perhaps two hundred mammoths along with those from bison, horse and reindeer. While doing so he found four flint artefacts within a scatter of bones a short distance from the main deposit. Yuri Mochanov identified them as belonging to the Dyuktai culture. And so the Prilensk Archaeological Expedition excavated the human settlement at Berelekh between 1971–3, and then again in 1981.

Their work discovered many tools made of stone, bone and ivory which had been discarded around 15,000 BC. Associated with these were mammoth, bison and reindeer bones; but those from arctic hare and partridge were far more numerous. So, just as Lubbock had found at Creswell Crags, the ice-age hunters at Berelekh seem to have preferred trapping small game to tackling mighty beasts. The mammoth tusks used to make knives and spears had most likely been scavenged from the 'cemetery' – just as people at Pushkari had collected from a similar accumulation to build their dwellings at the LGM. Mochanov thinks that a mammoth-bone house may have once been built at Berelekh, but after millennia of frost action and disturbance, not to mention the impact of Vereshchagin's water pump, no pattern amongst the bones can be discerned.

*

Soon after 13,000 BC, trees began to spread across the mammoth steppe. Guthrie believes that they were encouraged to do so not by higher temperatures but by increasing precipitation – the key to the mammoth steppe had been its aridity. Most of the new rainfall would have come as a persistent fine drizzle and mist, just as it does today. It would never have been substantial: modern-day Alaska receives the same annual rainfall as the Kalahari Desert. But because evaporation was, and still is, so low, the soils of the mammoth steppe soon became quite moist as a watery network of bogs, rivers and lakes seeped into existence.

The conifers that formed the new forests had plenty of water but struggled to acquire nutrients from the frozen ground. The same applies today, and growth can be remarkably slow: Guthrie describes how spruce trees might be one hundred years old but no more than 6 inches from one side to the other. Such trees cannot risk losing any new growth to hungry herbivores, and so they pack their leaves and needles with toxic compounds to make them quite inedible. When shed, they are extremely slow to decompose, resulting in a thick humic mat on the forest floor. This insulates the soil, raising the permafrost and further reducing the availability of nutrients to the trees. Thus growth is further inhibited and an even greater pressure is placed on the trees to make themselves unpleasant to eat.

Such trees also need extensive root systems to survive and this keeps almost the whole of their biomass below ground, safely away from browsing herbivores. The grasses, herbs and shrubs of the mammoth steppe had been quite different – quick growers, adapted to short seasonal bursts of rainfall and then dying back. As such, they could afford to be eaten; some even benefited from having their dead tissues grazed away so that sunlight could reach and warm the soil itself.

The spread of forests, bogs and lakes drove the animal herds to the far north where the mammoth steppe survived. But even there they were put under pressure by the increased snow cover that buried the grasses and shrubs and by the flooding of coastal lands by the rising sea. This combination of factors was sufficient to push the Siberian mammoth into extinction – no blame can be placed on the Dyuktai people as no kill sites have been found to compare with the Clovis sites of North America. Only one mammoth population is known to have survived the burst of global warming at 9600 BC – that which became trapped on Wrangel Island after the Siberian plain was inundated by the sea. They were the last of the woolly mammoths to walk upon planet earth.[11]

As Lubbock continues his northward journey in 6400 BC the trees become sparse and the idea that global warming has occurred seems a myth. When the air is still, clouds of mosquitoes settle upon his eyes, lips and nostrils and he wishes that the icy wind would blow. Midsummer arrives and the skies become pastel, often like the mother-of-pearl from inside a shell.

Strange haloes and coronas frequently appear around the sun and moon. The northern lights provide a distant celestial drapery of murmuring reds and green.

Eventually Lubbock finds himself on an extensive coastal plain. The few trees grow upon a variegated quilt of mosses, heather, lichens and fungi; they are stunted in size and battered by the wind. Lubbock trips over solid grassy hummocks and slips into boggy pools; but the moist-looking moss is surprisingly crisp beneath his feet.[12] The sky is grey and often delivers a sleet-laden wind that whips across the tundra. In the far distance there is the faint outline of snow-covered hills within which the village of Zhokhov is nestled.

An incongruous noise halts Lubbock's step; it is one that recalls other arrivals – those at 'Ain Mallaha, Skateholm and Koster. A dog's bark. Turning, he sees a sledge approach, pulled by four dogs and steered by a man dressed in thick hides and fur. It rattles slowly across the tundra, with a basket of bilberries, a bundle of sticks and a mammoth tusk carried upon its rear. Taking his chance, Lubbock leaps on board as the sledge passes by, gaining a lift for the last few kilometres to Zhokhov.

In 1989 a joint expedition by the Leningrad Institute of Archaeology and the Arctic and Antarctic Research Institute discovered a human settlement on the tiny island of Zhokhov. Initially this appeared as no more than a series of shallow round pits, scatters of animal bones and split driftwood within a small valley in the southwest of the island, close to the foot of an isolated hill. Excavations were undertaken by Vladimir Pitul'ko who found that the pits had once been dwellings and that the preservation of wood and bone was excellent due to the permafrost conditions. The settlement was revealed as the earliest evidence of human presence in the High Arctic.[13]

During his excavations, Pitul'ko found evidence for both sledges and dogs and guessed that these might go together,[14] pushing back the history of dog traction in the Arctic by several thousand years. That for the sledge was a fragment of wood, probably larch, which had been shaped and used as a runner. It was just over one metre long with striations and polish on the underside. With use it had become bevelled, indicating attachment to the left side of the sledge. A socket bored into the runner had once held part of the framework – the sledge had evidently been a substantial construction.

Although further fragments of the sledge were recovered, none provided direct evidence that it had been pulled by dogs. But dog bones were excavated, identified as such by being larger than those of the arctic fox and smaller than those of the wolf. Further evidence for canine domestication came from large quantities of 'small rounded deposits' – dog faeces – that were excavated from the permafrost. When pulled apart they were found to contain reindeer hair, fragments of bone and hoof. Having been found in discrete concentrations, the faeces indicated where dogs had been tethered to separate posts.

Dogs may have also been used for hunting. The animal bones recovered by Pitul'ko indicated that while the Zhokhov people hunted reindeer, geese, swans and the occasional seal, their primary food source had been the polar bear. This was a unique discovery – no other settlement in which polar bears were anything other than a minor supplement to the diet has ever been discovered by archaeologists or visited by anthropologists. This is not surprising as polar bears are extraordinarily strong and dangerous animals. The animal bones from Zhokhov also contradicted the pervasive view among archaeologists that the colonisation of the High Arctic had been by communities that specialised in the hunting of sea mammals.

All historically known Arctic cultures have held polar bears in the highest esteem, often attributing to them a key role in their mythological world. A pervasive belief among the Inuit of the Canadian Arctic is that there was once a time when bears and men could easily change into one another.[15] This may have arisen from the similarities between polar bears and humans: both are able to stand upright and to travel on land and sea; both are skilled in hunting and build winter dwellings, in the polar bears' case for giving birth. But respect never prevented killing; after all, polar bears have a lot to offer: good meat, warm pelts, fat for use in lamps; bones, claws and teeth for tool making.

When the Inuit people killed a male bear, its bladder, penis, spleen and tongue were hung up in an igloo with the harpoon and other weapons used in the hunt. If the animal was a she-bear the bladder and spleen were hung with the women's tools – needles and knives – so that the bear's soul would feel at home. The women were taught to fear the bear from an early age by stories about attacks from hungry bears appearing in camp while the men were away hunting. An Inuit boy's first bear hunt gave him adult status, and afterwards he would receive a dog whip with a handle made from the bear's penis bone.

Aleksey Kasparov from the Leningrad Institute of Archaeology made a meticulous study of the polar-bear bones that Vladimir Pitul'ko excavated at Zhokhov. He identified how initial butchery had taken place at the kill sites, where the lower legs and feet were discarded. Kasparov was able to recon-struct how the carcasses were butchered into joints of meat and the heads cut apart to allow the removal of canine teeth and brains. The size of the bones suggested that the Zhokhov people had mainly hunted females, most likely while the bears were searching for localities to make their winter dens.

A variety of hunting equipment was found, although exactly which had been used for polar bears and which for reindeer and geese remains unclear. There were needle-shaped bone projectile points, some of which might have been hafted on to wooden arrow shafts, fragments of which were also found. Larger bone points had slots along each side where flint blades would have been inset. Further pieces of bone had been carved into barbed points, most likely used for fishing. Ivory and antler had been used to make pickaxes, while a variety of stone types had been worked – flint, sandstone, chalcedony and obsidian. Some had been collected from the local beach; others, such as the obsidian, had been brought from a great distance and were used sparingly.

The Zhokhov people no longer used the bifacial technique to make their stone tools as had been favoured by those at Studenhoe, Dyuktai Cave and Berelekh. Neither did they produce the distinctive 'wedge-shaped' cores, preferring to turn stone nodules into conical or prismatic shapes before detaching their flakes and blades. Many were removed and used as knife blades, awls and engraving tools; larger pieces of stone were ground into axe-heads.

By the date of Zhokhov's occupation, people throughout Siberia had been using this new technology for several thousand years, that of the Dyuktai culture having been abandoned as the landscapes became covered with trees. Although Lubbock had failed to meet any people on his north-ward journey, hunter-gatherers were certainly living in the Siberian forests at 6400 BC as numerous sites have been found.[16] We know very little about their way of life as most sites yield no more than a small scatter of stone artefacts. This is why Pitul'ko's discovery and excavation at Zhokhov is so remarkable – the remnants of dwellings, dogs and sledges, belonging to a community of Stone Age polar bear hunters who had been living no less than 1,000 kilometres inside the Arctic Circle.

The sledge arrives at the village while Lubbock is picking bilberry seeds from between his teeth. He has enjoyed the ride, although feels disappointed that the runners of the sledge were made from wood rather than whale jaw-bones or frozen fish stuffed in skins like those described in *Prehistoric Times*.

Dusk also arrives at Zhokhov, the start of a protracted twilight that will subtly fade rather than darken, repainting the landscape in pale blues and misty purples. There are at least a dozen circular dwellings sheltering in the lee of a hill and close to a small brook within a thicket of willow. Each has split timbers for walls and a cone-shaped roof covered with turfs and moss. Several children had been waiting for the sledge; they help the driver tether his dogs, bringing them water in wooden bowls and bones to gnaw. The load of wood is stacked beside a dwelling, the tusk stood upright against a wall. The man takes a drink of water and then shares his now depleted bilberries with some of his family and friends all male – sitting around a smouldering fire.

Lubbock enters a dwelling, pushing through heavy drapes and stepping down into a conical-shaped room.[17] It is dark and warm inside; the air mordant with a blend of odours from fish, hide and blubber. The floor, like the walls, is made from split driftwood and covered with mats of knotted heather roots. In the middle there is a fireplace – a scatter of ash surrounded by stone blocks. Crouching, he examines a cluster of artefacts: a hollowed stone containing animal fat, a bone awl and blades of obsidian.

Surrounding these are scraps of cut hide, lengths of thread, fur and feathers. Shelves support wooden bowls; a variety of implements are hanging up – flint bladed knives, wooden spoons, harpoons, pieces of clothing, woven baskets. A pile of hides and furs suggest a sleeping place.

In a second dwelling Lubbock finds some of the women and children of Zhokhov – a dozen people crammed into the tiny space. They sit relieved of the thick heavy garments needed for outside wear. Two are breast-feeding, others hold sleeping infants. The air is even thicker than before, it now having the additional bouquet of semi-naked bodies and largely unwashed flesh.[18] They sit quietly, content to listen as one of the mothers hums to her child. Lubbock sits upon a pile of furs behind them; beyond the gentle song he can hear the wind, the chatter of men's voices and that noise which has followed him around the prehistoric world: the crack of one stone upon another. With this melody of Arctic village life he falls asleep.

Knowing that his final travels will be in lower latitudes – southern Asia and then Africa – Lubbock is conscious that his visit to Zhokhov is the last opportunity to learn about life in a frozen landscape. Having already learned how to trap hares at Creswell Crags, ambush reindeer in the Ahrensburg valley and butcher the kill at Verberie, he is aware that one very significant gap in his education remains: how to make suitable clothing for survival in an ice-age world. He knows a little from the passage about Esquimaux in *Prehistoric Times*, but he needs to learn through his own experience.

The people at Zhokhov wear garments made from reindeer skins and spend a great deal of time on their manufacture and care. And so throughout the next few days in the village Lubbock takes every opportunity to watch clothing being made, and whenever possible lends an unseen hand.[19] Most of this skilful and laborious work is carried out by the women and Lubbock recalls how the ice-age hunters of Gönnersdorf had appropriately celebrated their women by depicting them on stone.

The first task they undertake is cleaning reindeer hides – removing all the fat and sinews that remain after butchery. To do so, the skins are scraped with stone flakes set in bone handles. This is hard work and requires a deft hand to ensure that the skin itself isn't cut.

The skins are rinsed in water and then placed to soak in urine to remove any remaining traces of fat. While the skins are soaking, the women prepare thread from reindeer sinews. These are also washed and scraped to remove traces of blood and fat; they are soaked in sea water, hung to dry and then split into fine, strong threads. The women draw these repeatedly across their teeth until they become smooth and supple; Lubbock tries to do the same but without the rigours of an Arctic childhood his teeth are far too sharp to be of use. After a couple of days the skins are removed from the urine and rinsed. Next they are pegged out and stretched; then folded, rubbed and stretched some more until they too are completely soft.

Obsidian blades, as sharp as razors, are used to cut the skins into pieces. Thigh-length outer jackets require eight different segments – a front, a back, two pieces for the hood, two more for the shoulders and one for each arm. The skins are cut at angles so that the reindeer hairs will eventually overlap the seams and each piece is carefully shaped to allow both warmth and easy movement within the final garment. Holes are made around their edges using a bone awl and the pieces stitched tightly with the sinew-thread and bone needles; thick pieces of hide act as thimbles. Just as Victorian Lubbock had said of nineteenth-century Esquimaux, with such simple instruments 'they sew very strongly and well'. Ruffs of wolf fur are added – for fashion as much as warmth. Wolf fur is also particularly good at shedding ice crystals that form from breathing the icy-cold air. Trousers, which reach to the calves, are made in a similar fashion and are also worn with the caribou hair on the outside; leggings, in contrast, are made with the hair on the inside.

Two more items of clothing are essential: the inner-jacket and boots. The former is of most interest to Lubbock as, in all of his travels, he has never known what is worn under the outer clothing of ice-age hunters. In the case of the Zhokhov people it is stitched bird skins – just as Victorian Lubbock had described for the more recent peoples of the Arctic. Such inner jackets are made following the same pattern as the outer and with evident knowledge about the particular insulating effects of different types of feathers. He recognises the use of swan under-belly in some parts, and complete skins of eider ducks in others.

Stitched bird skins turned inside-out are also used for slippers worn inside the boots. The boots themselves are made from either reindeer or polar bear fur; soles are turned up around the side of the foot and stitched to ankle pieces which have straps attached and are sewn with a single central seam. Lubbock notices that the boots with polar-bear soles are principally used for stalking game, when it is essential to be as quiet as possible upon the snow.

Lubbock is fortunate to see such clothing being made. We lack any direct evidence for how the Zhokhov people dressed, but we do know sufficient about life at Zhokhov to be confident that clothing of this type was essential. To hunt polar bears and reindeer in the Arctic one needs insulation from the cold, especially when standing or sitting quite motionless while waiting for game; clothing must also allow sudden, energetic and precise movement for when the prey comes within range.

Not all of Lubbock's time is spent within the village. He frequently joins the groups that leave each day to travel across the tundra for different tasks. Fresh water has to be collected in bladder-skin bags from a spring about two kilometres away. Driftwood is gathered from the shore to use for house repairs, implements and fuel. During such trips the Zhokhov people are always on the lookout for animal bones, tusks, shed antlers and any other potentially useful items. All are collected, often with no specific purpose in mind. The village is littered with piles of such material, the dwellings cluttered with the bric-à-brac that nature provides.

As well as accompanying such trips Lubbock goes hunting with the men and boys. The summer is coming to an end, and with it their seasonal settlement at Zhokhov.[20] The villagers had arrived in the spring, following the herds of reindeer and the immense flocks of birds that come to nest upon the Arctic shore. Whereas summer had begun with a sudden burst of Arctic life, winter now approaches with a slow and quiet dying-away. The nights are lengthening and people know that a permanent darkness will soon arrive. The geese have already flown and the few reindeer that remain will soon be retreating south to avoid the Arctic winter. The Zhokhov people will follow, being as closely tied to the rhythms of nature as the animals themselves. But not quite yet. Drifts have accumulated with the new snowfalls and she-bears are now searching for sites to make their winter dens. It is time to hunt the polar bear.

The bears are well known; the Zhokhov people seem able to identify each one, knowing her age, where she had denned before, how many offspring she has produced, and even her personality. After a shortage of food over a period of several days, a decision is made to hunt a particular she-bear that has recently returned. This bear is familiar to all and the hunt begins with reminiscences about her life – times when she had been seen stalking seals on ice floes and gathering pawfuls of berries. The hunters recall seeing her the previous spring when she had sat with her cubs enjoying the sun after months in her winter den. The hunters set out from the village on foot and cross the hills to the fractured ice sheets of the northern coast. She is spotted in the water – an ivory-white head gliding through glassy blackness. Lubbock lies flat and perfectly still with the hunters as the bear effortlessly lifts her great bulk on to the ice. She takes a couple of steps and shakes herself; sea water whirls off in flat sheets amidst a fountain of spray. She raises her head and looks directly towards the hunters with questioning small, dark eyes. But any scent or movement that she had sensed must have been blown away. The great white bear begins to meander carelessly along the ice.

Lubbock has never seen a more beautiful beast. He remains lost in admiration as the hunters begin their stalk, departing silently with their bows and arrows. Lubbock lets them go, happy to miss this particular lesson in ice-age life.

The partly butchered carcass is brought back to the village where Lubbock watches its dismemberment until the head is tossed to the waiting dogs. With that, he leaves the Zhokhov people to whatever work and feast will follow. They will soon leave the village, only to return the following spring, as they have done for as long as anyone can recall. Such visits will only end when the peninsula is breached by the sea and the Zhokhov hills became one of many islands in the Arctic Ocean. The village will be forgotten until the year of 1989 when Vladimir Pitul'ko arrives to dig in this most unlikely place of human habitation.

SOUTH ASIA

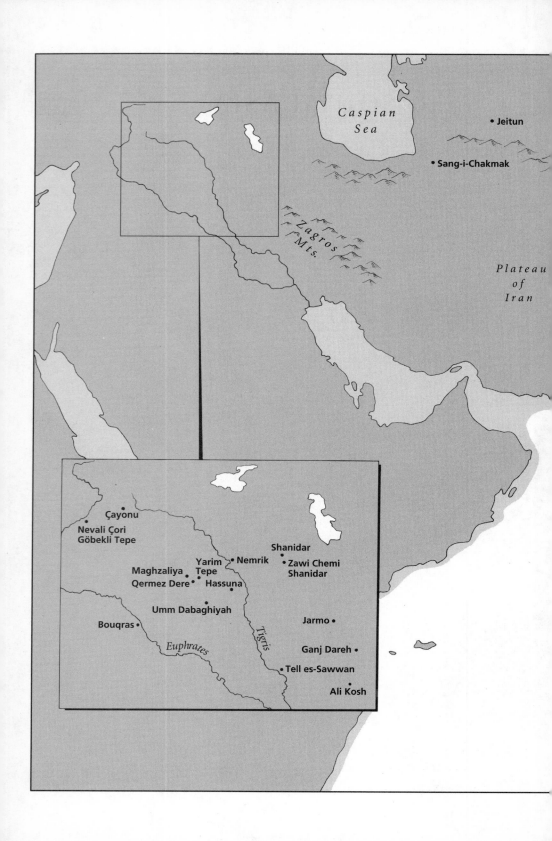

Caspian Sea

• Jeitun

• Sang-i-Chakmak

Zagros Mts.

Plateau of Iran

Çayönu •

Nevali Çori
Göbekli Tepe

Shanidar •

Yarim
Tepe • Nemrik

• Zawi Chemi
Shanidar

Maghzaliya •

Qermez Dere • • Hassuna

Umm Dabaghiyah •

Bouqras •

Euphrates

Tigris

Jarmo •

Ganj Dareh •

• Tell es-Sawwan

Ali Kosh •

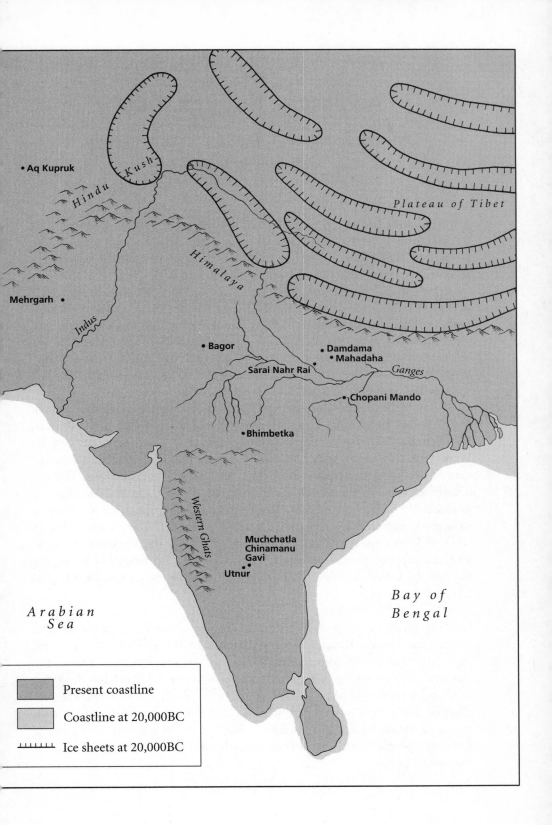

Aq Kupruk

Hindu

Kush

Mehrgarh •

Indus

Himalaya

Plateau of Tibet

• Bagor

Sarai Nahr Rai

• Damdama
• Mahadaha

Ganges

• Chopani Mando

•Bhimbetka

Western Ghats

Muchchatla
Chinamanu
Gavi
•
Utnur

*Arabian
Sea*

*Bay of
Bengal*

Present coastline

Coastline at 20,000BC

Ice sheets at 20,000BC

42

A Passage through India

Indian rock art and villages on the Ganges Plain,
20,000–8500 BC

John Lubbock begins his journey through the prehistory of southern Asia by standing in the rear of Muchchatla Chintamanu Gavi, one of the Kurnool Caves of central India. The brilliant patch of daylight that marks its entrance dazzles his eyes. The date is 17,000 BC.

As he approaches the light he hears voices and then briefly sees a number of bobbing silhouetted forms. But before he reaches them, the hunters have gathered their few belongings and left, disappearing into the woodland that surrounds the cave. Lubbock looks at what they have left behind: a few rocks around still-hot ashes, a scatter of greasy flint flakes and the unwanted parts of a small butchered deer, its head and hoofs. A pile of guts lies just outside the cave next to a patch of bloodstained ground.

As Lubbock wonders which way the hunters might have gone, a thick fog descends; he gives up hope of following and sits alone upon the floor of Muchchatla Chintamanu Gavi. Taking *Prehistoric Times* from his bag, he searches in vain for a passage on Indian archaeology, only finding a description of the 'modern savages' of Ceylon (Sri Lanka) – the Veddahs. There is a brief account of their huts made from bark and their skills at stalking game; a Mr Bailey is cited who 'thinks it would be impossible to conceive of a more barbarous race'. As if to distance himself from such views, in the very next sentence Victorian Lubbock describes the Veddahs as a kind and affectionate people.[1] Modern Lubbock looks up from his book; the fog has thickened and he decides to remain within the cave until it begins to clear.

Fleeting glimpses of people shrouded in fog convey the sense of our limited knowledge about ice-age settlement in the Indian subcontinent, especially that which comes after the last glacial maximum of 20,000 BC. Scatters of stone artefacts, assumed to date between the LGM and the spurt of global warming at 9600 BC, are widespread, providing an archaeological glimpse into people's lives. But there are few radiocarbon dates, no known traces of dwellings and no burials. From the whole subcontinent there is just one single Late Pleistocene hearth and very few collections of butchered bones.

*

With the exception of an extended coastal plain on its west, the topography of India at 20,000 BC was much the same as it is today. In the far north rose the heavily glaciated Himalayan mountain chain. Its great river systems drained into the Indus and the Ganges that flowed across vast alluvial plains. These merged in the northwest to form the Thar desert, where strong winds and extreme aridity created immense sand sheets and dunes. Ostriches thrived in such conditions but many other animals had to leave when ice-age conditions became severe. The landscapes remained dry far beyond the desert zone itself. Lake levels were low and rivers cut deep channels; with few trees and plants to hold the soil in place, erosion was severe.

The hills that sweep in great arcs across central India were covered in grassland with pockets of swamp and forest in the valleys. Their southern slopes leading to the Deccan plateau and the hills on either side of southern India – the Eastern and Western Ghats – were covered in woodland, probably little different to that of the present day. We know about some of the animals that lived within these varied habitats because their fossils have been recovered from river deposits: wild cattle and deer, rhino and boar, a variety of monkeys, snakes and small mammals. The hills of the far south were thickly forested, as were those of Sri Lanka that might have been joined to the mainland at the LGM.

The distribution of sites shows that people were living in many environmental settings throughout the continent during the turbulent ten millennia of climate change that brought the ice age to its close. They camped on sand dunes in the northwest, sometimes turning ostrich-egg shells into decorated beads;[2] they were drawn to the banks of any rivers that continued to flow and lakes that retained their water. Caves in central and southern India provided shelter, while campsites were made within the grasslands, woods and forests. The tools left behind are typical for ice-age hunters: nodules of chert, jasper and quartzite turned into flakes and blades, scrapers and arrowheads.[3] In Sri Lanka, however, the ice-age hunters had adopted microliths as the most effective use of stone, even before the time of the LGM.[4]

Much of their lifestyles is hidden from us so we must, in the absence of evidence itself, assume that these South Asian ice-age hunters also had tools, clothing and dwellings made from wood, bone, bark, fibres, hides, feathers and other materials that have left no trace. As elsewhere in the world where the archaeology is sparse, one is tempted to look at more recent hunter-gatherers to add greater substance to the otherwise vague picture of prehistoric life – just as Victorian John Lubbock had done when writing *Prehistoric Times*. The temptation is especially strong in India where so many people have lived by hunting and gathering into recent times. And hence Indian archaeologists such as V. N. Misra of Deccan College, Poona, have tried to lift the ice-age fog by using accounts of people such as the

Kanjars, hunter-gatherers of the Ganga valley in Uttar Pradesh, to interpret the archaeological remains.[5] Rather than just describing the size and shape of stone blades, Misra speculates about the use of hunting nets and baskets made from cane, about animal skins turned into drums and those of monitor lizards made into shoes. The risk, of course, is that the fog is lifted not to reveal the past, but simply the present imposed on a time to which it does not belong.

Archaeological study of the Kurnool Caves, found in the limestone crags of the Eastern Ghats in Andhra Pradesh state, began in 1884 when Robert Bruce Foote excavated the so-called Charnel-house. Foote, who was employed by the Geological Survey of India, undertook pioneering archaeological work especially in the south of the country where he found the first Pleistocene-aged stone implements. He introduced the terms 'Palaeolithic' and 'Neolithic' into Indian archaeology;[6] one must assume, therefore, that he had read John Lubbock's *Prehistoric Times* in which they were first coined. Foote's work was followed by that of his son who excavated two more caves, known intriguingly as 'Purgatory' and 'the Cathedral'. The sediments in all three were more than ten metres deep; although just one stone artefact was found, animal bones were abundant throughout.[7]

Foote believed that human hands had worked a great many of the bones. He describes finding barbed harpoons, arrow-heads, awls and knives of similarly elegant designs to those discovered by Lartet and Christy in the ice-age caves of France. Foote had little idea of how old such tools might have been; he suggested that the occupants of the Kurnool Caves had been at a 'low stage of civilisation'.

M. L. Krishna Murty of Deccan College began new excavations of the caves in the early 1970s.[8] He tackled Muchchatla Chintamanu Gavi and found similar bone-packed deposits, together with large quantities of stone artefacts. With the improved understanding of animal fauna that had arisen since Foote's time, it was now evident that many of the bones came from animals that were only present in Andhra Pradesh before the ice age had reached its close.

Murty believed that the bones, coming from a variety of carnivores, herbivores and small game, had all arrived in the cave by human hand, presumably while encased in meat and fat. Like Foote, he also thought that many had been shaped into tools. Both men's conclusions are open to doubt. None of the bone 'artefacts' illustrated in Murty's report have a clearly imposed form – certainly nothing to compare with the fine harpoons and carvings from ice-age France. And as Foote's collections have been lost, his claims cannot be appraised. Breakages caused by carnivore-gnawing, trampling and simple decay, can easily cause bones to look as if human hands have worked them. This leaves the stone blades, a hearth made with limestone blocks dating to between 17,000 and 14,000 BC, and a few burnt bones, as the only definite evidence of human activity close to the LGM. So even at Muchchatla Chintamanu Gavi we gain little more than a hint of what life was like in ice-age India.[9]

It was not until 9600 BC that the fog had lifted sufficiently for Lubbock to think it worth while to leave the cave. This coincides with the rapid global warming that brought the ice age to an end and accelerated the pace of environmental change that had begun soon after the LGM. Unfortunately, archaeologists have as yet gained little specific detail on the precise pattern of change that occurred in India, being unable to go beyond generalities about an overall increase in rainfall and the establishment of a vegetation little different to that of today – or rather, which existed before India's extensive deforestation.[10]

Lubbock travels northwards along animal paths and riverbanks. He passes many types of tree quite new to him – some are heavy with scarlet fruit, others have huge stems and roots that hang from branches to create cloister-like pillars and arches. There are feathery mimosas and acacias. Within the forest he sees many deer, some with spotted coats and others with spiky horns, wild boar, monkeys and rhino. All seem to be thriving in the warm, wet Holocene world, as are the crickets and cicadas whose constant chirping fills the sultry air – air that becomes hotter as the year passes from spring to summer.[11]

The modern rhythmical pattern of the Indian monsoon became established once the Holocene began: a relatively cold and dry start to the year, increasing temperatures through March to their peak in June, and then the arrival of the rains in late summer. Lubbock is crossing the Deccan plateau when he experiences his first Indian monsoon. For days the sky has been lurid, with heavy rain-charged clouds. When they begin to discharge torrents of drenching rain, Lubbock shelters in a cave to watch the dry streambed below become a great rushing sea of turbid water. Trees are uprooted, tons of earth and rock are whirled along, unlucky animals washed away. Thunder rolls around the sky as it is torn apart by lightning.

Archaeologists must assume that many other people also sought shelter from the monsoons of the early Holocene, as archaeological sites after 9600 BC are relatively abundant compared to those of the ice age. While this partly reflects better presentation and ease of discovery, the human population is likely to have risen substantially once the ice-age droughts came to an end. People continued to inhabit the same varied environments as their ice-age ancestors but were also able to settle upon newly available riverbanks and lakeshores, and within scrubland that had previously been desert.[12] But their presence is still indicated by little more than scatters of worked stone. As in so many other regions of the world, microliths become prevalent, most likely reflecting a more varied diet and a reliance on local stone.[13] Only on very rare occasions are the artefact scatters accompanied by collections of animal bones, traces of dwellings or human burials.[14] As in Europe, archaeologists refer to those who created such sites as Mesolithic hunter-gatherers.[15]

On a hot and dusty summer's day in 9000 BC Lubbock climbs into the hills now known as the Western Vindhyas. From one low summit he sees another topped by a line of turret-like stone boulders that rise above the trees. This striking hill is known as Bhimbetka; Lubbock finds its slopes covered by thick, thorny woodland through which there are many tiny paths. Some were made by wild pigs and deer and can only be crawled along; others have been cleared beyond head-height, the branches cut neatly with stone blades.[16]

The paths lead between small rockshelters that dot the hillside, gouged from its soft sandstone by millennia of wind and rain. Others are found below fallen boulders which balance precariously on rocky outcrops. Further paths lead to groves of fruit trees or muddy pools surrounded by animal tracks and human footprints.

After following a trail, Lubbock finds himself in a shelter where an artist is at work – the first he has seen since leaving northern Australia. The wall provides a rough surface, a few metres across and entirely open to daylight – quite unlike the deep underground cave walls that were painted in France at the LGM. A hunting scene is unfolding, but whether it is a myth, a memory or a wish is quite unclear. Eight stick-like and seemingly nude figures are already in place; two have armbands with tassels; one either wears a head-dress or has long flowing plaits. Most look male and a few are evidently so; others have wider hips and larger buttocks.

All the figures are busy; three of them are in a line, the first stalking prey with a bow and arrow, the second carrying small game from a pole across his shoulders, and the third, a woman, with baskets. Near by there is another group who bend, crouch and twist, perhaps while dancing in a circle. Further figures are scattered around, holding sticks and bags; one lies on the ground.

The artist takes his brush and begins to paint a deer immediately next to the hunter with the bow. With a few deft strokes, it is running across the rock-face with a swollen body, and then the tiny figure of its unborn young is painted inside. Lubbock moves closer and looks at the paint pots: dried and hollowed gourds, one containing a dark red paint, another black and a third white. Nearby are nodules of coloured rock which have been scraped into the gourds, the pigment then mixed with oily tree-sap to make a sticky paint. Some sticks and stone flakes lie on the ground, along with several brushes. As Lubbock watches, the painter reaches for one, dips its fine hairs into a pot of red and begins a new line upon the wall. But this is too thin and faint for his liking, the brush too soft. And so the artist takes a stick, pounds one end with a stone hammer and scrapes away the pith to leave a fan of stiff fibres. With this and a thicker paint he completes his line – the bold figure of a buffalo twice the size of the pregnant deer.

Bhimbetka has the greatest concentration of rock art in the whole of India, no less than 133 painted rockshelters and at least another hundred from which the paintings may have eroded away. This hill, with its distinctive pillars of stone is one of seven in the Western Vindhyas, across which more than four hundred painted rock-faces have been found. The date at which the paintings were made is open to debate – as is so frequently the case with rock art throughout the world. The local people attribute them to evil spirits – much as the Aborigines of Arnhem Land believe their 'Dynamic Figures' were painted by the mythical Mimi people – so the rock-faces of Bhimbetka were certainly painted before the time of living memory. Unfortunately, no attempt has been made to date the Bhimbetka paintings by taking carbon from the pigment itself, as has been done successfully in ice-age Europe. But circumstantial evidence suggests that many were made in the Early Holocene, at least by 8000 BC.

The most persuasive evidence comes from excavation. During the 1970s several rockshelters were dug to reveal a predominance of Mesolithic debris – stone artefacts, domestic refuse and a few buried bodies. Excavations by V. N. Misra of Deccan College in a rockshelter known as IIIF-23 revealed that it had been first occupied during the Late Pleistocene by people who left a collection of quartzite tools behind. Its Mesolithic occupants had used a larger array of tools, including microliths and querns, the latter reflecting the new-found importance of plant foods in the Holocene woodland. They paved its floor, built a wall within the cave and, as nodules of red and yellow ochre were found within the rubbish, most likely painted its walls.[17] Such pigments have been found in several Mesolithic deposits on Bhimbetka and leave little doubt that the Mesolithic people created many of the cave's paintings. Neolithic and later peoples seem to have hardly used it at all.

A second line of evidence comes from the paintings themselves. Yashodhar Mathpal of Deccan College has described them in exhaustive detail and identified two themes.[18] The first and most prominent is hunting and gathering – paintings of deer and boar hunts, of people collecting honey, dancing, beating drums, and a wide variety of jumping, running and leaping animals. The animals are typical of the surrounding forest – boar, deer, buffalo, monkeys and an assortment of smaller game; several are painted with their unborn young inside. The second theme differs in both subject matter and style: men riding or controlling horses and elephants, often armed with metal swords and shields. Some engage in warfare, others form royal processions. These paintings lack the vivacity of the hunter-gatherers and wild animals. None of the pictures relate to agriculture or animal herding – images readily seen elsewhere in India with the depiction of the distinctive zebu, the humped cattle.

Mathpal reasonably concludes that the first theme was the work of Early Holocene hunter-gatherers who lived in the hills either for all or part of the year. The second theme may have also been that of hunter-gatherers, but ones who lived in relatively recent times and had seen soldiers and royalty within towns and cities on the plains.

Mathpal tried to discover the motivation behind the artists' work. In contrast to those of ice-age Europe, the Bhimbetka paintings were made in places quite readily seen by all – a public rather than a private art. Its animals and people seem to be of the earthly rather than the supernatural world. For Mathpal, the paintings provide 'a record of the varied animal life which shared the forest environment with the prehistoric people, and of the various facets – economic and social – of the life of these people'. There is no reason, he suggests, to look for esoteric explanations for Bhimbetka's art.[18]

At daybreak Lubbock is on the summit of Bhimbetka. He climbs on to the pillars of rock so artfully sculptured by nature's hand and looks across a broad, flat valley towards the north. It is blanketed by a thick and vibrant woodland, with brilliant patches of red and orange from flowering trees that seem to have captured the sunset of the night before. He descends into the valley and once again travels through an exotic forest, finding shade below immense fig trees that look and sound like aviaries. The short, sharp whistles of golden orioles and the screeching of equally vibrant Indian rollers pierce the mixed melodies from insects and birds.

Lubbock continues travelling north, now on the flat alluvial plains of the River Ganges. Some trees are huge, both hardwoods, such as ebony and teak, and those with heavy loads of fruit; he passes through immense swathes of bamboo and crosses rocky ridges that rise abruptly from the plain. Signs of human activity are plentiful: remnants of fireplaces that suggest overnight hunting camps and clusters of stone along riverbanks that look too ordered to have been positioned by nature alone. Lubbock finds the still-warm carcass of a deer, its leg caught in a snare and death seeming to have ended a long and exhausting struggle. Other signs are also present: the fresh tracks of a tiger, the dung of elephant and rhino.

People start appearing – parties of women digging tubers, men inspecting deer tracks and checking snares. Lubbock travels with them, hitching rides on their canoes across the Ganges and other rivers, until he draws near to his next destination. A well-worn path then takes him to a hunter-gatherer village at 8500 BC.

He finds a dozen tent-shaped huts built on raised ground at the confluence of two small rivers. Their pitched roofs are made from stout branches and brushwood; each has a circular clay-lined pit containing ashes or burnt bone. Sitting by the nearest hut, Lubbock surveys the village and finds it similar to many others he has seen on his global travels. The hut floors are well swept but elsewhere the ground is littered with the material of hunter-gatherer life: piles of firewood, grinding stones, pegged-out skins. Something, however, is missing: those large piles of wasted stone flakes so often seen at hunter-gatherer camps elsewhere. The settlement looks deserted, except for a scraggy dog that is sniffing around and a flock of crows picking at a pile of bones. But inside one dwelling, Lubbock finds a young man, perhaps aged eighteen or twenty, lying upon its floor and seemingly in pain. One of his arms is deformed and he sweats profusely although the afternoon is cool and dry. All he wears is a loincloth and a white pendant around his neck.

Children running into the camp chase away the crows and announce the arrival of people from the forest. The adults who follow are physically big, looking strong and healthy. Some carry bundles of firewood, others have baskets with vegetables dug from the forest floor. One man has a deer draped across his shoulders, another carries an enormous white and weathered bone. On returning to her hut, a woman – presumably the mother – attends to the man on the floor, wiping his sweat with soft leaves and helping him to the fire which a young girl – his sister – stokes with dry wood.

Feeling like an intruder in the mother's grief, Lubbock steps outside again, and finds the other women grinding seeds, and the deer already being skinned. A quiver of arrows now stands against one of the hut walls. They are tipped with microliths almost identical to those he has seen at Azraq, Star Carr, Zhokhov and so many other places in the prehistoric world. But these are particularly small in size; Lubbock appreciates why when he sees the tiny pebbles being used as cores. Stone is evidently precious in this village – which explains the absence of knapping debris. Large points have to be made from bone, such as that scavenged from an elephant carcass which Lubbock had seen being carried into the village.

He follows a couple of the older children who head towards the river. They check fishing lines and nets and need Lubbock's help to haul a captured turtle to the riverbank. Together they drag it back to the camp alive and are shown how to slit its throat. When dusk arrives, Lubbock joins the family of the man who is ill while they share their food. When divided between all present, their portion of the roasted deer provides a mere morsel for each; all that Lubbock can sneak is a little marrow from a broken bone. He waits for some turtle meat but none arrives. They mainly eat coarse plants – pounded, roasted and mixed to a gruel in wooden bowls. The addition of honey makes it palatable but chewing is tough work and everybody finishes by picking their teeth with splinters of bone.

*

Damdama, as this Mesolithic site on the Ganges plain is known today, was discovered in 1978 close to the village of Warikalan and excavated until 1982 by J. N. Pal and his colleagues from Allahabad University.[20] Along with Mahadaha and Sarai-Nahar Rai, excavated in the early 1970s, it is one of three relatively well preserved Mesolithic settlements on the plain, now almost entirely cleared of its ancient forest. As both human and animal bones were eroding from the ground, these sites had become part of local mythology – Damdama and Mahadaha were believed to be where ancient warriors had been buried. The word 'Damdama', however, has a more prosaic origin: it means the sound which emanated from the ground when struck.

That may have been due to the richness of the archaeological remains below the surface. Damdama was found to have 1.5 metres of occupation deposits, containing large quantities of microliths and other stone tools, grinding and hammer-stones, charred plant remains and animal bones. Small pits and holes marked where posts had once stood to support walls and roofs; compacted floors were found along with fireplaces and many clay-lined pits. The dwellings may have been tent-like and thatched in design – as used by the recent Kanjars of the Ganga valley – or perhaps simple constructions from leaves and grass like those of the Pandaram people of southern India.

The deposits at the nearby sites of Mahadaha and Sarai-Nahar Rai, both located on the banks of horseshoe-shaped lakes, were almost as rich, contrasting dramatically with Early Holocene sites from elsewhere. With woods full of game and edible plants, and lakes brimming with fish and turtles, this was evidently a favoured locality. For although it was originally supposed that the Holocene hunter-gatherers had spent most of their year in the rocky Vindhyas, only visiting the Ganges plain for food and water during the summer months, it now appears that they had opted for a settled and sedentary way of life.

Studies of the excavated animal bones have shown a diverse range of species and that wild pigs, deer and possibly other game had been killed throughout the year.[21] Moreover, the bones of the bandicoot rat were found at Mahadaha and Damdama. This is a commensal animal – it cannot live without a constant supply of human waste to feed upon – and hence its presence has been used to argue for a permanent human presence in the same way as that of mice and sparrow remains at the Natufian sites of western Asia.[22]

Sedentism is further indicated by the eighty burials uncovered at the three sites – many more remain unexcavated. Most contained a single individual, almost always stretched out on its back with the head tilted to one side. The graves had mainly been dug close to the pit-hearths by the huts, suggesting that families kept their dead within their homes.

The skeletal remains provide some useful insight into social life, health and diet. About the same number of males and females were buried, with a possible bias towards the males. Most were quite young, suggesting that few people survived beyond the age of thirty-five. Children were rare. J. N. Pal – the excavator of Damdama – suggested that the very young had been buried outside the village. The same may have been the case with adults dying from an infectious disease, traces of which were rare in those buried between the fireplaces and hearths. Teeth were heavily worn, indicating a diet dominated by coarse plant material, and often carried tiny grooves reflecting habitual tooth-picking. Many teeth had hypoplasias: horizontal lines in the enamel showing periods of nutritional stress when young. But as almost all the people buried had acquired a substantial stature,[23] this does not appear to have inhibited growth.

Grave goods were scarce. Although a few contained arroweads, pendants and beads, nobody at Damdama, Sarai Nahar Rai or Mahadaha seemed to be particularly wealthy or to have been given a more impressive burial than others. The overall impression is a healthy population with few, if any, social distinctions. But just as Lubbock has seen elsewhere, social tensions are prone to arise among sedentary hunter-gatherers. This might explain the three skeletons from Sarai Nahar Rai with arrow-heads embedded in their ribs, hips and arm bones.[24]

Lubbock remains at Damdama for the autumn and winter months. When the monsoon arrives, the rivers flood and Damdama becomes an island within an extensive shallow lake. Once the waters subside Lubbock joins a party who trek southwards for 100 kilometres into the Vindhyas to find nodules of stone. On their return the young man with the deformed arm has died, his body remaining in the cave and already drained of blood. A grave is dug beside the fireplace where he had slowly withered away. Lubbock watches the burial ritual with little understanding: a fire is lit within the grave itself and left to burn out before the desiccated body is laid upon the hot ash, along with two arrow-heads and his ivory pendant. He is covered and left, only to be exposed when J. N. Pal excavates what he will describe as Grave VIII in AD 1974, recording that 'the left humerus presented some pathological deformity'.[25]

After a spring departure, Lubbock begins a journey westwards, heading towards the Indus valley where, for the first time since his travels in Europe, he will enter the world of farming.

In 8500 BC domesticated plants and animals were quite unknown to the people of Damdama; they had abundant supplies of wild foods and continued living as hunter-gatherers long into the Holocene. Lubbock had found them similar to several other groups he had visited during his travels – those of Uenohara in Japan, of Koster in North America and Skatelholm in Sweden. All became sedentary for at least part of the year when surrounded by abundant and diverse resources, and all used their dead to signify ownership of the land. But what Lubbock could not have anticipated is that the occupants of the Ganges plain would survive as hunter-gatherers long after those in Japan and North America had adopted a farming way of life.[26]

43

A Long Walk Across the Hindu Kush

Early farming in South and Central Asia; the domestication of cotton, 7500–5000 BC

Five adults, four children, three dogs and a flock of goats emerge from the wooded hills that mark what is today the end of the Bolan Pass in west Pakistan. It is 7500 BC and as Lubbock watches from his resting place by a river, the party of travellers search for a level area on which to dump the many bags and bedrolls they carry. A woman gently lays down her baby which had travelled wrapped tightly to its mother's body. Dusk is also arriving and this family looks exhausted after their journey from the west. Quite where they have come from Lubbock never discovers; but their goats and the bag that splits open to spill its barley seed announces them as the very first farmers on the Indus plains.[1] As people and animals alike quench their thirst, the region is set on a new historical course. Within 5,000 years the cities of Harappa and Mohenjo-Daro will be flourishing as centres of the Indus civilisation.

Lubbock remains seated to watch the gradual transformation of their camping site into a farming village. A second family of economic migrants arrive from the Bolan Pass, and then another. Woodland is cleared and barley sown in the fertile soils that are annually replenished with silt from winter flooding of the Bolan River. The riverbank provides clay for the bricks of rectangular houses and storage rooms; babies are born and the old die; harvests are good and more land is brought into cultivation.

Lubbock leaves his seat in 7000 BC, breaking through the dense mat of grass and shrubs that has bound him to the floor. He wades across freezing and fast-flowing waters to have a closer look at the cluster of buildings that now stand where twenty generations ago the first arrivals had dumped their bags. This is Mehrgarh, a farming village with more than a hundred inhabitants and the earliest known settlement of its type in southern Asia.[2]

Today, the archaeological remains of Mehrgarh are spread across several sites close to the Bolan River on the Kachi plain of Baluchistan – a parched landscape in the westernmost province of Pakistan that experiences the highest summer temperatures in the whole of southern Asia. The sites accumulated over a 4,000-year period as new settlements were established following the complete or partial abandonment of earlier ones. Throughout this time, the Bolan River kept changing its course; deserted dwellings became buried beneath its sediments and then exposed again as a new change of course cut through its deposits of silt and sand.

It was by one such shift of the river that the earliest settlement at Mehrgarh was revealed: 10 metres of superimposed mud-brick walls. Archaeologists discovered the site in the early 1970s, since when the French Archaeological Mission in Pakistan and the Pakistan Department of Archaeology have undertaken excavation. Jean-François Jarrige is the leading figure, having now excavated at Mehrgarh and its adjacent sites for almost thirty years.[3] The date of the original settlement remains unclear, but by 7000 BC several multi-roomed rectangular mud-brick houses with square storerooms were positioned on the riverbank. They were separated from each other by courtyards where most of the domestic work was done and beneath which the dead were buried. Initial finds of grinding stones and flint blades with the characteristic shine that comes from prolonged cutting of cereals, suggested a farming settlement; confirmation of this was soon obtained from a source similar to that which had first identified rice cultivation in the Yangtze valley.

The earliest people of Mehrgarh had mixed clay with chaff – the otherwise discarded waste from threshing – when making mud bricks. Although the walls they built later collapsed, became buried below new walls and then alluvium, were eroded by river water and finally excavated by archaeologists, the bricks still contained plant impressions – the chaff itself having almost entirely decayed. These were examined by Lorenzo Constantini of the National Museum of Oriental Art in Rome, a specialist on early plant remains who works with Jarrige. He identified several varieties of domesticated wheat and – in much larger quantities – barley. Wild plant foods had also been gathered from Mehrgarh; along with the cereals, Constantini identified the seeds of the plum-like jujube fruit and date stones. Such fruits suggest that the Kachi plain had been considerably wetter than it is today.

The only known archaeological remains in this region prior to Mehrgarh are scatters of microliths. These were left behind by hunter-gatherers who appear to have been neither cultivating wild plants nor living in permanent settlements.[4] And so the archaeological history of Baluchistan contrasts sharply with that of western Asia where the first farmers were preceded by village-based hunter-gatherers who lived in villages and cultivated wild cereals. We must conclude that farming arrived on the Indus plain as a ready-made package of wheat, barley, goats and mud-brick architecture, one brought by economic migrants from the west. The Bolan Pass seems the most likely point of arrival, this having been a route-way for traders and travellers throughout historic times.[5]

Migrations eastward from western Asia to the Indus plains are more difficult to explain than those westwards into Europe, as they involved crossing the immense Iranian plateau before fertile soils were found. But it should come as no surprise that people were prepared to make such journeys – this history has already recounted the remarkable travels of ice-age hunters through the Americas, Australia and the Arctic to reach the far corners of the earth. The migrant Neolithic farmers were simply following in a long tradition of *Homo sapiens*; they were incorrigibly curious about new lands and economically bold.

As Lubbock approaches the buildings of Mehrgarh in 7000 BC he notices penned animals other than goats – mainly the young calves of zebu, the local wild cattle that have humped backs, unlike those from western Asia.

A burial is taking place and one of the courtyards is crowded with people who circle a pit dug into its floor. Lubbock manages to squeeze to the front and sees the body of a young man positioned with knees tucked to his chest in a shallow grave. The dead man wears a red cloth shroud and a string of seashells around his neck. Having seen so many burials throughout the prehistoric world, Lubbock is more interested in looking at the people around him. Many are also wearing shells and he recognises some as dentalium – the tube-like shells that were so valued during the Natufian in western Asia and which he had also seen at Gönnersdorf in ice-age Europe. Their teeth are also rather striking as they are stained an unpleasant yellowish brown.

A priest-like figure nods to an assistant who comes forward dragging five young goats tugging at their leash. One by one they are held aloft; each has its throat slit and is drained of blood into bitumen-sealed baskets. The carcasses are placed at the dead man's feet. One of the blood-brimming baskets is placed within the grave. And then the man and goats are buried and the floor repaired with clay.

Burial within houses and courtyards is no longer a novelty for Lubbock. Many other features of Mehrgarh also have a familiar feel. As he explores the town he finds the same range of activities and daily rhythms, the same sounds and smells, as in the towns of western Asia which were also dependent upon cereals and goats. Just like at Jericho and 'Ain Ghazal, an assortment of wooden bowls, stone vessels and baskets take the place of pottery. But the stone artefacts – arrow points, knife blades, hide-scraping tools – are closer to those used by the hunter-gatherers who are still living on the Indus plains in 7000 BC. As both peoples rely on quartz nodules from the river-bed for their raw material, and as both go hunting for local game, this is hardly surprising. The hunter-gatherer population, however, has already felt the impact of the incoming farmers as many of their adolescent females have been taken for wives. The young women were quite willing to abandon their hunter-gatherer life for the perceived economic security of farming.

Lubbock's attention is suddenly drawn to heated voices from inside a house near by. He enters and squats behind two men sitting cross-legged upon the floor of its single room. One is dressed in a black woollen cloak and scarf quite different to the white and brown clothing worn at Mehrgarh. He has a pile of bright blue beads and is evidently a visiting trader. The other runs his fingers through the seashells that he keeps hidden within a leather pouch. The room is dingy and the air fetid. A smoky clay oven burns in a corner, above which hangs part of a butchered deer. Baskets, stone bowls and an assortment of hoes, digging sticks and other clutter are stacked against the walls. A woman sits upon a pile of hides and rush mats, breast-feeding her child while watching the bartering.

The deal takes several hours to complete. It is frequently interrupted by servings of herb tea, made by dropping hot stones from the oven into bowls of water and dried green leaves. Agreement is eventually reached long after nightfall. Bread and venison are shared, followed by milk drunk from wooden beakers. The man, his wife and child, the trader and Lubbock all sleep within the single room, completely filling its floor. When the trader rises at dawn, and departs to climb the Bolan Pass, Lubbock feels compelled to follow him, glad to escape the child that had cried throughout the night.

Lubbock's visit to Mehrgarh has been too brief for him to appreciate its arts and crafts; neither did he have time to witness its economic growth. He missed, for instance, the stylised clay figurines of seated people and animals that are found within some houses; while he saw the penned zebu calves, he was unable to appreciate their significance for the future economy of the town.

When Jean-François Jarrige and his colleagues examined the animal bones in successive layers of the archaeological deposit they found that those of cattle and sheep became progressively smaller, while those of goat and gazelle remained largely unchanged.[6] This indicated that the local wild sheep and humped cattle had slowly become domesticated, while gazelle remained wild throughout the town's history – although their numbers evidently fell as their bones become increasingly scarce. The gradual switch from a dependency on wild game to domesticated animals, especially cattle, is also reflected in the far smaller number of microliths – and hence hunting weapons – found in the later deposits of the town.

There were many burials at Mehrgarh. Most were found below the courtyards and contained a variety of grave-goods – quite unlike those of the hunter-gatherers at Damdama. Polished stone axes, elegant flint blades, stone vessels, nodules of ochre and polished stone beads were all placed with the dead. Several beads were made from turquoise and a few from lapis lazuli which had most likely originated far to the north in modern-day Afghanistan. Conversely, the seashells of Mehrgarh had come from the Arabian shore, 500 kilometres to the south. Some of the excavated bones were tinted red, suggesting that bodies had been covered by painted shrouds.

As the town expanded, a formal cemetery was created containing at least

150 burials. Many graves were now constructed as underground tombs, with bodies being placed in subterranean chambers divided by low mud-brick walls. These walls were periodically dismantled so that a new body could be placed within the chamber, requiring existing bones to be shifted aside. The wall was then rebuilt and the tomb buried once again. The appearance of such tombs must reflect the increasing importance of family ties but with what consequences for daily life, it is hard to know.

To date, little information on health and diet has been gleaned from the bones.[7] A dental study found the teeth of the Mehrgarh people to be similar to those of the indigenous Mesolithic people of southern Asia by being noticeably large. This appears to challenge the idea that their ancestors were immigrant farmers from the west rather than local people who had simply adopted the idea and means of farming. Most Neolithic farmers had poor dental health, due partly to a diet of coarse plant foods invariably mixed with grit from the grinding process, and partly due to the large quantity of carbohydrates they consumed that caused decay. But caries were practically absent among the Mehrgarh people, their teeth being as healthy as those of hunter-gatherers. This appears to have been due to the fluoride that was naturally present in the river water. This reduced decay. But it caused yellow and brown staining on their teeth.

One of the funerary chambers, dating to around 5500 BC, had contained an adult male lying on his side with legs flexed backward and a young child, approximately one or two years old, at his feet. Next to the adult's left wrist were eight copper beads which had once formed a bracelet. As such metal beads were only found in one other Neolithic burial at Mehrgarh, he must have been an extraordinarily wealthy and important person. Microscopic analysis showed that each bead had been made by beating and heating copper ore into a thin sheet which had then been rolled around a narrow rod. Substantial corrosion prevented a detailed technological study of the beads; yet this turned out to be a blessing as the corrosion had led to the preservation of something quite remarkable inside one of the beads – a piece of cotton.[8]

Christophe Moulherat and his colleagues at the Centre de Recherche et de Restauration des Musées de France made this astounding find. When one of the beads was cut in half, vegetable fibres were found – the remnants of the thread that had once strung the beads. These had survived because organic compounds had been replaced by metallic salts arising from corrosion of the copper. A section of fibre 5 millimetres square was isolated and covered with a fine layer of gold to allow a scanning electron microscope to reveal its structure. To make additional microscopic observations, the fibres had to be encased in resin and polished with a diamond paste.

After further microscopic study, the fibres were unquestionably identified as cotton; it was, in fact, a bundle of both unripe and ripe fibres that had been wound together to make a thread, these being differentiated by the thickness of their cell walls. As such, this copper bead contained the earliest known use of cotton in the world by at least a thousand years. The next earliest was also found at Mehrgarh: a collection of cotton seeds discovered amidst charred wheat and barley grains outside one of its mud-brick rooms.

Moulherat was unable to determine whether the cotton fibres at Mehrgarh came from wild or domesticated plants; but he strongly suspects the latter. Constantini thinks so too in light of the cotton seeds being found with domesticated cereals in what had likely been a storage area. It appears that the Mehrgarh farmers had been cultivating cotton not only for its fibres but also for its oil-rich seed.

Cotton is today the most important fibre crop in the world, cultivated in more than forty countries. More than fifty different species are known, all classified as members of the genus *Gossypium*. Only four of these are cultivated, each of which appears to have evolved quite independently, in a different part of the world. *Gossypium hirsutum* is the most widely grown species and is thought to have originated from its wild progenitors in Meso-America; a second New World domesticated cotton, *G. barbadense*, arose in South America. The most widespread African cotton is *G. herbaceum* which probably originated in South Africa as a likely ancestor has been found growing as an indigenous element in its open grasslands and forests. The fourth species, *G. arboreum*, is thought to have originated somewhere between India and eastern Africa.

Up until the Mehgarh discoveries, it was assumed that the domestication of *G. arboreum* occurred during the time of the Indus civilisation, not earlier than 2500 BC. But we should not be surprised if the farmers of this region had already been cultivating cotton at 5500 BC; we know that farmers of the Jordan valley, who had a similar economy and technology to those at Mehrgarh, had been making fabrics since at least 8000 BC. The evidence for that came from an unlikely source – the tiny cave of Nahal Hemar, located far from any known settlement. But even that now seems a mundane discovery compared with the use of gold leaf and diamond paste to reveal traces of cotton within a corroded copper bead.

By 5500 BC the occupied buildings of Mehrgarh were situated 200 metres from its original setting. Cattle had become the dominant animal, possibly being used for ploughing, transport and milk, as well as providing meat. Other developments included the production of pottery. This first appears in the form of rather fine vessels – pear-shaped, red-painted jars with outward-curving rims. Stone vessels and bitumen-covered baskets were evidently still catering for everyday needs; the new pottery seems most appropriate for display and impressing visitors. Perhaps it was used for drinking milk.

Mehrgarh continued to expand for several thousand years, repeatedly shifting its position on the Kachi plain and laying the foundations for the Indus civilisation. Jarrige's excavations have revealed a remarkable sequence of development. By 4000 BC, coarse pottery had been introduced for daily needs and become wheel-thrown for mass production; bow-drills were now tipped with green jasper for turning a variety of exotic stones into beads. By 3500 BC, the stylised clay figurines had been replaced by those of a more naturalistic appearance, which, together with pottery, would soon be produced on a massive scale. Clay and bone were used to make stamp seals. These attest not only to the growing importance of trade, but also to a new culture of private ownership, secrecy and wealth. Trade may have been the stimulus for developing copper work, evident from the discovery of crucibles used for smelting. By this date, similar farming towns are found throughout eastern Iran and western Pakistan. From these, the cities of Harappa and Mohenjo-Daro would eventually emerge – the culmination of a process set in train by the origin of farming in western Asia and then by economic migrants who found fertile soils on the Indus plains at 7500 BC.[9]

While these agricultural towns were flourishing, farming spread eastwards into India. But the West Asian 'package' of barley, wheat and goat had reached its environmental limit. Beyond the eastern extent of the Indus plains the climate changed from one with dry summers and wet winters to the precise converse, owing to the Indian monsoon. And so, rather than continuing to spread, selected elements of the Neolithic package were adopted in a piecemeal fashion – just as happened in southern Europe. The indigenous hunter-gatherers of southern Asia also soon began to cultivate their own local plants such as mung beans, urd and millet.

The site of Bagor in Rajasthan illustrates the type of hybrid economy that arose.[10] Located on a sand dune within a savannah-like environment, the site overlooks the Kotari River which only retains water today during the monsoon. It appears to have been a short-term camping site, one most likely used on an annual basis at around 6000 BC. The ground had been paved with slabs of schist, while roughly circular alignments of stone suggest wind-breaks or flimsy huts. There was one burial – an eighteen-year-old female laid on her back with her left arm resting across her body. The artefacts were all Mesolithic in character: large quantities of microliths made from local quartz and chert, together with fragments of grinding stones and pounders. The excavated animal bones came principally from wild cattle, deer, lizards, turtle and fish. But they also include those of domesticated sheep and goat. These may have been from feral animals that had escaped from flocks further west, or those taken by hunter-gatherer raids on farming settlements. Alternatively, the hunter-gatherers themselves might have begun to manage their own small herds.

Central India became an agricultural melting pot, especially from 5000 BC onwards, when domesticated rice began to arrive from southern China.

That, at least, is the most likely scenario for how rice came to be recovered from the site of Chopani Mando on the flood plain of the Belan River below the northern extent of the Vindhya hills.[11] Indigenous domestication of wild rice is another possibility.

The spread of farming to southern India did not occur until 3000 BC and principally took the form of cattle pastoralism. Many Neolithic settlements are known from the tops of granite outcrops across the Deccan plateau but acidic soils have destroyed plant remains and left animal bones extremely scarce. Complementing these sites are numerous 'ash mounds', sometimes located next to a settlement but often isolated within what would have been thick forest. These were formed by the periodic burning of cattle dung within palm-trunk enclosures, once used to protect cattle from wild animals and raiders.

Direct proof of penned cattle comes from hoofprints preserved in the deposits of burnt dung at the site of Utnur. This particular stockade was burnt and then rebuilt several times. In modern India, the burning of similar enclosures is associated with festivities either at the beginning or end of seasonal migrations of cattle to forest browsing grounds. Such fires also have a practical role: cattle are driven through the heat and smoke to kill off parasites, preventing the spread of disease.[12]

Back in 6500 BC, Lubbock's summer-time journey follows the trader from Mehrgarh and takes him through the mountains of Afghanistan. He has to climb over tumbled granite and pass through narrow gorges where thundering rivers suck and tug at boulders while their noise reverberates between canyon walls as if inside a tomb.[13] Such gorges open into wooded valleys edged by banks of scree which provide occasional glimpses of jagged snow-covered peaks. The high valleys are bounded by boulders that mark where glaciers had reached before global warming had made this land habitable to humankind. The trader visits several settlements, each with a patch of bright green sprouting cereals and goats foraging on an adjacent hillside. Some are based around large caves, often with brushwood huts built inside; others have small, oval, mud-brick dwellings roofed with leaves of the giant wild rhubarb that grows profusely in the valley bottoms. Several days are spent at each settlement while the trader exchanges a few of his seashells for coloured stone and renews his friendships. Food and water are swapped for news and gossip from Mehrgarh and the other villages he has passed through.

As Lubbock heads into central Afghanistan, he parts company with the trader to visit a settlement in the north where the high mountains and narrow passes give way to less dramatic but still rugged limestone hills and crags. He arrives at the entrance to a large cave. Two families are living within, along with their goats and dogs; it is dark and musty, the floor littered with debris from preparing food, making tools and clothing. The date is 6250 BC but there are no signs of pottery vessels, use still being made of wooden bowls and wickerwork baskets. Pockets of soil nearby are cultivated for cereals.

The cave's residents are sitting idly in the sun, drinking herb tea and reflecting on the beauty of their world. Lubbock sits with them; he admires the carpet of primulas that spreads around the cave, enjoys the scent of wild roses and the sounds of a nearby river that gushes between mulberry and walnut trees. Here in the heart of Central Asia – some would say at the heart of the world[14] – only the beetles are at work, carrying away goat droppings to their private store.

This particular cave, known locally as Ghar-i-Asp (Horse Cave) and located at Aq Kupruk (the White Bridge) on the terrace of the Balkh River, is one of a small number that has been archaeologically examined in Afghanistan.[15] It was excavated with the nearby Ghar-i-Mar (Snake Cave) by Louis Dupree in 1962 and 1965, working on behalf of the American Museum of Natural History and the National Museum of Afghanistan. Both caves had deep deposits showing near-continuous occupation from soon after the LCM of 20,000 BC into historic times, the uppermost levels containing Islamic glass of the thirteenth century AD. The ice-age occupants had used the cave for hunting ibex, wild goats and deer; they were followed by people with domesticated goats and sheep who later acquired pottery. Copper objects appear in the upper levels and then iron artefacts: many miscellaneous pieces along with knife blades, spear points, bronze bracelets and fragments of a Chinese coin.

Dupree placed the time at which Aq Kupruk's hunters started to become herders at the strikingly early date of about 10,000 BC. He was reliant, however, upon some very questionable identifications of goat bones as belonging to domestic rather than wild animals, together with some equally dubious radiocarbon dates.[16] If correct, it would be the earliest domestication of goats currently known, but we must be cautious. A new study of the Aq Kupruk Caves is required before any conclusions can be drawn. What is clear, however, is that by 6250 BC scattered communities were living throughout the high valleys of central Afghanistan, herding goats and tending small plots of wheat and barley.

After visiting Aq Kupruk, Lubbock continues heading northwest, until he reaches the edge of the mountainous plateau which we call today the Kopet Dag (the Dry Mountain) in modern-day Iran. A sharp drop leads to enormous fans of sediment, at first immensely steep then decreasing to pistachio-covered woodland. Lubbock stands upon its precipitous edge and looks towards the northeast, half-closing his eyes against the icy wind. Beyond the woods a grey savannah pimpled with hills and specks of red, silver and green stretches far into the distance, blending into the yellow of a seemingly infinite sandy desert.

Lubbock follows the scarp edge for another 200 kilometres, until he reaches a point at which he must descend to visit the next settlement in his travels: the farming village of Jeitun.[17] He chooses a steep valley, and clambers down towards the woodland, where fruit trees are laden with pomegranates, apples and pears ripe enough to eat.

A river that meanders between the poppy-covered foothills and dunes at the desert edge takes Lubbock to Jeitun. About twenty mud-brick houses are clustered on a small hill, encased in thick and acrid smoke from the dung being burned as fuel. There is a great deal here to remind him of Mehrgarh and the farming towns in western Asia, although Jeitun is much smaller in size. The houses each have a single rectangular room and are arranged around courtyards with outhouses and storage racks for grain. Lubbock walks around the village, watches a pair of goats being butchered in one courtyard and basket-weaving in another. Grinding stones lie unused but are surrounded by a thick patchwork carpet of coloured husks and chaff.

Pushing aside a hide drape to enter a house, Lubbock finds it hot, smoky and smelly inside. The walls are painted red, the floor no more than beaten earth and trampled ash. A large rectangular hearth burns dung in one corner, with partly-baked bread on its hot clay surround. In the opposite corner, a pile of hides, furs and mats are stacked upon a platform, presumably used for sleeping. In a third, a clay-lined pit is used for storing grain. Shiny-bladed sickles with bone handles hang upon the wall; a basket contains a variety of other stone-bladed tools. Several bowls are stacked upon the floor; Lubbock picks one up – a pottery vessel painted with wavy red lines.

A woman enters, dressed in thick layers of hides and woollens; she wears a necklace of seashells, much like those seen at Mehrgarh, and wraps her head up in a scarf. As she turns the bread, Lubbock notices two clay figurines close to the fire, one a goat, the other a human. But before he can take a closer look, three children giggle and stumble through the draped doorway; they stand patiently until a morsel of half-baked bread is placed within their dirty hands. And then they scarper away.

Lubbock visits several other houses, finding them almost identical in design, although most have plaster floors. As the Jeitun people are at work in the courtyards and surrounding fields, most of the occupants are either very old or very young. Lubbock sees a cluster of men and women by the river which ends just beyond the village in a marsh and goes to investigate. They are making mud bricks, eagerly helped by children who have, of course, coated themselves in mud. Some are digging from the riverbank, others are mixing clay with straw and then shaping it into bricks, each about the size of Lubbock's forearm but a little thicker. The straw is being cut in a nearby field, the ears of wheat having been harvested several weeks before.

That night Lubbock sits within a courtyard as a full moon rises above the mud-brick houses of Jeitun. It is 6000 BC and he imagines what is happening elsewhere in the world at this date in human history. He recalls those living at Damdama and hunting polar bears at Zhokhov in the Arctic; he thinks how canoes might be crossing the Torres Strait and arriving at Skateholm in southern Sweden; how ducks are being trapped at Koster; and finally, of those living face to face with bulls at Çatalhöyük. America, Europe, Australia, North, South, East and West Asia – Lubbock has visited them all. There is just one blank left to fill, one habitable continent in the world that he has yet to visit: Africa.

Jeitun is one of several archaeological sites in the piedmont zone at the base of the Kopet Dag in modern-day Turkmenistan which testify to the cultivation of cereals and herding of goats by 6000 BC. The similarities that Lubbock felt between Jeitun, Mehrgarh and the farming towns of western Asia are real and unsurprising – all have the same economy in similar environmental settings around the rim of the Iranian plateau. And just like the settlement of Mehrgarh, Jeitun raises the problem of whether the first farmers of Turkmenistan were immigrants from the west, indigenous hunter-gatherers who had acquired seed and animals by trade, or had their origins in the hills below the Kopet Dag where wheat and barley were already being cultivated some time before 6000 BC.[18]

Jeitun and its neighbouring sites exist as mounds referred to locally as Kurgans. The first excavations occurred at the turn of the century and demonstrated these to be the accumulated collapsed and weathered remains of mud-brick houses. In the 1950s the first systematic excavations took place at Jeitun, notably by the Soviet archaeologist V. M. Masson. This small mound was situated beyond the piedmont and among the sand dunes of the vast Kara Kum desert. Masson revealed a settlement of at least thirty small, rectangular one-roomed dwellings in the upper portion of the mound, along with hearths, storage areas and courtyards. Although no plant remains were recovered, the same signs of farming as those at Mehrgarh were found: flint sickles with the distinctive gloss from harvesting and impressions of barley and wheat within mud bricks.

Renewed excavations at Jeitun began in 1987 by the Turkmenian archaeologist Kakamurad Kurbansakhatov. In 1989 V. M. Masson invited David Harris from the Institute of Archaeology, London, to apply the latest techniques for extracting plant remains from the archaeological deposits and to recreate the landscape in which the Jeitun people had lived. Working with his colleague Gordon Hillman, Harris recovered grains of wheat and barley, along with those of many wild plants, confirming that Jeitun had become an established farming village by 6000 BC.[19] British involvement continued between 1990 and 1994 when a team of excavators joined those from Russia and Turkmenistan.

This renewed work resulted in a shift away from descriptions of architecture and stone artefacts to those of Jeitun's prehistoric economy and local ecology. But Harris and his colleagues faced a daunting task. Few clues existed about the prehistoric vegetation as excavated plant remains were rare, pollen was absent and the indigenous vegetation has been almost entirely destroyed by millennia of foraging goats. Similarly, modern irrigation schemes have radically altered the course of the Kara Su – the river Lubbock had followed – so that the timing, quantity and whereabouts of water for the Jeitun people remains unclear. Nevertheless, some progress has been made.

The trees and shrubs that still grow within the humid valleys of the Kopet Dag, such as the apples and plums that Lubbock enjoyed, are assumed to have once been more widespread. Woodland dominated by pistachio is thought to have covered the lower hills owing to the survival of climbing plants which are normally exclusively associated with this type of tree. As the rainfall regime at 6000 BC is likely to have been similar to that of today, with an effective summer drought, wheat could only have been grown on soils that held sufficient ground water to tide them through the summer months. Destructive spring floods caused by excessive rainfall and melting ice from the Kopet Dag were another problem facing the farmers of Jeitun. David Harris decided that the only viable fields must have been on the relatively high, flat, salty soils between the dunes, close to, but protected from, the active flood channels of the Kara Su. This was confirmed when Gordon Hillman found the seeds of sea club-rush among the cereal remains – a weed that infests wheat when grown on such soils and that cannot tolerate riverside situations.

Study of the excavated goat mandibles by Tony Legge – whose work on the animal bones of Abu Hureyra and Star Carr we have already encountered – showed that all stages of tooth growth and wear were present. This suggests that animals were killed throughout the year, implying that some people, at least, were permanently resident at Jeitun. As well as tending their herds, the Jeitun people hunted wild goats in the foothills of the Kopet Dag, along with wild boar, hare and fox. But gazelle was their favoured prey. Before the building of the railway that crosses Turkmenistan today, large herds of these animals had migrated seasonally from the mountains and high foothills to winter within the Kara Kum before returning in the spring. If they had done likewise at 6000 BC, Jeitun would have been near perfectly positioned for intercepting the migrating herds.

The recent excavations at Jeitun have failed to find any traces of pre-farming settlements at which hunter-gatherers might have begun to cultivate wild cereals themselves. Indeed, the wild ancestors of the wheat grown at Jeitun are unlikely to have been present in this part of central Asia. And so it seems that, just as in Baluchistan, fully-fledged farmers had arrived in the foothills and steppe that bordered the Kara Kum. To do so they must have descended from the Kopet Dag on to which they, or their ancestors, had climbed from western Asia.

Once again, Lubbock stands on the edge of the Kopet Dag and looks eastwards towards the steppe and desert. Spirals of smoke rise from Jeitun and neighbouring settlements nestled in the foothills and sand dunes far below. He now knows that the tiny patches of green are fields of wheat and their shiny edges the salt marsh glistening in the sun. During the year Lubbock remained at Jeitun he had helped build a new house using mud bricks, participated in the harvesting and threshing of wheat, joined in with the ambushing of gazelle and the collecting of almonds, walnuts and pistachios. Much of the summer was spent at campsites in the hills where the goats were taken to find pasture, leaving few people in the village itself. But now it is time for Lubbock to turn his back on Jeitun and the east; he is eager to reach Africa to complete his global travels.

But first he must return to western Asia, not to the Jordan valley where his travels began, but to the foothills of the Zagros mountains and the plains of Mesopotamia. The date is 6000 BC and the farming villages that once bordered the Tigris and Euphrates have long been replaced by substantial towns – the largest aggregations of people that have so far existed on planet earth.

44

Vultures of the Zagros

The roots of Mesopotamian civilisation, 11,000–9000 BC

The first civilisation of human history arose in Mesopotamia. This was the name of a Roman province lying between the Euphrates and the Tigris rivers, which is now called Iraq. By 'civilisation' I mean an entirely new scale of human society to any that had gone before: monumental architecture, urban centres, extensive trade, industrial production, centralised authority and expansionist tendencies. The Mesopotamian cities appeared at around 3500 BC, along with the invention of writing. While such developments fall outside the time frame of this history, their roots were laid much earlier in time. As from 11,000 BC, succession of remarkable hunter-gatherer settlements, farming villages and towns appear in Mesopotamia, associated with expanding trade networks, innovative technology and new religious ideas. By 6000 BC, Mesopotamia was home to flourishing agricultural communities that were set to create a new type of human experience: urban life.

Athough the first cities arose in the southern plains of Mesopotamia, in the vicinity of modern-day Baghdad, the cultural groundwork was done in the north – a varied landscape of plains, limestone ridges, deep wadis and imposing hills, most notably those known today as the Jebel Sinjar.[1] To their immediate south lies an extensive area of fertile soils, and it was on this so-called Sinjar plain that the first Mesopotamian villages and towns arose. These in turn developed from hunter-gatherer settlements which are found 300 kilometres further east, in the foothills of the Zagros mountains at 11,000 BC.

This is the date at which John Lubbock must begin his Mesopotamian travels. And so when he leaves Jeitun at 6000 BC, heading west to cross the Iranian plateau, time begins to go in reverse. At 7500 BC, he reaches a newly-built village on a small alluvial plain known to us today as Sang-i-Chakmak.[2] When he descends into the western flanks of the Zagros and approaches a hunter-gatherer settlement known today as Zawi Chemi Shanidar, located in the valley of the Greater Zab River, 11,000 BC has arrived.

Five hundred kilometres to the west, the hunter-gatherer village of Abu Hureyra is flourishing by the Euphrates; a further 400 kilometres away the people of 'Ain Mallaha are cutting wild wheat and hunting gazelles in the Mediterranean woodlands. Neither Mehrgarh nor Jeitun exist, nor do

Jericho and Göbekli Tepe: the whole of Asia, the whole world, is once again the sole domain of hunter-gatherers.

Zawi Chemi Shanidar consists of a cluster of brushwood huts, a spread of domestic debris, places for sitting, eating and talking, and a single circular stone structure. This campsite is on a riverbank and close to a spring; it nestles between steep valley walls and below a backdrop of dramatic mountain peaks. Even Lubbock, who has now seen so much of the world, finds it a spectacular setting. Both he and his new, unknowing hosts watch with awe as eagles and vultures circle overhead.

Despite the special beauty of his surroundings, Lubbock finds that life at Zawi Chemi Shanidar is little different to that of many other hunter-gatherer settlements in the prehistoric world. Beyond the valley itself the surrounding landscape is like that he had seen further west – steppe woodland with oak and pistachio. Lubbock spends several days collecting seeds and digging roots, grinding and pounding these into flour and paste using stone mortars similar to those at 'Ain Mallaha. He helps to ambush wild goats and trap wild boar; he accompanies some of the Zawi Chemi Shanidar people on long treks. One of these is 150 kilometres to the south, leaving the Zagros foothills and crossing desert to find a source of bitumen bubbling from the ground. His companions carry heavy bagfuls back to their campsite for lining baskets and securing knife blades into sockets. Another trek of an equal distance is made to the north, into the mountains to meet a party coming from the west with obsidian to exchange.[2]

On his return to Zawi Chemi Shanidar, Lubbock finds that preparations are under way for a dance. As dusk arrives he watches men and women adopting costumes; some tie vast wings to their arms, evidently cut from freshly killed vultures and eagles; others cover themselves in goat hides. A fire is lit and when darkness descends the whole community gathers to watch them perform.

Initially there is nothing but the flames, a slow beating of drums and a goat settled upon the grass. An eagle swoops from the darkness with talons extended; as it twists and turns, the goat runs into the night with the bird in chase. A herd of goats now arrive and quietly graze in the firelight. Having eaten, they cavort around the flames – head-butting, copulating, mothers prancing with their young. The drum beat begins again, this time faster and louder. The eagle returns followed by massive vultures that encircle the goats. The drumbeat quickens, the birds fly faster and the goats begin to panic; they attempt to leap over what has now become a swirling wall of feathers, with claws and hooked beaks ready to tear them apart. The drum-beating is now frenetic and with a final tumultuous strike the eagle attacks. Amid piercing cries it kills a goat and the vultures descend upon the others. And then there is silence – except for the crackle of flames and the panting of costumed human bodies lying exhausted upon the ground.

Zawi Chemi Shanidar means 'the field close to Shanidar' – Shanidar being the name of both a small Kurdish village and a large cave about four kilometres away.[4] The idea that its people had dressed in costumes to mimic vultures, eagles and goats is based on an intriguing discovery at this site. When Ralph Solecki of Columbia University, New York, made his excavations in the 1950s, he uncovered a dense mass of animal bones within a deposit of reddened earth, close to the stone structure. It was initially assumed to be a domestic rubbish dump, but was found to contain goat skulls and bird bones alone. The latter had come from the great bustard, along with various species of eagles and vultures, and were almost entirely restricted to wing bones. Fine slicing marks showed that the wings had been carefully detached from the birds; some had eventually been discarded still intact.[5]

Several bones had come from huge birds, such as bearded vultures, whose wins-span can reach 3 metres in breadth, and white-tailed sea eagles. Quite how such birds were caught, and what their wing bones were doing in a deposit with at least fifteen goat skulls, were not easy questions for Ralph Solecki and Rose, his colleague and wife, to answer. While vultures can occasionally become tame around settlements and hence be captured by using bait, eagles are more challenging – perhaps requiring young birds to be stolen from their nests and then hand-reared.

A ritualistic interpretation for the bone deposit seems likely, not only because of its peculiar contents but in light of discoveries elsewhere. When writing in 1977, Rose Solecki could cite the paintings and sculptures found by James Mellaart at Çatalhöyük in southern Turkey which associated animal skulls with birds of prey. Since then, the sites of Nevali Çori and Göbekli Tepe have been discovered, with further depictions of eagles and vultures, while talons are commonly found at Early Neolithic (PPNA) sites in western Asia. The bird bones from my own excavations in Wadi Faynan, for instance, are dominated by those from buzzards, vultures and eagles. And so there can be little doubt that birds of prey were held in high esteem throughout the Fertile Crescent, most likely having profound symbolic and religious significance. Rose Solecki suspected this in 1977, when she suggested that their wings had been used as costumes during a ritualistic dance at Zawi Chemi Shanidar.

Lubbock wakes beside smouldering ashes. The costumes have been left in a shallow pit near by – goat skulls and skins, bird wings and claws carved from wood. These are reddened by ochre that had rubbed off sweating bodies and which will now colour the earth around the bones. There is nobody to be seen. The sound of pounding from the nearby huts suggests that the dancers and spectators have returned to work – crushing acorns and hunting in the hills. Not that they will have left their sacred world behind: having travelled through prehistory, Lubbock knows there to be no distinction between the sacred and the profane – other than that invented for the modern world alone.

During his hunting and plant-gathering trips around the village, Lubbock had noticed a cave in the crags 4 kilometres to the northwest. He knows that the people of Zawi Chemi Shanidar still use the cave for shelter but has never been inside himself.

In the few hours it takes Lubbock to undertake the rugged climb to reach its entrance, two centuries of prehistoric time elapse, while vultures continue to glide between precipitous mountain peaks. Shanidar Cave, as it is known today, has a large chamber and grinding stones, baskets, hides and a variety of tools clustered on its floor. There are patches of paving and a few piles of cobbles that look as if they demarcate special areas or indicate something buried below. The interior is smelly – a blend of bats, damp animal hides, and the stale remnants of wood smoke.

While Lubbock stands at the entrance to admire the view and enjoy the fresh air, he sees a procession climbing towards the cave and guesses that it comes from Zawi Chemi Shanidar. The line of people approaches slowly, led by a man who carries a young child in his arms. They wear particularly elaborate beads made from bone, teeth and stone and their bodies are painted red.[6] A couple are hobbling, one with the aid of a stick. Lubbock sits upon a boulder within the cave to watch them arrive. The man lays the little boy's body on the floor; it is wrapped in strings of bone beads that almost entirely hide its blue and bloated form. Lubbock looks from face to face and detects signs of illness and disease. One has a wad of leaves once soaked in some glutinous material tied across an ear; another has a swollen jaw and looks to be suffering from severe toothache.

A fire is made on the cave floor. Lubbock listens to the prayers and watches strange poetic movements around the body, perhaps the miming of wild animals and flurries of snow. The man who carried it, presumably the child's father, digs a pit that exposes burnt wood from previous fires in the cave. The body, still clothed in beads, is laid to rest upon a scatter of ash and buried. A moment of silence. And then the people depart, the boy's father being the last to leave.

When Ralph Solecki excavated Shanidar Cave in the 1950s he discovered not only a cemetery of modern humans but also the bones of 50,000-year-old Neanderthals, for which the cave is better known.[7] While the Neanderthal remains were deeply buried below wind-blown sediment and roof-collapse, the cemetery was found just below the surface, a cluster of twenty-six graves together with domestic artefacts and debris similar to those excavated at Zawi Chemi Shanidar. Such similarities and a date of 10,800 BC suggest that the cave and riverside campsite had been used by the same people.[8] Many of the graves contained relatively young adults and children. Several had been buried with beads – one child had 1,500 within its grave, suggesting he had belonged to a family of high status. A further grave was found, isolated from the rest and containing a woman in a box-shaped pit with red ochre and a grinding stone.

Agelonakis Anagnostis analysed the human bones as part of a doctoral study at Columbia University.[9] She found that many of the adults had hypoplasias on their teeth – signs of malnutrition when young. Traces of ear infections and dental inflammations were frequent, as were limb bones that had been either cracked or broken, and signs of degenerative diseases such as arthritis. The bones as a whole had come from a remarkably unhealthy population – those who survived childhood had evidently struggled to reach what we would call middle-age.

This is quite different to the Early Natufian populations of the Jordan valley who appear to have been in a good state of health. Another contrast is the nature of their settlement. Although the presence of a cemetery suggests that Shanidar and the Greater Zab River valley were regularly visited, the absence of substantial stone-built dwellings either near caves or in riverside settlements suggests only temporary, most likely seasonal, occupancy.[10] In this regard the Zawi Chemi Shanidar people, together with those who had occupied the nearby and contemporary sites of Karim Shahir and M'lefaat, were quite unlike the Natufians who lived in permanent villages.[11] To find anything comparable in Mesopotamia, Lubbock has to leave Shanidar Cave and travel eastwards for 200 kilometres to the foothills of the Jebel Sinjar and the enigmatic village of Qermez Dere.

This journey requires Lubbock to cross the River Tigris and trek towards the Sinjar hills. He crosses a dry wilderness covered with spindly shrubs, tufts of grass and scattered trees. Among these lurk game of various kinds: troops of gazelle spring from low cover and bound across the plain, hares follow suit, while bustards with startling speckled plumage and ruffs of long feathers rise squawking from the grass. Herds of wild ass – onager – frequently graze in the distance. Lubbock's journey takes almost a millennium to complete, during which time temperatures fall and rains become less frequent as the Younger Dryas arrives. But its impact is far less severe than in the Jordan valley and Mediterranean lands, where the recurrent droughts force the abandonment of villages as Late Natufian people return to a life on the move.

Qermez Dere comes into sight as Lubbock reaches the summit of a low hill and gains an extensive view across the plain. At its edge he sees a cluster of huts next to the mouth of a shallow valley. From a distance the thatched roofs look very low and on arrival he discovers that these cover four subterranean dwellings accessed by ladders from above. It is late afternoon; work has evidently finished for the day and people sit lazily in scattered groups, some drinking from wooden cups, others seeming to be asleep. Around them is the familiar debris of hunter-gatherer life: grinding stones, piles of knapping debris, fragments of butchered bones and stained soil where blood has soaked away.[12]

Lubbock sits among them, feeling an empathy with their evident enjoyment of the view – southwards across the plain and westwards along the flanks of the rolling Sinjar hills. The only sounds are a gentle chatter of voices and water flowing along a nearby stream. The date is 10,000 BC and although the Younger Dryas is at its height in western Asia and Europe, the people of Qermez Dere are healthy and well fed. They have found an ideal place to live, one between the hills and the plain, each providing their own suite of animals to hunt and plants to gather. From the quantities of husks, stems, stalks and leaves heaped around the grinding stones, Lubbock suspects that 'wild gardens' are near by: stands of wild cereals and lentils that are watered, weeded and kept free of pests.

Aware that the light will soon begin to fade and the subterranean dwellings will then become pitch-dark inside, Lubbock leaves his seat and climbs down a ladder into a single room with plastered walls and floor. It is an odd shape, neither circular nor square, and dominated by four pillars in a row down its centre. Lubbock immediately recalls the pillars he had seen at Nevali Çori when travelling to Çatalhöyük – a village that, along with many others in the Fertile Crescent, has not yet been built.

The pillars at Qermez Dere are about chest-height; Lubbock examines them closely, finding they are made of clay and covered in plaster. Each rises smoothly from the floor and appears to depict human shoulders with abruptly truncated arms. Their surfaces lack decoration but seem to fluoresce in the increasing gloom. Lubbock walks around them, stroking the smooth plaster and pondering the purpose of their rather sensual forms.

Mats made from twisted fibres and luxuriant animal furs cover the floor. One side has a fireplace – several stone slabs around a pit cut through the plaster and containing ashes. The walls are bare, but are evidently cared for as the plaster has been thickly applied, polished and patched. Lubbock wonders what happens within this and the other subterranean rooms of Qermez Dere. They could hardly be more different to the cluttered, dirty and smelly rooms he has so frequently found at hunter-gatherer and early farming settlements throughout the world. He decides to wait and see. And so he gathers a couple of furs and settles down in comfort against a wall, positioning himself directly opposite the ladder from above.

During the next few days – or perhaps it is months, years or even centuries – many people enter the room, sometimes alone or in small groups: children, adults and the elderly. Lubbock soon begins to notice recurrent visitors and physical similarities. He notes postures and patterns of standing, touching and talking that suggest relationships – parent and child, man and wife, siblings, lovers. He guesses that all who come are members of an extended family to whom the dwelling belongs. When it is cold several come and sleep upon its floor, often making a fire in its hearth; when hot, they find shade below its thatch. It is a place where people come to sit quietly and alone or with others, to sing and maybe pray. Sometimes it is used for sex; babies are brought down the ladder for feeding; the sick come here to rest. Occasionally the room is packed for a family feast, or when visitors are being entertained.[13]

These varied uses continue until one spring morning when two women climb down the ladder and start to roll up the mats and furs. These are passed to others waiting outside, after which the women begin to sweep the floor, wipe the walls and polish the pillars, using brushes and leather rags. Only when the room is meticulously clean do they move on to their next task: its deliberate destruction.[14]

The roof is tackled first, timbers and thatch sending a great cloud of dust and dirt into the air as they crash to the floor. Once this is done, the family begins to fill the room with soil, using wooden shovels and baskets – this having been dug some distance away to avoid domestic refuse. After some ten minutes' work, when the collapsed roof timbers and thatch have been covered, one of the older men – whom Lubbock assumes to be the family head – halts the work. He unwraps a parcel and lifts each of its items in turn for all to see before throwing them into the partly buried house. First a large joint of meat – most likely from a wild cow, an animal rarely seen in the vicinity of Qermez Dere. Next, a handful of wild wheat, and then a finely made leather robe. A string of stone beads follows, and finally a selection of bone pins and needles.

When work resumes, the children help by throwing stones and handfuls of dirt into the hole. It continues all day until the room is completely buried, the fill slightly heaped above the surrounding ground. And so, as a final act, everybody jumps up and down to compact the soil – initially with much laughter and then with sagging energy and increasing fatigue.

During the next few days Lubbock watches the other subterranean dwellings destroyed in a similar fashion until all that is left of Qermez Dere are the clusters of querns, baskets and tools, scatters of domestic debris, fireplaces, and several collections of rugs and mats. Some patches of ground are swept clean of stones and kept clear of rubbish and artefacts for peaceful sitting, while a few simple brushwood shelters and windbreaks are hastily erected as protection from the wind and cold.[15] And then life at Qermez Dere continues much as before – except that any chance of privacy has now been lost. So Lubbock accompanies plant-gathering and hunting trips; he helps to clean hides and grind seeds, joins in with singing and dancing; he sleeps with others under the stars.

As the weeks pass he notices that a pile of firewood is gradually accumulating next to a growing collection of stone nodules; these are of gypsum and will be eventually crushed and mixed with water to make plaster. When autumn arrives young trees are felled, stripped of their branches and stored as timber. Grass is cut, for its stalks rather than seed; these are tied into bundles and stacked alongside the wood and stone. Within a few weeks the piles of firewood, gypsum and new roofing material are deemed sufficient. And so work begins on a new set of dwellings.

To Lubbock's surprise, each is built on practically the same spot as before, even though plenty of untouched ground is available near by. An approximate circle is marked out and then digging begins, removing much of the soil that had been so laboriously dumped just a few months ago. The marked lines are followed meticulously; when the old plaster walls are encountered they are simply cut through. Any old timbers and thatch are dumped – as are the objects that had once seemed so precious.

While the new pit is being dug the kilns are burning, rapidly using the store of firewood and reducing the gypsum nodules to powder. Pillars are moulded from clay and erected within the new subterranean room. These are plastered, along with the floor and walls, already prepared with a wash of red-brown clay. The roof is made with new timbers and thatch. Within a few days, the dwelling is complete – looking almost identical to its predecessor. The family gather inside, pleased with their work; Lubbock is left wondering why they had gone to all that trouble. Once again he appreciates the cultural barrier that so frequently intervenes between himself and those he visits on his travels, inhibiting his understanding of the past.

Why did those people of Qermez Dere repeatedly fill in their old dwellings and then construct them anew to the same design on precisely the same spot? Trevor Watkins of Edinburgh University, who excavated the room in which Lubbock had sat trying to discover its function, asked this question. He found that it had been rebuilt on at least two occasions. When backfilled for the last time, presumably just before the village was abandoned, six human crania had been placed upon its floor.

Watkins' excavations took place in 1986–7 in advance of the site's complete destruction by road building and quarrying. To him, Qermez Dere had initially appeared as a low mound adjacent to a deeply cut wadi. The scatters of grinding equipment, stone tools and butchered bones provided no surprises; but the subterranean houses with their fine plaster, pillars, and deliberate burial were different to anything found before.[16]

More than two decades after Watkins completed his work, Klaus Schmidt excavated Göbekli Tepe, located 300 kilometres to the northwest and a few centuries more recent in time. The similarities with Qermez Dere were striking: both sites had subterranean structures containing pillars but lacking in traces of domestic activity; at both sites the structures had been deliberately back-filled. Although those of Göbekli Tepe were on a far larger scale than those of Qermez Dere, having a grandeur that matched their massive pillars and dramatic setting, there is an unquestionable cultural link between the two sites, one that leads to Nevali Çori. Something deeply mysterious lies behind these sites and the societies that made them, something that must hold the key to the origin of the Neolithic world.

The third and last of the Mesopotamian hunter-gatherer settlements that Lubbock visits is also in the Zagros foothills and known today as Nemrik. Stefan Kozlowski of Warsaw University excavated it in conjunction with the Iraqi State Organisation of Antiquities and Heritage as a salvage project prior to the construction of 'Saddam's Dam'.[17] The work took place during the same years that Trevor Watkins was excavating at Qermez Dere, a mere sixty kilometres away on the far side of the River Tigris. The prehistoric occupation of Nemrik and Qermez Dere had overlapped in time, although the earliest dates for Nemrik place it just after 9600 BC. People were still living there almost two thousand years later; by then they had left their hunter-gatherer past behind to become farmers.

Lubbock left Qermez Dere at 9400 BC, after Holocene rain and warmth had arrived. That site would remain occupied for another thousand years until its residents joined, or perhaps created, one of the new farming settlements that had developed on the Sinjar plain by 8000 BC. But such developments are yet to occur as Lubbock treks northeast across a steppe now dotted with groves of ash and walnut, tamarisk and pistachio. In the distance the Zagros mountain slopes have been greened by oak forests and become home to deer, boar and wild cattle.

Nemrik sprawls across the end of a ridge that juts on to a plain; rivers run along gullies on either side, all the way into the River Tigris itself. Lubbock arrives at dawn. A few of its people have already left to go hunting in the hills, others remain sleeping within their circular dwellings – not subterranean, as at Qermez Dere, but with standing walls. There are eight of them, located in two clusters and surrounded by paved yards. These are evidently the working areas as Lubbock sees the familiar range of grinding stones, mortars and flint waste scattered across their slabs. Fireplaces and blackened stone bowls suggest that the yards are also used for cooking. They seem to be shared between the houses, as does a large and stinking refuse pit.

Lubbock looks closely at the sun-dried mud bricks from which each dwelling has been built – little different to those he had seen at Jericho and Jeitun. The entrance is hung with thick hides; pushing these aside, he enters a gloomy interior. It is partitioned by four posts, arranged in a square and supporting timber beams – the walls of mud bricks could never have supported such a weight.[18] The roof itself is made of latticed branches, interwoven with straw and plastered with clay. Raised platforms made from wood and clay have been built against the wall. These are beds and each supports a sleeping body covered with hide. Opposite, there is a cluster of domestic items and debris surrounding an embedded grinding stone. Between the sleeping and working areas of the house there are higher and narrower platforms that look like benches. Most of the floor is covered with mats and hides; the rest is trampled earth, especially around a stone slab that partially covers a pit. Lubbock peers down a hole and sees a skull staring back at him.

The detailed information about the structure and design of this dwelling derives from its excellent preservation and the quality of its excavation. Kozlowski, who called it 'House 1A', found charred lumps of clay from its collapsed roof which carried impressions of the lattice-work and straw. There were pits inside the remnants of walls where posts had stood. He also found the burial pit, an area where artefacts were concentrated, and the platforms that he thought were beds and benches.

Houses of this type were constructed at Nemrik around 9000 BC when its inhabitants lived by hunting and gathering. Kozlowski's excavations recovered the bones of wild animals and birds, along with the claws from crayfish which had been caught in the adjacent rivers. Although plant remains were scarce, traces of cereals, peas, lentils and vetch were found – all presumed to be from wild plants. Only towards the end of the lengthy occupation at Nemrik – at a date of around 8000 BC – were domestic varieties grown around the village. By that time the houses had taken on a more rectangular form, but practically all other aspects of life remained the same.

Kozlowski also made some more elaborate finds – one of which makes Lubbock recall the start of his Mesopotamian travels. He is still inside the house and intrigued by a series of small clay sculptures and carved stone pebbles that have been placed in little niches around the walls. Some are difficult to identify – one looks like the head of wild boar, another might be a goat and a third a human figure. Lubbock spends little time with these, prefering a far more impressive carving in stone. It rests within his palm; Lubbock enjoys its weight and feel as he runs his fingers along the smooth neck, around the eye-sockets and a sharp edge that forms a beak. It is the head of a vulture – just one of several such carvings prominently displayed at Nemrik two thousand years after people had worn eagle and vulture wings and swooped to kill at Zawi Chemi Shanidar in the valley of the Greater Zab.[19]

45

Approaching Civilisation in Mesopotamia

The development of towns and trade, 8500–6000 BC

On leaving Nemrik, Lubbock spent one thousand years travelling in northern Mesopotamia, observing the development of farming villages. Soon after 8000 BC he also watched family groups climbing the Zagros foothills to search for new grazing and arable lands on the Iranian plateau, the first steps in the spread of farming to South and Central Asia that would lead to Mehrgarh and Jeitun. But most people remained upon the Sinjar plain, cultivating the land and building more dwellings while unwittingly laying the foundations for a new type of urban world.

Lubbock began by looping back on himself, crossing the Tigris and then following a small tributary river as it wound its way through low oak-covered hills on the flanks of the Sinjar hills. The river valley was picturesque, with periodically steep, canyon-like sides. It was just after one such gorge that Lubbock found the village that we now know as Maghzaliyah[1] – ten rectangular and multi-roomed houses partly surrounded by what appeared to be a defensive wall. He was no more than twelve kilometres from the now abandoned site of Qermez Dere, whose debris had long ago been washed away by the rain and buried in the dirt.

Lubbock arrived at Maghzaliyah in the spring of 8000 BC, just as wheat was being harvested from small pockets of suitable soil around the village, each squeezed between outcrops of rock. It was cut with sickles made from obsidian blades and the grain stored in barrel-shaped clay bins. He discovered that obsidian was the main type of stone in use, no longer acquired by long treks from home, as at Zawi Chemi Shanidar, but from traders who arrived at Maghzaliyah from the north. Clay was extensively used for building, modelling figurines and making ovens; although pots were moulded into shape, no firing occurred to make brittle ceramic vessels. Lubbock doubted that this was from ignorance of the technique; it seemed more likely that plates, bowls and jars made of stone, wood and wickerwork were quite sufficient for people's needs.

Maghzaliyah was discovered by the Russian archaeologist Nikolai Ottovich Bader in the spring of 1977: a steeply conical tell, partly cut into on its northern edge by a road and destroyed on the eastern side by the Abra River. Otherwise the site was undisturbed. Bader's excavation revealed its dwellings to have had clay walls on stone foundations with thatched roofs and paved floors, both coated with plaster – fragments of which contained the imprints of reed matting. During the village's five-hundred-year history, between eight and ten houses had existed at any one time, suggesting a population of around a hundred people. But as each house had remained standing for no more than fifty years, and was rebuilt upon the same spot, the site was densely packed with architectural features. The animal bones and plant remains that Bader excavated indicated that the inhabitants of Maghzaliyah had been equally dependent upon wild and domestic foods; they hunted onagers on the steppe while managing flocks of sheep and cultivating fields of wheat.

Maghzaliyah was surrounded by a wall of massive stone slabs for much of its existence, possibly as a defence against wild animals, raiding parties or organised assaults by people from other villages – although no traces of violence were found on the bones of the dead. Adults and infants had been buried together in stone-lined tombs clustered within a discrete area of the settlement; these suggest family groups rather than warrior graves.[2] Perhaps the wall had not been for defence at all, but a means to delimit the world of human culture from that of nature, or even to distinguish the occupants as farmers from the hunter-gatherers that lived outside.

The origin of Maghzaliyah largely parallels that of early farming villages and small towns in the Jordan valley and beside the Euphrates, such as Beidha, 'Ain Ghazal and Bouqras. The descendants of the hunter-gatherer-cultivators who lived at Zawi Chemi Shanidar, Qermez Dere and Nemrik appear to have adopted cereal farming as soon as seed-grain became available. Whether domesticated cereals had originated in the north – perhaps at, or around, Çayönü – or in the west – perhaps at Jericho – remains as unclear as it is unimportant. Once present, the domesticated seed-grain had spread just as rapidly throughout northern Mesopotamia as it had in the Jordan valley, before being taken westwards into Europe and eastwards into central and southern Asia.

Maghzaliyah was just one of several farming villages that developed in the lands around the Tigris and in the Zagros foothills as soon as such grain became available. One of the first to be discovered is known as Jarmo, excavated by the American archaeologist Robert Braidwood during the 1950s.[3] Located 300 kilometres southeast of Maghzaliyah, Jarmo had about thirty houses at its peak, most of which were built with stone foundations and thick clay walls. Some of these had a striking similarity to contemporary houses built at Çayönü, 600 kilometres to the northwest. Further farming villages developed throughout the Zagros foothills. Two are known to the south of Jarmo: Ganj Dareh in the Kermanshah valley and Ali Kosh on the Deh Luran plains of modern-day Iran. Both have been claimed as having particularly early domesticated goats.[4]

This proliferation and rapid growth of farming settlements in northern Mesopotamia closely parallels that in the Jordan valley up until around 6500 BC. But after that date the two regions have an entirely different history. As Lubbock discovered at 'Ain Ghazal, a combination of farming-induced environmental degradation and renewed droughts drove some of its inhabitants into a nomadic lifestyle and others back to tiny villages scattered across the steppe. The town was abandoned and left to decay. While the same story of cultural collapse occurred throughout the Jordan valley, the precise opposite happened in the lands between the Euphrates and the Tigris. The soils, topography and climate of Mesopotamia were far more favourable to intensive cultivation. Rather than the economic boom and bust of the Jordan valley, its farming settlements proliferated in size and number. Sustained eonomic growth occurred, leading to that new scale of human society that we call 'civilisation'.

Umm Dabaghiyah, a settlement to the immediate south of the Sinjar plain, was one outcome of that economic growth.[5] It is here that Lubbock arrives in 7500 BC. To do so, he has crossed the fertile plain and found Umm Dabaghiyah's mud-brick buildings surounded by a dry steppe with no signs of cultivated crops. It looks quite different to anywhere else in the prehistoric world. While all other Neolithic settlements have been higgledy-piggledy affairs, with new houses and rooms added in a haphazard fashion, the whole of Umm Dabaghiyah looks to have been planned and built at once. It smells as bad, if not worse, than any other settlement Lubbock has visited – a rank stench of animal grease, fat, flesh and innards that lingers around its people and which has permeated its clay walls and plaster floors.

Exploring the settlement, Lubbock finds distinct areas for living, working and storage. Entry into any of the rectangular rooms is by an outside staircase on to its roof and then down an internal ladder, similar to those he found at Çatalhöyük. There are paintings on the walls – but thankfully no depictions of bulls, decapitations or sculptures of split female breasts. Instead, the paintings illustrate scenes of onager being stampeded into nets.

While only a few of the houses have these paintings, all are laid out in the same way: a small single room with plastered floors and walls. Although following a rigid plan, many appear hastily built by inexperienced hands as numerous repairs to crumbling clay walls and collapsing roofs are in progress. Each room has a hearth against a wall, surrounded by a kerb; they share chimneys with large clay ovens attached to the outside walls. Floors are covered by rush mats; there are stone bowls, wicker baskets and coarse pottery vessels lying untidily around the hearths. Overall, the houses lack a 'homely' feel; they are basic and functional, and seem more like workmen's quarters than family dwellings.

Two blocks of storerooms form the centrepiece of the settlement. These

Sir John Lubbock, Lord Avebury, from a drawing by George Richmond, R.A., in 1867.

Flint Scraper and microliths, c. 20,000 BC, from Wadi el-Uwaynid 14, Jordan.

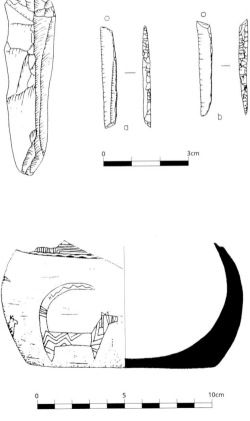

Stone bowl, c. 11,000 BC, from Hallan Çemi Tepesi, Turkey.

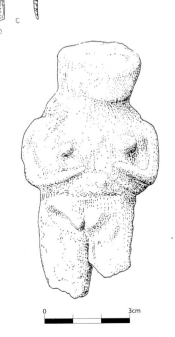

Female statuette, c. 9300 BC, from Mureybet, Syria.

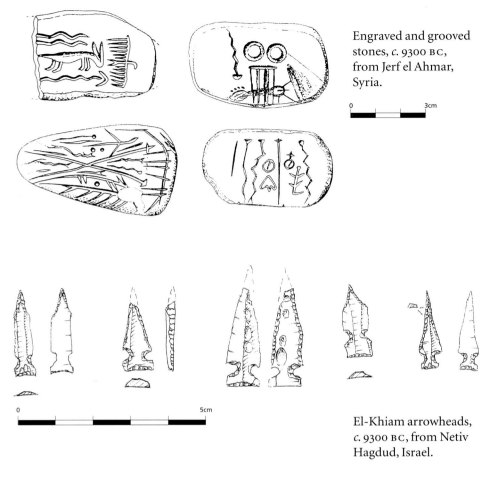

Engraved and grooved stones, *c.* 9300 BC, from Jerf el Ahmar, Syria.

0   3cm

El-Khiam arrowheads, *c.* 9300 BC, from Netiv Hagdud, Israel.

0   5cm

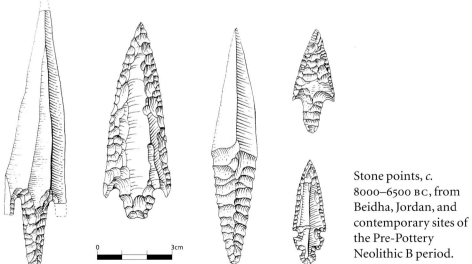

Stone points, *c.* 8000–6500 BC, from Beidha, Jordan, and contemporary sites of the Pre-Pottery Neolithic B period.

0   3cm

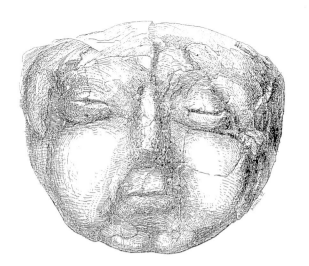

Modelled plaster skull, *c.* 7000 BC, from Kfar Hahoresh, Israel.

Painted fresco, *c.* 7000 BC, from Çatalhöyük, Turkey.

0   50cm

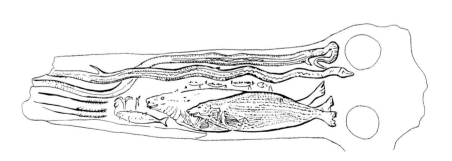

0   5cm

The Montgaudier Baton, France, *c.* 17,000 BC.

Engraved stone slab, *c.* 12,500 BC, showing four schematised women, one carrying a child, Gönnersdorf, Germany.

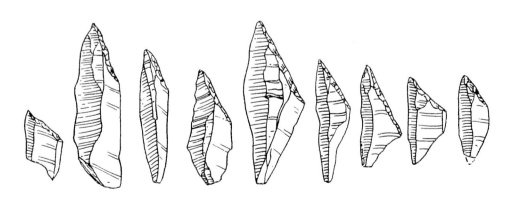

Microliths, *c.* 8800 BC, from Starr Carr, England.

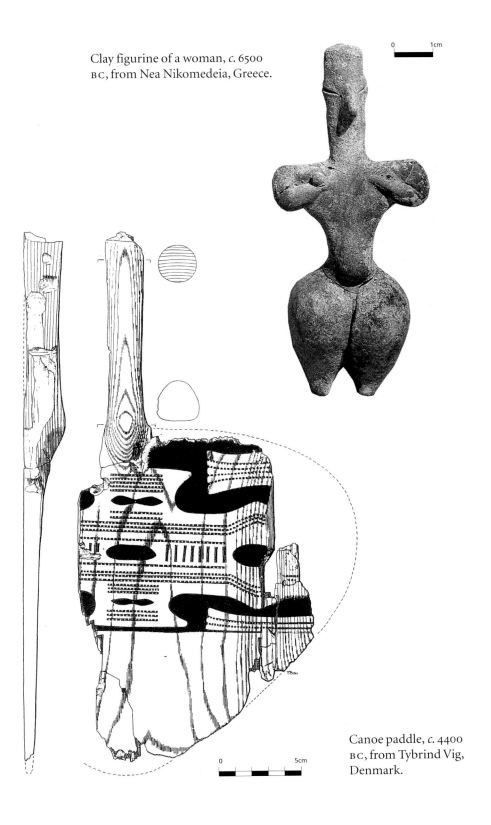

Clay figurine of a woman, *c.* 6500 BC, from Nea Nikomedeia, Greece.

0   1cm

Canoe paddle, *c.* 4400 BC, from Tybrind Vig, Denmark.

0   5cm

Folsom point,
c. 9000 BC, as found
in North America.

Clovis point,
c. 10,500 BC, from
Lehner site,
Arizona, USA.

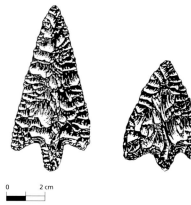

Triangular spear points, possibly
dating to 10,000 BC, from the Tapajós
river, Amazon.

Spear points from the Horner site, used
for bison hunting at *c.* 7000 BC.

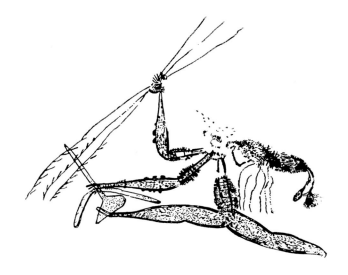

Male figure in the 'Dynamic' style, probably dating earlier than 10,000 BC, painted on a rock face in Arnhem Land, Australia. The hunter wears a long, tasselled ceremonial head-dress and holds barbed spears, a boomerang and a hafted stone axe.

Painted scene, c. 8000 BC, from Bhimbekta, India.

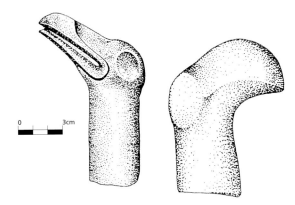

Heads of raptors carved in stone, c. 9000 BC, from Nemrik, Iraq.

Fragments of wall paintings, *c.* 7500 BC, from Umm Dabaghiyah, Iraq.

0   10 cm

Recent San rock paintings of a curing dance. The shaman kneels in the centre with his hands on the recumbent patient.

3cm

Rock engraving of long-horned cattle, dating prior to 3000 BC, from the Libyan Sahara.

are split into many small chambers which have been built with much better materials and techniques than the dwellings, having thick clay walls with internal buttresses and plaster footings. Most are entirely enclosed, lacking doors and with roofs made from hides and brushwood. When walking between the roofs – the thick walls provide a pathway – Lubbock widens tiny gaps in the roofing material to peer inside these stores, which are secure from rodents and the weather. In one he sees a pile of folded hides, in another a stack of salted meat, in a third bundles of onager tail hairs, and in a fourth hoofs and gazelle horns heaped in corners. Another has baskets of grain, roots and tubers. The rooms containing animal products are evidently becoming stocked during the hunting season, while those with stored vegetables are being slowly depleted.

Back in the courtyard a party of hunters have arrived with several onager carcasses. These have been caught in just the manner illustrated on the walls – by stampeding a small herd into nets that were suddenly raised from the ground to block their flight. Lubbock watches as the onagers are skinned; their hides are scraped clean of fat and sinews and then placed within clay-lined basins of salted water. Those from a previous kill have already been soaked and are draped across a series of low clay walls which form drying racks. The newly skinned carcasses are butchered with flint blades and basalt axes. Most joints will be rubbed with salt and left to dry before being salted again and put into store; the remainder will be roasted that night and eaten with some of the dwindling vegetable supplies.

Umm Dabaghiyah was discovered and excavated during the early 1970s by Diana Kirkbride while she was Director of the British School of Archaeology in Iraq. By this time, she had already excavated Beidha in southern Jordan; this led her to expect that Umm Dabaghiyah would be a similar type of farming village. As the site was a small tell, Kirkbride decided to attempt a 'total excavation'. Although that wasn't achieved, many buildings were exposed, several of which had been rebuilt on four separate occasions during five hundred years of occupation.

After three seasons of excavation, Kirkbride began to question the idea of a farming village. Her doubts were motivated by the finds themselves – the storerooms, plaster-lined basins and low walls of no structural value – along with what she didn't find: substantial traces of agricultural activity.

The near-desert environment in which Umm Dabaghiyah was located also now struck her as being 'singularly uninviting from the point of view of Stone Age settlement'.[6] The region was almost devoid of water; that available in a nearby swamp would have been saturated by salt owing to underlying deposits of gypsum. Such deposits inhibited tree growth, making wood for fuel and tools extremely scarce, if not entirely absent. The local flint had a coarse grain and many defects. It appeared that the inhabitants of Umm Dabaghiyah were denied almost all the key resources of Stone Age life. All except one: animals to hunt.

When Kirkbride excavated the site, the fauna of northern Mesopotamia was relatively impoverished, consisting of foxes, hares, desert rats and jerboas. In 7500 BC, however, onager and gazelle had grazed the plains, while wild boar and goats foraged in the distant Sinjar hills. Bones from onagers dominated those excavated from Umm Dabaghiyah, while fragments of wall paintings depicted hunting – animals surrounded by what Kirkbride had thought were hooks for holding nets.

When faced with her archaeological evidence and the bleakness of the site's contemporary landscape, Kirkbride changed her mind about Umm Dabaghiyah. Rather than being a small farming village it became a 'trading outpost', one specialising in onager and gazelle – a small satellite, she thought, to some nearby and as yet undiscovered 'magnificent' Çatalhöyük-like town.[7] Kirkbride suggested that Umm Dabaghiyah was a settlement of 'middlemen'. She envisaged desert-based hunter-gatherers bringing animal carcasses to the settlement and receiving obsidian, cereal grain and other commodities in return; these had, Kirkbride supposed, already been acquired by the middlemen of Umm Dabaghiyah by trading meat, hide, hair and horn at the as yet undiscovered town.

Kirkbride's interpretation has not been supported by further fieldwork. Archaeological surveys – most notably that by a Soviet Archaeological Expedition of 1969–80 – failed to discover that town, finding a scattering of small agricultural settlements in its place, one of which was Maghzaliyah. Some of these villages did indeed develop into the type of substantial town that Kirkbride imagined, but only after Umm Dabaghiyah had fallen into decay.

Consequently, my scenario for Lubbock's visit was a little different from that proposed by Kirkbride: Umm Dabaghiyah as the seasonal residence of specialist hunters from one or more farming settlements who arrived with supplies of stone, vegetables and cereal grain, and who killed and processed the animals themselves. I envisage them returning at the end of the hunting season with their produce, perhaps partly carried by tame wild asses.[8] The hair, hides, hoofs, meat and fat would have been exchanged for grain and stone, partly with other local inhabitants and partly with visiting traders.

Whichever scenario is correct, the specialised nature of Umm Dabaghiyah indicates a scale of organisation greater than that found in any previous Neolithic society. It illustrates the key role that trade and exchange were playing by 7500 BC in the gradual transition of farming villages into the towns that precipitated the urban centres of the first civilisation.

The Soviet Archaeological Expedition had been invited to undertake a programme of survey and excavation by the Iraqi government and made a remarkable contribution to our understanding of Mesopotamian prehistory.[9]

Before it began in 1969, our knowledge was restricted to the settlement of Jarmo in the Zagros foothills, dating to 8000 BC, and the town of Hassuna on the Sinjar plain, which dated to 6000 BC. Excavated in 1945 by the British archaeologist Seton Lloyd, Hassuna had produced complex, multi-roomed buildings, sophisticated painted pottery and a completely different scale of agriculture, craft activity and trade to that of Jarmo.

The two settlements seemed worlds apart in their culture and economy. Many archaeologists suspected that they were quite unrelated, the Hassuna people having spread into the region from outside, with their culture already formed. Kirkbride's discovery and excavation of Umm Dabaghiyah between 1970 and 1973 placed a settlement chronologically between Jarmo and Hassuna, but it was one quite anomalous to both, with its storeroom architecture and paintings of onager hunts.[10] The Soviet Expedition's extensive programme of survey and excavation on the Sinjar plain found further settlements, some contemporary with, some earlier and some later than Umm Dabaghiyah. When their discoveries were combined with the excavation of Qermez Dere by Trevor Watkins and of Nemrik by Stefan Kozlowski in the late 1980s, a complete sequence of economic development was established. The Hassuna towns had neither arrived on the plain fully fledged, nor derived entirely from the Jarmo-like villages of the Zagros foothills. They had developed from hunter-gatherer and small farming villages on the Sinjar plain itself.[11]

The Soviet Expedition had no difficulty finding sites to excavate – indeed there was an abundance of mounds in northern Mesopotamia. These had been known since Austen Henry Layard, the British diplomat and archaeologist, had travelled through Mesopotamia in the 1840s and brought its archaeology to public attention with his book *Nineveh and its Remains* – strangely unmentioned in Victorian John Lubbock's *Prehistoric Times* of 1865. He described how he had spent one evening in 1843 on the edge of the Sinjar plain watching the approach of night and counting 'above one hundred mounds, throwing their dark and lengthening shadows across the plain'.[12] Three years later he revised his estimate to double that number. When the first systematic archaeological survey of the Sinjar plain was undertaken almost a century later by Seton Lloyd working for Liverpool University, the two hundred mounds were recognised as 'but a small part of a great number which are spread over this once fertile plain'.[13]

One of the mounds excavated by the Soviet Expedition was fifty kilometres north of Umm Dabaghiyah and rose no higher than 2.5 metres above the surrounding plain. This was designated as Tell Sotto and excavated by Nikolai Bader between 1971 and 1974. He found a succession of single and multi-roomed houses showing the growth and then abandonment of a farming village, one that never had more than three or four houses at any one time.[14] As a series of pits large enough to be remnants of subterranean dwellings were found below the foundations of later buildings, the original settlement at Tell Sotto may have been a village much like that of Qermez Dere.

The houses of the first Sotto farmers were rectangular in shape; most had a single room, but one at least had several accessed by a corridor. While the walls of the Maghzaliyah buildings had been made from amorphous lumps of clay, those of Sotto were of sun-dried bricks. Some rooms had evidently been used for domestic tasks as they contained grinding stones, hearths, animal bones, pottery, ovens and racks for drying grain. In other rooms Bader found large pottery vessels, often set into the floor and used for storing grain. Similar vessels were used for another type of storage – that of deceased children whose tiny bodies had been squeezed inside, leaving Bader to find their bones.

Although small in size, Sotto appears to have been a thriving settlement to judge by the artefacts either made by its inhabitants or acquired by exchange: stone bracelets, beads, polished axes and clay figurines. Many of the dead were buried under floors and usually without any items in their graves. One burial, however, had clearly belonged to an extremely wealthy person; it contained a small clay basin with the remnants of a meal, a necklace of exotic stone beads including those of marble and lapis lazuli, and a small copper plate bent into a tube. The tube is one of the first signs of copper work in the world, only matched by a small awl from Maghzaliyah – both of these being a millennium older than the copper beads at Mehrgarh.

While Sotto's population never exceeded thirty or forty, the settlement is likely to have grown rapidly and given rise to several of the new villages that began to dot the Mesopotamian plain after 8000 BC.[15] Some of its inhabitants may have spent the winter season at Umm Dabaghiyah, kept warm by the large fireplaces and ovens. Others may have left Sotto to join a village that developed just two kilometres away and is known to us today as Yarim Tepe.[16] This continued to flourish long after the abandonment of Sotto, with an immense elaboration of architecture and pottery through twelve building levels. The result was a mound with 6 metres of archaeological deposits that was first described by Seton Lloyd in the 1930s, and then excavated by Nikolai Yakovlevich Merpert and Rauf Magomedovich Munchaev, two of Bader's colleagues on the Soviet Expedition.

Lubbock's northward journey from Umm Dabaghiyah was no longer than 40 kilometres but it took almost a millennium to complete – a period in which Maghzaliyah was completely abandoned and the population of Sotto declined. During this short journey Lubbock could see the distant Sinjar hills, furrowed with countless ravines, each marked by dark purple shadows that melted into the evening haze.[17] As he trekked north, arid steppe was replaced by tender grass with scattered scarlet tulips – the first of many spring flowers that would soon decorate the plain. Birds frequently sprang from the grass and Lubbock found several clusters of speckled eggs, laid simply upon the ground without any surrounding nest. He collected some eggs to eat and sat to rest among the tulips, remembering the other times he had sat among flowers on the steppe, once close to Ohalo and once outside Abu Hureyra during his West Asian travels.

Lubbock now sits somewhere quite different and feels disconsolate; he is within a small yard amidst the maze of mud-brick walls and alleys that constitutes Yarim Tepe. The date is 6400 BC, approximately halfway through the town's history, and although Lubbock only arrived a few days ago, he is already keen to leave. The town is bustling with adults attending to domestic chores; children run around in gangs, dogs scavenge rubbish and stray goats wander aimlessly in and out of houses. There are potters, stone craftsmen and weavers at work; right next to Lubbock a resident of Yarim Tepe is arguing with an itinerant trader about the relative worth of goats' wool and obsidian blades.

The noise, the smoke and the all-pervasive stink of human waste makes Lubbock wish to be elsewhere at this date in human history. He thinks of Zhokhov in the Siberian Arctic where he could be surrounded by an expanse of nature rather than the cultural claustrophobia of Yarim Tepe. Who, he thinks, would be a town-dwelling farmer rather than a hunter-gatherer? Having travelled through all but one of the world's continents he knows the answer: almost everyone in the prehistoric world. And yet, he reflects, there is a certain 'buzz' about the town. It is what some archaeologists describe as Mesopotamian civilisation in the making.

As he walks around Yarim Tepe, the pottery vessels being made and used are impressive. They come in a great variety of shapes and sizes – large storage vessels, jars, bowls, plates, beakers and trays. Some have been decorated by adding moulded figures or shapes, much as at Tell Sotto; others are painted with simple geometric motifs, quite different to the complex curved designs seen on the pots of Umm Dabaghiyah and Sotto. But while the pottery is striking, it is the copper work that impresses him most. Lubbock only sees a ring on someone's finger and a copper pendant dangling from a neck; he doesn't discover whether ore was actually smelted in the town or simply hammered into shape.

Yarim Tepe is easily more than twice the size of Sotto and is continuing to expand. Fields of wheat and barley surround its buildings; large flocks of sheep and goat are taken each day to graze on the nearby hills. Such agricultural activity provides surpluses for trade and to support the many craftsmen of the town. During his tour, Lubbock finds that narrow trenches have been dug for the foundations of a new building and lined with reed matting, followed by the partial construction of mud-brick walls. He helps gather broken pottery vessels from around the town and spreads their fragments between the newly built walls as a base for the plaster floor.

Most of the buildings at Yarim Tepe are rectangular structures with multiple rooms, sometimes grouped together to make distinct complexes within the town. Some, however, are quite different. These are round and a few metres across, with clay walls and domed roofs made from a lattice of branches and thatch. Several are dotted throughout the town, either within another building or in the corner of a yard. Lubbock learns the function of at least one such structure when he sees it surrounded by people eager for a view as the partly dismembered parts of a young woman's body are passed through an opening in its thatch and laid upon the floor.[18] Next came an assortment of objects which presumably the woman had owned: a wicker basket, strings of beads, fine stone and pottery vessels, bundles of flowers, the body of a baby goat. When watching this, Lubbock recalls the man at Qermez Dere who had thrown a similar collection of objects into a partly filled dwelling during its destruction, and the man buried with goats at Mehrgarh. Once her body parts and possessions are placed inside this tomb, the thatch is sealed and she is left alone with her parents and grand-parents, perhaps in wait for her children. But to join their mother they will need to achieve adulthood as only then will they be worthy of such dismemberment themselves.

Merpert and Munchaev found the skeletons of young children tucked into all sorts of places – beneath floors, between walls, in corners, nooks and crannies of the houses. A few had been buried with pottery vessels and animal horns, but most were seemingly left with little ceremony. Adult skeletons were rarely excavated; those found came predominantly in dis-membered parts from inside the circular structures, or 'tholoi' as the exca-vators described them. These were too few in number to represent the whole adult population and so a cemetery outside the town appears likely. Those who died as children qualified for neither the (hypothetical) ceme-tery nor the tholoi and were kept eternally within the home – or at least until archaeologists arrived and put them into boxes and museums.

The type of architecture, economy, artefacts, and society of Yarim Tepe – its culture – was the same as that found at Tell Hassuna when excavated by Seton Lloyd in the 1940s.[19] The Hassuna period, approximately 6800–5600 BC, marks the turning point of Mesopotamian prehistory. It leaves behind the world of hunter-gatherers and small farming villages and looks forward to the expansion of towns and trade.

As from 6000 BC, settlements appear in central and southern Mesopotamia, most likely created by people spreading from over-crowded northern towns into a landscape sparsely populated by hunter-gatherers.[20] While similar to those of Hassuna, the southern towns adopted their own pottery and architectural styles and are referred to as Samarra communi-ties. Some are quite spectacular, such as Tell es-Sawwan – a cliff-top settle-ment overlooking the River Tigris 110 kilometres north of modern-day Baghdad.[21]

By 5000 BC substantial towns are found throughout the whole of the Fertile Crescent, except in the extreme southwest where those of the Jordan valley had long been abandoned. In the lands surrounding the Tigris and Euphrates a new cultural unity had emerged, combining the Hassuna and Samarra cultures. Known as the Halaf period, this lasts for a whole millennium,[22] supported by the same crops that had sustained prehistoric farmers since the days of Jericho and Maghzaliyah: wheat and barley, peas and lentils. But a key development had occurred: the use of artificial irrigation. It had been this which enabled people to fully exploit the rich alluvial plains of southern Mesopotamia.

Although sheep and goats were pre-eminent at Sawwan, cattle were important, their significance reflected in cow figurines and pottery painted with a bull's-head motif. As the addition of rich milk fats to human diets can increase the birth rate,[23] cattle herding may have been a factor behind what appears to have been a population explosion. Many new settlements were founded during the Halaf period, while existing towns expanded, many reaching more than five times the size of Yarim Tepe at its peak.

The Halaf towns shared a distinctive architecture and style of painted pottery, some settlements supplying surrounding areas with their wares. Painted female clay figurines, stone pendants and stamp seals were also shared. The latter, often pierced and with linear designs, were used to secure baskets and pots, suggesting the movement and storage of valuable items. Both these and more mundane materials such as foodstuffs, pottery, and stone were extensively traded between the towns – trade was the root of prosperity, technological innovation and cultural unity.

The Halaf culture marks the end of Mesopotamian prehistory. During the Uruk period that followed, the first traces of writing are found. Within another thousand years the cities of the Mesopotamian civilisation begin to appear. But both these and the Halaf towns themselves will remain unseen by Lubbock – his time in Mesopotamia comes to an end at Yarim Tepe in 6400 BC.[24]

While sitting amidst the hubbub of that town, John Lubbock ponders where else he has been at this date in human history: not only at Zhokhov but also in the midden at Natsushima, the cemetery of Oleneostrovksi Mogilnik, the village of Koster, and within the mangrove swamps of Arnhem Land. He now recalls his astonishing journey through southern Asia – from Muchchatla Chintamanu Gavi at the LCM to Jeitun at 6000 BC, before travelling through Mesopotamian prehistory. That had been one of continual physical descent. It began in the highlands at 11,000 BC with the hunter-gatherers of Zawi Chemi Shanidar and continued in rolling foothills with visits to the sedentary villages of Qermez Dere and Nemrik; from these he had descended further into the lowlands to visit the small farming settlement of Maghzaliyah and the specialised hunting site of Umm Dabaghiyah which supplied the new towns with meat. Finally he came to Yarim Tepe with its craft specialists and constant stream of visiting tradesmen. No more than five thousand years have passed between the people who hunted gazelle and collected acorns in the Zagros foothills, and those around him now with their multi-roomed houses and tholos tombs, their pottery and metalwork, fields of wheat and flocks of sheep.

Lubbock wonders why Mesopotamia has been the scene for such rapid economic growth and cultural change. Climatic and environmental factors are evidently key – the presence of wild cereals, goats and sheep, a relatively mild Younger Dryas (if one at all), global warming at 9600 BC, fertile alluvial soils around the Euphrates and Tigris. And yet these factors only became significant in the 'rise of civilisation' due to the particular actions and choices made by people as they went about their daily lives. The inhabitants of Zawi Chemi Shanidar, Qermez Dere and Nemrik had been just as responsible for laying its foundations, as had those who lived at Maghzaliyah, Tell Sotto and Yarim Tepe. And none of these people had any foreknowledge of what was to come.

History, Lubbock thinks, is an extraordinary tangle of causes and consequences, of human ingenuity and complete accident, of environmental change and human response.[25] Understanding requires the knowledge of both local events and of the wider world in which these events occur. Nobody at 9600 BC could have known where history was heading as the final spurt of global warming arrived and the Neolithic world began.

AFRICA

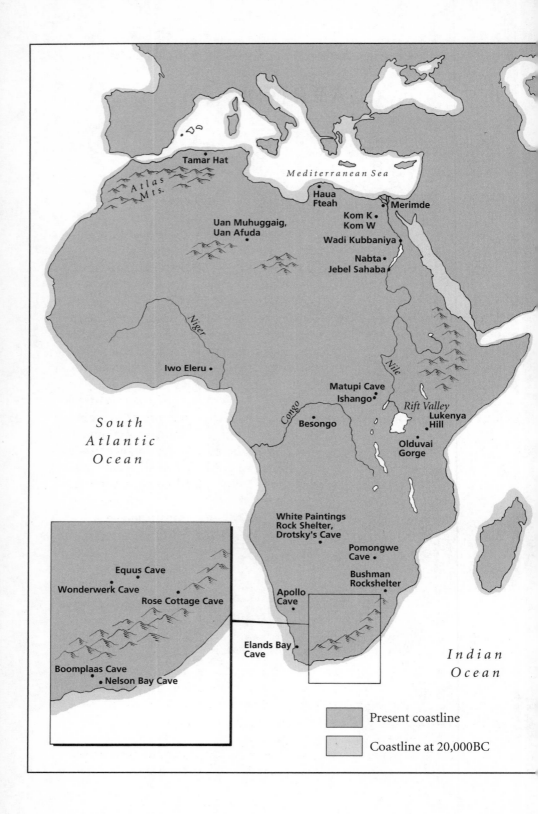

Tamar Hat

Atlas Mts.

Mediterranean Sea

Haua
Fteah

Merimde

Kom K
Kom W

Wadi Kubbaniya

Uan Muhuggaig,
Uan Afuda

Nabta
Jebel Sahaba

Niger

Iwo Eleru

Congo

Nile

Matupi Cave
Ishango

Rift Valley

Besongo

Lukenya
Hill

*South
Atlantic
Ocean*

Olduvai
Gorge

White Paintings
Rock Shelter,
Drotsky's Cave

Pomongwe
Cave

Equus Cave

Bushman
Rockshelter

Wonderwerk Cave

Rose Cottage Cave

Apollo
Cave

*Indian
Ocean*

Boomplaas Cave

Nelson Bay Cave

Elands Bay
Cave

Present coastline

Coastline at 20,000BC

46

Baked Fish by the Nile

Hunter-gatherers of North Africa and the Nile valley,
20,000–11,000 BC

A little naked girl toddles on the sandy floor. She falls, crawls, and then unsteadily stands again to the applause of the adults seated around her. John Lubbock sits among them, also enjoying her giggles and faltering steps. It is November in a year close to the LGM and he is visiting a group of families at their campsite in Wadi Kubbaniya, a tributary valley of the Nile. Their brushwood huts, grinding stones, rush mats and fireplaces are positioned on a sand dune below a sandstone cliff. Beyond these, the Sahara desert spreads west – far more extensive and arid than it is today. The campsite overlooks a scatter of trees amidst a mosaic of shrubs, reed-beds, ponds and the braided channels of the River Nile. The air is scented with wood smoke, camomile and baking fish.

The girl comes to stand in front of Lubbock and appears to stare him in the eye. Her hair is jet black and her skin a light chocolate brown; a sprinkling of sand covers her lips and nose from where she fell. Lubbock smiles and her face becomes a dimply grin – strange, because he cannot, of course, be seen. As the little girl turns away and heads for her mother, a nut-sized lump of light brown faeces falls from her bottom, landing right between Lubbock's feet. A man leans and flicks it with his finger, sending it spinning through the air to land within the fire. It hisses and soon turns black – a crucial piece of archaeological evidence in the making.[1]

Lubbock's last continental journey had begun a few hundred years earlier within a cave on the North African coast. At 20,000 BC he had woken to look out across a wide coastal plain, one covered by thick woodland that became grassland and then marsh before meeting the Mediterranean Sea. A scatter of hunting weapons, some hides, and the remnants of a still warm hearth surrounded him on the floor, all located behind a stone wall acting as a vital windbreak. Lubbock climbed the crags above the cave; looking south, towards the Sahara, he saw an expanse of low, rugged mountains; to the north, a party of hunters had just emerged from trees below the cave. They carried the carcass of a wild sheep, one with extravagant curly horns and a dark brown hairy coat.

Lubbock spent the next few months with the three families who passed the winter in this cave. Most days he went with the men to hunt wild sheep, a type known today as barbary sheep or *mouflon à manchettes*. Occasionally gazelle were hunted in the grasslands; wild cattle were stalked whenever their tracks were encountered among the trees. When not hunting, Lubbock accompanied the women to the nearby river, and on rare occasions to the distant shore to gather shellfish and seaweed.

Remnants from all of these activities were left within the cave, along with discarded tools and debris from manufacture and repair. The bones, baskets, shells, mats, ashes and flakes of stone, all became covered in rubbish left by later human occupants, by wind-blown sand, and by the decaying bodies, nest material and food remains of birds and animals who also sheltered within its walls. Roof-collapse added to the accumulating deposit. Once buried, the material left behind by Lubbock's unknowing hosts at 20,000 BC rotted, decayed and became mixed with both earlier and later debris by burrowing animals. That which survived eventually came to light in AD 1973, when excavations were undertaken in what had become known as Tamar Hat Cave in modern-day Algeria.[2]

Twenty years earlier, a far larger North African cave had been excavated by the Cambridge archaeologist Charles McBurney.[3] Known as the Haua Fteah, this is located 2,000 kilometres east of Tamar Hat on the slopes of the Gebel el-Akhdar – 'Green Mountain' – in northeast Libya. On his first visit in 1948, McBurney described its massive opening as 'distinctly awe-inspiring', the cave's huge domed roof dwarfing the shepherd's campsite situated within it. Lubbock had a similar reaction in 20,000 BC when, after travelling eastwards from Tamar Hat, he looked at the slopes of Gebel el-Akhdar from the coastal plain and saw the conspicuous dark oval entrance into the rock. The green scrub on the hillside lacked the lushness that McBurney would find and the desert to its south was even more inhospitable than that of Libya today. But the cave was just as large and, as the sea level was at its LGM low, overlooked an extensive coastal plan. Not surprisingly, the cave at Haua Fteah was as attractive to North African hunter-gatherers in prehistory as it was to McBurney as a site for excavation.

Just as at Tamar Hat, Lubbock remained with the occupants of the Haua Fteah long enough to discover how they lived. This required no more than a brief stay as their lifestyle was little different to that along the whole North African coast, with a reliance on the barbary sheep for meat, fat and hides. After leaving Haua Fteah, Lubbock continued his journey east until he reached the Nile delta – a vast expanse of lagoons, marshes and scrubby woodland, cut apart by a spider's web of streams. Spirals of smoke in the evening air told him that hunter-gatherers were scattered across the delta's many tiny islands. Borrowing a canoe that was drifting in the shallows, he began to paddle upstream.

At 20,000 BC, the River Nile was very different from that known today. Rather than a single, wide, sinuous-flowing channel, Lubbock found that it braided into several small streams which meandered slowly across a flood plain.⁴ Often there seemed to be hardly any water flowing at all. The small channels joined together when the river passed through gorges of steep rocky cliffs or massive dunes, and then divided once again. Some petered out entirely; others ended in ponds blocked by mounds of silt and sand.

Wild cattle and hartebeest grazed among the reeds, shrubs and thorny trees that grew at the river's edge. Once he passed crocodiles resting on a sandbank; plovers and snipe probed in the shallows while flocks of quail and lone herons flew overhead. But nature, in general, was quite impoverished compared to that seen by Lubbock on river journeys elsewhere in the prehistoric world. Moreover, it ended abruptly where the desolate desert began, on either side of the flood plain's narrow corridor.

Lubbock passed many small encampments of hunter-gatherers and paused to watch those fishing from canoes and fowling amidst the riverside reeds. He had travelled 500 kilometres from the delta before making a prolonged visit to a camping site; this was at the Nile's junction with its western tributary of Wadi Kubbaniya. By then it was July and the river had begun its annual rise, its waters swollen by rainfall in the highlands far to the south. Several families were in the midst of re-establishing their seasonal campsite on a dune nestled below the sandstone cliffs of the wadi.⁵ Some were busy putting the finishing touches to the small brushwood shelter that had been built on the crest of the dune; others were sweeping the camp clear of debris left from the previous year. The oval grinding stones that had also been left behind were almost entirely buried by blown sand. Lubbock helped a young man dig them free.

Those making the camp were all dark skinned and well built, wearing neat clothes made of hide. Two of the men were physically impaired, one limping from a once broken leg and the other with a stiff arm that carried substantial scars.⁶ No one individual seemed to assume the role of leader, and no one family seemed to have a grander hut or more possessions than any other. A few wore necklaces made with beads carved from ostrich-egg shells; others had smeared red pigment on their brows and cheeks.⁷ But these adornments were for vanity rather than to signify of status.

Lubbock soon discovered why the camp was situated on the dune itself. Within days of his arrival the annual Nile flood had nearly reached its peak; with an immense gush of water the river broke its banks, forming a network of interlinked ponds between the dunes. This was the signal for much activity in the camp: plants had to be gathered in the marshes before they became entirely submerged; stacks of firewood were built up; wooden racks were constructed from stout reeds; rushes woven into baskets. Meanwhile, the camp's children kept running to the ponds and back, evidently on the lookout for some greatly anticipated event. Lubbock sat beneath a tamarisk tree, watching the excited children and the adults at work.

Once again microliths were being manufactured in the prehistoric world. The blades of stone were chipped along one or both edges and then set into bone handles to make knives; some were used as the tips of arrows made from reeds, and as barbs in wooden spears[8] – yet another occurrence of the plug-in, pull-out technology, although one of the earliest that Lubbock had seen. Flint was also used but was evidently quite precious because it was not to be found in the immediate vicinity of the wadi. The only available nodules were brought to the dune in leather pouches and worked with immense care so as not to waste any flakes.[9]

When tired of watching sand gusting through the wadi and stone tools being made, Lubbock read his copy of *Prehistoric Times.* Although the site of Wadi Kubbaniya was not known in 1865, his Victorian namesake had written about the annual flooding of the Nile and the significance for archaeologists of the depth of silt deposited each year. Long before the invention of radiocarbon dating, the rate of sedimentation had seemed an ideal means to estimate the age of artefacts buried in the ground. The author quoted the research of a Mr Horner who had used the depth of sediment accumulated against ancient Egyptian monuments, such as the obelisk at Heliopolis, then believed to date to 2300 BC, to estimate that 3½ inches accumulated every century. Mr Homer had then dug pits and found shards of pottery 39 feet below the surface which would, he calculated, indicate an age of 13,000 BC. Modern John Lubbock was not surprised that Victorian Lubbock went on to note 'several reasons which render the calculations very doubtful'.[10] They were indeed quite wrong with regard to the pottery, which is now known to appear in the Nile valley only after 5000 BC.[11]

A sound of splashing woke Lubbock from an afternoon doze at the water's edge. He looked down to see a tangle of catfish thrashing in the shallows. They were tying themselves in knots while using their tails to slap each other in the face – the catfish way of looking sexy and attracting a mate.[12] These were the first of a vast number of catfish that arrived in the ponds of Wadi Kubbaniya each year to spawn. As the adults and children watched and waited, mating continued until almost every piece of underwater weed and much of the sand in the shallows was coated with glistening eggs. By this time, the fish were exhausted, hanging listlessly in the water. It was now that fishing could begin.

Lubbock had already done plenty of fishing during his travels – using poison in the Amazon at 10,500 BC, spearing salmon at Namu in 6500 BC and by moonlight close to Tybrind Vig in 4400 BC. This new ichthyological experience was as productive as any of those had been, but a lot less demanding of both effort and skill. The Wadi Kubbaniya people simply paddled ankle-deep in the water, scooped the fish up with baskets and tossed them on to the bank – the baskets having protected their hands from the fish's spines. The children waited eagerly for the fish, these often being more than a metre long: each was gleefully clubbed to death.

By dusk, when all the uncaught fish had returned to deeper and safer waters, Lubbock sat on the bank and helped with gutting the catch. The wooden racks were soon heavy with fish; they were placed over fires so that most of the catch could be smoked and hence preserved. That evening Lubbock joined in with the first 'fish feast' of the season, eaten with bread-like griddle-cakes that were cooked on hot stones around the campsite fire. As the moon rose and the singing and dancing began, he lay down to sleep and reflected on the delights of life in the Nile Valley at the LGM.

Lubbock returned to the ponds with his unknowing hosts on the following day and the day after that as a second and third flush of fish arrived to spawn. By then, however, the novelty of catching, clubbing and gutting had worn off for the children, and they played elsewhere. Their help wasn't missed – fish numbers had substantially declined as the short burst of spawning was almost over. As the weeks passed, the catfish were replaced by eels that came to feast upon the eggs and the small fry once they hatched. The Wadi Kubbaniya people tried to catch them, perhaps keen to preserve their future stocks of fish. As the eels slipped through Lubbock's fingers, men and women at the campsite were wrapping smoked and sun-dried fish within rushes before packing them into baskets to be eaten during the leaner days to come.

While the campsite was safe from even the highest reaches of the flood, it was exposed to the near constant wind that blew from the western desert; everything and everyone was frequently coated with a fine layer of sand. When the wind was strong, Lubbock sat behind a flimsy shelter on the dune and watched sand accumulate around the tamarisk and acacia trees that spread along the sides of the wadi; others did likewise while chipping small pebbles of chert.

By late summer the strong winds had relented and the flood waters had begun to recede. Lubbock decided to further his interest in Wadi Kubbaniya cuisine by working with the women to discover which plants were gathered and how they were converted into food.[13] As preparation, he collected a few discarded stone flakes from the campsite floor to shape a driftwood branch into a digging stick, one with a faint resemblance to those carried by the women wherever they went.

On most days the women left with empty baskets and infants tied upon their backs for the newly exposed marshy ground which now bordered the reedbeds and remaining water of the ponds. Lubbock acquired many lessons in plant gathering and food preparation: on some occasions he paddled in the ponds to pick flower buds from waterlilies; on others he helped dig the roots of bulrushes and papyrus and then to collect the seeds of camomile plants. There were several types of knee-high shrubs which provided either leaves, seeds or roots for food.

There was one plant, however, that dominated plant-gathering time. It grew just a few centimetres high, with purple flowers so thick that they made a carpet across the ground. Known today as wild purple nut-grass, it has been described as 'the worst weed in the world' owing to its ability to invade and proliferate in irrigated fields. But to the people of Wadi Kubbaniya at the LGM, it was the most valued food plant of all.[14]

On his first encounter with this plant, Lubbock knelt with the women and copied their actions as they thrust their digging sticks into the ground to lever up the boggy soil. Just below the surface there was a dense mat of interconnected swollen roots, each tuber no more than a few centimetres long. A few were black and hard; so these were dug out and thrown away; the rest were pale brown, torn from the ground and placed into baskets. The women dug continuously for several hours, gradually moving from one patch of nut-grass to the next. The tubers were so dense that many were left in the ground, their future growth enhanced by the removal of old tubers that had clogged the soil.

Once the baskets were full, the women sat by the pond and washed the dirt from themselves and the tubers before returning to their camp. Lubbock now witnessed the laborious process of turning knobbly nut-grass tubers into griddle-cakes – trying his hand at each step of the process. First, the tubers were laid out on hot stones within embers of the fire. After a few minutes of parching, the skins began to peel away and could be rubbed off by hand. Next, the now brittle tubers were ground into flour, although many pieces of peel and strands of tough fibres remained. These were removed by using sieves made from finely woven reeds, the clean flour collected into skin bags below.

This was still not ready for cooking; the Wadi Kubbaniya people knew that it would taste acrid and cause upset stomachs. And so Lubbock had to follow the women to a short stretch of fast-flowing water where the flour was repeatedly washed by filling the bags, swilling the contents, letting them stand, and then carefully pouring away the water. This removed the toxins contained in the flour. Finally the women returned to their camp and squeezed handfuls of the remaining soggy mush into small round cakes that were placed on the hot stones to cook. Not all of the mush was cooked in this manner. Some was saved in small wooden bowls for the young children, especially a small girl who had only recently finished feeding at her mother's breast.

The grinding stones were now in almost constant use for processing seeds. One fractured. To acquire a replacement, a couple of men went to the sandstone cliff behind the dune and spent a day flaking large slabs into oval shapes, closely watched by Lubbock. They also collected pebbles to use as rubbing and pounding stones. Each slab was pecked and ground to make it easier to hold, although most remained quite irregular in shape. All but one of the grinding stone rough-outs were left at the cliff-face for future use; the one carried back to the campsite was further flaked into the shape specified by the women who required it.[15]

Lubbock also went hunting with the men.[16] Their principal prey were the geese and ducks that arrived during the winter months. These were stalked from the reeds and shot with bow and arrow. Sometimes the hunters left the campsite at dusk and waited in ambush at a distant pond for wild cattle and hartebeest, striking them with stone-tipped spears. Gazelle couldn't be hunted in this manner: they gain all the moisture they need from vegetation alone and so had to be pursued through the scrubby woodland of the flood plain and into the edge of the desert itself. Kills, however, were rare and these two- or three-day hunting trips seemed more about gaining some freedom from the women and children of the camp than contributing to the food supply.

By now – November – the Nile waters had almost returned to their lowest level. The ponds were no longer connected and were merely shallow pools. This provided another chance for an easy catch as many fish were stranded and could once again be caught by hand as they swam hopelessly around in circles. A few still managed to escape to the River Nile. On some evenings Lubbock would leave the camp and watch the catfish as they struggled overland from one pond to another and finally to the river – this being one of the few types of fish that can take in oxygen from the air.

Within a few days the pools would be gone completely; the hollows between the dunes would then dry out, crack and become covered with blown sand until the Nile flooded its banks once again. As he sat at the campsite in Wadi Kubbaniya watching fish stuffed with camomile being baked upon the hot stones of the fire and the little girl toddling from person to person, sometimes leaving her faeces behind to be flicked into its glowing embers, Lubbock knew that the time had come for him to continue his prehistoric journey.

Gordon Hillman of the Institute of Archaeology, London, and doyen of archaeo-botany, identified the infant faeces when he studied the plant remains excavated from Wadi Kubbaniya. To him they appeared as tiny fragments, black on the outside and coffee-brown within. Some had a very fine clay-like texture which, to Hillman's expert eye, had evidently once been a finely ground plant 'mush'. He had to decide whether these charred lumps derived from food that had accidentally splashed on to a fire during preparation, vomit, or faeces from either a domesticated dog or a human donor. He chose the latter because one piece had been imprinted by the internal surface of a colon. The fine texture of the one-time food also suggested that this donor had not been canine. Hillman knew that many accounts of recent hunter-gatherers describe how children defecate on the spot whenever the need arises, with their faeces frequently scuffed on to campsite fires. He also found sand within the faeces, as one would expect from infants who spend their time crawling on the ground.[17]

The journey of that little brown lump from a fireplace in Wadi Kubbaniya at 20,000 BC to a slide below Hillman's microscope was due to the remarkable work of the Combined Prehistoric Expedition in the Nile valley. Led by Fred Wendorf and Angela Close of Southern Methodist University, Texas, and Romuald Schild of the Polish Academy of Sciences, this carried out a remarkable campaign of survey and excavation that has transformed our knowledge of North African prehistory.

It began in 1960 when the Egyptian government decided to construct a new dam at Aswan that would flood an extensive area to the south. The Combined Prehistoric Expedition, working with the Geological Survey of Egypt, was one of several international efforts to explore the archaeology of the threatened region. In 1967 it turned its attention to the Nile valley north of Aswan and almost immediately discovered dense scatters of chipped stone and grinding slabs on ancient dunes at the junction of Wadi Kubbaniya and the Nile. But with the outbreak of the Arab–Israeli War and continuing political turmoil, it wasn't until 1978 that Wendorf and his colleagues had the opportunity to excavate those sites.[18] They did so until 1984, finding that some were probably more than half a million years old while others dated to the LGM.[19]

The LGM sites were the most numerous and by far the best preserved. They were principally located on the dunes themselves, with a few found in the silty soils of the flood plain. Most contained tens of thousands of chipped stone artefacts, which had evidently accumulated from many visits to valued camping sites over an estimated 2,000 years. By meticulous excavation and the sieving of vast quantities of sand, many plant remains, fish-bones, mammal bones, ostrich-egg-shell beads and grinding slabs were recovered. Several years of study by many specialists led to the identification of particular species of plants and fish, and the reconstruction of those specific hunting, fishing and gathering practices that Lubbock had enjoyed. The archaeologists not only made their meticulous analysis of the remains themselves, but looked to modern studies of, say, the spawning behaviour of catfish, the use of tubers by living hunter-gatherers and the flooding regime of the Nile. Such was the extent of the work that publication only occurred in 1989 – more than twenty years after the initial discovery of these sites which provide such a detailed picture of life at the LGM.

Although the dunes at Wadi Kubbaniya were abandoned as annual campsites after 19,000 BC, most likely because wind-blown sand had blocked the wadi mouth, a similar lifestyle continued throughout the Nile valley until the end of the Pleistocene period. The Combined Prehistoric Expedition discovered many more scatters of stone tools in the dunes and flood plain of the Nile. Almost all the tools had been made on small blades just like those in Wadi Kubbaniya. But the specific manufacturing techniques and microlith shapes varied according to localities and dates. This suggested that several localised cultural traditions existed in the valley – families, and groups of families, had devised their own particular ways of making tools and passed these down from generation to generation.[20] Many of the sites had grinding stones, several had animal bones and plant remains, a few had burials. Whenever the dietary patterns could be established they looked similar to those in Wadi Kubbaniya with an emphasis on fishing in flood waters, hunting hartebeest and gathering a wide array of plants. Consequently this economy, so suited to the river's regime, appears to have remained unchanged long after the LGM – continuing, in fact, as late as 12,500 BC, when the dramatic effects of the late glacial interstadial were first felt.

Ever since 20,000 BC the river has maintained its braided appearance because it carried far less water than it does today – perhaps no more than ten or twenty per cent of its current flow. The modern Nile is fed by two main rivers: the White Nile and the Blue Nile. The former rises in modern-day Burundi and enters Lake Victoria which is the chief reservoir of the Nile itself. Between 20,000 and 12,500 BC it was blocked by sand dunes in southern Sudan and contributed no water to the main river at all.[21] The Blue Nile collects its water from the highlands of East Africa but the wet season between 20,000 and 12,500 BC was much shorter than that of today and so there was far less water for the River Nile to carry. Cooler temperatures, together with the presence of grasslands rather than trees and shrubs in the highlands, led to far higher levels of erosion. Hence, whatever water did flow in the Nile carried far more sediment than is currently the case. This was laid down throughout the river's course so that the Nile flood plain gradually rose in height, reaching as much as thirty metres above what it is at present. Without the constant flow from the White Nile, the annual rise and fall of the river is likely to have been even greater than today as its level was entirely dependent upon the highly seasonal rainfall in the East African highlands.

Between 12,700 and 10,800 BC, however, everything changed as the late glacial interstadial brought a sudden increase of temperature and rainfall. The East African highlands became covered in woodland and hence the extent of erosion and the sediment load carried by the river were markedly reduced. At the same time, the quantity of its water was vastly increased, partly due to the new rainfall and partly because the White Nile broke through its dune barrier. Rather than continuing to build up its flood plain, the Nile began to do the reverse: to cut down through its own sediments, those it had been depositing since the LGM. This had disastrous consequences for the valley's inhabitants.

The excessive floods of 12,500 BC deposited silt at far higher elevations than previously, and began a period of turmoil, during which the river has been described as the 'Wild Nile'. A vast amount of the marshes, with their edible plants and flood-plain woodlands in which the hartebeest and cattle had grazed, were lost completely. They remained so, as the river became a single fast-flowing channel with a far narrower flood plain than ever before.

Some, if not all, of the valley's inhabitants apparently chose to fight for the remaining campsites and those fishing, gathering and hunting grounds that survived. During the early 1960s Wendorf and his colleagues excavated a graveyard known as Jebel Sahaba, located 300 kilometres south of Wadi Kubbaniya. This dates to the period of the Wild Nile, between 13,000 and 11,000 BC. Of fifty-nine people buried in the graveyard, twenty-four had clearly suffered a violent death due to the presence of embedded arrow points and severe cut-marks on their bones and skulls. Men, women and children had all been killed. As violent acts can often leave no skeletal traces it is likely that many more had come to a brutal end.[22]

Whether this graveyard derived from the catastrophic slaughter of one group by another, or was a gradual accumulation of bodies during a period of endemic violence, remains unclear. But the inhabitants of the Nile valley appear never to have been entirely at peace. When excavating in Wadi Kubbaniya, Wendorf discovered a burial that dated to about 21,000 BC – a young man, aged twenty to twenty-five years, who had a slender muscular build. He had evidently died from arrows shot into his abdomen because two pointed blades were found within his pelvis. His right arm had been fractured when he was about fifteen years old, most likely while defending himself from attack, and his left arm had a partially healed wound.[23] Life in Wadi Kubbaniya might not, therefore, have been quite so idyllic as Lubbock had thought: its people may have had to use force to gain access to the dunes and the ponds that seethed with spawning fish.

Between 12,000 and 7000 BC archaeological sites become extremely rare throughout the Nile valley. Almost complete depopulation had occurred – most probably because mortality outweighed births due to the Western and Eastern Deserts remaining completely dry and uninhabitable. The few sites that are known suggest that relict groups had become reliant on hunting the hartebeest and wild cattle alone, there being no remains of grinding stones and few traces of winter birds or fish. Angela Close, who has studied hundreds of Nile valley sites and many thousands of stone tools, has used just three words to summarise the impact of global warming on the inhabitants of the Nile valley: 'an unmitigated disaster'.[24]

Lubbock left Wadi Kubbaniya soon after the LGM. He continued canoeing up the river, quite innocent of the catastrophe that was to come. By the time the floods of 12,500 BC and the slaughter at Jebel Sahaba had occurred he was far away in the southern reaches of the continent. When he returns to the Nile valley in 5000 BC he will find it densely populated, with people once again dependent upon plants growing on its flood plains. They will be farmers laying the basis for Egyptian civilisation.

47

On Lukenya Hill

*The development of East African landscapes and faunas
after 20,000 BC*

Ice takes on an absolute beauty when seen in the Tropics, when it appears to float above the savannah in defiance of nature's laws. That is Kilimanjaro at the LGM, just as it is Kilimanjaro today. Lubbock had not expected to be so enthralled as he climbed to the top of Lukenya Hill, found in today's southern Kenya. But the early-morning sky had a rare clarity and a faint, distant white peak – one quite contemptuous of its latitude – emerged from clouds that dissolved around its base.[1]

Mount Kilimanjaro has two peaks, known as Kibo and Mawenzi. At 20,000 BC both had been covered by ice which reached 1,000 metres lower than it does today – its past extent marked by the mounds of rock and sediment left behind when the glaciers retreated to their current diminutive size.[2] Now only the peak of Kibo is ice-covered; if our own global warming continues, this ice will have also entirely disappeared within the next twenty years.

Because of that forthcoming loss, what has been called 'Kilimanjaro's secret' has been extracted from its ice just in time – a record of tropical climate change between 10,000 BC and the present day. This has been derived by exactly the same methods that scientists use for the analysis of ice cores from Greenland and the Antarctic: by calculating changing ratios of oxygen isotopes that are a 'proxy' for temperature change and rainfall. A team led by Lonnie Thompson of Ohio State University drilled six ice cores from Kilimanjaro's summit in February 2000 and published their results in October 2002.[3]

Their key finding of relevance to this history was that between 10,000 and 5000 BC the African climate was much wetter and warmer than it is today. This confirmed evidence from other sources and is explained by a reduction in the intensity of the African monsoon; this, in turn, arose from a slight change in the earth's orbit around the sun. Thompson and his colleagues also confirmed evidence of a marked drought occurring at 6300 BC that lasted for a few decades, along with two further droughts happening in more recent – but still prehistoric – times. One of these occurred at around 2000 BC and has been related to major disturbances in the Mesopotamian and Indus valley civilisations. Although such droughts were previously suspected, the Kilimanjaro ice core has provided a new level of detail for climate change in the Tropics – it was the first, and most likely the last, ice-core climate record from Africa. Unfortunately it does not reach back to 20,000 BC, the date at which this chapter begins with Lubbock standing on Lukenya Hill.

Lukenya Hill is 200 kilometres northwest of Kilimanjaro. Two young men stand next to Lubbock, both of whom are also momentarily transfixed by the sight of floating ice and forget their task of watching for game. Tall and lean, they wear loincloths that match the tawny grass in colour. One carries a spear tipped with black obsidian. Turning to the surrounding plain, he nudges his companion and points towards an approaching herd of small antelope. As Lubbock follows, both turn and begin clambering across boulders and through thorny scrub, heading back to their camp – a shelter beneath a massive boulder perched on top of another at the base of the hill.

A twisted branch is burning in the middle of the shelter's floor, around which ten hunter-gatherers are variously squatting, sitting and lying, some using small mats of grass. The children wear nothing but strings of beads around their necks and waists; the adults little more. Although strong and healthy, the middle-aged already look old, their bodies having been ravaged by the rigours of life in East Africa at the LGM. Gourds and bags of arrows hang from wooden pegs forced into crevices in the cave wall. Having visited many hunter-gatherer caves before, Lubbock expected the air to be stale and smoky – but it smells of sweet jasmine, some leaves having just been crushed in a little wooden bowl.

The men's news is greeted with excitement. Spears are checked, one man chips a couple of tiny flakes from a stone point, while another shaves an imaginary bump from his spear's wooden shaft which might otherwise deflect its flight. Knives made from wooden handles and microliths are stuck into belts; fresh lines of red are smeared on to cheeks by fingers scraped across a stone palette of ochre paint. With that done, the hunters disperse to spread themselves along the edge of Lukenya Hill and the slopes to its immediate west. The approaching animals will have to pass through this natural trap and the hunters feel assured of making a kill. Lubbock remains with one of the lookouts who positions himself within a thicket of trees. Around him, the ground is littered with stone flakes and a few fragments of weathered bone – the slope has evidently been used for ambush and butchery many times before.

The innocent animals enter the pass. They catch the human scent, pause and then scatter in panic as one man stands to throw his spear. Three animals run directly into the path of waiting hunters; two drop down dead, one is wounded and escapes. The carcasses are dragged to the spot where Lubbock had watched the action. They are gutted and then draped across the hunters' shoulders, being small enough to be carried whole. Lubbock inspects them closely but cannot name the species. In fact, even if he could differentiate between wildebeest and hartebeest, between Thomson's gazelle, dik-dik, oribi, steinbok and duiker, he would still have failed to do so as the animals now being carried have no modern name at all.

Lukenya Hill, a mound of boulders approximately eight by two kilometres, earth and scrub vegetation upon a mass of granite, rises 200 metres above the Athi-Kapiti plains of Kenya. Excavations have occurred sporadically since the early 1970s; the many archaeological sites that have been discovered in its rockshelters, below its overhangs and in open settings at its base, provide the best picture we have of life in East Africa at the LGM and its immediate aftermath.

The most recent work has been done by Sibel Barut Kusimba of the Department of Anthropology, Lawrence University, Wisconsin, USA.[4] She excavated within a rockshelter known as GvJm62 – the first four letters being the code for locating the site in Kenya's national grid. Radiocarbon dating has placed occupation of this and four other sites, GvJm46, 16, 19, and 22, soon after the LGM – although Kusimba herself has suggested that some could in fact be much older.[5]

Many of the heavily fragmented bones recovered from Lukenya Hill were studied by Curtis Marean of Stony Brook University, New York. GvJm46 had the greatest number, but very few exceeded two centimetres in length and consequently they were of little value for species identification. Instead, Marean relied almost entirely on the size and shape of teeth, from which he identified numerous species that continue to graze on the African plains today, along with animals such as lions, aardvarks, baboons and hares. The majority, however, had come from an animal with no counterpart in the modern world. These teeth belonged to a type of small antelope which had evolved to graze on short, tough stalks of grass. The heavy wear upon the remaining teeth suggested that it had consumed its grass with copious amounts of grit from the dusty ground.

As this species was absent from the bone collections of Holocene date, it seems likely to have become extinct when global warming altered the landscape, providing the type of moist grass that favours eland, impala and gazelle. When writing in 1997, six years after announcing his discovery of a new species in the journal Nature, Marean thought it was still 'premature' to give this small extinct antelope a species name; perhaps it was, but 20,000 years does seem an extraordinarily long time to wait.[6]

Its presence in the earlier but not the later bone collections from Lukenya Hill is just one sign that the East African landscapes between 20,000 and 12,500 BC were much drier than those of today. Three other animals represented in the bones from Lukenya Hill are also very telling. Both the oryx and Grevy's zebra are still in existence, but only in landscapes far more arid than that which now surrounds Lukenya Hill – the oryx is in fact a desert-adapted antelope. Along with these, the giant buffalo had also grazed on dry, tall grasses close to Lukenya Hill at the LGM, as it had done throughout much of Africa. Like the unnamed antelope, this species could not survive the change in climate, becoming extinct in the south and east by 12,500 BC, although surviving in the north for another few thousand years. Each of these animals – the unnamed antelope, Grevy's zebra, oryx and giant bison – was excluded from the vicinity of Lukenya Hill by the change to moister grasslands.[7]

Lubbock had discovered the colder and drier nature of East Africa's climate at the LGM long before he arrived at Lukenya Hill. After completing his canoe trip up the Nile, he had crossed the dusty Ethiopian highlands, which lacked the forest on their lower slopes that we would see today. He then followed the western shore of Lake Turkana, its level severely reduced by the lack of rain. Nevertheless, its sea-blue waters and surrounding grasslands were a haven for flamingos, pelicans and many other wading birds. At night a host of hartebeest, zebra and antelope came to drink, while other animals came to hunt. Lubbock left the lake and headed due west for 800 kilometres, into the centre of the continent where the arid grasslands changed to scrubby savannah and would become rainforest in the Congo Basin.

This journey into Central Africa took him to the limestone massif of Mount Hoyo where he spent a winter sharing one of its forty caves with a group of hunter-gatherers. The one he chose is now called Matupi Cave;[8] it was spacious, with a low stone wall separating a cooking area at its front from a corridor leading to its dark interior. Fireplaces, grinding stones, digging sticks, spears and bows cluttered up its space, rubbish was simply discarded on the floor and occasionally brushed aside. Its people wore beads made from ostrich-egg shell and decorated themselves with ochre paint. During his visit, Lubbock went with the hunters to stalk antelope on the savannah and accompanied a party into the forest which began 20 kilometres to the west. The party returned triumphant carrying a porcupine and giant forest hog, to the immense delight of the children who had remained behind. Sometimes he dug tubers with the women whose digging sticks were weighted with pierced and decorated stones.

When the residents of Matupi Cave left to establish a fishing-camp on a nearby lakeshore, at a site to be known as Ishango,[9] Lubbock completed his journey to Lukenya Hill. This took him back into the drier lands of East Africa and around the shores of another much diminished lake, that we know today as Lake Victoria. There he watched egrets probe the same mud that would one day be cored by scientists studying the history of the lake.

The hunter-gatherers of Matupi Cave eventually lost, or left, their digging sticks within the cave; these tools joined an accumulation of stone flakes, microliths, grinding slabs and food remains. At 3000 BC this collection was entirely buried below the rubbish of new occupants, people who used iron for their tools.

Francis van Noten from Leiden University undertook excavations in 1974. The lower layers had the bones of savannah animals – antelopes, warthogs and ostriches – along with a few from porcupine and forest hog. Among these bones and the many pieces of chipped stone, Van Noten found fragments of decorated stones which he supposed had once been used as weights on digging sticks. The bones from the upper Iron Age layers came from quite different types of animals – those that occupy thick forest such as porcupines, mongoose and giant bats.

The collection of bones from Matupi Cave is one of several direct indicators of how the tropical forests of Central Africa changed in extent during the last glacial maximum and its immediate aftermath. Although the tropical forests of South America and Southeast Asia had remained largely intact during the LGM, those of Africa were markedly reduced in size, large areas being replaced by savannah and semi-desert. Such vegetation change is also apparent from the pollen grains sealed within cave and lake sediments that show how currently forested regions had once been covered by grass alone; if one digs below the forest soil, the sand of former savannah, if not of desert itself, can often be found.

Yet the forest in the central Congo basin survived intact throughout the period of most severe aridity. This resilient forest provided a refuge for the forest-adapted species which is still reflected in its immense wealth of flora and fauna today. When the rains returned as the Holocene began, some of its plants and animals spread east and west to reclaim what had become savannah and semi-desert at the LGM. Localities such as Matupi Cave became surrounded by forest, leading to the change in animal fauna within its deposits. This Early Holocene forest initially covered a much greater region than it does today, having been knocked back again as rainfall declined after 5000 BC and humans began to shape the African world themselves.[10]

Several weeks have passed since Lubbock watched the ambush of the unnamed antelope at Lukenya Hill. On this new day in his African travels he departs from the cave within an hour of sunrise, accompanying three hunters in their search for game. They walk slowly and quietly through the savannah woodland.[11] Always being alert for signs of animals – leaves and stems that have been nibbled, footprints and faeces, sleeping places and noises from the bush – the men are nevertheless frequently distracted from their task of hunting. A baobab tree with bees hovering at a hole leads to a prolonged stop. Large pebbles of quartz are searched for and broken apart, yielding sharp flakes and creating sparks, from which a smoky fire is lit to ward off the bees as the hole is enlarged. Honey, comb and larvae are eagerly discovered; Lubbock finds plenty to eat himself as the hunters take far more than they can manage. Satiated with honey, the hunters doze while Lubbock watches migratory plovers upon the plain, birds that will soon return to the northern tundras that he himself has visited.

Later in the day another pause is made at a shallow water-hole for drinking and bathing. A further hour of walking follows, before the party sit to eat berries they had found by chance. This time Lubbock goes to watch termites, remembering how the African past is said to lie within their belly.[12] And then, in mid-afternoon, he follows the hunters' slow meander back to camp.

This is the type of day often enjoyed by the modern-day Hadza of East Africa, those belonging to one of the few groups of surviving hunter-gatherers in the world. I suspect that it differs little from the days spent by hunters who occupied the caves of Lukenya Hill at 20,000 BC. The Hadza have been studied since the 1960s and despite the obvious problems involved in imposing a modern lifestyle on to the past, they provide a compelling vision of what life at the LGM may have been like.[13]

The prehistoric landscape around Lukenya Hill is likely to have been similar to the dry, tsetse-infested savannah, dominated by thorn scrub and acacia trees, which the Hadza now inhabit – although, just like the mammoth-steppe of the north, no exact modern analogue exists for African landscapes at the LGM. This is because the extensive short grasslands of modern-day Africa are as much a product of human activity as of climate change; they have been regularly and deliberately scorched by fire, a practice that may have been undertaken by pastoralists for several thousand years.

Regular burning clears the mature grass which is fibrous and unpalatable to their goats and cattle, producing the shorter types of grass that can support more animals; heavy grazing further inhibits the growth of tall grasses, trees and shrubs. The burning also helps to reduce the tsetse fly, which spreads sleeping sickness in humans and cattle. Whenever such burning and grazing is stopped, shrubs and trees readily return along with tall, tough grasses growing in their shade. Natural fires, as no doubt occurred around the LGM, are too infrequent to have the same impact on vegetation. And so, up until the arrival of pastoralists in East Africa at 2000 BC, the landscape around Lukenya Hill is likely to have had swards of long and tough grass, many more shrubs, and perhaps more trees than it does today.[14]

Throughout this subtly different landscape, a similar range and distribution of plant and animal foods would have been available throughout the year as are found today. This doesn't mean that the Lukenya Hill people had necessarily lived in a similar fashion to the modern-day Hadza, but the people living at 20,000 BC and its aftermath are likely to have made similar choices about which game to hunt and which plants to gather. The ambushing of herds, as envisaged by Marean, is likely to have been restricted to specific seasons, perhaps when rain was particularly sparse and mammals migrated in search of water. At other times, hunting would primarily have been done by searching for tracks and trails and then stalking individual game, or perhaps – as among the Hadza today – by scavenging from carnivore kills under cover of darkness.

Lubbock tried both methods, preferring to spend his time hunting rather than gathering roots, tubers, bulbs, berries and leaves with the women. While the Lukenya Hill group depended upon such plant foods for the vast majority of their diet, everyone longed for meat.[15] When in the bush and grasslands, Lubbock found his companions always alert for circling vultures and the sound of frenzied hyenas, either of which prompted a search for a newly available carcass. On one occasion, Lubbock and his companions encountered lions feeding upon a freshly killed zebra. The lions remained undaunted by the shouts and thrown stones but fled after arrows were shot, leaving their kill behind.

For the nocturnal hunt, Lubbock left the cave at Lukenya Hill with a hunting party late one afternoon. As they walked, spider's webs within the grass were illuminated by the setting sun, momentarily exposed in a narrow band between clouds and distant mountains. After two hours, they arrived at a rough circle of boulders which enclosed an area about three metres across and formed a hunting blind beside a game trail that led to a nearby water-hole. It was evidently in regular use in view of the many footprints in the sand.

A fire was lit and left to burn within the hide; later its embers would be periodically fanned into flame by a night-time breeze. The hunters ate some berries gathered on the way and then settled down to rest, with their arrows propped against the boulder wall. As the moon rose; Lubbock crouched down outside and watched for game but he failed to hear the faint clatter of hoofs on stony ground which alerted the hunters within the hide despite the constant chirruping of cicadas. Within a few minutes three impala had been shot with arrows; one was struck in its side, the other two escaped unharmed. The hunters returned to doze, waiting until dawn to track the wounded beast. They did so for several hours, following a trail of blood, broken stems and hoof-prints until these ceased at a patch of flattened, bloodstained grass. The near-dead impala had been taken by a leopard and was nowhere to be seen. When returning to Lukenya Hill the hunters picked up a few nodules of quartz, not wanting to arrive empty-handed once again.

Quartz, being easily found in the course of hunting or plant-gathering trips, was the most frequently used type of stone at Lukenya Hill.[16] Chert and obsidian were also used, but Kusimba found these in very small quantities when studying the excavated collections of stone artefacts. Although chert and obsidian have better flaking qualities than quartz, they were more difficult to come by. The closest source of chert to Lukenya Hill was a river-bed five kilometres away; this also provided small pieces of obsidian but any larger nodules had to be acquired from the Central Rift Valley 150 kilometres to the northwest, or from an escarpment 65 kilometres to the west. Because each outcrop has a specific chemical signature which is carried in every nodule, Kusimba was able to determine that most of the obsidian flakes had come from these distant sources rather than the local river-bed.[17]

The nodules of quartz, chert and obsidian were used to make a variety of tools; microliths were once again the most frequent type. Large flakes were frequently chipped around one edge to become what archaeologists call 'scrapers', most probably once hafted into short-handled tools and used for cleaning hides. Tools with a chisel-shaped edge were also made, these being known as burins. As such, the people at Lukenya Hill were making the same range of tools as were so many others in the world between 20,000 and 10,000 BC, although they had their own idiosyncratic forms such as a 'fan-shaped' scraper.

Lubbock has now travelled 250 kilometres southwest of Lukenya Hill and sits by the remnants of a seasonal stream. Time has moved on a thousand years to 19,000 BC but the African landscapes remain quite arid. This river flows whenever the summer rains arrive; indeed, it often floods to leave layers of silt across the valley floor that become sandwiched between dustings of wind-blown sand and ash. Rain last fell a month ago and the stream has become an irregular line of stagnant pools containing more rhino urine than drinking water. Soon these will be patches of mud and then gone altogether.

Lubbock is within Olduvai Gorge, explored and made famous by the Leakey family during their quest for the origins of humankind. The silt and sand left by the stream, together with the fine volcanic ash blown by the wind, will be mixed together to create the last of the geological layers that the Leakeys explored, that known as the Naisiusiu Beds. This forms throughout the gorge and across the nearby Serengeti plain, a capping for the two-million-years'-worth of geological strata below.[18]

Sitting on a boulder, Lubbock watches as two men butcher an antelope they had ambushed at dawn as it came to drink, shooting it with microlith-tipped arrows. Several other people sit near by, some resting idly in the early-morning sun, others chipping nodules of quartz to make new blades and butchery tools. One of the men curses as his greasy stone flake slips to gouge his thigh; blood spurts forth, and continues to do so as he places his hand in a futile attempt to stem the flow. He is made to lie down as a young girl darts away to search for a local healing plant. She returns within minutes carrying a handful of thick-ridged succulent leaves which are twisted above the wound. A clear liquid drips into the cut and has immediate effect as the bleeding ceases. The man is taken into the shade to rest, his bloody legs and hands washed with water from the pool.

Once the butchery is complete the party leaves, the injured man being helped to walk, others carrying the joints of meat. Lubbock looks at the ground before him – a scatter of stone flakes, unwanted microliths, spilled guts, antelope feet and head, and bloodstains from man as well as beast.

The scatter of microliths, stone flakes and broken bones was discovered and part-excavated by Louis Leakey in 1931 and more fully dug by his wife Mary in 1969. Many more artefacts were present because that shady spot had often been used for butchery. The Leakeys found several hundred tools and bones from numerous species, all broken into tiny fragments like those of Lukenya Hill. One imagines that after each killing, hyenas had come to chew the discarded bones. Flood waters would have washed some artefacts away and buried others below their silt deposits. Any wooden artefacts, woven baskets, and hide bags that had been left or forgotten rotted away. The scanty remains which the Leakeys recovered tell us little more than that some people had sat by Olduvai River around 19,000 BC and butchered their prey. We can also assume that they are unlikely to have remained there very long because the obsidian they used had come from a source 200 kilometres away and so they must have travelled extensively.

However, we have no idea whether they used medicinal plants. My guess is that they did, especially the one known today as sansaveria, a succulent growing in many parts of the Rift Valley. Its local name, olduvai, was given to the gorge itself. Richard Leakey has enthused about the healing properties of the plant, describing its use by the nomadic peoples of the Rift Valley and the Leakey family themselves whenever accidents occurred during their fieldwork.[19] Its juices act both as an antiseptic and as a natural bandage in binding the wound together. Richard Leakey believes sansaveria is far better than anything provided by modern pharmaceuticals and has questioned whether the earliest ape-like human ancestors who lived at Olduvai two million years ago knew of its properties. That we will never know, but we should not doubt that they were known by those modern humans who hunted within Olduvai Gorge soon after the LGM.

48

Frogs' Legs and Ostrich Eggs

Hunter-gatherers of the Kalahari Desert,
12,500 BC

A spider's web. Not strung airily between grass stalks or reeds but thickly woven across a tunnel in the dusty sand. Two women crouch down beside their find; John Lubbock is with them, wondering why they look so pleased. He had assumed they were searching for wispy stems from buried tubers or thicker and hollow stems with edible grubs inside. But both were ignored as the women pushed bushes aside, searching the broken ground around their roots. A digging stick is dipped into the hole and twisted to wind the web around its tip. Once the stick is wiped, the women begin to dig as the spider scuttles away. As soon as the sand becomes a little moist a hand is thrust into the hole and the women's next meal is dragged out by its leg, then swiftly struck with a digging stick before it has a chance to bite. A bullfrog.

The date is 12,500 BC and Lubbock is in the Gcwihaba Valley of the Western Kalahari Desert, Botswana.[1] He had arrived earlier that morning, tagging along behind the women as they walked down the well-worn path from their campsite. They had followed the dry river-bed to a thicket of bushes and begun their search, knowing that each web-covered hole might lead to a bullfrog hibernating below the ground. The Kalahari spiders like to take advantage of the bullfrogs' work by weaving their webs across the ready-made holes.

Lubbock looks at the women as they begin searching for another web, probing around a nearby bush. They have short black, tightly-curled hair and high cheekbones; their cocoa-coloured skin has been deliberately scarred on the face and thighs to leave parallel lines of bright red weals. Apart from the strands of white beads that adorn their necks and wrists, they wear nothing but hide capes and small tasselled aprons.[2]

By midday there are eight bullfrogs in their basket and the women have returned to their campsite outside what we call today Drotsky's Cave. The rest of the group are sitting and working in the open; two men are cleaning hides with quartz flakes hafted in bone handles, old women sit talking while twisting plant fibres into twine, children play with sticks. Inside the cave itself an elderly man pokes at the fire. Everyone stops when the women arrive, gathering round to see what they have found. Within minutes, the bullfrogs are spread across hot stones in the fire to cook; the small ones are allowed to turn crispy before being ground up with a wooden pestle and eaten as a mush;[3] the larger ones are simply pulled apart and shared between all present. Most adults get a frog's leg to eat, the soft bones being crunched up with the meat. Only the heads are wasted – discarded into the ashes after the skin and eyes have been nibbled away.

Lubbock manages to sneak a frog's leg, finding it tasty and filling to eat. While chewing the bones he thinks of what else he has eaten and drunk around the world at this date of 12,500 BC: bread from wild wheat at 'Ain Mallaha, arctic hare at Creswell Crags, tea made from boldo leaf at Monte Verde, a lizard and figs at Kulpi Mara Cave. He also thinks back over his journey from Olduvai Gorge that he had left at 19,000 BC. There is, however, little about human history to recall as the land had remained arid and largely uninhabited during that journey through modern-day Tanzania, Zambia and Zimbabwe. If people did exist within this region, Lubbock thought, they were most likely at the coast or living on productive grasslands around surviving lakes. Even when Lubbock passed through what seemed to him to be an attractive place to live, the most he found were men making transient camps on their way to more favoured hunting grounds.

There was, for instance, a striking set of hills containing numerous rock-shelters and caves in what we now call Matebeleland in western Zimbabwe.[4] Lubbock explored many of the caves and found stone artefacts scattered on the floors of some. But these were partly buried, and looked quite different to those he had seen at Wadi Kubbaniya and Lukenya Hill. The hills were not, however, completely deserted: Lubbock found a pair of hunters making overnight camp within the most impressive cave. It had a dome-shaped roof and looked across a small valley whose river-bed was dry. Lubbock sat by their fire, feeling just as hungry as the hunters themselves as their search for game had been unsuccessful. When Lubbock woke the next morning, the hunters had gone, leaving nothing more than a scatter of ashes and a few stone flakes behind.

This set of hills and caves were the setting for many hunter-gatherer camps long before the LGM, and would be so again once the Holocene began. Known as the Matopos, years of excavation have recovered traces of occupation that reach back 100,000 years, to a time when stone tools were made from large flakes rather than the small blades that Lubbock had come to know so well. The most recent study of the Matopos has been undertaken by Nicholas Walker of Uppsala University, Sweden, who focused on its use from the LGM until the present day. He found that while several caves had abundant remains from Holocene hunter-gatherers, just one – the impressive dome-shaped Pomongwe Cave – had signs of habitation between 20,000 and 10,000 BC. The few stone flakes that Walker found could only be tentatively dated to earlier than 13,000 BC.[5]

The history of occupation at the Matopos is likely to reflect that of sub-Saharan Africa as a whole. That vast areas were completely devoid of a human presence at the LGM and during its aftermath is certainly the impression we gain from the sparse number of archaeological sites that are known. If people were around, they must have been living in small and highly mobile groups, rather like the desert-adapted Kalahari Bushmen of recent times. By always being on the move, they would rarely have left sufficient debris for it to survive the ravages of time. My guess is that much of the continent was indeed a human desert – the cold and arid conditions must have had a debilitating impact on population numbers, increasing the chance of early mortality while reducing female fertility.

This absence of human company had ended when Lubbock reached Drotsky's Cave. Indeed, the region in which it is found appears to have broken the African rule of a relatively dry Pleistocene followed by a wet Holocene – the Gcwihaba valley seems to have done the precise reverse.

Ten creamy white spheres clustered in a shallow depression in the sand. A wonderful and unexpected find for Lubbock's three companions on a hunting trip in the low hills with rocky outcrops that surround the Gcwihaba valley. Until now, they had had little success. Hare tracks had led them to a burrow where they guessed the nocturnal animal would be asleep. The hunters searched the scrubby woodland for a straightish branch at least a couple of metres long. This was pushed down the burrow until the hunter could feel the hare; he thrust it forward with all his strength to hold the animal still while his companions began to dig. Gradually the coarse brown hair became exposed, the animal pinned down and quite unable to move. But as a rock was raised to deliver a lethal blow, the branch snapped and the hare escaped, its flight watched with dismay and delight in equal measure – the loss of a meal but an animal to admire running across the sands.

The chance discovery of an ostrich nest a little later in the day provided ample compensation. Each egg is pounded gently but firmly on the ground. This jars the contents, killing the embryo inside.[6] The hunters can carry three eggs each and agree that someone will be sent to collect the last.

The eggs are heavy. Several rests are taken on the walk back to Drotsky's Cave, during which fresh dung is gathered wherever it lies. On arrival, everyone is eager to see and touch the eggs and there is little delay in cooking the food. Two eggs are carefully cracked in half to make four cooking vessels, and their contents saved in a wooden bowl. Dung is coated thickly around the base of these newly made bowls, which are then positioned upon hot stones. Holes are carefully drilled into the ends of the remaining eggs and their contents poured out to cook. Ostrich egg omelette, strong and more gamey than that from a hen's egg, is shared by all – although Lubbock has to make do with scrapings from the bowls.

During the next few days he watches how the ostrich shells are used. The cooking bowls had become charred and were left to fragment within the fire. This was common practice with wasted food and other debris at

Drotsky's Cave; every few days the hearths were cleaned out, their ashes, burnt bones, shells and lumps of charcoal being dumped deep inside the cave. Of the ostrich eggs that remained whole, all but three were rinsed with water and flavoured by aromatic herbs to replace the odour of rotting egg. The addition of grass stoppers turned the ostrich-egg shells into water containers. The three remaining shells were used for making beads. An old woman – the mother of the man who first spotted the nest – broke them into jagged fragments and then drilled a hole in each by rotating a microlith-tipped stick between her palms.[7] Once drilled, the beads were strung tightly on a cord and then rubbed upon a stone to make them smooth and even. The woman wore many of the beads herself, giving others to her daughters and to their daughters in the camp.

Music, singing and dancing were essential to the people of Drotsky's Cave, just as Lubbock has so frequently found throughout the prehistoric world. And so were games, here most usually played by the women and children aged between eight and twelve. Lubbock enjoyed watching these games, but as he often felt utterly confused as to what was going on he resisted the temptation to join in.

We do not know, of course, whether games were really played outside of Drotsky's Cave in the Kalahari Desert at 12,500 BC. But they were definitely played just a few kilometres away at Nyae Nyae in AD 1952 by the !Kung bushmen, as they were observed by the anthropologist Lorna Marshall. Although not formally trained as an anthropologist, she made a seminal study of the !Kung of Nyae Nyae during the early 1950s.[8] Throughout the duration of one of the games, the !Kung children croaked in near perfect imitation of the bullfrogs which gathered to breed in the valley when the rains arrived.

When Marshall watched the game in 1952, it began with the players seated in a circle facing inwards; one girl was chosen to be mother and she started by tapping each of the others on the ankle with a stick. Once tapped, they croaked and lay back full-length as if asleep. When all were lying down she plucked a few hairs from her head and placed them on an imaginary fire in the centre of the circle – these represented the frogs that she was cooking for the meal. When these had cooked for long enough, her children were tapped again and they formed a circle around their mother. Each was asked in turn to fetch the pestle and mortar so that she could grind the crispy frogs, but each refused to go; and so, looking suitably annoyed, she went herself. As soon as the mother left the circle, her children stole the hairs – the frogs – and ran off to hide. The mother returned, scowling, making threatening noises and searching for her children. When found, they croaked, squealed and struggled before being struck on the head with her forefinger and pretending to cry. At this point, any semblance of order was lost; all the children ran chaotically around, shrieking and laughing in wild excitement.

In light of the apparent similarities in lifestyles between the Drotsky Cave inhabitants and the !Kung, as observed by Marshall, one is tempted to believe that such games were also played in 12,500 BC. The cave acquired its name from Martinus Drotsky, one of the first Europeans to travel widely in the Kalahari.[9] The first excavations were made by the American anthropologist John Yellen in 1969, who dug a trench close to where Drotsky had painted his name upon the wall. From the cave's sandy sediments Yellen acquired stone artefacts, fragments of ostrich-egg shell, animal bones and charcoal that dated to 12,500 BC – the first discovered trace of pre-Holocene settlement in the Kalahari Desert.[10]

New excavations were made in 1991 by Lawrence Robbins of Michigan State University and his colleagues. They dug deeper than Yellen had done and discovered a 30-centimetre-thick layer of charcoal and ash, beginning 50 centimetres below the surface. This contained many more artefacts and bones than the sandy sediments above and below, and was dated to have formed between 12,800 and 11,200 BC.[11]

This layer of charcoal and ash had arisen from many campfires within the cave, suggesting its intensive use for habitation. It contained a quantity of burnt bullfrog bones; these were primarily pieces of skull, which are ridged, robust and hence resistant to decay. Leg bones were markedly scarce, leading Robbins to suppose that they had been eaten with the meat. When Marshall lived with the !Kung in the 1950s she had heard that bullfrogs were eaten, although she never witnessed this; but in 1859 the missionary David Livingstone described how the Bushmen found bullfrogs by searching for spiders' webs, just as Lubbock had seen them doing.[12]

The !Kung of Nyae Nyae valued ostrich eggs as water containers and as material for making beads which the young girls particularly liked to wear. As Robbins excavated many ostrich-egg-shell fragments from the charcoal layer in Drotsky's Cave, both uses seem likely at 12,500 BC. Some were pierced to use as beads, although the layer lacked any debris from the process of manufacture itself. Other fragments were heavily burnt. The !Kung of Nyae Nyae had cooked their eggs in metal pots but the hunter-gatherers of 12,500 BC had lacked any containers to place over a fire. And so eggs might have been placed directly in the embers, perhaps having first been coated in dung. This is a method that Robbins himself had seen being used to cook chicken eggs by modern-day !Kung at Tsodilo, 50 kilometres north of Drotsky's Cave.

The bones of Kalahari spring hares and several small antelopes were also excavated from the layer of charcoal and ash. Such animals were regularly hunted by the recent !Kung. Richard Lee, an anthropologist who studied another group of the !Kung during the early 1960s, witnessed the use of long hooks to trap spring hares in their day-time burrows, in the same fashion that Lubbock had seen a branch being used.[13]

The accounts of Marshall and Lee can help us to imagine more readily the daily lives of those who discarded bullfrog bones and eggshells in Drotsky's Cave.[14] But we must rely on the archaeological evidence alone for information about the environmental history of the Kalahari and how changing climatic conditions impacted on the region's people. Some of the most telling evidence is smaller than the stone artefacts and animal bones, smaller even than fragments of frogs' skulls and eggshells. It is the sand itself, more specifically the particles of sand that accumulated within the cave. These can act as a gauge to the changing quantities of rainfall in the Kalahari Desert.

When Robbins and his colleagues excavated in Drotsky's Cave they took samples of sand at regular intervals from the surface to the bottom of their 130-centimetre-deep trench, most likely dating to 30,000 BC. Most of this sand had been blown inside – averaging a depth of 4.45 centimetres every 1,000 years. Some samples of the sand were largely made up from very fine particles, those less than 0.08 millimetres in size, which are easily carried on the wind; other samples were coarser in composition, with many particles more than 0.2 millimetres – the type of sand deposited by running water. Robbins and his colleagues reasoned that when outside conditions were very dry, all the sand entering the cave would be blown from nearby dunes and hence be extremely fine in composition. During wetter periods, vegetation would have grown across the dunes and stabilised their surface, providing very few particles of sand for the wind to carry. But in these conditions, run-off after heavy rain would wash the coarser grains into the cave.

The evidence indicated quite clearly that the period between 20,000 and 11,500 BC had been the wettest of the last 30,000 years as it contained the coarser samples of sand. And so, in complete contrast to so much of sub-Saharan Africa, the LGM and its aftermath had been wetter than the Holocene in the Kalahari. This result was confirmed by evidence from outside the cave. From the now dry bed of the Gcwihaba valley, sand and gravel dating to before 12,000 BC was found to contain diatoms that require substantial amounts of water to survive – diatoms being microscopic algae with silica-rich walls, each species having a distinctive form and particular habitat needs. So before 12,000 BC there had at least been a seasonal, and maybe even a permanent, stream within the valley. The remains of a turtle along with the many bullfrogs provide further evidence that a stream had flowed within the valley when fires were lit inside the cave.

As there were plenty of water sources around, Robbins and his colleagues concluded that between 20,000 and 12,500 BC the cave provided no special advantage over many other localities in the region. Consequently, it was used by hunting parties for no more than brief overnight stops, or perhaps simply for shelter during the day. When the climate began to change, when the rains began to fail, Drotsky's Cave became a focus for habitation – perhaps the Gcwihaba valley now provided one of the very few reliable water sources. For about a thousand years people regularly lit fires and made camp within the cave while they hunted antelope and hare, dug bullfrogs from their tunnels and caught them in the wet-season pools. But as aridity took hold and the valley became quite dry, Drotsky's Cave lost its attraction; once more it was just one of many places used by people continually on the move, searching for water in the Kalahari Desert. The layer of ash, bones and charcoal became covered by wind-blown sand. When, in 1969, John Yellen asked the modern-day !Kung about the cave, they believed it had only ever been used as a place to collect honey; they had never camped within the cave themselves.

After leaving Drotsky's Cave, Lubbock undertakes a journey of almost 2,000 kilometres to the Western Cape of South Africa, reaching the southern margins of the inhabited world for the third and final time in his travels – having already visited Tasmania and Tierra del Fuego. In front of him is a shallow river, known today as the Verlorenvlei, which flows westwards to reach the Atlantic Ocean a little under twenty kilometres away. A man stands knee-deep and immobile in its waters, a fishing spear poised above his head. As Lubbock watches, he strikes at the water, curses, and then tries again, before giving up and following the beaten trail back to a cliff-side cave a short way down river. Today we call it Elands Bay Cave – the first of four caves Lubbock must visit as he explores what happened in South Africa when global warming changed the world.

49

A South African Tour

Changing environments, diet and social life,
12,500–7000 BC

The fisherman now sits with two companions by the hot embers of a fire, observed by Lubbock who stands at the cave's entrance looking in. Each man has spears propped against the wall, a leather bag containing quartz nodules, a hammer-stone, knife and lengths of sinew.[1] Wads of grass have been placed on the floor, but these do little to cover the debris of this and many previous campsites in the cave.[2] After travelling most of the globe and visiting many similar sites, Lubbock's sense of smell has become finely tuned; this, together with the fisherman's lack of success, suggests that fishing is a new activity for the inhabitants of the cave.[3]

Elands Bay Cave is the Franchthi of the South. Its archaeological deposits show how people changed their lives as global warming changed their world, bringing the sea and its products to the doorstep of a once inland cave. Excavated by John Parkington and his colleagues from Cape Town University during the 1970s, it has yielded rich collections of animal, fish and bird bones, mollusc, ostrich and tortoise shells, tools made from a variety of materials, together with deposits of charcoal and ash. These date from around 30,000 BC to historic times and have, after three decades of study, provided a remarkable insight into human history in the Western Cape of South Africa, which Lubbock has stepped into at 12,500 BC.[4]

The use of Elands Bay Cave as a hunting camp was well under way at the LGM, when the sea lay some 35 kilometres away – 15 kilometres further than at the time of Lubbock's visit. The coastal plain was accordingly larger, but animals may have been scarce because of the colder and more arid conditions. Nevertheless, the now extinct Cape horse and giant buffalo, the eland, steenbok and grysbok are all present in the cave's deposits between the LGM and 9000 BC, after which the plain became entirely inundated by the rising sea and such animals were hunted no more.

Those who used Elands Bay Cave collected tortoises for food and ready-made bowls. One excavated layer from around 12,500 BC had so many carapaces that Parkington called it a 'tortoise midden'. This suggests that the annual visit to the cave may have been in the summer when tortoises and other reptiles were easiest to find. Other than wood charcoal from fire-places, no other plant remains were recovered. Whether this reflects a diet entirely based on game or the complete decay of vegetable matter remains unclear.

A lifestyle focused on big game in open grasslands appears widespread throughout South Africa at the LGM and its immediate aftermath. Pollen grains from cave sediments suggest a landscape of heaths and grasslands. Charcoal from fireplaces confirms this: that from Boomplaas Cave in the Southern Cape indicates that its LGM occupants had to find fuel in a completely treeless landscape.[5] Those using Rose Cottage Cave now located in the Orange Free State – further inland and at a higher elevation – were better off as they collected firewood from shrubs along the edge of a nearby valley.[6]

Herds of antelopes, eland, buffalo and horse grazed in both the uplands and lowlands and would have been available to hunt. The large mammals from Elands Bay Cave, however, are mainly represented by jaws and lower limb bones – carcass parts that suggest scavenging from carnivore kills. This may have been a sufficient means of acquiring meat as people are likely to have been thin on the ground, their numbers having suffered from the droughts of the LGM. Archaeological sites from this period are rare and, when found, suggest small mobile groups who remained at each of their camping sites for no more than a few weeks at a time. Nevertheless, communal hunts using spears may have been employed in the open landscapes, perhaps deploying beaters to chase animals into ambushes just as Lubbock has so often seen elsewhere.

By the time of Lubbock's arrival at Elands Bay Cave – 12,500 BC – landscapes and lifestyles had already begun to change. Ever since 16,000 BC annual temperatures and quantities of rainfall had been increasing, partly due to the arrival of winter rains to supplement those of summer. The new occupants of Boomplaas Cave collected their firewood from shrubs and trees. While doing so, they would have watched the gradual replacement of grazing herds by smaller-bodied and more solitary animals such as steenbok and klipspringer, ones that browsed within the scrubland.[7] New animals would have required new hunting methods; this in turn would have had consequences for social life.

The browsing animals had to be stalked by stealth; bows and arrows most likely replaced spears, as had been used in the communal grassland hunts. Such hunts would have been public affairs, probably involving the participation of women and children and often producing more than enough meat for all. Bows and arrows, on the other hand, served to 'privatise' the hunt, and with it the ownership of any acquired meat. Social rules for its distribution became essential, especially as relatively small quantities were available from the smaller, solitary animals now being stalked. Lyn Wadley from Witwatersrand University has suggested that the typical pattern seen among recent African hunter-gatherers, such as the !Kung, of women as plant gatherers excluded from the hunt, may date to the adoption of the bow and arrow for hunting, perhaps around 16,000 BC in this particular region of the world.[8]

While the changes in large mammals represented in Boomplaas and other caves are most evocative of changing human lifestyles, the rodents are just as telling about environmental change. During the LGM and its aftermath, the owls roosting in Boomplaas Cave had eaten shrews, which are known to inhabit open grasslands; after 12,500 BC their diet had changed to the mice and voles of a woodland habitat.[9] The dune molerat is a particularly useful rodent as it provides a rainfall gauge, rather like the particles of sand in Drotsky's Cave. Their size is known to vary with rainfall: when wet they grow larger, presumably because the roots they consume are more plentiful and nutritious; when dry they are relatively small; and when conditions become arid they disappear entirely from cave deposits. From measurements of their surviving bones, we know that the molerats trapped by the hunters of Elands Bay Cave between 12,500 and 7000 BC were substantially larger than those which come from both earlier and later deposits in the cave.[10]

Hunting parties keep coming and going every spring as Lubbock sits within Elands Bay Cave reading his copy of *Prehistoric Times* – knowing that he has little time left to finish the book. He looks up every time a new party arrives; sometimes they are empty-handed, at other times they have molerats tied to their waist or a partly butchered carcass in hand. Most years it is only men that arrive, but occasionally women and children accompany the hunters and their stay is extended from a few days to weeks. Lubbock has no idea where they spend the rest of the year but he notices that they often bring stone flakes made from a coarse black material unavailable in the vicinity of the cave. This stone is black hornfels and its nearest source is 200 kilometres east of Elands Bay.[11]

Once Lubbock has watched the new arrivals settle, clean out the fireplaces and eject any unwelcome insects and reptiles that had lodged within the cave, he returns to the pages of his book. The same annual routine of hunting and fishing, story-telling and singing, smoking, joking and toolmaking begins anew.

It is only when people arrive in the year of 12,000 BC that Lubbock realises he has been negligent of the changing world outside.[12] A pair of penguins have appeared within the cave – not entering by themselves but draped around a hunter's neck. This hunter is one of several new arrivals, soon followed by women and children carrying baskets of limpets and seaweed instead of roots or tortoises as in previous years. They look windswept and salty after foraging on the Atlantic shore. While Lubbock has been sitting reading, the tide has been coming in – not the daily tide but that which ebbs and flows with climate change. Global warming has been melting the northern glaciers; billions of litres of water have poured into the oceans; sea level has risen to bring the Atlantic shore to within daily walking distance of the cave. By 12,000 BC it is no more than five kilometres away and so a new type of debris will soon be discarded upon its floor.[13]

The following day Lubbock accompanies the women and children to the shore and watches a familiar scene, one he knows is being repeated throughout the world as the Holocene begins. Shellfish – in this case mainly limpets – are gathered. Rock pools are probed and boulders overturned in the search for crabs. As the women work and the children play, watchful seals are bobbing in the sea. At dusk, when the seals have come ashore, the tables will be turned as hunters creep stealthily towards them, ready to make a kill.

When Lubbock is once again left alone within the cave, debris from coastal foraging litters the floor: mollusc shells, discarded feathers from gulls, bones from seals, penguin and fish. The same happens the following year, and the next. As the same people keep returning, Lubbock watches them age and change. The young boys no longer go with the women to the shore but accompany the men on hunts; adolescent girls arrive newly pregnant or with their first child; some do not return – not just the old, who have died elsewhere, but those who have married and joined another group.[14]

The nature of the cave also begins to change. When Lubbock first arrived, it was a hunting camp with no signs of domestic work. But now there are grinding stones upon the floor. Hides are cleaned within the cave, clothing and ostrich-egg-shell beads are manufactured. Lubbock watches the burial of a young infant beneath the cave floor; when Parkington excavates the site, he will find another five.

Visits become both longer and more frequent, twice or three times a year, evidently designed to target resources at their very best: mussels in the late spring, limpets in the summer, and seals at the beginning of winter. The hunter-gatherers are always watching the clouds and the tides, continually enhancing their knowledge of the seascape – where the birds will nest, when the fish will spawn. Adjustments are made to the quantities and range of foods they gather; as soon as the mussels become more prolific on the shore – a consequence of changing offshore currents and sea temperatures[15] – time is spent collecting these rather than the tough and unpleasant-tasting limpets. As the years pass, as the sea encroaches ever nearer to the cave, the estuary of the Verlorenvlei – the river that flows past Elands Bay Cave – becomes their favoured foraging spot: pelicans and flamingos are shot with arrows, a variety of fish are caught in nets, rock lobsters are gathered, cormorants, gannets and gulls are snared.

As these new species enter the diet, others become neglected or can no longer be found. When Lubbock first arrived, the women and children would spend many hours searching for tortoises in the grasslands around the cave; now all their time is spent on the shore. The tortoises have become scarce as the soil and vegetation is now inundated by salt. A few small antelopes are hunted but the Cape horse has disappeared entirely from the remnants of the plain. This has become even more arid, its few freshwater springs have disappeared and knee-high succulents now grow across the former grassland.

By 10,000 BC the floor of the cave is a stinking shell midden; having already sat and slept upon such middens elsewhere in the prehistoric world, Lubbock has no wish to do so again. It is, in fact, time to make a tour, visiting other caves far inland before returning to the Western Cape at 7000 BC to see how much life at Elands Bay Cave has changed in the intervening millennia.

Having climbed the escarpment on to the high plains known today as the Great Karoo, Lubbock heads northeast across dry grassland scattered with stunted shrubs. For the most part it is dusty and dull, a mix of parched yellows and thirsty browns. The air is clear, and every direction is bounded with hills or mountain-tops. When the summer rain arrives, it falls in such torrents that water pours from the hard-baked ground into every fissure and gully before entering the streams and rushing towards the sea. It hardly seems to moisten the soil at all; and yet a short-term legacy is left in the sudden appearance of flowers of exquisite hue – purple, white, crimson and canary yellow – all glowing brightly upon a carpet of green.

After travelling almost 800 kilometres from Elands Bay Cave, and crossing high plains, hills, dry pans and lakes, Lubbock arrives at Wonderwerk Cave in the eastern flanks of the Kuruman hills. Night has fallen. He approaches beneath a starry sky to the sound of singing and clapping from within; on entering the cave he sees twenty or thirty women seated around a fire, swaying to the rhythm of their music; a similar number of men dance around the circle. Another set of figures, gigantic in size, perform chaotically upon the walls: human shadows thrown up by flickering flames. The music echoes in the dark chambers of the cave.

Lubbock watches for a moment and then joins the seated women, squeezing himself into the circle and picking up the rhythm with his hands. Several slabs of stone have been laid around the fire, each engraved with an animal form. The dancing men frequently burst through or even leap across the women, they reach down to examine the slabs, grasping them tightly and uttering incantations to the eland, horse and buffalo they depict. By now Lubbock is also sweating and swaying, he claps to the rhythm and sings, engulfed by the music and dancing, the flames and the hot, pungent, oxygen-drained air. The dancing becomes frenetic; several men begin to tremble, they shudder and shake and then, in a trance-like state, leave the earthly world within the cave. Two stagger around the circle, laying their trembling hands on each seated person in turn, fingers squeezing scalps in a call for sickness to depart. Others collapse, shaking uncontrollably on the ground, one bleeding profusely from the nose.

It ends. The clapping, singing and dancing come to a sudden halt. The shamans writhe upon the ground and then become still; the others lie flat upon their backs, panting deeply, relieved to be cured of all their ills.

Wonderwerk Cave has had a long history of study. Initial excavations were undertaken in the 1940s, followed by renewed work in the late 1970s, partly by Anne and J. Francis Thackeray of Yale University.[16] The cave has deposits with stone artefacts that reach back far beyond the LGM; the layers from 10,000 BC and after contain animal bones from grazing species such as zebra, hartebeest and wildebeest. The now extinct Cape horse is found in the lowest of the Holocene layers. In addition to stone artefacts and animal bones, the Thackerays found several engraved slabs of stone; all but one of these contained geometric images and dated to relatively recent Holocene times. One slab, however, was dated to 10,000 BC and has formed the basis for my elaborate scenario of the shamanistic medicine dance. It is no more than 8 centimetres across and shows the unfinished image of an unidentifiable mammal that looks like a horse or an antelope without a head.[17]

Many more art works may have been present within Wonderwerk Cave at 10,000 BC as its walls are covered by paintings of an unknown date. We know that artists were already at work in South Africa by 20,000 BC because of a collection of painted slabs from Apollo Cave, Namibia, that depict a giraffe-like creature, a rhino and a wild cat that some believe to have human legs. Archaeologists remain unsure whether these date closer to 20,000 or 30,000 BC; whichever is true, they establish that people had already begun to paint animals on rock-faces before 10,000 BC.[18]

We also know that pieces of ostrich-egg shell were being engraved by 12,000 BC – possibly much earlier – and that engravings were made on rock-faces throughout the Holocene.[19] Painting was widely practised by indigenous South African peoples – the San Bushmen – throughout historic times.

The most recent paintings have been extensively studied by archaeologists and are known to depict shamanistic practices: communication with, and travel to, a spirit world by the few individuals who have the ability to do so. In light of similarities between their imagery and the art of 10,000 BC and earlier, such as the presence of half-human and half-animal forms, it is quite possible that shamanistic practices also motivated the creation of South African rock art in prehistoric times. On this basis rests my scenario of a healing dance in Wonderwerk Cave at 10,000 BC.[20]

The first person to realise that trance dances, dreams, visions and shamans provide the key to understanding nineteenth- and twentieth-century South African rock art was David Lewis-Williams, Professor of Cognitive Archaeology at Witwatersrand University. By undertaking a detailed study of the historical records of San Bushmen and speaking to those who still survived, he found striking similarities between the San shamanistic practices and the imagery in their art.[21] He discovered that many paintings represent trance dances by showing groups of swaying bodies; others record the trance experience itself. Shamans themselves can be recognised in the paintings by blood pouring from a figure's nose or by their part-human/part-animal forms – transformation into another species being a key part of the trance experience. Paintings of eland are particularly significant as this animal contained the potency that shamans must harness to enter a trance. When shamans danced, they often turned to the depictions of eland on the rockshelter walls – just as I have imagined those in Wonderwerk Cave doing with the engraved slabs upon the floor. The written accounts record that when the trance was complete, the shamans would tell the group about their visit to the spirit world; the rock art indicates that they used paintings on cave walls to do the same.

Feeling in particularly good spirits after the dance, Lubbock leaves Wonderwerk Cave to continue his South African tour. The next locality he must visit is Rose Cottage Cave, 450 kilometres to the southeast, where he will arrive in 8500 BC. The country is now relatively lush; its grasslands and shrubs support more animals than Lubbock has previously seen in this region of the world. This partly reflects further increases in rainfall and temperature, and partly the fact that Lubbock has travelled further east, to a region that has always been a more productive landscape than the Great Karoo.[22] Lubbock now passes more campsites than ever before; he watches hunters stalking game and women digging tubers from the ground.[23]

There is indeed a great increase in the number of known archaeological sites in South Africa after 12,000 BC, which must reflect a substantial increase in the human population.[24] By 10,000 BC people had evidently begun to occupy all of the region's varied habitats. The majority of sites, however, are no more than small surface scatters of discarded stone tools and the waste from their manufacture.

Ever since the LGM, South African hunter-gatherers had shaped nodules of stone into cores that were often conical in shape and from which small, thin blades could be detached. Archaeologists use the term 'Robberg' sites to describe such collections of tools. Very few of the blades received any further chipping to turn them into specific shapes. Some may have been hafted on to spears, but would have been little more effective than tips made from hardened wood. This, though, was not the only type of stone tool being used in South Africa. Large flakes were also manufactured, many of which were further chipped into shapes referred to as scrapers, adzes and spokeshaves. Sites containing such flakes and tools – known by archaeologists as 'Oakhurst' sites – are found in large numbers across the open landscapes of South Africa's interior. Very few can be dated, but most are believed to lie between 12,000 and 7000 BC,[25] coinciding with a proliferation of bone points that implies a marked increase in hunting by bow and arrow.

John Parkington has suggested that the same people made both the Robberg and the Oakhurst types of tools – that these were in fact complementary. While the small blades seem appropriate for use in hunting and fishing, the large flakes and scrapers seem more useful for cleaning plant foods, preparing hides and working wood. And so different tools may have been made and discarded depending upon which activities were under way.[26] It could also have been a matter of simple geography, with the available raw materials dictating which type was made. In the interior, coarse-grained rocks, such as black hornfels, were found in big blocks, enabling large flakes to be easily detached. The quartzite nodules found in the lowlands of the Cape are more conducive to the manufacture of small and delicate blades.

Cave sites with long sequences of layered deposits, however, such as Rose Cottage Cave where Lubbock is about to arrive, suggest that Parkington's explanation of the two technologies is unlikely to be entirely correct. These consistently show that the large flakes and scrapers were made at a later date than the conical cores and small blades. It looks as if one tradition was completely replaced by another throughout the region – a marked change in tool manufacture that coincided with the expansion of human habitation into South Africa's interior. After another five thousand years, tool-making styles returned once again to the production of blades, which archaeologists call the Wilton tradition.[27]

A path beaten through a thicket of shrubs leads Lubbock to an unusual cave, one formed by a huge boulder that has fallen from a cliff-face to enclose a cavern behind. The sound of talking and laughing comes from inside, where at least twenty people sit around hearths in a spacious and warm interior, the boulder sheltering them from the cold wind outside. Extra light comes from a natural skylight in the roof. With this, Lubbock can see bundles of grass and leaves to be used for bedding stacked against the cave walls, and a niche crammed with firewood. Sticks have been wedged into crevices to act as pegs for bags, clothing, water-containers, bows and a butchered carcass. Everybody, except the very young, seems to be at work.

Close to the entrance some men are flaking stone. They use the black, coarse-grained type and let each new flake fall seemingly unwanted to the ground, although the odd one is picked from the debris and put aside for further work. Another group sits towards the rear, cleaning and preparing hides – scraping the fat away, stretching, twisting and pummelling to make them supple. On his journey from Elands Bay Cave Lubbock has learned that such leather work is always done by men – they hunt the animals and hence they work their skins, making clothing, belts and bags.[28] Three other hearths are surrounded by women, girls and the infants. At two of these, bulbous roots are being ground into a mush; at the third, two women sit together turning fragments of ostrich-egg shell into beads.

There is a constant hubbub of talk around each hearth; every now and then one person will take centre stage and relate a story to all.

Lyn Wadley of Witwatersrand University excavated the remnants of this scene, together with that of several others whose debris had all become intermixed.[29] She found concentrations of charcoal and burnt bone indicating where the hearths had been, dense scatters of chipped stone near the entrance and clustered fragments of ostrich-egg shells indicating a locus of bead manufacture. There was also a hearth surrounded by tools that suggests woodworking, and grinding stones where pigments had been prepared, while the chemistry of the cave sediments indicated that a great deal of plant material had been brought inside, eventually rotting upon the floor.[30]

Wadley's work built on a long history of excavation in what is a particularly striking cave – one that has continually attracted archaeologists just as it did hunter-gatherers in prehistory.[31] The layers dating to around 10,000 BC were formed above those which go back beyond 50,000 BC and below a sequence of layers that finished just a few hundred years ago. From the most recent layers, Wadley has discovered that the cave was a meeting place and ritual centre for the immediate ancestors of the historically known San Bushmen. One of their many wall-paintings depicts a medicine dance; another shows a lioness walking among a herd of eland. Wadley interprets the latter as depicting the ever-present threat of evil over goodness – the docile, gregarious eland representing the ideal of human behaviour amongst the San.[32]

Back in 8500 BC Lubbock enters the cave, tiptoeing between the hearths to the rear wall, where he finds some grass to sit on. Soon after he is settled, further visitors arrive; these call loudly from outside, causing a sudden silence before everyone rises to greet them. What looks like a family enters – a couple of young children, three adults, one of whom carries an infant, an old woman. Following many formal and informal greetings, everyone is seated again, the new arrivals having spread themselves between the hearths, each person sitting with their particular friends or relatives.

The visiting family only remains at Rose Cottage Cave for a couple of days. When they depart Lubbock notices how the young women are wearing new beads, while the men carry bone arrow-heads, gifts given in return for the leather garments they had brought.[33] Lubbock himself remains for a few more days, spending one of these on a hunt and another searching for edible plants, before departing very early one morning while the group remains sleeping within the cave.

Annual gatherings and regular visits between groups, families and individuals who spend most of the year apart were crucial to the modern Bushman way of life. It was by these that friendships were renewed, information shared, marriages and other rites of passage undertaken and gifts exchanged. The latter was essential, both creating and affirming bonds of friendship which could be called upon in times of need. Almost anything could be a gift but the most valued items were stone arrow-heads and ostrich-egg-shell beads.

Each individual, from the very young to the very old, had their own set of gift-giving partners, found within their own group and among others. Some partners may have seen each other just once a year, if that. No two people had exactly the same set of partners, producing a 'gift-giving network' that stretched for hundreds if not thousands of kilometres across the landscape.[34]

When the anthropologist Polly Wiessner studied gift-giving amongst Kalahari Bushmen in the early 1970s she found that more than two-thirds of each person's possessions had been received as gifts from their gift-giving partners. The remainder had been either made or purchased, and were destined to be given away.[35]

This gift-giving network turned out to be crucial to survival in the Kalahari Desert. With its unpredictable rainfall, every group faced a constant risk of insufficient food and water. If this did occur, its members were able to call on help from their gift-giving partners living elsewhere, as they were obliged to share their food. Wiessner describes how this worked from her own experiences in 1974. A group of !Kung faced severe food shortages: high winds throughout the spring had destroyed the crop of nuts they were hoping to collect, while exceptionally heavy rainfall had led to unusually tall grass, making snaring difficult and scattering the larger game. By August the !Kung were spending their time making handicrafts to serve as gifts and learning from passing visitors about conditions elsewhere. By September, the group had begun to disperse, people reporting that they wished to visit relatives 'because they missed them and wanted to do gift-giving'. Within two weeks, half of the population had departed, scattering thinly among other groups and relieving the pressure on those who remained.

Wadley believes that those who occupied Rose Cottage Cave at 10,000 BC were also concerned with gift-giving. As from 12,000 BC Rose Cottage Cave and other archaeological sites start to contain items that would have been ideal as gifts, notably bone arrow-heads and ostrich-egg-shell beads. It is no coincidence, Wadley thinks, that these appear in greater numbers just when people began to colonise the interior landscapes of South Africa – something reflected in the appearance of so many scatters of 'Oakhurst' tools. By having the security of gift-giving partners, people could risk exploring new landscapes and settle in those where sudden food shortages might arise.[36]

Lubbock has now travelled some 400 kilometres to the fourth cave of his South African tour, the last before he returns to the Western Cape. This is

Boomplaas Cave, located today in a limestone crag 60 metres above the floor of the Cango valley. Perched on a rock outside, Lubbock admires the view across the valley floor, and then once more opens *Prehistoric Times*.

Hilary Deacon, now at the University of Stellenbosch, South Africa, made a search for a cave like Boomplaas during the early 1970s. He wanted to excavate one that had deposits covering from at least 100,000 years ago to recent times; he also wanted a cave that contained well-preserved hearths, animal bones and other organic remains. Boomplaas almost fitted the bill – its earliest deposits were 'only' 80,000 years old and so Deacon had to dig elsewhere to go back in time beyond that date.[37]

Boomplaas provides valuable information about the changes in environment and human lifestyles as the Pleistocene reached its end and the Holocene began. But it is the most recent layers excavated by Deacon that are relevant to this history. Deacon found that burnt sheep dung formed the uppermost layers, a consequence of herders who used the cave as a byre during the last few hundred years. Such people were once described as 'Hottentots' and it is these that Lubbock now reads about in *Prehistoric Times*.[38]

For his account of the Hottentots, Victorian John Lubbock had drawn on a book written by a man called Kolben that aspired to be a history of the Cape. It contained the now familiar insults applied to so many of the 'modern savages' described in *Prehistoric Times*. The Hottentots were 'in many respects the filthiest people in the world'; one of their customs was to confine old people within a solitary hut where, 'without any one to comfort or assist 'em' they would 'die either of age or hunger, or be devoured by some wild beast'; unwanted children were – according to Kolben – 'buried alive'. Other customs were described as quite unfit for publication.

Victorian John Lubbock was evidently concerned about the accuracy of these claims, and noted their incompatibility with earlier descriptions of the Hottentots as 'the most friendly, the most liberal, and the most benevolent people to one another that ever appeared on earth'. Having visited so many 'savages' of the prehistoric world, modern John Lubbock knew that his namesake was quite right to question this latest barrage of Victorian racist abuse. He was more interested in the author's careful descriptions of Hottentot clothes and iron-working, of the animal bladders and baskets of tightly platted rushes they had used to store their milk.

Although the date is 8000 BC, similar containers are already being used within Boomplaas Cave, not for milk but for water and gathered plants. Domesticated animals and pastoralists will not arrive for another seven thousand years at least. Lubbock closes his book and takes shelter in the cave as rain begins to fall. On the floor are a scatter of mats made from tightly woven bulrushes, among which is the familiar clutter of a hunter-gatherer camp – several hearths, partly worked hides, stone flakes, baskets, bowls and firewood.[39] Underneath lie many layers of compacted earth made from washed-in silt and sand, weathered rock from the cave wall, and the decomposed remnants of mats, baskets and bags. This in turn covers the debris of those who used the cave before the Holocene began, hunting eland, Cape horse and giant buffalo when grasslands covered the Cango valley.

That had been before thorny shrubs and trees replaced those grasslands at 12,000 BC. And so when, in 8000 BC, a party of hunters arrive in Boomplaas Cave, they carry the partly butchered carcass of a small antelope that had lived by browsing in the bush rather than grazing upon the ground. It is a steenbok, an animal that can still be found in the Cango valley today. As this and other browsers spread with the new scrubland, the grazers had to leave to find their food elsewhere.[40]

Some, such as the white rhinoceros and black wildebeest, managed to do so and continue to survive today. But six species became extinct: the Cape horse, giant buffalo, giant hartebeest, Bond's springbok, the southern springbok and a large warthog-like pig. Richard Klein from the University of Chicago – who has studied the bones from South African caves for more than thirty years – has questioned whether the demise of these species can be attributed to the change of climate and its impact on vegetation alone.[41]

One of Klein's main concerns is that the fated species had already survived several previous periods of equivalent climate change. Moreover, as several survived to 10,000 BC, there seems to be a gap of at least two thousand years between the spread of woodland and their extinction. Bond's springbok had survived even longer, still being hunted at 6500 BC in light of bones found within another cave. And so Klein thinks that the hunter-gatherers of Boomplaas Cave and elsewhere played a role in the ultimate demise of these animals.

They need not have done very much – merely killing a few of each species every year might have had a devastating effect on populations that were already in a fragile state. The switch from spear hunting to the use of bow and arrow might been a significant factor. So too might the expansion of the human population into the interior, through the gift-giving network. During previous climatic periods, when the grasslands were diminished by the spread of trees, species such as the Cape horse and giant buffalo might have survived in the interior free from the threat of human predation. But by 12,000 BC such refugia had been lost in the face of the new expansion of human settlement. There was now no safe place to wait until more amenable conditions returned.

Thus, the situation in South Africa seems similar to that of North America where extinctions were far more extensive in scope. In both regions, environmental change alone appears insufficient to have caused extinction. So too was the extent of human hunting. But their combined impact seems to have been as fatal for the South African Cape horse and giant buffalo as it was for the North American mammoth and shasta ground sloth.

From Boomplaas Cave Lubbock heads west, travelling back to the cave in Elands Bay where his South African tour began. As he does so, the climate begins to change again. After at least eight thousand years of increasing rainfall, this trend was reversed, possibly with a return to summer rainfall alone – something that inhibited vegetation growth and caused the retreat of some browsing animals from the margins of their range.

When Lubbock arrives at Elands Bay Cave in 7000 BC, not only has the coastal plain entirely disappeared but also much of the rocky shore where he had watched molluscs, seaweed and crabs being gathered. Little more than an unproductive strip of sand remains. While he had been travelling inland, the sea level had continued to rise, reaching three metres higher than it does today. The cave is now isolated upon a headland, exposed to Atlantic gales and frequently smothered in fog, while the nearest source of freshwater lies some twenty kilometres away.

Elands Bay Cave is deserted inside.[42] A layer of blown sand covers the shells, animal bones and other debris that had once accumulated upon its floor. A pile of turds tells Lubbock that the cave is now used by animals; the sediments at its rear have been disturbed by a jackal's den. Lubbock sits upon the cold, damp floor, not surprised that people have left to live elsewhere. Neither was John Parkington when he found a chronological gap in the otherwise continuous use of Elands Bay Cave. He decided that people had gone to live inland where freshwater could readily be found.

With no one to watch and no light by which to read, Lubbock recalls what else is happening in the world close to this date in human history. In Jericho a young man is plastering the skull of his father, while at Nea Nikomedeia in Greece, the first farmers are clearing the land. At the other end of Europe, hunter-gatherers are roasting hazelnuts on a tiny Scottish island. A stampede of bison is taking place at Horner on the Great Plains of North America, while pumpkins are being gathered in the Oaxaca valley and vicuña herded in the Andes. On the other side of the world, the rock-faces of Arnhem Land in Australia are being painted with rainbow serpents and yams. In East Asia wild rice is being sown at Pengtoushan and pig traps are being dug in the Tama Hills of Japan. At Damdama on the Ganges plain, a turtle is being hauled from a nearby river.

Lubbock thinks about the newly settled farmers who are building mud-brick houses at Mehrgarh and Jeitun, and those of a longer standing who are making pots and arguing with visiting traders in the town of Yarim Tepe. But his thoughts are washed away as heavy rain begins to fall and Atlantic waves crash upon the shore, throwing salt-laden spray into the cave.[43] It is now completely dark. As there is no chance that moonlight will arrive on this wild stormy night, Lubbock huddles down to sleep on the cold cave floor.

Elands Bay Cave was destined to remain unused for another 4,000 years – a period in which the whole of the Western Cape would also be effectively deserted. It would only be after 2500 BC, once the sea level had fallen back, that this cave once again became a favoured shelter for those gathering molluscs on the shore.

50

Thunderbolts in the Tropics

Hunter-gatherers in Central and West Africa; environmental change in East Africa, 7000–5000 BC

John Lubbock takes shelter from relentless rain below a massive granite boulder. It is perched upon a jumble of rocks and covers the entrance of a small cave in which three other men are sitting, huddled around a small hearth. The date is 7000 BC and Lubbock is in western Nigeria. The cave will become known as Iwo Eleru – a local Yoruban name meaning 'the rock of ashes'. Leaning against a wall, Lubbock watches the men eating shoots taken from the surrounding forest; these are pulled through their teeth to strip away the flesh, leaving a tangle of stringy remnants on the floor. The men remain inside the cave, eating and talking until the rain begins to ease. And then, after a brief exchange of words, they disappear into the trees outside.

As at the start of his South Asian travels, Lubbock's glimpse of this region's Stone Age inhabitants must remain frustratingly brief because few archaeological remains are known between 20,000 and 5,000 BC. Sites of any sort are hard to find; and the ephemeral fireplaces and scatters of stone tools typically left by hunter-gatherers are near impossible to locate. Aerial survey cannot penetrate the rainforest canopy to identify monuments or ruins, while any items on the ground are hidden beneath thick vegetation. The great majority of campsites, once located on riverbanks, will have been either washed away by floods or buried by alluvium. And so archaeologists are largely dependent upon the chance finds by farmers and those making roads or digging wells.

Caves within the rockier parts of the forest provide the best chance of finding prehistoric occupation. But as airborne dust is scarce and as these caves are formed from resilient granite, they lack the floor deposits needed to seal and preserve human debris left within. Iwo Eleru is the one exception.

In the late 1960s Thurstan Shaw, then Professor of Archaeology at Ibadan University, wished to examine the late Stone Age archaeology of Nigeria: that coming after 15,000 BC. He was particularly interested in the antiquity of numerous ground stone axes that had been coming to light as stray finds throughout the West African forests. These were known locally as 'thunderbolts' and were frequently placed by local priests in venerated positions, such as on altars to Sango, the god of thunder.[1] Suspecting that they were in fact products of the Stone Age, Shaw began to search for a suitable cave to excavate, eventually finding Iwo Eleru which was located midway between the southern coast and the northern edge of the tropical forest.[2]

It had only ever been used as a temporary shelter. Each occupation is likely to have lasted little more than a few days and was separated by a long interval, perhaps of a century or more, from the next. The most recent had been by farmers from the local village 10 kilometres away – it was ashes from their fireplaces that gave the cave its name. Below this modern debris were pieces of pottery and fragments of axes – the former first being made around 3000 BC, the latter around one thousand years earlier. Both the pottery and the axe fragments were found in layers containing microliths and scrapers, together with a large number of cores and waste flakes. These continued right to the base of the cave deposit, dated at c. 10,000 BC. And so the chipped-stone technology remained unchanged throughout the Holocene.

Other than the appearances of axes and pottery, the only evidence Shaw discovered for changing lifestyles came from a gradual increase in the use of chert for tool manufacture. This stone is much better for flaking than the locally available quartz, but the nearest source would have been at least 50 kilometres from the cave. Only a tiny proportion of the tools in the lowest levels were made of chert; in the upper levels it was being used for more than 30 per cent of the tools. This could mean any number of things: that people were travelling longer distances in the course of their hunting and plant gathering, that trade networks had been established, that special trips were being made to collect chert nodules. Without more evidence it is hard to know which – if any – of these explanations is correct.

The only other discovery at Iwo Eleru was a poorly preserved male burial in the lower layers, dating to a few centuries before Lubbock's arrival.[3] Shaw was unable to locate a burial pit or any items deliberately placed within the grave; he thinks the body had been left tightly contracted and covered with a thin layer of soil alone. The man's teeth are described as being 'worn right down to the gums in great sweeping slopes and scallops, simply leaving little crescents of enamel round the edge'.[4] This is, in fact, a characteristic of the dental remains of hunter-gatherers in equatorial environments arising from pulling fibrous and sand-covered plants between the teeth to strip off the fleshy edible parts.

At the LGM, Iwo Eleru had been surrounded by savannah while the West African rainforest was restricted to small refugia along the coast and banks of major rivers. From 12,000 BC onwards, increased rainfall and temperature caused the forest spread to reach far beyond its current boundaries. Today there is a gap in an otherwise east–west continuity of West African forest, known as the Dahomey Gap, falling in the Republics of

Togo and Benin. The forest on either side has an identical range of animals and plants, indicating that they had once been joined. Elsewhere, the Early Holocene extent of the forest is evident from tree stumps of rainforest species found within buried soils of savannah that lie beyond the forest boundaries of today.[5]

Given the lack of animal bones or pollen grains in the deposits within Iwo Eleru, it is near impossible to tell exactly when the cave became surrounded by forest as it is today. The microliths and scrapers from Iwo Eleru are essentially the same as those found at sites in East and South Africa, such as Lukenya Hill and Rose Cottage Cave, sites known to have been in open woodland or savannah. Shaw suggested that the appearance of ground stone axes some time after 4000 BC might mark the date when Iwo Eleru became enclosed by rainforest, requiring its occupants to fashion new tools. But despite this, it seems unlikely that the shelter had remained in open savannah until then. Pollen diagrams from Lake Bosumtwi in Ghana suggest that substantial re-forestation had already begun by 10,000 BC.[6]

When making his journey to Iwo Eleru from Elands Bay Cave, Lubbock had initially revisited localities through which he had passed on his southward journey. He returned to Pomongwe Cave in the Matopos Hills of modern-day Zimbabwe where, at 15,000 BC, he had encountered the two hunters making an overnight camp. On his second visit to the cave, a party of women and children were spread around nearby bushes and seemed to be gathering berries. Lubbock paused to help and found that they were collecting caterpillars instead – altogether more nutritious. The bushes were heavily laden, allowing the women and children to eat as they worked and still fill the baskets they carried. These were then taken to the cave and emptied into storage pits at its rear, sealed under leaves weighted by stones.

The cave had been transformed since Lubbock's previous visit eight thousand years ago, having become a key settlement for the many families who now regularly hunted and gathered in the now well-watered Matopos Hills. Firewood and substantial piles of grass were stacked by the walls to use as bedding, while bunches of dried flowers and herbs hung from pegs. Near the entrance a large spread of glowing embers was turning to ash, protected from the outside breeze by a brushwood windbreak. This seemed to be a fireplace for communal use; around the walls there were smaller, private-looking hearths. The floor was covered by mats on which several craft activities had evidently taken place – pieces of cut leather, ostrich-egg shell, bone needles and grinding stones were scattered around. The women and children now sat on the mats to await the return of a hunting party. Lubbock looked inside the storage pits at the back of the cave. One was lined with roots and contained the berries, another was empty but had been fitted with a tortoise carapace, presumably to keep its contents dry.

From Pomongwe Cave, Lubbock retraced his past steps into the western Kalahari; Drotsky's Cave was empty, although there was recent debris on the floor. Fifty kilometres further north, however, he found a gathering of several families within the three striking Tsolido hills – known today as male, female and child. The people were based in an impressive-looking cave with a large overhanging roof, within which several racks of catfish were being dried, reminding Lubbock of Wadi Kubbaniya at 20,000 BC. He soon discovered that these Kalahari people were also catching spawning fish in a nearby lake immediately after the annual flood. Lubbock spent a few days fishing, once again using his hands to scoop docile fish from the shallows, although his new companions preferred to use spears tipped with barbed bone points.

Almost all the other activities under way at this cave were familiar to Lubbock. Women sat in small groups in the open air making ostrich-egg-shell beads and pounding various roots. Microliths and scraping tools were made and used to repair hunting weapons and to clean hides, new bone points were carved from the leg bones of antelope. The one new thing for Lubbock – in Africa at least – was to watch pigments being prepared. Lumps of white calcrete and red ochre were ground into a fine powder which was then mixed with water in tortoise-carapace bowls. Human figures and enigmatic signs were painted on the wall of what would appropriately become known as White Paintings Rockshelter.

After leaving the Tsolido hills, the final leg of Lubbock's journey to Iwo Eleru took him into the newly expanded rainforest of the Congo basin. Much of his time was spent on one river or another, having either 'hitched' a canoe ride or 'borrowed' a craft himself. He enjoyed being back in the tropics, feeling as overwhelmed by the extravagance of nature as when he had travelled in Southeast Asia and the Amazon. Great rapids foamed below high peaks with a beauty matched first by the vivid hornbills and kingfishers, and then by the orange, crimson and pure white blooms found upon the forest floor.

Wildlife, from hippos and gorillas to mangrove flies and mosquitoes, surrounded Lubbock in profusion. The only people he saw were in tiny groups along the riverbanks; they had always disappeared into the forest before he could reach them or paddled swiftly downstream in their canoes. Apart from a lost or discarded stone-bladed knife and a scatter of flakes from quartz nodules at a locality we now call Besongo, on the bank of the Busira River, they left no other traces.

As elsewhere in western Africa, archaeologists have had a frustrating time in the Congo basin – particularly when it comes to establishing how long people may have been living within the heart of the tropical forests. Although two stone flakes were discovered in 1945, the first formal report of stone tools from the Congo basin wasn't made until forty years later.[7] The

Dutch archaeologist Johannes Preuss conducted a systematic survey of the area in 1982–3, working with the National Museum of Zaire, as the region was then called. He worked around the shore of Lake Tumba, immediately next to the River Congo itself, and then along the banks of several tributary rivers in search of archaeological remains. The riverbanks were particularly challenging to survey, being either flat and entirely covered in vegetation, or open but very steep. Nevertheless, after surveying more than 1,000 kilometres of riverbank, nineteen scatters of artefacts were found to add to those from the lakeshore. Besongo on the Busira River was one of the most productive sites – it provided ninety-four flakes. Many others produced no more than two or three pieces.

The only clue to the age of the quartz flakes, and the few pieces chipped into scraping tools, is that they must be younger than the sediments on which they were found. Preuss dated these to 25,000 BC.[8] But whether the quartz flakes indicate that people were in the Congo basin at 20,000 BC, 15,000, 10,000 or 5,000 BC, or even just a few centuries ago, remains unknown. Their age makes a substantial difference to the type of lifestyle we should associate with them; if from 15,000 BC or earlier, for example, people would have been living within a savannah rather in than the rainforest habitat in which the stone flakes were discovered. Whatever their age, the people who discarded them were evidently travelling long distances as the nearest source of the stone they used is a least 200 kilometres away.

Another set of problems faced Lawrence Robbins, of Michigan State University, and his colleagues when analysing the finds from their excavations at White Paintings Rockshelter in the Tsodilo hills of Botswana.[9] Their work had revealed a remarkable depth of deposits, demonstrating that humans had been using the cave for at least 100,000 years. It is named after the great number of white paintings that cover its walls, including depictions of an elephant, snakes and figures on horseback. The latter cannot be much more than a century old as horses were not seen in the Kalahari until the mid-1800s. Local traditions attributed the paintings to recent Bushmen – a situation quite different to the paintings of Arnhem Land, Australia, and Bhimbetka, India, which were made before living memory and attributed to supernatural beings. Nevertheless, some of the paintings in White Paintings Rockshelter might be much older than others; those close to ground level are faded and were probably made when the cave floor was considerably lower than it is today.

Below the most recent cave deposits, Robbins and his colleagues found a layer of sand packed with catfish bones, microliths, ostrich-egg-shell fragments, grinding stones and barbed bone points. Unfortunately Robbins is unable to date this layer more accurately than placing it between 21,000 and 3000 BC. The problem is that the large quantities of fishbones suggest nearby lakes and ponds, the last of which are documented between 19,000 and 14,000 BC. The Tsodilo hills are supposed to have been quite dry in the

Holocene, just as they are today, with the nearest opportunities for fishing 45 kilometres away in the Okavango River. But radiocarbon dates indicate that the fishing had taken place between 9000 and 3000 BC, which fits with the style of the stone and bone artefacts.[10]

Robbins's dilemma is exacerbated by the strong likelihood of artefacts moving within the soft sand of the cave floor: fishbones and pieces of charcoal might have been dragged up or down by rodents in their burrows. This has in fact been demonstrated by one fragment of bone harpoon which was found to match another discovered 20 centimetres lower down. That depth of sand is likely to have taken 4,500 years to accumulate; it might have easily been penetrated by many other bones and charcoal fragments.[11]

The date at which a series of storage pits were made in the rear of Pomongwe Cave in the Matopos Hills is also rather vague. These were excavated in the early 1960s by Cran Cooke who undertook pioneering archaeological work in what was then Rhodesia. He found thick layers of ash within the entrance area and stone footings to suggest a windbreak.[12] The pits contained a host of interesting finds: one had charred caterpillars; several had been lined with grass, another with a tortoise carapace; one further pit contained the roots of a poisonous plant (*Boophone disticha*), presumably having been used to deter insects from attacking its original contents. Another pit had been used as a fireplace and still contained a heavily burnt piece of cord made from twisted bark fibre, preserved because it had been protected below a slab of stone.

When Nicholas Walker of Uppsala University made a new study of Pomongwe in the early 1980s, he had access to Cooke's unpublished notebooks. Several radiocarbon dates were available, ranging from 13,000 to 2000 BC. These were not always found to be in the correct order: a layer was dated to be younger than one directly above it, or quite different dates came from the same layer, or their aged seemed inappropriate for the types of tools they purported to date. Walker decided that the pits most likely dated to about 4000 BC, but the evidence remains contentious.[13] If he is correct, it does not preclude the possibility that caterpillars had also been collected three thousand years earlier when Lubbock had made his second visit to Pomongwe Cave.

By travelling into the Central and then West African rainforests, Lubbock was unable to appreciate the dramatic change that the lakes of East Africa had undergone. When he had passed along the shores of Lakes Turkana and Victoria at the LGM, the water was at levels far below that found today. Many smaller lakes had disappeared entirely. By 7000 BC the precise opposite was the case: for several thousand years the lakes had been far exceeding their present-day levels. Just as the increased rainfall after 12,000 BC enabled the rainforest to expand further than it does today, so too did it fill the lake basins of East Africa to unprecedented levels.[14]

The new shorelines are still quite visible as bands of shells and lake sediment stranded high and dry many metres above the present water level. Lake Turkana was 85 metres higher than it is now, doubling its current size and causing it to overflow its basin and feed water into the Nile river system. Numerous small basins became entirely flooded; many of the small lakes now found in the Rift Valley of southern Ethiopia had joined together to make one massive lake which spilled into the Awash River.

The lake edges had evidently proved attractive places for fishing as several sites containing microliths and barbed bone points are found around the exposed shorelines of Lake Turkana. One such site is Lowasera in Kenya, where the barbed points have thin grooves around their base, indicating that lines had once been attached. Fishbones, as well as those of crocodile and hippopotamus, were found.[15]

After 12,000 BC, tropical Africa enjoyed the wettest period of its recent history, perhaps receiving 50 per cent more rain than it does today.[16] The ultimate cause was a northward shift of the monsoon system which brought rainfall to the tropics while depriving more southerly areas such as the Kalahari.[17] This situation was not to last, however. Soon after 3000 BC, rainfall was reduced once again; lake levels fell and the forests retreated to their present positions. North Africa had a similar rainfall history, which temporarily gave the Sahara a very different landscape to that which we know today. This is what Lubbock will discover on the penultimate leg of his journey around the world.

51

Sheep and Cattle in the Sahara

The development of pastoralism in North Africa,
9600–5000 BC

The date is 6800 BC – no more than two hundred years have passed since Lubbock left Iwo Eleru and headed north into what is now the Sahara Desert. As he walked, the rainforest thinned and he encountered many parties of hunter-gatherers, resting within their campsites and caves. But Lubbock wasted little time in reaching the eastern extent of the Sahara's central massif, known today as the Tadrart Acacus. This is a mass of ancient sandstone and schist rising from a surrounding sea of sand to both east and west.

The wadis of the Acacus are dry when Lubbock arrives, but the region is evidently well watered by summer rains. Rather than empty sand, the cliffs and crags are surrounded by a scrubby savannah, with tamarisk and acacia trees clustering around shallow lakes and ponds. The cliff-like sides of the wadis house numerous caves and rockshelters, outside of which people have made their camps. Like many that Lubbock has seen around the world there are windbreaks and small brushwood shelters, fireplaces, grinding stones, piles of stone flakes, the debris from making baskets and cleaning hides. Lubbock watches hunters returning empty-handed from nearby crags; the women, who carry baskets of seed knocked from the heads of wild grass, have been more productive. At first, life seems to have changed little since Lubbock had begun his global journey at Ohalo. But he soon changes his mind when he visits two caves, both of which have something strikingly different to offer.[1]

The first appears as little more than a recess below an extensive overhang of the cliff. The ground outside is quite clean of human debris, and Lubbock notices that people seem to give the cave's entrance a wide berth as they pass along the wadi. Inside, the floor is bare: solid rock with a few patches of wind-blown sand. On the western wall there is a painting – a procession of schematic figures positioned along a wavy line. Painted in outline alone, the figures have exaggerated and rounded heads and wear head-dresses decorated with parallel bands and feathers. All face east, some seemingly in positions of worship – bending over or with arms raised and opened wide. Two figures are anomalous; one is painted solid red and the other stands upon his head with legs wide apart.[2]

On leaving this cave, which will become known as Uan Muhuggiag,

Lubbock has walked no more than a few kilometres before he passes a second one that he feels compelled to visit. It has an enormously high and wide arch-like entrance and is surrounded by a hunter-gatherer camp. A few occupants are present, sitting in a group and talking animatedly about some issue that Lubbock does not understand. As he passes, he sees a vessel filled with water on the ground; the first pottery he has seen since leaving Yarim Tepe in Mesopotamia. Picking it up, Lubbock runs his figures over the wavy lines incised on its walls.

On entering the second cave, the smell of dung and urine announces the presence of sheep. Five of them are penned in the rear; not domestic, white woolly sheep but wild animals – the same animals, in fact, that Lubbock had seen hunted from the caves of Tamar Hat and Haua Fteah at the start of his African travels. They stand on layers of trampled, hardened dung and nibble the forage stuffed between the stout branches that restrain them. They are strong, distinguished creatures, but with bruised and bloodied legs from attempts to escape the pen. Animals under human control is something else that Lubbock hasn't yet seen on his African journey.

As he turns to leave the stinking cave, Lubbock notices paintings of round-headed figures similar to those he has just been looking at. These are faded and partly covered with dirt. Uan Afuda, as this cave is known today, has evidently lost any religious significance it might once have had. In the place of gods and ghosts are sheep – less spiritual beings but of more practical benefit in times of need.[3]

Uan Afuda was excavated in 1993–4 by Mauro Cremaschi and Savino di Lernia from the Universities of Milan and Rome, who found that both the cave itself and the area immediately outside had been used as a campsite from 9500 BC. Several other sites had already been excavated in the region, and Uan Afuda initially seemed to fit with an existing pattern of hunter-gatherer base camps in the Acacus and overnight campsites in the surrounding lowlands. But Uan Afuda contained one very puzzling find: a 40-centimetre-thick layer of hardened dung in the rear of the cave, dating to 7000 BC.[4]

This was first thought to derive from wild sheep sheltering in the cave when it was unoccupied by humans. But after studying the floors of caves where wild animals shelter in the Acacus today, di Lernia realised that such animals produce no more than loose and scattered droppings. Compared to these, the thick, compacted layer of dung in Uan Afuda seemed unnatural. When excavated, it was found to contain human debris: chipped stone, lumps of charcoal, butchered bones. It also contained pollen and fragments from a narrow range of plants including wild cereals, figs and *Echium* – a species known for being toxic. This range of plants could not have accumulated on its own and no animal would have chosen such a diet.

The animal that had left the dung was identified as the Barbary sheep, partly by the size and shape of its dung pellets and partly because no other candidates could be found. A few bones of other species were excavated – jackal, hartebeest, porcupine – but those from Barbary sheep were by far the most numerous. And so di Lernia concluded that at around 7000 BC animals had been corralled within the cave and provided with fodder. Toxic plants such as *Echium* might have been included to act as a soporific to keep excitable animals under control – much as modern Turkish farmers feed their sheep willow leaves when they want to subdue them.

The management of wild sheep at Uan Afuda Cave arose as a consequence of fluctuations between relatively wet and dry conditions in the central Sahara. By 12,000 BC, substantial summer rains had produced freshwater lakes and plentiful ponds and swamps within and around the Acacus. This drew both animals and people back to the central Sahara after the extreme aridity of the LGM; a lifestyle based around hunting Barbary sheep arose, supplemented by the gathering of plants and tubers. The first paintings within Uan Afuda, Uan Muhuggiag and other caves were made at this relatively affluent time – depictions of wild animals that preceded the round-headed figures that Lubbock had seen upon the walls.

Di Lernia thinks the shift from hunting to the corralling of Barbary sheep was due to a marked decline in their availability in the wild. As from 8000 BC – perhaps a little earlier – rainfall began to diminish once again, ponds dried up and the quantity of vegetation declined.[5] Several millennia of hunting may well have already severely reduced numbers of wild animals in and around the Acacus, but even if not, this return to aridity required a substantial change in human lifestyle. Rather than abandoning the region as a whole – as earlier inhabitants had done – people began to exploit a wider range of resources and started using existing ones in novel ways. The first grinding stones are found, indicating a greater use of wild grasses which were laborious to collect and process. The first pottery vessels also appear, their surfaces decorated with zig-zags and wavy lines. Perhaps their primary purpose was to make a more effective use of increasingly scarce water supplies.

The most important innovation, however, was the capture and penning of Barbary sheep. Slaughter most likely happened only when need arose, providing an insurance against seasons of drought and potentially scarce resources. Di Lernia thinks the animals were communally owned, and hence corralling would not have interfered with the hunter-gatherer sharing ethic. But the potential, at least, had now arisen for the private ownership of a valuable resource.

A similar process may have once led to the domestication of goats and sheep in western Asia. But, as genetic studies have confirmed, the Barbary sheep never produced a domesticated cousin. This might be because the slow transition from wild to domestic was halted when the people of Uan

Afuda had to change their lifestyle once again soon after 7000 BC. This date marks the arrival of a new people within their lands, one who came from the east, bringing a fully domesticated stock – not sheep but cattle.

Before the cattle herders arrived, the Acacus hunter-gatherers had developed a distinctive style of art involving the round-headed figures Lubbock has seen painted on their cave walls. This art has been studied since the 1950s by Fabrizio Mori of Rome University, whose work culminated in a magnificent corpus published in 1998.[6] By painstakingly recording paintings and engravings made in a variety of styles, Mori established three successive periods of art before 5000 BC: large wild animals, 'round heads', and 'pastoral' in which cattle predominate. Traces of pigments on grinding stones, depictions of Barbary sheep and the absence of cattle from the 'round-head' paintings, led Mori to believe that these were made between 9500 and 7000 BC.[7]

Mori believes that the round-headed figures in Uan Muhuggiag are worshipping at sunrise, and that the wavy line below depicts water flowing in the wadi. There are other 'round-head' paintings within the cave, one of which includes two elongated shapes that appear to be wrapped corpses ready for burial. An actual burial was indeed found close to the entrance of the cave – a man lying on his back with his hands drawn up to his face as if in self-defence.[8] Mori thinks that Uan Muhuggiag, which was kept quite clean of human debris, had been a place of deep religious significance for those who hunted and then corralled Barbary sheep in the Acacus.

The date is 6700 BC and Lubbock stands amidst a crowd that has quickly gathered in the vicinity of Uan Afuda. They stare at a boy who has appeared upon the crest of a nearby dune. He, however, is of less interest than the cattle by his side. These look like the animals Lubbock had seen at Yarim Tepe in Mesopotamia, having flat backs rather than the distinctive hump of the South Asian Zebu that became domesticated at Mehrgarh.[9] Although the people who use Uan Afuda and other caves have known about the westward spread of cattle herders for several years, this is the first time the new pastoral lifestyle has been seen within the Acacus itself.

The boy – about ten years of age – is joined by a couple of older youths. For several minutes the hunter-gatherers and cattle herders stare at each other, before the boys turn on their heels and disappear behind the dune. The crowd disperses to campfires and caves where they will no doubt discuss how they should respond to these new people within their midst. Lubbock already knows what he has to do: he must now visit this new world of African pastoralism that will continue in the continent long after his global tour has come to an end.

He travels due east through a landscape of scrubby woodland and semi-desert punctuated by shallow seasonal lakes.[10] An abandoned campsite is soon encountered – small rings of stones that had been used as fireplaces[11] and a variety of domestic debris including the bones of butchered gazelle and hare. Among this clutter are several standing stones with rope still attached where cattle had once been tethered, and most likely will be again.[12]

His next stop is Nabta in the eastern Sahara, a cattle herder's camp located some 2,000 kilometres from Uan Afuda and no more than 100 kilometres from Wadi Kubbaniya in the Nile valley where he had once gathered tubers at the LGM.

Lubbock arrives at dusk on a summer's day in 6700 BC, pushing his way through knee-high shrubs to find about a dozen circular and oblong huts clustered by the edge of a shallow lake. A small herd of cattle are settled upon the ground within an enclosure made by a thorn-branch fence. A group of men and adolescent boys are sitting outside the huts enjoying the evening sun, while the women are talking in little groups around the huts and the children are playing near by. As Lubbock approaches, fires are lit and the dusk suddenly turns into night. He is so exhausted that he enters the nearest hut and falls asleep upon a rush mat on its floor.[13]

The lowing of cattle as they are led from the village for grazing wakes Lubbock before dawn.[14] His resting place turns out to be a cooking hut; next to him a woman is preparing food. She is tall and sleek, her body draped with a finely cut hide and her black hair tied inside a scarf. She tends to a pottery vessel half buried within the sandy floor amidst hot embers which heat the gruel-like mixture inside. All the hut contains, apart from this hearth and several mats, is a small stack of firewood and a bundle of herbs hanging from the roof. The hut itself is a simple but robust construction – a circle of tamarisk branches stuck into the ground, tied at the apex and covered by animal skins to make a dome. Lubbock watches the woman ladle the gruel into several dried gourd bowls. She takes them outside where her husband, mother and children are waiting to eat.

Lubbock spends the day watching life at this herders' camp. He encounters this elegant woman again within a nearby oblong hut which has niches for sleeping along its sides and beds made from stacks of thin twigs and hides. She is squatting by the fire, singing to herself as she waits for some lumps of charcoal to begin smouldering within a hearth. Once they give off a strong aromatic scent, she drops the charcoal into a couple of buckets made from hide stretched across wooden frames. It is swilled around and then emptied back into the hearth thus preparing the buckets to receive that morning's milk.

Soon after sunrise the cattle return, led by several young men and boys. There are twenty animals in all but the herd disperses into four smaller groups, each owned by one of the families at the camp. It is the job of the young girls to lead their calves from a small enclosure and allow them to suckle for a short time before the women come to milk the cows into the fumigated buckets.

Once this has been done, the family gathers in a circle by the oblong hut, each holding a cup made from half a gourd. Lubbock sits with them and observes that no one drinks until the woman's husband has spoken, perhaps a prayer or a blessing. Each person in turn then scoops up a little milk and begins to drink.

After everyone has fed and rested the boys take the cattle to find more grazing; as it is the wet season there is a plentiful supply of both grass and nourishing acacia pods nearby. The calves are fed with fodder and taken by the girls to drink at the water's edge, but otherwise remain within the camp. Lubbock does likewise, following the woman around as she takes surplus milk into her cooking hut and performs domestic chores. The sandy hut floors are sprinkled with water to guard against dust; water and firewood are collected; aromatic branches for cleaning the milk-buckets gathered, along with bark fibres and roots for the repair of mats. The woman's aged mother helps with the work and keeps an eye on her two young children who are continually on the verge of crawling into the open fireplace.

A little later, Lubbock finds himself at the lakeside watching the children at play: hunting lizards, throwing stones, playing the role of a herd owner and his wife. They all look under ten years of age, which seems to be when their adult role begins.

As the older boys and men who are not required to herd the cattle have left to hunt gazelle and check their snares, the camp becomes very quiet during the midday heat. Children rest while adults undertake their tasks within the shade. Old men engage in rope-making and leatherwork, the women knot roots into mats. In the late afternoon Lubbock helps with cleaning and smoking the milk pots in preparation for the return of the cattle.

As the day draws to a close, any available young men leave to meet the herdsmen and help bring the cattle home. These are milked once again before it becomes too dark for manual work, and then the men are joined by visitors from nearby camps who bring some leaves to chew. The women and children initially hang around listening to the conversation of the men and then make their own gatherings for gossip and story-telling. People leave one by one to find their beds. Lubbock returns to the cooking hut where he again sleeps upon the floor.

Whether Lubbock would have actually seen domesticated cattle at Nabta and enjoyed a day such as this – similar to that of recent cattle herders in eastern Africa – are matters of some dispute. The site was excavated by the same team that worked at Wadi Kubbaniya: the Combined Prehistoric Expedition led by Fred Wendorf, Angela Close and Romuald Schild. Several sites were discovered around the ancient lake deposits of Nabta between 1974 and 1977. One of these – named as E-75-6 – provided particularly rich collections of plant remains and animal bones. It was further examined between 1990 and 1992 when the huts and hearths on which Lubbock's visit is based were discovered. Wells were also found, suggesting that people eventually chose to remain at Nabta throughout the winter months when the lake would have been quite dry.

The most important discovery was cattle bones, some of which dated to 9000 BC when no more than short-term camps were made beside the lake during the rainy season.[15] Wendorf and his colleagues also found cattle bones of a similar date at other desert sites, notably Bir Kiseiba, fifty kilometres to the north-east of Nabta.[16] Neither the shape nor the size of these bones precluded the possibility that they came from wild cattle. But Wendorf and his colleagues thought the landscape around these sites would have been far too dry for them to survive. All the other animals represented in their bone collections – gazelle, hare, tortoise and jackal – were small in size and had adapted to desert conditions. Unlike such species, cattle need to drink every day and would therefore have required human assistance to survive in the eastern Sahara.

The significance of this claim is that it makes the date of cattle domestication in North Africa earlier than that of western Asia, generally agreed at around 7500 BC. Before the excavation of Nabta and Bir Kiseiba there had been a consensus that cattle herding spread into North Africa from western Asia at around 7000 BC – just as it had spread into Europe – followed a millennium later by domesticated sheep and goats. Consensual views are not easily overturned and Wendorf's claims were quickly disputed by several critics, all of whom were acknowledged experts on cattle domestication.[18] They questioned the date and identification of the small number of fragmented 'cattle' bones that Wendorf had found; they asked why desert antelopes were absent from the bone collections if conditions were so severe, and suggested that the wells were recent constructions accidentally dug into archaeological sites.

Wendorf and his colleagues countered such criticisms, and so the debate ground to a halt. It wasn't until 1996 that new evidence suddenly appeared, strongly supporting Wendorf's case – evidence that came from modern-day cattle. A team of geneticists from Trinity College Dublin, led by Daniel Bradley and Ronan Loftus, compared the DNA of African and European cattle to identify when they had last shared a common ancestor.[19] They measured the extent of difference between the two samples of DNA, thereby measuring the number of mutations that had occurred since the two lineages diverged. Using an estimate for the rate at which new genetic mutations arise, an actual date for divergence could be proposed.

Bradley and Loftus concluded that the European and African strains had been evolving quite separately for at least 20,000 years. And so domestic cattle in Africa must have had a quite independent origin from those of Europe, which are known to have originated in western Asia. Thus, African domestication could indeed have occurred by 9000 BC. In other words,

Wendorf's interpretation of the bones from Nabta and Bir Kiseiba was entirely validated by the genetics of modern cattle.

It is, however, harder to say precisely where and exactly when the first African domestic cattle appeared. One possibility is that this occurred within the Nile valley at some date before 9000 BC.[20] It may have been only with the support of domestic cattle that people were able to spread into the more precarious landscapes of the eastern Sahara. Although substantially wetter than today, any lakes were dry throughout the winter months and drought was frequent. Unfortunately there is a dearth of archaeological sites in the Nile valley between 12,000 and 9,000 BC. But as no site from before 6000 BC has yielded bones of domestic animals, it seems likely that domestication had arisen elsewhere.

This might have been within the eastern Sahara itself. In this scenario, people had dispersed from the Nile valley to live an entirely hunting-and-gathering lifestyle on the shores of the desert lakes by 10,000 BC.[21] Wild cattle might have been available to hunt during periods of relatively high rainfall – although no such animals are known. Calves might have been captured, tethered and sheltered as an insurance against food shortages in future years of drought – in just the same fashion that people in the Acacus penned up a few wild sheep within their caves.[22]

Over time, as the climate became drier, winter droughts more frequent and lake waters less reliable, people would have become as dependent upon their cattle as the cattle were on humans for access to grazing and water. People would have been able to use their cattle's milk and blood, only slaughtering them for meat when conditions became severe. And when times were desperate, the eastern Sahara must have been abandoned altogether. In this manner, domestic stock and a new herding lifestyle could easily have evolved within the eastern Sahara by 9000 BC, to spread into – rather than out of – the Nile valley at around 5000 BC. Here, their milk, meat and traction would eventually become one factor that underpinned the Egyptian civilisation.

Whether domesticated cattle developed in the Nile valley or in the eastern Sahara, cattle herders were occupying the caves of the Acacus by 6500 BC[23] – some two hundred years after Lubbock's visit. The original hunter-gatherers may have moved to live elsewhere or become intermixed with the eastern migrants. Whatever the case, Uan Muhuggiag and other sites were used as cattle shelters, their floors becoming coated with dung, their walls marked with a new and flourishing art that replaced the round-headed figures. The depictions of cattle serve to remind us that the animals of pastoralists were far more than merely economic assets supplying milk, blood, meat and hides: their social lives and rituals, and some would say their manner of thought itself,[24] were intimately entwined with their beasts.

In 6700 BC Lubbock remained at Nabta throughout the summer and into the more challenging winter months when the lake dried and a well was dug. He learned more about the lives of these first African cattle herders – how they cultivated wild millet and sorghum,[25] and how cattle veins were cut by stone blades to provide nutritious blood. Lubbock participated in a sequence of ceremonies throughout the year as children passed into puberty, marriages were made and the elderly passed away.[26]

Whenever successive years of drought occurred, the Nabta campsite was abandoned for the Nile valley or surviving lakes elsewhere. Visitors were constantly arriving, just as the people of Nabta visited their own friends and relatives elsewhere. Nabta's population grew and families left to establish new campsites, gradually edging their way eastwards towards the Acacus. At around 5800 BC visitors from the north brought a small flock of sheep and goats, some of which were soon being herded along with their cattle.[27] After a prolonged period of drought the Nabta basin was abandoned altogether, this occurring at around 4000 BC.[28] Lubbock, however, had departed more than a thousand years before – heading northwards for the Nile delta where not only his African travels, but his entire journey around the world, would reach its end.

52

Farmers in the Nile Valley and Beyond

The arrival of cereal agriculture in North Africa,
5500–4000 BC

Clouds have been blown to tattered threads and a lone heron flies lazily across a sky turned vermilion and orange, violet, mauve and the palest green. John Lubbock stands at the edge of a promontory that rises above the lowlands as the sun sets behind the reed-beds of the Nile delta on a summer's day in 4500 BC. It is silent, other than the faint croaking of frogs that comes from a distant marsh. Nature has put on a marvellous display for Lubbock's last few hours in the prehistoric world. He turns and looks towards the cluster of dwellings behind him and wonders whether culture will do the same.

A single plume of smoke spirals upwards from within the village, one that is known as Merimde to archaeologists today. Lubbock approaches and steps into a range of cooking smells: roasted meat, mint and bread baking upon hot stones. He follows an alley that winds between mud-walled dwellings with floors sunk so low that his shoulders brush against the reed-thatched roofs. He hears a murmur of voices and a crackle of flame; turning a corner, he enters a courtyard where the villagers are gathered, one hundred of them at least. They wear elegant robes, headscarves, beads and bangles. They sit or stand in groups around fireplaces where the food is being cooked.

Lubbock stands amidst this crowd as they look expectantly around. And then another traveller enters the courtyard, this one visible to all and accompanied by an elderly local man, perhaps his father. As soon as he appears, a shout goes up. Everyone turns and raises their hands; formulaic greetings are voiced, followed by more informal words of welcome to their long-awaited guest. Children rush to him and he is dragged towards an empty space prepared with cushions beside a fire where a whole goat has been roasted on a spit. As he sits down, others do likewise. Mint tea is served. Now that this traveller has arrived, the feast and celebrations can begin. Lubbock never discovers who he is, where he has been and why he is so revered. He sneaks a little bread and sits in a corner, unobserved.

After leaving the cattle herders of Nabta, Lubbock had followed the Nile valley northwards, retracing on foot the southward journey he had made by canoe at 20,000 BC. Life for many people had hardly changed at all since then: wild cattle and hartebeest were still hunted; catfish were still caught in vast numbers whenever they spawned; wild plants were still gathered. A few families also engaged in cultivation and managed small flocks of sheep and goat. But Lubbock remained at a distance from any campsite or village until he reached a large lake fed by the Nile, less than fifty kilometres from where the delta began. This was within what is now called the Fayum Depression where the earliest-known farming settlements of the Nile valley are found. These were quite unlike the farming villages that Lubbock had seen in Europe and Asia, as cultivated crops and domesticated animals remained as mere supplements to a hunter-gatherer diet.

Lubbock spent two centuries exploring the settlements located around the lake after his arrival at Fayum in 5000 BC.[1] None had any dwellings more substantial than brushwood huts or were used for longer than a few months at any one time. Their occupants had small flocks of sheep, goats and sometimes cattle that were often taken to graze on the surrounding plateau. Barley and wheat were sown in small plots on the flood plain of the lake, and then left unattended while people hunted for game and fished elsewhere, both at Fayum and beyond. Immediately after the summer rains, catfish were obtained in large quantities from marshes and pools that appeared around the lake. When winter arrived, people turned their attention to the wildfowl, hunting and trapping them within the marsh.

Cereals were cultivated and many wild plant foods were gathered[2] – often in such quantities that stores could be made in case of hardships later in the year. On one occasion Lubbock helped fill about twenty large, basket-lined pits with cereal grain and other seed. These were located upon a small but prominent hill some distance from the lakeside settlement where the people were based in a cluster of simple huts. Lubbock remained unsure whether the ridge was used to protect the stores from dampness and the risk of flooding from the lake, or to conceal them from the many visitors who came to Fayum on journeys up and down the Nile.

In 4800 BC Lubbock had sat by the lake's shore and thought about his journey around the world, from Ohalo through innumerable campsites, caves, villages and towns as he travelled through 15,000 years of human history within each continent of the world. Now only the settlement of Merimde in the Nile delta was left to visit. It was no more than 100 kilometres further north and would be where his travels would end.

The Fayum Depression has been more intensively explored for Neolithic settlement than any other region in North Africa. Today it contains a small brackish and saline lake covering about 200 square kilometres. When the Greek historian Herodotus visited in 450 BC he marvelled at a lake that must have been ten times greater in extent; at 5000 BC it covered more than 20,000 square kilometres.[2] These ancient shorelines were first mapped in the nineteenth century and then surveyed for archaeological sites in the

1920s by the Cambridge archaeologists Gertrude Caton-Thompson and Elizabeth Gardner.³ One of their first finds was a low, elongated mound which they called Kom W. This proved to be an accumulation of debris from a mixed hunting-gathering and farming lifestyle – charcoal, animal bones, fishbones, pot shards, stone artefacts and so forth. Around its edge, holes had been hollowed in the bedrock for use as cooking places; some still had cooking pots in place containing fish and other bones. Signs of architecture were surprisingly absent – only simple shelters must have been used while the rubbish mound accumulated over many brief visits to the lakeshore.

Kom K, a slightly smaller site, was discovered a short distance away. It was just under one kilometre from here that Caton-Thompson and Gardner made their most spectacular discovery: fifty-six grain silos, dug into a small ridge, nine of which still contained cereal grains and other seeds. A further 109 silos were discovered on an adjacent ridge, one of which provided charred grain dating to just before 5000 BC.⁴

These silos are suggestive of the manner in which recent pastoralists of East Africa, such as the Kel Tamasheq people of Mali, have stored the seed from wild grass.⁵ They do so as an insurance against future scarcity. The grain is dried and stored in leather sacks or holes in the sand. If the following harvest provides sufficient grain, the stores will be replaced or replenished. Otherwise it is kept and said to remain quite edible for two or three years at least.

Following Caton-Thompson and Gardner's work, several archaeological projects have been conducted within the Fayum Depression by British, American and Egyptian teams – including a survey by the Combined Prehistoric Expedition. As a consequence, many new sites have been discovered, including dense clusters of lakeside hearths where fish had once been dried. But no more silos have been found and neither has any evidence of architecture more substantial than a brushwood hut. Farming had evidently remained a marginal activity – the wild resources of the Fayum appear to have been so abundant and diverse that the laborious work of tending to domestic plants and animals could be largely ignored.

The earliest farming village of the type we know from western Asia, one with mud-brick buildings and courtyards, is found at Merimde. This site is located 45 kilometres northwest of Cairo on the western edge of the Nile delta and rises as a small tell upon a spur of desert jutting into the flood plain. Discovered and excavated in the 1930s, Merimde then received further study between 1978 and 1988,⁷ revealing almost 1,000 years of occupation between 5000 and 4100 BC. It had begun life as a hunter-gatherer campsite, and its early phases suggest a lifestyle much like that occurring around the Fayum lake, with substantial amounts of fishing, hunting and gathering of wild plants. Cereal cultivation and domestic animals were used as mere supplements to the diet. But as it evolved into a farming village, its cluster of simple hide-covered huts were eventually replaced by dome-shaped dwellings built with blocks of mud mixed with straw. Granaries were constructed, and life at Merimde became structured by the cultivation of grain and management of herds.

Unlike cattle, the ultimate source of the sheep and goats, wheat and barley at Merimde, Fayum and Nabta was western Asia. There are no signs that these were independently domesticated in the Nile valley where they first appear long after farming had become established in the Jordan valley and beyond. Quite how the sheep, goats and cereals spread westwards into Africa remains unclear. Arid spells may have driven pastoralists out of the Negev and Sinai deserts towards the Nile valley. Excavations at Merimde and Fayum have recovered many types of tools that are found in western Asia, such as distinctively notched arrow points and pear-shaped mace heads.[8] The arts of spinning and weaving also appear to have spread from the east.

Both the migration of people and of trade are likely to have played a role in the arrival of Asian-style Neolithic villages in the Nile valley, just as they did in the spread of farming into Europe. But why the goats, sheep and cereals took so long to arrive remains unclear. By 5000 BC substantial farming towns were already thriving in Europe and southern Asia, to where the sheep, goat and cereals of western Asia had spread at least two thousand years before. That had required migrants or traders to travel far greater distances than is needed to reach the Nile delta from the Jordan valley. The Sinai desert may have provided a barrier, but this could hardly have been more severe than the Iranian plateau which had to be crossed for farming to reach southern Asia.

Once present in North Africa, farming settlements similar to that of Merimde soon spread along the Nile valley. They formed small dispersed communities with huts, storage pits and animal enclosures. It took another thousand years before more substantial settlements arose, with mud-brick houses. Soon after 3500 BC the first traces of canals are found – the beginning of an irrigation system that would be the key to crop cultivation, on which Egyptian civilisation would be based as it emerged during the next two thousand years.[9]

The impact of cereal farming and pastoralism on African history is beyond the chronological remit of this book.[10] Suffice it to say that as from 3500 BC North Africa became severely arid, just as it remains today. Pastoralists were driven from the Sahara and their lifestyle gradually spread into the south[11] as people migrated into the savannah landscapes of West, East and South Africa. The indigenous hunter-gatherers probably played a role by acquiring cattle, sheep and goats themselves – perhaps by thieving animals, or gaining them by trade or as bride-wealth when marriages were arranged.

By 3000 BC cattle pastoralism was present in the West African river basins and on the savannahs around Lukenya Hill; it took at least another 3,000 years to reach the Cape. This southward dispersal was a far more challenging affair than the western spread of farming economies across Europe several thousand years before. The African herders had to contend with hot, drought-ridden landscapes, a multitude of predators and – worst of all – a host of parasites and endemic diseases.

A final aspect of African farming that requires brief comment is the cultivation of indigenous plants, some of which evolved into domesticated forms. A great many of these have been known from historic times, including water melons, millet and sorghum from savannah regions, together with the cola nut, oil palm and cow pea from the forest margins. But we have almost no idea as to when the cultivation of such plants began. As Jack Harlan, the acknowledged authority on native African crops, has explained: 'African agriculture could be as old as any or it could be younger than most.'[12]

A shroud of sweet-smelling smoke hangs over the Merimde courtyard where the feast has reached its end. A few people are already sleeping around their fires, others talk quietly while still drinking tea. Lubbock sits in his corner and watches the other traveller to Merimde rise to say farewell. He knows the correct procedure: he bows his head, hugs and kisses his hosts, says the appropriate words. And then he leaves the courtyard, accompanied by the elderly man with whom he arrived.

It is also time for John Lubbock to depart. Unseen by all, he also bows his head in thanks, not just to the people of Merimde but to all of those he has seen in the prehistoric world. He too then leaves the courtyard, walking alone into the darkness.

Epilogue: 'The Blessings of Civilisation'

Past, present and future impacts of global warming on human history

In each continent he visited, John Lubbock stepped into the history of the world at 20,000 BC and left it 15,000 years later. His travels have enabled me to write a narrative about human lives rather than a catalogue of archaeological finds. When they began, it was a time of global economic equality when everyone lived as hunter-gatherers in a world of extensive ice sheets, tundra and desert. By their end, many were living as farmers. Some people grew wheat and barley, others rice, taro or squash. Some lived by herding animals, some by trade and others by making crafts. A world of temporary campsites had been replaced by one with villages and towns, a world with mammoths had been transformed into one with domesticated sheep and cattle. The path towards the huge global disparities of wealth with which we live today had been set.

Many hunter-gatherers survived but their fate had been sealed when agriculture began. The new farmers, eager for land and trade, continued to disrupt hunter-gatherer lives. They were followed by warlords and then nation-states building empires in every corner of the world. Some hunter-gatherers survived until recent times by living in those places where farmers could not go: the Inuit, the Kalahari Bushmen and the Desert Aborigines. But even these communities are no more, effectively killed off by the twentieth century.

It is no coincidence that human history reached a turning point during a period of global warming. All communities were faced with the impact of environmental change – sudden catastrophic floods, the gradual loss of coastal lands, the failure of migratory herds, the spread of thick and often unproductive forest. And along with the problems, all communities faced new opportunities to develop, discover, explore and colonise.

The consequences were different on each continent. Western Asia, for example, happened to have a suite of wild plants suited to cultivation. North America had wild animals that were liable to extinction once human hunting combined with climate change. Africa was so well endowed with edible wild plants that this cultivation had not even begun there by 5000 BC. Australia likewise. Europe lacked its own potential cultivars but it had the soils and climate in which the cereals and animals domesticated elsewhere would thrive. South America had its vicuña and North Africa its wild cattle; Mexico its squash and teosinte, the Yangtze valley its wild rice.

Continents, and regions within continents, also had their own particular environmental history, defined by their size, shape and place within the world. The people who lived in Europe and western Asia had the most challenging roller-coaster ride of environmental change. Those living in the central Australian desert and the Amazonian forest had the least. The type of woodland that spread in northern Europe favoured human settlement, while that in Tasmania caused the abandonment of its valleys. The melting of the northern ice sheets caused the loss of coastal plains throughout the world with the exception of the far north, where precisely the opposite occurred when the land, freed from its burden of ice, rose faster than the sea.

Although the history of any region was conditioned by the type of wild resources it possessed and the specific character of its environmental change, neither of these determined the historical events that occurred. People always had choices and made decisions from day to day, albeit with little thought or knowledge of what consequences might follow. No one planting wild seed in the vicinity of Jericho or Pengtoushan, tending squash close to Guilá Naquitz or digging ditches at Kuk Swamp, anticipated the type of world that farming would create.

Human history arose from accident as much as by design, and the paths of historical change were many and varied. In western Asia, hunter-gatherers settled down to live in permanent villages before they began to farm, just as they did in Japan and on the Ganges plain. Conversely, plant cultivation in Mexico and New Guinea led to domesticated plants and farming long before permanent settlement appeared. In North Africa, cattle came before crops, just as vicuña came before quinua in the Andes. In Japan and the Sahara the invention of pottery preceded the start of farming, whereas it occurred simultaneously with the origin of rice farming in China; its invention in western Asia came about long after farming towns had begun to flourish.

Who could have predicted the course that history would take? At 20,000 BC, Southwest Europe set the cultural pace with its ice-age art, by 8000 BC it was an entirely undistinguished region. At 7500 BC, western Asia had towns housing more than a thousand people, but within a millennium itinerant pastoralists were making campsites within their ruins. Who would have imagined that the Americas, the last continent to be colonised, the last to begin a history of its own, would have become the most powerful nation on planet earth today, its culture pervading every corner of the world? Or that the very first civilisation would have arisen in Mesopotamia? Or that Australia would remain a land of hunter-gatherers while farming flourished in New Guinea?

While the history of each continent was unique, and has required its own specific mix of narrative and causal argument to explain, some forces of historical change were common to all. Global warming was one. Human population growth was another; this occurred throughout the world as people were freed from the high mortality imposed by ice-age droughts and cold and required new forms of society and economy irrespective of environmental change.

A third common factor was species identity. All people in all continents at 20,000 BC were members of *Homo sapiens*, a single and recently evolved species of humankind. As such, they shared the same biological drives and the means to achieve them – a mix of co-operation and competition, sharing and selfishness, virtue and violence. All possessed a peculiar type of mind, one with an insatiable curiosity and new-found creativity. This mind – one quite different to that of any human ancestor – enabled people to colonise, to invent, to solve problems, and to create new religious beliefs and styles of art. Without it, there would have been no human history but merely a continuous cycle of the adaptation and readaptation to environmental change that had begun several million years ago when our genus first evolved. Instead, all of these common factors combined, engaging with each continent's unique conditions and a succession of historical contingencies and events, to create a world that included farmers, towns, craftsmen and traders. Indeed, by 5000 BC there was very little left for later history to do; all the groundwork for the modern world had been completed. History had simply to unfold until it reached the present day.

John Lubbock sits on a hilltop in southern England, one close to where I myself live and work.[1] It is a summer's day in 2003. He reads the final chapter of *Prehistoric Times* and finds his Victorian namesake extolling the 'blessings of civilisation' over the life of a savage, one who was 'a slave to his own wants, his own passions…', one who can 'depend on no one, and no one can depend on him'[2]. As my own book has shown, the development of modern-day archaeology has proved such views to be entirely wrong. Prehistoric hunter-gatherers were no more the starving, morally decrepit savages depicted in *Prehistoric Times* than they were the Noble Savages proposed by Jean-Jacques Rousseau a century before.

There are two main reasons for archaeology's success in exposing the error of such views and revealing the true nature of prehistoric times.[3] First and foremost is the commitment of its practitioners, all the way from those distinguished academics I have named within my text to the thousands of volunteers who have dug holes and washed finds ever since the discipline begun. Second, and not far behind, is the use of science: that which allows us to identify cotton inside a corroded copper bead, reconstruct the pattern of prehistoric migrations from the genes of people alive today, specify ice-age temperatures from beetle wings and – most especially – establish the order of events by the use of radiocarbon dating.

Victorian John Lubbock had valued science, not only for its role in the nascent discipline of archaeology which he himself helped to create, but as one of the great 'blessings of civilisation' that farming and industry had delivered to humankind. He lavished praise on the telescope and the microscope as having improved the eye and provided 'fresh sources of interest' for enquiring minds. He praised the printing press, which 'brings all who choose into communion with … the thoughts of a Shakespeare or a Tennyson, the discoveries of a Newton or a Darwin … the common property of mankind'. He cited chloroform to illustrate how the progress of science has diminished the extent of human suffering.[4]

We have no cause to challenge such claims – the idea of living permanently in a hunter-gatherer world without books and medicines is quite appalling. But when one sits upon a hilltop in southern England and looks across the devastated landscape that modern farming has delivered, one must be less sanguine than Victorian John Lubbock. At 12,500 BC southern England had been an ice-age tundra frequented by reindeer, snowy owl and arctic hare; by 8000 BC it was smothered in lush woodland within which red deer browsed and wild boar rooted on the forest floor. Even in 1950 it had been a richly textured landscape of woods and fields, of ponds, paths and pastures. But in 2003, there are vast expanses of southern England where hardly a tree or bush exists, from which wild animals and birds have been almost entirely expelled by the industry of modern farming. There are very few hills from which traffic below and aeroplanes above cannot be heard.

Its polluted air requires one to ponder the circularity of history. Farming and industry were products of a history brought about by global warming. Now they themselves are the cause of renewed global warming that has already had a sizeable impact upon the world and will condition the future history of humankind. Mass deforestation and the burning of fossil fuels have increased the level of greenhouse gases and planet earth is becoming warmer than nature intends. During the last few decades, glaciers on all continents have receded, snow cover in the Northern Hemisphere has reduced dramatically, and the Antarctic ice shelf is on the verge of collapse.[5]

Just as in prehistoric times, the natural world is undergoing change. The flowering dates of many plants have already advanced, birds are breeding earlier and changing their habitats. Once again insects have been some of the first species to respond: flights of aphids are arriving earlier in the United Kingdom while the butterflies in North America and Britain are being found at higher altitudes and further north.

The next century of human-made global warming is predicted to be far less extreme than that which occurred at 9600 BC. At the end of the Younger Dryas, mean global temperature had risen by 7°C in fifty years, whereas the predicted rise for the next hundred years is less than 3°C; the end of the last ice age led to a 120-metre increase in sea level, whereas that predicted for the next fifty years is a paltry 32 centimetres at most, rising to 88 centimetres by AD 2100.[6] However, while future global warming may be less extreme than that of 9600 BC, the modern world is in a far more fragile state owing to environmental pollution and the resource requirements of six billion people. As a consequence, the threats to human communities and natural ecosystems are far more severe than those of prehistoric times. When the vast low-lying regions of the ice-age world were flooded, many were uninhabited; those settlements that did exist – such as the 7000-BC town of Atlit-Yam on the Israeli coast – housed a few hundred people at most. Today, 120 million people live in the delta regions of Bangladesh, six million of them on land less than one metre above current sea level, and 30 million below three metres. Rising sea level will be accompanied by devastating storms and the penetration of salt into their freshwater supplies.[7]

When global warming made the Tasmanian valleys uninhabitable after 14,000 BC and the Sahara Desert after 5000 BC, their people found other places to live – the world was still quite empty of human settlement. But where will the new displaced populations be able to go? Those from the flooded delta regions; those from inundated low-lying islands in the Pacific and Indian Oceans[8]; those from Sub-Saharan Africa where the frequency and intensity of drought will become too severe to be relieved by any amount of international aid?

The global warming that brought the ice age to its close created localities of abundant resource which people claimed as their own and were prepared to fight for, such as in the Nile valley at 14,000 BC, northern Australia at 6000 BC and southern Scandinavia at 5000 BC. Such conflicts were trivial affairs in comparison to those that we know today; but our modern world seems destined to become yet more violent as the impacts of renewed global warming are felt.

Shortage of fresh water will become a major source of conflict. Its supplies are already under pressure owing to the demands of modern farming and daily human need. Such pressure will become severe with the predicted reductions of rainfall and increased evaporation in the key catchments of the world. Water will eclipse land, politics and even religion as the source of dispute between Middle Eastern states – a development that has already begun.[9] Moreover, global warming will likely exacerbate the existing extremes of wealth and poverty in the world: agricultural productivity in the developed nations is predicted to increase, while the reverse will happen in the developing world. Global terrorism is bound to thrive.

It is ironic that the continent that became habitable as a consequence of the natural global warming after the LGM, is now the one doing most to make vast areas of the world uninhabitable for others by its excessive contribution to the cause of renewed global warming: America is the main polluter of our skies.

John Lubbock looks beyond the traffic at the countryside of southern England. It is bleak. Much of the Early Holocene oak woodland had already been cleared in prehistoric times. But this region only took on its now desolate appearance during the last fifty years: ponds were left to silt up and soon disappeared, copses were removed, hedges grubbed-up, small farms replaced by factory-like enterprises that specialised in growing wheat and harvesting subsidies.[10] Today's prairie-like landscape suffers from soil erosion and has been polluted by an excess of fertiliser and pesticide.[11] As with so much other farmland in the Western world, it produces far more food than we require.[12] And yet we live within a world blighted by hunger. Eight hundred million people live close to starvation – a number predicted to increase with the new global warming. Over the next hundred years, an additional 80 million people are likely to become hungry and malnourished because of environmental change.[13] Some believe that the only way to end world hunger is by genetically engineering existing crops to increase their yields, improve their pest resistance and make them tolerant of salt-ridden soils.[14]

Human-induced genetic modification of plants first arose from the attempts of hunter-gatherers in western Asia to cope with the droughts of the Younger Dryas and to feed the gatherings at Göbekli Tepe and elsewhere. Their cultivation of wild cereals unknowingly created genetic change and produced the domesticated wheat and barley we grow today. The genetics of other species were also changed by human action, creating domesticated squash, maize and beans, rice, quinua, taro and potatoes. Such plants supported the Early Holocene increase in human population, and now, via plant breeding and crop management, support our vast global population. But a further two billion people will need feeding during the next quarter-century.[15]

Some scientists believe that the genetic engineering of plants at the molecular level – the deliberate insertion of DNA from one species into another – is simply the next step forward in this history of plant manipulation for human need.[16] Because new genetic variants solved a food crisis brought about by past climate change, they argue, additional genetic variants might do the same for us today.

This may indeed be the case but archaeology has given us another, and perhaps a far more important, lesson from the past. As soon as farming had begun, the surpluses arising from the new, high-yielding genetic variants had come under centralised control, as is evident from the buildings at Jerf el Ahmar in 9300 BC, Beidha in 8200 BC and Kom K in 5000 BC. From the very start of farming, food had become a commodity, a source of wealth and power for those who controlled its distribution. And so one should suspect that the already existing inequities of global food supply are likely to become enhanced by the creation of yet more genetic variants with even higher yields. Those who guarded the grain silos in prehistoric times are being reincarnated as the biotechnology companies who patent such plants and distribute their seed.[17]

The defiled landscape of southern England, and that of so many other regions of the modern world, poses another question about biotechnology. As has been evident from this history, when archaeologists study a past environment they invariably find a far greater diversity of plants and animals than are known in the same locality today. The flora of the forest steppe in the vicinity of Ohalo at 20,000 BC and the fauna of North America at 15,000 BC are just the most obvious examples of a far richer and more varied natural world in prehistoric times. Biodiversity was reduced by climate change – the increasing zonation of vegetation types in northern latitudes favoured the few specialists over the many generalists. But the consequences of farming for biodiversity have been far more severe, as can be appreciated by either imagining the devastated landscape around 'Ain Ghazal in 6500 BC or by looking at that of any intensively farmed region of the world today.

Will the cultivation of new genetic variants, plants unnaturally resistant to pests and disease, take the loss of biodiversity to a new extreme? Will such plants invade and overrun the communities of wild species that still survive? Will the remaining refuges of the natural world, especially the precious wetlands and salt marsh, also be turned into agricultural land, just as happened to the woodlands of southern England when people had the first genetic variants to sow?[18]

There are no answers. Biotechnology might be the greatest blessing we have and lead to the end of world hunger; disease-resistant, genetically engineered crops might protect biodiversity by reducing the need for chemical sprays. A common need for water might unite the warring factions of the Middle East. The predicted extent and impact of global warming might be quite wrong. Our politicians might devise both the will and the means to curb pollution, to distribute resources fairly throughout the world, to provide new homes for displaced populations, and to preserve the natural world. They might do all these things. But they probably won't.

So what about the 'blessings of civilisation'? Are the delights of the microscope, the thoughts of Darwin, the poetry of Shakespeare and the advances of medical science, sufficient recompense for the environmental degradation, social conflict and human suffering that ultimately derive from the origin of farming 10,000 years ago? Would it have been better if we had remained as Stone Age hunter-gatherers forsaking the development of literature and science? The answer is in our hands; it depends upon what we choose to do during the next hundred years of global warming – our future, that of planet earth, remains within our control. All we can know for sure is that by the end of the twenty-first century the world will be quite different from how it is today – perhaps as different as the world of 5000 BC was from that of the LGM.

John Lubbock turns his page and reads the final paragraph of *Prehistoric Times*. He finds words that remain entirely appropriate for today:

> Even in our own time we may hope to see some improvement, but the unselfish mind will find its highest gratification in the belief that, whatever may be the case with ourselves, our descendants will understand many things which are hidden from us now, will better appreciate the beautiful world in which we live, avoid much of the suffering to which we are subject, enjoy many blessings of which we are not yet worthy, and escape many of those temptations which we deplore, but cannot wholly resist.

John Lubbock, Prehistoric Times, 1865, p. 492

NOTES

1: The Birth of History

1. Unfortunately I lack the space within this book to provide definitions for 'farming', 'towns', 'civilisation' and many of the other terms I use, such as 'village' or 'hunter-gatherer'. My adoption of these simply follows common usage. 'Civilisation' is perhaps the most contentious; my reference is to societies with a state organisation, monumental architecture, social and labour differentiation. I do not mean to imply that such societies had 'civilised' values, or that such societies are the result of a progressive social evolution, as the term was used to suggest by prehistorians and social theorists in the early twentieth century (see Trigger, 1989). My use of 'town' also requires a brief comment. I use this simply to refer to a settlement that is significantly larger than those of the very first sedentary communities, whether they be of hunter-gatherers, cultivators or farmers – whose settlements I refer to as villages. Such 'towns' might remain very small in comparison with settlements of recent history and would be referred to as villages by later prehistoric or historic archaeologists. I do not mean to imply any particular form of social or economic organisation different to that within a village.

2. I have decided to use 'BC' (Before Christ) in this book rather than the more scientific 'BP' (Before Present) – to my mind both are equally arbitrary. The 'Present' in BP is, in fact, 1950 and so a BC date is converted to a BP date by simply adding 1950. Within my main text I give dates as approximate BC dates – in calendar years rather than 'radiocarbon' years – the difference between these being explained in chapter 2. In my endnotes I provide specific dates in uncalibrated radiocarbon years and, when possible, calibrated years BC at one standard deviation (calculated using OxCal version 3.5). With very few exceptions, all dates I refer to are based on radiocarbon dating, and many have utilised the AMS, accelerator mass spectrometry technique. The technique of radiocarbon dating is explained in chapter 2.

3. Mithen (1998).

4. Owing to the problems of calibrating radiocarbon dates as described in chapter 2, and securing accurate details from ice cores, as described below, the precise date at which glacial conditions reached their peak cannot be specified. It most likely fell at 22,000 or 21,000 BC rather than the nice round number that I have chosen to use for convenience.

5. The reasons for the growth of ice sheets, and cyclical climate change in general, are examined in chapter 2.

6. See Petit et al. (1999) for a demonstration of c. 100,000-year oscillations in earth's climate, which draws on evidence from the Vostok ice core, Antarctica.

7. This is, I appreciate a contentious statement and we cannot remove the possibility that some of the current global warming (and associated changes in climate) have arisen from natural rather than anthropogenic causes – for the past 130 years solar output has been increasing (Parker, 1999). We can be confident, however, that human activities are a major contributor to the current phase of global warming. For an exhaustive treatment of this topic, see *Climate Change 2001, The Report of the Intergovernmental Panel on Climate Change* (3 vols.), published by Cambridge University Press.

8. Greenhouse gases are those in the atmosphere which, by absorbing thermal radiation emitted by the earth's surface, have a blanketing effect upon it. The most important of these gases is water vapour, but its amount in the atmosphere is not directly changed by human activities. These, however, can influence the amount of carbon dioxide, nitrous oxide, the chloroflurocarbons and ozone. Once increased, such gases have the effect of a greenhouse, warming that encased within. The role of greenhouse gases and issues concerning global warming in general are described by Houghton (1997).

9. A key concern of archaeologists throughout much of the twentieth century was the identification of archaeological cultures which many implicitly assumed to relate directly to an ethnically defined group of people. Childe (e. g. 1929, 1958) championed this view, using recurring association of artefact types (e.g. specific styles of pottery, swords, burial practices and architecture) to identify prehistoric cultures. The most popularly known culture of this type is the 'Celts'. Human history then became no more than the replacement of one culture by another, and the emergence of new cultures, the origin of which was often assumed to be in some distant land by some undefined mechanism. Many archaeologists believed that there was no necessary direct relationship between such archaeological cultures and human groups – archaeological cultures were assumed to have their own evolutionary dynamic, a position developed by David Clarke. This 'culture history' view of the past came under serious question during the 1960s with the rise of 'processual' archaeology, as in the work of Binford and Renfrew, which was itself criticised by the 'post-processualists' such as Ian Hodder. Trigger (1989) provides a review of such developments in

archaeological thought. I find the identification of past 'cultures' through specific types of material culture to be of little value in attempting to reconstruct past human behaviour, societies and history. There are, however, a few exceptions: cases in which traditions of artefact manufacture appear so strong that they suggest the people recognised themselves as some form of cultural entity. Consequently I use the terms 'Natufian' and 'Clovis' to imply both 'archaeological cultures', in Childe's terms, and to refer to people who had a degree of cultural self-identity. But in the majority of cases I have deliberately avoided invoking past cultures, as I have no belief that such cultures existed.

10. John Lubbock was one of the most influential Victorians involved in the establishment of archaeology as a discipline and the nineteenth-century debates on evolutionary theory, especially as regards humans and culture. Hutchinson (1914) provided a two-volume biography, but Lubbock deserves a modern treatment to assess his contribution to the development of archaeological and evolutionary thought, expanding on the brief treatment he receives from Trigger (1989). Janet Owen from the University of Durham is engaged on research regarding his collections of archaeological and ethnographic material; much of the short bibliographic note that follows draws on her recent publication (Owen, 1999).

John Lubbock was born in 1834, the son of a City banker and liberal-minded mother. They lived at the High Elms estate near Down in Kent, where they were neighbours of Charles Darwin. This appears to have been a close and stimulating relationship that developed Lubbock's passion for science and evolutionary theory. He followed his father by becoming a banker in the family firm and was elected as an MP in 1870. As a Victorian polymath, Lubbock was involved in entomology, botany, geology, archaeology and ethnography. In 1865 he published *Prehistoric Times*, which became a best-seller and standard textbook, with the seventh and final edition appearing in 1913. His second book, *On the Origin of Civilisation*, was first published in 1870 and also went into several editions.

Lubbock spoke in support of Huxley in the famous British Association meeting in Oxford in 1860. He sought to use archaeological evidence to support Darwin's theory, publishing many articles in the 1860s which culminated in his two books. He was one of the founding members of the elite X Club established in 1864 in defence of evolutionary theory; other members included Thomas Huxley, Joseph Hooker, John Tyndall and Herbert Spencer. Lubbock held many influential positions: President of the Ethnological Society, 1864–5; President of the International Association for Prehistoric Archaeology, 1868; first President of the Royal Anthropological Society, 1871–3; Vice-President of the Linnean Society, 1865; Vice President of the Royal Society

on several occasions between 1871 and 1894; President of the Society of Antiquaries, 1904. During this period he worked closely with John Evans, the other key figure in the establishment of archaeology as a discipline. He also knew Lieut.-Gen. Henry Lane Fox Pitt-Rivers who was engaged in making a substantial collection of archaeological and ethnographic artefacts from around the world and addressing the mechanism of cultural change. John Lubbock made his own important collection.

As from 1870, Lubbock began to invest his time and energies in politics and natural science rather than archaeology and ethnography. He published numerous articles on botany, zoology and geology and a book entitled *Ants, Bees and Wasps* in 1882.

As Liberal MP for Maidstone, Kent, Lubbock had a distinguished political career. He had four main interests: the promotion of the study of science in primary and secondary schools; the national debt, free trade and related economic issues; the protection of ancient monuments; the securing of additional holidays and shorter working hours for the working classes. In 1871 he purchased part of the Avebury estate to protect the stone circle from impending destruction. He steered the Ancient Monuments Act of 1882 through Parliament. When made a peer in 1890, he took the title of Lord Avebury. He also passed the Bank Holidays Act of 1871, along with another 28 Acts of Parliament. He was a founder member of the London County Council in 1888, becoming its Chair from 1890 to 1892. His first wife, Ellen Frances Hordern died in 1879. Five years later he married Alice Lane Fox, the daughter of Pitt-Rivers. John Lubbock died in 1913.

11. The extent to which cultural and historical change are explained by reference to the actions of specific individuals is a long-debated topic in the humanities. My own position is that archaeological explanation needs to make specific reference to the activities of individuals (Mithen, 1990, 1993b) and produce narratives that weave together long-term global developments with day-to-day human experience. In writing this specific book I have been particulary influenced by Hobsbawm's (1997) essay 'On History from Below' and Evans's (1997) book entitled *In Defence of History* that discusses the nature of historical explanation in response to the Post-Modernist agenda.

12. These quotes are taken from Theroux's essay 'Being a Stranger', the introduction to his collection of 1985–2000 travel writings, *Fresh-Air Fiend* (London, Penguin Books, 2001).

13. W. Thesiger, *The Marsh Arabs* (London, Penguin Books, 1967, p. 23).

2: The World at 20,000 BC

1. Pushkari is described in Soffer (1990) and has a radiocarbon date of 19,010±300 BP. It is not a well-preserved site and much of my reconstruction scenario is based on the better preserved and

younger sites of Mezin and Mezerich, as described in Soffer (1985).

2. For those requiring further information about human evolution, see Johanson & Edgar (1996) for a well-illustrated work on the fossil record, Stringer & McKie (1996) for the origin of modern humans and Mithen (1998) for the evolution of mind.

3. The 2002 discovery of a seven-million-year-old fossil specimen is described in *Nature* (vol. 404, pp. 145–9, 11 July 2002, with a commentary by Bernard Wood on pp. 133–4).

4. The precise timing that hominids left Africa and arrived at different localities in Asia and Europe is subject to considerable debate by palaeoanthropologists. For recent reviews and a selection of the arguments, see the edited volume by Straus & Bar-Yosef (2001). My own computer simulation work explores the problems in establishing the timing and nature of hominid dispersals from Africa (Mithen & Reed, 2002).

5. Hot Springs, South Dakota, USA, is one of the most important mammoth-bone localities in the world. At least 100 mammoths met their end within a natural sink-hole and have been extraordinarily well preserved within the sediments. Uncalibrated radiocarbon dates for the mammoth bones include 26,075±975 BP and 21,000+700,-640 BP (the accuracy of these are questionable, Haynes 1991, p. 225) with the assumption that most of the mammoths met their deaths around 26,000 years ago. They apparently came to feed on vegetation at the edge of the pond, or perhaps to drink, and then slipped or became trapped within the mud to die of either starvation or drowning. Lister & Bahn (1995) describe the site and provide spectacular illustrations.

6. The following text about the causes of long-term climate change caused by variation in the earth's orbit draws on Dawson (1992) and Lowe & Walker (1997). Milankovitch's theory has been validated because several of the warm peaks identified by the ocean-core and ice-core records (as described below) correlate with the predicted periods of Milankovitch-driven global warming, such as that of OIS5e at 125,000, and that which came between 20,000 and 10,000 years ago (*see* note 8). Similarly, the global cooling that led to the ice sheets of 20,000 years ago also correlates with a period of decreased spring and increased winter exposure to solar radiation within the Milankovitch cycle – just the conditions that would lead to the growth of ice sheets in the Northern Hemisphere. The new data from the Vostok ice core revealed in 1999 confirmed the significance of the 100,000 and 41,000-year cycles, while the 21,000-cycle is also of significance for the short-term fluctuations within the major climatic cycles.

The Milankovitch cycles are not the only influence on global climatic change. Another cyclic phenomenon appears to be variations in solar output – the sun seems to get hotter, and then cooler and hotter again. This may account for a 1,500-year periodicity in global climate evident from the last 15,000 years (Campbell et al., 1998). For the last 130 years there certainly has been an increase in output from the sun that has had a significant effect on global temperatures, although anthropogenic warming has become dominant in the last two decades (Parker, 1999).

Not all the influences on global climate derive from cyclic phenomena. The classic aperiodic influence is impact by meteors, the most famous being that which struck the earth *c.* 65 million years ago, creating a long, long winter by pushing vast quantities of dust into the atmosphere. Volcanic eruptions have also had an influence. The eruption of Toba in Sumatra about 75,000 years ago was most probably the largest volcanic explosion the planet has known for the last million years and is likely to have been a major influence over the short but intense cold period of OIS4.

7. There are two key problems with invoking variation in earth's orbital pattern as the cause of climate change. The first is that on the basis of our knowledge of its influence on seasonality, the 100,000-year cycle should be having a much weaker effect on the earth's climate than the shorter cycles, but nevertheless it is this long-term cycle which is of most significance. Secondly, while the changes in orbital patterns arise gradually, those changes in the earth's climate arise suddenly, flipping from one state to another.

In light of these two problems, substantial effort has been made to understand how small changes in seasonal temperatures and hemispheric contrasts between the seasons might be amplified to have such dramatic climatic consequences. Probably the most significant amplifying mechanism is an alteration in ocean currents (Ruddiman & McIntyre, 1981). During glacial phases these appear to have had a different pattern to those of interglacials, with the absence of the formation of deep water in the North Atlantic. The consequence of this is that western Europe is denied its warm winters. It may be the case that relatively slight variations in seasonality caused by the Milankovitch cycles change the prevailing winds sufficiently to transfer water evaporation from one part of the ocean to another. The part of the ocean from where water is evaporated becomes relatively more saline, and hence more susceptible to sinking, while that which receives transported water vapour as precipitation becomes less saline and hence less susceptible to sinking. There may be threshold levels in the relative degree of salinity in different parts of the oceans that result in sudden transitions of ocean currents from one state to another. Indeed, it is evident from the changes in carbon dioxide levels in the earth's atmosphere, as detected from bubbles of gas trapped within the ice sheets, that such changes have happened in the past and this may be why gradual developments in orbital patterns result in sudden transitions of the earth's climate.

Ocean currents are likely to be just one of

several amplifying mechanisms. By themselves they seem incapable of explaining global climatic change, as opposed to that of the North Atlantic region where the sudden end of deep-water formation would have had its influence. Additional amplifying mechanisms seem significant. One is the build-up of greenhouses gases, principally carbon dioxide, that may itself be largely a consequence of the changes in ocean currents. Just as is happening today, these greenhouse gases would warm up the earth and may lead to a switch from glacial to interglacial conditions. The growth of ice sheets may itself have constituted an amplifying mechanism. As these extended in size, the degree of albedo would have increased – that is, the amount of radiation reflected by their whiteness. Hence, as they began to grow under the influence of the Milankovitch cycle, their very presence would have further amplified the changes in temperatures and made relatively mild climatic influences quite severe. Conversely, as soon as some global warming began and the ice sheets began to melt, reduced albedo would have amplified the global warming.

8. To explain how ice cores from Greenland and the Antarctic provide information about past climate I will begin by describing how such information is derived from ocean sediments. These are principally composed of the calcium-rich skeletal remains of micro-organisms, notably those known as foraminifera. The chemical composition of the sediments reflects the chemistry of the water within which the foraminifera had lived. Oxygen within the ocean comes in two principal isotopes, ^{18}O and ^{16}O (atoms with different numbers of neutrons). As water temperature falls, there is a relative enrichment of ^{18}O, because the lighter isotopes are preferentially removed by evaporation. Conversely, as water temperature increases, there is a relative depletion of ^{18}O. So, as the remains of organisms accumulate gradually on the sea bed, they create a trace of how the relatives levels of ^{18}O and ^{16}O have fluctuated, and thereby provide a record of temperature change. By taking a core of sediment – from a region where there has been minimal disturbance to the seabed – and measuring the relative concentrations of ^{18}O and ^{16}O in a series of successive slices through the core, one can monitor how our global climate has changed. Many such cores have been taken from all of the world's oceans and these provide similar curves of changing isotope frequencies.

Perhaps the most important, V28-238, comes from a region known as the Soloman Plateau of the equatorial Pacific (Shackleton & Opdyke, 1973). About one million years is recorded in the 1,500-cm of sediment of this core, and the often jagged fluctuations in ^{18}O and ^{16}O concentrations inform us about four major features of our climatic history. First, during the last million years there have been at least ten major glacial–interglacial cycles, each cycle of which took about 100,000 years to complete. Second, within these

cycles there have been many smaller fluctuations between relatively warm and relatively cold temperatures – scientists refer to these as stadials (relatively cold phases within an interglacial) and interstadials (the converse situation). Third, the transition from a glacial to an interglacial state often occurred very rapidly – a sudden transformation of global climate in the timescale of decades rather than centuries or millennia. Fourth, the present interglacial is particularly warm, as indeed was the preceding interglacial 125,000 years ago. The volume of ice has been lower in these interglacials than at any time in the earth's history.

The alternating periods of warm and cold in the global climate as identified by the oxygen isotopes are denoted by numbers. Any warm phase has an odd number, and the numbers go back in time in ascending order. Thus our present interglacial is referred to as Oxygen Isotope Stage (OIS) 1, and the last ice age, which peaked 20,000 years ago as OIS2. The warm phase that preceded the latter between 59,000 and 24,000 years ago and is known as OIS3, while the last full interglacial that reached its peak at 125,000 years ago is OIS5. Moreover, that interglacial is itself broken up into five sub-stages of relatively warmer and cold periods, which are denoted by letters, OIS5a–OIS5e, with the latter marking the time of the highest sea level. The oxygen isotope curves also indicate glacial periods when ice sheets may have been as large and sea levels as low as at the LGM. OIS12, for instance, which lies between 478,000 and 423,000, was a period of major ice advances across North America and Eurasia.

Ice cores can provide a more detailed picture than marine sediments of how global climate has varied during the last half-million years as individual annual layers can be examined. The moisture that evaporates from oceans is eventually precipitated within snow and becomes preserved within glacier ice. Hence as ice layers gradually build up, just like the layers of sediment on the ocean floor, they will also contain a record of fluctuating ^{18}O and ^{16}O concentrations. The relationship of these within the ice to global temperatures will, however, be the inverse of that within ocean sediments: when ^{18}O is relatively low, this will be denoting a period of relative warmth. The longest ice-core sequence so far secured was published in Petit et al., (1999), providing a dramatic illustration of the regular oscillation from glacial to interglacial conditions. Ice cores also contain a great deal of other information. Trapped bubbles of gas, for instance, tell us about the state of the atmosphere, while the electrical conductivity of the ice tells us about its dust content and hence the quantity in the past atmosphere, which reflects storminess.

9. J. Lewis-Williams (2002) has provided an interpretation of Upper Palaeolithic art as resulting from shamanistic trance visions which may have been drug induced.

10. I may be taking a slight artistic licence with

time in this case. The horse panel from Pech Merle has been dated to prior to the LGM at 24,840±340 BP (Bahn & Vertut, 1997) – although the large deviation in the date places the LGM within the 95% confidence level. The paintings in Pech Merle are described by Lorblanchet (1984) who has himself made a replica of the panel using ice-age techniques.

11. The advent of radiocarbon dating soon after the last war transformed archaeology, with the first radiocarbon dates being published in 1949 by Willard Libby. The techniques involved are described by Bowman (1990) while the significance of radiocarbon dating for archaeology was most fully explained by Renfrew (1973). Archaeologists today prefer to use the Accelerator Mass Spectrometry (AMS) technique as described by Hedges (1981) as this allows for the greatest degree of accuracy. The key feature of the AMS technique is that it counts ¹⁴C atoms directly, disregarding their radioactivity. This allows minute samples to be dated, enabling the technique to be applied to precious relics, such as the Turin shroud and Palaeolithic cave paintings. It also allows a much greater degree of precision. Any further developments in the radiocarbon-dating technique are unlikely to reduce the magnitude of standard deviations below 50 years. Hence there will always remain some degree of imprecision.

12. For tree-ring-based calibration curves, see Kromer & Becker (1993), Kromer & Spurk, (1998). The absence of tree rings before 11,000 years ago means that radiocarbon dates cannot be calibrated by the use of dendrochronology. This is unfortunate as it is precisely during the few thousand years before 11,000 years ago that some of the most important cultural and environmental events occurred and without accurate dating the association between these cannot be established. Fortunately, other means to calibrate dates have been found – although the term 'correction' is generally used to distinguish these methods from that which uses tree rings.

One means of correction has been by securing what are known as paired radiocarbon uranium-thorium dates from coral (Bard et al., 1990). Uranium-thorium dating operates on the same principle as radiocarbon dating – in this case the decay of uranium into thorium – but returns calendar dates. In that sense it is equivalent to the counting of tree rings. As with using tree rings, one can examine the deviations between the U/Th (i.e. calendar) and the radiocarbon dates and hence provide a means to correct dates coming from archaeological sites. This method has shown that at 20,000 calendar years ago, a radiocarbon date is about 3,000 years too young – so if a bone was dated to 17,000 BP, then the animal died at about 20,000 years ago. By the time we reach 12,500 years ago, radiocarbon dates are about 2,000 years too young.

13. All radiocarbon calibrations in this book make use of the OxCal ver. 3.0 programme.

14. The following text describing activities at Ohalo is based on material in Nadel & Hershkovitz (1991) and Nadel & Werker (1999). Further information about Ohalo, including radiocarbon dates, is provided in chapter 3.

3: Fires and Flowers

1. The Ohalo I refer to is in fact properly known as Ohalo II. There is a series of publications by Nadel and his colleagues about specific aspects of the site. Nadel & Hershkovitz (1991) provided the first reports on subsistence data; Nadel et al. (1994) describe twisted fibres; Nadel (1996) the organisation of space within the settlement; Nadel (1994) the burial from Ohalo; Nadel & Werker (1999) describe the brushwood huts. Nadel et al. (1995) provide 26 AMS radiocarbon dates which lie between 21,050±330 and 17,500±200 (with one aberrant date of 15,500±130), which suggest that occupation had most likely occurred at 19,400 BP. Belitzky & Nadel (2002) consider the environmental and possible tectonic reasons for the rapid flooding of the site.

2. Moore et al. (2000) report that the coastal plain of the Levant would have been extended by 5 km from Latakia south to Mt Carmel, and by 15 km along the coast of Palestine.

3. For an exposition of the techniques of pollen analysis with regard to reconstructing past environments, as is briefly summarised in this chapter, see Lowe & Walker (1997).

4. That, at least, is the theory. In practice, there are many complicating factors. Different species produce different quantities of pollen: willow trees are a renowned 'over-producer' while mugwort – one of the first colonisers of tundra as the climate warms – is a notable 'under-producer'. So a large number of pollen grains from willow does not necessarily mean a large number of willow trees, and mugwort may have been abundant even though its pollen was all but absent in the core. The pollen of some species, such as alder, is deposited in its immediate vicinity, while that of others, such as pine, can be carried for many miles on the wind. In view of these differences between trees, it requires immense botanical knowledge and an appreciation of many local environmental factors to accurately translate a collection of pollen grains into a plant community. Fortunately, the study of pollen grains began more than a hundred years ago and is now one of the most sophisticated methods by which prehistoric environments are reconstructed.

5. The palynological sequence from the Hula core is described by Baruch & Bottema (1991), along with that from other pollen cores in the region. Of these, the Ghab core from northwestern Syria is important but suggests contrasting developments to those recorded in the Hula core – an expansion of woodland at the late-glacial maximum and Younger Dryas. Hillman (1996) suggests that while this might reflect localised developments, the limited number of radiocarbon dates which provide the chronology for the

Ghab core are most likely erroneous. Hillman also summarises the evidence from the Zeribar core that comes from the northern Zagros Mountains.

6. Hillman (2000, fig. 12.2) provides a sense of the colourful late-glacial steppe via a photograph of the flowering steppe of central Syria taken in April 1983.

7. Hillman (2000) provides a detailed account of his reconstructions of the steppe, available plant foods and a review of how such plants have been traditionally exploited; a shorter version of selected aspects is available in Hillman (1996) and Hillman et al. (1989). His work in this regard is of as much importance as archaeological excavations themselves in terms of understanding prehistoric hunter-gathering and the origin of agriculture.

8. Zohary & Hopf (2000) discusses the wild progenitors of the Neolithic crop assemblages and the key differences between these and the domesticated variants.

9. In *The Seven Pillars of Wisdom* T.E. Lawrence (1935, pp. 591–2) wrote: 'Also Azrak was a famous place, queen of these oases, more beautiful than Amruh, with its verdure and running springs … Next day we walked gently to Azrak. When we were over the last ridge of lava-pebbles and saw the king of the Mejabar graves, that most beautifully put of cemeteries … Azrak was empty of Arabs, beautiful as ever, and even more beautiful a little later when its shining pools were brilliant with the white bodies of our men swimming, and the slow drift of the wind through its reeds was pointed by their gay shouts and splashing echoed off the water.'

10. Lubbock (1865, p. 67).

11. Archaeologists, of course, have typological names for all such artefacts. The ones I envisage in this scenario are the microliths manufactured at Wadi el-Uwaynid (Garrard et al., 1987) that have been described as including 'double truncated backed pieces', 'arch backed curved pointed pieces', 'La Mouillah points', and burins (the chisel-like objects).

12. A variety of manufacturing techniques and shapes of microliths have been found in these collections. These seem unlikely to relate to specialised hunting or plant-gathering tools; they were probably local traditions, passed from generation to generation within families, just as we unthinkingly pass on our own habits to our children. Such traditions spread between the families and groups that regularly associated with each other and so leave us with a record of their social lives. That several different traditions are found suggest that the landscape may have been sparsely populated, with people living in small, scattered groups – not surprising in light of the cold and dry conditions at the LGM and following millennia. Some archaeologists, notably Nigel Goring-Morris (1995), believe that the differences between manufacturing techniques and shapes of microliths evident from stone artefact collections

reflect different cultures – ethnic groups – with exotic names such as Nebekian, Qalkan and Nizzanan. The most widespread is known as the Kebaran, which is often used for all these late-glacial hunter-gatherers. Goring-Morris (1995) describes how the period can be divided into four phases on the basis of microlith typology. But it seems unlikely to me that the past people divided themselves into such cultures; if they had done so, the tiny microliths would hardly have been an effective expression of identity.

13. These sites are referred to as Uwaynid 14 and 18, both of which seem to be isolated remains of a one-time continuous spread of material close to a freshwater spring (Garrard et al., 1987). Uwaynid 14 has dates of 18,400±250 BP and 18,900±250 BP, while Uwaynid 18 is dated to 19,800±350 BP and 19,500±250 BP (Garrard et al., 1988).

14. The sites Garrard studied ranged in date from the Upper Palaeolithic to the Late Neolithic; some had originally been located during a survey by Waechter in the 1930s. The sites Garrard explored in Wadi el-Jilat, about 55 km southwest of the Azraq basin, are particularly impressive, notably the huge site of Jilat 6 which covers 18,200 sq. m. with three distinct phases, the earliest of which is likely to be contemporary with the sites in Wadi el Uwaynid (Garrard et al., 1986, 1987, 1988).

15. Garrard et al. (1986) reports finding tortoise shells at several of his sites and suggests that they had been used as bowls.

16. The following draws on Hillman (1996).

17. I am referring here to the 'Geometric Kebaran' which introduces a degree of uniformity into the late-glacial chipped stone assemblages. Goring-Morris (1995) also distinguishes two further cultures that existed in the Negev desert, the Mushabian and the Ramonian, both defined by particular manufacturing techniques and shapes of microliths.

18. Neve David is described by Kaufman (1986).

4: Village Life in the Oak Woodland

1. 'Ain Mallaha was discovered in 1954 and initially tested in 1955 and 1956 by Jean Perrot, who then undertook full excavations between 1959 and 1961. Further excavation was undertaken by Monique Lechevallier in 1971–2 and then by François Valla from 1973 to 1976, and once again between 1996–7. An account of the earlier work is provided by Valla (1991) and of his final excavations by Valla et al. (1999).

2. Bar-Yosef (1998a) and Valla (1995) provide reviews of the Natufian culture. The edited volume by Bar-Yosef & Valla (1991) has a fine collection of papers and is heavily drawn upon within this chapter.

3. Bar-Yosef & Belfer-Cohen (1989) describe the Natufian as the point of no turning back towards agriculture on account of the sedentary nature of some Early Natufian villages. It is not a position that I necessarily agree with.

4. My description of structure no. 131 draws on the study by Boyd (1995).

5. The Natufian, particularly the Early Natufian, is rich in art objects, both the decoration and carving of utilitarian items and those with no evident functional purpose. A review of Natufian art is provided by Bar-Yosef and Belfer-Cohen (1998), while Belfer-Cohen (1991) describes art objects from Hayonim Cave, Noy (1991) those from Nahal Oren and Weinstein-Evron & Belfer-Cohen (1993) objects from recent excavations at El-Wad. Sickle hafts carved into ungulates have been found at Kebara Cave and El-Wad (see Bar-Yosef & Belfer-Cohen 1998, fig. 5) but not (as far as I know) at 'Ain Mallaha – and hence I have taken an artistic liberty.

6. Both the specific burial practices at 'Ain Mallaha and those of the Natufian in general have been subject to considerable debate and differing interpretation. Wright (1978) argued that these reflected social stratification within Natufian society but this position has since been questioned by Belfer-Cohen (1995) and Byrd & Monahan (1995) who have made a more careful consideration of the data, paying particular attention to the changes in burial customs between the Early and Late Natufian which had been neglected by Wright.

7. The Early Natufian have given us the earliest evidence for dog domestication from anywhere in the world. My imaginary picture of an elderly woman and puppy at 'Ain Mallaha is based on the burial from that site showing a puppy curled by the head of an elderly individual whose left hand rested on its body (Davis & Valla, 1978). Clutton-Brock (1995) reviews existing knowledge about the origin of the domestic dog.

8. This is illustrated in Bar-Yosef & Belfer-Cohen (1998, fig. 4).

9. D. E. Bar-Yosef (1989) describes and interprets shells at Palaeolithic and Neolithic sites in the southern Levant.

10. Lubbock (1865, p. 183). The passage relates to evidence from Europe, especially the Danish shell-mounds.

11. Lubbock (1865, p. 484).

12. The Natufian archaeology at Hayonim Cave is described by Bar-Yosef (1991) while Belfer-Cohen (1988) makes a specific study of its burials. This has two radiocarbon dates, 12,360±160 BP (13,123–12,155 cal BC) and 12,010±180 BP (12,974–11,615 cal BC), which places it in the Early Natufian but not at the start of that period. The Late Natufian occupation on Hayonim Terrace is described by Henry et al. (1981) and Valla (1991).

13. Biological data about Natufian populations in the Levant are described by Belfer-Cohen (1991).

14. Bar-Yosef & Belfer-Cohen (1999) described limestone and bone Natufian objects from Hayonim Cave which have a strikingly similar incised pattern to that on a bone object from Kebara Cave.

15. Garrod (1932) 'announced' the discovery of the Natufian. Her excavations at El-Wad at Mount Carmel are described in Garrod & Bate (1937), while Belfer-Cohen (1995) provides a critical discussion of the decorated burials from El-Wad. New excavations at El-Wad have been described by Valla et al. (1986).

16. The following draws on Lieberman (1993). Campana & Crabtree (1990) have discussed the evidence for communal gazelle hunting in the Natufian and its social and economic implications.

17. For a critque of Natufian sedentism, see Edwards (1989).

18. As it is feasible that mobile hunter-gatherers might invest time, labour and resources in constructing dwellings which are only used for part of the year, the evidence from 'commensuals' provided by Tchernov (1991) – the 'wild' animals that are dependent upon human presence – has been taken as the key evidence for sedentism. The use of such remains as a sign of sedentism has, however, been seriously questioned by Tangri & Wyncoll (1989).

19. Tchernov & Valla (1997) describe dog burials from the Late Natufian deposits of Hayonim Terrace and provide a discussion about dog domestication in the Natufian.

20. The Natufian settlement at Beidha is described by Byrd (1989) and that of Wadi Tabqa by Byrd & Colledge (1991).

21. The following draws on Hastorf (1998).

22. Hastorf (1998, p. 779).

23. Bar-Yosef & Belfer-Cohen (1999, p. 409).

24. Hillman (2000) notes that his experimental work had shown that using a pestle and mortar for dehusking wild wheat was almost impossible due to the tough and tight husks, unless parching had taken place to make the husks quite brittle. Unlike wild rye, in which the chaff could be winnowed away, the chaff from wild wheat is heavy and can only be separated by sieving or agitating on a wooden tray or dish.

25. A substantial study of Natufian plant husbandry involving studies of artefacts and experimental work is provided by Unger-Hamilton (1991).

26. Hillman & Davies (1990) provide a seminal and detailed study regarding the domestication rates of wild cereals.

27. The following draws on Unger-Hamilton (1991).

28. The following draws on Anderson (1991).

5: On the Banks of the Euphrates

1. Abu Hureyra was excavated by Andrew Moore as a salvage operation in advance of the dam that created Lake Assad and which flooded the site. The following text concerns Abu Hureyra 1, the epi-palaeolithic settlement located below the more substantial Neolithic village whose collapsed mud-brick walls formed the tell. I draw on both the summary (Moore, 1991) and the final (Moore, 2000) excavation report, together with the description of the village and excavations by Moore (1979). With regard to chronology, Abu

Hureyra 1 has 26 AMS radiocarbon dates which form a tight series between 11,500 and 10,000 BP.

2. Moore (2000) provides two alternative reconstructions for the dwellings at Abu Hureyra, one in which they are roofed individually as dome-shaped dwellings, and a second in which the pits are covered by a single continuous roof rather like a Bedouin tent. Moore finds the latter more likely on the basis of the arrangement of post holes.

3. This was a different type of gazelle to that hunted by the Natufian people, one that formed larger herds and made annual migrations. Each year, in the early summer, the herds reached the Euphrates having travelled northwards from the deserts of today's eastern Jordan and Saudi Arabia. Many of them turned west to find summer grazing in northern Syria. But not all, because every year hunters were waiting for them. The following text regarding gazelle-hunting from Abu Hureyra draws on Legge & Rowley-Conwy (1987). The Persian gazelle is *Gazella subgutturosa*.

4. Hillman's seminal study and results are described in Hillman (1996) and Hillman (2000). In light of the plants that would have left no archaeological trace, he suggests that more than 250 species had been exploited by the people of Abu Hureyra.

5. Legge & Rowley-Conwy (1987) provide a summary of their results and interpretation, while an extended discussion about hunting practices at Abu Hureyra is found in Moore et al. (2000).

6. Unfortunately there are no human remains from Abu Hureyra 1. For the palaeopathology of the Early Natufian people, see Belfer-Cohen et al. (1991) and see Smith (1991) for dental evidence for the nutritional status of the Natufian populations.

7. For Valla's views regarding Natufian sedentism and reference to Mauss, see Valla (1998).

8. The relevant passage is Lubbock (1865, pp. 296–9). For current theories of climate change, see Dawson (1992) and endnotes to chapter 1.

6: One Thousand Years of Drought

1. For Late Natufian settlement in the Negev, see Goring-Morris (1989, 1999). Henry (1976) describes excavations at Rosh Zin.

2. For Nahel Oren, see Noy et al. (1973).

3. For Mureybet, see Cauvin (1977, 2000).

4. Cope (1991) describes her studies on gazelle-hunting in the Natufian.

5. Bar-Yosef (1991) describes occupation in Hayonim Cave stratified below the Natufian that dates back to the early Upper Palaeolithic. Two dates, 16,240±640 BP and 15,700±230 BP, relate to the Kebaran period of occupation. Below these layers there are thick deposits with Middle Palaeolithic occupation.

6. For dental evidence on the state of Natufian health, see Smith (1991).

7. The evidence for such physical differences in Natufian populations is described in Belfer-Cohen et al. (1991).

8. For the Hula core and its interpretation, see Baruch & Bottema (1991) and Hillman (1996).

9. Hallan Çemi is described by Rosenberg & Davis (1992) and Rosenberg & Redding (2000). Five radiocarbon dates are cited lying between 11,700±460 BP (12,344–11,184 cal BC) and 9,700±300 BP (9490–8625 cal BC). The majority of the architecture is believed to date to midway through this period at c. 10,400 BP.

10. The following text regarding changing burial practices during the Natufian draws on Byrd & Monahan (1995).

11. Anderson (1991).

12. Goring-Morris (1991) makes a comprehensive description and interpretation of archaeological sites in the Negev that he refers to as the Harifian culture.

13. For instance, at Hatula (Ronen & Lechevallier, 1991) in the Judaean hills, which although undated appears to be Late Natufian due to similarities between the Late Natufian and PPNA faunal assemblages at the site and the absence of traces of sedentary lifestyle. Hare, polecat, badger, wild cat, and fox are found in addition to gazelle, sheep, aurochs, wild boar and equid. The importance of the small game increases markedly in the Early Neolithic. Salibiya I in the Jordan valley (Crabtree et al., 1991) also shows a diverse range of small game, and has a substantial number of immature gazelle, which suggests pressue on those herds leading to over-exploitation. Salibiya I is associated with a radiocarbon date of 11,530±1550 BP from a nearby deposit, while its Late Natufian date is confirmed by the particular form of the lunate microliths.

14. For a discussion regarding the impact of low carbon dioxide levels during the Pleistocene on cereal productivity and agricultural origins in general, see Sage (1995).

15. Hillman (2000, Hillman et al., 2001) provides an extremely detailed and careful argument as to the status of the rye grains from Abu Hureyra. He suggests that some forms of pulses had also become cultigens at the same time as the rye. The specific dates on the rye grains are 11,140–100 BP (11,372–11,323 cal BC), 10,930±120 BP (11,183–10,928 cal BC) and 10,610±100BP (10,925±10,417 cal BC).

16. Heun et al. (1997) made a phylogenetic analysis of wild and domesticated einkorn wheat and identified the Karacadağ hills of southern Turkey as the locality of domestication. They begin their paper with a series of caveats regarding assumptions they had to make to undertake the study, which should be carefully attended to when considering their results.

7: The Founding of Jericho

1. Kenyon's (1957) popular account of her work, *Digging Up Jericho*, remains a classic and contains a summary of the previous work on the tell. Radiocarbon dates for the PPNA settlement at Jericho are summarised in Bar-Yosef & Gopher (1997). They list fifteen dates from the western trench that range from 10,300±500 (10,856–9351

cal BC) to 9230±220 (8796–8205 cal BC), and three from the northern section between 9582±89 BP (9160±8800 cal BC) and 9200±70 BP (8521–8292 cal BC).

2. Kenyon (1957, p. 25).

3. Kenyon (1957, p. 70).

4. For a brief biography of Kenyon, see Champion (1998).

5. For the architecture and stratigraphy of Jericho, see Kenyon & Holland (1981); for the pottery and other finds, see Kenyon & Holland (1982, 1983).

6. Kenyon (1957, p. 68).

7. Bar-Yosef (1996) puts forward the argument that the walls of Jericho were for defence against floods and mud-slides.

8. For Childe's views about the Neolithic see, for instance, Childe (1925, 1928).

9. Although Kenyon referred to the skull cults of the Sepik River valley in New Guinea, she did not develop her argument that these might provide useful analogies for those of the PPNA. In the Sepik River region, clan ancestors were normally represented by masks, often of people supposed to have played a key role in the formation and history of the clan. Just as Kenyon suggests, the PPNA plastered skulls may have been of people who played a key role in the foundation of the village. In the Sepik valley, decorated skulls and shrunken heads were frequently made from the severed heads of enemies; Baxter Riley (1923) provides particularly evocative descriptions of how the heads and skulls were prepared. Head-hunting practices and the use of heads as trophies, as practised in Oceania, might also provide useful analogies for the PPNA practices and have been described by Hutton (1922, 1928) and Von Furer-Haimendorf (1938).

10. El-Khiam points are symmetrical points made on small blades with two basal notches. They were originally defined from the excavations on the terrace of El-Khiam by Echegaray (1963). For twenty years this point was the only defined type for the PPNA but as more extensive collections became available, further type artefacts were proposed, notably the Jordan valley point and the Salibiya point (Nadel et al., 1991). All three are triangular in shape with a narrow base. Other types of flint artefacts have also been recognised as unique to the PPNA, notably the Hagdud truncation, as described by Bar-Yosef et al. (1987). For those who enjoy the intricacies of Neolithic chipped stone typology from the Fertile Crescent, Gebel and Kozlowski (1994) is an essential read. The relative frequencies of El-Khiam points, Hagdud truncations, microliths and small bifacial pieces have been used to define two facies of the PPNA, the Khiamian and the Sultanian, with the latter having low frequencies of microliths and the presence of Hagdud truncations and bifacial picks. There is an ongoing debate as to whether the Khiamian and Sultanian represent functionally diverse toolkits from the same culture, either found at different sites (Nadel, 1990) or within the same settlement (Mithen et al., 2000) or chronologically successive phases of the PPNA (Bar-Yosef 1998b). Some argue that the Khiamian is merely a post-depositional mixture of the Sultanian and underlying Natufian (Garfinkel, 1996).

11. This is evident from the microwear traces present on the points, many of which indicate a circular motion charcteristic of drilling or boring rather than the impact fractures that arise on projectile points. Such microwear studies are being conducted by Sam Smith as doctoral research at the University of Reading. A preliminary report on the points from Dhra' is provided in Goodale & Smith (2001).

8: Pictograms and Pillars

1. For a full description of Netiv Hagdud, see Bar-Yosef & Gopher (eds., 1997). They provide ten radiocarbon dates that range between 9400±180 BP (9115–8340 cal BC) and 9970±150 BP (9746–8922 cal BC) with the majority tightly clustered around 9700 BP. The excavations at Netiv Hagdud recovered a much larger sample of plant remains than had come from Jericho. This included a substantial amount of barley grains that, after studies by Kislev (1989, Kislev et al., 1986), are known to have been from a biologically wild rather than a domesticated variant. The large quantity of harvesting and plant processing equipment, however, suggests that substantial and productive cultivation was undertaken. Gilgal is described by Noy et al. (1980) and Noy (1989) and has at least five radiocarbon dates ranging between 9950±150 BP (9743–9246 cal BC) and 9710±70 BP (9250–8922 cal BC). Other PPNA sites in this region include Salibiya IX described by Enoch-Shiloh & Bar-Yosef (1997). The two radiocarbon dates for this settlement, 18,500±140 and 12,300±47 BP (13,072–12,159 cal BC) are far too old for the cultural remains, indicating contamination of the samples. Limited information is available about the PPNA settlement of Gesher; Garfinkel & Nadel (1989) described its chipped stone assemblage. Four radiocarbon dates are available between 9790±140 BP (9597–8839 cal BC) and 10,020±100 BP (9741–9309 cal BC).

2. Edwards (2000) provides a report on the PPNA site of Zad (more accurately known as Zad 2 to distinguish it from a nearby Bronze Age site). He provides a single radiocarbon date of 9500 BP (9100–8550 cal BC).

3. Dhra' is described by Kuijt & Mahasneh (1998) and has three radiocarbon dates between 9960±110 BP (9684–9276 cal BC) and 9610±170 BP (9220–8750 cal BC). This report does not include the mud-wall building with pillars that was discovered during the 2000 excavation season (Finlayson, pers. comm.).

4. For a preliminary report on the site of WF16, see Mithen et al. (2000). This site currently has seven radiocarbon dates on wood charcoal ranging between 10,220±60 BP (10,326–9748 cal BC) and 9180±60 BP (8451–8290 cal BC).

5. For an overview of the PPNA in the Jordan valley, see Kuijt (1995) who suggests a settlement hierarchy. Site summaries are also provided in Bar-Yosef & Gopher (1997). Another important site is Iraq Ed-Dubb, described by Kuijt et al (1991). This has Late Natufian occupation dated to 11,415–120 (11,528–11,222 cal BC) and 10,785±285 BP (11,197–10,393 cal BC), and a single date for the PPNA deposits of 9950±100 BP (9678–9255 cal BC) (Bar-Yosef & Gopher, 1997).

6. In the following text, space precludes me from making reference to Tell Aswad, which is another key site of this period. Bar-Yosef & Gopher (1997) provide a brief summary of its PPNA archaeology, while van Zeist & Bakker-Heeres (1985) describe its important assemblage of plant remains. Its basal levels have been dated to 9730±120 BP (9283–8835 cal BC) and 9340±120 BP (8776–8338 cal BC). It is found in the Damascus basin and was originally a small village of round houses by the edge of a lake – today called Lake Ateibe. People lived for many thousands of years at this location and eventually a tell developed, known today as Tell Aswad. Relatively little is known about the early village but it is currently undergoing new excavations by Danielle Stordeur of Lyons University. Very few plant remains were originally uncovered, but those analysed from the earliest levels, dating to 9000–8500 BC, included domesticated wheat – one of the very earliest discoveries. Lentils and peas had also been cultivated, and may have been some of the very earliest domesticated strains.

7. Excavations at Mureybet are described in Cauvin (1977). The earliest Neolithic is found in Mureybet Phase III with radiocarbon dates between 10,000 and 9600 BP. Its plant remains have been described by van Zeist and Bakker-Heeres (1986).

8. See Cauvin (2000) for his arguments about the nature of Neolithic religion, its deities, and the claim that ideological change preceded economic change.

9. For descriptions of Jerf el Ahmar, see Stordeur et al. (1996, 1997). Two of its radiocarbon dates are 9690±90 (9249–8840 cal BC) and 9790±80 BP (9345–9167 cal BC).

10. This building at Hallan Çemi Tepesi is described by Rosenberg (1999).

11. Stordeur et al. (1996, p. 2).

12. Göbekli Tepe is described by Hauptmann (1999), while Schmidt (2001) provides a report on his excavations undertaken between 1995 and 1999. Owing to the monumental architecture, accurate dating of the site is essential, but its very nature makes this difficult. The absence of domestic deposits such as hearths and pits means that charcoal from well-sealed contexts for dating is absent. Two radiocarbon dates, indicating a PPNA age, have been acquired from charcoal found within the fill of the structures. But as this fill is redeposited the origin of the charcoal, and hence its relationship with the walls and pillars, is unclear. Nevertheless, Schmidt has stratigraphic evidence for a PPNA age for the structures and massive pillars. After the circular structures had been infilled, many PPNB rectangular buildings were constructed around the edge of the depression that remained. This depression was marked by a terrace wall contemporary with the PPNB structures and which was built directly on the fill (Schmidt, pers. comm.).

13. For descriptions of the artworks and other finds from excavations by Schmidt during the 1990s, together with some interpretation, see Schmidt (1994, 1996, 1998, 1999).

14. Heun et al. (1997) made a phylogenetic analysis of wild and domesticated einkorn wheat and identified the Karacadağ hills of southern Turkey as the locality of domestication. They begin their paper with a series of caveats regarding assumptions they had to make to undertake the study, which should be carefully attended to when considering their results.

15. Ghuwayr I has been described by Simmons & Najjar (1996, 1998).

9: In the Valley of Ravens

1. I am simply using the term 'town' in this and following chapters to contrast the PPNB settlements with those of the PPNA and do not imply any particular social and economic distinctions by use of that term.

2. The following text concerning Beidha draws on three principal publications: two reports by Kirkbride (1966, 1968) concerning her excavations, and the analysis of the architecture and layout by Byrd (1994). As of 2001, the final report of Kirkbride's excavations of the PPNB settlement at Beidha has not been published. Weinstein (1984) lists seventeen radiocarbon dates from Beidha which lie between 9128±103 BP (8521–8242 cal BC) and 8546±7100 BP (7729–7482 cal BC).

3. Kirkbride (1968) provides a brief background to her work at Beidha, while biographical details are covered by Champion (1998).

4. See Byrd (1994) for a specific study regarding Beidha, together with Byrd (2000), Banning & Byrd (1987) and Byrd & Banning (1988) for related and important studies on Neolithic architecture and town layout.

5. Kuijt (2000) reviews the limited evidence for social differentiation during the PPNB, which effectively comes from the burial. He summarises this by stating that 'certain individuals and groups were selected from the community and treated differently during life with skull deformation and again distinguished in death through skull caching and plastering' (p. 157). Byrd (2000) suggests that the similarity in size and outward appearance of PPNB domestic structures, and general uniformity of burial practices, may have served to create a community-wide egalitarian ethos, even though there would have been emergent inequality between households. He suggests that elders may have controlled prestige goods, postmarital residence choices and other items, including marriage costs.

6. Wright (2000) provides an excellent study of cooking and dining in the early villages and towns of western Asia, discussing where food preparation and consumption would have taken place and its social origins and consequences. She stresses that in PPNB towns such as Beidha, preparation was likely to have been a publicly observable activity taking place in courtyards while some meals would have been eaten within the houses.

7. The excavations in Nahal Hemar Cave are described by Bar-Yosef & Alon (1988). The substantial disturbance caused to the deposit have inhibited accurate dating. Charcoal from a hearth provided three dates between 8100±100 BP (7309–6830 cal BC) and 8270±80 BP (7472–7143 cal BC), while three dates have been acquired from organic artefacts which are systematically older: 8600±120 BP (7797–7523 cal BC) for knotted net, 8500±220 BP (7913–7185 cal BC) for twined fabric and 8690±70 BP (7794–7599 cal BC) for cordage.

8. The organic remains from Nahal Hemar Cave are described by Bar-Yosef & Schick (1989).

9. The other insight we gain into such materials is from imprints of matting on plaster floors as found at Jericho (Kenyon, 1957) and 'Ain Ghazal (Rollefson & Simmons, 1987).

10. Kirkbride used the term 'corridor building' for this construction at Beidha. Similar structures have not (as far as I am aware) been found in other PPNB settlements.

11. Although Beidha has circular structures below the rectangular buildings, this site and other PPNB settlements in the Jordan valley lack signs of any gradual transition between the two types of architecture. Such architectural developments are present, however, at the sites of Mureybet (Cauvin, 1977, 2000) and Jerf el Ahmar (Stordeur et al., 1996, 1997), leading some to think that this is where the PPNB originated.

12. The changing nature of domestic architecture between the PPNA and PPNB is one of the most dramatic features of the Early Holocene archaeological record. The key transition is between relatively small, circular and separate dwellings and two-storey, rectangular buildings, as also seen in the development of complex societies elsewhere in the world. Flannery (1972) interpreted this change, arguing on the basis of ethnographic analogy that the former settlements may have been occupied by patrilineal and polygynous extended families, while the later rectangular houses were occupied by individual families. This study came under criticism by Saidel (1993, rebutted by Flannery, 1993) and further discussed by Byrd (2000). He sees the major change being not so much one of social organisation as the movement of various activities to the inside of buildings – although this itself is likely to have many implications for social knowledge and interaction. Flannery (2002) revisited the issue of architectural change and places greater emphasis on a change in the pattern of risk management from a group to a family basis.

13. Both Byrd (2000) and Goring-Morris (2000) stress the likely tensions that existed within the PPNB towns and suggest that the emergence of social hierarchies and ritual ideologies were necessary to regulate increasingly complex social relationships.

14. Legge (1996) and Uerpmann (1996) discuss issues concerning caprine domestication in Southwest Asia. There are immense problems with identifying the transition from wild to domestic forms of goats and other animals. One of these is that the morphological criteria to distinguish the two forms remain rather subjective, and need to be adjusted to account for local variability in animal size and form arising from ecological conditions. Substantial progress is likely to be made by the use of genetic evidence in light of recent studies by Kahila Bar-Gal et al. (2002a, 2002b). These studies have confirmed that morphological criteria alone are liable to give a false impression about the species identification and domesticated status of animals represented by faunal remains.

15. There is some discrepency in dating regarding the start of sheep- and goat-herding at Abu Hureyra. Legge & Rowley-Conwy (1987) place the start of phase 2 at Abu Hureyra at 7500 BC, with the switch to goat and sheep happening at c. 6500 BC. Hedges et al. (1991), however, cite a date of 8330±100 (7522–7189 cal BC) for Trench E, which was associated with the switch to sheep and goat. Legge (1996) further complicates the situation with his statement that goat bones are found in the phase 2A that he dates to between 9400–8300 BP.

16. The following text about goat domestication in general draws on Hole (1996) and Legge (1996).

17. There is some dispute about the dating of Ganj Dareh. Hole (1996) reports that a date of 12,200 calendar years BP has been attributed to the basal layer, but he believes that a date between 10,000 and 9400 calendar years BP is more appropriate. Legge (1996) appears to prefer dates that cluster between 9000 and 8450 BP (radiocarbon years), seeming to reject the earlier dates as being invalid but without providing his reasons. Hedges et al. (1991) provide four radiocarbon dates between 9010±110 BP (8292–7967 cal BC) and 8690±110 BP (7940–7593 cal BC), but also refer to the problems associated with their interpretation.

18. Hesse (1984) describes his study of the goat bones from Ganj Dareh. His argument that there was also a significant size reduction from wild populations has now been rejected following a more detailed study by Zeder (Zeder & Hesse, 2000) that has confirmed the significance of the mortality profile. Zeder & Hesse (2000) also provide radiocarbon dates that confirm a date for domesticated goats at 8000 BC.

19. Hole (1996). For a review of recent research on goat domestication, see Zeder (1999).

20. The abandonment of Beidha, and indeed all the PPNB towns, is subject to much debate. General environmental degradation seems

central, but whether this arose from climatic change, deforestation for creating fields or deforestation for generating fuel, especially for plaster production, remains unclear. The key issues and possibilities are discussed in Rollefson & Köhler-Rollefson (1989) and Simmons (2000).

21. Excavations at Basta undertaken between 1986–9 are described by Nissen (1990).

10: The Town of Ghosts

1. Bar-Yosef & Meadow (1995) refer to the possibility of exchange between members of the PPNB farming communities and hunter-gatherers of the desert regions.

2. Abu Salem is located in the central Negev highlands and is described by Gopher & Goring-Morris (1998). Another important PPNB settlement is Ein Qadis I in the eastern Sinai (Gopher et al. 1995).

3. The PPNB saw a proliferation of new arrow-head and spear types, many of which were elegantly made. Classic types include the 'Byblos', 'Jericho' and 'Amuq' points, each of which have a slightly different design after having been made from a long blade. The key work for such artefacts is Gebel & Kozlowski (1994). The changing significance of wild animals is also apparent from their use in burial ritual at Kfar HaHoresh (Goring-Morris, 2000) and in the animal figurines from sites such as 'Ain Ghazal (Schmandt-Besserat, 1997).

4. Rollefson & Simmons (1987) refer to 45 different species of wild animals represented at 'Ain Ghazal, which they estimate as providing 50% of the meat eaten. They assume these wild animals were all hunted from 'Ain Ghazal itself.

5. Reese (1991) and D. E. Bar-Yosef (1991) describe the movement of seashells in the Levant from the Epi-Palaeolithic to the Neolithic. D. E. Bar-Yosef argues that the trend away from the dentalium shells had begun in the PPNA and notes that it is unclear whether this arose from cultural preference or due to changing availability on the shores of the eastern Mediterranean and Red Sea.

6. The following scenario about PPNB Jericho is based on Kenyon (1957). A list of 21 radiocarbon dates for the PPNB town at Jericho has been provided by Weinstein (1984). These range from 9140±200 BP (8687–7972 cal BC) for site E to 7800±160 BP (6981–6461 cal BC) for site F, with the majority clustered around 8500 BP. Waterbolk (1987) discusses radiocarbon dates from Southwest Asia, commenting on the quality of dates from different laboratories and how the value of dates can be maximised.

7. There is considerable intersite architectural variability during the PPNB. The unique presence of the corridor buildings at Beidha is just one aspect of this. Byrd & Banning (1988) discuss other features, focusing on the contrast between what they term 'pier' houses at Jericho and 'Ain Ghazal and the multicellular dwellings found at Bouqras and Abu Hureyra.

8. Although skulls may have been removed after having been buried for a substantial time, so that the flesh and other matter had decayed by natural processes, decapitation before burial remains a possibility. For a detailed description of known manufacturing techniques for plastered skulls from Jericho, Kfar HaHoresh and Beisamoun, see Goren et al. (2001), and for 'Ain Ghazal, see Griffin et al. (1998).

9. Goren et al. (2001) conclude a comparative study of plastered skulls from Jericho, Kfar HaHoresh and Beisamoun by arguing for pronounced intersite variability in the methods of skull modelling as well as in the iconographic details, although there was a common basic technological approach. They suggest that there was a dissemination of the required technology in the form of communicated general knowledge rather than through the movement of artisans from one site to another.

10. For a description of the objects from Nahal Hemar, see Bar-Yosef & Schick (1989).

11. Excavations at Kfar HaHoresh are described by Goring-Morris et al. (1994, 1995) and it is dated to between 9200–8500 BP. Goring-Morris (2000) interprets the ritual practices at Kfar HaHoresh in their broader social context. He notes that there were at least two and possibly four burials that were accompanied by the almost complete carcasses of wild animals.

12. Excavations at Atlit-Yam are described by Galili et al. (1993). This is a late PPNB/PPNC site with five radiocarbon dates between 8140±120 BP (7448–6862 cal BC) and 7550±80 BP (6461–6260 cal BC).

13. In the following text I draw on the general overview about 'Ain Ghazal provided by Rollefson & Simmons (1987) as well as various specialist reports specified below. The town is divided into three chronological phases: Middle PPNB, 7250–6500 BC, to which the majority of finds belong, Late PPNB 6500–6000 BC, and PPNC, 6000–5500 BC (Rollefson, 1989).

14. Banning & Byrd (1987) make a detailed study of house-building techniques at 'Ain Ghazal, inferring frequent remodelling of houses and a trend to smaller residential units.

15. Schmandt-Besserat (1997) describes the animal models at 'Ain Ghazal and interprets them in the general context of zoomorphic imagery from the PPNB. The most interesting of the 126 recovered animal figurines are two bovids that had been stabbed with microliths in the throat, abdomen, chest or eye.

16. Schmandt-Besserat (1992) believes these clay tokens may have played an important role in the earliest stages of the development of writing. Their function, however, remains very unclear and many believe her arguments are tenuous.

17. This scenario refers to the first of two caches of monumental figures discovered at 'Ain Ghazal, as described by Rollefson (1983). Their method of manufacture has been identified during the conservation process (Tubb & Grissom, 1995).

Rollefson (2000) reviews the nature of ritual and social structure at 'Ain Ghazal during the course of its existence from Middle PPNB to the Yarmoukian. I am most grateful to Kathryn Tubb (UCL) for discussions about the statues.

18. Schmandt-Besserat (1998) discusses the 'Ain Ghazal statues in the context of fragments of similar statues from elsewhere in the Near East and the plastered skulls, and interprets them by making comparisons to Babylonian texts and statues. Schuster (1995) had suggested that the 'Ain Ghazal statues represented ghosts.

19. Rollefson (1998) describes and interprets these new structures at 'Ain Ghazal.

20. The final stages of occupation at 'Ain Ghazal are described by Rollefson (1989, 1993). He identifies a PPNC phase with distinctive architectural features and argues that these were inherited by pottery-using Neolithic people, referred to as the Yarmoukian culture.

21. Banning et al. (1994) argue that archaeologists have underestimated the population size of the Neolithic immediately following the PPNB. They suggest that a change in settlement pattern has resulted in many later Neolithic sites becoming buried by sediments at the foot of slopes and hence being undetected during surveys.

22. As noted in the previous chapter, general environmental degradation seems central to the abandonment of PPNB towns, but whether this arose from climatic change, deforestation for creating fields or deforestation or generating fuel, especially for plaster production, remains unclear. The key issues and possibilities are discussed in Rollefson & Köhler-Rollefson (1989, 1993), Rollefson (1993) and Simmons (2000).

23. Rollefson & Köhler-Rollefson (1993) argue that owing to the environmental degradation caused by a combined farming and herding system, the subsistence base was reconstructed into segregated farming and herding sectors, the latter involving migratory pastoralism. Goring-Morris (1993) discusses the emergence of herding economies in the Negev and Sinai.

11: Heaven and Hell at Çatalhöyük

1. My text about Bouqras draws on the summary and interpretation provided by Matthews (2000). He cites radiocarbon dates from the settlement that span the period 6400–5900 BC.

2. My text about Nevali Çori draws on the summary provided by Hauptmann (1999). He cites three radiocarbon dates for levels I/II at the site: 9212±76 BP (8526–8294 cal BC), 9243±55 BP (8548–8324 cal BC) and 9261±181 BP (8738–8272 cal BC), and one from pit 277 of 9882±224 BP (9956–8919 cal BC). Hauptmann's report is in an excellent edited volume by Özdoğan & Başgelen (1999), which covers the Neolithic in Turkey.

3. For a comparative study of cult-buildings at Çayönü, Hallan Çemi Tepsi and Nevali Çori, and intriguing ideas about the cult of buildings, see Özdoğan & Özdoğan (1998).

4. The first excavation of the low mound was undertaken in 1962, partly under the direction of Robert Braidwood from the University of Chicago. By 1991, sixteen seasons of excavation had taken place, involving archaeologists from the universities of Istanbul, Karlsruhe and Rome, in addition to that of Chicago. In 1985, work at Çayönü came under the overall direction of Özdoğan, University of Istanbul, who has undertaken the enormous task of piecing together the discoveries from all excavations to reveal the history of this settlement. A summary of the excavation history and the development of the settlement is provided by Özdoğan (1999). Braidwood was a pioneer of prehistoric archaeology, being one of the first to bring together teams of archaeologists, botanists, zoologists and geologists. He excavated many sites in addition to Çayönü, including Jarmo, as described in chapter 45. Robert Braidwood died on 15 January 2003 at the age of ninety-five. Linda, his wife and constant companion of sixty-six years died eighteen hours later.

5. The immense obsidian workshops of central Anatolia are described by Balkan-Atli et al. (1999).

6. Aşıklı Höyük is described by Esin & Harmankaya (1999). This is a substantial tell site that had undergone extensive excavation of the uppermost layers to reveal a highly ordered layout of rectangular mud-walled structures partitioned by alleyways.

7. Çatalhöyük was excavated during the 1960s by James Mellaart and much of the following text draws on his general book about the site (Mellaart 1967). New excavations were initiated by Hodder, applying a wide range of modern scientific techniques and what he describes as a 'reflexive' methodology (Hodder, 1997). The new excavations have led to the development of a very informative website (catal.archaeology.cam.ac.uk/catal/) and two volumes of articles, one about the surface archaeology (Hodder, 1996) and one focusing on methodological issues (Hodder, 2000). Hodder (1999a) is a useful short summary of the new approach to interpretation of the symbolism at the site. My scenario of a visit to Çatalhöyük has been influenced by a lecture given by Hodder at the University of East Anglia in August 2000. Cessford (2001) has provided a new series of AMS radiocarbon dates for the earliest sequence at Çatalhöyük and assessed those available from the 1960s for the later phases of settlement. Below the known buildings, a series of middens exist and sheep/goat pens have been identified and dated by 14 AMS determinations between 8155±50 BP (7300–7070 cal BC) and 7935+50 (7030–6960 cal BC). Cessford has assessed the existing dates for the later period of occupation that Mellaart had divided into several building phases, suggesting this lies between 8092±98 BP (7310–6820 cal BC) and 7521±77 BP (6440–6250 cal BC).

8. My description of this room is based on the reconstruction of a Çatalhöyük building in Hodder (1999b).

9. This figurine is described by Mellaart (1967, p. 184) as a goddess. It was found within a grain bin in what Mellaart describes as a shrine at Çatalhöyük and is just one of a great number of figurines from the site. He believed that the Mother Goddess was at the centre of the mythological world of the Çatalhöyük people; she was 'the only source of life … became associated with the processes of agriculture, with the taming and nourishing of domesticated animals, with the ideas of increase, abundance and fertility' (Mellaart, 1967, p. 202). More recently he has described this deity as the 'source and mistress of all life, the Creatress, the Great Mother, the symbol of life itself' (Mellaart et al., 1989, p. 23). These quotes were also cited by Voigt (2000) who describes Hodder's (1990) interpretation of the symbolism and her own, neither of which use the notion of a Mother Goddess deity.

10. There is a remarkable array of paintings and sculptures from Çatalhöyük as described by Mellaart (1967), of which only a small fraction are referred to in the following text.

11. Hodder was the main proponent of what became known as post-processual archaeology during the late 1970s and 1980s and has been highly influential on the development of archaeological theory in general and our understanding of the Neolithic period. His key books include Hodder (1985, 1990, 1991, 1999c). Since 2000, Hodder has been based at Stanford University.

12. Some aspects of the micro-stratigraphic work are discussed in Matthews et al. (1996, 1997).

13. Özdoğan & Özdoğan (1998) have drawn an interesting distinction between the Neolithic settlements in eastern Turkey such as Çayönü, Hallan Çemi Tepsi and Nevali Çori that have cult buildings clearly separated from those of a domestic nature, and settlements in central Turkey such as Çatalhöyük where ritual and domestic activities were entirely integrated within the same space.

14. Asouti & Fairbairn (2001) summarise and interpret the plant remains from Çatalhöyük and other central Anatolian sites, while Martin et al. (2001) do likewise for animal bones.

15. This was a 1999 interview given to the Society for Californian Archaeology that can be read at www. scanet. org/hodder. html. Hodder has indicated that he intends his project at Çatalhöyük to last for 25 years.

12: Three Days on Cyprus

1. The names of archaeological sites on Cyprus are formally given with a prefix of the locality in which they are found, hence Aetokremnos Cave is Akrotiri-Aetokremnos. As several of the site names are already polysyllabic I have dispensed with this formality for the chapter. For those who wish to have the full names, the other sites referred to are: Kissonerga-Mylouthkia, Parekklisha-Shillourokambos and Kalvasos-Tenta. As far as I can deduce, Khirokitia is not normally preceded by a locality prefix.

2. A full description of the Akrotiri-Aetokremnos Cave and the excavations by Simmons is provided in Simmons (1999). I am very grateful to Alan Simmons for discussing his work and interpretations and responding to my critical comments in such a constructive fashion. This chapter has also benefited from discussion with Sue Colledge, to whom I am also grateful.

3. Thirty-one radiocarbon dates had been acquired on a variety of materials from the cave, which lay between 3700±60 BP (2196–1980 cal BC) and 12,150±500 BP (13,256–11,579 cal BC). The three dates on bone were deemed unreliable and the weighted average of the remaining 28 gave a calibrated date of 9703 BC (Simmons, 1999). A mean date of 10,500 BC is also frequently quoted, which I assume includes the bone dates. The radiocarbon dates have been critically assessed by Manning (1991).

4. Unfortunately there has been very limited study of the palaeoecology of Cyprus. My text draws on material in Simmons (1999). The status of the indigenous flora at 10,000 BC is very unclear. The early floras of Cyprus do not document wild wheat, although they do note the presence of wild barley which has also been recovered from early Neolithic contexts (Colledge, pers. comm.).

5. There is very little evidence as to when the hippos and elephants first arrived on Cyprus or the date at which dwarf forms emerged. Further discussion of these issues can be found in Sondaar (1977, 1986).

6. We have no evidence for the type of wood, if any, that was used as fuel. Driftwood poses a problem for establishing the chronology of a site as it might already be of considerable antiquity before being burned. This might help explain the 300-year spread of dates from Aetokremnos.

7. For a flavour of this debate and detailed discussion of the problematic issues, see the exchange of papers by Bunimovitz & Barkai (1996), Strasser (1996), Simmons (1996) and Reese (1996) in issue 9 of the *Journal of Mediterranean Archaeology*. Vigne (1996) makes a valuable contribution by reflecting on the evidence from Corsica.

8. There were many types of birds represented in the faunal assemblage, several most likely arriving by natural processes alone. The most abundant species, the great bustard, appears to have been the key target of the hunters, this being easy prey due to living in gregarious flocks and being unfamiliar with human predators (Simmons, 1999).

9. It is to Simmons's credit that he included Olsen's (1999) report within his 1999 volume – tackling each of her criticisms with an editorial footnote.

10. The hippo bones had not contained any collagen – the key compound used for radiocarbon dating. Hence, as the dates were made on bone apatite, this is generally considered unreliable. The bones might easily have become contaminated with charcoal from much younger wood.

11. Unfortunately we have little idea about the chronology of extinction for the pygmy elephants and hippos on Cyprus – my text is pure speculation. There are substantial collections of hippo and elephant bones from many caves on Cyprus with which this question could be addressed using dating programmes. The possible role of humans in the extinction of island fauna during the Pleistocene is discussed by Sondaar (1987).

12. The wells from Mylouthkia are described within Peltenburg et al. (2000) and, at greater length, in Peltenburg et al. (2001) from which I draw information for the rest of this chapter. The pre-pottery Neolithic dates for Mylouthkia include 9315±60 BP, 9235±70 BP (8545–8298 cal BC) and 9110±70 BP (8446–8242 cal BC). I am very grateful to Paul Croft and Eddie Peltenburg for discussion about the wells and their interpretation while on Cyprus in September 2001.

13. Paul Croft (pers. comm.) suggests that the wells had been dug because people wished to be located close to the bay with its natural harbour. There were plenty of freshwater streams on the island so that the digging of wells was not absolutely necessary.

14. This is pure speculation. We have no evidence for the nature of boats at this date in Mediterranean prehistory.

15. Excavations at Shillourokambos are described in Guilaine et al. (1998) and summarised in Peltenburg et al. (2001). Key radiocarbon dates are 9310±80 BP (8717–8340 cal BC), 9205±75 BP (8524–8293 cal BC) and 9110±90 BP (8451–8239 cal BC).

16. Excavations at Tenta are described in Todd (1987) and in an academically useful guidebook to the site, Todd (1998). The one radiocarbon date Todd acquired from the summit structure suggested that it had been built at around 8300 BC (9240±130 BP) (8605–8292 cal BC). This was at least 1,000 years earlier than all his other dates and hence he disregarded it as unreliable. But since Mylouthkia and Shillourokambos have been discovered, that early date has now been reinstated as quite valid.

17. These similarities are covered in detail within Peltenburg et al. (2001), in which illustrations of the Jerf el Ahmar structures are also provided.

18. The cover was designed with the name of the site – Tenta – in mind. And that, according to local legend, was because St Helena, mother of Constantine the Great, pitched her tent on the site when she returned from Jerusalem to Cyprus in AD 327 bearing the Cross of the Crucifixion, prior to the construction of the Stavrovouni Monastery about 20 km northeast of Tenta (Todd, 1998).

19. For excavations at Khirokitia, see Le Brun (1994), and also the academically useful guidebook to the site (Le Brun, 1997).

13: Pioneers in Northern Lands

1. Gough's Cave is part of an underground system truncated by the Cheddar Gorge which forms part of a dry valley system deeply incised into the limestone on the western edge of the Mendip Hills in Somerset. Jacobi's excavations are described in Currant et al. (1989). Radiocarbon dates on human bone and artefacts range between 12,300±160 BP (13,178–12,132 cal BC) and 12,800±170 BP (13,797–12,444 cal BC). Gough's Cave and others in the Cheddar Gorge, together with Creswell Crags in Derbyshire, are the most important locations for late-glacial settlement in Britain and have given their names to distinctive artefacts: Cheddar and Creswell points. Jacobi (1991) provides an overview of the late glacial in Britain.

2. Cook (1991). These human bones were not the first to come from the cave. Specimens had been found in the early excavations but their surfaces had been damaged by the diggers' tools and then covered in preservatives. Such treatment – unthinkable today – removed the possibility of any detailed study. Cook was also able to reveal that butchery had taken place very soon after death.

3. Parkin et al. (1986) analyse the animal bones from Gough's Cave, a collection dominated by horse and red deer. In addition to the evidence for tendon and ligament removal, cut-marks indicated skinning, dismembering and filleting. Carnivores had used the rear of the cave, where bones had been heavily chewed, perhaps dragged from the human occupation in the entrance area. The red deer jaws suggested that the cave had been used during the winter months.

4. Reindeer-dominated assemblages from the LGM of southwest France are described by Delpech (1983) and Bahn (1984). Many of these, such as from Gourdon in the Pyrenees, are heavily fragmented.

5. There is some ambiguity in Lubbock's text (1865, pp. 243–6) as to whether he actually accompanied Lartet and Christy when they explored caves in 1863. Lubbock describes his own visit to the Dordogne in the context of their discoveries and uses the term 'we' when describing places visited.

6. Marshack (1972) describes the Montgaudier baton. The fish is identified as a male salmon at the time of spawning because of a 'kype' or hook on its lower jaw. The seals may be following the salmon upstream or gathering at estuaries or coasts, as they do in the spring; one of the eels is clearly a male and these emerge from hibernation in the spring. As Marshack describes, several other works of art have seasonally specific imagery; Mithen (1990) describes how these may have been used in decision-making during the Upper Palaeolithic.

7. Both quotes are from Lubbock (1865, p. 255).

8. Atkinson et al. (1987) describe the reconstruction of seasonal temperatures in Britain during the last 22,000 years by the use of beetle remains.

9. Cordy (1991).

10. Chaleux Cave is found in the Namur region

of Belgium and was excavated by Edouard Dupont in the 1860s. Charles (1993) re-evaluated the fauna he recovered, while Cordy (1991) describes the small mammals.

11. Lubbock (1865, p. 295).

12. Pollen analysis as a means to reconstruct vegetation history did not develop until the early twentieth century, notably through the work of Von Post and Godwin in the 1930s. In 1865 Lubbock would, I am sure, have been quite aware that plants produced pollen which was species distinct.

13. Lubbock (1865, p. 316).

14. Who became Sir Joseph Prestwich, Professor of Geology at the University of Oxford.

15. Lubbock (1865, p. 295).

16. Although cut-marked hare bones came from Creswell Crags in England, we do not know how those hares had been caught. My little scenario draws on the trapping methods of the Eskimo, as briefly described by Birket-Smith (1959) and Graburn (1969).

17. For a reconstruction of the landscapes of Doggerland, the history of its development and loss below the North Sea, see Coles (1998).

18. Campbell (1977).

19. Charles & Jacobi (1994).

20. While radiocarbon dates from Robin Hood Cave range from 42,900±2400 BP to 2020±80 BP, the five dates from hare bones cluster between 12,290±120 (13,138–12,139 cal BC) and 12,600±170 BP (13,546–12,360 cal BC) and are most likely indistinguishable (Charles & Jacobi, 1994).

21. This dilemma is nicely illustrated by attempts to establish when people first used the small cave known as Trou de Blaireaux near Namur in Belgium (Housley et al., 1997). The stone artefacts from the lower layer of this cave are scarce, but those which exist were once believed to be about 16,000 years old, owing to radiocarbon dates on animal bones from the same layer. But the dated animal bones are found within a collection of female and juvenile reindeer antlers which is just the type of material collected by wolves for their young to gnaw upon. It seems most likely that the cave was once used as a wolf den and only later utilised for human occupation, the rubbish from which became mixed in with that of the wolves. The cause of this was most likely badgers burrowing into the cave in recent times – it is, after all, called 'Badger's Hole'.

22. Lubbock (1865, pp. 244–7). Whether he really had seen cut marks is unclear; we know today that bones can acquire many natural grooves that look almost identical to marks from flint knives until seen under scanning electron microscopes.

23. Lubbock (1865, p. 183).

24. Lubbock (1865, p. 260).

25. Lubbock (1865, pp. 184–5).

26. As used in radiocarbon dating, accelerator mass spectrometry (AMS) actually selects and counts the ^{14}C atoms in a sample relative to the ^{13}C and ^{12}C atoms. It requires only 1 mg of carbon, the amount that can be derived from about 0. 5 g of bone. This technique has allowed not only tiny pieces of cut-marked bones to be individually dated but also samples taken from carved objects and even cave paintings. Grove (1992) explains the advantages of AMS dating over conventional methods.

27. Housley et al. (1997). Charles (1996) has also made an important contribution to the study of recolonisation using AMS dates from cut-marked bones.

28. In some cases the ideal specimens, pieces of bone or antler that had been carved into tools, could not in fact be dated (Housley et al., 1997). Preservative coatings that had been applied long before the AMS dating technique became available had changed the chemical composition of the bone and consequently any radiocarbon date would be questionable. But there were many other humanly modified specimens available.

14: With Reindeer Hunters

1. The following text about the Ahrensburg valley and my reconstruction scenario draws on Bokelmann (1991) and Bratlund (1991). For further information about hunting strategies in late glacial northern Europe, see Bratlund (1996).

2. Reindeer had been a key species hunted by Neanderthals in Europe as long ago as 250,000 BC. But with the arrival of anatomically modern humans not long before 30,000 BC the intensity of reindeer hunting increased markedly, with the first mass slaughters. The contrast between Middle and Upper Palaeolithic reindeer hunting, and the role of reindeer in Upper Palaeolithic economies, remains a subject of debate (e. g. Chase, 1989; Mellars, 1989; Mithen, 1990, chapter 7).

3. Lubbock (1865, pp. 243–5) outlines Lartet's phases based on dominant animal species and considers the chronological overlap between these species.

4. Audouze (1987) provides a review of the late-glacial settlement in the Paris basin. Verberie has a date of 10,640±180 BP (10,974–10,390 cal BC) but its technology and fauna suggest that much of the occupation deposit may date to c. 12,000 BP.

5. The particular scenario I describe for reindeer butchery is taken from Binford's (1978) study of the methods used by the Nunamiut. Audouze & Enloe (1991) argue that this appears an excellent model for activities at Verberie.

6. For a detailed description of Pincevent, see Leroi-Gourhan & Brézillon (1972). Enloe et al. (1994) interpret the spatial patterning of bone fragments at Pincevent. Housley et al. (1997) provide six AMS radiocarbon dates ranging between 11,870±130 BP (12,141–11,582 cal BC) and 12,600±200 BP (13,556–12,354 cal BC).

7. Enloe et al. (1994); Audouze & Enloe (1991).

8. For a detailed description of the stone-tool technology at Etiolles on which the following text is based, see Pigeot (1987). Housley et al. (1997) provide five AMS radiocarbon dates, four of which are between 12,800±220 BP (13,811–12,435

cal BC) and 13,000±300 BP; the other is an outlier at 11,900±250 BP (12,318–11,524 cal BC).

9. For this particular technology the knappers first shaped the nodule, making it symmetrical, thinner than it is wide, and with a flat upper surface that will act as the striking platform. The prepared core must have a crest the complete length of the nodule. This will guide the fracture which runs through the stone when the first blow to the platform is made. The long thin flake, when removed, will take with it the complete apex of the crest, creating a blade that may be up to 60 cm long. It will leave a 'scar' on the nodule, one with two parallel ridges which will then guide the second and third blows of the hammer. By this means, one nodule of flint is turned into twenty or thirty blades, each becoming progressively smaller. The Etiolles knappers were quite spoilt by their large and high-quality nodules of stone. With such flint, they abandon cores when 15-cm-long blades could still have been removed; such cores would have been highly valued at almost any other ice age settlement (Pigeot, 1987).

10. Pigeot (1990) provides a succinct summary of her refitting and spatial study. Fischer (1990) has been able to make a similar study of cores from a late-glacial site at Trollesgave, Denmark.

11. The following text draws heavily on material from Straus & Otte (1998).

12. A detailed study of Bois Laiterie is provided in Otte & Straus (1997).

13. This refers to mating networks. Birdsell (1958) wrote a seminal paper about population structure among hunter-gatherers, while Wobst (1974, 1976) developed influential mathematical models. The number of 500 effectively means that there are enough women to bear sufficient children to keep the numbers steady without the risk of inbreeding.

14. The significance of the fluctuations in reindeer numbers for Upper Palaeolithic hunter-gatherers is discussed by Mithen (1990). He suggests that human hunting may have caused an exaggeration in the size of the fluctuations.

15. For a review of late-glacial settlement in western Germany, see Weniger (1989).

16. Bosinski & Fischer (1974) describe excavations at Gönnersdorf. Housley et al. (1997) provide nine AMS radiocarbon dates ranging between 12,790±120 BP (13,760–12,458 cal BC) and 10,540±210 BP (10,927–10,342 cal BC).

17. There is no evidence that these engraved slates were created in drug-induced states. But that shamanism, art and altered states of consciousness were interrelated in prehistoric Europe has been proposed by Lewis-Williams & Dowson (1988). Similar relationships have been proposed for several other art traditions, notably the rock art of North America (e. g. Whitley, 1992).

18. For a description of the mammoth-bone drawings from Gönnersdorf, see Bosinski (1984).

19. Lubbock (1865, p. 460).

20. Lubbock (1865, p. 363).

21. Lubbock (1865, p. 437). This was with regard to the Fuegians.

22. Bosinski (1991) describes the female imagery from Gönnersdorf.

23. One might draw a comparison here between the innovation of Ahrensburgian spear points used to promote efficiency of reindeer hunting during the Younger Dryas in Europe, and that of the Haraf point, innovated at a similar time to hunt gazelle in the Negev desert.

15: At Star Carr

1. See the foreword to Clark's (1954) excavation report about Star Carr.

2. This risks exaggerating the case; Clark's excavations at Star Carr were critical for the development of an economic approach to the Mesolithic (and prehistory in general) rather than the typological approach which he had himself pioneered in his earlier Mesolithic studies (Clark, 1932).

3. Lubbock (1865, p. 2).

4. Lubbock (1865, p. 2).

5. Lubbock (1865, p. 2).

6. Lubbock was drawing on the three-age system of stone-bronze-iron, as had already been proposed by the Danish scholar, Christian Thomsen (1788–1865). For a study of how this arose and its profound influence on archaeological thought, see Trigger (1989).

7. The key passage of text is Lubbock (1865, pp. 191–7).

8. Clark (1932).

9. For further information about Thomsen, Worsaae, Steenstrup and the significance of the nineteenth-century work at the Kjökkenmöddings, see Klindt-Jensen (1975).

10. Clark excavated Star Carr in three field seasons 1949–51 and published the results in a seminal monograph (Clark, 1954), followed almost 20 years later by his interpretation of the site (Clark, 1972). Mellars & Dark (1998) provide six AMS radiocarbon dates on artefacts from Clark's excavation which range between 9060±220 BP (8552–7599 cal BC) and 9670±100 BP (9243–8836 cal BC). Their own excavations revealed an earlier phase of occupation with AMS radiocarbon dates of 9700±160 BP (9280–8802 cal BC) and 9500±120 BP (9136–8631 cal BC). Dark (2000) provides some fine-tuning for the absolute date of Star Carr, suggesting that the above dates may be two centuries too young.

11. The constant stream of new interpretations of Star Carr, and new types of study on its material, reflects both changing theoretical attitudes in archaeology and the appearance of new techniques, especially those of archaeological science. It might also reflect the dearth of well-preserved Mesolithic sites in Britain and a rather unhealthy obsession with the site of Star Carr that has inhibited the development of Mesolithic archaeology. After Clark's (1972) own work, key contributions have included the following: Jacobi (1978) suggested that the site may have been occupied in the early summer; Pitts (1979) proposed that it had been a specialised industrial site used for antler and skin working; Andersen et al. (1981)

addressed site formation at Star Carr and proposed multiple occupations occurring at different seasons; Dumont (1988) undertook a microwear study of the chipped stone. The most important recent studies have been that of the fauna by Legge & Rowley-Conwy (1988) and the palaeoenvironment studies by Dark (in Mellars & Dark, 1998).

12. Legge & Rowley-Conwy (1988).

13. See contributions by Dark and by Law in Mellars & Dark (1998). Petra Dark's work is crucial because it informs us not only about past environments and human interaction with vegetation, but also about site-formation activity, demonstrating several occupation events by the changing densities of microscopic particles of charcoal in the sediments of the lake.

14. For a more detailed description of European vegetation history during the Late Pleistocene and Holocene, see Huntley & Webb (1988).

15. For a review of hunting methods used in Mesolithic Europe, together with other aspects of the Mesolithic period, see Mithen (1994). Bonsall (1989) and Vermeersch & Van Peer (1990) provide important collections of papers. Zvelebil (1986a) deals with the Later Mesolithic and the transition to farming.

16. The function of microliths has been much debated in Mesolithic studies. Traditionally assumed to be points and barbs for arrows, Clarke (1976) challenged this by proposing that they had been used in plant-processing technology, possibly as grater boards. Strong associations of microliths with plant remains have come from Mount Sandel (Woodman, 1985) and Staosnaig (Mithen et al., 2000) and wear traces have suggested a variety of uses (e. g. Finlayson, 1990; Finlayson & Mithen, 1997). Nevertheless, the majority of microliths are likely to have been used in hunting weapons, probably in the fashion suggested by Zvelebil (1986b) and Mithen (1990).

17. For hafted microliths, see Clark (1975). The Vig specimen is described by Noe-Nygaard (1973) and the Prejlerup by Aaris-Sørensen (1984), while Noe-Nygaard (1974) reviews Mesolithic hunting with regard to hunting injuries on bone.

18. One of the best examples of basketry comes from the site of Ageröd V in Scania and has 48 branches still woven together with pine roots (Larsson, 1983). It is difficult to identify, however, whether the basketry was for fish-traps, baskets themselves or some other function.

19. Fragments of fishnet, floats and sinkers have also been recovered from Tybrind Vig, Denmark. Andersen (1995) provides a review of the wide range of fishing equipment that has been recovered from the Late Mesolithic in Denmark, while papers in Fischer (1995) deal with many features of marine and freshwater fishing. Burov (1998) reviews the use of vegetable material for manufacture during the Mesolithic period of northeast Europe.

20. A canoe hollowed from lime with ash-wood paddles has been found at Tybrind Vig, Denmark (Andersen, 1985).

21. Good examples of wood structures used in fishing have come from Halsskov, Denmark. For these and other wooden structures used for Mesolithic fishing, see Pedersen (1995). Burov (1998) describes birch-bark bags.

22. This broken bow has been reconstructed and described by Larsson (1983) from remains recovered from Ageröd, Scania.

23. Clarke (1976) speculated about the significance of plant food in Mesolithic Europe, and Zvelebil (1994) has made a comprehensive summary of existing evidence.

24. The plant remains from Franchthi Cave are summarised in Hansen & Renfew (1978).

25. Excavations at Staosnaig are described in Mithen et al. (2000), while the plant remains are summarised in Mithen et al. (2001). The hazelnut-rich deposit has seven AMS radiocarbon dates that range between 7935±55 BP (7029–6697 cal BC) and 7040±55 BP (5985–5842 cal BC).

16: Last of the Cave Painters

1. Of the AMS radiocarbon dates from cave paintings cited in Bahn & Vertut (1997), the most recent were from a black horse painted in Las Monedas, Santander, Spain at 11,950±120 (12,317–11,671 cal BC), and in Le Portel, Ariège, France at 11,600±150 (11,861–11,491 cal BC).

2. The extent of fishing during the late Pleistocene in southwest France is a matter of contention. Very few fishbones have come from the cave excavations which provided so many reindeer bones, but this might be explained by the paucity of recovery methods in the early twentieth century. Jochim (1983) speculated that the cave-painting societies were in fact largely dependent upon fish, using an analogy with the complex hunter-gatherer groups of the northwest coast of America. A study of diet by examining the chemical composition of human bone, however, found the first evidence for a substantial use of aquatic resources only at the very end of the Pleistocene, after 12,000 BP (Hayden et al., 1987).

3. Although direct dating of the spotted-horse panel from Pech Merle has given a radiocarbon date of 24,840±340 (Bahn & Vertut, 1997), charcoal on the floor in front of the paintings gave a date of 11,380±390 BP (11,873±11,024 cal BC), and that from in front of another panel of paintings 11,200±800 BP (12,185–9820 cal BC) (Lorblanchet, 1984). Various explanations are possible for the difference in these dates, one of which is that visitors entered the cave long after the paintings had been made.

4. Bahn (1984, pp. 250–60) provides a concise summary of Mas d'Azil's excavation and complex stratigraphy, while many of its art objects are illustrated in Bahn & Vertut (1997).

5. Bahn & Vertut (1997) describe how a flat cake of red ochre pitted with holes and associated with a sharp bone needle was found within the cave and interpreted by the excavators as evidence of tattooing.

6. Bahn (1984) refers to the Pyrenean sites of Mas d'Azil and Isturitz as 'super-sites' on account of the quantity and quality of their art works and artefacts.

7. At the very end of the Pleistocene, small, flat and frequently perforated harpoons were manufactured, replacing the longer and cylindrical harpoons of the Magdalenian. Although quite out of date with regard to chronology and the available sample, Thompson (1954) describes these new 'Azilian' harpoons, providing a typology and speculation on how they were used.

8. Couraud (1985) has made a detailed study of Azilian pebbles, key results of which are summarised by Bahn & Couraud (1984).

9. Straus (1986) describes Late Pleistocene settlement systems in Cantabrian Spain, suggesting that these involved a series of residential base camps and specialised task-specific sites at the coast and in the uplands.

10. My understanding is that there are no Azilian horizons within Altamira Cave, but I have been unable to check this with reference to the original excavation reports. Beltrán (1999) makes no reference to Azilian material in his recent study of the cave (one with stunning photographs of the paintings) and Straus (1992) has no reference to Altamira in his text about the Azilian and list of Azilian radiocarbon dates.

11. Excavations at La Riera are described in detail by Straus & Clark (1986) who provide a comprehensive review of 19th-century research in Cantabrian Spain. The Conde de la Vega del Sella had excavated the rockshelter of La Llera in 1914 and the small cave of Cueto de la Mina in 1915, the latter revealing a long sequence of human occupation through the Late Pleistocene and Early Holocene.

12. La Riera cave has 29 levels, many separated into several horizons with radiocarbon dates between 20,860±410 (level 1) and 6500±200 (5638–5260 cal BC) (level 29, top) (Straus & Clark, 1986).

13. Archaeologists face severe problems when they attempt to estimate either absolute or relative population levels for prehistoric periods, and differentiating whether dietary change arose from environmental pressures or population growth. Straus & Clark (1986, pp. 351–66) interpret the subsistence changes through the ice age at La Riera and conclude that increasing population levels played a critical role in the hunting intensification and resource diversification they recognise. A succinct account is provided in Straus et al. (1980).

14. Straus (1992) has suggested that cave paintings known as 'tectiforms', which are broadly rectangular in shape, may be depictions of such brushwood fences.

15. For an overview of changing environments and society across the Pleistocene–Holocene transition in northern Spain, see Straus (1992).

16. Recent AMS radiocarbon dates from pigments of the Altamira paintings indicate that the

paintings had been made gradually over a long period of time. Bahn & Vertut (1997) cite seven dates which range between 16,480±210 and 13,570±190 BP.

17. See Bahn & Vertut (1997) for a review of Upper Palaeolithic art.

18. This is forwarding the 'adaptive' interpretation of Palaeolithic art which has been expressed in several different forms by archaeologists such as Pfeiffer (1982), Jochim (1983), Rice & Patterson (1985) and Mithen (1988, 1989, 1991).

19. Palaeolithic art as information underlies the work of Gamble (1991) on the social context of the art, and those who adopt an explicitly adaptive viewpoint (e. g. Jochim 1983, Mithen 1991).

20. This is an argument proposed by Mithen (1988) who claims that there are many explicit references in the art to the means by which hunter-gatherers acquire information about their game and about environments in general.

21. Of course we do not know the stories that were told by Palaeolithic hunter-gatherers; the claim that they contained survival information is based on an analogy with the stories of the Inuit as interpreted by Minc (1986).

17: Coastal Catastrophe

1. Christensen et al. (1997) cite various estimates for sea-level rise in northern Europe ranging from 4.0 m. /100 years in the western Baltic to 2.3 m. /100 years on the North Sea coast of Germany.

2. Dawson (1992) summarises the complex patterns of Early Holocene sea-level change. He explains that the largest catastrophic floods occurred at around 8000 BP due to the disintegration of the Laurentide ice sheet, which led to an almost instantaneous rise in global sea level of between 0.2 and 0.4 m.

3. Coles (1998) attempts to reconstruct the late-glacial and Early Holocene landscapes of Doggerland.

4. Coles (1998, p. 47) describes how Clark's (1936) synthesis of Mesolithic Europe conveyed a sense that 'the submerged land had been the heartland of an early Mesolithic culture'.

5. An account of the discovery of this barbed antler point is provided by Clark in his introduction to his Star Carr monograph (Clark, 1954), while he stresses its significance for the development of Mesolithic studies in Clark (1972). For early finds of Mesolithic harpoons, including that from the Ower bank, see Godwin & Godwin (1933).

6. The point was dated to 11,740±150 BP (12,077–11,527 cal BC) (Housley, 1991). Coles (1998) suggests that it might derive from southern-based hunter-gatherers making occasional forays north for game, furs and seasonally abundant wildfowl.

7. Fischer (1997) provides a detailed scenario for the drowning of forests based on evidence from underwater stumps from the Storebaelt region of Denmark.

8. Van Andel & Lionos (1984) reconstructed the changing location of Franchthi Cave with respect to the seashore by plotting sea-floor depths and correlating these with known sea-level fluctuations.

9. Excavations at Franchthi Cave are described by Jacobsen & Farrand (1987).

10. Wordsworth (1985).

11. Dawson et al. (1990).

12. The following text is based on material in Ryan et al. (1997). Bill Ryan and Walt Pitman, the marine geologists who documented that catastrophic flood, have attempted to connect it with Noah's flood as related in the Old Testament (Mestel, 1997).

13. Lubbock (1865, p. 177).

14. Sir Charles Lyell (1797–1875) published his three-volume work *Principles of Geology* between 1830–3. This put forward the notion of uniformitarianism: that geological change in the past had happened by the same processes and at the same rate as observable in the present. This work, promoting the idea of slow, continuous change, had a profound influence on Charles Darwin and the development of his notion of evolution by natural selection. As it implied a substantial age for deposits containing human artefacts and the bones of extinct animals, it also opened up the question of human antiquity.

15. Prestwich (1893).

16. Pirazzoli (1991) provides a brief account of the history of understanding sea-level change.

17. The following text regarding the complex sea-level changes in the Baltic region draws on Björck (1995).

18: Two Villages in Southeast Europe

1. The following text is based on the description of Lepenski Vir I, drawing on the basic text by Srejović (1972) and the regional study of the Iron Gates by Radovanović (1996). Lepenski Vir I is itself broken down into five phases (a–e). Radovanović (1996, appendix 3) provides eleven radiocarbon dates for Lepenski Vir I, ranging from 7360±100 BP (6376–6083 cal BC) to 6900±100 BP (5885–5666 cal BC), with two outliers at 6620±100 BP (5625–5478 cal BC) and 6200±210 BP (5362–4854 cal BC).

2. Balma Margineda has a long stratified sequence beginning at the very end of the Pleistocene at 11,000 BP (Geddes et al., 1989). My reference was to the Late Mesolithic levels with dates of 8530±420 BP (8200–7081 cal BC) and 8390±150 BP (7582–7186 cal BC).

3. The plant remains at Roc del Migdia are described by Holden et al. (1995). Although no traces of acorns were present, they attribute this to the poor preservation of what is likely to have been a key food resource. Four radiocarbon dates from the Mesolithic levels range between 7280±370 (6463–5744 cal BC) and 8800±240 BP (8202–7609 cal BC).

4. This imaginary journey across southern Europe has been inspired by Nicholas Crane's

(1996) account of his mountain walk across Europe. Similar inspiration has come from Patrick Leigh Fermor's (1986) account of his walk from the Hook of Holland to Constantinople, especially his accounts of walking through the forests of Transylvania.

5. I am influenced here by Baring-Gould's (1905) description of the Riviera just after the turn of the twentieth century.

6. Excavations at Mondeval de Sora are described in Alciati et al. (1993). The Mesolithic in northern Italy is referred to as the Castelnovian and that at Mondeval de Sora has two radiocarbon dates, 8380±70 BP (7539–7349 cal BC) and 7330±59 BP (6229–6087 cal BC).

7. Excavations in one such cave, Šebrn Abri, are described by Miracle et al. (2000). With three radiocarbon dates ranging between 9280±40 BP (8604–8342 cal BC) and 8810±80 BP (8198–7984 cal BC), it is rather too early for my narrative. But there are most likely to be similar rockshelters with slightly later occupation in the vicinity.

8. This refers to House 54, located centrally in Phase 2 of Lepenski Vir I (Radovanović 1996, p. 109). Garašanin & Radovanović (2001) have recently discussed the significance of a pottery vessel in this house for the nature and timing of contact between the Mesolithic people of the Iron Gates and Early Neolithic groups in the Balkans.

9. These remarks about the health status of children at Lepenski Vir are in fact based on reports from the contemporary settlement of Vlasac from which data is available. Meiklejohn & Zvelebil (1991) cite studies which have identified rickets in 44% of child skeletons and osteomalacia in 15% of males and 25% of females. Both of these are signs of vitamin D and/or calcium deficiency. This seems surprising in a population heavily dependent upon fish. They also cite research that has identified enamel hypoplasia on 70% of all teeth. I assume that the health status of Lepenski Vir was similar.

10. This is based on the location of the burial and jawbone in House 40 of Lepenski Vir I (Srejović, 1972, 119). Radovanović (2000) has reanalysed the range and chronological sequence of burial practices at Lepenski Vir in light of a reassessment of the archaeological remains.

11. See Radovanović (1997) for her interpretation of symbolism at Lepenski Vir that links the flow of the river, human life cycle and the annual movements of the fish, especially the beluga.

12. The following draws on Srejović (1972) and the regional study of the Iron Gates by Radovanović (1996).

13. All of the key sites in the Iron Gates are described in Radovanović (1996). Whittle (1996) suggests that Lepenski Vir may have been a sacred centre and is sceptical that sedentary hunter-gatherer settlements appeared within the Iron Gates prior to contact with the first farmers. He doubts that Lepenski Vir and other sites had a long pre-Neolithic development.

14. Srejović (1989) was unable to cite any

Mesolithic sites in Bulgaria and southern Yugoslavia, while Chapman (1989) stressed the lack of a Mesolithic population in nearly all of southeastern Europe.

15. Perlès (2001) provides a comprehensive study of Neolithic Greece and its Mesolithic background. As well as concluding that the Mesolithic population was sparse, she also argued that it was isolated from the widespread trends of Mesolithic Europe in view of its very distinctive technological traditions.

16. The reconstruction of the settlement and lifestyle at Nea Nikomedeia in the preceding and following text draws on Rodden (1962, 1965). He provides a single radiocarbon date of 6220±150 BC (5319–4959 cal BC).

17. Perlès (2001) examines the evidence that might indicate where the farming colonists of Greece originated from. She concludes that no satisfactory link has been made with any specific region of Turkey or western Asia. One of the key issues is the extent to which colonising people maintain or lose their original cultural identity. Those arriving in Greece appear to have rapidly lost any strong cultural affiliation to their 'homeland' this being quite different to the migration of LBK farmers across Central Europe.

18. For the Neolithic colonisation of Crete, see Broodbank & Strasser (1991). Whittle (1996) discusses the complicated situation of southern Italy. Early Neolithic sites which appear to have the whole 'Neolithic package' of domesticated animals and cereals have encouraged the idea of colonisation. The enclosures on the Tavoliere plain have been particularly influential on this idea. Whittle, however, stresses the lack of knowledge about Mesolithic settlement and is generally cautious about the idea of colonising farmers originating from either Greece or western Asia.

19. My text here rejects the idea that the Neolithic in Southeast Europe may have emerged from the local Mesolithic without the influx of new people, a position that had been favoured by Dennell (1983). Halstead (1996) and more recently Perlès (2001) review the arguments for Mesolithic continuity into the Neolithic, with Perlès concluding: 'That farming was introduced by immigrant groups now seems an inescapable conclusion' (2000, p. 45).

20. The chronology of the earliest Neolithic in Greece is poorly defined. Van Andel & Runnels (1995) summarised the available radiocarbon dates and give the Early Neolithic as lasting between 9000 and 6000 BP, which fits with Halstead's (1996) characterisation of the Aceramic Neolithic. Perlès (2001) has provided the most detailed study of the available radiocarbon dates, especially for those sites claimed to be from a pre-pottery Neolithic. Fourteen dates exist from such sites, with modal values ranging from 8130 to 7250 BP (7500–6500 BC).

21. Perlès (1990) describes and analyses the chipped stone from Franchthi Cave, showing that the major change in the sequence occurs only with the appearance of the Ceramic Neolithic. Shackleton (1988) was able to show that the species of marine molluscs collected by inhabitants of the cave also continued unchanged when the first domesticated animals appeared, suggesting a continuity in coastal foraging patterns.

22. The reliance of the Early Neolithic farmers on the flood plains has been discussed in detail by Van Andel and Runnels (1995). In doing so, they reject what had been a prevailing idea: that Early Neolithic farming had similarities to the traditional farming methods witnessed in the Mediterranean during historic periods, as had been argued by Barker (1985).

23. Rodden (1965) describes various items of personal adornment from Nea Nikomedeia and contemporary settlements in Southeast Europe that have similarities to those from Çatalhöyük. He claims that both European and Asiatic characteristics were present.

24. Archaeologists are none the wiser and have sometimes concocted elaborated scenarios of religious ideologies during the Neolithic, largely based on the clay figurines (e. g. Gimbutas, 1974).

25. Halstead (1996) describes how production may have been organised within Early Neolithic villages and how households may have guarded against subsistence failure.

26. Ammerman and Cavalli-Sforza (1979, 1984) developed a very influential 'wave of advance' model for the spread of farmers (or farming) through Europe. Their original model implied a continuous movement driven by a steady population growth behind the front. When making a detailed review and interpretation of the Early Neolithic in southeastern Europe, Van Andel and Runnels (1995) preferred later versions of the wave of advance model, that included discontinuities in time and space. They argued that the first farmers effectively leap-frogged from one fertile flood plain to the next, with periods of rapid movement interspersed with relative stasis as the current flood plain gradually filled up with settlements. But, as they acknowledge, current models are frustrated by an inadequate radiocarbon chronology.

27. Whittle (1996) sees the major cultural developments in the Danube gorges as happening in response to the spread of farming communities, describing these as 'indigenous resistance'.

28. See chapter 17, 'Coastal Catastrophe'. The abrupt drowning of the Black Sea shelf is described by Ryan et al. (1997).

29. Lillie (1998) describes a large set of AMS radiocarbon dates from Mesolithic and Neolithic cemeteries from the Dnieper Rapids region of the Ukraine, several of which have in excess of 100 internments. Twenty such cemeteries are now known, some of which lie wholly within the Mesolithic while others span both cultural periods. That of Marievka, for instance, has three AMS dates between 7955±55 BP (7033–6708 cal BC) and 7630±110 BP (6636–6384 cal BC), while Derievka I has five dates between 7270±110 BP

(6226–6018 cal BC) and 6110±120 BP (5209–4853 cal BC). Other cemeteries span much longer periods, with youngest dates of c. 2500 BP. Unfortunately there are very few settlement remains associated with these cemeteries.

19: Islands of the Dead

1. Oleneostrovski Mogilnik, deer island cemetery, is found in Lake Onega, Karelia. Price & Jacobs (1990) provide eleven AMS radiocarbon dates on human bone. Eight of these were tightly clustered between 7280±80 BP (6218–6032 cal BC) and 7750±110 BP (6689–6444 cal BC). There were three outliers (two younger and one older) which were explained away as a consequence of contamination. Jacobs (1995) cites a large series of conventional radiocarbon dates that average 7050 BP.

2. The following text draws on the historical account of work at Oleneostrovski Mogilnik provided by Jacobs (1995). For the development of archaeology in Stalinist Russia, see Trigger (1989).

3. Gurina (1956).

4. With this burial, I am thinking of that illustrated by Jacobs (1995, fig. 6) which is based on an original drawing in Gurina (1956).

5. The following draws on O'Shea and Zvelebil (1984).

6. There is a possibility that such a hypothesis could be tested today by the study of ancient DNA extracted from the human skeletons. This requires that specimens are excavated in laboratory-like conditions, quite different to those employed in 1936, and indeed on almost any dig today. Although the techniques for extracting ancient DNA from human bone have been available for more than a decade, successful applications have been limited, largely owing to the immense methodological problems involved (see the review of such studies by Renfrew, 1998). These were underestimated when the technique first became available, and appeared to have an astonishing potential to address population history and biological relationships. Ancient DNA studies are subsumed within biomolecular archaeology (Hedges & Sykes, 1992) and archaeogenetics which includes the use of DNA from living people to make inferences about past population history (Renfrew & Boyle, 2000).

7. Jacobs (1995).

8. Coles & Orme (1983) noted the significant transformation to landscapes made by beavers and how these might have been taken advantage of during the Mesolithic and Neolithic.

9. In thinking and writing about this journey I have been inspired by Ransome's (1927) account of *Racundra*'s first cruise in the Baltic Sea.

10. Zvelebil (1981) and articles in Zvelebil et al. (1998) cover Mesolithic settlement in the Baltic region in the context of the transition to the Neolithic. Matiskainen (1990) summarises Mesolithic subsistence in Finland.

11. The following account of Skateholm draws on Larsson (1984). Radiocarbon dates for the settlement and cemeteries range from 6240±95 BP

(5304–5060 cal BC) to 5930±125 BP (4959–4618 cal BC).

12. A detailed reconstruction of the local environment of Skateholm and likely subsistence patterns are provided in Larsson (1988).

13. Rowley-Conwy (1998).

14. There is no direct evidence for dwellings of any kind at Skateholm, and we have no traces of clothing. My suggestion of such diversity is based on that of the diversity in burial practices.

15. Separate dog burials had, however, been clustered together within one area of the cemetery (Larsson, 1984).

16. There has not been a detailed study of the Skateholm cemeteries to compare with that by O'Shea and Zvelebil (1984) for Oleneostrovski Mogilnik. Clark & Neeley (1987) addressed the Skateholm data in the context of a general study of social differentiation in the European Mesolithic.

17. A complex symbolic code that we are simply unable to read may have been used in the Skateholm cemetery to identify shamans and other distinguished persons. Perhaps the decision as to whether a person should be buried sitting or lying, with an otter skull or with a wooden structure, was indeed dictated by strict rules reflecting the type of person, the role they played in society and the one waiting for them in the afterworld. We simply do not know.

18. Larsson (1989, 1990) specifically addresses the dog burials at Skateholm.

19. Newell et al.'s (1979) catalogue of skeletal remains from Mesolithic Europe includes references to specimens with signs of injury. Bennike (1985) has reviewed the evidence for traumatic injury from Mesolithic specimens in Denmark, finding this present in 44% of her skull sample, as compared with a mere 10% in the Neolithic. This would suggest a remarkably high level of violence for small-scale societies. Schulting (1998) has reappraised her data and combined it with that from Sweden and France to conclude that evidence of injury is found on about 20% of specimens – still a notably high figure.

20. For descriptions of violence and warfare among the Yanomamö, see Chagnon (1988, 1997).

21. Chagnon (1997, p. 187).

22. The Ofnet skull 'nests' are dated to c. 7500 BP and have been interpreted as evidence for a Mesolithic massacre by Frayer (1997).

23. For this population/resource disequilibrium argument, see Price (1985).

24. Zvelebil (2000) argues that the Mesolithic people would have suffered six types of disruptive influence following contact with Neolithic farmers: (1) internal social disruption caused by the circulation of prestige items and increased social competition; (2) opportunistic use of hunter-gatherer lands by farmers causing disruption to Mesolithic foraging strategies; (3) direct loss of hunting lands to farmers; (4) ecological change and over-exploitation of wild resources caused by the supplying of forest products to

farmers; (5) hypergyny – the loss of women to the farming communities; (6) transmission of new diseases.

20: At the Frontier

1. Bradley (1997) has proposed ideological differences between Mesolithic and Neolithic people which may have inhibited the adoption of farming by the former. Domestication is, he claims, 'a state of mind'.

2. The following text about the Linearbandkeramik draws on material in Whittle (1996), Price et al. (1995) and Coudart (1991). The last of these provides a particularly interesting discussion about social structure and cultural conformity within the LBK. LBK migration has most recently been considered by Price et al. (2001) who make an innovative use of human bone chemistry to explore the frequency with which individuals changed their place of residence during their life.

3. There has been a long debate regarding the extent to which the agricultural/Neolithic transition in Europe derives from the spread of people, and if so whether these were immigrants or transformed hunter-gatherers, or by the spread of ideas. Zvelebil (2000) provides an excellent review of the current arguments for the agricultural transition in Europe, placing great emphasis on the internal social dynamics of the Mesolithic communities and their social relations with Neolithic people within 'frontier' zones. In this article, he argues that the LBK was created by Mesolithic communities on the periphery of the Hungarian plain.

4. I am grateful to Richard Bradley for information about such sites and the issue of 'dead houses'. He discusses the issues and evidence in Bradley (1998).

5. Van de Velde (1997) discusses issues concerning LBK burial practices and the attempts to deduce social organisation from LBK graveyards.

6. The following description of Grave 8 at the Bøgebakken cemetery of Vedbaek draws on the description in Albrethsen & Brinch Petersen (1976). The cemetery has three radiocarbon dates: 6290±75 BP (5360–5081 cal BC), 6050±75 BP (5042–4809 cal BC) and 5810±105 BP (4779–4540 cal BC).

7. For the ideology of the Saami, see Ahlbäck (1987). Zvelebil (1997) has drawn several direct analogies between shamanistic practices ethnographically documented in western Siberia and aspects of the Mesolithic archaeological record.

8. Due to the different photosynthetic pathways used by terrestrial and marine plants, they differ in the ratio of ^{12}C to ^{13}C, this ratio being significantly lower in marine plants. Its level is maintained throughout the food chain. As human bone is remodelled on a ten-year cycle, its chemistry provides some indication as to the nature of diet during the last decade of life. Specifically, the ratio of ^{12}C to ^{13}C can inform as to the relative proportions of marine and terrestrial foods within

the diet. Price (1989) provides a review of this and other techniques for extracting dietary information from the chemistry of human bone. Tauber (1981) provided the first results for Mesolithic Denmark and demonstrated a dramatic difference between Mesolithic and Neolithic diets. Schulting (1998) has further explored this theme, drawing together evidence from Northwest Europe to show how the Mesolithic diet had been dominated by marine foods that appear to have been entirely dropped from the diet during the Neolithic.

9. This is indeed what most archaeologists had thought before the chemical analysis of bone was applied to Mesolithic specimens.

10. The health status of later Mesolithic populations has been described by Meiklejohn and Zvelebil (1991).

11. The following text about Tybrind Vig draws on the report by Andersen (1985). The site was excavated in 1978 as a submerged settlement. It provided a rich inventory of artefacts including fishing gear. At least one burial was located at the site, which included both activity and rubbish disposal areas. Radiocarbon dates range from 6740±80 BP (5717–5562 cal BC) and 5260±95 BP (4222–3977 cal BC).

12. Two dugout canoes and paddles were found at Tybrind Vig, as described by Andersen (1987).

13. The following citations from *Prehistoric Times* are taken from Lubbock (1865, pp. 171–97).

14. The following text about Ertebølle draws on the report by Andersen & Johansen (1986). There is a large set of dates from the site, ranging between 6010±95 BP (5025–4741 cal BC) and 5070±90 BP (3963–3774 cal BC). Enghoff (1986) has made a very detailed study of fishing activities from Ertebølle, with the surprising discovery that most of the fish at this coastal settlement came from freshwater. She interpreted this as a preference for eels. She made a similar study of the fishbones from the Norsminde midden on the east coast of Jutland and found not a single freshwater fish. People from that midden had focused on catching flatfish, most likely reflecting the local ecology of the midden (Enghoff, 1989).

15. The site of Aggersund is described by Andersen (1978). This has three radiocarbon dates with extremes of 5460±95 BP (4448–4113 cal BC) and 5410±100 BP (4244–4050 cal BC).

16. The reconstruction of foraging activities around the assumed permanent settlement of Ertebølle, including proposals for specific activities undertaken at Dyrholm and Vaengo Sø, has been made by Rowley-Conwy (1983).

17. Rowley-Conwy (1984a).

18. The ground stone axes being referred to are Danubian shaft-hole axes and perforated axe hammers, as reported from Mesolithic contexts in Denmark by Fischer (1982). The Mesolithic inhabitants of Denmark were also making T-shaped antler axes, bone combs and rings as imitations of Neolithic artefacts (Zvelebi, 1998).

19. The following text draws on the excavation

report of Ringkloster by Andersen (1994). Rasmussen (1994) provides thirteen radiocarbon dates which range between 5820±95 BP (4776–4549 cal BC) and 4800±65 BP (3652–3519 cal BC). Rowley-Conwy (1994) analyses and interprets the animal bones and Enghoff (1994) the fishbones from the site.

20. Rowley-Conwy (pers. comm.)

21. Vang Petersen (1984) describes spatial variation in artefact distributions which most likely relate to territorial and social boundaries. Bone combs and a special T-shaped axe made from red deer antler are not be found east of Fyn, while a distinctive type of stone axe and curved harpoons are absent from Jutland where only straight varieties are found. Three different types of flint axes have been found on the island of Zealand, each within a discrete area of the island; those in the southeast have a flared cutting edge, while those in the northeast have almost symmetrical sides. Verhart (1990) has attempted to identify social territories based on the distribution of bone and antler point types across the whole of northern Europe.

22. Evidence for exchange between Neolithic farmers and Mesolithic hunter-gatherers was first presented by Fischer (1982). Zvelebil (1998) provides an excellent review of this evidence and a discussion of forager and farmer interactions. He stresses how, in ethnographically documented cases of forager-farmer contact, women frequently marry into the farming society, a phenomenon known as hypergyny. Verhart & Wansleeben (1997) discuss Mesolithic–Neolithic interactions and transition in the Netherlands by drawing on ethnographic parallels from New Guinea and stress the exchange of prestige objects.

23. A brief description of Esbeck can be found in Whittle (1996). This has a square double-ditched enclosure associated with eroded house remains which are confined within an inner ditch. Whittle suggests that the ditch is too shallow to be defensive and is dated to the end of the LBK sequence, whereas confrontation is to be expected at the time of initial LBK settlement.

21: A Mesolithic Legacy

1. See Coles (1998) for a description of the final flooding of Doggerland, with maps indicating the last surviving islands.

2. Excavations at Téviec are reported in Péquart et al. (1937), and those at Hoëdic by Péquart & Péquart (1954). My text also draws on Schulting (1996) who provides a summary of the sites and makes an analysis of the distribution of grave goods. He provides eight radiocarbon dates ranging between 6740±60 BP (5712–5564 cal BC) and 5680±50 BP (4582–4408 cal BC).

3. In both graves H and K at Téviec the skeletal remains of previous interments had clearly been pushed aside to make room for later interments. Grave K contained a total of six individuals, the first of which had remained in position rather than being moved aside (Péquart et al., 1937).

4. Péquart et al. (1937) classified stone-lined hearths at Téviec into three types: domestic, feasting and ritual. The feasting and ritual hearths appear to be directly related to the mortuary activities; the feasting hearths are close to the larger graves, while the ritual hearths are often found on top of the grave slabs themselves (Schulting, 1996). The significance of the feasting was stressed by Thomas & Tilley (1993) who believed that this set a precedent for Neolithic practices of the same type. Schulting (1996), however, argues that the feasting was of less importance than they claim and that the midden material was first and foremost routine domestic rubbish rather than a reflection of large social gatherings.

5. Lewthwaite (1986) rejects suggestions that people had been on Corsica prior to 10,000 BC and were responsible for the extinction of the endemic deer. The first human colonisation occurred after 7000 BC. Occupations at sites such as Araguina-Sennola indicate predation on a wide range of small game and coastal foods but an absolute lack of any indigenous medium-sized game.

6. This pottery is referred to as cardial ware. It is often rather poorly made and survives as small fragments. Examples are described and illustrated in Whittle (1996).

7. Excavations at Arene Candide have been reported by Maggi (1997). This volume includes a final report on the animal bones by Rowley-Conwy, who also summarises his interpretation of the pig and sheep bones in Rowley-Conwy (2000).

8. The following draws on Zilhão (1993), which provides an excellent summary of existing data from southern Europe and a critical review of the acculturation interpretations.

9. For the Mesolithic communities of the Sado valley, Portugal, see Morais Arnaud (1989) and for a more general review of Mesolithic archaeology in Portugal, see Gonzalez Morales & Arnaud (1990).

10. Excavations at Gruta do Caldeirão are described in Zilhão (1992).

11. Lubell et al. (1989) examined the skeletal remains of the late Mesolithic populations from the Portuguese middens and the earliest Neolithic people from the region, finding that they they all appeared to be in good health and thus rejecting the notion that the Mesolithic people had been attracted to farming for reasons of nutrition and health.

12. For a review of the potential, techniques and problems involved in using human genetics to address issues of population history, see Renfrew & Boyle (eds, 2000) for Europe, and Renfrew (ed., 2000) for the Americas.

13. Cavalli-Sforza et al. (1994). This volume may well have the same relationship to the development of historical genetics as the works of the great German historian Leopold von Ranke, in the mid-nineteenth century, had on the

development of traditional historical scholarship. Leopold von Ranke (1795–1886) authored over sixty books including histories of the Popes, Germany at the time of the Reformation, and a history of the world that he began at the age of 83, completing 17 volumes before his death eight years later. His *History of the Latin and Teutonic Nations 1494–1535* (1824) is generally regarded as the first critical historical work. Evans (1997) describes how Ranke helped establish history as a separate discipline from literature and philosophy, wanting not only to collect facts but to understand the inner being of the past.

14. Cavalli-Sforza began work on the genetics of Europeans in the 1970s. He originally worked with blood proteins that he took as proxy for genes, and then looked directly at gene sequences with his classic study based on thirty-nine genes from nuclear DNA (Lewin, 1997; Sykes, 2000; Cavalli-Sforza et al., 1994). The key to his study was a principal components analysis of his data. The quoted gradient of gene frequencies from the southeast to the northwest of Europe was produced by the first principal component of the analysis, which accounted for 26–28% of the total variance.

15. Renfrew put his arguments forward in his 1987 book, *Archaelogy and Language*. A concern with the origin of Indo-European also figured highly in the interests of archaeologists in the late nineteenth and early twentieth century, especially Gordon Childe (e.g. his 1926 volume, *The Aryans: A Study of Indo-European Origins*). Until Renfrew reinvigorated this debate, a consensus existed that Indo-European had originated on the Russian steppes in the third millennium BC and spread into Europe by invading tribesmen. Renfrew demonstrated that such views are quite incompatible with the archaeological record.

16. Lewin (1997) provides an accessible account of how Renfrew's and Cavalli-Sforza's ideas fitted neatly together.

17. In the year after publication of Renfrew's *Archaeology and Language*, the journal *Antiquity* ran a special section on this theme, with three papers, Zvelebil & Zvelebil (1988), Sherrat & Sherrat (1988) and Ehret (1988), all of which applauded Renfrew's attempt to relate archaeology and language but made substantial criticisms of his conclusion about Indo-European. Zvelebil & Zvelebil stressed that prior to very recent times the distribution of non Indo-European languages had been substantially more widespread, while Sherrat & Sherrat argued that language evolution in Europe must have been a much more gradual process than Renfrew suggested. Ehret focused on the complex relationship between language, ethnicity and material culture.

18. The key paper for Sykes's work is Richards et al. (1996). Sykes also summarises this work in Sykes (1999, 2000), while Lewin (1997) provides a popular account which makes clear the significance it has for the archaeology of Europe. Sykes (2001) has also produced his own popular account of his work.

19. Sykes (1999) suggests that lineages reaching back to the early Upper Palaeolithic (50,000–20,000 BC) have contributed 10% to the modern gene pool, and those from the later Upper Palaeolithic (20–10,000 BC) 70%. One of the most interesting developments has been by Torroni et al. (1998), who have used mtDNA to show that there was a major movement of people from the southwest of Europe to the northeast at around 15,000 BC. This fits precisely with the archaeological evidence for late-glacial expansion out of the LGM refugia.

20. Key papers in this debate are Cavalli-Sforza & Minch (1997) and Richards et al. (1997).

21. New research is being undertaken on the male Y chromosome in an attempt to identify male population history (Sykes, 2000). Sykes (1999) acknowledges the possible biasing impact of the mtDNA evidence by citing that from Polynesia. In this case 99% of the mtDNA predates European arrivals but at least a third of the Y chromosomes come from Europeans. He also makes explicit several other potential problems with the mtDNA work, notably estimating the mutation rate. Zvelebil (2000) makes a comprehensive critique of the genetic studies as a whole.

22. Sykes (1999) emphasises the increasing convergence between his own and Cavalli-Sforza's conclusions, while Renfrew (2000) argues that the two sets of results are compatible with each other.

23. For studies of the Mesolithic–Neolithic transition in the northern Baltic regions, see those within Zvelebil et al. (eds, 1998).

24. The earliest Neolithic in Scandinavia is referred to as the Funnel Beaker culture, otherwise known as the TRB. The idea that long mounds are mortuary equivalents of LBK long houses goes back to Childe and has been developed by Hodder (1984) and most recently by Bradley (1998). It is likely, however, that the LBK farmers themselves were the first to construct long barrows (Scarre, 1992) as domestic architecture gradually disappeared from northern Europe.

25. Zvelebil & Rowley-Conwy (1986) review the evidence for the final Mesolithic and earliest Neolithic in Atlantic Europe.

26. For studies of Neolithic and megalithic origins in Northwest and Atlantic Europe, see Sherratt (1995) and Scarre (1992). As Thomas & Tilley (1993) have argued, the association between feasting and burial that appears evident in the earliest Neolithic may also have originated in the Mesolithic traditions apparent at Téviec.

22: A Scottish Envoi

1. Up until 1992, the earliest radiocarbon-dated settlements in Scotland were Kinloch on the Isle of Rum with radiocarbon dates of 8590±95 BP (7742–7540 cal BC) and 8515±190 BP (7810–7207 cal BC) (Wickham-Jones, 1990) and Fife Ness in Fife with dates of 8545±65 BP (7603–7524 cal BC) and 8510±65 BP (7592–7523 cal BC). Since 1992, two slightly earlier sites have been discovered: Daer in

the Lowther Hills of Clydesdale with a date of 9075±80 BP (8446–8206 cal BC) (Ward, pers. comm.) and Cramond, Edinburgh, with a date of 9250±60 BP (Saville, pers. comm.)

2. The entire collection of artefacts from this field (referred to as BRG3), an illustration of the stone point, and the Islay survey as a whole, is described in Mithen, Finlayson, Mathews & Woodman (2000).

3. These points are discussed in Morrison & Bonsall (1989) who describe them as Ahrensburgian; they are also discussed in Mithen (2000b) and Edwards & Mithen (1995).

4. This was *The Southern Hebrides Mesolithic Project* and is fully published in Mithen (ed., 2000).

5. Edwards (2000) reviews the vegetation history of Islay and adjacent islands.

6. This work was done in conjunction with Sue Dawson and is described in Dawson, S. & Dawson, A. G. (2000b) along with a reconstruction of the sea-level changes on Islay.

7. Dawson, A. G. & Dawson, S. (2000a) describe the glaciomarine sedimentation of the Rinns and the origin of the flint pebbles. Their restriction to the west coast of Islay and Colonsay was demonstrated by Marshall (2000a, 2000b) who undertook a complete survey of the Hebridean coastlines.

8. Excavations and analysis of the artefacts from Coulererach are described in Mithen & Finlay (2000b). The site was particulary difficult to work on as any trenches flooded very rapidly. As these were excavated through the limited pasture of the croft, our excavations were constrained in area. Just one radiocarbon date was acquired: 7530±80 BP (6530–6210 cal BC) I suspect a well-preserved Mesolithic site survives below the peat.

9. Bunting et al. (2000) describe the palynological study of peat deposits in the vicinity of Lake Gorm. The peat from Coulererach itself was of limited value for the Mesolithic as there was a hiatus between the artefact spread and the base of the peat which was dated to 4700–100 BP.

10. For excavations and study of artefacts at Gleann Mor, see Mithen & Finlayson (2000). One Mesolithic radiocarbon date was acquired of 7100±125 BP (6154–5810 cal BC).

11. For excavations and study of artefacts at Aoradh, see Mithen, Woodman, Finlay & Finlayson (2000). This site remains undated.

12. Microliths have traditionally been assumed to have been used as the points and barbs on arrows. This came into question when Clarke (1976) suggested that many might have been used in plant-processing equipment. The application of microwear analysis to the microliths from Bolsay has indicated that while many were used as arrow-heads, traces of cutting and boring motions in others suggested that these had been used for other tasks (Finlayson & Mithen, 2000). The distinctive nature of the Bolsay assemblage is not only the high frequency of microliths but the fact that these are dominated by a single type: scalene triangles.

13. For excavations and study of artefacts at Bolsay, see Mithen, Lake & Finlay (2000a, b). Mesolithic radiocarbon dates for this site are 7250±145 BP (6242–5923 cal BC) and 7400±55 BP (6379–6118 cal BC).

14. John Mercer and Susan Searight undertook a substantial number of excavations of Mesolithic sites on Jura during the 1960s and 1970s. The most important of their sites were Glenbatrick (Mercer, 1974) which may have early Mesolithic microliths, similar in design to those from Star Carr, and Lussa Wood I (Mercer, 1980), which might have a late-glacial component and a radiocarbon date of 8195±350 BP (7573–6699 cal BC). All of the Jura sites had dense scatters of chipped-stone artefacts and are reviewed with complete bibliographic references in Mithen (2000b).

15. Mithen (2000c) describes the archaeological survey undertaken on Colonsay that involved both field-walking and test-pitting.

16. This initial survey of Staosnaig and the following excavations that took place between 1989 and 1994 are described in Mithen & Finlay (2000a).

17. Sarah Mason and Jon Hather provide an extensive ethnohistorical study of the use of lesser celandine within Mithen & Finlay (2000a).

18. Several specialists were involved in the study of the material from Staosnaig: Nyree Finlay (chipped stone), Clare Whitehead (coarse stone), Wendy Carruthers (hazelnut shells), Sarah Mason & Jon Hather (other plant material) and Stephen Carter (sediments). Radiocarbon dates for the Mesolithic features at the site ranged from 8110±60 BP (7294–7050 cal BC) to 7040±55 BP (5985–5842 cal BC). The rapid accumulation of the fill most likely occurred at c. 7700 BP. The plant remains are summarised in Mithen, Finlay, Carruthers, Carter & Ashmore (2001).

19. Roasting hazelnuts had been a common activity throughout Mesolithic times. This may have been used to reduce nuts into a paste for ease of storage and travel; roasting may also have made large quantities of nuts more palatable. Further reasons for roasting hazelnuts are discussed in Mithen & Finlay (2000a). For experimental hazelnut roasting, see Score & Mithen (2000).

20. This pollen evidence comes from Loch Cholla on Colonsay and is summarised in Edwards (2000). It remains unclear whether the reduction in tree pollen was indeed the consequence of human activity or merely a reflection of changing climatic conditions.

21. The principal excavations of the Oronsay middens were undertaken by Mellars (1987), although important excavations had also taken place at the turn of the century, as Mellars describes in his volume.

22. The original study on 'otoliths' was published in Mellars & Wilkinson (1980). Mellars (1987) provides several scenarios for possible settlement patterns but has a clear preference for the sedentary model. It is most unfortunate that seasonality

evidence from bird bones has not been published as this might confirm, or perhaps counter, that from the otoliths.

23. Mithen (2000e) summarises the radiocarbon dates from his excavations and their implications for the interpretation of the Oronsay middens. The 'gap' in the occupation record on Islay is also evident from the palaeoenvironmental evidence.

24. Carbon isotope studies of human bone fragments from the middens are reported in Richards & Mellars (1998). As I describe in Mithen (2000e), there remain other possibilities than this permanent residency on Oronsay; if this was the case, we should allow for visits to Islay, Colonsay and Jura, and perhaps further afield. These would have been necessary to ensure population viability and prevent inbreeding among the group.

25. The tradition of Neolithic stone-built houses on Orkney is described by Richards (1990): the site of Stonehall suggests that it may reach back to 5000 BP. A timber hall dating to between 5200 and 4700 BP has been found at Balbridie (Fairweather & Ralston, 1993) and has provided a large assemblage of cereal grain. Mithen (2000b) reviews the Mesolithic/Neolithic transition in Scotland.

26. Bolsay has more Neolithic than Mesolithic dates, ranging between 4740±50 BP (3633–3383 cal BC) and 3535±80 BP (1952–1744 cal BC). It also has a considerable quantity of Neolithic pottery and one ground stone axe; in contrast, very few pieces of typologically distinct Neolithic chipped stone are found within the assemblage. On this basis, it seems that the microlithic technology had continued to be used by the Neolithic occupants of the site (Mithen, Lake & Finlay, 2000b). Port Charlotte burial tomb on Islay has a radiocarbon date of 5020±90 BP (3940–3709 cal BC), with a scatter of probable sheep bones below the structure – some have claimed that these are deer bones; unfortunately the original collection is no longer available for study.

27. Schulting (1999) compares the carbon isotope frequencies of Mesolithic and Neolithic human bones in western Scotland to find evidence of a substantial contrast in diet, a picture repeated throughout Northwest Europe.

23: Searching for the First Americans

1. Figgins (1927) describes his work at Folsom. The following text about Folsom also draws on Meltzer (1993a), and it is from photographs within that work that comments about the appearance of the main protagonists are made. Meltzer (2000) describes renewed investigations at the Folsom site.

2. Quoted in Adovasio (1993, p. 200).

3. From Bonnichsen & Gentry Steele (1994).

4. Meltzer (1993a) provides a beautifully written and illustrated account of the history of the search for the first Americans.

5. Chapter VII of Prehistoric Times considered 'North American Archaeology' (the following quotes are taken from pp. 198–236). Victorian John Lubbock had not been to the Americas himself and relied on 'four excellent memoirs' recently published by the Smithsonian Institution. Most of the chapter described fortifications, enclosures, temples and mounds. A variety of 'implements' of stone and metal were also described, with several comments about their similarity to those found in Europe.

Throughout the chapter, Victorian John Lubbock constantly sought clues as to the age of the monuments and artefacts; he noted how trees which were at least 300 years old had grown on top of waste heaps from copper mines, and that the living Indian savages could not throw any light on the archaeological remains. He thought the wide variety of trees within the woodland covering the burial mounds suggested considerable age. Arguments for the antiquity of burials based on the state or amount of skeleton surviving were treated with caution – Lubbock knew that in Britain Saxon burials were frequently entirely perished whereas many prehistoric ones had survived intact.

Towards the end of the chapter, some comments on the antiquity of the First Americans were made. Victorian John Lubbock was aware that prehistoric Indians had independently invented agriculture, which took them out of their 'original barbarism'; after that, he believed, they had erected burial mounds only to 'relapse into partial barbarism' again. Such developments, he wrote, did not 'require an antiquity of more than 3000 years. I do not, of course, deny that the period may have been very much greater, but in my opinion at least, it *need* not be greater. At the same time there are other observations which, if they eventually prove to be correct, would indicate a very much higher antiquity.'

These 'other observations' were human artefacts found with the bones of extinct animals, of which he had two accounts, both involving the mastodon, a prehistoric relative of the elephant. Victorian Lubbock was sceptical, concluding that 'there does not as yet appear to be any satisfactory proof that man co-existed with the mammoth and mastodon'.

6. See Fiedel (1999) for most recent dating of the Folsom culture in light of new methods of radiocarbon calibration.

7. Dent is described in Cassells (1983). Haynes (1991) comments that the association between mammoth bones and Clovis points at Dent may have arisen by post-depositional movement of sediments.

8. Warnica (1966) describes the excavations at Blackwater Draw, while Saunders (1992) provides an interpretation of its evidence with regard to mammoth hunting.

9. The chronological relationship between Folsom and Clovis in light of stratigraphic relationships and radiocarbon determinations is discussed by Taylor et al. (1996).

10. Haury et al. (1953) describe the Naco mammoth and Clovis points.

11. Haury et al. (1959) describe the initial excava-

tions at Lehner Ranch. Traces of mammoth bones at this site had first been seen in 1952 by Edward Lehner when inspecting the property he wished to purchase. He carefully removed a few fragments, which were identified as coming from mammoths by the Arizona State Museum. When many more bones became exposed after the heavy summer rains of 1955, Emil W. Haury of the museum began excavations, having already excavated at the Naco site. Thirteen spear points were found among the bones of eight mammoths, together with an assortment of other stone tools. Continued excavation in 1956 found the jaw of a ninth mammoth, together with bones from other animals including a horse and tapir. Jeffrey Saunders (1977) from Illinois State Museum made a detailed study of the mammoth-bone collection and concluded that a complete family of mammoths had been killed en masse as they had huddled together in defence of their young and injured – an interpretation contested by many others (Haynes, 1991). It is evident that Lehner Ranch had not been a kill site alone. Further excavations in 1974–5 by Haury and Vance Haynes from Arizona University revealed bones from a wider range of animals: birds, rabbits, bears and camels. Lehner Ranch began to look more like a hunter-gatherer base camp to which hunting parties returned year after year.

12. This date of 11,500 BC is not necessarily the one understood in the 1970s. For the latest thinking about the date of the Clovis culture, see Fiedel (1999).

13. Martin's arguments will be covered in detail in chapter 27. Here we can simply note that he used the relative rarity of Clovis sites, and especially kill sites, as evidence for the very rapid dispersal of these hunters through the continent. His arguments have been made clearly in Martin (1984, 1999) and by use of a simulation model in Mosimann & Martin (1975).

14. The Mojave Desert lies to the north of the Colorado River in southeast California. Stone artefacts had been collected from the gravels of the Calico Hills in 1948. They had attracted the attention of Louis Leakey, famed discoverer of human ancestors in East Africa and who believed that he might repeat the act here; accounts of his work at Calico can be found in Leakey et al. (1968, 1970). In May 1963 Leakey had visited the region with Dee Simpson, an archaeologist from Los Angeles. Impressed with the evidence for ancient lakes and rivers, he thought it a suitable habitat for the First Americans. 'Dee, dig here,' Leakey had boldly stated (quoted in Leakey et al., 1970, p. 72), quickly grabbing large cobbles to build four cairns to mark the spot.

Excavations began and further stone artefacts were recovered – much cruder in style than those found upon the surface. Leakey declared that these had a 'primitive' appearance and must have been made by humans many tens, probably hundreds, of thousands of years ago. Others immediately doubted such 'artefacts', notably Vance

Haynes (1973). He made several visits to the site and remained unpersuaded that any of the other pieces were true artefacts. Several stones had certainly been broken by being hit either by another stone or by smashing on to a hard surface. But nature alone could have been responsible. Haynes examined the gravels from which the supposed artefacts had come. The ancient river had been fast flowing; the stones it carried would have been violently knocked around. Some of these knocks could have produced what looked like human-made artefacts; with enough searching, such stones would eventually be found. And that, Haynes, argued, is exactly what had happened in the Calico Hills.

In her autobiography, Mary Leakey (1984, pp. 142–4) provides her views about the Calico excavations and the role it played in her estrangement from her husband. She explains how his enthusiasm for the Calico site led to the loss of her academic respect for him, due to his quite uncritical approach to what were evidently naturally fractured cobbles. Louis, she explains, could count on adulation in southern California where he was a 'visiting super-star' and had 'personal infallibility'. According to Mary Leakey, the Calico excavation was 'catastrophic to his professional career and was largely responsible for the parting of our ways' (p. 142).

15. The following text about Bluefish Caves draws on Cinq-Mars (1979), Adovasio (1993) and Ackerman (1996). The latter provides dates of 24,000 BP for a split caribou tibia that could have been a broken fleshing tool and a date of 23,500 BP for a mammoth-bone core.

16. Particularly important clusters of sites are found in the Nenana and the Tanana valleys, sites with names that evoke the affinity of hunter-gatherers with the natural world: Dry Creek (11,120±85 BP; 11,238–11,020 cal BC), Broken Mammoth (11,770±210 BP; 12,112–11,524 cal BC), Swan Point (11,660±60 BP; 11,868–11,521 cal BC); Owl Ridge (11,340±150 BP; 11,521–11,191 cal BC); and Walker Road (11,120±180 BP; 11,389–10,968 cal BC). While these sites have early dates, it is often difficult to be confident that the material being dated is definitely associated with, or is a product of, human activity. But their evidence suggests that by 11,500 BC people were hunting bison and elk in birch, pine and spruce woodland, fishing and fowling, and trapping otters and foxes for their pelts. The earliest of these Alaskan foragers used stone tools referred to as the Nenana culture, some aspects of which are very similar to Clovis, although fluted points are missing. After that date, a new technology appears which relied on making very small blades of stone: the Denali culture as found at Bluefish Caves. This never spread into North America. Site summaries for western and eastern Beringia are provided in West (1996).

17. The date of 12,700 BC for the opening of the ice-free corridor is the one favoured by Fiedel (1999) who drew on arguments by Jackson & Duk-Rodkin (1996) and Mandryk (1996). The

most recent discussion is by Mandryk et al. (2001).

18. The following text about Meadowcroft Rockshelter draws on the excavation reports by Adovasio et al. (1978, 1990), the palaeoenvironmental reconstruction described by Adovasio et al. (1985), and Adovasio's (1993) overview. Adovasio et al. (1978) provide a list of almost fifty radiocarbon dates. Our concern is with those from the lower strata, which has seven dates between 19,600± 2400 BP and 13,240±1010BP. Not all of these have such large deviations: 15,120±165BP and 13,270±340 BP. The earliest of these dates is associated with bark-like material that might be basketry. Below this set of dates are two others, from which there are no definite cultural associations: 21,380±800 BP and 21,070±475BP.

19. Adovasio (1993, p. 205).

20. A micromorphological analysis of the sediments published in 1999 confirmed the evidence of the 1970s excavations, finding no evidence that ground water could have contaminated the charcoal samples (Goldberg & Arpin, 1999).

21. The idea of a coastal route had been first proposed in the 1960s by Chard. Fladmark was the first, however, to develop this into a viable hypothesis, such as in Fladmark (1979).

22. An overview of the coastal route scenario is provided by Gruhn (1994). Mounting palaeoenvironmental evidence has provided further support for the feasibility of a coastal route and further called into question the viability of the 'ice-free corridor' land route until 11,500 BP – far too late for the First Americans.

23. I will address the significance of linguistic diversity among Native Americans in the following chapter. Here I simply note that Bryan and Gruhn's argument is likely to be entirely fallacious (Meltzer, 1993b; see Nettle, 1999, for alternative explanations of linguistic diversity).

24. One problem with the coastal entry scenario is that it appears to harbour a technological contradiction: if the First Americans were clever enough to construct vessels for coastal migration, why is the only possible evidence of their actual presence crude stone artefacts, such as those from Pedra Furada, which are comparable to those used by our ape-like ancestors rather than technologically sophisticated modern humans? Ruth Gruhn (1994) defends her position by pointing to some of the Native American groups themselves. Just look at the Yahgan people of Tierra del Fuego, she asks. They were people who lived in cold, rugged and stormy environments with hardly any material culture at all – a fact that had impressed Charles Darwin when he encountered them during his Beagle voyages. Any archaeological record they left would not be dissimilar to that of the claimed pre-Clovis Americans.

25. The following text about Pedra Furada draws on Guidon & Delibrias (1986), Guidon (1989), Bahn (1991), Meltzer et al. (1994) and Guidon et al. (1996).

26. Stated in Bahn (1991)

27. According to Meltzer et al. (1994), these flakes that looked near identical to those that had been detached by a hammer-stone and the broken cobbles themselves had become embedded with the sediments of the cave and mistakenly interpreted as true stone artefacts. Guidon herself accepts that eroded cobbles were indeed the source of the artefacts, but rejects the claim that the fractures were purely natural in origin. It is, however, a very persuasive argument. If the broken cobbles were indeed artefacts, one must again ask why the Pedra Furada people made tools no more complex than those of our ancestors on the African savannah more than 2 million years ago? No one questions that the earliest Americans were anything other than Homo sapiens, a species that had been making complex stone tools in Africa, Asia and Europe for more than a million years. Why revert to the most primitive technology when in the Americas, and why keep making the same types of tools for more than 30,000 years? There is no evidence for technological developments at Pedra Furada, whereas in all other regions of the world modern human culture is characterised by constant change. And why should such artefacts be absent from all other caves in the region? Most probably this is because they lack a naturally eroding deposit of quartzite pebbles.

28. Several other aspects of the site were also questioned by Meltzer et al. (1994), such as the circular stone features which could easily have been created by swirling water currents.

29. From Meltzer et al. (1994).

30. From Guidon et al. (1996).

24: American Past in the Present

1. Turner (1994). Meltzer (1993a) provides an excellent summary of Turner's work.

2. Quoted in Ruhlen (1994).

3. Greenberg (1987).

4. Greenberg et al. (1986).

5. The following draws upon Goddard & Campbell (1994).

6. Christy Turner, for instance, had identified a cluster of Native American tribes on the northwest coast sharing some specific dental features; but this did not overlap at all well with the Na-Dene linguistic group as mapped by Greenberg.

7. Nichols (1990).

8. Nettle (1999).

9. According to Nettle, European contact came at a time before the expected reduction in languages had begun to take place. That contact itself caused a severe reduction in Native American languages, especially on the east coast. Indeed, the relatively high number of languages on the west coast that Alan Bryan has used as evidence of early colonisation of America is, according to David Meltzer, simply because 'it is one of the areas on the continent where indigenous populations weathered the deadly effects of European

contact and disease and survived ... until the end of the nineteenth century when intensive linguistic fieldwork began' (quoted in Meltzer, 1993b).

10. See Wallace (1995) for a discussion of the virtues of mitochondrial DNA with particular regard to the study of the First Americans.

11. Torroni (2000). The technical term is haplogroup: a group of well-defined haplotypes which is itself a group that shares a set of genetic markers when analysed by restriction fragment polymorphism. For more details, see Torroni (2000, pp. 78–80).

12. Horai et al. (1993).

13. Torroni et al (1994).

14. Bonatto & Salzano (1997). Stone & Stoneking (1998) reached a similar conclusion, drawing on samples of ancient DNA from a prehistoric Native American cemetery, and dated the single migration to 23–37,000 years ago. Torroni (2000) reviews all studies of mitochondrial DNA and attempts to find areas of agreement.

15. Historical genetics and linguistics face similar problems and require their studies to be integrated in order to be mutually supporting, as exemplified in Renfrew (2000).

16. These problems are more serious when addressing recent events in human history, such as migrations, rather than those long time spans during which human evolution takes place. Slight differences in assumed mutation rates will change estimates for the date of colonisation by several thousand years – perhaps altering this from 12,000 to 15,000, or from 20,000 to 30,000 years ago. Such differences of a few thousand years may not be of great significance if one is attempting to date events that occurred hundreds of thousands of years ago, such as the origin of modern humans (c. 130,000 years ago), or the date of the last common ancestor to modern humans and apes (c. 5–6 million years ago). But a few thousand years make a whole world of difference when attempting to understand the peopling of the Americas. The required level of accuracy may still be far beyond that possible with our limited understanding of mutation rates and how these vary between genes.

17. Figures from Chatters (2000).

18. Steele & Powell (1994).

19. Chatters (2000). A fragment of the fifth left metacarpal from Kennewick Man has been dated to 8410±60 BP (7574–7377 cal BC).

25: On the Banks of the Chinchihuapi

1. This chapter draws on Dillehay's (1989, 1997) final reports on his excavation at Monte Verde and his two summary articles (Dillehay 1984, 1987). My reconstructions are based on his evidence unless stated otherwise. Dillehay (1987, 12) describes himself as being confused and overwhelmed when beginning work at the site.

2. As there are no human remains from Monte Verde, any ideas about the physical appearance of the site's inhabitants are pure conjecture, drawing on the evidence from other pre-10,000 BP skeletal material (Steele & Powell, 1994; Chatters, 2000).

3. Meltzer (1997), with his profound knowledge of the history of American archaeology, describes Dillehay's (1989, 1997) volumes about Monte Verde as marking a milestone in American archaeology.

4. There are eleven radiocarbon dates for MV-II which range between 12,780±240 BP (13,802–13,188 cal BC) and 11,990±200 BP (12,365–11,578 cal BC). Dillehay favours a date of 12,570 BP (which calibrates to approximately 12,500 BC).

5. MV-I has a date of 33,370±530 BP and one >33,020 BP. It is currently impossible to calibrate such dates but one must assume that they are likely to refer to a date of at least 36,000 BC.

6. It is not clear whether the mastodon remains at Monte Verde were acquired by hunting or scavenging. My suggestions for the use of footpads and internal organs are pure speculation, based on ethnographic analogy. Dillehay (1992) discusses the relationship between humans and mastodons at Monte Verde.

7. Lubbock (1865, pp. 234–5). The original account was published by Dr A. C. Koch in The Transactions of the Academy of Science of St Louis in 1857, p. 61.

8. Adovasio & Pedler (1997).

9. From Meltzer (1993b, pp. 159–60).

26: Explorers in a Restless Landscape

1. My text regarding the nature and evolution of the North American fauna draws on material in Sutcliffe (1986).

2. Rancho La Brea is an abundant fossil locality now in Los Angeles, California, with Pleistocene fauna dating between 36,000 BP and 10,000 BP. Throughout that time, natural seeps of tar trapped animals resulting in a remarkable collection of fossils within natural asphalt. These were first recognised in 1875, since when over 100 tons of fossils have been recovered ranging from mammoths to birds and invertebrates. Detailed study is provided by Stock (1992) and a summary by Sutcliffe (1986).

3. In conditions of low humidity and uniform temperature, as found in caves in the American Southwest, dung escapes fungal decay, bacterial and insect attack. Rampart Cave, found within the Grand Canyon, has the best-preserved dung balls and been described by Martin et al. (1961) and Hansen (1978).

4. Martin et al. (1985).

5. Descriptions of extinct species of mega-fauna from North America and elsewhere in the world can be found in Martin & Klein (1984).

6. The term 'mega-fauna' is used to refer to animals over 40 kg in weight (Martin, 1984). A review of extinctions in North America can be found in Stuart (1991), Mead & Meltzer (ed., 1985) and Grayson (1989).

7. Martin & Klein (1984) provided global coverage for mega-faunal extinctions. Quite why Africa lost so few of its species remains unclear. One possibility is that because humans had evolved in Africa its mega-fauna had developed patterns of

social and migratory behaviour to minimise the risks of human predation. The most severe extinctions occurred in the continents that were most recently colonised and where animals may have never had need to develop avoidance or defensive mechanisms against human predators. Mega-faunal extinctions in Australia are considered in chapter 34, and in Africa in chapter 49.

8. The following text concerning environmental change in North America draws heavily on the fabulous book by Pielou (1991).

9. This is Pielou's (1991) thought about the ice sheets.

10. The impact of the Younger Dryas in North America remains unclear. From my study of the literature, it appears to have been substantial but David Meltzer (pers. comm.), with his more comprehensive and in-depth knowledge of the archaeological and palaeoenvironmental data, cautions against exaggerating the impact of the Younger Dryas on both natural communities and human culture in North America.

11. Anderson & Gillam (2000) propose specific routes that colonising Americans may have taken, using least-cost solution scenarios for entry through the ice-free corridor and northwest coast.

12. The apparently rapid colonisation of the Americas suggests that the first Americans had both high mobility and high fertility. Surovell (2000) explains how highly mobile hunter-gatherers are usually assumed to have low reproduction rates, partly due to the problem of transporting young children, but suggests that both high fertility and mobility were indeed feasible for the First Americans. Meltzer (n.d.a) also discusses the demographic issues surrounding the initial colonisation of the Americas.

13. Meltzer (n.d.b) has discussed the issue of 'landscape learning' in the context of the peopling of the Americas, an issue that has unfortunately been otherwise neglected in the vast amount of literature devoted to New World colonisation.

14. The following text regarding the melt-water lakes draws on Dawson (1992).

15. Broecker et al. (1989) argued that a change in the routing of the melt waters from the Laurentide ice sheet was the cause of the Younger Dryas. Up until 13,000 years ago, warm water – about 10°C – flowing northwards from the South Atlantic began to sink when it reached approximately 60° latitude, the level of Labrador or northern Scotland. It flowed back south at a lower depth and with a temperature of about 2°C. As the water sank, its warmth had been released into the atmosphere. The first consequence was that warm air blew across the whole of Europe. The second was that Europeans of 14,000 years ago had no need to dress in clothes as thick as those of their counterparts at the same latitudes in North America. The same holds true today: anyone from England had better take extra clothes when they head directly east for a holiday in Newfoundland. The great influx of the water from Lake Agassiz at 13,000 years ago may have disrupted this so-called 'conveyer belt' system. As the water was fresh, it diluted the salty water flowing up from the South Atlantic; this reduced its density and prevented it from sinking, and hence no warmth was released into the atmosphere. The result – or at least that claimed by some scientists – was the Younger Dryas when the Natufian hunter-gatherers had to start cultivating rather than just gathering wild plants. The Younger Dryas lasted as long as Lake Agassiz continued to drain into the North Atlantic.

16. For a succinct summary of Bechan Cave, diet and the lifestyle of the Columbian mammoth, see Lister & Bahn (1995).

17. Dillehay (1991) examines disease ecology and human migration into the Americas.

18. Meltzer (1993a).

19. The origin of the Clovis tradition has been debated for many years (Stanford, 1991). This was a particular problem when the Clovis people were thought to be the First Americans: bifacially made, fluted, spear points are absent from Beringia other than in very rare specimens that may be quite unrelated to the Clovis points themselves. Goebel et al. (1991) argue that the Nenana complex of Alaska is the forerunner of the Clovis; even though this lacks the fluted points, it involves a similar range of knapping techniques and tool types to those found in Clovis assemblages. In their scenario, Clovis technology would have arrived in North America by a second wave of migrants travelling south. This seems to conflict with the lack of a chronological trend from north to south, and the highest density of Clovis points being found in the eastern, woodland region. Since 1997, Dennis Stanford and Bruce Bradley have proposed the idea that Clovis had European origins, believing that Clovis points derive from Solutrean points of Southwest Europe, which were also made by bifacial knapping although they lacked a flute. Hence they argue that Solutrean descendants spent 5,000 years crossing the Atlantic by travelling along the edge of the ice sheets and presumably living on marine resources. Straus (2000) not only describes fundamental flaws in this idea but concludes by stating: 'It seems to me particularly irresponsible – in the absence of any credible scientific evidence for prehistoric European settlement of the New World – for some professional archaeologists to be suggesting that Native Americans are not the descendants of the first colonizers of this land.' I agree with those sentiments.

20. Storck (1991).

21. Dunbar (1991).

22. Frison (1991).

23. Bryan (1991) describes the fluted-point tradition as a whole, focusing on their diversity.

27: Clovis Hunters on Trial

1. Meltzer & Mead (1985).

2. Grayson (1989).

3. There is inevitable inaccuracy partly because all the radiocarbon dates themselves have deviations of at least a hundred years and partly due to the uncertainties of calibration.

4. Martin's claim is, in fact, even more substantial – that humans were responsible for mega-faunal extinctions throughout the world (Martin, 1984). A recent summary of his views regarding mammoths in North America can be found in Martin (1999).

5. Saunders (1977) relied upon the age distribution of the mammoths, which suggested that an entire herd had been killed at Lehner Ranch. He lacked, however, any cut-mark evidence and there are no strong reasons to believe that the mammoths were killed at the same time. His interpretation is contested by others such as Meltzer (pers. comm.) and Haynes (1991).

6. Animal bones and plant remains are rarely preserved on Clovis sites. The traditional focus on big (mega) game hunting is most likely a reflection of the chance survival of mammoth bones on a few sites and the fact that these were the first Clovis sites to be discovered. When Clovis points were found elsewhere in the continent, it was assumed that these had also been used for big-game hunting. The distribution of Clovis sites is also most likely biased to those in big-game hunting locations. Many sites are likely to be deeply buried by alluvium in river valleys, where the focus of activities may have been plant gathering. The Aubrey site, for instance, on the edge of the Trinity River in northeast Texas has plant remains but had been buried by 8 metres of river sediments since the Holocene began. Meltzer (1993c) provides a review of Clovis adaptations and discusses the biased nature of the archaeological record. Dincauze (1993) reviews Clovis economy in the woodlands of eastern America and Tankersley (1998) does likewise for the northeast.

7. Shawnee-Minisnik in Pennsylvania is another site deeply buried in alluvium. It provided unspecified fish remains and a variety of plants, which indicates foraging in a temperate forest (Dincauze, 1993). Bloodstains on artefacts from the Debert site have been identified as from caribou (Tankersley, 1998). Evidence for big-game hunting – mammoth, horse and camel – was found at Lubbock Lake in addition to the smaller animals (Johnson, 1991). For the Old Humboldt site, see Willig (1991) who also describes fishbones from, aptly, Fishbone Cave also in Nevada.

8. Little Salt Spring near Charlotte harbour in southwest Florida was once a freshwater spring and is now a sink-hole. Excavations in 1959 uncovered the shell of a giant land tortoise with a pointed wooden stake between the upper and lower shells, showing how the animal had been stabbed in the back of the right foreleg. Several of the bones were burnt, suggesting that the animal had been upturned and roasted on the spot (Dunbar, 1991). Kimmswick is located in the

confluence area of the Mississippi, Missouri and Illinois rivers. Stone artefacts were found in association with the remains of a cow and calf mastodon, peccary, whitetailed deer, ground sloth and a variety of small mammals (Tankersley, 1998).

9. Meltzer (1993c).

10. Haynes's (1987, 1991) work is a classic example of how some of the most valuable research in archaeology is done by studying the present, not the past. It has led Haynes to claim that the Clovis hunters in the southwest were doing little more than killing off animals which were already emaciated by the drought. He spent many years in Africa examining the natural die-off sites of elephants. The 1980s were a good time for this research because they were a bad time for elephants – several years of drought leading to widespread starvation. Haynes observed how the elephants that gathered and died at the dried-up water-holes were often left quite untouched by any scavenging carnivores. Hence, as they became buried, many of the bones remained joined together. As such, these remains are quite different to those known from the few accounts of elephant hunting and butchery by traditional peoples. In those cases, the carcasses were thoroughly broken up, the bones smashed for marrow, the remains widely dispersed. Artefacts were rarely lost or discarded with these remains, largely because valuable steel knives were the principal butchery implements. Fireplaces may have been the only trace of a human presence, other than the tell-tale cut and butchery marks on the bones.

Armed with this knowledge, Haynes examined the Clovis mammoth sites and found a surprising, and rather paradoxical, pattern. On the one hand, the mammoth remains looked remarkably similar to those from the natural die-off elephant sites: they were located at water-holes, many of the bones were still joined together, and cut-marks and bone smashing were virtually absent. Moreover, at several sites the mammoth bones were principally those of young adults and females, in the most susceptible age range among the elephants at the African water-holes. As such, the Clovis sites are quite different from any known examples of elephant kill and butchery sites. Yet the presence of artefacts, especially the large Clovis points, was a clear indication of human activity.

11. The distribution of Clovis archaeological sites throughout the American south and west suggests that finding reliable fresh water was a priority for Clovis people as well as the game. Dunbar (1991) describes how Clovis sites in Florida are predominantly found around low-lying areas and 'sink-holes' – natural hollows in the ground due either to the erosion of limestone or to rock collapse. These are likely to have acted as oases in a region which was becoming increasingly arid during the Younger Dryas. A similar focus can be recognised on the southern plains (Johnson, 1991)

and in the far west (Willig, 1991). Nevertheless, the Clovis people may have been living in an environment with far more surface water available than their Folsom descendants would find. Meltzer (pers. comm.) doubts the existence of a Clovis drought, the evidence for which has been critically reviewed by Holliday (2000). As the LGM had been a wet/cool period in the American southwest, with numerous lakes in now arid environments (Li et al., 1996), a consequence of changes in the polar-front jet stream (Mock & Bartlein, 1995), the same may have been the case in the Younger Dryas: while other regions of the Old World were suffering from renewed drought, the southwest was receiving increased rainfall. The idea of a Clovis drought has been most forcefully argued by Vance Haynes (1991). Key evidence for this is the 'black mat' at Murray Springs – a horizon of compacted spring-laid deposits – that indicates a rapid rise in the water table, above which no mammoth bones are found. Haynes once thought this to mark the end of the Younger Dryas but revised his views to suggest that it marks the start, which is more in tune with the chronology of Clovis coming to an end at c. 10,900 BC just before the start of the Younger Dryas at 10,800 BC (Fiedel, 1999).

12. Some of the most obvious burial places, like the caves in the Appalachian Mountains, appear not to have been used by the Clovis people at all. Walthall (1998) discusses the apparent absence of any Clovis or Early Holocene use of cave sites.

13. Remains of fish, marmot, horse, camel and bird bones were found associated with the burial in Fishbone Cave, Nevada, which has been dated to between 10,900±300 BP and 11,250±260 BP (Willig, 1991).

14. Lahren & Bonnichsen (1974).

15. The Anzick cache included several bone foreshafts for spears; these were the parts of a spear to which the points themselves were attached and which broke off when the animal was struck, allowing the hunter to retain the main spear shaft (Lahren & Bonnichsen, 1974).

16. Numerous other caches of Clovis artefacts are known throughout the continent (Stanford, 1991). Another cache from Montana known as the Simon site contained some particularly large projectile points which were also covered with red ochre – it may have been another burial. The most spectacular is that known as the Ritchie-Roberts cache, found in central Washington. Here fourteen exquisite fluted points were found, ranging in length from 10 cm to a remarkable 23 cm. At that size it seems doubtful if the point could have ever been used effectively and its manufacture was perhaps largely for the display of tool-making skills. The Drake cache from Colorado had thirteen newly made or resharpened points, and tiny fragments of ivory, possibly the remains of foreshafts.

17. Taçon (1991) describes the symbolic aspects of stone use and tool development in western Arnhem Land, Australia. The Rainbow Serpent (see chapter 36), one of the most important figures in the Dreamtime mythology, swallowed other Ancestral Beings and was then forced to vomit their bones. These formed the rocky sandstone ridges and quartz escarpment of the Australian landscape, from which the Aborigines acquired material for making stone points. As such, the stone points embodied the essence of Ancestral Beings, becoming prestigious objects imbued with mystical properties. Stone artefacts were also tied into gender relations. Within the Aboriginal societies, stone axes and points belonged to men and were attributed with masculine properties (Taçon, 1991). In the Yorant tribe of northern Queensland, women and young men had to borrow stone axes from the older men and, by doing so, reinforced the power of those men in the society. Stone points among many Aboriginal groups were considered metaphors for the penis, not only because of their shape and hardness, but because both were used to penetrate flesh.

18. MacPhee & Marx (1999).

19. The key problem has been with contamination, either from the organisms within the ground in which the bones were buried, from the excavators or during the stages of post-excavation study.

20. Lundelius & Graham (1999) and Guthrie (1984) give environmental explanations focussed on changing seasonality and vegetation for Late Pleistocene extinctions.

21. Some species may have effectively held the ecological communities together – remove them and the community would collapse. The ecologist Norman Owen-Smith (1987) has suggested that mammoths played this role. As they were critical in maintaining the conditions for many other species to survive, they were in his terms the 'keystone' species. We can certainly see this with elephants today. These animals maintain their habitat by dismembering trees and uprooting seedlings. By doing so, they ensure that many types of plants can flourish and allow an array of grazers and browsers to survive. When the elephants are lost, the landscape becomes uniform bushland or woodland supporting far fewer species. Hence Richard Leakey has written that if the elephant becomes extinct, many more species will inevitably follow. Perhaps this was the case in North America as the ice age came to its end. The extinction of the mammoth due to increased seasonality may have set in motion a whole train of consequences, leading to a massive loss of biodiversity.

22. Pielou (1991).

23. We might also draw on our own modern experience to question the role of habitat loss in ice-age extinctions. During the last 500 years about 90 mammals have become extinct in the world, the vast majority due to destruction of their habitats rather than to hunting or disease. Yet these animals are precisely the converse of those which were lost at the end of the ice age: they are dominated by rodents, shrews and bats, and more than 75% of them lived on small

islands. Nothing could be more different to the loss of large animals from continental land masses.

24. S. L. Vartanyan et al. (1993). Lister (1993) provides a useful commentary about the significance of this find.

25. Since undertaking this work in the early 1990s, the evidence for drought has become more contested (Meltzer, pers. comm.; Holliday, 2000).

26. These skills are also of use to ecologists studying the likely growth and decline of animal populations today. In the early 1980s I spent some time writing a program for the Cambridge ecologists Steve Albon and Tim Clutton-Brock regarding the red-deer herds on the Scottish island of Rum. While in Cambridge I was approached by an elephant ecologist, Keith Lindsey, who wanted to know about the likely effect of climate change and poaching on the herds of African elephants he was studying in Botswana. He and other elephant ecologists were able to supply me with information about the rate at which elephants reproduce and how this is effected by drought. Some of the figures were quite startling, such as the duration of gestation (24 months), and the late onset of sexual maturity (9–13 years). During periods of water shortage, a calf may have had as little as a 50:50 chance of reaching its first birthday. These effects of stress become magnified if drought occurs in two or more successive years. Armed with such data, I worked out the mathematics and developed a computer simulation for elephant population dynamics.

27. Mithen (1993, 1996).

28. I am grateful to David Meltzer for reminding me once again about these uncomfortable facts for those who favour humans having played a causal role in mega-faunal extinctions.

28: Virginity Reconsidered

1. This site has dates of 10,420±100 BP (10,828–50,162 cal BC) and 10,280±110 BP (10,620–9751 cal BC). It has the bones of guanaco, fox, horse, camelid, birds and rodents and a lithic assemblage of edge-trimmed flakes (Dillehay et al., 1992).

2. Lubbock (1865, pp. 189–91). All the following quotes are taken from these pages.

3. The following is taken from Lubbock (1865, pp. 432–9).

4. Lubbock (1865, p. 440).

5. Bird (1938).

6. For a review of fishtail points in southern South America, see Politis (1991).

7. The ground sloth species is otherwise known as mylodon (Mylodon darwinii). Quite how long this species survived in Patagonia remains unclear. It gained some notoriety when Bruce Chatwin (1977) described his journey to Mylodon Cave in southern Chile, in his quest to add to the piece of mylodon skin that supposedly once had been found in the cave. He describes finding more hairs within the cave, but the reliability of his account can be questioned – his basic description of the cave is, for instance, quite inaccurate. Borrero (1996) argues that mylodon was scavenged rather hunted in the Late Pleistocene.

8. Radiocarbon dates for Fell's Cave range between 11,000±170 BP (11,222–10,914 cal BC) and 10,080±160 BP (9987–9310 cal BC) (Politis 1991).

9. His dates from Palli-Aike were about 1,000 years younger. Bird has also excavated several human skeletons from that cave which may have been of the people who had made the fishtail points (Dillehay et al., 1992).

10. Alas, I have not been to the Amazon. Any description of the Amazonian environments and the practices of recent Amazonian people in the following text is taken from the accounts of two travellers: Alfred Russel Wallace (1889), co-discoverer with Charles Darwin of natural selection, who published his Travels on the Amazon and Rio Negro in 1889, and Nick Gordon (1997), a wildlife cameraman who published his own Amazonian diary more than a hundred years later.

11. At least that is what appears to be the case from the only three pollen sequences available from this vast area, two from the Amazonian lowlands at Carajas and Lake Pata, and one from marine deposits off the mouth of the Amazonian River (Colinvaux et al., 2000).

12. Fifty-six radiocarbon dates were secured on wood and carbonised plants at the site, covering 1,200 radiocarbon years between 10,000±60 BP (9677–9310 cal BC) and 11,145±135 BP (11,394–11,022 cal BC) (Roosevelt et al., 1996). Vance Haynes and Dina Dincauze have disputed the earliest dates, suggesting that a date of 10,500 BP, rather than 11,200 BP, is most reliable for the first occupation due to the large standard errors on the earliest dates. Roosevelt challenges this, pointing to the stratigraphic sequence of the dates, with the earliest in the lowest levels (Gibbons, 1996).

13. Fish have always been one of the gastronomic pleasures of the Amazon, with the eyeballs of the massive fruit-eating tambaqui acknowledged as a delicacy (Gordon, 1997).

14. For a review of early pottery in South America, see Roosevelt (1995).

15. A brief summary of Holocene developments in Amazonian prehistory is provided in Roosevelt (1999); for a more extensive review of prehistoric and recent Amazonian Indians, see Roosevelt (1994).

16. Roosevelt et al. (1996).

17. This possibility has been raised by Dina Dincauze, as cited in Gibbons (1996).

29: Herders and the 'Christ-Child'

1. When people travel above 2,500 m they suffer from hypoxia, a decrease in the availability of oxygen caused by decreasing air pressure. Symptoms can include nausea, fatigue, hyperventilation, mental disorientation and dizziness, and typically last between 24 and 48 hours. Residents of upland areas become physiologically adapted (Aldenderfer, 1998).

2. My descriptions of the puna and its resources are taken from Rick (1980, 1988).

3. Other archaeologists had already excavated in Pachamachay Cave in 1969, 1970 and 1973. Rick (1980) excavated relatively small areas, a 1 m. by 1 m. trench within the cave in 1974 and a 3 m. by 3m. trench in the area immediately outside the cave in 1975. He cites a date of 11,800±930 BP for the second lowest of 33 strata (Rick, 1988), one of limited value due to its large deviation.

4. There are size distinctions between the llama and the alpaca, and between the guanaco and the vicuña. The shape of the incisors may also be used as a diagnostic criterion: vicuña incisors are parallel-sided with open roots, guanaco/llama incisors are spatulate-sided with closed roots; alpaca incisors are somewhere in between (Browman, 1989).

5. Smith (1995) provides a summary of the changes in faunal remains within the caves of the Jumin basin.

6. Browman (1989).

7. See Smith (1995) for a discussion about the domestication of plants in the central Andes.

8. Pearsall (1980) provides a detailed description of the plant remains from Pachamachay Cave and reviews the uses of the plants by recent and contemporary people.

9. Cormorants and other sea birds, anchovy and other fish were exploited at the 12,500-year-old site of Quebrada Tacahuay on the Peruvian coast (Keefer et al., 1998). There is no reason to doubt that these resources were also exploited during the Early Holocene.

10. Quebrada Jaguay is described by Sandweiss et al. (1998). It has a Late Pleistocene component, with the earliest radiocarbon date of 11,105±260 BP (11,459–10,944 cal BC) and an Early Holocene component reaching to 7,500±130 BP (6458–6226 cal BC). Obsidian is found in the Late Pleistocene horizons and has been sourced by its trace elements to a locality in the highlands, 130 km away.

11. Keefer et al. (1998).

12. Keefer et al. (1998). Nine radiocarbon dates have been published, ranging from 7990±80 BP (7057–6771 cal BC) to 10,770±150 BP (11,051–10,487 cal BC), with one outlier at 4,550±60 BP (3367–3101 cal BC). The report provides insufficient information to be confident that all, or any, of these samples directly date the archaeological materials. The date of 10,530±140 BP (10,891–10,228 cal BC) was, for instance, made on a charcoal fragment taken from a bulk sample that happened to be interspersed with chipped stone artefacts. The archaeological material is also highly dispersed and does not provide conclusive evidence for a discrete habitation or processing site (Meltzer, pers. comm.).

13. The following description of El Niño is taken from Houghton (1997).

14. The 1997–8 impact of El Niño is described in detail in the 1999 World Disasters Report.

30: A Double-Take in the Oaxaca Valley

1. Flannery (1986) contains a comprehensive study of the modern and past environment around Guilá Naquitz, his excavations and their implications for the origin of farming. All references to Flannery's excavations and interpretations in this chapter draw on this volume. Marcus and Flannery (1996) provide an excellent account of the landscapes of the Oaxaca valley and the development of agriculture and urban society.

2. Lubbock (1865, p. 233).

3. The following draws on Smith (1995) which provides a succinct summary about the origins of agriculture in Central America.

4. Richard 'Scotty' MacNeish spent a total of 5,683 days digging in the field, mainly in Central and South America. He ended his career as Director of the Robert S. Peabody Foundation for Archaeology in Andover, Massachusetts. He was the classic field archaeologist: hard-working, hard drinking, fast driving, and it was the latter that cost him his life at the age of 82 following a road accident in Belize on 16 January 2001. MacNeish was passionate about archaeology – apparently he talked 'shop' all the way to the hospital as the driver happened to be an interested amateur archaeologist.

5. Maize cobs from Guilá Naquitz, which indicate that the domestication of teosinte was under way, have been dated to 5410±40 BP (4340–4220 cal BC) and 5420±60 BP (4355–4065 cal BC) (Piperno & Flannery, 2001). Benze (2001) discusses how these cobs support the argument that maize originated from teosinte, while Smith (2001) discusses the more general significance of these dates for the origin of farming in the New World, stressing the value of converging data from archaeology and biology.

6. Matsuoka et al. (2002) provide a phylogenetic study of modern maize varieties to establish the likely date of a single domestication event, which was then followed by a diversification of this species into several varieties.

7. Smith (1997). He provides nine radiocarbon dates on cucurbita seeds and peduncle specimens from Guilá Naquitz that display morphological features indicating domestication ranging between 6980±50 BP (5970–5790 cal BC) and 8990±60 BP (8207–7970 cal BC).

8. For full accounts of the theories that I will summarise and explore, see Flannery (1986; Marcus & Flannery, 1996) and Hayden (1990).

9. For a study of hunter-gatherer decision-making, see Mithen (1990).

10. Flannery (pers. comm.) stresses that, as far as we know, only the seeds of squash were eaten at this date (8000 BC). Try to imagine, he asks, competitive feasting on squash seeds, which come from fruits about the size of an orange.

11. Gheo-Shih was studied in 1967 by Frank Hole and is described in Flannery & Marcus (1983). Charcoal for radiocarbon dating was lacking and on typological grounds it is placed between 5000 and 4000 BC. The most common type of projec-

tile point is known as the Pedernales type, which is also present in the uppermost levels of Guilá Naquitz. Animal and plant remains were poorly preserved. One area was quite clean of artefacts and boulders, looking as if it had been used for meetings or for dance. Flannery (pers. comm.) has explained that he and other archaeologists have found more than 2,000 sites on the valley floors and is dismissive of the idea that there might remain a substantial class of settlement undiscovered. He feels that Hayden's arguments suffer from an inadequate knowledge of the geomorphology and archaeology of the region gained from first-hand fieldwork.

12. I am grateful to Kent Flannery (pers. comm.) for explaining his view, reflected in my text, that the competitive feasting as recorded among Indians of the northwest coast is an inappropriate model for the Oaxaca valley at 8000 BC. He suggests that the historically documented Indians of the West Desert and Great Basin provide much better analogies in light of their food resources and known lifestyles. There is no evidence for ranking or competition in the Oaxaca valley until 1150 BC, more than 6,000 years after agriculture begins. The oldest evidence for a feast is 850–700 BC and involved dogs. Such developments are covered in Marcus and Flannery's (1996) excellent account of the development of agriculture and urban society in the Oaxaca valley.

31: To Koster

1. A summary of Early Holocene environments and archaeology in the southwest is provided in Cordell (1985).

2. The following material about sandals and Sandal Shelter is from Geib (2000). His set of AMS dates range between 8300±60 BP (7514–7196 cal BC) to 5575±50 BP (4454–4417 cal BC), with the majority at around 7500 BP.

3. Mock & Bartlein (1995).

4. A detailed review of the terminal Pleistocene and Early Holocene environments and archaeology of the Great Basin is provided by Beck & Jones (1997).

5. The only structure known is from the Pauline Lake site where there is a rock-cleared oval, 4 m. in diameter, with a heath in the centre and thought to be the remains of a dwelling (Beck & Jones, 1997).

6. Hogup Cave appears to have been used sporadically over a long period of time. It has radiocarbon dates ranging from 8350±160 BP (7576–7181 cal BC) to c. 3700 BP (Beck & Jones, 1997).

7. Frison (1978) describes the Bighorn basin and provides scenarios for the creation of the Horner site. He provides three radiocarbon dates: 7880±1300 BP, 8750±120 BP (8156–7605 cal BC) and 8840±120 BP (8201–7798 cal BC). The large deviations detract from the value of these dates and Frison states (without reasons) that the older date should be preferred to the younger. The narrative of my text, however, relies on the younger date.

The following text about bison hunting on the High Plains draws on Frison (1978) and Bamforth (1988).

8. The term 'altithermal' was introduced by Antev in 1948 and now sits rather awkwardly with our new knowledge about substantial climatic fluctuations during the Holocene. Whether it was a single regional event, or simply the amalgam of many small fluctuations that cannot be divided on the basis of terrestrial evidence, remains unclear. Meltzer (1999) provides an assessment of human responses to the altithermal on the plains.

9. There was a brief stint of agriculture on the southern plains c. 1250–1450 AD, as well as on the northern plains and in the Missouri River valley (Meltzer, pers. comm.).

10. The Koster project was co-directed by Stuart Struever and James Brown, with excavations lasting until 1979. Although there are several summary reports, a final report of the project remains unpublished. There is a good popular account of the excavations and interpretations by Struever and Holton (1979), on which most of the following text is based. Brown & Vierra (1983) provide an academic account, in an ecological framework, of the basic stratigraphy and cultural developments at the site.

11. The first occupation at Koster is referred to as phase 11 and has a radiocarbon date of 8730±90 BP (7940–7605 cal BC).

12. While Koster is the best-known settlement of the Archaic in the midwest, a wide range of other types of settlements have been found reflecting a diversity of lifestyles of people exploiting specific ecological niches. There are, for instance, cave occupations and shell mounds. A range of sites and an overview of the period is provided in Phillips & Brown (1983).

13. Dates for phase 8 at Koster range from 7670±110 BP (6639–6421 cal BC) to 6860±80 BP (5836–5664 cal BC) (Brown & Vierra, 1983). This is also referred to as the Middle Archaic 2.

14. Phase 7a at Koster is dated to 5825±80 BP (4775–5552 cal BC), while the end of phase 6 is dated at 4880±250 BP (3960–3485 cal BC). As with other dates from Koster, the larger standard deviations detract from their value. This phase is also referred to Middle Archaic 3 (Helton) phase.

15. The human remains from Koster have been studied by Buikstra (1981). The remnants of only 25 individuals came from phases 6 and 7, most of which were fragmented, redeposited and isolated bones. She found an unusually high frequency of evidence for traumatic injury and degenerative disease in this sample, which matched that in another sample from a Middle Archaic domestic site in the region of Koster, Modoc Rockshelter. In contrast, a sample from a Middle Archaic cemetery located below a later Hopewell-phase cemetery, the Gibson site on the crest of a bluff, provided little evidence of either traumas or disease. Consequently, Buikstra concluded that any individuals unable to perform the normal range of activities, due either to disease or injury,

were buried in a quite different location to healthy individuals. Neither sample included infants and children, which were presumably buried in a third type of location. One must be cautious about Buikstra's interpretation, due to the small samples involved; I have been unable to locate an ethnographic analogy for hunter-gatherers or horticulturalists burying physically constrained individuals in a discrete area away from other members of the community.

16. The development of agriculture in eastern America, involving indigenous domestication, is described in Smith (1995). The complex societies in this region are referred to as belonging to the Hopewell culture.

32: Salmon Fishing and the Gift of History

1. Unfortunately the 'traders' settlement' I refer to here is pure speculation. Chicago was founded in 1803 close to Fort Dearborn, became a city in 1837 and expanded with the construction of the railways. I have been unable to locate evidence for an Archaic settlement at the same locality, but the environmental situation would appear to be ideal for post-glacial hunter-gatherers.

2. The following text concerning the hunter-gatherers of the northwest coast draws upon Ames & Maschner (1999).

3. Cannon (2000) has studied the changing sea levels on the central coast of British Columbia and its relationship to human settlement. He finds a strong linear correlation between the dates of shell middens and their elevation above current sea levels. This indicates a gradual fall in sea level beween 10,000 and 8,000 BP.

4. Lubbock (1865, pp. 412–25).

5. Carlson (1996) describes the excavations and finds from the earliest occupations at Namu. Initial excavations had been undertaken in 1969–70, and further excavations in 1994. Those of 1977–8 had the agreement of the Bella Bella Band Council and those of 1994 were under the joint control of Simon Fraser University and the Heilsuk Tribal Council. Cannon (1996) describes the animal and fishbones from the site, drawing inferences about the economy. He provides a date for the basal levels of Namu as 9720±140 BP (9282–8811 cal BC) (Cannon 2000).

6. This is a modern Dene story told by Blondin (cited in Driver et al., 1996) and my attribution of it to the people of Namu is mere speculation.

7. It is, of course, no more than speculation that the 6,000-year-old inhabitants of Namu had similar ideological views to the historically recorded northwest-coast Indians. Evidence that the Raven was invested with symbolic meaning as early as 12,000 years ago has, however, come from Charlie Lake Cave in British Columbia (Driver et al., 1996). This has provided two raven skeletons (one at c. 10,500 BP and one at c. 9500 BP) which hint at ritual. Both were relatively complete, with no traces of cut-marks or carnivore scavenging. The younger specimen appears to have been deposited in a depression with a microblade core.

Driver et al. doubt that these birds had died naturally and allude to the mythological significance of ravens in later traditions.

33: A Lost World Revealed

1. The following chapters about Australia draw heavily on two excellent recent syntheses of Australian prehistory by Flood (1995) and Mulvaney & Kamminga (1999).

2. The earliest dates for occupation in Australia currently come from two rockshelters in Kakadu, Nauwalabila and Malakunanja, in which traces of occupation have been dated by TL methods to 50,000–60,000 years ago, and a burial at Lake Mungo claimed to date to 60,000 BP (Thorne et al., 1999). All three of these are open to serious question with regard to both the reliability of the dates and whether they actually relate to human activity. O'Connell & Allen (1998) provide an excellent discussion of this issue, while chapter 9 of Mulvaney & Kamminga (1999) provides a more general but nevertheless useful review of Australian colonisation.

3. Quoted in Flood (1995, p. 121). Rhys Jones died on 12 October 2001. Having been educated at Cambridge, he made a substantial contribution to Australian prehistory, and indeed to the world-wide study of hunter-gatherers.

4. The archaeological fieldwork was partly the result of the plans by the Tasmanian Hydro-Electric Commission for a series of dams on the lower Gordon River system, even though this had been declared as a World Heritage area in 1972. The dams would have led to the flooding of the valley and its many limestone caves. Major protests occurred during the summer of 1982, with the arrest of over 1,400 demonstrators. The discovery of archaeological sites made a major contribution to the cultural data base that was influential in the newly elected federal Labour government intervening on behalf of the conservationists and preventing the dams. Further archaeological fieldwork was stimulated by the struggle to extend the World Heritage area to the east (Jones, 1990).

5. Jones (1987, p. 30).

6. Kiernan et al. (1983) describe the excavations in Kutikina Cave, while Jones (1981, 1987) provides a more popular account of the discovery of Tasmania's ice-age hunters. The top of the occupation debris was dated to 14,840±930 BP.

7. The research was undertaken as the Southern Forests Archaeological Project and reported in Allen (1996). Cosgrove (1999) provides a succinct overview, stressing that there is no evidence for the traditionally conceived development from 'simple' Pleistocene hunter-gatherers to 'complex' Holocene hunter-gatherers.

8. The paintings of Wargata Cave are described in Jones et al. (1988). The use of blood as a pigment was identified by the presence of blood proteins and cells in the pigment. These were dated using AMS to 10,730±810 and 9240±820 BP.

9. Jones's comparison is stated by Flood (1995, p. 125). It seems a rather generous comparison with regard to the art, but Jones is really referring to the general lifestyle of being dependent upon hunting herds of mammals, using caves and creating art. As he stresses, the intriguing contrast is how similar these two regions were at 18,000 BP and how different they are today.

10. I am grateful to Jim O'Connell for pointing out the limited value of Jones's comparison. The rock art of southwest France is far richer than that of Tasmania and it is likely that people lived at far higher densities. The key resources – reindeers in France and wallabies in Tasmania – had very different behavioural patterns, which would have led to different types of hunting behaviour.

11. The following text draws on the detailed study of wallaby hunting by Cosgrove & Allen (2001). There is limited evidence for seasonality; the assumption of winter, spring and early summer occupation is largely based on the absence of very young wallabies which, on the basis of modern wallaby reproduction, would have been born in the late summer and autumn. There is no direct evidence on hunting techniques. Cosgrove and Allen draw on ethnographic records of wallaby and kangaroo hunting that refer to the use of drives.

12. Lubbock (1865, p. 354, quoting vol. I, p. 100, of *Cook's Third Voyage*).

13. Lubbock (1865, p. 465, quoting Dove from the *Tasmanian Journal of Natural Science*, vol. I, p. 249).

14. Darwin glass is otherwise known as imbracite. Thomas Loy has identified blood residues from red-necked wallaby surviving on one glass artefact (Flood, 1995).

15. Cave Bay Cave was excavated by Bowdler (1984) following a visit in 1973. Flood (1995) cites radiocarbon dates of 22,750±420 BP, a bone point associated with a date of 18,550 BP, and one hearth dated to 15,000 years ago.

16. For archaeological work on King Island, see Sim & Thorne (1990) and Sim (1990).

17. The pandemelon is a tiny wallaby, now extinct elsewhere. Quolls are marsupial carnivores, sometimes referred to as native cats. Several species exist, including the Eastern quoll which has white spots on black or fawn fur, and its larger cousin the tiger, or spotted-tailed quoll, which reaches up to 78 cm in length. Both are ferocious little animals eating grubs, insects, birds and small mammals. For descriptions and pictures of Tasmanian wildlife, see http://www.talune. com. au.

18. The relationship between environmental change and settlement change in southwest Tasmania is discussed by Porch & Allen (1995).

19. Cosgrove (1995) argues that southeast and southwest Tasmania were quite different cultural provinces, partly on the basis of the distribution of Darwin glass. The two key southwestern sites which show continuity of settlement into the Holocene are ORS7 in the Shannon River valley and Parmerpar Meethaner in the Forth River valley.

34: Body Sculpture at Kow Swamp

1 An account of Thorne's 'discovery' is provided in Mulvaney & Kamminga (1999).

2. The chronology of the cemetery at Kow Swamp remains poorly understood. Pardoe (1995) is only able to confidently accept three radiocarbon dates: Kow Swamp specimen 1, 10,070±250 BP (10,910–8720 cal BC), KS9, 9300±220 BP (9092–8268 cal BC) and KS14 8700±220 BP (8199–7550 cal BC). He questions the reliability of dates of KS5 at 13,000±280 BP and KS17 of 11,350±160 BP. But most authors (e. g. Flood, 1995, Mulvaney & Kamminga, 1999) are prepared to accept that the cemetery had begun by 13,000 BP. Pardoe (1995) accepts slightly older dates for burials from the nearby cemeteries of Coobool Creek, 14,300±1000 BP and Nacurrie 11,440±160 BP.

3. Mr George Murray Black 'excavated' several concentrations of burials in southeastern Australia between 1929 and 1950 (Sunderland & Ray, 1959). The precise location of these remains unclear; Pardoe (1995) assumes that he must have been excavating cemeteries due to the large number of burials he discovered in a short period of time.

4. For Thorne's description and interpretation of Pleistocene skeletal remains, see Thorne & Macumber (1972), Thorne (1971, 1977). Summaries are provided in Flood (1995) and Mulvaney & Kamminga (1999). Thorne also drew specimens from elsewhere in Australia into his 'robust' type, such as the burial from King Island in the Bass Strait.

5. The 'origins of modern humans' debate dominated palaeoanthropology during the 1980s and 1990s. Thorne was in fact simply providing a modern formulation of the multi-regional evolution scenario originally proposed in the 1940s by Weidenreich and also recently supported by Frayer and Wolpoff – see Frayer et al. (1993). For a review of the whole debate and arguments that support a single African origin, see Stringer & McKie (1996).

6. Lahr (1994) has most convincingly demonstrated that Thorne's argument for a *Homo erectus* ancestor to Australian *H. sapiens* is unfounded.

7. Brothwell initially raised the possibility of cranial deformation in an editorial in the edition of *Nature* in which the Kow Swamp skulls were published (1972, vol. 238) and later developed this into a short paper (Brothwell, 1975). Brown (1981) undertook a more detailed study using comparative material.

8. The following draws on Pardoe (1988, 1995).

9. Radcliffe-Brown (1918, p. 231).

10. Mulvaney & Kamminga (1999, pp. 158, 162) describe the entire Kow Swamp material being returned to the Echuca Aboriginal community in 1990 and that 'its fate remains obscure'.

11. Lubbock (1865, pp. 414–16).

12. Flood (1995, chapter 12) reviews the extinction of the Australian mega-fauna. The thylacine should not be considered with the other extinctions as this occurred in much more recent times (c. 3000 BP), most likely as a direct consequence of the introduction of the dingo. There is a chance that the thylacine still survives in Tasmania. The Tasmanian devil has been extinct for only a few hundred years.

13. This figure of 90 kg is taken from Flood (1995). O'Connell (pers. comm.) has noted that an animal of this size would be exceptional. During the 1970s he studied hunting amongst the Alyawarra Aboriginal community and saw more than a hundred red kangaroos ('boomers') shot, the largest of which was 60 kg.

14. The most provocative work has been by T. Flannery (1990, 1994) who adopted Paul Martin's blitzkrieg thesis for the extinction of Australian mega-fauna. In contrast, Horton (1984, 1986) has strongly argued for a climatic change explanation. Webb (1995) follows Flannery in attributing a causal role to humans but suggests that this was indirect – the Australian ecosystems were already quite fragile when humans arrived and the extra predator unbalanced them, resulting in the loss of the mega-fauna that was already under considerable environmental stress.

15. Excavations at Cuddie Springs are described by Dodson et al. (1993) and Field and Dodson (1999). The latter also reviews theories regarding mega-faunal extinction, favouring climatic change as the major cause. The site has three main phases: a long period during which the bones of mega-fauna accumulated before any human presence, which probably begins substantially earlier than 35,000 years ago; a phase between 35,000 and 28,000 years ago when mega-fauna bones are found associated with cultural material; and a post-mega-fauna phase during which cultural remains continue to be uncovered. Flood (1995) cites studies regarding hair and blood residues on stone artefacts. Cuddie Springs is also important as an example of the involvement of an Aboriginal community in a major archaeological research project (Field et al., 2000).

16. Cosgrove & Allen (2001) comment on the extinctions with regard to Tasmania, while Miller et al. (1999) and Roberts et al. (2001) provide the most recent reviews of this issue.

17. Pardoe (1995). Mulvaney and Kamminga (1999) cite arguments by Horton and Wright that some mega-fauna species, such as Diprotodon, may have survived in refuge areas such as the Liverpool Plains of central New South Wales as recently as 6000 years BP.

35: Across the Arid Zone

1. 'Gibber' is an Aboriginal word for stone (the 'g' is pronounced hard) and gibber fields refers to plains covered with small stones (Spencer & Gillen, 1912, p. 40).

2. Spencer & Gillen (1912, p. 43).

3. For a recent description of the Arunta – now referred to as the Arrente, see Morton (1999).

4. Spencer & Gillen (1912, pp. 6–7).

5. The following summary of the arid zone draws on Edwards & O'Connell (1995).

6. Kulpi Mara is described by Thorley (1998). There are three layers containing artefacts and bone fragments (not identified in his report). The base of layer 3 has a date of 29,510±230 BP; a date of 24,250±620 BP was gained for the upper part. Layer 2 has three dates: base, 12,060±240 BP (13,075–11,621 cal BC); lower, 12,790±150 BP (13,774–12,446 cal BC); and middle 12,800±260 BP. The middle of layer 1 has a date of 2500±60 BP (785–521 cal BC).

7. Puritjarra Rockshelter and the excavations are described by Smith (1987, 1989). Flood (1995, pp. 102–3) provides a succinct summary.

8. Smith acquired twelve radiocarbon dates on charcoal and six thermoluminesence dates (TL). The base of the sediment gave a TL date of 30,000 years; above this there was a radiocarbon date of 21,950±270 BP (Smith, 1987).

9. Puritjarra and Kulpi Mara are the only sites in central Australia with dates for Pleistocene occupation. Northwestern Australia – wholly within the arid zone – is much better served with 197 radiocarbon dates coming from 58 occupation sites and might provide a different occupation history (Veth, 1995). Not one of those dates falls in the gap between 19,000 BC (17,900 BP) (17,900 BP) and 9800 BC (9870 BP) when environmental conditions would have been severe. Veth believes that this indicates the arid zone was completely abandoned during the LGM; there was either a collapse in population numbers as drought conditions impacted on human fertility and mortality, or people shifted their settlement to the still tolerable margins of the desert, most likely to the coastal plains now drowned by the higher sea level. He has developed a model for colonisation and occupation of the arid zone which divides it into three habitat types: refuges, corridors and barriers (Veth, 1989, 1995). While he believes that the first two were occupied intermittently since 30,000 years ago, barrier deserts posed severe problems due to their limited rain and sources of food. These were mainly the dunefield areas of the Great Sandy, Gibson and Simpson deserts. Veth argues that these were only occupied after 5,000 years ago due to the invention/adoption at that time of technology for grinding seeds and working hardwoods, and the development of extended social networks and long-distance trade. Edwards & O'Connell (1995) provide a critical summary of his views.

10. Gould (1980) provides a wide-ranging study of arid-zone adaptation, addressing issues about how archaeologists can most effectively use ethnographic studies of living people.

11. A diet consisting of such a wide range of foodstuffs, many involving substantial processing, is referred to by anthropologists as a broad-

spectrum diet. Edwards and O'Connell (1995) argue that the emergence of broad-spectrum diets of hunter-gatherers occurred in all continents soon after the end of the last ice age. In some regions it may have been a precondition of the emergence of farming. As the current evidence suggests that a broad-spectrum diet may not have been adopted until 5–6,000 years ago, substantially later than elsewhere in the world, they describe Australia as providing a problem case. Their paper provides an excellent discussion of the issues involved, reviewing recent work on arid-zone colonisation and occupation. O'Connell & Hawkes (1981) have provided a quantified study of plant use by the Alyawara, another Aboriginal group of the Central Desert.

12. The kinship systems of recent Aborigines might be a very recent development in their societies, possibly being no more than a few centuries old (O'Connell, pers. comm.). Lourandas (1997) has suggested that the Mid-Holocene is a time of fundamental change in the social life of Aborigines throughout the continent.

13. See Edwards & O'Connell (1995) who were unable to cite any grinding stones older than 5,000 years old.

14. Fullagar & Field (1997).

15. Lubbock (1865, pp. 346–54).

36: Fighting Men and a Serpent's Birth

1. My descriptions of the above paintings are taken from Taçon & Chippindale (1994); see Layton (1992) for a general review and interpretation of Australian Aboriginal art. The paintings show men in elaborate clothing and head-dresses but my description of tunics and trousers being made of animal hide and head-dresses of plumes, furs, bones and bark is pure supposition. Chippindale et al. (2000) provide a further important study of the Dynamic Figures, in which they argue that this art contains an important visionary element, created while the artists were in altered states of consciousness, or a record of visions while they had previously been in that state.

2. This, and the following text regarding dating the rock art, draws on Chippindale and Taçon (1998).

3. Chippindale et al. (2000) provide a review of the activities of Dynamic Figures. In some depictions the specific activity cannot be identified.

4. Although these deposits have been well dated, they provide very little information about past lifestyles; the stone artefacts are no more than pieces of flaked quartz, axes made from volcanic stone and occasional pestles and mortars. There have been no discoveries of animal bones or plant remains to tell us what the people ate, or human bones to tell us what they looked like. Moreover, the rate of deposition was often very slow – in some rockshelters no more than one centimetre of sediment was laid down every thousand years. For further details, see Taçon & Brockwell (1995).

5. Taçon & Brockwell (1995) provide a synthesis of the archaeological evidence from rockshelters and the paintings of Arnhem Land. Peaks of red ochre within the deposits occur at 2000 BP, between 3–4000 BP, at 6000 BP, and three times between 6000 and 12,000 BP. Chippindale et al. (2000) place the Dynamic Figures at around 10,000 years ago.

6. For other views, see the commentary that follows Taçon & Chippindale (1994), especially that by Davidson.

7. Lubbock (1867, pp. 347–8).

8. Alas, I have not had the pleasure of sitting within a mangrove swamp in Arnhem Land. But there is a rich description of doing so by Searcy (1909, pp. 30–1).

9. The impact of sea-level rise in Arnhem Land, including the flooding of the Arafura plains, is described by Taçon & Brockwell (1995). There remains considerable uncertainty about the specific dates at which New Guinea and Australia became separated.

10. The oldest shell midden in Arnhem Land has a date of 6240±100 BP (5315–5058 cal BC). This is buried three metres below mangrove muds (Allen, 1989). It suggests that there are many shell-middens buried in the open plain and that the continuing dominance of rockshelter occupation in the archaeological record gives a false impression of land use. For an excellent study of shellfish-gathering by recent Aborigines, and the manner in which shell middens accumulate, see Meehan (1982).

11. The lack of change in Australian lithic technology across the Pleistocene/Holocene transition is surprising. By 6500 BC a new technology does emerge, and becomes widespread throughout the continent; it is known as the small tool tradition and thought to relate to an intensification of resource exploitation.

12. This painting, and the developments within Arnhem Land art described in the following text, are described in Taçon & Chippindale (1994) and Taçon & Brockwell (1995).

13. Warner (1937).

14. Lloyd Warner (1937, p. 157) tells of one occasion when the contestants' friends did not hold them back; the two men rushed at each other while hurling death threats and obscenities but then stood breast to breast, obviously feeling rather ridiculous.

15. Warner (1937, p. 147).

16. This follows Taçon & Chippindale (1994).

17. Taçon et al. (1996) review the beliefs about the Rainbow Serpent, explaining how there were in fact two mythological beings, Yingarna and Ngalyod. They describe various examples of Rainbow Serpent depictions and make statistical comparison of over a hundred different images, finding limited variation across Arnhem Land, but a trend to increased variation and complexity through time. They argue that the ribboned pipefish might be a better source for the Rainbow Serpent than the sea horse, although both animals are very similar.

18. Flood (1995, p. 215).

19. Flood (1995, pp. 140–1).

20. Flood (1995, p. 174)

21. Flood (1995, p. 213). The story goes like this 'Gumuduk was a tall, thin, medicine man, who belonged to the hills country. He owned a magical bone of such power that he could use it to make the rain fall in season, the trees bear much fruit, the animals increase and the fish multiply. Because of such good fortune the hills people always had plenty of food. However, the tribe that lived on the fertile plain below the Kiti range captured the medicine man and his bone, convinced that they, too, would in future have more food. But instead of bringing them prosperity, the theft resulted in a calamity which totally destroyed their country. For the medicine man escaped and was so angry over the indignity he had suffered that, plunging his magical bone into the ground, Gumuduk decreed that wherever he walked in the country of his enemies salt water would rise in his footsteps. Those waters not only contaminated the rivers and lagoons, but completely inundated the tribal lands. And when the waters dried up, the whole area was changed to an inhospitable desert of salt lakes, useless to both the creatures and the Aborigines.'

22. The following description of seasonal changes in the Aboriginal lifestyle in Cape York draws on Thomson's (1939) description of the Wik Monkan of western Cape York, succinctly summarised by Lourandas (1997, pp. 44–5).

37: Pigs and Gardens in the Highlands

1. Descriptions of the diversity of island types, the physiography of the straits, and resources available in prehistory are provided by Harris (1977) and Barham & Harris (1983, 1985).

2. Barham & Harris (1985) describe fieldwork on a relict field system on the island of Saibai 4 km south of the Papua New Guinea coast which proved to be about 700 years old.

3. The history of study of the Torres Strait is summarised in Barham & Harris (1983). Banks had been accompanied by another naturalist, Solander, and their observations were supplemented by those from later voyages of exploration prior to the arrival of the first Christian missionaries. By the time that Haddon made his study there had been three centuries of intermittent European contact.

4. Harris (1977, 1979) provides detailed descriptions of how pre-contact subsistence strategies are likely to have varied from south to north across the Torres Strait.

5. Turtle was the other key prey species. Along with dugong, fish and shellfish these were more abundant in the clear seas around the southern islands than in the muddy waters of the Papua New Guinea coast. Haddon (1901–35) describes the hunting tactics using harpoons for the dugong.

6. Quoted in Harris (1995, p. 848).

7. As described by Harris (1977) who also suggests that cycads had been a managed resource in Cape York.

8. White (1971, pp. 182–4). While Harris (1995) generally supports this view, he also suggests that the nature of root- and tree-crop agriculture as practised in New Guinea may have been inherently less prone to expansion when compared to, say, the cereal-based farming of Southwest Asia. This would have been especially the case if pigs were a later addition to the farming practices, i.e. within the last 500 years (as discussed below).

9. I believe this term was first used by Marshall Sahlins in his 1968 essay 'La première société d'abondance' (in Les Temps Modernes, no. 268, October 1968, pp. 641–80) before becoming popularised in his seminal book, Stone Age Economics (Sahlins, 1974).

10. Barham & Harris (1985) describe relict mounds and field systems close to the present village of Waidoro, currently 6 km inland from the Papua New Guinea coast. But the date of such settlement remains unclear. Gorecki (1989) describes work at Ruti which lies at an altitude of 500 m. This provides evidence of forest clearance and swamp management beginning at 5000 BP.

11. A. F. R. Wollaston, who led the British Ornithologists Union Expedition of 1910, published an account entitled Pygmies and Papuans, the Stone Age Today in New Guinea (Wollaston, 1912).

12. Quoted by Tree (1996, p. 116), who also describes the exposure in the Australian newspapers of the existence of the New Guinea highlanders.

13. Much of the following description of travelling on the rivers and the wildlife of New Guinea is based on that provided by Wollaston (1912).

14. The following description of the forest and footpaths is drawn from that provided by Lewis (1975, pp. 46–62).

15. The history of environmental changes in the highlands is summarised by Hope et al. (1983).

16. Excavations at Kosipe are described by White et al. (1970) while Golson (1982) suggests that the current contemporary stands of pandanus close to the site might reflect past conditions and have been the key resource attracting people to Kosipe.

17. Mountain (1993) describes the Nombe Rockshelter which has a rich array of terrestrial and arboreal animals, including the only association in New Guinea between extinct animals, one diprotodontid and three macropodids, and human debris. But with the presence of thylacine, the predator–prey relationships remain unclear. Hope & Golson (1995) summarise additional archaeological evidence regarding Late Pleistocene human lifestyles in the highlands of New Guinea.

18. Bellwood (1996).

19. The description of the New Guinea highlands at the time of the first European contact, and the impact of the missionaries on the indigenous society, draws on Golson (1982). For Strathern's work, see Strathern (1971), while Rappaport (1967) provides another classic study of highland society.

20. The recent history of Kuk Swamp and its reclamation by the Kawelka tribe is described in Gorecki (1985).

21. Traditional tools used in New Guinea highland agriculture during the last 500 years are described by Golson & Steensberg (1985). A wooden spade dating to 4000 BP has been found at Tambul (Bayliss-Smith, 1996).

22. Golson's excavations are described in a large sequence of publications, notably Golson (1977, 1982, 1989; Golson & Hughes, 1976). All of these lack detailed archaeological descriptions of the features, stratigraphic sections, and contextual information regarding the radiocarbon dates. Golson cites a date of 9000 BP (that I assume is uncalibrated radiocarbon years) for the initial work at Kuk Swamp, and dates of 6000–5000 BP for what he calls phase two. But without published details and independent evaluation Golson's claim is severely constrained.

23. Golson (1982) suggests that conditions in the swamp were deteriorating, possibly as a result of the human activities. What had been wetland management in the early phases of work at Kuk, had become a major problem in swamp drainage with a transition to the specialised cultivation of a single species, initially taro after 2000 BP and then sweet potato in the last 300 years.

24. Pollen evidence from numerous sites throughout the highlands supports the claim that clearances had been happening prior to 9000 BP due to the loss of tree pollen and presence of charcoal in the sediments (Haberle, 1994). It was not until 5000 BP, however, that a significant reduction in forest cover occurred. It is still unclear whether the early clearances had been undertaken to enable plant cultivation or simply as a means to regenerate wild plants and attract game to new shoots, as undertaken by Australian Aborigines (Bayliss-Smith, 1996).

25. The phytoliths from Australimusa bananas were recovered from the sediments between 9000 and 6000 BP at Kuk Swamp (Wilson, 1985).

26. Golson (1977, 1982) describes the sweet potato having a 'revolutionary' impact on New Guinea society. The importance of sweet potato was that it could grow at higher latitudes than taro, up to 2,700 m, the level at which persistent cloud formations occurred. Sweet potatoes were often grown in fields by themselves, segregated from mixed plantings of other plants such as taro, sugar cane, bananas and yams. They also provided better fodder for pigs.

27. Golson (1977) suggested that taro was grown at Kuk 9000 BP and, as Yen (1995) notes, most later commentators have agreed with him. Bayliss-Smith (1996), however, argues that taro was not cultivated in 'anything like its current form' until after 4500BP.

28. Jones and Meehan (1989) described Aborigines of Arnhem Land collecting wild tarot, which appeared to be known to them as one of their native plants; Matthews (1991) has described native New Guinea wild taro, while tissues and starch grains of taro were found on stone artefacts from Kilu Cave on Buka Island in the Solomons dating to 28,000 BP (Loy et al., 1992); and Bayliss-Smith (1996) makes the general case for indigenous taro on New Guinea.

29. Yen (1995) provides a review of all possible New Guinea staple crop- and tree-plants.

30. A wide range of contrasting interpretations have been forwarded for the type of plant cultivation occurring at Kuk Swamp at 6000 BP, and indeed throughout the highlands. These have been reviewed and critically evaluated by Bayliss-Smith (1996).

31. Les Groube (1989; Groube et al., 1986) has found a great many axeheads embedded in the riverbanks of the Huon peninsula on the northeast side of the island. He has been able to date these to at least 40,000 years ago by finding that they come from below a layer of volcanic ash which has this date: tectonic uplift led to the survival of a relict Pleistocene coastline. Many of the axes are broken and have damage scars, showing that they had been used for heavy work. Groube suggests that they had been deployed for a variety of tasks: ring-barking, branch trimming, root clearance and the felling of small trees. Fire was also used, as is evident from charcoal grains in sediments dating to 30,000 years ago (Hope at al., 1983). Unfortunately there are no swamp deposits from which pollen cores could be extracted to examine vegetation history. So from the very earliest occupation in New Guinea, people may have been making subtle modifications to the forest to encourage the growth of some plants and to remove or inhibit others. This is precisely what continues to happen in many regions of New Guinea today with plants such as pandanus which remain in that ambiguous zone between wild and domestic. Groube (1989) explains how only minimal forest management is needed for the cultivation of sago. And so the developments at Kuk Swamp from 8200 BC onwards appear to have been a natural extension of such activities rather than a dramatic break with the past – no Neolithic Revolution, merely an evolution of plant gathering through plant management towards horticulture. Bellwood (1996, p. 486), however, claims that this 'gradualist stance' is more an 'epiphenomenon of ideology rather than a product of hard data'. He stresses that all pollen diagrams with convincing evidence of clearance for horticulture come from the Holocene.

32. Bellwood (1996) suggests that environmental stress in the Holocene, such as long periods of drought or frost, may have been a factor that encouraged people to develop the swamps for plant cultivation.

33. Golson (1982) summarises the limited evidence from elsewhere in the highlands for the swamp drainage at 6,000 years ago. It is assumed by most archaeologists that cultivation began in the lowlands and then spread to higher altitudes; Golson & Hughes (1976, p. 301) stated that 'one thing of which we can be certain is that the agri-

culture we see at Kuk did not originate in the New Guinea Highlands … Obviously that regime had an earlier history at lower latitudes.' The limited and ambiguous evidence for this has been summarised by Hope & Golson (1995) but Bellwood (1996) and Haberle (1994) find this evidence unconvincing and doubt that New Guinea agriculture had started in the lowlands.

34. Jing & Flad (2002) provide evidence for pig domestication in China by 6000 BC.

35. Claims for pigs at 10,000 BP have been made by Golson & Hughes (1976), while Golson (1982) states that it is certain that pigs were present by 6000 BP. The alternative view of a much more recent presence has been favoured by Bayliss-Smith (1996) and Harris (1995) following radiocarbon dates reported by Hedges et al. (1995). Sue Bulmer (pers. comm.) argues that these dates are likely to be in error in light of the firm stratigraphic position of pig bones in Late Pleistocene or Early Holocene contexts within at least four sites. She also contends that the transport of pigs to New Guinea and other islands of southeast Indonesia does not necessarily imply domestication, and that pigs might have arrived on New Guinea without human assistance.

36. Feral pigs remain as a major game animal in lowland New Guinea but are not found above 1,525 m. (Golson, 1982) where all pigs are in domestic contexts. Groube (1989) stresses how pigs might have provided the first substantial competition with humans for many of the forest and cultivated plants.

37. Gosden (1995) provides a review of the colonisation and late-pleistocene developments on the Bismarck Archipelago and Solomon Islands. A key site is Matenbek Rockshelter on New Ireland, where phalanger bones are from 20,000 years ago, along with obsidian that had been transported from a source on New Britain 350 km away. Balof 2 and Panakiwuk on New Ireland are also important sites during the Late Pleistocene, both being used sporadically but showing evidence for shark fishing and shellfish gathering and the arrival of new animals such as the rat. The site of Pamwak on Manus Island suggests that bandicoots and the Pacific almond might have also been deliberately taken to the islands from the mainland, and provides axes made from shell.

38: Lonesome in Sundaland

1. *National Geographic* (1971). This was followed by a second and influential article in the magazine by MacLeish (1972), who wrote of the Tasaday 'as perhaps the simplest of living humans, and those closest to nature … gentle and affectionate … Our friends have given me a new measure of man. If our ancient ancestors were like the Tasaday, we come from far better stock than I had thought' (1972, p. 248).

2. Berreman (1999) provides a succinct overview of the Tasaday controversy. The role of the Tasaday in providing a vision of human nature that challenged that emerging from the experience of Vietnam has been examined by Dumont (1988). Sponsel (1990) further explored the Tasaday as a symbol of peace, the living embodiment of Rousseau's Noble Savage.

3. The lithic record is supplemented by three other types of material – charcoal, plant remains and marine shells, but these are found in too few cases to help reconstruct behaviour and long-term change. Lang Kamnan Rockshelter provides samples of shell and charcoal and has been interestingly interpreted by Shoocongdej (2000). The Ban Kao Caves, Thailand, provide 28 samples of possible food or medicinal plants from levels between 1215 and 5000 BC (Pyramarn, 1989).

4. Here I am taking a 'lumping' rather than a 'splitting' view of the Hoabinhian culture, the classic artefact of which is a pebble tool which has been flaked across one or both surfaces. Some variation in chipped stone assemblages occurs both through time and across space in Southeast Asia. Much of this, however, is most likely explained by variation in raw material availability. One of the best overviews is by Anderson (1990) who described four geographical clusters of the Hoabinhian: subtle variations in artefact types and assemblage composition from different regions. His excavations in Lang Rongrien Rockshelter recovered the classic Hoabinhian pebble tools from its upper layers (post 7000 BC) but tools made on flakes from its lower, pre-20,000 BC layers. He argued that the latter did not provide the precursors for the Hoabinhian.

5. To my deep regret I have no personal experiences of watching a rainforest dawn on which to draw upon in my text. As second best I have drawn upon material in Alfred Russel Wallace's (1869) account of his travels through the Malay archipelago. I have also drawn upon descriptions of the rainforest and events in O'Hanlon's (1985) account of his journey, *Into the Heart of Borneo*.

6. Harrisson provided numerous short reports on his work (notably Harrisson, 1957, 1959a,b, 1965) but did not complete an overall report. His work lacks any plans and drawings of stratigraphic sections. Bellwood (1997) provides a summary of his finds, as far as they can be understood at all.

7. Harrisson (1959c) provides radiocarbon dates ranging between 39,600±1000 and 2025±60 BP (cal 108 BC–AD 54), with one date at 19,570±190 BP. This short note provides limited information on the material dated and its excavated context; I have been unsuccessful in my attempts to relate the dated samples to excavated material described in his reports (Harrisson, 1957, 1959a,b).

8. The *palang* is a rod of bamboo, bone or wood with which the end of the penis is pierced, this being a custom among several of the Indonesian tribes. O'Hanlon (1985) cites Harrisson describing the palang, noting how knobs, points or even blades of suitable material may be attached and that some men have two *palang* at right angles through the penis tip. Harrisson went on to state that 'the function of this device is, superficially, to add to the sexual pleasure of the women by

stimulating and extending the inner walls of the vagina. It is, in this, in my experience decidedly successful.' This passage is quoted at greater length by O'Hanlon and with regard to the natural *palang* of the Borneo rhino. It originates in a 1957 issue of the *Sarawak Museum Journal* that I have been unable to consult to check for its authenticity.

9. Barker provides an overview of his Niah Cave project at www.le.ac.uk/archaeology/niah.htm, from which the quote is taken.

10. Pope (1989) has extolled the use of bamboo as a raw material and used this to explain the poverty of lithic technology in Southeast Asia. I remain sceptical as to its value for prehistoric hunter-gatherers working without metal tools.

11. The following text about environmental change in Southeast Asia draws on Anderson (1990) and Bellwood (1997).

12. Bellwood (1997, pp. 168–9) describes such middens, some of which had been up to 5 m. thick and contained hearths, secondary burials dusted with red ochre, pig and estuarine fishbones.

13. Excavations in Gua Sireh are described in Datan (1993). He undertook two field seasons, the first directed jointly with Peter Bellwood while Datan was a graduate student at Australian National University.

14. Excavations in Lang Rongrien are described in Anderson (1990).

15. The date for the charcoal from layer 7 in Lang Rongrien was in fact given as >43,000 BP, which effectively means an 'infinite' date, the true age being beyond the scope of radiocarbon dating (Anderson, 1990). Other key dates for Lang Rongrien include 8300±85 BP (7517–7184 cal BC) for the layer immediately above the rubble and 27,350±570 BP for that below. The basal layer is dated to 37,000±1780 BP and the uppermost layer to 7580±70 BP (6497–6370 cal BC). To reach the layer of rubble, Anderson had dug through a succession of floor layers, each containing Hoabinhian pebble tools. The artefacts from the pre-20,000 BC layers were principally made on flakes, leading Anderson (1990) to doubt that they were a direct precursor of the Hoabinhian pebble tools.

16. Shoocongdej (2000) describes excavations in Lang Kamnan and provides six radiocarbon dates ranging between 27,100±500 and 7990±100 BP (7058–6708 cal BC). These come from dating land snails and consequently their accuracy is questionable, as snails can collect 'old carbon' from the ingestion of limestone. See also the information on subsistence from material in Ban Kao Caves as reported by Pyramarn (1989).

17. For claims that people cannot survive by hunting and gathering alone within rainforests, see Bailey et al. (1989) and Headland (1987).

18. The first trace of rice cultivation comes from husks dated from Gua Sireh Cave in western Sarawak (Bellwood, 1997).

19. Endicott & Bellwood (1991) describe the subsistence practices of the Batek in a rebuttal to

Bailey et al. (1989). A succinct account of the Batek is also provided by Endicott (1999).

20. Brosius (1991, 1999) describes the foraging practices of the Penan and makes a damming critique of Headland (1987). His 1986 account of how the Penan invest their landscape with cultural meaning (Brosius, 1986) is of particular interest.

21. Bellwood (1997) described how wild cattle are at least ten times more abundant in open monsoonal forest than in the equatorial rainforest itself.

22. Bellwood (1997, p. 158)

23. The following speculations on religious practices draw on those of the Penan and Batek as described in Brosius (1999) and Endicott (1999).

24. The following draws on Berreman (1999). As he recounts, there has been a reluctance to 'call a hoax a hoax' and Berremen criticises the American Anthropological Association who, by stating that the word 'hoax' has an ambiguous meaning, served to help vindicate Elizalde and Marcos.

25. This was stated by Balangan, a Tasaday, in a Central Television documentary of 1988 and is quoted in Berreman (1999).

26. Bellwood (1997) suggests that the Batek may indeed be direct descendants of the Hoabinhian people. The Penan, however, are most probably descendants of the farmers who penetrated Borneo after 4000 BC. Some members of these communities, Bellwood suggests, turned to foraging in the highland areas. He suggests that if the Penan had a longer history in Borneo we should expect to find groups in the interior, which continues to be uninhabited.

39: Down the Yangtze

1. Stegodon was a genus of mastodont which ranged from Africa to southern Asia. The late Miocene forms are believed to be ancestral to modern elephants. Some species survived into the Pleistocene and produced dwarfed forms on the Indonesian islands (Lister & Bahn 1995). My text about ice-age environments in China draws on Chen & Olsen (1990).

2. Baiyanjiao Cave was excavated in 1979 and 1982 and provided an assemblage of 1,576 stone artefacts, two bone tools and the remains from 22 animal species. Stone artefacts had been made from limestone, chert, sandstone and quartz with a high proportion turned into scrapers. The bone implements had been polished. The fauna contained the typical mix for this region and period, known as the Ailuropoda-Stegodon fauna, including bear, tapir, deer, rhino, pig, stegodon, tiger and hyena. Radiocarbon dates for occupation vary between 11,740±200 BP (12,103–11,510 cal BC) and 14,220±200 BP (Chen & Olsen 1990).

3. For information about the Three Gorges Dam, and comment regarding the severe environmental and social destruction it is likely to cause, see the web pages of the International Rivers Network, www.irn.org.

4. My description of a journey through the Ichang Gorge draws on that provided by Mrs J. F. Bishop (1899) who made a journey down the Yangtze in the 1890s and produced a detailed description of its landscapes and people, with a focus on its upper reaches.

5. Evidence for environmental change in China comes from pollen cores taken from lake sediments, animal bones from cave deposits and geomorphological evidence relating to the rise and fall of sea, lake and river levels. Lu (1999) provides a comprehensive summary of this evidence, only a small amount of which is available in English.

6. I am cautious about describing this as the Younger Dryas which may have been primarily an event in the region of western Asia, Europe and the Atlantic. It is evident that the end of the Pleistocene was characterised by several fluctuations of climate which may have been quite independent of the Younger Dryas event. Lu (1999) provides evidence for this cold spell in China beginning at c. 10,800 BC and is willing to use the Younger Dryas term. Quite how these Late Pleistocene environmental changes impacted upon human settlement remains unclear. There are many scatters of chipped stone that probably relate to the Late Pleistocene but few of these have absolute dates or are associated with faunal remains, features or other material which may aid interpretation. The development of chipped stone technology during this period involved the spread of a microblade and microlithic technology originating in northern China. Wu & Olsen (1985) provide an overview of the whole Palaeolithic, Chen & Olsen (1990) focus on the last glacial maximum and Lu (1999) provides a review of Late Pleistocene and Early Holocene settlement.

7. Pei (1990) describes his 1988 excavations at Pengtoushan, located in the middle of the Liyang plain amidst branches of the Li River. Lu (1999) provides a list of 24 radiocarbon dates for the site, mainly calculated from charred cereal grain embedded in pottery sherds. These range from 9875±180 BP (9746–8958 cal BC) to 6252±100 BP (5318–5061 cal BC) with the majority between 8,000 and 7,500 BP.

8. *Oryza sativa* comes in two varieties, the long-grained *O. sativa indica*, and the short-grained *O. sativa japonica*. *Indica* dominates the crops in temperate and subtropical south China while *japonica* tolerates the colder winters and less unreliable summer rainfall of northern regions. Smith (1995) discusses scenarios for their evolution while Ahn (1992) provides a detailed discussion of rice phylogeny.

9. Gordon (1999) provides a succinct summary of the rise of Chinese civilisation based on rice cultivation.

10. Ahn (1992) provides a detailed overview of the many varieties of rice and the complexities of attempting to produce a definitive classification. One of the problems is the extent of cross-fertilisation between wild and domestic varieties resulting in the blurring of genetic distinction (Smith, 1995).

11. Ahn (1992) provides a detailed description of the morphological and physiological differences between wild and domesticated rice varieties.

12. Reviews of the evidence for rice cultivation in South, Southeast and East Asia, including the initial interpretations for Khok Phanom Di and Banyan Valley Cave, are provided by Glover & Higham (1996) and Higham & Lu (1998). The earliest currently accepted date for rice cultivation in Southeast Asia is about 5,000 BP. Smith (1995) provides a succinct summary of the history of the archaeological study of rice cultivation.

13. Smith (1995).

14. MacNeish and Wenning were co-directors of the Sino-American Jiangxi Origin of Rice Project as summarised in Zhijun (1998). MacNeish died in a car crash in Belize in January 2001.

15. Pearsall et al. (1995).

16. One does, however, need a multivariate statistical test of large samples to distinguish wild from domestic rice as a single measure is inadequate and individual grains cannot be confidently assigned as either wild or domestic. Once measurements on the glume cell phytoliths have been made, Pearsall et al. (1995, p. 95) describe what must be done: 'once these data are available, Bayesian calculation of joint probability obtained from multiple linear discriminant function classification will allow relatively unambiguous judgement as to whether domesticated rice is present in an assemblage.' One must assume that such methods were used by Zhijun (1998) when classifying the phytoliths from Diaotonghuan Cave.

17. My description of Diaotonghuan Cave draws on that by Zhijun (1998).

18. Evocative descriptions of the annual flooding of the Yangtze basin are provided by Bishop (1899).

19. Pei (1990) explains that the dwellings at Pengtoushan had not been well preserved but describes large surface structures with substantial post holes and two types of smaller semi-subterranean structures.

20. The sherds from more than 100 vessels were recovered from Pengtoushan (Pei, 1990) reflecting a wide variety of forms and decoration. The coiling technique had been the main method of manufacture. Pei (1990) also describes the chipped and ground stone assemblage.

21. This appears to have been an impressive mound covering 10,000 sq. m. and rising 3–4 m. above the surrounding plain (Smith, 1995).

22. Pottery of a similar date has been found elsewhere in China, notably in Yuchan Cave on the southern edge of Hunan Province (Lu, 1999).

23. The link between the origin of pottery and development of rice agriculture is considered by Higham & Lu (1998) and Lu (1999).

24. This scenario is based on Van Liere's (1980) description of 'floodland farming', as practised in historic times in Southeast Asia.

25. Van Liere (1980) describes the use of floodwater farming in the Mekong delta of Southeast Asia, together with a range of water management methods.

26. As Pei (n.d.) appears to have recovered wooden shovels and remnants of a plough from the contemporary and nearby site of Bashidang it seems likely that they had once existed at Pengtoushan.

27. Gordon (1999) suggests that the experimental work on wheat of Hillman & Davies (1990) might also be relevant to the evolution of rice in China.

28. A brief description of the Bashidang excavations is provided in Pei (n.d.). The dwellings included semi-subterranean structures and the burials took various forms. The whole settlement appears to have been surrounded by a protective ditch, presumably a guard against floodwaters. Pei also claims to have found wooden and bamboo tablets that had been used for divination. He provides the time frame of 7,000–8,000 years ago, but without quoting any specific radiocarbon dates. He also describes an earlier occupation at Bashidang dating to 15,000 BP.

29. Pei (1998) describes the rice grains from Bashidang.

30. Hemudu is just one of many settlements in the Yangtze delta and Hang-Chou Bay region after 7000 BP. Those north of the bay have different types of ceramics and artefacts to those on the southern side, suggesting some form of cultural boundary, although the way of life – a mixture of plant cultivation and hunting-and-gathering was quite similar (Smith, 1995). In addition to rice, water caltrop and fox nut, both aquatic plants, were also cultivated. Hemudu was excavated in the 1970s and provided four metres of deposits indicating occupation for at least 1,000 years (Smith, 1995). Lu (1999) provides a description of the site and a list of 13 dates from the first horizon which range between 5975±100 BP (4990–4720 cal BC) and 6310±170 BP (5470–5062 cal BC), with an outlier of 5320±100 BP (4311–4002 cal BC).

31. Very little is known about the domestication of water buffalo but there seems little doubt that these were present at Hemudu (Smith, 1995). Pei (n.d.) describes a complete water buffalo skull from Pengtoushan which he claims was from a domesticated animal, while a newspaper report about Pei's excavations at Bashidang claims he found evidence for domesticated water buffalo and pig at that settlement (Zhongguo, 1998)

32. Hsiao-Tung (1939) provides a detailed description of Chinese peasant life in the village of Kaihsienkung, south of Lake Tai, during the early twentieth century which is likely to share many features of that of the Neolithic.

33. A detailed chronology for sea-level rise around the coast of Japan and the precise date for when its connection with the mainland was breached are currently unavailable; Aikens & Higuchi (1982) and Imamura (1996) summarise currently available information. This issue is complicated by the tectonic activity around the coasts of Japan that has also had a major influence on changing sea levels and interpretation of sedimentary evidence.

40: With the Jomon

1. For this chapter I am indebted to Naoko Matsumoto of Okayama University and Visiting Scholar at Reading University 2001–2 for information, literature, translations and discussion.

2. Uenohara is described by Minaminihon (1997), a (Japanese) text with an excellent series of photographs. Izumi & Nishida (1999) carries a reconstruction drawing of Uenohara, on which my own description is based.

3. Although the earliest dates for rice grains are associated with Late Jomon sites in northern Honshu between 1000 and 800 BC, rice phytoliths have been found in southwestern Japan in Early and Middle Jomon contexts (Crawford & Chen, 1998), such as at Okayama at 6000 BP (Matsumoto, pers. comm.).

4. Tsukada (1986) provides a detailed synthesis of the vegetation changes in Japan during the last 20,000 years, largely based on pollen evidence; 70% of Japan is still covered by forests, much of which is similar in composition to that of the Early Holocene.

5. This design of construction contrasts with that found on the majority of Jomon sites in which pit dwellings have a single central post (Matsumoto, pers. comm.; Imamura, 1996).

6. The Jomon technique of treating and decorating the surface of pots produced an immense variety of designs as different types of knots, twists and means of application were used. One of these was to wrap the cord around a dowel and then roll it across the surface, creating what Japanese archaeologists call the Yoriitomon type of pottery. See Imamura (1996) for a description of pottery designs and decorative styles.

7. In contrast to Imamura (1996), Trigger (1989) states that none of Morse's students became professional archaeologists. He provides a brief but interesting history of Japanese archaeology.

8. Imamura (1996) summarises the history of archaeology in Japan and describes the development of relative and absolute schemes for Jomon pottery styles and periods.

9. For overviews of Jomon subsistence, all of which focus on the Middle Jomon period owing to its number of sites with organic preservation, see Imamura (1996), Watanabe (1986) and Rowley-Conwy (1984b).

10. Aikens & Higuchi (1982) describe Fukui Cave. The uppermost layers containing the pottery shards have radiocarbon dates of 12,400±350 BP and 12,700±500 BP. The earliest levels contain large flakes and blades of flint together with stone axes, while later levels contain micro-blades and the first pottery shards.

11. The history and still continuing debate about the age of Jomon pottery is covered by Imamura (1996).

12. Senpukuji, a cave in northwestern Kyushu's port city of Sasebo, also has particularly early pottery. This may even precede that from Fukui as it has shards with a further variety of the linear-relief decoration below a layer containing pottery

of the same design as that from the earliest layers at Fukui Cave. Unfortunately, reliable radiocarbon dates are not available. Particularly early pottery has also been found at the rockshelter of Kamikuroiwa in western Shikoku, where it is dated to 12,165 BP. Aikens and Higuchi (1982) provide succinct summaries of these sites.

13. Stone tools with intentionally ground edges are found at Palaeolithic sites in Japan dating as early as 30,000 BP. Reviews of Palaeolithic sites are provided by Aikens & Higuchi (1982) and Barnes & Reynolds (1984). There continues to be a substantial debate as to the date of the earliest sites on Japan.

14. Matsumoto (pers. comm.).

15. Aikens (1995) argues for the direct association between the spread of pottery and woodland through Japan and a utilitarian origin for pottery manufacture.

16. Matsumoto (pers. comm.).

17. Hayden (1995) suggests that pottery together with a range of other technologies emerged for prestige reasons.

18. Matsumoto (pers. comm.).

19. Aikens (1995) and Imamura (1996) describe the development of Jomon pottery, the last providing illustrations of the remarkable vessels of the Middle Jomon period.

20. I am taking some archaeological artistic licence here. The thick clay earrings are only known from the materials at Uenohara that date to 7500 BP. These are found with buried pots and clay figurines, but with a complete absence of domestic debris. This suggests that the site may have acquired a ritualistic rather than domestic function.

21. As far as I understand, there is no direct evidence that pits at Uenohara were used for storage of acorns. But this type of storage was certainly underway by its date of occupation in light of the discovery of storage pits at Higashi-Kurotsuchida in the Kagoshima region dating to 11,300±130 BP (11,492–11,192 cal BC) (Miyaji, 1999) which had contained acorns from Japanese oak. Further storage pits are known from Middle Jomon sites after 5000 BP. My specific description of storage using layers of crushed rock and reed is based on an illustration in Miyaji (1999). As he describes, some kinds of acorns contain large amounts of tanin or saponin which has a bitter taste and can have an astringent effect on the mouth. North American Indians reduced the bitterness by soaking acorns in ashes or burying them in the ground for several months.

22. Sakura-jima continues to billow smoke and ash today. Its summit reaches more than 1,000 m. above the waters in Kagosima Bay. There were no less than 132 eruptions during 2000, the last on 7 October when a column of ash was sent five kilometres into the air amidst volcanic lightning. Gritty ash fell on to the city of Kagoshima and smashed 35 car windscreens. Detailed reports about recent activity of Sakura-jima can be found at http://www.nmnh.si.edu/gvp/volcano/regiono8/kyushu/sakura.

23. The date of this eruption is placed at 6300 BP (Matsumoto, pers. comm.).

24. The remnant of the Kikai volcano is a 19-km-wide submerged caldera visible by a series of islands. Eruptions in 1934 and 1935 created further small islands. Activity has continued until the present day, as documented at http//www.nmnh.si.edu/gvp/volcano/regiono8/kyushu/kikai.

25. Matsui (1999) provides a brief description of Awazu in the context of a survey of key waterlogged sites in Japan. No radiocarbon dates are provided.

26. Imamura (1996) describes his work at Kirigaoka, together with that at Tama Hills and the role of pig traps within the Jomon economy.

27. I have not dealt with the issue of rising sea level and how this had conditioned the coastal archaeology of Japan. The most detailed study has been undertaken in Utsumi Bay, which has shown a complex series of fluctuations, changing coastal environments and foraging opportunities, as described within Imamura (1996).

28. My description of shellfish gathering and cooking is based on that in Meehan (1982) relating to the Anbarra people of Australia and the collection of *Tapes hiantina*.

29. Natsushima midden is described within Aitkins & Higuchi (1982) and Imamura (1996). Charcoal below the midden associated with pottery shards gave dates of 9450±400 BP (9310–8227 cal BC) and 9240±500 BP (9217–7827 cal BC).

30. Kamo is described within Aikens & Higuchi (1982). The canoe had been hollowed out from a split log of apananthe wood; it was shallow with squarish ends. Two of the paddles had broad blades and four were more slender. A fragment of wood from the canoe was dated to about 5100 BP (Aikens & Higuchi do not provide a standard deviation).

31. This is not meant to be dismissive of the very excellent studies that have been undertaken on many Jomon sites, especially those of more recent periods than Natsushima. Koike (1986), for instance, describes a detailed study of shell-midden remains from the Murata River area including seasonality and ageing studies on a range of animal species. Watanabe (1986) has made excellent use of ethnographic data to interpret Jomon remains. Although there are no burials at Natsushima, numerous burials are known from Initial and Early Jomon sites such as in the rockshelters of Futsukaichi (Kyushu), Tochihara (Honshu) and Oyaji (Honshu), and the shell-midden site of Ishiyama (Honshu). The burials are quite variable: some are the secondary burial of individual body parts, notably skulls, others are primary burials with necklaces of shell beads, or have stones placed within their hands or upon their heads (Matsumoto, pers. comm.).

32. The nature and extent, if any, of Jomon cultivation has been long debated in Japanese archaeology (Imamura, 1996). Gourds, Asian bean, perilla and paper mulberry are possible candidates for having been cultivated (Akazawa, 1986).

33. Like cultivation, the role of salmon in the Jomon economy has been much debated – the key issue being whether the absence of bones reflects poor quality excavation, poor survival or simply the lack of salmon fishing (Akazawa, 1986; Imamura, 1996).

34. The start of substantial rice farming is referred to as the beginning of the Yanoi period. Imamura (1996) summarises a long debate as to whether this arose from immigrant peoples or the adoption of agricultural methods by the indigenous Jomon. I have followed the first possibility but the situation is likely to have involved a complex mix of immigration and indigenous development, as has become apparent for the development of farming in Europe.

35. For an introductory description of the Ainu, see Svensson (1999). A classic study of their environment and economy of value to archaeological interpretation was undertaken by Watanabe (1973).

41: Summer in the Arctic

1. Reconstructions of vegetation history of the Russian far east are provided by Kuzmin (1996), that of Siberia by Ukraintseva et al. (1996) and Guthrie (1990).

2. Excavations in Dyuktai Cave are described by Mochanov & Fedoseeva (1996a) who identify three discrete Pleistocene horizons each containing stone artefacts and faunal remains dated between 16,000 BP and 12,000 BP. The uppermost level has a radiocarbon date of 740±40 BP, while the Pleistocene levels have six radiocarbon dates ranging between 14,000±100 and 12,100±120 BP.

3. Mochanov & Fedoseeva (1996a,b) provide a brief history of archaeological research in Siberia, including the establishment and aims of the Prilensk Archaeological Expedition.

4. I am not aware that a proper taphonomic study of the faunal assemblage from Dyuktai Cave has been undertaken. Without that, it is premature to conclude which of the animals had been hunted by humans, which were taken there by carnivores using the cave as their den, and which had lived and died in the cave by their own accord. As explained elsewhere in this book (such as with regard to Creswell Crags), human activity is frequently 'down-sized' from big-game hunting to the trapping of small game once such taphonomic studies are completed.

5. The bifacial tools used by the Dyuktai people are unlikely to have been the forerunners of those lethal projectile points used by the Clovis people. Their similarity most probably arose from quite independent discovery – the two groups simply reached the same solution as to how to make sharp robust tools from flint. As explained in chapter 26, Clovis points most likely originated in the east of North America. Precisely the same solution had also been arrived at by the Solutrean people who had painted the horses in the French cave of Pech Merle at the LGM.

6. Studenoe-2 is described by Goebel et al. (2000) in an article that summarises other early instances of microblade technology. Studenoe-2 has a large series of radiocarbon dates including four earlier than 17,000 BP, the earliest of which are 18,830±300 BP and 17,885±120 BP.

7. Lubbock (1865, pp. 392–412).

8. Guthrie (1990) provides a historical review of the discovery and study of the frozen fauna from Siberia and Alaska, including the Berezovka mammoth. Important studies with regard to palaeoecology and extinction are provided by Vereshchagin & Baryshnikov (1982, 1984) and Ukraintseva et al. (1996). Guthrie made a particularly important study of 'Blue Babe', the frozen body of a young bison that had died 36,000 years ago in northern Alaska. The carcass had become coated with blue vivianite crystals, leading to it being named after the mythical, immense blue ox that had roamed the northern woods with a giant man known as Paul Bunyan.

9. In the following text I will follow Guthrie's (1990) reconstruction of the mammoth steppe as a landscape rich in flora and herbivores, one that he originally proposed during the late 1960s. There has, however, been considerable disagreement about this reconstruction from palynologists such as Ritchie & Cwynar (1982) and Colinvaux (1986). They argue that it had been a far harsher environment than Guthrie proposes, one that was only able to support a large mammal fauna during interglacials. Guthrie (1990) discusses and persuasively rejects their criticisms of his reconstruction.

10. Berelekh is primarily known as a large natural accumulation of mammoth bones, but a palaeolithic site in its vicinity has also been located with radiocarbon dates of 12,930±80 BP, 13,420±200 BP, and 12,240±160 BP (13,150–11,907 cal BC). Excavations were undertaken by Mochanov between 1971–73 and in 1981 and are summarised in Mochanov & Fedoseeva (1996c).

11. I provide a brief summary of the discovery of the Wrangel Island mammoths in chapter 27, 'Clovis Hunters on Trial'. They are described by Vartanyan et al. (1993). The date at which Wrangel and Zhokhov became islands is unclear; Pitul'ko suggests a date of 4500 BP.

12. For these remarks about walking on the tundra I have drawn upon a description in Thubron (2000).

13. The following text regarding the settlement on Zhokhov island draws on reports by Pitul'ko (1993, 2001) and Pitul'ko & Kasparov (1996). The latter provides 22 radiocarbon dates for the settlement, the majority of which are derived from samples of excavated driftwood and lie between 8930±180 BP (8286–7802 cal BC) and 7450+170 BP (6476–6030 cal BC) with two outliers (12,600±250 BP and 10,810±390 BP [11,348–10,150 cal BC]). Pitul'ko suggests that 8000 BP is the best estimate for the age of the site. The descriptions of polar bears in this chapter draw on the material in Lopez (1986).

14. Pitul'ko & Kasparov (1996) provide a brief

summary of the existing evidence for the appearance of dog traction in the Arctic. They note that the dog sledge from Zhokhov seems quite different in design from the rather simpler peat-bog sledges that have been found in northern Europe and Russia between 8000 and 6000 BP.

15. The following text about human–polar bear relations draws on D'Anglure (1990). He explains that the Inuit men use their mythology about the polar bear as an ideological means to control their women's behaviour.

16. Pitul'ko (2001) provides a brief summary of the cultural developments and known sites of the terminal Pleistocene and Early Holocene in Northeast Asia, all of which are grouped together as the Sumnagin culture, in which the Zhokhov material is also placed.

17. There is no information within the Zhokhov reports regarding what the interior of dwellings may have been like. My text has been inspired by the descriptions of Eskimo dwellings contained within the books by Weyer (1932) and Birket-Smith (1959).

18. When writing about Eskimo snow-houses, Birket-Smith (1936, p. 127) states that "It goes without saying that the air in these small rooms, heated by blubber lamps and heavy with the effluvia of many more or less naked and more or less clean people, is not exactly attractive to a sensitive nature".

19. The following description of clothing and manufacturing techniques is based on that of the clothing found on the mummified Inuit at Qilakitsoq dating to 1475, as described in Hansen et al. (1991), and on general descriptions of Eskimo clothing within Lopez (1986). The Qilakitsoq clothing was principally made from seal-skin; as Zhokhov people appear to have been hunters of polar bear and reindeer alone I have replaced this with reindeer skins which were also widely used throughout the Arctic. Obsidian blades, bone awls, bone needles and the bones of swans and ducks were found at Zhokhov.

20. Seasonality evidence at Zhokhov comes from reindeer mandibles by examining the eruption of teeth (Pitul'ko & Kasparov, 1996). Most specimens suggested killing in the early summer, while a few suggested that occupation had continued through to October. Pitul'ko & Kasparov concluded that this evidence implies the historically known pattern of pursuing reindeer during their spring migrations to the north.

42: A Passage through India

1. Lubbock (1865, pp. 343–5). Lubbock was citing Bailey from the *Transactions of the Ethnological Society*, vol. II, p. 278.

2. Sahni et al. (1990) reviews the evidence for Late Pleistocene ostriches in India, while Kumar et al. (1990) review beads and other ornaments made from ostrich-egg shell during the Late Pleistocene.

3. For reviews of Upper Palaeolithic archaeology in India, see Kennedy (2000), Chakrabarti (1999), Misra (1989a) and Datta (2000). The latter provides a list of Upper Palaeolithic dates from the subcontinent, of which only 5 from a total of 20 fall after 20,000 BC.

4. Microlithic technology in Sri Lanka appears to reach back to 34,000 BC and continued into historic times. Kennedy (2000) provides a succinct summary of the palaeoenvironmental and archaeological evidence from Sri Lanka.

5. Nagar & Misra (1990) describe the Kanjars, and the role of ethnographic analogy in Indian archaeology.

6. Fuller (pers. comm.). For Foote's contribution to the study of the Neolithic in India see Korisettar et al. (2000).

7. Foote (1884) describes his work in the Kurnool Caves. A brief summary is provided in Murty (1974).

8. Murty (1974) provides a detailed description of his excavations in Muchchatla Chintamanu Gavi. A TL date of 17,390±10% BP was derived from the hearth.

9. The change-over from excavations undertaken by Robert Foote to those by M. L. Krishna Murty illustrates a general switch that occurred in the 1940s from an archaeology undertaken by the British to that by Indians themselves. One of the greatest figures was Hasmukh Dhirajlal Sankalia (1908–89), on whom Misra (1989b) provides a detailed biographical article. He led Deccan College to become the premier archaeological research centre in South Asia, and guided two generations of Indian archaeologists to prominence. Sankalia produced his monumental work *Prehistory and Protohistory of India and Pakistan* in 1963. This provided the first compendium of artefact scatters but within it, and indeed within archaeology to the present day, the colonial legacy remains. In their willingness to find comparisons between Indian and European sites, Foote, his contemporaries and early-twentieth-century archaeologists such as the Cambridge prehistorian Miles Burkitt, have left a terminology of Upper Palaeolithic, Mesolithic and Neolithic that now seems quite inappropriate for Indian prehistory. Many undated scatters of stone tools have been given such names simply because that is what they would be called if found in a European context. As the range of raw materials in India, and hence their knapping characteristics and resulting tools, are different from the fine quality flint found throughout most of Europe, such assumptions may have led to gross errors about the nature of Indian prehistory. For instance, it is evident that microlithic technology – the defining element of European Mesolithic, begins in South Asia before 20,000 BC. As well as sites in Sri Lanka, that of Patne in Maharashtra has microliths in a horizon dated to 23,050±200 BC (Chakrabarti, 1999). This is more similar to the pattern in Africa and western Asia than Europe; it also continues into historic times among modern hunter-gatherers. I am grateful to Bishnupriya Basak for discussion about typological schemes for Late Pleistocene

and Holocene lithics and the continuing colonial legacy. Kennedy (2000) and Morrison (1999) also discuss the imposition of an Upper Palaeolithic and Mesolithic terminology, the former appearing to be in favour of this.

10. For overviews of the climatic changes at the start and during the Early Holocene, see Allchin & Allchin (1982), Misra (1989a) and Kennedy (2000). Chakrabarti (1999, p. 98) summarises the state of knowledge by stating that "the story of climate change in the Early Holocene and Holocene in general in the Indian subcontinent is not particularly well understood beyond some stray patches of scientific research". It is generally acknowledged that the earlier part of the Holocene was substantially wetter than the latter part – but ice-core evidence suggests that many more fluctuations had occurred than can be currently accounted for by the terrestrial evidence alone.

11. For evocative descriptions of Indian forests before much of the modern deforestation had occurred, see Webber (1902).

12. For reviews of the Mesolithic record in India, see Misra (1989a), Chakrabarti (1999) and Kennedy (2000). For a typical Mesolithic cave occupation, see the description of Vangasari Cave in the Eastern Ghats by Prakash (1998) – a dense scatter of chipped stone with many microliths and grinding stones, but no organic materials to provide information about economy or for dating. Prakash comments about the large number of Mesolithic sites on the coastal plain and the lack of Neolithic and latter occupation within the hills.

13. There are some excellent studies of Late Pleistocene and Early Holocene lithic technology in India which frequently examine the significance of changing raw materials. Datta (1991), for instance, has compared Upper Palaeolithic and Mesolithic technology in West Bengal and shown that the technological changes accompany a switch to a greater use of a chertz and quartz. Khanna (1993) made an interesting study of the use of chalcedony at Bagor in Rajasthan, comparing how this non-local material was preferentially used when available. Basak (1997) has also made an important contribution by comparing a large number of assemblages in terms of raw materials and technology from the Tarafeni valley in West Bengal. Unfortunately many of these studies suffer from the lack of detailed chronology based on absolute dates.

14. Kennedy (2000) reviews the burial record and skeletal evidence for the Mesolithic period. Other than the Ganges plain sites that are discussed below, the key site is Lekhahia Ki Pahari in Uttar Pradesh which has a date of 8370±75 BP (7538–7334 cal BC). This is a rockshelter with a paved floor and painted walls from which 21 skeletons were excavated in the mid-1960s. The earliest feature is a pit dug into the bedrock into which two human skulls and the mandible of an animal were placed.

15. See note 9 regarding the use of this European terminology for Indian archaeology.

16. My description of Bhimbetka, its archaeology and paintings draws on Mathpal (1984).

17. Misra's excavations in IIIF-23 are described in Mathpal (1984) and Kennedy (2000). Important excavations were also undertaken by Wakanker (1973).

18. Mathpal (1984).

19. Mathpal (1984, p. 202).

20. Excavations at Damdama are described in Varma et al. (1985), with general reviews about Mesolithic settlement on the Ganges plain in Sharma (1973) and Pal (1994). Kennedy (2000) cites radiocarbon dates of 8640±65 BP (7733–7585 cal BC) and 8865±65 BP (8202–7850 cal BC) made on bone from Damdama.

21. Thomas et al. (1995) and Chattopadhyaya (1999) summarise the faunal remains from Damdama. Thomas et al. argue that there had been a cyclical trend in resource management which increases/decreases in mammalian fauna, compensated for by an inverse change in avian and aquatic fauna. I suspect that this is more likely a reflection of environmental change rather than resource depletion/recovery or management.

22. Chattopadhyaya (1999) reviews changing views about the nature of settlement on the plain and provides the evidence and arguments for sedentary settlement.

23. Kennedy (2000) summarises skeletal evidence from Damdama, Mahadaha and Sarai Nahar Rai. Lukacs & Pal (1992) provide a report on the dentition from the latter two of these sites.

24. These burials are described in Sharma (1973). Several additional burials also contained microliths which may have been arrow-heads but it remains unclear whether these had been deliberately placed grave goods, chance inclusions within the burial fill, or had once been embedded within the bodies.

25. This burial is described in Varma et al. (1985, p. 56, from where the quote is taken) and Pal (1992).

26. The chronology of the settlements of the Ganges plain remains rather unclear; any existing evidence has been summarised by Kennedy (2000). We know that people were using the Ganges plain before the end of the ice age as scatters of their artefacts have been found. The settled community of Damdama had arisen by 9000 BC, and probably did start as a seasonal camp that gradually turned into a permanent village. Those of Mahadaha and Sarai Nahar Rai most likely arose soon afterwards in light of the similarities in their technology, diet and economy. They appear to have been thriving in much the same fashion no less than six or even seven thousand years later, long after farming economies had arisen throughout the subcontinent and just prior to the first urban centres of the Ganges plain. Mahadaha has dates of 2675–2515 BC and 2250–2125 BC, while Sarai Nahar Rai has a TL date on charred bone of 995 BC, cited in Kennedy, and a radiocarbon date

of 8400±115 BC (uncalibrated) cited in Chakrabarti (1999) Both sites have near identical remains, and are also extremely similar to Damdama. It appears, therefore, that there was a long period of stable culture and economy on the Ganges plain.

43: A Long Walk Across the Hindu Kush

- 1 The area of Baluchistan south of the Bolan Pass is encompassed by the Indus plains, although this does not drain directly into the Indus itself.

2. For the following account of Mehrgarh I have largely drawn on Jarrige & Meadow (1980), Chakrabarti (1999), Possehl (1999) and Kennedy (2000). I am grateful to Greg Possehl and Dorian Fuller for answering my questions about this site.

3. The excavation reports of Jarrige and his colleagues are found in Jarrige et al (1995).

4. Possehl (1999) describes sites with large numbers of microliths in southern Baluchistan. Unfortunately there has been a very limited survey for such sites, and even less excavation.

5. The Bolan Pass is one of the key routes into southern Asia, used by traders and others through ancient and medieval times. Although Alexander arrived in India via another of the key passes, the Kyber Pass, he returned by the Bolan Pass.

6. The animal bones from Mehrgarh were studied by Meadow and are described in Jarrige & Meadow (1980) and Meadow (1996). While the goat bones in the earliest levels are recognised as being from domesticated animals, these also show some reduction in size through the history of the town.

7. All currently available information about the palaeoanthropology at Mehrgarh has been summarised in Kennedy (2000).

8. I am grateful to Margaritta Tengberg (Paris) for information about the cotton threads within the copper bead at Mehrgarh, which she originally described in a seminar at the Institute of Archaeology, London, in November 2001. Since then, a publication has become available with useful technical details and a discussion of cotton domestication (Moulherat et al., 2002).

9. Before the discovery of Mehrgarh little was known about the origin of the Indus civilisation. Mortimer Wheeler suggested that it arose from the diffusion to a backward area of an "idea" that was "in the air" once the towns of western Asia had begun to flourish (Jarrige & Meadow, 1980).

10. Bagor I is described by Misra (1973).

11. Excavations at Chopani Mando are described in Sharma et al. (1980) and briefly summarised in Chakrabarti (1999). I am grateful for further information about this site from Dorian Fuller.

12. The Neolithic of southern India has most recently been described in Korisettar et al. (2000) while Allchin (1963) made a study of the ash mounds and describes the site of Utnur, also briefly covered in Allchin & Allchin (1982).

13. This particular image is taken from the description of walking in the Hindu Kush within Newby (1954). I have also drawn on Thesiger (2000) for imagining Lubbock's journey across central Afghanistan.

14. Colin Thubron (1994) describes Central Asia as 'the World's heart' – which has become a particularly apt description in light of the suffering of the Afghan peoples throughout the late twentieth and early twenty-first centuries.

15. Excavations at Aq Kupruk are described in Dupree (1972).

16. Dupree (1972) provides the following dates but without comment on the material dated nor the context: Horse Cave: 16,615±215 BP for an Upper Palaeolithic flint industry with ibex, wild goat and deer; 10,210±235 BP (10,385–9394 cal BC) for aceramic Neolithic with domesticated sheep/goat, 4500±60 BP (3342–3099 cal BC) for ceramic Neolithic. Snake Cave: 8650±100 BP (7909–7586 cal BC) for aceramic Neolithic with domesticated sheep and goat. Perkins identified the sheep/goat as domesticated or wild, as reported in Dupree (1972) but few seem to have confidence in his results (e.g. see Harris & Gosden, 1996).

17. The following text about Jeitun draws on Masson & Sarianidi (1972), Harris et al. (1993) and Harris et al. (1996).

18. Harris & Gosden (1996) provide a useful overview of the origin of agriculture in western and Central Asia, together with the problems of interpreting the currently sparse information. The pre-farming settlements in Turkmenistan are described in Masson & Sarianidi (1972), the best known of which are Mesolithic settlements in the vicinity of the Caspian Sea.

19. Harris et al. (1996) provide eleven AMS radiocarbon dates which range between 7000±70 BP (5980–5801 cal BC) and 7270±90 BP (6218–6028 cal BC). Although Masson believed there to be at least three distinct phases of the village, these could not be distinguished by the radiocarbon dating.

44: Vultures of the Zagros

1. A brief but evocative description of the landscapes of Mesopotamia is provided by Postgate (1992).

2. A brief note about Sang-i-Chakmak is included in Harris & Gosden (1996). They comment on its similarity to Jeitun which it is believed to post-date. But no radiocarbon dates are available.

3. While both obsidian and bitumen are known from both Zawi Chemi Shanidar or from contemporary deposits in Shanidar Cave, there are no indications as to whether these had been acquired directly or by trade and exchange.

4. Zawi Chemi Shanidar is fully described by Solecki (1981). Solecki & Rubin (1958) provide a date of 10,870±300 BP (11,236–10,399 cal BC). Its full name is in fact Zawi Chemi Daraw Shanidar, meaning 'the field by the gully of Shanidar'. An excellent summary of this site, and all others referred to in this chapter, can be found in Matthews' (2000) synthesis of the early prehistory of Mesopotamia.

5. This feature is fully described in R. L. Solecki (1977). The 17 identified birds were as follows: 4 bearded vultures, 1 griffon vulture, 7 white-tailed sea eagles, 4 small eagles and 1 great bustard. Of the 107 identified bird bones, 96 were from wings, 2 from legs and 9 cervical vertebrae. The discard of complete wings is indicated by articulated bones within the deposit. There is some inconsistency in reports of R. L. Solecki (1977), R. S. Solecki (1963) and Matthews (2000) as to whether the animal bones were from goat or sheep. Matthews summarises recent debate as to whether these had been from domesticated animals, a proposition that seems most unlikely.

6. R. L. Solecki (1981) stresses the particularly wide range of beads and polished stones found at Zawi Chemi Shanidar. Further examples were excavated in Shanidar Cave.

7. R. S. Solecki (1963) provides a review of his work at Shanidar and is drawn upon in the following text; the excavations have never been fully published. See Trinkaus (1983) for a description and interpretation of the Shanidar Neanderthals.

8. Solecki & Rubin (1958) provide a date of 10,600±300 BP (11,011–10,026 cal BC) from charcoal associated with the burials.

9. Anagnostis (1989). The study was undertaken with a study of the bones from the Neolithic site of Ganj Dareh. Both showed a similar range of pathologies which are generally typical for early farming, but not hunter-gatherer populations.

10. We must be cautious here as only a small proportion of Zawi Chemi Shanidar has been excavated and substantial dwellings might have existed at the site. Some might think that this is likely in light of the unhealthy nature of the population, suggesting stress that might have come from resource depletion arising from sedentism.

11. Matthews (2000) provides a summary of Karim Shahir and M'lefaat. The first of these is an open-air settlement close to the summit of a flat-topped hill in the Chemchemal valley, that in which Jarmo is located. Two flat depressions at this site might constitute the remnants of dwellings; several cooking pits with fire-cracked rocks were excavated, along with a 3-metre deep pit, the sides of which had been coated with bright red ochre. This may have had a ritual function. Ground stone artefacts were found, together with large quantities of chipped stone, beads and pendants. Animal bones indicated the hunting of sheep/goat, wild boar, wild cattle, deer and gazelle. Complete publication is provided by Howe (1983). M'lefaat is a low mound with ten round or oval houses, some built with the earliest mud bricks from Mesopotamia. Some dwellings were subterranean, and these surrounded a central open area with a pebble floor with grinding stones and hearths. As at the other sites of these periods, animal bones implied the hunting of a wide range, including sheep/goat, cattle, pig, fox and wolf. Further details are contained in Dittemore (1983). Watkins (1998) provides four

radiocarbon dates clustered between 9890±140 BP (9686–9215 cal BC) and 9660±250 BP (9348–8628 cal BC).

12. The following text about Qermez Dere draws on Watkins (1990; Watkins et al, 1989). Radiocarbon dates are provided in Watkins (1998); five are clustered between 10,145±90 BP (10,115–9411 cal BC) and 9580±95 BP (9160–8799 cal BC), with an early outlier at 11,990±100 (12,335–11,714 cal BC). Unfortunately no contextual information for the dates is provided and hence it is unclear how these relate to the sequence of building and destruction at the site.

13. As Watkins (1990, Watkins et al., 1989) describes, there is no clear indication of what the dwellings were used for other than the negative evidence of an absence of domestic equipment and refuse. The use of the rooms for feasting, caring for babies, resting and sex is purely speculative.

14. The preceding description of a room and the following text is an imaginative development of the nature and sequence of destruction and rebuilding of what Watkins (1990; Watkins et al., 1989) describes as room RAB.

15. There is no archaeological evidence for these structures, nor that the destruction and rebuilding of houses took part at the seasonal times I have suggested.

16. Watkins (1990) stressed the exclusion of everyday activities from the Qermez Dere dwellings in terms of the lack of domestic debris. Whereas the Jordan valley Natufian and Neolithic dwellings contained domestic debris on their floors, those of Qermez Dere were quite empty and clean. Such activities appear to have been excluded, presumably having been conducted either in the open air or below simple shelters that have left no trace. Watkins believed that the 'house' had become the 'home': what had once been a shelter for everyday activities was now the locus for the social and private aspects of family life. He interprets this as being "the centre of the family and the focus for the representation of appropriate symbolic values" (1990, p. 337).

17. The following text about Nemrik draws on Kozlowski (1989) and Kozlowski & Kempisty (1990). Kozlowski (1994) provides radiocarbon dates which indicate that the site was occupied between 10,150 and 8500 BP. Kozlowski (1989) divides the site into three main phases, between which there may have been periods of abandonment.

18. Kozlowski (1989) suggests that drapes might have been hung from these internal posts to create areas of private space, echoing the thoughts of Watkins regarding the role of dwellings at Qermez Dere.

19. Art objects have been found from all phases of occupation at Nemrik. The stone sculptures include representations of a woman, a phallus, a snake and seventeen finely carved bird heads including those which are clearly a vulture and a bustard (Kozlowski, 1989; Matthews, 2000).

45: Approaching Civilisation in Mesopotamia

1. My text about Maghzaliyah draws on the excavation report of Bader (1993a), which is an English version of a Russian publication of 1979, and an English language publication from the journal *Sumer* of 1984. I also draw on Bader's (1993b) overview of early agricultural sites in northern Mesopotamia, and the summaries and synthesis provided in Matthews (2000).

2. There have been no palaeopathological reports contained with the publications cited above; it is possible, therefore, that arrow wounds and axe blows might be found on the bodies to counter the notion of family groups rather than the graves of people who had died by violence.

3. Matthews (2000) provides a succinct summary of Jarmo while full reports of the excavations, analytical studies and interpretations are found in Braidwood et al. (1983).

4. Both Ali Gosh and Ganj Dareh appear to have been occupied between 8500 and 8000 BC, but both suffer from poor dating which has made their evidence very difficult to interpret. For Ali Kosh, see Hole et al. (1969); for evidence regarding domesticated goats at Ganj Dareh, see Hesse (1984) and further discussion in Legge (1996), Hole (1996) and Smith (1995).

5. The following text about Umm Dabaghiyah draws on Kirkbride (1974, 1982).

6. Kirkbride (1982, p. 13).

7. Kirkbride (1974) describes the 'trading outpost' interpretation for Umm Dabaghiyah.

8. Matthews (2000) raises the possibility that tame animals were used for transportation.

9. An overview of the Soviet work as a whole was published in an edited volume by Yoffe and Clark (1993). This contained previous excavation reports that had appeared in a variety of Russian and English language journals over a period of twenty years, together with new summaries and review articles. The significance of the Soviet work can be readily appreciated from this volume and its review by Oates (1994), who described it as having added exponentially to our knowledge of northern Mesopotamia.

10. It should be noted here that a Japanese team excavated an Early Hassuna mound known as Telul eth-Thalathat during the late 1960s and early 1970s which provided important new evidence for prehistoric settlement. This tell provides what is, I believe, the only radiocarbon date for this period – 5850±80 BC (uncalibrated). The final excavations are described in Fukai & Matsutani (1981) and key results summarised in Matthews (2000).

11. This course of development had been anticipated by Oates (1973).

12. Layard (1854, vol. 1, p. 315).

13. Lloyd (1938, 123).

14. My text about Tell Sotto draws on Bader (1993c, originally published in Russian in 1975) and Bader (1993b).

15. Another of these is Kültepe (Bader, 1993d).

16. Yarim Tepe is in fact a cluster of six different mounds, covering a period that included the whole of the Hassuna, Halaf and Ubaid periods. My reference is to Yarim Tepe I, the Hassuna mound, and draws on Merpert & Munchaev (1993) – a publication originally appearing as two parts in the journal *Iraq* in 1973 and 1987. Matthews (2000) provides a useful summary of this and Hassuna sites in general.

17. This is the description of Layard (1853, p. 246).

18. This little scenario is based on the finds from tholos 319 at Yarim Tepe (Merpert & Munchaev, 1993).

19. Lloyd's excavations at Hassuna are described in Lloyd & Safar (1945). He had also made one of the first surveys of the Sinjar plain (Lloyd, 1938) and noted the potential of the Yarim Tepe mounds for excavation.

20. Matthews (2000) does not list any known sites in southern Mesopotamia before 6000 BC. It is conceivable that early prehistoric settlements may remain buried below alluvium.

21. For Tell es-Sawwan, see Matthews (2000).

22. Matthews (2000) provides excellent summaries of sites of the Halaf period and makes a general review of its economy and society.

23. This is suggested in Matthews (2000) who notes that cow's milk can lead to an earlier onset of menstruation and ovulation after breastfeeding.

24. For those wishing to follow the later developments of Mesopotamian pre- and proto-history, see Postgate (1992).

25. Matthews (2000) makes similar reflections at the end of his excellent review and synthesis of Mesopotamian prehistory, emphasising that while this may look like a predestined 'Rise of Civilisation', there was no set plan or goal. He argues that "what happened in prehistory is a complex and quirky assembly of short-term idiosyncratic actions and reactions, each of which is comprehensible within its historical context, as far as that is knowable." (Matthews, 2000, p. 113).

46: Baked Fish by the Nile

1. This chapter focuses on the work in Wadi Kubbaniya as described within Wendorf et al. (1980, 1989a, 1989b).

2. Excavations in Tamar Hat Cave are described in Saxon et al. (1974). Five radiocarbon dates are provided, ranging between 20,600±500 BP and 16,100±360 BP. Saxon et al. suggest that the sheep remains within the cave had arisen from managed herds due to the sex and age profile of the kill, but the identifications have since been questioned (Close & Wendorf, 1990). Winter occupation is indicated by oxygen isotope analysis of marine shells in the deposit. The chipped stone within this and other sites of North African coastal regions at the LGM is referred to as the Iberomaurusian culture.

3. Excavations in the Haua Fteah are described in McBurney (1967). His main interest was with the stone artefacts, which are meticulously described and placed into a series of succeeding

cultures that range from the Middle Palaeolithic to the Neolithic. The chronology of the cave deposits remain little understood, but Close & Wendorf (1990) are confident that it was occupied at the LGM. The animal fauna from the cave was described by Higgs (within McBurney, 1967) and showed remarkable consistency throughout the cave's occupation, with a dominance of Barbary sheep, and a significant presence of horse, bovids and gazelle. But the frequency of these animals changed through time, which is most likely explained by changing climate and landscapes around the cave.

4. Wendorf and his colleagues have proposed this interpretation for the Nile in Upper Egypt and Nubia during the Late Pleistocene, which is succinctly summarised in Close (1996) and Wendorf & Schild (1989). The state of the Nile in Lower Egypt is quite unknown and may have been very different (Close, pers. comm.).

5. The following text is based around excavations at site E-78-3 in Wadi Kubbaniya (Wendorf et al., 1980). This has radiocarbon dates ranging between 17,930±380 BP and 16,960±210 BP. This is just one of many sites dating to this period excavated in Wadi Kubbaniya. A total of 54 radiocarbon dates are available, which indicate occupation occurred over a 2,000-year period, begun between 19,500–19,000 BP and ended at around 17,000 BP.

6. Unfortunately there were no human remains from sites of this period in Wadi Kubbaniya. But one burial was found dating to a slightly earlier period, of a man who had died from injuries (Wendorf et al., 1996) while the Jebel Sahaba cemetery of Nubia indicated substantial violence in the Nile valley dating to c. 13,000–11,000 BP (Wendorf, 1968). Consequently, as the Wadi Kubbaniya site falls between these two discoveries, its own people probably lived in a state of social tension and perhaps interpersonal violence.

7. Ostrich-egg-shell beads and grinding stones with smears of red ochre are described in Wendorf et al. (1980).

8. Close (pers. comm.) points out that there is no evidence for bone handles, or any other kind of haft, in North Africa at this period (or for many thousands of years after).

9. Wendorf & Schild (1989a) suggest that the flint had originated 150 km to the north of Wadi Kubbaniya. It was worked primarily with the levallois technique and very few debitage flakes were recovered. Flint was also preferably used for the manufacture of retouched tools in general, and in particular burins and scaled pieces.

10. The relevant passage in Lubbock (1865, pp. 320–3).

11. Pottery does, however, appear in the Sahara desert by 9000 BP.

12. The following text about fishing at Wadi Kubbaniya is based on the study of fish remains by Gautier & Van Neer (1989), while summaries of their work are found in Wendorf & Schild (1989) and Close & Wendorf (1990).

13. The following text is based on Hillman (1989, Hillman et al., 1989) who provides an extensive and detailed description of the plant remains from Wadi Kubbaniya, their analysis and interpretation.

14. Hillman et al. (1989) cite the 'worst weed in the world' quote and describe how their experimental exploitation of purple nut-grass produced 21,200 tubers weighing 3.3 kg from a mere 1 sq. m.

15. Wendorf et al. (1989b) describe several quarries or workshops at which grinding stones were made along the sandstone escarpment of Wadi Kubbaniya.

16. Animal bones and reconstructed hunting behaviour at Wadi Kubbaniya are described by Gautier and Van Neer (1989). The best preserved Late Pleistocene site with animal bones in the Nile valley dates to 21,000–19,500 BP, attributed to the Fakhurian culture, and is called E71K12, discovered in 1962 but not fully excavated until 1995. This provides a similar picture of hunting hartebeest and wild cattle at ponds that accumulated behind dunes (Wendorf et al., 1997).

17. Hillman (1989; Hillman et al., 1989) describes the methods used to identify the faeces and provides several accounts of defecation in hunter-gatherer camps. Some other specimens of faeces included coarser material and may have derived from slightly older children.

18. The Arab-Israeli War was just one of the political events that impacted upon the research of the Combined Prehistoric Expedition. Wendorf et al. (1997) describe how the legislation passed by the Egyptian government in 1991, offering land titles to anyone who reclaimed and cultivated desert land, led to an immense land rush in some areas with the levelling of dunes, digging and spreading of silt. This destroyed many known but unexcavated sites and provided the need to pursue excavations such as at that site known as E71R12 which had a substantial faunal assemblage.

19. Wendorf & Schild (1989) provide a summary of the archaeology of Wadi Kubbaniya, described in detail within Wendorf et al. (1989b). The oldest material is Late Acheulean, which is followed by three Middle Palaeolithic complexes, the Late Pleistocene Fakhurian material and then the LGM sites described as the Kubbaniyan.

20. As in the comparable time period in western Asia, several distinct 'cultures' have been identified by variations in chipped-stone technology, these having names such as the Gemaian, Fakhurian, Halfan, Idfuan, Qadan and Afian (as summarised in Wendorf & Schild, 1989, and Close, 1996). All of these were based on the production of bladelets. As they appear to have the same economic basis, variations in the stone-tool technology seems unlikely to relate to functional activities but to stylistic choices by the toolmakers. This occurs within Wadi Kubbaniya itself as the sites found on the flood plain and associated with hunting game had the same range of artefacts as those found on the dunes associated with processing fish and preparing plant foods. There

is just one Late Pleistocene technology that is notably different, that of the Sebilian. This used large blocks of sandstone and quartzite to produce large flakes, frequently using discoidal or levallois core techniques. In this regard it is very different to all other industries which are based on bladelet production. Two dates place it at *c.* 11,000 BP but Close (1996) appears to have little confidence in these. As such, it has been suggested as coming from intrusive groups moving into the Nile valley, or even belonging to the Middle Palaeolithic period.

21. The following text about the Nile draws on Wendorf & Schild (1989) and Close (1996).

22. The graveyard of Jebel Sahaba is described in Wendorf (1968), and is just one of three grave-yards that are associated with Qadan industry (Wendorf & Schild, 1989).

23. This burial is described in Wendorf et al. (1986).

24. Close (1996, p. 54).

47: On Lukenya Hill

1. In this view of Kilimanjaro, and in several places in the following chapter when imagining the wildlife and landscapes of East Africa, I have drawn on the writings of Peter Matthiessen as collected his astounding book, *African Trilogy* (Matthiessen, 2000).

2. Environmental reconstructions for East Africa based upon pollen, lake sediments and glacial moraines are described in Hamilton (1982) and summarised in Brooks & Robertshaw (1990).

3. Thompson et al. (2002) describe the results from the Kilimanjaro cores, while a commentary on their significance, headlined with 'Kilimanjaro's secrets revealed', is provided by Gasse (2002).

4. As far as I know, no single source exists for the history of excavation at Lukenya Hill. The articles I have drawn on in the following text, and which provide details about stratigraphy, site formation and excavation method, are Gramly & Rightmire (1973), Gramly (1976), Miller (1979) and Kusimba (2001). The papers about the Lukenya Hill lithics (Kusimba, 1999; Barut, 1994) and fauna (Marean, 1992, 1997) also include brief summaries of site locations and excavations.

5. Kusimba (1999; Barut, 1994) tabulates radio-carbon dates from sites at Lukenya Hill, all having been made on bone. Those with late Stone Age technology range from 20,780±1050 BP for GvJm46 to 13,705±430 for GvJm19; all of the dates have standard deviations greater that 400 years and hence they are all rather problematic. Kusimba's main concern is that the dates from GvJm46 and GvJm19 were made on bone apatite, rather than collagen, which is often known to be inaccurate. She cites a radiocarbon date on the Naisiusiu Beds from the Olduvai Gorge of 17,550+1000BP made on bone apatite, while the beds were later dated by other methods to at least 42,000 BP. Consequently she assumes that her own apatite dates might be 20,000 years too young.

Marean (1997) does not address this issue, but draws on the typology of the microliths to suggest that several of the sites, or rather layers within the sites, date to the LGM. It is evident from the site reports and the lithics that most of the sites have multiple occupations, and without contextual information for the dated materials the association between a cited date and a specific collection of lithics and bones remains unclear. My text, therefore, simply assumes that there was occupation at Lukenya Hill at 20,000 BC while recognising the need for a new dating programme. Lifestyles at 40,000 BC and 13,000 BC are likely to have been very similar to those at the LGM.

6. Marean's studies of the Lukenya Hill animal bones are described in Marean (1992, 1997). The identification of a now extinct species was announced in *Nature* by Marean & Gifford-Gonzalez (1991) where the details about dental anatomy are provided.

7. As Marean (1992) describes, just as important as the presence of dry-grassland-adapted species in the fauna from Lukenya Hill is the rarity of those species that prefer moister, shorter grasses, such as the impala, Thomson's gazelle and eland. He also rightfully comments on the problem of establishing the fauna of a habitat when relying on archaeological finds, as the animals represented are those selected by human hunters. Surprisingly, the bone collections lack any sign of animal-gnawing.

8. My description of Matupi Cave draws on the excavation reports of Van Noten (1977, 1982).

9. The open-air site of Ishango is located on a beach where the present Semliki River exits from Lake Rutanzige. Excavated by Heinzelin de Braucourt (1961), this site has multiple horizons from the Iron Age to a date just prior to the LGM. This earliest horizon has abundant mammal and fish remains and bone harpoons made with two rows of barbs. Peters (1989) has restudied the animal remains following new excavations. A brief summary of Ishango is provided in Brooks & Robertshaw (1990).

10. Useful papers summarising pollen and sedimentary evidence about the changing extent of the African forests are Maley (1993), Grove (1993) and Moeyersons & Roche (1982). Brooks & Robertshaw (1990) have also provided a useful summary.

11. The following scenario of a day's hunting is based on the description of a Hadza day found in Bunn et al. (1988).

12. "The African past lies in the belly of the termite, which has eaten all trace of past tropical civilisations and will do as much for the greater part of what now stands" (Matthiessen, 2000, p. 90).

13. A succinct summary of the Hadza is provided in Woodburn (1968) while detailed descriptions of their hunting and butchery practices are provided by Bunn et al. (1988) and O'Connell et al. (1988). These recent studies have been undertaken to examine how specific hunting, scavenging and butchery practices are reflected in animal bone

assemblages with specific regard to the interpretation of those from the Plio-Pleistocene of East Africa. Further detailed studies on plant gathering and child care have been undertaken (e. g. Hawkes et al., 1997), geared towards addressing the evolution of human life history and social organisation.

14. The impact of the burning of East African grasslands and proposals for how those around Lukenya Hill might have looked at 20,000 BC are provided by Marean (1992, 1997).

15. This is the situation among the modern Hadza, as described by Woodburn (1968).

16. The following text draws on the studies described in Kusimba (1999, 2001).

17. Merrick & Brown (1984) describe the sourcing of obsidian in Kenya and Tanzania by the use of X-ray fluorescence analysis for 12 elements which led to the recognition of 35 petrologically distinct sources. Not all of the obsidian at Lukenya Hill had come from distant sources; some was from a local source. Kusimba (1999) briefly describes an additional study which identified a further chemical variant of the local Lukenya Hill obsidian.

18. The formation and the archaeology of the Naisiusiu Beds are described in Leakey et al. (1972). They provide a date of 17,000±1000 BP from ostrich-egg shell located at the level of a bone concentration within the type section. Kusimba (1999), however, has noted that the Naisiusiu Beds have been redated to 42,000±1000 BP based on a single crystal of ^{40}Ar/^{39}Ar dating of volcanic tuffs capping the LSA material.

19. Richard Leakey's description of sansaveria is in Leakey & Lewin (1979, p. 48).

48: Frogs' Legs and Ostrich Eggs

1. This chapter draws on the study of the paleoenvironment and archaeology of Drotsky's Cave by Robbins et al. (1996).

2. This description is based on the women of the !Kung of Nyae Nyae in the early 1950s, as provided by Marshall (1976). My suggestion of similar physical features and use of deliberate scarification to that found among the !Kung of the 1950s has no evidence in its support. Among the recent !Kung, scarification was made by one woman pinching up a fold of skin and cutting a line of vertical cuts along it with a knife. A mixture of charcoal and fat was rubbed into the bleeding cut. Skin formed around the fragments of charcoal and the lines remained dark for a lifetime (Marshall, 1976, pp. 34–5).

3. Marshall (1976, p. 358) suggests this is how bullfrogs might have been eaten, although she herself had no direct evidence.

4. The Matopos Hills of Zimbabwe, lying some 25 kilometres south of Bulawayo, are described by Walker (1995) in his detailed study of their Late Pleistocene and Holocene archaeology.

5. Excavations in Pomongwe Cave are described by Walker (1985). Its name derives from the local word for melon in reference to the dome-shaped hill in which it is found.

6. Marshall (1976) describes this method for killing the embryos within ostrich-egg shells. I have drawn upon her text, and that of Lee (1979) for further information about the use of ostrich eggs by the !Kung to make speculations about what may have happened at Drotsky's Cave.

7. While microliths themselves were not recovered from Drotsky's Cave, Robbins et al. (1996) describe the presence of several bladelet scars which demonstrate the use of a sophisticated microlith technology. This counters a suggestion by Yellen et al. (1987) that Drotsky's Cave had been part of a non-microlithic tradition based on the results of his initial test excavation.

8. Marshall (1976) devotes two fascinating chapters (pp. 313–81) to the topics of play, games and music among the !Kung of Nyae Nyae. The children, she explains, play all their waking hours while a great deal of leisure time by the adults is spent making music.

9. Martinus Drotsky was a farmer from the Ghanzi area in Botswana who was led to the cave by !Kung bushmen in 1934 (Robbins, pers. com.).

10. Charcoal from Yellen's excavation yielded a radiocarbon date of 12,200±150 BP (13,111–11,896 cal BC) (Robbins et al., 1996).

11. Robbins et al. (1996) acquired dates of: 5470±90 BP (4448–4169 cal BC) for charcoal within sand between 20–30 cm below the surface; 11,240±60 BP (11,439–11,096 cal BC) for the top of the charcoal layer; 12,450±80 BP (13,294–12,210 cal BC) for the base of the charcoal layer.

12. Livingstone's account is cited in Robbins et al. (1996, pp. 15–16).

13. Lee (1979, pp. 139–41). He notes that the spring-hare probe used by the !Kung was an unusual tool because it was dedicated to the one specific task of catching spring hares. With the use of this, they achieved about a 50% success rate in finding and killing a hare on the days that they went hunting. This compares with a 20–25% success rate for other animals.

14. We must, of course, be extremely cautious about using the !Kung as a direct analogy for Kalahari hunter-gatherers of 12,500 BC. I am aware of no evidence that indicates a direct historical link. The ancestry of recent African hunter-gatherers is a matter of considerable dispute and research among anthropologists. Some hunter-gatherer groups may represent recent readaptations to hunting and gathering from a pastoral and farming lifestyle due to social and economic oppression and environmental change. Such issues are discussed in Clark & Brandt (1984) and Schrire (1984).

49: A South African Tour

1. These are the typical contents of a !Kung Bushman hunters' bag (Lee, 1979).

2. The Later Holocene levels of Elands Bay Cave have more or less fragmented wads of Zostera, an estuarine grass, but there are no such remains from the Late Pleistocene levels (Parkington, 1980).

3. The history of fishing at Elands Bay Cave has been described by Poggenpoel (1987). His study of fishbones from Elands Bay Cave and the nearby Tortoise Cave describes how the species represented change through time, coming to include large quantities of white steenbras and white stumpnose. He discusses changing fish availability due to sea-level rise and the likely fishing techniques, drawing on the size distribution of fish and the surviving artefacts such as bone fish gorges – double-ended polished bone slithers. At 12,500 BC, just one species of fish was caught, *Mugil cephalus*. This is a marine species but one known to swim long distances upstream. At 12,500 BC, Elands Bay Cave was approximately 20 km from the coast.

4. Parkington has published a substantial number of articles concerning the excavations at Elands Bay Cave since 1980, which reflect both the continuing study of its materials and how his own interpretations have changed. My text has drawn on several of these, hoping to reach a position concurrent with his current views. Parkington (1980) provides a succinct description of the cave's stratigraphy and subsistence remains; Parkington (1984) places his work at Elands Bay Cave into the context of changing views of the Later Stone Age in South Africa since serious study began in the late 1920s; Parkington (1986, 1988) places the cave into its landscape context of the Western Cape, while Parkington (1987) reflects upon his own previous interpretations of the cave; Parkington et al. (1988) focuses on the Holocene settlement of the Western Cape, the most recent of which is further considered by dietary studies of human bones leading to differing interpretations by Sealy & Van der Merwe (1988, 1992) and Parkington (1991). Several reports are available on specific organic remains from the cave, notably fishbones (Poggenpoel 1987), wood charcoal (Cartwright & Parkington, 1997), shellfish (Buchanan, 1988) and micromammals (Matthews, 1999).

5. General overviews of climate and vegetation change in South Africa are provided by J. Deacon (1987, 1990), Mitchell (1990), and Mitchell et al. (1996). A study of the charcoal and vegetation around Boomplaas Cave is found within H. J. Deacon et al. (1984).

6. A study of the charcoal from Rose Cottage Cave is reported by Wadley et al. (1992).

7. Klein (1978) describes the changes in animal fauna from Boomplaas Cave and relates these to changing environments. Those from Rose Cottage Cave are described by Plug & Engela (1992).

8. Wadley (1987, 1989, 1993) elaborates on the social impact of bow-and-arrow hunting with regard to new gender relations. She suggests that wives and meat might have been simultaneously privatised.

9. H. J. Deacon (1995) provides some information about the rodent remains from Boomplaas Cave.

10. Klein (1991) has made a detailed study of the relationship between dune molerat size and rainfall in modern and prehistoric environments of South Africa. Further palaeoenvironmental information regarding Late Pleistocene environments can be gained from the large mammal fauna that I have referred to in my text. Of particular value are sites where the bones have accumulated by non-human processes alone, notably Equus Cave (Klein et al., 1991).

11. Parkington (1984) describes how rock types might be used to reconstruct settlement patterns in the Late Pleistocene and Early Holocene.

12. The specific chronology of the economic changes evident at Elands Bay Cave is less well known than is desirable. The Late Pleistocene and Early Holocene layers have a large series of radiocarbon dates; Mitchell et al. (1996) cite 21 of these ranging from 12,450±280 BP (13,356–12,167 cal BC) to 8000±95 BP (7060–6710 cal BC). But how they relate to specific horizons is not easy to discern from the available literature. Parkington (1980) states that at 13,000 years ago the large mammal fauna begins to change, reflecting the contraction of the coastal plain, and that marine mammals make their first appearance somewhere between 11,000 and 12,000 years ago. Soon after 10,000 years ago, marine elements begin to dominate the faunal assemblage, while between 8,000 and 9,000 years ago Parkington suggests there was a rescheduling of occupation, with visits in the early spring and late winter.

13. Van Andel (1989) has made a specific study of Late Pleistocene sea levels and the human exploitation of coastal plains, while Poggenpoel (1987) provides a particularly useful set of diagrams showing the changing distance between Elands Bay Cave and the coast.

14. Pleistocene and Early Holocene burials in South Africa are relatively rare and so we have limited knowledge about their location and character. Wadley (1997) has provided a useful summary of existing information.

15. The impact of changing currents on mussel availability is explained by Parkington (1986). He argues that prior to 10,000 BP mussel populations had died off along the coast due to the loss of 'upwelling' conditions in the sea, a consequence of changes in the wind patterns at the LGM and its immediate aftermath. After 10,000 BP these were re-established: mussels recolonised the rocky coast and became the preferred shellfish. An alternative explanation for the shift from limpets to mussels is a change in the time of year that visits were made to Elands Bay Cave.

16. Thackeray et al. (1981) and Wadley (1993) provide brief summaries of the excavations at Wonderwerk cave.

17. The engraved slab is described by Thackeray et al. (1981) where it is assigned to a context dated to 10,200±90 BP (10,333–9650 cal BC).

18. The Apollo Cave slabs are described by Wendt (1976) and have been dated to 27,000 BP. Wadley (1993), however, explains that a date closer to 19,000 BP is equally plausible.

Lewis-Williams (1984) has proposed that the feline has human legs and hence sees a continuity with the very recent painted images of combined human and animal forms that he believes are directly related to shamanistic practices.

19. Mitchell (1997) summarises the existing dating evidence for rock paintings and rock engravings in South Africa. In addition to those I have cited in my text, painted slabs have been dated to 3600 BP at Steenbokfontein, while Mitchell explains that a range of studies indicate that engravings were produced throughout the Holocene, with pecked and scraped engravings made only in the last 2,700 years. Wadley (1993) describes and illustrates several engraved pieces of eggshell from Late Pleistocene sites in South Africa, notably Boomplaas Cave. The earliest of these is 14,200 BP, while at the site of Melkhoutboom these have been dated slightly earlier, to 15,400 BP. Fine-lined Holocene engravings are found across the interior of South Africa and often match the distribution of stone artefact scatters dating to 12,000 BP and after, suggesting the engravings have a similar date.

20. For my scenario I drew on descriptions of trance-dances within Lewis-Williams (1987) and Wadley (1987).

21. Lewis-Williams (1981, 1982, 1987) shows the successive development and refinement of his shamanistic interpretation of South African rock art, while Lewis-Williams & Dowson (1988) sought to extend the application to the rock art of the Upper Palaeolithic. Since the mid-1980s similar interpretations have been applied to prehistoric rock art throughout the world, as illustrated by the papers found within Chippindale & Taçon (eds., 1998). Unfortunately these often lack the direct historical analogy that Lewis-Williams is able to use.

22. Klein (1980) describes the modern ecozones of South Africa. These have been by used by him and other archaeologists (e.g. Wadley 1993) to make inferences about vegetation and animal abundance in prehistory.

23. There is very little evidence for the role of plant foods in Late Pleistocene and Early Holocene economies. H. J. Deacon (1976, 1993) has argued that the environmental changes that marked the start of the Holocene may have led to a major switch from big-game hunting to the trapping of smaller game and the exploitation of plant foods. But evidence has not been forthcoming and Parkington (1984) suggests that any intensive use of underground plant foods only occurred in the Late Holocene. As such, the historically documented economic system of the San Bushmen might have very little time-depth, questioning many of the analogies that have been drawn.

24. Wadley (1993) quantifies the numbers of sites known at successive segments of Late Pleistocene to demonstrate this substantial population growth after 13,000 BP; Mitchell et al. (1996) do likewise and claim that another spurt of

population growth occurred between 10,000 and 9000 BP. There are immense difficulties in trying to estimate human population levels by counting the numbers of sites. Changing settlement patterns can, for instance, increase the number of sites created by the same number of people, while a great many lithic scatters throughout South Africa remain undated.

25. I am greatly simplifying the complex issues regarding the cultural sequences within South Africa. I use the term 'Oakhurst' in the same manner as Wadley (2000), to embrace a number of regional industries that have been referred to as Oakhurst, Albany and Kuruman, among others. These all share a relative lack of bladelets. The chronological switch between Robberg- and Oakhurst-type assemblages is regionally variable, happening particularly late at Rose Cottage Cave (Wadley & Vogel, 1991). Parkington (1984) provides a comprehensive review of how the terminological frameworks for South African Late Pleistocene and Holocene industries arose; a good summary is also provided by Wadley (1993).

26. Parkington (1984) suggested that the open-air non-microlithic sites and cave microlithic sites might be contemporary, a position challenged by Wadley (1993). Parkington (1984) also notes that Robberg and Oakhurst assemblages share a similar type of tool, the naturally backed knife, and that some Oakhurst assemblages also contain small blades. It seems likely that the distinctions between these two industries are more subtle than is often portrayed.

27. Many of the small blades in Wilton assemblages are chipped into specifically shaped microliths, suggesting a more formal range of tools; this industry also sees a shift from the use of bone to stone for arrow-heads (Wadley, 1993).

28. This is based on the case among the !Kung of recent times (Lee, 1979; Wadley, 1987).

29. Wadley (2000) provides a detailed description of the contents and spatial distribution of artefacts within the Early Holocene layers at Rose Cottage Cave. These contain Oakhurst-type artefacts and are dated to between 9250±70 BP (8595–8320 cal BC) and 8160±70 BP (7303–7064 cal BC).

30. Study of carbon isotopes indicated plants in the cave used the C3 photosynthetic pathway, contrasting with the dominance of C4 outside, which reflects the grassland environment of the hill slope. The C3 values are interpreted as reflecting leaves, firewood and edible plants which had been brought into the cave (Wadley, 2000).

31. Wadley (1991) provides a brief history of work at Rose Cottage Cave.

32. Ouzman & Wadley (1997) describe and interpret the most recent Holocene archaeology and wall paintings of Rose Cottage Cave. The spatial organisation appears strikingly similar to that of the Oakhurst and Robberg levels, and contrasts significantly with that from the Middle Stone Age. Wadley (2001) has used this as a basis for discussing the emergence of modern cognition.

33. Wadley (1987) notes that the majority of men's gifts are made of organic materials and unlikely to survive into the archaeological record.
34. Lee (1979) and Marshall (1976) describe the significance of the !Kung gift-giving system, known as *hxaro*, as well as their aggregations and frequent visiting. Wadley (1987) has provided a succinct summary and discussed the relevance of this to prehistoric studies in South Africa.
35. For the following text I draw on Wiessner (1982).
36. See Wadley (1987, 1993) for a discussion of possible gift-giving networks, along with other social aspects, of Late Pleistocene and Early Holocene lifestyles in South Africa.
37. H. J. Deacon (1995) briefly summarises the history of his work at Boomplaas and Klasies River Mouth – the site that contained deposits reaching back to 125,000 years ago – as well as the stratigraphic sequences, changes in environment, economy and artefacts at these two sites. H. J. Deacon (1979) is also a useful article for background information regarding the work at Boomplaas. Wadley (1993) cites six radiocarbon dates for the Late Pleistocene occupation at Boomplaas, ranging from 21,220±195 BP to 12,060±105 BP (12,982–11,871 cal BC), while Mitchell (1997) provides two Holocene dates – 9100±135 BP (8545–8023 cal BC) and 6400±75 BP (5470–5317 cal BC). The first of these refers to the Albany horizon in which I have situated Lubbock.
38. The relevant passage is Lubbock (1865, pp. 338–43). Kolben's book is *History of the Cape of Good Hope*.
39. H. J. Deacon (1995) suggests that changing clothing styles during South African prehistory might be inferred from changes in scraper technology. The Wilton industry contains small convex scrapers which seem suitable for preparing the thin supple leather of small antelopes and repairing garments made from such material. The scrapers found in the Albany assemblage of the Early Holocene layers at Boomplaas Cave suggest a different emphasis on skin working and that skin underclothing may not have been worn.
40. Klein (1978) summarises the large mammal bones from Boomplaas Cave.
41. The following draws on Klein (1984a, 1984b). Mitchell et al. (1996) question his conclusions by stating that we lack firm evidence that the environmental changes that began the Holocene were not actually more severe than those of earlier interglacials. They further argue that the species that became extinct were the most specialised grazers, implying that this supports a purely environmental explanation. They also note that arguments have been made that the Cape horse evolved into Grevy's zebra and the giant bison into the Cape buffalo. What is less contentious is that there is little evidence for selective hunting of the extinct species and no evidence for major kill sites.
42. Parkington et al. (1988) date this period of abandonment between 7800 and 3500 BP, attributing it equally to the combined impacts of Mid-Holocene aridity and the high level of the sea. Mitchell (1997) has since cited dates for sites in the Western Cape within this period – such as 5130±50 BP (3980–3804 cal BC) for a shell from Doorspring midden found to the north of Elands Bay Cave – and suggests that the Western Cape may not have been as arid as Parkington has proposed.
43. Parkington (1984) interprets gypsum deposits in the cave as a consequence of salt-laden mists and sprays bringing water into the cave. The gypsum evaporated out as the water penetrated down into the Pleistocene layers.

50: Thunderbolts in the Tropics
1. Shaw's (1969) anecdote about such 'thunderbolts' is worth repeating: "In Western Nigeria they [stone axes/thunderbolts] are associated with the god of thunder (Sango). Whenever a house is struck by lightning the Sango priest is called in and he looks around to try and find the thunderbolt that is responsible. Having brought this [an axe] along with him concealed in his robes, he finally points to a spot and tells his assistant to dig in order to find the thunderbolt. They dig, and of course duly find it; it probably goes back into the Sango altar." (Shaw, 1969, p. 365).
2. Shaw (1969) describes his excavations within Iwo Eleru.
3. Brothwell & Shaw (1971) describe the skeletal remains. They cite a date of 9250±200 BC (presumaby uncalibrated) derived from charcoal close to the skeleton; another piece of charcoal 'from another low level' in the excavation gave a date of 7200±150 BC (6224–5895 cal BC) (Shaw, 1969). Brothwell and Shaw (1971) cite a date of 1515±65 BC (438–618 cal AD) near the top of the excavation and indicate that a further three other dates are available – none of which I have been able to locate.
4. Shaw (1969, p. 371).
5. Maley (1993) reviews evidence for the vegetational history of equatorial Africa during the Late Pleistocene and Early Holocene. He provides the example of Pointe-Noire in the coastal zone of the Gabon that is currently covered by savannah vegetation as a locality where the stumps of rainforest trees can be found *in situ* in palaeosols and dated 6500–3000 BP.
6. Maley (1993) provides brief comments about the pollen cores from Lake Bosumtwi, which show that the first stages of reforestation had begun between 13,000 and 12,000 BP.
7. The following text about artefacts from the Congo basin draws on Fiedler & Preuss (1985).
8. Preuss relied on radiocarbon dates of organic remains sealed within the sediments; a key date is 24,860±290 BP on sands from the Busira River (Fiedler & Preuss, 1985).
9. Robbins et al. (2000) provide a detailed description of excavations at White Paintings Rockshelter. In addition to the Early Holocene levels that I describe, the site is also of particular interest because its use is still remembered in oral tradition, and has well preserved lower levels

indicating intensive fishing and manufacture of ostrich-egg-shell beads earlier than 40,000 BP.

10. The dating evidence for these layers is particularly complicated (Robbins et al., 2000). Radiocarbon dates suggest a date of 5.7/8–4.1 ka BP, but OSL (optical spin luminesence) dates suggest an age of 20.6±1.9 ka BP, which would fit rather better with the known history of palaeoenvironmental conditions. Both the barbed bone points and microliths are described by Robbins et al. as being more in keeping with a Mid-Holocene age.

11. The time taken for sand to accumulate in White Paintings Rockshelter is based on the rate that Robbins et al. (1996) estimate sand accumulation within Drotsky's Cave – which may not, however, be applicable to another site. There are two hints from the fishbone layer that pigments may have been prepared at a contemporary date. First, two of the grinding-stone fragments had a red tint which suggests their use for ochre; second, a piece of bone had been engraved with a spiky design that is also found on the wall of a nearby cave.

12. Cooke's excavations in Pomongwe Cave are described by Walker (1985) in the context of his renewed excavations and interpretation.

13. I have been unable to make sense of the radiocarbon dates provided by Walker (1985, p.136 and table 30), partly due to the different layer terminology used by Cooke and Walker.

14. The history of lake levels in East Africa is described by Grove (1993) and Hamilton (1982).

15. Lowasera is described by Phillipson (1977), who provides further comments about additional sites located on ancient shorelines in Phillipson (1985).

16. Grove (1993) provides various estimates for the extent of past rainfall based on two alternative methods. The first involves calculating the water balance of a palaeolake, making assumptions about evaporation and run-off coefficients, while the second attempts to derive values for evaporation losses by reconstructing energy flows in a palaeolake and its basin. Several results calculated by slightly different methods by different authors are provided, ranging from increases in rainfall of 15% to 54%. In October 2002, new evidence became available from the ice cores taken from Kilimanjaro which has provided a detailed record of changing temperature/rainfall but has not, so far as I understand, been integrated with that from other sources.

17. This is taken from Hamilton (1982). As he notes, atmospheric circulation over Africa during the Quaternary is incompletely understood.

51: Sheep and Cattle in the Sahara

1. Barich (1987, 1992) provides a study of the Holocene archaeology in the Tadrart Acacus, on which much of the following text is based.

2. This description is based on the illustration and text provided in Mori (1998, pp. 152–3).

3. Excavations within and immediately outside Uan Afuda are described in Mori (1998) and di Lernia (2001).

4. The following text concerning interpretation of the material in Uan Afuda is based on di Lernia (2001).

5. The Holocene environment of the Sahara suffered a great number of fluctuations between relatively wet and dry periods. The dating of these is difficult to establish; different authors specify different periods of aridity (e. g. compare Hassan, 1997, with Wendorf & Schild, 1994). This may partly reflect the problems associated with the calibration of Early Holocene radiocarbon dates, and partly with establishing the local severity of the climatic fluctuations which are apparent from the ice-core record.

6. Mori (1998), *The Great Civilisations of the Ancient Sahara*.

7. Mori (1998, pp. 171–89) provides a detailed discussion of all dating evidence available, including the radiocarbon dating of organic materials used within the paint and of the patinas that have formed over the paintings.

8. The 'self-defence' interpretation is that of Mori (1998, p. 64) who explains that the burial was discovered close to a 'child mummy'. The burial was found in layers that has dates of 7550±120 BP (6470–6241 cal BC) and 7823±95 BP (6891–6502 cal BC). Mori suggests that inhumations are numerous within the Acacus.

9. The majority of cattle in Africa today have the humped back – Zebu cattle – and derive from Mid- to Late Holocene introductions into the continent. Blench & MacDonald (2000) provide a set of essays which cover the origins and development of African livestock with a focus on cattle.

10. For vegetation history of the Sahara during the Early Holocene, see Ritchie & Haynes (1987).

11. Rings of stone thought to be Neolithic fireplaces are found throughout the Sahara and can provide valuable palaeoecological information (Gabriel, 1987).

12. Pachur (1991) provides a study of tethering stones in the Sahara and discusses their palaeoenvironmental implications.

13. The discovery and excavation of archaeological sites around the ancient lake of Nabta are described in a detailed academic study in Wendorf & Schild (1980) and in a more accessible form in Wendorf et al. (1985). The following text is based on the specific site of E-75-6 which has a series of 22 radiocarbon dates with a central value of 8000 BP (Wendorf & Schild, 1980).

14. The following scenario of a day at Nabta is heavily based on that of the Boran pastoralists of Kenya as described by Dahl (1979). The details about pits in the floors used for cooking and hut constructions are based on descriptions within Wendorf & Schild (1980) and Schild et al. (1996).

15. The earliest radiocarbon date associated with cattle bones, claimed to be from domestic animals, is 8840±90 BP (8201–7816 cal BC) (Wendorf & Schild 1980). Gautier (1984) has suggested that cattle bones from Bir Kiseiba most

likely dated to 9500 BP. Gautier (1987) provided a summary of all available data up until the mid-1980s on the earliest domesticated cattle throughout North Africa.

16. Excavations and the cattle bones at Bir Kiseiba are described by Wendorf et al. (1984).

17. The date for this hinges on when domestic cattle first became present in Southwest Asia, which has proved difficult to establish. The available data has been summarised in MacDonald (2000).

18. Key papers in this debate with Wendorf et al. about the date of cattle domestication in Africa are Clutton-Brock (1989), Smith (1986, 1992) and Muzzolini (1989). A summary of the debate is provided in MacDonald (2000).

19. The study of cattle DNA is provided in Bradley et al. (1996).

20. This is the hypothesis proposed by Wendorf & Schild (1994) and Close & Wendorf (1992) who suggest that the first stages of domestication may have occurred in the Late Pleistocene. They note that cattle skulls had been used as grave markers in Qadan cemeteries at c. 14,500 BP and that what had been thought to be a sexually dimorphic size differentiation in cattle bones from the Late Pleistocene might in fact reflect wild cattle (the larger) and those undergoing the first steps towards domestication (the smaller).

21. This eastern Sahara origin for domestication is proposed by Hassan (2000).

22. This type of scenario for the domestication of sheep and cattle in the Sahara has recently been supported by Marshall & Hildeband (2002) within a review of the beginning of food production in Africa. They stress the fluctuations between relatively wet and dry periods as being of crucial importance for cattle domestication, favouring the notion of 'storage on the hoof'. Their publication appeared too late in 2002 for their ideas to be fully integrated into my text.

23. Gautier (1987) provides a date for cattle pastoralists in the Acacus of 7440±220, coming from the cave of Ti-n-Torha North. This cave had a sequence of deposits that match those within Uan Muhuggiag (Barich, 1987) where the lowest level with domestic cattle has been dated as 7438±1200 BP (Wendorf & Schild, 1994).

24. See, for instance, Galaty (1989) for a study of Maasai practical reasoning.

25. The plant remains from E-75-6 are described in Wasylikowa et al. (1993) and Wendorf et al. (1992). They argue that although the sorghum is morphologically wild, the lipid fractions (fatty acids extracted from the seeds) show a close resemblance to domesticated forms. They imply that sorghum might have been indigenously domesticated at an early date in Africa. This seems unlikely in light of recent studies of ancient DNA (Rowley-Conwy et al., 1997).

26. There is no direct evidence for the extraction of blood from cattle at Nabta (just as there is no direct evidence for milking). But blood extraction is a common practice among recent and modern pastoralists, as described by Cagnolo (1933). Similarly, there is no direct evidence for any of the ceremonies associated with life-stages, as commonly found among pastoralists. The only trace of ritual activity is a megalith complex that was constructed at Nabta at c. 6000 BP, consisting of nine large stone slabs embedded in the ancient lake sediments that appear to have once been part of a circle. It may "indicate the emerging combination of religious phenomena with leaders who could organise the construction of small-scale public architecture" (Wendorf et al., 1996, p. 132).

27. Wendorf & Schild (1994, p. 121) provide a date of "around 7000 BP" for the appearance of sheep and goats at Nabta.

28. This is thought to have happened at c. 5500 BP, following early intervals of short abandonments of Nabta. Wendorf & Schild (1994) describe significant differences in material culture between the Early, Middle and Later Neolithic phases of settlement.

52: Farmers in the Nile Valley and Beyond

1. The following text draws on studies of the Fayum Neolithic by Hassan (1986, 1988), Wenke et al. (1988) and Wetterstrom (1993). This has been divided into an early phase, 5200–4500 BC and a late phase as from 4000 BC. When placed together these are referred to as Fayum A. Fayum B refers to occupation sites that date between 8–7000 BC and are otherwise known as Qarunian.

2. Harlan (1989) provides an excellent overview of the use of wild grass seeds as food in the Sahara and Sub-Sahara.

3. Hassan (1986) provides a brief summary of the history of studies at the Fayum Depression as a prelude to a detailed study of the fluctuating lake levels. After Herodotus had been the first to record the lake, its existence was also commented upon by Strabo, Diodorus and Pliny. Caton-Thompson & Gardner (1934) provide a detailed description of their research and the discovery of the granaries.

4. Hassan (1985) cites the date as 5145±155 cal BC.

5. This comparison has been made by Wetterstrom (1993).

6. Wendorf & Schild (1976) and Hassan (1986) describe geological studies relating to fluctuations of the lake levels; Wendorf & Schild (1976) also describe numerous sites found during their archaeological survey; Ginter & Kozlowski (1983) undertook excavations at several sites, while Wenke et al. (1988) summarise considerable field-work on the southwest shore of the lake. Brewer (1989) has made an important archaeo-zoological study of the fauna from Fayum, concluding that people may have remained within the basin all year round.

7. Wetterstom (1993) provides a succinct summary of the work at Merimde.

8. Hassan (1988) stresses the similarities in artefact types between Fayum/Merimde and

Southwest Asia. Wenke et al. (1988), in contrast, have stressed that the technology at these Nile valley sites is basically macrolithic in character, quite different to the microlithic nature of sites in the Sinai and Negev.

9. For the pre-dynastic farming developments in the Nile valley, see Hassan (1988). Haaland (1995) provides a review of developments regarding sedentism and farming in the Middle Nile region.

10. For an excellent review of the origin and spread of food production in Africa, see Marshall & Hildebrand (2002).

11. Clutton-Brock (2000) provides a study of the southward spread of African pastoralism, stressing the many difficulties it faced.

12. Harlan (1992, p. 69) provides a review of indigenous African agriculture.

Epilogue: 'The Blessings of Civilisation'

1. The specific hill is of no consequence, but I am thinking of one close to my home in Berkshire, England.

2. Lubbock (1865, p. 484).

3. I recognise the controversial nature of the word 'true' within this sentence. Thankfully it is too late in my book to get into discussions about the nature or otherwise of historical truth. For those who wish to pursue this topic, see Evans (1997) for a critique of postmodernist history.

4. Lubbock (1865, pp. 487–8).

5. McCarthy et al. (2001) document a vast range of environmental and ecological changes that have occurred during the last fifty years that can be directly attributed to global warming, ranging from the melting of glaciers to the changing distributions of butterflies and birds. Barnacle geese, for instance, have invaded agricultural land as they move further north in Norway, while in Antarctica penguins have reduced in numbers and altered where they live in response to a warmer climate.

6. These predicted figures are taken from McCarthy et al. (2001, p. 27, table TS-1) – the volume of the 2001 report of the Intergovernmental Panel on Climate Change that is concerned with impacts, adaptation and vulnerability. More specifically, the predicted rise of temperature for the next hundred years is between 0.8 and 2.6°C, and the rise of sea level between 0.05 and 0.32 m, rising to a maximum estimate of 0.88 m. by AD 2100.

7. These figures regarding population numbers and farming land in delta regions are taken from Houghton (1997). As they are at least five years old they are likely to be under-estimates.

8. McCarthy et al. (2001) evaluate the impact of sea-level rise on small island states. As an example, an 80-cm sea-level rise could inundate 66% of the Marshall Islands and Kiribati in the Pacific, and a 90-cm rise 85% of Male, the capital of the Maldives.

9. Houghton (1997) provides a particularly succinct summary of the likely impact of global warming on freshwater supplies, which is examined at length in McCarthy et al. (2001). The Ataturk Dam in southeast Turkey has substantial impacts on freshwater supplies in Syria.

10. This has, of course, been common in much of southern England and beyond. For a study of how the countryside has changed in a typical area, a 20-sq. km area of west Berkshire, see Bowers & Cheshire (1983, chapter 2).

11. This is not my subjective opinion but that coming from the government-supported Environment Agency, as detailed in their report on the state of the environment in England and Wales (Environment Agency, 2000).

12. There is a vast literature that details the crisis in food production and supply. I have found the most informative work to be the anthology entitled *The Paradox of Plenty, Hunger in a Bountiful World* (Boucher, 1999).

13. This figure is quoted from McCarthy et al. (2001, p. 938).

14. See Borlaug (2000). Norman Borlaug is a US plant breeder who developed new strains of rice and wheat for the underdeveloped countries. He received the Nobel Peace Prize in 1970 for his part in the 'green revolution' and seems as ready to extol the new science of biotechnology as was Victorian John Lubbock to praise the new science of his day.

15. Borlaug (2000) quotes a figure of 8.5 billion for the expected world population in 25 years' time. McCarthy et al. (2001) quote figures of 8.4–11.3 billion for 2050, and 7.1–15.1 billion for 2100.

16. See Borlaug (2000, p. 489). Some would vehemently disagree with this, believing that the new genetically modified organisms are qualitatively different from anything that has come before. As far as we know, the first cultivators/farmers did not engage in any plant breeding at all; they simply (unconsciously) favoured some existing genetic variants over others. Moreover, biotechnology often moves genes between very different organisms, something which could not have been done by conventional plant breeding or unintended selection. Also, a single gene, or a small number, are often moved between organisms; in plant breeding (deliberate or unintended) this is impossible and whole chromosomes containing many thousands of unknown genes are transferred.

17. I do not mean to imply that Borlaug (2000) is unaware of the seriousness of this issue. Indeed, he himself writes that as so much of biotechnology is being undertaken in the private sector, the issue of intellectual property rights must be addressed and accorded adequate safeguards by national government: "The more important matters of concern by civil societies should be equity issues related to genetic ownership, control, and access to transgenic agricultural products" (p. 489).

18. For a debate about the ecological impacts of genetically modified organisms see www.nature.com/nature/debates/gmfoods.

BIBLIOGRAPHY

Aaris-Sørensen, K. 1984. *Uroksen fra Prejlerup. Et arkæozoologisk fund.* Copenhagen: Zoological Museum (guidebook).

Ackerman, R.E. 1996. Bluefish Caves. In *American Beginnings* (ed. F. West), pp. 511–13. Chicago: University of Chicago Press.

Adhikary, A.K. The Birhor. In *The Cambridge Encyclopedia of Hunters and Gatherers* (eds. R.B. Lee & R. Daly), pp. 248–51. Cambridge: Cambridge University Press.

Adovasio, J.M. 1993. The ones that will not go away, a biased view of pre-Clovis populations in the New World. In *From Kostenki to Clovis* (eds. O. Soffer & N.D. Praslov), pp. 199–218. New York: Plenum Press.

Adovasio, J.M. & Pedler, D.R. 1997. Monte Verde and the antiquity of humankind in the Americas. *Antiquity* 71, 573–80.

Adovasio, J.M., Carlisle, R.C., Cushman, K.A., Donahue, J., Guilday, J.E., Johnson, W.C., Lord, K., Parmalee, P.W., Stuckenrath, R. & Wiegman, P.W. 1985. Palaeoenvironmental reconstruction at Meadowcroft Rockshelter, Washington County, Pennsylvania. In *Environments and Extinctions: Man in Late Glacial North America* (eds. J.I. Mead & D.J. Meltzer), pp. 73–110. Orono, ME: Centre for the Study of Early Man.

Adovasio, J.M., Donahue, J. & Stuckenrath, R. 1990. The Meadowcroft Rockshelter radiocarbon chronology 1975–1990. *American Antiquity* 55, 348–54.

Adovasio, J.M., Gunn, J.D., Donahue, J. & Stuckenrath, R. 1978. Meadowcroft Rockshelter, 1977: An overview. *American Antiquity* 43, 632–51.

Ahlbäck, T. (ed.) 1987. *Saami Religion.* Uppsala.

Ahn, S.M. 1992. *Origin and differentiation of domesticated rice in Asia – a review of archaeological and botanical evidence.* Unpublished Ph.D. dissertation, Institute of Archaeology, University College London.

Aikens, C.M. 1995. First in the world: The Jomon pottery of early Japan. In *The Emergence of Pottery: Technology and Innovation in Ancient Societies* (eds. W.K. Barnett & J.W. Hoopes), pp. 11–21. Washington: Smithsonian Institution Press.

Aikens, C.M. & Higuchi, T. 1982. *Prehistory of Japan.* New York: Academic Press.

Akazawa, T. 1986. Regional variation in procurement systems of Jomon hunter-gatherers. In *Prehistoric Hunter-Gatherers in Japan: New Research Methods* (eds. T. Akazawa & C.M. Aikens), pp. 73–89. Tokyo: University of Tokyo Press.

Albrethsen, S.E. & Brinch Petersen, E. 1976. Excavation of a Mesolithic cemetery at Vedbæk, Denmark. *Acta Archaeologica* 47, 1–28.

Alciati, G., Cattani, L., Fontana, F., Gerhardinger, E., Guerreschi, A., Milliken, S., Mozzi, P. & Rowley-Conwy, P. 1993. Mondeval de Sora: A high altitude Mesolithic campsite in the Italian Dolomites. *Prehistoria Alpina* 28, 351–66.

Aldenderfer, M. 1998. *Montane Foragers. Asana and the South-Central Andean Archaic.* Iowa City: University of Iowa Press.

Allchin, B. & Allchin, F.R. 1982. *The Rise of Civilization in India and Pakistan.* Cambridge: Cambridge University Press.

Allchin, F.R. 1963. *Neolithic Cattle Keepers of South India.* Cambridge: Cambridge University Press.

Allen, H. 1989. Late Pleistocene and Holocene settlement patterns and environment, Kakadu, Northern Territory, Australia. *Indo-Pacific Prehistory Association Bulletin* 9, 92–117.

Allen, J. (ed.) 1996. *Report of the Southern Forests Archaeological Project,* Vol. 1. Bundoora: School of Archaeology, La Trobe University.

Alley, R.B., Mayewski, P.A., Sowers, T., Stuiver, M., Taylor, K.C. & Clark, P.U. 1997. Holocene climatic instability: A prominent widespread event at 8,200 years ago. *Geology* 25, 483–6.

Ames, K.M. & Maschner, H.D.G. 1999. *Peoples of the Northwest Coast: Their Archaeology and Prehistory.* London: Thames & Hudson.

Ammerman, A.J. & Cavalli-Sforza, L.L. 1979. The wave of advance model for the spread of agriculture in Europe. In *Transformations: Mathematical Approaches to Culture Change* (eds. C. Renfrew & K.L. Cooke), pp. 275–94. New York: Academic Press.

Ammerman, A.J. & Cavalli-Sforza, L.L. 1984. *The Neolithic Transition and the Genetics of Population in Europe.* Princeton NJ: Princeton University Press.

Anagnostis, A. 1989. *The Palaeopathological Evidence, Indicators of Stress of the Shanidar Proto-Neolithic and the Ganj Dareh Early Neolithic Human Skeletal Collections.* Unpublished Ph.D. thesis, Columbia University, NY.

Andersen, S.H. 1978. Aggersund. En Ertebølleboplads ved Limfjorden. *Kuml* 1978, 7–56.

Andersen, S.H. 1985. Tybrind Vig. A preliminary report on a submerged Ertebølle settlement on the west coast of Fyn. *Journal of Danish Archaeology* 4, 52–69.

Andersen, S.H. 1987. Mesolithic dug-outs and paddles from Tybrind Vig, Denmark. *Acta Archaeologica* 57, 87–106.

Andersen, S.H. 1994. Ringkloster: Ertebølle trappers and wild boar hunters in eastern Jutland. *Journal of Danish Archaeology* 12, 13–59.

Andersen, S.H. 1995. Coastal adaptation and marine exploitation in Late Mesolithic Denmark – with special emphasis on the Limfjord region. In *Man & Sea in the Mesolithic* (ed. A. Fischer), pp. 41–66. Oxford: Oxbow Monograph, No. 53.

Andersen, S.H. & Johansen, E. 1986. Ertebølle revisited. *Journal of Danish Archaeology* 5, 31–61.

Anderson, D.D. 1990. *Lang Rongrien Rockshelter: A Pleistocene–Early Holocene Archaeological Site from Krabi, Southwestern Thailand.* Philadelphia: The University Museum, University of Pennsylvania.

Anderson, D.G. & Gillam, J.C. 2000. Paleoindian colonization of the Americas: Implications from an examination of physiography, demography and artifact distribution. *American Antiquity* 65, 43–66.

Anderson, P. 1991. Harvesting of wild cereals during the Natufian as seen from the experimental cultivation and harvest of wild einkorn wheat and microwear analysis of stone tools. In *The Natufian Culture in the Levant* (eds. O. Bar-Yosef & F.R. Valla), pp. 521–6. Ann Arbor, MI: International Monographs in Prehistory.

Andresen, J.M., Byrd, B.F., Elson, M.D., McGuire, R.H., Mendoza, R.G., Staski, E. & White, J.P. 1981. The deer hunters: Star Carr reconsidered. *World Archaeology* 13, 31–46.

Andrews, M.V., Beck, R.B., Birks, H.J.B., Gilbertson, D.D. & Switsur, V.R. 1987. The past and present vegetation of Oronsay and Colonsay. In *Excavations on Oronsay* (ed. P. Mellars), pp. 52–77. Edinburgh: Edinburgh University Press.

Asouti, E. & Fairbairn, A. 2001. Subsistence economy in Central Anatolia during the Neolithic: The archaeobotanical evidence. In *The Neolithic of Central Anatolia* (eds. F. Gerard & L. Thissen), pp. 181–92. Istanbul: Yayinlari.

Atkinson, T.C., Briffa, K.R., & Coope, G.R. 1987. Seasonal temperatures in Britain during the past 22,000 years, reconstructed using beetle remains. *Nature* 325, 587–92.

Audouze, F. 1987. The Paris Basin in Magdalenian times. In *The Pleistocene Old World* (ed. O. Soffer), pp. 183–200. New York: Plenum Press.

Audouze, F. & Enloe, J. 1991. Subsistence strategies and economy in the Magdalenian of the Paris Basin, France. In *The Late Glacial in North-West Europe: Human Adaptation and Environmental Change at the End of the Pleistocene* (eds, N. Barton, A.J. Roberts & D.A. Roe), pp. 63–71. London: Council for British Archaeology, Research Report No. 77.

Bader, N.O. 1993a. Tell Maghzaliyah: An early Neolithic site in northern Iraq. In *Early Stages in the Evolution of Mesopotamian Civilization. Soviet Excavations in Northern Iraq* (eds. N. Yoffee & J.J. Clarke), pp. 7–40. Tucson: University of Arizona Press.

Bader, N.O. 1993b. Summary of the Earliest Agriculturalists of Northern Mesopotamia (1989). In *Early Stages in the Evolution of Mesopotamian Civilization. Soviet Excavations in Northern Iraq* (eds. N. Yoffee & J.J. Clarke), pp. 63–71. Tucson: University of Arizona Press.

Bader, N.O. 1993c. The early agricultural settlement of Tell Sotto. In *Early Stages in the Evolution of Mesopotamian Civilization. Soviet Excavations in Northern Iraq* (eds. N. Yoffee & J.J. Clarke), pp. 41–54. Tucson: University of Arizona Press.

Bader, N.O. 1993d. Results of the excavations at the early agricultural site of Kültepe in northern Iraq. In *Early Stages in the Evolution of Mesopotamian Civilization. Soviet Excavations in Northern Iraq* (eds. N. Yoffee & J.J. Clarke), pp. 55–61. Tucson: University of Arizona Press.

Bahn, P. 1984. *Pyrenean Prehistory.* Warminster: Aris & Phillips.

Bahn, P. 1991. Dating the first Americans. *New Scientist* 131, 26–8.

Bahn, P. & Couraud, C. 1984. Azilian pebbles: An unsolved mystery. *Endeavour* 8, 156–8.

Bahn, P. & Vertut, J. 1997. *Journey Through the Ice Age.* London: Weidenfeld & Nicolson.

Bailey, R., Head, G., Jerike, M., Owen, B., Rechtman, R. & Zechenter, E. 1989. Hunting and gathering in the tropical rainforest: Is it possible? *American Anthropologist* 91, 59–82.

Baird, D., Garrard, A., Martin, L. & Wright, K. 1992. Prehistoric environment and settlement in the Azraq basin: An interim report on the 1989 excavation season. *Levant* XXIV, 1-31.

Balkan-Atli, Binder, D., Cauvin, M.C. 1999. Obsidian: Sources, workshops and trade in Central Anatolia. In *Neolithic in Turkey. The Cradle of Civilization, New Discoveries* (eds. M. Özdoğan & N. Başgelen), pp. 133–46. Istanbul: Arkeoloji ve Sanat Yayinlari.

Bamforth, D.R. 1988. *Ecology and Human Organization on the Great Plains.* New York: Plenum Press.

Banning, E.B. & Byrd, B.F. 1987. Houses and changing residential unit: Domestic architecture at PPNB 'Ain Ghazal. *Proceedings of the Prehistoric Society* 53, 309–25.

Banning, E.B., Rahimi, D., & Siggers, J. 1994. The late Neolithic of the southern Levant: Hiatus, settlement shift or observer bias? The perspective from Wadi Ziqlab. *Paléorient* 20, 151–64.

Bard, E., Hamelin, B., & Fairbanks, R.G. 1990. U-Th ages obtained by mass spectrometry in corals from Barbados: Sea level during the past 130,000 years. *Nature* 346, 456–8.

Barham, A.J. & Harris, D.R. 1983. Prehistory and palaeoecology of Torres Strait. In *Quaternary Coastlines and Marine Archaeology: Towards a Prehistory of Land Bridges and Continental Shelves* (eds. P.M. Masters & N.C. Fleming), pp. 529–57. London: Academic Press.

Barham, A.J. & Harris, D.R. 1985. Relict field systems in the Torres Strait region. In *Prehistoric Agriculture in the Tropics* (ed. I.S.

Farrington), pp. 247–83. Oxford: British Archaeological Reports, International Series, 232.

Barich, B.E. 1987. *Archaeology and Environment in the Libyan Sahara. The Excavations in the Tadrat Acacus, 1978–83.* Oxford: British Archaeological Reports, International Series 368.

Barich, B.E. 1992. Holocene communities of western and central Sahara: A reappraisal. In *New Lights on the Northeast African Past* (eds. F. Klees & R. Kuper), pp. 185–204. Africa Praehistorica 5. Köln: Heinrich-Barth Institut.

Baring-Gould, S. 1905. *A Book of the Riviera.* London: Methuen.

Barker, G. 1985. *Prehistoric Farming in Europe.* Cambridge: Cambridge University Press.

Barnes, G. & Reynolds, T. 1984. The Palaeolithic of Japan: A Review. *Proceedings of the Prehistoric Society* 50, 49–62.

Baruch, U. & Bottema, S. 1991. Palynological evidence for climatic changes in the Levant ca. 17,000–9,000 BP. In *The Natufian Culture in the Levant* (eds. O. Bar-Yosef & F. Valla), pp. 11–20. Ann Arbor, MI: International Monographs in Prehistory.

Barut, S. 1994. Middle and Later Stone Age lithic technology and land use in East African savannas. *African Archaeological Review* 12, 43–70.

Bar-Yosef, D.E. 1989. Late Palaeolithic and Neolithic marine shells in the southern Levant as cultural markers. In *Shell Bead Conference* (ed. C.F. Hayes), pp. 167–74. Rochester, NY: Rochester Museum and Science Centre.

Bar-Yosef, D.E. 1991. Changes in the selection of marine shells from the Natufian to the Neolithic. In *The Natufian Culture in the Levant* (eds. O. Bar-Yosef & F. Valla), pp. 629–36. Ann Arbor, MI: International Monographs in Prehistory.

Bar-Yosef, O. 1991. The archaeology of the Natufian layer at Hayonim Cave. In *The Natufian Culture in the Levant* (eds. O. Bar-Yosef & F. Valla), pp. 81–93. Ann Arbor, MI: International Monographs in Prehistory.

Bar-Yosef, O. 1996. The walls of Jericho: An alternative explanation. *Current Anthropology* 27, 157–62.

Bar-Yosef, O. 1998a. The Natufian culture in the Levant, theshold to the origins of agriculture. *Evolutionary Anthropology* 6, 159–77.

Bar-Yosef, O. 1998b. Jordan prehistory: A view from the west. In *The Prehistoric Archaeology of Jordan* (ed. D.O. Henry), pp. 162–74. Oxford: British Archaeological Reports, International Series, 705.

Bar-Yosef, O. & Alon, D. 1988. Excavations in Nahal Hemar cave. *'Atiqot* 18, 1–30.

Bar-Yosef, O. & Belfer-Cohen, A. 1989. The origins of sedentism and farming communities in the Levant. *Journal of World Prehistory* 3, 477–98.

Bar-Yosef, O. & Belfer-Cohen, A. 1998. Natufian imagery in perspective. *Rivista di Scienze Preistoriche* XLII, 247–63.

Bar-Yosef, O. & Belfer-Cohen, A. 1999. Encoding information: Unique Natufian objects from Hayonim Cave, western Galilee, Israel. *Antiquity* 73, 402–10.

Bar-Yosef, O. & Gopher, A. 1997. Discussion. In *An Early Neolithic Village in the Jordan Valley. Part I: The Archaeology of Netiv Hagdud* (eds. O. Bar-Yosef & A. Gopher), pp. 247–66. Cambridge, MA: Peabody Museum of Archaeology and Ethnology, Harvard University.

Bar-Yosef, O. & Gopher, A. (eds.) 1997. *An Early Neolithic Village in the Jordan Valley. Part I. The Archaeology of Netiv Hagdud.* Cambridge, MA: Peabody Museum of Archaeology and Ethnology, Harvard University.

Bar-Yosef, O., Gopher, A. & Nadel, D. 1987. The 'Hagdud Truncation' – a new tool type from the Sultanian industry at Netiv Hagdud, Jordan Valley. *Mitekufat Haeven* 20, 151–7.

Bar-Yosef, O. & Meadow, R.H. 1995. The origins of agriculture in the Near East. In *Last Hunters-First Farmers: New Perspectives on the Transition to Agriculture* (eds. T.D. Price & A.B. Gebauer), pp. 39–94. Santa Fe, NM: School of American Research Press.

Bar-Yosef, O. & Schick, T. 1989. Early Neolithic organic remains from Nahal Hemar Cave. *National Geographic Research* 5, 176–90.

Bar-Yosef, O. & Valla, F.R. (eds.) 1991. *The Natufian Culture in the Levant.* Ann Arbor, MI: International Monographs in Prehistory.

Basak, B. 1997. Microlithic sites in the Tarafeni Valley, Midnapur District, West Bengal: A discussion. *Man and Environment* XXII, 12–28.

Baxter Riley, E. 1923. Dorro head hunters. *Man* 23, 33–5.

Bayliss-Smith, T. 1996. People–plant interactions in the New Guinea highlands: Agricultural heartland or horticultural backwater? In *The Origin and Spread of Agriculture and Pastoralism in Eurasia* (ed. D.R. Harris), pp. 499–523. London: University College London Press.

Beck, C. & Jones, G.T. 1997. The terminal Pleistocene/Early Holocene archaeology of the Great Basin. *Journal of World Prehistory* 11, 161–236.

Belfer-Cohen A. 1988. The Natufian graveyard in Hayonim Cave. *Paléorient* 14, 297–308.

Belfer-Cohen, A. 1991. Art items from layer B, Hayonim Cave: A case study of art in a Natufian context. In *The Natufian Culture in the Levant* (eds. O. Bar-Yosef & F.R. Valla), pp. 569–88. Ann Arbor, MI: International Monographs in Prehistory.

Belfer-Cohen, A. 1995. Rethinking social stratification in the Natufian culture: The evidence from burials. In *The Archaeology of Death in the Ancient Near East* (eds. S. Campbell & A. Green), pp. 9–16. Oxford: Oxbow Books, Monograph No. 51.

Belfer-Cohen, A., Schepartz, A. & Arensburg, B. 1991. New biological data for the Natufian populations in Israel. In *The Natufian Culture in the Levant* (eds. O. Bar-Yosef & F. Valla), pp.

411–24. Ann Arbor, MI: International Monographs in Prehistory.

Belitzky, S. & Nadel, D. 2002. The Ohalo II Prehistoric camp (19.5 Ky): New evidence for environmental and tectonic changes at the Sea of Galilee. *Geoarchaeology* 17, 453–64.

Bellwood, P. 1996. The origin and spread of agriculture in the Indo-Pacific region: gradualism and diffusion or revolution and colonisation. In *The Origin and Spread of Agriculture and Pastoralism in Eurasia* (ed. D.R. Harris), pp. 465–98. London: University College London Press.

Bellwood, P. 1997 *Prehistory of the Indo-Malaysian Archipelago*. Rev. ed. Honolulu: University of Hawaii Press.

Beltrán, A. 1999. *The Cave of Altamira*. New York: Harry N. Abrams Inc.

Bender, B. 1978. Gatherer-hunter to farmer: A social perspective. *World Archaeology* 10, 204–22.

Bennike, P. 1995. *Palaeopathology of Danish Skeletons*. Copenhagen: Akademisk Forlag.

Benze, B.F. 2001. Archaeological evidence of teosinte domestication from Guilá Naquitz, Oaxaca. *Proceedings of the National Academy of Sciences* 98, 2104–6.

Berreman, G. 1999. The Tasaday controversy. In *The Cambridge Encyclopedia of Hunters and Gatherers* (eds. R.B. Lee & R. Daly), pp. 457–64. Cambridge: Cambridge University Press.

Betts, A. 1989. The Pre-Pottery Neolithic B in eastern Jordan. *Paléorient* 15, 147–53.

Betts, A. 1998. The Black Desert survey. Prehistoric sites and subsistence strategies in eastern Jordan. In *Prehistory of Jordan. The State of Research in 1986* (eds. A. Garrard & H. Gebel), pp. 369–91. Oxford: British Archaeological Reports, International Series 396.

Binford, L. 1968. Post-Pleistocene adaptations. In *New Perspectives in Archaeology* (eds. S. Binford & L. Binford), pp. 313–42. Chicago: Aldine.

Binford, L. 1978. *Nunamiut Ethnoarchaeology*. New York: Academic Press.

Bird, J.B. 1938. Antiquity and migrations of the early inhabitants of Patagonia. *Geographical Review* 28, 250–75.

Bird-David, N. 1999. The Nayaka of the Wynaad, South India. In *The Cambridge Encyclopedia of Hunters and Gatherers* (eds. R.B. Lee & R. Daly), pp. 257–60. Cambridge: Cambridge University Press.

Birdsell, J.B. 1958. On population structure in generalized hunting and collecting populations. *Evolution* 12, 189–205.

Birket-Smith, K. 1959. *The Eskimos*. 2nd edn. London: Methuen & Co. Ltd.

Bishop, J.F. 1899. *The Yangtze River and Beyond*. London: John Murray.

Björck, S. 1995. Late Weichselian to Early Holocene development of the Baltic sea – with implications for coastal settlement in the southern Baltic region. In *Man & Sea in the Mesolithic* (ed. A. Fischer), pp. 23–34. Oxford: Oxbow Monograph 53.

Blench, R.M. & K.C. MacDonald, (eds) 2000. *The Origins and Development of African Livestock. Archaeology, Genetics, Linguistics and Ethnography*. London: University College London Press.

Bokelmann, K. 1991. Some new thoughts on old data on humans and reindeer in the Ahrensburgian Tunnel Valley in Schleswig-Holstein, Germany. In *The Late Glacial in North-West Europe: Human Adaptation and Environmental Change, at the End of the Pleistocene* (eds. N. Barton, A.J. Roberts & D.A. Roe), pp. 72–81 London: Council for British Archaeology, Research Report No. 77.

Bonatto, S.L. & Salzano, F.M. 1997. Diversity and age of the four major haplogroups, and their implications for the peopling of the New World. *American Journal of Human Genetics* 61, 1413–23.

Bonnichsen, R. & Gentry Steele, D. 1984. Introducing First American Research. In *Method and Theory for Investigating the Peopling of the Americas* (eds. R. Bonnichsen and D. Gentry Steele), pp. 1–6. Corvallis, OR: Centre for the Study of the First Americans.

Bonsall, C. (ed.) 1989. *The Mesolithic in Europe*. Edinburgh: Edinburgh University Press.

Borlaug, N. 2000. Ending world hunger. The promise of biotechnology and the threat of anti-science zealotry. *Plant Physiology* 124, 487–90.

Borrero, L.A. 1996. The Pleistocene-Holocene transition in southern South America. In *Humans at the End of the Ice Age* (eds. L.G. Straus, B.V. Eriksen, J.M. Erlandson & D.R. Yesner), pp. 339–54. New York: Plenum Press.

Bosinski, G. 1984. The mammoth engravings of the Magdalenian site of Gönnersdorf (Rhineland, Germany). In *La Contribution de la Zoologie et de l'Ethologie a l'Interprétation de l'Art des Peuples Chasseurs Préhistorique* (eds. H.-G. Bandi et al.), pp. 295–322. Fribourg: Editions Universitaires.

Bosinski, G. 1991. The representation of female figures in the Rhineland Magdalenian. *Proceedings of the Prehistoric Society* 57, 51 -64.

Bosinski, G. & Fischer, G. 1974. *Die Menschendarstellungen von Gönnersdorf der Ausgrabung von 1968*. Steiner: Wiesbaden.

Boucher, D.H. 1999. *The Paradox of Plenty: Hunger in a Bountiful World*. Oakland, CA: Food First Books.

Bowdler, S. 1984. Hunter Hill, Hunter Island. *Terra Australis* 8, Canberra: Prehistory Department, Australian National University.

Bowers, J.K. & Chesire, P. 1983. *Agriculture, The Countryside and Land Use*. London: Methuen.

Bowman, S. 1990. *Radiocarbon Dating*. London: British Museum Publications.

Boyd, B. 1995. Houses and hearths, pits and burials: Natufian mortuary practices at Mallaha (Eyan), Upper Jordan Valley. In *The Archaeology of Death in the Ancient Near East* (eds. S. Campbell & A. Green), pp. 17–23. Oxford: Oxbow Books, Monograph No. 51.

Bradley, D.G., MacHugh, D.E., Cunningham, P., Loftus, R.T. 1996. Mitochrondial diversity and the origins of African and European cattle. *Proceedings of the National Academy of Sciences USA* 93, 5131–5.

Bradley, R. 1997. Domestication as state of mind. *Analecta Praehistorica Leidensa* 29, 13–17.

Bradley, R. 1998. *The Significance of Monuments.* London: Routledge.

Braidwood, L., Braidwood, R., Howe, B., Reed, C. & Watson, P.J. (eds.) 1983. *Prehistoric Archaeology along the Zagros Flanks.* Chicago: The University of Chicago Oriental Institute Publication, Vol. 105.

Brantingham, P.J., Olsen, J.W. & Schaller, G.B. 2001. Lithic assemblages from the Chang Tang region, Northern Tibet. *Antiquity* 75, 319–27.

Bratlund, B. 1991. A study of hunting lesions containing flint fragments on reindeer bones at Stellmoor, Schleswig-Holstein, Germany. In *The Late Glacial in North-West Europe: Human Adaptation and Environmental Change at the End of the Pleistocene* (eds. N. Barton, A.J. Roberts & D.A. Roe), pp. 193–207. London: Council for British Archaeology, Research Report No. 77.

Bratlund, B. 1996. Hunting strategies in the late glacial of northern Europe: A survey of the faunal evidence. *Journal of World Prehistory* 10, 1–48.

Breuil, H. 1952. *Four Hundred Centuries of Cave Art.* Centre d'Etudes et de Documentation Préhistoriques: Montignac.

Brewer, D.J. 1989. *Fishermen, Hunters and Herders. Zooarchaeology in the Fayum, Egypt (ca. 8200–5000 bp).* Oxford: British Archaeological Reports, International Series 478.

Brey, H. & Muller, C. 1992. *Cyprus, Insight Guide.* London: APA Publications (HK) Ltd.

Brinch Petersen. E. 1990. Nye grave fra jægerstenaldren, Strøby Egede og Vedbæk. *Nationalmuseets Arbefdsmark* 1990, 19–33.

Broecker, W.S. & Denton, G.H. 1990. What drives glacial cycles? *Scientific American,* Jan. 1990, 43–50.

Broecker, W.S., Kennett, J.P., Flower, B.P., Teller, J.T., Trumboe, S., Bonani, G. & Wolfli, W. 1989. Routing of meltwater from the Laurentide ice sheet during the Younger Dryas cold episode. *Nature* 341, 318–21.

Broodbank, C. & Strasser, T.F. 1991. Migrant farmers and the Neolithic colonization of Crete. *Antiquity* 65, 233–45.

Brooks, A.S. & Robertshaw, P. 1990. The glacial maximum in tropical Africa: 22,000–12,000 BP. In *The World at 18,000 BP, Vol. Two, Low Latitudes* (eds. C. Gamble & O. Soffer), pp. 121–69. London: Unwin Hyman.

Brosius, J.P. 1986. River, forest and mountain: The Penan Gang landscape. *Sarawak Museum Journal* 36, 173–84.

Brosius, J.P. 1991. Foraging in tropical rainforests: The case of the Penan of Sarawak, east Malaysia (Borneo). *Human Ecology* 19, 123–50.

Brosius, J.P. 1999. The Western Penan of Borneo. In *The Cambridge Encyclopedia of Hunters and Gatherers* (ed. R.B. Lee & R. Daly), pp. 312–16. Cambridge: Cambridge University Press.

Brothwell, D. 1975. Possible evidence of a cultural practice affecting head growth in some Late Pleistocene East Asian and Australasian populations. *Journal of Archaeological Science* 2, 75–77.

Brothwell, D. & Shaw, T. 1971. A late Upper Pleistocene proto-West African Negro from Nigeria. *Man* (N.S.) 6, 221–7.

Browman, D.L. 1989. Origins and development of Andean pastoralism: an overview of the past 6000 years. In *The Walking Larder* (ed. J. Clutton-Brock), pp. 256–68. London: Unwin Hyman.

Brown, J.A. & Vierra, R.K. 1983. What happened in the Middle Archaic? Introduction to an ecological approach to Koster Site archaeology. In *Archaic Hunters and Gatherers in the American Midwest* (eds. J.L. Phillips & J.A. Brown), pp. 165–96. New York: Academic Press.

Brown. M.D., Hosseini, S.H., Torroni, A., Bandelt, H.-S., Allen, J.C., Schurr, T.G., Scozzari, R., Cruciani, F. & Wallace, D.C. 1998. MtDNA haplogroup X: an ancient link between Europe/West Asia and North America? *American Journal of Human Genetics* 63, 1852–61.

Brown, P. 1981. Artificial cranial deformation: a component in the variation in Pleistocene Australian Aboriginal crania. *Archaeology in Oceania* 16, 156–67.

Bryan, A.L. 1991. The fluted-point tradition in the Americas – one of several adaptations to Late Pleistocene American environments. In *Clovis: Origins and Adaptations* (eds. R. Bonnichsen & K.L. Turnmire), pp. 15–34. Corvallis, OR: Centre for the Study of the First Americans.

Buchanan, W.F. 1988. *Shellfsh in Prehistoric Diet, Elands Bay, S.W. Cape Coast, South Africa.* Oxford: British Archaeological Reports, International Series 455.

Buikstra, J.E. 1981. Mortuary practices, palaeodemography and paleopathology: a case study from the Koster site (Illinois). In *Archaeology of Death* (eds. R. Chapman, I. Kinnes & K. Randsborg), pp. 123–32. Cambridge: Cambridge University Press.

Bunimovitz, S. & Barkai, R. 1996. Ancient bones and modern myths: Ninth millennium BC hippopotamus hunters at Akrotiri Aetokremnos, Cyprus. *Journal of Mediterranean Archaeology* 9, 85–96.

Bunn, H.T., Bartram, L.E., & Kroll, E.M. 1988. Variability in bone assemblage formation from Hadza hunting, scavenging, and carcass processing. *Journal of Anthropological Archaeology* 7, 412–57.

Bunting, M.J., Davies, A., Edwards, K. & Keith-Lucas, M. 2000. A palaeoecological investigation of the vegetational and environmental history of the Loch Gorm area, Northwest Islay. In *Hunter-Gatherer Landscape Archaeology, The Southern Hebrides Mesolithic Project 1988–98*, Vol. 1. (ed. S. Mithen), pp. 137–48. Cambridge: McDonald Institute for Archaeological Research.

Burov, G.M. 1998. The use of vegetable materials in the Mesolithic of Northeast Europe. In *Harvesting the Sea, Farming the Forest* (eds. M. Zvelebil, R. Dennell & L. Domańska), pp. 53–64. Sheffield: Sheffield Academic Press.

Byrd, B.F. 1989. *The Natufian Encampment at Beidha: Late Pleistocene Adaptations in the Southern Levant.* Aarhus: Denmark, Jutland Archaeological Society Publications, Vol. 23.

Byrd, B.F. 1994. Public and private, domestic and corporate: The emergence of the southwest Asian village. *American Antiquity* 59, 639–66.

Byrd, B.F. 2000. Households in transition: Neolithic social organization within southwest Asia. In *Life in Neolithic Farming Communities. Social Organization, Identity and Differentiation* (ed, I. Kuijt), pp. 63–102. New York: Kluwer/Plenum Publications.

Byrd, B.F. & Banning, E.B. 1988. Southern Levantine pier houses: Intersite architectural patterning during the Pre-Pottery Neolithic B. *Paléorient* 14, 65–72.

Byrd, B.F. & Colledge, S.M. 1991. Early Natufian occupation along the edge of the southern Jordanian steppe. In *The Natufian Culture in the Levant* (eds. O. Bar-Yosef & F. Valla), pp. 265–76. Ann Arbor, MI: International Monographs in Prehistory.

Byrd, B.F. & Monahan, C.M. 1995. Death, mortuary ritual and Natufian social structure. *Journal of Anthropological Archaeology* 14, 251–87.

Cagnolo, I.M.C. 1933. *The Akikuyu, Their Customs, Traditions and Folklore.* Nyeri: Catholic Mission of the Consolata Fathers.

Campana, D.V. & Crabtree, P.J. 1990. Communal hunting in the Natufian of the southern Levant: The social and economic implications. *Journal of Mediterranean Archaeology* 3, 223–43.

Campbell, I.D., Campbell, C. Apps, M.J., Rutter, N.W., Bush, A.B.G. 1998. Late Holocene – 1500-year climatic periodicities and their implications. *Geology* 26, 471–3.

Campbell, J.B. 1977. *The Upper Palaeolithic of Britain. A Study of Man and Nature, during the Late Ice Age.* Oxford: Clarendon Press.

Cannon, A. 1996. The Early Namu archaeofauna. In *Early Human Occupation in British Columbia* (eds. R.L. Carlson & L.D. Bona), pp. 103–10. Vancouver: University of British Columbia Press.

Cannon, A. 2000. Settlement and sea-levels on the central coast of British Columbia: evidence from shell midden cores. *American Antiquity* 65, 67–77.

Caratini, C. & Tissot, C. 1988. Palaeogeographic evolution of the Mahakom Delta in Kalimanatan, Indonesia. *Review of Palaeobotany and Palynology* 55, 217–28.

Carlson, R.L. 1996. Early Namu. In *Early Human Occupation in British Columbia* (eds. R.L. Carlson & L.D. Bona), pp. 83–102. Vancouver: University of British Columbia Press.

Cartwright, C. & Parkington, J.E. 1997. The wood charcoal assemblages from Elands Bay Cave, southwestern Cape: Principles, procedures and preliminary interpretation. *South African Archaeological Bulletin* 52, 59–72.

Cassells, E.S. 1983. *The Archaeology of Colorado.* Boulder, CO: Johnson Publishing.

Caton-Thompson, G. & Gardner, E.W. 1934. *The Desert Fayum.* London: The Royal Anthropological Institute of Great Britain and Ireland.

Cauvin, J. 1977. Les fouilles de Mureybet (1971–1974) et leur significance pour les origines de la sedentarisation au Proche-Orient. *Annual of the American Schools of Oriental Research* 44, 19–48.

Cauvin, J. 2000. *The Birth of the Gods and the Origins of Agriculture.* Cambridge: Cambridge University Press.

Cavalli-Sforza, L.L., Menozzi, P., & Piazza, A. 1994. *History and Geography of Human Genes.* Princeton, NY: Princeton University Press.

Cavalli-Sforza, L.L. & Minch, E. 1997. Paleolithic and Neolithic lineages in the European mitochondrial gene pool. *American Journal of Human Genetics* 19, 233–57.

Cessford, C. 2001. A new dating sequence for Çatalhöyük. *Antiquity* 75, 717–25.

Chagnon, N. 1988. Life histories, blood revenge and warfare in a tribal population. *Science* 239, 985–92.

Chagnon, N. 1997. *Yanomamö.* Oxford: Harcourt Brace (5th edn).

Chakrabarti, D. 1999. *India, An Archaeological History.* Oxford: Oxford University Press .

Champion, S. 1998. Women in British Archaeology, visible and invisible. In *Excavating Women. A History of Women in European Archaeology* (eds. M. Diaz-Andreu & M.L.S. Sørenson), pp. 175–97. London: Routledge.

Chapman, J. 1989. Demographic trends in neothermal south-east Europe. In *The Mesolithic in Europe* (ed. C. Bonsall), pp. 500–15. Edinburgh: John Donald.

Charles, R. 1993. Evidence for faunal exploitation during the Belgian lateglacial: recent research on the Dupont collection from the Trou de Chaleux. In *Exploitation des Animaux Sauvages à Travers le Temps*, pp. 103–14. Juan-les-Pins: XIIIe Recontres Internationales d'Archéologie et d'Histoire d'Antibes IVe Colloque international de l'Homme et l'Animal, Société de Recherche Inter-disciplinaire Éditions APDCA.

Charles, R. 1996. Back in the north: The radiocarbon evidence for the human recolonisation of the north-west Ardennes after the last glacial maximum. *Proceedings of the Prehistoric Society* 62, 1–19.

Charles, R. & Jacobi, R.M. 1994. The lateglacial fauna from the Robin Hood Cave, Creswell

Crags: A re-assessment. *Oxford Journal of Archaeology* 13, 1–32.

Chase, P. 1989. How different was Middle Palaeolithic subsistence? A zooarchaeological approach to the Middle Upper Palaeolithic transition. In *The Human Revolution* (eds. P. Mellars & C. Stringer), pp. 321–37. Edinburgh: Edinburgh University Press.

Chatters, J.C. 2000. The recovery and first analysis of an early Holocene human skeleton from Kennewick, Washington. *American Antiquity* 65, 291–316.

Chattopadhyaya, U. 1999. Settlement pattern and the spatial organization of subsistence and mortuary practices in the Mesolithic Ganges Valley, North-Central India. *World Archaeology* 27, 461–76.

Chatwin, B. 1977. *In Patagonia.* London: Jonathan Cape.

Chen, C. & Olsen, J.W. 1990. China at the last glacial maximum. In *The World at 18,000 BP, Vol. 1: High Latitudes* (eds. O. Soffer & C. Gamble), pp. 276–95. London: Unwin Hyman.

Childe, V.G. 1925. *The Dawn of European Civilisation.* London: Kegan Paul.

Childe, V.G. 1928. *The Most Ancient Near East. The Oriental Prelude to European Prehistory.* London: Kegan Paul.

Childe, V.G. 1929. *The Danube in Prehistory.* Oxford: Clarendon Press.

Childe, V.G. 1958. *The Prehistory of European Society.* London: Penguin.

Chippindale, C., Smith, B. & Taçon, P. 2000. Visions of dynamic power: Archaic rock-paintings, altered states of consciousness and 'clever men' in Western Arnhem Land (NT), Australia. *Cambridge Archaeological Journal* 10, 63–101.

Chippindale, C. & Taçon, P. 1998. The many ways of dating Arnhem Land rock art, north Australia. In *The Archaeology of Rock Art* (eds. C. Chippendale & P. Taçon), pp. 90–111. Cambridge: Cambridge University Press.

Chippindale, C. & Taçon, P. (eds) 1998. *The Archaeology of Rock Art.* Cambridge: Cambridge University Press.

Christensen, C., Fischer, A., & Mathiassen, D.R. 1997. The great sea rise in the Storebælt. In *The Danish Storebælt since the Ice Age* (eds. L. Pedersen, A. Fischer & B. Aaby), pp. 45–54. Copenhagen: A/S Storebælt Fixed Link.

Cinq-Mars, J. 1979. Bluefish Cave I: A Late Pleistocene Eastern Beringian cave deposit in the northern Yukon. *Canadian Journal of Archaeology* 3, 1–33.

Clark, G.A. & Neeley, M. 1987. Social differentiation in European Mesolithic burial data. In *Mesolithic North West Europe: Recent Trends* (eds. P. Rowley-Conwy, M. Zvelebil & P. Blankholm), pp. 121–27. Sheffield: Department of Archaeology & Prehistory.

Clark, J.D. & Brandt, S.A. (eds.) 1984. *From Hunters to Farmers: Causes and Consequences of Food Production in Africa.* Berkeley: University of Los Angeles Press.

Clark, J.G.D. 1932. *The Mesolithic Age in Britain.* Cambridge: Cambridge University Press.

Clark, J.G.D. 1936. *The Mesolithic Settlement of Northern Europe.* Cambridge: Cambridge University Press.

Clark, J.G.D. 1954. *Excavations at Star Carr.* Cambridge: Cambridge University Press.

Clark, J.G.D. 1972. *Star Carr: A Case Study in Bioarchaeology.* Addison-Wesley module in Anthropology 10.

Clark, J.G.D. 1975. *The Earlier Stone Age Settlement of Scandinavia.* Cambridge: Cambridge University Press.

Clarke, D. 1976. Mesolithic Europe: The Economic Basis. In *Problems in Economic and Social Archaeology* (eds. G. de G. Sieveking, I.H. Longworth & K.E. Wilson), pp. 449–81. London: Duckworth.

Close, A.E. 1996. Plus ça change: The Pleistocene-Holocene transition in Northeast Africa. In *Humans at the End of the Ice Age* (eds. L.G. Straus, B.V. Eriksen, J.M. Erlandson & D.R. Yesner), pp. 43–60. New York: Plenum Press.

Close, A.E. & Wendorf, F. 1990. North Africa at 18,000 BP. In *The World at 18,000 BP, Vol. Two, Low Latitudes* (eds. C. Gamble & O. Soffer), pp. 41–57. London: Unwin Hyman.

Close, A.E. & Wendorf, F. 1992. The beginnings of food production in the Eastern Sahara. In *Transitions to Agriculture in Prehistory* (eds. A. Gebauer & T.D. Price) pp. 63–72. Madison, WI: Prehistory Press.

Clutton-Brock, J. 1987. *A Natural History of domesticated Animals.* Cambridge: Cambridge University Press & British Museum.

Clutton-Brock, J. 1989. Cattle in ancient North Africa. In *The Walking Larder: Patterns of Domestication, Pastoralism and Predation* (ed. J. Clutton-Brock), pp. 200–6. London: Unwin Hyman.

Clutton-Brock, J. 1995. Origins of the dog: Domestication and early history. In *The Domestic Dog: Its Evolution, Behaviour and Interactions with People* (ed. J. Serpell), pp. 7–20. Cambridge: Cambridge University Press.

Clutton-Brock, J. 2000. Cattle, sheep, and goats south of the Sahara: An archaeozoological perspective. In *The Origins and Development of African Livestock* (eds. R.M. Blench & K.C. MacDonald), pp. 30–8. London: University College London.

Cohen, M. 1977. *The Food Crisis in Prehistory.* New Haven, CT: Yale University Press.

Coles, B. 1998. Doggerland: A speculative survey. *Proceedings of the Prehistoric Society* 64, 45–81.

Coles, J.M. & Orme, B.J. 1983. Homo sapiens or *Castor fibre*? *Antiquity* LVII, 95–101.

Colinvaux, P.A. 1986. Plain thinking on Bering land bridge vegetation and mammoth populations. *Quarterly Review of Archaeology* 7, 8–9.

Colinvaux, P.A., De Oliveira, P.E. & Bush, M.B. (2000). Amazonian and neotropical plant communities on glacial time-scales: The failure of the aridity and refuge hypotheses. *Quaternary Science Reviews* 19, 141–69.

Cook, J. 1991. Preliminary report on marked human bones from the 1986–1987 excavations at Gough's Cave, Somerset, England. In *The Late Glacial in North-West Europe: Human Adaptation and Environmental Change at the End of the Pleistocene* (eds. N. Barton, A.J. Roberts & D.A. Roe), pp. 160–8. London: Council for British Archaeology, Research Report No. 77.

Cope, C. 1991. Gazelle hunting strategies in the Natufian. In *The Natufian Culture in the Levant* (eds. O. Bar-Yosef & F. Valla), pp. 341–58. Ann Arbor, MI: International Monographs in Prehistory.

Cordell, L. 1985. *Prehistory of the Southwest*. New York: Academic Press.

Cordy, J.-M. 1991. Palaeoecology of the late glacial and early postglacial of Belgium and neighbouring areas. In *The Late Glacial in North-West Europe. Human Adaptation and Environmental Change at the End of the Pleistocene* (eds. N. Barton, A.J. Roberts & D.A. Roe), pp. 40–7. London: Council for British Archaeology, Research Report No. 77.

Cosgrove, R. 1995. Late Pleistocene behavioural variation and time trends: the case from Tasmania. *Archaeology in Oceania* 30, 83–104.

Cosgrove, R. 1999. Forty-two degrees south: The archaeology of Late Pleistocene Tasmania. *Journal of World Prehistory* 13, 357–402.

Cosgrove, R. & Allen, J. 2001. Prey choice and hunting strategies in the Late Pleistocene: Evidence from Southwest Tasmania. In *Histories of Old Ages: Essays in Honour of Rhys Jones* (eds. A. Anderson, S. O'Connor & I. Lilley), pp. 397–429. Canberra: Coombs Academic Publishing, Australian National University.

Coudart, A. 1991. Social structure and relationships in prehistoric small-scale sedentary societies: The Bandkeramik groups in Neolithic Europe. In *Between Bands and States* (ed. S.A. Gregg), pp. 395–420. Carbondale: Centre for Archaeological Investigations, Southern Illinois University Occasional Paper No. 9.

Couraud, C. 1985. *L'Art Azilien. Origine – Survivance*. XXe Supplément à Gallia Préhistoire. Paris: CNRS.

Crabtree, P.J., Campana, D.V., Belfer-Cohen, A. & Bar-Yosef, D.E. 1991. First results of the excavations at Salibiya I, Lower Jordan Valley. In *The Natufian Culture in the Levant* (eds. O. Bar-Yosef & F. Valla), pp. 161–72. Ann Arbor, MI: International Monographs in Prehistory.

Crane, N. 1996. *Clear Waters Rising*. London: Penguin.

Crawford. G.W. & Chen S. 1998. The origins of rice agriculture: Recent progress in East Asia. *Antiquity* 72, 858–66.

Currant, A.P., Jacobi, R.M. & Stringer, C.B. 1989. Excavations of Gough's Cave, Somerset, 1986–87. *Antiquity* 63, 131–6.

Dahl, G. 1979. *Suffering Grass. Subsistence and Society of Waso Borano*. Stockholm: Department of Social Anthropology, University of Stockholm.

D'Anglure, B.S. 1990. Nanook, super-male: The polar bear in the imaginary space and social time of the Inuit of the Canadian Arctic. In *Signifying Animals: Human Meaning in the Natural World* (ed. R. Willis), pp. 178–95. London: Unwin Hyman.

Daniel, G. & Renfrew, C. 1988. *The Idea of Prehistory*. Edinburgh: Edinburgh University Press.

Dansgaard, W., White, J.W.C., Johnsen, S.J. (1989). The abrupt termination of the Younger Dryas climatic event. *Nature* 33, 532–4.

Dark, P. 2000. Revised 'absolute' dating of the early Mesolithic site of Star Carr, North Yorkshire, in light of changes in the Early Holocene tree-ring chronology. *Antiquity* 74, 304–7.

Datan, I. 1993. Archaeological Excavations at Gua Sireh (serian) and Lubang Angin (Gunung Mulu National Park). *Sarawak Museum Journal*, Special Monograph No. 6.

Datta, A. 1991. Blade and blade tool assemblages of the Upper Palaeolithic and Mesolithic periods – A case study from the mid-Kasai Valley in the Jhargram sub-division of Midnapur district, West Bengal. *Man and Environment* XVI, 23–31.

Datta, A. 2000. The context and definition of Upper Palaeolithic industries in Panchpir, Orissa, India. *Proceedings of the Prehistoric Society* 66, 47–59.

Davis, S.J.M. & Valla, F.R. 1978. Evidence for the domestication of the dog 12,000 years ago in the Natufian of Israel. *Nature* 276, 608–10.

Dawson, A.G. 1992. *Ice Age Earth*. London: Routledge.

Dawson A.G. & Dawson, S. 2000a. Late Quaternary glaciomarine sedimentation in the Rinns of Islay, Scottish Inner Hebrides and the geological origin of flint nodules. In *Hunter-Gatherer Landscape Archaeology, The Southern Hebrides Mesolithic Project 1988–98, Vol. 1* (ed. S. Mithen), pp. 91–7. Cambridge: McDonald Institute for Archaeological Research.

Dawson, S. & Dawson, A.G. 2000b. Late Pleistocene and Holocene relative sea-level changes in Gruinart, Isle of Islay. In *Hunter-Gatherer Landscape Archaeology, The Southern Hebrides Mesolithic Project 1988–98 Vol. 1* (ed. S. Mithen), pp. 99–113. Cambridge: McDonald Institute for Archaeological Research.

Dawson, A.G., Smith, D.E. & Long, D. 1990. Evidence for a Tsunami from a Mesolithic site in Inverness, Scotland. *Journal of Archaeological Science* 17, 509–12.

Dawson, W.H. 1925. *South Africa. People, Places and Problems*. London: Longmans, Green & Co.

Deacon, H.J. 1976. *Where Hunters Gathered. A Study of Holocene Stone Age People in the Eastern Cape*. South African Archaeological Society Monograph Series 1. Cape Town: Claremont.

Deacon, H.J. 1979. Excavations at Boomplaas Cave – A sequence through the Upper Pleistocene and Holocene in South Africa. *World Archaeology* 10, 241–57.

Deacon, H.J. 1993. Planting an idea: An archaeology of Stone Age gatherers in South Africa. *South African Archaeological Bulletin* 48, 86–93.

Deacon, H.J. 1995. Two Late Pleistocene-Holocene archaeological depositories from the Southern Cape, South Africa. *South African Archaeological Bulletin* 50, 121–31.

Deacon, H.J., Deacon. J., Scholtz, A., Thackeray, J.F., Brink, J.S. & Vogel, J.C. 1984. Correlation of palaeoenvironmental data from the Late Pleistocene and Holocene deposits at Boomplaas Cave, Southern Cape. In *Late Cainozoic Palaeoclimates of the Southern Hemisphere* (ed. J. Vogel), pp. 339–51. Rotterdam: Balkema.

Deacon, J. 1987. Holocene and Pleistocene palaeoclimates in the Western Cape. In *Papers in the Prehistory of the Western Cape, South Africa* (eds. J.E. Parkington & M. Hall), pp. 24–32. Oxford: British Archaeological Reports, International Series 332.

Deacon, J. 1990. Changes in the archaeological record in South Africa at 18,000 BP. In *The World at 18,000 B.P., Vol.: Two Low Latitudes* (eds. C. Gamble & O. Soffer), pp. 170–88. London: Unwin Hyman.

Delpech, F. 1983. *Les Faunas du Paléolithique Supérieur dans le Sud Ouest de la France*. Paris: CNRS.

Dennell, R. 1983. *European Economic Prehistory*. London: Academic Press.

Diamond, J. 1997. *Guns, Germs & Steel*. London: Chatto & Windus.

Dikov, N.N. 1996. The Ushki sites, Kamchatka peninsula. In *American Beginnings* (ed. F. West), pp. 244–50. Chicago: University of Chicago Press.

di Lernia, S. 2001. Dismantling dung: Delayed use of food resources among Early Holocene of the Libyan Sahara. *Journal of Anthropological Archaeology* 20, 408–41.

Dillehay, T.D. 1984. A late ice age settlement in southern Chile. *Scientific American* 251, 106–17.

Dillehay, T.D. 1987. By the banks of the Chinchihuapi. *Natural History* 4/87, 8–12.

Dillehay T.D. 1989. *Monte Verde. A Late Pleistocene Settlement in Chile. 1: Palaeoenvironmental and Site Context*. Washington, DC: Smithsonian Institution Press.

Dillehay, T.D. 1991. Disease ecology and initial human migration. In *The First Americans: Search and Research* (eds. T.D. Dillehay & D.J. Meltzer), pp. 231–64. Boca Raton: CRC Press.

Dillehay, T.D. 1992. Humans and proboscideans at Monte Verde, Chile: Analytical problems and explanatory scenarios. In *Proboscidean and Palaeoindian Interactions* (eds. J.W. Fox, C.B. Smith & K.T. Wilkins), pp. 191–210. Waco, TX: Baylor University Press.

Dillehay, T.D. 1997. *Monte Verde. A Late Pleistocene Settlement in Chile. 2: The Archaeological Context*. Washington, DC: Smithsonian Institution Press.

Dillehay, T.D., Calderon, G.A., Politis, G., Beltrao, M.C. 1992. Earliest hunters and gatherers of South America. *Journal of World Prehistory* 6, 145–204.

Dincauze, D.F. 1993. Fluted points in the eastern forests. In *From Kostenki to Clovis* (eds. O. Soffer & N.D. Praslov), pp. 279–92. New York: Plenum Press.

Dittemore, M. 1983. The soundings at M'lefaat. In *Prehistoric Archaeology along the Zagros Flanks* (eds. L.S. Braidwood, R.J. Braidwood, B. Howe, C.A. Reed & P.J. Watson), pp. 671–92. Chicago: Chicago University Press.

Dodson, J.R., Fullagar, R.K.L., Furby, J.H., Jones, R. & Prosser, I. 1993. Humans and megafauna in a Late Pleistocene environment from Cuddie Springs, northwestern New South Wales. *Archaeology in Oceania* 28, 94–9.

Driver, J.C., Handly, M., Fladmark, K.R., Nelson, D.E., Sullivan, G.M. & Preston, R. 1996. Stratigraphy, radiocarbon dating and culture history of Charlie Lake Cave, British Columbia. *Arctic* 49, 265–77.

Dumont, J.P. 1988. The Tasaday, which and whose? Toward the political economy of an ethnographic sign. *Cultural Anthropology* 3, 261–75.

Dumont, J.V. 1988. *A Microwear Analysis of Selected Artefact Types from the Mesolithic Sites of Star Carr and Mount Sandel*. Oxford: British Archaeological Reports, British Series 187.

Dunbar, J.S. 1991. Resource orientation of Clovis and Suwannee age paleoindian sites in Florida. In *Clovis: Origins and Adaptations* (eds. R. Bonnichsen & K.L. Turnmire), pp. 185–214. Corvallis, OR: Centre for the Study of the First Americans.

Dupree, L. (ed.) 1972. *Prehistoric Research in Afghanistan (1959–1965)*. Philadelphia: Transactions of the American Philosophical Society 62.

Echegaray, G.J. 1963. Nouvelles fouilles à El-Khiam. *Revue Biblique* 70, 94–119.

Edwards, D. & O'Connell, J.F. 1995. Broad spectrum diets in arid Australia. *Antiquity* 69, 769–83.

Edwards, K.J. 2000. Vegetation history of the Southern Inner Hebrides during the Mesolithic period. In *Hunter-Gatherer Landscape Archaeology, The Southern Hebrides Mesolithic Project 1988-98, Vol. 1* (ed. S. Mithen), pp. 115–27. Cambridge: McDonald Institute for Archaeological Research.

Edwards, K.J. & Mithen, S.J. 1995. The colonization of the Hebridean islands of western Scotland: Evidence from the palynological and archaeological records. *World Archaeology* 26, 348–61.

Edwards, P.C. 1989. Problems of recognizing earliest sedentism: The Natufian example. *Journal of Mediterranean Archaeology* 2, 5–48.

Edwards, P.C. 1991. Wadi Hammeh 27: An Early Natufian site at Pella. In *The Natufian Culture in the Levant* (eds. O. Bar-Yosef & F. Valla), pp. 123–48. Ann Arbor, MI: International Monographs in Prehistory.

Edwards, P.C. 2000. Archaeology and environment of the Dead Sea plain: Excavations at the PPNA site of ZAD 2. *ACOR Newsletter* 12.2, 7–9.

Edwards, P.C., Bourke, S.J., Colledge, S.M., Head, J. & Macumber, P.G. 1988. Late Pleistocene prehistory in the Wadi al-Hammeh, Jordan Valley. In *The Prehistory of Jordan* (eds. A.N. Garrard & H.G. Gebel), pp. 525–65. British Archaeological Reports, International Series 396.

Edwards, P.C., Meadows, J., Metzger, M.C. & Sayei, G. 2002. Results from the first season at Zahrat adh-Dhra' 2: A new Pre-Pottery Neolithic A site on the Dead Sea plain in Jordan. *Neo-lithics* 1:02, 11–16.

Ehret, C. 1988. Language change and the material correlates of language and ethnic shift. *Antiquity* 62, 564–74.

Endicott, K. 1999. The Batek of peninsular Malaysia. In *The Cambridge Encyclopedia of Hunters and Gatherers* (ed. R.B. Lee & R. Daly), pp. 298–302. Cambridge: Cambridge University Press.

Endicott, K. & Bellwood, P. 1991. The possibility of independent foraging in the rainforest of peninsular Malaysia. *Human Ecology* 19, 151–85 .

Enghoff, I. 1986. Freshwater fishing from a sea-coast settlement – The Ertebølle locus classicus revisited. *Journal of Danish Archaeology* 5, 62–76.

Enghoff, I. 1989. Fishing from the stone age settlement of Norsminde. *Journal of Danish Archaeology* 8, 41–50.

Enghoff, I. 1994. Freshwater fishing at Ringkloster, with a supplement of marine fish. *Journal of Danish Archaeology* 12, 99–106.

Enloe, J.G., David, F. & Hare, T.S. 1994. Patterns of faunal processing at section 27 of Pincevent: The use of spatial analysis and ethnoarchaeological data in the interpretation of archaeological site structure. *Journal of Anthropological Archaeology* 13, 105–24.

Enoch-Shiloh, D. & Bar-Yosef, O. 1997. Salibiya IX. In *An Early Neolithic Village in the Jordan Valley. Part 1: The Archaeology of Netiv Hagdud* (eds. O. Bar-Yosef & A. Gopher), pp. 13–40. Cambridge, MA: Peabody Museum of Archaeology and Ethnology, Harvard University.

Environment Agency (2000). *The State of the Environment of England and Wales: The Land.* London: The Stationery Office Ltd.

Esin, U. & Harmankaya, S. 1999. Aşıklı. In *Neolithic in Turkey. The Cradle of Civilization, New Discoveries* (eds. M. Özdoğan & N. Başgelen), pp. 115–32. Istanbul: Arkeoloji ve Sanat Yayinlari.

Evans, R.J. 1997. *In Defence of History.* London: Granta.

Fairweather, A.D. & Ralston, I.B. 1993. The

Neolithic timber hall at Balbridie, Grampian region, Scotland: The building, the date and plant macrofossils. *Antiquity* 67, 313–23.

Fermor, P.L. 1986. *Between the Woods and the Water.* London: John Murray.

Fiedel, S.J. 1999. Older than we thought: Implications of corrected dates for Palaeoindians. *American Antiquity* 64, 95–115.

Fiedler, L. & Preuss, J. 1985. Stone tools from the Inner Zaïre Basin (Région de l'equateur, Zaïre). *The African Archaeological Review* 3, 179–87.

Field, J. & Dodson, J. 1999. Late Pleistocene megafauna and archaeology from Cuddie Springs, South-eastern Australia. *Proceedings of the Prehistoric Society* 65, 275–301.

Field, J. et al. (10 authors) 2000. 'Coming back'. Aborigines and archaeologists at Cuddie Springs. *Journal of Public Archaeology* 1, 35–48.

Figgins, J.D. 1927. The antiquity of Man in America. *Natural History* 27, 229–39.

Finlayson, B. 1990. The function of microliths: Evidence from Smittons and Starr, SW Scotland. *Mesolithic Miscellany* 11, 2–6.

Finlayson, B. & Mithen, S.J. 1997. The microwear and morphology of microliths from Gleann Mor, Islay, Scotland. In *Projectile Technology* (ed. H. Knecht), pp. 107–29. New York: Plenum Press.

Finlayson, B. & Mithen, S.J. 2000. The morphology and microwear of microliths from Bolsay Farm and Gleann Mor: A comparative study. In *Hunter-Gatherer Landscape Archaeology, The Southern Hebrides Mesolithic Project 1988–98, Vol 2* (ed. S. Mithen), pp. 589–93. Cambridge: McDonald Institute for Archaeological Research.

Fischer, A. 1982. Trade in Danubian shaft-hole axes and the introduction of Neolithic economy in Denmark. *Journal of Danish Archaeology* 1, 7–12.

Fischer, A. 1990. On being a pupil of a flintknapper 11,000 years ago. A preliminary analysis of settlement organization and flint technology based on conjoined flint artefacts from the Trollesgave site. In *The Big Puzzle: International Symposium on Refitting Stone Artefacts* (eds. E. Cziesla, S. Eickhoff, N. Arts & D. Winter), pp. 447–64. Bonn: Holos.

Fischer, A. (ed.) 1995. *Man & Sea in the Mesolithic.* Oxford: Oxbow Monograph, No. 53.

Fischer, A. 1997. Drowned forests from the stone age. In *The Danish Storebælt Since the Ice Age* (eds. L. Pedersen, A. Fischer & B. Aaby), pp. 29–36. Copenhagen: A/S Storebælt Fixed Link.

Fladmark, K.R. 1979. Routes: Alternate migration corridors for Early Man in North America. *American Antiquity* 44, 55–69.

Flannery, K. 1972, The origin of the village as a settlement type in Mesoamerica and the Near East: A comparative study. In *Man, Settlement and Urbanization* (eds. P. Ucko, R. Tringham & G. Dimbleby), pp. 23–53. London: Duckworth.

Flannery, K. 1973. The origins of agriculture. *Annual Review of Anthropology* 2, 271–310.

Flannery, K. 1986. *Guilá Naquitz*. New York: Academic Press.

Flannery, K. 1993. Comments on Saidel's 'round house or square?'. *Journal of Mediterranean Archaeology* 6, 109–17.

Flannery, K. 2002. The origins of the village revisited: From nuclear to extended households. *American Antiquity* 67, 417–33.

Flannery, K. & Marcus, J. 1983. *The Cloud People: Divergent Evolution of the Zapotec and Mixtec Civilisations*. New York: Academic Press.

Flannery, T. 1990. Pleistocene faunal loss: implications of the aftershock for Australia's past and future. *Archaeology in Oceania* 25, 45–67.

Flannery, T. 1994. *The Future Eaters*. Port Melbourne: Reed.

Flood, J. 1995. *Archaeology of the Dreamtime*, rev. edn. Sydney: HarperCollins.

Foote, R.B. 1884. Rough notes on Billa Surgam and other caves in the Kurnool district. *Records of the Geological Survey of India* 17, 27–34.

Frayer, D.W. 1997. Ofnet: Evidence for a Mesolithic massacre. In *Troubled Times: Violence and Warfare in the Past* (eds. D.L. Martin & D.W. Frayer), pp. 181–216. Amsterdam: Gordon & Breach.

Frayer, D.W., Wolpoff, M.H., Thorne, A.G., Smith, F.H. & Pope, G.G. 1993. Theories of modern human origins: The paleontological test. *American Antiquity* 95, 14–50.

Frison, G.C. 1978. *Prehistoric Hunters on the High Plains*. New York: Academic Press.

Frison, G.C. 1991. The Goshen paleoindian complex: New data for paleoindian research. In *Clovis. Origins and Adaptations* (eds. R. Bonnichsen & K.L. Turnmire), pp. 133–52. Corvallis, OR: Centre for the Study of the First Americans.

Fukai, S. & Matsutani, T. 1981. *Telul eth-Thalathat. The Excavations of Tell II. The Fifth Season (1976), Vol. IV*. Tokyo.

Fullagar, R. & Field, J. 1997. Pleistocene seed-grinding implements from the Australian arid zone. *Antiquity* 71, 300–7.

Gabriel, B. 1987. Palaeoecological evidence from Neolithic fireplaces in the Sahara. *African Archaeological Review* 5, 93–103.

Galaty, J.G. 1989. Cattle and cognition: Aspects of Maasai practical reasoning. In *The Walking Larder: Patterns of Domestication, Pastoralism and Predation* (ed. J. Clutton-Brock), pp. 215–30. London: Unwin Hyman.

Galili, E., Weinstein-Evron, M., Hershkovitz, I., Gopher, A., Kislev, M., Lernau, O, Kolska-Horwitz, L. & Lernau, H. 1993. Atlit-Yam: A prehistoric site on the sea floor off the Israeli coast. *Journal of Field Archaeology* 20, 133–57.

Gamble, C. 1991. The social context for European Palaeolithic art. *Proceedings of the Prehistoric Society* 57, 3–15.

Gamble, C. & Soffer, O. (eds.) 1990. *The World at 18,000 BP. Vol. Two: Low Latitudes*. London: Unwin Hyman.

Garašanin, M. & Radovanović, I. 2001. A pot in house 54 at Lepenski Vir I. *Antiquity* 75, 118–25.

Garfinkel, Y. 1996. Critical observations on the so-called Khiamian flint industry In *Neolithic Chipped Stone Industries of the Fertile Crescent and their Contemporaries in Adjacent Regions* (eds. H.G. Gebel & S. Kozlowski), pp. 15–21. Berlin: Ex Oriente.

Garfinkel, Y. & Nadel, N. 1989. The Sultanian flint assemblage from Gesher and its implications for recognizing early Neolithic entities in the Levant. *Paléorient* 15, 139–51.

Garrard, A., Baird, D., Colledge, S., Martin. L. & Wright, K. 1994. Prehistoric environment and settlement in the Azraq basin: An interim report on the 1987 and 1988 excavation season. *Levant* XXVI, 73–109.

Garrard, A., Betts, A., Byrd, B. & Hunt, C. 1985. Prehistoric environment and settlement in the Azraq basin: An interim report on the 1984 excavation season. *Levant* XIX, 5–25.

Garrard, A., Byrd, B. & Betts, A. 1987 Prehistoric environment and settlement in the Azraq basin: An interim report on the 1985 excavation season. *Levant* XVIII, 5–24.

Garrard, A., Colledge, S, Hunt, C. & Montague, R. 1988. Environment and subsistence during the late Pleistocene and Early Holocene in the Azraq basin. *Paléorient* 14, 40–49.

Garrod, D.A.E. 1932. A new Mesolithic industry: The Natufian of Palestine. *Journal of the Royal Anthropological Institute* 62, 257–70.

Garrod, D.A.E. & Bate, D.M.A. 1937. *The Stone Age of Mount Carmel*. Oxford: Clarendon Press.

Gasse, F. 2002. Kilimanjaro's secrets revealed. *Science* 298, 548–9.

Gautier, A. 1984. Archaeozoology of Bir Kiseiba region, Eastern Sahara. In *Cattle Keepers of the Eastern Sahara: The Neolithic of Bir Kiseiba* (eds. F. Wendorf, R. Schild & A.E. Close), pp. 49–72. Dallas: Southern Methodist University Press.

Gautier, A. 1987. Prehistoric men and cattle in North Africa: A dearth of data and surfeit of models. In *Prehistory of Arid North Africa: Essays in Honor of Fred Wendorf* (ed . A. Close), pp. 163–187. Dallas, Texas: SMU Press.

Gautier, A. & Van Neer, W. 1989. Animal remains from the Late Palaeolithic sequence at Wadi Kubbaniya. In *The Prehistory of Wadi Kubbaniya, Vol. 2. Stratigraphy, Paleoeconomy, and Environment* (eds. F. Wendorf, R. Schild & A.E. Close), pp. 119–63. Dallas: Southern Methodist University Press.

Gebel, H.G. & Kozlowski, S. 1994. *Neolithic Chipped Stone Industries of the Fertile Crescent and their Contemporaries in Adjacent Regions*. Berlin: Ex Oriente.

Geddes, D., Guilaine, J., Coularou, J., Le Gall, O. & Martzluff, M. 1989. Postglacial environments, settlement and subsistence in the Pyrenees: The Balma Margineda, Andorra. In *The Mesolithic in Europe* (ed. C. Bonsall), pp. 561–71. Edinburgh: John Donald.

Geib, P. 2000. Sandal types and Archaic prehistory

on the Colorado Plateau. *American Antiquity* 65, 509–24.

Gibbons, A. 1996. First Americans: Not mammoth hunters, but forest dwellers. *Science* 272, 346–7.

Gimbutas, M. 1974. *The Goddesses and Gods of Old Europe*. London: Thames & Hudson.

Ginter, B. & Kozlowski, J.K. 1983. Investigations on Neolithic settlement. In *Qasr el-Sagha 1980* (ed. J. Kozlowski), pp. 37–74. Warszaw: Panstwowe Wydawnicto Naukowe.

Glover, I.C. & Higham, C.F.W. 1996. New evidence for early rice cultivation in south, southeast and east Asia. In *The Origins and Spread of Agriculture and Pastoralism in Eurasia* (ed. D. Harris), pp. 413–41. London: University College London Press.

Goddard, I. & Campbell, L. 1994. The history and classification of American Indian languages: What are the implications for the peopling of the Americas? In *Method and Theory for Investigating the Peopling of the Americas* (eds. R. Bonnichsen & D. Gentry Steele), pp. 189–207. Corvallis, OR: Centre for the Study of the First Americans.

Godwin, H. & Godwin, M.E. 1933. British Maglemose harpoon sites. *Antiquity* 7, 36–48.

Goebel, T., Powers, R. & Biglow, N. 1991. The Nenana complex of Alaska and Clovis origins. In *Clovis: Origins and Adaptations* (eds. R. Bonnichsen & K.L. Turnmire), pp. 49–80. Corvallis, OR: Centre for the Study of the First Americans.

Goebel, T., Waters, M.R., Buvit, I., Konstantinov, M.V. & Konstantinov, A.V. 2000. Studenoe-2 and the origins of microblade technologies in the Transbaikal, Siberia. *Antiquity* 74, 567–75.

Goldberg, P. & Arpin, T.L. 1999. Micromorphological analysis of sediments from Meadowcroft Rockshelter, Pennsylvania: Implications for radiocarbon dating. *Journal of Field Archaeology* 26, 325–43.

Golson, J. 1977. No room at the top: Agricultural intensification in the New Guinea highlands. In *Sunda and Sahul: Prehistoric Studies in Southeast Asia, Melanesia and Australia* (eds. J. Allen, J. Golson & R. Jones), pp. 601–38. London: Academic Press.

Golson, J. 1982. The Ipomoean revolution revisited: society and the sweet potato in the upper Wahgi valley. In *Inequality in New Guinea Highland Societies* (ed. A. Strathern), pp. 109–36. Cambridge: Cambridge University Press.

Golson, J. 1989. The origin and development of New Guinea Agriculture. In *Foraging and Farming. The Evolution of Plant Exploitation* (eds. D.R. Harris & G.C. Hillman), pp. 678–87. London: Unwin Hyman.

Golson, J. & Hughes, P.J. 1976. The appearance of plant and animal domestication in New Guinea. *Journal de la Société des Océanistes* 36, 294–303.

Golson, J. & Steensberg, A. 1985. The tools of agricultural intensification in the New Guinea highlands. In *Prehistoric Intensive Agriculture in the Tropics* (ed. I.S. Farrington), pp. 347–84.

Oxford: British Archaeological Reports, International Series 232.

Gonzalez Morales, M.R. & Morais Arnaud, J.E. 1990. Recent research on the Mesolithic in the Iberian peninsula: Problems and prospects. In *Contributions to the Mesolithic in Europe* (eds. P.M. Vermeersch & P. Van Peer), pp. 451–61. Leuven: Leuven University Press.

Goodale, N. & Smith, S. 2001. Pre-Pottery Neolithic A projectile points at Dhra', Jordan: Preliminary thoughts on form, function and site interpretation. *Neo-lithics* 2:01, 1–5.

Gopher, A. & Goring-Morris, N. 1998. Abu Salem: A Pre-Pottery Neolithic B camp in the Central Negev desert highland, Israel. *Bulletin of the American Schools of Oriental Research* 312, 1–18.

Gopher, A., Goring-Morris, N. & Rosen, S.A. 1995. 'Ein Qadis I: A Pre-Pottery Neolithic B occupation in eastern Sinai. *'Atiqot* XXVII, 15–33.

Gordon. B.C. 1999. Preliminary report on the study of the rise of Chinese civilization based on paddy rice agriculture. www.carleton.ca/~bgordon/rice/papers

Gordon, N. 1997. *Tarantulas and Marmosets, An Amazon Diary*. London: Metro.

Gorecki, P. 1985. The conquest of a new 'wet' and 'dry' territory: Its mechanism and its archaeological consequence. In *Prehistoric Intensive Agriculture in the Tropics* (ed. I.S. Farrington), pp. 321–45. Oxford: British Archaeological Reports, International Series 232.

Gorecki, P. 1989. Prehistory of the Jimi Valley. In *A Crack in the Spine: Prehistory and Ecology of the Jimi-Yuat Valley, Papua New Guinea* (eds. P. Gorecki & D. Gillieson), pp. 130–87. Townsville: Division of Anthropology & Archaeology, School of Behavioural Science, James Cook University of North Queensland.

Goren, Y., Goring-Morris, N. & Segal, I. 2001. The technology of skull modelling in the Pre-Pottery Neolithic B (PPNB): Regional variability, the relation of technology and iconography and their archaeological implications. *Journal of Archaeological Science* 28, 671–90.

Goring-Morris, N. 1987. *At the Edge: Terminal Pleistocene Hunter-Gatherers in the Negev and Sinai*. Oxford: British Archaeological Reports, International Series 361.

Goring-Morris, N. 1989. The Natufian of the Negev and the Rosh Horesha-Saflulim site complex. *Mitekufat Haeven* 22, 48–60.

Goring-Morris, N. 1991. The Harifian of the southern Levant. In *The Natufian Culture in the Levant* (eds. O. Bar-Yosef & F. Valla), pp. 173–216. Ann Arbor, MI: International Monographs in Prehistory.

Goring-Morris, N. 1993. From foraging to herding in the Negev and Sinai: The early to late Neolithic transition. *Paléorient* 19, 65–89.

Goring-Morris, N. 1995. Complex hunter/gatherers at the end of the Palaeolithic (20,000–10,000 BP). In *The Archaeology of Society in the Holy Land* (ed. T. Levy), pp. 141–68. New York: Facts on File.

Goring-Morris, N. 1999. Saflulim: A Late Natufian base camp in the Central Negev higlands, Israel. *Palestine Exploration Quarterly* 131, 36–64.

Goring-Morris, N. 2000. The quick and the dead: The social context of aceramic Neolithic mortuary practices as seen from Kfar Hahoresh. In *Life in Neolithic Farming Communities. Social Organization, Identity and Differentiation* (ed, I. Kuijt), pp. 103–36. New York: Kluwer/Plenum Publications.

Goring-Morris, N., Goren, Y., Horwitz, L.K., Hershkovitz, I., Lieberman, R., Sarel, J. & Bar-Yosef, D. 1994. The 1992 season of excavations at the Pre-Pottery Neolithic B settlement of Kfar Hahoresh. *Journal of the Israel Prehistoric Society* 26, 74–121.

Goring-Morris, N., Goren, Y., Horwitz, L.K., Bar-Yosef, D. & Hershkovitz, I. 1995. Investigations at an early Neolithic settlement in the Lower Galilee: Results of the 1991 season at Kefar HaHoresh. '*Antiqot* XXVII, 37–62.

Gosden, C. 1995. Arboriculture and agriculture in coastal New Guinea. *Antiquity* 69, 807–17.

Gove, H.E. 1992. The history of AMS, its advantages over decay counting: applications and prospects. In *Radiocarbon after Four Decades: An Inter-disciplinary Perspective* (eds. R.E. Taylor, A. Long & R.S. Kra), pp. 214–229. Berlin and New York: Springer Verlag.

Gould, R. 1980. *Living Archaeology.* Cambridge: Cambridge University Press.

Graburn, N.H. 1969. *Eskimos without Igloos, Social and Economic Developments in Sugluk.* Boston: Little, Brown & Co.

Gramly, R.M. 1976. Upper Pleistocene archaeological occurrences at site GvJm/22, Lukenya Hill, Kenya. *Man* 11, 319–44.

Gramly, R.M. & Rightmire, G.P. 1973. A fragmentary cranium and dated Later Stone Age assemblage from Lukenya Hill, Kenya. *Man* 8, 571–9.

Grayson, D.K. 1989. The chronology of North American Late Pleistocene extinctions. *Journal of Archaeological Science* 16, 153–65.

Greenberg, J.H. 1987. *Language in the Americas.* Stanford, CA : Stanford University Press.

Greenberg, J.H., Turner, C.H. II., Zegura, S.L. 1986. The settlement of the Americas: A comparison of the linguistic, dental and genetic evidence. *Current Anthropology* 27, 477–97.

Griffin, P.S., Grissom, C.A. & Rollefsom, G.O. 1998. Three late eights millennium plastered faces from 'Ain Ghazal, Jordan. *Paléorient* 24, 59–70.

Grøn, O. & Skaarup, J. 1991. Møllegabet II - A submerged Mesolithic site and a 'boat burial' from Ærø. *Journal of Danish Archaeology* 10, 38–50.

Groube, L. 1989. The taming of the rainforests: A model for late Pleistocene exploitation in New Guinea. In *Foraging and Farming. The Evolution of Plant Exploitation* (eds. D.R. Harris & G.C. Hillman), pp. 292–317. London: Unwin Hyman.

Groube, L., Chappell, J., Muke, J. & Price, D. 1986. A 40,000-year-old human occupation site at Huon peninsula, Papua New Guinea. *Nature* 324, 453–5.

Grove, A.T. 1993. Africa's Climate in the Holocene. In *The Archaeology of Africa, Food, Metals and Towns* (eds. T. Shaw, P. Sinclair, B. Andah & A. Okpoko) pp. 32–42. London: Routledge.

Grühn, R. 1994. The Pacific coastal route of initial entry: An overview. In *Method and Theory for Investigating the Peopling of the Americas* (eds. R. Bonnichsen & D. Gentry Steele), pp. 249–56. Corvallis, OR: Centre for the Study of the First Americans.

Guidon, N. 1989. On stratigraphy and chronology at Pedra Furada. *Current Anthropology* 30, 641–2.

Guidon, N. & Delibrias, G. 1986. Carbon-14 dates point to man in the Americas 32,000 years ago. *Nature* 321, 69–71.

Guidon, N., Pessis, A.-M., Parenti, F., Fontugue, M. & Guérin, C. 1996. Pedra Furada in Brazil and its 'presumed' evidence: limitations and potential of the available data. *Antiquity* 70, 416–21.

Guilaine, J., Briois, F., Coularou, J., Devèze, P., Philibert, S., Vigne, J.-D., & Carrère, I. 1998. La site Néolithique précéramique de Shillourokambos (Parekklisha, Chypre). *Bulletin de Correspondance Hellénique* 122, 603–10.

Gurina, I.I. 1956. *Oleneostrovski' Mogilnik.* Materialy I issledovaniya po arheologi' SSSR, No. 47. Akademiya nauk, Moscow.

Guthrie, R.D. 1984. Mosaics, allelochemics and nutrients, an ecological theory of Late Pleistocene megafaunal extinction. In *Quaternary Extinctions* (eds. P.S. Martin & R.G. Klein), pp. 259–98. Tucson: University of Arizona Press.

Guthrie, R.D. 1990. *Frozen Fauna of the Mammoth Steppe. The Story of Blue Babe.* Chicago: University of Chicago Press.

Haaland, R. 1995. Sedentism, cultivation, and plant domestication in the Holocene Middle Nile region. *Journal of Field Archaeology* 22, 157–74.

Haberle, S.G. 1994. Anthropogenic indicators in pollen diagrams: Problems and prospects for late Quaternary palynology in New Guinea. In *Tropical Palynology. Applications and New Developments* (ed. J. Hather), pp. 172–201. London: Routledge.

Haddon, A.C. 1901–35. *Report of the Cambridge Anthropological Expedition to the Torres Straits.* Cambridge: Cambridge University Press.

Halstead, P. 1996. The development of agriculture and pastoralism in Greece: When, how, who and what? In *The Origins and Spread of Agriculture and Pastoralism in Eurasia* (ed. D. Harris), pp. 296–309. London: University College London Press.

Hamilton, A.C. 1982. *Environmental History of East Africa. A Study of the Quaternary.* London: Academic Press.

Hansen, J. & Renfrew, J.M. 1978. Palaeolithic–Neolithic seed remains at Franchthi Cave, Greece. *Nature* 271, 349–52.

Hansen, J.P.H., Meldgaard, J. & Nordqvist, J. 1991. *The Greenland Mummies.* Washington DC: Smithsonian Institution Press.

Hansen, R.M. 1978. Shasta ground sloth food habits, Rampart Cave, Arizona. *Palaeobiology* 4, 302–19.

Harlan, J. 1989. Wild grass seeds as food sources in the Sahara and Sub-Sahara. *Sahara* 2, 69–74.

Harlan, J. 1992. Indigenous African agriculture. In *The Origins of Agriculture, An International Perspective* (eds. C. Wesley Cowan & P.J. Watson), pp 59–70. Washington DC: Smithsonian Institution Press.

Harris, D.R. 1977. Subsistence strategies across the Torres Strait. In *Sunda and Sahul: Prehistoric Studies in Southeast Asia, Melanesia and Australia* (eds. J. Allen, J. Golson & R. Jones), pp. 421–63. London: Academic Press.

Harris, D.R. 1979. Foragers and farmers in the Western Torres Strait islands: An historical analysis of economic, demographic, and spatial differentiation. In *Social and Ecological Systems* (eds. P.C. Burnham & R.F. Ellen), pp. 76–109. New York: Academic Press.

Harris, D.R. 1989. An evolutionary continuum of people-plant interaction. In *Foraging and Farming: The Evolution of Plant Exploitation* (eds. D.R. Harris & G.C. Hillman), pp. 11–26. London: Unwin Hyman.

Harris, D.R. 1995. Early agriculture in New Guinea and the Torres Strait divide. *Antiquity* 69, 848–54.

Harris, D.R. 1996. Domesticatory relationships of people, plants and animals. In *Redefining Nature: Ecology, Culture and Domestication* (eds. R. Ellen & K. Fukui), pp. 437–63. Oxford: Berg.

Harris, D.R. & Gosden, C. 1996. The beginnings of agriculture in western Central Asia. In *The Origins and Spread of Agriculture and Pastoralism in Eurasia* (ed. D.R. Harris), pp. 370–99. London: University College London Press.

Harris, D.R., Gosden, C. & Charles, M.P. 1996. Jeitun: Recent excavations at an early Neolithic site in Southern Turkmenistan. *Proceedings of the Prehistoric Society* 62, 423–42.

Harris, D.R., Masson, V.M., Berezkin, Y.E., Charles, M.P., Gosden, C., Hillman, G.C., Kasparov, A.K., Korobkova, G.F., Kurbansakhatov, K., Legge, A.J. & Limbrey, S. 1993. Investigating early agriculture in Central Asia: New research at Jeitun, Turkmenistan. *Antiquity* 67, 324–38.

Harrison, T. 1957. The Great Cave of Niah: A preliminary report on Borneo prehistory. *Man* 57, 161–6.

Harrison, T. 1959a. New archaeological and ethnographical results from Niah Caves, Sarawak. *Man* 59, 1–8.

Harrison, T. 1959b. The caves of Niah: A history of prehistory. *Sarawak Museum Journal* 7, 549–94.

Harrison, T. 1959c. Radiocarbon C-14 datings from Niah: A note. *Sarawak Museum Journal* 9, 136–8.

Harrison, T. 1965. 50,000 years of stone age culture in Borneo. *Smithsonian Institution Annual Report* 1964, 521–30.

Hassan, F.A. 1985. Radiocarbon chronology of Neolithic and predynastic sites in Upper Egypt and the delta. *African Archaeological Review* 3, 95–116.

Hassan, F.A. 1986. Holocene lakes and prehistoric settlements of the western Faiyum, Egypt. *Journal of Archaeological Science* 13, 483–501.

Hassan, F.A. 1988. The Predynastic of Egypt. *Journal of World Prehistory* 2, 135–50.

Hassan, F.A. 1997. Holocene palaeoclimates of Africa. *African Archaeological Review* 14, 213–229.

Hassan, F.A. 2000. Climate and cattle in North Africa: A first approximation. In *The Origins and Development of African Livestock* (eds. R.M. Blench & K.C. MacDonald), pp. 61–85. London: University College London Press.

Hastorf, C.A. 1998. The cultural life of early domestic plants. *Antiquity* 72, 773–82.

Hauptmann, H. 1999. The Urfa region. In Neolithic in *Turkey: The Cradle of Civilization, New Discoveries* (eds. M. Özdoğan & N. Başgelen), pp. 65–86. Istanbul: Arkeoloji ve Sanat Yayınları.

Haury, E.M., Antevs, E. & Lance, J.F. 1953. Artefacts with mammoth remains, Naco, AZ: Parts I–III. *American Antiquity* 19, 1–24.

Haury, E.M., Sayles, E.B. & Wasley W.W. 1959. The Lehner mammoth site, Southeastern Arizona. *American Antiquity* 25, 2–30.

Hawkes, K., O'Connell, J.F. & Blurton Jones, N.G. 1997. Hadza women's time allocation, offspring provisioning, and the evolution of long postmenopausal life spans. *Current Anthropology* 38, 551–74

Hayden, B. 1990. Nimrods, piscators, pluckers and planters: The emergence of food production. *Journal of Anthropological Archaeology* 9, 31–69.

Hayden, B. 1995. The emergence of prestige technologies and pottery. In *The Emergence of Pottery. Technology and Innovation in Ancient Societies* (eds. W.K. Barnett & J.W. Hoopes), pp. 257–65. Washington DC: Smithsonian Institution Press.

Hayden, B., Chisholm, B. & Schwarz, H.P. 1987. Fishing and foraging: Marine resources in the Upper Palaeolithic of France. In *The Pleistocene Old World* (ed. O. Soffer), pp. 279–91. New York: Plenum Press.

Haynes, C.V. 1973. The Calico site: Artifacts or geofacts? *Science* 181, 305–10.

Haynes, C.V. 1991. Geoarchaeological and palaeo-hydrological evidence for a Clovis-age drought in North America and its bearing on extinction. *Quaternary Research* 35, 438–50.

Haynes, G. 1987. Proboscidean die-offs and die-outs: Age profiles in fossil collections. *Journal of Archaeological Science* 14, 659–68.

Haynes, G. 1991. *Mammoths, Mastodonts and Elephants: Biology, Behaviour and the Fossil Record.* Cambridge: Cambridge University Press.

Haynes, G. 1992. The Waco mammoths: Possible clues to herd size, demography and reproductive health. In *Proboscidean and Palaeoindian Interactions* (eds. J.W. Fox, C.B. Smith & K.T. Wilkins), pp. 111–23. Waco, TX: Baylor University Press.

Headland, T.N. 1987. The wild yam question: How well could independent hunter-gatherers live in a tropical rainforest environment? *Human Ecology* 15, 463–91.

Hedges, R.E.M. 1981. Radiocarbon dating with an accelerator: Review and preview. *Archaeometry* 23, 3–18.

Hedges, R.E.M., Housley, R.A., Bronk, C.R. & Van Klinken, G.J. 1990. Radiocarbon dates from the Oxford AMS system: Archaeometry datelist 11. *Archaeometry* 32, 211–27.

Hedges, R.E.M., Housley, R.A., Bronk, C.R; Van Klinken, G.J. 1995. Radiocarbon dates from the Oxford AMS system: Archaeometry datelist 20. *Archaeometry* 37, 195–214.

Hedges, R.E.M. & Sykes, B.C. 1992. Biomolecular archaeology: Past, present and future. *Proceedings of the British Academy* 77, 267–84.

Heinzelin de Braucourt, J. de. 1961. Ishango. *Scientific American* 206, 105–16.

Henry, D.O. 1976. Rosh Zin: A Natufian settlement near Ein Avdat. In *Prehistory and Palaeoenvironments in the Central Negev* (ed. A.E. Marks), pp. 317–47. Dallas: Southern Methodist University Press.

Henry, D.O. 1989. *From Foraging to Agriculture. The Levant at the End of the Ice Age.* Philadelphia: University of Pennsylvania Press.

Henry, D.O., Leroi-Gourhan, A. & Davis, S. 1981. The excavation of Hayonim terrace: An examination of terminal Pleistocene climatic and adaptive changes. *Journal of Archaeological Science* 8, 33–58.

Hershkovitz, I., Zohar, I., Segal, I., Speirs, M.S., Meirav, O., Sherter, U., Feldman, H., & Goring-Morris, N. 1995. Remedy for an 8500 year-old plastered human skull from Kfar Hahoresh, Israel. *Journal of Archaeological Science* 22, 779–88.

Hesse, B. 1984. These are our goats: The origins of herding in west central Iran. In *Animals and Archaeology* 3: *Early Herders and their Flocks* (eds. J. Clutton-Brock & C. Grigson), pp. 243–64. Oxford: British Archaeological Reports, International Series 202.

Heun, M., Schafer-Pregl, R., Klawan, D., Castagna, R., Accerbi, M., Borghi, B. & Salamini, F. 1997. Site of einkorn wheat domestication identified by DNA fingerprinting. *Science* 278, 1312–14.

Higham, C. & Lu, T.L.-D. 1998. The origins and dispersal of rice cultivation. *Antiquity* 72, 867–77.

Hillman, G.C. 1989. Late Palaeolithic plant foods from Wadi Kubbaniya in Upper Egypt: Dietary diversity, infant weaning, and seasonality in a riverine environment. In *Foraging and Farming: The Evolution of Plant Exploitation* (eds. D.R.

Harris & G.C. Hillman), pp. 207–39. London: Unwin Hyman.

Hillman, G.C. 1996. Late Pleistocene changes in wild plant-foods available to hunter-gatherers of the northern Fertile Crescent: Possible preludes to cereal cultivation. In *The Origins and Spread of Agriculture and Pastoralism in Eurasia* (ed. D. Harris), pp. 159–203. London: University College London Press.

Hillman, G.C. 2000. The plant food economy of Abu Hureyra 1 and 2. In *Village on the Euphrates* (by A.M.T. Moore, G.C. Hillman & A.J. Legge), pp. 327–99. Oxford: Oxford University Press.

Hillman, G.C., Colledge, S.M., Harris, D.R. 1989. Plant food economy during the Epi-Palaeolithic period at Tell Abu Hureyra, Syria: Dietary diversity, seasonality, and modes of exploitation. In *Foraging and Farming. The Evolution of Plant Exploitation* (eds. D.R. Harris & G.C. Hillman), pp. 240–68. London: Unwin Hyman.

Hillman, G.C. & Davies, M.S. 1990. Measured domestication rates in wild wheats and barley under primitive cultivation, and their archaeological implications. *Journal of World Prehistory* 4, 157–222.

Hillman, G.C. Hedges, R. Moore, A., Colledge, S. & Pettitt, P. 2001. New evidence of lateglacial cereal cultivation at Abu Hureyra on the Euphrates. *The Holocene* 11, 383–93.

Hillman, G.C., Madeyska, E. & Hather, J. 1989. Wild plant foods and diet at Late Palaeolithic Wadi Kubbaniya: The evidence from charred remains. In *The Prehistory of Wadi Kubbaniya, Vol. 2: Stratigraphy, Paleoeconomy, and Environment* (eds. F. Wendorf, R. Schild & A.E. Close), pp. 162–242. Dallas: Southern Methodist University Press.

Hobsbawm, E. 1997. *On History.* London: Weidenfeld & Nicolson.

Hodder, I. 1982. *The Present Past. An Introduction to Anthropology for Archaeologists.* London: Batsford.

Hodder, I. 1984. Burials, houses, women and men in the European Neolithic. In *Ideology, Power and Prehistory* (eds. D. Miller & C. Tilley), pp. 51–68. Cambridge: Cambridge University Press.

Hodder, I. 1985. *Symbols in Action.* Cambridge: Cambridge University Press.

Hodder, I. 1990. *The Domestication of Europe.* Oxford: Blackwell.

Hodder, I. 1991. *Reading the Past.* 2nd edn. Cambridge: Cambridge University Press.

Hodder, I. (ed.) 1996. *On the Surface: Çatalhöyük 1993–95.* Cambridge: McDonald Institute for Archaeological Research.

Hodder, I. 1997. 'Always momentary, fluid and flexible': Towards a reflexive excavation methodology. *Antiquity* 71, 691–700.

Hodder, I. 1999a. Symbolism at Çatalhöyük. In *World Prehistory. Studies in Memory of Grahame Clark* (eds. J. Coles, R. Bewley & P. Mellars), pp. 171–99. London: *Proceedings of the British Academy* 99.

Hodder, I. 1999b. Renewed work at Çatalhöyük. In

Neolithic in Turkey: The Cradle of Civilization, New Discoveries (eds. M. Özdoğan & N. Başgelen), pp. 153–64. Istanbul: Arkeoloji ve Sanat Yayinlari.

Hodder, I. 1999c. *The Archaeological Process. An Introduction.* Oxford: Blackwell.

Hodder, I. (ed.) 2000. *Towards a Reflexive Method in Archaeology: The Example at Çatalhöyük.* Cambridge: McDonald Institute for Archaeological Research.

Hodder, I. (ed) 2001. *Archaeological Theory Today.* Cambridge: Polity Press.

Holden, T.G., Hather, J.G., & Watson, J.P.N. 1995. Mesolithic plant exploitation at the Roc del Migdia, Catalonia. *Journal of Archaeological Science* 22, 769–78.

Hole, F. 1996. The context of caprine domestication in the Zagros region. In *The Origins and Spread of Agriculture and Pastoralism in Eurasia* (ed. D. Harris), pp. 263–81. London: University College London Press.

Hole, F., Flannery, K. & Neely, J. (eds.) 1969. *Prehistory and Human Ecology of the Deh Luran Plain.* Memoir 1 of the Museum of Anthropology, University of Michigan. Ann Arbor, MI: University of Michigan Press.

Holliday, V. 2000. Folsom drought and episodic drying on the southern high plains from 10,900–10,200 ^{14}C yr B.P. *Quaternary Research* 53, 1–12.

Hoopes, J. & Barnett, W. 1995. *The Emergence of Pottery.* Washington DC: Smithsonian Institution Press.

Hope, G.S. & Golson, J. 1995. Late Quaternary change in the mountains of New Guinea. *Antiquity* 69, 818–30.

Hope, G.S., Golson, J. & Allen, J. 1983. Palaeoecology and prehistory in New Guinea. *Journal of Human Evolution* 12, 37–60.

Horai, S., Kondo, R., Nakagawa-Hattori, Y., Hayashi, S., Sonoda, S. & Tajima, K. 1993. Peopling of the Americas, founded by four major lineages of mitochondrial DNA. *Journal of Molecular Biology and Evolution* 10, 23–47.

Horton, D.R. 1984. Red kangaroos: Last of the megafauna. In *Quaternary Extinctions. A Prehistoric Revolution* (eds. P.S. Martin & R.G. Klein), pp. 639–79. Tucson: University of Arizona Press.

Horton, D.R. 1986. Seasons of repose: Environment and culture in the late Pleistocene of Australia. In *Pleistocene Perspectives* (ed. A. Aspimon), pp. 1–14. London: Allen & Unwin.

Houghton, J. 1997. *Global Warming. The Complete Briefing.* Cambridge: Cambridge University Press.

Housley, R.A. 1991. AMS dates from the Late Glacial and early Postglacial in north-west Europe: A review. In *The Late Glacial in North-West Europe: Human Adaptation and Environmental Change at the End of the Pleistocene* (eds. N. Barton, A.J. Roberts & D.A Roe), pp. 25–39. London: Council for British Archaeology, Research Report No. 77.

Housley, R.A., Gamble, C.S., Street, M. & Pettitt, P. 1997. Radiocarbon evidence for the lateglacial re-colonisation of northern Europe. *Proceedings of the Prehistoric Society* 63, 25–54.

Howe, B. 1983. Karim Shahir. In *Prehistoric Archaeology along the Zagros Flanks* (eds. L.S. Braidwood, R.J. Braidwood, B. Howe, C.A. Reed & P.J. Watson), pp. 23–154. Chicago: Chicago University Press.

Hsiao-Tung, F. 1939. *Peasant Life in China. A Field Study of Country Life in the Yangtze Valley.* London: George Routledge & Sons, Ltd.

Huntley, B. & Webb, T. 1988. *Vegetation History.* Dordrecht: Kluwer.

Hutchinson, H.G. 1914. *Life of Sir John Lubbock, Lord Avebury.* London: Macmillan.

Hutton, J.H. 1922. Divided and decorated heads as trophies. *Man* 22, 113–14.

Hutton, J.H. 1928. The significance of head-hunting in Assam. *Journal of the Royal Anthropological Institute of Great Britain and Ireland* 58, 399–408.

Imamura, K. 1996. *Prehistoric Japan. New Perspectives on Insular East Asia.* Honolulu: University of Hawaii Press.

Izumi, T. & Nishida, Y. 1999. *Jomon Sekai no Ichimannen* (The Thousand Years of the Jomon World). Tokyo: Shueisha.

Jackson, L.E., Jr, & Duk-Rodkin, A. 1996. Quaternary geology of the ice-free corridor: Glacial controls on the peopling of the New World. In *Prehistoric Mongoloid Dispersals* (eds. T. Akazawa & E.J.E. Szathmáry), pp. 214–27. Oxford: Oxford University Press.

Jacobi, R. 1978. Northern England in the eighth millennium BC: an essay. In *The Early Postglacial Settlement of Northern Europe: An Ecological Perspective* (ed. P. Mellars), pp. 295–332. London: Duckworth.

Jacobi, R. 1991. The Creswellian, Creswell and Cheddar. In *The Late Glacial in North-West Europe. Human Adaptation and Environmental Change at the End of the Pleistocene* (edited by N. Barton, A.J. Roberts & D.A. Roe), pp. 128–40. London: Council for British Archaeology, Research Report No. 77.

Jacobs, K. 1995. Returning to Oleni' ostrov: Social, economic and skeletal dimensions of a boreal forest Mesolithic cemetery. *Journal of Anthropological Archaeology* 14, 359–403.

Jacobsen, T.W. & Farrand, W.R. 1987. *Excavations at Franchthi Cave, Greece. Fascicle 1: Franchthi Cave and Paralia. Maps, Plans and Sections.* Bloomington: Indiana University Press.

Jarrige, C., Jarrige, J.-F., Meadow, R.H. & Quivron, G. 1995. Mehrgarh. *Field Reports 1974–1985, from Neolithic Times to the Indus Civilization.* Karachi: Department of Culture and Tourism of Sindh Pakistan, Department of Archaeology and Museums, French Ministry of Foreign Affairs.

Jarrige, J.-F. & Meadow, R.H. 1980. The antecedents of civilization in the Indus Valley. *Scientific American* 243, 102–10.

Jenkinson, R.D.S. 1984. *Creswell Crags. Late Pleistocene Sites in the East Midlands.* Oxford: British Archaeological Reports, British Series 122.

Jenkinson, R.D.S. & Gilbertson, D.D. 1984. *In the Shadow of Extinction. A Quaternary Archaeology and Palaeoecology of the Lake, Fissures and Smaller Caves at Creswell Crags SSSI.* Sheffield: Department of Prehistory and Archaeology, University of Sheffield.

Jespen, G.L. 1953. Ancient buffalo hunters of northwestern Wyoming. *Southwestern Lore* 19, 19–25.

Jing, Y. & Flad, R.K. 2002. Pig domestication in China. *Antiquity* 76, 724–32.

Jochim, M. 1983. Palaeolithic cave art in ecological perspective. In *Hunter-Gatherer Economy in Prehistory* (ed. G. Bailey), p. 212–19. Cambridge: Cambridge University Press.

Johanson, D. & Edgar B. 1996. *From Lucy to Language.* London: Weidenfeld & Nicolson.

Johanson, E. 1991. Late Pleistocene cultural occupation on the southern plains. In *Clovis: Origins and Adaptations* (eds. R. Bonnichsen & K.L. Turnmire), pp. 215–36. Corvallis, OR: Centre for the Study of the First Americans.

Jones, R. 1981. The extreme climatic place? *Hemisphere* 26, 54–9.

Jones, R. 1987. Ice-age hunters of the Tasmanian wilderness. *Australian Geographic* 8, 26–45.

Jones, R. 1990. From Kakadu to Kutikina: The southern continent at 18,000 years ago. In *The World at 18,000 BP, Vol. Two, Low Latitudes* (eds. C. Gamble & O. Soffer), pp. 264–95. London: Unwin Hyman.

Jones, R., Cosgrove, R., Allen, J., Cane, S., Kieran, K., Webb, S., Loy, T., West, D. & Stadler, E. 1988. An archaeological reconnaissance of karst caves within the southern forest region of Tasmania. *Australian Archaeology* 26, 1–23.

Jones R. & Meehan, B. 1989. Plant foods of the Gidjingali: Ethnographic and archaeological perspectives from northern Australia on tuber and seed exploitation. In *Foraging and Farming. The Evolution of Plant Exploitation* (eds. D.R. Harris & G.C. Hillman), pp. 120–34. London: Unwin Hyman.

Kahila Bar-Gal, G., Khalaily, H., Mader, O., Ducos, P. & Horwitz, L.K. 2002. Ancient DNA evidence for the transition from wild to domestic status in Neolithic goats: A case study from the site of Abu Gosh, Israel. *Ancient Biomolecules* 4, 9–17.

Kahila Bar-Gal, G., Smith, P., Tchernov, E., Greenblatt, C., Ducos, P., Gardeisen, A. and Horwitz, L.K. 2002. Genetic evidence for the origin of the agrimi goat (*Capra aegagrus cretica*). *Journal of the Zoological Society of London* 256, 269–377.

Kaufman, D. 1986. A reconsideration of adaptive change in the Levantine Epipalaeolithic. In *The End of the Palaeolithic in the Old World* (ed. L.G. Straus), pp. 117–28. Oxford: British Archaeological Reports, International Series 284.

Keefer, D.K. et al. 1998. Early maritime economy and El Niño events at Quebrada Tacahuay, Peru. *Science* 281, 1833–5.

Kendrick, D.M. 1995. *Jomon of Japan: The World's Oldest Pottery.* London: Kegan Paul International.

Kennedy, K.A.R. 2000. *God-Apes and Fossil Men, Paleoanthropology of South Asia.* Ann Arbor, MI: University of Michigan Press.

Kenyon, K. 1957. *Digging Up Jericho.* London: Ernest Benn Ltd.

Kenyon, K. & Holland, T. 1981. *Excavations at Jericho, Vol. III: The Architecture and Stratigraphy of the Tell.* London: British School of Archaeology in Jerusalem.

Kenyon, K. & Holland, T. 1982. *Excavations at Jericho, Vol. IV. The Pottery Type Series and Other Finds.* London: British School of Archaeology in Jerusalem.

Kenyon, K. & Holland, T. 1983. *Excavations at Jericho, Vol. V: The Pottery Phases of the Tell and Other Finds.* London: British School of Archaeology in Jerusalem.

Khanna, G.S. 1993. Patterns of mobility in the Mesolithic of Rajasthan. *Man and Environment* XVIII, 49–55.

Kiernan, K., Jones, R. & Ranson, D. 1983. New evidence from Fraser Cave for glacial man in southwest Tasmania. *Nature* 301, 28–32.

Kingsley, M. 1987. *Travels in West Africa.* London: J.M. Dent.

Kirkbride, D. 1966. Five seasons at the Prepottery Neolithic village of Beidha in Jordan. *Palestine Exploration Quarterly* 98, 5–61.

Kikbride, D. 1968. Beidha: Early Neolithic village life south of the Dead Sea. *Antiquity* XLII, 263–74.

Kirkbride, D. 1972. Umm Dabaghiyah 1971: A preliminary report. *Iraq* 34, 3–15.

Kirkbride, D. 1973a. Umm Dabaghiyah 1972: A second report. *Iraq* 35, 1–7.

Kirkbride, D. 1973b. Umm Dabaghiyah 1973: A third report. *Iraq* 35, 205–9.

Kirkbride, D. 1974. Umm Dabaghiyah: A trading outpost? *Iraq* 36, 85–92.

Kirkbride, D. 1975. Umm Dabaghiyah 1974: A fourth report. *Iraq* 37, 3–10.

Kirkbride, D. 1982. Umm Dabaghiyah. In *Fifty Years of Mesopotamian Discovery* (ed. J. Curtis), pp. 11–21. London: British School in Iraq.

Kislev, M.E. 1989. Pre-domesticated cereals in the Pre-Pottery Neolithic A period. In *People and Culture Change* (ed. I. Hershkovitz), pp. 147–52. Oxford: British Archaeological Reports, International Series 508.

Kislev, M.E., Bar-Yosef, O. & Gopher, A. 1986. Early domestication and wild barley from the Netiv Hagdud region in the Jordan Valley. *Israel Journal of Botany* 35, 197–201.

Klein, R.G. 1978. A preliminary report on the larger mammals from the Boomplaas stone age cave site, Cango Valley, Oudtshoorn District, South Africa. *South African Archaeological Bulletin* 33, 66–75.

Klein, R.G. 1980. Environmental and ecological implications of large mammals from Upper Pleistocene and Holocene sites in southern Africa. *Annals of the South African Museum* 81, 223–83.

Klein, R.G. 1984a. The large mammals of Southern Africa: Late Pleistocene to recent. In *Southern African Prehistory and Palaeoenvironments* (ed. R. Klein), pp. 107-46. Rotterdam: Balkema.

Klein, R.G. 1984b. Mammalian extinctions and stone age people in Africa. In *Quaternary Extinctions. A Prehistoric Revolution* (eds. P.S. Martin & R.G. Klein), pp. 553–70. Tucson: University of Arizona Press.

Klein, R.G. 1991. Size variation in the Cape dune molerat (*Bathyergus suillus*) and Late Quaternary climatic change in the southwestern Cape province, South Africa. *Quaternary Research* 36, 243–56.

R.G., Cruz-Uribe, K., & Beaumont, P.B. 1991. Environmental, ecological, and palaeoanthropological implications of Late Pleistocene mammalian fauna from Equus Cave, northern Cape Province, South Africa. *Quaternary Research* 36, 94–119.

Klindt-Jensen, O. 1975. *A History of Scandinavian Archaeology.* London: Thames & Hudson.

Koike, H. 1986. Prehistoric hunting pressure and palaeobiomass: An environmental reconstruction and archaeozoological analysis of a Jomon shellmound area. In *Prehistoric Hunter-Gatherers in Japan. New Research Methods* (eds. T. Akazawa & C.M. Aikens), pp. 27–53. Tokyo: University of Tokyo Press.

Korisettar, R., Venkatasubbaiah, P.C. & Fuller, D.Q. 2000. Brahmagiri and beyond: The archaeology of the Southern Neolithic. In *Indian Archaeology in Retrospect, Vol. 1.* (eds. S. Settar & R. Korisettar), pp. 151–237. New Delhi: Manohar.

Kozlowski, S.K. 1989. Nemrik 9, a PPN site in northern Iraq. *Paléorient* 15, 25–31.

Kozlowski, S.K. 1994. Radiocarbon dates from aceramic Iraq. In *Late Quaternary chronology and paleoclimates of the Eastern Mediterranean,* (ed. O. Bar-Yosef & R.S. Kra), pp. 255–64. Tucson and Cambridge, MA: The University of Arizona and Peabody Museum of Archaeology and Ethnology, Harvard University.

Kozlowski, S.K. & Kempisty, A. 1990. Architecture of the pre-pottery neolithic settlement in Nemrik, Iraq. *World Archaeology* 21, 348–62.

Kromer, B., Becker, B. 1993. German oak and pine ¹⁴C calibration, 7200–9439 BC. *Radiocarbon* 35, 125–35.

Kromer, B. & Spurk, M. 1998. Revision and tentative extension of the tree-ring based ¹⁴C calibration 9200–11,955 cal BP. *Radiocarbon* 40, 1117–25.

Kuijt, I. 1994. Pre-Pottery Neolithic A settlement variability: Evidence for sociopolitical developments in the southern Levant. *Journal of Mediterranean Archaeology* 7, 165–92.

Kuijt, I. 1996. Negotiating equality through ritual: A consideration of Late Natufian and Pre-Pottery Neolithic A period mortuary practices. *Journal of Anthropological Archaeology* 15, 313–36.

Kuijt, I. 2000. Keeping the peace: Ritual, skull caching and community integration in the Levantine Neolithic. In *Life in Neolithic Farming Communities. Social Organization, Identity and Differentiation* (ed. I. Kuijt), pp. 137–62. New York: Kluwer/ Plenum Publications.

Kuijt, I., Mabry, J. & Palumbo, G. 1991. Early Neolithic use of upland areas of Wadi El-Yabis: Preliminary evidence from the excavations of 'Iraq Ed-Dubb, Jordan. *Paléorient* 17, 99–108.

Kuijt, I. & Mahasneh, H. 1998. Dhra': An early Neolithic village in the southern Jordan Valley. *Journal of Field Archaeology* 25, 153–61.

Kumar, G., Sahni, A., Pancholi, R.K. & Narvare, G. 1990. Archaeological discoveries and a study of Late Pleistocene ostrich egg shells and egg shell objects in India. *Man and Environment* XV, 29–40.

Kusimba, S.B. 1999. Hunter-gatherer land use patterns in Late Stone Age East Africa. *Journal of Anthropological Archaeology* 18, 165–200.

Kusimba, S.B. 2001. The early Later Stone Age in East Africa: Excavations and lithic assemblages from Lukenya Hill. *African Archaeological Review* 18, 77–120.

Kutzbach, J.E., Guetter, P.J., Behling, P.J. & Selin, R. 1993. Simulated climatic changes: Results of the COHMAP climate-model experiments. In *Global Climates Since the Last Glacial Maximum* (eds. H.E. Wright, Jr, J.E. Kutzbach, T. Webb III, W.F. Rudimann, F.A. Street-Perrott & P.J. Bartlein), pp 24–93. Minneapolis. University of Minnesota Press.

Kuzmin, Y.V. 1996. Palaeoecology of the Palaeolithic of the Russian Far East. In *American Beginnings: The Prehistory and Palaeoecology of Beringia* (ed. F.H. West), pp. 136–46. Chicago: University of Chicago Press.

Lahr, M. 1994. The multiregional model of modern human origins. *Journal of Human Evolution* 26, 23–56.

Lahr, M. & Foley, R.A. 1994. Multiple dispersals and modern human origins. *Evolutionary Anthropology* 3, 48–60.

Lahren, L. & Bonnichsen, R. 1974. Bone foreshafts from a Clovis burial in southwestern Montana. *Science* 186, 147–50.

Larsson. L. 1983. *Ageröd V. An Atlantic Bog Site in Central Scania.* Acta Archaeologica Lundensia Series In 8 no. 12.

Larsson, L. 1984. The Skateholm project. A late Mesolithic settlement and cemetery complex at a southern Swedish bay. *Meddelanden från Lunds Universitetets Historiska Museum,* 5–3. New Series 58.

Larsson, L. (ed.) 1988. *The Skateholm Project: I. Man and Environment.* Stockholm: Almqvist & Wiksell.

Larsson, L. 1989. Big dog and poor man: Mortuary practices in Mesolithic societies in southern Sweden. In *Approaches to Swedish Prehistory* (eds. T.B Larsson & H. Lundmark), pp. 211–23. Oxford: British Archaeological Reports, International Series 500.

Larsson, L. 1990. Dogs in traction – symbols in action. In *Contributions to the Mesolithic in Europe* (eds. P.M. Vermeersch & P. van Peer), pp. 153–60. Leuven: Leuven University Press.

Larsson, L. & Bartholin, T.S. 1978. A longbow found at the Mesolithic bog site Ageröd V in Central Scania. *Meddelanden från Lunds Universitets Historiska Museum*, 1977–78.

Layard, A.H. 1853. *Discoveries in the Ruins of Nineveh and Babylon.* London: John Murray.

Layard, A.H. 1854. *Nineveh and its Remains.* 6th edn. London: John Murray.

Layton, R. 1992. *Australian Rock Art. A New Synthesis.* Cambridge: Cambridge University Press.

Le Brun, A. 1994. *Fouilles Récentes à Khirokitia (Chypre), 1988–1991.* Paris: Editions Recherche sur les Civilisations.

Le Brun, A. 1997. *Khirokitia, A Neolithic Site.* Nicosia: Bank of Cultural Foundation.

Leakey, L.S.B., Simpson, R.d.E. & Clements, T. 1968. Archaeological excavations in the Calico Mountains, California: Preliminary report. *Science* 160, 1022–3.

Leakey, L.S.B., Simpson, R.d.E. & Clements, T. 1970. Man in America: The Calico Mountains excavations. *Britannica Yearbook of Science and the Future*, 65–79.

Leakey, M.D. 1984. *Disclosing the Past: An Autobiography.* London: Weidenfeld & Nicolson.

Leakey, M.D., Hay, R.L., Thurber, D.L., Protsch, R., & Berger, R. 1972. Stratigraphy, archaeology and age of the Ndutu and Naisiusiu Beds, Olduvai Gorge, Tanzania. *World Archaeology* 3, 328–41.

Leakey, R. & Lewin, R. 1979. *The People of the Lake.* London: Penguin.

Leakey, R. & Lewin, R. 1996. *The Sixth Extinction, Biodiversity and its Survival.* London: Phoenix.

Lee, R.B. 1979. *The !Kung San: Men, Women, and Work in a Foraging Society.* Cambridge: Cambridge University Press.

Legge, A.J. 1996. The beginning of caprine domestication in Southwest Asia. In *The Origins and Spread of Agriculture and Pastoralism in Eurasia* (ed. D. Harris), pp. 238–62. London: University College London Press.

Legge, A.J. & Rowley-Conwy, P.A. 1987. Gazelle killing in stone age Syria. *Scientific American* 255, 88–95.

Legge, A.J. & Rowley-Conwy, P.A. 1988. *Star Carr Revisited. A Re-analysis of the Large Mammals.* London: Birkbeck College.

Leroi-Gourhan, A. & Brézillon, M. 1972. *Fouilles de Pincevent: Essai d'Analyse Ethnographique d'un Habitat Magdalénien.* Paris: Gallia Préhistoire, supplément 7.

Lewin, R. 1997. Ancestral echoes. *New Scientist* 2089, 32–37.

Lewis, G. 1975. *Knowledge of Illness in a Sepik Society: A Study of Gnau, New Guinea.* New Jersey: Humanities Press Inc.

Lewis-Williams, J.D. 1981. *Believing and Seeing. Symbolic Meanings in Southern San Rock Paintings.* Cambridge: Cambridge University Press.

Lewis-Williams, J.D. 1982. The economic and social context of southern San rock art. *Current Anthropology* 23, 429–49.

Lewis-Williams, J.D. 1984. Ideological continuities in prehistoric southern Africa: The evidence of rock art. In *Past and Present in Hunter-Gatherer Studies* (ed. C. Schrire), pp. 225–52. New York: Academic Press.

Lewis-Williams, J.D. 1987. A dream of eland: An unexplored component of San shamanism and rock art. *World Archaeology* 19, 165–76.

Lewis-Williams, J.D. 2002. *The Mind in the Cave.* London: Thames & Hudson.

Lewis-Williams, J.D. & Dowson, T.A. 1988. The signs of all times: entoptic phenomena in Upper Palaeolithic art. *Current Anthropology* 29, 201–45.

Lewthwaite, J. 1986. The transition to food production: A Mediterranean perspective. In *Hunters in Transitions* (ed. M. Zvelebil), pp. 53–66. Cambridge: Cambridge University Press.

Li, J., Lowenstein, T.K., Brown, C.B., Ku, T.-L. & Luo, S. 1996. A 100 KA record of water tables and paleoclimates from salt cores, Death Valley, California. *Palaeogeography, Palaeoclimatology, Palaeoecology* 123, 179–203.

Lieberman, D.E. 1993. The rise and fall of seasonal mobility among hunter-gatherers: The case of the Southern Levant. *Current Anthropology* 34, 599–631.

Liere, van W.J. 1980. Traditional water management in the lower Mekong Basin. *World Archaeology* 11, 265–80.

Lillie, M.C. 1998. The Mesolithic-Neolithic transition in Ukraine: New radiocarbon determinations for the cemeteries of the Dnieper Rapids region. *Antiquity* 72, 184–8.

Lister, A.M. 1993. Mammoths in miniature. *Nature* 362, 288–9.

Lister, A.M. & Bahn, P. 1995. *Mammoths.* London: Boxtree Press.

Lloyd, S. 1938. Some ancient sites in the Sinjar district. *Iraq* 5, 123–42.

Lloyd, S. & Safar, F. 1945. Tell Hassuna. Excavations by the Iraq Government Directorate General of Antiquities in 1943 and 1944. *Journal of Near Eastern Studies* 4, 255–89.

Lopez, B. 1986. *Arctic Dreams. Imagination and Desire in a Northern Landscape.* New York: Charles Scribner's Sons.

Lorblanchet, M. 1984. Grotte de Pech Merle. In *L'Art des Cavernes: Atlas Grottes Ornées Paléolithique Francaise*, pp. 467–4. Paris: Imprimerie Nationale.

Lourandas, H. 1997. *Continent of Hunter-Gatherers. New Perspectives in Australian Prehistory.* Cambridge: Cambridge University Press.

Lovelock, J, 1979. *Gaia: A New Look at Life in Earth.* Oxford: Oxford University Press.

Lowe, J.J. & Walker, M.J.C. 1997. *Reconstructing Quaternary Environments.* 2nd edn. Harlow: Prentice-Hall.

Loy, T., Spiggs, M. & Wickler, S. 1992. Direct evidence for human use of plants 28,000 years ago: Starch residues on stone artefacts from the northern Solomon islands. *Antiquity* 66, 898–912.

Lu, T. Li Dan, 1999. *The Transition from Foraging to Farming and the Origin of Agriculture in China.* Oxford: British Archaeological Reports, International Series 774.

Lubbock, John. 1865. *Pre-historic Times, as Illustrated by Ancient Remains, and the Manners and Customs of Modern Savages.* London: Williams & Norgate.

Lubell, D., Jackes, M. & Meiklejohn, C. 1989. Archaeology and human biology of the Mesolithic-Neolithic transition in South Portugal. In *The Mesolithic in Europe* (ed. C. Bonsall), pp. 632–40. Edinburgh: John Donald.

Lukacs, J.R. & Pal, J.N. 1992. Dental anthropology of Mesolithic hunter-gatherers: A preliminary report on the Mahadaha and Sarai Nahar Rai dentition. *Man and Environment* XVII, 45–55.

Lundelius, E.L., Jr, & Graham, R. 1999. The weather changed: Shifting climate dissolved ancient animal alliances. *Discovering Archaeology,* Sept. /Oct. 1999, 48–53.

MacDonald, K.C. 2000. The origins of African livestock: Indigenous or imported? In *The Origins and Development of African Livestock* (eds. R.M. Blench & K.C. MacDonald), pp. 2–17. London: University College London Press.

MacLeish, K. 1972. The Tasadays: Stone age cavemen of Mindanao. *National Geographic* 142, 219–49.

MacPhee, R.D.E. & Marx, P.A. 1999. Mammoths and microbes: Hyperdisease attacked the New World. *Discovering Archaeology,* Sept. /Oct. 1999, 54–9.

Maggi, R. 1997. *Arene Candide. Functional and Environmental Assessment of the Holocene Sequence.* Rome: Ministero per i Beni Culturali e Ambientali (Memorie dell' Instituto Italiano di Paleontologia Umana V).

Maley, J. 1993. The climatic and vegetational history of the equatorial regions of Africa during the Upper Quaternary. In *The Archaeology of Africa, Food, Metals and Towns* (eds. T. Shaw, P. Sinclair, B. Andah & A. Okpoko), pp. 43–52. London: Routledge.

Mandryk, C.A.S. 1996. Late glacial vegetation and environment on the eastern foothills of the Rocky Mountains, Alberta, Canada. *Journal of Paleolimnology* 16, 37–57.

Mandryk, C.A.S., Josenhans, H., Fedje, D.W. & Mathews, R.W. 2001. Late Quaternary palaeoenvironments in Northwestern North America: Implications for inland versus coastal migration routes. *Quaternary Science Reviews* 20, 301–14.

Manning, S. 1991. Approximate calendar date for the first human settlement on Cyprus. *Antiquity* 65, 870–8.

Marcus, J. & Flannery, K. 1996. *Zapotec Civilization: How Urban Society Evolved in Mexico's Oaxaca Valley.* London: Thames & Hudson.

Marean, C. 1992. Implications of Late Quaternary mammalian fauna from Lukenya Hill (South-Central Kenya) for palaeoenvironmental change and faunal extinctions. *Quaternary Research* 37, 239–55.

Marean, C. 1997. Hunter-gatherer foraging strategies in tropical grasslands: Model building and testing in the East African Middle and Later Stone Age. *Journal of Anthropological Archaeology* 16, 189–225.

Marean, C. & Gifford-Gonzalez, D. 1991. Late Quaternary extinct ungulates of East Africa and palaeoenvironmental implications. *Nature* 350, 418–20.

Marks, A.E. & Larson, P.A. 1977. Test excavations at the Natufian site of Rosh Horesha. In *Prehistory and Palaeoenvironments in the Central Negev, Israel II* (ed. A.E. Marks), pp. 181–232. Dallas: Southern Methodist University Press.

Marshack, A. 1972. *The Roots of Civilization.* London: Weidenfeld & Nicolson.

Marshall, F. & Hildebrand, E. 2002. Cattle before crops: The beginnings of food production in Africa. *Journal of World Prehistory* 16, 99–143.

Marshall, G. 2000a. The distribution of beach pebble flint in Western Scotland with reference to raw material use during the Mesolithic. In *Hunter-Gatherer Landscape Archaeology, The Southern Hebrides Mesolithic Project 1988–98* Vol. 1 (ed. S. Mithen), pp. 75–7. Cambridge: McDonald Institute for Archaeological Research.

Marshall, G. 2000b. The distribution and character of flint beach pebbles on Islay as a source for Mesolithic chipped stone artefact production. In *Hunter-Gatherer Landscape Archaeology, The Southern Hebrides Mesolithic Project 1988–98* Vol. 1, (ed. S. Mithen), pp. 79–90. Cambridge: McDonald Institute for Archaeological Research.

Marshall, L. 1976. *The !Kung of Nyae Nyae.* Cambridge, MA: Harvard University Press.

Martin, L., Russell, N. & Carruthers, D. 2001. Animal remains from the Central Anatolian Neolithic. In *The Neolithic of Central Anatolia* (eds. F. Gerard & L. Thissen), pp. 193–206. Istanbul: Yayinlari.

Martin, P.S. 1984. Prehistoric overkill: The global model. In *Quaternary Extinctions* (eds. P.S. Martin & R.G. Klein), pp. 354–403. Tucson: University of Arizona Press.

Martin, P.S. 1999. The time of the hunters. *Discovering Archaeology,* Sept./Oct. 1999, 41–7.

Martin, P.S. & Klein, R.G. (eds.) 1984. *Quaternary Extinctions. A Prehistoric Revolution.* Tucson: Arizona University Press.

Martin, P.S., Sabels, B.E. & Shulter, R., Jr, 1961. Rampart Cave coprolite and ecology of the shasta ground sloth. *American Journal of Science* 259, 102–27.

Martin, P.S., Thompson, R.S. & Long, A. 1985. Shasta ground sloth extinction: A test of the Blitzkrieg model. In *Environments and Extinctions. Man in Late Glacial North America* (eds. J.I. Mead & D.J. Meltzer), pp. 5–14. Orono, ME: Centre for the Study of Early Man.

Masson, V.M. & Sarianidi, V.I. 1972. Central Asia, *Turkmenia Before the Achaemenids*. London: Thames & Hudson.

Mathpal, Y. 1984. *Prehistoric Rock Paintings of Bhimbetka*. New Delhi: Abhinar Publications.

Matiskainen, H. 1990. Mesolithic subsistence in Finland. In *Contributions to the Mesolithic in Europe* (eds. P.M. Vermeersch & P. van Peer), pp. 211–14. Leuven: Leuven University Press.

Matsui, A. 1999. Wetland archaeology in Japan: Key sites and features in the research history. In *Bog Bodies, Sacred Sites and Wetland Archaeology* (eds. B. Coles, J. Coles & M.S. Jørgensen), pp. 147–56. University of Exeter, Dept. of Archaeology: WARP, Occasional Paper 12.

Matsuoka, Y., Vigouroux, Y., Goodman, M.M., Sanchez, J., Buckler, E. & Doebley, J. 2002. A single domestication for maize shown by multi-locus microsatellite genotyping. *Proceedings of the National Academy of Sciences* 99, 6080–4.

Matthews, P. 1991. A possible tropical wildtype taro: *Colocasia esculenta var. aquatilis*. In *Indo-Pacific Prehistory, 1990*, Vol. 2, (ed. P. Bellwood), pp. 69–81. *Bulletin of the Indo-Pacific Prehistory Association* 11.

Matthews, R. 2000. The *Early Prehistory of Mesopotamia 500,000 to 4,500 BC. Subartu* V. Turnhout: Brepols publishers.

Matthews, T. 1999. Taphonomy and the micro-mammals from Elands Bay Cave. *South African Archaeological Bulletin* 54, 133–40.

Matthews, W., French, C.A.I., Lawrence, T. & Cutler, D. 1996. Multiple surfaces: The micromorphology. In *On the Surface: Çatalhöyük 1993–95* (ed. I. Hodder), pp. 79–100. Cambridge: McDonald Inst. for Archaeological Research.

Matthews, W., French, C.A.I., Lawrence, T., Cutler, D.F. & Jones, M.K. 1997. Microstratigraphic traces of site formation processes and human activities. *World Archaeology* 29, 281–308.

Matthiessen, P. 2000. *An African Trilogy*. London: The Harvill Press.

Mattison, C. 1992. *Frogs and Toads of the World*. London: Blandford.

McBurney, C.B.M. 1967. The *Haua Fteah (Cyrenaïca) and the Stone Age of the South-East Mediterranean*. Cambridge: Cambridge University Press.

McCarthy, J.J., Canziani, O.F., Leary, N.A., Dokken, D.J. & White, K.S. 2001. *Climate Change 2001: Impacts, Adaptation, and Vulnerability*. Cambridge: Cambridge University Press.

Mead, J.I. & Meltzer, D.J (eds.) 1985. *Environments and Extinctions. Man in Late Glacial North America*. Orono, ME: Centre for the Study of the Early Man.

Meadow, R.H. 1996. The origins and spread of agriculture and pastoralism in northwestern South Asia. In *The Origins and Spread of Agriculture and Pastoralism in Eurasia* (ed. D.R. Harris), pp. 390–412. London: University College London Press.

Meehan, B. 1982. *From Shell Bed to Shell Midden*. Canberra: Institute of Aboriginal Studies.

Meiklejohn, C. & Zvelebil, M. 1991. Health status of European populations at the agricultural transition and the implications for the adoption of farming. In *Health in Past Societies* (eds. H. Bush & M. Zvelebil), pp. 129–43. Oxford: British Archaeological Reports, International Series 567.

Mellaart, J. 1967. *Çatal Höyük. A Neolithic Town in Turkey in Anatolia*. London: Thames & Hudson.

Mellaart, J., Hirsch, U. & Balpinar, B. 1989. *The Goddess from Anatolia*. Milan: Eskenazi.

Mellars, P. 1987. *Excavations on Oronsay*. Edinburgh: University Press.

Mellars, P. 1989. Major issues in the emergence of modern humans. *Current Anthropology* 30, 349–85.

Mellars, P. 1996. *The Neanderthal Legacy*. Princeton, NJ: Princeton University Press.

Mellars, P. & Dark, P. 1998. *Star Carr in Context*. Cambridge: McDonald Institute of Archaeological Research.

Mellars, P. & Wilkinson, M.R. 1980. Fish otoliths as evidence of seasonality in prehistoric shell middens: The evidence from Oronsay (Inner Hebrides). *Proceedings of the Prehistoric Society* 46, 19–44.

Meltzer, D.J. 1989. Why we don't know when the first people came to North America. *American Antiquity* 54, 471–90.

Meltzer, D.J. 1993a. *Search for the First Americans*. Washington, DC: Smithsonian Institution Press.

Meltzer, D.J. 1993b. Pleistocene peopling of the Americas. *Evolutionary Anthropology* 117, 15–69.

Meltzer, D.J. 1993c. Is there a Clovis adaptation? In *From Kostenki to Clovis* (eds. O. Soffer & N.D. Praslov), pp. 293–307. New York: Plenum Press.

Meltzer, D.J. 1994. The discovery of deep time: A history of views on the peopling of the Americas. In *Method and Theory for Investigating the Peopling of the Americas* (eds. R. Bonnichsen & D. Gentry Steele), pp. 7–26. Corvallis, OR: Centre for the Study of the First Americans.

Meltzer, D.J. 1997. Monte Verde and the Pleistocene peopling of the Americas. *Science* 276, 754–5.

Meltzer, D.J. 1999. Human responses to Middle Holocene (Altithermal) climates on the North American Great Plains. *Quaternary Research* 52, 404–16.

Meltzer, D.J. 2000. Renewed investigations at the Folsom Palaeoindian type site. *Antiquity* 74, 35–6.

Meltzer, D.J. n.d.a. Modelling the initial colonization of the Americas: issues of scale, demography and landscape learning. In *Pioneers of the Land. The Initial Human Colonization of the Americas* (eds. G.A. Clark & C. Michael Barton). Tucson: University of Arizona Press.

Meltzer. D.J. n.d.b. What do you do when no one's been there before? Thoughts on the exploration and colonization of new lands. In *The First Americans. The Pleistocene Colonization of the New World* (ed. N. Jablonski), *Memoirs of the California Academy of Sciences*, 27, 25–56.

Meltzer, D.J., Adovasio, J.M. & Dillehay, T.D. 1994. On a Pleistocene occupation at Pedra Furada, Brazil. *Antiquity* 68, 695–714.

Meltzer, D.J. & Mead, J.I. 1985. Dating Late Pleistocene extinctions: Theoretical issues, analytical bias and substantive results. In *Environments and Extinctions. Man in Late Glacial North America* (eds. J.I. Mead & D.J. Meltzer), pp. 145–74. Orono, ME: Centre for the Study of Early Man.

Mercer, J. 1974. Glenbatrick Waterhole, a microlithic site on the Isle of Jura. *Proceedings of the Society of Antiquaries of Scotland* 105, 9–32.

Mercer, J. 1980. Lussa Wood I: The late glacial and early postglacial occupation of Jura. *Proceedings of the Society of Antiquaries of Scotland* 110, 1–31.

Merpert, N.Y. & Munchaev, R.M. 1993. Yarim Tepe I. In *Early Stages in the Evolution of Mesopotamian Civilization. Soviet Excavations in Northern Iraq* (eds. N. Yoffee & J.J. Clarke), pp. 73–114. Tucson: University of Arizona Press.

Merrick, H.V. & Brown, F.H. 1984. Obsidian sources and patterns of source utilization in Kenya and northern Tanzania: Some initial findings. *African Archaeological Review* 2, 129–52.

Mestel, R. 1997. Noah's Flood. *New Scientist* 1156, 24–7.

Miller, S. 1979. Lukenya Hill, GvJm46, excavation report. *Nyame Akuma* 14, 31–4.

Miller, S. et al. 1999. Pleistocene extinction of *Genyornis newtoni*: human impact on Australian megafauna. *Science* 205–8.

Minaminihon, S. 1997. *Hakkutsu!! Uehorara Iseki* (The Excavation of Uenohara Site). Kagoshima: Minaminihon Shinbunsha.

Minc, L.D. 1986. Scarcity and survival: The role of oral tradition in mediating subsistence crisis. *Journal of Anthroplogical Archaeology* 5, 39–113.

Miracle, P., Galanidou, N. & Forenbaher, S. 2000. Pioneers in the hills: Early Mesolithic foragers at Šebrn Abri (Istria Croatia). *European Journal of Archaeology* 3, 293–329.

Misra, V.N. 1973. Bagor: A late Mesolithic settlement in north-west India. *World Archaeology* 5, 92–100.

Misra, V.N. 1989a. Stone age India: An ecological perspective. *Man and Environment* XIV, 17–33.

Misra, V.N. 1989b. Hasmukh Dhirajlal Sankalia (1908–1989): Scholar and Man. *Man and Environment* XIV, 1–20.

Mitchell, P. 1990. A palaeoecological model for archaeological site distribution in southern Africa during the Upper Pleniglacial and Late Glacial. In *The World at 18,000 B.P., Vol. Two: Low Latitudes* (eds. C. Gamble & O. Soffer), pp. 189–205. London: Unwin Hyman.

Mitchell, P. 1997. Holocene later stone age hunter-gatherers south of the Limpopo River, ca. 10,000–2000 B.P. *Journal of World Prehistory* 11, 359–424.

Mitchell, P.J., Yates, R. & Parkington, J.E. 1996. At the transition. The Archaeology of the Pleistocene-Holocene boundary in Southern Africa. In *Humans at the End of the Ice Age, The Archaeology of the Pleistocene-Holocene Transition* (eds. L.G. Straus, B.V. Eriksen, J.M. Erlandson & D.R. Yesner), pp. 15–41. New York: Plenum Press.

Mithen, S.J. 1988. Looking and learning: Upper Palaeolithic art and information gathering. *World Archaeology* 19, 297–327.

Mithen, S.J. 1989. To hunt or to paint? Animals and art in the Upper Palaeolithic. *Man* (N.S.) 23, 671–95

Mithen, S.J. 1990. *Thoughtful Foragers. A Study of Prehistoric Decision Making.* Cambridge: Cambridge University Press.

Mithen, S.J. 1991. Ecological interpretations of Palaeolithic art. *Proceedings of the Prehistoric Society* 57, 103–14.

Mithen, S.J. 1993a. Simulating mammoth hunting and extinction: Implications for the Late Pleistocene of the Central Russian Plain. In *Hunting and Animal Exploitation in the Later Palaeolithic and Mesolithic of Eurasia* (eds. G.L. Petersen, H. Bricker & P. Mellars), pp. 163–78. Tucson: Archaeological Papers of the American Anthropological Association.

Mithen, S.J. 1993b. Individuals, groups and the Palaeolithic record: A reply to Clark. *Proceedings of the Prehistoric Society* 59, 393–8.

Mithen, S.J. 1994. The Mesolithic Age. In *The Oxford Illustrated Prehistory of Europe* (ed. B. Cunliffe), pp. 79–135. Oxford: Oxford University Press.

Mithen, S.J. 1996b. Simulating mammoth hunting and extinctions: Implications for North America. In *Time, Process and Structured Transformation in Archaeology* (eds. S. van der Leeuw & J. McGlade), pp. 176–215. London: Routledge.

Mithen, S.J. 1998. *The Prehistory of the Mind. A Search for the Origins of Art, Science and Religion.* New edn. London: Orion.

Mithen, S.J. 1999. Hunter-Gatherers of the Mesolithic. In *The Archaeology of Britain* (ed. J. Hunter & I. Ralston), pp. 35–57. London: Routledge.

Mithen, S.J. (ed.) 2000a. *Hunter-Gatherer Landscape Archaeology, The Southern Hebrides Mesolithic Project 1988–98* (2 vols). Cambridge: McDonald Institute for Archaeological Research.

Mithen, S.J. 2000b. The Scottish Mesolithic: problems, prospects and the rationale for the Southern Hebrides Mesolithic Project. In *Hunter-Gatherer Landscape Archaeology, The Southern Hebrides Mesolithic Project 1988–98, Vol. 1* (ed. S. Mithen), pp. 9–37. Cambridge: McDonald Institute for Archaeological Research.

Mithen, S.J. 2000c. The Colonsay Survey. In *Hunter-Gatherer Landscape Archaeology, The Southern Hebrides Mesolithic Project 1988-9, Vol. 2* (ed. S. Mithen), pp. 349–58. Cambridge: McDonald Institute for Archaeological Research.

Mithen, S.J. 2000d. The Mesolithic in the Southern Hebrides: Issues of colonization, settlement and the transitions to the Neolithic and farming. In *Hunter-Gatherer Landscape Archaeology, The Southern Hebrides Mesolithic Project, 1988–98, Vol. 2* (ed. S. Mithen), pp. 597–626. Cambridge: McDonald Institute for Archaeological Research.

Mithen, S.J. 2000e. Mesolithic sedentism on Oronsay: Chronological evidence from adjacent islands in the southern Hebrides. *Antiquity* 74, 298–304.

Mithen, S.J. & Finlay, N. (& twelve contributors) 2000a. Staosnaig, Colonsay: excavations 1989–1995. In *Hunter-Gatherer Landscape Archaeology, The Southern Hebrides Mesolithic Project, 1988–98, Vol. 2* (ed. S. Mithen), pp. 359–441. Cambridge: McDonald Institute for Archaeological Research.

Mithen, S.J. & Finlay, N. (& two contributors) 2000b. Coulererach, Islay: test-pit survey and trial excavation. In *Hunter-Gatherer Landscape Archaeology, The Southern Hebrides Mesolithic Projet, 1988–98, Vol. 1* (ed. S. Mithen), pp. 217–29. Cambridge: McDonald Institute for Archaeological Research.

Mithen, S.J., Finlay, N., Carruthers, W., Carter, S. & Ashmore, P. 2001. Plant use in the Mesolithic: Evidence from Staosnaig, Isle of Colonsay. *Journal of Archaeological Science* 28, 223–34.

Mithen, S.J. & Finlayson, B. (& four contributors) 2000. Gleann Mor, Islay: Test-pit survey and trial excavation. In *Hunter-Gatherer Landscape Archaeology, The Southern Hebrides Mesolithic Project, 1988–98, Vol. 2* (ed. S. Mithen), pp. 187–205. Cambridge: McDonald Institute for Archaeological Research.

Mithen, S.J., Finlayson, B., Pirie, A., Carruthers, D. & Kennedy, A. 2000. New evidence for economic and technological diversity-in the Pre-Pottery Neolithic A: Wadi Faynan 16. *Current Anthropology* 41, 655–63.

Mithen, S.J., Finlayson, B., Mathews, M. & Woodman, P.E. 2000. The Islay Survey. In *Hunter-Gatherer Landscape Archaeology, The Southern Hebrides Mesolithic Project, 1988–98, Vol. 2* (ed. S. Mithen), pp. 153–86. Cambridge: McDonald Institute for Archaeological Research.

Mithen, S.J., Lake, M. & Finlay, N. (& six contributors) 2000a. Bolsay Farm, Islay: test-pit survey and trial excavation. In *Hunter-Gatherer Landscape Archaeology, The Southern Hebrides Mesolithic Project, 1988–89, Vol. 1* (ed. S, Mithen), pp. 259–89. Cambridge: McDonald Institute for Archaeological Research.

Mithen, S.J., Lake, M. & Finlay, N. (& six contributors) 2000b. Bolsay Farm, Islay: area excavation. In *Hunter-Gatherer Landscape Archaeology, The Southern Hebrides Mesolithic Project, 1988–98, vol. 1* (ed. S. Mithen), pp. 291–328. Cambridge: McDonald Institute for Archaeological Research.

Mithen, S.J., Marshall, G., Dopel, B. & Lake, M. 2000. The experimental knapping of flint beach pebbles. In *Hunter-Gatherer Landscape Archaeology, The Southern Hebrides Mesolithic Project, 1988–98, Vol. 2* (ed. S. Mithen), pp. 529–40. Cambridge: McDonald Institute for Archaeological Research.

Mithen, S.J. & Reed, M. 2002. Stepping Out: A computer simulation of hominid dispersal. *Journal of Human Evolution* 43, 433–62.

Mithen, S.J., Woodman, P.E., Finlay, N. & Finlayson, B. 2000. Aoradh, Islay: test-pit survey and trial excavation. In *Hunter-Gatherer Landscape Archaeology, The Southern Hebrides Mesolithic Project, 1988–98, Vol. 1* (ed. S. Mithen), pp. 231–9. Cambridge: McDonald Institute for Archaeological Research.

Miyaji, A. 1999. Storage pits and the development of plant food management in Japan during the Jomon period. In *Bog Bodies, Sacred Sites and Wetland Archaeology* (eds. B. Coles, J. Coles & M.S. Jørgensen), pp. 165–70. University of Exeter, Dept. of Archaeology: WARP, Occasional Paper 12.

Mochanov, Y.A. & Fedoseeva, S.A. 1996a. Dyuktai Cave. In *American Beginnings: The Prehistory and Palaeoecology of Beringia* (ed. F.H. West), pp. 164–74. Chicago: University of Chicago Press.

Mochanov, Y.A. & Fedoseeva, S.A. 1996b. Introduction (to Aldansk: Adlan River Valley, Sakha Republic). In *American Beginnings. The Prehistory and Palaeoecology of Beringia* (ed. F.H. West), pp. 157–63. Chicago: University of Chicago Press.

Mochanov, Y.A. & Fedoseeva, S.A. 1996c. Berelekh, Allakhovsk region. In *American Beginnings. The Prehistory and Palaeoecology of Beringia* (ed. F.H. West), pp. 218–21. Chicago: University of Chicago Press.

Mock, C.J. & Bartlein, P.J. 1995. Spatial variability of Late Quaternary palaeoclimates in the western United States. *Quaternary Research* 44, 425–33.

Moore, A.M.T. 1979. A pre-Neolithic farmers' village on the Euphrates. *Scientific American* 241, 50–8.

Moore, A.M.T. 1991. Abu Hureyra I and the antecedents of agriculture on the Euphrates. In *The Natufian Culture in the Levant* (eds. O. Bar-Yosef & F. Valla), pp. 277–94. Ann Arbor, MI: International Monographs in Prehistory.

Moore, A.M.T. 2000. The excavation of Abu Hureyra 1. In *Village on the Euphrates* (by A.M.T. Moore, G.C. Hillman & A.J. Legge), pp. 105–31. Oxford: Oxford University Press.

Moore, A.M.T., Hillman, G. & Legge, A.J. 2000. *Village on the Euphrates.* Oxford: Oxford University Press.

Morais Arnaud, J.E. 1989. The Mesolithic communities of the Sado Valley, Portugal, in their ecological setting. In *The Mesolithic in Europe* (ed. C. Bonsall), pp. 614–31. Edinburgh: John Donald.

Mori, F. 1998. *The Great Civilisations of the Ancient Sahara.* Rome: L'Erma, di Bretschneider.

Morley, R. & Fenley, J. 1987. Late Cainozoic vegetation and environmental change in the Malay archipelago. In *Biogeographical Evolution of the Malay Archipelago* (ed. T.C. Whitmore). Oxford: Clarendon Press.

Morris, B. 1999. The Hill Pandaram of Kerala. In *The Cambridge Encyclopedia of Hunters and Gatherers* (eds. R.B. Lee & R. Daly), pp. 265–8. Cambridge: Cambridge University Press.

Morrison, A. & Bonsall, C. 1989. The early postglacial settlement of Scotland, a review. In *The Mesolithic in Europe* (ed. C. Bonsall), pp. 134–42. Edinburgh: John Donald.

Morrison, K. 1999. Archaeology of South Asian hunters and gatherers. In *The Cambridge Encyclopedia of Hunters and Gatherers* (eds. R.B. Lee & R. Daly), pp. 238–42. Cambridge: Cambridge University Press.

Morton, J. 1999. The Arrernte of Central Australia. In *The Cambridge Encyclopedia of Hunter-Gatherers* (eds. R.B. Lee & R. Daly), pp. 329–34. Cambridge: Cambridge University Press.

Mosimann, J.E. & Martin, P.S. 1975. Simulating overkill by Palaeoindians. *American Scientist* 63, 304–13.

Moulherat, C., Tengberg, A., Haquet, J-F. & Mille, B. 2002. First evidence of cotton at Neolithic Mehrgarh, Pakistan: Analysis of mineralised fibres from a copper bead. *Journal of Archaeological Science* 29, 1393–1401.

Mountain, M.-J. 1993. Bones, hunting and predation in the Pleistocene of northern Sahul. In *Sahul in Review* (eds. M.A. Smith, M. Spriggs & B. Frankhauser), pp. 123–30. Canberra: Department of Prehistory, Occasional Papers in Prehistory 24.

Moeyersons, J. & Roche, E. 1982. Past and present environments. In *The Archaeology of Central Africa* (ed. F. van Noten), pp. 15–26. Graf: Akademische Drück und Verlagsanstalt.

Moyle, P.B. & Cech, J.J., Jr, 1996. *Fishes: An Introduction to Icthyology.* 3rd edn. London: Prentice-Hall International Ltd.

Mulvaney, J. & Kamminga, J. 1999. *Prehistory of Australia.* Washington, DC: Smithsonian Institution Press.

Murty, M.L.K. 1974. A Late Pleistocene cave site in Southern India. *Proceedings of the American Philosophical Society* 118, 196–230.

Muzzolini, A. 1989. Les débuts de la domestication des animaux en Afrique: Faits et problèmes. *Ethnozootechnie* 42, 7–22.

Nadel, D. 1990. The Khiamian as a case of Sultanian intersite variability. *Journal of the Israel Prehistoric Society* 23, 86–99.

Nadel, D. 1994. Levantine Upper Palaeolithic – Early Epi-palaeolithic burial customs: Ohalo II as a case study. *Paléorient* 20, 113–21.

Nadel, D. 1996. The organisation of space in a fisher-hunter-gatherers' camp at Ohalo II, Israel. In *Nature et Culture* (ed. M. Otte), pp. 373–88. Liège: University of Liège E.R.A.U.L. 69.

Nadel, D., Bar-Yosef, O., Gopher, A. 1991. Early Neolithic arrowhead types in the southern Levant: A typological suggestion. *Paléorient* 17, 109–19.

Nadel, D., Carmi, I., & Segal, D. 1995. Radiocarbon dating of Ohalo II: Archaeological and methodological implications. *Journal of Archaeological Science* 22, 811–22.

Nadel, D., Danin, A., Werker, E., Schick, T., Kislev, M.E. & Stewart, K. 1994. 19,000 years-old twisted fibres from Ohalo II. *Current Anthropology* 35, 451–8.

Nadel, D. & Hershkovitz, I. 1991. New subsistence data and human remains from the earliest Levantine Epipalaeolithic. *Current Anthropology* 32, 631–5.

Nadel, D. & Werker, E. 1999. The oldest ever brush hut plant remains from Ohalo II, Jordan Valley, Israel (19,000 BP). *Antiquity* 73, 755–64.

Nagar, M. & Misra, V.N. 1990. The Kanjars – A hunting-gathering community of the Ganga Valley, Uttar Pradesh. *Man and Environment* XV, 71–88.

National Geographic 1971. First glimpse of a stone age tribe. *National Geographic* 140, 882.

Nettle, D. 1999. *Linguistic Diversity.* Oxford: Oxford University Press.

Newby, E. 1954. *A Short Walk in the Hindu Kush.* London: Secker & Warburg.

Newell, R.R., Constandse-Westermann, T.S. & Meiklejohn, C. 1979. The skeletal remains of Mesolithic man in western Europe: An evaluative catalogue. *Journal of Human Evolution* 81, 1–228.

Nichols, J. 1990. Linguistic diversity and the first settlement of the New World. *Language* 66, 475–521.

Nissen, H. 1990. Basta: Excavations of 1986–89. *The Near East in Antiquity* 4, 75–85.

Noe-Nygaard, N. 1973. The Vig bull: New information on the final hunt. *Bulletin of the Geological Society of Denmark* 22, 244–8.

Noe-Nygaard, N. 1974. Mesolithic hunting in Denmark illustrated by bone injuries caused by human weapons. *Journal of Archaeological Science* 1, 217–48.

Noy, T. 1989. Gilgal I: A Pre-pottery Neolithic site. *Paléorient* 15, 11–18.

Noy, T. 1991. Art and decoration of the Natufian at Nahal Oren. In *The Natufian Culture in the Levant* (eds. O. Bar-Yosef & F.R. Valla), pp.

557–68. Ann Arbor, MI: International Monographs in Prehistory.

Noy, T., Legge, A.J. & Higgs, E.S. 1973. Recent excavations at Nahal Oren, Israel. *Proceedings of the Prehistoric Society* 39, 75–99.

Noy, T., Schuldrenrein, J. & Tchernov, E. 1980. Gilgal, a Pre-pottery Neolithic A site in the Lower Jordan Valley. *Israel Exploration Journal* 30, 63–82.

Oates, J. 1973. The background and development of early farming communities in Mesopotamia and the Zagros. *Proceedings of the Prehistoric Society* 39, 147–81.

Oates, J. 1994. 'An extraordinarily ungrateful conceit': A western publication of important Soviet field studies. *Antiquity* 68, 882–5.

O'Connell, J.F. & Allen, J. 1998. When did humans first arrive in greater Australia and why is it important to know? *Evolutionary Anthropology* 6, 132–46.

O'Connell, J.F. & Hawkes, K. 1981. Alyawara plant use and optimal foraging theory. In *Hunter-Gatherer Foraging Strategies: Ethnographic and Archaeological Analysis* (eds. B. Winterhalder & E.A. Smith), pp. 99–125. Chicago: University of Chicago Press.

O'Connell, J.F., Hawkes, K. & Blurton-Jones, N. 1988. Hadza hunting, butchering, and bone transport and their archaeological implications. *Journal of Anthropological Research* 44, 113–61.

O'Hanlon, R. 1985. *Into the Heart of Borneo*. London: Penguin.

Olsen, S. 1999. Investigation of the Phanourios bones for evidence of cultural modification. In *Faunal Extinction in and Island Society* (ed. A. Simmons), pp. 230–7. New York: Plenum Press.

Ortea, J. 1986. The Malacology of La Riera Cave. In *La Riera Cave-Stone Age Hunter-Gatherer Adaptations in Northern Spain* (eds. L.G. Straus & G.A. Clark), pp. 289–98. Arizona State University. Anthropological research papers, No. 36.

O'Shea, J.M. & Zvelebil, M. 1984. Oleneostrovski Mogilnik: Reconstructing the social and economic organization of prehistoric foragers in northern Russia. *Journal of Anthropological Archaeology* 3, 1–140.

Otte, M. & Straus, L.G. 1997. *La Grotte du Bois Laiterie*. Liège: Études et Recherches Archéologiques de l'Université de l'Université de Liège, No. 80.

Ouzman, S. & Wadley, L. 1997. A history in paint and stone from Rose Cottage Cave, South Africa. *Antiquity* 71, 386–404.

Owen, J. 1999. The collections of Sir John Lubbock, the first Lord Avebury (1834–1913). *Journal of Material Culture* 4, 282–302.

Owen-Smith, N. 1987. Pleistocene extinctions: The pivotal role of mega-herbivores. *Palaeobiology* 13, 351–62.

Özdoğan, A. 1999. Çayönü. In *Neolithic in Turkey. The Cradle of Civilization, New Discoveries* (eds. M. Özdoğan & N. Başgelen), pp. 35–64. Istanbul: Arkeoloji ve Sanat Yayinlari.

Özdoğan, M. & Başgelen, N. (eds) 1999. *Neolithic in Turkey: The Cradle of Civilization, New Discoveries*. Istanbul: Arkeoloji ve Sanat Yayinlari.

Özdoğan, M. & Özdoğan, A. 1998. Buildings of cult and the cult of buildings. In *Light on Top of the Black Hill* (eds. G. Arsebuk et al.), pp. 581–93. Istanbul: Ege Yayinlari.

Pachur, H.-J. 1991. Tethering stones as palaeoenvironmental indicators. *Sahara* 4, 13–32.

Pal, J.N. 1992. Mesolithic human burials in the Ganga Plain, North India. *Man and Environment* XVII, 35–44.

Pal, J.N. 1994. Mesolithic settlements in the Ganga Plain. *Man and Environment* XIX, 91–101.

Pardoe, C. 1988. The cemetery as symbol: the distribution of Aboriginal burial grounds in southeastern Australia. *Archaeology in Oceania* 23, 1–16.

Pardoe, C. 1995. Riverine, biological and cultural evolution in southeastern Australia. *Antiquity* 69, 696–713.

Parker, E.N. 1999. Sunny side of global warming. *Nature* 399, 416–17.

Parkin, R.A., Rowley-Conwy, P. & Serjeantson, D. 1986. Late Palaeolithic exploitation of horse and red deer at Gough's Cave, Cheddar, Somerset. *Proceedings of the University of Bristol Speleological Society* 17, 311–30.

Parkington, J.E. 1980. The Elands Bay cave sequence: Cultural stratigraphy and subsistence strategies. *Proceedings of the 8th Pan-African Congress of Prehistory and Quaternary Studies*, Nairobi, pp. 315–20.

Parkington, J.E. 1984. Changing views of the Later Stone Age of South Africa. *Advances in World Archaeology* 3, 89–142.

Parkington, J.E. 1986. Landscape and subsistence changes since the last glacial maximum along the Western Cape coast. In *The End of the Palaeolithic in the Old World* (ed. L.G. Straus), pp. 201–27. Oxford: British Archaeological Reports, International Series 284.

Parkington, J.E. 1987. Changing views of prehistoric settlement in the Western Cape. In *Papers in the Prehistory of the Western Cape, South Africa* (eds. J.E. Parkington & M. Hall), pp. 4–20. Oxford: British Archaeological Reports, International Series 332.

Parkington, J.E. 1988. The Pleistocene/Holocene transition in the Western Cape, South Africa: Observations from Verlorenvlei. *In Prehistoric Cultures and Environments in the Late Quaternary of Africa* (eds. J. Bower & D. Lubell), pp. 349–63. Oxford: British Archaeological Reports, International Series 405.

Parkington, J.E. 1989. Interpreting paintings without a commentary. *Antiquity* 63, 13–26.

Parkington, J.E. 1990. A view from the south: Southern Africa before, during and after the Last Glacial Maximum. In *The World at 18,000 B.P., Vol. Two: Low Latitudes* (eds. C. Gamble & O. Soffer), pp. 214–28. London: Unwin Hyman.

Parkington, J.E. 1991. Approaches to dietary

reconstruction in the Western Cape: Are you what you have eaten? *Journal of Archaeological Science* 18, 331–42.

Parkington, J.E., Poggenpoel, C.A., Buchanan, W.F., Robey, T.S., Manhire, A.H. & Sealy, J.C. 1988. Holocene coastal settlement patterns in the Western Cape. In *The Archaeology of Prehistoric Coastlines* (eds. G.N. Bailey & J.E. Parkington), pp. 22–41. Cambridge: Cambridge University Press.

Pearsall, D.M 1980. Pachamachay ethnobotanical report: Plant utilization at a hunting base camp. In *Prehistoric Hunters of the High Andes* (ed. J. Rick), pp. 191–231. New York: Academic Press.

Pearsall, D.M., Piperno, D.R., Dinan, M.V., Umlauf, M., Zhao, Z. & Benfer R.A., Jr, 1995. Distinguishing rice (*Oryza sativa poaceae*) from wild *Oryza* species through phytolith analysis: results of preliminary research. *Economic Botany* 49, 183–96.

Pedersen, L. 1995. 7000 years of fishing. In *Man & Sea in the Mesolithic* (ed. A. Fischer), pp. 75–86. Oxford: Oxbow Monograph, No. 53.

Pei, A. 1990. Brief excavation report of an early Neolithic site at Pengtoushan in Lixian County, Hunan. Wenwu (Cultural Relics) 8, 17–29 (available in English translation at www.carleton.ca/~bgordon/rice/papers).

Pei, A. 1998. Notes on new advancements and revelations in the agricultural archaeology of early rice cultivation in the Dongting Lake region. *Antiquity* 72, 878–85.

Pei, A. n.d. New progress in rice agriculture and the origin of civilization: summary of results on the excavation of three major sites on the Liyang plain in Hunan, China (English translation at www.carleton.ca/~bgordon/rice/papers).

Peltenburg, E., Colledge, S., Croft, P., Jackson, A., McCartney, C. & Murray, M-A. 2000. Agro-pastoralist colonization of Cyprus in the 10th millennium BP: Initial assessments. *Antiquity* 74, 844–53.

Peltenburg, E., Colledge, S., Croft, P., Jackson, A., McCartney, C. & Murray, M-A. 2001. Neolithic dispersals from the Levantine corridor: A Mediterranean perspective. *Levant* 33, 35–64.

Penck, A. & Brückner, E. 1909. *Die Alpen im Eiszitalter*. Leipzig: Tachnitz.

Péquart, M. & Péquart S-J. 1954. *Hoëdic, Deuxième Station-Nécropole du Mésolithique Côtier Armoricain*. Anvers: De Sikkel.

Péquart, M., Péquart S-J., Boule, M. & Vallois, H. 1937. *Téviec, Station-Nécropole du Mésolithique u Morbihan*. Paris: Archives de L'Institut de Paléontologie Humaine XVIII.

Perlès, C. 1990. *Excavations at Franchthi Cave, Greece. Fascicle 5. Les Industries Lithiques Tailées de Francthi 2. Les Industries de Mésolithiques et du Néolithique Initial*. Bloomington: Indiana University Press.

Perlès, C. 2001. *The Early Neolithic in Greece. The First Farming Communities in Europe*. Cambridge: Cambridge University Press.

Peters, J. 1989. Late Pleistocene hunter-gatherers at

Ishango (eastern Zaire): The faunal evidence. *Revue de Paléobiologie* 8, 1.

Petit, J.R. et al. (eighteen additional authors). 1999. Climate and atmospheric history of the past 420,000 years from the Vostok ice core, Antarctica. *Nature* 399, 429–35.

Pfeiffer, J. 1982. *The Creative Explosion: An Enquiry into the Origins of Art and Religion*. New York: Harper & Row.

Phillips, J.L. & Brown, J.A. (eds.) 1983. *Archaic Hunters and Gatherers in the American Midwest*. New York: Academic Press.

Phillipson, D.W. 1977. Lowasera. *Azania* 12, 53–82.

Phillipson, D.W. 1985. *African Archaeology*. Cambridge: Cambridge University Press.

Pielou, E.C. 1991. *After the Ice Age, The Return of Life to Glaciated North America*. Chicago: University Chicago Press.

Piette, E. 1889. L'époque de transition intermédiaire entre l'age du renne et l'époque de la pierre polie. Paris: *Comptes rendus du 10e Congress Internationale d'Anthropologie et de l'Archaeologie Préhistorique*, pp. 203–13.

Pigeot, N. 1987. *Magdaléniens d'Etiolles. Économie de Débitage et Organisation Sociale*. Paris: CNRS.

Pigeot, N. 1990. Technical and social actors: Flint knapping specialists and apprentices at Magdalenian Etiolles. *Archaeological Review from Cambridge* 9, 126–41.

Piperno, D.R. & Flannery, K.V. 2001. The earliest archaeological maize (*Zea mays L.*) from highland Mexico: New accelerator mass spectometry dates and their implications. *Proceedings of the National Academy of Sciences* 98, 2101–3.

Piperno, D.R. & Pearsall, D.M. 1998. *The Origins of Agriculture in Lowland Neotropics*. San Diego: Academic Press.

Pirazzoli, P.A. 1991. *World Atlas of Holocene Sea Level Change*. Amsterdam: Elsevier.

Pitts, M. 1979. Hides and antlers: A new look at the gatherer-hunter site at Star Carr, North Yorkshire, England. *World Archaeology* 11, 32–42.

Pitul'ko, V. 1993. An early Holocene site in the Siberian high Arctic. *Arctic Anthropology* 30, 13–21.

Pitul'ko, V. 2001. Terminal Pleistocene–Early Holocene occupation in northeast Asia and the Zhokhov assemblage. *Quaternary Science Review* 20, 267–75.

Pitul'ko, V. & Kasparov, A. 1996. Ancient Arctic hunters: Material culture and survival strategy. *Arctic Anthropology* 33, 1–36.

Plug, I. & Engela, R. 1992. The macrofaunal remains from recent excavations at Rose Cottage Cave, Orange Free State. *South African Archaeological Bulletin* 47, 16–25.

Poggenpoel, C.A. 1987. The implications of fish bone assemblages from Elands Bay Cave, Tortoise Cave and Diepkloof for changes in the Holocene history of Verlorenvlei. In *Papers in the Prehistory of the Western Cape, South Africa* (eds. J.E. Parkington & M. Hall), pp. 212–36.

Oxford: British Archaeological Reports, International Series 332.

Politis, G. 1991. Fishtail projectile points in the southern cone of South America: An overview. In Clovis: Origins and Adaptations (eds. R. Bonnichsen & K.L. Turnmire), pp. 287–301. Corvallis, OR: Centre for the Study of the First Americans.

Pope, G. 1989. Bamboo and human evolution. Natural History 10, 49–56.

Porch, N. & Allen, J. 1995. Tasmania: archaeological and palaeoecological perspectives. Antiquity 69, 714–32.

Posseh, G. 1999. Indus Age: The Beginnings. Philadelphia: University of Pennsylvania Press.

Postgate, N. 1992. Early Mesopotamia: Society and Economy at the Dawn of History. London: Routledge.

Prakash, P.V. 1998. Vangasari: A Mesolithic cave in the Eastern Ghats, Andhra Pradesh. Man and Environment XXIII, 1–16.

Prestwich, J. 1893. On the evidence of a submergence of Western Europe and of the Mediterranean coasts at the close of the glacial or so-called post-glacial period and immediately preceding the Neolithic or recent period. Philosophical Transactions of the Royal Society, Series A, 184, 903–84.

Price, T.D. 1985. Affluent foragers of Southern Scandinavia. In Prehistoric Hunter-Gatherers, the Emergence of Cultural Complexity (eds. T.D. Price & S.A. Brown), pp. 341–60. New York: Adademic Press.

Price, T.D. 1989. The reconstruction of Mesolithic diet. In The Mesolithic in Europe (ed. C. Bonsall), pp. 48–59. Edinburgh: John Donald.

Price, T.D., Bentley, R.A., Luning, J., Gronenborn, D. & Wahl, J. 2001. Prehistoric human migration in the Linearbandkeramik of Central Europe. Antiquity 75, 593–603.

Price, T.D., Gebauer, A.B., & Keeley, L.H. 1995. Spread of farming into Europe north of the Alps. In Last Hunters, First Farmers. New Perspectives on the Prehistoric Transition to Agriculture (eds. T.D. Price & A.B. Gebauer), pp. 95–126. Sante Fe, NM: School of American Research.

Price, T.D. & Jacobs, K. 1990. Oleni' ostrov: First radiocarbon dates from a major Mesolithic cemetery in Karelia, USSR. Antiquity 64, 849–53.

Pyramarn, K. 1989. New evidence on plant exploitation and environment during the Hoabinhian (Late Stone Age) from Ban Kao Caves, Thailand. In Foraging and Farming: The Evolution of Plant Exploitation (eds. D.R. Harris & G.C. Hillman), pp. 283–91. London: Unwin Hyman.

Radcliffe-Brown, A.R. 1918. Notes on the social organisation of Australian Tribes. Journal of the Royal Anthropological Institute 48, 222–53.

Radovanović, I. 1996. The Iron Gates Mesolithic. Ann Arbor, MI: International Monographs in Prehistory, Archaeological Series, No. 11.

Radovanović, I. 1997. The Lepenski Vir culture: A contribution to interpretation of its ideological aspects. In Antidoron Dragoslavo Srejović Completis LXV Annis ad Amicus, Collegis, Discipulis Oblatum, pp. 87–93. Centre for Archaeological Research, Faculty of Philosophy, Belgrade.

Radovanović, I. 2000. Houses and burials at Lepenski Vir. European Journal of Archaeology 3, 330–49.

Ransome, A. 1927. 'Racundra's' First Cruise. London: Jonathan Cape.

Rappaport, R. 1967. Pigs for the Ancestors: Ritual in the Ecology of a New Guinea People. New Haven, CT: Yale University Press.

Rasmussen, K.L. 1994. Radiocarbon datings at Ringkloster. Journal of Danish Archaeology 12, 61–3.

Reese, D. 1991. Marine shells in the Levant: Upper Palaeolithic, Epipalaeolithic and Neolithic. In The Natufian Culture in the Levant (eds. O. Bar-Yosef & F. Valla), pp. 613–28. Ann Arbor, MI: International Monographs in Prehistory.

Reese, D.S. 1996. Cypriot hippo hunters no myth. Journal of Mediterranean Archaeology 9, 107–12.

Renfrew, C. 1973. Before Civilization. London: Jonathan Cape.

Renfrew, C. 1987. Archaeology, and Language: The Puzzle of Indo-European Origins. London: Jonathan Cape.

Renfrew, C. 1991. Before Babel: Speculations on the origins of linguistic diversity. Cambridge Archaeological Journal 1, 3–23.

Renfrew, C. 1998. Applications of DNA in archaeology: A review of the DNA studies in the Ancient Biomolecules Initiative. Ancient Biomolecules 2, 107–16.

Renfrew, C. (ed.) 2000. America Past and Present: Genes and Languages in the Americas and Beyond. Cambridge: McDonald Institute for Archaeological Research.

Renfrew, C. 2000. Archaeogenetics: Towards a population history of Europe. In Archaeogenetics. DNA and the Population Prehistory of Europe (eds. C. Renfrew & K. Boyle), pp. 3–11. Cambridge: McDonald Institute for Archaeological Research.

Renfrew, C. & Boyle, K. (eds.) 2000. Archaeogenetics: DNA and the population prehistory of Europe. Cambridge: McDonald Institute for Archaeological Research.

Rice, P.C. & Patterson, A.L. 1985. Cave art and bones: Exploring the inter-relationships. American Anthropologist 87, 94–100.

Richards, C. 1990. The late Neolithic settlement complex at Barnhouse Farm, Stennes. In The Prehistory of Orkney (ed. A.C. Renfrew), 2nd edn., pp. 305–16. Edinburgh: Edinburgh University Press.

Richards, M. & Mellars, P.A. 1998. Stable isotopes and the seasonality of the Oronsay middens. Antiquity 72, 178–84.

Richards, M.R., Côrte-Real, H., Forster, P., Macaulay, V., Wilkinson-Herbots, H.,

Demaine, A., Papiha, S., Hedges, R., Bandelt, H.-J. & Sykes, B.C. 1996. Palaeolithic and Neolithic lineages in the European mitochondrial gene pool. *American Journal of Human Genetics* 59, 185–203.

Richards, M.R., Macaulay, V., Sykes, B., Pettitt, P., Hedges, R., Forster, P. & Bandelt, H.-J. 1997. Reply to Cavalli-Sforza and Minch. *American Journal of Human Genetics* 61, 251–4.

Rick, J.W. 1980. *Prehistoric Hunters of the High Andes*. New York: Academic Press.

Rick, J.W. 1988. The character and context of highland preceramic society. In *Peruvian Prehistory* (ed. R.W. Keatinge), pp. 3–40. Cambridge: Cambridge University Press.

Ritchie, J.C. & Cwynar, L.C. 1982. The late Quaternary vegetation of the northern Yukon. In *Paleoecology of Beringia* (ed. D.M. Hopkins et al.), pp. 113–26. New York: Academic Press.

Ritchie, J.C. & Haynes, C.V. 1987. Holocene vegetation zonation in the eastern Sahara. *Nature* 330, 645–7.

Rival, L. 1999. The Huaorani. In *The Cambridge Encyclopedia of Hunters and Gatherers* (eds. R.B. Lee & R. Daly), pp. 101–4. Cambridge: Cambridge University Press.

Robbins, L.H., Murphy, M.L., Stevens, N.J., Brook, G.A., Ivester, A.H., Haberyan, K.A., Klein, R.G., Milo, R., Stewart, K.M., Matthiesen, D.G., Winkler, A.J. 1996. Palaeoenvironment and archaeology of Drotsky's Cave: Western Kalahari Desert, Botswana. *Journal of Archaeological Science* 23, 7–22.

Robbins, L.H., Murphy, M.L., Brook, G.A., Ivester, A.H., Campbell, A.C., Klein, R.G., Milo, R., Stewart, K.M., Downey, W.S., & Stevens, N.J. 2000. Archaeology, palaeoenvironment, and chronology of the Tsodilo Hills White Paintings Rock Shelter, Northwest Kalahari Desert, Botswana. *Journal of Archaeological Science* 27, 1085–13.

Roberts, R.L. (and ten authors) 2001. New ages for the last Australian mega-fauna: Continent wide extinctions about 46,000 years ago. *Science* 292, 1888–92.

Rodden, R. 1962. Excavations at the early Neolithic site of Nea Nikomedeia, Greek Macedonia. *Proceedings of the Prehistoric Society* 28, 267–88.

Rodden, R. 1965. An early Neolithic village in Greece. *Scientific American* 212/4, 82–92.

Rollefson, G.O. 1983. Ritual and ceremony at Neolithic 'Ain Ghazal. *Paléorient* 9, 29–38.

Rollefson, G.O. 1989. The aceramic neolithic of the southern Levant: The view from 'Ain Ghazal. *Paléorient* 15, 135–40.

Rollesfon, G.O. 1993. The origins of the Yarmoukian at 'Ain Ghazal. *Paléorient* 19, 91–100.

Rollefson, G.O. 1998. 'Ain Ghazal (Jordan): Ritual and ceremony III. *Paléorient* 24, 43-58.

Rollefson, G.O. 2000. Ritual and social structure at Neolithic 'Ain Ghazal. In *Life in Neolithic Farming Communities: Social Organization, Identity and Differentiation* (ed. I. Kuijt),

pp. 163–90. New York: Kluwer/Plenum Publications.

Rollefson, G.O. & Köhler-Rollefson, I. 1989. The collapse of early Neolithic settlements in the southern Levant. In *People and Culture Change: Proceedings of the Second Symposium on Upper Palaeolithic, Mesolithic and Neolithic Populations of Europe and the Mediterranean Basin* (ed. I. Hershkovitz), pp. 59–72. Oxford: British Archaeological Reports, International Series 508.

Rollefson, G.O. & Köhler-Rollefson, I. 1993. PPNC adaptations in the first half of the 6th millennium B.C. *Paléorient* 19, 33–42.

Rollefson, G.O. & Simmons, A.H. 1987. The life and death of 'Ain Ghazal. *Archaeology* Nov./Dec. 1987, 38–45.

Ronen, A. & Lechevallier, M. 1991. The Natufian at Hatula. In *The Natufian Culture in the Levant* (eds. O. Bar-Yosef & F. Valla), pp. 149–60. Ann Arbor, MI: International Monographs in Prehistory.

Roosevelt, A.C. 1994. *Amazonian Indians from Prehistory to the Present: Anthropological Perspectives*. Tucson: University of Arizona Press.

Roosevelt, A.C. 1995. Early pottery in the Amazon. In *The Emergence of Pottery, Technology and Innovation in Ancient Societies* (eds. W.K. Barnett & J.W. Hoopes), pp. 115–31. Washington, DC: Smithsonisan Institution Press.

Roosevelt, A.C. 1999. Archaeology of South American Hunters and Gatherers. In *The Cambridge Encyclopedia of Hunters and Gatherers* (eds. R.B. Lee & R. Daly), pp. 86–91. Cambridge: Cambridge University Press.

Roosevelt, A.C. et al. 1996. Palaeoindian cave dwellers in the Amazon: The peopling of the Americas. *Science* 272, 373–84.

Rosenberg, M. 1999. Hallan Çemi. In *Neolithic Turkey* (eds. M. Özdoğan & N Başgelen pp. 25–33. Istanbul: Arkeoloji ve Sanat Yayinlari.

Rosenberg, M. & Davis, M. 1992. Hallan Çemi Tepesi: Some preliminary observations concerning material culture. *Anatolica* 18, 1–18.

Rosenberg, M. & Redding, R.W. 2000. Hallan Çemi and early village organization in eastern Anatolia. In *Life in Neolithic Farming Communities* (ed. I. Kuijt), pp. 39–61. New York: Kluwer Academic/Plenum Publishers.

Rowley-Conwy, P.A. 1983. Sedentary hunters: The Ertebølle example. In *Hunter-Gatherer Economy in Prehistory* (ed. G. Bailey), pp. 111–26. Cambridge: Cambridge University Press.

Rowley-Conwy, P.A. 1984a. The laziness of the short distance hunter: The origins of agriculture in Western Denmark. *Journal of Anthropological Archaeology* 3, 300–24.

Rowley-Conwy, P.A. 1984b. Postglacial foraging and early farming economies in Japan and Korea: A west European perspective. *World Archaeology* 16, 28–41.

Rowley-Conwy, P.A. 1994. Meat, furs and skins:

Mesolithic animal bones from Ringkloster, a seasonal hunting camp in Jutland. *Journal of Danish Archaeology* 12, 87–98.

Rowley-Conwy, P.A. 1998. Cemeteries, seasonality and complexity in the Ertebølle of southern Scandinavia. In *Harvesting the Sea, Farming the Forest* (eds. M. Zvelebil, R. Dennell & L. Domańska), pp. 193–202. Sheffield: Sheffield Academic Press.

Rowley-Conwy, P.A. 2000. Milking caprines, hunting pigs: The Neolithic economy of Arene Candide in its west Mediterranean context. In *Animal Bones, Human Societies* (ed. P. Rowley-Conwy), pp. 124–32. Oxford: Oxbow Books.

Rowley-Conwy, P.A., Deakin, W.J. & Shaw, C.H. 1997. Ancient DNA from archaeological sorghum (*Sorghum bicolor*) from Qasr Ibrim, Nubia. *Sahara* 9, 23–30.

Ruddiman, W.F. & McIntyre, A. 1981. Oceanic mechanisms for amplication of the 23,000-year ice volume cycle. *Science* 212, 617–21.

Ruhlen, M. 1994. Linguistic evidence for the peopling of the Americas. In *Method and Theory for Investigating the Peopling of the Americas* (eds. R. Bonnichsen & D. Gentry Steele), pp. 177–88. Corvallis, OR: Centre for the Study of the First Americans.

Ryan, W.B.F. et al. (ten authors) 1997. An abrupt drowning of the Black Sea shelf. *Marine Geology* 138, 119–26.

Sage, R.F. 1995. Was low atmospheric CO_2 during the Pleistocene a limiting factor for the origin of agriculture? *Global Change Biology* 1, 93–106.

Sahlins, M. *Stone Age Economics*. 1974. London: Tavistock.

Sahni, A., Kumar, G., Bajpaj, S. & Srinivasan 1990. A review of late Pleistocene ostriches (*Struthio sp.*) in India. *Man and Environment* XV, 41–52.

Saidel, B.A. 1993. Round house or square? Architectural form and socio-economic organization in the PPNB. *Journal of Mediterranean Archaeology* 6, 65–108.

Sandweiss, D.H. et al. 1998. Quebrada Jaguay: Early South American maritime adaptations. *Science* 281, 1830–2.

Saunders, J.J. 1977. Lehner Ranch revisited. In *Palaeoindian Lifeways* (ed. E. Johnson), pp. 48–64. Lubbock: West Texas Museum Association.

Saunders, J.J. 1992. Blackwater Draw: mammoths and mammoth hunters in the terminal Pleistocene. In *Proboscidean and Paleoindian Interactions* (eds. J.W. Fox, C.B. Smith & K.T. Wilkins), pp. 123–47. Waco, TX: Baylor University Press.

Saxon, E.C., Close, A.E., Cluzel, C., Morse, V. & Shackleton, N.J. 1974. Results of recent investigations at Tamar Hat. *Libya* 22, 49–91.

Scarre, C. 1992. The early Neolithic of western France and Megalithic origins in Atlantic Europe. *Oxford Journal of Archaeology* 11, 121–54.

Schild, R., Królik, H., Wendorf, F. & Close, A.E. 1996. Architecture of Early Neolithic huts at Nabta Playa. In *Interregional Contacts in the Later Prehistory of Northeastern Africa* (eds. L. Krzyzaniak, K. Kroeper & M. Kobusiewicz), pp. 101–14. Poznan: Poznan Archaeological Museum.

Schilling, H. 1997. The Korsør Nor site. The permanent dwelling place of a hunting and fishing people in life and death. In *The Danish Storebælt since the Ice Age* (eds. L. Pedersen, A. Fischer & B. Aaby), pp. 93–8. Copenhagen: A/S Storebælt Fixed Link.

Schmandt-Besserat, D. 1992. *Before Writing* (2 vols.) Austin: University of Texas Press.

Schmandt-Besserat, D. 1997. Animal symbols at 'Ain Ghazal. *Expedition* 39, 48–58.

Schmandt-Besserat, D. 1998. 'Ain Ghazal 'monumental' figures. *Bulletin of the American Schools of Oriental Research* 310, 1–17.

Schmidt, K. 1994. Investigations in the Upper Mesopotamian Early Neolithic: Göbekli Tepe and Gücütepe. *Neo-lithics* 2/95, 9–10.

Schmidt, K. 1996. The Urfa-Project 1996. *Neo-lithics* 2/96, 2–3.

Schmidt, K. 1998. Beyond daily bread: Evidence of Early Neolithic ritual from Göbekli Tepe. *Neo-lithics* 2/98, 1–5.

Schmidt, K. 1999. Boars, ducks and foxes – the Urfa-Project 99. *Neo-lithics* 3/99, 12–15.

Schmidt, K. 2001. Göbekli Tepe, Southeastern Turkey. A preliminary report on the 1995–1999 excavations. *Paléorient* 26, 45–54.

Schrire, C. (ed.) 1984. *Past and Present in Hunter-Gatherer Studies*. New York: Academic Press.

Schulting, R. 1996. Antlers, bone pins and flint blades: The Mesolithic cemeteries of Téviec and Höedic, Brittany, *Antiquity* 70, 335–50.

Schulting, R. 1998. *Slighting the Sea: The Mesolithic-Neolithic Transition in Northwest Europe*. Unpublished Ph.D. thesis, University of Reading.

Schulting, R. 1999. Slighting the sea: Stable isotope evidence for the transition to farming in Northwestern Europe. *Documenta Praehistorica* XXV, 203–18.

Schuster, A.H.M. 1995. Ghosts of 'Ain Ghazal. *Archaeology* 49, 65–6.

Score, D. & Mithen, S.J. 2000. The experimental roasting of hazelnuts. In *Hunter-Gatherer Landscape Archaeology, The Southern Hebrides Mesolithic Project, 1988–98, Vol. 2* (ed. S. Mithen), pp. 507–21. Cambridge: McDonald Institute for Archaeological Research.

Sealy, J.C. & van der Merwe, N.J. 1988. Social, spatial and chronological patterning in marine food use as determined by d13C measurements of Holocene human skeletons from the south-western Cape, South Africa. *World Archaeology* 20, 87–102.

Sealy, J.C. & van der Merwe, N.J. 1992. On 'Approaches to dietary reconstruction in the Western Cape: Are you what you have eaten?' – A reply to Parkington. *Journal of Archaeological Science* 19, 459–66.

Searcy, A. 1909. *In Australian Tropics*. London: Keegan Paul, Trench, Trübner & Co.

Shackleton, J. 1988. *Excavations at Franchthi Cave, Greece. Fascicle 4. Marine Molluscan Remains from Franchthi Cave*. Bloomington: Indiana University Press.

Shackleton, N.J. 1987. Oxygen isotopes, ice volumes and sea level. *Quaternary Science Reviews* 6, 183–90.

Shackleton, N.J. & Opdyke, N.D. 1973. Oxygen isotope and palaeomagnetic stratigraphy of equatorial Pacific core V28–238: oxygen isotope temperatures and ice volume on a 10^5 and 10^6 year scale. *Quaternary Research* 3, 39–55.

Sharma, G.R. 1973. Mesolithic lake cultures in the Ganga Valley, India. *Proceedings of the Prehistoric Society* 39, 129–46

Sharma, G.R. et al. 1980. *Beginnings of Agriculture (Epi-Palaeolithic to Neolithic). Excavations at Chopani-Mando, Mahadaha and Mahagara*. Allahabad.

Shaw, T. 1969. The Late Stone Age in the Nigerian forest. *Actes 1e Colloque International d'Archéologie Africaine*, Fort Lamy, pp. 364–73.

Shaw, T. 1978. *Nigeria, Its Archaeology and Early History*. London: Thames & Hudson.

Sherratt, A. 1995. Instruments of conversion? The role of megaliths in the Mesolithic/Neolithic transition in north-west Europe. *Oxford Journal of Archaeology* 14, 245–61.

Sherratt, A. & Sherrat, S. 1988. The archaeology of Indo-European: An alternate view. *Antiquity* 62, 584–95.

Shoocongdej, R. 2000, Forager mobility organization in seasonal tropical environments of western Thailand. *World Archaeology* 32, 14–40.

Sillen, A. & Lee-Thorp, J.A. 1991. Dietary change in the Late Natufian. In *The Natufian Culture in the Levant* (eds. O. Bar-Yosef & F. Valla), pp. 399–410. Ann Arbor, MI: International Monographs in Prehistory.

Sim, R. 1990. Prehistoric sites on King Island in the Bass Straits: Results of an archaeological survey. *Australian Archaeology* 31, 34–43.

Sim, R. & Thorne, A. 1990. Pleistocene human remains from King Island, Southeastern Australia. *Australian Archaeology* 31, 44–51.

Simmons, A.L. 1996. Whose myth? Archaeological data, interpretations, and implications for the human association with extinct Pleistocene fauna at Akrotiri Aetokremnos, Cyprus. *Journal of Mediterranean Archaeology* 9, 97–105.

Simmons, A.L. 1999. *Faunal Extinctions in an Island Society. Hippo Hunters of the Akrotiri Peninsula, Cyprus*. New York: Plenum.

Simmons, A. 2000. Villages on the edge. Regional settlement change and the end of the Levantine Pre-Pottery Neolithic. In *Life in Neolithic Farming Communities: Social Organization, Identity and Differentiation* (ed. I. Kuijt), pp. 211–30. New York: Kluwer/Plenum Publications.

Simmons, A. & Najjar, M. 1996. Current investigations at Ghwair I, a Neolithic settlement in southern Jordan. *Neo-Lithics* 2, 6–7.

Simmons, A. & Najjar, M. 1998, Al-Ghuwayr I. A pre-pottery Neolithic village in Wadi Faynan, Southern Jordan: A preliminary report on the 1996 and 1997/98 seasons. *Annual Report of the Department of Antiquities of Jordan* 42, 91–101.

Smith, A.B. 1986. Review article: Cattle domestication in North Africa. *African Archaeological Review* 4, 197–203.

Smith, A.B. 1992. *Pastoralism in Africa. Origins, Development and Ecology*. Athens: Ohio University Press.

Smith, B.D. 1995. *The Emergence of Agriculture*. New York: Scientific American Library.

Smith, B.D. 1997. The initial domestication of *Cucurbita pepo* in the Americas 10,000 years ago. *Science* 276, 932–4.

Smith, B.D. 2001. Documenting plant domestication: The consilience of biological and archaeological approaches. *Proceedings of the National Academy of Sciences* 98, 1324–6.

Smith, M.A. 1987. Pleistocene occupation in arid Australia. *Nature* 328, 710–11.

Smith, M.A. 1989. The case for a resident human population in the Central Australian Ranges during full glacial aridity. *Archaeology in Oceania* 24, 93–105.

Smith, P. 1991. Dental evidence for nutritional status in the Natufians. In *The Natufian Culture in the Levant* (eds. O. Bar-Yosef & F.R.Valla), pp. 425–33. Ann Arbor, MI: International Monographs in Prehistory.

Soffer, O. 1985. *The Upper Palaeolithic of the Central Russian Plain*. Orlando: Academic Press.

Soffer, O. 1990. The Russian plain at the last glacial maximum. In *The World at 18,000 BP. Vol. One: High Latitudes* (eds. O. Soffer & C. Gamble), pp. 228–52. London: Unwin Hyman.

Soffer, O. & Gamble, C. (eds.) 1990. *The World at 18,000 BP. Vol. One: High Latitudes*. London: Unwin Hyman.

Solecki, R.S. 1963. Prehistory in Shanidar Valley, Northern Iraq. *Science* 139, 179–93.

Solecki, R.L. 1977. Predatory bird rituals at Zawi Chemi Shanidar. *Sumer* 33, 42–7.

Solecki, R.L. 1981. *An Early Village Site at Zawi Chemi Shanidar*. Malibu: Undena Publications.

Solecki, R.S. & Rubin, M. 1958. Dating of Zawi Chemi Shanidar, Northern Iraq. *Science* 127, 1446.

Sondaar, P. 1977. Insularity and its effects on mammal evolution. In *Major Patterns in Vertebrate Evolution* (eds. M. Hecht, P. Goody & B. Hecht), pp. 671–707. New York: Plenum Press.

Sondaar, P. 1986. The island sweepstakes. *Natural History* 95, 50–7.

Sondaar, P. 1987. Pleistocene Man and extinctions of island endemics. *Mémoire Société Géologique de France* (N.S.) 150, 159–65.

Spencer, W.B. & Gillen, F.J. 1912. *Across Australia*. London: Macmillan.

Sponsel, L.E. 1990.. Ultraprimitive pacifists. The Tasaday as a symbol of peace. *Anthroplogy Today* 6, 3–5.

Srejović, D. 1972. *Lepenski Vir*. London: Thames & Hudson.

Srejović, D. 1989. The Mesolithic of Serbia and Montenegro. In *The Mesolithic in Europe* (ed. C. Bonsall), pp. 481–91. Edinburgh: John Donald.

Stanford, D. 1991. Clovis origins and adaptations: An introductory perspective. In *Clovis: Origins and Adaptations* (eds. R. Bonnichsen & K.L. Turnmire), pp. 1–14. Corvallis, OR: Centre for the Study of the First Americans.

Steele, D.G. & Powell, J.P. 1994. Paleobiological evidence of the peopling of the Americas: A morphometric view. In *Method and Theory for Investigating the Peopling of the Americas* (eds. R. Bonnichsen & D. Gentry Steele), pp. 141–63 . Corvallis, OR: Centre for the Study of the First Americans.

Stegeborn, W. The Wanniyala-aetto (Veddahs) of Sri Lanka. In *The Cambridge Encyclopedia of Hunters and Gatherers* (eds. R.B. Lee & R. Daly), pp. 269–73 . Cambridge: Cambridge University Press.

Stekelis, M. & Yizraeli, T. 1963. Excavations at Nahal Oren (preliminary report). *Israel Exploration Journal* 13, 1–12.

Stock, C. 1992. *Rancho La Brea. A Record of Pleistocene Life in Calfornia.* 7th edn. Los Angeles: Natural History Museum of Los Angeles.

Stone, A.C. & Stoneking, M. 1998. MtDNA analysis of a prehistoric Oneota population: Implications for the peopling of the New World. *American Journal of Human Genetics* 62, 1153–70.

Storck, P.L. 1991. Imperialists without a state: The cultural dynamics of early paleoindian colonization as seen from the Great Lakes region. In *Clovis: Origins and Adaptations* (eds. R. Bonnichsen & K.L. Turnmire), pp. 153–62. Corvallis, OR: Centre for the Study of the First Americans.

Stordeur, D., Helmer, D. & Willcox, G. 1997. Jerf el-Ahmar, un nouveau site de l'horizon PPNA sur le moyen Euphrate Syrien. *Bulletin de la Société Préhistorique Française* 94, 282–5.

Stordeur, D., Jammous, B., Helmer, D. & Willcox, G. 1996. Jerf el-Ahmar: A new Mureybetian site (PPNA) on the Middle Euphrates. *Neo-lithics* 2/96, 1–2.

Strasser, T. 1996. Archaeological myths and the overkill hypothesis in Cypriot prehistory. *Journal of Mediterranean Archaeology* 9, 113–16.

Strathern, A. 1971. *The Rope of Moka*. Cambridge: Cambridge University Press.

Straus, L.G. 1986. Late Würm adaptive systems in Cantabrian Spain. *Journal of Anthropological Archaeology* 5, 330–68.

Straus, L.G. 1992. *Iberia Before the Iberians. The Stone Age Prehistory of Cantabrian Spain.* Albuquerque: University of New Mexico Press.

Straus, L.G. 2000. Solutrean settlement of North America? A review of reality. *American Antiquity* 65, 219–26.

Straus, L.G. & Bar-Yosef, O. (eds.) 2001. Out of Africa in the Pleistocene. *Quaternary International* 75.

Straus, L.G. & Clark, G.A. 1986. *La Riera Cave: Stone Age Hunter-Gatherer Adaptations in Northern Spain.* Arizona State University, Anthropological Research Papers No. 36.

Straus, L.G., Clark, G., Altuna, J. & Ortea, J. 1980. Ice age subsistence in northern Spain. *Scientific American* 242, 142–52.

Straus, L.G. & Otte, M. 1998. Bois Laiterie cave and the Magdalenian of Belgium. *Antiquity* 72, 253–68.

Stringer, C. & McKie, R. 1996. *African Exodus*. London: Jonathan Cape.

Struever, S. & Holton, F.A. 1979. *Koster: Americans in Search of their Prehistoric Past.* New York: Anchor Press.

Stuart, A.J. 1986. Who (or what) killed the giant armadillo? *New Scientist* 17, 29–32.

Stuart, A.J. 1991 . Mammalian extinctions in the Late Pleistocene of Northern Eurasia and North America. *Biological Reviews* 66, 453–62.

Sugden, H. & Edwards, K. 2000. The early Holocene vegetational history of Loch a'Bhogaidh, Southern Rinns, Islay, with special reference to hazel (*Corylus avellana L.*). In *Hunter-Gatherer Landscape Archaeology, The Southern Hebrides Mesolithic Project, 1988–98, Vol. 1* (ed. S. Mithen), pp. 129–48. Cambridge: McDonald Institute for Archaeological Research.

Sunderland, S. & Ray, L.J. 1959. A note on the Murray Black collection of Australian Aboriginal skeletons. *Royal Society of Victoria Proceedings* 71, 45–8.

Surovell, T.A. 2000. Early Paleoindian women, children, mobility, and fertility. *American Antiquity* 65, 493–508.

Sutcliffe, A.J. 1986. *On the Track of Ice Age Mammals*. London: British Museum.

Svensson, T.G. 1999. The Ainu. In *The Cambridge Encyclopedia of Hunter-Gatherers* (eds. R.B. Lee & R. Daly), pp. 132–6. Cambridge: Cambridge University Press.

Sykes, B. 1999. The molecular genetics of European ancestry. *Philosophical Transactions of the Royal Society of London* B. 354, 131–9.

Sykes, B. 2000. Human diversity in Europe and beyond: From blood groups to genes. In *Archaeogenetics: DNA and the Population Prehistory of Europe* (eds. C. Renfrew & K. Boyle), pp. 23–8. Cambridge: McDonald Institute for Archaeological Research.

Sykes, B. 2001. *The Seven Daughters of Eve.* London: Transworld Publishers.

Szathmary, E.J.E. 1993. Genetics of aboriginal North Americans. *Evolutionary Anthropology* 2, 202–20.

Taçon, P. 1991. The power of stone: symbolic aspects of stone use and tool development in western Arnhem Land, Australia. *Antiquity* 65, 192-207.

Taçon, P. & Brockwell, S. 1995. Arnhem Land prehistory in landscape, stone and paint. *Antiquity* 69, 676–95.

Taçon, P. & Chippindale, C. 1994. Australia's ancient warriors: Changing depictions of fighting in the rock art of Arnhem Land, N.T. *Cambridge Archaeological Journal* 4, 211–48.

Taçon, P., Wilson, M. & Chippindale, C. 1996. Birth of the Rainbow Serpent in Arnhem Land rock art and oral history. *Archaeology in Oceania* 31, 103–24.

Tangri, D. & Wyncoll, G. 1989. Of mice and men: Is the presence of commensal animals in archaeological sites a positive correlation of sedentism? *Paléorient* 15, 85–94.

Tankersley, K.B. 1998. Variation in the early paleoindian economies of Late Pleistocene eastern North America. *American Antiquity* 63, 7–20.

Tauber, H. 1981. 13^c evidence of dietary habits of prehistoric man in Denmark. *Nature* 292, 332–3.

Taylor, R.E., Haynes, C.V. & Stuiver, M. 1996. Clovis and Folsom age estimates: stratigraphic context and radiocarbon calibration. *American Antiquity* 70, 515–25.

Tchernov, E. 1991. Biological evidence for human sedentism in southwest Asia during the Natufian. In *The Natufian Culture in the Levant* (eds. O. Bar-Yosef & F. Valla), pp. 315–40. Ann Arbor, MI: International Monographs in Prehistory.

Tchernov, E. & Valla, F.R. 1997. Two new dogs, and other Natufian dogs, from the southern Levant. *Journal of Archaeological Science* 24, 65–95.

Thackeray, A.I., Thackeray, J.F., Beaumont, P.B. & Vogel, J.C. 1981. Dated rock engravings from Wonderwerk Cave, South Africa. *Science* 214, 64–7.

Thesiger, W. 2000. *Among the Mountains, Travels through Asia.* London: Flamingo.

Thomas, J. & Tilley, C. 1993. The axe and the torso: Symbolic structures in the Neolithic of Brittany. In *Interpretative Archaeology* (ed. C. Tilley), pp. 225–324. Oxford: Berg.

Thomas, P.K., Joglekar, P.P., Mishra, V.D., Pandey, J.N. & Pal, J.N. 1995. A preliminary report of the faunal remains from Damdama. *Man and Environment* XX, 29–36.

Thompson, L.G. et al. (eleven authors). 2002. Kilimanjaro ice core records: Evidence of Holocene climate change in tropical Africa. *Science* 298, 589–93.

Thompson, M.W. 1954. Azilian harpoons. *Proceedings of the Prehistoric Society* XX, 193–211.

Thomson, D.F. 1939. The seasonal factor in human culture. *Proceedings of the Prehistoric Society* 5, 209–21.

Thorley, P. 1998. Pleistocene settlement in the Australian arid zone: Occupation of an inland riverine landscape in the central Australian ranges. *Antiquity* 72, 34–45.

Thorne, A.G. 1971. Mungo and Kow Swamp: Morphological variation in Pleistocene Australians. *Mankind* 8, 85–9.

Thorne, A.G. 1977. Separation or reconciliation? Biological clues to the development of Australian society. In *Sunda and Sahul* (eds. J.

Allen, J. Golson & R. Jones), pp. 187–204. London: Academic Press.

Thorne, A.G., Grun, R., Mortimer, G., Spooner, N.A., Simpson, J.J., McCulloch, M., Taylor, L. & Curnoe, D. 1999. Australia's oldest human remains: Age of Lake Mungo 3 skeleton. *Journal of Human Evolution* 36, 591–612.

Thorne, A.G. & Macumber, P.G. 1972. Discoveries of Late Pleistocene man at Kow Swamp, Australia. *Nature* 238, 316–19.

Thubron, C. 1994. *The Lost Heart of Asia.* London: Penguin.

Thubron, C. 2000. *In Siberia.* London: Penguin.

Todd, I.A., 1987. *Vasilikos Valley Project 6: Excavations at Kalavasos-Tenta, Vol. I.* SIMA 71:6. Åström:Göteborg.

Todd, I.A. 1998. *Kalavasos-Tenta.* Nicosia: The Bank of Cyprus Cultural Foundation.

Torroni, A. 2000. Mitochondrial DNA and the origin of Native Americans. In *America Past, America Present* (ed. C. Renfrew), pp. 77–87. Cambridge: McDonald Institute for Archaeological Research.

Torroni, A., Bandelt, H.-J., D'Urbano, L., Lahermo, P., Moral, P., Sellito, D., Rengo, C., Forster, P., Savontaus, M.L., Bonné-Tamir, B. & Scozzari, R. 1998. MtDNA analysis reveals a major Palaeolithic population expansion from southwestern to northeastern Europe. *American Journal of Human Genetics* 62, 1137–52.

Torroni, A., Neel, J.V., Barrantes, R., Schurr, T.G. & Wallace, D.C. 1994. A Mitochondrial DNA 'clock' for the Amerinds and its implications for timing their entry into North America. *Proceedings of the National Academy of Sciences* 91, 1158–62.

Tree, I. 1996. *Islands in the Clouds: Travels in the Highlands of New Guinea.* London: Lonely Planet Publications.

Trigger, B. 1989. *A History of Archaeological Thought.* Cambridge: Cambridge University Press.

Trinkaus, E. 1983. *The Shanidar Neanderthals.* New York: Academic Press.

Tsukada, M. 1986. Vegetation in prehistoric Japan: The last 20,000 years. In *Windows on the Japanese Past: Studies in Archaeology and Prehistory* (ed. R.J. Pearson), pp. 11–56. Ann Arbor: Centre for Japanese Studies, University of Michigan.

Tubb, K. & Grissom. C. 1995. 'Ain Ghazal: A comparative study of the 1983 and 1985 statuary caches. In *Studies in the History and Archaeology of Jordan V* (eds. K. 'Amr, F. Zayadine & M. Zaghloul), pp. 437–47. Amman: Jordan Press Foundation.

Turner, C.G. II. 1994. Relating Eurasian and Native American populations through dental morphology. In *Method and Theory for Investigating the Peopling of the Americas* (eds. R. Bonnichsen & D. Gentry Steele), pp. 131–40. Corvallis, OR: Centre for the Study of the First Americans.

Ukraintseva, V.V., Agenbroad, L.D. & Mead, J.

1996. A palaeoenvironmental reconstruction of the 'Mammoth Epoch' of Siberia. In *American Beginnings: The Prehistory and Palaeoecology of Beringia* (ed. F.H. West), pp. 129–35 Chicago: University of Chicago Press.

Uerpmann, H.-P. 1996. Animal domestication – accident or intention? In *The Origins and Spread of Agriculture and Pastoralism in Eurasia* (ed. D. Harris), pp. 227–37. London: University College London Press.

Unger-Hamilton, R. 1991. Natufian plant husbandry in the southern Levant and comparison with that of the Neolithic periods: The lithic perspective. In *The Natufian Culture in the Levant* (eds. O. Bar-Yosef & F.R.Valla), pp. 483–520. Ann Arbor, MI: International Monographs in Prehistory.

Valla, F.R. 1991. Les Natoufiens de Mallaha et l'espace. In *The Natufian Culture in the Levant* (eds. O. Bar-Yosef & F.R. Valla), pp. 111–22. Ann Arbor, MI: International Monographs in Prehistory.

Valla, F.R. 1995. The first settled societies – Natufian (12,500–10,200 BP). In *The Archaeology of Society in the Holy Land* (ed. T. Levy), pp. 169–87. New York: Facts on File.

Valla, F.R. 1998. Natufian seasonality: A guess. In *Seasonality and Sedentism: Archaeological Perspectives from Old and New World Sites* (eds. T.R. Rocek & O. Bar-Yosef), pp. 93–108. Cambridge, MA: Harvard University, Peabody Museum of Archaeology and Ethnology.

Valla, F.R., Bar-Yosef, O., Smith, P., Tchernov, E. & Desse, J. 1986. Un nouveau sondage sur la terrace d'El-Ouad, Israël (1980–81). *Paléorient* 12, 21–38.

Valla, FR., Le Mort, F. & Plisson, H. 1991. Les fouilles en cours sur la terrasse d'Hayonim. In *The Natufian Culture in the Levant* (eds. O. Bar-Yosef & F.R. Valla), pp. 93–110. Ann Arbor, MI: International Monographs in Prehistory.

Valla, F.R. et al (eight additional authors) 1999. Le Natufien final et les nouvelles fouilles à Mallaha (Eynan), Israel 1996–1997. *Journal of the Israel Prehistoric Society* 28, 105–76.

van Andel, T.H. 1989. Late Pleistocene sea levels and the human exploitation of the shore and shelf of southern South Africa. *Journal of Field Archaeology* 16, 133–53.

van Andel, T.H. & Lionos, N. 1984. High resolution seismic reflection profiles for the reconstruction of post-glacial transgressive shorelines: An example from Greece. *Quaternary Research* 22, 31–45.

van Andel, T.H. & Runnels, C.N. 1995. The earliest farmers in Europe. *Antiquity* 69, 481–500.

van Noten, F. 1977. Excavations at Matupi Cave. *Antiquity* 51, 35–40.

van Noten, F. 1982. *The Archaeology of Central Africa*. Graf: Akademische Drück-und Verlagsanstalt.

van Zeist, W. & Bakker-Heeres, J.A.H. 1985. Archaeobotanical studies in the Levant: Neolithic sites in the Damascus Basin, Aswad, Ghoraife, Ramad. *Praehistoria* 24, 165–256.

van Zeist, W. & Bakker-Heeres, J.A.H. 1986. Archaeobotanical studies in the Levant III. Late Paleolithic Mureybet. *Palaeohistoria* 26, 171–99.

Vang Petersen, P. 1984. Chronological and regional variation in the late Mesolithic of eastern Denmark. *Journal of Danish Archaeology* 3, 7–18.

Varma, R.K., Misra, V.D., Pandey, J.N. & Pal, J.N. 1985. A preliminary report on the excavations at Damdama. *Man and Environment* IX, 45–65.

Vartanyan, S.L., Garutt, V.E. & Sher, A.V. 1993. Holocene mammoths from Wrangel Island in the Siberian Arctic. *Nature* 362, 337–40.

Velde, P. van de 1997. Much ado about nothing: Bandkeramik funerary ritual. *Analetica Prahistorica Leidensia* 29, 83–90.

Vereshchagin, N.K. & Baryshnikov, G.F. 1982. Paleoecology of the mammoth fauna in the Eurasian Arctic. In *Paleoecology of Beringia* (ed. D.M. Hopkins et al.), pp. 267–80. New York: Academic Press.

Vereshchagin, N.K. & Baryshnikov, G.F. 1984. Quaternary mammalian extinctions in northern Eurasia. In *Quaternary Extinctions: A Prehistoric Revolution* (eds. P.S. Martin & R.G. Klein), pp. 483–516. Tucson: University of Arizona Press.

Verhart, L.B.M. 1990. Stone age bone and antler points as indicators for 'social territories' in the European Mesolithic. In *Contributions to the Mesolithic in Europe* (eds. P.M. Vermeersch & P. Van Peer), pp. 139–51. Leuven: Leuven University Press.

Verhart, L.B.M. & Wansleeben, M. 1997. Waste and prestige; The Mesolithic-Neolithic transition in the Netherlands from a social perspective. *Analecta Praehistorica Leidensia* 29, 65–73.

Vermeersch, P.M. & Van Peer, P. (eds.) 1990. *Contributions to the Mesolithic in Europe*. Leuven: Leuven University Press.

Veth, P. 1989. Islands in the interior: A model for the colonistion of Australia's arid zone. *Archaeology in Oceania* 24, 81–92.

Veth, P. 1995. Aridity and settlement in Northwestern Australia. *Antiquity* 69, 733–46.

Vigne, J.-D. 1996. Did man provoke extinctions of endemic large mammals on the Mediterranean islands? The view from Corsica. *Journal of Mediterranean Archaeology* 9, 117–20.

Voigt, M.M. 2000. Çatalhöyük in context: Ritual at early Neolithic sites in central and eastern Turkey. In *Life in Neolithic Farming Communities. Social Organization, Identity and Differentiation* (ed. I. Kuijt), pp. 253–93. New York: Kluwer/Plenum Publications.

von Furer-Haimendorf, C. 1938. The head-hunting ceremonies of the Konyak Nagas of Assam. *Man* 38, 25.

Wadley, L. 1987. *Later Stone Age Hunters and Gatherers of the Southern Transvaal*. Oxford: British Archaeological Reports, International Series 380.

Wadley, L. 1989. Legacies from the Late Stone Age. *South African Archaeological Society Goodwin Series* 6, 42–53.

Wadley, L. 1991. Rose Cottage Cave: Background and a preliminary report on the recent excavations. *South African Archaeological Bulletin* 46, 125–30.

Wadley, L. 1993. The Pleistocene Late Stone Age south of the Limpopo River. *Journal of World Prehistory* 7, 243–96.

Wadley, L. 1997. Where have all the dead men gone? In *Our Gendered Past, Archaeological Studies of Gender in Southern Africa* (ed. L. Wadley), pp. 107–33. Witwaterstand: University of Witwaterstand Press.

Wadley, L. 2000. The early Holocene layers of Rose Cottage Cave, eastern Orange Free State: Technology, spatial patterns and environment. *South African Archaeological Bulletin* 55, 18–31.

Wadley, L. 2001. What is cultural modernity? A general view and a South African perspective from Rose Cottage Cave. *Cambridge Archaeological Journal* 11, 201–21.

Wadley, L., Esterhuysen, A. & Jeannerat, C. 1992. Vegetation changes in the eastern Orange Free State: The Holocene and later Pleistocene evidence from charcoal studies at Rose Cottage Cave. *South African Journal of Science* 88, 558–63.

Wadley, L. & Vogel, J.C. 1991. New dates from Rose Cottage Cave, Ladybrand, eastern Orange Free State. *South African Journal of Science* 87, 605–7.

Wakankar, V.S. 1973. Bhimetka excavation. *Journal of Indian History*, Trivandrum, 23–32.

Walker, N.J. 1985. Late Pleistocene and Holocene Hunter-Gatherers of the Matopos: An Archaeological Study of Change and Continuity in Zimbabwe. *Studies in African Archaeology* 10, Uppsala University.

Wallace, A.R. 1869. *The Malay Archipelago: The Land of the Orang-Utan and the Bird of Paradise. A Narrative of Travel, with Studies of Men and Nature.* 2 vols. London: Macmillan & Co. Ltd.

Wallace, A.R. 1889. *Travels on the Amazon and Rio Negro.* London: Ward, Lock & Co.

Wallace, D.C. 1995. Mitochondrial DNA variation in human evolution, degenerative disease and ageing. *American Journal of Human Genetics* 57, 201–23.

Walthall, J.A. 1998. Rockshelters and hunter-gatherer adaptation to the Pleistocene/Holocene transition. *American Antiquity* 63, 223–38.

Wang, J. 1983. *Taro – A review of Colocasia esculenta and its potentials.* Honolulu: University of Hawaii Press.

Warner, W.L. 1937. *A Black Civilization: A Social Study of an Australian Tribe.* London: Harper & Row.

Warnica, J.M. 1966. New discoveries at the Clovis site. *American Antiquity* 31, 345–57.

Wasylikowa, K., Harlan, J.R., Evans, J., Wendorf, F., Schild, R., Close, A.E., Krolik, H. & Housley, R.A. 1993. Examination of botanical remains from Early Neolithic houses at Nabta Playa, Western Desert, with special reference to sorghum grains. In *The Archaeology of Africa,*

Food, Metals and Towns (eds. T. Shaw, P. Sinclair, B. Andah & A. Okpoko), pp. 154–64. London: Routledge.

Watanabe, H. 1973. *The Ainu Ecosystem: Environment and Group Structure.* Seattle: University of Washington Press.

Watanabe, H. 1986. Community habitation and food gathering in prehistoric Japan: An ethnographic interpretation of the archaeological evidence. In *Windows on the Japanese Past: Studies in Archaeology and Prehistory* (ed. R.J. Pearson), pp. 229–54. Ann Arbor: Centre for Japanese Studies, University of Michigan.

Waterbolk, H.T. 1987. Working with radiocarbon dates in southwestern Asia. In *Chronologies in the Near East* (eds. O. Aurenche, J. Evin, & F. Hours), pp. 39–59. Oxford: British Archaeological Reports, International Series.

Watkins, T. 1990. The origins of the house and home? *World Archaeology* 21, 336–47.

Watkins, T. 1992. The beginnings of the Neolithic: Searching for meaning in material culture change. *Paléorient* 18, 63–75.

Watkins, T. 1998. Centres and peripheries: The beginnings of sedentary communities in N. Mesopotamia. *Subartu* IV, 1–11.

Watkins, T., Baird, D. & Betts, A. 1989. Qermez Dere and the early Aceramic Neolithic of Northern Iraq. *Paléorient* 15, 19–24.

Webb, E. 1998. Megamarsupial extinction: the carrying capacity argument. *Antiquity* 72, 46–55.

Webber, T.W. 1902. *The Forests of Upper India and their Inhabitants.* London: Edward Arnold.

Weinstein, J.M. 1984. Radiocarbon dating in the southern Levant. *Radiocarbon* 26, 297–366.

Weinstein-Evron, M. & Belfer-Cohen, A. 1993. Natufian figurines from the new excavations of the El-Wad cave, Mt Carmel, Israel. *Rock Art Research* 10, 102–6.

Wendorf, F. 1968. Site 117: A Nubian final Palaeolithic graveyard near Jebel Sahaba Sudan. In *Prehistory of Nubia* (ed. F. Wendorf), pp. 945–95. Dallas: Fort Burgwin Research Centre and Southern Methodist Press.

Wendorf, F., Close, A.E., & Schild, R. 1985. Prehistoric settlements in the Nubian Desert. *American Scientist* 73, 132–41.

Wendorf, F., Close, A.E., Schild, R., Wasylikowa, K., Housley, R.A., Harlan, J.R. & Krolik, H. 1992. Saharan exploitation of plants 8,000 years BP. *Nature* 359, 721–4.

Wendorf, F. & Schild, R. 1976. *Prehistory of the Nile Valley.* New York: Academic Press.

Wendorf, F. & Schild, R. 1980. *Prehistory of the Eastern Sahara.* New York: Academic Press.

Wendorf, F. & Schild, R. 1989. Summary and synthesis. In *The Prehistory of Wadi Kubbaniya, Vol. 3: Late Paleolithic Archaeology* (eds. F. Wendorf, R. Schild & A.E. Close), pp. 768–824. Dallas: Southern Methodist University Press.

Wendorf, F. & Schild, R. 1994. Are the Early Holocene cattle in the Eastern Sahara domestic or wild? *Evolutionary Anthropology* 13, 118–27.

Wendorf, F., Schild, R., Baker, P., Gautier, A.,

Longu, L. & Mohamed, A. 1997. A *Late Palaeolithic Kill-Butchery Camp in Upper Egypt*. Dallas: Southern Methodist University Press.

Wendorf, F., Schild, R. & Close, A.E. (eds.) 1980. *Loaves and Fishes: The Prehistory of Wadi Kubbaniya*. Dallas: Department of Anthropology, Institute for the Study of Earth and Man, Southern Methodist University Press.

Wendorf, F., Schild, R. & Close, A.E. (eds.) 1984. *Cattle Keepers of the Eastern Sahara: The Neolithic of Bir Kiseiba*. Dallas: Southern Methodist University Press.

Wendorf, F., Schild, R. & Close, A.E. (eds.) 1986. *The Prehistory of Wadi Kubbaniya, Vol. 1: The Wadi Kubbaniya Skeleton: A Late Palaeolithic Burial from Southern Egypt*. Dallas: Southern Methodist University Press.

Wendorf, F., Schild, R. & Close, A.E. (eds.) 1989a. *The Prehistory of Wadi Kubbaniya, vol. 2: Stratigraphy, Paleoeconomy and Environment*. Dallas: Southern Methodist University Press.

Wendorf, F., Schild, R. & Close, A.E. (eds.) 1989b. *The Prehistory of Wadi Kubbaniya, vol. 3: Late Paleolithic Archaeology*. Dallas: Southern Methodist University Press.

Wendorf, F., Schild, R. & Zedeno, N. 1996. A Late Neolithic megalithic complex in the Eastern Sahara: A preliminary report. In *Interregional Contacts in the Later Prehistory of Northeastern Africa* (eds. L. Krzyaniak, K. Kroeper & M. Kobusiewicz), pp. 125–32. Poznan: Poznan Archaeological Museum.

Wendt, W.E. 1976. 'Art Mobilier' from Apollo 11 Cave, South West Africa: Africa's oldest dated works of art. *South African Archaeological Bulletin* 31, 5–11.

Weniger, G.-R. 1989. The Magdalenian in Western Central Europe: Settlement patterns and regionality. *Journal of World Prehistory* 3, 323–72.

Wenke, R.J., Long, J.E. & Buck, P.E. 1988. Epipalaeolithic and Neolithic subsistence and settlement in the Fayyum oasis of Egypt. *Journal of Field Archaeology* 15 , 29–51.

West, F. (ed.) 1996. *American Beginnings: The Prehistory and Palaeoecology of Beringia*. Chicago: University of Chicago Press.

Wetterstrom, W. 1993. Foraging and farming in Egypt: The transition from hunting and gathering to horticulture in the Nile Valley. In *The Archaeology of Africa, Food, Metals and Towns* (eds. T. Shaw, P. Sinclair, B. Andah & A. Okpoko), pp. 165–226. London: Routledge.

Weyer, E.M. 1932. *The Eskimos: Their Environment and Folkways*. New Haven, CT: Yale University Press.

White, J.P. 1971. New Guinea and Australian prehistory: the 'Neolithic Problem'. In *Aboriginal Man and Environment in Australia* (eds. D.J. Mulvaney & J. Golson), pp 182–95. Canberra: Australian National University Press.

White, J.P., Crook, K.A.W. & Ruxton, B.P. 1970. Kosipe: A Late Pleistocene site in the Papuan higlands. *Proceedings of the Prehistoric Society* 36, 152–70.

Whitley, D.S. 1992. Shamanism and rock art in far western north America. *Cambridge Archaeological Journal* 2, 89–113.

Whitley, D.S. 1998. Finding rain in the desert: Landscape, gender and far western North American rock art. In *The Archaeology of Rock Art* (eds. C. Chippendale & P. Taçon), pp. 11–29. Cambridge: Cambridge Archaeological Press.

Whittaker, J. 1994. *Flint Knapping, Making and Understanding Stone Tools*. Austin: University of Texas Press.

Whittle, A. 1996. *Europe in the Neolithic: The Creation of New Worlds*. Cambridge: Cambridge University Press.

Wickham-Jones, C. 1990. *Rhum: Mesolithic and Later Sites at Kinloch, Excavations 1984–1986*. Edinburgh: Society of Antiquaries, Monograph Series No. 7.

Wickham-Jones, C. 1994. *Scotland's First Settlers*. London: Batsford.

Wickham-Jones, C. & Dalland, M. 1998. A small Mesolithic site at Craigford golf course, Fife Ness, Fife. *Internet Archaeology* 5 (http://intarch.ac.uk/journal/issue 5).

Wiessner, P. 1982. Risk, reciprocity and social influences on !Kung San economics. In *Politics and History in Band Societies* (eds. E. Leacock & R. Lee), pp. 61–84. Cambridge: Cambridge University Press.

Willig, J.A. 1991. Clovis technology and adaptation in far western North America: Regional patterning and environmental context. In *Clovis: Origins and Adaptations* (eds. R. Bonnichsen & K.L. Turnmire), pp. 91–118. Corvallis, OR: Centre for the Study of the First Americans.

Wilson, S.M. 1985. Phytolith evidence from Kuk, an early agricultural site in Papua New Guinea. *Archaeology in Oceania* 20, 90–97.

Wobst, H.M. 1974. Boundary conditions for palaeolithic social systems: A simulation approach. *American Antiquity* 39, 147–78.

Wobst, H.M. 1976. Locational relationships in Palaeolithic society. *Journal of Human Evolution* 5, 49–58.

Wobst, H.M. 1978. The archaeo-ethnology of hunter-gatherers or the tyranny of the ethnographic record in archaeology. *American Antiquity* 43, 303–9.

Wollaston, A.F.R. 1912. *Pygmies & Papuans, The Dutch Stone Age To-Day in Dutch New Guinea*. London: Smith, Elder & Co.

Woodburn, J.C. 1968. An introduction to Hadza Ecology. In *Man the Hunter* (eds. R.B. Lee & I. DeVore), pp. 49–55. Chicago: Aldine.

Woodman, P.C. 1985. *Excavations at Mount Sandel 1973–77*. Belfast: HMSO.

Wordsworth, J. 1985. The excavation of a Mesolithic horizon at 13–24 Castle Street, Inverness. *Proceedings of the Antiquaries of Scotland* 115, 89–103.

World Disasters Report 1999. Geneva: International Federation of Red Cross and Red Crescent Societies.

Wright, GA. 1978. Social differentiation in the

Early Natufian. In *Social Archaeology, Beyond Subsistence and Dating* (eds. C. Redman et al.), pp. 201–33. London: Academic Press.

Wright, K.I. 2000. The social origins of cooking and dining in early villages of Western Asia. *Proceedings of the Prehistoric Society* 66, 89–121.

Wu, R. & Olsen, J.W. 1985. *Palaeoanthropology and Palaeolithic Archaeology in the People's Republic of China.* New York: Academic Press.

Yakar, R. & Hershkovitz, I. 1988. The modelled skulls from the Nahal Hemar Cave. '*Atiqot* 18, 59–63.

Yellen, J.E., Brooks, A.S., Stuckenrath, T. & Welbourne, R. 1987. A terminal Pleistocene assemblage from Drotsky's Cave, western Ngamiland, Botswana. *Botswana Notes and Records* 19, 1–6.

Yen, D.E. 1995. The development of Sahul agriculture with Australia as bystander. *Antiquity* 69, 831–47.

Yoffe, N. & Clarke, J.J. (eds.) 1993. *Early Stages in the Evolution of Mesopotamian Civilisation: Soviet Excavations in Northern Iraq.* Tucson: University of Arizona Press.

Zeder, M. 1999. Animal domestication in the Zagros: A review of past and current research. *Paléorient* 25, 11–25.

Zeder, M. & Hesse. B. 2000. The initial domestication of goats (*Capra hircus*) in the Zagros mountains 10,000 years ago. *Science* 287, 2254–7.

Zhijun, Z. 1998. The middle Yangtze region in China is one place where rice was domesticated: phytolith evidence from the Diaotonghuan Cave, northern Jiangxi. *Antiquity* 72, 885–97.

Zhongguo, L. 1998. Another discovery in Neolithic research of early civilization near Dongting Lake. www.carleton.ca/~bgordon/rice/papers

Zilhão, J. 1992. *Gruta do Caldeirao. O Neolítico Antigo.* Trabalhos de Arqueologia 6. Lisboa: Instituto Português do Património Arquitectónico e Arqueológico.

Zilhão, J. 1993. The spread of agro-pastoral economies across Mediterranean Europe. *Journal of Mediterranean Archaeology* 6, 5–63.

Zohary, D. 1989. Domestication of the southwest Asian Neolithic crop assemblage of cereals, pulses and flax: The evidence from the living plants. In *Foraging and Farming: The Evolution of Plant Exploitation* (eds. D.R. Harris & G.C. Hillman), pp. 358–73. London: Unwin Hyman.

Zohary, D. & Hopf, M. 2000. *Domestication of Plants in the Old World.* 3rd edn. Oxford: Oxford University Press.

Zvelebil, M. 1981. *From Forager to Farmer in the Boreal Zone.* Oxford: British Archaeological Reports, International Series 115.

Zvelebil, M. (ed.) 1986a. *Hunters in Transition.* Cambridge: Cambridge University Press.

Zvelebil, M. 1986b. Postglacial foraging in the forests of Europe. *Scientific American*, May, pp. 86–93.

Zvelebil, M. 1994. Plant use in the Mesolithic and its role in the transition to farming. *Proceedings of the Prehistoric Society* 60, 35–74.

Zvelebil, M. 1997. Hunter-gatherer ritual landscapes: Spatial organisation, social structure and ideology among hunter-gatherers of northern Europe and western Siberia. *Analetica Praehistorica Leidensia* 29, 33–50.

Zvelebil, M. 1998. Agricultural frontiers, Neolithic origins and the transition to farming in the Baltic basin. In *Harvesting the Sea, Farming the Forest* (eds. M. Zvelebil, R. Dennell, & L. Domanska), pp. 9–28. Sheffield: Sheffield Academic Press.

Zvelebil, M. 2000. The social context of the agricultural transition in Europe. In *Archaeogenetics: DNA and the Population Prehistory of Europe* (eds. C. Renfrew & K. Boyle), pp. 57–79. Cambridge: McDonald Institute for Archaeological Research.

Zvelebil, M., Dennell, R. & Domańska, L. (eds.). 1998. *Harvesting the Sea, Farming the Forest.* Sheffield: Sheffield Academic Press.

Zvelebil, M. & Rowley-Conwy, P.A. 1986. Foragers and Farmers in Atlantic Europe. In *Hunters in Transition* (ed. M. Zvelebil), pp. 67–94. Cambridge: Cambridge University Press.

Zvelebil, M. & Zvelebil, K.V. 1988. Agricultural transition and Indo-European dispersals. *Antiquity* 62, 574–83.

PICTURE ACKNOWLEDGEMENTS

Excavations at Ohalo, Sea of Galilee (© Steven Mithen)

Tell Abu Hureyra, Syria, and the remains of its hunter-gatherer dwellings (© Gordon Hillman [Tell] and © Andrew Moore [floor])

Tell es-Sultan surrounded by the modern town of Jericho (© Steven Mithen)

Wadi Faynan, Jordan (© Steven Mithen)

Excavations of hunter-gatherer-cultivator dwellings at WF16 (© Steven Mithen)

Excavations at Göbekli Tepe, southern Turkey (© Steven Mithen)

Plaster figure from 'Ain Ghazal, Jordan (© Kathy Tubb)

The site of Ghuwayr I, Wadi Faynan, Jordan (© Steven Mithen)

Dr Alan Simmons at the remains of Aetokremnos Cave, Cyprus, and a sample of the excavated pygmy hippopotamus bones (© Steven Mithen)

Excavations at Verberie, River Oise, France, showing a typical hearth (© Françoise Audoze)

La Riera Cave, Asturias, Spain: entrance and layers of occupation debris (© Lawrence Straus)

Carved human/fish stone figure from Lepenski Vir, Danube River, Serbia (from Srejović, D. 1972)

Burial of young woman with new-born baby at Vedbaek, Denmark (© National Museum of Denmark)

Excavation of the Ertebølle shell midden, Denmark (© National Museum of Denmark)

Underwater excavation at Tybrind Vig, Denmark (© National Museum of Denmark)

Excavations at Bolsay Farm, Isle of Islay, Scotland (© Steven Mithen)

Excavations at Bluefish Caves, Alaska, USA (© Jaques Cinq-Mars)

Meadowcroft rockshelter, Pennsylvania, USA (©Bradley T. Lepper)

Monte Verde, Chile, and excavations showing preserved wooden timbers from hunter-gatherer dwellings (© Tom Dillehay)

The Puna landscape of the Peruvian Andes (© John Rick)

Pachamachay Cave, Peru (© John Rick)

Excavations in Panaulauca Cave, Peru (© John Rick)

Excavations at Guilá Naquitiz rockshelter, Mexico (© Kent Flannery)

Sandal Shelter, Arizona, USA, and woven sandal made from Yucca leaves (© Phil R. Geib)

Excavations at the Koster site, Illinois, USA (© James Brown)

Inside Kutikina Cave, Tasmania (© Richard Cosgrove)

Excavations at Puritijarra rockshelter in the Central Australian Desert (© Mike Smith)

Rock painting located in Kakadu National Park, Australia (© Paul Tauçon)

Excavations at Kuk Swamp in New Guinea (© Jack Golson/ANU)

View from the entrance of Niah Cave, Sarawak (© Graeme Barker)

Excavations at Uenohara, Kyushu, Japan with the distant volcano of Sakura-jima (© Minami Nihon Shinbun)

Excavation on Zhokhov Island, Siberian Arctic (© Vladimir Pitul'ko)

Excavations at Jeitun, Turkmenistan (© David Harris)

Excavations at Umm Dabaghiyah, Iraq (© John Curtis)

Mud-walled dwellings at Yarim Tepe, Iraq (© Roger Matthews)

Excavations in Wadi Kubbaniya, Nile valley (© Angela Close)

Site of GvJm19 below an overhang of rock on Lukenya Hill, Kenya (© Curtis W. Marean)

Location of Drotsky's Cave, Kalahari Desert, Botswana (© Lawrence Robbins)

Excavation and entrance of Rose Cottage Cave, South Africa (© Lyn Wadley)

Sir John Lubbock, Lord Avebury (from Hutchinson 1914)

Flint scraper and microliths, Wadi el-Uwaynid 14, Jordan (from Garrard et al. 1986, with permission from A. Garrard)

Stone bowl, Hallan Çemi Tepesi, Turkey (From Rosenberg & Davis 1992, with permission from M. Rosenberg)

Female statuette, Mureybet, Syria (from Cauvin 2000, with permission from Cambridge University Press)

Engraved and grooved stones, Jerf el Ahmar, Syria (from Stordeur et al. 1997)

El-Khiam arrowheads, Netiv Hagdud, Israel (Figure 4.5 [13-17] from Ofer Bar-Yosef and Avi Gopher, eds., *An Early Neolithic Village in the Jordan valley, Part 1: The Archaeology of Netiv Hagdud*, American School of Prehistoric Research, Bulletin 43. © 1997 by the President and Fellows of Harvard College)

Stone points, Beidha, Jordan (from Cauvin 2000)

Modelled plaster skull, Kfar Hahoresh, Israel (from Gorring-Morris et al. 1994, with permission from N. Gorring-Morris)

Painted fresco, Çatalhöyük, Turkey (from Mellaart 1967, with permission from J. Mellaart)

The Montgaudier Baton, France (from Marshack 1972)

Engraved stone slab, Gönnersdorf, Germany (from Bahn and Vertut 1997)

Microliths, Starr Carr, England (from Clark 1954, with permission from Cambridge University Press)

Clay figurine of a woman, Nea Nikomedeia, Greece (from Rodden 1965)

Canoe paddle, Tybrind Vig, Denmark (from Anderson 1985, with permission of S. Anderson)

Folsom point as found in North America (Whittaker 1994, with permission from Texas University Press)

Clovis point, the Lehner site, Arizona, USA (from Haury et al. 1959)

Triangular spear points, the Tapajós river, Amazon (from Roosevelt et al. 1996)

Spear points, the Horner site (reprinted from Frison 1978, *Prehistoric Hunters of the High Plains*, with permission from Elsevier)

Male figure in the 'Dynamic' style, Arnhem Land, Australia (from Flood 1995)

Painted scene, Bhimbekta, India (from Mathpal 1984, with permission from Abhinav publications)

Heads of raptors carved in stone, Nemrik, Iraq (from Kozlowski 1989, by permission of CNRS-*Paléorient*)

Fragments of wall paintings, Umm Dabaghiyah, Iraq (from Matthews 2000)

Recent San rock paintings of a curing dance (from Lewis-Williams 1987, with permission from D. Lewis Williams)

Rock engraving of long-horned cattle, Libyan Sahara (from Mori 1998, with permission from L'Erma di Bretschneider)

INDEX

Abbott, Charles 211
Abu Hureyra 40–5, 46, 63, 75, 100, 158, 290,
    360, 418, 420, 519–20
  farming 38, 41, 42, 53, 66
  gazelle hunting 41, 42, 44, 47, 520
  herding 77, 523
  sedentism 43–4
Abu Salem 80
Adovasio, James 216–17, 218, 219–20, 233
Aetokremnos Cave 97–100, 104, 526
Agassiz, Lake 242, 543
Aggersund 184
'Ain Ghazal 79, 80, 83–7, 88, 91, 92, 102, 158,
    409, 431, 432, 510, 524
  architecture 84
  burial rituals 84–5, 96, 102
  figurines 84, 524
  religious buildings 86, 105
'Ain Mallaha 29–32, 33, 37, 42, 43, 46, 47, 48,
    50, 100, 130, 141, 158, 231, 261, 279, 330,
    345, 372–3, 374, 420, 421, 463, 518
  burials 30–1, 34, 51–2
  domesticated dogs 31–2
  microliths 31, 40
  sedentism 44
Ainu people 227, 380
Aitkins, Melvin 372–3
Ali Kosh 431, 565
Allen, Jim 307
Alon, David 75, 82–3
Altamira cave paintings 112, 144–6, 149, 307,
    531
Ama__ ___ __46
      262
      6

      24

_____ 249
  Aoradh 201
  Apollo Cave slabs 474, 569–70
  Aq Kupruk Caves 415

Arawe skull binding 314–15
archaeo-botany 22–3
archaeo-zoology 34, 42, 137, 184 see also
    dental evidence
Arene Candide 189
Arnhem Land 327–33
Arrente (Arunta) people 319–20
arrow-heads 80, 524
  Ahrensburgian points 123, 129, 197–8
  Harif points 53
  el-Khiam points 61, 69, 521;
art
  Altamira 112, 114–16, 149, 307, 531
  Çatalhöyük bull paintings 92–3, 422
  cave/rock engraving/painting 13, 112, 131,
      143–5, 144–5, 149, 218, 307, 322, 331, 332,
      400–2, 432, 474–5, 477, 486–7, 490, 491,
      493, 519, 530, 531, 569–70
  clay figurines 63, 81, 84, 416, 429, 436,
      524
  decorative artefacts 30, 31, 32, 33, 49–50,
      519
  Dynamic Figures 327–9, 331, 401, 552
  Göbekli Tepe pillars 65–7, 69, 103, 104
  Gönnersdorf artists 130, 131–2, 135, 390,
      529
  Jerf el Ahmar 65
  as mapping 36
  Nevali Çori 89
  as noticeboard 148–9
  pictograms 65, 66
  Rainbow Serpent 333, 481
  Wondewerk Cave 474, 570
Aşıklı Höyük 91, 525
Atlit-Yam 83, 100, 508
Audouze, Françoise 124
Australian Aborigines 23, 25, 35, 67, 78, 249,
    312–35, 552
  Dreamtime mythology 304, 323, 324, 325,
      333, 334–5
  Flood stories 334–5
  Homo erectus claimed descent 314–15, 550
  lack of farming incentive 338–9
  Rainbow Serpent 333, 335, 552
  in Tasmania 304–11, 325, 335, 549–50
Awazu 376

Azraq basin 22, 24–5, 26–7, 28, 29, 30, 126, 518
Aztec civilisation 275

Babylonian religion 86
Bader, Nikolai Ottovich 430–1, 435–6
Bagor 413
Baiyanjiao Cave 359, 556
Ballawinne Cave 307
Bailey, Robert 354
Balma Margineda 159, 532
Baltic ice lake 155–6, 157
Banks, Joseph 337
Banyan Valley Cave 362
Bar-Yosef, Ofer 29, 32, 36, 46, 59–60, 75, 82–3, 520
Barasana people 36
Barker, Graeme 350
Bashidang 368, 369
Basta 79
Batek people 354, 355, 358
Bechan Cave 244
Beidha 35, 72, 73, 75, 76, 79, 80, 431
    domesticated animals 77
    town architecture 73–4, 76, 81, 86. 102, 105, 509, 523, 524
    use of woven fabric 74–5
Beinn Tart a'Mhill 197
Belfer-Cohen, Anna 36, 43
Bellwood, Peter 355
Berelekh 383, 385, 389
Berezovka mammoth 384–5, 560
Beringia 213, 214–16, 239–40, 383
Besongo 486–7
Bhimbetka 400–2
Bir Kiseiba 496, 497
Bird, Junius 260
Björck, Svante 155
Black, Murray 314
Black Sea 153, 166
Blackwater Draw 213
Bluefish Caves 214–15, 223, 232, 233, 234, 383
Bois Laiterie Cave 128, 130
Bøgebakken cemetery 181
Bølling 113
Bolsay 201, 205, 206
Bonatto, Sandro 226
bone analysis 114–15, 118–19, 122, 147, 528
Bonnichsen, Robson 211, 235
Boomplaas Cave 470, 471, 479–80
Bordes, François 112
Bosinski, Gerhard 131

Bouqras 88, 96, 431
Bradley, Daniel 496
Braidwood, Robert 431
Bratlund, Bodil 123
Bridgend point 197–8
Brosius, Peter 354–5
Brown, Barnum 211
Bryan, Alan 217–18, 541
bull worship 64, 92–3, 146
burial practices
    'Ain Ghazal 84–5, 86, 96, 102, 105
    'Ain Mallaha 30–1, 34, 51–2, 519
    Bagor 413
    Bøgebakken cemetery 181
    Cyprus 101
    El Wad cemetery 32, 44
    Gruta do Caldeirão 191
    Iwo Eleru 485
    Jerf el Ahmar 64
    Jericho 60–1, 81–2
    Kfar HaHoresh 83
    Koster 292, 294
    Kow Swamp cemetery 312–13
    LBK 180–1, 535
    Lepenski Vir 161–2
    Megalithic tombs 195, 205
    Mahadaha and Damdama 404–5
    Mehrgarh 409, 410–11
    Mesolithic cemeteries 166, 533–4
    Natufian 32, 46, 50–1, 60–1
    Neve David 28
    Ofnet skull nests 176–7
    Oleneostrovski Mogilnik island cemetery 168–71, 174, 188, 358
    PPNB 522, 524
    Shanidar Cave 423–4
    Skateholm cemeteries 172, 174–5
    Tasmanian 309–10
    Tell Sotto 436
    Téviec and Hoëdic 187–8, 195, 536
    WF16 69, 70
    Yarim Tepe 438
Byrd, Brian 73–4

Calico Hills 214, 232, 540
Campbell, John 118
Campbell, Lyle 223, 225
Campbell, Sue 199–200
Carlson, Roy 299
Cascadia 297–8
Çatalhöyük 91, 92–6, 101, 105, 164, 417, 432, 525–6

architecture 92, 94–5
  bull paintings 92–3, 422
Caton-Thompson, Gertrude 501
Cauvin, Jacques 63–4, 67, 522
Cavalli-Sforza, Luca 192, 193, 194, 536–7
Cave Bay Cave 309–10
Çayönü 90–1, 431, 525
Chagnon, Napolean 175–6
Chaleux Cave 115, 128
Champlain Sea 243
Chatters, James 227
Chauvet 148
Childe, Gordon 60, 190, 513
Chippindale, Christopher 328–9, 332
Chopani Mando 414
Christy, Henry 111, 398
Cinq-Mars, Jacques 214–15, 223, 233
Clark, Geoffrey 146–7
Clark, Sir Grahame 134, 135–6, 137, 141, 150,
  167
Clarke, David 513
Close, Angela 450, 452, 495
Clovis people 222, 223, 239, 245, 246–9,
  253–4, 256, 286, 296, 382, 386, 544–5
  'Clovis First' 213–14, 216, 225, 231
    Clovis points 213–14, 245, 248, 249, 256,
      258, 263, 286, 543
    implication of Monte Verde 231–2, 233–4
    putative pre-Clovis sites 214, 215, 216–20
Colonsay 196, 201–3, 204
Constantini, Lorenzo 408
Coobool Creek skulls 314–16
Cook, Captain James 308, 311, 337, 338
Cook, Jill 111
Cooke, Cran 488
Cope, Carol 47
Cordy, Jean-Marie 115
Cosgrove, Richard 307
Coulerarach 199–200
Couraud, Claude 145
Coxcatlán Cave 277
Cramond 199
Cremaschi, Mauro 491
Creswell Crags 117–18, 119, 197, 231, 379, 385,
  390, 463
Croft, Paul 100, 527
Cuddie Springs 317, 325
Cuiry-les-Chaudardes 180
Cyprus 97–106, 180

Damdama 402–5, 410
Danger Cave 288

Dark, Petra 137–8
Darwin, Charles 5, 258–9
Darwin Crater 309
Datan, Ipoi 352–3
Davies, Stuart 38
Dawson, Alistair 198–9
Deacon, Hilary 479, 571
de Acosta, Fray Joseph 211, 213
Dead Sea 56, 81
Dead Sea Scrolls 74
Deaf Adder Gorge 327
Denali culture 223, 540
dendrochronology 14–15
Dent 212–13
dental evidence 32, 34, 43, 48,128, 180, 221–2,
  223, 227, 405, 411, 424
Dhra' 62, 521
Diatonghuan Cave 363–4
  pottery 366
di Lernia, Savino 491–2
Dillehay, Tom 219–20, 229, 231, 233–4, 542
Dincauze, Dena 233, 546
Dirty Shame Rock 288
Doggerland 118, 150–1, 152, 154, 155, 187
  Ower bank 150
domesticated animals
  cattle 414, 493–7, 573
  dogs 29, 30–1, 32, 34–5, 174, 292, 378,
    387–8, 389, 519
  guinea pigs 269
  llamas 268–9
  pigs 342, 344, 345–6
  sheep and goats 77–8, 85, 417, 418, 440,
    431, 491–2, 523
  zebu 409, 410, 414, 493
domesticated plants
  beans, maize and squash 23–4, 276–8,
    280–1, 282, 283
  grain 23–4, 38, 41, 53–4, 67, 345, 417, 431,
    437, 440, 501–2
  quinua and potato 269
  rice 361–4, 366–8, 380, 414, 557
  tropical root crops 338, 343–5
Drotsky's Cave 462, 464–8, 471, 486, 568,
  572
Drotsky, Martinus 466, 568
Dryholm 184
Dupree, Louis 415
Dyuktai Cave culture 382, 383, 385, 386, 389,
  560

Edwards, Kevin 198

Edwards, Philip 62, 521
Elands Bay Cave 469–73, 481–2, 569
Elizalde, Manuel 348, 357
El-Wad cemetery 32–3, 46, 519
Endicott, Kirk and Karen 354
Enloe, James 126, 127
Ertebølle midden 183–4, 190, 194, 204, 379,
    535
  pottery 184
Etiolles 124, 126–7, 139, 200
Euphrates, River 40, 47, 63, 88, 439

fauna
  African survival and extinction 239, 480,
    542–3, 571
  American 236–9, 244, 246
  American mega-fauna extinction 238–9,
    245, 246–56, 289, 480, 545
  Australian mega-fauna extinction 317–18
  Berezovka mammoth 384–5, 560
  Chinese mega-fauna 359
  computer simulated population
    dynamics 254, 546
  European survival and extinction 97–8,
    114, 139
  Great Interchange 237
  mammoth cemetery 385
  mammoth steppe 385, 386
  Natufian 33–4
  polar bears 388, 392, 561
  Siberian mammoth extinction 386
  Wrangel Island mammoths 252–3, 386
Fayum Depression 500–1, 502
Fell's Cave 259, 260
fertility symbols 67, 69
Field, Judith 325
Figgins, Jesse 210, 212, 286
Finlay, Nyree 197, 200
Finlayson, Bill 62, 68, 197
Fishbone Cave 249, 288, 545
Fladmark, Knut 217, 541
Flannery, Kent 76, 274–6, 278, 281, 282, 284,
    345, 547–8, 551
flint knapping 26, 28, 127, 518 see also
    microliths
floatation 42
Flood, Josephine 334–5, 553
Folsom 210–11, 212–13, 234, 286
Foote, Robert Bruce 398
Forchhammer, Professor 183
forest steppe 21–3, 24–5, 27–8, 518
Franchthi Cave 141, 151, 163–4, 177, 469

Fuegians 259–60, 299
Fukui Cave 372, 373, 379, 558
Fullagar, Richard 325

Ganj Dareh 77–8, 431, 523, 565
Gardner, Elizabeth 501
Garrard, Andy 26–7, 518
Garrod, Dorothy 32–3, 36, 57–8, 519
Garstang, John 56
Gcwihaba valley 464, 467–8
Geib, Philip 287
genetically engineered crops 4, 509, 574, 510
genetic prehistory 191–4, 223, 225–6, 496,
    534, 537
  mtDNA 193–4, 225–6
  difficulty of recovering DNA from
    ancient bone 99, 250, 545
Ghar-i-Asp 415, 563
Ghar-i-Mar 415, 563
Gheo-Shih 279, 282, 284, 547–8
Gilgal 62, 521
Gillen, Frank 319–20, 323
Gleann Mor 200–1
global temperature change 4, 11, 12, 15, 54,
    211, 239, 242–3, 250–2, 272, 332, 341, 386,
    453, 469, 470, 471–2, 504, 507–8, 513,
    515–16, 574
  Allerød 12, 113, 115
  Bølling 12, 113, 114, 115, 120, 123, 124, 130
  see also sea level change, Younger
    Dryas
Göbekli Tepe 64, 66, 522
  cultivation of wild wheat 67, 345
  pillars 65–7, 69, 103, 104
  as ritual centre 66–7, 89–90, 91, 96, 422,
    427
Goddard, Ives 223, 225
Godwin, Harry 150–1
Golson, Jack 342, 343–4, 554
Gönnersdorf 130, 131–2, 135, 390, 409
Goring-Morris, Nigel 83
Gough's Cave 110–11, 118, 187, 527
  suggestion of cannibalism 110–11, 197
Gould, Richard 323–5
Graham, Russell 250
Grayson, Donald 246
Greenberg, Joseph 222–4
greenhouse gases 4, 12, 513
Gruhn, Ruth 217–18
Gruinart 198–9, 201
Gruta do Caldeirão 190–1
Gua Sireh 351–3

Guidon, Niède 218–20, 224, 233, 541
Guilá Naquitz 274–84
  domesticated plants 276–8, 280–1, 282, 283, 345, 362
Guilaine, Jean 102
Gurina, I.I. 168–9, 170
Guthrie, Dale 250–1, 385, 386

Haddon, A.C. 337, 553
Hadza people 458, 459
Halaf culture 439
Hallan Çemi Tepesi 49, 64, 90, 522, 525
Harlan, Jack 503
Harris, David 237–8, 417–18, 553
Harrisson, Tom 349–50, 352, 555
Hassuna 435, 438, 439, 565
Hastorf, Christine 35–6
Haua Fteah 444, 491
Hauptmann, Harald 89
Hayden, Brian 278, 281, 282, 284, 373, 548
Haynes, Gary 248, 254, 544
Haynes, Vance 233, 255–6, 546
Hayonim Cave 32, 34, 36, 46, 47, 100, 128, 141, 519
Hemudu 369
Henry, Donald 33
Herz, Otto F. 384
Hesse, Brian 78
Hides, Jack 339
Hillman, Gordon 23, 38, 42, 53, 368, 385, 417–18, 449, 518, 519, 520
Hoabinhian culture 349–50, 354, 355, 358, 555
Hodder, Ian 94–5, 526
Hoëdic 188, 194, 195
Hogup Cave 288, 548
Hole, Frank 78
Holmes, William Henry 212
Homo erectus 4, 10, 314
Homo ergaster 10
Homo heidelbergensis 4, 10
Homo neaderthalensis 4, 10, 68, 191
Homo sapiens 10, 191, 227, 506
Horai, Satoshi 226
Horner site 288–9
Hot Springs 11, 515
Hottentots 479
Housley, Rupert 119, 120
Hrdlička, Aleš 210
Hula basin 28, 35, 36–7, 46
  Hula core 22, 27, 48, 54, 517

Imamura, Keiji 377
Inca civilisation 266, 268
Intirtekwerle rockshelter 324
Inuit 25, 383–4, 388
  Eskimo-Aleut languages 222, 225
Inverness 152
Ishango 456, 567
Islay 196–200, 202, 204, 205
Iwo Eleru Cave 483–5

Jacobi, Roger 110–11
Jacobs, Ken 171
Jacobsen, Thomas W. 141
Jarmo 431, 435
Jarrige, Jean-François 408, 410
Jebel Sahaba 452
Jeitun 416–19, 481
Jefferson, Thomas 222
Jerf el Ahmar 64, 360
  architecture 64, 66, 71, 103, 104, 509
  artwork 64–5, 66, 69
  burial 64
  ritual 66, 67
Jericho 6, 38, 56–61, 63, 69, 75, 76, 80, 81, 91, 92, 409, 439, 481
  burials 60–1, 81–2
  figurines 81
  mud brick building 58, 61
  plastered skulls 81–2, 102, 481
  'temple' 86
  Wall of 59, 63
Jomon culture 371–80
  boar pit traps 376–8
  lacquer use 372, 373
  pottery 371–4, 380, 558–9
Jones, Rhys 306–7, 311, 549, 550
Jordan, River and valley 53, 57, 62, 63, 78, 80, 83, 522
Jura 196, 197, 201, 202, 204

Kakinoshima comb 372
Kalahari Bushmen 478
Kalahari desert 478
Kamo shell midden 379, 559
Karacadağ 54, 67, 520, 522
Karim Shahir 424, 564
Kaufman, Daniel 28
Kawelka tribe 341–2
Kebaran period 26, 32, 43, 47, 48, 50, 52, 53, 139
Keefer, David 271–2
Kel Tamasheq 501

Kennewick Man 227, 228, 358
Kenyon, Kathleen 56–8, 59, 60, 63, 68, 71, 82, 520–1
Kermanshah valley 77–8
Kfar HaHoresh 83, 524
Khabur, River 88
Khirokita 102–3, 104–5
Khok Phanom Di 362
Kidder, A.V. 211
Kiernan, Kevin 306
Kikai eruption 375, 559
Kilimanjaro ice cores 453–4
Kirigaoka 377
Kirkbride, Diana 72–3, 76, 433–4, 435
Kjøkkenmøddinger (kitchen middens) 135, 136, 183–4, 190, 203, 331, 378, 552
Klein, Richard 480
Kom W and Kom K grain silos 501–2, 509
Konstantinov, Mikhail 383
Kosipe 340–1, 553
Koster 291–5, 374, 405, 417, 548–9
Kow Swamp skulls 312–16
Kozlowski, Stefan 428, 429, 435, 564
Kuijt, Ian 62, 521, 522
Kuk Swamp 341–5, 554
Kulpi Mara Cave 322–3, 324, 325, 463, 551
!Kung bushmen 465–6, 468, 470, 478, 568
Kurbansakhatov, Karamurad 417
Kurnool Caves 396, 398
Kusimba, Sibel Barut 455, 459–60, 567
Kutikina Cave 305–8, 310, 311

Lang Kamnan 353–4, 556
Lang Rongrien 352, 353, 556
Larrson, Lars 172, 173, 174, 175
Lartet, Edouard 111, 112, 122, 398
Lascaux 6, 134, 148, 307
LBK (Linearbandkeramik) 179–80, 186, 188–9, 194
  Timber long house building 178, 179, 180, 189, 195, 205
LGM (last glacial maximum) 3, 4, 8, 11, 12, 13, 48, 111, 114, 120, 166, 214, 235, 237, 239, 261, 287, 296, 304, 305, 309, 317, 321, 323, 337, 340, 346, 397, 450, 457, 467, 470, 488
Last Supper Cave 288
Lawrence, T.E. 24, 518
Layard, Austen Henry 435
Leakey, Louis 214, 233, 460–1, 540
Leakey, Mary 461
Leakey, Richard 460–1, 545

Lee, Richard 466–7, 568
Legge, Tony 42, 137, 141, 418
Lehner Ranch 213, 214, 246, 248, 253, 255–6, 286, 540
Lepenski Vir 158, 160–2, 164, 166, 177, 532
Leroi-Gourhan, André 126
Lewis-Williams, David 474–5
Lewthwaite, James 189, 191, 194, 536
Lieberman, Daniel 34, 128
linguistic prehistory 222, 223–6
  historical linguistics 223–4
Livingstone, David 466
Lloyd, Seton 435, 436, 438
Loftus, Ronan 496
Lowasera 489
Lubbock, Sir John (Lord Avebury) 5–6, 25, 26, 31, 44, 111–12, 116, 119, 122–3, 131, 135, 153–4, 183, 184, 185, 212, 233, 259–60, 276, 299, 308, 316, 325, 329–30, 333, 371, 383–4, 389, 390, 396, 397, 435, 446, 471, 479, 506–7, 511, 514, 527, 528, 539
Lukenya Hill 454–6, 458, 459, 463, 485, 503
Lundelius, Ernest 250
Lyell, Sir Charles 153–4
Lynch, Thomas 233

Magens Mello, Rev. J. 118
Maghzaliyah 430–1, 434, 436, 439
Mahadaha 404–5
Marean, Curtis 455, 458, 567
Marshall, Lorna 465–6, 567
Martin, Paul 213, 238, 246, 247, 249, 255–6, 540, 544
Marx, Professor 250
Mas d'Azil 143–5, 148, 149
Masson, V.M. 417
Mathpal, Yashodhar 401–2
Matopos hills 463–4, 485, 488
Matthews, Wendy 95
Matupi Cave 456–7
Mauss, Marcel 43
McBurney, Charles 444
MacNeish, Richard 277, 362–3, 547
MacPhee, Ross 250
Mead, Jim 246
Meadowcroft Rockshelter 216–18, 220, 233, 234
Mehrgarh 407–13, 417, 436, 481, 493, 563
  burial 409, 410–11
  cotton thread 411–12
Meiendorf 122–3, 139
Mellaart, James 94, 95, 422

Mellars, Paul 203–4
Meltzer, David 211, 212, 219–20, 233, 234–5, 238, 245, 246, 541
Mercer, John 201, 538
Merimde 499, 501–2
Merpert, Nikolai Yakovlevich 436, 438
microliths 26, 28, 31, 40, 43, 47, 139–40, 446, 450–1, 475–6, 484, 518
Milankovitch, Milutin 11, 515–16
Mimi people 328
Miskovice 180
Misra, V.N. 397–8, 401, 561
Missoula, Lake 242
M'lefaat 424, 564
Mochanov, Yuri 382, 385
Mondeval de Sora 159
Monte Alban 274, 283
Monte Alegre 262
Monte Verde 229–35, 247, 258, 280, 290, 463, 542
Montgaudier baton 112, 527
Moore, Andrew 42, 520
Mori, Fabrizio 493, 572
Morse, Edward S. 371
'mother goddess' cults 63–4, 164
Moulherat, Christophe 411
Muchchatla Chinlamanu Gavi Cave 396, 398–9
Munchaev, Rauf Magomedovich 436, 438
Mureybet 47, 63, 67, 522
    architecture 63, 71
    artefacts 63
    worship 63–4
Murngin people 332, 333, 552
Murray River people 314–16
Murray Springs 248, 253, 255–6, 286
Murty, M.L. Krishna 398, 561
Mylouthkia wells 100–2, 105

Na-Dene 222, 223, 225
Nabta 494–6, 497–8
Naco 213, 253, 255–6, 540
Nadel, Dani 20–1, 517
Nahal Hemar Cave 74–5, 82, 84, 412, 523
Nahal Oren 47, 48
Najjar, Mohammed 70–1
Namu 299–300, 446
Natsushima shell midden 378–80, 559
Natufian culture 29–39, 54, 80, 424
    animal domestication 30–1, 34–5, 78
    cultivation 35–6, 38, 53
    harvesting cereals 30, 37–9, 519

Late Natufians 46–9, 50–4, 57, 61
    sedentism 34, 36, 39, 43–4, 53, 113, 519
Nea Nikomedeia 162–7, 180, 188, 533
    farming 165, 481
    pottery 164, 184
    shrine building 164, 165
Negev desert 47, 72, 74, 80
Nemrik 103, 428–9, 431, 435, 564
Nenana culture 540
Netiv Hagdud 62, 63, 76, 103, 362, 521
Nettle, Daniel 224–5, 541
Nevali Çori 88–90, 103, 360
    cult building 89–90, 91, 96, 422, 425, 427
Neve David 28, 44
New Guinea 8, 342, 343–5, 345–6, 553–4, 555
Niah Cave 349–51, 352
Nichols, Johanna 224–5
Nile, River 15, 444–5, 446, 449, 451–2, 497–8, 499–500, 501, 502
Nombe Rockshelter 341, 553
Nyae Nyae 465–6

Oakhurst sites 475, 570, 476, 478
obsidian as trade indicator 41, 50, 68, 69, 84, 85, 91, 94, 101, 271, 299, 391, 430, 459, 460, 461
Odaiyamamoto 373
Ofnet skull nests 176–7
Ohalo 15–16, 20–2, 24, 26, 28, 29, 56, 517
Olduvai Gorge 460–1
Oleneostrovski Mogilnik island cemetery 168–71, 174, 188, 358
Olmec civilisation 275
Olsen, Sandi 99
O'Malley, Jim 339
Omo Kibish 10
orbital variation 11–12, 515
Oronsay middens 203–4, 205–6, 539
O'Shea, John 170–1
ostrich shell 464–5, 466, 474
Owen-Smith, Norman 545
Özdoğan, Asli 90

Pachamachay Cave 267–8, 269–70, 547
Pal, J.N. 404, 405
palaeoentomology 114, 116
Palli Aike 259, 260
Panaulauca Cave 268–9
Pandaram people 404
Pardoe, Colin 315, 318
Parkington, John 469, 472, 476, 481
Pearsall, Deborah 270, 363

Pech Merle 13, 15, 93, 111, 143, 149
Pedra Furada 218–20, 224, 232, 233, 234, 262, 541
Pedra Pintada cave 262–4, 354
  fishing with poison 263–4, 446
  pottery 264
Pei, Anping 362, 366–8, 558
Peltenburg, Eddie 103–4
Penan people 354–5, 358
Pengtoushan
  rice cultivation 361–2, 366, 367–8, 369, 481, 557
  pottery 365–6, 367, 557
Péquart, M. and S.J. 188
Perlès, Catherine 162, 533
Perrot, Jean 29–30
phytolithic evidence 363–4
Pielou, E.C. 251
Piette, Edouard 144
Pigeot, Nicole 124, 127
Pincevent 124, 125–6, 127, 130
Pitul'ko, Vladimir 387–8, 389, 560
Pleistocene period 13, 238, 329, 350, 359, 396, 398
pollen analysis (palynology) 21–2, 113–14, 116, 138, 363, 491, 517, 554
Polynesian people 227
Pomongwe Cave 463, 485, 488
pottery
  Diatonghuan Cave 366
  earliest Chinese 361, 366–7
  earliest European 163–4, 165
  Ertebølle midden 184
  Jamon 371–4, 380, 558–9
  LBK 178–9, 505
  Nea Nikomedeia 164, 184
  Pedra Pintada 264
  proto-pottery in West Asia 63
  Saharan 491, 492
  Sotto 436–7
  Yarim Tepe 437
Powell, Joseph 226
Prejlerup 140
Pre-Pottery Neolithic A (PPNA) 60, 62–71, 73, 78, 523
Pre-Pottery Neolithic B (PPNB) 68, 71, 73, 76 87, 523
Prestwich, Sir Joseph 116, 154
Preuss, Johannes 487
proto-Indo-European language 193
Puntutjarpa rockshelter 324
Puritjarra Cave 322–3, 324, 325

Pushkari 8–11, 13, 15, 385, 514–15

Qermez Dere 424–7, 430, 431, 435, 436
  building 103, 425, 426–7, 564
Quebrada Jaguay 270–1, 330, 547
Quebrada Tacahuay 271–2
Qurayqira 68

Radcliffe-Brown, Alfred 315, 316
radiocarbon dating 14–15, 116, 119, 517
  accelerator mass spectrometry (AMS) 119, 528
  pioneering use at Star Carr 135
Radovanović, Ivana 161
Rampart Cave 236, 238, 542
Rancho La Brea tar-pits 236, 238, 241, 246, 542
Ranson, Don 306
Ravdonikas, Vladislav Iosifovich 168, 169, 171, 358
Red Sea 80
Reed, Melissa 255
Renfrew, Colin 192–3, 194, 222
rice cultivation 361–4, 366–8, 380, 414, 557
Rick, John 267–9
Riera, La 146–8, 531
Ringkloster 185–6, 200
Rinns, the 197, 199
Robberg sites 475, 476, 570
Robbins, Laurence 466, 467, 487–8
Roberts, Frank 211
Roc del Migdia 159, 532
Rodden, Robert 167
Rollefson, Gary 85, 86
Roosevelt, Anna 262, 264–5
Rose Cottage Cave 470, 475, 476–8, 485, 570
Rosh Horesha 47
Rosh Zin 47
Rowley-Conwy, Peter 42, 137, 141, 173, 184, 186, 189, 191, 194, 200
Rust, Alfred 122, 123

Saami people 181
Sahara desert 492, 496–7
Sahelanthropus tchadensis 10
Sahlins, Marshall 338
Salazar, Zeus 348, 357
Salzano, Francisco 226
Samarra communities 438–9
San Bushmen 474, 477
Sandal Shelter 286–7
Sandweiss, Daniel 271

Sankalia, Hasmukh Dhirajlal 561
Sarai-Nahar Rai 404–5
Sato, Hiroyuki 372
Saunders, Jeffrey 247, 249, 254
Schild, Romuald 450, 495
Schmandt-Besserat, Denise 85–6
Schmidt, Klaus 65–6, 67, 89–90, 427
sea level change 150–7, 166, 190, 198–9, 240, 330, 346
  El Nino 271–2
sedentism 43, 46, 50, 268, 373, 404
Sella, Conde de la Vega del 146
Sepik River 61, 521
shamanism 130–1, 473–5, 529
Shaw, Thurstan 483–4, 485, 571
Shawnee-Minisnik 247, 544
Shillourokambos 102, 105
Shinto, Koichi 375
Shoocongdej, R. 354, 556
Simmons, Alan 70–1, 97–9
Sinai desert 80
Skara Brae 205
Skateholm 172–5, 194, 200, 405, 534
  cemeteries 174–5
  community violence 175
  domesticated dogs 174, 387–8
Smith, Bruce 267–8, 269, 278
Smith, Mike 322–3
Solecki, Ralph and Rose 422
Spencer, Baldwin 319–20, 323
Spirit Cave 288
Srejović, Dragoslav 161
Staosnaig 141, 202–3, 538
Star Carr 134–8, 186, 200, 372–3, 418, 529–30
Steele, D. Gentry 226
Steenstrup, Professor 135–6, 183
Stellmoor 123, 129, 197, 261
Stordeur, Danielle 64, 65, 103
Strathern, Andrew 341
Straus, Lawrence 146–7
Studenhoe 383, 389
Suess, Eduard 154
Sugihara, Sosuke 379
Sundaland 351
Sykes, Bryan 193–4, 537

Tabqa 35
Taçon, Paul 328–9, 332, 333, 552
Tadrart Acacus 490–1, 493, 497
Tama Hills pig traps 378, 481
Tamar Hat Cave 443–4, 491, 565
Tasaday hoax 348–9, 357–8, 555, 556

Tasmania 8, 10, 15, 305–11, 549
Taurus Mountains 49, 88, 90
Tell Aswad 38, 75, 522
Tell es-Sawwan 438, 439
Tell es-Sultan see also Jericho
Tell Sotto 435–6
Tenta 102–3, 104, 527
Téviec 187–8, 194, 195, 536
Thackeray, Anne and J. Francis 474
Thesiger, Wilfred 6–7
Thompson, Lonnie 453
Thorley, Peter 322
Thorne, Alan 313–14
Tigris, River 438–9, 440
Titicaca, Lake basin 266, 269, 270
Todd, Ian 103
Torroni, Antonio 226
Troncoso, Carlos 231
Tros Arroyos 259
Tsodilo hills 466, 486, 487–8
Turner II, Christy G. 221–2, 223, 227
Tybrind Vig 182, 194, 446, 535

Uan Afuda Cave 490–2, 493
Uan Muhuggiag Cave 490, 492, 493
Uenohara 370–1, 373–5, 377, 405
Umm Dabaghiyah 432–5, 436
Unger-Hamilton, Romana 38–9
Uruk period 439
Utnur 414

Vaengo Sø 184
Valla, François 31, 43
van de Maele, Mauricio 231
van Noten, Francis 457
Vedbaek 181, 194
Veddah people 396
Verberie 124, 126, 289, 390
Vereshchagin, N.K. 385
Vig 140

Wadi Faynan (WF16) 62–3, 68–70, 76, 96, 521
Wadi Gharab 72, 79
Wadi Ghuwayr 70–1
Wadi Kubbaniya 443, 445–52, 463, 486
Wadi el-Uwaynid 26–7, 518
Wadi Zarqa 83–4, 87
Wadley, Lyn 470–1, 477–8, 569
Walker, Nicholas 463, 488
Wallace, Alfred Russel 265
  Wallace's Line 351

Wargata Cave 307, 549
Warner, Trevor 427–8, 435
Warren, Captain Charles 56
Watkins, Lloyd 332, 552
Wendorf, Fred 450, 452, 495, 496, 497
Wenming, Yan 362, 363
White Paintings Rockshelter 486, 487, 572
Wiessner, Polly 478
Wilton tradition 476, 570
Wollaston, A.F.R. 339
Wonderwerk Cave 473–5
    paintings 474, 570
Worsaae, Professor 135–6, 183
woven material 24, 74–5, 81, 140, 282, 530
Wrangel Island mammoths 252–3, 386

Yahgan people 541
Yamanouchi, Suago 372
Yanomamö people 175–6, 177
Yarim Tepe 436, 437–9, 440, 481, 493, 565
    architecture 437–8
    burial 438

pottery 437
Yellen, John 466, 468
Younger Dryas 13, 41, 44, 48–9, 50, 52–3, 67,
    80, 100, 104, 113–14, 115, 123, 132, 138, 139,
    143, 239, 242, 244, 255, 261, 364, 424, 425,
    507, 543

Zad 62, 521
Zagros Mountains 49, 420, 421
Zapotec civilisation 274, 275, 283
Zawi Chemi Shanidar 412–4, 431, 563–4
    ritual dancing 422
    Shanidar Cave burial 423–4
Zeder, Melinda 78
Zegura, Stephen 223
Zhokhov 381, 387–92
    clothing manufacture 390–1
    polar bear hunting 388, 392, 417, 561
Zilhão, João 190–1, 194
Zohary, Daniel 23–4, 68
Zvelebil, Marek 170, 171, 179, 194, 537